# The Developing Person

## Through Childhood and Adolescence

**LaunchPad** macmillan learning     **LearningCurve**

## for *The Developing Person Through Childhood and Adolescence*, Eleventh Edition

### Available March 2018 at launchpadworks.com

Each chapter in LaunchPad for *The Developing Person Through Childhood and Adolescence,* Eleventh Edition, features a collection of activities carefully chosen to help master the major concepts. The site serves students as a comprehensive online study guide, available any time, with opportunities for self-quizzing with instant feedback, exam preparation, and further explorations of topics from the textbook. For instructors, all units and activities can be instantly assigned and students' results and analytics are collected in the Gradebook.

### For Students

- Full e-Book of *The Developing Person Through Childhood and Adolescence,* Eleventh Edition
- *Developing Lives* interactive simulation
- Data Connections activities
- LearningCurve Quizzing
- Student Video Activities
- DSM 5 Appendix
- *Scientific American* Newsfeed

### For Instructors

- Gradebook
- Worth Video Collection for Human Development
- Presentation Slides
- Instructor's Resource Guide
- Test Bank
- Electronic Figures, Photos, and Tables
- Correlation of *The Developing Person Through Childhood and Adolescence,* Eleventh Edition, to NCLEX-RN Test and NAEYC Standards

## LearningCurve

*What Is LearningCurve?* LearningCurve is a cutting-edge study tool designed to increase your understanding and memory of the core concepts in every chapter. Based on insights from the latest learning and memory research, the LearningCurve system pairs multiple-choice and fill-in-the-blank questions with instantaneous feedback and a rich array of study tools including videos, animations, and lab simulations. The LearningCurve system is adaptive, so the quiz you take is customized to your level of understanding. The more questions you answer correctly, the more challenging the questions become. Best of all, the e-Book of *The Developing Person Through Childhood and Adolescence,* Eleventh Edition, is fully integrated, so you can easily review the text as you study and answer questions. LearningCurve is a smart and fun way to study each chapter.

**LearningCurve** is available as part of **LaunchPad** for *The Developing Person Through Childhood and Adolescence,* **Eleventh Edition.** To find out more or purchase access, go to **launchpadworks.com.**

ELEVENTH EDITION

# The Developing Person

## Through Childhood and Adolescence

### Kathleen Stassen Berger

Bronx Community College
City University of New York

worth publishers
Macmillan Learning
New York

*Vice President, Social Sciences and High School:* Charles Linsmeier
*Director of Content and Assessment, Social Sciences:* Shani Fisher
*Executive Program Manager:* Christine Cardone
*Developmental Editor:* Andrea Musick Page
*Assistant Editor:* Melissa Rostek
*Executive Marketing Manager:* Katherine Nurre
*Marketing Assistant:* Morgan Ratner
*Director of Media Editorial, Social Sciences:* Noel Hohnstine
*Senior Media Editor:* Laura Burden
*Assistant Media Editor:* Nik Toner
*Director, Content Management Enhancement:* Tracey Kuehn
*Managing Editor:* Lisa Kinne
*Senior Content Project Manager:* Peter Jacoby
*Senior Project Manager:* Andrea Stefanowicz, Lumina Datamatics, Inc.
*Media Producer:* Joseph Tomasso
*Senior Workflow Supervisor:* Susan Wein
*Photo Editor:* Sheena Goldstein
*Photo Researcher:* Candice Cheesman
*Director of Design, Content Management:* Diana Blume
*Cover design:* Blake Logan
*Interior design:* Lumina Datamatics, Inc.
*Art Manager:* Matthew McAdams
*Illustrations:* Lumina Datamatics, Charles Yuen
*Composition:* Lumina Datamatics, Inc.
*Printing and Binding:* LSC Communications
*Cover Photograph:* Images By Tang Ming Tung/DigitalVision/Getty Images

*Library of Congress Control Number:* 2017936099
ISBN-13: 978-1-319-05813-5
ISBN-10: 1-319-05813-2

Printed in the United States of America
Second printing

WORTH PUBLISHERS

One New York Plaza
Suite 4500
New York, NY 10004-1562
www.macmillanlearning.com

**Kathleen Stassen Berger** received her undergraduate education at Stanford University and Radcliffe College, and then she earned an MAT from Harvard University and an M.S. and Ph.D. from Yeshiva University. Her broad experience as an educator includes directing a preschool, serving as chair of philosophy at the United Nations International School, and teaching child and adolescent development at Fordham University graduate school, Montclair State University, and Quinnipiac University. She also taught social psychology to inmates at Sing Sing Prison who were earning paralegal degrees.

Currently, Berger is a professor at Bronx Community College of the City University of New York, as she has been for most of her professional career. She began there as an adjunct in English and for the past decades has been a full professor in the Social Sciences Department, which includes psychology, sociology, economics, anthropology, political science, and human services. She has taught introduction to psychology, child and adolescent development, adulthood and aging, social psychology, abnormal psychology, and human motivation. Her students—from diverse ethnic, economic, and educational backgrounds, of many ages, ambitions, and interests—honor her with the highest teaching evaluations.

Berger is also the author of *Invitation to the Life Span* and *The Developing Person Through the Life Span*. Her developmental texts are used at more than 700 colleges and universities worldwide and are available in Spanish, French, Italian, and Portuguese as well as English. Her research interests include adolescent identity, immigration, bullying, and grandparents, and she has published articles on developmental topics in the *Wiley Encyclopedia of Psychology, Developmental Review*, and in publications of the American Association for Higher Education and the National Education Association for Higher Education. She continues teaching and learning from her students as well as from her four daughters and three grandsons.

© 2016 Macmillan

# BRIEF CONTENTS

Preface   xiii

## PART I The Beginnings
**CHAPTER 1** The Science of Human Development   3
**CHAPTER 2** Theories   35
**CHAPTER 3** The New Genetics   67
**CHAPTER 4** Prenatal Development and Birth   97

## PART II The First Two Years
**CHAPTER 5** The First Two Years: Biosocial Development   135
**CHAPTER 6** The First Two Years: Cognitive Development   163
**CHAPTER 7** The First Two Years: Psychosocial Development   189

## PART III Early Childhood
**CHAPTER 8** Early Childhood: Biosocial Development   223
**CHAPTER 9** Early Childhood: Cognitive Development   251
**CHAPTER 10** Early Childhood: Psychosocial Development   281

## PART IV Middle Childhood
**CHAPTER 11** Middle Childhood: Biosocial Development   311
**CHAPTER 12** Middle Childhood: Cognitive Development   339
**CHAPTER 13** Middle Childhood: Psychosocial Development   367

## PART V Adolescence
**CHAPTER 14** Adolescence: Biosocial Development   403
**CHAPTER 15** Adolescence: Cognitive Development   429
**CHAPTER 16** Adolescence: Psychosocial Development   457

**EPILOGUE** Emerging Adulthood   487
**APPENDIX** More About Research Methods   503

Glossary   G-1
References   R-1
Name Index   NI-1
Subject Index   SI-1

# CONTENTS

Preface    xiii

# PART I

# The Beginnings

## Chapter 1    The Science of Human Development    3

**Understanding How and Why    4**
The Scientific Method    4
**A VIEW FROM SCIENCE:** Overweight Children and Adult Health    5
The Nature–Nurture Controversy    6

**The Life-Span Perspective    8**
Development Is Multidirectional    9
Development Is Multicontextual    10
**INSIDE THE BRAIN:** Thinking About Marijuana    10
Development Is Multicultural    14
Development Is Multidisciplinary    17
Development Is Plastic    19
**A CASE TO STUDY:** David    20

**Designing Science    22**
Observation    22
The Experiment    23
The Survey    24
Studying Development over the Life Span    25

**Cautions and Challenges from Science    29**
Correlation and Causation    29
Quantity and Quality    30
Ethics    30

## Chapter 2    Theories    35

**What Theories Do    36**
Questions and Answers    37
Past and Future    37

**Grand Theories    38**
Psychoanalytic Theory: Freud and Erikson    39
Behaviorism: Conditioning and Learning    41
Cognitive Theory: Piaget and Information Processing    45
**INSIDE THE BRAIN:** Measuring Mental Activity    49

**Newer Theories    51**
Sociocultural Theory: Vygotsky and Beyond    51

Evolutionary Theory    54
**OPPOSING PERSPECTIVES:** Toilet Training—How and When?    56

**What Theories Contribute    62**

## Chapter 3    The New Genetics    67

**The Genetic Code    68**
46 to 21,000 to 3 Billion    68
Same and Different    69
Matching Genes and Chromosomes    71
**OPPOSING PERSPECTIVES:** Too Many Boys?    73

**New Cells, New People    75**
Cells and Identity    75
Twins and More    77

**From Genotype to Phenotype    80**
Many Factors    80
Gene–Gene Interactions    80
Nature and Nurture    83
Practical Applications    85

**Chromosomal and Genetic Problems    86**
Spontaneous Mutations    86
Not Exactly 46    86
Gene Disorders    88
Genetic Counseling and Testing    89
**A CASE TO STUDY:** Raising Healthy Children    90

## Chapter 4    Prenatal Development and Birth    97

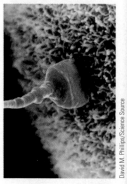

**Prenatal Development    98**
Germinal: The First 14 Days    98
Embryo: From the Third Week Through the Eighth Week    98
Fetus: From the Ninth Week Until Birth    100
**INSIDE THE BRAIN:** Neuronal Birth and Death    101

**Birth    105**
The Newborn's First Minutes    106
Medical Assistance    107

**Problems and Solutions    112**
Harmful Substances    112
Applying the Research    116
**A VIEW FROM SCIENCE:** What Is Safe?    117
Prenatal Diagnosis    119
Low Birthweight: Causes and Consequences    119
**OPPOSING PERSPECTIVES:** "What Do People Live to Do?"    120
Complications During Birth    124

**The New Family   125**
The Newborn   125
New Mothers   126
New Fathers   127
Parental Alliance   128
Family Bonding   128

# PART II
# The First Two Years

**Chapter 5   The First Two Years: Biosocial Development   135**

**Body Changes   135**
Body Size   136
Sleep   137
Brain Development   139
**INSIDE THE BRAIN:** Neuroscience Vocabulary   140
Harming the Infant Body and Brain   144
**A VIEW FROM SCIENCE:** Face Recognition   145

**Perceiving and Moving   147**
The Senses   147
Motor Skills   150
Cultural Variations   152

**Surviving in Good Health   153**
Better Days Ahead   153
**A CASE TO STUDY:** Scientist at Work   155
Immunization   156
Nutrition   157

**Chapter 6   The First Two Years: Cognitive Development   163**

**Sensorimotor Intelligence   164**
Stages One and Two: Primary Circular Reactions   165
Stages Three and Four: Secondary Circular Reactions   166
Stages Five and Six: Tertiary Circular Reactions   166
**A VIEW FROM SCIENCE:** Object Permanence   167

**Information Processing   169**
Affordances   170
Memory   171

**Language: What Develops in the First Two Years?   174**
The Universal Sequence   174
**INSIDE THE BRAIN:** Understanding Speech   176
Cultural Differences   178
Theories of Language Learning   179
**OPPOSING PERSPECTIVES:**
Language and Video   182

**Chapter 7   The First Two Years: Psychosocial Development   189**

**Emotional Development   189**
Early Emotions   190
Toddlers' Emotions   191
Temperament   192
**INSIDE THE BRAIN:** Expressing Emotions   193

**The Development of Social Bonds   196**
Synchrony   196
Attachment   198
Insecure Attachment and the Social Setting   202
**A CASE TO STUDY:** Can We Bear This Commitment?   205
Social Referencing   205
Fathers as Social Partners   206

**Theories of Infant Psychosocial Development   208**
Psychoanalytic Theory   208
Behaviorism   208
Cognitive Theory   210
Evolutionary Theory   210
Sociocultural Theory   211
Conclusion   216

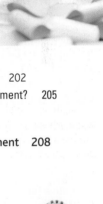

# PART III
# Early Childhood

**Chapter 8   Early Childhood: Biosocial Development   223**

**Body Changes   223**
Growth Patterns   223
Nutrition   224
Brain Growth   226

**INSIDE THE BRAIN:** Connected Hemispheres    228

**Advancing Motor Skills    231**

Gross Motor Skills    231

**A VIEW FROM SCIENCE:** Eliminating Lead    234

Fine Motor Skills    236

**Injuries and Abuse    237**

Avoidable Injury    238

**A CASE TO STUDY:** "My Baby Swallowed Poison"    239

Prevention    240

**Child Maltreatment    241**

Definitions and Statistics    242

Frequency of Maltreatment    243

Consequences of Maltreatment    244

Preventing Maltreatment    246

**Chapter 9    Early Childhood:
                    Cognitive
                    Development    251**

**Thinking During Early
Childhood    251**

Piaget: Preoperational Thought    251

**A CASE TO STUDY:** Stones
in the Belly    254

Vygotsky: Social Learning    255

Children's Theories    260

Brain and Context    261

**Language Learning    263**

A Sensitive Time    263

The Vocabulary Explosion    263

Acquiring Grammar    265

Learning Two Languages    267

**Early-Childhood Schooling    268**

Homes and Schools    269

Child-Centered Programs    270

Teacher-Directed Programs    272

Intervention Programs    273

Long-Term Gains from Intensive Programs    275

**Chapter 10    Early Childhood:
                    Psychosocial
                    Development    281**

**Emotional Development    281**

Initiative Versus Guilt    282

Motivation    284

**Play    286**

Playmates    286

Active Play    288

Learning Emotional Regulation    290

**Challenges for Caregivers    293**

Styles of Caregiving    293

**A VIEW FROM SCIENCE:** Culture and Parenting Style    296

Discipline    296

**OPPOSING PERSPECTIVES:** Is Spanking OK?    298

Becoming Boys or Girls: Sex and Gender    300

**A CASE TO STUDY:** The Berger Daughters    303

What Is Best?    305

# PART IV
# Middle Childhood

**Chapter 11    Middle Childhood:
                     Biosocial
                     Development    311**

**A Healthy Time    312**

Slower Growth, Greater Strength    312

Physical Activity    313

Health Problems in Middle
Childhood    315

**A VIEW FROM SCIENCE:** What Causes
Childhood Obesity?    317

**Children with Special Brains and
Bodies    320**

Measuring the Mind    320

Special Needs in Middle Childhood    323

Specific Learning Disorders    325

**OPPOSING PERSPECTIVES:** Drug Treatment for ADHD and Other
Disorders    326

**Special Education    329**

**A CASE TO STUDY:** Unexpected and Odd    330

Labels, Laws, and Learning    331

Early Intervention    332

Gifted and Talented    333

**Chapter 12** Middle Childhood: Cognitive Development 339

**Building on Theory 339**
Piaget and Concrete Thought 339
Vygotsky and Culture 341
**A CASE TO STUDY:** Is She Going to Die? 342
Information Processing 342
**INSIDE THE BRAIN:** Coordination and Capacity 344
Memory 345
Control Processes 346

**Language 348**
Vocabulary 348
Speaking Two Languages 349
Differences in Language Learning 350
**OPPOSING PERSPECTIVES:** Happiness or High Grades? 352

**Teaching and Learning 353**
International Schooling 353
Schooling in the United States 359
Choices and Complications 360

**Chapter 13** Middle Childhood: Psychosocial Development 367

**The Nature of the Child 368**
Self-Concept 369
**OPPOSING PERSPECTIVES:** Protect or Puncture Self-Esteem? 371
Resilience and Stress 372

**Families and Children 375**
Shared and Nonshared Environments 375
Family Structure and Family Function 376
**A VIEW FROM SCIENCE:** "I Always Dressed One in Blue Stuff..." 377
Connecting Structure and Function 380
Family Trouble 383

**The Peer Group 386**
The Culture of Children 386
**A CASE TO STUDY:** Ignorance All Around 391

**Children's Moral Values 392**
Moral Reasoning 393
What Children Value 395

# PART V
# Adolescence

**Chapter 14** Adolescence: Biosocial Development 403

**Puberty Begins 403**
Unseen Beginnings 404
Brain Growth 407
When Will Puberty Begin? 408
**INSIDE THE BRAIN:** Lopsided Growth 409
**A VIEW FROM SCIENCE:** Stress and Puberty 412
Too Early, Too Late 412

**Growth and Nutrition 414**
Growing Bigger and Stronger 414
Diet Deficiencies 415
Eating Disorders 418

**Sexual Maturation 420**
Sexual Characteristics 420
Sexual Activity 421
Sexual Problems in Adolescence 422

**Chapter 15** Adolescence: Cognitive Development 429

**Logic and Self 430**
Egocentrism 430
Formal Operational Thought 432
Two Modes of Thinking 434
**A CASE TO STUDY:** Biting the Policeman 437
**INSIDE THE BRAIN:** Impulses, Rewards, and Reflection 439

**Digital Natives 440**
Technology and Cognition 441
Sexual Abuse? 441
Addiction 442
Cyber Danger 443

**Secondary Education** 445

Definitions and Facts 446

Middle School 447

High School 449

**OPPOSING PERSPECTIVES**: Testing 450

Variability 454


**Chapter 16** Adolescence: Psychosocial Development 457

Stuart Hughs/Getty Images

**Identity** 457

Not Yet Achieved 458

Four Arenas of Identity Formation 458

**Relationships with Adults** 461

**A VIEW FROM SCIENCE**: Teenagers, Genes, and Drug Use 462

Parents 463

**Peer Power** 465

Peer Pressure 465

**A CASE TO STUDY**: The Naiveté of Your Author 467

Romance 468

Sex Education 469

**Sadness and Anger** 471

Depression 472

Delinquency and Defiance 474

**Drug Use and Abuse** 477

Variations in Drug Use 477

**OPPOSING PERSPECTIVES**: E-Cigarettes: Path to Addiction or Healthy Choice? 478

Harm from Drugs 479

Preventing Drug Abuse: What Works? 480


**Epilogue** Emerging Adulthood 487

Hero Images/Getty Images

**Biosocial Development** 487

Strong and Active Bodies 487

Taking Risks 488

**Cognitive Development** 489

Countering Stereotypes 490

Cognitive Growth and Higher Education 491

**Psychosocial Development** 495

Identity Achievement 495

Intimacy Needs 496

Concluding Questions and Hopes 500

**Appendix** More About Research Methods 503

**Make It Personal** 503

**Read the Research** 503

Professional Journals and Books 503

The Internet 504

**Additional Terms and Concepts** 505

Who Participates? 505

Research and Design 506

Reporting Results 506


Glossary G-1

References R-1

Name Index NI-1

Subject Index SI-1

If human development were simple, universal, and unchanging, there would be no need for a new edition of this textbook. Nor would anyone need to learn anything about human growth. But human development is complex, varied, and never the same.

This is evident to me in small ways as well as large ones. Yesterday, I made the mistake of taking two of my grandsons, aged 6 and 7, to the grocery store, asking them what they wanted for dinner. I immediately rejected their first suggestions—doughnuts or store-made sandwiches. But we lingered over the meat counter. Asa wanted hot dogs and Caleb wanted chicken. Neither would concede.

At least one universal is apparent in this anecdote: Grandmothers seek to nourish grandchildren. But complexity and variability were evident in two stubborn cousins and one confused grandmother.

This small incident is not unlike the headlines in today's newspaper. Indeed, other developmental questions seem more urgent now, interweaving what is universally true about humans with what is new and immediate, balancing them in order to move forward with our public and personal lives. I found a compromise for dinner—chicken hot dogs, which both boys ate, with whole wheat bread and lots of ketchup. I do not know the solutions to public dilemmas such as climate change, immigration, gun violence, and systemic racism, but I believe that a deeper and more accurate understanding of human development might help.

That is why I wrote this eleventh edition, which presents both the enduring and the current findings from the study of child and adolescent development. Some of those findings have been recognized for decades, even centuries, and some are new, as thousands of scientists study how humans grow and change with new circumstances. I hope they will help us with the public and private aspects of our lives.

## What's New in the Eleventh Edition?
### New Material

Every year, scientists discover and explain more concepts and research. The best of these are integrated into the text, with hundreds of new references on many topics, including epigenetics at conception, prenatal protections, infant nutrition, autism spectrum disorder, attachment, high-stakes testing, drug addiction and opioid-related deaths, sex education, and diversity of all kinds—ethnic, economic, gender, and cultural. Cognizant of the interdisciplinary nature of human development, I include recent research in biology, sociology, education, anthropology, political science, and more—as well as my home discipline, psychology.

Genetics and social contexts are noted throughout. The interaction of nature and nurture is discussed in many chapters, because neuroscience relates to every aspect of life. Among the many topics described with new research are the variations, benefits, and hazards of breast-feeding, infant day

Rick Friedman/Corbis via Getty Images

**What Can You Learn?** Scientists first establish what is, and then they try to change it. In one recent experiment, Deb Kelemen (shown here) established that few children under age 12 understand a central concept of evolution (natural selection). Then she showed an experimental group a picture book illustrating the idea. Success! The independent variable (the book) affected the dependent variable (the children's ideas), which confirmed Kelemen's hypothesis: Children can understand natural selection if instruction is tailored to their ability.

care, preschool education, single parenthood, exercise, vaccination, same-sex marriage—always noting differences, deficits, and resilience.

No paragraph in this edition is exactly what it was in the tenth edition. To help professors who taught with the earlier texts, or students who have friends who took the course a few years ago, here are some highlights of the updates:

- Updated examples illustrating replication, race and ethnicity, and cross-sequential study (Chapter 1).
- New feature on childhood obesity illustrating the scientific method (Chapter 1).
- New feature on marijuana use and sensitive periods (Chapter 1).
- Expanded discussion and new examples of what theories do (Chapter 2).
- New example and figure on opioid-related deaths illustrating classical conditioning (Chapter 2).
- Descriptions of newer brain imaging techniques such as DTI (diffusion tensor imaging) (Chapter 2).
- *Grandmother hypothesis* added to the discussion of evolutionary theory (Chapter 2).
- New coverage on the impact of the microbiome (Chapter 3).
- Updated material on stem cells and the use of CRISPR (Chapter 3).
- New feature on genetic counseling (Chapter 3).
- New feature on neurogenesis in the developing fetus (Chapter 4).
- Updated coverage and data on cesarean sections, the utilization of midwives, and alternatives to hospital birth (Chapter 4).
- Added discussion of teratogens, including recent research and data on Zika virus (Chapter 4).
- New research and data on international trends in low birthweight (Chapter 4).
- Updated coverage and research examples of infant sleep, bed-sharing, and co-sleeping (Chapter 5).
- New feature explaining neuroscience terms and brain structures (Chapter 5).
- New research on newborn vision and experience of pain (Chapter 5).
- Added coverage of motor-skill development, including walking (Chapter 5).
- New research on memory in infancy (Chapter 6).
- New coverage of bilingualism in babies (Chapter 6).
- Added discussion of attachment and the work of Bowlby and Ainsworth (Chapter 7).
- New features on emotional expression and adoptive parents' attachment to their children (Chapter 7).
- Expanded coverage and research on infant day care, including new data on international trends in paid family leave (Chapter 7).
- Updated research on childhood obesity and nutrition (Chapter 8).
- Added discussion and research on childhood allergies (Chapter 8).
- New research on dangers of environmental pollutants in early childhood (Chapter 8).
- New research examples in discussion of young children's logic (Chapter 9).
- Expanded discussion and new research on STEM learning, educational software use, and bilingualism in early childhood (Chapter 9).
- New research on brain plasticity and emotional regulation (Chapter 10).
- New coverage and data on screen time (Chapter 10).
- New research on gender development and gender differences (Chapter 10).
- Added discussion of embodied cognition and the importance of physical activity for overall health (Chapter 11).
- Added coverage on Sternberg, Gardner, and multiple intelligences (Chapter 11).

Images By Tang Ming Tung/Taxi/Getty Images

**Is She Awake?** This 36-year-old mother in Hong Kong put her 7-month-old baby on her back, protecting her from SIDS as the Chinese have done for centuries. However, the soft pillow and comforter are hazards. Will she carry the baby to a safe place before she falls asleep?

- Updated coverage of childhood psychopathology, including ADHD, autism spectrum disorder, and specific learning disorders, and special education (Chapter 11).
- New feature on cognition in middle childhood (Chapter 12).
- Added discussion of Vygotsky and the role of instruction (Chapter 12).
- New discussion of the U.S. Common Core standards and of Finland's recent education reform (Chapter 12).
- Added discussion and research on social comparison in middle childhood (Chapter 13).
- New U.S. and international research on various family structures (Chapter 13).
- New feature and research on bullying (Chapter 13).
- Added discussion of the benefits of psychotherapy for emotional problems during adolescence (Chapter 14).
- New coverage and research on executive function (Chapter 14).
- New research on eating disorders and sexual activity during adolescence (Chapter 14).
- Added discussion and research on advances in cognition during adolescence (Chapter 15).
- Updated coverage of media use among adolescents (Chapter 15).
- New research on adolescents' experience of middle school (Chapter 15).
- Updated coverage of ethnic and gender development, as well as sexual orientation (Chapter 16).
- Updated coverage of teenage drug use, including e-cigarettes (Chapter 16).
- More coverage on exercise and new data on family-planning trends worldwide (Epilogue).
- Updated material on college completion and debt, including a new infographic (Epilogue).
- Updated material and new research on dating, cohabitation, and romance in emerging adults (Epilogue).

Steve Russell/Getty Images

**Universal Morality** Remarkable? Not really. By the end of middle childhood, many children are eager to express their moral convictions, especially with a friend. Chaim Ifrah and Shai Reef believe that welcoming refugees is part of being a patriotic Canadian and a devout Jew, so they brought a welcoming sign to the Toronto airport where Syrian refugees (mostly Muslim) will soon deplane.

## New *Inside the Brain* Feature

Since new discoveries abound almost daily in the field of neuroscience, I have added *Inside the Brain* features to several chapters, exploring topics such as the intricacies of prenatal and infant brain development, brain specialization and speech development, and brain maturation and emotional development.

## New and Updated Coverage of Neuroscience

Inclusion of neuroscience is a familiar feature of this book. In addition to the new *Inside the Brain* features, I include the latest, cutting-edge research on the brain in virtually every chapter, often enhancing it with charts, figures, and photos to help students understand the brain's inner workings. A list highlighting this material is available at macmillanlearning.com.

## New *Developing Lives*

*Developing Lives* is a robust and sophisticated interactive experience in which each student "raises" a virtual child from sperm-and-egg to teenager—fully integrated into LaunchPad. With *Developing Lives*, each student creates a personal profile, selects a virtual partner (or chooses to be a single parent), and marks the arrival of their newborn (represented by a unique avatar based on the parents' characteristics). As the child grows, the student responds to events both planned and unforeseen, making important decisions (nutrition choices, doctor visits, sleeping location) and facing uncertain moments (illness, divorce, a new baby), with each choice affecting how the child grows. Throughout, *Developing Lives* deepens each student's attachment and understanding of key concepts in the field with immediate, customized feedback based on child development research. It integrates more than 200 videos and animations and includes quizzes and essay questions that are easy to assign and assess.

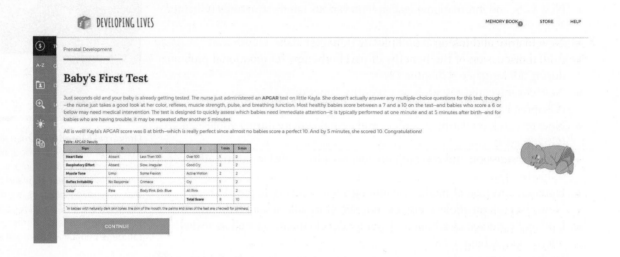

## New Integration with LaunchPad

Throughout the book, the margins include LaunchPad call-outs to online videos about people in a particular context or key scientists who might become role models. For example, Susan Beal, the Australian scientist who revolutionized our understanding of SIDS (sudden infant death syndrome) and infant sleep is shown. The video demonstrates that she is not an aloof expert, but a wife and mother, like many students and their relatives. Application to *Developing Lives* (described above) and Data Connections activities (described below) are also highlighted for the reader.

**LaunchPad**
macmillan learning

**Video: Newborn Reflexes** shows several infants displaying the reflexes discussed in this section.

Inna Astakhova/Shutterstock

## Renewed Emphasis on Critical Thinking and Application in the Pedagogical Program

We all need to be critical thinkers. Virtually every page of this book presents questions as well as facts. A new marginal feature, *Think Critically*, encourages student reflection and analysis. There are no pat answers to these questions: They could be used to start a class discussion or begin a long essay.

Every chapter begins with a few *What Will You Know?* questions, one for each major heading. Of course, much of what readers will learn will be reflected in new attitudes and perspectives—hard to quantify. But these *What Will You Know?* questions are intended to be provocative and to pose issues that the students will remember for decades.

In addition, after every major section, *What Have You Learned?* questions appear. They are designed to help students review what they have just read, a pedagogical technique proven to help retention. Ideally, students will answer these learning objective questions in sentences, with specifics that demonstrate knowledge. Some items on the new lists are straightforward, requiring only close attention to the chapter content. Others require comparisons, implications, or evaluations.

Key terms are indicated with bold print and are defined in the margins as well as in the glossary, because expanded vocabulary aids expanded understanding. To help students become better observers, occasional *Observation Quizzes* accompany a photo or figure. And, since many students reading this book are preparing to be teachers, health care professionals, police officers, or parents, every chapter contains *Especially For* questions that encourage students to apply important developmental concepts just as experts in the field do.

As a professor myself, I continue to seek ways to deepen knowledge. Cognitive psychology and research on pedagogy finds that vocabulary, specific applications details, and critical thinking are all part of learning. These features are designed to foster all four.

# Updated Features

## Online *Data Connections* Activities

Understanding how scientists use data helps students realize that the study of human development is much more than personal experience and common sense. Evidence sometimes contradicts myths and assumptions, and sometimes it confirms them. This edition continues to offer interactive activities—many of which have been updated with the latest available data—to allow students to interpret data on topics ranging from infant breast-feeding to adolescent risk-taking.

For example, students discover how U.S. poverty rates are worse for children than for adults, data that may be surprising. These interactive activities advance active thinking, deepening their understanding of the need for data. Instructors can assign these activities in the online LaunchPad that accompanies this book.

## *Opposing Perspectives, A View from Science*, and *A Case to Study*

Special topics and new research abound in childhood and adolescent development. This edition of *The Developing Person Through Childhood and Adolescence* includes boxed features in every chapter. *Opposing Perspectives* focuses on controversial topics—from prenatal sex selection to e-cigarettes. Information and opinions on both sides of each issue are presented, so students can weigh evidence, assess arguments, and reach their own conclusions while appreciating that an opposite conclusion also has merit. *A View from Science* explains research in more detail, illustrating the benefits of the scientific method. *A Case to Study* focuses on particular individuals, helping students to recognize the personal implications of what they learn.

## Infographics

Information is sometimes better understood visually and graphically. Carefully chosen, updated photos and figures appear on almost every page, with captions that explain and increase knowledge. In addition, every chapter includes a full-page, graphical depiction.

These infographics explain key concepts, from brain development to school attendance rates, often with data that encourage students to think of other nations, other cultures, other times. My two awesome editors and I have worked closely with noted designer Charles Yuen to create these infographics, hoping they reinforce key ideas.

## Child Development and Nursing Career Correlation Guides

Many students taking this course will become nurses or early-childhood educators. This book and accompanying testing material are fully correlated to the NAEYC (National Association for the Education of Young Children) career preparation goals and the NCLEX (nursing) licensure exam. These two supplements are available in LaunchPad.

# Ongoing Features

## Writing That Communicates the Excitement and Challenge of the Field

Writing about the science of human development should be lively, just as people are. Each sentence conveys attitude as well as content. Chapter-opening vignettes describe real-life situations. Examples and clear explanations abound, helping students connect theory, research, and experiences.

## Coverage of Diversity

Cross-cultural, international, multiethnic, sexual orientation, poverty, age, family structure, gender—all these words and ideas are vital to appreciating how children develop. Research uncovers surprising similarities and notable differences: All people have much in common, yet each human is unique. From the discussion of social contexts in Chapter 1 to the coverage of cultural differences among emerging adults in the Epilogue, each chapter explains that no one is average; each of us is diverse.

New research on family structures, immigrants, bilingualism, and ethnic differences in health are among the many topics that illustrate human diversity. Respect for human differences is evident throughout. Examples and research findings from many parts of the world are not add-ons but are integral to our understanding of child development. A list of these examples and research is available at macmillanlearning.com.

## Current Research from the Field

My mentors encouraged curiosity, creativity, and skepticism; as a result, I read and analyze thousands of articles and books on everything from the genetic alleles that predispose children to autism spectrum disorder to the complications of ethnic identity. The recent explosion of research in neuroscience has challenged me, once again, first to understand and then to explain many complex

Hero Images/DigitalVision/Getty Images

**Learning to Button** Most shirts for 4-year-olds are wide-necked without buttons, so preschoolers can put the shirts on themselves. But the skill of buttoning is best learned from a mentor, who knows how to increase motivation.

findings and speculative leaps. My students continue to ask questions and share their experiences, providing new perspectives and concerns.

## Topical Organization Within a Chronological Framework

The book's basic organization remains unchanged. Four chapters begin the book with coverage of definitions, theories, genetics, and prenatal development. These chapters function not only as a developmental foundation but also as the structure for explaining plasticity, nature and nurture, multicultural awareness, risk analysis, gains and losses, family bonding, and many other concepts that yield insights for all of human development.

The other three parts correspond to the major periods of development. Each age is discussed in three chapters, one for the biological, one for the cognitive, and one for the social world. I believe that this topical organization within a chronological framework provides a scaffold for students' understanding of the interplay between chronological age and specific topics.

**Sisters and Brothers** Gender equality has become important to both sexes, as evidenced by the thousands of men who joined the Women's March on January 21, 2017—the day after President Trump's inauguration. Many who attended took exception with his positions on sex and gender issues, and the result was one of the largest protest marches ever: an estimated 4 million people in more than one hundred towns and cities. This shows Washington, D.C., where more than half a million gathered.

## Photographs, Tables, and Graphs That Are Integral to the Text

Students learn a great deal from this book's illustrations because Worth Publishers encourages authors to choose the photographs, tables, and graphs and to write captions that extend the content. *Observation Quizzes* that accompany many of them inspire readers to look more closely at certain photographs, tables, and figures. The online *Data Connections* further this process by presenting numerous charts and tables that contain detailed data for further study.

## Media and Supplements

After teaching for many years, I know personally that supplements can make or break a class, and that some publisher's representatives are helpful in explaining how to use them while others are not. Many new quizzes, videos, and other aids are available for both students and professors. Ask your publisher's representative how these might be used. I have taught with texts from many publishers; I expect you will find that Worth representatives are among the best, and you will be glad you asked for help.

**Global Decay** Thousands of children in Bangalore, India, gathered to brush their teeth together, part of an oral health campaign. Music, fast food, candy bars, and technology have been exported from the United States, and many developing nations have their own versions (Bollywood replaces Hollywood). Western diseases have also reached many nations; preventive health now follows.

## LaunchPad with *Developing Lives*, LearningCurve Quizzing, and *Data Connections* Activities

Built to solve key challenges in the course, LaunchPad gives students what they need to prepare for class and gives instructors what they need to set up a course, shape the content, craft presentations and lectures, assign and assess homework, and guide the learning of every student.

**Observation Quiz** Beyond toothbrushes, what other health tools do most children here have that their parents did not? (see answer, p. 314)

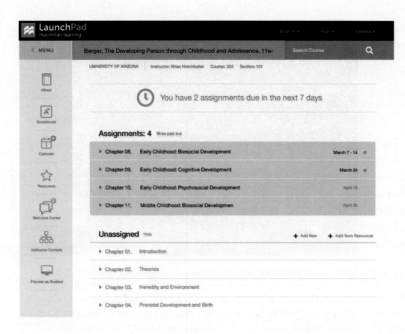

LaunchPad, which can be previewed at launchpad-works.com, includes the following:

- An **interactive e-Book,** which integrates the text with videos that aid student learning.
- **Developing Lives,** the sophisticated interactive experience in which students "raise" their own virtual child. This fascinating simulation integrates more than 200 videos and animations and includes quizzes and essay questions that are easy to assign and assess.
- **Data Connections,** interactive activities that allow students to interpret data on topics ranging from breast-feeding to risk-taking.
- The **LearningCurve adaptive quizzing system,** which is based on the latest findings from learning and memory research. It combines adaptive question selection, immediate and valuable feedback, and a gamelike interface to engage students in a learning experience that is unique to them. Each LearningCurve quiz is fully integrated with other resources in LaunchPad through the Personalized Study Plan, so students can review using Worth's extensive library of videos and activities. And state-of-the-art question analysis reports allow instructors to track the progress of individual students as well as their class as a whole.
- Worth's **Video Collection for Human Development,** which covers the full range of the course, from classic experiments (like the Strange Situation and Piaget's conservation tasks) to investigations of children's play to adolescent risk-taking. Instructors can assign these videos to students through LaunchPad or choose 1 of 50 popular video activities that combine videos with short-answer and multiple-choice questions. (For presentation purposes, our videos are also available on flash drive.)
- **Instructor's Resources,** which has been hailed as the richest collection of instructor's resources in developmental psychology. They include learning objectives, springboard topics for discussion and debate, handouts for student projects, course-planning suggestions, ideas for term projects, and a guide to audiovisual and online materials.
- **Lecture Slides,** which include two sets of prebuilt slides: one comprised of chapter art and illustrations, and another consisting of comprehensive, book-specific lectures. These slides can be used as-is or customized to fit your course needs.
- A **Test Bank** containing at least 100 multiple-choice and 70 fill-in-the-blank, true-false, and essay questions per chapter. Good test questions are critical to every course, and we have gone through each and every one of these test questions with care. We have added more challenging questions, and questions are keyed to the textbook by topic, page number, and level of difficulty. Questions can be organized by NCLEX, NAEYC, and APA goals and Bloom's taxonomy. We have also written rubrics for grading all of the essay questions in the test bank.

The Diploma computerized test bank guides instructors step by step through the process of creating a test. It also allows them to quickly add an unlimited number of questions; edit, scramble, or re-sequence items; format a test; and include pictures, equations, and media links. The accompanying gradebook enables instructors to record students' grades throughout the course and includes the capacity to sort student records, view detailed analyses of test items, curve tests, generate reports, and add weights to grades.

## Thanks

I would like to thank the academic reviewers who have read this book in every edition and who have provided suggestions, criticisms, references, and encouragement. They have all made this a better book.

I want to mention especially those who have reviewed this edition:

Chris Alas, Houston Community College
Adrienne Armstrong, Lone Star College
William Robert Aronson, Florida International University
T. M. Barratt, Arizona State University
Daniel Benkendorf, The City University of New York–Baruch College
Gina Brelsford, Pennsylvania State University–Harrisburg
Melissa A. Bright, University of Florida
Alda Cekrezi, Lone Star College
Kristi Cordell-McNulty, Angelo State University
Barbara Crosby, Baylor University
Faith T. Edwards, University of Wisconsin—Oshkosh
Naomi Ekas, Texas Christian University
Michael A. Erickson, Hawaii Pacific University
Diane Klieger Feibel, University of Cincinnati—Blue Ash College
Lori Neal Fernald, The Citadel Military College of South Carolina
Valerie C. Flores, Loyola University Chicago
Stacie Foster, Arizona State University
Kathryn Frazier, Northeastern University
Christopher Gade, Berkeley City College
Dan Grangaard, Austin Community College
Jiansheng Guo, California State University—East Bay
Pinar Gurkas, Clayton State University
E. Allison Hagood, Arapahoe Community College
Toni Stepter Harris, Virginia State University
Raquel Henry, Lone Star College—Kingwood
Danelle Hodge, California State University—San Bernadino
Vernell D. Larkin, Hopkinsville Community College
Richard Marmer, American River College
Jerry Marshall, Green River College
T. Darin Matthews, The Citadel Military College of South Carolina
Elizabeth McCarroll, Texas Woman's University
Alejandra Albarran Moses, California State University–Los Angeles
Kelly A. Warmuth, Providence College

The editorial, production, and marketing people at Worth Publishers are dedicated to meeting the highest standards of excellence. Their devotion of time, effort, and talent to every aspect of publishing is a model for the industry, and the names of all those who helped with this edition are listed on the second page of this book. I particularly would like to thank Andrea, Chris, and Chuck.

New York
July 2017

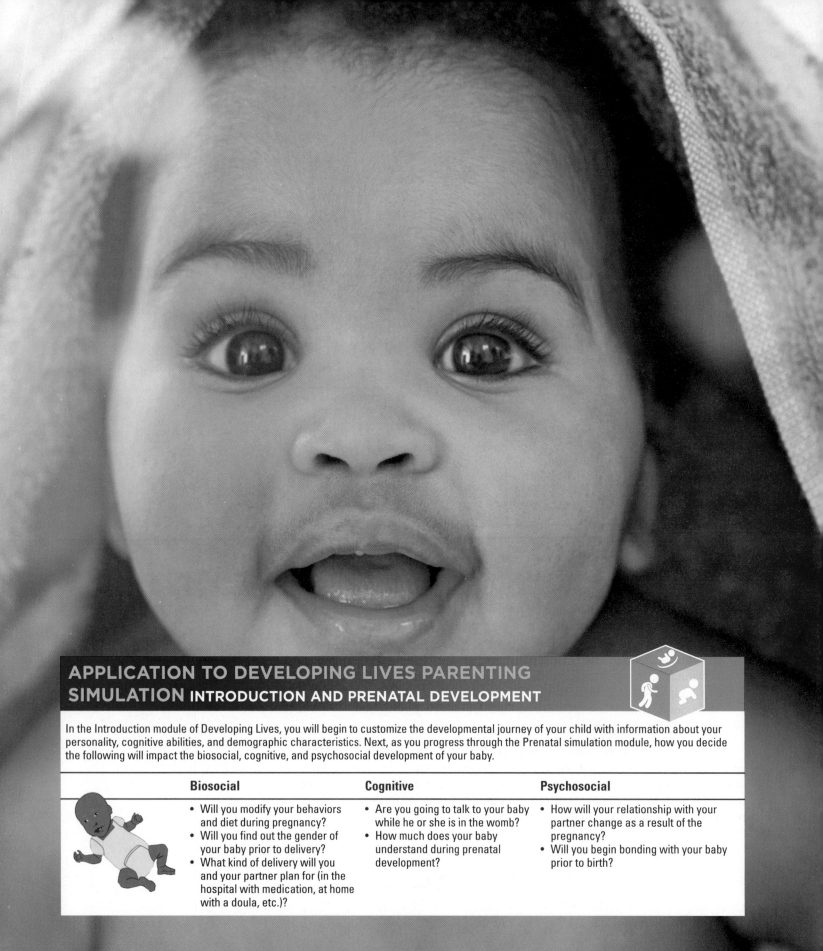

# APPLICATION TO DEVELOPING LIVES PARENTING
## SIMULATION INTRODUCTION AND PRENATAL DEVELOPMENT

In the Introduction module of Developing Lives, you will begin to customize the developmental journey of your child with information about your personality, cognitive abilities, and demographic characteristics. Next, as you progress through the Prenatal simulation module, how you decide the following will impact the biosocial, cognitive, and psychosocial development of your baby.

| | Biosocial | Cognitive | Psychosocial |
|---|---|---|---|
| | • Will you modify your behaviors and diet during pregnancy?<br>• Will you find out the gender of your baby prior to delivery?<br>• What kind of delivery will you and your partner plan for (in the hospital with medication, at home with a doula, etc.)? | • Are you going to talk to your baby while he or she is in the womb?<br>• How much does your baby understand during prenatal development? | • How will your relationship with your partner change as a result of the pregnancy?<br>• Will you begin bonding with your baby prior to birth? |

# The Beginnings

**T**he science of human development includes many beginnings. Each of the first four chapters of this text forms one corner of a solid foundation for our study.

Chapter 1 introduces definitions and dimensions, explaining research strategies and methods that help us understand how people develop. The need for science, the power of culture, and the necessity of an ecological approach are all explained.

Without ideas, our study would be only a jumble of observations. Chapter 2 provides organizing guideposts: Five major theories, each leading to many other theories and hypotheses, are described.

Chapter 3 explains heredity. Genes never act alone, yet no development—whether in body or brain, at any time, in anyone—is unaffected by DNA.

Chapter 4 details the prenatal growth of each developing person from a single cell to a breathing, grasping, crying newborn. Many circumstances—from the mother's diet to the father's care to the culture's values—affect development during every day of embryonic and fetal growth.

As you see, the science and the wonder of human life begin long before birth. These four chapters provide the basic ideas and concepts that enable us to understand each developing child—and all of the rest of us. ●●

# The Science of Human Development

## What Will You Know?*

1. Why is science especially crucial for understanding how people develop?
2. Are children always and everywhere the same, or is each child unique, changing from day to day and place to place?
3. What methods are used to study development?
4. What must scientists do to make their conclusions valid and ethical?

When I was 4 years old, professional photographers came to our house to take pictures of my mother and me, wearing matching dresses. I was bathed and dressed for the occasion, and my mother wore lipstick and perfume. Right before they came, I found a scissors and cut my hair. My mother stopped me before I could finish, but some tufts were short. She laughed, tying bows to make my hair presentable. I do not remember any of this, but my mother has told this anecdote many times. There are photographs to prove it.

What surprises you most about this memory? Is it normal for children to misbehave, or does my hair-cutting suggest something pathological—maybe defiance, or antisocial behavior? Would you have punished me if I were your child?

What about this incident reflects culture and history—maybe photographers coming to homes, mother–daughter dresses, lipstick, ribbons, scissors within a child's reach? Why did my mother laugh and cherish the memory?

This chapter introduces the developmental perspective, which seeks to answer questions like these. Every action of each child could be natural, could be cultural, or could reflect something odd about their genes or upbringing. To really understand this incident, we need research—on other 4-year-olds, on other mothers, and on my mother and me over the years.

Perhaps my mother did not want those photographers, but, as expected of wives at the time, she may have agreed to please my father. But perhaps she resented the pressure on appearance, so she was glad that I cut my hair. Does that interpretation come from my current viewpoint, not from hers? Maybe, maybe not.

You, and everyone who was ever a child, experienced dozens of incidents like this one. Are you the product of genes, culture, context, or child rearing? This chapter suggests how to find answers.

---

*What Will You Know? questions are a preview *before* each chapter, one for each major heading. They are big ideas that you will still know a decade from now, unlike the What Have You Learned? questions, which are more specific and appear *after* each major heading.

✦ **Understanding How and Why**
The Scientific Method
A VIEW FROM SCIENCE:
   Overweight Children and
   Adult Health
The Nature–Nurture
   Controversy

✦ **The Life-Span Perspective**
Development Is
   Multidirectional
Development Is
   Multicontextual
INSIDE THE BRAIN: Thinking About
   Marijuana
Development Is Multicultural
Development Is
   Multidisciplinary
Development Is Plastic
A CASE TO STUDY: David

✦ **Designing Science**
Observation
The Experiment
The Survey
Studying Development over
   the Life Span

✦ **Cautions and Challenges
   from Science**
Correlation and Causation
Quantity and Quality
Ethics

**science of human development** The science that seeks to understand how and why people of all ages change or remain the same over time.

# Understanding How and Why

The **science of human development** *seeks to understand how and why people—all kinds of people, everywhere, of every age—change or remain the same over time.* The goal is for the 7.6 billion people on Earth to fulfill their potential. Their development is *multidirectional, multicontextual, multicultural, multidisciplinary,* and *plastic*, five terms that will be explained soon.

First, however, we need to emphasize that developmental study is a *science*. It depends on theories, data, analysis, critical thinking, and sound methodology, just like every other science. All scientists ask questions and seek answers in order to ascertain "how?" and "why?"

Science is especially useful when we study people: Lives depend on it. What should pregnant women eat? How much should babies cry? When should children be punished, how, and for what? Should schools be coed or single-sex, public or private? Should education encourage independence or obedience, be optional or required, through eighth grade or twelfth grade? People disagree about all this and more, sometimes vehemently.

## The Scientific Method

Almost everyone cares about children, yet many people respond to children without understanding them. Disputes occur often because facts are unknown, and applications spring from assumptions, not from data.

### Five Crucial Steps

**scientific method** A way to answer questions using empirical research and data-based conclusions.

**hypothesis** A specific prediction that can be tested.

**empirical evidence** Evidence that is based on observation, experience, or experiment; not theoretical.

To avoid unexamined opinions, to rein in personal biases, and to discover new truths, researchers follow the five steps of the **scientific method** (see Figure 1.1):

1. *Begin with curiosity.* On the basis of theory, prior research, or a personal observation, pose a question.
2. *Develop a hypothesis.* Shape the question into a **hypothesis,** a specific prediction to be examined.
3. *Test the hypothesis.* Design and conduct research to gather **empirical evidence** (data).
4. *Analyze the evidence.* Conclude whether the hypothesis is supported or not.
5. *Report the results.* Share the data, conclusions, and alternative explanations.

## Replication

**replication** Repeating a study, usually using different participants, sometimes of another age, socioeconomic status (SES), or culture.

As you see, developmental scientists begin with curiosity and then seek the facts, drawing conclusions after careful research. Reports are written so that other scientists can examine the procedures, analyze the data, check the conclusions, and then replicate the results.

**Replication**—repeating the study with different participants—is needed before conclusions are considered solid. Scientists study the reports (Step 5) of other

**FIGURE 1.1**
**Process, Not Proof** Built into the scientific method—in questions, hypotheses, tests, and replication—is a passion for possibilities, especially unexpected ones.

1. Curiosity

2. Hypothesis

3. Test

4. Analyze data and draw conclusions

5. Report the results

scientists and build on what has gone before. Sometimes they try to duplicate a study exactly, using the same methods; often they follow up with related research (Stroebe & Strack, 2014). Conclusions are then revised, refined, rejected, or confirmed.

Obviously, the scientific method is not foolproof. Scientists may draw conclusions too hastily, misinterpret data, or ignore alternative perspectives. The results from one group of people may differ from the results from another group. Sometimes scientists discover outright fraud (Bouter, 2015). Ideally, results are replicated, not only by conducting the same research again but also by designing other research that will verify and extend the same hypothesis (Larzelere et al., 2015).

An effort to replicate 100 published studies in psychology found that about one-third did not produce the same results and another one-third were less conclusive than the original (Open Science Collaboration, 2015). Problems often arose from the research design (Step 3) of the original studies and the pressure to publish.

The push for replication is welcomed by scientists in many disciplines. For instance, educators reevaluated the effects of preschool education paid by state taxes in Virginia. They confirmed that children who attended preschool recognized nine more letters, on average, than children of the same age who did not (Huang, 2017). Since replication reveals that some well-intentioned programs are not effective, it is good to know that this one was.

Asking questions and testing hypotheses are crucial for every aspect of child development. A View from Science shows this process in more detail.

---

**A VIEW FROM SCIENCE**

## Overweight Children and Adult Health*

Obesity is a serious problem. Over the life span, from infancy to age 60, rates of obesity increase, and with it, rates of diabetes, heart disease, and stroke. The connection between overweight and disease was not always known. Indeed, the opposite seemed true.

Since tiny newborns and underweight children are more likely to die, people made a logical, but false, assumption: Heavier children must be healthier (Laraway et al., 2010).

That assumption had fatal consequences. Adults were proud of their pudgy babies and overfed their children. Not until the middle of the twentieth century, in the famous Framingham Heart Study, did scientists discover that obese adults risked premature death—of heart disease, stroke, diabetes, and many other ailments.

This discovery sparked a new question (Step 1): Was childhood obesity a health risk when those children grew up? That led to a hypothesis (Step 2) that overweight in childhood impairs health in adulthood.

This hypothesis is now widely assumed to be true. For instance, a poll found that most Californians consider childhood obesity "very serious," with one-third of them rating poor eating habits as a worse risk to child health than drug use or violence (Hennessy-Fiske, 2011). But is their assumption valid?

The best way to test that hypothesis (Step 3) is to examine adult health in people who had been weighed and measured

**What Will Become of Her?** This happy, beautiful girl in Sweden may become an overweight woman . . . or she may not. Research finds that if she slims down by adulthood, she is likely to be healthier than the average woman who was never overweight.

in childhood. Several researchers did exactly that, using data on children's height and weight—and their measurements as adults—from four studies. A summary of those studies (Juonala et al., 2011) found that most people (83 percent) maintained their relative weight. Thus most overweight children became overweight adults. (See Figure 1.2a.) Analysis of those data led to a strong conclusion (Step 4), which was then published (Step 5): Overweight children are likely to become obese adults.

---

*Many chapters of this text feature A View from Science, which explains surprising insights from recent scientific research.

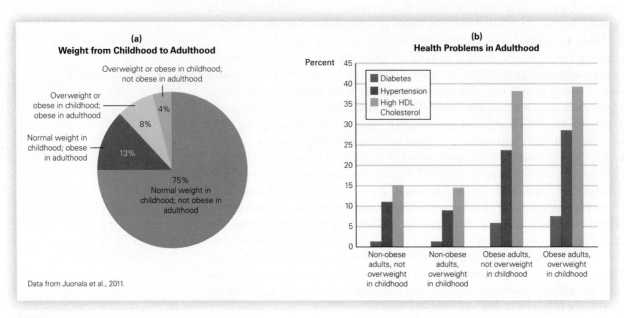

**FIGURE 1.2**

**Not Yet Obese** You probably know that more than half of all adults in the United States are overweight, so this chart—with only 21 percent of adults obese—may seem inaccurate. However, three facts explain why the data are accurate: (1) "Obese" is much heavier than overweight; (2) the average adult in this study was 34 years old (middle-aged and older adults are more often obese); and (3) one of the studies that provided much of the longitudinal data was in Finland, where rates of obesity are lower than in the United States.

Other research finds that childhood obesity is increasing in almost every nation of the world, including those countries where, in the past, malnutrition and infectious diseases were prime causes of child death. That is no longer true: Very few children die of malnutrition, but many become overweight adults, a health hazard that can be traced to childhood. As one review states it:

> The prevalence of overweight and obesity in children and adults continues to increase worldwide and, because of their association with cardiovascular disorders, diabetes, and dyslipidemia, are becoming one of the major health issues.
>
> *[Susic & Varagic, 2017, p. 139]*

For instance, in those four studies, 29 percent of the adults who were overweight all their lives had high blood pressure, compared to 11 percent of those who were never overweight (Juonala et al., 2011). Hypertension is a proven risk factor for heart disease and strokes, which are becoming the most common cause of death in poor nations (Mozaffarian et al., 2016).

A new question arose (Step 1), building on those earlier findings. What about overweight children who become normal-weight adults? Have they already harmed their health? That led to another hypothesis (Step 2): Overweight children will have a higher rate of heart attacks, strokes, diabetes, and death in adulthood, even if they slim down. The research design (Step 3) was to measure indications of health in adults who had been overweight as children but who now were normal weight.

The data (Step 4) *disproved* the hypothesis (see Figure 1.2b): As normal-weight adults, those who had been overweight as children were *not* at high risk of disease, a conclusion replicated by several studies with quite different populations (Juonala et al., 2011). Scientists were happy with that conclusion—disproving a commonly believed hypothesis may be even more welcome than proving it, because science ideally uncovers false assumptions as well as confirms true ones.

Many other issues, complications, and conclusions regarding diet are discussed later in this book. For now, all you need to remember are the steps of the scientific method and that developmentalists are right: Significant "change over time" is possible.

## The Nature–Nurture Controversy

**nature** In development, nature refers to the traits, capacities, and limitations that each individual inherits genetically from his or her parents at the moment of conception.

An easy example of the need for science concerns a great puzzle of life, the *nature–nurture debate*. **Nature** refers to the influence of the genes that people inherit. **Nurture** refers to influences from the environment, which is broadly interpreted to include the entire context of development. The environment begins with the health and diet of the embryo's mother and continues lifelong, including experiences in the family, school, community, and nation.

The nature–nurture debate has many manifestations, among them *heredity–environment, maturation–learning,* and *sex–gender.* Under whatever name, the basic question is, "How much of any characteristic, behavior, or emotion is the result of genes, and how much is the result of experience?"

Some people believe that most traits are inborn, that children are innately good ("an innocent child") or bad ("beat the devil out of them"). Others stress nurture, crediting or blaming parents, neighborhood, drugs, or even food, when someone is good or bad, a hero or a scoundrel.

Neither belief is accurate. The question is "how much," not "which," because *both* genes and the environment affect every characteristic: Nature always affects nurture, and then nurture affects nature. Even "how much" is misleading, because it implies that nature and nurture each contribute a fixed amount. Instead, the dynamic interaction between them shapes the person (Eagly & Wood, 2013; Lock, 2013; Shulman, 2016).

A further complication is that the impact of any good or bad experience—a beating, or a beer, or a blessing—is magnified or inconsequential because of the particular genes or events. Thus, every aspect of nature and nurture depends on other aspects of nature and nurture in ways that vary for each person.

## Epigenetics

The science of this interaction is explored in **epigenetics,** the study of the many ways in which the environment alters genetic expression. Epigenetics begins with methylation at conception and continues lifelong. For example, brain formation is directed by genes inherited at conception, but those genes are not alone. Soon, nutrients and toxins affect the prenatal brain, nurture affecting nature.

Not only do biological influences shape the brain, social experiences do as well. Chronic loneliness, for example, changes brain structures (Cacioppo et al., 2014). More than that, over thousands of years, human experiences shape genes. We are affected not only by our own nature and nurture but also by the nature and nurture of our parents, grandparents, and so on (Young, 2016).

Sometimes protective factors, in either nature or nurture, outweigh our liabilities. As one review explains, "there are, indeed, individuals whose genetics indicate exceptionally high risk of disease, yet they never show any signs of the disorder" (Friend & Schadt, 2014, p. 970). Why? Epigenetics. [**Developmental Link:** More discussion of epigenetics occurs in Chapter 3.]

## Dandelions and Orchids

There is increasing evidence of **differential susceptibility**—that sensitivity to any particular experience differs from one person to another because of the particular genes each person has inherited, or because of events that the person experienced years earlier.

Some people are like *dandelions*—hardy, growing and thriving in good soil or bad, with or without ample sun and rain. Other people are like *orchids*—quite wonderful, but only when ideal growing conditions are met (Ellis & Boyce, 2008; Laurent, 2014).

For example, in one study, depression in pregnant women was assessed and then the emotional maturity of their children was measured. Those children who had a particular version of the serotonin transporter gene (5-HTTLPR) were likely

**nurture** In development, nurture includes all of the environmental influences that affect the individual after conception. This includes everything from the mother's nutrition while pregnant to the cultural influences in the nation.

JANEK SKARZYNSKI/AFP/Getty Images

**Chopin's First Concert** Frederick Chopin, at age 8, played his first public concert in 1818, before photographs. But this photo shows Piotr Pawlak, a contemporary prodigy playing Chopin's music in the same Polish Palace where that famous composer played as a boy. How much of talent is genetic and how much is cultural—a nature–nurture question that applies to both boys, 200 years apart.

**epigenetics** The study of how environmental factors affect genes and genetic expression—enhancing, halting, shaping, or altering the expression of genes.

**differential susceptibility** The idea that people vary in how sensitive they are to particular experiences. Often such differences are genetic, which makes some people affected "for better or for worse" by life events. (Also called *differential sensitivity.*)

*Think Critically questions occur several times in each chapter. They are intended to provoke thought, not simple responses, and hence have no obvious answers.

**LaunchPad**
macmillan learning

**Video Activity: The Boy Who Was a Girl** examines the case of David/Brenda Reimer and what it means to be a boy or a girl.*

*Throughout the book, the margins contain descriptions of relevant online videos and activities available in LaunchPad.

**life-span perspective** An approach to the study of human development that takes into account all phases of life, not just childhood or adulthood.

to be emotionally immature *if* their mothers were depressed, but *more* mature than average if their mothers were *not* depressed (Babineau et al., 2015).

Each of us carries both joys and scars from childhood experiences that would not have affected another person. Think about your favorite teacher. What about you—either in your genes or in your experiences—made that particular teacher wonderful for you? Could that same teacher be hated, or ignored, by another student? That's differential susceptibility.

## Male and Female

The nature–nurture debate is not merely academic. In a tragic case, an infant's penis was mistakenly destroyed in 1966. At that time, sex differences were thought to originate from the genitals and child rearing, not from the genes. So his parents had his testicles removed and renamed him Brenda. They raised him as a girl (Money & Ehrhardt, 1972).

But we now know that some male–female differences are genetic and hormonal—in the brain, not the body; in nature, not nurture. After a troubled childhood, Brenda chose to become David, a man, at age 15. That was too late; David killed himself at age 38 (Diamond & Sigmundson, 1997; Associated Press, 2004).

From this example, it is tempting to conclude that all male–female differences are due to nature, but that would be incorrect. For instance, it was once believed that biology made females inferior in math. Girls who wanted to be physicists or engineers were told to choose another career. But in the 1960s millions of women insisted that nurture, not nature, kept women from excelling in math.

Consequently, more girls were allowed to study calculus. Recent international tests find that math scores of the two sexes have become quite similar: In some nations (Russia, Singapore, Algeria, and Iran) girls are ahead of boys! The practical implications of that research are that college women are encouraged to become engineers, physicists, or chemists (Brown & Lent, 2016). The scientific implications are, again, that nature and nurture interact, in sex differences and in everything else.

**WHAT HAVE YOU LEARNED?***

1. What are the five steps of the scientific method?
2. What is the difference between asking a question (Step 1) and developing a hypothesis (Step 2)?
3. Why is replication important for scientific progress?
4. What basic question is at the heart of the nature–nurture controversy?
5. When in development does nature begin to influence nurture?
6. What is the difference between genetics and epigenetics?
7. How might differential susceptibility be evident when students respond to a low exam grade?

# The Life-Span Perspective

The **life-span perspective** (Baltes, 1987; Fingerman et al., 2011; Lerner et al., 2014) began as a lens through which to view the entire human life span, particularly adult development. Insights from that perspective soon transformed our

---

*The best way to remember what you have learned is to ask yourself questions as you go along and then write the answers. These questions are a guide, but better questions are ones you write yourself.

understanding of development at every age. The crucial idea is that, at every moment in life, context and culture affect each person's past and shape their future. The life-span perspective views development as multidirectional, multicontextual, multicultural, multidisciplinary, and plastic (Baltes et al., 2006; Barrett & Montepare, 2015; Raz & Lindenberger, 2013).

## Development Is Multidirectional

Multiple changes, in every direction, characterize development. Traits appear and disappear, with increases, decreases, and zigzags (see Figure 1.3). An earlier assumption—that all development advances until about age 18, steadies, and then declines—has been soundly disproven by life-span research.

### Patterns of Change

Sometimes *discontinuity* is evident: Change can occur rapidly and dramatically, as when caterpillars become butterflies. Sometimes *continuity* is found: Growth can be gradual, as when redwoods add rings over hundreds of years. Some characteristics do not seem to change at all: The person I am now is an older version of the person I was as an infant. The same is true of you.

Children experience simple growth, radical transformation, improvement, and decline as well as stability, stages, and continuity—day to day, year to year, and generation to generation. Not only do the pace and direction of change vary, but each characteristic follows its own trajectory.

Losses in some abilities occur simultaneously with gains in others. For example, babies lose some ability to distinguish sounds from other languages when they begin talking in whatever language they hear; school-age children become quite realistic, losing some of the magical imagination of younger children.

### Critical and Sensitive Periods

The timing of losses and gains, impairments or improvements, varies as well. Some changes are sudden and profound because of a **critical period,** which is either when something *must* occur to ensure normal development or the only time when an abnormality might occur. For instance, the human embryo grows arms and legs, hands and feet, fingers and toes, each over a critical period between 28 and 54 days after conception. After that, it is too late: Unlike some insects, humans never grow replacement limbs.

We know this fact because of a tragic episode. Between 1957 and 1961, thousands of newly pregnant women in 30 nations took *thalidomide,* an antinausea drug. This change in nurture (via the mother's bloodstream) disrupted nature (the embryo's genetic program).

If an expectant woman ingested thalidomide during the critical period for limb formation, her newborn's arms or legs were malformed or absent (Moore et al., 2015, p. 480). Whether all four limbs, or just arms, hands, or fingers were missing depended on exactly when the drug was taken. If thalidomide was ingested only after day 54, no harm occurred.

Life has few such dramatic critical periods. Often, however, a particular development occurs more easily—but not exclusively—at a certain time. That is called a **sensitive period.**

An example is learning language. If children do not communicate in their first language between ages 1 and 3, they might do so later (hence, these years are

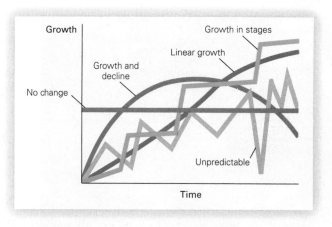

**FIGURE 1.3**

**Patterns of Developmental Growth** Many patterns of developmental growth have been discovered by careful research. Although linear (or nonlinear) progress seems most common, scientists now find that almost no aspect of human change follows the linear pattern exactly.

**critical period** A crucial time when a particular type of developmental growth (in body or behavior) must happen for normal development to occur, or when harm (such as a toxic substance or destructive event) can occur.

**sensitive period** A time when a certain type of development is most likely, although it may still happen later with more difficulty. For example, early childhood is considered a sensitive period for language learning.

John Moore/Getty Images

**I Love You, Mommy** We do not know what words, in what language, her son is using, but we do know that Sobia Akbar speaks English well, a requirement for naturalized U.S. citizens. Here she obtains citizenship for her two children born in Pakistan. Chances are they will speak unaccented American English, unlike Sobia, whose accent might indicate that she learned British English as a second language.

not critical), but their grammar is impaired (hence, these years are sensitive).

Similarly, childhood is a sensitive period for learning to speak a second or third language with native pronunciation. Adults who master new languages are asked, "Where are you from?" by those who can detect an accent, even when the speaker does not. Indeed, adults born in the United States whose first language was English reveal whether they grew up in Boston, Brooklyn, or Boise. The same is true within every other nation, as the tone, timing, and pronunciation of every language varies by region and social class.

Sometimes the multidirectional nature of development shows the influence of national culture. Childhood and adolescence are a sensitive period for attitudes about psychosocial drugs, as evident from changes in acceptance of marijuana. This is discussed further in Inside the Brain.

## Development Is Multicontextual

The second insight from the life-span perspective is that "human development is fundamentally contextual" (Pluess, 2015, p. 138). Some of the many contexts that affect development are physical (climate, noise, population density, etc.); some relate to family (parents' relationship, siblings' values, income, other relatives, etc.); and some to community (urban, suburban, or rural; multiethnic or not; etc.).

**INSIDE THE BRAIN**

## Thinking About Marijuana*

Brains are affected by drugs, for better or worse, in two ways. First, structural changes are possible in the size and activity of particular regions. Second, the links between neurons are strengthened or weakened. These findings again reveal differential susceptibility, as well as multidirectional development.

The most studied drug is alcohol, which (1) reshapes the brain during fetal development and (2) strengthens desire. As a result, (1) some newborns are brain damaged lifelong, and (2) some social drinkers suddenly find that a drink awakens neuronal links that make another drink impossible to refuse.

Now consider marijuana. Links between fear from part of the brain (the amygdala) or pleasure from other parts of the brain (especially in the basal ganglia) precede drug use. Both are multidirectional, powerfully affected by childhood. Consequently, attitudes change because of the rise and fall of fear (see Figure 1.4).

In the United States in the 1930s, marijuana was declared illegal. The 1936 movie *Reefer Madness* was shown until

about 1960, with vivid images connecting marijuana with a warped brain, suicide, and insanity. Most adolescents feared and shunned marijuana. However, marijuana was part of the jazz and popular music scene: In the 1960s, the Beatles, Bob Dylan, James Brown, and Bob Marley smoked it and sang about it.

Young adolescents listened to that music, resisted adult rules, and increasingly tried marijuana themselves. By 1980, half of all high school seniors had smoked "weed" in the previous year, according to *Monitoring the Future*, an annual report (Miech et al., 2016).

That worried older adults, whose emotional reactions to marijuana had been formed decades earlier. They believed it would permanently damage vulnerable teenage brains, leading to psychological disorders and drug addiction (Estroff & Gold, 1986).

President Nixon declared that drug abuse (especially marijuana, but not cigarettes or alcohol) was "Public Enemy Number One." A decade later, Nancy Reagan (first lady from 1981 to 1989) advocated, "Just say no to drugs." That affected the attitudes and behavior of the next cohort: By 1991, the rate of high school seniors who had *ever* tried marijuana (21 percent) was only one-third of what it had been.

---

*Inside the Brain features are new to this edition. The brain is crucial for all of development, so many findings from the study of the brain appear as regular text. Sometimes, however, more details from neurology add to our understanding. This feature presents these details.

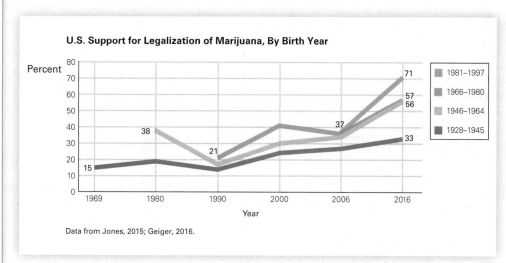

**FIGURE 1.4**

**Double Trends** Both cohort and generational trends are evident. Note that people of every age are becoming more accepting of marijuana, but the effect is most obvious for adults who never heard about "reefer madness."

**Observation Quiz** Why is the line for the 1981–1997 cohort much shorter than the line for the older cohorts? (see answer, p. 14)* ←

Attitudes, politics, and behavior are multidirectional, and so another shift has occurred. The parents of current adolescents are not from the generation that most feared the drug. One result is that far fewer (30 percent) of their teenagers think regular use of marijuana is "a great risk," compared to about 80 percent in the early 1980s. Behavior has shifted as well: In 2016, 38 percent of high school students reported smoking marijuana in the past year.

This signifies changes in the neurological links to marijuana use—irrational fears and desires. Some evidence finds that marijuana smoking alters the brain (Mandelbaum & de la Monte, 2017), but many scientists are not convinced. Some question research that finds a correlation between marijuana use and "structural abnormalities in the brains of young people," but we lack good "scientific evidence about the effects of marijuana on the adolescent brain." As a result, we are "gambling with the health and safety of our youth" (DuPont & Lieberman, 2014, p. 557).

It may be that pregnant women who use marijuana damage the brains of their fetus (Alpár et al., 2016; Volkow et al., 2017). On the other hand, some find that marijuana relieves pain, with fewer dangerous side effects (addiction and death) than prescribed opiates (Miller, 2016).

The best we have longitudinally may be from Australians who were regular users of marijuana from age 18 on. By midlife, they had more financial and relationship problems than those who were drug-free—but not more than those who abused alcohol (Cerdá et al., 2016). However, data on Australians who smoked an illegal drug 20 years ago may not apply to Americans now.

Unfortunately, federal laws passed decades ago impede current research: Longitudinal, unbiased studies on brain benefits and costs of marijuana have not been published, and earlier data may confuse correlation with causation (a topic discussed at the end of this chapter).

We know that the effects of the drug on the brain vary, and that just thinking about marijuana triggers extreme brain reactions, including phobia and ecstasy. Are current attitudes (mostly positive) more rational than the mostly negative ones of our great-grandparents? More science needed.

---

*Observation Quizzes are designed to help students practice a crucial skill, specifically to notice small details that indicate something about human development. Answers appear on the next page or two.

For example, a student might decide on a whim to stop by a social gathering instead of heading straight to the library. The social context of the party (perhaps free drinks and food, lively music, many friends, ample room, and interesting strangers) is influential, affecting that student's performance in class the next morning, and perhaps his or her future. We each encounter several contexts each day, some by choice and some not; they all could affect our later thoughts and actions.

## Ecological Systems

Leading developmentalist Urie Bronfenbrenner (1917–2005) emphasized the importance of considering contexts. Just as a naturalist studying an organism examines the ecology (the relationship between the organism and its

BartCo/E+/Getty Images

**Where in the World?** Like every child, this boy is influenced by dozens of contexts from each of Bronfenbrenner's systems, some quite direct and some in the macro- and exosystems. His cap (called a *kopiah*), diligence, all-boys school, and slanted desk each affects his learning, but those could occur in many nations—in the Americas, Europe, or Africa. In fact, this is in Asia, in Kota Bharu, Malaysia.

**ecological-systems approach** A perspective on human development that considers all of the influences from the various contexts of development. (Later renamed *bioecological theory*.)

environment) of a tiger, or a tree, or a trout, Bronfenbrenner recommended an **ecological-systems approach** (Bronfenbrenner & Morris, 2006) to study humans.

This approach recognizes three nested levels (see Figure 1.5). Most obvious are *microsystems*—each person's immediate social contexts, such as family and peer group. Next are *exosystems* (local institutions such as school and church, temple, or mosque) and then *macrosystems* (the larger social setting, including cultural values, economic conditions, and political processes).

Two more systems affect these three. One is the *chronosystem* (literally, "time system"), which is the historical context. The other is the *mesosystem,* consisting of the connections among the other systems.

Toward the end of his life, Bronfenbrenner renamed his approach *bioecological theory* to highlight the role of a sixth set of systems, those within the body (e.g., the sexual-reproductive system, the cardiovascular system) that affect the external systems (Bronfenbrenner & Morris, 2006).

Bronfenbrenner's perspective remains useful. For example, a puzzling fact is that children who have been sexually abused are likely to be abused again, in childhood and adulthood. Why? Fault of the family? The culture?

Perhaps all three and more. Psychologists using the bioecological approach to analyze repeated sexual victimization conclude that the micro-, macro-, and exosystems each have an impact (Pittenger et al., 2016).

## History and Social Class

Two contexts—the historical and the socioeconomic—are basic to understanding everyone, from conception onward. Since they are relevant to every stage, we explain them now.

**FIGURE 1.5**

**The Ecological Model** According to developmental researcher Urie Bronfenbrenner, each person is significantly affected by interactions among a number of overlapping systems, which provide the context of development. *Microsystems*—family, peer group, classroom, neighborhood, house of worship—intimately and immediately shape human development. Surrounding and supporting the microsystems are the *exosystems*, which include all the external networks, such as community structures and local educational, medical, employment, and communications systems, that affect the microsystems. Influencing both of these systems is the *macrosystem*, which includes cultural patterns, political philosophies, economic policies, and social conditions. *Mesosystems* refer to interactions among systems, as when parents and teachers coordinate to educate a child. Bronfenbrenner eventually added a fifth system, the *chronosystem*, to emphasize the importance of historical time.

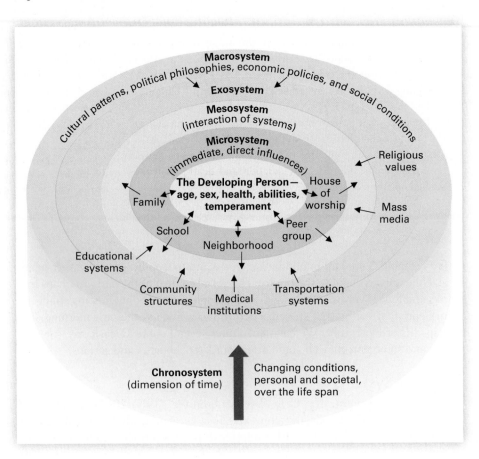

People born within a few years of one another are called a **cohort,** a group defined by its members' shared age. Cohorts travel through life together, affected by the values, events, technologies, and culture of the historical period as it interacts with their age at the time. From the moment of birth, when parents name their baby, historical context affects what may seem like a private and personal choice (see Table 1.1).

If you know someone named Emma, she is probably young: Emma is the most common name for girls born in 2015 but was not in the top 100 until 1996, and not even in the top 1,000 in 1990. If you know someone named Mary, she is probably old: About 10 percent of all girls born from 1900 to 1965 were named Mary, but now Mary is unusual.

Two of my daughters, Rachel and Sarah, have names that were common when they were born. One wishes she had a more unusual name; the other is glad she does not. That is differential susceptibility, which applies to you as well as to my daughters. Your name is influenced by history; your reaction is yours.

The second pervasive context is economic, reflected in a person's **socioeconomic status,** abbreviated **SES:** (Sometimes SES is called *social class,* as in *middle class* or *working class.*) SES reflects education, occupation, and neighborhood, as well as income.

Measuring SES is complex, especially internationally. The United Nations rates the United States and Canada as wealthy nations, but most North Americans do not consider themselves rich. (See Figure 1.6.)

SES is not just about money. Suppose a U.S. family is comprised of an infant, an unemployed mother, and a father who earns less than $17,000 a year. Their SES would be low if they live in a violent, drug-infested neighborhood and the wage earner is a high school dropout working 45 hours a week for minimum wage (in 2016, the federal minimum wage was $7.25 an hour). But SES would be much higher if the wage earner is a postdoctoral student living on campus and teaching part time. Both of these families are below the official poverty line for a family of three ($19,790), but only one is low-SES.

SES brings advantages and disadvantages, opportunities and limitations—all affecting housing, health, nutrition, knowledge, and habits. Although low income

| TABLE 1.1 |
| --- |
| **Popular First Names** |
| **Girls** |
| 2015: Emma, Olivia, Sophia, Isabella, Ava |
| 1995: Jessica, Ashley, Emily, Samantha, Sarah |
| 1975: Jennifer, Amy, Heather, Melissa, Angela |
| 1955: Mary, Deborah, Linda, Debra, Susan |
| 1935: Mary, Shirley, Barbara, Betty, Patricia |
| **Boys** |
| 2015: Noah, Liam, Mason, Jacob, William |
| 1995: Michael, Matthew, Christopher, Jacob, Joshua |
| 1975: Michael, Jason, Christopher, James, David |
| 1955: Michael, David, James, Robert, John |
| 1935: Robert, James, John, William, Richard |
| Information from U.S. Social Security Administration. |

**cohort** People born within the same historical period who therefore move through life together, experiencing the same events, new technologies, and cultural shifts at the same ages. For example, the effect of the Internet varies depending on what cohort a person belongs to.

**socioeconomic status (SES)** A person's position in society as determined by income, occupation, education, and place of residence. (Sometimes called *social class.*)

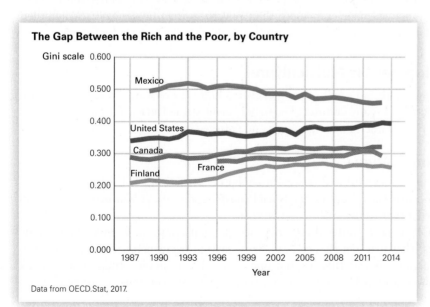

**The Gap Between the Rich and the Poor, by Country**

Data from OECD.Stat, 2017.

**FIGURE 1.6**

**Children of the Future** The United States is an exception to a general rule: the wealthier a nation, the smaller the income gap. Since young families tend to be the least wealthy, and since education and health care are affected by neighborhood and employment, a wide gap bodes ill for children. Particularly troubling are the trend lines—unless changes occur, the United States will be worse than Mexico by 2035.

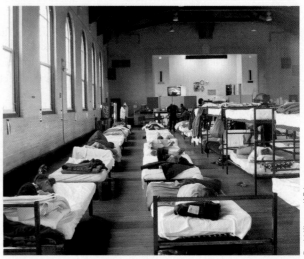

**Same Situation, Far Apart: Shelter Rules** The homeless shelter in Paris, France *(left)* allows dogs, Christmas trees, and flat-screen televisions for couples in private rooms. The one in Cranston, Rhode Island *(right)* is only for men (no women, children, or dogs), who must leave each morning and wait in line each night for one of the 88 beds. Both places share one characteristic: Some of the homeless are turned away, as there is not room for everyone.

**● Answer to Observation Quiz** (from p. 11) Because surveys rarely ask children their opinions, and the youngest cohort on this graph did not reach adulthood until about 2005.

**culture** A system of shared beliefs, norms, behaviors, and expectations that persist over time and prescribe social behavior and assumptions.

**social construction** An idea that arises from shared perceptions, not on objective reality. Many age-related terms (such as *childhood, adolescence, yuppie,* and *senior citizen*) are social constructions, strongly influenced by social assumptions.

obviously limits a child, other factors are pivotal, especially education and national policy.

For example, the nations of northern Europe seek to eliminate SES disparities as much as possible, and the health and school achievement of children from their low-income families are not far behind the richest children. By contrast, developing nations, especially in Latin America, tend to have large SES achievement gaps (Ravallion, 2014). Among advanced nations, the United States has "recently earned the distinction of being the most unequal of all developed countries" (Aizer & Currie, 2014, p. 856). Such differences by nation are a result of the macrosystem, not the microsystem.

Income differences are not only found by ethnic group but also by age. Young children with young parents are poorest, and poverty in early childhood reduces academic achievement even more than poverty during adolescence (Wagmiller, 2015). The reason probably relates to the quality of education before age 5.

## Development Is Multicultural

In order to study "all kinds of people, everywhere, at every age," research must include people of many cultures. For social scientists, **culture** is far more than food or clothes; it is a set of ideas, beliefs, and patterns of behavior.

### Creating Culture

Culture is a powerful and pervasive **social construction,** that is, a concept created, or *constructed,* by a society. Social constructions affect how people think and act—what they value, ignore, and punish.

Although most adults think they accept, appreciate, and understand many cultures, that may not be accurate. It is easy to overgeneralize, becoming simplistic about cultures that are not one's own. For example, when people speak of Asian culture or Hispanic culture, they may be stereotyping, ignoring cultural differences between people from Korea and Japan, for instance, or those from Mexico and Guatemala.

Every generalization risks harming individuals. For example, the idea that Asian children are the "model minority" increases the pressure on children to excel, and then to be teased when they do. Further, some people in every group deliberately rebel against the expected beliefs and behaviors from their culture.

Thus, the words *culture* and *multicultural* need to be used carefully, especially when they are applied to individuals, lest one slides from awareness to stereotype.

In a diverse nation such as the United States, everyone is multicultural. Within each person, ethnic, national, school, and family cultures sometimes clash, with no one a pristine exemplar of only one culture. One of my students, whose parents had immigrated to the United States, wrote:

> My mom was outside on the porch talking to my aunt. I decided to go outside; I guess I was being nosey. While they were talking I jumped into their conversation which was very rude. When I realized what I did it was too late. My mother slapped me in my face so hard that it took a couple of seconds to feel my face again.
>
> *[C., personal communication]*

Notice how my student reflects her mother's culture; she labels herself "nosey" and "very rude." She later wrote that she expects children to be seen, not heard. Her son makes her "very angry" when he interrupts.

In this example, she and her son both reflect U.S. culture, where talkative children are encouraged, as well as the culture of her mother's homeland, where they are not. Do you think my student was nosey or, on the contrary, that her mother should not have slapped her? Or do you hesitate to choose either option? Your answer—or non-answer—reflects your culture.

As with my student's mother, people tend to believe that their culture is better than others. This belief has benefits: People who endorse their culture's attitudes and habits tend to be happy, proud, and willing to help strangers. However, that belief becomes destructive if it reduces respect for people from other groups. Thoughtlessly, differences are assumed to be inferior (Akhtar & Jaswal, 2013).

**Hard Floor, Hard Life** These are among the thousands of unaccompanied minors who fled Latin America and arrived in Arizona and Texas in 2014. Developmentalists predict that the effects of their hazardous journey will stay with them, unless sources of resilience—such as caring family and supportive community—are quickly found. Culture and context affect everyone lifelong.

**Observation Quiz** How many children are sleeping here in this photograph? (see answer, p. 16) ↑

## Difference and Deficit

Developmentalists recognize the **difference-equals-deficit error,** which is the assumption that people unlike us (difference) are inferior (deficit). Sadly, when humans notice that someone else does not think or act as they do, the human tendency is to believe that such a person is to be pitied, feared, or encouraged to change. Even 3-year-olds assume that the way things are done by their parents, or in their community, is the right way (Schmidt et al., 2016).

The difference-equals-deficit error is one reason that a careful multicultural approach is necessary. Never assume that another culture is wrong and inferior—or the opposite, right and superior. Assumptions can be harmful.

For example, one Japanese child, on her first day in a U.S. school, was teased for the food she brought for lunch. The next day, when she arrived at school, she dumped the contents of her lunchbox in the garbage—she would rather go hungry than be considered deficient.

This example illustrates the problem with judging another culture: A Japanese lunch might, or might not, be healthier than a typical American one. The children

**difference-equals-deficit error** The mistaken belief that a deviation from some norm is necessarily inferior to behavior or characteristics that meet the standard.

**Video: Research of Geoffrey Saxe** further explores how difference does not equal deficit.

did not know or care about nutrition; they assumed that their usual lunch was best. Meanwhile, the Japanese child's mother may have thought she was packing a better lunch than the standard U.S. one.

To further develop a multicultural perspective, we need to differentiate *culture, ethnicity,* and *race*. Members of an **ethnic group** almost always share ancestral heritage and often have the same national origin, religion, and language. That shared history affects them when they are far from their original home.

Consequently, ethnic groups often share a culture, but this is not always true (see Figure 1.7). There are "multiple intersecting and interacting dimensions" to ethnic identity (Sanchez & Vargas, 2016, p. 161). People may share ethnicity but differ culturally, especially if they left their original home long ago and adopted the culture of their new place, such as people of Irish descent in Ireland, Australia, and North America. The opposite is also true: People of many ethnic groups may all share a culture, as evident in all the people who identify with British, American, or Canadian culture.

Ethnicity is a social construction, a product of the social context, not biology. It is nurture, not nature, with specifics dependent on the other people nearby. For example, African-born people in North America typically consider themselves African, but African-born people in Africa identify with a more specific ethnic group. Awareness of ethnicity has increased in the United States, in part because the recent influx of immigrants has awakened an interest in family history among many Americans. People in the United States are more aware of ethnicity and race than people elsewhere (Verkuyten, 2016). That itself is cultural.

Some Americans are puzzled by civil wars in distant nations (e.g., in Syria, or Sri Lanka, or Kenya), where bitter enemies may appear to be of the same ethnicity. Do not be surprised: Within every nation, people recognize ethnic differences that outsiders do not see. Social constructions are potent.

Ethnic identity flourishes when co-ethnics are nearby, when ethnic distinctions are visible, and people of other groups emphasize differences (Sanchez & Vargas, 2016). For those reasons, **race,** thought to signify biological distinctions, may be confused with ethnicity.

That mistake was made in South Africa. Apartheid separated the population into four distinct groups, supposedly racial ones: White, Black, Coloured, and Asian. This simple division was one reason that the end of apartheid was called a "bloodless revolution," with no violence between Whites and Blacks. However, there was extensive violence among Black groups, not noted at first in the press because Westerners did not expect or understand it (Thompson & Berat, 2014).

Social scientists are convinced that race is a social construction, without biological usefulness. Skin color is particularly misleading, because dark-skinned people with African ancestors have the "highest levels of genetic diversity" (Tishkoff et al., 2009, p. 1035), and because many dark-skinned people whose ancestors were not African share neither culture nor ethnicity with Africans.

Concern that the word *race* is inaccurate and misleading is expressed by biologists as well as social scientists. As one team writes:

> We believe the use of biological concepts of race in human genetic research—so disputed and so mired in confusion—is problematic at best and harmful at worst. It is time for biologists to find a better way.
>
> *[Yudell et al., 2016, p. 564]*

---

**ethnic group** People whose ancestors were born in the same region and who often share a language, culture, and religion.

**Answer to Observation Quiz** (from p. 15) Nine—not counting the standing boy or the possible tenth one whose head is under the blanket. Rumpled blankets suggest that eight more are elsewhere at the moment. Each night hundreds of children sleep in this Border Protection Processing Facility in Brownsville, Texas. They are detained while authorities decide whether to send them back to the countries they fled or to a safe place in the United States.

**THINK CRITICALLY:** To fight racism, must race be named and recognized?

**race** A group of people who are regarded by themselves or by others as distinct from other groups on the basis of physical appearance, typically skin color. Social scientists think race is a misleading concept, as biological differences are not signified by outward appearance.

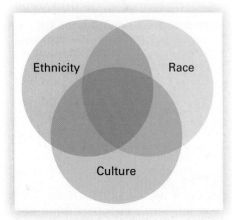

**FIGURE 1.7**
**Overlap—But How Much?** Ethnicity, culture, and race are three distinct concepts, but they often—though not always—overlap.

However, the fact that race is a social construction does not make it irrelevant. African American adolescents who are proud of their race are likely to achieve academically, resist drug addiction, and feel better about themselves (Zimmerman et al., 2013). Thousands of medical, educational, and economic conditions—from low birthweight to college graduation, from home ownership to marriage rates—reflect racial disparities.

Thus, some social scientists believe that, in order to overcome racism, race must be recognized. They say that to be "color-blind" is to be racist (Neville et al., 2016). Perhaps. In any case, remember that race is a social construction, not a biological one, and that it indicates neither culture nor ethnicity.

## Development Is Multidisciplinary

Historically, the various specialities within universities were each called a *discipline*. This continues, but developmental science is increasingly multidisciplinary (Lerner et al., 2014). The reason is that every academic discipline risks becoming a *silo*, a storage tank for research in that discipline, isolated from other disciplines. Breaking out of silos is crucial for understanding the whole person.

Nonetheless, scientists need to burrow into specific aspects of human life in order to fully grasp the developmental process. For that reason, development is often divided into three domains—*biosocial, cognitive*, and *psychosocial*. (Figure 1.8 describes each domain.) Each domain is the focus of several academic disciplines: Biosocial includes biology, neuroscience, and medicine; cognitive includes psychology, linguistics, and education; and psychosocial includes sociology, economics, and history.

## Genetics

The need for multidisciplinary research is obvious when considering genetic analysis. When the human genome was first mapped in 2003, some people assumed that humans became whatever their genes destined them to be—heroes, killers, or

Mike Coppola/Getty Images

**Fitting In** The best comedians are simultaneously outsider and insider, giving them a perspective that helps people laugh at the absurdity of their lives. Trevor Noah—son of a Xhosa South African mother and a German Swiss father—grew up within, yet outside, his native culture. For instance, he was seen as "Coloured" in his homeland, but as "White" on a video, which once let him escape arrest!

● **Observation Quiz** What four aspects of Noah's attire signify that he belongs at this fashion gala? (see answer, p. 19) ↑

---

**DOMAINS OF HUMAN DEVELOPMENT**

| Biosocial | Cognitive | Psychosocial |
|---|---|---|
| Includes all the growth and change that occur in a person's body and the genetic, nutritional, and health factors that affect that growth and change. Motor skills—everything from grasping a rattle to driving a car—are also part of the biological domain. In this book, this domain is called biosocial, rather than physical or biological. | Includes all the mental processes that a person uses to obtain knowledge or to think about the environment. Cognition encompasses perception, imagination, judgment, memory, and language—the processes people use to think, decide, and learn. Education—not only the formal curriculum in schools but also informal learning—is part of this domain as well. | Includes development of emotions, temperament, and social skills. Family, friends, the community, the culture, and the larger society are particularly central to the psychosocial domain. For example, cultural differences in gender roles or in family structures are part of this domain. |

**FIGURE 1.8**

**The Three Domains** The division of human development into three domains makes it easier to study, but remember that very few factors belong exclusively to one domain or another. Development is not piecemeal but holistic: Each aspect of development is related to all three domains.

# Diverse Complexities

It is often repeated that "the United States is becoming more diverse," a phrase that usually refers only to ethnic diversity and not to economic and religious diversity (which are also increasing and merit attention). From a developmental perspective, two other diversities are also important—age and region, as shown below. What are the implications for schools, colleges, employment, health care, and nursing homes in the notable differences in the ages of people of various groups? And are attitudes about immigration, or segregation, or multiracial identity affected by the ethnicity of one's neighbors?

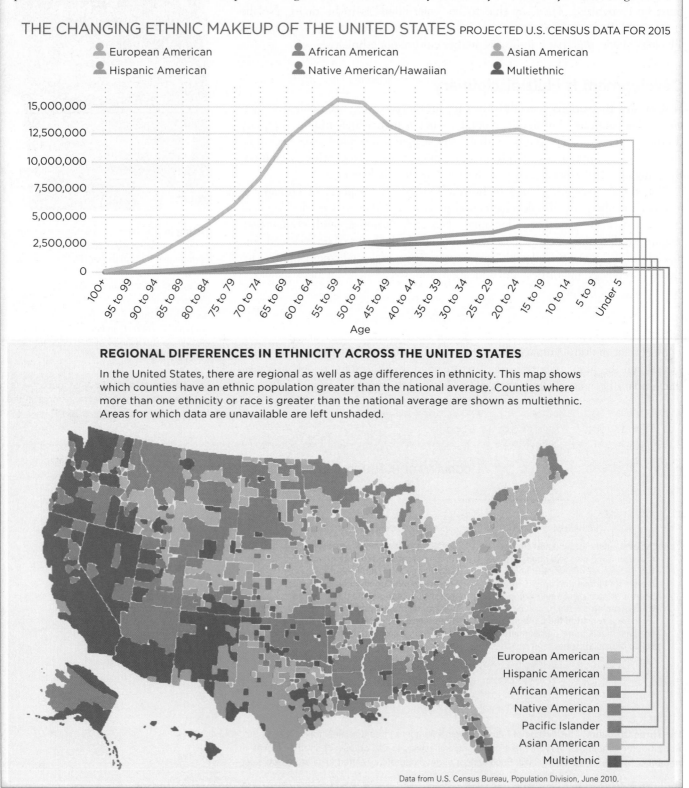

## THE CHANGING ETHNIC MAKEUP OF THE UNITED STATES PROJECTED U.S. CENSUS DATA FOR 2015

European American    African American    Asian American
Hispanic American    Native American/Hawaiian    Multiethnic

Age

## REGIONAL DIFFERENCES IN ETHNICITY ACROSS THE UNITED STATES

In the United States, there are regional as well as age differences in ethnicity. This map shows which counties have an ethnic population greater than the national average. Counties where more than one ethnicity or race is greater than the national average are shown as multiethnic. Areas for which data are unavailable are left unshaded.

European American
Hispanic American
African American
Native American
Pacific Islander
Asian American
Multiethnic

Data from U.S. Census Bureau, Population Division, June 2010.

ordinary people. Biology was thought to be destiny: For example, thousands of scientists searched for a particular gene that would make a person develop alcohol use disorder, schizophrenia, or diabetes. And those thousands failed. Multidisciplinary research shows that many influences from many domains make a person more, or less, likely to have specific traits.

Yes, genes affect every aspect of behavior. But even identical twins, with identical genes, differ physically, cognitively, and socially. The reasons abound, including non-DNA influences in utero and their position in the womb, both of which affect birthweight and birth order, and dozens of other epigenetic influences throughout life (Carey, 2012). [**Developmental Link:** Mapping of the human genome is discussed in Chapter 3.] The need for many disciplines to understand the effect of genes is evident in our discussion of dandelions and orchids, and of nature and nurture.

Overall, multidisciplinary research broadens and deepens our knowledge. People are complex. A proper grasp of all of the systems—from the workings of the microbiome in the gut to the effects of climate change in the entire world—requires scientific insights from many disciplines. Adding to this complexity, people change over time. That leads to the final theme of the life-span perspective, plasticity.

## Development Is Plastic

The term **plasticity** denotes two complementary aspects of development: (1) Human traits can be molded (as plastic can be), yet (2) people maintain a certain durability of identity (as plastic does). The concept of plasticity in development provides both hope and realism—hope because change is possible, and realism because development builds on what has come before.

## Dynamic Systems

Plasticity is basic to our contemporary understanding of human development (Lerner, 2009). This is evident in the **dynamic-systems approach.** The idea is that human development is an ongoing, ever-changing interaction between the body and mind and between the individual and every aspect of the environment, including all of the systems described in the ecological-systems approach.

Note the word *dynamic*: Physical contexts, emotional influences, the passage of time, each person, and every aspect of the ecosystem are always interacting, always in flux, always in motion. For instance, a new approach to developing the motor skills of children with autism spectrum disorder stresses the dynamic systems that undergird movement—the changing aspects of the physical and social contexts (Lee & Porretta, 2013). [**Developmental Link:** Autism spectrum disorder is discussed in Chapter 11.]

Similarly, a dynamic-systems approach to understanding the role of fathers in child development takes into account the sex and age of the child, the role of the mother, and the cultural norms of fatherhood. The result is a complex mix of complementary effects—and, dynamically, this affects the child in diverse ways as plasticity of family systems would predict (Cabrera, 2015).

The dynamic-systems approach builds on the multidirectional, multicontextual, multicultural, and multidisciplinary nature of development. With any developmental topic, stage, or problem, the dynamic-systems approach urges consideration of all the interrelated aspects, every social and cultural factor, over days and years. Plasticity and the need for a dynamic-systems approach are most evident

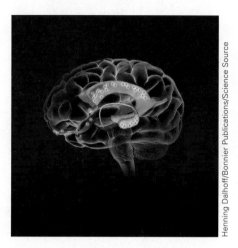

Henning Dalhoff/Bonnier Publications/Science Source

**Birth of a Neuron** A decade ago, neuroscientists thought that adult brains lost neurons, with age or alcohol, but never gained them. Now we know that precursors of neurons arise in the lateral ventricles (bright blue, center) to become functioning neurons in the olfactory bulb (for smell, far left) and the hippocampus (for memory, the brown structure just above the brain stem). Adult neurogenesis is much less prolific than earlier in life, but the fact that it occurs at all is astounding.

**plasticity** The idea that abilities, personality, and other human characteristics can change over time. Plasticity is particularly evident during childhood, but even older adults are not always "set in their ways."

**dynamic-systems approach** A view of human development as an ongoing, ever-changing interaction between the physical, cognitive, and psychosocial influences. The crucial understanding is that development is never static but is always affected by, and affects, many systems of development.

when considering the actual lived experience of each individual. My nephew David (A Case to Study, below) is one example.

Plasticity emphasizes that people can and do change, that predictions are not always accurate. Even "brain anatomy can change noticeably as a function of learning" (Zatorre, 2013, p. 587).

The early months and years are especially plastic, "for better or for worse" (Hartman & Belsky, 2015). Parent responses, early education, nutrition, and exercise put each child on a path. With each year, it is increasingly difficult to change direction. However, plasticity means that even adults can chart a new course.

**Comfortable Routine?** This 37-year-old father in Stockholm, Sweden, uses his strong tattooed arm to buckle his daughter's sandals—caregiving as millions of contemporary men do. Plasticity means that many sex differences that were thought to be innate are actually the result of culture and experience. Is this an example?

---

## A CASE TO STUDY

# David*

My sister-in-law contracted rubella (also called German measles) early in her third pregnancy; it was not diagnosed until David was born, blind and dying. Immediate heart surgery saved his life, but surgery to remove a cataract activated a hidden virus and destroyed that eye.

The eye doctor was horrified at the unexpected results of surgery, and he decided that the cataract on the other eye should not be removed until the virus was finally gone. But one dead eye and one thick cataract meant that David's visual system was severely impaired for the first five years of his life. That affected all of his other systems.

For instance, he interacted with other children by pulling their hair. Fortunately, the virus that had damaged the embryo occurred after the critical period for hearing. As dynamic systems might predict, David developed extraordinary listening ability in response to his diminished sight.

The virus harmed many other aspects of fetal development—thumbs, ankles, teeth, toes, spine, and brain. David attended three special preschools—for the blind, for children with cerebral palsy, for children who were intellectually disabled. At age 6, when some sight was restored, he entered regular public school, learning academics but not social skills—partly because he was excluded from physical education and recess.

By age 10, David had blossomed intellectually: He had skipped a year of school and was in fifth grade, reading at the

**My Brother's Children** Michael, Bill, and David (left to right) are adults now, with quite different personalities, abilities, numbers of offspring (4, 2, and none), and contexts (in Massachusetts, Pennsylvania, and California). Yet despite genes, prenatal life, and contexts, I see the shared influence of Glen and Dot, my brother and sister-in-law—evident here in their similar, friendly smiles.

eleventh-grade level. Before age 20, he learned to speak a second and a third language. In emerging adulthood, he enrolled in college.

As development unfolded, the interplay of systems was evident. David's family context allowed him to become a productive and happy adult. He told me, "I try to stay in a positive mood." This was especially important when David's father died in 2014. David accepted the death (he said, "Dad is in a better place") and comforted his mother.

---

*Many chapters include the feature A Case to Study. Each person is unique, which means that generalities cannot be validly drawn from one case, but sometimes one example makes a general concept clear.

Remember, plasticity cannot erase a person's genes, childhood, or permanent damage. The brain destruction and compensation from that critical period of prenatal development remain. David is now 50. He still lives with his widowed mother. They both need each other.

Despite David's lifelong disabilities, his listening skills continue to be impressive. He once told me:

> I am generally quite happy, but secretly a little happier lately, especially since November, because I have been consistently getting a pretty good vibrato when I am singing, not only by myself

but also in congregational hymns in church. [*He explained vibrato:*] When a note bounces up and down within a quartertone either way of concert pitch, optimally between 5.5 and 8.2 times per second.

David works as a translator of German texts, which he enjoys because, as he says, "I like providing a service to scholars, giving them access to something they would otherwise not have." As his aunt, I have seen him repeatedly overcome disabilities. Plasticity is dramatically evident. This case illustrates all five aspects of the life-span perspective (see Table 1.2).

## TABLE 1.2

### Five Characteristics of Development

| Characteristic | Application in David's Story |
|---|---|
| *Multidirectional.* Change occurs in every direction, not always in a straight line. Gains and losses, predictable growth, and unexpected transformations are evident. | David's development seemed static (or even regressive, as when early surgery destroyed one eye), but then it accelerated each time he entered a new school or college. |
| *Multidisciplinary.* Numerous academic fields—especially psychology, biology, education, and sociology, but also neuroscience, economics, religion, anthropology, history, medicine, genetics, and many more—contribute insights. | Two disciplines were particularly critical: medicine (David would have died without advances in surgery on newborns) and education (special educators guided him and his parents many times). |
| *Multicontextual.* Human lives are embedded in many contexts, including historical conditions, economic constraints, and family patterns. | The high SES of David's family made it possible for him to receive daily medical and educational care. His two older brothers protected him. |
| *Multicultural.* Many cultures—not just between nations but also within them—affect how people develop. | Appalachia, where David lived, is more accepting of people with disabilities. |
| *Plasticity.* Every individual, and every trait within each individual, can be altered at any point in the life span. Change is ongoing, although it is neither random nor easy. | David's measured IQ changed from about 40 (severely intellectually disabled) to about 130 (far above average), and his physical disabilities became less crippling as he matured. |

## WHAT HAVE YOU LEARNED?

1. What aspects of development show continuity?

2. What is the difference between a critical period and a sensitive period?

3. Why is it useful to know when sensitive periods occur?

4. What did Bronfenbrenner emphasize in his ecological-systems approach?

5. What are some of the social contexts of life?

6. How does cohort differ from age group?

7. What factors comprise a person's SES?

8. How might male–female differences be examples of the difference-equals-deficit error?

9. What is the difference between race and ethnicity?

10. What is the problem with each discipline having its own silo?

11. How is human development plastic?

**scientific observation** A method of testing a hypothesis by unobtrusively watching and recording participants' behavior in a systematic and objective manner—in a natural setting, in a laboratory, or in searches of archival data.

## Designing Science

To verify or refute a hypothesis (Step 2), researchers must choose among hundreds of research designs and decide who, what, how, and when to study (Step 3) in order to gather results that will lead to valid conclusions (Step 4) that are worth publishing (Step 5). Often they use statistics to discover relationships between various aspects of the data. (See Table 1.3.)

Every research design, method, and statistic has strengths as well as weaknesses. Understanding these helps people assess whether the conclusions of a particular study are solid or flimsy, believable or open to doubt. To help you evaluate what you learn, here are three basic research strategies and three ways to study change over time.

## Observation

Yogi Berra famously said, "You can observe a lot just by watching." Like many of his sayings, that quote is amusing but also deep. Scientists agree with Berra.

**Scientific observation** requires researchers to record behavior systematically and objectively. Observations often occur in a naturalistic setting such as a public park or a home, as people go about their daily lives. Scientific observation can also

### TABLE 1.3

**Statistical Measures Often Used to Analyze Search Results**

| Measure | Use |
| --- | --- |
| Effect size | There are many kinds, but the most useful in reporting studies of development is called *Cohen's d*, which can indicate the power of an intervention. An effect size of 0.2 is called small, 0.5 moderate, and 0.8 large. |
| Significance | Indicates whether the results might have occurred by chance. If chance would produce the results only 5 times in 100, that is significant at the 0.05 level; once in 100 times is 0.01; once in 1,000 is 0.001. |
| Cost-benefit analysis | Calculates how much a particular independent variable costs versus how much it saves. This is useful for analyzing public spending, finding that preschool education, or preventative health measures, save money. |
| Odds ratio | Indicates how a particular variable compares to a standard, set at 1. For example, one study found that, although less than 1 percent of all child homicides occurred at school, the odds were similar for public and private schools. The odds of it in high schools, however, were 18.47 times that of elementary or middle schools (set at 1.0) (MMWR, January 18, 2008). |
| Factor analysis | Hundreds of variables could affect any given behavior. In addition, many variables (such as family income and parental education) overlap. To take this into account, analysis reveals variables that can be clustered together to form a factor, which is a composite of many variables. For example, SES might become one factor, child personality another. |
| Meta-analysis | A "study of studies." Researchers use statistical tools to synthesize the results of previous, separate studies. Then they analyze the accumulated results, using criteria that weigh each study fairly. This approach improves data analysis by combining studies that were too small, or too narrow, to lead to solid conclusions. |

be done in a laboratory, where scientists record human reactions, often with wall-mounted video cameras and the scientist in another room.

Observation is crucial to develop hypotheses. However, observation does not prove a hypothesis.

For example, in one study of children arriving at a preschool, several weeks after the start of the year, scientists observed how long parents stayed to hug and kiss their children before saying goodbye. When parents lingered three minutes or more, their "children spent less time involved in the preschool peer social environment," measured by whether the child looked at or played with other children (Grady et al., 2012, p. 1690).

The authors suggest that this "has implications for not only children's later peer interactions and peer status, but also for children's engagement in school and, ultimately, academic achievement" (J. Grady et al., 2012, p. 1690). Perhaps, by staying, the parents made the children anxious about school.

But those implications are not proven. Perhaps parents of shy children stayed to help the children become more comfortable with school. Contrary to the researchers' speculation, those children might become academically strong later on. Thus, the data led to two alternative hypotheses: (1) Parental anxiety impairs child social engagement, or (2) shy children are given parental support. More research is needed.

## The Experiment

The **experiment** proves what causes what. In the social sciences, experimenters typically do something to a group of participants or expose them to something and then note their reaction.

In technical terms, the experimenters manipulate an **independent variable,** which is the imposed treatment or special condition (also called the *experimental variable*; a *variable* is anything that can vary). They note whether and how the independent variable affects whatever they are studying, called the **dependent variable** (which *depends* on the independent variable).

Thus, the independent variable is the possible cause; the dependent variable is the result. The purpose of an experiment is to see whether the independent variable affects the dependent variable. In other words, *what* (independent variable) causes *what* (dependent variable).

**experiment** A research method in which the researcher tries to determine the cause-and-effect relationship between two variables by manipulating one (called the *independent variable*) and then observing and recording the ensuing changes in the other (called the *dependent variable*).

**independent variable** In an experiment, the variable that is introduced to see what effect it has on the dependent variable. (Also called *experimental variable*.)

**dependent variable** In an experiment, the variable that may change as a result of whatever new condition or situation the experimenter adds. In other words, the dependent variable *depends* on the independent variable.

**What Can You Learn?** Scientists first establish what is, and then they try to change it. In one recent experiment, Deb Kelemen (shown here) established that few children under age 12 understand a central concept of evolution (natural selection). Then she showed an experimental group a picture book illustrating the idea. Success! The independent variable (the book) affected the dependent variable (the children's ideas), which confirmed Kelemen's hypothesis: Children can understand natural selection if instruction is tailored to their ability.

Rick Friedman/Corbis via Getty Images

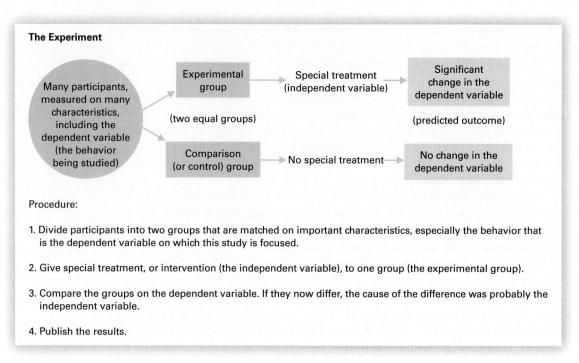

**FIGURE 1.9**

**How to Conduct an Experiment** The basic sequence diagrammed here applies to all experiments. Many additional features, especially the statistical measures listed in Table 1.3 and various ways of reducing experimenter bias, affect whether publication occurs. (Scientific journals reject reports of experiments that were not rigorous in method and analysis.)

🔵 **Especially for Nurses\*** In the field of medicine, why are experiments conducted to test new drugs and treatments? (see response, p. 26)

\*Since many students reading this book are preparing to be teachers, health care professionals, police officers, or parents, every chapter contains Especially For questions, which encourage students to apply important developmental concepts.

**survey** A research method in which information is collected from a large number of people by interviews, written questionnaires, or some other means.

In a typical experiment (as diagrammed in Figure 1.9), at least two groups of participants are studied. One group, the *experimental group,* receives the particular treatment or condition (the independent variable); the other group, the *comparison group* (also called the *control group*), does not.

To follow up on the observation study above, researchers could experiment. For example, they could assess the social skills (dependent variable) of hundreds of children in the first week of school and then require parents in half of the classes to linger at drop-off (independent variable, experimental group), and in the other classes, ask the parents to leave immediately or let the parents do whatever they thought best (both control or comparison groups).

Several months later, the social skills (dependent variable) of the children could be measured again. A few years later, their school achievement (another dependent variable) could be recorded. Would this experiment prove that lingering at drop-off caused later academic success?

## The Survey

A third research method is the **survey,** in which information is collected from a large number of people by interview, questionnaire, or some other means. This is a quick, direct way to obtain data. It avoids assuming that the people we know are representative of people in general.

For example, perhaps you know an 8-year-old boy who is a bully, or a 16-year-old girl who is pregnant. Some people might jump to the conclusion that boys are bullies and that many teenagers have babies. But one of the lessons from science is that *one case proves nothing.* At best, it raises questions, or provides an example of something found in research that included hundreds of participants.

If you surveyed several hundred people, you would discover that most boys are not bullies and that the birth rate of 15- to 19-year-old women has fallen steadily in past decades, from a peak of 96 per 1,000 in 1957 to 22 per 1,000 in 2015. Births are increasing in only one group, those over age 35. For instance, in 2015, the birth rate for women aged 35 to 39 was 52 per 1,000, more than twice that of the birth rate for women aged 15 to 19 (Martin et al., 2016).

These birth data come from birth certificates, which are more accurate than surveys. Indeed, although surveys are quick and direct, they are not always accurate. People sometimes lie to please the researcher, and answers are influenced by the wording and the sequence of the questions.

Survey respondents may even lie to themselves. For instance, every two years since 1991, high school students in the United States have been surveyed confidentially. The most recent survey included 15,713 students from all 50 states and from schools large and small, public and private (MMWR, June 10, 2016).

Students are asked whether they had sexual intercourse *before* age 13. Every year, more ninth-grade boys than eleventh-grade boys say they had sex before age 13, yet those eleventh-graders were ninth-graders a few years before (see Figure 1.10).

Why? Do ninth-graders lie because they want to appear sexually active? Or do eleventh-graders lie because they are embarrassed by their earlier actions? Or do some students forget, or misunderstand the question? The survey cannot tell us.

> **THINK CRITICALLY:** If you want to predict who will win the next U.S. presidential race, what survey question would you ask, and who would you ask?

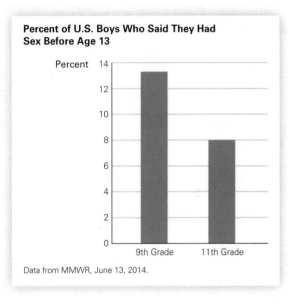

**Percent of U.S. Boys Who Said They Had Sex Before Age 13**

Data from MMWR, June 13, 2014.

## Studying Development over the Life Span

In addition to conducting observations, experiments, and surveys, developmentalists must measure how people *change or remain the same over time,* as our definition explains. Remember that systems are dynamic, ever-changing. To capture that dynamism, developmental researchers use one of three basic research designs: cross-sectional, longitudinal, and cross-sequential.

### Cross-Sectional Versus Longitudinal Research

The quickest and least expensive way to study development over time is with **cross-sectional research,** in which groups of people of one age are compared with people of another age. Cross-sectional design seems simple. However, the people being compared may differ in more ways than just age.

**FIGURE 1.10**

**I Forgot?** If these were the only data available, you might conclude that ninth-graders have suddenly become more sexually active than eleventh-graders. But we have 20 years of data—those who are ninth-graders now will answer differently by eleventh grade.

**cross-sectional research** A research design that compares groups of people who differ in age but are similar in other important characteristics.

**All Smiling, All Multiethnic, All the Same?** Cross-sectional research comparing these people would find age differences, but there might be cohort differences as well. Only longitudinal research could find them.

**longitudinal research** A research design in which the same individuals are followed over time, as their development is repeatedly assessed.

**Response for Nurses** (from p. 24) Experiments are the only way to determine cause-and-effect relationships. If we want to be sure that a new drug or treatment is safe and effective, an experiment must be conducted to establish that the drug or treatment improves health.

For example, because most women now in their 50s gained an average of a pound every year throughout their adulthood, does this mean that women now age 20 who weigh 140 pounds will, on average, weigh 170 pounds at age 50? Not necessarily.

To help discover whether age itself rather than cohort causes a developmental change, scientists undertake **longitudinal research.** This requires collecting data repeatedly on the same individuals as they age. The current cohort of young women, aware of the risks of overweight and the need for exercise, may not gain as much weight as older generations did (Arigo et al., 2016).

For insight about the life span, the best longitudinal research follows the same individuals from infancy to old age. Long-term research requires patience and dedication from a team of scientists, but it can pay off. As you read in A View from Science on page 6, longitudinal research was needed to reveal that one-third of overweight children become normal-weight adults.

Consider another example. A longitudinal study of 790 low-SES children in Baltimore found that only 4 percent graduated from college by age 28 (Alexander et al., 2014). Without scientific data, a person might think that the problem was not enough counselors in high school or too many teenagers making poor choices.

However, because this was a longitudinal study, the data pinpointed when those children were pushed toward, or away from, higher education. Surprisingly, it was long before adolescence. The strongest influences on college attendance were good early education and encouraging, friendly neighbors.

Good as it is, longitudinal research has a problem, something already mentioned—the historical context. Science, popular culture, and politics change over time, and each alters the experiences of a child. Data collected on children born decades ago may not be relevant today.

**Seven Times of Life** These photos show Sarah-Maria, born in 1980 in Switzerland, at seven periods of her life: infancy (age 1), early childhood (age 3), middle childhood (age 8), adolescence (age 15), emerging adulthood (age 19), and adulthood (ages 30 and 36).

**Observation Quiz** Longitudinal research best illustrates continuity and discontinuity. For Sarah-Maria, what changed over 30 years and what didn't? (see answer, p. 28) ←

For instance, many recent substances that were once thought to be beneficial might be harmful, among them *phthalates* and *bisphenol A* (BPA) (chemicals used in manufacturing in plastic baby bottles), *hydrofracking* (a process used to get gas for fuel from rocks), *e-waste* (from old computers and cell phones), and more. Some nations and states ban or regulate each of these; others do not. Verified, longitudinal data are not yet possible.

Because of the outcry among parents, bisphenol A has been replaced with bisphenol S (BPS). But we do not know if BPS is better, or worse, than BPA, because we do not have data on babies who drank from both kinds of bottles and are now adults (Zimmerman & Anastas, 2015).

A new example is *e-cigarettes*. They are less toxic (how much less?) to the heart and lungs than combustible cigarettes. Some (how many?) smokers reduce their risk of cancer and heart disease by switching to e-cigs (Bhatnagar et al., 2014). But some teenagers (how many?) are more likely to smoke cigarettes if they start by vaping.

The best research shows that nonsmoking teenagers who use e-cigarettes are almost four times as likely to say they "will try a cigarette soon," an ominous result. But that is a survey, not longitudinal proof (Park et al., 2016).

Until longitudinal data on addiction and death for e-cig smokers are known, 10 or 20 years from now, no one can be certain whether the harm outweighs the benefits (Dutra & Glantz, 2014; Hajek et al., 2014; Ramo et al., 2015). [**Developmental Link:** The major discussion of e-cigarette use is in Chapter 16.] Do we need to wait until e-cig smokers die of lung disease, or not?

## Cross-Sequential Research

Scientists have discovered a third strategy, a sequence of data collection that combines cross-sectional and longitudinal research. This combination is called **cross-sequential research** (also referred to as *cohort-sequential* or *time-sequential research*). In sequential designs, researchers study people of different ages (a cross-sectional approach), follow them for years (a longitudinal approach), and then combine the results.

A cross-sequential design lets researchers compare findings for, say, 7-year-olds with findings for the same individuals at age 1 as well as with data from people who were 7 long ago, who are now ages 13, 19, or even much older (see Figure 1.11). Cross-sequential research is complicated, in recruitment and analysis, but it lets scientists disentangle age from history.

The first well-known cross-sequential study (the *Seattle Longitudinal Study*) found that some intellectual abilities (vocabulary) increase even after age 60, whereas others (speed) start to decline at age 30 (Schaie, 2005/2013), confirming that development is multidirectional. This study also discovered that declines in adult math ability are more closely related to education than to age, something neither cross-sectional nor longitudinal research could reveal.

The advantages of cross-sequential research are now evident. Accordingly, many researchers combine cross-sectional and longitudinal data collected by other scientists, thus using cross-sequential analysis without needing to do all of the data collection themselves.

For example, six scientists combined data from 14 longitudinal studies. They found that adolescent optimism about the future predicted health in middle age (Kern et al., 2016). Without a cross-sequential analysis, would people know that teenagers who say "life will be better when I grow up" are likely to be in good health decades later?

**cross-sequential research** A hybrid research design in which researchers first study several groups of people of different ages (a cross-sectional approach) and then follow those groups over the years (a longitudinal approach). (Also called *cohort-sequential research* or *time-sequential research*.)

**Especially for Future Researchers** What is the best method for collecting data? (see response, p. 29)

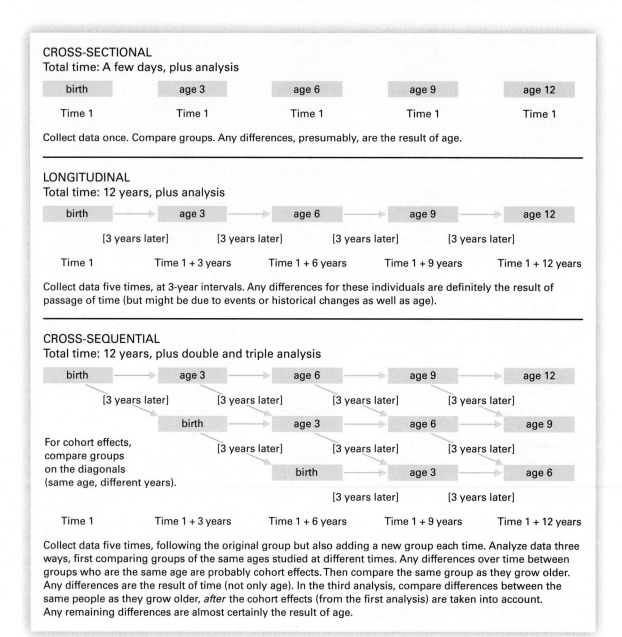

CROSS-SECTIONAL
Total time: A few days, plus analysis

| birth | age 3 | age 6 | age 9 | age 12 |
|-------|-------|-------|-------|--------|
| Time 1 | Time 1 | Time 1 | Time 1 | Time 1 |

Collect data once. Compare groups. Any differences, presumably, are the result of age.

LONGITUDINAL
Total time: 12 years, plus analysis

birth → age 3 → age 6 → age 9 → age 12

[3 years later]    [3 years later]    [3 years later]    [3 years later]

Time 1    Time 1 + 3 years    Time 1 + 6 years    Time 1 + 9 years    Time 1 + 12 years

Collect data five times, at 3-year intervals. Any differences for these individuals are definitely the result of passage of time (but might be due to events or historical changes as well as age).

CROSS-SEQUENTIAL
Total time: 12 years, plus double and triple analysis

birth → age 3 → age 6 → age 9 → age 12

[3 years later]    [3 years later]    [3 years later]    [3 years later]

birth → age 3 → age 6 → age 9

For cohort effects, compare groups on the diagonals (same age, different years).

[3 years later]    [3 years later]    [3 years later]

birth → age 3 → age 6

[3 years later]    [3 years later]

Time 1    Time 1 + 3 years    Time 1 + 6 years    Time 1 + 9 years    Time 1 + 12 years

Collect data five times, following the original group but also adding a new group each time. Analyze data three ways, first comparing groups of the same ages studied at different times. Any differences over time between groups who are the same age are probably cohort effects. Then compare the same group as they grow older. Any differences are the result of time (not only age). In the third analysis, compare differences between the same people as they grow older, *after* the cohort effects (from the first analysis) are taken into account. Any remaining differences are almost certainly the result of age.

**FIGURE 1.11**
**Which Approach Is Best?** Cross-sequential research is the most time-consuming and complex, but it yields the best information. One reason that hundreds of scientists conduct research on the same topics, replicating one another's work, is to gain some advantages of cohort-sequential research without waiting for decades.

**Answer to Observation Quiz** (from p. 26) Of course, much changed and much did not change, but evident in the photos is continuity in Sarah-Maria's happy smile and discontinuity in her hairstyle and color, which shows dramatic age and cohort changes.

**WHAT HAVE YOU LEARNED?**

1. Why does observation NOT prove "what causes what"?
2. Why do experimenters use a control (or comparison) group as well as an experimental group?
3. What are the strengths and weaknesses of the survey method?
4. Why would a scientist conduct a cross-sectional study?
5. What are the advantages and disadvantages of longitudinal research?
6. What current substances or practices might be found to be harmful in the future?
7. Why do developmentalists use cross-sequential research?

# Cautions and Challenges from Science

The scientific method illuminates and illustrates human development as nothing else does. Facts, consequences, and possibilities have emerged that would not be known without science—and people of all ages are healthier, happier, and more capable because of it.

For example, death of newborns, measles in children, girls not sent to school, and boys being bullied are all less prevalent today than a century ago. Science deserves credit. Even violent death—in war, from homicide, or as punishment for a crime—is less likely in recent centuries than in past ones: Inventions, discoveries, and education are reasons (Pinker, 2011).

Developmental scientists have also discovered unexpected sources of harm. Video games, cigarettes, television, shift work, asbestos, and even artificial respiration are all less benign than people first thought.

As evident in these examples, the benefits of science are many. However, there are also serious pitfalls. We now discuss three potential hazards: misinterpreting correlation, depending too heavily on numbers, and ignoring ethics.

## Correlation and Causation

Probably the most common mistake in interpreting research is confusing correlation with causation. That was evident in Inside the Brain on page 10. It is true that 14-year-olds who regularly smoke marijuana are less likely to graduate from high school. But marijuana may not be the cause: It may be a symptom of academic problems that predated the first use of marijuana.

A **correlation** exists between two variables if one variable is more (or less) likely to occur when the other does. A correlation is *positive* if both variables tend to increase together or decrease together, *negative* if one variable tends to increase while the other decreases, and *zero* if no connection is evident. (Try the quiz in Table 1.4.)

Expressed in numerical terms, correlations vary from +1.0 (the most positive) to −1.0 (the most negative). Correlations are almost never that extreme; a correlation of +0.3 or −0.3 is noteworthy; a correlation of +0.8 or −0.8 is astonishing.

Many correlations are unexpected. For instance, a positive correlation is evident in being a first-born child and having asthma, in being a teenage girl and attempting suicide, and in living in a county with few dentists and being obese. The dentist study found that surprising correlation even after taking into account community poverty and the number of medical doctors. The authors suggest that dentists provide information about nutrition, which improves health (Holzer et al., 2014).

Remember that *correlation is not causation*. Just because two variables are correlated does not mean that one causes the other—even if it seems logical that it does. Can you think of other possible explanations for the correlation between dentists and obesity?

**Response for Future Researchers** (from p. 27) There is no best method for collecting data. The method used depends on many factors, such as the age of participants (infants can't complete questionnaires), the question being researched, and the time frame.

**correlation** A number between +1.0 and −1.0 that indicates the degree of relationship between two variables, expressed in terms of the likelihood that one variable will (or will not) occur when the other variable does (or does not). A correlation indicates only that two variables are somehow related, not that one variable causes the other to occur.

---

### TABLE 1.4

**Quiz on Correlation**

| Two Variables | Positive, Negative, or Zero Correlation? | Why? (Third Variable) |
|---|---|---|
| 1. Ice cream sales and murder rate | _____ | _____ |
| 2. Reading ability and number of baby teeth | _____ | _____ |
| 3. Sex of adult and his or her average number of offspring | _____ | _____ |

For each of these three pairs of variables, indicate whether the correlation between them is positive, negative, or nonexistent. Then try to think of a third variable that might determine the direction of the correlation. The correct answers are printed upside down below.

Answers:
1. Positive; third variable: heat
2. Negative; third variable: age
3. Zero; each child must have a parent of each sex; no third variable

**A Pesky Third Variable** Correlation is often misleading. In this case, a third variable (the supply of fossil fuels, a crack in the window, or the profit of the corporation) may be relevant.

**quantitative research** Research that provides data that can be expressed with numbers, such as ranks or scales.

**qualitative research** Research that considers qualities instead of quantities. Descriptions of particular conditions and participants' expressed ideas are often part of qualitative studies.

**Especially for Future Researchers and Science Writers** Do any ethical guidelines apply when an author writes about the experiences of family members, friends, or research participants? (see response, p. 31)

**LaunchPad**
macmillan learning

**Video Activity: Eugenics and the "Feebleminded": A Shameful History** illustrates what can happen when scientists fail to follow a code of ethics.

## Quantity and Quality

A second caution concerns **quantitative research** (from the word *quantity*). Quantitative research data can be categorized, ranked, or numbered and thus can be easily translated across cultures and for diverse populations. One example of quantitative research is the use of children's school achievement scores to compare the effectiveness of education within a school or a nation.

Since quantities can be easily summarized, compared, charted, and replicated, many scientists prefer quantitative research. Statistics require numbers. Quantitative data are easier to replicate (Creswell, 2009). However, when data are presented in categories and numbers, some nuances and individual distinctions are lost.

Many developmental researchers thus turn to **qualitative research** (from the word *quality*)—asking open-ended questions, reporting answers in narrative (not numerical) form. Qualitative researchers are interested in understanding how people interpret their experiences and how they construct their worlds (Merriam, 2009, p. 24).

Qualitative research reflects cultural and contextual diversity, but it is also more vulnerable to bias and harder to replicate. Both types of research, and research that combines the two, are needed (Mertens, 2014).

## Ethics

The most important caution for all scientists, especially for those studying humans, is to uphold ethical standards. Each academic discipline and professional society involved in the study of human development has a *code of ethics* (a set of moral principles).

Ethical standards and codes are increasingly stringent. Most educational and medical institutions have an *Institutional Review Board* (IRB), a group that permits only research that follows certain guidelines. One crucial focus is on the well-being of the participants in a study: They must understand and consent to their involvement, and the researcher must keep results confidential and must ensure that no one is harmed.

Although IRBs slow down science, some research conducted before IRBs was clearly unethical, especially when the participants were children, members of minority groups, prisoners, or animals. Even so, some ethical dilemmas remain (Leiter & Herman, 2015).

Many ethical issues arose in the 2014–2016 Ebola epidemic in West Africa (Gillon, 2015; Rothstein, 2015). Among them: Is it fair to use vaccines whose safety is unproven when such proof would take months? What kind of informed consent is needed to avoid both false hope and false fear? Is it best to keep relatives away from people who have Ebola, even though social isolation makes it more likely that a sick person will die?

More broadly, is justice served by a health care system that is inadequate in some countries and high-tech in others? Medicine has tended to focus on individuals, ignoring the customs and systems that make some people more vulnerable. One observer noted:

> When people from the United States and Europe working in West Africa have developed Ebola, time and again the first thing they wanted to take was not an experimental drug. It was an airplane that would cart them home.
>
> *[Cohen, 2014, p. 911]*

As stressed early in this chapter, scientists, like all other humans, have strong opinions, which they expect research to confirm. They might try (sometimes without noticing it) to achieve the results they want. As one team explains:

> Our job as scientists is to discover truths about the world. We generate hypotheses, collect data, and examine whether or not the data are consistent with those hypotheses . . . . [but we] often lose sight of this goal, yielding to pressure to do whatever is justifiable to compile a set of studies we can publish. This is not driven by a willingness to deceive but by the self-serving interpretation of ambiguity . . .
>
> *[Simmons et al., 2011, pp. 1359, 1365]*

Obviously, collaboration, replication, and transparency are essential ethical safeguards. Hundreds of questions regarding human development need answers, and researchers have yet to find them. That is the most important ethical mandate of all. For instance:

- Do we know enough about prenatal drugs to protect every fetus?
- Do we know enough about preschool to ensure that every 6-year-old will read?
- Do we know enough about poverty to enable every child to be healthy?
- Do we know enough about transgender children, or single parenthood, or divorce, or same-sex marriages to ensure optimal development?

The answer to all of these questions is a resounding *NO*.

Scientists and funders tend to avoid questions that might produce unwanted answers. People have strong opinions about drugs, preschool, income, sex, and families that may conflict with what science discovers. Religion, politics, and ethics shape scientific research, sometimes stopping investigation before it begins.

For instance, in 1996, the U.S. Congress, in allocating funds for the Centers for Disease Control, passed a law stating, "None of the funds made available for injury prevention and control at the Centers for Disease Control and Prevention may be used to advocate or promote gun control." Some believe that this prohibition is one reason that the rate of gun death in the United States is higher than in any other nation. What laws—if any—would change that? Scientists do not agree on the answer, partly because solid research with a national sample has not been done (Gostin, 2016).

An even greater question is about the "unknown unknowns," the topics that we assume we understand but do not, hypotheses that have not yet occurred to anyone because our thinking is limited by our cultures and contexts. This probably applies to both sides of the gun debate.

We hope that the next cohort of developmental scientists will tackle these ethical problems—building on what is known, mindful of what needs to be explored, and raising questions that no one has thought of before. Remember that the goal is to help everyone fulfill their potential. Much more needs to be learned. The next 15 chapters are only a beginning.

*John Moore/Getty Images*

**Science and Ebola** Ebola was halted as much because of social science as medicine, which has not yet found an effective vaccine. Fortunately, social workers taught practices that were contrary to West African culture—no more hugging, touching, or visiting from one neighborhood to another. Psychologists advised health workers, like this one from Doctors Without Borders, to hold, reassure, and comfort children as much as possible. This girl was *not* among the 5,000 Liberians who died.

---

**THINK CRITICALLY:** Can you think of an additional question that researchers should answer?

---

**WHAT HAVE YOU LEARNED?**

1. Why does correlation not prove causation?
2. What are the advantages and disadvantages of quantitative research?
3. What are the advantages and disadvantages of qualitative research?
4. What is the role of the IRB?
5. Why might a political leader avoid funding developmental research?
6. What questions about human development remain to be answered?

**Response for Future Researchers and Science Writers** (from p. 30) Yes. Anyone you write about must give consent and be fully informed about your intentions. They can be identified by name only if they give permission. For example, family members gave permission before anecdotes about them were included in this text. My nephew David read the first draft of his story (see pp. 20–21) and is proud to have his experiences used to teach others.

# SUMMARY

## Understanding How and Why

**1.** The study of human development is a science that seeks to understand how people change or remain the same over time. As a science, it begins with questions and hypotheses and then gathers empirical data.

**2.** Replication confirms, modifies, or refutes conclusions, which are not considered solid until they are confirmed by several studies.

**3.** The universality of human development and the uniqueness of each individual's development are evident in both nature (the genes) and nurture (the environment); no person is quite like another. Nature and nurture always interact, and each human characteristic is affected by that interaction.

**4.** Crucial to the study of nature and nurture is the concept of differential susceptibility—that genes or experiences affect the likelihood that a person will be affected by the environment.

## The Life-Span Perspective

**5.** The assumption that growth is linear and that progress is inevitable has been replaced by the idea that both continuity (sameness) and discontinuity (sudden shifts) are part of every life and that gains and losses are apparent at every age.

**6.** Time is a crucial variable in studying human development. A critical period is a time when something *must* occur or when an abnormality might occur. Often a particular development can occur more easily at a particular time, called a sensitive period.

**7.** Urie Bronfenbrenner's ecological-systems approach notes that each of us is situated within larger systems of family, school, community, and culture, as well as part of a historical cohort. Changes in the context affect all other aspects of the system.

**8.** Certain experiences or innovations shape people of each cohort because they share the experience of significant historical events. Socioeconomic status (SES) affects each child's opportunities, health, and education.

**9.** *Culture, ethnicity*, and *race* are social constructions, concepts created by society. Culture includes beliefs and patterns; ethnicity refers to ancestral heritage. Race is also a social construction, not a biological one.

**10.** Developmentalists try to avoid the difference-equals-deficit error. Differences are alternate ways to think or act. They are not necessarily harmful.

**11.** Within each person, every aspect of development interacts with the others, but development can be divided into three domains—biosocial, cognitive, and psychosocial. A multidisciplinary, dynamic-systems approach is needed.

**12.** Throughout life, human development is plastic. Brains and behaviors may change over time. Plasticity means that change is possible, not that everything can change.

## Designing Science

**13.** Commonly used research methods are scientific observation, the experiment, and the survey. Each can provide insight and discoveries, yet each is limited.

**14.** Developmentalists study change over time, often with cross-sectional and longitudinal research. Ideally, results from both methods are combined in cross-sequential analysis.

## Cautions and Challenges from Science

**15.** A correlation shows that two variables are related not that one *causes* the other: Both may be caused by a third variable.

**16.** Quantitative research provides numerical data. This makes it best for comparing contexts and cultures via verified statistics. By contrast, more nuanced data come from qualitative research, which reports on individual lives.

**17.** Ethical behavior is crucial in all of the sciences. Results must be fairly gathered, reported, and interpreted. Participants must understand and consent to their involvement.

**18.** The most important ethical question is whether scientists are designing, conducting, analyzing, publishing, and applying the research that is most critically needed.

# KEY TERMS

science of human development (p. 4)
scientific method (p. 4)
hypothesis (p. 4)
empirical evidence (p. 4)
replication (p. 4)
nature (p. 6)
nurture (p. 7)
epigenetics (p. 7)
differential susceptibility (p. 7)

life-span perspective (p. 8)
critical period (p. 9)
sensitive period (p. 9)
ecological-systems approach (p. 12)
cohort (p. 13)
socioeconomic status (SES) (p. 13)
culture (p. 14)
social construction (p. 14)

difference-equals-deficit error (p. 15)
ethnic group (p. 16)
race (p. 16)
plasticity (p. 19)
dynamic-systems approach (p. 19)
scientific observation (p. 22)
experiment (p. 23)
independent variable (p. 23)

dependent variable (p. 23)
survey (p. 24)
cross-sectional research (p. 25)
longitudinal research (p. 26)
cross-sequential research (p. 27)
correlation (p. 29)
quantitative research (p. 30)
qualitative research (p. 30)

results, but none is adequate by itself (Carlson & Lynch, 2017, p. 212). More research and better theories are needed.

A **developmental theory** is a systematic statement of general principles that provides a framework for understanding how and why people change over time. Facts and observations connect to patterns, weaving details into a meaningful whole.

A developmental theory is more than a hunch or a hypothesis; it is more comprehensive than a folk theory. Developmental theories provide insights that are both broad and deep, connecting the distant past and the far-off future.

**developmental theory** A group of ideas, assumptions, and generalizations that interpret and illuminate the thousands of observations that have been made about human growth. A developmental theory provides a framework for explaining the patterns and problems of development.

## Questions and Answers

As you remember from Chapter 1, the first step in the science of human development is to pose a question, which often springs from theory. Among the thousands of important questions are the following, each central to one of the five theories in this chapter:

1. Do early experiences—of breast-feeding or attachment or abuse—shape adult personality?
2. Does learning depend on encouragement, punishment, and/or role models?
3. Do morals develop spontaneously in childhood so children do not need to be taught right from wrong?
4. Does culture determine parents' behavior, such as how to respond to an infant's cry?
5. Is survival an inborn instinct, underlying all personal and social decisions?

The answer to each of these questions is "yes" when examined in order by the following theories: psychoanalytic, behaviorism, cognitive, sociocultural, and evolutionary. Each question is answered "no" or "not necessarily" by several others. For every answer, more questions arise: Why or why not? When and how? SO WHAT? This last question is crucial; implications and applications affect everyone's daily life.

To be more specific about what theories do:

- Theories produce *hypotheses*.
- Theories generate *discoveries*.
- Theories offer *practical guidance*.

## Past and Future

Humans spontaneously develop theories about everything they observe. Scientists have realized this for centuries. Charles Darwin wrote, "As soon as the important faculties of the imagination, wonder, and curiosity, together with some power of reasoning, had become partially developed, man would naturally crave to understand what was passing around him, and would have vaguely speculated on his own existence" (Darwin, 1871, quoted in Thomson, 2015, p. 104; Culotta, 2009, and many others).

**Give My Regards to Broadway** Those lyrics written by George Cohan (1878–1942) are inscribed on his bronze statue overlooking thousands of twenty-first-century tourists from every state and nation in Times Square in New York City. Like all five theories in this chapter, this scene depicts the dynamic interaction of old insights and new realities.

Quoting Darwin (a controversial figure) evokes theories about creation and evolution, including the theory that science and religion are opposing worldviews, a theory not held by most scientists. Most agree with the theologian and civil rights leader Martin Luther King Jr., who said:

> Science investigates; religion interprets. Science gives man knowledge, which is power; religion gives man wisdom, which is control. Science deals mainly with facts; religion deals mainly with values. The two are not rivals.
>
> [King, 1977, p. 4]

**Backpacks or Bouquets?** Children worldwide are nervous on their first day of school, but their coping reflects implicit cultural theories. Kindergartner Madelyn Ricker in Georgia shows her new backpack to her teacher, and elementary school students in Russia bring flowers to their teachers.

Theories are meant to be useful. That is why we need them. Without developmental theories, we would be reactive and bewildered, blindly following our culture and our prejudices to the detriment of anyone who wonders about their children, their childhood, their future.

Not surprisingly, given that history and culture shape perspectives (as stressed in Chapter 1), each of the major theories in this chapter became ascendant in a particular decade during the past 100 years. Of course, all five shed light on current issues—otherwise, they would not still be useful. All were developed primarily by European and North American scientists, another limitation.

But that perspective is not a reason to reject them. In fact, all of these theories echo ideas written by ancient sages, in Greece, China, India, and elsewhere, since humans always "naturally crave to understand," and since humans everywhere and always are one species. Consider them a benchmark, useful for understanding human development. Also remember that none of them is the final theoretical word: As explained in Chapter 1, human growth is dynamic, always affected by cohort and culture.

---

### WHAT HAVE YOU LEARNED?

1. What are the similarities and differences between folk theories and scientific theories?
2. What three things do theories do?
3. Why do people need theories to move forward with their lives?
4. Who develops theories—everyone or just scientists?
5. What is the focus of a developmental theory?

---

## Grand Theories

In the first half of the twentieth century, two opposing theories—psychoanalytic and behaviorism—dominated the discipline of psychology, each with extensive applications to human development. In about 1960, a third theory—cognitive—arose, and it too was widely applied to development.

These three are called "grand theories" and explained here because they are comprehensive, enduring, and far-reaching. In developmental studies, these theories continue to be useful. But be forewarned: None of them is now considered as grand as developmentalists once believed.

## Psychoanalytic Theory: Freud and Erikson

Inner drives, deep motives, and unconscious needs rooted in childhood—especially the first six years—are the focus of **psychoanalytic theory.** These unconscious forces are thought to influence every aspect of thinking and behavior, from the smallest details of daily life to the crucial choices of a lifetime.

### Freud's Ideas

Psychoanalytic theory originated with Sigmund Freud (1856–1939), an Austrian physician who treated patients suffering from mental illness. He listened to their remembered dreams and uncensored streams of thought. From that, he constructed an elaborate, multifaceted theory.

**Freud at Work** In addition to being the world's first psychoanalyst, Sigmund Freud was a prolific writer. His many papers and case histories, primarily descriptions of his patients' symptoms and sexual urges, helped make the psychoanalytic perspective a dominant force for much of the twentieth century.

**psychoanalytic theory** A grand theory of human development that holds that irrational, unconscious drives and motives, often originating in childhood, underlie human behavior.

According to Freud, development in the first six years of life occurs in three stages, each characterized by sexual interest and pleasure arising from a particular part of the body. In infancy, the erotic body part is the mouth (the *oral stage*); in early childhood, it is the anus (the *anal stage*); in the preschool years, it is the penis (the *phallic stage*), a source of pride and fear among boys and a reason for sorrow and envy among girls. Then, after a quiet period (*latency*), the *genital stage* arrives at puberty, lasting throughout adulthood. (Table 2.1 describes stages in Freud's theory.)

Freud maintained that sensual satisfaction (from stimulation of the mouth, anus, or penis) is linked to major developmental stages, needs, and challenges. During the oral stage, for example, sucking provides not only nourishment for the infant but also erotic joy and attachment to the mother. Kissing between lovers is a vestige of the oral stage. Next, during the anal stage, pleasures arise from self-control, initially with toileting but later with wanting everything to be clean, neat, and regular (an "anal personality").

One of Freud's most influential ideas was that each stage includes its own struggles. Conflict occurs, for instance, when parents wean their babies (oral stage), toilet train their toddlers (anal stage), deflect the sexual curiosity and fantasies of their 5-year-olds (phallic stage), and limit the sexual interests of adolescents (genital stage). Freud thought that the experiences surrounding these conflicts determine later personality.

Freud did not believe that any new stage occurred after puberty; rather, he believed that adult personalities and habits were influenced by childhood. Unconscious conflicts rooted in early life are evident in adult behavior—for instance, cigarette smoking (oral) or meticulous housecleaning (anal) or falling in love with a much older partner (phallic).

### Erikson's Ideas

Many of Freud's followers became famous theorists themselves—Carl Jung, Alfred Adler, and Karen Horney among them. They agreed with Freud that early-childhood experiences affect everyone, often unconsciously, but they also expanded and modified his ideas. For scholars in human development, one neo-Freudian, Erik Erikson (1902–1994), is particularly insightful. He proposed a comprehensive developmental theory of the entire life span.

Erikson described eight developmental stages, each characterized by a particular challenge, or *developmental crisis*. Although Erikson named two polarities

**No Choking** During the oral stage, children put everything in their mouths, as Freud recognized and as 12-month-old Harper Vasquez does here. Toy manufacturers and lawyers know this, too, which is why many toy packages read "Choking hazard: small parts, not appropriate for children under age 3."

**TABLE 2.1**

Comparison of Freud's Psychosexual and Erikson's Psychosocial Stages

| Approximate Age | Freud (psychosexual) | Erikson (psychosocial) |
|---|---|---|
| Birth to 1 year | *Oral Stage*<br>The lips, tongue, and gums are the focus of pleasurable sensations in the baby's body, and sucking and feeding are the most stimulating activities. | *Trust vs. Mistrust*<br>Babies either trust that others will satisfy their basic needs, including nourishment, warmth, cleanliness, and physical contact, **or** develop mistrust about the care of others. |
| 1–3 years | *Anal Stage*<br>The anus is the focus of pleasurable sensations in the baby's body, and toilet training is the most important activity. | *Autonomy vs. Shame and Doubt*<br>Children either become self-sufficient in many activities, including toileting, feeding, walking, exploring, and talking, **or** doubt their own abilities. |
| 3–6 years | *Phallic Stage*<br>The phallus, or penis, is the most important body part, and pleasure is derived from genital stimulation. Boys are proud of their penises; girls wonder why they don't have them. | *Initiative vs. Guilt*<br>Children either try to undertake many adultlike activities **or** internalize the limits and prohibitions set by parents. They feel either adventurous **or** guilty. |
| 6–11 years | *Latency*<br>Not really a stage, latency is an interlude. Sexual needs are quiet; psychic energy flows into sports, schoolwork, and friendship. | *Industry vs. Inferiority*<br>Children busily practice and then master new skills **or** feel inferior, unable to do anything well. |
| Adolescence | *Genital Stage*<br>The genitals are the focus of pleasurable sensations, and the young person seeks sexual stimulation and satisfaction in heterosexual relationships. | *Identity vs. Role Confusion*<br>Adolescents ask themselves "Who am I?" They establish sexual, political, religious, and vocational identities **or** are confused about their roles. |
| Adulthood | Freud believed that the genital stage lasts throughout adulthood. He also said that the goal of a healthy life is "to love and to work." | *Intimacy vs. Isolation*<br>Emerging adults seek companionship and love **or** become isolated from others, fearing rejection.<br><br>*Generativity vs. Stagnation*<br>Adults contribute to future generations through work, creative activities, and parenthood **or** they stagnate.<br><br>*Integrity vs. Despair*<br>Older adults try to make sense of their lives, either seeing life as a meaningful whole **or** despairing at goals never reached. |

**A Legendary Couple** In his first 30 years, Erikson never fit into a particular local community, since he frequently changed nations, schools, and professions. Then he met Joan. In their first five decades of marriage, they raised a family and wrote several books. If Erikson had published his theory at age 73 (when this photograph was taken) instead of in his 40s, would he still have described life as a series of crises?

at each crisis, he recognized a wide range of outcomes between those opposites. Typically, development at each stage leads to neither extreme but to something in between.

In the stage of *initiative versus guilt*, for example, 3- to 6-year-olds undertake activities that exceed the limits set by their parents and their culture. They leap into swimming pools, pull their pants on backward, make cakes according to their own recipes, and wander off alone.

Erikson thought that those preschool initiatives produce feelings of pride or failure, depending on adult reactions. Should adults pretend to like the cake that a preschooler made or, instead, punish that child for wasting food and messing up the kitchen? According to Erikson's theory, a child will feel guilty lifelong if adults are too critical or if social norms are too strict regarding the young child's initiatives.

As you can see from Table 2.1, Erikson's first five stages are closely related to Freud's stages. Like Freud, Erikson believed that unresolved childhood conflicts echo throughout life, causing problems in adulthood.

Erikson considered the first stage, *trust versus mistrust*, particularly crucial. For example, an adult who has difficulty establishing a secure, mutual relationship with a life partner may never have resolved that first crisis of early infancy. If you know people who are "too trusting" or "too suspicious," Erikson would suggest that you ask them about their care when they were infants.

In his emphasis on childhood, Erikson agreed with Freud. However, in two crucial aspects, Erikson's stages differ significantly from those of his mentor.

1. Erikson's stages emphasized family and culture, not sexual urges.
2. Erikson recognized adult development, with three stages after adolescence.

## Behaviorism: Conditioning and Learning

The comprehensive theory that dominated psychology in the United States for most of the twentieth century was **behaviorism.** This theory began in Russia, with Pavlov, who first described conditioning.

### Classical Conditioning

More than a century ago, Ivan Pavlov (1849–1936) did hundreds of experiments to examine the link between something that affected a living creature (such as a sight, a sound, a touch) and how that creature reacted. Technically, he was interested in how a *stimulus* affects a *response*.

While studying salivation in his laboratory, Pavlov noticed that his research dogs drooled (response) not only at the smell of food (stimulus) but also, eventually, at the sound of the footsteps of the people bringing food. This observation led Pavlov to perform a famous experiment: He conditioned dogs to salivate (response) when hearing a particular noise (stimulus).

Pavlov began by sounding a tone just before presenting food. After a number of repetitions of the tone-then-food sequence, dogs began salivating at the sound even when there was no food. This simple experiment demonstrated **classical conditioning** (also called *respondent conditioning*).

In classical conditioning, a person or animal learns to associate a neutral stimulus with a meaningful one, gradually responding to the neutral stimulus in the same way as to the meaningful one. In Pavlov's original experiment, the dog associated the tone (the neutral stimulus) with food (the meaningful stimulus) and eventually responded to the tone as if it were the food itself. The conditioned response to the tone, no longer neutral but now a conditioned stimulus, was evidence that learning had occurred.

Behaviorists see dozens of examples of classical conditioning. Infants learn to smile at their parents because they associate them with food and play; toddlers learn to fear busy streets if the noise of traffic repeatedly frightens them; students learn to enjoy—or hate—school, depending on their kindergarten experience.

One current application of this theory is to explain the sudden increase of opioid overdose deaths in the United States (see Figure 2.1). (Opioids include heroin, morphine, and many prescription painkillers.) Many such deaths may not really be caused by an excessive quantity of the drug, because the deadly dose may be far less than others consume with no ill effect. Indeed, an "overdose" might be the same quantity as what that very person had taken before.

Nor is every overdose death the consequence of some hidden "extra" within the drug. Indeed, people die of legally prescribed and carefully produced pills at doses they have taken before. One hypothesis is that the person died because of a conditioned response (Siegel, 2016).

This is how the stimulus–response link might work. When people habitually take a certain drug, they become conditioned to it—their body and mind tolerate it, protecting them from serious side effects. That explains craving: Those with substance use disorder (SUD) are conditioned to seek the drug when they feel

Mai Chen/Alamy Stock Photo

**Just Like Her Grandparents** She sits on London Bridge, establishing her identity via hair, shoes, and clothes. Erikson would say she is quite conventional, doing what adolescents have always done!

**Especially for Teachers** Your kindergartners are talkative and always moving. They almost never sit quietly and listen to you. What would Erik Erikson recommend? (see response, p. 43)

**behaviorism** A grand theory of human development that studies observable behavior. Behaviorism is also called *learning theory* because it describes the laws and processes by which behavior is learned.

**classical conditioning** The learning process in which a meaningful stimulus (such as the smell of food to a hungry animal) is connected with a neutral stimulus (such as the sound of a tone) that had no special meaning before conditioning. (Also called *respondent conditioning*.)

**Overdose Deaths Due to Opioids in the United States, 2002–2015**

Legend:
- Female
- Male
- Total

Y-axis: 0; 5,000; 10,000; 15,000; 20,000; 25,000; 30,000; 35,000
X-axis: 2002, 2003, 2004, 2005, 2006, 2007, 2008, 2009, 2010, 2011, 2012, 2013, 2014, 2015

Data from National Center on Health Statistics, CDC Wonder, various years.

**FIGURE 2.1**

**A Deadly Response** The epidemic of opioid deaths is most notable among white, middle-aged men. There are many explanations for this demographic, but one that arises from behaviorism is that these drug-users are not conditioned to heroin. Tolerance may be psychological as well as physical; novice substance abusers have not acquired it.

**A Contemporary of Freud** Ivan Pavlov was a physiologist who received the Nobel Prize in 1904 for his research on digestive processes. It was this line of study that led to his discovery of classical conditioning, when his research on dog saliva led to insight about learning.

⬤ **Observation Quiz** How is Pavlov similar to Freud in appearance, and how do both look different from the other theorists pictured? (see answer, p. 44) ↑

anxious, or in pain, or lonely. They connect relief of those feelings (response) with the drug (stimulus).

However, that same dose might be too much if the circumstances have not allowed the body and mind to prepare to adjust to it. A relatively small dose in a new context might be too much. A study of 44 "overdose" victims who survived (they were hospitalized and treated immediately, usually with naloxone, a potent antidote to opioid poisoning) found that often the dose was usual but conditioning made the response extreme (Neale et al., 2017). Two examples:

> Alan (23 years) . . . had been told to leave the hostel where he had been staying because he had taken drugs and was intoxicated. . . . He had then taken more heroin and was wandering around outside, but could not remember overdosing. He was found unconscious . . .
>
> *[2017, p. 171]*

Thus he was tolerant of heroin taken in his hostel room, but the same dose outside made him unconscious.

> James (38 years) reported . . . [that] a friend had injected him. He stated that he could not remember anything about the effects of the heroin as he had instantly "blacked out" as the needle "went in".
>
> *[2017, p. 172]*

Of course, the friend did not know that James had been psychologically conditioned to instantly connect injection—even before any physiological effects in the bloodstream—with blacking out. Thus, a relatively small dose (the friend thought he was being helpful) could have killed him.

Behaviorists notice many reactions linked to stimuli that once were neutral. Think of how some people react to the buzzing of a bumble bee or the sight of a police car in the rearview mirror. Such reactions are learned. The announcement of a final exam makes some students sweat—as no young child would.

## Behaviorism in the United States

Pavlov's ideas seemed to bypass most Western European developmentalists but were welcomed in the United States, because many North Americans disputed the psychoanalytic emphasis on the unconscious.

The first of three famous Americans who championed behaviorism was John B. Watson (1878–1958). He argued that if psychology was to be a true science, psychologists should examine only what they could see and measure, not invisible unconscious impulses. In his words:

> Why don't we make what we can *observe* the real field of psychology? Let us limit ourselves to things that can be observed, and formulate laws concerning only those things. . . . We can observe *behavior—what the organism does or says.*

[*Watson, 1924/1998, p. 6*]

According to Watson, if the focus is on behavior, it is apparent that everything is learned. He wrote:

> Give me a dozen healthy infants, well-formed, and my own specified world to bring them up in and I'll guarantee to take any one at random and train him to become any type of specialist I might select—doctor, lawyer, artist, merchant-chief, and yes, even beggar-man and thief, regardless of his talents, penchants, tendencies, abilities, vocations, and race of his ancestors.

[*Watson, 1924/1998, p. 82*]

Other American psychologists agreed. They chose to study observable behavior, objectively and scientifically. For everyone at every age, behaviorists believe there are natural laws of human behavior. They experiment with mice and pigeons, as well as with people, to discover the laws that apply to all living creatures. Such laws explain how simple actions become complex competencies, because stimuli in the environment affect each action. Children are taught how to act, whether parents know it or not.

Learning in behaviorism is far more comprehensive than the narrow definition of learning, which focuses on academics, such as learning to read or multiply. Instead, for behaviorists, everything that people think, do, and feel is learned, step by step, via conditioning.

For example, newborns *learn* to suck on a nipple; infants *learn* to smile at a caregiver; preschoolers *learn* to hold hands when crossing the street. Such learning is conditioned and can endure when no longer useful. That explains why children suck lollipops, adults smile at strangers, and I still grab my children's hands in traffic. My children laugh and say, "Mom, I know how to avoid cars now." Of course, I understand that they are adults, quite able to walk the city by themselves, but I have been conditioned by the years when they were children.

## Operant Conditioning

The most influential North American proponent of behaviorism was B. F. Skinner (1904–1990). Skinner agreed with Watson that psychology should focus on observable behavior. He did not dispute Pavlov's classical conditioning, but, as a good scientist, he built on Pavlov's conclusions. His most famous contribution was to recognize another type of conditioning—**operant conditioning** (also called *instrumental conditioning*)—in which animals (including people) act and then something follows that action.

In other words, Skinner went beyond learning by association, in which one stimulus is paired with another stimulus (in Pavlov's experiment, the tone with the food). He focused instead on what happens *after* the response. If the consequence that follows is enjoyable, the creature (any living thing—a bird, a mouse, a child) tends to repeat the behavior; if the consequence is unpleasant, the creature does not do it again.

Consequences that increase the frequency or strength of a particular action are called *reinforcers*; the process is called **reinforcement** (Skinner, 1953). According

**An Early Behaviorist** John Watson was an early proponent of learning theory. His ideas are still influential and controversial today.

**Response for Teachers** (from p. 41) Erikson would note that the behavior of 5-year-olds is affected by their developmental stage and by their culture. Therefore, you might design your curriculum to accommodate active, noisy children.

**operant conditioning** The learning process by which a particular action is followed by something desired (which makes the person or animal more likely to repeat the action) or by something unwanted (which makes the action less likely to be repeated). (Also called *instrumental conditioning.*)

**reinforcement** When a behavior is followed by something desired, such as food for a hungry animal or a welcoming smile for a lonely person.

AP Images

**Rats, Pigeons, and People** B. F. Skinner is best known for his experiments with rats and pigeons, but he also applied his knowledge to human behavior. For his daughter, he designed a glass-enclosed crib in which temperature, humidity, and perceptual stimulation could be controlled to make her time in the crib enjoyable and educational. He encouraged her first attempts to talk by smiling and responding with words, affection, or other positive reinforcement.

**Answer to Observation Quiz** (from p. 42) Both are balding, with white beards. Note also that none of the other theorists in this chapter have beards—a cohort difference, not an ideological one.

to behaviorism, almost all of our daily behavior, from saying "Good morning" to earning a paycheck, is the result of past reinforcement.

Pleasant consequences are sometimes called *rewards*, but behaviorists do not call them that because they want to avoid the confusion of the word "reward." What some people consider a reward may actually be a *punishment,* an unpleasant consequence. For instance, a teacher might reward good behavior by giving the class extra recess time, but some children hate recess. For them, recess is not a reinforcer.

The opposite is true as well: Something thought to be a punishment may actually be reinforcing. For example, parents "punish" their children by withholding dessert. But a particular child might dislike the dessert, so being deprived of it is no punishment.

Culture matters, too. Japanese parents threaten to punish their children by refusing to let them come home; American parents threaten to make the children stay home. Whether these opposite strategies are really punishments depends on the child as well as the culture (Bornstein, 2017).

The crucial question is "What works as a reinforcement or punishment for that individual?" The answer varies by age, as developmentalists have shown. For instance, adolescents find risk and excitement particularly reinforcing, and they consider punishments much less painful than adults do. That was one conclusion of a study of teenagers who were violent: For them, the thrill of breaking the law was reinforcing, outweighing the pain of getting caught (Shulman et al., 2017).

Consider a common practice in schools: Teachers send misbehaving children out of the classroom. Then principals suspend the worst violators from school.

However, if a child hates the teacher, leaving class is rewarding; and if a child hates school, suspension is a reinforcement. Indeed, research on school discipline finds that some measures, including school suspension, *increase* later disobedience (Osher et al., 2010). Educators have learned that, to stop misbehavior, it is often more effective to encourage good behavior, to "catch them being good" (Polirstok, 2015, p. 932).

In the United States, the chance of an African American child being suspended from school is three times higher than for a European American child. The rate is also higher than average for children designated as needing special education. Those statistics raise a troubling question: Is suspension a punishment for the child, or is it a reinforcer for the teacher? (Tajalli & Garba, 2014; Shah, 2011).

The data show that children who are suspended from school are more likely than other children to be imprisoned years later. That is a correlation; it does not prove that suspension *causes* later imprisonment. But behaviorists suggest that it might (Mallett, 2016). **[Developmental Link:** Correlation and causation are discussed in Chapter 1.]

Remember, behaviorists focus on the *effect* that a consequence has on future behavior, not whether it is intended to be a reward or not. Children who misbehave again and again have been reinforced, not punished, for their actions—perhaps by their parents or teachers, perhaps by their friends or themselves.

**TABLE 2.2**

**Three Types of Learning**

Behaviorism is also called *learning theory* because it emphasizes the learning process, as shown here.

| Type of Learning | Learning Process | Result |
|---|---|---|
| Classical Conditioning | Learning occurs through association. | Neutral stimulus becomes conditioned response. |
| Operant Conditioning | Learning occurs through reinforcement and punishment. | Weak or rare responses become strong and frequent—or, with punishment, unwanted responses become extinct. |
| Social Learning | Learning occurs through modeling what others do. | Observed behaviors become copied behaviors. |

## Social Learning

At first, behaviorists thought all behavior arose from a chain of learned responses, the result of (1) the association between one stimulus and another (classical conditioning) or (2) past reinforcement (operant conditioning). Thousands of experiments inspired by learning theory have demonstrated that both classical conditioning and operant conditioning occur in everyday life. We are all conditioned to react as we do.

However, people at every age are social and active, not just reactive. Instead of responding merely to their own direct experiences, "people act on the environment. They create it, preserve it, transform it, and even destroy it . . . [in] a socially embedded interplay" (Bandura, 2006, p. 167).

That social interplay is the foundation of **social learning theory** (see Table 2.2), which holds that humans sometimes learn without personal reinforcement. As Albert Bandura, the primary proponent of this theory, explains, this learning often occurs through **modeling,** when people copy what they see others do (also called *observational learning*) (Bandura, 1986, 1997).

Modeling is not simple imitation: Some people are more likely to follow or to be role models than others. Indeed, people model only some actions, of some individuals, in some contexts. Sometimes people do the opposite of what they have seen.

Generally, modeling is most likely when the observer is uncertain or inexperienced (which explains why modeling is especially powerful in childhood) and when the model is admired, powerful, nurturing, or similar to the observer. Social learning occurs not only for behavior and preferences (why do teenagers wear their hair as they do?) but also for morals, which may appear to be decided by each individual but also are affected by what people learn from others (Bandura, 2016).

## Cognitive Theory: Piaget and Information Processing

According to **cognitive theory,** thoughts and expectations profoundly affect attitudes, values, emotions, and actions. This may seem obvious now, but it was not always so clear. Social scientists recognize a "cognitive revolution," which occurred around 1980. Suddenly *how* and *what* people think became important. This added to psychoanalysis (which emphasized hidden impulses) and behaviorism (which emphasized observed actions). Thoughts come between impulses and actions, and they are crucial.

The cognitive revolution is ongoing: Contemporary researchers use new tools to study cognition, with neuroscience, large data, and body–mind connections (e.g., Glenberg et al., 2013; Griffiths, 2015). To understand the impact of cognitive theory on development, we begin with Piaget.

### Piaget's Stages of Development

Jean Piaget (1896–1980) transformed our understanding of cognition, leading some people to consider him "the greatest developmental psychologist of all time" (Haidt, 2013, p. 6). His academic training was in biology, with a focus on shellfish—a background that taught him to look closely at small details.

Before Piaget, most scientists believed that babies could not yet think. But Piaget used scientific observation with his own three infants. He took meticulous notes, finding infants curious and thoughtful.

**LaunchPad**
macmillan learning

**Video Activity: Modeling: Learning by Observation** features the original footage of Albert Bandura's famous experiment.

**social learning theory** An extension of behaviorism that emphasizes the influence that other people have over a person's behavior. Even without specific reinforcement, every individual learns many things through observation and imitation of other people. (Also called *observational learning*.)

**modeling** The central process of social learning, by which a person observes the actions of others and then copies them.

**THINK CRITICALLY:** Is your speech, hairstyle, or choice of shoes similar to those of your peers, or of an entertainer, or a sports hero? Why?

**cognitive theory** A grand theory of human development that focuses on changes in how people think over time. According to this theory, our thoughts shape our attitudes, beliefs, and behaviors.

**TABLE 2.3**

Piaget's Periods of Cognitive Development

|  | Name of Period | Characteristics of the Period | Major Gains During the Period |
|---|---|---|---|
| Birth to 2 years | Sensorimotor | Infants use senses and motor abilities to understand the world. Learning is active, without reflection. | Infants learn that objects still exist when out of sight (*object permanence*) and begin to think through mental actions. (The sensorimotor period is discussed further in Chapter 6.) |
| 2–6 years | Preoperational | Children think symbolically, with language, yet children are *egocentric,* perceiving from their own perspective. | The imagination flourishes, and language becomes a significant means of self-expression and social influence. (The preoperational period is discussed further in Chapter 9.) |
| 6–11 years | Concrete operational | Children understand and apply logic. Thinking is limited by direct experience. | By applying logic, children grasp concepts of conservation, number, classification, and many other scientific ideas. (The concrete-operational period is discussed further in Chapter 12.) |
| 12 years through adulthood | Formal operational | Adolescents and adults use abstract and hypothetical concepts. They can use analysis, not only emotion. | Ethics, politics, and social and moral issues become fascinating as adolescents and adults use abstract, theoretical reasoning. (The formal-operational period is discussed further in Chapter 15.) |

Patrick Grehan/CORBIS/Corbis via Getty Images

**Would You Talk to This Man?** Children loved talking to Jean Piaget, and he learned by listening carefully—especially to their incorrect explanations, which no one had paid much attention to before. All his life, Piaget was absorbed with studying the way children think. He called himself a "genetic epistemologist"—one who studies how children gain knowledge about the world as they grow.

**cognitive equilibrium** In cognitive theory, a state of mental balance in which people are not confused because they can use their existing thought processes to understand current experiences and ideas.

Later he studied hundreds of schoolchildren. From this work emerged the central thesis of cognitive theory: *How* children think changes with time and experience, and their thought processes affect behavior. According to cognitive theory, to understand people, one must understand their thinking.

Piaget maintained that cognitive development occurs in four age-related periods, or stages: *sensorimotor, preoperational, concrete operational*, and *formal operational* (see Table 2.3). Each period fosters certain cognitive processes: Infants think via their senses; preschoolers have language but not logic; school-age children have simple logic; adolescents and adults can use formal, abstract logic (Inhelder & Piaget, 1958/2013b; Piaget, 1952/2011).

Piaget found that intellectual advancement occurs because humans at every age seek **cognitive equilibrium**—a state of mental balance. The easiest way to achieve this balance is to interpret new experiences through the lens of preexisting ideas. For example, infants grab new objects in the same way that they grasp familiar objects; a child's concept of God as loving or punishing depends on their experience with their own parents. That is why people of many faiths call themselves "a child of God."

At every age, people interpret other people's behavior by assuming that everyone thinks as they themselves do. Once a child gets an idea, he or she sticks to it—even when logic or adults say it is wrong.

Cognition is easier when the mind simplifies ideas. For instance, once children grasp the concept of "dog," they can see unfamiliar animals on the street, from Great Danes to Chihuahuas, and say "doggie." They also expect dogs to sniff, bark, wag tails, and so on. Some children want to pet every dog they see; some fear them all—but in either case, generalities of "dogness" are evident.

Achieving cognitive equilibrium is not always easy, however. Sometimes a new experience or question is jarring or incomprehensible—such as learning that some dogs (Basenjis) do not bark. Then the individual experiences *cognitive disequilibrium*, an imbalance that creates confusion.

(a)

(b)

(c)

**How to Think About Flowers** A person's stage of cognitive growth influences how he or she thinks about everything, including flowers. *(a)* To an infant in the sensorimotor stage, flowers are "known" through pulling, smelling, and even biting. *(b)* At the concrete operational stage, children become more logical. This boy can understand that flowers need sunlight, water, and time to grow. *(c)* At the adult's formal operational stage, flowers can be part of a larger, logical scheme—for instance, to earn money while cultivating beauty. As illustrated by all three photos, thinking is an active process from the beginning of life until the end.

As Figure 2.2 illustrates, disequilibrium advances cognition if it leads to adaptive thinking. Piaget describes two types of adaptation:

- **Assimilation:** New experiences are reinterpreted to fit, or *assimilate*, into old ideas. [A Basenji could bark if it wanted to, or Basenjis are not really dogs.]
- **Accommodation:** Old ideas are restructured to include, or *accommodate*, new experiences. [Some dogs do not bark.]

Ideally, when two people disagree, adaptation is mutual. Think of a lovers' quarrel. If both parties listen sympathetically to the other, they both accommodate. Then the quarrel strengthens their relationship, and they reach a new, better equilibrium.

Accommodation requires more effort than assimilation, but it advances thought. Children—and everyone else—actively develop new concepts when the old ones fail. In Piagetian terms, they *construct* ideas based on their experiences.

## Information Processing

Piaget is credited with discovering that each person's mental constructs affect what they do. This *constructionist* idea of cognition is now accepted by most social scientists. However, many think Piaget's theories were limited. Neuroscience, cross-cultural studies, and detailed research have revealed problems in Piaget's theory.

A newer version of cognitive theory is called **information-processing theory,** inspired by the input, programming, memory, and output of the computer. When conceptualized in that way, thinking is affected by the neurons, synapses, and neurotransmitters of the brain.

Information processing is "a framework characterizing a large number of research programs" (Miller, 2011, p. 266). Instead of interpreting *responses* by infants and children, as Piaget did, this cognitive theory focuses on the *processes* of thought—that is, when, why, and how neurons fire to activate a thought.

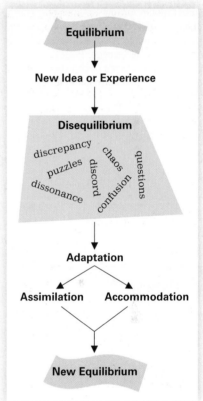

**FIGURE 2.2**

**Challenge Me** Most of us, most of the time, prefer the comfort of our conventional conclusions. According to Piaget, however, when new ideas disturb our thinking, we have an opportunity to expand our cognition with a broader and deeper understanding.

**assimilation** The reinterpretation of new experiences to fit into old ideas.

**accommodation** The restructuring of old ideas to include new experiences.

**information-processing theory** A perspective that compares human thinking processes, by analogy, to computer analysis of data, including sensory input, connections, stored memories, and output.

**Brain Cells in Action** Neurons reach out to other neurons, shown here in an expansion microscopy photo that was impossible even a decade ago. No wonder Piaget's description of the four stages of cognition needs revision from the information-processing perspective.

Brain activity is traced back to what activated those neurons. Information-processing theorists examine stimuli from the senses, body movements, hormones, and organs, all of which affect thinking (Glenberg et al., 2013). These scientists believe that details of cognitive processes shed light on the outcome.

Information-processing theorists contend that cognition begins when *input* is picked up by one of the senses. It proceeds to brain reactions, connections, and stored memories, and it concludes with some form of *output*. For infants, output consists of moving a hand, making a sound, or staring a split second longer at one stimulus than at another. As children mature, information-processing scientists examine words, hesitations, neuronal activity, and bodily reactions (heartbeat, blood pressure, hormones, and the like).

The latest techniques to study the brain have produced insights from neuroscience on the sequence and strength of neuronal communication. This research has uncovered patterns beyond those traced by early information-processing theory. Combining brain research and cognitive insights leads to new understanding of cognition, as detailed in an article titled "Could a Neuroscientist Understand a Microprocessor?" The answer is yes; the two streams of research are better together (Jonas & Kording, 2017).

With the aid of sensitive technology, information-processing research has overturned some of Piaget's findings, as you will later read. However, the basic tenet of cognitive theory is equally true for Piaget, neuroscience, and information processing: *Ideas matter.*

Thus, how children interpret a hypothetical social situation, such as whether they anticipate acceptance or rejection, affects their actual friendships; how teenagers conceptualize heaven and hell influences their sexual activity. For everyone, ideas frame situations and affect actions.

**Healthy Control Adults**

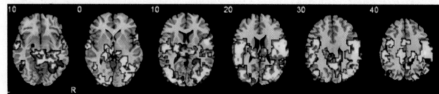

**Adults with Childhood ADHD**

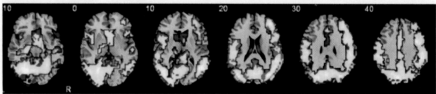

**They Try Harder** Details of brain scans require interpretation from neurologists, but even the novice can see that adults who have been diagnosed with ADHD (second line of images) reacted differently in this experiment when they were required to push a button only if certain letters appeared on a screen. Sustained attention to this task required more brain power (the lit areas) for those with ADHD. Notice also that certain parts of the brain were activated by the healthy adults and not by those with ADHD. Apparently, adults who had problems paying attention when they were children have learned to focus when they need to, but they do it in their own way and with more effort.

DR TORSTEN WITTMANN/SCIENCE PHOTO LIBRARY/Getty Images

# Measuring Mental Activity

A hundred years ago, people thought that emotions came from the heart. That's why we still send hearts on Valentine's Day, why we speak of broken hearts or of people who are soft- or hard-hearted.

But now we know that everything begins inside the brain. It is foolish to dismiss a sensation with "It's all in your head." Of course it is in your head; everything is.

Until quite recently, the only way scientists could estimate brain activity was to measure heads. Measuring produced some obvious discoveries—babies with shrunken brains (*microcephaly*) suffered severe intellectual disability; brains grew bigger as children matured.

Measuring also led to some obvious errors, now discredited. In the nineteenth and early twentieth centuries, many scientists believed the theory that bumps on the head reflected intelligence and character, a theory known as *phrenology*. Psychiatrists would run their hands over a person's skull to measure 27 traits, including spirituality, loyalty, and aggression. Another example was that some scientists said that women could never be professors because their brains were too small (Swaab & Hofman, 1984).

Within the past half-century, neuroscientists developed ways to use electrodes, magnets, light, and computers to measure brain activity, not just brain size (see Table 2.4). Bumps on the head and head size (within limits) were proven irrelevant to intellectual processes. Researchers now study cognitive processes between input and output. Some results are cited later. In this feature we describe methods.

## TABLE 2.4

### Some Techniques Used by Neuroscientists to Understand Brain Function

**EEG (electroencephalogram)**

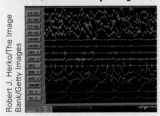

Robert J. Herko/The Image Bank/Getty Images

The EEG measures electrical activity in the cortex. This can differentiate active brains (beta brain waves—very rapid, 12 to 30 per second) from sleeping brains (delta waves—1 to 3 per second) and brain states that are half-awake, or dreaming. Complete lack of brain waves, called flat-line, indicates brain death.

**ERP (event-related potential)**

Langlois Social Development Lab

The amplitude and frequency of brain electrical activity changes when a particular stimulus (called an event) occurs. First, the ERP establishes the usual patterns, and then researchers present a stimulus (such as a sound, an image, a word) that causes a blip in electrical activity. ERP indicates how quickly and extensively people react—although this method requires many repetitions to distinguish the response from the usual brain activity.

**MRI (magnetic resonance imaging)**

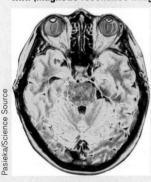

Pasieka/Science Source

The water molecules in various parts of the brain each have a magnetic current, and measuring that current allows measurement of myelin, neurons, and fluid in the brain.

**fMRI (functional magnetic resonance imaging)**

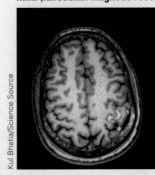

Kul Bhatia/Science Source

In advanced MRI, function is measured as more oxygen is added to the blood flow when specific neurons are activated. The presumption is that increased blood flow means that the person is using that part of the brain. fMRI has revealed that several parts of the brain are active at once—seeing something activates parts of the visual cortex, but it also may activate other parts of the brain far from the visual areas.

**PET (positron emission tomography)**

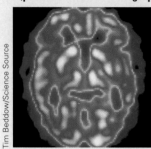

Tim Beddow/Science Source

When a specific part of the brain is active, the blood flows more rapidly in that part. If radioactive dye is injected into the bloodstream and a person lies very still within a scanner while seeing pictures or other stimuli, changes in blood flow indicate thought. PET can reveal the volume of neurotransmitters; the rise or fall of brain oxygen, glucose, amino acids; and more. PET is almost impossible to use with children (who cannot stay still) and is very expensive with adults.

**fNIRS (functional near-infrared spectroscopy)**

Pat Greenhouse/The Boston Globe via Getty Images

This method also measures changes in blood flow. But, it depends on light rather than magnetic charge and can be done with children, who merely wear a special cap connected to electrodes and do not need to lie still in a noisy machine (as they do for PET or fMRI). By measuring how each area of the brain absorbs light, neuroscientists infer activity of the brain (Ferrari & Quaresima, 2012).

**DTI (diffusion tensor imaging)**

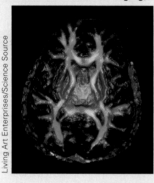

Living Art Enterprises/Science Source

DTI is another technique that builds on the MRI. It measures the flow (diffusion) of water molecules within the brain, which shows connections between one area and another. This is particularly interesting to developmentalists because life experiences affect which brain areas connect with which other ones. Thus, DTI is increasingly used by clinicians who want to individualize treatment and monitor progress (Van Hecke et al., 2016).

For both practical and ethical reasons, it is difficult to use these techniques on large, representative samples. One of the challenges of neuroscience is to develop methods that are harmless, quick, acceptable to parents and babies, and comprehensive. A more immediate challenge is to depict the data in ways that are easy to interpret and understand.

Brain imagery has revealed many surprises. For example, fNIRS finds that the brains of newborns are more active when they hear the language that their mother spoke when they were in the womb than when they hear another language (May et al., 2011). fMRI on adolescents has found that a fully grown brain does not mean a fully functioning brain: The prefrontal cortex is not completely connected to the rest of the brain until about age 25. Brain scans of new mothers reveal that babies change their mothers' brains (P. Kim et al., 2016).

All the tools indicated on these two pages have discovered brain plasticity and variations not imagined in earlier decades. However, sensitive machines and advanced computer analysis are required for accurate readings. Even then, all we know is whether parts of the brain are functioning and active—or not. Changes in light absorption, or magnetism, or oxygenated blood flow in the brain are miniscule from one moment to the next. Interpreting what that means is more complex.

For example, it would be good to replace the conventional lie detector, which is unreliable, with brain imaging. But current technology is not ready (Rose, 2016).

Variations within and between people make it difficult to know what someone is thinking via brain scans. Once again, this confirms the need for theory: Without an idea of what to look for, or what it might mean, the millions of data points from all brain images might lead naive scientists to the same trap as earlier measurements of the skull—their own bias.

# Newer Theories

You have surely noticed that the seminal grand theorists—Freud, Pavlov, Piaget— were all men, scientists who were born in the late nineteenth century and who lived and died in Europe. These background variables are limiting. (Of course, female, non-European, and contemporary theorists have other background limitations.)

A new wave of research and understanding from scientists with more varied experiences is described now. As you will see, contemporary researchers benefit from extensive global and historical research. The multidisciplinary nature of developmental study is now apparent. Sociocultural theorists incorporate research from anthropologists who report on cultures in every nation; evolutionary psychologists use data from archeologists who examine the bones of humans who died 100,000 years ago.

## Sociocultural Theory: Vygotsky and Beyond

One hallmark of newer theories is that they are decidedly multicultural, influenced by recognition that cultures shape experiences and attitudes. Whereas *culture* once referred primarily to oddities outside the normative Western experience, it is now apparent that many cultural differences occur within each nation.

Some cultural differences within the United States arise from ethnic and national origins—people whose grandparents lived in Pakistan versus those with grandparents from Poland, for instance. Some arise from socioeconomic status (SES), when college graduates are contrasted with those who dropped out of high school.

Developmental researchers also appreciate the many cultural differences related to region, age, and gender: An 80-year-old woman in Montana might have a different sociocultural perspective than a 15-year-old boy in Mississippi, even if both have the same SES and ethnic background. [**Developmental Link:** The concept of SES is introduced in Chapter 1.]

The central thesis of **sociocultural theory** is that human development results from the dynamic interaction between developing persons and their surrounding society. Culture is not something external that impinges on developing persons but is internalized, integral to everyday attitudes and actions. This idea is so central to our current understanding of human development that it was already stressed in Chapter 1. Now we explain the terms and implications of sociocultural theory in more detail.

**sociocultural theory** A newer theory which holds that development results from the dynamic interaction of each person with the surrounding social and cultural forces.

Dr. James Wertsch

**Affection for Children** Vygotsky lived in Russia from 1896 to 1934, when war, starvation, and revolution led to the deaths of millions. Throughout this turmoil, Vygotsky focused on learning. His love of children is suggested by this portrait: He and his daughter have their arms around each other.

**apprenticeship in thinking** Vygotsky's term for how cognition is stimulated and developed in people by more skilled members of society.

**guided participation** The process by which people learn from others who guide their experiences and explorations.

**zone of proximal development** In sociocultural theory, a metaphorical area, or "zone," surrounding a learner that includes all of the skills, knowledge, and concepts that the person is close ("proximal") to acquiring but cannot yet master without help.

## Teaching and Guidance

The pioneer of the sociocultural perspective was Lev Vygotsky (1896–1934). Like the other theorists, he was born at the end of the nineteenth century, but unlike them, he traveled extensively within his native Russia, studying Asian and European groups of many faiths, languages, and social contexts.

Vygotsky noted that people everywhere were taught whatever beliefs and habits were valued within their community. He noted many variations. For example, his research included how farmers used tools, how illiterate people thought of abstract ideas, and how children with disabilities learned in school.

In Vygotsky's view, everyone, schooled or not, develops with the guidance of more skilled members of their society. Those skilled people become mentors in an **apprenticeship in thinking** (Vygotsky, 2012).

The word *apprentice* once had a quite specific meaning, sometimes spelled out in a legal contract that detailed what an apprentice would learn from a master. For example, in earlier centuries, a boy wanting to repair shoes would apprentice himself to a cobbler, learning the trade while assisting his teacher.

Vygotsky believed that children become apprentices, sometimes deliberately, but more often guided by knowledgeable parents, teachers, and other people. Mentors teach children how to think within their culture, explaining ideas, asking questions, and reinforcing values.

To describe this process, Vygotsky developed the concept of **guided participation,** the method used by parents, teachers, and entire societies to teach skills and habits. Tutors engage learners (*apprentices*) in joint activities, offering "mutual involvement in several widespread cultural practices with great importance for learning: narratives, routines, and play" (Rogoff, 2003, p. 285).

Active apprenticeship and sensitive guidance are central to sociocultural theory because everyone depends on others to learn. All cultural beliefs are social constructions, not natural laws, according to sociocultural theorists, and thus they need to be taught.

Customs protect and unify a community, yet some cultural assumptions need to change. Because they are social constructions, communities can reconstruct them.

For example, Vygotsky thought that children with disabilities should be educated (Vygotsky, 1994b). This belief has been enshrined in U.S. law since about 1970, a sociocultural shift. Many other social constructions—about the role of women, about professional sports, about family—have been revised in the past half century. Sociocultural theory stresses that customs reflect people, as well as vice versa.

## The Zone of Proximal Development

According to sociocultural theory, all learning is social, whether people are learning a manual skill, a social custom, or a language. As part of the apprenticeship of thinking, a mentor (parent, peer, or professional) finds the learner's **zone of proximal development,** an imaginary area surrounding the learner that contains the skills, knowledge, and concepts that are close (proximal) to being grasped but not yet reached.

Through sensitive assessment of each learner, mentors engage mentees within their zone. Together, in a "process of joint construction," new knowledge is attained (Valsiner, 2006). The mentor must avoid two opposite dangers: boredom and failure. Some frustration is permitted, but the learner must be actively engaged, neither passive nor overwhelmed (see Figure 2.3).

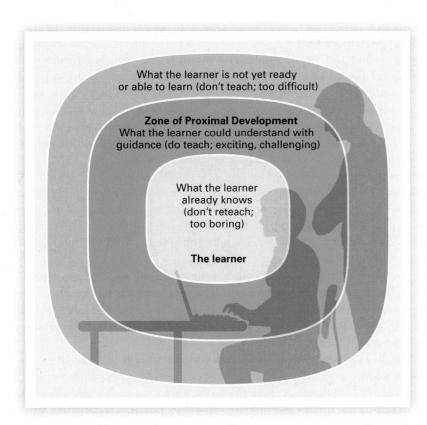

What the learner is not yet ready
or able to learn (don't teach; too difficult)

**Zone of Proximal Development**
What the learner could understand with
guidance (do teach; exciting, challenging)

What the learner
already knows
(don't reteach;
too boring)

**The learner**

FIGURE 2.3
**The Magic Middle** Somewhere between the boring and the impossible is the zone of proximal development, where interaction between teacher and learner results in knowledge never before grasped or skills not already mastered. The intellectual excitement of that zone is the origin of the joy that both instruction and study can bring.

A mentor must sense whether support or freedom is needed and how peers can help (they may be the best mentors). Skilled teachers know when a person's zone of proximal development expands and shifts.

Excursions into and through the zone of proximal development are everywhere. For example, at thousands of science museums in the United States, children ask numerous questions, and adults guide their scientific knowledge (Haden, 2010).

Consider a more common example: a father teaching his daughter to ride a bicycle. He begins by rolling her along, supporting her weight. He tells her to keep her hands on the handlebars, to push the right and left pedals in rhythm, and to look straight ahead. As she becomes more comfortable and confident, he begins to roll her along more quickly, praising her for steadily pedaling.

In later days or weeks, he jogs beside her, holding only the handlebars. When he senses that she can maintain her balance, he urges her to pedal faster while he loosens his grip. Perhaps without realizing it, she rides on her own. Soon she waves goodbye and bikes around the block.

Note that this is not instruction by preset rules. Sociocultural learning is active: No one learns to ride a bike by reading and memorizing written instructions, and no good teacher merely repeats a prepared lesson.

Role models and cultural tools also teach, according to sociocultural theory. The bicycle-riding child wants to learn because she has seen other children biking, and stores sell tricycles, training wheels, and small bikes without pedals. Thus, cultural artifacts guide learning.

In another culture, everything might be different. Perhaps no one rides bicycles, or no fathers teach their daughters—or even allow them outside the house unsupervised. Recognizing such cultural differences is crucial for understanding development, according to this theory.

Bruno De Hogues/The Image Bank/Getty Images

**Zone of Excitement** Vygotsky believed that other people, especially slightly older peers, and all the artifacts of the culture, teach everyone within their zone of proximal development. What lessons are these children learning about emotions, via frightening yet thrilling experiences? Much depends on the design of the amusement park rides, on the adults who paid, and, here, on the big sister, who encourages the hesitant younger child.

## Universals and Specifics

By emphasizing the impact of all of the specific aspects of each culture, sociocultural theory aims to apply universally to everyone, everywhere. Thus, mentors, attuned to ever-shifting abilities and motivation, continually urge new competence—the next level, not the moon. For their part, learners ask questions, show interest, and demonstrate progress that informs and inspires the mentors. When education goes well, both mentor and learner are fully engaged and productive within the zone. Particular skills and lessons vary enormously, but the overall process is the same.

Within each culture, learners have personal traits, experiences, and aspirations. Consequently, education must be attuned to the individual. Some people need more assurance; some seek independence. However, the idea that each person has a particular learning style (e.g., through listening or watching) is more myth than fact (Kirschner, 2017).

Mentors need to be sensitive to the needs, abilities, and motives of the learner, but they must not pigeonhole anyone's learning mode. The sociocultural perspective likewise notes that it is shortsighted to consider any culture exclusively one type or another; everyone, and every culture, expresses common humanity, albeit in various ways.

In another example, every Western child must learn to sit at the table and eat with a knife and fork. This is a long process. Parents neither spoon-feed their 3-year-olds nor expect them to cut their own meat. Instead they find the proper zone of proximal development, and they provide appropriate tools and guidance.

However, given that about one-third of the world's people eat with knives and forks, about one-third with chopsticks, and about one-third with their hands, it would be foolish to measure 3-year-olds' dexterity by noting how they used utensils. Cultural differences must be considered first, before measuring skill.

Likewise, children universally grow up within families, but the specifics of family type and family relationships vary a great deal. Because of insights from sociocultural theory, a Western analysis of children's family drawings is now thought to be inadequate for children in non-Western cultures (Rübeling et al., 2011).

Specifically, some psychologists thought that children who drew their families with small people, neutral facial expressions, and arms downward were less securely attached to their families than those who drew smiling families with arms up (Fury et al., 1997). However, a comparison of drawings from children in Berlin and from children in Cameroon finds that culture influences drawings more than the child's psyche (see Figure 2.4) (Gernhardt et al., 2016).

Remember that all theories are designed to be useful, yet each is distinct. The Opposing Perspectives feature on page 56 is one illustration of the way psychoanalytic, behaviorist, cognitive, and sociocultural theory might apply to common parental concerns.

## Evolutionary Theory

You are familiar with Charles Darwin and his ideas, first published over 150 years ago, regarding the evolution of plants, insects, and birds over billions of years (Darwin, 1859). But you may not realize that serious research on human development inspired by this theory is quite recent (Simpson & Kenrick, 2013). As a proponent of this theory recently wrote:

> Evolutionary psychology . . . is a revolutionary new science, a true synthesis of modern principles of psychology and evolutionary biology.

*[Buss, 2015, p. xv]*

This perspective is not universally accepted by social scientists, but nonetheless this theory has led to new hypotheses and provocative ideas relevant to human development. A leading psycholinguist wrote, "there are major spheres of

**FIGURE 2.4**

**Standing Firm** When children draw their families, many child therapists look for signs of trouble—such as small, frowning people (with hands down) not standing on solid ground. But cross-cultural research shows that such depictions reflect local norms. As their drawings demonstrate, the Cameroonian 6-year-olds were as well adjusted in their local community as the three German children.

A. Nso Boy, 6;6 Years

B. Nso Girl, 6;5 Years

C. Nso Girl, 6;0 Years

D. Berlin Boy, 6;5 Years

E. Berlin Girl, 6;6 Years

F. Berlin Girl, 6;5 Years

human experience—beauty, motherhood, kinship, morality, cooperation, sexuality, violence—in which evolutionary psychology provides the only coherent theory" (Pinker, 2003, p. 135).

The basic idea of evolutionary psychology is that in order to understand the emotions, impulses, and habits of humans over the life span, we must appreciate how those same emotions, impulses, and habits developed within *Homo sapiens* over the past 100,000 years.

## Why We Fear Snakes More Than Cars

Evolutionary theory has intriguing explanations for many issues in human development, including pregnant women's nausea, 1-year-olds' attachment to their parents, and the obesity epidemic. All of these may have evolved to help child survival many millennia ago.

For example, many people are terrified of snakes; they scream and sweat upon seeing one. Yet snakes currently cause less than one death in a million, while cars

## Toilet Training—How and When?

Parents hear conflicting advice about almost everything regarding infant care, including feeding, responding to cries, bathing, and exercise. Often a particular parental response springs from one of the theories explained in this chapter—no wonder advice is sometimes contradictory.

One practical example is toilet training. In the nineteenth century, many parents believed that bodily functions should be controlled as soon as possible in order to distinguish humans from lower animals. Consequently, they began toilet training in the first months of life (Accardo, 2006). Then, psychoanalytic theory pegged the first year as the oral stage (Freud) or the time when trust was crucial (Erikson), before the toddler's anal stage (Freud) began or autonomy needs (Erikson) emerged.

Consequently, psychoanalytic theory led to postponing toilet training to avoid serious personality problems later on. This was soon part of many manuals on child rearing. For example, a leading pediatrician, Barry Brazelton, wrote a popular book for parents advising that toilet training should not begin until the child is cognitively, emotionally, and biologically ready—around age 2 for daytime training and age 3 for nighttime dryness.

> As a society, we are far too concerned about pushing children to be toilet trained early. I don't even like the phrase "toilet training." It really should be toilet learning.
>
> [Brazelton & Sparrow, 2006, p. 193]

By the middle of the twentieth century, many U.S. psychologists had rejected psychoanalytic theory and become behaviorists. Since they believed that learning depends primarily on conditioning, some suggested that toilet training occur whenever the parent wished, not at a particular age.

In one application of behaviorism, children drank quantities of their favorite juice, sat on the potty with a parent nearby to keep them entertained, and then, when the inevitable occurred, the parent praised and rewarded them—a powerful reinforcement. Children were conditioned (in one day, according to some behaviorists) to head for the potty whenever the need arose (Azrin & Foxx, 1974).

Cognitive theorists would consider such a concerted effort, with immediate reinforcement, unnecessary, and they might wonder why any parent would think toilet training should occur before the child understands what is happening. Instead, cognitive theory suggests that parents wait until the child can understand reasons to urinate and defecate in the toilet.

Sociocultural theory might reject all of these theories. Instead, the cultural context is crucial, which is why the advent of disposable diapers in modern society has pushed the age of toilet training later and later in the twenty-first century.

Context is also the explanation for some African cultures in which children toilet train themselves by following slightly older children to the surrounding trees and bushes. This is easier, of course, if toddlers wear no diapers—which makes sense in some climates. Sociocultural theory explains that practices differ because of the ecological context, and infants adjust.

Meanwhile, some Western parents prefer to start potty training very early. One U.S. mother began training her baby just 33 days after birth. She noticed when her son was about to defecate, held him above the toilet, and had trained him by 6 months (Sun & Rugolotto, 2004).

Such early training is criticized by all of the theories, each in their own way:

- Psychoanalysts would wonder what made her such an anal person, valuing cleanliness and order without considering the child's needs.
- Behaviorists would say that the mother was trained, not the son. She taught herself to be sensitive to his body; she was reinforced when she read his clues correctly.
- Cognitive theory would question the mother's thinking. For instance, did she have an odd fear of normal body functions?
- Sociocultural theorists would be aghast that the U.S. drive for personal control took such a bizarre turn.
- Evolutionary theory would criticize this attempt to go against human nature.

What is best? Some parents are reluctant to train, and according to one book, the result is that many children are still in diapers at age 5 (Barone, 2015). Dueling theories and diverse parental practices have led the authors of an article for pediatricians to conclude that "despite families and physicians having addressed this issue for generations, there still is no consensus regarding the best method or even a standard definition of toilet training" (Howell et al., 2010, p. 262).

Many sources explain that because each child is different, there is no "right" way: "the best strategy for implementing training is still unknown" (Colaco et al., 2013, p. 49).

That may suggest sociocultural theory, which notes vast differences from one community to another. A study of parents' opinions in Belgium found that mothers without a partner and without much education were more likely to wait too long, until age 3 or so (van Nunen et al., 2015). Of course, both "too soon" and "too late" are matters of opinion.

What values are embedded in each practice? Psychoanalytic theory focuses on later personality, behaviorism stresses conditioning of body impulses, cognitive theory considers variation in the child's intellectual capacity, sociocultural theory allows vast diversity, and evolutionary theory respects human nature.

There is no easy answer, but many parents firmly believe in one approach or another. That confirms the statement at the beginning of this chapter: We all have theories, sometimes strongly held, whether we know it or not.

---

cause more than a thousand times that (OECD, 2014). Why is virtually no one terrified of automobiles? The explanation is that human fears have evolved since ancient times, when snakes were common killers. Thus,

> ancient dangers such as snakes, spiders, heights, and strangers appear on lists of common phobias far more often than do evolutionarily modern dangers such as cars and guns, even though cars and guns are more dangerous to survival in the modern environment.
>
> *[Confer et al., 2010, p. 111]*

Since our fears have not caught up to automobiles, we must use our minds to pass laws regarding infant seats, child-safety restraints, seat belts, red lights, and speed limits. North Americans are succeeding in such measures: The 2015 U.S. motor-vehicle death rate was 11 per 100,000, half the rate of 25 years ago (Highway Traffic Reporting System, various years).

Other modern killers—climate change, drug addiction, obesity, pollution—also require social management because instincts are contrary to what we now know about the dangers of each of these. Evolutionary theory contends that recognizing the ancient origins of destructive urges—such as the deadly desire to eat calorie-dense whipped cream—is the first step in controlling them (King, 2013).

## Why We Protect Babies

According to evolutionary theory, every species has two long-standing, biologically based drives: survival and reproduction. Understanding these two drives provides insight into protective parenthood, the death of newborns, infant dependency, child immaturity, the onset of puberty, the formation of families, and much more (Konner, 2010).

Here is one example. Adults see babies as cute, despite the reality that babies have little hair, no chins, stubby legs, and round stomachs—none of which is considered attractive in adults. The reason, evolutionary theory contends, is that adults are instinctually attuned to protect and cherish infants more than adults. That was essential 100,000 years ago, when survival of the species was in doubt.

But humans do not always protect every baby. Indeed, another evolutionary instinct is that all creatures seek to perpetuate their own descendants more than those who are unrelated. That might lead to infanticide of infants who are not one's own.

Some primates do exactly that: Chimpanzee males who take over a troop kill babies of the deposed male. This occurred among ancient humans as well. The Bible chronicles at least three examples, two in the story of Moses and one in the birth of Jesus. Modern humans, of course, have created laws against infanticide—a necessity because evolutionary instincts might be murderous (Hrdy, 2009).

An application of evolutionary theory is found in research on grandmothers. Recently, grandmothers have been studied extensively by women (evidence of the wider perspective of newer theories). Historic data from every continent led to the *grandmother hypothesis*, that menopause and female longevity were evolutionary adaptations arising from children's survival needs (Hawkes & Coxworth, 2013). Older women needed to stop childbearing and live on for decades, because they were needed to protect the young.

## Genetic Links

This inborn urge to protect is explained by another concept from evolutionary theory: **selective adaptation.** The idea is that humans today react in ways that promoted survival and reproduction long ago. According to one version of selective adaptation, genes for traits that aided survival and reproduction are favored to allow the species to thrive (see Figure 2.5). Some of the best qualities of people—cooperation, spirituality, and self-sacrifice—may have originated thousands of years ago when tribes and then nations became prosperous because they took care of one another (Rand & Nowak, 2016).

Selective adaptation works as follows: If one person happens to have a trait that makes survival more likely, the gene (or combination of genes) responsible for that trait is passed on to the next generation because that

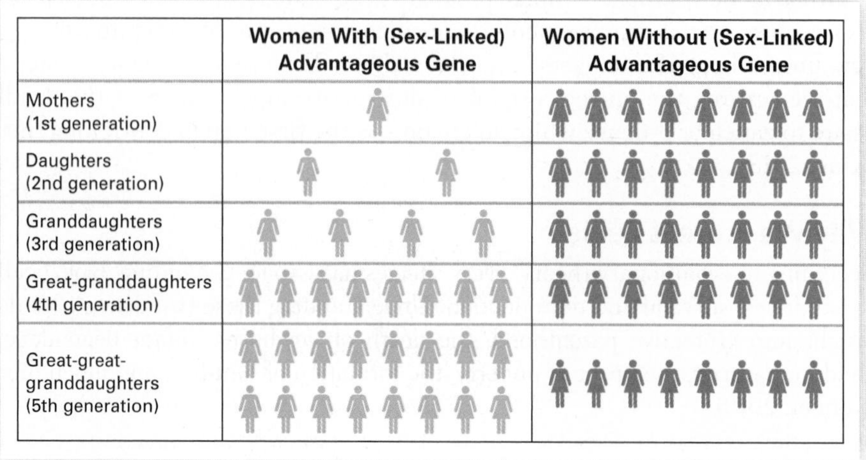

---

**Especially for Teachers and Counselors of Teenagers** Teen pregnancy is destructive of adolescent education, family life, and sometimes even health. According to evolutionary theory, what can be done about this? (see response, p. 62)

**selective adaptation** The process by which living creatures (including people) adjust to their environment. Genes that enhance survival and reproductive ability are selected, over the generations, to become more prevalent.

---

**FIGURE 2.5**

**Selective Adaptation Illustrated** Suppose only one of nine mothers happened to have a gene that improved survival (top row). Suppose, the average woman had only one surviving daughter, but this gene mutation might allow each woman who had the gene bore two girls who survived to womanhood instead of one. As you see, in 100 years, the "odd" gene becomes more common, making it a new normal.

| | Women With (Sex-Linked) Advantageous Gene | Women Without (Sex-Linked) Advantageous Gene |
|---|---|---|
| Mothers (1st generation) | 1 | 8 |
| Daughters (2nd generation) | 2 | 8 |
| Granddaughters (3rd generation) | 4 | 8 |
| Great-granddaughters (4th generation) | 8 | 8 |
| Great-great-granddaughters (5th generation) | 16 | 8 |

person will live long enough to reproduce. Anyone with such a fortunate genetic inheritance has a better chance than those without that gene to survive, mate, and bear many children—half of whom would inherit genes for that desirable trait.

For example, originally almost all human babies lost the ability to digest lactose at about age 2, when they were weaned from breast milk. Older children and adults were all *lactose-intolerant*, unable to digest milk (Suchy et al., 2010). In a few regions thousands of years ago, cattle were domesticated and raised for their meat. In those places, "killing the fatted calf" provided a rare feast for the entire community.

As you will see in the next chapter, genes are not always copied exactly from one generation to the next; spontaneous mutations occur. In those cattle-raising regions, occasionally a young woman would chance to have an aberrant but beneficial gene for the enzyme that allows digestion of cow's milk. If she drank milk intended for a calf, she not only could digest it but she also would not be malnourished like most other young women. Her weight gain would allow earlier puberty, successful pregnancies, and then ample breast milk.

For all of those reasons, her mutant gene would spread to more descendants than the genes of her less-fortunate sisters. Thus, the next generation would include more people who inherited that odd gene, becoming lactose-tolerant unlike most of their peers. Because of the reproductive advantages, with each generation their numbers would increase. Eventually, that gene would become the new norm.

Interestingly, there are several distinct genetic versions of lactose tolerance: Apparently in each cattle-raising region, when a mutant gene allowed digestion of milk, selective adaptation increased the prevalence of that gene (Ranciaro et al., 2014).

This process of selective adaptation has taken centuries. Currently, many people can digest milk, enhancing survival in cattle-raising communities. That is why few Scandinavians are lactose-intolerant but many Africans are—but not those Africans in regions of Kenya and Tanzania where cattle were raised (Ranciaro et al., 2014).

Once it was understood that milk might make some African and Asian children sick, better ways to relieve hunger were found. Although malnutrition is still a global problem, fewer children are malnourished today than decades ago, partly because nutritionists know which foods are digestible, nourishing, and tasty for whom. Evolutionary psychology has helped with that.

For groups as well as individuals, evolutionary theory notices how the interaction of genes and environment affects survival and reproduction. Genetic variations are particularly beneficial when the environment changes, which is one reason genetic diversity benefits humanity as a whole. Compared to other species, human genes have evolved rapidly, in part because people have had to adapt to many climates (Tattersall, 2017).

If a species' gene pool does not include variants that allow survival in difficult circumstances (such as exposure to a new disease or to an environmental toxin), the entire species becomes extinct. One example is HIV/AIDS, which was deadly in most untreated people but not in a few who were genetically protected. The same is true for Ebola. Some people have inborn protection plus genetic influences on lifestyle that make catching Ebola unlikely (Kilgore et al., 2015). No wonder biologists worry when a particular species becomes inbred. Inbreeding eliminates protective diversity.

Critics point out that people do not always act as evolutionary theory predicts: Parents sometimes abandon newborns, adults sometimes handle snakes, and so

**Got Milk!** Many people in Sweden (like this barefoot preschooler at her summer cottage) drink cow's milk and eat many kinds of cheese. That may be because selective adaptation allowed individuals who could digest lactose to survive in the long northern winters when no crops grew.

**THINK CRITICALLY:** What would happen if lust were the only reason one person would mate with another?

## Highlights of the Science of Human Development

As evident throughout this textbook, much more research and appreciation of the brain, social context, and the non-Western world has expanded our understanding of human development in the 21st century. This timeline lists a few highlights of the past.

**200,000-50,000 BCE** With their large brains, long period of child development, and extensive social and family support, early humans were able to sustain life and raise children more effectively than other primates.

**c. 400 BCE** In ancient Greece, ideas about children from philosophers like Plato (c. 428-348 BCE) and Aristotle (384-322 BCE) influenced further thoughts about children. Plato believed children were born with knowledge. Aristotle believed children learn from experience.

©2016 MACMILLAN

**1650-1800** European philosophers like John Locke (1632-1704) and Jean Jacques Rousseau (1712-1778) debate whether children are born as "blank slates" and how much control parents should take in raising them.

©2016 MACMILLAN

**1797** First European vaccination: Edward Jenner (1749-1823) publicizes smallpox inoculation, building on vaccination against smallpox in Asia, the Middle East, and Africa.

**1750-1850** Beginning of Western laws regulating child labor and protecting the rights of children.

**1879** First experimental psychology laboratory established in Leipzig, Germany.

**1885** Sigmund Freud (1856-1939) publishes *Studies on Hysteria*, one of the first works establishing the importance of the subconscious and marking the beginning of the theories of psychoanalytic theory.

©2016 MACMILLAN

**1895** Ivan Pavlov (1849-1936) begins research on dogs salivation response.

AGENCY ANIMAL PICTURE/STOCKBYTE/GETTY IMAGES

**1905** Max Weber (1864-1920), the founder of sociology, writes *The Protestant Work Ethic*, about human values and adult work.

**1905** Alfred Binet's (1857-1911) intelligence test published.

**1907** Maria Montessori (1870-1952) opens her first school in Rome.

HARVEY WATTS PHOTOGRAPHY/MOMENT/GETTY IMAGES

**1913** John B. Watson (1878-1958) publishes *Psychology As the Behaviorist Views It*.

**140 BCE** In China, imperial examinations are one of the first times cognitive testing is used on young people.

**500-1500** During the Middle Ages in Europe, many adults believed that children were miniature adults.

SCALA/ART RESOURCE, NY

**1100-1200** First universities founded in Europe. Young people pay to be educated together.

RALF HETTLER/GRAFISSIMO/GETTY IMAGES

**1837** First kindergarten opens in Germany, part of a movement to teach young children before they entered the primary school system.

**1859** Charles Darwin (1809-1882) publishes *On the Origin of Species*, sparking debates about what is genetic and what is environmental.

NICHOLAS VEASEY/PHOTOGRAPHER'S CHOICE/GETTY IMAGES

**1900** Compulsory schooling for children is established for most children in the United States and Europe.

RALF HETTLER/GRAFISSIMO/GETTY IMAGES

**1903** The term "gerontology," the branch of developmental science devoted to studying aging, first coined.

FUSE/CORBIS/GETTY IMAGES

**1920** Lev Vygotsky (1896-1934) develops sociocultural theory in the former Soviet Union.

**1923** Jean Piaget (1896-1980) publishes *The Language and Thought of the Child*.

©2016 MACMILLAN

**1933** Society for Research on Child Development, the preeminent organization for research on child development, founded.

**1939** Mamie (1917-1983) and Kenneth Clark (1914-2005) receive their research grants to study race in early childhood.

JGI/JAMIE GRILL/BLEND IMAGES/GETTY IMAGES

Timeline: 50,000 BCE | 400 BCE | 0 | 500 | 1000 | 1500 | 1650 | 1700

**1943** Abraham Maslow (1908–1970) publishes *A Theory of Motivation*, establishing the hierarchy of needs.

**1950** Erik Erikson (1902–1994) expands on Freud's theory to include social aspects of personality development with the publication of *Childhood and Society*.

©2016 MACMILLAN

**1951** John Bowlby (1907–1990) publishes *Maternal Care and Mental Health*, one of his first works on the importance of parent–child attachment.

MONKEY BUSINESS IMAGES/SHUTTERSTOCK

**1953** Publication of the first papers describing DNA, our genetic blueprint.

ALONZODESIGN/DIGITALVISION VECTORS/GETTY IMAGES

**1957** Harry Harlow (1905–1981) publishes *Love in Infant Monkeys*, describing his research on attachment in rhesus monkeys.

MARTIN ROGERS/THE IMAGE BANK/GETTY IMAGES

**1961** The morning sickness drug Thalidomide is banned after children are born with serious birth defects, calling attention to the problem of teratogens during pregnancy.

**1961** Alfred Bandura (b. 1925) conducts the Bobo Doll experiments, leading to the development of social learning theory.

**1979** Urie Bronfenbrenner (1917–2005) publishes his work on ecological systems theory

**1986** John Gottman (b. 1942) founded the "Love Lab" at the University of Washington to study what makes relationships work.

**1987** Carolyn Rovee-Collier (1942–2014) shows that even young infants can remember in her classic mobile experiments.

FOTOSEARCH/FOTOSEARCH/SUPERSTOCK

**1990** The United Nations treaty *Convention on the Rights of the Child* in effect, requiring the best interests of children be considered, and stating that they are not solely the possession of their parents. All UN nations have signed on, except Somalia, South Sudan, and the United States.

TONGRO/GETTY IMAGES

**1993** Howard Gardner (b. 1943) publishes *Multiple Intelligences*, a major new understanding of the diversity of human intellectual abilities. Gardner has since revised and expanded his ideas in many ways.

**1994** Steven Pinker (b. 1954) publishes *The Language Instinct*, focusing attention on the interaction between neuroscience and behavior, helping developmentalists understand the need for physiological understanding as part of human growth. These themes continue in his later work, such as *How the Mind Works* in 1997.

| 1800 | | 1900 | 2000 |

ANYAIVANOVA/ISTOCK/THINKSTOCK

**1953** B.F. Skinner (1904–1990) conducts experiments on rats and establishes operant conditioning.

**1955** Emmy Werner (b. 1929) begins her Kauai study, which focuses on the power of resilience.

DONNA DAY/EXACTOSTOCK-1598/SUPERSTOCK

**1956** K. Warner Schaie's (b. 1928) Seattle Longitudinal Study of Adult Intelligence begins.

**1965** Head Start, an early childhood education program, launched in the United States.

**1965** Mary Ainsworth (1913–1999) starts using the "Strange Situation" to measure attachment.

©2016 MACMILLAN

**1966** Diana Baumrind (b. 1928) publishes her first work on parenting styles.

**1972** Beginning of the Dunedin, New Zealand, study—one of the first longitudinal studies to include genetic markers.

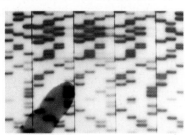
TETRA IMAGES/GETTY IMAGES

**1990–Present** New brain imaging technology allows pinpointing of brain areas involved in everything from executive function to Alzheimer's disease.

ADVENTTR/E+/BARIS SIMSEK/GETTY IMAGES

**1990** Barbara Rogoff (b. 1950) publishes *Apprenticeship in Thinking*, making developmentalists more aware of the significance of culture and context. Rogoff provided new insights and appreciation of child-rearing in Latin America.

**1996** Giacomo Rizzolatti publishes his discovery of mirror neurons.

**2000** Jeffrey Arnett conceptualizes emerging adulthood.

**2003** Mapping of the human genome is completed.

**2013** DSM-5, which emphasizes the role of context in understanding mental health problems, is published.

**Present** Onward. There are many more discoveries and research chronicled in this book.

BLEND IMAGES/BLEND IMAGES/SUPERSTOCK

on. However, evolutionary theorists contend that humans need to understand ancient impulses within our species in order to control them. For instance, we can make cars and guns safer—in part because we know that risk-taking adolescents find them irrationally attractive rather than instinctively frightening.

---

**WHAT HAVE YOU LEARNED?**

**1.** Why is the sociocultural perspective particularly relevant within the United States?

**2.** How do mentors and mentees interact within the zone of proximal development?

**3.** How do the customs and manufactured items in a society affect human development?

**4.** Why are behaviors and emotions that benefited ancient humans still apparent today?

**5.** How are human tastes affected by what people ate 100,000 years ago?

**6.** How does an understanding of ancient people help protect modern humans?

---

## What Theories Contribute

Each major theory discussed in this chapter has contributed to our understanding of human development (see Table 2.5):

- *Psychoanalytic theories* make us aware of the impact of early-childhood experiences, remembered or not, on subsequent development.
- *Behaviorism* shows the effect that immediate responses, associations, and examples have on learning, moment by moment and over time.
- *Cognitive theories* bring an understanding of intellectual processes, including the fact that thoughts and beliefs affect every aspect of our development.
- *Sociocultural theories* remind us that development is embedded in a rich and multifaceted cultural context, evident in every social interaction.
- *Evolutionary theories* suggest that human impulses need to be recognized before they can be guided.

No comprehensive view of development can ignore any of these theories, yet each has encountered severe criticism: *psychoanalytic theory* for being too subjective; *behaviorism* for being too mechanistic; *cognitive theory* for undervaluing emotions; *sociocultural theory* for neglecting individual choice; *evolutionary theory* for ignoring the power of current morals, laws, and norms.

Most developmentalists prefer an **eclectic perspective,** choosing what they consider to be the best aspects of each theory. Rather than adopt any one of these theories exclusively, they make selective use of all of them.

Obviously, all theories reflect the personal background of the theorist, as do all criticisms of theories. Being eclectic, not tied to any one theory, is beneficial because everyone, scientist as well as layperson, is biased. But even being eclectic may be criticized: Choosing the best from each theory may be too picky or the opposite, too tolerant.

For developmentalists, all of these theories merit study and respect. It is easy to dismiss any one of them, but using several perspectives opens our eyes

---

**Response for Teachers and Counselors of Teenagers** (from p. 58) Evolutionary theory stresses the basic human drive for reproduction, which gives teenagers a powerful sex drive. Thus, merely informing teenagers of the difficulty of caring for a newborn (some high school sex-education programs simply give teenagers a chicken egg to nurture) is not likely to work. A better method would be to structure teenagers' lives so that pregnancy is unlikely—for instance, with careful supervision or readily available contraception.

**eclectic perspective** The approach taken by most developmentalists, in which they apply aspects of each of the various theories of development rather than adhering exclusively to one theory.

**TABLE 2.5**

### Five Perspectives on Human Development

| Theory | Area of Focus | Fundamental Depiction of What People Do | Relative Emphasis on Nature or Nurture |
|---|---|---|---|
| Psychoanalytic | Psychosexual (Freud) or psychosocial (Erikson) stages | Battle unconscious impulses and overcome major crises. | More nature (biological, sexual impulses, and parent–child bonds) |
| Behaviorist | Conditioning through stimulus and response | Respond to stimuli, reinforcement, and models. | More nurture (direct environment produces various behaviors) |
| Cognitive | Thinking, remembering, analyzing | Seek to understand experiences while forming concepts. | More nature (mental activity and motivation are key) |
| Sociocultural | Social control, expressed through people, language, customs | Learn the tools, skills, and values of society through apprenticeships. | More nurture (interaction of mentor and learner, within cultures) |
| Evolutionary | Needs and impulses that originated in ancient times | Develop impulses, interests, and patterns to survive and reproduce. | More nature (needs and impulses apply to all humans) |

and minds to aspects of development that we might otherwise ignore. As one overview of seven developmental theories (including those explained here) concludes,

> Because no one theory satisfactorily explains development, it is critical that developmentalists be able to draw on the content, methods, and theoretical concepts of many theories.
>
> *[Miller, 2016, p. 434]*

As you will see in many later chapters, theories provide a fresh look at behavior. Imagine a mother, father, teacher, coach, and grandparent discussing the problems of a particular child. Each might suggest a possible explanation that makes the others say, "I never thought of that." If they listen to each other with an open mind, together they might understand the child better and agree on a beneficial strategy.

Using five theories is like having five perceptive observers. All five are not always on target, but it is better to use theory to consider alternate possibilities than to stay in one narrow groove. A hand functions best with five fingers, although each finger is different and some fingers are more useful than others.

**LaunchPad**
macmillan learning

The Data Connections activity **Historical Highlights of the Science of Human Development** explores the events and individuals that helped establish the field of developmental psychology.

### WHAT HAVE YOU LEARNED?

1. What are the criticisms of each of the five theories?

2. Why are most developmentalists eclectic in regard to theories?

3. Why is it useful to know more than one theory to explain human behavior?

# SUMMARY

## What Theories Do

**1.** A theory provides general principles to guide research and explain observations. Each of the five major developmental theories—psychoanalytic, behaviorist, cognitive, sociocultural, and evolutionary—interprets human development from a distinct perspective, providing a framework for understanding human emotions, experiences, and actions.

**2.** Theories are neither true nor false. They are not facts; they suggest hypotheses to be tested and interpretations of the myriad human behaviors. Good theories are practical: They aid inquiry, interpretation, and daily life.

**3.** A developmental theory focuses on changes that occur over time, uncovering the links between past, present, and future. Developmental theories attempt to answer the crucial questions of the life span.

## Grand Theories

**4.** Psychoanalytic theory emphasizes that adult actions and thoughts originate from unconscious impulses and childhood conflicts. Freud theorized that sexual urges arise during three stages of childhood—oral, anal, and phallic—and continue, after latency, in the genital stage.

**5.** Erikson described eight successive stages of development, each involving a crisis to be resolved. The early stages are crucial, with lifelong effects, but the emphasis is not only on the body and sexual needs. Instead, Erikson stressed that societies, cultures, and family shape each person's development.

**6.** Behaviorists, or learning theorists, believe that scientists should study observable and measurable behavior. Behaviorism emphasizes conditioning—a lifelong learning process in which an association between one stimulus and another (classical conditioning) or the consequences of reinforcement and punishment (operant conditioning) guide behavior.

**7.** Social learning theory recognizes that people learn by observing others, even if they themselves have not been reinforced or punished. Children are particularly susceptible to social learning, but all humans are affected by what they notice in other people.

**8.** Cognitive theorists believe that thoughts and beliefs powerfully affect attitudes, actions, and perceptions, which in turn affect behavior. Piaget proposed four age-related periods of cognition, each propelled by an active search for cognitive equilibrium.

**9.** Information processing focuses on each aspect of cognition—input, processing, and output. This perspective has benefited from technology, first from understanding computer functioning and more recently by the many ways scientists monitor the brain.

## Newer Theories

**10.** Sociocultural theory explains human development in terms of the guidance, support, and structure provided by each social group through culture and mentoring. Vygotsky described how learning occurs through social interactions in which mentors guide learners through their zone of proximal development.

**11.** Sociocultural learning is also encouraged by the examples and tools that each society provides. These are social constructions, which guide everyone but also which can change.

**12.** Evolutionary theory contends that contemporary humans inherit genetic tendencies that have fostered survival and reproduction of the human species for tens of thousands of years. Through selective adaptation, the fears, impulses, and reactions that were useful 100,000 years ago for *Homo sapiens* continue to this day.

**13.** Evolutionary theory provides explanations for many human traits, from lactose intolerance to the love of babies. Selective adaptation is the process by which genes enhance human development over thousands of years. Societies use laws and customs to protect people from some genetic impulses.

## What Theories Contribute

**14.** Psychoanalytic, behavioral, cognitive, sociocultural, and evolutionary theories have aided our understanding of human development. However, no single theory describes the full complexity and diversity of human experience. Most developmentalists are eclectic, drawing on many theories.

# KEY TERMS

developmental theory (p. 37)
psychoanalytic theory (p. 39)
behaviorism (p. 41)
classical conditioning (p. 41)
operant conditioning (p. 43)
reinforcement (p. 43)

social learning theory (p. 45)
modeling (p. 45)
cognitive theory (p. 45)
cognitive equilibrium (p. 46)
assimilation (p. 47)
accommodation (p. 47)

information-processing theory (p. 47)
sociocultural theory (p. 51)
apprenticeship in thinking (p. 52)
guided participation (p. 52)

zone of proximal development (p. 52)
selective adaptation (p. 58)
eclectic perspective (p. 62)

## APPLICATIONS

**1.** Developmentalists sometimes talk about "folk theories," which are developed by ordinary people. Choose three sayings in your culture, such as (from the dominant U.S. culture) "A penny saved is a penny earned" or "As the twig is bent, so grows the tree." Explain the underlying assumptions, or theory, that each saying reflects. Why might the theory be wrong?

**2.** Cognitive theory suggests the power of thoughts, and sociocultural theory emphasizes the power of context. Find someone who disagrees with you about some basic issue (e.g., abortion, immigration, socialism) and listen carefully to their ideas and reasons (encourage them to explain; don't contradict). Then analyze how cognition and experience shaped their ideas *and* your own.

**3.** Ask three people to tell you their theories about male–female differences in mating and sexual behaviors. Which of the theories described in this chapter is closest to each explanation, and which theory is not mentioned?

# The New Genetics

## What Will You Know?

1. Genetically, how is each zygote unique?
2. How do twins differ from other siblings?
3. Who is likely to carry genes that they do not know they have?
4. Why are far more abnormal zygotes created than abnormal babies born?

"**S**he needs a special school. She cannot come back next year," Elissa's middle school principal told us.

We were stunned. Apparently her teachers thought that our wonderful daughter, bright and bubbly (Martin called her "frothy"), was learning-disabled. They had a label for it, "severely spatially disorganized."

Perhaps we should not have been surprised. We knew she misplaced homework, got lost, left books at school, forgot where each class met on which day. But we focused on her strengths in reading, analyzing, and friendship.

I knew the first lesson from genetics: Genes affect everything, not just physical appearance, intellect, and diseases. It dawned on me that Elissa had inherited our behavior. Our desks were covered with papers; our home was cluttered. If we needed masking tape, or working scissors, or silver candlesticks, we had to search in several places. Elissa seemed quite normal to us, but were we spatially disorganized, too?

The second lesson from genetics is that nurture always matters. We had learned to compensate. Since he often got lost, Martin readily asked for directions; since I mislaid documents, I kept my students' papers in clearly marked folders at my office.

There is a third lesson. Whether or not a gene is *expressed,* that is, whether or not it actively affects a person, depends partly on the social context as that person develops. We did not want our genes and habits to impair Elissa. Now that we were aware of her problems, we got help. I consulted a friend who is a professor of special education; Martin found a tutor who knew about disorganized 12-year-olds. Elissa learned to list her homework assignments, check them off when done, put papers carefully in her backpack (not crumpled in the bottom).

We all did our part. We double-checked the list and made sure Elissa had everything when she left for school; Martin attached her bus pass to her backpack; I wrote an impassioned letter telling the principal it would be unethical to expel her; we bought more textbooks so that she could leave one set at school and one at home. The three of us toured other schools, exploring options. Elissa studied diligently, hoping she would stay with her friends.

Success! Elissa aced her final exams, and the principal reluctantly allowed her to return. She became a stellar student and is now a gifted strategist, master organizer, and accomplished professional.

+ **The Genetic Code**
  46 to 21,000 to 3 Billion
  Same and Different
  Matching Genes and
    Chromosomes
  OPPOSING PERSPECTIVES: Too Many
    Boys?

+ **New Cells, New People**
  Cells and Identity
  Twins and More

+ **From Genotype to
  Phenotype**
  Many Factors
  Gene–Gene Interactions
  Nature and Nurture
  Practical Applications

+ **Chromosomal and Genetic
  Problems**
  Spontaneous Mutations
  Not Exactly 46
  Gene Disorders
  Genetic Counseling and Testing
  A CASE TO STUDY: Raising Healthy
    Children

Left: Philip Nealey/Photodisc/Getty Images
Top: shapecharge/E+/Getty Images

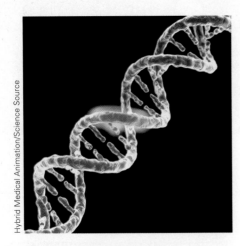

**Twelve of 3 Billion Pairs** This is a computer illustration of a small segment of one gene. Even a small difference in one gene can cause major changes in a person's phenotype.

**deoxyribonucleic acid (DNA)** The chemical composition of the molecules that contain the genes, which are the chemical instructions for cells to manufacture various proteins.

**chromosome** One of the 46 molecules of DNA (in 23 pairs) that virtually every cell of the human body contains and that, together, contain all the genes. Other species have more or fewer chromosomes.

**gene** A small section of a chromosome; the basic unit for the transmission of heredity. A gene consists of a string of chemicals that provide instructions for the cell to manufacture certain proteins.

**genome** The full set of genes that are the instructions to make an individual member of a certain species.

This chapter explains these three lessons. New discoveries about genes are published every day, leading to many surprises, dilemmas, and choices. I hope your understanding of human genetics will mean that you will never be stunned by what a professional says about your child.

## The Genetic Code

First, we review some biology. All living things are composed of cells. The work of cells is done by *proteins.* Each cell manufactures certain proteins according to a code of instructions stored by molecules of **deoxyribonucleic acid (DNA)** at the heart of the cell. These coding DNA molecules are on a **chromosome.**

### 46 to 21,000 to 3 Billion

Humans have 23 pairs of chromosomes (46 in all), which contain the instructions to make the proteins needed for life and growth (see Figure 3.1). The instructions in the 46 chromosomes are organized into genes, with each **gene** usually at a precise location on a particular chromosome.

Individuals have about 21,000 genes, each directing the formation of specific proteins made from a string of 20 amino acids. The genes themselves are a collection of about 3 billion *base pairs,* which are pairs of four chemicals (adenine paired with thymine, and guanine paired with cytosine).

The entire packet of instructions to make a living organism is called the **genome.** There is a genome for every species and variety of plant and animal— even for every bacterium and virus. Genes also define each species, with many genes shared among humans that are not present in other mammals. For example, humans are the only species that talks as we do, an innovation that may have originated from genes handed down by Neanderthal ancestors (Frayer, 2017).

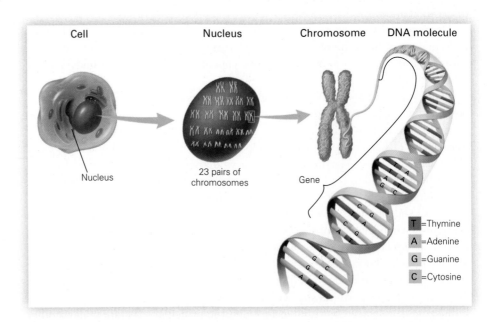

**FIGURE 3.1**

**How Proteins Are Made** The genes on the chromosomes in the nucleus of each cell instruct the cell to manufacture the proteins needed to sustain life and development. The code for a protein is the particular combination of four bases, T-A-G-C (thymine, adenine, guanine, and cytosine).

Members of the same species are quite similar genetically—it is estimated that more than 99 percent of any person's base pairs are identical to those of any other person. Knowing the usual genome of *Homo sapiens,* which was decoded in 2001, is only the start of understanding human genetics because everyone has a slightly different set of genetic instructions.

## Same and Different

It is human nature for people to notice differences more than commonalities. For that reason, before we focus on genetic differences, keep in mind the most important truth: All people are the same in a multitude of ways.

Not only do we all have very similar bodies (two eyes, hands, and feet; the same organs, blood vessels, and bones), but we also all use words and gestures to communicate. We all love and hate; we all hope and fear, not only for ourselves but also for our descendants, our friends, and everyone else.

But, we also have many differences; none of us is exactly like anyone else. Our differences start with our genes. Any gene that varies in the precise sequence of those 3 billion base pairs—sometimes with a seemingly minor transposition, deletion, or repetition—is called an **allele.**

Most alleles cause small differences (such as the shape of an eyebrow), but some are crucial. Another way to state this is to say that some genes are *polymorphic* (literally, "many forms"). They may have *single-nucleotide polymorphisms* (abbreviated SNPs, pronounced "snips"), which is a variation in only one part of the code.

Because each person's variations differ from every other person's variations, each of us is unique. You can recognize at a glance that two people are not identical, even if both are the same age, sex, and ethnicity.

When you search for a well-known friend among a crowd of thousands, you do not mistakenly greet someone who superficially looks like your friend. Even so-called identical twins differ—although few people can see the differences. Tiny variations in SNPs distinguish each face and each body—inside and out.

> **allele** A variation that makes a gene different in some way from other genes for the same characteristics. Many genes never vary; others have several possible alleles.

## Beyond the Genes

RNA (ribonucleic acid, another molecule) and additional DNA surround each gene. In a process called *methylation,* this additional material enhances, transcribes, connects, empowers, silences, and alters genetic instructions.

This noncoding material used to be called *junk*—but no longer. The influences of this surrounding material "alter not the gene itself, but rather, the regulatory elements that control the process of gene expression" (Furey & Sethupathy, 2013, p. 705). Methylation continues throughout life, from conception until death.

Obviously, genes are crucial, but even more crucial is whether or not a gene is expressed. RNA regulates and transcribes genetic instructions, turning some genes and alleles on or off. In other words, a person can have the genetic tendency for a particular trait, disease, or behavior, but that tendency might never appear because it was never turned on. The work of about 120 alleles is to inactivate certain genes (Macosko & McCarroll, 2013). Think of a light switch: A lamp might have a new bulb and an electricity source, but the room stays dark unless the switch is flipped.

Some genetic activation occurs because of prenatal RNA, and some occurs later because of biological factors (such as pollution) and psychological ones (as with social rejection). As already mentioned in Chapter 1, the study of exactly how, why, and when genes change in form and expression is called **epigenetics,** with the Greek root *epi-,* meaning "around, above, below." Epigenetic changes are crucial: Events and circumstances surrounding (around, above, below) the genes determine whether genes are expressed or silenced (Ayyanathan, 2014).

> **epigenetics** The study of how environmental factors affect genes and genetic expression—enhancing, halting, shaping, or altering the expression of genes.

**microbiome** All of the microbes (bacteria, viruses, and so on) with all of their genes in a community; here, the millions of microbes of the human body.

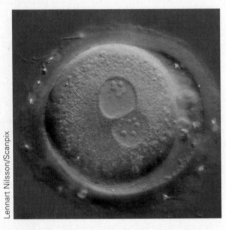

**The Moment of Conception** This ovum is about to become a zygote. It has been penetrated by a single sperm, whose nucleus now lies next to the nucleus of the ovum. Soon, the two nuclei will fuse, bringing together about 21,000 genes to guide development.

**zygote** The single cell formed from the union of two gametes, a sperm and an ovum.

**copy number variations** Genes with various repeats or deletions of base pairs.

## The Microbiome

One aspect of both nature and nurture that profoundly affects each person is the **microbiome,** which refers to all of the microbes (bacteria, viruses, fungi, archaea, and yeasts) that live within every part of the body. The microbiome includes what people call "germs," which they douse with disinfectant and antibiotics. However, most microbes are helpful, not harmful. Microbes have their own DNA, reproducing throughout life.

There are thousands of varieties of these microbes. Together they have an estimated 3 million different genes—influencing immunity, weight, diseases, moods, and much else that affects us every day (Dugas et al., 2016; Koch, 2015). Particularly intriguing is the relationship between the microbiome and nutrition, since bacteria in the gut break down food for nourishment (Devaraj et al., 2013; Pennisi, 2016).

In one telling study, researchers in Malawi studied identical (*monozygotic*) and fraternal (*dizygotic*) twins when one twin was malnourished and the other was not, even though both lived in the same home and were fed the same food. Some suspected that in such cases the greedier twin grabbed food from the other. But, the scientists analyzed each twin's microbiome and found differences that might explain why only one suffered from life-threatening malnutrition (Smith et al., 2013).

Experiments find that obese or thin mice change body size when the microbiome from another mouse with the opposite problem is implanted (Dugas et al., 2016). All of this research suggests that when a child is too thin or overweight, the microbiome—more than the parents—may be to blame.

## Siblings Not Alike

The differences between siblings are not only in the microbiome but also in the genes themselves. Each reproductive cell (sperm or ovum, called *gametes*) has only one of the two chromosomes that a man or a woman has at each of the 23 locations. This means that each man or woman can produce $2^{23}$ different gametes—more than 8 million versions of their chromosomes (actually 8,388,608).

When a sperm and an ovum combine, they create a new single cell called a **zygote.** The genes on one of those 8 million possible sperm from the father interact with the genes on one of the 8 million possible ova from the mother. Thus, your parents could have given you an astronomical number of unique siblings.

Each parent contributes 23 chromosomes, or half the genetic material. When the man's chromosomes pair with the woman's (chromosome 1 from the sperm with chromosome 1 from the ovum, chromosome 2 with chromosome 2, and so on), each gene from each parent connects with its counterpart from the other parent, and the interaction between the two determines the inherited traits of the future person. Since some alleles from the father differ from the alleles from the mother, their combination produces a zygote unlike either parent. Thus, each new person is a product of two parents but is unlike either one.

Even more than that, each zygote carries genes that "are themselves transmitted to individual cells with large apparent mistakes—somatically acquired deletions, duplications, and other mutations" (Macosko & McCarroll, 2013, p. 564). Small variations, mutations, or repetitions in the 3 billion base pairs could make a notable difference in the proteins and thus, eventually, in the person.

Attention has focused on **copy number variations,** which are genes with repeats or deletions (from one to hundreds) of base pairs. Copy number variations are widespread—everyone has them—and they correlate with almost every disease and condition, including heart disease, intellectual disability, mental illness, and many cancers. Most, however, are insignificant: About 30 percent of our skin cells include copy number variations (Macosko & McCarrol, 2013). No matter; our skin still protects us just fine.

Genetic diversity helps the species, because creativity, prosperity, and survival are enhanced when one person is unlike another. There is an optimal balance between diversity and similarity for each species: Human societies are close to that optimal level (Ashraf & Galor, 2013).

## Matching Genes and Chromosomes

The genes on the chromosomes constitute an organism's genetic inheritance, or **genotype,** which endures throughout life. Growth requires duplication of the code of the original cell again and again.

### Autosomes

In 22 of the 23 pairs of chromosomes, both members of the pair (one from each parent) are closely matched. As already explained, some of the specific genes have alternate alleles, but each chromosome finds its comparable chromosome, making a pair. Those 44 chromosomes are called *autosomes,* which means that they are independent (*auto* means "self") of the sex chromosomes (the 23rd pair).

Each autosome, from number 1 to number 22, contains hundreds of genes in the same positions and sequence. If the code of a gene from one parent is exactly like the code on the same gene from the other parent, the gene pair is **homozygous** (literally, "same-zygote").

However, the match is not always letter-perfect because the mother might have a different allele of a particular gene than the father has. If a gene's code differs from that of its counterpart, the two genes still pair up, but the zygote (and, later, the person) is **heterozygous.** This can occur with any of the gene pairs on any of the autosomes.

Given that only half of a man's genes are on each sperm and only half of a woman's genes are on each ovum, the combination creates siblings who will be, genetically, similar and different. Thus, which particular homozygous or heterozygous genes my brother and I inherited from our parents is a matter of chance, and it has no connection to the fact that I am a younger sister, not an older brother.

### Sex Chromosomes

However, for the **23rd pair** of chromosomes, a marked difference is apparent between my brother and me. My 23rd pair matched, but his did not. In that, he is like all males: When gametes combine to form the zygote, half of the time a dramatic mismatch occurs, because some sperm carry an X and some a Y.

This is how it happens. In males, the 23rd pair has one X-shaped chromosome and one Y-shaped chromosome. It is called **XY.** In females, the 23rd pair is composed of two X-shaped chromosomes. Accordingly, it is called **XX.**

Because a female's 23rd pair is XX, when her 46 chromosomes split to make ova, each ovum contains either one X or the other—but always an X. And because a male's 23rd pair is XY, half of a father's sperm carry an X chromosome and half a Y.

The X chromosome is bigger and has more genes, but the Y chromosome has a crucial gene, called *SRY,* that directs the embryo to make male hormones and organs. Thus, sex depends on which sperm penetrates the ovum—a Y sperm with the SRY gene, creating a boy (XY), or an X sperm, creating a girl (XX) (see Figure 3.2).

### Male–Female Variations

To further complicate matters, sometimes one-half of a gene pair switches off completely, which may cause a problem if that remaining gene is destructive. For girls, one X of the 23rd pair is deactivated early in prenatal life. The implications of that shutoff are not well understood, but it is known that sometimes that X is

---

**Especially for Medical Doctors** Can you look at a person and then write a prescription that will personalize medicine to that person's particular genetic susceptibility? (see response, p. 72)

**genotype** An organism's entire genetic inheritance, or genetic potential.

**homozygous** Referring to two genes of one pair that are exactly the same in every letter of their code. Most gene pairs are homozygous.

**heterozygous** Referring to two genes of one pair that differ in some way. Typically one allele has only a few base pairs that differ from the other member of the pair.

**23rd pair** The chromosome pair that, in humans, determines sex. The other 22 pairs are autosomes, inherited equally by males and females.

**XY** A 23rd chromosome pair that consists of an X-shaped chromosome from the mother and a Y-shaped chromosome from the father. XY zygotes become males.

**XX** A 23rd chromosome pair that consists of two X-shaped chromosomes, one each from the mother and the father. XX zygotes become females.

●● **Response for Medical Doctors** (from p. 71): No. Personalized medicine is the hope of many physicians, but appearance (the phenotype) does not indicate alleles, recessive genes, copy number variations, and other genetic factors that affect drug reactions. Many medical researchers seek to personalize chemotherapy for cancer, but although this is urgently needed, success is still experimental, even when the genotype is known.

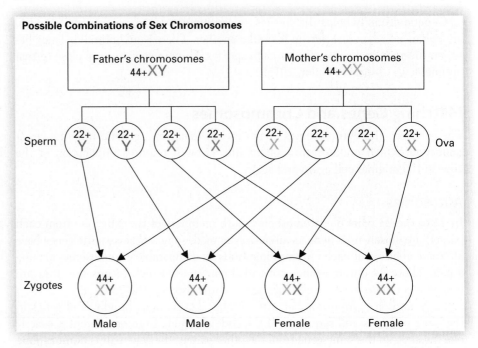

**Possible Combinations of Sex Chromosomes**

**FIGURE 3.2**

**Determining a Zygote's Sex**  Any given couple can produce four possible combinations of sex chromosomes; two lead to female children and two lead to male children. In terms of the future person's sex, it does not matter which of the mother's Xs the zygote inherited. All that matters is whether the father's Y sperm or X sperm fertilized the ovum. However, for X-linked conditions it matters a great deal because typically one, but not both, of the mother's Xs carries the trait.

**She Laughs Too Much**  No, not the smiling sister, but the 10-year-old on the right, who has Angelman syndrome. She inherited it from her mother's chromosome 15. Fortunately, her two siblings inherited the mother's other chromosome 15. If the 10-year-old had inherited the identical deletion on her father's chromosome 15, she would have Prader-Willi syndrome, which would cause her to be overweight, always hungry, and often angry. With Angelman syndrome, however, laughing, even at someone's pain, is a symptom.

from the ovum and sometimes it is from the sperm. Boys, of course, have only one X; it is always activated.

The fact that X deactivation occurs in girls but not in boys is only one example of the significance of the embryo's sex. Sometimes the same allele affects male and female embryos differently. For instance, women develop multiple sclerosis more often than men, and they usually inherit it from their mothers, not their fathers, probably for genetic as well as epigenetic reasons (Huynh & Casaccia, 2013).

It sometimes matters whether a gene came from the mother or the father, a phenomenon called *parental imprinting*. The best-known example occurs with a small deletion on chromosome 15. If that deletion came from the father's chromosome 15, the child may develop Prader-Willi syndrome and be obese, slow-moving, and stubborn. If that deletion came from the mother's chromosome 15, the child will have Angelman syndrome and be thin, hyperactive, and happy—sometimes too happy, laughing when no one else does. Other diseases and conditions are affected by imprinting, again sometimes in opposite ways (Couzin-Frankel, 2017).

Although sex is determined at conception, for most of history no one knew it until a baby was born and someone shouted "It's a ------!" In former times, millions of pregnant women ate special foods, slept on one side, or repeated certain prayers, all to control the sex of the fetus—which was already male or female.

## More Than Sex Organs

That SRY gene directs the embryo to grow a penis, and much more. The Y chromosome causes male hormone production that affects the brain, skeleton, body fat, and muscles, beginning in the first weeks of prenatal

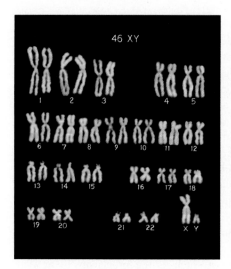

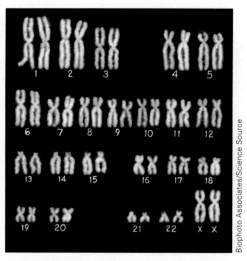

**Uncertain Sex** Every now and then, a baby is born with "ambiguous genitals," meaning that the child's sex is not abundantly clear. When this happens, a quick analysis of the chromosomes is needed to make sure that there are exactly 46 and to see whether the 23rd pair is XY or XX. The karyotypes shown here indicate a normal baby boy *(left)* and girl *(right)*.

Biophoto Associates/Science Source

development and continuing to the last breath in old age. At conception, there are about 120 males for every 100 females, perhaps because Y sperm swim faster and reach the ovum first (remember, they carry fewer genes, so they are lighter than the X sperm).

However, male embryos are more vulnerable than female ones (because of fewer genes, again?), so they are less likely to survive. The United Nations reports that, at birth, the natural male/female ratio worldwide is about 104:100; in developed nations, it is 105:100, but it is only 103:100 in the poorest nations. Maternal nutrition and prenatal care are the probable reasons.

Biological differences become cultural differences as soon as a newborn is named and wrapped in blue or pink. Thousands of gender differences throughout the life span—from toy trucks given to 1-day-old boys to the survival rates of old women—begin with that SRY gene. In fact, cultural differences can begin soon after conception, as soon as parents know the sex of the embryo. If they want a boy, or want a girl, that SRY gene may mean life or death, as the following explains.

**OPPOSING PERSPECTIVES**

## Too Many Boys?

In past centuries, millions of newborns were killed because they were the wrong sex, a practice that would be considered murder today. Now the same goal is achieved long before birth in three ways: (1) inactivating X or Y sperm before conception, (2) inserting only male or female zygotes after in vitro conception, or (3) aborting XX or XY fetuses.

Recently, millions of couples have used these methods to choose their newborn's sex. Should this be illegal? It is in at least 36 nations. It is legal in the United States (Murray, 2014).

To some prospective parents, those 36 nations are unfair—they allow similar measures to avoid severely disabled newborns. Why is that legal but sex selection is not? There are moral reasons. But should governments legislate morals? People disagree (Wilkinson, 2015).

One nation that forbids prenatal sex selection is China. This was not always so. In about 1979, China began a "one-child" policy, urging and sometimes forcing couples to have only one child. That achieved the intended goal: fewer children to feed . . . or starve. Severe poverty was almost eliminated.

But advances in prenatal testing, combined with the Chinese tradition that sons, not daughters, care for aging parents, led many couples to want their only child to be male. Among the unanticipated results of the one-child policy:

- Since 1980, an estimated 9 million abortions of female fetuses
- Adoption of thousands of newborn Chinese girls by Western families
- By 2010, far more unmarried young men than women

MANISH SWARUP/AP Images

**My Strength, My Daughter** That's the slogan these girls in New Delhi are shouting at a demonstration against abortion of female fetuses in India. The current sex ratio of children in India suggests that this campaign has not convinced every couple.

In 1993, the Chinese government forbade prenatal testing for sex selection. In 2013, China rescinded the one-child policy. Yet from 2005 to 2010, the ratio of preschool boys to girls was 117:100, an imbalance that continues (United Nations, Department of Economic and Social Affairs, Population Division, 2015). Despite government policies, many Chinese couples still prefer to have only one child, a boy, and are willing to abort female embryos.

The argument in favor of sex selection is freedom from government interference. Some fertility doctors and many individuals believe that each couple should be able to decide how many children to have and what sex they should be (Murray, 2014).

Why would anyone object to personal choice? One reason is social harm. For instance, 30 years after the one-child policy began, many more young Chinese men than women die, and the 2010 Chinese census found that women lived an average of eight years longer than men.

The developmental explanation is that unmarried young men take risks to attract women. They become depressed if they remain alone. Thus, the skewed sex ratio among young adults in China increases early death, from accidents and suicide, from drug overdoses and poor health practices, in young men. That affects the overall averages, harming society.

This is a warning to every nation. A society with an excess of males might also have an excess of problems, since males are more likely to be drug addicts, commit crimes, kill each other, die of heart attacks, and start wars than females. For instance, the U.S. Department of Justice reports that, since 1980, 85 percent of the prison population are men, and, primarily because of heart disease and violence, men are about twice as likely as women to die before age 50 (Centers for Disease Control and Prevention, 2014).

But wait: Chromosomes and genes do not *determine* behavior. Every sex difference is influenced by culture. Even traits that originate with biology, such as the propensity to heart attacks, are affected more by environment (in this case, diet and cigarettes) than by XX or XY chromosomes. Perhaps nurture would change if nature produced more males than females, and then societies would adapt.

Already, medical measures and smoking declines have reduced heart attacks in men. In 1950, four times as many middle-aged men as women died of heart disease; by 2010, the rate was lower for both sexes, but especially for men (2:1, not 4:1). Lifelong, rates of cardiovascular deaths in the United States are currently close to sex-neutral (Centers for Disease Control and Prevention, 2015).

Indeed, every sex difference is strongly influenced by culture and policy. It is thought that one reason some cultures accept divorce and remarriage, or polygamy, is that some communities have an excess of women and in this way most women will have husbands and children. Societies could change customs to adapt to an excess of males as well. But is that what should happen?

> **THINK CRITICALLY:** Might laws against prenatal sex selection be unnecessary if culture shifted?

## WHAT HAVE YOU LEARNED?

1.  How many chromosomes and genes do people have?

2.  What is an allele?

3.  What is the effect of the microbiome?

4.  Why is each zygote unique, genetically?

5.  What determines whether a zygote will become a boy or a girl?

# New Cells, New People

Within hours after conception, the zygote begins *duplication* and *division*. First, the 23 pairs of chromosomes (carrying all the genes) duplicate to form two complete sets of the genome. These two sets move toward opposite sides of the zygote, and the single cell splits neatly down the middle into two cells, each containing the original genetic code.

These first two cells duplicate and divide, becoming four, which duplicate and divide, becoming eight, and so on. The name of the developing mass changes as cells multiply—the zygote (one cell) becomes a *morula*, then a *blastocyst*, then an *embryo*, then a *fetus*—and then, at birth, a *baby*. [**Developmental Link:** Prenatal growth is detailed in Chapter 4.]

## Cells and Identity

Nine months after conception, a newborn has about 26 billion cells, all influenced by nutrients, drugs, hormones, viruses, microbes, and so on from the pregnant woman. Almost every human cell carries a complete copy of the genetic instructions of the one-celled zygote. About half of those genetic instructions came from each parent, but every zygote also has a few spontaneous mutations—about 40 base pair variations that were not inherited.

Adults have about 37 trillion cells, each with the same 46 chromosomes and the same thousands of genes of the original zygote (Bianconi et al., 2013). This explains why DNA testing of any body cell, even from a drop of blood or a snip of hair, can identify "the biological father," "the guilty criminal," "the long-lost brother." DNA lingers long after death. Several living African Americans claimed Thomas Jefferson as an ancestor: DNA proved some right and some wrong (Foster et al., 1998).

Indeed, because the Y chromosome is passed down to every male descendant, and because the Y changes very little from one generation to the next, men today have the Y of their male ancestors who died thousands of years ago. Female ancestors also live on. Each zygote has *mitochondria*, biological material that provides energy for the cell. The mitochondria come from the mother, and her mother, and her mother, and thus each person carries evidence of maternal lineage.

### Stem Cells

The cells that result from the early duplication and division are called **stem cells.** Stem cells are able to produce any other cell and thus become a complete person.

After about the eight-cell stage, although duplication and division continue, a third process, *differentiation*, begins. In differentiation, cells specialize, taking different forms and reproducing at various rates depending on where they are located. For instance, some cells become part of an eye, others part of a finger, still others part of the brain. They are no longer stem cells.

Scientists have discovered ways to add genes to certain differentiated cells in a laboratory process that reprograms those cells, making them like stem cells again (Papapetrou, 2016). However, it is not yet known how to reprogram stem cells to cure genetic conditions without risking harm to patients.

Another new method, called CRISPR, has been developed to edit genes (Lander, 2016), and it is now being used to control the mosquitos that spread malaria, Zika virus, and other diseases. Although human genes could theoretically

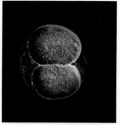

(a)

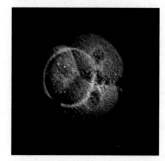

(b)

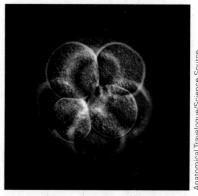

(c)

Anatomical Travelogue/Science Source

**First Stages of the Germinal Period** The original zygote as it divides into *(a)* two cells, *(b)* four cells, and *(c)* eight cells. Occasionally at this early stage, the cells separate completely, forming the beginning of monozygotic twins, quadruplets, or octuplets.

**stem cells** Cells from which any other specialized type of cell can form.

be edited with CRISPR, the prospect of "designer babies" raises serious ethical questions. Therefore, at least at the moment, CRISPR is forbidden for human organisms (Lander, 2016; Green, 2015).

## In Vitro Fertilization

**in vitro fertilization (IVF)** Fertilization that takes place outside a woman's body (as in a glass laboratory dish). The procedure involves mixing sperm with ova that have been surgically removed from the woman's ovary. If a zygote is produced, it is inserted into a woman's uterus, where it may implant and develop into a baby.

The ethical implications of CRISPR raise the issue of **in vitro fertilization (IVF),** which was pronounced "sacrilegious" and against God when first attempted in 1960. That did not stop the scientists, who finally succeeded with a live baby, Louise Brown, in 1978.

Over the past half-century, IVF has become "a relatively routine way to have children" (C. Thompson, 2014, p. 361). An estimated 6 million IVF babies have been born, some from every nation of the world, among them the younger sister of Louise Brown. Both Brown daughters have now grown up and had babies of their own, conceived naturally. Brown was teased by other children, but she says she would have used IVF to have her son if it were needed.

IVF differs markedly from the typical conception, which is often unintended—almost one-half of the time in the United States and about one-third of the time in western Europe (Finer & Zolna, 2016). By contrast, IVF couples desperately want a baby and must undertake difficult and expensive measures to conceive.

In IVF, the woman first takes hormones to increase the number of fully developed ova. On the scheduled day, surgeons remove several ova from her ovaries, the man ejaculates into a sterile container, and then technicians combine ova and sperm in a laboratory dish (*in vitro* means "in glass"). Often the technicians choose the ova and sperm that look most viable and then insert one active sperm into each ovum.

**Especially for Poor College Students** Your friend wants to pay for college by selling sperm or ova. Should he or she do it? (see response, p. 79)

Zygotes that fail to duplicate, or blastocysts that test positive for serious genetic diseases, are rejected, but one or more of the others are inserted into the uterus. About half of the inserted blastocysts implant and grow. Fertility decreases with age, so some young women freeze their ova for IVF years later (Mac Dougall et al., 2013). A slightly higher risk of congenital malformations may occur (Qin et al., 2015).

If IVF newborns are not low birthweight, they do as well or better than other babies, not only in childhood health, intelligence, and school achievement but also in emotional development as teenagers (Wagenaar et al., 2011). Compared to the average parent, IVF parents are older and of higher SES, and the pregnancies are always wanted—all reasons that their children develop well (Golombok, 2015).

Thanks to IVF, millions of couples who would have been infertile now have children. Indeed, some parents have children who are neither genetically nor biologically theirs if others have donated the sperm, the ova, and/or the womb. The word *donate* is misleading, since most donors—often college students—are paid. Since up to three strangers could create a baby for someone else, the "real" parents are considered those who raise a child, not those who conceive it (Franklin, 2013).

Some nations forbid IVF unless a couple provides proof of heterosexual marriage, of infertility, and even of financial and emotional health. Several European nations limit the numbers of blastocysts inserted into the uterus at one time, partly because national health care pays for both IVF and newborn care.

The United States has no legal restrictions, although not every infertile couple has the money and the determination that are required. The cost is about $20,000 for all the drugs, the monitoring, and the procedure itself, which results in successful pregnancy about half the time. Some insurance pays for part of the cost, and medical societies provide some oversight. For example, the California Medical Board removed the medical license from the physician who inserted 12 blastocysts in Nadya Suleman. She gave birth to eight surviving babies in 2009, a medical miracle but a developmental disaster.

STR/AFP/Getty Images

**Mama Is 60** Wu Jingzhou holds his newborn twin daughters, born to his 60-year-old wife after in vitro fertilization. Ordinarily, it is illegal in China, as in most other nations, for women to have children after menopause. But an exception was made for this couple because the death of their only child, a young woman named Tingling, was partly the government's fault.

## Twins and More

Thus far we have described conception as if one sperm and one ovum resulted in one baby. That is typical, but there are many exceptions. To understand this, you need to understand the difference between monozygotic and dizygotic twins (see Visualizing Development, p. 78).

### Monozygotic Twins

Remember that each stem cell contains the entire genetic code. If parents who carry destructive genes use IVF, at about the eight-cell stage, before implantation, one cell can be removed and analyzed. If the destructive gene is present, that seven-cell blastocyst is not implanted, but otherwise it is inserted into the uterus, where it might grow normally. Removing one stem cell does not harm development, because every one of the remaining cells has all of the instructions needed to create a person. Ideally, a healthy baby is born nine months later.

With lower animals, scientists have separated stem cells and allowed two identical animals to develop. This is illegal for humans—each IVF zygote becomes one embryo. However, about once in every 250 pregnancies, nature in the woman's body within 24 hours after conception does what scientists are forbidden to do—it splits those early cells. If each separated cell duplicates, divides, differentiates, implants, grows, and survives, multiple births occur, as with the triplets on p. 66.

One separation results in **monozygotic (MZ) twins,** from one (*mono*) zygote (also called *identical twins*). Separations at the four- or eight-cell stage create monozygotic quadruplets or octuplets. Because monozygotic multiples originate from one zygote, they have identical genetic instructions for appearance, psychological traits, disease vulnerability, and everything else genetic.

Remember, however, that epigenetic influences begin as soon as conception occurs: Monozygotic twins look and act very much alike, but their environments are not identical. Epigenesis begins within hours after conception, and thus the developing blastocysts may differ. Then, the particular spot in the uterus where each twin implants may make one fetus heavier than the other, which again may affect that person lifelong. At birth, one is born first, and from that moment on each twin will have a slightly different experience.

Monozygotic twins are fortunate in some ways. They can donate a kidney or other organ to their twin with no organ rejection. They can also befuddle their parents and teachers, who may need ways (such as different earrings) to tell them apart.

Usually, the twins themselves establish their own identities. For instance, both might inherit athletic ability, but one decides to join the basketball team while the other plays soccer.

As one monozygotic twin writes:

> Twins put into high relief *the* central challenge for all of us: self-definition. How do we each plant our stake in the ground, decide how sensitive, callous, ambitious, conciliatory, or cautious we want to be every day? . . . Twins come with a built-in constant comparison, but defining oneself against one's twin is just an amped-up version of every person's life-long challenge: to individuate—to create a distinctive persona in the world.

*[Pogrebin, 2010, p. 9]*

AP Photo/Antelope Valley Press, Ron Siddle

**Perfectly Legal** Nadya Suleman was a medical miracle when her eight newborns all survived, thanks to expert care in a Los Angeles hospital. Soon thereafter, however, considerable controversy began: She was dubbed "Octomom" because—even though already a single mother of six children, including twins—she still opted to undergo in vitro fertilization, which resulted in implantation of her octuplets.

**monozygotic (MZ) twins** Twins who originate from one zygote that splits apart very early in development. (Also called *identical twins*.) Other monozygotic multiple births (such as triplets and quadruplets) can occur as well.

**LaunchPad**
macmillan learning

**Video Activity: Identical Twins: Growing Up Apart** gives a real-life example of how genes play a significant role in people's physical, social, and cognitive development.

# One Baby or More

Humans usually have one baby at a time, but sometimes twins are born. Most often they are from two ova fertilized by two sperm (*lower left*), resulting in dizygotic twins.

Sometimes, however, one zygote splits in two (*lower right*), resulting in monozygotic twins; if each of these zygotes splits again, the result is monozygotic quadruplets.

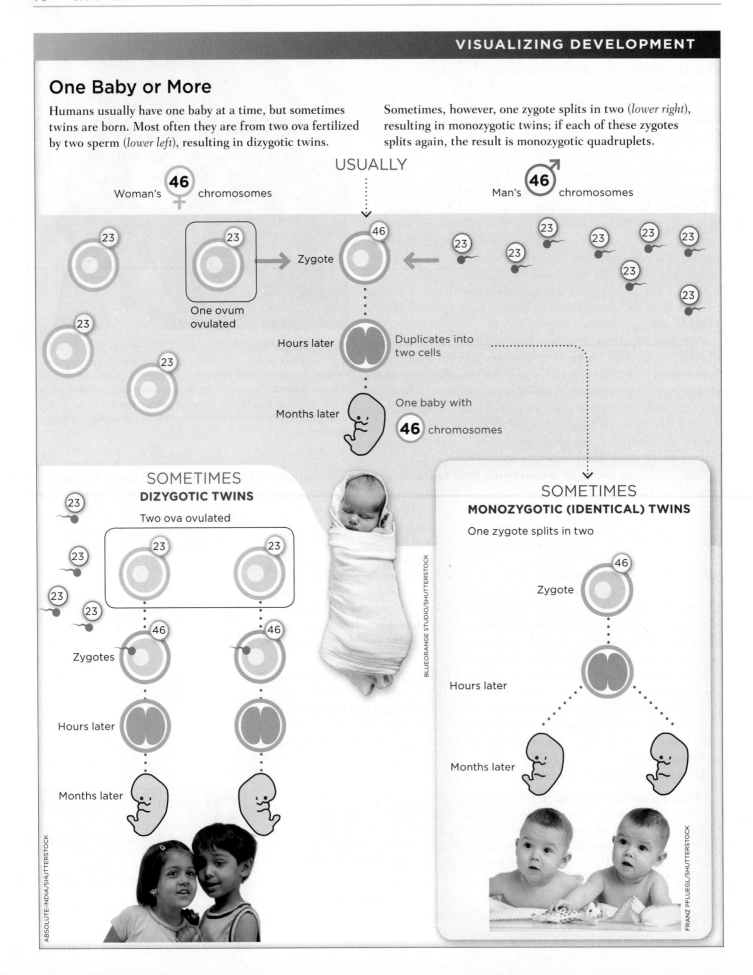

USUALLY

Woman's **46** chromosomes

Man's **46** chromosomes

One ovum ovulated

Zygote

Hours later — Duplicates into two cells

Months later — One baby with **46** chromosomes

## SOMETIMES
### DIZYGOTIC TWINS

Two ova ovulated

Zygotes

Hours later

Months later

ABSOLUTE-INDIA/SHUTTERSTOCK

BLUEORANGE STUDIO/SHUTTERSTOCK

## SOMETIMES
### MONOZYGOTIC (IDENTICAL) TWINS

One zygote splits in two

Zygote

Hours later

Months later

FRANZ PFLUEGL/SHUTTERSTOCK

That twin and her monozygotic sister both married and had a son and a daughter within months of each other. Coincidence? Genetics? Sister pressure?

## Dizygotic Twins

Most twins are <u>not</u> monozygotic. About once in 60 conceptions, **dizygotic (DZ) twins** are conceived. They are also called *fraternal twins*, although because *fraternal* means "brotherly" (as in *fraternity*), fraternal is inaccurate. MZ twins are always the same sex (their 23rd chromosomes are either XX or XY), but for DZ twins one-fourth are both girls, one-fourth are both boys, and one-half are a boy and a girl.

DZ twins begin life when two ova are fertilized by two sperm at about the same time. Usually, women release only one ovum per month, so most human newborns are singletons. However, sometimes multiple ovulation occurs.

People say that twinning "skips a generation," but that is not completely accurate. It skips fathers, not mothers. Since dizygotic twinning requires multiple ovulation, the likelihood of a woman ovulating two ova and thus conceiving twins depends on her genes from her parents. Her husband's genes are irrelevant. However, a man has half his genes from his mother. If she had genes for multiple ovulation, there is a 50 percent chance that the X that created him is the double-ovulating X. Then his daughters (who always get his X) are likely to have twins.

When dizygotic twinning occurs naturally, the incidence varies by ethnicity. For example, about 1 in 11 Yorubas in Nigeria is a twin, as are about 1 in 45 European Americans, 1 in 75 Japanese and Koreans, and 1 in 150 Chinese. Age matters, too: Older women more often double-ovulate and thus have more twins.

IVF often produces twins, because prospective parents are so eager to have babies that they ignore medical advice to implant only one zygote: The result is more underweight, preterm DZ twins. [**Developmental Link:** The problems of low birthweight are detailed in Chapter 4.]

After twins are conceived, prenatal growth is hazardous. Sometimes an early sonogram reveals two developing organisms, but only one embryo continues to develop. This *vanishing twin* phenomenon may occur in about 12 percent of pregnancies (Giuffrè et al., 2012).

Like all children from the same parents, DZ twins have about half of their genes in common. They can differ markedly in appearance, or they can look so much alike that only genetic tests determine whether they are MZ or DZ twins. In the rare incidence that a woman releases two ova at once *and* has sex with two men over a short period, twins can have different fathers. Then they share only one-fourth of their genes.

**dizygotic (DZ) twins** Twins who are formed when two separate ova are fertilized by two separate sperm at roughly the same time. (Also called *fraternal twins*.)

**Response for Poor College Students** (from p. 76) Selling gametes is profitable and easier for men than women, since "harvesting" ova requires taking drugs, a medical procedure, and sometimes side effects. More troubling may be the psychic costs: possible rejection after genetic testing and lifelong worries about unseen offspring. Ask your friend to think it over with a psychologist, clergyperson, and/or another trusted advisor.

**Especially for Twins** Your friend is scheduled for IVF and wants several zygotes implanted, but her doctor advises only one. She knows that you loved being a twin. What do you tell her? (see response, p. 81)

---

### WHAT HAVE YOU LEARNED?

**1.** What makes a cell a "stem cell"?

**2.** How does DNA establish identity?

**3.** What is similar and different in an IVF and a traditional pregnancy?

**4.** Why is CRISPR almost always illegal for humans?

**5.** What is the difference between monozygotic and dizygotic twins?

**6.** Are some pregnancies more likely to be twins than others?

**phenotype** The observable characteristics of a person, including appearance, personality, intelligence, and all other traits.

**polygenic** Referring to a trait that is influenced by many genes.

**multifactorial** Referring to a trait that is affected by many factors, both genetic and environmental, that enhance, halt, shape, or alter the expression of genes, resulting in a phenotype that may differ markedly from the genotype.

**Sisters, But Not Twins, in Iowa** From their phenotype, it is obvious that these two girls share many of the same genes, as their blond hair and facial features are strikingly similar. And you can see that they are not twins; Lucy is 7 years old and Ellie is only 4. It may not be obvious that they have the same parents, but they do—and they are both very bright and happy because of it. This photo also shows that their genotypes differ in one crucial way: One of them has a dominant gene for a serious condition.

**⬤⬤ Especially for Scientists** A hundred years ago, it was believed that humans had 48 chromosomes, not 46; 20 years ago, it was thought that humans had 100,000 genes, not 21,000 or so. Why? (see response, p. 82)

**Human Genome Project** An international effort to map the complete human genetic code. This effort was essentially completed in 2001, though analysis is ongoing.

# From Genotype to Phenotype

As already explained, when a sperm and an ovum create a zygote, the *genotype* (all the genes of the developing person) is established. This initiates several complex processes that form the **phenotype**—the person's actual appearance, behavior, and brain and body functions.

Nothing is totally genetic, not even physical traits such as height or hair color, but nothing is wholly untouched by genes, either. Genes affect behavior as well as bodies: People who work overtime, get divorced, or spank their children do so partly for genetic reasons (Knopik et al., 2017)!

## Many Factors

The phenotype depends on the combination of the genotype and the environment, from the moment of conception until the moment of death. The environment changes genes directly, in epigenesis. It also affects the phenotype via culture and context. As you remember, human development is remarkably plastic.

Almost every trait is **polygenic** (affected by many genes) and **multifactorial** (influenced by many factors). A zygote might have the alleles for becoming, say, a musical genius, but that potential may never be expressed. Completely accurate prediction of the phenotype is impossible, even if the genotype is entirely known (Lehner, 2013). One reason is *differential susceptibility,* as explained in Chapter 1. Because of a seemingly minor allele, or a transient environmental influence, a particular person may be profoundly changed—or not affected at all—by experiences.

Remember that all important human characteristics are epigenetic. This is easiest to see with conditions that are known to be inherited, such as cancer, schizophrenia, and autism spectrum disorder (Kundu, 2013; Knopik et al., 2017). It is also apparent with cognitive abilities and personality traits.

Diabetes is a notable example. People who inherit genes that put them at risk do not always become diabetic. Lifestyle factors—including overweight and lack of exercise—activate that genetic risk. But some people have the lifestyle factors and never become diabetic because they do not have diabetes in their genotype.

The same may be true for other developmental changes over the life span. Substance abuse—cocaine, cigarettes, alcohol, and so on—may produce epigenetic changes. Once addicted, a person who has not used the drug for years is still vulnerable and can never use the drug again as an unaffected person could (Bannon et al., 2014). The brain has changed; so the person is "clean" but still an addict.

In general, some bio-psycho-social influences (such as injury, temperature extremes, drug abuse, and overcrowding) can impede healthy development, whereas others (nourishing food, loving care, meditation) can facilitate it, all because of differential susceptibility and epigenetic changes. For example, if a person feels lonely and rejected, that feeling affects the RNA, which allows genetic potential for heart disease or social anxiety to be expressed (Slavich & Cole, 2013).

## Gene–Gene Interactions

Many discoveries have followed the completion of the **Human Genome Project** in 2001. One of the first surprises was that humans have far fewer than 100,000 genes, the number often cited in the twentieth century.

Each person has about 21,000 genes on the 46 chromosomes. The precise number is elusive because it is not obvious where one gene starts and another ends, or even if a particular stretch of DNA is actually a gene. Nor can we predict exactly how the genes from one parent will interact with the genes from the other: The interaction is affected by other genes. Some basics are known, however, and are described now.

## Additive Heredity

Some genes and alleles are *additive* because their effects *add up* to influence the phenotype. The phenotype then reflects the contributions of every additive gene. Height, hair curliness, and skin color, for instance, are usually the result of additive genes. Indeed, height is probably influenced by 180 genes, each contributing a very small amount (Enserink, 2011).

Most Americans have ancestors of varied height, hair curliness, skin color, and so on, so their children's phenotype does not mirror the parents' phenotypes (although the phenotype always reflects the genotype). I see this in my family: Our daughter Rachel is of average height, shorter than her father and me, but taller than either of our mothers. She apparently inherited some of her grandmothers' height genes via our gametes. And none of my children has exactly my skin color—apparent when we borrow clothes from each other and are distressed that a particular shade is attractive on one but ugly on another.

How any additive trait turns out depends partly on all the genes a child happens to inherit (half from each parent, which means one-fourth from each grandparent, one-eighth from each great-grandparent, and so on). Some of those genes amplify or dampen the effects of other genes, aided by all the other DNA and RNA (not junk!) in the zygote.

Genetic diversity is apparent in every family, but it is particularly apparent in African Americans. This is because genes from many parts of Africa, Europe, and the Americas have been passed down to the next generation for over 400 years.

## Dominant–Recessive Heredity

Not all genes are additive. In one nonadditive form, called **dominant–recessive,** alleles differ markedly in their contribution to a trait. The *dominant gene* is more powerful, and the recessive gene is much less influential. If a gene pair has one dominant and one recessive allele, the recessive gene is not on the phenotype, even though it is on the genotype. However, when both halves of a gene pair are recessive, and thus there is no dominant gene for that trait, the two recessive genes acting together affect the phenotype.

Most recessive genes are harmless. For example, blue eyes are determined by a recessive allele and brown eyes by a dominant one, so a child conceived by a blue-eyed parent (who always has two recessive blue-eye genes) and a brown-eyed parent will usually have brown eyes.

"Usually," but not always. Sometimes a brown-eyed person is a carrier of the blue-eye gene. In that case, in a blue-eye/brown-eye couple, every child has at least one blue-eye gene (from the blue-eyed parent), and half of the children will have another blue-eye recessive gene (from the brown-eyed parent). That half will have blue eyes because they have no dominant brown-eye gene. The other half will have a brown-eye dominant gene and thus have brown eyes but carry the blue-eye gene, like their brown-eyed parent.

This gets tricky if both parents are carriers. If two brown-eyed parents both carry the blue-eye recessive gene, the chances are one in four that their child will have blue eyes (see Figure 3.3). This example is simple because it presumes that only one pair of genes determines eye color. However, as with almost every trait, eye color is polygenic, with other genes having some influence. Eyes are various shades of blue and brown, and sometimes green or hazel, because of many genes.

**Response for Twins** (from p. 79)
Most people appreciate who they are—male or female, of a particular ethnicity, single-born or twin. But you should convey the downsides of twinship, not only for you but for your parents. Caring for one newborn is difficult; twins are more often low birthweight and medically fragile.

**dominant–recessive pattern** The interaction of a heterozygous pair of alleles in such a way that the phenotype reflects one allele (the dominant gene) more than the other (the recessive gene).

© 2016 Macmillan

**Genetic Mix** Dizygotic twins Olivia and Harrison have half their genes in common, as do all siblings from the same parents. If the parents are close relatives who themselves share most alleles, the nonshared half is likely to include many similar genes. That is not the case here, as their mother (Nicola) is from Wales and their father (Gleb) is from the nation of Georgia, which includes many people of Asian ancestry. Their phenotypes, and the family photos on the wall, show many additive genetic influences.

**Especially for Future Parents** Suppose you wanted your daughters to be short and your sons to be tall. Could you achieve that? (see response, p. 82)

● ● **Response for Scientists** (from p. 80): There was some scientific evidence for the wrong numbers (e.g., chimpanzees have 48 chromosomes), but the reality is that humans tend to overestimate many things, from the number of genes to their grade on the next test. Scientists are very human: They tend to overestimate until the data prove them wrong.

● ● **Observation Quiz** Why do these four offspring look identical except for eye color? (see answer, p. 85) ➜

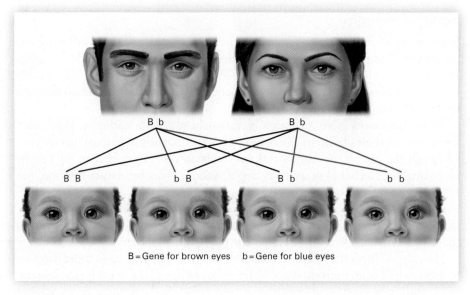

B = Gene for brown eyes    b = Gene for blue eyes

**FIGURE 3.3**

**Changeling?** No. If two brown-eyed parents both carry the blue-eye gene, they have one chance in four of having a blue-eyed child. Other recessive genes include the genes for red hair, Rh-negative blood, and many genetic diseases.

**carrier** A person whose genotype includes a gene that is not expressed in the phenotype. The carried gene occurs in half of the carrier's gametes and thus is passed on to half of the carrier's children. If such a gene is inherited from both parents, the characteristic appears in the phenotype.

Everyone is a **carrier** of recessive genes, which are *carried* on the genotype but not apparent in their phenotype. For instance, no one would guess by looking at me that my mother had to stretch to reach 5 feet, 4 inches tall. But Rachel has half of her genes from me, and one of my height genes may be recessive.

Again, most recessive genes are carried on the genotype but hidden on the phenotype. A recessive trait appears on the phenotype *only* when a person inherits the same recessive gene from both parents. Understanding the double recessive might prevent parents from blaming each other if their child has a recessive disease, and it might prevent a brown-eyed father from suspecting infidelity if a child is unexpectedly blue-eyed.

## Mother to Son

**X-linked** A gene carried on the X chromosome. If a male inherits an X-linked recessive trait from his mother, he expresses that trait because the Y from his father has no counteracting gene. Females are more likely to be carriers of X-linked traits but are less likely to express them.

A special case of the dominant–recessive pattern occurs with genes that are **X-linked** (located on the X chromosome). If an X-linked gene is recessive—as are the genes for red–green color blindness (by far the most common type of color blindness), several allergies, a few diseases, and some learning disorders—the fact that it is on the X chromosome is critical (see Table 3.1). Boys might have the phenotype; girls are usually only carriers.

To understand this, remember that the Y chromosome is much smaller than the X, containing far fewer genes. For that reason, many genes on the X have no match on the Y. Therefore, most X-linked recessive genes have no dominant gene on the Y. If a boy (XY) inherits a recessive gene on his X from his mother, he will have no corresponding dominant gene on his Y from his father to counteract it, so his phenotype will be affected. A girl will be affected only if she has the recessive trait on both of her X chromosomes, the X from her father and the X from her mother.

● ● **Response for Future Parents** (from p. 81): Possibly, but you wouldn't want to. You would have to choose one mate for your sons and another for your daughters, and you would have to use sex-selection methods. Even so, it might not work, given all the genes on your genotype. More important, the effort would be unethical, unnatural, and possibly illegal.

This explains why males inherit X-linked disorders from their mothers, not their fathers. A study of children from six ethnic groups in northern India found nine red–green color-blind boys for every one such girl, but it also found marked

## TABLE 3.1

### The 23rd Pair and X-Linked Color Blindness

| 23rd Pair | Phenotype | Genotype | Next Generation |
|---|---|---|---|
| **1.** XX | Normal woman | Not a carrier | No color blindness from mother |
| **2.** XY | Normal man | Normal X from mother | No color blindness from father |
| **3.** ⊗X | Normal woman | Carrier from father | Half of her children will inherit her ⊗. The girls with her ⊗ will be carriers; the boys with her ⊗ will be color-blind. |
| **4.** X⊗ | Normal woman | Carrier from mother | Half of her children will inherit her ⊗. The girls with her ⊗ will be carriers; the boys with her ⊗ will be color-blind. |
| **5.** ⊗Y | Color-blind man | Inherited from mother | All of his daughters will have his ⊗. None of his sons will have his X. All of his children will have normal vision unless their mother also had an ⊗ for color blindness. |
| **6.** ⊗⊗ | Color-blind woman (rare) | Inherited from both parents | Every child will have one ⊗ from her. Therefore, every son will be color-blind. Daughters will only be carriers unless they also inherit an ⊗ from the father, as their mother did. |

⊗ = X that carries recessive gene for color-blindness

variation (3 to 7 percent) in rates of color blindness from one ethnic group to another (Fareed et al., 2015).

This confirms that color blindness is genetic and that communities in which individuals typically marry someone within their group (as was the case in those six Indian groups) have a particular genetic frequency. Thus, worldwide, ethnic groups vary in incidence of every disorder—some nations are high in stomach cancer, others in breast cancer, others in lung cancer, and so on (Torre et al., 2015). Part of the reason is genetic frequency, although diet and pollution also affect regional incidence.

> **THINK CRITICALLY:** If a woman has a color-blind brother, will her sons be color-blind?

## Nature and Nurture

One goal of this chapter is for readers to grasp the complex interaction between genotype and phenotype. This is not easy. For decades, millions of scientists have struggled to understand this complexity. Each year brings advances in statistics and molecular analysis, new data to uncover various patterns, all resulting in hypotheses to be explored.

Now we examine two complex traits, addiction and visual acuity, in two specific manifestations, alcohol use disorder and nearsightedness. As you will see, understanding the progression from genotype to phenotype has many practical implications.

## Alcohol Use Disorder

At various times throughout history, people have considered the abuse of alcohol and other drugs to be a moral weakness, a social scourge, or a personality defect. Historically and internationally, the main focus has been on alcohol, since people everywhere discovered fermentation thousands of years ago, to the joy of many and the addiction of some. Alcohol has been declared illegal (as in the United States from 1919 to 1933) or considered sacred (as in many Judeo-Christian rituals). Addicts have been jailed, jeered, or burned at the stake.

Hero Images Inc./Alamy

**Welcome Home** For many women in the United States, white wine is part of the celebration and joy of a house party, as shown here. Most people can drink alcohol harmlessly; there is no sign that these women are problem drinkers. However, danger lurks. Women get drunk on less alcohol than men, and females with alcohol use disorder tend to drink more privately and secretly, often at home, feeling more shame than bravado. All that makes their addiction more difficult to recognize.

⬤ **Especially for Drug Counselors** Is the wish for excitement likely to lead to addiction? (see response, p. 86)

**heritability** A statistic that indicates what percentage of the variation in a particular trait within a particular population, in a particular context and era, can be traced to genes.

We now know that inherited biochemistry affects alcohol metabolism. Punishing those with the genes does not stop addiction. There is no single "alcoholic gene," but alleles that make alcoholism more likely have been identified on every chromosome except the Y (Epps & Holt, 2011).

To be more specific, alleles create an addictive pull that can be overpowering, extremely weak, or somewhere in between. Each person's biochemistry reacts to alcohol by causing sleep, nausea, aggression, joy, relaxation, forgetfulness, or tears.

If metabolism allows people to "hold their liquor," they might drink too much; others (including many East Asians) sweat and become red-faced after just a few sips. That embarrassing response may lead to abstinence. This inherited "flushing" tendency not only makes alcohol addiction rare but also improves metabolism (Kuwahara et al., 2014).

Although genes for biological addiction were the focus of early research, we now know that inherited personality traits (including a quick temper, sensation seeking, and high anxiety) may be pivotal (Macgregor et al., 2009).

Yet social contexts may be equally crucial. Some (such as fraternity parties) make it hard to avoid alcohol; others (such as a church social in a "dry" county) make it difficult to drink anything stronger than lemonade.

Sex (biological—either XX or XY) and gender (cultural) also matter. For biological reasons (body size, fat composition, metabolism), women become drunk on less alcohol than men. Heavy-drinking females double their risk of mortality compared to heavy-drinking males (Wang et al., 2014). Many cultures encourage men to drink but not women (Chartier et al., 2014). Again, phenotype is affected by both genotype and environment.

## Nearsightedness

Age, genes, and culture affect vision as well. The effects of age are straightforward. Newborns focus only on things within 1 to 3 feet of their eyes; vision improves steadily until about age 10. The eyeball changes shape at puberty, increasing myopia (nearsightedness), and again in middle age, decreasing myopia.

Most research finds many genetic influences on nearsightedness. The heritability is about 75 percent—which is quite high (Williams & Hammond, 2016). If one monozygotic twin is nearsighted, the other twin is virtually always nearsighted, too.

However, **heritability** indicates only how much of the variation in a particular trait, *within a particular population, in a particular context and era,* can be traced to genes. For example, the heritability of height is very high (about 95 percent) when children receive good medical care and nutrition, but it is low (about 20 percent) when children are severely malnourished. Children who are chronically underfed are quite short, no matter what their genes. Thus, in some places, nearsightedness may not be inherited.

Indeed, it is not. In some African and Asian communities, vision heritability is close to zero because some children are severely deprived of vitamin A. For them, eyesight depends less on nature (genes) than nurture: "Because of vitamin A deficiency, more than 250,000 children become blind every year, and half of them die within a year of losing their sight" (Ehrenberg, 2016, p. 25).

To prevent blindness, scientists have developed strains of local staples such as "golden rice" that are high in vitamin A, although widespread use is restricted because of fears of genetically modified food (Ehrenberg, 2016). This can be seen as an economic issue, as the nations that most need geneticially modified (GMO) additives, such as bananas with iron or plants with omega-3 fatty acids, are the poorest ones, while anti-GMO sentiment is strongest in rich nations.

Some nations (Zambia and Cameroon) avoid GMOs by adding vitamin A directly to cooking oil and sugar. This must be carefully done—excessive, nonfood vitamin A causes health problems, but the risks are far less serious than blindness (Tanumihardjo et al., 2016).

What about children who consume adequate vitamin A in a balanced diet? Is their vision entirely inherited? Cross-cultural research suggests that it is not (Seppa, 2013a).

One ophthalmologist predicted "an epidemic of pathological myopia and associated blindness in the next few decades in Asia" (Saw, quoted in Seppa, 2013a, p. 23). The first published research on this phenomenon appeared in 1992, when scholars noticed that in army-mandated medical exams of all 17-year-old males in Singapore in 1980, 26 percent were nearsighted but 43 percent were nearsighted in 1990 (Tay et al., 1992). Another summary says that myopia is "out of control" in the United States (Holden, 2010).

An article in the leading British medical journal *The Lancet* suggests that although genes are usually to blame for severe myopia, "any genetic differences may be small" for common nearsightedness (I. Morgan et al., 2012, p. 1739). Nurture must somehow be involved. But how?

One possible culprit is homework. As Chapter 12 describes, contemporary East Asian children are amazingly proficient in math and science. Fifty years ago, most Asian children were working outside; now almost all are diligent students. As their developing eyes focus on their books, those with a genetic vulnerability to myopia may lose acuity for objects far away—which is exactly what nearsightedness means.

A study of Singaporean 10- to 12-year-olds found a positive correlation between nearsightedness (measured by optometric exams) and high academic achievement, especially in language, which correlates with extensive reading. Correlation is not proof, but the odds ratio was 2:5 and the significance was 0.001, which makes these data impossible to ignore (Saw et al., 2007).

Another possible culprit is too much time indoors. Data from the United States on children playing sports have led some ophthalmologists to suggest that the underlying cause is inadequate exposure to daylight (I. Morgan et al., 2012). If children spent more time outside playing, would fewer need glasses?

Between the early 1970s and the early 2000s, nearsightedness in the U.S. population increased from 25 to 42 percent (Vitale et al., 2009). Urbanization, television, and fear of strangers have kept many U.S. children indoors most of the time, unlike children of earlier generations. One ophthalmologist comments that "we're kind of a dim indoors people nowadays" (Mutti, quoted in Holden, 2010, p. 17). Decades ago, genetically vulnerable children did not necessarily become nearsighted; now they do. Nurture affecting nature, again.

## Practical Applications

Since genes affect every disorder, no one should be blamed or punished for inherited problems. However, knowing that genes never act in isolation allows prevention. For instance, if alcohol use disorder is in the genes, parents can keep alcohol out of their home, hoping their children become cognitively and socially mature before imbibing. If nearsightedness runs in the family, parents can play outdoors with their children every day.

Of course, playing outdoors and avoiding alcohol are recommended for all children, as are dozens of other behaviors, such as flossing twice a day, saying "please," sleeping 10 hours each night, eating five servings of vegetables each day, and promptly writing thank-you notes. It is unrealistic to expect parents to make their children do all of these, but awareness of genetic risks can guide priorities.

*© Imaginechina/Corbis*

**Applauding Success** These eager young men are freshmen at the opening convocation of Shanghai Jiao Tong University. They have studied hard in high school, scoring high on the national college entrance exam. Now their education is heavily subsidized by the government. Although China has more college students than the United States, the proportions are far lower, since the population of China is more than four times that of the United States.

**Observation Quiz** Name three visible attributes of these young men that differ from a typical group of freshmen in North America. (see answer, p. 88) ↑

**Answer to Observation Quiz** (from p. 82): This is a figure drawn to illustrate the recessive inheritance of blue eyes, and thus eyes are the only difference shown. If this were a real family, each child would have a distinct appearance.

**LaunchPad**
macmillan learning

**Video: Genetic Disorders** offers an
overview of various genetic disorders.

**Response for Drug
Counselors** (from p. 84): Maybe. Some
people who love risk become addicts; others
develop a healthy lifestyle that includes
adventure, new people, and exotic places.
Any trait can lead in various directions. You
need to be aware of the connections so that
you can steer your clients toward healthy
adventures.

> **WHAT HAVE YOU LEARNED?**
>
> **1.** Why do humans vary so much in skin color and height?
>
> **2.** What is the difference between additive and dominant–recessive inheritance?
>
> **3.** Why don't children always look like their parents?
>
> **4.** Why are sons more likely to inherit recessive conditions from their mothers instead of their fathers?
>
> **5.** What genes increase the risk of alcohol use disorder?
>
> **6.** What suggests that nearsightedness is affected by nurture?
>
> **7.** What does *heritability* mean?

## Chromosomal and Genetic Problems

We now focus on conditions caused by an extra chromosome or a single destructive gene. Each person carries about 40 alleles that *could* cause serious disease—including some very common ones such as strokes, heart disease, and cancer—but most of those require at least two SNPs, plus particular environmental conditions, before they appear.

If all notable anomalies and disorders are included, 92 percent of people do not develop a serious genetic condition by early adulthood—but that means 8 percent have a serious condition in their phenotype as well as their genotype (Chong et al., 2015). Study of such problems is relevant because:

1. They provide insight into the complexities of nature and nurture.
2. Knowing their origins helps avoid or limit their effects.
3. Information combats prejudice: Difference is not always deficit.

## Spontaneous Mutations

Many genetic and chromosomal problems are spontaneous mutations (Reilly & Noonan 2016; Arnheim & Calabrese, 2016). They are not present in the parents' genes and thus could not be predicted in advance. Nor are they likely to reappear in future embryos. Spontaneous mutations are more likely if the parents have been exposed to various pollutants or radiation, which then affects the sperm, ova, or zygote (Cassina et al., 2017).

Age matters, too: The frequency of chromosomal miscounts rises when the mother is over age 35; genetic mutations increase in the sperm when the father is over age 40. This does not mean that older parents should not have children: Serious problems are unusual no matter how old the parents are.

Nature aborts many embryos early in pregnancy (one reason an early miscarriage is not necessarily a tragedy). Many other mutations are harmless. Some mutations are helpful and become more common in later generations, as with lactose tolerance described in Chapter 2.

However, some spontaneous mutations result in severe disabilities that are indistinguishable, except with genetic analysis, from disabilities that are inherited directly. It is helpful to know when the problem is not in the parent's genes, because then the couple could have another child without worrying about a repeat.

## Not Exactly 46

As you know, each sperm or ovum usually has 23 chromosomes, creating a zygote with 46 chromosomes and eventually a person. However, sperm and ova do not always split exactly in half to make gametes.

Miscounts are not rare. About half of all zygotes have more than or fewer than 46 chromosomes (Milunsky & Milunsky, 2016). Almost all of them fail to duplicate, divide, differentiate, and implant, or they are spontaneously aborted before anyone knows that conception occurred.

If implantation does occur, many embryos with chromosomal miscounts are aborted, either by nature (miscarried) or by choice. Ninety-nine percent of fetuses that survive until birth have the usual 46 chromosomes. For the remaining 1 percent, birth is hazardous. Only 1 newborn in 166 births survives with 45, 47, or, rarely, 48 or 49 chromosomes (Benn, 2016).

Survival is more common if only some cells have 47 chromosomes and the others 46 (a condition called *mosaicism*), or if only a piece of a chromosome is missing or extra. Advanced analysis suggests that mosaicism of some sort "may represent the rule rather than the exception" (Lupski, 2013, p. 358). Usually mosaicism has no marked effect, although cancer is more likely with extra or missing genetic material.

## Down Syndrome

If an entire chromosome is missing or added, that leads to a recognizable *syndrome,* a cluster of distinct characteristics that tend to occur together. Usually the cause is three chromosomes at a particular location instead of the typical two (a condition called a *trisomy*). One in 10,000 newborns has three chromosomes at the 13th site (called Patau syndrome), and one in 5,000 has three at the 18th (called Edwards syndrome). Most trisomies die in the womb; those who are born usually die soon after except for trisomy 21 and trisomies at the 23rd pair (Archarya et al., 2017).

The most common extra-chromosome condition that results in a surviving child is **Down syndrome.** In 1868, Dr. Langdon Down and his wife opened a home for children with three chromosomes at the 21st site (then called "Mongolian Idiots"), demonstrating that such children could be quite capable. The World Health Organization officially named trisomy-21 *Down syndrome* in 1965.

Some 300 distinct characteristics can result from trisomy-21. No individual with Down syndrome is identical to another, but this trisomy usually produces telltale physical characteristics—a thick tongue, round face, and slanted eyes, as well as distinctive hands, feet, and fingerprints. The brain is somewhat smaller, with the hippocampus (important for memory) especially affected.

Many people with Down syndrome also have hearing problems, heart abnormalities, muscle weakness, and short stature. They are slow to develop intellectually, especially in language, with a notable deficit in hearing sounds that rhyme (Næss, 2016).

However, the impact of that third chromosome varies with every step of development, from genetics to epigenetics to child rearing to adulthood (Karmiloff-Smith et al., 2016). One specific is the gene for APP, a precursor for Alzheimer's disease, which is on chromosome 21. People with Down syndrome sometimes inherit three copies of that gene (one on each chromosome) and are more likely to develop major neurocognitive disorder (dementia), sometimes before age 40. However, not every individual with Down syndrome inherits three copies, and not everyone who expresses it develops major neurocognitive disorder.

That extra chromosome always affects the brain and other organs lifelong, but family context, education, and possibly medication can decrease the harm (Kuehn, 2011). Although drugs to advance cognition are still experimental, already "people with Down syndrome are achieving success in school and employment and are very satisfied with their lives" (Skotko, quoted in Underwood, 2014, p. 965).

## Problems of the 23rd Pair

Every human has at least 44 autosomes and one X chromosome; an embryo cannot develop without those 45. However, about 1 in every 300 infants is born with

REUTERS/Claudia Daut

**Universal Happiness** All young children delight in painting brightly colored pictures on a big canvas, but this scene is unusual for two reasons: Daniel has trisomy-21, and this photograph was taken at the only school in Chile where typical children and those with special needs share classrooms.

**Observation Quiz** How many characteristics can you see that indicate Daniel has Down syndrome? (see answer, p. 89) ↑

**Down syndrome** A condition in which a person has 47 chromosomes instead of the usual 46, with 3 rather than 2 chromosomes at the 21st site. People with Down syndrome typically have distinctive characteristics, including unusual facial features, heart abnormalities, and language difficulties. (Also called *trisomy-21*.)

**Especially for Teachers** Suppose you know that one of your students has a sibling who has Down syndrome. What special actions should you take? (see response, p. 89)

⬤ **Answer to Observation Quiz** (from p. 85): Glasses, not nearsightedness! Rates of corrective lenses (estimated at 85 percent) are as high among university students in the United States, but Americans are more likely to wear contacts. Two other visible differences: uniforms and gender. Except for the military, no U.S. university issues uniforms and the majority of North American students are women. A fourth difference may be inferred from their attentiveness: The graduation rate of incoming college students in China is about 90 percent, compared to about 50 percent in the United States.

only one sex chromosome (no Y) or with three or more (not just two) (Benn, 2016). Each particular combination of sex chromosomes results in specific syndromes (see Table 3.2).

Having an odd number of sex chromosomes impairs cognition and sexual maturation, with varied specifics depending on epigenetics (Hong & Reiss, 2014). It is not unusual for an affected child to seem to be developing typically until adulthood, when they consult a doctor because they are infertile. This problem is more common in men than women.

## Gene Disorders

Everyone carries alleles that *could* produce serious diseases or disabilities in the next generation. Most such genes have no serious consequences because they are recessive. The phenotype is affected only when the inherited gene is dominant or when a zygote has received the same recessive gene from both parents.

### Dominant Disorders

Most of the 7,000 *known* single-gene disorders are dominant (always expressed) (Milunsky & Milunsky, 2016). Most dominant disorders are relatively mild; severe ones are infrequent because children who inherited a severe disorder often died before puberty and thus never passed on that lethal dominant gene.

However, a few dominant disorders do not appear until adulthood. One such condition is *Huntington's disease,* a fatal central nervous system disorder caused by a copy number variation—more than 35 repetitions of a particular set of three base pairs. Although children with the dominant gene sometimes are affected (Milunsky & Milunsky, 2016), definite symptoms first appear in midlife. By then, an affected person could have had several children, as did the original Mr. Huntington. Half of his children inherited his dominant gene, which is why the disease is named after him.

Another exception to the general rule that serious dominant diseases are not inherited is a rare but severe form of Alzheimer's disease. It causes major neurocognitive disorder (formerly called *dementia*) before age 60. (Most forms of Alzheimer's begin after age 70 and are additive, not dominant.)

---

### TABLE 3.2

**Common Abnormalities Involving the Sex Chromosomes**

| Chromosomal Pattern | Physical Appearance | Psychological Characteristics | Incidence* |
|---|---|---|---|
| XXY (Klinefelter Syndrome) | Males. Usual male characteristics at puberty do not develop—penis does not grow, voice does not deepen. Usually sterile. Breasts may develop. | Can have some learning disabilities, especially in language skills. | 1 in 700 males |
| XYY (Jacob's Syndrome) | Males. Typically tall. | Risk of intellectual impairment, especially in language skills. | 1 in 1,000 males |
| XXX (Triple X Syndrome) | Females. Normal appearance. | Impaired in most intellectual skills. | 1 in 1,000 females |
| XO (only one sex chromosome) (Turner Syndrome) | Females. Short, often "webbed" neck. Secondary sex characteristics (breasts, menstruation) do not develop. | Some learning disabilities, especially related to math and spatial understanding; difficulty recognizing facial expressions of emotion. | 1 in 6,000 females |

*Incidence is approximate at birth.
Information from Hamerton & Evans, 2005; Aksglaede et al., 2013; Powell, 2013; Benn, 2016.

## Recessive Disorders

Recessive diseases are more numerous than dominant ones because they are passed down by carriers. Most recessive disorders are on the autosomes and thus are not X-linked, which means that either parent could be a carrier (Milunsky & Milunsky, 2016). Only in the rare case when two carriers have a child who inherits the double recessive (true for one child in four from such a couple) is it apparent that something is amiss. There are thousands of recessive diseases, but advance carrier detection is currently possible for only several hundred.

Some recessive conditions are X-linked, including hemophilia, Duchenne muscular dystrophy, and **fragile X syndrome,** the last of which is caused by more than 200 repetitions on one gene (Plomin et al., 2013). (Some repetitions are normal, but not this many.) The cognitive deficits caused by fragile X syndrome are the most common form of *inherited* intellectual disability. (Many other forms, such as trisomy-21, are not usually inherited.) Boys are more often impaired by fragile X than are girls, again because they have only one X.

## The Most Common Disorders

About 1 in 12 North American men and women carries an allele for cystic fibrosis, thalassemia, or sickle-cell disease, all devastating in children who inherit the recessive gene from both parents. These conditions are common because carriers have benefited from the gene.

Consider the most studied example: sickle-cell disease. Carriers of the sickle-cell gene die less often from malaria, which is prevalent and lethal in parts of Africa. Indeed, four distinct alleles cause sickle-cell disease, each originating in a malaria-prone region.

Selective adaptation allowed the gene to become widespread because it protected more people (the carriers) than it killed (those who inherited the recessive gene from both parents). Odds were that if a couple were both carriers and had four children, one would die of sickle-cell disease, one would not be a carrier and thus might die of malaria, but two would be carriers. They would be protected against a common, fatal disease. Consequently, they would likely become parents themselves. In that way, the recessive trait became widespread.

Almost every disease and risk of death is more common in one group than in another (Weiss & Koepsell, 2014). Whenever a particular genetic condition is common, there are benefits for those who are carriers. About 11 percent of Americans with African ancestors have the recessive gene for sickle-cell disease—they are protected against malaria. Cystic fibrosis is more common among Americans with ancestors from northern Europe, because carriers may have been protected from cholera.

Benefits are apparent for additive genes as well. Dark skin is protective against skin cancer, and light skin allows more vitamin D to be absorbed from the sun—a benefit if a baby lives where sunlight is scarce.

Modern Europeans inherited between 1 and 4 percent of their genes from Neanderthals, who became extinct about 30,000 years ago. Neanderthal genes protect contemporary humans against some diseases but may also make them more vulnerable to allergies and depression—depending on which bits of Neanderthal genes they happen to inherit (Saey, 2016).

## Genetic Counseling and Testing

Until recently, after the birth of a child with a severe disorder, couples blamed witches or fate, not genes or chromosomes. That has changed. Many young adults are concerned about their genes long before parenthood. Virtually everyone has a relative with a serious condition that is partly genetic.

**fragile X syndrome** A genetic disorder in which part of the X chromosome seems to be attached to the rest of it by a very thin string of molecules. The cause is a single gene that has more than 200 repetitions of one triplet.

**Answer to Observation Quiz** (from p. 87): Individuals with Down syndrome vary in many traits, but visible here are five common ones. Compared to most children his age, including his classmate beside him, Daniel has a rounder face, narrower eyes, shorter stature, larger teeth and tongue, and—best of all—a happier temperament.

**Response for Teachers** (from p. 87): As the text says, "information combats prejudice." Your first step would be to make sure you know about Down syndrome, reading material about it. You would learn, among other things, that it is not usually inherited (your student need not worry about his or her progeny) and that some children with Down syndrome need extra medical and educational attention. This might mean that you need to pay special attention to your student, whose parents might focus on the sibling.

**LaunchPad**
macmillan learning

Visit the Data Connections activity **Common Genetic Diseases and Conditions** to learn about several different types of genetic disorders.

Knowing the entire genome of a particular individual takes extensive analysis, but the cost has plummeted in recent years from more than a million dollars to less than a thousand. The results sometimes help find the best treatment for a disease, but experts hesitate to recommend full genome screening because most SNPs are "variants of unknown significance" (Couzin-Frankel, 2016, p. 442). In other words, it is not hard for a technician to find something unusual, but no one knows what all the oddities signify.

Some people pay for commercial genetic testing, which may provide misleading information. From the perspective of genetic counselors, even worse is that the emotional needs of the person are not addressed. For instance, some people who *might* be carriers of Huntington's disease commit suicide—before symptoms appear and without treatment that might reduce symptoms and allow years of normal life (Dayalu & Albin, 2015).

On the other hand, some diseases can be detected with almost 100 percent accuracy, which may help couples plan their future childbearing. That itself creates difficult choices as well as new opportunites, as shown in A Case To Study.

---

**A CASE TO STUDY**

# Raising Healthy Children

Twenty-six-year-old Amanda Kalinsky "screamed . . . became primal . . . shut down" when she heard the news she had chosen to hear (Aleccia, 2014). She wanted to know whether she carried the allele (F198S) for a rare, prion disease.

The answer was yes. There are three lethal prion diseases: Gerstmann-Straussler-Scheinker (GSS), Creutzfeldt-Jakob (CJ), and fatal familial insomnia. All are genetic and fatal, all strike in middle age, and all have no known cure.

Amanda's grandfather had no reason to scream: He died of GSS never knowing why his muscles and his brain stopped working. Her father was unaware until middle age that he also inherited GSS. He had already fathered three children. Amanda and her two siblings watched their father, beginning at age 52, lose his ability to move, to think, and finally to breathe. He died at age 58, hoping that none of his offspring would suffer as he did.

The odds were not good: Half of his sperm carried his dominant GSS gene. That made it likely that at least one of his children would inherit it. As it happened, his son was tested and was disease-free, and one daughter does not know. She is among many who might carry deadly genes but reject testing. Some say that everyone dies of something; they do not want to know, years before, what their death will be.

But Amanda had recently married Bradley, also in his 20s. Their shared vision of a large, healthy family was dashed when she learned that half of her children would die of GSS. She did not want to bring another generation of suffering into the world.

Her genetic counselor offered hope that would have been impossible a decade earlier. She could choose IVF with pre-implantation diagnosis. She became the first GSS carrier to do so (Uflacker et al., 2014).

At age 26, Amanda took drugs to stimulate her ovaries and then had 14 ova surgically removed. Meanwhile, Bradley ejaculated into a laboratory dish. Twelve of the 14 ova seemed viable; technicians inserted one sperm into each. Fertilization succeeded for nine of them, and they were tested twice, the second time after three days of duplication. Three of them carried the deadly allele and were destroyed.

Nathan Morgan/The New York Times/Redux

**Who Has the Fatal Dominant Disease?** The mother, but not the children. Unless a cure is found, Amanda Kalinsky will grow weak and experience significant cognitive decline, dying before age 60. She and her husband, Bradley, wanted children without Amanda's dominant gene for a rare disorder, Gerstmann-Straussler-Scheinker disease. Accordingly, they used IVF and pre-implantation testing. Only zygotes without the dominant gene were implanted. This photo shows the happy result.

Two of the remaining five were inserted, and both grew—a 100-percent success rate, perhaps because the parents were young and the zygotes were carefully chosen. The other three were frozen (*cryopreservation*) for later use. One became Tatum, the younger brother of twins Ava and Cole (see photo). Amanda and Bradley might soon try for a fourth child with the remaining blastocysts—they want to have children quickly so that Amanda will be alive and well while the children grow.

Amanda considers it a miracle that she is able to raise a healthy family, although she said that destroying three potential babies because they might develop GSS in middle age was "one of the hardest parts of the process."

Comfort comes, ironically, from the fact that this particular allele has very high *penetrance,* which means it almost always causes the disease. That is unlike many other alleles that increase risk but might be harmless. Each of us carries about 50 of those—and usually they do not attack us (Hayden, 2016).

As already noted, IVF raises many ethical issues—not only the possibility of sex selection but also temptation to choose "designer babies" who are "tall, dark, and handsome," or "blue-eyed blonds," or intellectual geniuses, or athletic stars (Murray, 2014). Not only can zygotes be tested and selectively inserted, as in this case, but CRISPR technology now allows genes to be added or deleted in the first days of prenatal life. At the moment, only when a genetic condition is very severe, with no reasonable alternative, is germline editing allowed (Kaiser, 2017).

Removing a gene before implantation is controversial, since the specter of designer babies looms. One genome scientist says we need "to put friction tape on the slope so the slope isn't slippery" (Lander, quoted in Kaiser, 2017).

Nevertheless, it is hard not to be grateful that recent genetic breakthroughs allow decades of happy family life for Amanda, Bradley, Ava, Cole, and Tatum.

## Psychological Disorders

Misinformation and mistaken fears are particularly destructive for those with psychological disorders, such as depression, schizophrenia, and autism spectrum disorder. No doubt genes are a factor in all of these conditions (Knopik et al., 2017). Yet, as with addiction and vision, the environment is crucial—not only the microsystem but also the macrosystem and exosystem.

This was confirmed by a study of the entire population of Denmark, where good medical records and decades of free public health care make research accurate. If *both* Danish parents developed schizophrenia, 27 percent of their children developed it; if one parent had it, 7 percent of their children developed it. These same statistics can be presented in another way: Even if both parents had schizophrenia, almost three-fourths (73 percent) of their children did not (Gottesman et al., 2010). (Some of them developed other psychological disorders, again providing evidence for epigenetics and additive genes.)

Even more persuasive is evidence for monozygotic twins. If one identical twin develops schizophrenia, often—but not always—the other twin also develops a psychological disorder of some sort. Two conclusions are obvious: (1) Genes are powerful, and (2) schizophrenia is not entirely genetic.

Numerous studies have identified environmental influences on schizophrenia, including fetal malnutrition, birth in the summer, adolescent use of psychoactive drugs, emigration in young adulthood, and family emotionality during adulthood.

Because environment is crucial, few scientists advocate genetic testing prenatally or in childhood for schizophrenia or any psychological condition. They fear that a positive test would lead to needless abortion or parental depression and stress, which might cause a disorder that would not have occurred otherwise. Even in adulthood, a positive genetic diagnosis might add to discrimination against the mentally ill (Mitchell et al., 2010).

## The Need for Counseling

The problems with testing for genes that cause psychological disorders are only one of several complications with genetic testing. Scientists—and the general

**genetic counseling** Consultation and testing by trained experts that enables individuals to learn about their genetic heritage, including harmful conditions that they might pass along to any children they may conceive.

public—have many opinions about genetic testing, and nations have varying policies (Plows, 2011). The problem is that science has revealed much more about genes than anyone imagined a decade ago. Laws and ethics have not kept up, and few prospective parents can interpret their own genetic history or laboratory results without help.

Professionals who have been trained to provide **genetic counseling** help prospective parents understand their genetic risk so that they can make informed decisions, not impulsive, irrational ones. Genetic counselors can advise about special hazards, precautions, and treatments that can occur before as well as after birth.

The genetic counselor's task is complicated for many reasons. One is that new genetic disorders—and treatments—are revealed almost weekly. An inherited disorder that once meant lifelong neurological impairment (e.g., phenylketonuria, or PKU) might now mean a normal life. A second reason is that the accuracy, effect, and interpretation of testing varies: Sometimes a particular gene increases the risk of a problem by only a tiny amount, perhaps 0.1 percent. A third reason is that the emotional stress of the clients must be respected and incorporated in the counseling process.

Even doctors may be poor at counseling. Consider the experience of one of my students. A month before she became pregnant, Jeannette's employer required her to have a rubella vaccination. Hearing that Jeannette had had the shot, her obstetrician gave her the following prognosis:

> My baby would be born with many defects, his ears would not be normal, he would be intellectually disabled. . . . I went home and cried for hours and hours. . . . I finally went to see a genetic counselor. Everything was fine, thank the Lord, thank you, my beautiful baby is okay.
>
> *[Jeannette, personal communication]*

Jeannette may have misunderstood what she was told, but that is exactly why the doctor should not have spoken. Genetic counselors are trained to make information clear. If sensitive counseling is available, then preconception, prenatal, or even prenuptial (before marriage) testing is especially useful for:

- individuals who have a parent, sibling, or child with a serious genetic condition
- couples who have had several spontaneous abortions or stillbirths
- couples who are infertile
- women over age 35 and men over age 40
- couples from the same ethnic group, particularly if they are relatives

The last listed item above is especially crucial among populations who often intermarry. This is true for Greeks in Cyprus, where about one-third of the population carries the recessive gene for thalassemia (either A or B). In the 1970s, 1 in every 158 babies was born with serious thalassemia, which led to repeated hospitalization and premature death. Then Cyprus encouraged everyone to be tested, before conception or at least prenatally. Now virtually no newborns in Cyprus have the condition (Hvistendahl, 2013).

Genetic counselors follow two ethical rules: (1) Tests are confidential, beyond the reach of insurance companies and public records, and (2) decisions are made by the clients, not by the counselors.

These guidelines are not always easy to follow (A. Parker, 2012). One quandary arises when parents already have a child with a recessive disease but tests reveal that the husband does not carry that gene. Should the counselor tell the couple that their next child will not have this disease because the husband is not the biological father of the first?

Another quandary arises when DNA is collected for one purpose—say, to assess the risk of sickle-cell disease—and analysis reveals another quite different problem, such as an extra sex chromosome or a high risk of breast cancer. This problem is new: Even a few years ago, testing was so expensive that it focused on only one specific, high-risk disease. Now counselors learn about thousands of conditions that were not suspected. If no treatment is available, must the person be told?

The current consensus is that information should be shared if:

1. the person wants to hear it;
2. the risk is severe and verified;
3. an experienced counselor explains the data; and
4. treatment is available.

That is not as straightforward as it appears. Scientists and physicians disagree about severity, certainty, and treatment. Some experts advocate informing patients of any serious genetic disorder, even when the person does not want to know and when the information might be harmful (Couzin-Frankel, 2013a).

An added complication is that individuals differ in their willingness to hear bad news. What if one person wants to know but other family members—perhaps a parent or a monozygotic twin who has the same condition—do not? We all are carriers. Do we all want specifics?

Sometimes couples make a decision (such as to begin or to abort a pregnancy) that reflects a mistaken calculation of the risk, at least as the professional interprets it (A. Parker, 2012). Even with careful counseling, people with identical genetic conditions make opposite choices.

For instance, 108 women who already had one child with fragile X syndrome were told that they had a 50 percent chance of having another such child. Most (77 percent) decided to avoid pregnancy with sterilization or excellent contraception, but some (20 percent) intentionally had another child (Raspberry & Skinner, 2011). Always the professional explains probabilities; always the clients decide.

Many developmentalists believe that public health is most likely to benefit from changes in the environment, not in genetic testing. Some fear that the twenty-first-century emphasis on genes is a way to avoid focusing on public health issues (poverty, pollution, pesticides, and so on), which cause more health problems than genes do (Plows, 2011).

A wise genetic counselor notes the many relevant factors in nature and nurture. Then, they write a letter explaining the genetic facts and future possibilities. Finally, they follow up months and years later to find out what needs more explanation.

Developmentalists now recognize the power of genes, but they also know that context and culture have a major effect, since plasticity is characteristic of child development. As you have read many times in this chapter, genes are part of the human story, influencing every page, but they do not determine the plot or the final paragraph. The remaining chapters describe the rest of the story.

**Double Trouble or Genetic Joy?** Six-year-old Ethan Dean inherited two recessive genes for cystic fibrosis. That may prevent him from fulfilling his wish—to become a garbage man. But another genetic trait is evident: Humans want to care for children, especially those with deadly conditions. The Sacramento Department of Sanitation, and the Make-a-Wish foundation, gave Ethan a day collecting trash, to his apparent delight.

**THINK CRITICALLY:** Instead of genetic counseling, should we advocate health counseling?

## WHAT HAVE YOU LEARNED?

1. What chromosomal miscounts might result in a surviving child?

2. What is the cause and consequence of Down syndrome?

3. How common are recessive conditions?

4. Why is sickle-cell disease very common in some parts of Africa?

5. What is the role of the genetic counselor?

6. What ethical mandates are required of genetic counselors?

# SUMMARY

## The Genetic Code

**1.** Genes are the foundation for all development, first instructing the developing creature to form the body and brain, and then affecting thought, behavior, and health lifelong. Human conception occurs when two gametes (a sperm with 23 chromosomes and an ovum with 23 chromosomes) combine to form a single cell called a zygote.

**2.** A zygote usually has 46 chromosomes (half from each parent), which carry a total of about 21,000 genes. Genes and chromosomes from each parent match up to make the zygote, but the match is not always letter-perfect because of genetic variations called alleles, or polymorphisms.

**3.** Genetic variations occur in many ways, from the chromosomes of the parent to the epigenetic material surrounding the zygote and the microbiome of every body part. Spontaneous mutations, changing the number or sequences of base pairs, also make each person unique.

**4.** The most notable mismatch is in the 23rd pair of chromosomes, which is XX in females and XY in males. The sex of the embryo depends on the sperm, since only men have a Y chromosome and thus can make Y gametes.

## New Cells, New People

**5.** The first duplications of the one-celled zygote create stem cells, each of which could become a person if it developed. Monozygotic twins occur if those first stem cells split completely, which rarely occurs. Usually, the cluster of cells continues dividing and duplicating throughout development, creating a baby with 26 billion cells and eventually an adult with 37 trillion cells.

**6.** Dizygotic twins occur if two ova are fertilized by two sperm at about the same time. Genetically, they have half their genes in common, as do all full siblings.

**7.** In vitro fertilization (IVF) has led to millions of much-wanted babies and also to an increase in multiple births, who often are preterm and of low birthweight. Ethical concerns regarding IVF have quieted, but new dilemmas appear with stem cells and CRISPR.

## From Genotype to Phenotype

**8.** Genes interact in many ways, sometimes additively with each gene contributing to development and sometimes in a dominant–recessive pattern. The environment interacts with the genetic instructions for every trait, making every characteristic polygenic and multifactorial.

**9.** Genetic makeup can make a person susceptible to many conditions. Examples include substance use disorder (especially alcohol use disorder) and poor vision (especially nearsightedness). Culture and family affect both of these conditions dramatically.

**10.** Knowing the impact of genes and the environment can help in several ways, including guiding parents to protect their children from potentially harmful genes.

## Chromosomal and Genetic Problems

**11.** Often a gamete has fewer or more than 23 chromosomes, which may create a zygote with 45, 47, or 48 chromosomes. Usually such zygotes do not duplicate, implant, or grow.

**12.** Infants may survive if they have three chromosomes at the 21st site (Down syndrome) or extra sex chromosomes. They may have intellectual and sexual problems, but they may have a fulfilling life.

**13.** Everyone is a carrier for genetic abnormalities. Usually these conditions are recessive, not apparent unless the mother and the father both carry the gene. Serious dominant disorders usually do not appear until midlife. Serious recessive diseases can become common if carriers have a health advantage.

**14.** Genetic testing and counseling can help many couples. Testing provides information about possibilities, but the final decision rests with the couple.

# KEY TERMS

deoxyribonucleic acid (DNA) (p. 68)
chromosome (p. 68)
gene (p. 68)
genome (p. 68)
allele (p. 69)
epigenetics (p. 69)
microbiome (p. 70)
zygote (p. 70)

copy number variations (p. 70)
genotype (p. 71)
homozygous (p. 71)
heterozygous (p. 71)
23rd pair (p. 71)
XY (p. 71)
XX (p. 71)
stem cells (p. 75)

in vitro fertilization (IVF) (p. 76)
monozygotic (MZ) twins (p. 77)
dizygotic (DZ) twins (p. 79)
phenotype (p. 80)
polygenic (p. 80)
multifactorial (p. 80)
Human Genome Project (p. 80)

dominant–recessive pattern (p. 81)
carrier (p. 82)
X-linked (p. 82)
heritability (p. 84)
Down syndrome (p. 87)
fragile X syndrome (p. 89)
genetic counseling (p. 92)

## APPLICATIONS

**1.** Pick one of your traits, and explain the influences that both nature *and* nurture have on it. For example, if you have a short temper, explain its origins in your genetics, your culture, and your childhood experiences.

**2.** Many adults have a preference for having a son or a daughter. Interview adults of several ages and backgrounds about their preferences. If they give the socially preferable answer ("It does not matter"), ask how they think the two sexes differ. Listen and take notes—don't debate. Analyze the implications of the responses you get.

**3.** Draw a genetic chart of your biological relatives, going back as many generations as you can, listing all serious illnesses and causes of death. Include ancestors who died in infancy. Do you see any genetic susceptibility? If so, how can you overcome it?

**4.** Given what is known about the genetics of substance use disorders, ask several people how addiction can be prevented. Discuss why answers differ.

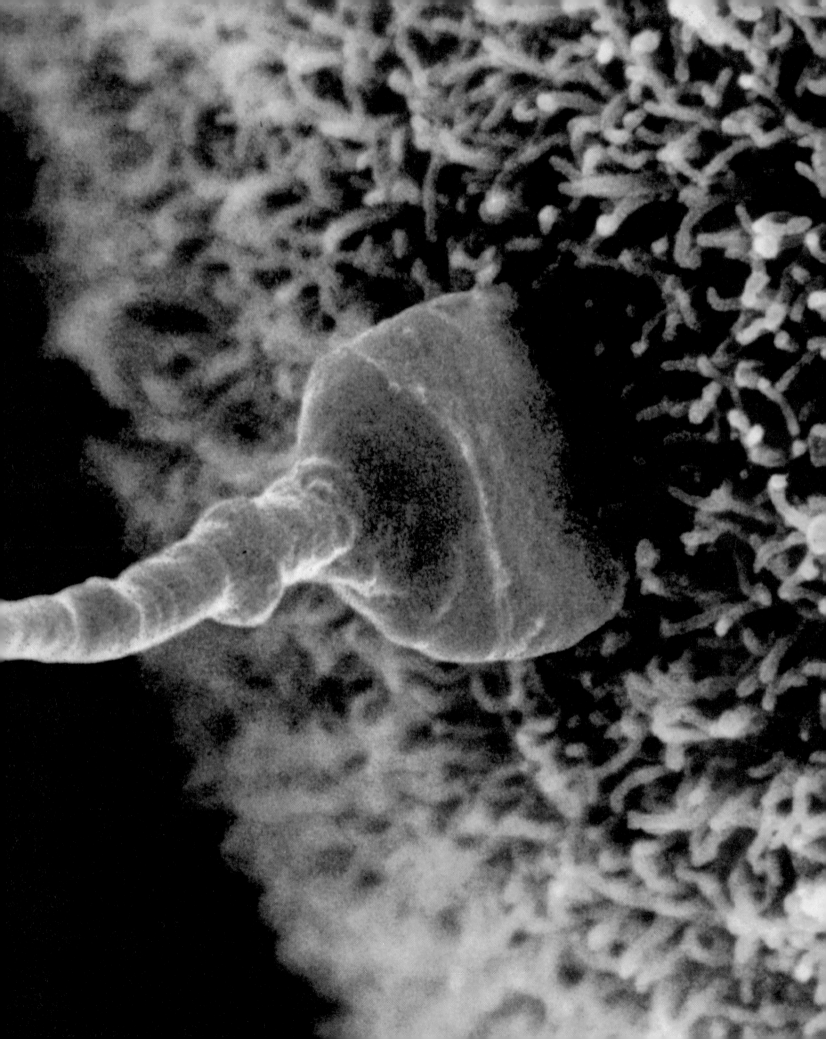

# Prenatal Development and Birth

## What Will You Know?

1. Why do most zygotes never become babies?
2. Are home births ever best?
3. What can a pregnant woman do to ensure a healthy newborn?
4. Why do new mothers and fathers sometimes become severely depressed?

**M**y daughter Elissa had a second child. At 6 A.M., she and her husband were in the labor room of the birthing center; I was with Asa, age 5, in the family waiting room. Several times, Asa walked down the hall to see his parents. Usually the midwife opened the labor room door to let us in. Sometimes we had to wait until a contraction was over. Then parents and son smiled at each other again.

When the baby was born, a nurse came to say, "There's a new person who wants to meet you."

"Let me put this last Lego piece in," Asa said. He then brought his new creation to show his parents, who introduced him to his brother, Isaac, sucking on his mother's breast.

The scientific study of human development is not only about how individuals change over time, it is about historical change—Bronfenbrenner's chronosystem. We will explore many aspects of historical and cultural variations in pregnancy and birth in this chapter, the thought of which struck me forcefully as I remembered when Elissa was born.

Back then, midwives were banned and fathers were relegated to waiting rooms, as my husband, Martin, had been for our first two babies. Newly inspired by feminism, I convinced my obstetrician to let Martin stay with me. He wept when he held Elissa, wet and wide-eyed, moments old. Then she was wiped, weighed, wrapped, and wheeled away.

The nurses did not let me touch her for 24 hours. They said that I had no milk, that I needed rest, that she was tired, too. By contrast, six hours after Isaac was born, his entire family was home again. I know that my experience is limited to my nation and culture: Elissa and Isaac were both born in New York City. Elsewhere, millions of other newborns arrive in homes—as did my own mother.

This chapter describes what we now know about prenatal growth and birth, and some of the vast differences from one era, one culture, even one family to another. Possible harm is noted: causes and consequences of diseases, malnutrition, drugs, pollution, stress. Fathers, particularly, have become more active partners, and everyone—medical professionals, governments, and family members—affects the early life of each developing person. This chapter will help all of us be a positive influence on the estimated one and a half million babies born next year.

+ **Prenatal Development**
Germinal: The First 14 Days
Embryo: From the Third Week Through the Eighth Week
Fetus: From the Ninth Week Until Birth
INSIDE THE BRAIN: Neuronal Birth and Death

+ **Birth**
The Newborn's First Minutes
Medical Assistance

+ **Problems and Solutions**
Harmful Substances
Applying the Research
A VIEW FROM SCIENCE: What Is Safe?
Prenatal Diagnosis
Low Birthweight: Causes and Consequences
OPPOSING PERSPECTIVES: "What Do People Live to Do?"
Complications During Birth

+ **The New Family**
The Newborn
New Mothers
New Fathers
Parental Alliance
Family Bonding

Left: David M. Phillips/Science Source
Top: shapecharge/E+/Getty Images

# Prenatal Development

The most dramatic and extensive transformation of the life span occurs before birth. To make it easier to study, prenatal development is often divided into three main periods. The first two weeks are called the **germinal period;** the third week through the eighth week is the **embryonic period;** from then until birth is the **fetal period.** (Alternative terms are presented in Table 4.1.)

## Germinal: The First 14 Days

You learned in Chapter 3 that the one-celled zygote duplicates, divides, and multiplies. Soon after the 16-cell stage, a fourth crucial process, *differentiation,* begins: The early cells take on distinct characteristics. About one week after conception, the mass of about 100 cells, called a *blastocyst,* forms two distinct parts—a shell that will become the *placenta* and a nucleus that will become the *embryo.* That is the first differentiation. In the next 20 weeks, every cell will differentiate, becoming what the genetic instructions dictate, from the many parts of the brain to the tiny toenails.

The placenta, an understudied "throwaway organ" (Kaiser, 2014a, p. 1073), must achieve **implantation**—that is, it must embed into the nurturing lining of the uterus (see Figure 4.1). This process is far from automatic; more than half of natural conceptions and an even larger proportion of in vitro conceptions never implant, usually because of a chromosomal or genetic abnormality (Niakan et al., 2012). Most new life ends before an embryo begins (see Table 4.2).

## Embryo: From the Third Week Through the Eighth Week

The start of the third week after conception initiates the *embryonic period,* during which the mass of cells takes shape—not yet recognizably human but worthy of a new name, **embryo.** (The word *embryo* is often used loosely, but each early stage has a particular name; here, "embryo" refers to day 14 to day 56.)

**germinal period** The first two weeks of prenatal development after conception, characterized by rapid cell division and the beginning of cell differentiation.

**embryonic period** The stage of prenatal development from approximately the third week through the eighth week after conception. The basic forms of all body structures, including internal organs, develop.

**fetal period** The stage of prenatal development from the ninth week after conception until birth. The fetus gains about 7 pounds (more than 3,000 grams) and organs become more mature, gradually able to function on their own.

**implantation** The process, beginning about 10 days after conception, in which the developing organism burrows into the uterus, where it can be nourished and protected as it continues to develop.

**embryo** The name for a developing human organism from about the third week through the eighth week after conception.

| TABLE 4.1 |
|---|
| **Timing and Terminology** |
| Popular and professional books use various phrases to segment the stages of pregnancy. The following comments may help to clarify the phrases used. |
| *Beginning of pregnancy:* Pregnancy begins at conception, which is also the starting point of *gestational age.* However, the organism does not become an *embryo* until about two weeks later, and pregnancy does not affect the woman (and is not confirmed by blood or urine testing) until implantation. Perhaps because the exact date of conception is usually unknown, some obstetricians and publications count from the woman's last menstrual period (LMP), usually about 14 days *before* conception. |
| *Length of pregnancy:* Full-term pregnancies last 266 days, or 38 weeks, or 9 months. If the LMP is used as the starting time, pregnancy lasts 40 weeks, sometimes expressed as 10 lunar months. (A lunar month is 28 days long.) |
| *Trimesters:* Instead of *germinal period, embryonic period,* and *fetal period,* as used in this text, some writers divide pregnancy into three-month periods called *trimesters.* Months 1, 2, and 3 are called the *first trimester;* months 4, 5, and 6, the *second trimester;* and months 7, 8, and 9, the *third trimester.* |
| *Due date:* Although a specific due date based on the LMP is calculated, only 5 percent of babies are born on that exact day. Babies born between two weeks before and one week after that date are considered *full term.* [This is recent; until 2012, three weeks before and two weeks after were considered full term.] Because of increased risks for postmature babies, labor is often induced if the baby has not arrived within seven days after the due date, although many midwives and doctors prefer to wait to see whether labor begins spontaneously. |

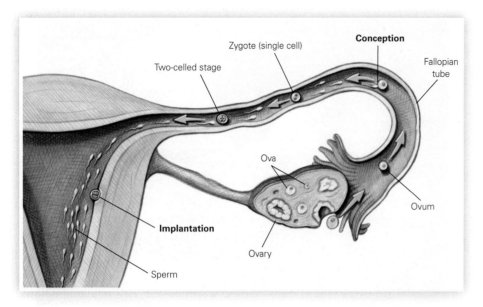

**FIGURE 4.1**
**The Most Dangerous Journey** In the first 10 days after conception, the organism does not increase in size because it is not yet nourished by the mother. However, the number of cells increases rapidly as the organism prepares for implantation, which occurs successfully not quite half of the time.

| TABLE 4.2 |
| --- |
| **Vulnerability During Prenatal Development** |
| **The Germinal Period** |
| An estimated 60 percent of all zygotes do not grow or implant properly and thus do not survive the germinal period. Many of these organisms are abnormal; few women realize they were pregnant. |
| **The Embryonic Period** |
| About 20 percent of all embryos are aborted spontaneously. This is usually called an early *miscarriage,* a term that implies something wrong with the woman when in fact the most common reason for a spontaneous abortion is a chromosomal abnormality. |
| **The Fetal Period** |
| About 5 percent of all fetuses are aborted spontaneously before viability at 22 weeks or are *stillborn,* defined as born dead after 22 weeks. This is much more common in poor nations. |
| **Birth** |
| Because of all these factors, only about 31 percent of all zygotes grow and survive to become living newborn babies. Age of the mother is crucial, with survival of the newborn most likely if the pregnancy lasted at least 36 weeks and the mother was in her early 20s. |
| Information from Bentley & Mascie-Taylor, 2000; Laurino et al., 2005; Cunningham et al., 2014. |

First, a thin line (called the *primitive streak*) appears down the middle of the inner mass of cells; it will become the *neural tube* 20 to 27 days after conception and develop into the central nervous system (CNS, the brain and spinal column). The head appears in the fourth week, as eyes, ears, nose, and mouth start to form, and a minuscule blood vessel that will become the heart begins to pulsate.

By the fifth week, buds that will become arms and legs emerge. The upper arms and then forearms, palms, and webbed fingers grow. Legs, knees, feet, and

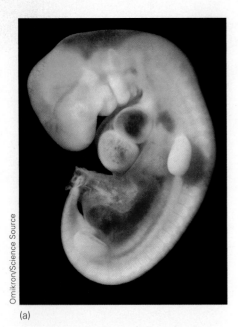

(a)

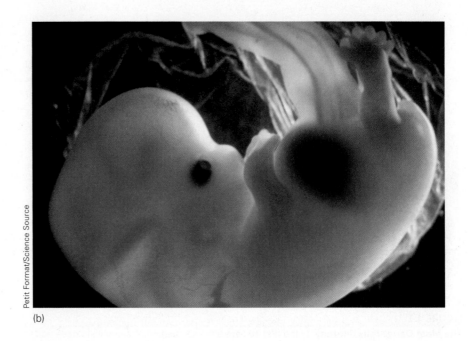

(b)

**The Embryonic Period** *(a)* At 4 weeks past conception, the embryo is only about 1/8 inch (3 millimeters) long, but already the head has taken shape. *(b)* By 7 weeks, the organism is somewhat less than an inch (2 centimeters) long. Eyes, nose, the digestive system, and even the first stage of toe formation can be seen.

**cephalocaudal development** Growth and development that occurs from the head down.

**proximodistal development** Growth or development that occurs from the center or core in an outward direction.

**fetus** The name for a developing human organism from the start of the ninth week after conception until birth.

**ultrasound** An image of a fetus (or an internal organ) produced by using high-frequency sound waves. (Also called *sonogram*.)

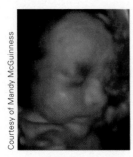

**Meet Your Baby** The sonogram above shows Elisa Clare McGuinness at 22 weeks post-conception. She continued to develop well for the next four months, becoming a healthy, 3,572-gram newborn, finally able to meet her family—two parents and an older brother.

webbed toes, in that order, emerge a few days later, each with a distinct cluster of differentiated cells that begin to form the skeleton. Then, 52 and 54 days after conception, respectively, the fingers and toes separate.

As you can see, growth occurs in a **cephalocaudal** (literally, "head-to-tail") pattern, and also in a **proximodistal** (literally, "near-to-far") pattern, with the extremities forming last. This directional pattern continues until puberty, when it reverses. (The feet of a young teenager grow first—the brain last!)

At the end of the eighth week after conception (56 days), the embryo weighs just one-thirtieth of an ounce (1 gram) and is about 1 inch (2½ centimeters) long. It has all the basic organs and body parts (except sex organs) of a human being, including elbows and knees. It moves frequently, about 150 times per hour, but this movement is imperceptible and random; it will be many months before deliberate movement occurs.

## Fetus: From the Ninth Week Until Birth

The organism is called a **fetus** from the beginning of the ninth week after conception until birth. The fetal period encompasses dramatic change, from a tiny, apparently sexless creature smaller than the final joint of your thumb to a boy or girl about 20 inches (51 centimeters) long.

### The Third Month

If the 23rd pair of chromosomes are XY, the SRY gene on the Y triggers the development of male sex organs. Otherwise, female organs develop. The male fetus experiences a rush of the hormone testosterone, affecting many structures and connections in the brain (Filová et al., 2013).

By the end of the third month, the sex organs may be visible via **ultrasound** (in a *sonogram*), which is similar to an X-ray but uses sound waves instead of radiation. The 3-month-old fetus weighs about 3 ounces (87 grams) and is about 3 inches (7.5 centimeters) long. Early prenatal growth is very rapid, with considerable variation, especially in body weight. The numbers just given—3 months, 3 ounces, 3 inches—are rounded off for easy recollection. (Metric measures—100 days, 100 grams, 100 millimeters—are similarly imprecise yet useful.)

# Neuronal Birth and Death

In earlier decades, a newborn's chance of survival was pegged to how much the baby weighed. Today, we know that weight is a crude predictor—some 1-pound babies live and some 3-pound ones die. The crucial factor is maturation of the brain.

As you now know, the central nervous system is the first body system to begin development. The embryonic stage starts with the primitive streak, which becomes the neural tube even before the facial features are formed and the first pulsating blood vessel appears.

Already in the third week after conception, some cells specialize to become *neural progenitor cells,* which duplicate and multiply many times until some of them create neurons (brain cells). Neurons do not duplicate, but some endure lifelong. Those early neurons migrate to a particular part of the brain (brain stem, cerebellum, hypothalamus, visual cortex, and so on) and specialize. For example, some neurons are dedicated to seeing faces, others to seeing red and green, others to blue and yellow, and so on.

By mid-pregnancy, the brain has developed billions of neurons (*neurogenesis*). Earlier, the cortex (the outer part of the brain) had been smooth, but now folds and wrinkles (ridges and depressions, called *gyri* and *sulci*) allow the human brain to be larger and more complex than the brains of other animals (Stiles & Jernigan, 2010). [**Developmental Link:** The cortex and other brain structures are described in Chapter 5.]

Following the proximodistal (near-to-far) sequence, the six layers of the cortex are produced, with the bottom (sixth) layer first and then each new layer above the previous one. The top, outer layer is the last to form. Similarly, the brain stem above the back of the neck, then the midbrain, and finally the forebrain develop and connect.

Synchronized connections between parts of the brain indicate that they are working together—as in an adult who sees something delicious that awakens hunger and promotes reaching, all in a flash. Each of these three actions arises together from different parts of the brain. Such synchrony begins prenatally.

One study found that a relative lack of synchronized coordination after 20 weeks predicted preterm delivery, perhaps because something was amiss in the prenatal environment (Thomason et al., 2017). This finding awaits replication, and much early brain development remains mysterious, but advances in MRIs open new windows to the study of the fetal brain (Miller, 2017).

A detailed study of one crucial brain region, the *hippocampus* (the major site for memory formation), reveals an explosion of new cells in that area during the fourth month, followed by a gradual slowdown of new cell formation (Ge et al., 2015). Although this mid-gestation burst of neurogenesis and then its

slowing is generally true of the entire brain, each area follows a timetable that reflects specific brain function.

By full term, human brain growth is so extensive that the cortex has many gyri and sulci (see Figure 4.2). Although some huge mammals (whales, for instance) have bigger brains than humans, no other creature needs as many folds because, relative to body size, the human brain is much larger.

Beyond brain growth, with an estimated 86 billion neurons at birth, another process occurs in the final three months of a normal pregnancy—cell death. Programmed cell death, called *apoptosis,* occurs in two prenatal waves. The first wave is easy to understand: Abnormal and immature neurons, such as those with missing or extra chromosomes, are lost. Later in development, however, seemingly normal neurons die: Almost half of all newly formed brain cells are gone before birth (Underwood, 2013). Why?

Perhaps the final three months are the best time for normal cell death, allowing the remaining neurons to establish connections for thinking, remembering, and responding. Surviving preterm babies often have subtle intellectual and emotional deficits. There are many plausible hypotheses for this correlation; less time for prenatal apoptosis is one of them.

In the final months of pregnancy, the various lobes and areas of the brain are established, and pathways between one area and another are forged. For instance, sound and sight become coordinated: Newborns quickly connect voices heard during pregnancy with faces. That may be why they recognize their mother after seeing her only once or twice. That phenomenal accomplishment occurs within a day or two after birth. Indeed, the fetal brain is attuned to the voices much more than to other

N. Bromhall/Science Source

**Can He Hear?** A fetus, just about at the age of viability, is shown fingering his ear. Such gestures are probably random; but yes, he can hear.

noises: Neurological plasticity is designed to recognize the voices of familiar people by the sixth month after conception (Webb et al., 2015).

The final months of pregnancy are crucial for the brain in another way: The membranes and bones covering the brain thicken, which helps prevent "brain bleeds," a hazard of preterm birth if paper-thin blood vessels in the cortex collapse.

Newborns have two areas on the top of their heads (*fontanels*) where the bones of the skull have not yet fused. Fontanels enable the fetal head to become narrower as it moves through the vagina during birth, and then they gradually close during infancy. Fontanels are larger in preterm babies, making them more vulnerable to brain damage.

Curiously, some areas of chimpanzee brains are packed with more neurons than human brains, allowing less room for dendrites and axons. Furthermore, *myelination,* which speeds transmission from one neuron to another, is already about 20 percent complete for the newborn chimp but virtually absent for the newborn human (Gash & Dean, 2015). Thus, brains of human fetuses are ready to be molded by experience after birth.

Although many connections form in the brain before birth, this process continues for years—the human brain is not fully connected until early adulthood. One distinguishing difference between human brains and those of other primates is the extensive prenatal and postnatal growth of axons and dendrites, the connecting fibers between one neuron and another (Gash & Dean, 2015; Collins et al., 2016). More than any other creature, humans learn before birth and lifelong: Our brains are evidence of that.

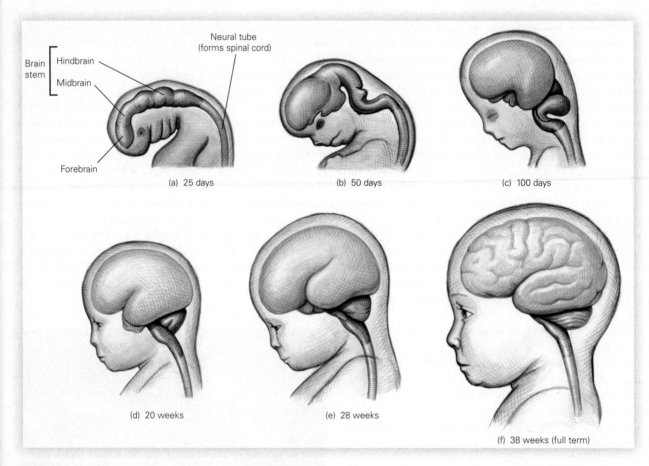

**FIGURE 4.2**

**Prenatal Growth of the Brain** Just 25 days after conception *(a)*, the central nervous system is already evident. The brain looks distinctly human by day 100 *(c)*. By the 28th week of gestation *(e)*, at the very time brain activity begins, the various sections of the brain are recognizable. When the fetus is full term *(f)*, all parts of the brain, including the cortex (the outer layers), are formed, folding over one another and becoming more convoluted, or wrinkled, as the number of brain cells increases.

## The Middle Three Months

Although movement begins earlier, in the fourth month it is evident in all body parts, with "stretching, yawning, hand to face contact, swallowing and tongue protrusion" (DiPietro et al., 2015, p. 33). Indeed, "Large body movements—whole body flexion and extension, stretching and writhing, and vigorous leg kicks that somersault the fetus through the amniotic fluid—peak at 14–16 weeks gestation" (Adolph & Franchek, 2017). No wonder this is the time when many future mothers experience *quickening*, the fetus's first palpable movement. The heartbeat becomes stronger and speeds up when the fetus is awake and moving. Digestion and elimination develop. Fingernails, toenails, and buds for teeth form, and hair grows (including eyelashes).

All of those developments inspire awe, but the crucial mid-pregnancy development is that the entire central nervous system becomes active, regulating heart rate, breathing, and sucking. Brain advances allow the fetus to reach the **age of viability** at the end of this trimester, when a fetus born far too early can survive.

Survival is far from automatic. A century ago, if a fetus was born before 30 weeks of gestation, it soon died. Currently, if birth occurs in an advanced neonatal unit, some very preterm babies survive.

In Japan, which has excellent neonatal care, 20 percent of 22-week-old newborns survive without major neurological impairment (Ishii et al., 2013). However, the age of viability is stuck at 22 weeks because even the most advanced technology cannot maintain life without some brain response. (Reports of survivors born before 22 weeks are suspect because the date of conception is unknown.)

**Video: Brain Development Animation: Prenatal** shows how the brain develops from just after conception until birth.

**age of viability** The age (about 22 weeks after conception) at which a fetus might survive outside the mother's uterus if specialized medical care is available.

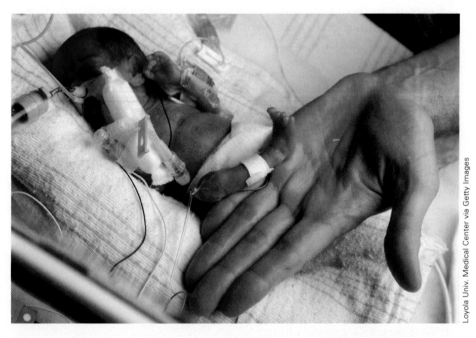

**One of the Tiniest** Rumaisa Rahman was born after 26 weeks and 6 days, weighing only 8.6 ounces (244 grams). Nevertheless, she has a good chance of living a full, normal life. Rumaisa gained 5 pounds (2,270 grams) in the hospital and then, six months after her birth, went home. Her twin sister, Hiba, who weighed 1.3 pounds (590 grams) at birth, had gone home two months earlier. At their one-year birthday, the twins seemed normal, with Rumaisa weighing 15 pounds (6,800 grams) and Hiba 17 pounds (7,711 grams) (Nanji, 2005).

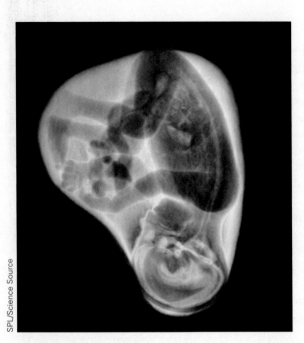

SPL/Science Source

**Ready for Birth?** We hope not, but this fetus at 27 weeks postconception is viable, although very small. At full term (38 weeks), weight gain would mean that the limbs are folded close to the body, and the uterus is almost completely full.

## The Final Three Months

Reaching the age of viability simply means that life outside the womb is *possible*. Many babies born between 22 and 24 weeks die, and survivors born before 27 weeks often develop slowly because they have missed some essential brain development in the uterus (Månsson & Stjernqvist, 2014).

Each day of the final three months improves the odds not only of survival but also of healthy life and normal cognition. (More on preterm birth appears later in this chapter.) Many aspects of prenatal life are awe-inspiring; the fact that an ordinary woman provides a far better home for a fetus than the most advanced medical technology is one of them.

The critical difference between life and death—or between a fragile, preterm newborn and a robust full-term one—is maturation of the neurological, respiratory, and cardiovascular systems. In the final three prenatal months, the lungs expand and contract, and breathing muscles strengthen as the fetus swallows and spits out amniotic fluid. The valves of the heart go through a final maturation, as do the arteries and veins throughout the body; the testicles of the male fetus descend; brain pathways form.

The fetus usually gains at least 4½ pounds (2.1 kilograms) in the third trimester, increasing to about 7½ pounds (about 3.4 kilograms) at birth, with boys a few ounces heavier than girls. The weight of 7½ pounds is an average: Some well-nourished mothers give birth to healthy newborns weighing 6 pounds, others 10 pounds, although small or large newborns are examined more carefully to ensure that nothing is amiss.

Generally, northern European newborns tend to be heavy and northern African ones tend to be light, a difference that might be selective adaptation in an ecosystem where people survived best if they were relatively tall or short. It does seem that people who live in savannahs (open spaces with a few small trees) are relatively tall for genetic reasons (Migliano & Guillon, 2012).

Of course, smaller newborns and shorter adults may be affected by malnutrition, not adaptive growth. National variations are evident; what they indicate is disputed (de Vrieze, 2017).

Reflexes (see pp. 125–126) are a better indication of health than weight. Unless something is amiss, by 36 weeks, most newborns are ready to thrive at home on mother's milk—no expert help, oxygenated air, or special feeding required. For thousands of years, that is how humans survived: We would not be alive if any of our ancestors had required intensive newborn care.

### WHAT HAVE YOU LEARNED?

1. What are the three stages of prenatal development?

2. Why are the first days of life the most hazardous?

3. What parts of the embryo form first?

4. When do sex organs appear?

5. What distinguishes a fetus from a baby?

6. What is the prognosis of a baby born before 25 weeks of gestation?

7. What occurs in the final three months of pregnancy?

# Birth

About 266 days or 38 weeks (36–39 weeks is considered full term) after conception, the fetal brain signals the release of the hormone *oxytocin,* which prepares the fetus for delivery and starts labor. Oxytocin also strengthens the mother's urge to nurture her baby, and it increases when she breast-feeds. In both mothers and fathers, oxytocin continues to encourage caregiving for months and years (Swain et al., 2014).

The average baby is born after 14 hours of active labor for first births and 7 hours for subsequent births, although often birth takes twice or half as long, depending on the woman's body and her surroundings. The definition of "active" labor varies, which is one reason some women believe they are in labor for days and others 10 minutes. Doctors consider active labor as beginning with regular contractions and ending when the fetal head passes through the cervix (Cunningham et al., 2014). (Figure 4.3 shows the universal stages of birth.)

Birthing positions and places vary. Some cultures expect women to sit or squat upright, supported by family members; some doctors insist that women be lying down on their backs; some women give birth in a warm "birthing tub" of water.

Most U.S. births now take place in hospital labor rooms with high-tech operating rooms nearby. Another 1 to 6 percent of U.S. births occur in *birthing centers* (not in a hospital), with the rate varying by state. Less than 1 percent occur at home (MacDorman et al., 2014). (Home births are illegal in some U.S. states.)

**FIGURE 4.3**

**A Typical, Uncomplicated Birth** *(a)* The baby's position as the birth process begins. *(b)* The first stage of labor: The cervix dilates to allow passage of the baby's head. *(c)* Transition: The baby's head moves into the "birth canal," the vagina. *(d)* The second stage of labor: The baby's head moves through the opening of the vagina (the baby's head "crowns") and *(e)* emerges completely. *(f)* The third stage of labor is the expulsion of the placenta. This usually occurs naturally, but the entire placenta must be expelled; so birth attendants check carefully. In some cultures, the placenta is ceremonially buried to commemorate its life-giving role.

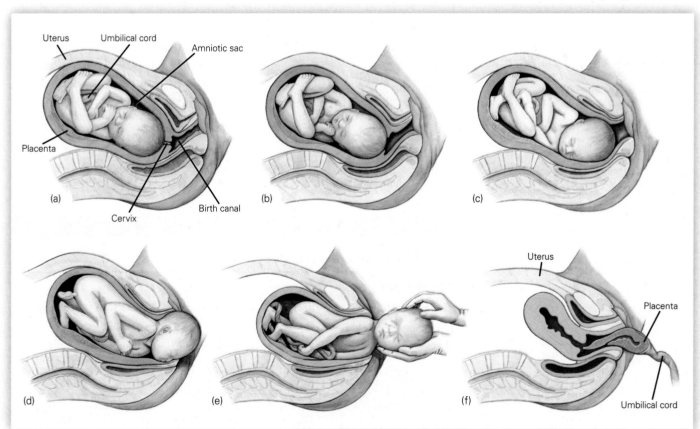

**Choice, Culture, or Cohort?** Why do it that way? Both of these women (in Peru, on the *left,* in England, on the *right*) chose methods of labor that are unusual in the United States, where birth stools and birthing pools are uncommon. However, in all three nations, most births occur in hospitals—a rare choice a century ago.

**Apgar scale** A quick assessment of a newborn's health, from 0 to 10. Below 5 is an emergency—a neonatal pediatrician is summoned immediately. Most babies are at 7, 8, or 9—almost never a perfect 10.

## The Newborn's First Minutes

Newborns usually breathe and cry on their own. Between spontaneous cries, the first breaths of air bring oxygen to the lungs and blood, and the infant's color changes from bluish to pinkish. ("Pinkish" refers to blood color, visible beneath the skin, and applies to newborns of all hues.) Eyes open wide; tiny fingers grab; even tinier toes stretch and retract. The newborn is instantly, zestfully, ready for life.

Nevertheless, a birth attendant has important work to do. Mucus in the baby's throat is removed, especially if the first breaths seem shallow or strained. The baby is given to the mother to preserve its body heat and to breast-feed a first meal of *colostrum,* a thick substance that helps the newborn's digestive and immune systems. Either before or after that, the umbilical cord is cut and the baby is weighed, measured, and examined.

One widely used assessment of infant health is the **Apgar scale** (see Table 4.3) (1953/2015). In 1933, when Virginia Apgar earned her M.D. from Columbia University Medical School, she wanted to work in a hospital but was told that only men did surgery. So, she became an anesthesiologist instead of a surgeon. She was troubled to see that "delivery room doctors focused on mothers and paid little attention to babies. Those who were small and struggling were often left to die" (Beck, 2009, p. D1).

To save those young lives, Apgar developed a simple rating scale of five vital signs—color, heart rate, cry, muscle tone, and breathing—to alert doctors when a

### TABLE 4.3

#### Criteria and Scoring of the Apgar Scale

**Five Vital Signs**

| Score | Color | Heartbeat | Reflex Irritability | Muscle Tone | Respiratory Effort |
|---|---|---|---|---|---|
| 0 | Blue, pale | Absent | No response | Flaccid, limp | Absent |
| 1 | Body pink, extremities blue | Slow (below 100) | Grimace | Weak, inactive | Irregular, slow |
| 2 | Entirely pink | Rapid (over 100) | Coughing, sneezing, crying | Strong, active | Good; baby is crying |

Information from Apgar, 1953/2015.

newborn was in trouble. Birth attendants worldwide use the Apgar (using the acronym, Appearance, Pulse, Grimace, Activity, and Respiration) at one minute and again at five minutes after birth, assigning each vital sign a score of 0, 1, or 2. (See Visualizing Development, p. 108.)

## Medical Assistance

How closely any particular birth matches the foregoing depends on many factors. One is whether or not the woman has support and encouragement during labor, provided by the father, other relatives, or a **doula,** who is trained and dedicated to helping mothers in the entire birth process. A doula provides massage, encouragement, information, and reassurance—all of which relieve stress.

Especially if a woman feels intimidated by medical professionals, a doula can be very helpful (Kang, 2014). When a doula is part of the medical team, women use less medication and are less likely to have extensive medical intervention. According to most studies, women who choose a midwife rather than a physician also have better birth outcomes (McRae et al., 2016).

**doula** A woman who helps with the birth process. Traditionally in Latin America, a doula was the only professional who attended childbirth. Now doulas are likely to arrive at the woman's home during early labor and later work alongside a hospital's staff.

## Surgery

One-third of U.S. births occur via **cesarean section (c-section,** or simply *section*), whereby the fetus is surgically removed through incisions in the mother's abdomen. The World Health Organization suggested that c-sections are medically indicated in about 15 percent of births (such as when the pelvis is too small and the fetal head too big for a vaginal birth). Midwives are as skilled at delivering babies as physicians, but in most nations only medical doctors can perform surgery.

In some nations, cesareans are rare—less than 5 percent. In those nations, birth may be hazardous for mother and child. Public health workers find that training midwives to perform cesareans and implementing good newborn care saves many lives (Pucher et al., 2013).

Other nations have far more cesareans than the recommended 15 percent. Dramatic increases have occurred in China, where the rate was 5 percent in 1991, 20 percent by 2001, and about 50 percent in 2014 (Hellerstein et al., 2015).

**cesarean section (c-section)** A surgical birth, in which incisions through the mother's abdomen and uterus allow the fetus to be removed quickly, instead of being delivered through the vagina. (Also called *section*.)

BEA KALLOS/Newscom/European Pressphoto Agency/ BUDAPEST/Budapest/HUNGARY

**Mother Laboring, Doula Working** In many nations, doulas work to help the birth process, providing massage, timing contractions, and preparing for birth. In the United States, doulas typically help couples decide when to leave home, avoiding long waits between hospital admittance and birth. Here, in Budapest, this expectant mother will have her baby with a licensed midwife at home. Nora Schimcsig is her doula; the two women will be together from this moment in early labor to the first breast-feeding of the newborn.

# A Healthy Newborn

Just moments after birth, babies are administered their very first test. The APGAR score is an assessment tool used by doctors and nurses to determine whether a newborn requires any medical intervention. It tests five specific criteria of health, and the medical professional assigns a score of 0, 1, or 2 for each category. A perfect score of 10 is rare—most babies will show some minor deficits at the 1-minute mark, and many will still lose points at the 5-minute mark.

### GRIMACE RESPONSE/REFLEXES

**(2)** A healthy baby will indicate his displeasure when his airways are suctioned—he or she will grimace, pull away, cough, or sneeze.

**(1)** Baby will grimace during suctioning.

**(0)** Baby shows no response to being suctioned and requires immediate medical attention.

### RESPIRATION

**(2)** A good strong cry indicates a normal breathing rate.

**(1)** Baby has a weak cry or whimper, or slow/irregular breathing.

**(0)** Baby is not breathing and requires immediate medical intervention.

### PULSE

**(2)** A pulse of 100 or more beats per minute is healthy for a newborn.

**(1)** Baby's pulse is less than 100 beats per minute.

**(0)** A baby with no heartbeat requires immediate medical attention.

### APPEARANCE/COLOR

**(2)** Body and extremities should show good color, with pink undertones indicating good circulation.

**(1)** Baby has some blueness in the palms and soles of the feet. Many babies exhibit some blueness at both the 1- and 5-minute marks; most warm up soon after.

**(0)** A baby whose entire body is blue, grey, or very pale requires immediate medical intervention.

### ACTIVITY AND MUSCLE TONE

**(2)** Baby exhibits active motion of arms, legs, and body.

**(1)** Baby shows some movement of arms and legs.

**(0)** A baby who is limp and motionless requires immediate medical attention.

## REFLEXES IN INFANTS

Never underestimate the power of a reflex. For developmentalists, newborn reflexes are mechanisms for survival, indicators of brain maturation, and vestiges of evolutionary history. For parents, they are mostly delightful and sometimes amazing.

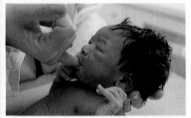

**THE SUCKING REFLEX** A newborn, just a few minutes old, demonstrates that he is ready to nurse by sucking on a doctor's finger.

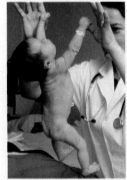

**THE GRASPING REFLEX** When the doctor places a finger on the palm of a healthy infant, he or she will grasp so tightly that the baby's legs can dangle in space.

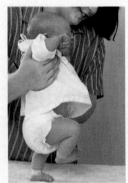

**THE STEP REFLEX** A 1-day-old girl steps eagerly forward on legs too tiny to support her body.

In the United States, the c-section rate rose between 1996 and 2008 (from 21 percent to 34 percent) and has held steady for the past decade. Variation is stark from one hospital to another—from 7 to 70 percent (Kozhimannil et al., 2013). Why?

Many suspect nonmedical reasons depending on the patient's insurance (Jolles, 2017). Cesareans are easier to schedule, quicker, and bring more income to hospitals and doctors; they require surgeons, anesthesiologists, and several hospital days.

With current technology, cesareans are safe and quick, and welcomed by many women. Disadvantages appear later: more medical complications after birth and less breast-feeding of the newborn (Malloy, 2009).

By age 3, children born by cesarean are twice as likely to be obese (16 percent compared to 8 percent) (Huh et al., 2012). The reason may be that babies delivered vaginally have more beneficial bacteria in their microbiome (Wallis, 2014). An innovation is to rub the c-section newborn with a cloth that carries vaginal secretions from the mother (Dominguez-Bello et al., 2016).

**Pick Up Your Baby!** Probably she can't. In this maternity ward in Beijing, China, most patients are recovering from cesarean sections, making it difficult to cradle, breast-feed, or carry a newborn until the incision heals.

## Drugs

In the United States, drugs are usually part of the birth process. The goal is to balance the needs of the mother, the fetus, and the hospital—and people disagree about how best to do that. In about half of U.S. hospital births, doctors use an *epidural,* an injection in the spine that numbs the lower half of the body while keeping the mother awake. One woman, named Resch, had an epidural and a cesarean because her fetus was in a breech position (buttocks first, not head first).

> Resch felt "a lot of rough pushing and pulling" and "a painless suction sensation" as if her body were "a tar pit the baby was wrestled from". She heard the doctor say to the resident: "Hold her up by the hips", and Resch peered down. She saw her daughter for the first time, wet and squirming . . . Resch's husband held the baby next to Resch's cheek. Resch felt "overwhelmed by emotions"—"joy, awe, anxiety, relief, surprise." She gave thanks for her healthy baby, and for modern obstetrical care.
>
> *[Lake, 2012, p. 21]*

Resch was grateful, but critics would not be. Sometimes headaches or other side effects are caused by an epidural, but the most common problem is that contractions weaken. On average, an epidural adds more than two hours to the time required for a vaginal birth (Cheng et al., 2014). In addition, any anesthetic that enters the woman's bloodstream slows down the baby's reflexes, including sucking and breathing.

Another drug-based intervention is *induced labor,* in which labor is started, speeded up, or strengthened with Pitocin, which is artificial oxytocin. Three decades ago, 1 in 20 U.S. births involved Pitocin; now 1 in 5 does.

Like cesareans, good obstetric practice sometimes requires induction, but many nurses think Pitocin is overused—especially when it is used to start labor before 37 weeks of gestation (Striley & Field-Springer, 2016). When labor is artificially induced, that increases the likelihood of an epidural, because the contractions are more painful. After an epidural, cesareans are more likely (Jonsson et al., 2013).

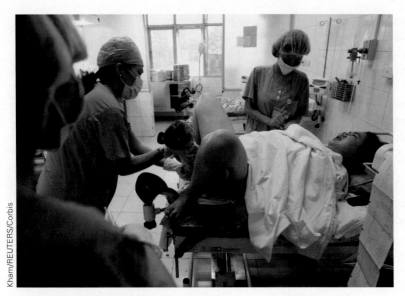

Kham/REUTERS/Corbis

**Everyone Healthy and Happy** A few decades ago in the developing world and a century ago in advanced nations, hospital births were only for birthing women who were near death, and only half of the fetuses survived. That has changed, particularly in Asia, where women prefer to give birth in hospitals. Hospital births themselves are not what they once were. Most new mothers participate in the process: Here, Le Thi Nga is about to greet her newborn after pulling with all her strength on the belt that helped her push out the head.

**Observation Quiz** What evidence shows that, even in Hanoi, technology is part of this birth? (see answer, p. 112) ↑

# Newborn Survival

The benefits of modern medical measures at birth are evident. A century ago, at least 1 of every 20 newborns in the United States died (De Lee, 1938), as did more than half of those born in developing nations. Birth was hazardous for women as well: It was the most common cause of death for young women.

In poor nations even today, complications of pregnancy and birth may be serious. Worldwide, about 2 million newborns (1 in 70) die each year, with the first hours after birth the most critical (Baqui et al., 2016), and almost 300,000 women die in pregnancy or birth. In the poorest nations, the rates may be higher: Some newborn deaths are not recorded and some maternal deaths—from an illegal abortion, for instance—are not attributed to pregnancy.

Currently in the United States, neonatal mortality is rare: Less than 1 newborn in 250 dies, most of whom were born far too soon. About 40 other nations have even better rates of newborn survival. In developed nations, women almost never die from complications of pregnancy, abortion, or birth—the rate is less than 1 in 10,000.

As you can see from Figure 4.4, U.S. rates have risen as rates have fallen in other nations, but that may be attributed to a change in data collection. A death during pregnancy or within 42 days after birth is now tallied as maternal mortality (Maron, 2015).

Critics point out, however, that survival is not the only measure of success. A particular issue in medically advanced nations is the attention lavished on "miracle babies" who require high-tech medical support, microsurgery, and weeks in the hospital before they go home (Longo, 2013).

Miracle babies often need special care all their lives. The unusual, happy outcomes are published; the public cost of hospital care and the private burden life-

**FIGURE 4.4**

**Could Be Better** Maternal mortality in developed nations is very low—about one birth in 10,000, and almost always the mother was ill before birth. These rates are much better than in poor nations, where birth itself can still be hazardous. Prenatal care makes a difference: The United States is the only advanced nation here that does not provide free prenatal care for everyone.

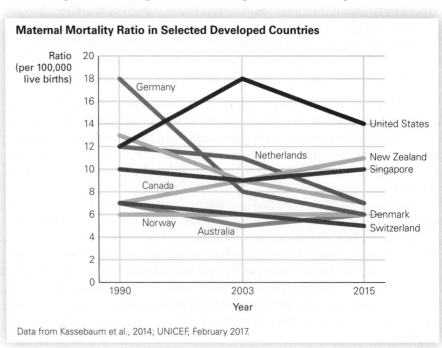

**Maternal Mortality Ratio in Selected Developed Countries**

Ratio (per 100,000 live births)

Germany

United States

Netherlands

New Zealand
Singapore

Canada

Norway

Australia

Denmark
Switzerland

1990    2003    2015

Year

Data from Kassebaum et al., 2014; UNICEF, February 2017.

To learn what medications are safe in pregnancy, women often consult the Internet. However, a study of 25 Web sites that, together, listed 235 medications as safe found that TERSIS (a group of expert teratologists who analyze drug safety) had declared only 60 (25 percent) safe. The rest were not *proven* harmful, but TERSIS found insufficient evidence to confirm safety (Peters et al., 2013). The Internet sites sometimes used unreliable data: Some drugs on the safe list of one site were on the danger list of another.

Laws that criminalize substance abuse during pregnancy may be more likely to keep women away from prenatal care than to get them clean. A particular problem is that using drugs (including alcohol) during pregnancy is a crime for which women are arrested and jailed in five states (Minnesota, North Dakota, Oklahoma, South Dakota, and Wisconsin). Sadly, these states happen to have many Native Americans and a history of removing land and civil rights from them. Other states wait until birth: Several new Alabama mothers have been jailed because the hospital discovered illegal substances in their babies (Eckholm, 2013).

## Prenatal Diagnosis

Early prenatal care has many benefits: Women learn what to eat, what to do, and what to avoid. Some serious conditions, syphilis and HIV among them, can be diagnosed and treated in the first prenatal months before they harm the fetus.

Tests of blood, urine, fetal heart rate, and ultrasound reassure parents, facilitating the crucial parent–child bond. It is now possible to know the sex of the fetus within the first few months. This allows parents to name the fetus, considering him or her a person long before birth.

In general, early care protects fetal growth, connects women to their future child, makes birth easier, and renders parents better able to cope. When complications (such as twins, gestational diabetes, and infections) arise, early recognition increases the chance of a healthy birth.

Unfortunately, however, about 20 percent of early pregnancy tests *raise* anxiety instead of reducing it. For instance, the level of alpha-fetoprotein (AFP) may be too high or too low, or ultrasound may indicate multiple fetuses, abnormal growth, Down syndrome, or a mother's narrow pelvis. Many such warnings are **false positives;** that is, they falsely suggest a problem that does not exist. Any warning, whether false or true, requires further testing but also leads to worry and soul-searching. Some choose to abort; some do not. Neither decision is easy. Consider John and Martha in Opposing Perspectives (see p. 120).

## Low Birthweight: Causes and Consequences

Some newborns are small and immature. With modern hospital care, they usually survive, but it would be better for everyone—mother, father, baby, and society—if all newborns were in the womb for at least 36 weeks and weighed more than 2,500 grams (5½ pounds). (Usually, this text gives pounds before grams. But hospitals worldwide report birthweight using the metric system, so grams precede pounds and ounces here.)

The World Health Organization defines **low birthweight (LBW)** as less than 2,500 grams. LBW babies are further grouped into **very low birthweight (VLBW),** under 1,500 grams (3 pounds, 5 ounces), and **extremely low birthweight (ELBW),** under 1,000 grams (2 pounds, 3 ounces). Some newborns weigh as little as 500 grams: About one-half of them die even with excellent care (Lau et al., 2013).

**Especially for Social Workers** When is it most important to convince women to be tested for HIV: before pregnancy, after conception, or immediately after birth? (see response, p. 121)

**Response for Nutritionists** (from p. 116): Useful, yes; optimal, no. Some essential vitamins are missing (too expensive), and individual nutritional needs differ, depending on age, sex, health, genes, and eating habits. The reduction in neural-tube defects is good, but many women don't eat cereal or take vitamin supplements before becoming pregnant.

**false positive** The result of a laboratory test that reports something as true when in fact it is not true. This can occur for pregnancy tests, when a woman might not be pregnant even though the test says she is, or during pregnancy, when a problem is reported that actually does not exist.

**low birthweight (LBW)** A body weight at birth of less than 2,500 grams (5½ pounds).

**very low birthweight (VLBW)** A body weight at birth of less than 1,500 grams (3 pounds, 5 ounces).

**extremely low birthweight (ELBW)** A body weight at birth of less than 1,000 grams (2 pounds, 3 ounces).

# "What Do People Live to Do?"

John and Martha, both under age 35, were expecting their second child. Martha's initial prenatal screening revealed low alpha-fetoprotein, which could indicate Down syndrome.

Another blood test was scheduled. . . . John asked:

"What exactly is the problem?" . . .

"We've got a one in eight hundred and ninety-five shot at a retarded baby."

John smiled, "I can live with those odds."

"I'm still a little scared."

He reached across the table for my hand. "Sure," he said, "that's understandable. But even if there is a problem, we've caught it in time. . . . The worst-case scenario is that you might have to have an abortion, and that's a long shot. Everything's going to be fine." . . .

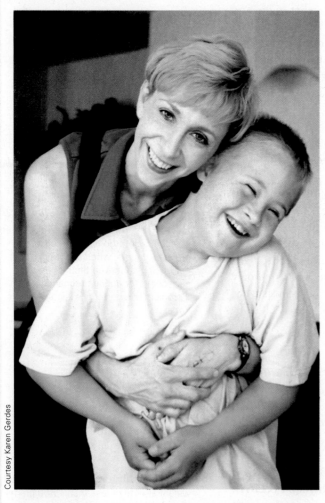

**Happy Boy** Martha Beck not only loves her son Adam (shown here), but she also writes about the special experiences he has brought into the whole family's life—hers, John's, and their other children's. She is "pro-choice"; he is a chosen child.

"I might *have to have* an abortion?" The chill inside me was gone. Instead I could feel my face flushing hot with anger. "Since when do you decide what I *have* to do with my body?"

John looked surprised. "I never said I was going to decide anything," he protested. "It's just that if the tests show something wrong with the baby, of course we'll abort. We've talked about this."

"What we've talked about," I told John in a low, dangerous voice, "is that I am pro-choice. That means I decide whether or not I'd abort a baby with a birth defect. . . . I'm not so sure of this."

"You used to be," said John.

"I know I used to be." I rubbed my eyes. I felt terribly confused. "But now . . . look, John, it's not as though we're deciding whether or not to have a baby. We're deciding what *kind* of baby we're willing to accept. If it's perfect in every way, we keep it. If it doesn't fit the right specifications, whoosh! Out it goes.". . .

John was looking more and more confused. "Martha, why are you on this soapbox? What's your point?"

"My point is," I said, "that I'm trying to get you to tell me what you think constitutes a 'defective' baby. What about . . . oh, I don't know, a hyperactive baby? Or an ugly one?"

"They can't test for those things and—"

"Well, what if they could?" I said. "Medicine can do all kinds of magical tricks these days. Pretty soon we're going to be aborting babies because they have the gene for alcoholism, or homosexuality, or manic depression. . . . Did you know that in China they abort a lot of fetuses just because they're female?" I growled. "Is being a girl 'defective' enough for you?"

"Look," he said, "I know I can't always see things from your perspective. And I'm sorry about that. But the way I see it, if a baby is going to be deformed or something, abortion is a way to keep everyone from suffering—*especially* the baby. It's like shooting a horse that's broken its leg. . . . A lame horse dies slowly, you know? . . . It dies in terrible pain. And it can't run anymore. So it can't enjoy life even if it doesn't die. Horses live to run; that's what they do. If a baby is born not being able to do what other people do, I think it's better not to prolong its suffering."

". . . And what is it," I said softly, more to myself than to John, "what is it that people do? What do we live to do, the way a horse lives to run?"

[Beck, 1999, pp. 132–133, 135]

The second AFP test was in the normal range, "meaning there was no reason to fear . . . Down syndrome" (Beck, 1999, p. 137).

As you read in Chapter 3, genetic counselors help couples weigh options *before* becoming pregnant. John and Martha had had no counseling because the pregnancy was unplanned and their risk for Down syndrome was low. The opposite of a false positive is a false negative, a mistaken assurance that all is well. Amniocentesis later revealed that the second AFP was a false negative. Their fetus had Down syndrome after all. Martha decided against abortion.

Most new mothers try to nurse their newborn, finding it painful and noting that their baby does not immediately latch on and suck successfully. That can make the mother feel worse. Successful breast-feeding mitigates maternal depression, one of the many reasons every first-time mother needs a lactation consultant.

## New Fathers

As we have seen, fathers-to-be help mothers-to-be stay healthy, nourished, and drug-free. Then, at birth, fathers may be crucial. I observed this when Elissa delivered Asa (the big brother of Isaac, whose birth began this chapter). Asa's birth took 48 hours in the hospital. Elissa's anxiety rose when the doctor and midwife discussed a possible cesarean for "failure to progress" without asking her opinion. Her husband told her, "All you need to do is relax between contractions and push when a contraction comes. I will do the rest." She listened. He did. No cesarean.

Whether or not he is present at birth, the father's legal acceptance of the baby has an impact. A study of all live single births in Milwaukee from 1993 to 2006 (151,869 babies!) found that complications correlated with several expected variables (e.g., maternal smoking) and one unexpected one—no father listed on the birth record. This correlation was especially apparent for European Americans: When mothers did not name the father, they had longer labors, and, more often, cesareans (Ngui et al., 2009).

Currently, about half of all U.S. women are not married when their baby is born (U.S. Census Bureau, 2014), but fathers may still be on the birth certificate. When fathers acknowledge their role, birth is better for mother and child.

Fathers may experience pregnancy and birth biologically, not just psychologically. Many fathers have symptoms of pregnancy and birth, including weight gain and indigestion during pregnancy and pain during labor (Leavitt, 2009). Father activity prenatally can be very positive for the baby (Bribiescas & Burke, 2017). Among the Papua in New Guinea and the Basques in Spain, husbands used to build a hut when birth was imminent and then lie down to writhe in mock labor (Klein, 1991).

Paternal experiences of pregnancy and birth are called **couvade,** expected in some cultures, a normal variation in many, and considered pathological in others (M. Sloan, 2009). A study in India found that couvade was common (Ganapathy, 2014). In the United States, couvade is unnoticed and unstudied, but many fathers are intensely involved during prenatal development, birth, and infancy (Brennan et al., 2007; Raeburn, 2014).

Fathers are usually the first responders when the mother experiences postpartum depression; they may be instrumental in getting the support that the mother and baby need. But fathers are vulnerable to depression, too, with the same stresses that mothers feel (Gutierrez-Galve et al., 2015). Indeed, sometimes the father experiences more emotional problems than the mother (Bradley & Slade, 2011). Friends and relatives need to help both parents in the first weeks after birth.

A study of fathers found that many men not only felt stressed but also felt troubled that they felt stressed, and they avoided talking about it. Many thought that their partner had good reason to be stressed and that they should be strong and supportive, not stressed themselves (Darwin et al., 2017).

At the same time, in modern marriages, both partners feel the effects of pregnancy and birth. One father acknowledged that he did not sleep well during pregnancy; several fathers worried intensely about the birth, their partner, and the baby, and yet many men felt they had no right to complain. One said, "I'm always conscious that my wife has it a lot worse"; another said at the birth, "I felt a bit more like a spare part, but then again they were very good with [partner]. I just felt in the way."

Nathan Allred/Alamy

**Mutual Joy** Ignore this dad's tattoo and earring, and the newborn's head wet with amniotic fluid. Instead recognize that for thousands of years hormones and instincts have propelled fathers and babies to reach out to each other, developing lifelong connections.

**couvade** Symptoms of pregnancy and birth experienced by fathers.

**Especially for Nurses in Obstetrics** Can the father be of any practical help in the birth process? (see response, p. 128)

"Of course I know what he wants when he cries. He wants you."

Marty Bucella/CartoonStock

● **Response for Nurses in Obstetrics** (from p. 127): Usually not, unless they are experienced, well taught, or have expert guidance. But their presence provides emotional support for the woman, which makes the birth process easier and healthier for mother and newborn.

**parental alliance** Cooperation between a mother and a father based on their mutual commitment to their children. In a parental alliance, the parents support each other in their shared parental roles.

**parent–infant bond** The strong, loving connection between parents and their baby.

Several men found relief at work, where they could put the stress of fatherhood behind them or talk about their feelings with other men. A man who is part of a group of engineers said, "we probably spend half the day talking about babies and kids and that sort of thing. . . . I know that there's guys there that have had similar experiences or they know what it's like. They know how I'm feeling if I say, oh, we've had a rough night. . . . Some people have had worse experiences, so you think, what we're going through is normal" (quoted in Darwin et al., 2017).

## Parental Alliance

Remember John and Martha, the young couple whose AFP was a false negative but amniocentesis revealed that their fetus had trisomy-21 (Down syndrome)? One night at 3:00 A.M., after about seven months of pregnancy, Martha was crying uncontrollably. She told John she was scared.

"Scared of what?" he said. "Of a little baby who's not as perfect as you think he ought to be?"

"I didn't say I wanted him to be perfect," I said. "I just want him to be normal. That's all I want. Just normal."

"That is total bullshit. . . . You don't want this baby to be normal. You'd throw him in a dumpster if he just turned out to be normal. What you really want is for him to be superhuman."

"For your information," I said in my most acid tone, "I was the one who decided to keep this baby, even though he's got Down's. You were the one who wanted to throw him in a dumpster."

"How would you know?" John's voice was still gaining volume. "You never asked me what I wanted, did you? No. You never even asked me."

[Beck, 1999, p. 255]

This episode ended well, with a long, warm, and honest conversation between the two prospective parents. Each learned what their fetus meant to the other, a taboo topic until that night.

Their lack of communication up to this point, and the sudden eruption of sorrow and anger, is not unusual, because pregnancy itself raises memories from childhood and fears about the future. Yet honest and intimate communication is crucial throughout pregnancy, birth, and child rearing. Such early communication between new parents helps to form a **parental alliance,** a commitment by both parents to cooperate in raising their child.

The parental alliance is especially beneficial, yet depression in both parents especially likely, when the infant is physically vulnerable, such as having a low birthweight (Helle et al., 2016). Family conflict when a newborn needs extra care increases the risk of child maladjustment and parental divorce (Whiteside-Mansell et al., 2009).

## Family Bonding

To what extent are the first hours after birth crucial for the **parent–infant bond,** the strong, loving connection that forms as parents hold, examine, and feed their newborn? It has been claimed that this bond develops in the first hours after birth when a mother touches her naked baby, just as sheep and goats must immediately smell and nuzzle their newborns if they are to nurture them (Klaus & Kennell, 1976).

However, the hypothesis that early skin-to-skin contact is *essential* for human nurturance is false (Eyer, 1992; Lamb, 1982). Substantial research on monkeys

**Better Care** Kangaroo care benefits mothers, babies, and hospitals, saving space and medical costs in this ward in Manila. Kangaroo care is one reason Filipino infant mortality in 2010 was only one-fifth of what it was in 1950.

begins with *cross-fostering,* a strategy in which newborns are removed from their biological mothers in the first days of life and raised by another female or even a male monkey. A strong and beneficial relationship sometimes develops (Suomi, 2002). Parents may begin to bond with their children before birth, and/or they may bond in the months after birth.

This finding does not contradict the generalization that prospective parents' active involvement in pregnancy, birth, and care of the newborn benefits all three. Factors that encourage parents (biological or adoptive) to nurture their newborns have lifelong benefits, proven with mice, monkeys, and humans (Champagne & Curley, 2010). Beneficial, but not essential.

The benefits of early contact are evident with **kangaroo care,** in which the newborn lies between the mother's breasts, skin-to-skin, listening to her heartbeat and feeling her body heat. A review of 124 studies confirms that kangaroo-care newborns sleep more deeply, gain weight more quickly, and spend more time alert than do infants with standard care, as well as being healthier overall (Boundy et al., 2016). Father involvement may also be important for the newborn's health, including father–infant kangaroo care (Feeley et al., 2013).

Kangaroo care benefits babies, not only in the hospital but months later, either because of improved infant adjustment to life outside the womb or because of increased parental sensitivity and effectiveness. Which of these two is the explanation? Probably both.

As we will see in later chapters, the relationship between parent and child develops over months, not merely hours. Parental alliance continues to be influential. Birth is one step of a lifelong journey, not only for the baby but for the mother and father as well.

**kangaroo care** A form of newborn care in which mothers (and sometimes fathers) rest their babies on their naked chests, like kangaroo mothers that carry their immature newborns in a pouch on their abdomen.

## WHAT HAVE YOU LEARNED?

**1.** How can a newborn be socially interactive?

**2.** What causes postpartum depression?

**3.** How are fathers affected by birth?

**4.** Why is kangaroo care beneficial?

**5.** When does the parent–infant bond form?

# SUMMARY

## Prenatal Development

**1.** The first two weeks of prenatal growth are called the germinal period. Soon the single-celled *zygote* multiplies into many cells, becoming a *blastocyst,* with more than 100 cells that will eventually form both the placenta and the embryo. The growing organism travels down the fallopian tube and implants in the uterus. More than half the time, implantation fails.

**2.** The embryonic period, from the third week through the eighth week after conception, begins with the first signs of the future central nervous system. The future heart begins to beat, and the eyes, ears, nose, mouth, and brain form.

**3.** Hormones, including sex hormones, and genes affect development of the embryo. By the eighth week, the embryo has all of the basic organs and features, except for sex organs. At that point, the embryo becomes a fetus.

**4.** The fetal period extends from the ninth week until birth. In the ninth week, the sex organs develop. By the end of the third month, all of the organs and body structures have formed and can function, although the tiny fetus could not survive outside the womb.

**5.** At 22 weeks, when the brain can regulate basic body functions, viability is possible but unlikely. Babies born before the 26th week are at high risk of death or disability.

**6.** The average fetus gains approximately 4½ pounds (2,040 grams) from the sixth month to the ninth month, weighing 7½ pounds (3,400 grams) at birth. Maturation of brain, lungs, and heart ensures survival of more than 99 percent of all full-term babies.

## Birth

**7.** Birth typically begins with contractions that push the fetus out of the uterus and then through the vagina. The Apgar scale, which rates the newborn at one minute and again at five minutes after birth, provides a quick evaluation of the infant's health.

**8.** Medical assistance speeds contractions, dulls pain, and saves lives. However, many aspects of medicalized birth may be unnecessary, including about half of the cesareans performed in the United States and many induced labors that occur before 37 weeks. Contemporary birthing practices are aimed at balancing the needs of baby, parents, and medical personnel.

## Problems and Solutions

**9.** Some teratogens cause physical impairment. Others, called behavioral teratogens, harm the brain and therefore impair cognitive abilities and affect personality. About 20 percent of children have learning or emotional problems that *could* be traced to behavioral teratogens.

**10.** Whether a teratogen harms an embryo or fetus depends on timing, dose, and genes. Public and personal health practices can protect against prenatal complications, with some specifics debatable. Always, however, family members affect the pregnant woman's health.

**11.** Low birthweight (under 5½ pounds, or 2,500 grams) may arise from early or multiple births, placental problems, maternal illness, malnutrition, smoking, drinking, illicit drug use, and age. Underweight babies experience more medical difficulties and psychological problems for many years. Babies that are small for gestational age (SGA) are especially vulnerable.

**12.** Every birth complication, such as unusually long and stressful labor that includes anoxia (a lack of oxygen to the fetus), has a combination of causes. Long-term handicaps are not inevitable, but careful nurturing from parents and society may be essential.

## The New Family

**13.** Newborns are primed for social interaction. The Brazelton Neonatal Behavioral Assessment Scale measures 46 newborn behaviors, 20 of which are reflexes.

**14.** Many women feel unhappy, incompetent, or unwell after giving birth, with the most vulnerable time when the baby is 2 or 3 months old. Postpartum depression gradually disappears with appropriate help.

**15.** Fathers can be crucial in birth events and newborn care. Sometimes fathers experience symptoms of pregnancy and birth, as well as postpartum depression. Ideally, a parental alliance forms to help the child develop well.

**16.** Kangaroo care benefits all babies, but especially those who are vulnerable. Mother–newborn and father–newborn contact is beneficial, although the parent–infant bond depends on many factors in addition to birth circumstances.

## KEY TERMS

germinal period (p. 98)
embryonic period (p. 98)
fetal period (p. 98)
implantation (p. 98)
embryo (p. 98)
cephalocaudal development
  (p. 100)
proximodistal development
  (p. 100)
fetus (p. 100)
ultrasound (p. 100)

age of viability (p. 103)
Apgar scale (p. 106)
doula (p. 107)
cesarean section (c-section)
  (p. 107)
teratogen (p. 112)
behavioral teratogens (p. 112)
teratology (p. 114)
threshold effect (p. 114)
fetal alcohol syndrome (FAS)
  (p. 115)

false positive (p. 119)
low birthweight (LBW) (p. 119)
very low birthweight (VLBW)
  (p. 119)
extremely low birthweight
  (ELBW) (p. 119)
preterm (p. 121)
small for gestational age (SGA)
  (p. 121)
immigrant paradox (p. 121)
cerebral palsy (p. 124)

anoxia (p. 124)
Brazelton Neonatal Behavioral
  Assessment Scale (NBAS)
  (p. 125)
reflex (p. 125)
postpartum depression (p. 126)
couvade (p. 127)
parental alliance (p. 128)
parent–infant bond (p. 128)
kangaroo care (p. 129)

## APPLICATIONS

**1.** Go to a nearby greeting-card store and analyze the cards about pregnancy and birth. Do you see any cultural attitudes (e.g., variations depending on the sex of the newborn or of the parent)? If possible, compare those cards with cards from a store that caters to another economic or ethnic group.

**2.** Interview three mothers of varied backgrounds about their birth experiences. Make your interviews open-ended—let the mothers choose what to tell you, as long as they give at least a 10-minute description. Then compare and contrast the three accounts, noting especially any influences of culture, personality, circumstances, and cohort.

**3.** People sometimes wonder how any pregnant woman could jeopardize the health of her fetus. Consider your own health-related behavior in the past month—exercise, sleep, nutrition, drug use, medical and dental care, disease avoidance, and so on. Would you change your behavior if you were pregnant? Would it make a difference if you, your family, and your partner did not want a baby?

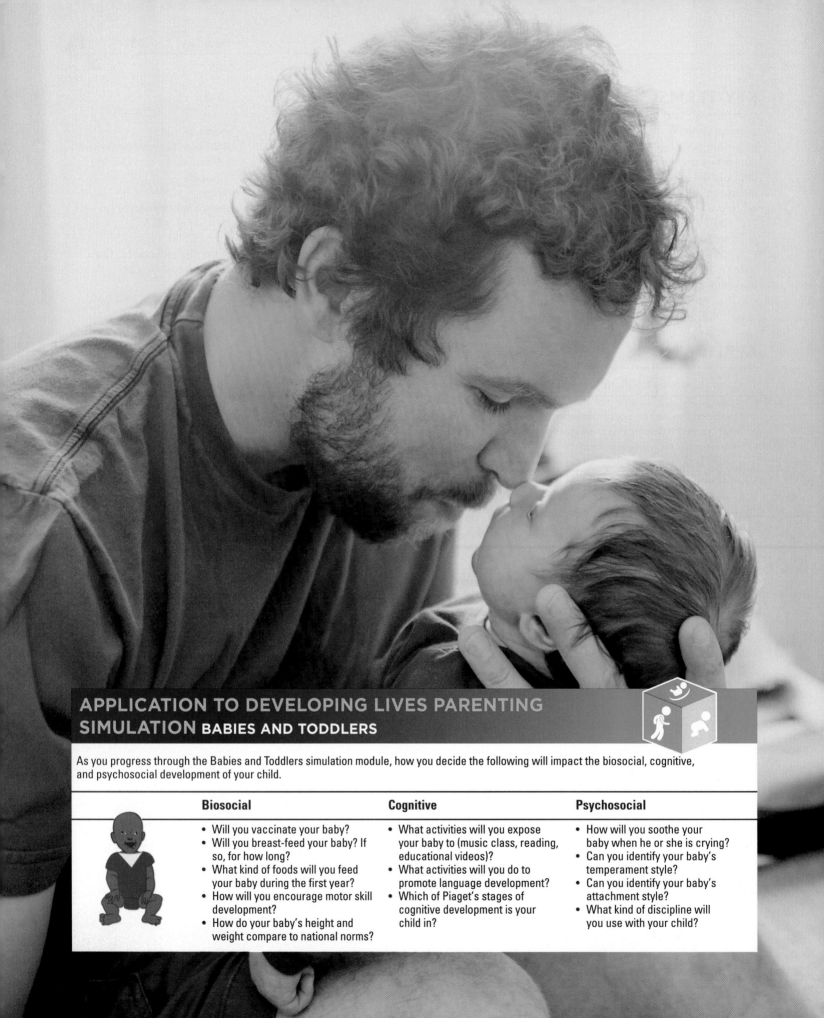

## APPLICATION TO DEVELOPING LIVES PARENTING SIMULATION BABIES AND TODDLERS

As you progress through the Babies and Toddlers simulation module, how you decide the following will impact the biosocial, cognitive, and psychosocial development of your child.

| | Biosocial | Cognitive | Psychosocial |
|---|---|---|---|
| | • Will you vaccinate your baby?<br>• Will you breast-feed your baby? If so, for how long?<br>• What kind of foods will you feed your baby during the first year?<br>• How will you encourage motor skill development?<br>• How do your baby's height and weight compare to national norms? | • What activities will you expose your baby to (music class, reading, educational videos)?<br>• What activities will you do to promote language development?<br>• Which of Piaget's stages of cognitive development is your child in? | • How will you soothe your baby when he or she is crying?<br>• Can you identify your baby's temperament style?<br>• Can you identify your baby's attachment style?<br>• What kind of discipline will you use with your child? |

# The First Two Years

**A**dults don't change much in a year or two. They might have longer, grayer, or thinner hair; they might gain or lose weight; they might learn something new. But if you saw friends you hadn't seen for two years, you'd recognize them immediately.

Imagine caring for your newborn niece or nephew every day for a month. You would learn everything about that baby—how to dress, when to play, what to feed, where to sleep. Then imagine you moved to a distant city for two years. When you returned and your sister asked you to pick up the child at a day-care center, you would have to ask which child to take! In those two years, the child's weight would have quadrupled, height increased by a foot, and hair grew. Emotions would have changed, too—less crying, new fear—including fear of you, now a stranger.

Two years are a tiny part of the average human life. However, in those 24 months, people reach one-half of their adult height, learn to run, climb, and talk in sentences, and express every emotion—not just joy and fear but also love, jealousy, and shame. Invisible growth of the brain is even more awesome; plasticity is extraordinary during infancy, enabling all of these changes and more. The next three chapters describe this transformation. ●●

# The First Two Years:
## Biosocial Development

## What Will You Know?

1. What part of an infant grows most in the first two years?
2. Are babies essentially blind and deaf at birth?
3. What happens if a baby does not get his or her vaccinations?

**O**ur first child, Bethany, was born when I was in graduate school. At 14 months, she was growing well and talking but had not yet taken her first step. I told my husband that genes are more influential than anything we did. I had read that babies in Paris are late to walk, and my grandmother was French.

To my relief, Bethany soon began walking, and she became the fastest runner in her kindergarten class. My genetic explanation was bolstered when our next two children, Rachel and Elissa, were also slow to walk. My students with Guatemalan and Ghanaian ancestors bragged about their infants who walked before a year; those from China and France had later walkers. Genetic, I thought.

Fourteen years after Bethany, Sarah was born. I could finally afford a full-time caregiver, Mrs. Todd. She thought Sarah was the most advanced baby she had ever known, except for her own daughter, Gillian.

"She'll be walking by a year," Mrs. Todd told me. "Gillian walked at 10 months."

"We'll see," I graciously replied.

I underestimated Mrs. Todd. She bounced my delighted baby on her lap, day after day, and spent hours giving her "walking practice." Sarah took her first step at 12 months—late for a Todd, early for a Berger, and a humbling lesson for me.

As a scientist, I know that a single case proves nothing. My genetic explanation might be valid, especially since Sarah shares only half her genes with Bethany and since my daughters are only one-eighth French, a fraction I had conveniently ignored when I sought reassurance about my late-walking first-born.

Nonetheless, I now know that caretakers influence every aspect of biosocial growth. You will soon read many examples of caregiving that enables babies to grow, move, see, and learn. Nurture is at least as important as nature. Genes provide the scaffold, but every day shapes and guides each infant to become a distinct—and special—human being.

+ **Body Changes**
  Body Size
  Sleep
  Brain Development
  INSIDE THE BRAIN: Neuroscience Vocabulary
  Harming the Infant Body and Brain
  A VIEW FROM SCIENCE: Face Recognition

+ **Perceiving and Moving**
  The Senses
  Motor Skills
  Cultural Variations

+ **Surviving in Good Health**
  Better Days Ahead
  A CASE TO STUDY: Scientist at Work
  Immunization
  Nutrition

## Body Changes

In infancy, growth is so rapid and the consequences of neglect so severe that gains are closely monitored. Medical checkups, including measurement of height, weight, and head circumference, provide the first clues as to whether an infant is progressing as expected—or not.

Left: Jose Luis Pelaez Inc/Getty Images
Top: twomeows/Moment/Getty Images

**LaunchPad**
macmillan learning

**Video: Physical Development in Infancy and Toddlerhood** offers a quick review of the physical changes that occur during a child's first two years.

**percentile** A point on a ranking scale of 0 to 100. The 50th percentile is the midpoint; half the people in the population being studied rank higher and half rank lower.

# Body Size

Newborns lose several ounces in the first three days and then gain an ounce a day for months. Birthweight doubles by 4 months and triples by a year, so a 7-pound newborn might be 21 pounds at 12 months (9,525 grams, up from 3,175 grams at birth). That is an average, but variation is substantial, depending not only on genes and nutrition but also on birthweight—small babies may double their weight in two months and quadruple by age 1. Height also increases rapidly: A typical newborn grows 10 inches (25 centimeters) by age 1, measuring about 30 inches (76 centimeters).

Physical growth then slows, but not by much. Most 24-month-olds weigh about 28 pounds (13 kilograms) and have added another 4 inches (10 centimeters) in the previous year. Typically, 2-year-olds are one-half their adult height and about one-fifth their adult weight (see Figure 5.1).

Growth is often expressed in a **percentile,** indicating how one person compares to another. Thus, a 12-month-old's weight at the 30th percentile means that 29 percent of 12-month-old babies weigh less and 69 percent weigh more. Healthy babies vary in size, so any percentile between 10 and 90 is okay, as long as the percentile is close to the previous one for that individual.

When an infant's percentile moves markedly up or down, that could signify trouble. A notable drop, say from the 50th to the 20th percentile, suggests poor nutrition. A sudden increase, perhaps from the 30th to the 60th percentile, signifies overfeeding.

Parents were once blamed. Especially when the percentile dropped, it was thought that parents made feeding stressful, leading to *failure to thrive.* Now pediatricians consider it "outmoded" to blame parents, because failure to thrive may be caused by allergies, the microbiome, or other medical conditions (Jaffe, 2011, p. 100). Similarly, obesity is now thought to be cultural and genetic, as well as familial. Overweight babies are still problematic, but blaming parents alone is neither fair nor helpful.

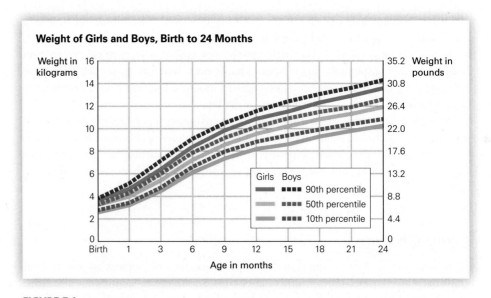

**FIGURE 5.1**

**Averages and Individuals** Norms and percentiles are useful—most 1-month-old girls who weigh 10 pounds should be at least 25 pounds by age 2. But although females weigh less than males on average lifelong, individuals do not always follow the norms. Do you know a 200-pound woman married to a 150-pound man?

**Same Boy, Much Changed** All three photos show Conor: first at 3 months, then at 12 months, and finally at 24 months. Note the rapid growth in the first two years, especially apparent in changing proportions.

## Sleep

Throughout childhood, regular and ample sleep correlates with normal brain maturation, learning, emotional regulation, academic success, and psychological adjustment (Maski & Kothare, 2013). Sleep deprivation can cause poor health, and vice versa. As with many health habits, sleep patterns begin in the first year.

**Especially for New Parents** You are aware of cultural differences in sleeping practices, which raises a very practical issue: Should your newborn sleep in bed with you? (see response, p. 138)

### Patterns of Infant Sleep

Newborns spend most of their time sleeping, about 15 to 17 hours a day. Hours of sleep decrease rapidly with maturity: The norm per day for the first two months is 14¼ hours; for the next three months, 13¼ hours; for 6 to 17 months, 12¾ hours. Remember that norms are simply averages. Among every 20 young infants, their parents report, one baby sleeps nine hours or fewer per day and another one sleeps 19 hours or more (Sadeh et al., 2009).

Over the first few months, the time spent in each stage of sleep changes. For instance, babies born preterm often seem to be dozing most of the time, never in deep sleep, but that may be caused partially by the constant bright lights and frequent feedings in the traditional NICU (neonatal intensive care unit). When they come home, preterm babies usually adjust to a day–night schedule (Bueno & Menna-Barreto, 2016).

Newborns dream a lot: About half of their sleep is **REM (rapid eye movement) sleep.** REM sleep declines over the early weeks, as does "transitional sleep," the dozing, half-awake stage. At 3 or 4 months, quiet sleep (also called *slow-wave sleep*) increases markedly.

**REM (rapid eye movement) sleep** A stage of sleep characterized by flickering eyes behind closed lids, dreaming, and rapid brain waves.

Sleep varies not only because of biology (maturation and genes) but also because of caregivers. Infants who are fed cow's milk and cereal may sleep more soundly—easier for parents but bad for the baby. Social environment matters: If parents respond to predawn cries with food and play, babies wake up early and often, night after night (Sadeh et al., 2009).

Insufficient sleep becomes a problem for parents as well as for infants, because "[p]arents are rarely well-prepared for the degree of sleep disruption a newborn infant engenders, and many have unrealistic expectations about the first few postnatal months." As a result, many parents become "desperate" and institute patterns they may later regret (C. Russell et al., 2013, p. 68).

Cecilia Varas

**co-sleeping** A custom in which parents and their children (usually infants) sleep together in the same room.

**bed-sharing** When two or more people sleep in the same bed.

**Response for New Parents** (from p. 137): From the psychological and cultural perspectives, babies can sleep anywhere as long as the parents can hear them if they cry. The main consideration is safety: Infants should not sleep near comforters and pillows or on a too-soft mattress, nor beside an adult who is drunk or on drugs. Otherwise, families should decide for themselves, remembering that early learning tends to endure.

## Where Should Babies Sleep?

Traditionally, most middle-class North American infants slept in cribs in their own rooms; it was feared that they would be traumatized if their parents had sex in the same room. By contrast, most infants in Asia, Africa, and Latin America slept near their parents, a practice called **co-sleeping,** and sometimes in their parents' bed, called **bed-sharing.** In those cultures, nighttime parent–child separation was considered cruel.

Today, Asian and African mothers still worry more about separation, whereas European and North American mothers worry more about privacy. A 19-nation survey found that parents act on these fears: The extremes were 82 percent of Vietnamese babies co-sleeping compared with 6 percent in New Zealand (Mindell et al., 2010) (see Figure 5.2). Although in general co-sleeping is more common in nations with high poverty rates, income is not the main determinant: In Japan—one of the wealthiest nations in the world—families often sleep together.

Cohort is significant: In the United States, bed-sharing doubled from 1993 to 2010, from 6.5 percent to 13.5 percent (Colson et al., 2013). The infant's feeding patterns also have an effect: Bed-sharing is more common in breast-feeding mothers and in babies who wake often at night. A study in Sweden of preterm infants (who need to be fed every two or three hours) found that most slept with their mothers—especially if the mother had trouble getting back to sleep if she got up to feed her infant (Blomqvist et al., 2017).

The argument for co-sleeping is that the parents can quickly respond to a hungry or frightened baby. Indeed, a popular book on infant care advocates "attachment parenting," advising keeping the infant nearby day and night (Sears & Sears, 2001). Responsive attachment correlates with co-sleeping (Kim et al., 2017).

However, when co-sleeping results in bed-sharing, that doubles the risk of sudden infant death syndrome (SIDS), when a baby dies unexpectedly while asleep (Vennemann et al., 2012). Some pediatricians therefore advise against co-sleeping, although such advice may be ignored by tired mothers, especially those in cultures where bed-sharing is the norm.

Consequently, many experts seek ways to safeguard the practice of bed-sharing (Ball & Volpe, 2013). Their advice includes *never* sleeping beside a baby if the parent has been drinking, and *never* using a soft comforter, pillow, or mattress near a sleeping infant.

**FIGURE 5.2**

**Awake at Night** Why the disparity between Asian and non-Asian rates of co-sleeping? It may be that Western parents use a variety of gadgets and objects—monitors, night-lights, pacifiers, cuddle cloths, sound machines—to accomplish some of what Asian parents do by having their infant next to them.

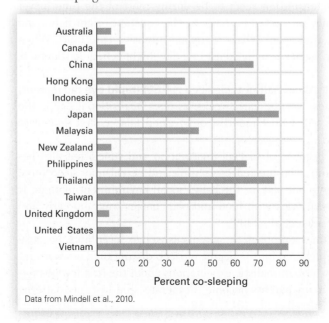

Percent co-sleeping

Data from Mindell et al., 2010.

**Is She Awake?** This 36-year-old mother in Hong Kong put her 7-month-old baby on her back, protecting her from SIDS as the Chinese have done for centuries. However, the soft pillow and comforter are hazards. Will she carry the baby to a safe place before she falls asleep?

Developmentalists remind parents that babies learn from experience. If they become accustomed to bed-sharing, they may crawl into their parents' bed long past infancy. Parents might lose sleep for years because they wanted more sleep when their babies were small. Sleeping alone may encourage independence—a trait appreciated in some cultures, abhorred in others.

## Brain Development

From two weeks after conception to two years after birth, the brain grows more rapidly than any other organ, from about 25 percent of adult weight at birth to 75 percent at age 2 (see Figure 5.3). Prenatal and postnatal brain growth (measured by head circumference) affects later cognition (Gilles & Nelson, 2012). If teething or a stuffed-up nose temporarily slows eating, body weight is affected before brain weight, a phenomenon called **head-sparing.** That term expresses well what nature does—protect the brain.

Many other terms in neuroscience are not as self-explanatory, but they are useful to understand the brain. Accordingly, they are explained in the following.

### Exuberance and Pruning

At birth, the brain contains far more neurons than a person needs. Some neurons disappear in programmed cell death, and a few new ones develop. By contrast, the newborn's brain has far fewer dendrites, axons, and synapses than the person will eventually have, and much less myelin. Because of all that, the brain at birth is only half as large as at age 1 (Gao et al., 2016).

To be specific, an estimated fivefold increase in dendrites in the cortex occurs in the 24 months after birth, with about 100 trillion synapses present at age 2. According to one expert, "40,000 new synapses are formed every second in the infant's brain" (Schore & McIntosh, 2011, p. 502).

Extensive *postnatal* brain growth is highly unusual for mammals. It occurs in humans because birth would be impossible if the fetal head were large enough to contain the brain networks humans need. (As it is, the head is by far the most difficult part of the human birth process.) Because the human brain grows so much after birth, humans must nurture and protect children for many years (Konner, 2010).

**head-sparing** A biological mechanism that protects the brain when malnutrition disrupts body growth. The brain is the last part of the body to be damaged by malnutrition.

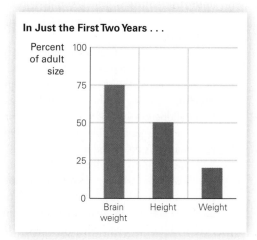

**FIGURE 5.3**

**Growing Up** Two-year-olds are totally dependent on adults, but they have already reached half their adult height and three-fourths of their adult brain size.

# Neuroscience Vocabulary

To understand the impressive brain growth that occurs throughout childhood, it is helpful to know some basic terms of neurological development (see Visualizing Development, p. 143).

Communication within the *central nervous system (CNS)*—the brain and spinal cord—begins with nerve cells, called **neurons.** At birth, the human brain has about 86 billion.

Within and between areas of the CNS, neurons are connected to other neurons by intricate networks of nerve fibers called **axons** and **dendrites.** Each neuron has a single axon and numerous dendrites, which spread out like the branches of a tree. Most of the brain growth in infancy consists of increases in dendrites.

The axon of one neuron meets the dendrites of other neurons at intersections called **synapses,** which are critical communication links within the brain. Brain development in infancy is "characterized by overproduction of synapses followed by a period of gradual pruning" (Bernier et al., 2016, p. 1159). Synapse formation and demise is remarkably plastic and is heavily dependent on experience.

Neurons communicate by *firing,* or sending electrochemical impulses through their axons to synapses to be picked up by the dendrites of other neurons. The dendrites bring the message to the cell bodies of their neurons, which, in turn, may fire, conveying messages via their axons to the dendrites of other neurons. Some firing is involuntary—such as the reflexes cited in Chapter 4. Most infant brain development requires new connections between one neuron and another, as dendrites grow (Gao et al., 2016).

Axons and dendrites do not touch at synapses. Instead, the electrical impulses in axons typically cause the release of **neurotransmitters,** which stimulate other neurons. There are more than 100 neurotransmitters, although the exact number is not known.

Neurotransmitters carry information from the axon of the sending neuron, across a pathway called the *synaptic gap,* to the dendrites of the receiving neuron, a process speeded up by **myelin,** a coating on the outside of the axon. Myelin increases over childhood—lack of it is one reason infants are slow to react to something pleasurable or painful. [**Developmental Link:** Myelination is discussed in Chapter 8.]

Some neurons are deep inside the brain in a region called the *hindbrain,* which controls automatic responses such as heartbeat, breathing, temperature, and arousal. Others are in the *midbrain,* in areas that affect emotions and memory. And in humans most neurons (about 70 percent) are in the *forebrain,* especially the **cortex,** the brain's six outer layers (sometimes called the *neocortex*). Most thinking, feeling, and sensing occur in the cortex (Johnson & de Haan, 2015; Kolb & Whishaw, 2015).

The forebrain has two halves and four lobes, which are general regions, each containing many parts. No important human activity is exclusively left- or right-brain, or in one lobe or another. Although each lobe and hemisphere has specialized functions, thousands of connections transmit information among the parts, and much of the specialization is the result of various constraints and experiences, not foreordained by genes (Johnson & de Haan, 2015).

The back of the forebrain is the *occipital lobe,* where vision is located; the sides of the brain are the *temporal lobes,* for hearing; the top is the *parietal lobe,* which includes smell, touch, and spatial understanding; and the front is the *frontal lobe,* which enables people to plan, imagine, coordinate, decide, and create. Humans have a much larger frontal cortex relative to body size than any other animal.

The very front of the frontal lobe is called the **prefrontal cortex.** It is not, as once thought, "functionally silent during most of infancy" (Grossmann, 2013, p. 303), although the prefrontal cortex is very immature at birth.

Pleasure and pain may arise from the **limbic system,** a cluster of brain areas deep in the forebrain that is heavily involved in emotions and motivation. Two crucial parts of the limbic system are the amygdala and the hippocampus.

**neuron**  One of billions of nerve cells in the central nervous system, especially in the brain.

**axon**  A fiber that extends from a neuron and transmits electrochemical impulses from that neuron to the dendrites of other neurons.

**dendrite**  A fiber that extends from a neuron and receives electrochemical impulses transmitted from other neurons via their axons.

**synapse**  The intersection between the axon of one neuron and the dendrites of other neurons.

**neurotransmitter**  A brain chemical that carries information from the axon of a sending neuron to the dendrites of a receiving neuron.

**myelin**  The coating on axons that speeds transmission of signals from one neuron to another.

**cortex**  The outer layers of the brain in humans and other mammals. Most thinking, feeling, and sensing involves the cortex.

**prefrontal cortex**  The area of the cortex at the very front of the brain that specializes in anticipation, planning, and impulse control.

**limbic system**  The parts of the brain that interact to produce emotions, including the amygdala, the hypothalamus, and the hippocampus. Many other parts of the brain also are involved with emotions.

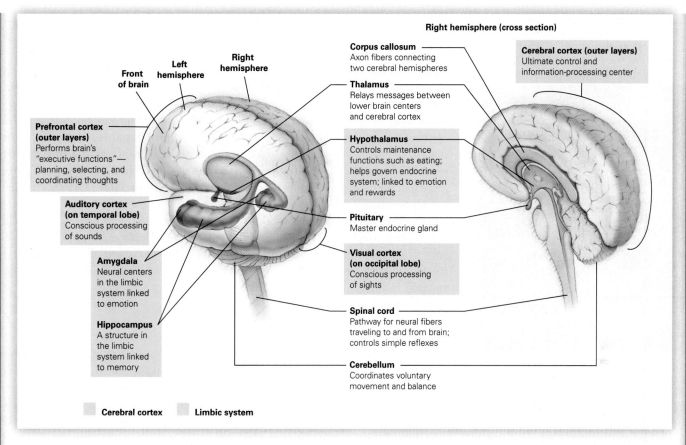

**FIGURE 5.4**

**Connections**  A few of the hundreds of named parts of the brain are shown here. Although each area has particular functions, the entire brain is interconnected. The processing of emotions, for example, occurs primarily in the limbic system, where many brain areas are involved, including the amygdala, hippocampus, and hypothalamus.

The **amygdala** is a tiny structure, about the same shape and size as an almond. It registers strong emotions, both positive and negative, especially fear. The amygdala is present in infancy, but growth depends partly on early experience. Increased amygdala activity may cause terrifying nightmares or sudden terrors.

Another structure in the emotional network is the **hippocampus,** located next to the amygdala. A central processor of memory, especially memory for locations, the hippocampus responds to the amygdala by summoning memory. Some places feel comforting (perhaps a childhood room) and others evoke fear (perhaps a doctor's office), even when the experiences that originated those emotions are long gone.

Sometimes considered part of the limbic system is the **hypothalamus,** which responds to signals from the amygdala and to memories from the hippocampus by producing hormones, especially **cortisol,** a hormone that increases with stress (see Figure 5.4). Another nearby brain structure, the **pituitary,** responds to the hypothalamus by sending out hormones to various body parts.

Brain research is one area of extensive international collaboration. For example, a 5-billion-dollar, 12-year project in the United States called BRAIN (Brain Research Through Advancing Innovative Neurotechnologies) began in 2014 and is developing new tools

(Huang & Luo, 2015). Given new methods and thousands of neuroscientists worldwide, the names and functions of various parts of the brain may be described differently from one source to another.

Thus, the descriptions here are only a beginning. From a developmental perspective, what is crucial to know is that all human thoughts and actions originate in the complexity of the brain, and that understanding the brain adds insight to our effort to understand how humans live their lives. Extensive neurological plasticity is evident as all these parts of the infant brain adapt to experience (Gao et al., 2016).

**amygdala**  A tiny brain structure that registers emotions, particularly fear and anxiety.

**hippocampus**  A brain structure that is a central processor of memory, especially memory for locations.

**hypothalamus**  A brain area that responds to the amygdala and the hippocampus to produce hormones that activate other parts of the brain and body.

**cortisol**  The primary stress hormone; fluctuations in the body's cortisol level affect human emotions.

**pituitary**  A gland in the brain that responds to a signal from the hypothalamus by producing many hormones, including those that regulate growth and that control other glands, among them the adrenal and sex glands.

**transient exuberance** The great but temporary increase in the number of dendrites that develop in an infant's brain during the first two years of life.

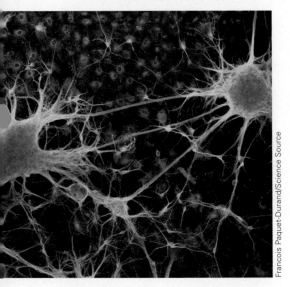

**Connecting** The color staining on this photo makes it obvious that the two cell bodies of neurons (stained chartreuse) grow axons and dendrites to each other's neurons. This tangle is repeated thousands of times in every human brain. Throughout life, those fragile dendrites will grow or disappear as the person continues thinking.

**pruning** When applied to brain development, the process by which unused connections in the brain atrophy and die.

**experience-expectant** Brain functions that require certain basic common experiences (which an infant can be expected to have) in order to develop normally.

**experience-dependent** Brain functions that depend on particular, variable experiences and therefore may or may not develop in a particular infant.

Early dendrite growth is called **transient exuberance:** *exuberant* because it is so rapid and *transient* because some of it is temporary. Thinking and learning require connections among many parts of the brain, a more efficient process because some potential connections are pruned (Gao et al., 2016). Just as a gardener might prune a rose bush by cutting away some growth to enable more, or more beautiful, roses to bloom, unused brain connections atrophy and die.

As one expert explains it, there is an "exuberant overproduction of cells and connections followed by a several year long sculpting of pathways by massive elimination" (Insel, 2014, p. 1727). Notice the word "sculpting," as if a gifted artist created an intricate sculpture from raw marble or wood. Human infants are gifted artists, developing their brains to adjust to whatever family, culture, or society they are born into.

For example, to understand any sentence in this text, you need to know the letters, the words, the surrounding text, the ideas they convey, and how they relate to your other thoughts and experiences. Those connections are essential for your comprehension, which differs from other people whose infant brains developed in homes unlike yours. Thus, your brain automatically interprets these roman letters, and, for most of you, is befuddled when viewing Arabic, Cyrillic, or Chinese.

Further evidence of the benefit of cell death comes from a sad symptom of fragile X syndrome (described in Chapter 3), "a persistent failure of normal synapse pruning" (Irwin et al., 2002, p. 194). Without **pruning,** the dendrites of children with fragile X are too dense and long, making thinking difficult. Similar problems occur for children with autism spectrum disorder: Their brains are unusually large and full, making communication between neurons less efficient and some sounds and sights overwhelming (Lewis et al., 2013).

Thus, pruning is essential. Normally, as brains mature, the process of extending and eliminating dendrites is exquisitely attuned to experience, as the appropriate links in the brain are established, protected, and strengthened (Gao et al., 2016). As with the rose bush, pruning needs to be done carefully, allowing further growth.

## Necessary and Possible Experiences

A scientist named William Greenough identified two experience-related aspects of brain development (Greenough et al., 1987). Adults who understand them avoid the difference-equals-deficit error explained in Chapter 1, while still providing the experiences every baby needs.

- **Experience-expectant growth.** Certain functions require basic experiences in order to develop, just as a tree requires water. Those experiences are part of almost every infant's life, and thus, almost all human brains grow as their genes direct. Brains *expect* such experiences; development suffers without them.
- **Experience-dependent growth.** Human brains are quite plastic, as was also explained in Chapter 1. Particular brain connections grow as specific experiences occur. These experiences are not essential: They happen in some families and cultures but not in others.

The basic, expected experiences *must* happen for normal brain maturation to occur, and they almost always do. For example, in deserts and in the Arctic, on isolated farms and in crowded cities, almost all babies have things to see, objects to manipulate, and people to love them. Babies everywhere welcome expected experiences: They look around, they grab for objects, they smile at people. As a result, babies' brains develop. Without such expected experiences, their brains wither.

# Nature, Nurture, and the Brain

The mechanics of neurological functioning are varied and complex; neuroscientists hypothesize, experiment, and discover more each day. Brain development begins with genes and other biological elements, but hundreds of epigenetic factors affect brain development from the first to the final minutes of life. Particularly important in human development are experiences: Plasticity means that dendrites form or atrophy in response to nutrients and events. The effects of early nurturing experiences are lifelong, as proven many times in mice; research on humans suggests similar effects.

## NATURE

Human brains are three times as large per body weight and take years longer to mature than the brains of any other mammal, but the basics of brains are the same from mouse to elephant. New dendrites form and unused ones die—especially in infancy and adolescence. Brain plasticity is lifelong.

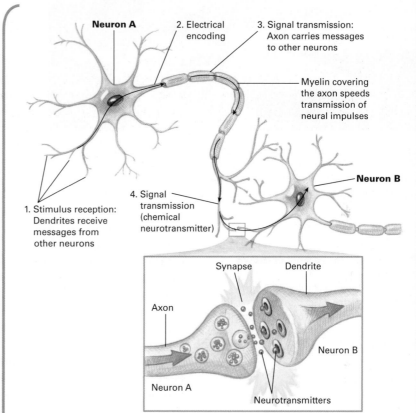

**Neuron A**

2. Electrical encoding

3. Signal transmission: Axon carries messages to other neurons

Myelin covering the axon speeds transmission of neural impulses

**Neuron B**

1. Stimulus reception: Dendrites receive messages from other neurons

4. Signal transmission (chemical neurotransmitter)

Synapse    Dendrite

Axon

Neuron B

Neuron A

Neurotransmitters

In the synapse—an intersection between axon and dendrite—neurotransmitters carry information from one neuron to another.

Stockbyte/Getty Images

## NURTURE

In the developing brain, connections from axon to dendrite reflect how a baby is treated. In studies of mice, scientists learned that when a mother mouse licks her newborn its methylation of a gene (called Nr3c1) is reduced, allowing increased serotonin to be released by the hypothalamus and reducing stress hormones. Baby mice who were frequently licked and nuzzled by their mothers developed bigger and better brains!

Researchers believe that, just as in rodents, the human mothers who cuddle, cradle, and caress their babies shape their brains for decades.

| Low Maternal Licking and Grooming | High Maternal Licking and Grooming |
| --- | --- |
| • High stress hormone levels<br>• High anxiety | • Low stress hormone levels<br>• Low anxiety |

Anyaivanova/iStock/Getty Images

Nicole Hill/RubberBall/Alamy

Aaron McCoy/Photolibrary/Getty Images

**Face Lit Up, Brain Too** Thanks to scientists at the University of Washington, this young boy enjoys the EEG of his brain activity. Such research has found that babies respond to language long before they speak. Experiences of all sorts connect neurons and grow dendrites.

◐ **Especially for Parents of Grown Children** Suppose you realize that you seldom talked to your children until they talked to you and that you often put them in cribs and playpens. Did you limit their brain growth and their sensory capacity? (see response, p. 147)

In contrast, dependent experiences *might* happen; because of them, one brain differs from another, even though both brains are developing normally. Babies' experiences vary, in the languages they hear, the faces they see, the emotions their caregivers express, and, as you just read, where they sleep. *Depending* on those particulars, infant brains are structured and connected one way or another; some dendrites grow and some neurons thrive while others die (Stiles & Jernigan, 2010).

Consequently, experience-expectant and experience-dependent events make all people both similar and unique, because each of us undergoes particular events.

The distinction between essential and variable input to the brain's networks can be made for all creatures. But some of the most persuasive research has been done with birds. All male songbirds have a brain region dedicated to listening and reproducing sounds (experience-expectant), but birds of the same species produce slightly different songs depending on where they live (experience-dependent) (Konner, 2010).

Birds inherit genes that produce the neurons they need, perhaps dedicated to learning new songs (canaries) or to finding hidden seeds (chickadees). That is experience-expectant: Songs and seeds are essential for those species. Then, depending on their ecological niche, birds *depend* on specific experiences with learning songs or finding seeds.

Indeed, human babies learn language in much the same way as birds learn songs (Prather et al., 2017). Unless something is seriously wrong, adults talk to babies, whose brains *expect* language. But the particular language *depends* on the specific culture.

Another human example comes from face recognition: All infants need to see faces (experience-expectant), but which particular face differences they notice depends on who they see (experience-dependent), as the following box explains.

## Harming the Infant Body and Brain

Thus far, we have focused on the many harmless variations that families offer babies; most infants develop well. Feeding and health care vary, but every family tries to ensure that their children survive in good health and thrive within their culture.

For brain development, it does not matter whether a person learns French or Farsi, or expresses emotions dramatically or subtly (e.g., throwing themselves to the floor or merely pursing their lips, a cultural difference). However, infant brains do not grow normally if they lack basic, expected experiences.

### Necessary Stimulation

Some adults imagine that babies need quiet, perhaps in a room painted one neutral color. That is a mistake. Babies need stimulation—sights and sounds, emotional expression, and social interaction that encourages movement (arm waving, then crawling, grabbing, and walking). Severe lack of stimulation stunts the brain. As one review explains, "enrichment and deprivation studies provide powerful evidence of . . . widespread effects of experience on the complexity and function of the developing system" of the brain (Stiles & Jernigan, 2010, p. 345).

# Face Recognition

Unless you have prosopagnosia (face blindness), the *fusiform face area* of your brain is astonishingly adept. Newborns are even quicker to recognize a face that they have seen just once than are older children and adults (Zeifman, 2013). They have no idea which faces are important, so they are primed to stare intently at all of them—unlike adults, who know they can glance at hundreds in a crowd without paying much attention, unless they happen to recognize someone.

Because of experience-expectancies, every face is fascinating early in life: Babies stare at pictures of monkey faces and photos of human ones, at drawings and toys with faces, as well as at live faces. Soon, experience-dependent learning begins (de Heering et al., 2010). By 3 months, babies smile readily at familiar people, differentiate men and women, and distinguish among faces from their own ethnic group (called the *own-race effect*). The own-race effect results from limited multiethnic experience. Indeed, children of one ethnicity, adopted and raised exclusively among people of another ethnicity, recognize differences among people of their adopted group more readily than differences among people of their biological group.

The importance of experience is confirmed by two studies. In the first study, infants from 6 to 9 months of age were repeatedly shown a book with pictures of six monkey faces, each with a name written on the page. One-third of the infants' parents read the names while showing the pictures; another one-third said only "monkey" as they turned each page; the final one-third simply turned the pages with no labeling. (The six named monkeys are below.)

At 9 months, infants in all three groups viewed pictures of six *unfamiliar* monkeys. The infants who had heard names of monkeys were better at distinguishing one new monkey from another than were the infants who saw the same picture book but did not hear each monkey's name (Scott & Monesson, 2010).

Now consider the second study. Most people do not notice the individuality of newborns. However, 3-year-olds with younger siblings were found to be much better at recognizing differences in unfamiliar newborns than were 3-year-olds with no younger brothers or sisters (Cassia et al., 2009). This finding shows, again, that experience matters, contributing to development of dendrites in the fusiform face area.

As with almost every infant development, experience combines with inborn instincts, evident not only in newborn humans but also in all primates. Researchers prevented macaque monkeys from seeing faces (including those of other monkeys and of humans) for the first three months of life. They found that, even without experience, 3-month-old monkeys looked more attentively at photos of faces than photos of other objects (Simpson et al., 2017). Every face—of chimpanzees, otters, as well as monkeys—was almost equally interesting.

By 6 months—when they had some experiences with other macaques—they paid more attention to the faces of their own species (Simpson et al., 2017). That is just what human babies do: They look intently at every face-like image at first but zero in on the faces that are most important to them.

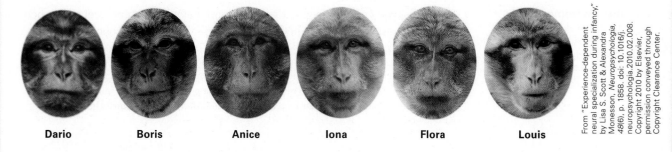

**Dario**    **Boris**    **Anice**    **Iona**    **Flora**    **Louis**

From "Experience-dependent neural specialization during infancy," by Lisa S. Scott & Alexandra Monesson, *Neuropsychologia*, 48(6), p. 1858. doi: 10.1016/j. neuropsychologia.2010.02.008. Copyright 2010 by Elsevier, permission conveyed through Copyright Clearance Center.

**Iona Is Not Flora** If you heard that Dario was not Louis or Boris, would you stare at unfamiliar monkey faces more closely in the future? For 6-month-olds, the answer is yes.

Proof came first from rodents! Some "deprived" rats (raised alone in small, barren cages) were compared with "enriched" rats (raised in large cages with toys and other rats). At autopsy, the brains of the enriched rats were larger, with more dendrites (Diamond, 1988; Greenough & Volkmar, 1973). Subsequent research with other mammals confirms that isolation and sensory deprivation

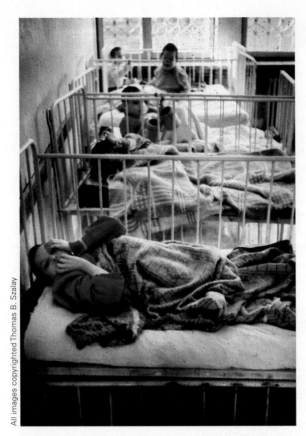

All images copyrighted Thomas B. Szalay

**Hands on Head** These children in Romania, here older than age 2, probably spent most of their infancy in their cribs, never with the varied stimulation that infant brains need. The sad results are evident—that boy is fingering his own face, because the feel of his own touch is most likely one of the few sensations he knows. The girl sitting up in the back is a teenager. This photo was taken in 1982; Romania no longer destroys children so dramatically.

**shaken baby syndrome** A life-threatening injury that occurs when an infant is forcefully shaken back and forth, a motion that ruptures blood vessels in the brain and breaks neural connections.

**self-righting** The inborn drive to remedy a developmental deficit; literally, to return to sitting or standing upright after being tipped over. People of all ages have self-righting impulses, for emotional as well as physical imbalance.

stunt development. That is now sadly evident in longitudinal studies of orphans from Romania, described in Chapter 7.

## Stress and the Brain

Some infants experience the opposite problem, too much of the wrong kind of stimulation. If the brain produces an overabundance of *cortisol* (the stress hormone) early in life (as when an infant is frequently terrified), that derails the connections from parts of the brain, causing atypical responses to stress lifelong. Years later, that child or adult may be hypervigilant (always on the alert) or emotionally flat (never happy or sad).

Note that these infants respond to emotions, even without physical pain. Occasional pains or stresses—from routine inoculations, brief hunger, an unwanted bath or diaper change—are part of normal infant life. High intensity and frequency of pains or stresses are *not* normal, and they can lead to a harmful flood of stress hormones (Propper & Holochwost, 2013).

Understanding this distinction is crucial for caregivers. All babies cry. Because the prefrontal cortex has not yet developed, infants cannot *decide* to stop crying on command.

In this case, the stress hormones are in the adults, who might react without thinking because of their stress. Some adults yell at their babies (which may terrify the baby), or even worse, shake them. The ruptured blood vessels and broken neural connections that result are referred to as **shaken baby syndrome,** an example of *abusive head trauma* (Christian & Block, 2009). Death is the worst consequence of shaken baby syndrome; lifelong intellectual impairment is the more likely one.

Not every infant who has neurological symptoms of head trauma is the victim of abuse: Legal experts worry about false accusations (Byard, 2014). Nonetheless, infants are vulnerable, so the response to a screaming, frustrating baby should be to comfort or walk away, never to shake, yell, or hit.

Lest you cannot imagine the frustration that some parents feel when their baby cries, consider what one mother in Sweden said about her colicky baby, now age 5 and much beloved.

> There were moments when, both me and my husband . . . when she was apoplectic and howling so much that I almost got this thought, "now I'll take a pillow and put over her face just until she quietens down, until the screaming stops."
>
> [*quoted in Landgren et al., 2012, p. 55*]

Developmental discoveries about early development have many implications. First, since early growth is so rapid, well-baby checkups are needed often in order to spot and treat any problems. Vision and hearing are springboards for growth, so sensory impairments should be remedied.

Fortunately, one characteristic of infants is **self-righting,** an inborn drive to compensate and overcome problems. Infants with few toys develop their brains by using sticks, or empty boxes, or whatever is available. Malnourished newborns have *catch-up growth*, so a 5-pound newborn who is now well-fed gains weight faster than an 8-pound one. Plasticity is apparent from the beginning (Tomalski & Johnson, 2010).

## WHAT HAVE YOU LEARNED?

1. What facts indicate that infants grow rapidly in the first year?

2. Why are pediatricians not troubled when an infant is consistently small, say at the 20th percentile in height and weight?

3. How do sleep patterns change from birth to 18 months?

4. What are the arguments for and against bed-sharing?

5. How can pruning increase brain potential?

6. What is the difference between experience-expectant and experience-dependent growth?

7. What is the effect of stress or social deprivation on early development?

8. What should caregivers remember about brain development when an infant cries?

# Perceiving and Moving

Young human infants combine motor ineptness with sensory acuteness (Konner, 2010). What a contrast to kittens, for instance, who are born deaf, with eyes sealed shut, and who can walk immediately. For humans, senses are crucial from birth on; movement skills take months and years.

Thus, newborns listen and look from day 1, and then they gradually develop skill movements by practicing whatever they can do. The interaction between the senses and movement is continuous in the early months, with every sensation propelling the infant to attempt new motor skills. Here are the specifics.

## The Senses

All the senses function at birth. Newborns have open eyes, sensitive ears, and responsive noses, tongues, and skin. Indeed, very young babies use all their senses to attend to everything. For instance, in the first months of life, they smile at everyone and suck almost anything in their mouths.

**Sensation** occurs when a sensory system detects a stimulus, as when the inner ear reverberates with sound, or the eye's retina and pupil intercept light. Thus, sensations begin when an outer organ (eye, ear, nose, tongue, or skin) meets anything that can be seen, heard, smelled, tasted, or touched.

Genetic selection over more than 100,000 years affects all the senses. Humans cannot hear what mice hear, or see what bats see, or smell what puppies smell; humans do not need those sensory abilities. However, survival requires babies to respond to people, and newborns innately do so with every sense they have (Konner, 2010; Zeifman, 2013).

**sensation** The response of a sensory organ (eyes, ears, skin, tongue, nose) when it detects a stimulus.

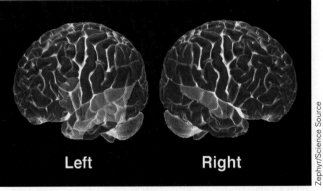

Zephyr/Science Source

**From Sound to Language** Hearing occurs in the temporal lobe, in both hemispheres, the green and some of the red parts of the brain. Language comprehension, however, is mostly in the left hemisphere, here shown in the brown region that responds to known words, and Broca's area, the red bulb that produces speech. A person could hear but not understand (a baby) or understand but not speak (if Broca's area is damaged).

## Hearing

The sense of hearing develops during the last trimester of pregnancy. At birth, certain sounds trigger reflexes, even without conscious perception. Sudden noises startle newborns, making them cry.

Familiar, rhythmic sounds such as a heartbeat are soothing: That is one reason kangaroo care reduces newborn stress, as the infant's ear rests on the mother's chest. [**Developmental Link:** Kangaroo care is explained in Chapter 4.] Soon, infants turn their heads to see the source of a voice—an ability that

**THINK CRITICALLY:** Which is most important in the first year of life, accurate hearing or seeing?

requires instant calculation of the difference between when the sound reaches the left and right ears.

Newborn hearing is routinely checked at most hospitals in North America and Europe, since early remediation benefits deaf infants. If they have cochlear implants early in life, their ability to understand and produce language is not delayed—unlike for those whose deafness is remedied after age 2 (Tobey et al., 2013).

## Seeing

By contrast, vision is immature at birth. Although in mid-pregnancy the eyes open and are sensitive to bright light (if the pregnant woman is sunbathing in a bikini, for instance), the fetus has nothing much to see. Consequently, newborns are legally blind; they focus only on things between 4 and 30 inches (10 and 75 centimeters) away (Bornstein et al., 2005).

Almost immediately, experience combines with maturation of the visual cortex to improve the ability to see shapes and notice details. Movement captures attention, as does contrast. For example, by 6 weeks when babies can see a person, they focus on the eyes—those colorful dots in a plain surface.

Vision improves so rapidly that researchers are hard-pressed to describe the day-by-day improvements (Dobson et al., 2009). By 2 months, infants not only stare at faces but also, with perception and cognition, smile. (Smiling can occur earlier but not because of perception.) In many ways, the vision of the new infant is attracted to the eyes of other people, and by age 1 infants interpret emotions, follow gaze, and use their own eyes to communicate (Grossmann, 2017).

Because **binocular vision** (coordinating both eyes to see one image) is impossible in the womb (nothing is far enough away), many newborns seem to use their two eyes independently, momentarily appearing wall-eyed or cross-eyed. Typically, experience leads to rapid focus and binocular vision. Usually between 2 and 4 months, both eyes can focus on a single thing (Wang & Candy, 2010). Early screening for visual ability is as important as screening for hearing, because good vision is crucial for learning (Brémond-Gignac et al., 2011).

Binocular vision allows depth perception, which has been demonstrated in 3-month-olds, although it was once thought to develop much later. Toddlers who are experienced crawlers and walkers are very adept at deciding whether a given path is safe to cross upright or is best traversed sitting or crawling. This illustrates early coordination of the senses and motor skills (Kretch & Adolph, 2013). (This does *not* mean that toddlers can be trusted not to fall off tables or out of windows.)

**binocular vision** The ability to focus the two eyes in a coordinated manner in order to see one image.

**Who's This?** Newborns don't know much, but they look intensely at faces. Repeated sensations become perceptions, so in about six weeks this baby will smile at Dad, Mom, a stranger, the dog, and every other face. If this father in Utah responds like typical fathers everywhere, by 6 months cognition will be apparent: The baby will chortle with joy at seeing him but become wary of unfamiliar faces.

## Tasting and Smelling

As with vision and hearing, smell and taste rapidly adapt to the social context. Babies appreciate what their mothers eat, prenatally through amniotic fluid, then through breast milk, and finally through smells and spoonfuls of the family dinner.

The foods of a particular culture may aid survival because some natural substances are medicinal. For example, bitter foods provide some defense against malaria; hot spices help preserve food and thus work against food poisoning (Krebs, 2009). Thus, a taste for the family cuisine may save young lives.

Families pass on cultural taste preferences despite immigration or changing historical circumstances. Thus, a feeding pattern that was protective may no longer be so. Indeed, when starvation was a threat, humans developed a taste for high-fat foods; now their descendants enjoy French fries, whipped cream, and bacon, jeopardizing their health.

Adaptation also occurs for the sense of smell. When breast-feeding mothers used a chamomile balm to ease cracked nipples during the first days of their babies' lives, those babies preferred that smell almost two years later, compared with babies whose mothers used an odorless ointment (Delaunay-El Allam et al., 2010).

As babies learn to recognize each person's scent, they prefer to sleep next to their caregivers, and they nuzzle into their caregivers' chests—especially when the adults are shirtless. One way to help infants who are frightened of the bath (some love bathing, some hate it) is for the parent to join the baby in the tub. The smells of the adult's body mixed with the smell of soap, and the pleasant touch, sight, and voice of the caregiver make the entire experience comforting.

**Learning About a Lime** As with every other normal infant, Jacqueline's curiosity leads to taste and then to a slow reaction, from puzzlement to tongue-out disgust. Jacqueline's responses demonstrate that the sense of taste is acute in infancy and that quick brain perceptions are still to come.

## Touch and Pain

The sense of touch is acute in infants. Wrapping, rubbing, massaging, and cradling are each soothing to many new babies. Even when their eyes are closed, some infants stop crying and visibly relax when held securely by their caregivers. The newborn's ability to be comforted by touch is tested in the Brazelton NBAS, described in Chapter 4. In the first year of life, infants' heart rates slow and they relax when stroked gently and rhythmically on the arm (Fairhurst et al., 2014).

Pain and temperature are not among the traditional five senses, but they are often connected to touch. Some babies cry when being changed, distressed at the sudden coldness on their skin. Some touches are unpleasant—a poke, pinch, or pat—although this varies from one baby to another.

Scientists are not certain about infant pain (Fitzgerald, 2015). Some experiences that are painful to adults (circumcision, the setting of a broken bone) are much less so to newborns, although that does not mean that newborns never feel pain (Reavey et al., 2014). For many newborn medical procedures, from a pinprick to minor surgery, a taste of sugar right before the event is an anesthetic. Doctors hesitate to use drugs, because that may slow down breathing.

Babies born very early experience many medical procedures that would be painful for adults. The more procedures they undergo, the more impaired their development at age 1, but that outcome could be related to the reasons for those procedures rather than the pain of them (Valeri et al., 2015).

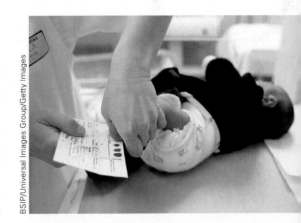

**The First Blood Test** This baby will cry, but most experts believe the heel prick shown here is well worth it. The drops of blood will reveal the presence of any of several genetic diseases, including sickle-cell disease, cystic fibrosis, and phenylketonuria. Early diagnosis allows early treatment, and the cries subside quickly with a drop of sugar water or a suck of breast milk.

**THINK CRITICALLY:** What political controversy makes objective research on newborn pain difficult?

Many hospital NICUs have adopted practices that make the first days of life better for babies, including allowing parents to touch their fragile infants, reducing or eliminating bright lights and noisy monitors, reducing pain and distress through careful swaddling, positioning, and so on. The result is improved social and cognitive development later on (Montirosso et al., 2017).

Physiological measures, including hormones, heartbeat, and rapid brain waves, are studied to assess infant pain, but the conclusions are mixed. Infant brains are immature: They have some similar responses to pain and some dissimilar ones when compared to adults (Moultrie et al., 2016).

## Motor Skills

**motor skill** The learned abilities to move some part of the body, in actions ranging from a large leap to a flicker of the eyelid. (The word *motor* here refers to movement of muscles.)

The most dramatic **motor skill** (any movement ability) is independent walking, which explains why I worried when my 14-month-old daughter had not yet taken a step (as described in the introduction to this chapter). All the basic motor skills, from the newborn's head-lifting to the toddler's stair-climbing, develop in infancy.

Motor skills begin with reflexes, explained in Chapter 4. Reflexes become skills if they are practiced and encouraged. As you saw in the chapter's beginning, Mrs. Todd set the foundation for my fourth child's walking when Sarah was only a few months old. Similarly, some very young babies can swim—if adults build on the swimming reflex by floating with them in calm, warm water.

### Gross Motor Skills

**gross motor skills** Physical abilities involving large body movements, such as walking and jumping. (The word *gross* here means "big.")

Deliberate actions that coordinate many parts of the body, producing large movements, are called **gross motor skills.** These skills emerge directly from reflexes and proceed in a *cephalocaudal* (head-down) and *proximodistal* (center-out) direction. Infants first control their heads, lifting them up to look around. Then they control their upper bodies, their arms, and finally their legs and feet. (See At About This Time, which shows age norms for gross motor skills.)

**Observation Quiz** Which of these skills has the greatest variation in age of acquisition? Why? (see answer, p. 152) ➔

onebluelight/E+/Getty Images

**Advancing and Advanced** At 8 months, she is already an adept crawler, alternating hands and knees, intent on progress. She will probably be walking before a year.

### AT ABOUT THIS TIME

**Age Norms (in Months) for Gross Motor Skills**

|  | When 50% of All Babies Master the Skill | When 90% of All Babies Master the Skill |
|---|---|---|
| Sit unsupported | 6 | 7.5 |
| Stands holding on | 7.4 | 9.4 |
| Crawls (creeps) | 8 | 10 |
| Stands not holding | 10.8 | 13.4 |
| Walking well | 12.0 | 14.4 |
| Walk backward | 15 | 17 |
| Run | 18 | 20 |
| Jump up | 26 | 29 |

*Note:* As the text explains, age norms are affected by culture and cohort. The first five norms are based on babies from five continents [Brazil, Ghana, Norway, United States, Oman, and India] (World Health Organization, 2006). The next three are from a U.S.-only source [Coovadia & Wittenberg, 2004; based on Denver II (Frankenburg et al., 1992)]. Mastering skills a few weeks earlier or later does not indicate health or intelligence. Being very late, however, is a cause for concern.

Sitting requires muscles to steady the torso, no simple feat. By 3 months, most babies can sit propped up in a lap. By 6 months, they can usually sit unsupported, but "novice sitting and standing infants lose balance just from turning their heads or lifting their arms" (Adolph & Franchak, 2017). Babies never propped up (as in some institutions for orphaned children) sit much later, as do babies who cannot use vision to adjust their balance.

Crawling is another example of the head-down and center-out direction of skill mastery. As they gain muscle strength, infants wiggle, attempting to move forward by pushing their arms, shoulders, and upper bodies against whatever surface they are lying on. Motivation is crucial: Babies want to move forward to explore objects just out of reach.

Usually by 5 months, infants add their legs to this effort, inching forward (or backward) on their bellies. Exactly when this occurs depends partly on how much "tummy time" the infant has had to develop the muscles, and that, of course, is affected by the caregiver's culture (Zachry & Kitzmann, 2011).

Between 8 and 10 months after birth, most infants can lift their midsections and move forward—or sometimes backward first. Some babies never crawl, but they all find some way to move before they can walk (inching, bear-walking, scooting, creeping, or crawling). As soon as they are able, babies walk (falling frequently but getting up undaunted and trying again), since walking is quicker than crawling, and has another advantage—free hands (Adolph et al., 2012). That illustrates the drive that underlies every motor skill: Babies are powerfully motivated to do whatever they can as soon as they can.

Beyond motivation, the dynamic-systems perspective highlights the interaction of strength, maturation, and practice. We illustrate these three with walking.

1. *Muscle strength.* Newborns with skinny legs and 3-month-olds buoyed by water make stepping movements, but 6-month-olds on dry land do not; their legs are too chubby for their underdeveloped muscles. As they gain strength, they stand and then walk—easier for thin babies than heavy ones (Slining et al., 2010).
2. *Brain maturation.* The first leg movements—kicking (alternating legs at birth and then both legs together or one leg repeatedly at about 3 months)—occur without much thought. As the brain matures, deliberate and coordinated leg action becomes possible.
3. *Practice.* Unbalanced, wide-legged, short strides become a steady, smooth gait.

Once toddlers are able to walk by themselves, they practice obsessively, barefoot or not, at home or in stores, on sidewalks or streets, on lawns or in mud. This depends a great deal on caregivers providing the opportunity—holding them to walk—in the bath, after diapering, around the house, on the sidewalk. Indeed, "practice, not merely maturation, underlies improvements. . . . In 1 hour of free play, the average toddler takes about 2400 steps, travels the length of about 8 U.S. football fields, and falls 17 times" (Adolph & Franchak, 2017).

## Fine Motor Skills

Small body movements are called **fine motor skills.** The most valued fine motor skills are finger movements, enabling humans to write, draw, type, tie, and so on. Movements of the tongue, jaw, lips, and toes are fine movements, too.

Regarding hand skills, newborns have a strong reflexive grasp but lack control. During their first two months, babies excitedly stare and wave their arms at objects dangling within reach. By 3 months, they can usually touch such objects, but because of limited eye–hand coordination, they cannot yet grab and hold on unless an object is placed in their hands.

**About to Fall** This girl in Brazil is new to walking and needs her whole body to balance. Fortunately, falls are common but harmless in infancy, because bodies are padded, bones are flexible, and the floor is nearby. In late adulthood, falls can be fatal.

**fine motor skills** Physical abilities involving small body movements, especially of the hands and fingers, such as drawing and picking up a coin. (The word *fine* here means "small.")

**Video: Fine Motor Skills in Infancy and Toddlerhood** shows the sequence in which babies and toddlers acquire fine motor skills.

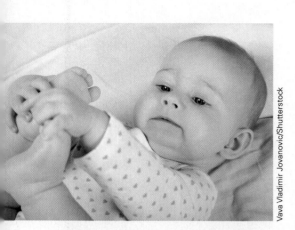

Vava Vladimir Jovanovic/Shutterstock

**Success** At 6 months, this baby is finally able to grab her toes. From a developmental perspective, this achievement is as significant as walking, as it requires coordination of feet and fingers. Note her expression of determination and concentration.

**◑ Answer to Observation Quiz** (from p. 150): Jumping up, with a three-month age range for acquisition. The reason is that the older an infant is, the more impact both nature and nurture have.

| AT ABOUT THIS TIME | | |
|---|---|---|
| **Age Norms (in Months) for Fine Motor Skills** | | |
| | **When 50% of All Babies Master the Skill** | **When 90% of All Babies Master the Skill** |
| Grasps rattle when placed in hand | 3 | 4 |
| Reaches to hold an object | 4.5 | 6 |
| Thumb and finger grasp | 8 | 10 |
| Stacks two blocks | 15 | 21 |
| Imitates vertical line (drawing) | 30 | 39 |
| Data from World Health Organization, 2006. | | |

By 4 months, infants sometimes grab, but their timing is off: They close their hands too early or too late. Finally, by 6 months, with a concentrated, deliberate stare, most babies can reach, grab, and grasp almost any object that is the right size. Some can even transfer an object from one hand to the other.

Toward the end of the first year and throughout the second, finger skills improve as babies master the pincer movement (using thumb and forefinger to pick up tiny objects) and self-feeding (first with hands, then fingers, then utensils) (Ho, 2010). (See At About This Time.)

As with gross motor skills, fine motor skills are shaped by practice, which is relentless from the third month of prenatal development throughout childhood. Practice is especially obvious in the first year, when "infants flap their arms, rotate their hands, and wiggle their fingers, and exhibit bouts of rhythmical waving, rubbing, and banging while holding objects" (Adolph & Franchak, 2017).

As with every motor skill, progress depends not only on maturation and practice but also on culture and opportunity. For example, when given "sticky mittens" (with Velcro) that allow grabbing, infants master hand skills sooner than usual. Their perception advances as well (Libertus & Needham, 2010; Soska et al., 2010). More generally, all senses and motor skills expand the baby's cognitive awareness, with practice advancing both skill and cognition (Leonard & Hill, 2014).

## Cultural Variations

The importance of context is illustrated by follow-up studies on the "sticky mittens" experiments. Some researchers have given 2-month-olds practice in reaching for toys without sticky mittens. The infants advanced as much as those with special mittens (Williams et al., 2015). It seems that practice of every motor skill advances development, not only of the skill but overall (Leonard & Hill, 2014).

When U.S. infants are grouped by ethnicity, generally African American babies are ahead of Hispanic American babies when it comes to walking. In turn, Hispanic American babies are ahead of those of European descent. Internationally, the earliest walkers are in sub-Saharan Africa, where many well-nourished and healthy babies walk at 10 months.

As found in detailed studies in Senegal and Kenya, babies in many African communities are massaged and stretched from birth onward and are encouraged to walk as soon as possible (Super et al., 2011). They do so long before a year after birth (Adolph & Franchak, 2017). The latest walkers may be in rural China (15 months), where infants are bundled up against the cold (Adolph & Robinson,

2013). The other reason some cultures discourage walking is that some places are rife with danger (poisonous snakes, open fires), so toddlers are safer if they cannot wander. By contrast, some cultures encourage running over long distances: Their children can run marathons (Adolph & Franchak, 2017).

Remember that difference is not deficit. However, slow development *relative to local norms* may indicate a problem that needs attention; lags are much easier to remedy during infancy than later on.

Also remember the dynamic systems of senses and motor skills: If one sense or motor skill is impaired, other parts are affected as well. This is true throughout childhood: Fine motor skills are aided by the ability to sit; language development depends on hearing; reading depends on vision—so careful monitoring of basic sensory and motor skills in infancy is part of good infant care.

---

### WHAT HAVE YOU LEARNED?

**1.** What particular sounds and patterns do infants pay attention to?

**2.** How does an infant's vision change over the first year?

**3.** Why is hearing more acute than vision in the early weeks?

**4.** Why do some babies prefer certain tastes and smells that others dislike?

**5.** What is known and unknown about infant pain?

**6.** What is universal and what is cultural in the development of gross motor skills?

**7.** What is the relationship between motor skills and the senses?

**8.** Why do caregivers vary in which motor skills they encourage?

---

# Surviving in Good Health

Public health measures have dramatically reduced infant death. In 1950, worldwide, one infant in six died before age 1; in 2015, the rate was about 1 in 28. Income is significant; the rate is 1 in 200 in the most developed nations, 1 in 6 in the poorest ones (United Nations, 2015). Progress is most dramatic in large developing nations (China and India). All told, about 2 million people are alive today who would have died if they had been born 70 years ago. As you can see from Figure 5.5 on the following page, improvement is evident everywhere. Infant mortality has been reduced by 900 percent in Poland, Japan, Chile, China, and Finland.

## Better Days Ahead

Most child deaths occur in the first month. In the twenty-first century in developed nations, 99.9 percent of 1-month-olds live to adulthood. Public health measures (clean water, nourishing food, immunization) deserve most of the credit.

Both survival and life itself are better for children, because parents have fewer births and thus attend more to each one. Maternal education is pivotal. Especially in low-income nations, educated women have far fewer, but much healthier, children than women who never went to school (de la Croix, 2013).

## Considering Culture

Many cultural variations are simply alternative ways to raise a healthy child—a difference, not a deficit. Sometimes, however, one mode of infant care is much better

Louise Gubb/Corbis via Getty Images

**Well Protected**  Disease and early death are common in Ethiopia, where this photo was taken, but neither is likely for 2-year-old Salem. He is protected not only by the nutrition and antibodies in his mother's milk but also by the large blue net that surrounds them. Treated bed nets, like this one provided by the Carter Center and the Ethiopian Health Ministry, are often large enough for families to eat, read, as well as sleep in together, without fear of malaria-infected mosquitoes.

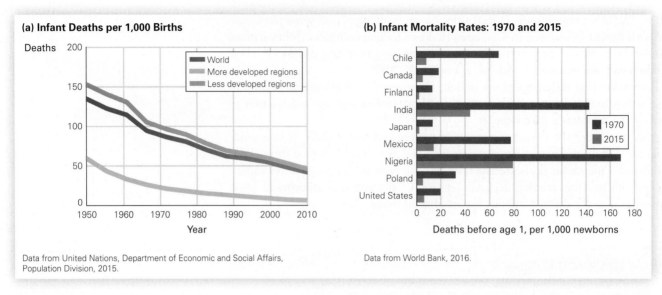

**(a) Infant Deaths per 1,000 Births**

Legend:
- World
- More developed regions
- Less developed regions

Data from United Nations, Department of Economic and Social Affairs, Population Division, 2015.

**(b) Infant Mortality Rates: 1970 and 2015**

Countries listed: Chile, Canada, Finland, India, Japan, Mexico, Nigeria, Poland, United States

Legend: 1970, 2015

Deaths before age 1, per 1,000 newborns

Data from World Bank, 2016.

**FIGURE 5.5**

**More Babies Are Surviving**  Improvements in public health—better nutrition, cleaner water, more widespread immunization—over the past three decades have meant millions of survivors.

**sudden infant death syndrome (SIDS)**  A situation in which a seemingly healthy infant, usually between 2 and 6 months old, suddenly stops breathing and dies unexpectedly while asleep.

than another. To identify them, international comparisons become useful. Consider the dramatic worldwide reduction in **sudden infant death syndrome (SIDS)**.

Every year until the mid-1990s, tens of thousands of infants died of SIDS, called *crib death* in North America and *cot death* in England. Tiny infants smiled at their caregivers, waved their arms at rattles that their small fingers could not yet grasp, went to sleep, and never woke up. Scientists tested hypotheses (the cat? the quilt? natural honey? homicide? spoiled milk?) to no avail. Grief-ridden parents were sometimes falsely arrested. Sudden infant death was a mystery. Finally, one major risk factor—sleeping on the stomach—was discovered, thanks to the work of one scientist, described in A Case to Study on the following page.

**Public Service Victory**  Sometimes data and discoveries produce widespread improvements—as in the thousands of lives saved by the "Back to Sleep" mantra. The private grief of mystified parents in Australia is separated by merely 30 years from this subway poster viewed by hundreds of thousands of commuters. Despite many developmental problems—some described in this chapter—the average human life is longer and healthier than it was a few decades ago.

# Scientist at Work

Susan Beal, a 35-year-old scientist with five young children, began to study SIDS deaths in South Australia. She responded to phone calls, often at 5 or 6 A.M., reporting that another baby had died. Her husband supported her work, often becoming the sole child-care provider when she needed to leave home at a moment's notice.

Sometimes Beal was the first professional to arrive, before the police or the coroner. Initially, she was reluctant to question the grieving parents. But soon she learned that parents were grateful to talk, in part because they tended to blame themselves and needed to express that emotion to someone who was not likely to accuse them. Beal reassured them that scientists shared their bewilderment. (Visit the link to watch a short interview with Susan Beal.)

> **LaunchPad**
> macmillan learning
>
> **Interview with Susan Beal**
> http://www.youtube.com/watch?v=ZIPt5q2QJ91

Beal was as much a scientist as a sympathetic listener, so she took detailed, careful notes on dozens of circumstances at each of more than 500 deaths. She found that some things did not matter (such as birth order), and some increased the risk (maternal smoking and lambskin blankets).

A breakthrough came when Beal noticed an ethnic variation: There were far more SIDS victims of European descent than of Chinese descent, which was surprising given the proportions of European and Chinese babies in that part of Australia. Genetic? Most experts thought so. But Beal's notes revealed that almost all SIDS babies died while sleeping on their stomachs, contrary to the Chinese custom of placing infants on their backs to sleep. She developed a new hypothesis: Sleeping position mattered.

To test her hypothesis, Beal convinced a large group of non-Chinese parents to put their newborns to sleep on their backs. Almost none of them died suddenly.

After several years of gathering data, she drew a surprising conclusion: Back-sleeping protected against SIDS. Her published report (Beal, 1988) caught the attention of doctors in the Netherlands, where pediatricians had told parents to put their babies to sleep on their stomachs. Two Dutch scientists (Engelberts & de Jonge, 1990) recommended back-sleeping; thousands of parents took heed. SIDS was reduced in the Netherlands by 40 percent in one year—a stunning replication.

In the United States, Benjamin Spock's *Baby and Child Care,* first published in 1946, sold more copies than any book other than the Bible. He advised stomach-sleeping, and millions of parents followed that advice. In 1984, SIDS killed 5,245 babies in the United States.

But Beal's 1988 article and the Netherlands' 1990 data caught on in the United States. By 1994, a "Back to Sleep" campaign cut the SIDS rate dramatically (Kinney & Thach, 2009; Mitchell, 2009). By 1996, the U.S. SIDS rate was one-half what it had been.

In 2015, the U.S. Centers for Disease Control and Prevention reported just 1,600 SIDS deaths, even though the population of infants has increased over the past decades (see Figure 5.6). Consequently, in the United States alone, about 100,000 people are alive who would be dead if they had been born before 1990.

Stomach-sleeping is a proven, replicated risk, but it is not the only one. Other risks include low birthweight, winter, being male, exposure to cigarettes, soft blankets or pillows, bed-sharing, and physical abnormalities (in the brain stem, heart, mitochondria, microbiome) (Neary & Breckenridge, 2013; Ostfeld et al., 2010). Most SIDS victims experience several risks, a cascade of biological and social circumstances.

That does not surprise Susan Beal. She sifted through all the evidence and found the main risk—stomach-sleeping—but she continues to study other factors. She praises the courage of the hundreds of parents who talked with her just hours after their baby died. The entire world praises her.

**SIDS Deaths per 100,000 Live Births—United States**

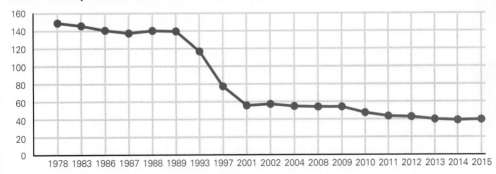

Data from Xu et al., December 2016; Murphy et al., December 2015; Hoyert & Xu, 2012; Murphy et al., 2012; Kochanek et al., 2011; Miniño et al., 2007; Hoyert et al., 2005; Mathews et al., 2003; Gardner & Hudson, 1996; Macdorman & Rosenberg, 1993; Monthly Vital Statistics Report, 1980.

**FIGURE 5.6**

**Alive Today** As more parents learn that a baby should be on his or her "back to sleep," the SIDS rate continues to decrease. Other factors are also responsible for the decline—fewer parents smoke cigarettes in the baby's room.

**immunization** A process that stimulates the body's immune system by causing production of antibodies to defend against attack by a particular contagious disease. Creation of antibodies may be accomplished either naturally (by having the disease), by injection, by drops that are swallowed, or by a nasal spray.

# Immunization

Diseases that could be deadly (including measles, chicken pox, polio, mumps, rotavirus, and whooping cough) are now rare because of **immunization,** which primes the body's immune system to resist a particular disease. Immunization (often via *vaccination*) is said to have had "a greater impact on human mortality reduction and population growth than any other public health intervention besides clean water" (Baker, 2000, p. 199).

In the first half of the twentieth century, almost every child had at least one of these diseases. Usually they recovered, and then they were immune. Indeed, some parents took their toddlers to play with a child who had an active case of chicken pox, for instance, hoping their child would catch the disease and then become immune. This protected that child later in life.

## Success and Survival

Beginning with smallpox in the nineteenth century, doctors discovered that giving a small dose of a virus to healthy people stimulates antibodies and provides protection. Stunning successes in immunization include the following:

- Smallpox, the most lethal disease for children in the past, was eradicated worldwide as of 1980. Vaccination against smallpox is no longer needed.
- Polio, a crippling and sometimes fatal disease, has been virtually eliminated in the Americas. Only 784 cases were reported anywhere in the world in 2003. However, false rumors halted immunization in northern Nigeria. Polio reappeared, sickening 1,948 people in 2005, almost all of them in West Africa. Public health workers and community leaders rallied and Nigeria's polio rate fell again, to six cases in 2014. However, poverty and wars in South Asia prevented immunization there: Worldwide, 359 cases were reported in 2014, almost all in Pakistan and Afghanistan (Hagan et al., 2015) (see Figure 5.7).
- Measles (rubeola, not rubella) is disappearing, thanks to a vaccine developed in 1963. Prior to that time, 3 to 4 million cases occurred each year in the United States alone (Centers for Disease Control and Prevention, May 15, 2015). In 2012 in the United States, only 55 people had measles, although globally about 20 million measles cases occurred that year. If a traveler brings measles back to the United States, unimmunized children and adults may catch the disease. That happened in 2014, when 667 people in the United States had measles—the highest rate since 1994 (MMWR, January 8, 2016).

Immunization protects not only from temporary sickness but also from complications, including deafness, blindness, sterility, and meningitis. Sometimes such damage from illness is not apparent until decades later. Having mumps in childhood, for instance, can cause sterility and doubles the risk of schizophrenia in adulthood (Dalman et al., 2008).

Immunization also protects those who cannot be safely vaccinated, such as infants under 3 months and people with impaired immune systems (HIV-positive, aged, or undergoing chemotherapy). Fortunately, each vaccinated child stops transmission of the disease, a phenomenon called *herd immunity*. Usually, if 90 percent of the people in a community (a herd) are immunized, no one dies of that disease.

Everywhere, some children are not vaccinated for valid medical reasons, but in 20 of the U.S. states, parents may refuse vaccination for their children because of "personal belief" (Blad, 2014). One such state is Colorado, where only 81 percent of 1- to 3-year-olds were fully immunized in 2013, a rate far below herd immunity. This horrifies public health workers, who know that the risks of the diseases—especially to babies—are far greater than the risks from immunization.

Scott Eels/Redux

**True Dedication** This young Buddhist monk lives in a remote region of Nepal, where until recently measles was a common, fatal disease. Fortunately, a UNICEF porter carried the vaccine over mountain trails for two days so that this boy—and his whole community—could be immunized.

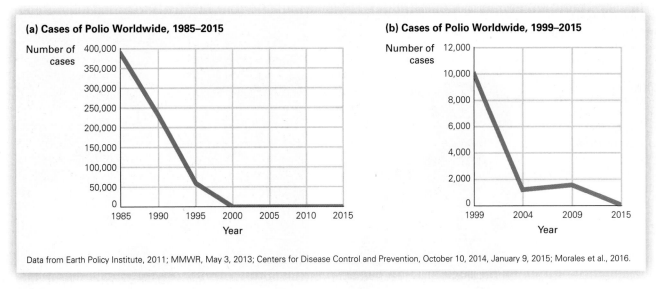

**FIGURE 5.7**

**Not Yet Zero**  Many public health advocates hope polio will be the next infectious disease to be eliminated worldwide, as is the case in almost all of North America. The number of cases has fallen dramatically worldwide *(a)*. However, there was a discouraging increase in polio rates from 2004 to 2009 *(b)*.

Children may react to immunization by being irritable or even feverish for a day, to the distress of their parents. However, parents do not notice if their child does *not* get polio, measles, or so on. Before the varicella (chicken pox) vaccine, more than 100 people in the United States died each year from that disease, and 1 million were itchy and feverish for a week. Now, far fewer people get chicken pox, and almost no one dies of it.

Many parents are concerned about the potential side effects of vaccines, in part because the rare event of one person sickened by vaccination is broadcast widely. Psychologists find that a common source of irrational thinking is overestimating the frequency of a memorable case (Ariely, 2010). As a result, the rate of missed vaccinations in the United States has been rising over the past decade, and epidemics of childhood diseases, such as one that occurred at Disneyland in Anaheim, California, in 2014, are feared.

An example of the benefits of immunization comes from Connecticut. In 2012, flu vaccination was required for all 6- to 59-month-olds in licensed day-care centers. Most children were not in centers, but many home-care parents became aware of the law and immunized their children. That winter, far fewer Connecticut children were hospitalized for flu, although rates rose everywhere else. Meanwhile, Colorado had the highest rate of flu hospitalizations (MMWR, March 7, 2014).

## Nutrition

As already explained, infant mortality worldwide has plummeted in recent years for several reasons: fewer sudden infant deaths, advances in prenatal and newborn care, and, as you just read, immunization. One other measure is making a huge difference: better nutrition.

### Breast Is Best

Ideally, nutrition starts with *colostrum,* a thick, high-calorie fluid secreted by the mother's breasts at birth. This benefit is not understood in some cultures, where the mother is not allowed to breast-feed until her milk "comes in" two or three days after birth. (Sometimes other women nurse the newborn; sometimes herbal

**⬤⬤  Especially for Nurses and Pediatricians**  A mother refuses to have her baby immunized because she wants to prevent side effects. She wants your signature for a religious exemption. In some jurisdictions, that allows the mother to refuse vaccination. What should you do? (see response, p. 159)

**Video: Nutritional Needs of Infants and Children: Breast-Feeding Promotion** shows UNICEF's efforts to educate women on the benefits of breast-feeding.

**Same Situation, Far Apart: Breast-Feeding** Breast-feeding is universal. None of us would exist if our fore mothers had not successfully breast-fed their babies for millennia. Currently, breast-feeding is practiced world-wide, but it is no longer the only way to feed infants, and each culture has particular practices.

tea is given.) Worldwide research confirmed that colostrum saves infant lives, especially if the infant is preterm (Moles et al., 2015; Andreas et al., 2015).

Compared with formula using cow's milk, human milk is sterile, more digestible, and rich in nutrients (Wambach & Riordan, 2014). Allergies and asthma are less common in children who were breast-fed, and in adulthood, their obesity, diabetes, and heart disease rates are lower.

The composition of breast milk adjusts to the age of the baby, with milk for premature babies distinct from that for older infants. Quantity increases to meet the demand: Twins and even triplets can be exclusively breast-fed for months.

Formula is preferable only in unusual cases, such as when the mother uses toxic drugs or is HIV-positive. Even with HIV, however, breast milk without supplementation may be advised by the World Health Organization. In some nations, the infants' risk of catching HIV from their mothers is lower than the risk of dying from infections, diarrhea, or malnutrition as a result of bottle-feeding (A. Williams et al., 2016).

Doctors worldwide recommend breast-feeding with no other foods—not even juice—for the first months of life. (Table 5.1 lists some of the benefits of breast-feeding.) Some pediatricians suggest adding foods (rice cereal and bananas) at 4 months; others want mothers to wait until 6 months (Fewtrell et al., 2011).

Breast-feeding was once universal, but by the mid-twentieth century many mothers thought formula was better. Fortunately, that has changed again. In 2015, 81 percent of U.S. newborns were breast-fed, as were one-half of all 6-month-olds and one-fourth of all 1-year-olds (Centers for Disease Control and Prevention, August, 2016).

## TABLE 5.1

### The Benefits of Breast-Feeding

| For the Baby | For the Mother |
|---|---|
| Balance of nutrition (fat, protein, etc.) adjusts to age of baby | Easier bonding with baby |
| Breast milk has more microbiome micronutrients | Reduced risk of breast cancer and osteoporosis |
| Less infant illness, including allergies, ear infections, stomach upsets | Natural contraception (with exclusive breast-feeding, for several months) |
| Less childhood asthma | Pleasure of breast stimulation |
| Better childhood vision | Satisfaction of meeting infant's basic need |
| Less adult illness, including diabetes, cancer, heart disease | No formula to prepare; no sterilization |
| Protection against many childhood diseases, since breast milk contains antibodies from the mother | Easier travel with the baby |
| Stronger jaws, fewer cavities, advanced breathing reflexes (less SIDS) | **For the Family** |
| Higher IQ, less likely to drop out of school, more likely to attend college | Increased survival of other children (because of spacing of births) |
| Later puberty, fewer teenage pregnancies | Increased family income (because formula and medical care are expensive) |
| Less likely to become obese or hypertensive by age 12 | Less stress on father, especially at night |

Information from Beilin & Huang, 2008; Riordan & Wambach, 2009; Schanler, 2011; U.S. Department of Health and Human Services, 2011.

Encouragement of breast-feeding from family members, especially fathers, is crucial. In addition, nurses ideally visit new mothers weekly at home; such visits (routine in some nations, rare in others) increase the likelihood that breast-feeding will continue.

Although every expert agrees that breast milk is beneficial, given the complexity and variation of human families, mothers should not feel guilty for feeding their babies formula. No single behavior—breast-feeding, co-sleeping, hand-washing, exercising, family planning—defines good motherhood.

## Malnutrition

**Protein-calorie malnutrition** occurs when a person does not consume enough food to sustain normal growth. Children may suffer from **stunting**, being short for their age because chronic malnutrition reduced their growth, or from **wasting**, being severely underweight for their age and height (2 or more standard deviations below average). Many nations, especially in East Asia, Latin America, and Central Europe, have seen improvement in child nutrition in the past decades, with an accompanying decrease in wasting and stunting (see Figure 5.8).

In other nations, however, primarily in Africa, wasting has increased (Black et al., 2013). Explanations include high birth rate, maternal AIDS deaths, climate change, and civil wars.

Chronically malnourished infants and children suffer in three ways:

1. Learning suffers. If malnutrition continues long enough to affect height, it also affects the brain. If hunger reduces energy and curiosity, learning suffers.
2. Diseases are more serious. About half of all childhood deaths occur because malnutrition makes a childhood disease lethal, especially the leading causes of childhood deaths—diarrhea and pneumonia—but also milder diseases such as measles (Walker et al., 2013; Roberts, 2017).
3. Some diseases result directly from malnutrition—including both *marasmus* during the first year, when body tissues waste away, and *kwashiorkor* after age 1, when growth slows down, hair becomes thin, skin becomes splotchy, and the face, legs, and abdomen swell with fluid (edema).

Prevention, more than treatment, is needed. Sadly, some children hospitalized for marasmus or kwashiorkor die even after being fed because their digestive systems were already failing (M. Smith et al., 2013). Ideally, prenatal nutrition, then

**THINK CRITICALLY:** For new mothers in your community, why do some use formula and others breast-feed exclusively for six months?

**protein-calorie malnutrition** A condition in which a person does not consume sufficient food of any kind. This deprivation can result in several illnesses, severe weight loss, and even death.

**stunting** The failure of children to grow to a normal height for their age due to severe and chronic malnutrition.

**wasting** The tendency for children to be severely underweight for their age as a result of malnutrition.

**Response for Nurses and Pediatricians** (from p. 157): It is difficult to convince people that their method of child rearing is wrong, although you should try. In this case, listen respectfully and then describe specific instances of serious illness or death from a childhood disease. Suggest that the mother ask her grandparents whether they knew anyone who had polio, tuberculosis, or tetanus (they probably did). If you cannot convince this mother, do not despair: Vaccination of 95 percent of toddlers helps protect the other 5 percent. If the mother has genuine religious reasons, talk to her clergy adviser.

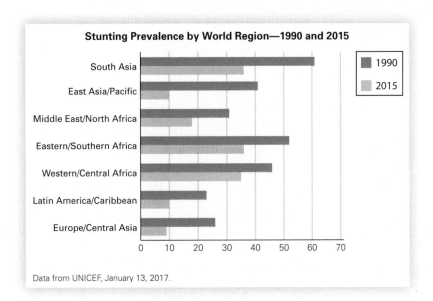

Data from UNICEF, January 13, 2017.

**FIGURE 5.8**

**Evidence Matters** Genes were thought to explain height differences among Asians and Scandanavians, until data on hunger and malnutrition proved otherwise. The result: starvation down and height up almost everywhere—especially in Asia. Despite increased world population, far fewer young children are stunted (255 million in 1970; 156 million in 2015). Evidence also identifies problems: Civil war, climate change, and limited access to contraception have increased stunting in East and Central Africa, from 20 to 28 million in the past 50 years.

**Same Situation, Far Apart: Children Still Malnourished** Infant malnutrition is still common in some nations. The 16-month-old at the left is from South Sudan, a nation suffering from civil war for decades. The 7-month-old boy in India on the right is a twin—a risk for malnutrition. Fortunately, they are getting medical help, and their brains are somewhat protected because of head-sparing.

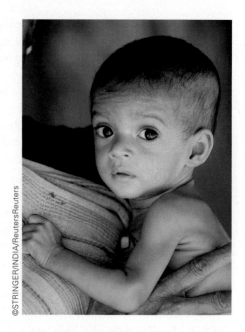

breast-feeding, and then supplemental iron and vitamin A stop malnutrition before it starts. Once malnutrition is apparent, highly nutritious formula (usually fortified peanut butter) often restores weight—but not always.

A combination of factors—genetic susceptibility, poor nutrition, infection, and abnormal bacteria in the digestive system (the microbiome)—may be fatal (M. Smith et al., 2013). Giving severely ill children an antibiotic to stop infection saves lives—but always, prevention is best (Gough et al., 2014).

## WHAT HAVE YOU LEARNED?

1. Why is polio still a problem in some nations?

2. Why do doctors worry about immunization rates in the United States?

3. What are the reasons for and against breast-feeding until a child is at least 1 year old?

4. When is it advisable that a woman not breast-feed?

5. What is the relationship between malnutrition and disease?

6. Which is worse, stunting or wasting? Why?

# SUMMARY

## Body Changes

**1.** In the first two years of life, infants grow taller, gain weight, and increase in head circumference—all indicative of development. On average, birthweight doubles by 4 months, triples by 1 year, and quadruples by 2 years.

**2.** By age 2, the average well-nourished child weighs about 28 pounds (12.7 kilograms) and has gained more than a foot in height since birth, reaching about one-half of adult height.

**3.** Medical checkups in the first months of a child's life focus especially on weight, height, and head circumference because

early detection of slow growth can halt later problems. Percentile changes can signify difficulties.

**4.** The amount of time a child sleeps decreases over the first two years. Variations in sleep patterns are normal, caused by both nature and nurture. Bed-sharing is the norm in many developing nations, although it increases the risk of SIDS. Co-sleeping is increasingly common in developed nations.

**5.** Brain size increases dramatically, from about 25 to about 75 percent of adult brain weight in the first two years. Complexity increases as well, with cell growth, development of dendrites, and formation of synapses.

**6.** Some stimulation is experience-expectant, needed for normal brain development. Both exuberant growth and pruning aid cognition, as the connections that are experience-dependent are strengthened.

**7.** Experience is vital for brain development. An infant who is socially isolated, overstressed, or deprived of stimulation may be impaired lifelong.

### Perceiving and Moving

**8.** At birth, the senses already respond to stimuli. Prenatal experience makes hearing the most mature sense. Vision is the least mature sense at birth, but it improves quickly with experience. Infants use all their senses to strengthen their early social interactions.

**9.** The senses of smell, taste, and touch are present at birth, and they help infants respond to their social world. Pain is experienced, but infant pain is not identical to adult pain.

**10.** Infants gradually improve their motor skills as they begin to grow and brain maturation continues. Control of the body proceeds from the head downward (cephalocaudal) and from the core to the extremities (proximodistal).

**11.** Gross motor skills are mastered throughout infancy, depending on practice, motivation, and maturation. Major advances are

sitting up (at about 6 months), walking (at about 1 year), and running (before age 2).

**12.** Fine motor skills also improve, as infants learn to grab, aim, and manipulate almost anything within reach. Development of the senses and motor skills are mutually reinforcing.

### Surviving in Good Health

**13.** About 2 billion infant deaths have been prevented in the past half-century because of improved health care. One major innovation is immunization, which has eradicated smallpox and almost eliminated polio and measles.

**14.** Public health workers are concerned that some regions of the world, and some states of the United States, have immunization rates that are below herd immunity. Young infants may be most vulnerable to viruses, although deaths from childhood diseases can occur at any age.

**15.** Breast milk helps infants resist disease and promotes growth of every kind. Most babies are breast-fed at birth, but rates over the first year vary depending on family and culture. Pediatricians now recommend breast milk as the only nourishment for the first four to six months.

**16.** Severe malnutrition stunts growth and can cause death, both directly through marasmus or kwashiorkor and indirectly if a child becomes sick. Stunting and wasting are both signs of malnutrition, which has become less common worldwide except in some nations of sub-Saharan Africa.

## KEY TERMS

percentile (p. 136)
REM (rapid eye movement)
  sleep (p. 137)
co-sleeping (p. 138)
bed-sharing (p. 138)
head-sparing (p. 139)
neuron (p. 140)
axon (p. 140)
dendrite (p. 140)
synapse (p. 140)

neurotransmitter (p. 140)
myelin (p. 140)
cortex (p. 140)
prefrontal cortex (p. 140)
limbic system (p. 140)
amygdala (p. 141)
hippocampus (p. 141)
hypothalamus (p. 141)
cortisol (p. 141)
pituitary (p. 141)

transient exuberance (p. 142)
pruning (p. 142)
experience-expectant (p. 142)
experience-dependent (p. 142)
shaken baby syndrome (p. 146)
self-righting (p. 146)
sensation (p. 147)
binocular vision (p. 148)
motor skill (p. 150)
gross motor skills (p. 150)

fine motor skills (p. 151)
sudden infant death syndrome
  (SIDS) (p. 154)
immunization (p. 156)
protein-calorie malnutrition
  (p. 159)
stunting (p. 159)
wasting (p. 159)

## APPLICATIONS

**1.** Immunization regulations and practices vary, partly for social and political reasons. Ask at least two faculty or administrative staff members what immunizations the students at your college must have and why. If you hear "It's a law," ask why.

**2.** Observe three infants (whom you do not know) in public places such as a store, playground, or bus. Look closely at body size and motor skills, especially how much control each baby has over his or her legs and hands. From that, estimate the

baby's age in months. Then ask the caregiver how old the infant is. Explain your accuracy.

**3.** *This project can be done alone, but it is more informative if several students pool responses.* Ask 3 to 10 adults whether they were bottle-fed or breast-fed and, if breast-fed, for how long. If someone does not know, or expresses embarrassment, that itself is worth noting. Do you see any correlation between adult body size and infant feeding?

# The First Two Years:
## Cognitive Development

## What Will You Know?

1. Why did Piaget compare 1-year-olds to scientists?
2. What factors influence whether infants remember what happens to them before they can talk?
3. When and how do infants learn to talk?

✦ **Sensorimotor Intelligence**
Stages One and Two: Primary Circular Reactions
Stages Three and Four: Secondary Circular Reactions
Stages Five and Six: Tertiary Circular Reactions
A VIEW FROM SCIENCE: Object Permanence

✦ **Information Processing**
Affordances
Memory

✦ **Language: What Develops in the First Two Years?**
The Universal Sequence
INSIDE THE BRAIN: Understanding Speech
Cultural Differences
Theories of Language Learning
OPPOSING PERSPECTIVES: Language and Video

"You've been flossing more," my dental hygienist told me approvingly. I am proud. I never flossed as a child (did flossing exist then?), but lately I have flossed every morning. This change was the result of cognition: I read that heart disease and flossing were negatively correlated, and I applied what I know about behavior modification—keeping daily track, with check marks, of when I flossed. But my hygienist was not satisfied.

"You need to brush three minutes each time, and floss twice a day."

"Why?"

"You will have less tartar."

"What is wrong with tartar?"

"It causes gingivitis."

"What is wrong with gingivitis?"

"It causes periodontitis."

"What is wrong with periodontitis?"

She looked at me as if I were incredibly stupid, and replied, "It is terrible, it is expensive, it is time-consuming. You could lose a tooth."

I thought of asking "What's wrong with losing a tooth?" I did not.

How does this apply to infant cognitive development? The negative cascade of daily events, from another minute of brushing to a lost tooth, is not unlike the positive cascade that transforms a newborn into a talking, goal-directed 2-year-old. As you will see, infants learn rapidly, from their first attempt to suck and swallow to their comprehension of some laws of physics, from recognition of their mother's voice to their memory for action sequences that they have witnessed, from a reflexive cry to spoken sentences with several words.

Each day of looking and learning seems insignificant, yet caregiver actions accumulate to turn a newborn into a toddler who thinks, understands, pretends, and explains. This chapter describes in detail those early days and months, which build the intellectual foundation for the later thinking and talking. Everyday actions of infants' caregivers lead to these accomplishments.

The conversation with my dental hygienist is relevant in another way as well. My repeated questioning is similar to infants' drive for new understanding, evident in the six stages of intellectual progression that Piaget describes, and the gradual improvement of infant memory detailed by information-processing theorists. Babies, too, are curious, questioning explorers.

The final topic of this chapter may be most important. How do infants learn so much? What is the best way to nurture early cognition?

## Sensorimotor Intelligence

Jean Piaget earned his doctorate in biology in 1918, when most scientists thought infants only ate, cried, and slept. When Piaget became a father, his own babies became the subjects of his scientific observation skills. Contrary to conventional wisdom, he detailed their active learning. [**Developmental Link:** Piaget's theory of cognitive development is introduced in Chapter 2.]

Piaget called cognition in the first two years **sensorimotor intelligence.** Early reflexes, senses, and body movements are the raw materials for infant cognition, as described in Table 6.1.

**sensorimotor intelligence** Piaget's term for the way infants think—by using their senses and motor skills—during the first period of cognitive development.

**LaunchPad**
macmillan learning

**Video: Sensorimotor Intelligence in Infancy and Toddlerhood** shows how senses and motor skills fuel infant cognition.

### TABLE 6.1

**The Six Stages of Sensorimotor Intelligence**

For an overview of the stages of sensorimotor thought, it helps to group the six stages into pairs.

**Primary Circular Reactions**

The first two stages involve the infant's responses to its own body.

| | |
|---|---|
| *Stage One* (birth to 1 month) | *Reflexes:* sucking, grasping, staring, listening |
| | *Example:* sucking anything that touches the lips or cheek |
| *Stage Two* (1–4 months) | *The first acquired adaptations:* accommodation and coordination of reflexes |
| | *Examples:* sucking a pacifier differently from a nipple; attempting to hold a bottle to suck it |

**Secondary Circular Reactions**

The next two stages involve the infant's responses to objects and people.

| | |
|---|---|
| *Stage Three* (4–8 months) | *Making interesting sights last:* responding to people and objects |
| | *Example:* clapping hands when mother says "patty-cake" |
| *Stage Four* (8–12 months) | *New adaptation and anticipation:* becoming more deliberate and purposeful in responding to people and objects |
| | *Example:* putting mother's hands together in order to make her start playing patty-cake |

**Tertiary Circular Reactions**

The last two stages are the most creative, first with action and then with ideas.

| | |
|---|---|
| *Stage Five* (12–18 months) | *New means through active experimentation:* experimentation and creativity in the actions of the "little scientist" |
| | *Example:* putting a teddy bear in the toilet and flushing it |
| *Stage Six* (18–24 months) | *New means through mental combinations:* thinking before doing, new ways of achieving a goal without resorting to trial and error |
| | *Example:* before flushing the teddy bear again, hesitating because of the memory of the toilet overflowing and mother's anger |

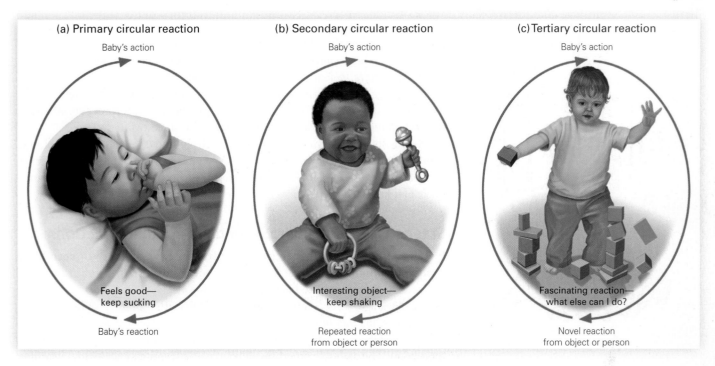

(a) Primary circular reaction

Baby's action

Feels good—
keep sucking

Baby's reaction

(b) Secondary circular reaction

Baby's action

Interesting object—
keep shaking

Repeated reaction
from object or person

(c) Tertiary circular reaction

Baby's action

Fascinating reaction—
what else can I do?

Novel reaction
from object or person

**FIGURE 6.1**
**Never Ending**  Circular reactions keep going because each action produces pleasure that encourages more action.

## Stages One and Two: Primary Circular Reactions

Piaget described the interplay of sensation, perception, action, and cognition as *circular reactions,* emphasizing that, as in a circle, there is no beginning and no end. Each experience leads to the next, which loops back (see Figure 6.1). In **primary circular reactions,** the circle is within the infant's body. Stage one, called the *stage of reflexes,* lasts only a month, as reflexes become deliberate actions; sensation leads to perception, perception leads to cognition, and then cognition leads back to sensation.

Stage two, *first acquired adaptations* (also called *stage of first habits*), begins because reflexes adjust to whatever responses they elicit. Adaptation is cognitive; it includes repeating old patterns (assimilation) and developing new ones (accommodation). [**Developmental Link:** Assimilation and accommodation are explained in Chapter 2.]

**primary circular reactions**  The first of three types of feedback loops in sensorimotor intelligence, this one involving the infant's own body. The infant senses motion, sucking, noise, and other stimuli and tries to understand them.

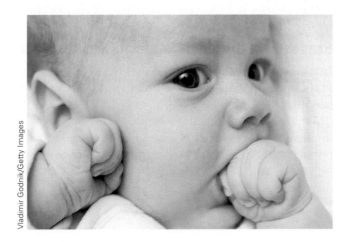

Vladimir Godnik/Getty Images

**Time for Adaptation**  Sucking is a reflex at first, but adaptation begins as soon as an infant differentiates a pacifier from her mother's breast or realizes that a hand has grown too big to fit into the mouth. This infant's expression of concentration suggests that she is about to make that adaptation and suck just her thumb from now on.

"IS THIS THE WAY YOU PLAN TO SPEND YOUR PEAK LEARNING YEARS?"

**Still Wrong** Parents used to ignore infant cognition. Now some make the opposite mistake, assuming infants learn via active study.

**secondary circular reactions** The second of three types of feedback loops in sensorimotor intelligence, this one involving people and objects. Infants respond to other people, to toys, and to any other object that they can touch or move.

**Especially for Parents** When should parents decide whether to feed their baby only by breast, only by bottle, or using some combination of the two? When should they decide whether or not to let their baby use a pacifier? (see response, p. 168)

**tertiary circular reactions** The third of three types of feedback loops in sensorimotor intelligence, this one involving active exploration and experimentation. Infants explore a range of new activities, varying their responses as a way of learning about the world.

Here is one example. In a powerful reflex, full-term newborns suck anything that touches their lips (stage one). They must learn to suck, swallow, and suck again without spitting up too much—a major circular reaction that often takes a few days to learn. Then, infants *adapt* their sucking reflex to bottles or breasts, pacifiers or fingers, each requiring specific types of tongue pushing. This adaptation signifies that infants have begun to interpret sensations; as they accommodate, they are thinking—ready for stage two.

During stage two, which Piaget pegged from about 1 to 4 months of age, additional adaptation of the sucking reflex begins. Infant cognition leads babies to suck in some ways for hunger, in other ways for comfort—and not to suck fuzzy blankets or hard plastic. Once adaptation occurs, it sticks.

## Stages Three and Four: Secondary Circular Reactions

In stages three and four, development advances from primary to **secondary circular reactions.** These reactions extend beyond the infant's body; this circular reaction is between the baby and something else.

During stage three (4 to 8 months), infants attempt to produce exciting experiences, *making interesting sights last*. Realizing that rattles make noise, for example, infants wave their arms and laugh whenever someone puts a rattle in their hand. The sight of something delightful—a favorite squeaky toy, a smiling parent—can trigger active efforts for interaction.

Next comes stage four (8 months to 1 year), *new adaptation and anticipation* (also called the *means to the end*). Babies may ask for help (fussing, pointing, gesturing) to accomplish what they want. Thinking is more innovative as adaptation becomes more complex. For instance, instead of always smiling at Grandpa, an infant might first assess his mood. Stage-three babies continue an experience; stage-four babies initiate and anticipate.

### Pursuing a Goal

An impressive attribute of stage four is that babies work to achieve their goals. Suppose a 10-month-old girl might crawl over to her mother, bringing a bar of soap as a signal that she loves baths, and then start to remove her clothes to make her wishes crystal clear—finally squealing with delight when the bath water is turned on. Similarly, if a 10-month-old boy sees his father putting on a coat to leave, he might drag over his own jacket to signal that he wants to go along.

In both cases, the infant has learned from repeated experience—Daddy sometimes brought the baby along when he went out. With a combination of experience and brain maturation, babies become attuned to the goals of others, an ability that is more evident at 10 months than 8 months (Brandone et al., 2014).

## Stages Five and Six: Tertiary Circular Reactions

In their second year, infants start experimenting in thought and deed—or, rather, in the opposite sequence, deed and thought. They act first (stage five) and think later (stage six).

**Tertiary circular reactions** begin when 1-year-olds take independent actions to discover the properties of other people, animals, and things. Infants no longer respond only to their own bodies (primary reactions) or to other people or objects (secondary reactions). Their cognition is more like a spiral than a closed circle, increasingly creative with each discovery.

# Object Permanence

Piaget discovered that, until about 8 months, babies do not search for an object that is momentarily out of sight. He thought they did not understand **object permanence**—the concept that objects or people continue to exist when they are not visible. At about 8 months—not before—infants look for toys that have fallen from the crib, rolled under a couch, or disappeared under a blanket.

As another scholar explains:

> Many parents in our typical American middle-class households have tried out Piaget's experiment in situ: Take an adorable, drooling 7-month-old baby, show her a toy she loves to play with, then cover it with a piece of cloth right in front of her eyes. What do you observe next? The baby does not know what to do to get the toy! She looks around, oblivious to the object's continuing existence under the cloth cover, and turns her attention to something else interesting in her environment. A few months later, the same baby will readily reach out and yank away the cloth cover to retrieve the highly desirable toy. This experiment has been done thousands of times and the phenomenon remains one of the most compelling in all of developmental psychology.
>
> *[Xu, 2013, p. 167]*

Piaget and his colleagues studied the development of object permanence. They found:

- Infants younger than 8 months do *not* search for an attractive object momentarily covered by a cloth.
- At about 8 months, infants remove the cloth immediately after an object is covered but *not* if they have to wait for a few seconds.
- At 18 months, they search after a wait but *not* if they have seen the object hidden in one place and then moved to another. They search in the first place, not the second, a mistake called *A-not-B*. They look where they remember seeing it (A), not where they saw it moved (to B).
- By 2 years, children fully understand object permanence, progressing through several stages of ever-advanced cognition (Piaget, 1954/2013a).

This research provides many practical suggestions. If young infants fuss because they see something they cannot have (keys, a cell phone, candy), caregivers can put the coveted object out of sight. Fussing stops if object permanence has not yet appeared.

By contrast, for toddlers, hiding a forbidden object is not enough. It must be securely locked away lest the child later get

**object permanence** The realization that objects (including people) still exist when they can no longer be seen, touched, or heard.

it, climbing onto the kitchen counter or under the bathroom sink to do so.

Piaget believed that failure to search before 8 months meant that infants had no concept of object permanence—that "out of sight" literally means "out of mind." However, a series of clever experiments in which objects seemed to disappear while researchers traced babies' eye movements and brain activity revealed that infants much younger than 8 months are surprised if an object vanishes (Baillargeon & DeVos, 1991; Spelke, 1993).

Further research on object permanence continues to question some of Piaget's conclusions. Many other creatures (cats, monkeys, dogs, birds) develop object permanence faster than human infants. The animal ability seems to be innate, not learned, as wolves can develop it as well as dogs—but neither is adept at A-not-B displacement, as when an object is moved by a hand underneath a cloth that covers it (Fiset & Plourde, 2013). By age 2, children figure this out; dogs do not.

**Family Fun** Peek-a-boo makes all three happy, each for cognitive reasons. The 9-month-old is discovering object permanence, his sister (at the concrete operational stage) enjoys making Brother laugh, and their mother understands more abstract ideas—such as family bonding.

**Imitation Is Lifelong** As this photo illustrates, at every age, people copy what others do—often to their mutual joy. The new ability at stage six is "deferred imitation"— this boy may have seen another child lie on a tire a few days earlier.

BruesWu/MomentOpen/Getty Images

Piaget's stage five (12 to 18 months), *new means through active experimentation,* builds on the accomplishments of stage four. Now goal-directed and purposeful activities become more expansive.

Toddlers delight in squeezing all the toothpaste out of the tube, drawing on the wall, or uncovering an anthill—activities they have never observed. Piaget referred to the stage-five toddler as a **"little scientist"** who "experiments in order to see."

**"little scientist"** The stage-five toddler (age 12 to 18 months) who experiments without anticipating the results, using trial and error in active and creative exploration.

A 1-year-old's research method is trial and error. Their devotion to discovery is familiar to every adult scientist—and to every parent. Watch out: protection needed.

Finally, in the sixth stage (18 to 24 months), toddlers use *mental combinations,* intellectual experimentation via imagination that can supersede the active experimentation of stage five. Because they combine ideas, stage-six toddlers think about consequences, hesitating a moment before yanking the cat's tail or dropping a raw egg on the floor. They store what they have seen in memory and do it later, an ability Piaget called *deferred imitation.*

The ability to combine ideas allows stage-six toddlers to pretend. For instance, they know that a doll is not a real baby, but they can belt it into a stroller and take it for a walk. Newer research finds that some accomplishments that Piaget pegged for stage six—including pretending and imitation—begin much earlier.

Piaget was right to describe babies as avid and active learners who "learn so fast and so well" (Xu & Kushnir, 2013, p. 28). His main mistake was underestimating how rapidly their learning occurs.

● **Especially for Parents** One parent wants to put all the breakable or dangerous objects away because the toddler is able to move around independently. The other parent says that the baby should learn not to touch certain things. Who is right? (see response, p. 170)

◑ **Response for Parents** (from p. 166): Both decisions should be made within the first month, during the stage of reflexes. If parents wait until the infant is 4 months or older, they may discover that they are too late. It is difficult to introduce a bottle to a 4-month-old who has never sucked on an artificial nipple or a pacifier to a baby who has already adapted the sucking reflex to a thumb.

### WHAT HAVE YOU LEARNED?

1. What is a circular reaction?

2. Why did Piaget call his first stage of cognition *sensorimotor* intelligence?

3. How do the first two sensorimotor stages illustrate primary circular reactions?

4. How does a stage-three infant make interesting events last?

5. How is object permanence an example of stage four of sensorimotor intelligence?

6. In sensorimotor intelligence, what is the difference between stages five and six?

7. What implications for caregivers come from Piaget's description of sensorimotor intelligence?

8. What evidence suggests that infants are thinking, not just reacting, before age 1?

# Information Processing

To understand cognition, many researchers consider the workings of a computer, including input, memory, programs, analysis, and output. An emphasis on how the human brain uses experience to advance cognition is basic to an *information-processing approach* to cognition, as described in Chapter 2. This approach is insightful in understanding infant cognition, since babies cannot yet use words to show their knowledge.

For infants, output might be uncovering a hidden toy, uttering a sound, or simply staring at one photo longer than another. More recently, infants' brain activity has been studied as they gaze at a picture (Kouider et al., 2013).

To better understand information processing in infancy, consider a baby's reaction to his empty stomach. As a newborn, he simply cries as a reflex—no cognition needed. Soon, however, when hunger makes him fussy, he might hear his mother's voice, look for her, reach to be picked up, and then nuzzle her breast—all without crying because of new cognition. In a few months, information from the stomach (hunger) will be processed, leading to new output: a gesture or a word.

The information-processing perspective, aided by modern technology, has uncovered many aspects of infant cognition. As one researcher summarizes, "Rather than bumbling babies, they are individuals who . . . can learn surprisingly fast about the patterns of nature" (Keil, 2011, p. 1023). Concepts and categories seem to develop in infants' brains by 6 months or earlier (Mandler & DeLoach, 2012).

The information-processing perspective helps tie together many aspects of infant cognition. In earlier decades, infant intelligence was measured via age of sitting up, grasping, and so on, but we now know that the age at which infants achieve motor skills does not predict later intellectual achievement.

Instead, information-processing research has found that signs of attention correlate with later cognitive ability. Babies who focus intently on new stimuli and then turn away are more intelligent than babies who stare aimlessly (Bornstein & Colombo, 2012). Smart babies like novelty and try to understand it (Schulz, 2015).

**Video: Event-Related Potential (ERP) Research** shows a procedure in which the electrical activity of an infant's brain is recorded to see whether it responds differently to familiar versus unfamiliar words.

GILKIS - Emielke van Wyk/Gallo Images/Getty Images

**What Next?** Information-processing research asks what these babies are thinking as they both pull on the same block. Will those thoughts lead to hitting, crying, or sharing?

**Response for Parents** (from p. 168):
It is easier and safer to babyproof the house because toddlers, being "little scientists," want to explore. However, it is important for both parents to encourage and guide the baby. If having untouchable items prevents a major conflict between the adults, that might be the best choice.

**affordance** An opportunity for perception and interaction that is offered by a person, place, or object in the environment.

Mark Richards/PhotoEdit

**Depth Perception** This toddler in a laboratory in Berkeley, California, is crawling on the experimental apparatus called a visual cliff. She stops at the edge of what she perceives as a drop-off.

**visual cliff** An experimental apparatus that gives the illusion of a sudden drop-off between one horizontal surface and another.

Now let us look at two specific aspects of infant cognition that illustrate the information-processing approach: affordances and memory. Affordances concern perception or, by analogy, input. Memory concerns brain organization and output—that is, storage and retrieval.

## Affordances

Perception, remember, requires processing of information that arrives at the brain from the sense organs. Decades of thought and research led Eleanor and James Gibson to conclude that perception is far from automatic (E. Gibson, 1969; J. Gibson, 1979). Perception—for infants, as for the rest of us—is a cognitive accomplishment that requires selectivity: "Perceiving is active, a process of *obtaining* information about the world. . . . We don't simply see, we look" (E. Gibson, 1988, p. 5).

The environment (people, places, and objects) *affords*, or offers, many opportunities to interact with whatever is perceived (E. Gibson, 1997). Each of these opportunities is called an **affordance.** Which particular affordance is perceived depends on four factors: (1) the senses, (2) motivation, (3) maturation, and (4) experience.

For example, imagine that you find yourself lost in an unfamiliar city (factor 1). Motivation is high: You need directions (factor 2). Who should you ask? Not the first person you see, because maturation (factor 3) and experience (factor 4) have taught you that finding good directions (an affordance) depends on choosing well. You seek someone knowledgeable and approachable, so you evaluate facial expressions, body language, gender, dress, and so on of passersby (Miles, 2009).

Developmentalists studying children emphasize that age, motivation, and experience affect what affordances a child perceives. Infants look around every waking moment—listening, grabbing, tasting, and touching. They are developing their understanding of how the world works, relying on their senses to do so. That shapes their brains. Early cognition springs from accurate perception—unlike adults who may ignore perceptions because prior beliefs led them astray (McCabe, 2014).

For example, since toddlers need to practice running, every open space affords locomotion: a meadow, a building's long hall, a city street. For adults, affordance is more limited. They imagine a bull grazing in the meadow, neighbors behind the hallway doors, or traffic on the street. Because motivation and experience are pivotal in affordances, toddlers move when adults are immobilized. We might all be healthier if we paid more attention to perceptions than to assumptions, seeking places to run more than reasons not to.

Variation in affordance is apparent between and within cultures. City-dwellers complain that visitors from rural areas walk too slowly, yet visitors complain that urbanites are always in a hurry. Sidewalks afford either fast travel or views of architecture, depending on the perceiver.

### Research on Early Affordances

Experience always affects which affordances are perceived. This is obvious in studies of depth perception. Research demonstrating this began with an apparatus called the **visual cliff,** designed to provide the illusion of a sudden drop-off between one horizontal surface and another. In a classic research study, 6-month-olds, urged forward by their mothers, wiggled toward Mom over the supposed edge of the cliff, but 10-month-olds, even with their mothers' encouragement, fearfully refused to budge (E. Gibson & Walk, 1960).

Scientists once thought that a visual deficit—specifically, inadequate depth perception—prevented 6-month-olds from seeing the drop, which was why they moved forward. According to this hypothesis, as the visual cortex matured, 10-month-olds perceived that crawling over a cliff afforded falling.

Later research, benefiting from advanced technology and an information-processing approach, found that some 3-month-olds noticed the drop: Their heart rate slowed, and their eyes opened wide when they were placed over the cliff.

Thus, depth perception was not the problem, but until they can crawl, infants need not know that crawling over an edge affords falling. The difference is in processing affordances, not visual input. Those conclusions were drawn by Eleanor Gibson herself, the scientist who did the early visual cliff research and who explained the concept of affordances (Adolph & Kretch, 2012).

A similar sequence happens with fear. Infants at 9 months pay close attention to snakes and spiders, but they do not yet fear them. A few months later, perhaps because they have learned from others, they are afraid of those creatures (LoBue, 2013).

Very young babies are particularly attuned to emotional affordances, using their limited perceptual abilities and intellectual understanding to respond to smiles, shouts, and so on. Indeed, in one study, babies watched a three-second video demonstration by an actor whose face was covered (so no visual expression could be seen) as he acted out happiness, anger, or indifference. The results: 6-month-olds could distinguish whether a person is happy or angry by body movements alone (Zieber et al., 2014). Hundreds of information-processing experiments have found that infants are able to connect emotions with movement, facial expression, and tone of voice, an impressive example of early affordances.

**Especially for Parents of Infants** When should you be particularly worried that your baby will fall off the bed or down the stairs? (see response, p. 172)

## Memory

Information-processing research, with detailed behavioral and neurological measures, traces memory in very young babies. Within the first weeks after birth, infants recognize their caregivers by face, voice, and smell.

Memory improves with maturation. In one study, after 6-month-olds had had only two half-hour sessions with a novel puppet, they remembered the experience a month later—an amazing feat of memory for babies who could not talk or even stand up (Giles & Rovee-Collier, 2011).

Instead of noting the many "faults and shortcomings relative to an adult standard," it may be more appropriate to realize that children of all ages remember what they need to remember (Bjorklund & Sellers, 2014, p. 142). Sensory and caregiver memories are apparent in the first month, motor memories by 3 months, and then, at about 9 months, more complex memories (Mullally & Maguire, 2014).

## Forget About Infant Amnesia

Before information-processing research, many scientists hypothesized *infant amnesia,* that infants remember nothing. Their evidence was that adults rarely remember events that occurred before they were 3. But the fact that memories fade with time, and that children cannot verbalize what happened when they were babies, does not mean amnesia.

For example, you may not remember your third-grade teacher's name, but that does not mean you had no memory of it when you were in fifth grade; it just means that you do not now remember what you once knew. If you saw a photo of your third-grade teacher, your brain would register that you knew that person, although you might not remember the teacher's name. Then, if presented with four possible names, you probably could choose correctly.

Indeed, if you saw a photo of a grandmother who cared for you every day when you were an infant and who died when you were 2, your brain would still react. Information-processing research finds evidence of very early memories, with visual memories particularly strong (Leung et al., 2016; Gao et al., 2016).

© 1989 Universal Press Syndicate

**Selective Amnesia** As we grow older, we forget about spitting up, nursing, crying, and almost everything else from our early years. However, strong emotions (love, fear, mistrust) may leave lifelong traces.

 **Response for Parents of**
**Infants** (from p. 171): Constant vigilance is necessary for the first few years of a child's life, but the most dangerous age is from about 4 to 8 months, when infants can move but do not yet fear falling over an edge.

No doubt memory is fragile in the first months of life and improves with age. A certain amount of both experience and brain maturation are required to process and recall what happens (Bauer et al., 2010). But some of that experience happens on day 1—or even in the womb, and some memories may begin long before a baby can verbalize them.

One important insight regarding infant amnesia begins with the distinction between *implicit* and *explicit* memory. Implicit memory is not verbal; it is memory for movement or thoughts that are not put into words. Implicit memory begins by 3 months, is stable by 9 months, continues to improve for the first two years, and varies from one infant to another (Vöhringer et al., 2017). Explicit memory takes longer to emerge, as it depends on language.

Thus, when people say "I don't remember," they mean "I cannot recall it," because it is not in explicit memory. Unconsciously and implicitly, a memory might be present. A person might have an irrational fear of doctors or hospitals, for instance, because of terrifying and painful experiences in the first year.

## Conditions of Memory

Many studies seek to understand what infants *can* remember, even if they cannot later put memories into words. Memories are particularly evident if:

- Motivation and emotion is high.
- Retrieval is strengthened by reminders and repetition.

The most dramatic proof of infant memory comes from innovative experiments in which 3-month-old infants learned to move a mobile by kicking their legs (Rovee-Collier, 1987, 1990). Babies were laid on their backs and were connected to a mobile by means of a ribbon tied to one foot. Virtually every baby began making occasional kicks (as well as arm movements and noises) and realized that kicking made the mobile move. They then kicked more vigorously and frequently, happy at their accomplishment. So far, this is no surprise—self-activated movement is highly reinforcing to infants.

When some 3-month-olds had the mobile-and-ribbon apparatus reinstalled and reconnected *one week later*, most started to kick immediately. They remembered! But when other 3-month-old infants were retested *two weeks later*, they began with only random kicks. Apparently they had forgotten.

### Reminders and Repetition

The lead researcher, Carolyn Rovee-Collier, then developed another experiment demonstrating that 3-month-old infants *could* remember after two weeks *if they*

**LaunchPad**
macmillan learning

**Video: Contingency Learning in Young Infants** shows Carolyn Rovee-Collier's procedure for studying instrumental learning during infancy.

Ian Boddy/Science Source

**He Remembers!** Infants are fascinated by moving objects within a few feet of their eyes—that's why parents buy mobiles for cribs and why Rovee-Collier tied a string to a mobile and a baby's leg to test memory. Babies not in her experiment, like this one, sometimes flail their limbs to make their cribs shake and thus make their mobiles move. Piaget's stage of "making interesting sights last" is evident to every careful observer.

had a brief **reminder session** (Rovee-Collier & Hayne, 1987). In the reminder session, *two weeks* after the initial training, the infants watched the mobile move but were *not* tied to it and were positioned so that they could *not* kick. The next day, they were again connected to the mobile and positioned so that they could move their legs. Then they kicked as they had learned to do two weeks earlier.

Apparently, watching the mobile move on the previous day had revived their faded memory. The information about making the mobile move was stored in their brains, but they needed processing time to retrieve it. Other research similarly finds that repeated reminders are more powerful than single reminders and that context is crucial, especially for infants younger than 9 months: Being tested in the same room as the initial experience aids memory (Rovee-Collier & Cuevas, 2009).

**reminder session** A perceptual experience that helps a person recollect an idea, a thing, or an experience.

## A Little Older, a Little More Memory

Older infants retain information for a longer time than younger babies do, with less training or reminding. Many researchers have found that memory improves markedly by 9 months (Mullally & Maguire, 2014). At that age, babies who watch someone else play with a new toy will, the next day, play with it in the same way as he or she had observed. Infants younger than 9 months do not usually do this.

One-year-olds can transfer learning from one object or experience to another, can learn from strangers, and can copy what they see in books and videos. The dendrites and neurons of several areas of the brain change to reflect remembered experiences. Overall, infants remember not only specific events but also patterns (Keil, 2011). Babies know what to expect from a parent or a babysitter, which foods are delicious, or what details indicate bedtime. Every day of their young lives, infants are processing information and storing conclusions.

**Especially for Teachers** People of every age remember best when they are active learners. If you had to teach fractions to a class of 8-year-olds, how would you do it? (see response, p. 174)

---

### WHAT HAVE YOU LEARNED?

1. How do affordances differ for infants and adults?
2. Why do 10-month-olds refuse to crawl over visual cliffs?
3. What suggests that very young infants have some memory?
4. What conditions help 3-month-olds remember something?
5. How does memory improve between 6 months and 2 years?

# Language: What Develops in the First Two Years?

The human linguistic ability at age 2 far surpasses that of full-grown adults from every other species. Very young infants listen intensely, figuring out speech. One scholar explains, "infants are acquiring much of their native language before they utter their first word" (Aslin, 2012, p. 191). How do they do it?

## The Universal Sequence

The sequence of language development is the same worldwide (see At About This Time). Some children learn several languages, some only one; some learn rapidly, others slowly. But, all follow the same path. Even deaf infants who become able to hear (thanks to cochlear implants) follow the sequence, catching up to their age-mates unless they have other disabilities (Fazzi et al., 2011). Those who learn sign language also follow the same path as hearing infants, at first learning one word at a time and then longer and more complex sentences.

### Listening and Responding

Newborns prefer to listen to the language their mother spoke when they were in the womb. They do not understand the words, of course, but they like the familiar rhythm, sounds, and cadence.

Surprisingly, newborns of bilingual mothers differentiate between the two languages (Byers-Heinlein et al., 2010). Data were collected on 94 newborns (age 0 to 5 days) in a large hospital in Vancouver, Canada. Half were born to mothers who spoke both English and Tagalog (a language native to the Philippines), one-third to mothers who spoke only English, and one-sixth to mothers who spoke English and Chinese. The bilingual mothers used English in more formal contexts and Chinese or Tagalog with family.

The infants in all three groups sucked on a pacifier connected to a recording of 10 minutes of English or Tagalog matched for pitch, duration, and number of syllables. As evident in the frequency and strength of their sucking, most of the infants with bilingual mothers preferred Tagalog. For the Filipino babies, this was probably because their mothers spoke English in formal settings but not when with family and friends, so Tagalog was associated with more animated talk. Those babies with monolingual mothers preferred English, as both formal and informal English sounds were familiar (Byers-Heinlein et al., 2010).

Curiously, the Chinese bilingual mothers' babies (who had never heard Tagalog) nonetheless preferred it to English. The researchers believe that they liked Tagalog because the rhythm of that language is similar to Chinese (Byers-Heinlein et al., 2010).

The same conclusion (that babies prefer familiar language) comes from everyday life. Newborns attend to voices more than to mechanical sounds (a clock ticking) and look closely at the facial expressions of whoever is talking to them (Minagawa-Kawai et al., 2011). By 1 year, they are more likely to imitate the actions of a stranger who speaks their native language than the actions of someone who speaks another language (Buttelmann et al., 2013).

**Response for Teachers** (from p. 173): Remember the three principles of infant memory: real life, motivation, and repetition. Find something children already enjoy that involves fractions—even if they don't realize it. Perhaps get a pizza and ask them to divide it in half, quarters, eighths, sixteenths, and so on.

Ariel Skelley/Getty Images

**Who Is Babbling?** Maybe both the 6-month-old and the 27-year-old. During every day of infancy, mothers and babies communicate with noises, movements, and expressions.

**The Development of Spoken Language in the First Two Years**

| Age* | Means of Communication |
| --- | --- |
| Newborn | Reflexive communication—cries, movements, facial expressions. |
| 2 months | A range of meaningful noises—cooing, fussing, crying, laughing. |
| 3–6 months | New sounds, including squeals, growls, croons, trills, vowel sounds. |
| 6–10 months | Babbling, including both consonant and vowel sounds repeated in syllables. |
| 10–12 months | Comprehension of simple words; speechlike intonations; specific vocalizations that have meaning to those who know the infant well. Deaf babies express their first signs; hearing babies also use specific gestures (e.g., pointing) to communicate. |
| 12 months | First spoken words that are recognizably part of the native language. |
| 13–18 months | Slow growth of vocabulary, up to about 50 words. |
| 18 months | Naming explosion—three or more words learned per day. Much variation: Some toddlers do not yet speak. |
| 21 months | First two-word sentence. |
| 24 months | Multiword sentences. Half the toddler's utterances are two or more words long. |

*The ages in this table reflect norms. Many healthy, intelligent children attain each linguistic accomplishment earlier or later than indicated here.

Infants' ability to distinguish sounds in the language they hear improves, whereas the ability to hear sounds never spoken in their native language (such as a foreign way to pronounce "r" or "l") deteriorates (Narayan et al., 2010). If parents want a child to speak two languages, they should speak both of them to their baby from birth on.

In every language, adults use higher pitch, simple words, repetition, varied speed, and exaggerated emotional tone when talking to infants. This is sometimes called *baby talk,* since it is directed to babies, and sometimes called *motherese,* since mothers universally speak it. But nonmothers speak it as well. Scientists prefer a more formal term, **child-directed speech.**

No matter what term is used, child-directed speech fosters learning, and babies communicate as best they can.

- By 4 months, babies squeal, growl, gurgle, grunt, croon, and yell, telling everyone what is on their minds in response to both their own internal state and their caregivers' words.
- At 7 months, infants begin to recognize words that are highly distinctive (Singh, 2008): *Bottle, doggie,* and *mama,* for instance, might be differentiated, but not *baby, Bobbie,* and *Barbie.*

Infants also like alliteration, rhymes, repetition, melody, rhythm, and varied pitch. Think of your favorite lullaby (itself an alliterative word); obviously, babies prefer sounds over content. Early listening abilities and preferences are the result of brain function, as the following explains.

**child-directed speech** The high-pitched, simplified, and repetitive way adults speak to infants and children. (Also called *baby talk* or *motherese.*)

# Understanding Speech

One particular research strategy has been a boon to scientists, confirming the powerful curiosity of very young babies. That research method is called **habituation** (from the word *habit*).

Habituation refers to getting accustomed to an experience after repeated exposure, as when the school cafeteria serves macaroni day after day or when infants repeatedly encounter the same sound, sight, toy, or so on. Evidence of habituation is loss of interest (or, for macaroni, loss of appetite). The idea is that the pathways in the brain are well established, and thus attention is no longer needed.

Using habituation with infants involves repeating one stimulus until the babies lose interest and then presenting another slightly different stimulus (a new sound, sight, or other sensation). Babies indicate that they detect a difference between the two stimuli with

- a longer or more focused gaze;
- a faster or slower heart rate;
- more or less muscle tension around the lips;
- a change in the rate, rhythm, or pressure of suction on a nipple;
- brain activation as reflected by the fMRI or DTI.

[**Developmental Link:** DTI, fMRI, ERP, and other types of neuroimaging techniques are described in Chapter 2.]

For example, decades ago scientists used habituation to discover that 1-month-olds can detect the difference between certain sounds, such as *pah* and *bah* (Eimas et al., 1971). More recently, methods of measuring brain activity reveal that infants respond to some aspects of speech before observable evidence is found (Johnson & de Haan, 2015; Dehaene-Lambertz, 2017). Newborns—even if born before full term—can discriminate one syllable from another, evident by a burst of neuronal activity in their frontal lobes (Mahmoudzadeh et al., 2013).

Other research finds that infants not only hear differences between sounds but also begin learning language very early. For instance, one study found that when infants hear speech, their

**habituation** The process of becoming accustomed to an object or event through repeated exposure to it, and thus becoming less interested in it.

brains react more notably (registered on ERP, or event-related potential) at the same time that their gaze tends to focus on the mouth more than the eyes (Kushnerenko et al., 2013).

Evidence from DTI (diffusion tensor imaging) has found that the processes for one of the most complex aspects of learning to talk—specifically, activating axons that become pathways within the brain to connect the lobes in order for speech to occur—are bundled over infancy. Axons are connected to the temporal lobe for hearing, the parietal lobe for moving the mouth, the occipital lobe for seeing, and the frontal lobe for thinking (Dubois et al., 2016).

Those "crucial circuits that are required to develop a language system in humans" are similar in structure for infants and adults (Dubois et al., 2016, p. 2295). Although the early brain pathways are immature, with scant myelination, advances are evident between 6 and 22 weeks after birth.

Because of maturation of the language areas of the cortex, even 4-month-old infants attend to voices, developing expectations of the rhythm, segmentation, and cadence of spoken words long before comprehension (Minagawa-Kawai et al., 2011).

Soon, infants use their brains to deduce the rules of their native language, such as which syllable is stressed, whether changing inflection matters (as in Chinese), whether certain sound combinations are repeated, and so on. All of this is based on very careful listening to human speech, including speech not directed toward them with words they do not yet understand (Buttelmann et al., 2013).

As you read, Piaget was innovative because he realized that babies can think. Over the past century, and increasingly with brain imagery, it is now apparent that the human brain, even in the first year of life, does more than think. It works hard to enable people to communicate, interact, and create—supporting all the functions that we consider the pinnacle of human intellectual achievement.

## Babbling and Gesturing

**babbling** An infant's repetition of certain syllables, such as *ba-ba-ba,* that begins when babies are between 6 and 9 months old.

Between 6 and 9 months, babies repeat certain syllables (*ma-ma-ma, da-da-da, ba-ba-ba*), a vocalization called **babbling** because of the way it sounds. Babbling is experience-expectant; all babies babble, even deaf ones. Babbling should be encouraged: Caregivers need to respond to those early sounds. Research finds that babbling is a crucial predictor of later vocabulary, even more than the other major influence—education of the mother (McGillion et al., 2017).

Expectations appear early. Before infants start talking, they become aware of the patterns of speech, such as which sounds are commonly spoken together.

A baby who often hears that something is "pretty" expects the sound of *prit* to be followed by *tee* (MacWhinney, 2015) and is startled if someone says "prit-if."

Infants notice the relationship between mouth movements and sound. In one study, 8-month-olds watched a film of someone speaking, with the audio a fraction of a second ahead of the video. Even when the actor spoke an unknown language, babies noticed the mistiming (Pons & Lewkowicz, 2014).

Toward the end of the first year, babbling begins to imitate the accent, cadence, consonants, and so on of whatever language caregivers utter. By 12 months, analysis of brain waves finds that babies attend to sounds of their native language; unlike 6-month-olds, their brains seem indifferent to sounds of languages they never hear. The brains of bilingual 1-year-olds respond to both languages (Ramírez et al., 2017).

Some caregivers, recognizing the power of gestures, teach "baby signs" to their 6- to 12-month-olds, who communicate with hand signs months before they move their tongues, lips, and jaws to make words. There is no evidence that baby signing accelerates talking (as had been claimed), but it may make parents more responsive, which itself is an advantage (Kirk et al., 2013). For deaf babies, sign language is crucial in the first year: It not only predicts later ability to communicate with signs, it also advances crucial cognitive development (Hall et al., 2017).

Even without adult signing, gestures become a powerful means of communication (Goldin-Meadow, 2015). One early gesture is pointing and responding to someone else who is pointing, which requires something quite sophisticated—understanding another person's view.

Most animals cannot interpret pointing; most 10-month-old humans look in the direction that someone else points and already point with their tiny index fingers (not just a full hand). Pointing is well developed by 12 months, especially when the person who is pointing also speaks (e.g., "look at that") (Daum et al., 2013).

**Are You Hungry?** Pronunciation is far more difficult than hand skills, but parents want to know when their baby wants more to eat. One solution is evident here. This mother is teaching her 12-month-old daughter the sign for "more," a word most toddlers say several months later.

**holophrase** A single word that is used to express a complete, meaningful thought.

## First Words

Finally, at about a year, the average baby utters a few words, understood by caregivers if not by strangers. In the first months of the second year, spoken vocabulary increases gradually (perhaps one new word a week).

Meanings are learned rapidly; babies understand about 10 times more than they can say. Initially, the first words are merely labels for familiar things (*mama* and *dada*). But each early word soon becomes a **holophrase,** a single word that expresses an entire thought. That is accompanied by gestures, facial expressions, and nuances of tone, loudness, and cadence (Saxton, 2010). Imagine meaningful communication in "Dada," "Dada?" and "Dada!": Each is a holophrase.

Of course, the thought in the baby's mind may not be what the adult understands. I know this personally. I was caring for my 16-month-old grandson when he said "Mama, mama." He looked directly at me, and he didn't seem wistful.

**Show Me Where** Pointing is one of the earliest forms of communication, emerging at about 10 months. As you see here, pointing is useful lifelong for humans.

Isaac spoke few words that I recognized, but I thought I knew what he meant. "Mommy's not here," I told him. That didn't interest him; he repeated "mama, mama," more as a command than a complaint. I tried again. I know that *mama* means milk in Japanese baby talk (*miruku* is Japanese for milk), so I offered Isaac milk in his sippy cup. He said, "No, no."

When his father, Oscar, appeared, Isaac grinned broadly, said "mama," and went to be lifted and cuddled in his father's arms. I asked Oscar what "mama" means. His answer: "Pick me up." That makes logical sense. When Isaac sees his mother, he says "mama" and she picks him up.

## The Naming Explosion

Between 12 and 18 months, almost every infant learns the name of each significant caregiver (often *dada, mama, nana, papa, baba, tata*) and sibling (and sometimes each pet). (See Visualizing Development, p. 180.) Other frequently uttered words refer to the child's favorite foods (*nana* can mean "banana" as well as "grandma") and to elimination (*pee-pee, wee-wee, poo-poo, ka-ka, doo-doo*).

Notice that all of these words have two identical syllables, each a consonant followed by a vowel. Many words follow that pattern—not just *baba* but also *bobo, bebe, bubu, bibi*. Other early words are only slightly more complicated—*ma-me, ama*, and so on. The meaning of these words varies by language, but every baby says such words, and every culture assigns meaning to them.

Spoken vocabulary builds rapidly once the first 50 words are mastered, with 21-month-olds typically saying twice as many words as 18-month-olds (Adamson & Bakeman, 2006). This language spurt is called the **naming explosion** because many early words are nouns, that is, names of persons, places, or things.

## Cultural Differences

Cultures and families vary in how much child-directed speech children hear. Some parents read to their infants, teach them signs, and respond to every burp or fart as if it were an attempt to talk. Other parents are much less verbal. They use gestures and touch; they say "hush" and "no" instead of expanding vocabulary.

**Especially for Caregivers** A toddler calls two people "Mama." Is this a sign of confusion? (see response, p. 181)

**naming explosion** A sudden increase in an infant's vocabulary, especially in the number of nouns, that begins at about 18 months of age.

**Universal or Culture-Specific?** Both. All children enjoy music and like to bang on everything from furniture to people. Making noise is fun, but even infants prefer the noises of their community and do their best to repeat them. This boy has learned to play the bongo drums (notice the skilled angle of his hands) thanks to his grandfather.

Jupiterimages/Photolibrary/Getty Images

## Theory One: Infants Need to Be Taught

The seeds of the first perspective were planted in the middle of the twentieth century, when behaviorism dominated North American psychology. The essential idea was that learning is acquired, step by step, through association and reinforcement.

B. F. Skinner (1957) noticed that spontaneous babbling is usually reinforced. Typically, when a baby says "ma-ma-ma-ma," a grinning mother appears, repeating the sound and showering the baby with attention, praise, and perhaps food. The baby learns affordances and repeats "ma-ma-ma-ma" when lonely or hungry; through operant conditioning, talking begins.

Skinner believed that most parents are excellent instructors, responding to their infants' gestures and sounds, thus reinforcing speech. Even in preliterate societies, parents use child-directed speech, responding quickly with high pitch, short sentences, stressed nouns, and simple grammar—exactly the techniques that behaviorists would recommend.

The core ideas of Skinner's theory are the following:

- Parents are expert teachers.
- Repetition strengthens associations, especially when linked to daily life.
- Well-taught infants become articulate, highly verbal children.

In every culture, infants learn language faster if parents speak to them often. Few parents know the theory of behaviorism, but many use behaviorist techniques. Skinner believed that proved his theory, because these methods succeed (Tamis-LeMonda et al., 2014).

Behaviorists note that some 3-year-olds converse in elaborate sentences; others just barely put one simple word with another. Such variations correlate with the amount of language each child has heard. Parents of the most verbal children teach language throughout infancy—singing, explaining, listening, responding, and reading to their children every day, long before the first spoken word (Forget-Dubois et al., 2009) (see Figure 6.2).

According to behaviorists, if adults want children who speak, understand, and (later) read well, they must talk to their infants. A recent application of this theory comes from commercial videos designed to advance toddlers' vocabulary. Typically, such videos use repetition and attention-grabbing measures (sound, tone, color) to encourage babies to learn new words (Vaala et al., 2010). Such videos, and Skinner's theories, have come under attack from many developmentalists, as explained on the following page.

**Response for Caregivers** (from p. 178): Not at all. Toddlers hear several people called "Mama" (their own mother, their grandmothers, their cousins' and friends' mothers) and experience mothering from several people, so it is not surprising if they use "Mama" too broadly. They will eventually narrow the label down to one person, unless both of their parents are women. Usually such parents differentiate, such as one called Mama and the other Mom, or both by their first names.

**Especially for Educators** An infant day-care center has a new child whose parents speak a language other than the one the teachers speak. Should the teachers learn basic words in the new language, or should they expect the baby to learn the teachers' language? (see response, p. 183)

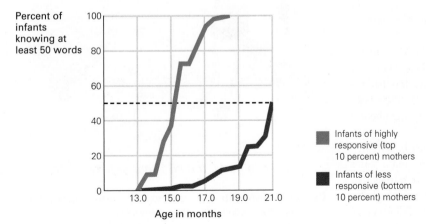

Infants of highly responsive (top 10 percent) mothers

Infants of less responsive (bottom 10 percent) mothers

Data from Tamis-LeMonda et al., 2001, p. 761.

**FIGURE 6.2**

**Maternal Responsiveness and Infants' Language Acquisition** Learning the first 50 words is a milestone in early language acquisition, as it predicts the arrival of the naming explosion and the multiword sentence a few weeks later. Researchers found that half of the infants of highly responsive mothers (top 10 percent) reached this milestone at 15 months. The infants of nonresponsive mothers (bottom 10 percent) lagged significantly behind, with half of them at the 50-word level at 21 months.

# Language and Video

Toddlers can learn to swim in the ocean, throw a ball into a basket, walk on a narrow path beside a precipice, call on a smartphone, cut with a sharp knife, play a guitar, say a word on a flashcard, recite a poem, utter a curse, and much else—if provided appropriate opportunity, encouragement, and practice. Indeed, toddlers in some parts of the world do each of these things—sometimes to the dismay, disapproval, and even shock of adults from elsewhere.

Infants do what others do, a trait that fosters rapid learning. For language learning, parents are advised to read books, sing songs, and talk to their babies. But active curiosity challenges caregivers, who want to keep "little scientists" quiet and in one place. Many weary caregivers covet some free time when their infants do not need them and will not get into danger.

Commercial companies cater to parents' wishes, advertising ways to further the young intellect without demanding more of the caregivers. Cognitive research has proven that infants are fascinated by movement, sound, and people, advancing their knowledge every day. Building on that research, corporations have created child-directed videos, CDs, MP3 downloads, and more that mesmerize, even in the first year. "It's crack for babies," as one mother said (quoted in DeLoache et al., 2010, p. 1572).

Products were named to appeal to parents (*Baby Einstein, Brainy Baby*, and *Mozart for Mommies and Daddies—Jumpstart your Newborn's I.Q.*) and were advertised with testimonials. Scientists deplored such advertisements, since one case proves nothing. [**Developmental Link:** Chapter 1 describes the importance of replication.] Moreover, since every baby improves communication skills every month, parents could easily be misled into believing that their baby's rapid learning was caused by a video, not normal maturation.

Researchers fought back. A famous study found that infants watching *Baby Einstein* were delayed in language compared to other infants (Zimmerman et al., 2007). One product, *My Baby Can Read*, was pulled off the market in 2012 after experts repeatedly attacked its claims (Ryan, 2012).

A lawsuit was threatened regarding the *Baby Einstein* series, and in 2009 the company dropped misleading claims and offered refunds to purchasers (Lewin, 2009). But few parents asked for their money back. Instead, at least through 2016, *Baby Einstein* videos remained popular, with parents raving about a package with 26 *Baby Einstein* DVDs.

Commercial apps for tablets and smartphones have joined the market, with *Shapes Game HD, VocabuLarry*, and a series called *Laugh and Learn*. Most toddler apps offer free trials that babies enjoy, which prompts parents to pay for more content. All of this is predictable, based on what you know. Babies enjoy doing something—like touching a screen—to "make interesting sights last," parents are sometimes overwhelmed with infant care, and corporations seek a profit.

Developmental research continues to find that screen time during infancy is useless at best, perhaps even harmful for early learning. One recent study found that toddlers could learn a word from either a book or a video but that only book-learning, not video-learning, enabled children to use the new word in another context (Strouse & Ganea, 2017).

Another study focused particularly on teaching "baby signs," 18 hand gestures that refer to particular objects (Dayanim & Namy, 2015). The babies in this study were 15 months old, an age at which all babies use gestures and are poised to learn object names. The 18 signs referred to common early words, such as *baby, ball, banana, bird, cat*, and *dog*.

In this study, the toddlers were divided into four groups: video only, video with parent watching and reinforcing, book instruction with parent reading and reinforcing, and no instruction. Not surprisingly, the no-instruction group learned words but not signs, and the other three groups learned some signs.

*"Keep in mind, this all counts as screen time."*

**Caught in the Middle** Parents try to limit screen time, but children are beguiled and bombarded from many sides.

The two groups with parent instruction learned most, with the book-reading group remembering signs better than either video group.

When parents watch a video with their infants, they talk less than they do when they read a book or play with toys (Anderson & Hanson, 2016). Since adult input is essential for language learning, cognitive development is reduced by video time. Infants are most likely to understand and apply what they have learned when they learn directly from another person (R. Barr, 2013).

No wonder the American Association of Pediatricians suggests no screen time (including television, tablets, smartphones, and videos) for children under age 2. Some other sources are less absolute, suggesting that screen time is useful under some circumstances (Cantor & Cornish, 2016).

However, Canadian research finds that toddlers who are allowed the most screen time are from low-income families and usually do not attend day-care centers, factors that put them at risk for slow language development (Carson & Kuzik, 2017).

Research on infants and toddlers from Spanish-speaking homes is particularly distressing. Researchers studying 119 Hispanic American children under age 3 in New York City found that some watched television or some other screen almost constantly when they were at home. The mean was 3.5 hours per day and the median was 2.5 hours per day; 56 percent were watching at least 2 hours daily. They were six times as likely to be slow in language development when compared to the 44 percent who watched less than 2 hours (Duch et al., 2013).

Under some circumstances, older children can learn from screens, but developmentalists find that, because infants need direct and meaningful communication to learn those early words, screen time cannot "substitute for *responsive*, loving face-to-face relationships" (Lemish & Kolucki, 2013, p. 335). Screen time during infancy is worthless as an educational tool. Then why does almost every parent use it?

## Theory Two: Social Impulses Foster Infant Language

The second theory is called *social-pragmatic*. It arises from the sociocultural reason for language: communication. According to this perspective, infants communicate because humans are social beings, dependent on one another for survival and joy. All human infants (and no chimpanzees) seek to master words and grammar in order to join the social world (Tomasello & Herrmann, 2010).

According to this perspective, it is the emotional messages of speech, not the words, that propel communication. Evidence for social learning comes from educational programs for children. Many 1-year-olds enjoy watching television and videos, as the Opposing Perspectives feature explains, but they learn best when adults are actively involved in teaching. In a controlled experiment, 1-year-olds learned vocabulary much better when someone taught them directly than when the same person gave the same lesson on video (Roseberry et al., 2009).

## Theory Three: Infants Teach Themselves

A third theory holds that language learning is genetically programmed to begin at a certain age; adults need not teach it (theory one), nor is it a by-product of social interaction (theory two). Instead, it arises from the genetic impulse to imitate. That impulse has been characteristic of the human species for 100,000 years.

For example, English articles (*the, an, a*) signal that the next word will be the name of an object, and since babies have "an innate base" that primes them to learn, articles facilitate learning nouns (Shi, 2014, p. 9). Article use is a helpful clue for infants learning English, but it is frustrating for anyone who learns English as an adult. Many such adults speak English well but omit articles; they may say "Here is book" instead of "Here is a book." That is an example of the power of centuries of humanity: We imitate for survival, and until a few millennia ago, humans had no need to learn languages other than their own.

Infants and toddlers have always imitated what they hear—not slavishly but according to their own concepts and intentions. Theory three proposes that this is exactly how they learn language (Saxton, 2010). This theory is buttressed by

**Response for Educators** (from p. 181): Probably both. Infants love to communicate, and they seek every possible way to do so. Therefore, the teachers should try to understand the baby and the baby's parents, but they should also start teaching the baby the majority language of the school.

**Especially for Nurses and Pediatricians** Eric and Jennifer have been reading about language development in children. They are convinced that because language develops naturally, they need not talk to their 6-month-old son. How do you respond? (see response, p. 184)

● **Response for Nurses and Pediatricians** (from p. 183): Although humans may be naturally inclined to communicate with words, exposure to language is necessary. You may not convince Eric and Jennifer, but at least convince them that their baby will be happier if they talk to him.

**language acquisition device (LAD)** Chomsky's term for a hypothesized mental structure that enables humans to learn language, including the basic aspects of grammar, vocabulary, and intonation.

research which finds that variations in children's language ability correlate with differences in brain activity and perceptual ability, evident months before the first words are spoken and apart from the particulars of parental input (Cristia et al., 2014). Some 5-year-olds are far more verbal than others because they were born to be so.

This perspective began soon after Skinner proposed his theory of verbal learning. Noam Chomsky (1968, 1980) and his followers felt that language is too complex to be mastered merely through step-by-step conditioning. Although behaviorists focus on variations among children in vocabulary size, Chomsky focused on similarities in language acquisition—the evolutionary universals, not the differences.

Noting that all young children master basic grammar according to a schedule, Chomsky cited *universal grammar* as evidence that humans are born with a mental structure that prepares them to seek some elements of human language. For example, everywhere, a raised tone indicates a question, and infants prefer questions to declarative statements (Soderstrom et al., 2011). This suggests that infants are wired to have conversations, and caregivers universally ask them questions long before they can answer back.

Chomsky labeled this hypothesized mental structure the **language acquisition device (LAD).** The LAD enables children, as their brains develop, to derive the rules of grammar quickly and effectively from the speech they hear every day, regardless of whether their native language is English, Thai, or Urdu.

According to theory three, language is experience-expectant, as the developing brain quickly and efficiently connects neurons to support whichever language the infant hears. Because of this experience expectancy, the various languages of the world are all logical, coherent, and systematic. Then some experience-dependent learning occurs as each brain adjusts to a particular language.

Research supports this perspective as well. As you remember, newborns are primed to listen to speech, and all infants babble *ma-ma* and *da-da* sounds (not yet referring to mother or father). No reinforcement or teaching is required; all a baby needs is time for dendrites to grow, mouth muscles to strengthen, neurons to connect, and speech to be heard. This theory might explain why poets put together phrases that they have never heard to produce novel understanding, and why people hear words in their dreams that make no sense. Thus, the language impulse may arise from the brain, not from other people.

**Same Situation, Far Apart: Before Words** The Polish babies learning sign language *(left)* and the New York infant interpreting a smile *(right)* are all doing what babies do: trying to understand communication long before they are able to talk.

Nature even provides for deaf infants. All 6-month-olds, hearing or not, prefer to look at sign language over nonlinguistic pantomime. For hearing infants, this preference disappears by 10 months, but deaf infants begin signing at that time, which is their particular expression of the universal LAD.

## A Hybrid Theory

Which of these three perspectives is correct? Perhaps all of them. In one monograph that included details and results of 12 experiments, the authors presented a hybrid (which literally means "a new creature, formed by combining other living things") of previous theories (Hollich et al., 2000). Since infants learn language to do numerous things—indicate intention, name objects, combine words, talk with caregivers, sing to themselves, express wishes, remember the past, and much more—some aspects of language learning are best explained by one theory at one age and other aspects by another theory at another age.

Since every human must learn language, nature allows variations so that the goal is attained. Ideally, caregivers talk often to infants (theory one), encourage social interaction (theory two), and appreciate innate impulses (theory three). There is no single critical period or exclusive mode for language acquisition, but rather various linguistic accomplishments are attained at many times and in many ways (Balari & Lorenzo, 2015).

A master linguist explains that "the human mind is a hybrid system," perhaps using different parts of the brain for each kind of learning (Pinker, 1999, p. 279). Another expert agrees:

> our best hope for unraveling some of the mysteries of language acquisition rests with approaches that incorporate multiple factors, that is, with approaches that incorporate not only some explicit linguistic model, but also the full range of biological, cultural, and psycholinguistic processes involved.
>
> [Tomasello, 2006, pp. 292–293]

The idea that every theory is correct may seem idealistic. However, many scientists who are working on extending and interpreting research on language acquisition arrived at a similar conclusion. They contend that language learning is neither the direct product of repeated input (behaviorism) nor the result of a specific human neurological capacity (LAD). Rather, from an evolutionary perspective, "different elements of the language apparatus may have evolved in different ways," and thus, a "piecemeal and empirical" approach is needed (Marcus & Rabagliati, 2009, p. 281).

Neuroscience is the most recent method for understanding the development of language. Many parts of the infant brain, including both hemispheres and the prefrontal cortex, some acting hierarchically and some in parallel, are involved in language learning. This again suggests a hybrid approach. One neuroscientist who details the multiple brain pathways that infants use for language begins with the same amazement that traditional linguists have expressed for decades:

> For thousands of years and across numerous cultures, human infants are able to perfectly master oral or signed language in only a few years. No other machine, be it silicon or carbon based, is able to reach the same level of expertise.
>
> [Dehaene-Lambertz, 2017, p. 48]

What conclusion can we draw from all the research on infant cognition? It is clear that infants are amazing and active learners who use many methods to advance cognition—including an understanding of objects, of affordances, and of communication. Remember that before Piaget many experts assumed that babies did not yet learn or think. How wrong they were!

Steven J. Kazlowski/Alamy

**Family Values** Every family encourages the values and abilities that their children need to be successful adults. For this family in Ecuador, that means strong legs and lungs to climb the Andes, respecting their parents, and keeping quiet unless spoken to. A "man of few words" is admired. By contrast, many North American parents babble in response to infant babble, celebrate the first spoken word, and stop their conversation to listen to an interrupting child. If a student never talks in class, or another student blurts out irrelevant questions, perhaps the professor should consider cultural background.

**WHAT HAVE YOU LEARNED?**

1. What communication abilities do infants have before they talk?

2. What aspects of early language development are universal, apparent in every culture?

3. What is typical of the first words that infants speak and the rate at which they acquire them?

4. What are the early signs of grammar in infant speech?

5. According to behaviorism, how do adults teach infants to talk?

6. According to sociocultural theory, why do infants try to communicate?

7. What is the language acquisition device?

8. What does the idea that child speech results from brain maturation imply for caregivers?

# SUMMARY

## Sensorimotor Intelligence

1. Piaget realized that very young infants are active learners who seek to understand their complex observations and experiences. The six stages of sensorimotor intelligence involve early adaptation to experience.

2. Sensorimotor intelligence begins with reflexes and ends with mental combinations. The six stages occur in pairs, with each pair characterized by a circular reaction; infants first react to their own bodies (primary), then respond to other people and things (secondary), and finally, in the stage of tertiary circular reactions, infants become more goal-oriented, creative, and experimental as "little scientists."

3. Infants gradually develop an understanding of objects. According to Piaget's classic experiments, infants understand object permanence and begin to search for hidden objects at about 8 months. Newer research, using brain scans and other new methods, finds that Piaget underestimated infant cognition.

## Information Processing

4. Another approach to understanding infant cognition involves information-processing theory, which looks at each step of the thinking process, from input to output. The perceptions of a young infant are attuned to the particular affordances, or opportunities for action, that are present in the infant's world.

5. From a baby's perspective, the world is filled with exciting affordances, and babies are eager to experience all of the opportunities for learning available to them. Adults are more cautious, and perhaps less perceptive.

6. Infant memory is fragile but not completely absent. Reminder sessions help trigger memories, and young brains learn motor sequences and respond to repeated emotions (their own and those of other people) long before explicit memory, using words.

7. Memory is multifaceted; infant amnesia is a myth. At about 9 months, many aspects of implicit memory are evident. One-year-olds can apply what they have learned to new situations.

## Language: What Develops in the First Two Years?

8. Language learning, which distinguishes the human species from other animals, is an amazing accomplishment. Many researchers try to explain how language develops.

9. Attempts to communicate are apparent in the first weeks and months, beginning with noises, facial expressions, and avid listening. Infants babble at about 6 months, understand words and gestures by 10 months, and speak their first words at about 1 year. Deaf infants make their first signs before 1 year.

10. Vocabulary builds slowly until the infant knows approximately 50 words. Then the naming explosion begins. Grammar is evident in the first holophrases, and combining words together in proper sequence is further evidence that babies learn grammar as well as vocabulary.

11. Toward the end of the second year, toddlers express wishes and emotions in short sentences. Variation is evident, in part because of caregiver attention. Some babies are already bilingual.

12. Various theories explain how infants learn language. Each major theory emphasizes different aspects of learning: that infants must be taught, that their social impulses foster language learning, and that their brains are genetically attuned to language as soon as the requisite maturation has occurred.

13. Each theory of language learning is confirmed by research. Developmental scientists find that many parts of the brain, and many strategies for learning, result in early language accomplishments.

## KEY TERMS

sensorimotor intelligence
  (p. 164)

primary circular reactions
  (p. 165)

secondary circular reactions
  (p. 166)

tertiary circular reactions
  (p. 166)

object permanence (p. 167)

"little scientist" (p. 168)

affordance (p. 170)

visual cliff (p. 170)

reminder session (p. 173)

child-directed speech (p. 175)

habituation (p. 176)

babbling (p. 176)

holophrase (p. 177)

naming explosion (p. 178)

grammar (p. 179)

mean length of utterance
  (MLU) (p. 179)

language acquisition device
  (LAD) (p. 184)

## APPLICATIONS

**1.** Elicit vocalizations from an infant—babbling if the baby is under age 1, using words if the baby is older. Write down all of the baby's communication for 10 minutes. Then ask the primary caregiver to elicit vocalizations for 10 minutes, and write these down. What differences are apparent between the baby's two attempts at communication? Compare your findings with the norms described in the chapter.

**2.** Many educators recommend that parents read to babies every day, even before 1 year of age. What theory of language develop-

ment does this reflect and why? Ask several parents whether they did so, and why or why not.

**3.** Test a toddler's ability to pretend and to imitate, as Piaget would expect. Use a doll or a toy car and pretend with it, such as feeding the doll or making the car travel. Then see whether the child will do it. This experiment can be more elaborate if the child succeeds.

# The First Two Years:
## Psychosocial Development

## What Will You Know?

1. Does a difficult newborn become a difficult child?
2. What do babies do to indicate how responsive their parents are?
3. Do infants benefit or suffer when cared for by someone other than their mother?

+ **Emotional Development**
  Early Emotions
  Toddlers' Emotions
  Temperament
  INSIDE THE BRAIN: Expressing
  Emotions

+ **The Development of Social Bonds**
  Synchrony
  Attachment
  Insecure Attachment and the
  Social Setting
  A CASE TO STUDY: Can We Bear
  This Commitment?
  Social Referencing
  Fathers as Social Partners

+ **Theories of Infant Psychosocial Development**
  Psychoanalytic Theory
  Behaviorism
  Cognitive Theory
  Evolutionary Theory
  Sociocultural Theory
  Conclusion

**M**y daughter Bethany came to visit her newest nephew, Isaac, 7 months old. She had visited him many times before, expressing joy and excitement with her voice, face, and hands. By 2 months, he always responded in kind, with big smiles and waving arms. Although this is typical behavior for babies and aunts, they both seemed overjoyed with their interaction. But at 7 months, Isaac was more hesitant and looked away, nuzzling into his mother. Later Bethany tried again, and this time Isaac kept looking and smiling.

"You like me now," she said.

"He always liked you; he was just tired," said Elissa, his mother.

"I know," Bethany told her. "I didn't take it personally."

I appreciated both daughters. Elissa sought to reassure Bethany, and Bethany knew that Isaac's reaction was not really to her. But the person I appreciated most was Isaac, responsive to people as well-loved babies should be, but newly wary and seeking maternal comfort as he grew closer to a year. Emotions change month by month in the first two years; ideally caregivers change with them.

We open this chapter by tracing infants' emotions as their brains mature and their experiences accumulate. Next we explore caregiver–infant interaction, particularly *synchrony*, *attachment*, and *social referencing*, and some theories that explain those developments.

Finally, we explore a controversy: Who should be infant caregivers and how should they respond? Families and cultures answer this question in many ways. Fortunately, as this chapter explains, despite diversity of temperament and caregiving, most people thrive, as long as their basic physical and emotional needs are met. Isaac, Elissa, and Bethany are all thriving.

## Emotional Development

In their first two years, infants progress from reactive pain and pleasure to complex patterns of social awareness (see At About This Time), a movement from basic instinctual emotions to learned emotions and then to thoughtful ones (Panksepp & Watt, 2011).

## AT ABOUT THIS TIME

### Developing Emotions

| | |
|---|---|
| Birth | Distress; Contentment |
| 6 weeks | Social smile |
| 3 months | Laughter; curiosity |
| 4 months | Full, responsive smiles |
| 4–8 months | Anger |
| 9–14 months | Fear of social events (strangers, separation from caregiver) |
| 12 months | Fear of unexpected sights and sounds |
| 18 months | Self-awareness; pride; shame; embarrassment |

As always, culture and experience influence the norms of development. This is especially true for emotional development after the first 8 months.

**Grandpa Knows Best** Does her tongue sticking out signify something wrong with her mouth or mind? Some parents might worry, but one advantage of grandparents is that they have been through it before: All babies do something with their fingers, toes, or, as here, tongue (sometimes all three together!) that seems odd but is only a temporary exploration of how their body works.

**social smile** A smile evoked by a human face, normally first evident in infants about 6 weeks after birth.

**separation anxiety** An infant's distress when a familiar caregiver leaves; most obvious between 9 and 14 months.

**stranger wariness** An infant's expression of concern—a quiet stare while clinging to a familiar person, or a look of fear—when a stranger appears.

## Early Emotions

At first, there is comfort and pain. Newborns are happy and relaxed when fed and drifting off to sleep. They cry when they are hurt or hungry, tired or frightened (as by a loud noise or a sudden loss of support).

Some infants have bouts of uncontrollable crying, called *colic*, probably the result of immature digestion; some have *reflux*, probably the result of immature swallowing. About 20 percent of babies cry "excessively," defined as more than three hours a day, more than three days a week, for more than three weeks (J. Kim, 2011).

### Smiling and Laughing

Soon, crying decreases and additional emotions become recognizable. Curiosity is evident: Infants respond to objects and experiences that are new but not too novel. Happiness is expressed by the **social smile,** evoked by a human face at about 6 weeks. (Preterm babies smile later because the social smile is affected by age since conception, not age since birth.)

Laughter builds as curiosity does; a typical 6-month-old laughs loudly upon discovering new things, particularly social experiences that balance familiarity and surprise, such as Daddy making a funny face. They prefer looking at happy faces over sad ones, even if the happy faces are not looking at them (Kim & Johnson, 2013).

### Anger and Sadness

Reactive crying and the positive emotions of joy and contentment are soon joined by negative emotions. Anger is notable at 6 months, usually triggered by frustration, such as when infants are prevented from moving or grabbing.

To investigate infants' response to frustration, researchers "crouched behind the child and gently restrained his or her arms for 2 min[utes] or until 20 s[econds] of hard crying ensued" (Mills-Koonce et al., 2011, p. 390). "Hard crying" is not rare: Infants hate to be strapped in, caged in, closed in, or even just held in place when they want to explore.

In infancy, anger is a healthy response to frustration, unlike sadness, which also appears in the first months. Sadness indicates withdrawal and is accompanied by a greater increase in the body's production of cortisol.

Since sadness produces physiological stress (measured by cortisol levels), sorrow negatively impacts the infant. All social emotions, particularly sadness and fear, affect the brain. Caregiving matters. Sad and angry infants whose mothers are depressed become fearful toddlers and depressed children (Dix & Yan, 2014). Abuse and unpredictable responses are likely among the "early adverse influences [that] have lasting effects on developing neurobiological systems in the brain" (van Goozen, 2015, p. 208).

### Fear

Fear in response to some person, thing, or situation (not just being startled) soon becomes more frequent and obvious. Two kinds of social fear are typical:

- **Separation anxiety**—clinging and crying when a familiar caregiver is about to leave. Separation anxiety is normal at age 1, intensifies by age 2, and usually subsides after that.
- **Stranger wariness**—fear of unfamiliar people, especially when they move too close, too quickly. Wariness indicates memory, so it is a positive sign.

Christopher Hope-Fitch/Getty Images

If separation anxiety remains intense after age 3, impairing a child's ability to leave home, to go to school, or to play with other children, it is considered an emotional disorder. Separation anxiety as a disorder can be diagnosed up to age 18 (American Psychiatric Association, 2013); some clinicians diagnose it in adults as well (Bögels et al., 2013).

Many typical 1-year-olds fear anything unexpected, from a flushing toilet to a popping jack-in-the-box, from closing elevator doors to the tail-wagging approach of a dog. With repeated experience and reassurance, older infants might enjoy flushing the toilet (again and again) or calling the dog (becoming angry if the dog does *not* come). Note the transition from instinct to learning to expectation (Panksepp & Watt, 2011).

Unexpected and unfamiliar human actions attract attention from infants in the second half of the first year. Often, fear changes to joy, as evident in Isaac's reaction to Bethany in this chapter's opening. In another example, infants were first acclimated to dancing to music as it normally occurs, on the beat. Then infants saw a video in which the soundtrack was mismatched with dancing. Eight- to 12-month-old babies, but not younger ones, were curious about offbeat dancing, which led the researchers to conclude that "babies know bad dancing when they see it" (Hannon et al., 2017).

**Developmentally Correct** Both Santa's smile and Olivia's grimace are appropriate reactions for people of their age. Adults playing Santa must smile no matter what, and if Olivia smiled, that would be troubling to anyone who knows about 7-month-olds. Yet every Christmas, thousands of parents wait in line to put their infants on the laps of oddly dressed, bearded strangers.

## Toddlers' Emotions

Emotions take on new strength during toddlerhood, as both memory and mobility advance. For example, throughout the second year and beyond, anger and fear become less frequent but more focused, targeted toward infuriating or terrifying experiences. Similarly, laughing and crying are louder and more discriminating.

The new strength of emotions is apparent in temper tantrums. Toddlers are famous for fury. When something angers them, they might yell, scream, cry, hit, and throw themselves on the floor. Logic is beyond them; if adults respond with anger or teasing, that makes it worse.

One child said, "I don't want my feet. Take my feet off. I don't want my feet." Her mother tried logic, which didn't work, and then said she could get a pair of scissors and cut off the offending feet. A new wail of tantrum erupted, with a loud shriek "Nooooo!" (Katrina, quoted in Vedantam, 2011).

With temper tantrums, soon sadness comes to the fore, at which time comfort—rather than acquiescence or punishment—is helpful (Green et al., 2011).

**Especially for Nurses and Pediatricians** Parents come to you concerned that their 1-year-old hides her face and holds onto them tightly whenever a stranger appears. What do you tell them? (see response, p. 192)

## Social Awareness

Temper can be seen as an expression of selfhood, as can other common toddler emotions: pride, shame, jealousy, embarrassment, disgust, and guilt. These emotions require social awareness.

Such awareness typically emerges from family interactions. For instance, in a study of infant jealousy, when mothers deliberately paid attention to another infant, babies moved closer to their mothers, bidding for attention. Their brain activity also registered social emotions (Mize et al., 2014).

Culture is crucial here, with independence valued in some families but not in others. Many North American parents encourage toddler pride (saying, "You did it yourself"—even when that is untrue), but Asian families typically cultivate modesty and shame. Such differences may still be apparent in adult personality and judgment.

**THINK CRITICALLY:** Which does your culture consider more annoying, people who brag or people who put themselves down?

**self-awareness** A person's realization that he or she is a distinct individual whose body, mind, and actions are separate from those of other people.

**LaunchPad**
macmillan learning

**Video Activity: Self-Awareness and the Rouge Test** shows the famous assessment of how and when self-awareness appears in infancy.

**My Finger, My Body, and Me** Mirror self-recognition is particularly important in her case, as this 2-year-old has a twin sister. Parents may enjoy dressing twins alike and giving them rhyming names, but each baby needs to know she is an individual, not just a twin.

**temperament** Inborn differences between one person and another in emotions, activity, and self-regulation. It is measured by the person's typical responses to the environment.

Disgust is also strongly influenced by other people as well as by maturation. According to a study that involved children of various ages, many 18-month-olds (but not younger infants) expressed disgust at touching a dead animal. No toddlers or young children, however, were yet disgusted when a teenager cursed at an elderly person—something that parents and older children often find disgusting (Stevenson et al., 2010).

Positive emotions also show social awareness in toddlerhood. For instance, toddlers spontaneously try to help a stranger who has dropped something or who is searching for a hidden object. This empathy and generosity emerges quite apart from any selfish motives (Warneken, 2015).

## Self-Awareness

In addition to social awareness, another foundation for emotional growth is **self-awareness,** the realization that one's body, mind, and activities are distinct from those of other people (Kopp, 2011). Closely following the new mobility that results from walking is an emerging sense of "me" and "mine" that leads infants to develop a new consciousness of others at about age 1.

In a classic experiment (Lewis & Brooks, 1978), 9- to 24-month-olds looked into a mirror after a dot of rouge had been surreptitiously put on their noses. If they reacted by touching the red dot on their noses, that meant they knew the mirror showed their own faces. None of the babies younger than 12 months did that, although they sometimes smiled and touched the dot on the "other" baby in the mirror.

Between 15 and 24 months, babies become self-aware, touching their own red noses with curiosity and puzzlement. Self-recognition in the mirror/rouge test (and in photographs) usually emerges with two other advances: pretending and using first-person pronouns (*I, me, mine, myself, my*) (Lewis, 2010). Thus, "an explicit and hence reflective conception of the self is apparent at the early stage of language acquisition at around the same age that infants begin to recognize themselves in mirrors" (Rochat, 2013, p. 388).

This is another example of the interplay of all the infant abilities—walking, talking, and emotional self-understanding all work together to make the 18-month-old quite unlike the 8-month-old.

## Temperament

**Temperament** is defined as the "biologically based core of individual differences in style of approach and response to the environment that is stable across time and situations" (van den Akker et al., 2010, p. 485). "Biologically based" means that these traits originate with nature, not nurture. Confirmation that temperament arises from the inborn brain comes from an analysis of the tone, duration, and intensity of infant cries after the first inoculation, before much experience outside the womb. Cry variations at this very early stage correlate with later temperament (Jong et al., 2010).

Temperament is *not* the same as personality, although temperamental inclinations may lead to personality differences. Generally, personality traits (e.g., honesty and humility) are learned, whereas temperamental traits (e.g., shyness and aggression) are genetic. [**Developmental Link:** The three domains are discussed in Chapter 1.] Of course, for every trait, nature and nurture interact as the following makes clear.

# Expressing Emotions

Brain maturation is crucial for emotional development, particularly for emotions that are in response to other people. Experience connects the amygdala and the prefrontal cortex (van Goozen, 2015), and it helps infants connect their feelings with those of other people (Missana et al., 2014).

Maturation of the cortex is crucial for the social smile and laughter in the first months of life (Konner, 2010). Jealously may arise before 6 months, when the brain expects maternal attention and the infant sees mother paying heed to another baby (Legerstee, 2013). Similar expectations and reactions occur for fear, self-awareness, and anger. Infant experience may form an adult who cries, laughs, or angers quickly.

An example of the connection between brain development and caregiving came from a study of "highly reactive" infants (i.e., those whose brains naturally reacted with intense fear, anger, and other emotions). Highly reactive 15-month-olds with responsive caregivers (not hostile or neglectful) became less fearful, less angry, and so on. By age 4, they were able to regulate their emotions, presumably because they had developed neurological links between brain excitement and emotional response. However, highly reactive toddlers whose caregivers were less responsive were often overwhelmed by later emotions (Ursache et al., 2013).

Differential susceptibility is apparent here: Innate reactions and caregiver actions *together* sculpt the brain. Both are affected by ethnicity and culture, with some parents fearful of spoiling and others sympathetic to every sign of distress.

The social smile, for instance, is tentative for almost every face at 2 months, but it soon becomes a quicker and fuller smile at the sight of a familiar, loving caregiver. This occurs because, with repeated experience, the neurons that fire together become more closely and quickly connected to each other (via dendrites).

Every experience activates and prunes neurons. Remember this with baby mice in Chapter 5: Some were licked and nuzzled by their mothers almost constantly, and some were neglected. A mother mouse's licking of her newborn babies allowed more serotonin (a neurotransmitter) to be released by the hypothalamus. That not only increased momentary pleasure (mice love being licked) but also started a chain of epigenetic responses to reduce cortisol from many parts of the brain and body, including the adrenal glands. The effects on both brain and behavior are lifelong.

For optimal development of the brain, parents need to be comforting (as with the nuzzled baby mice) but not overprotective. Fearful mothers tend to raise fearful children, but fathers who offer their infants exciting but not dangerous challenges (such as a game of chase, crawling on the floor) reduce later anxiety (Majdandžić et al., 2013).

By contrast, excessive fear and stress harms the hypothalamus, which grows more slowly if an infant is often frightened. Brain scans of children who were maltreated in infancy show abnormal responses to stress, anger, and other emotions later on, including to photographs. Some children seem resilient, but many areas of the brain (the hypothalamus, the amygdala, the HPA axis, the hippocampus, and the prefrontal cortex) are affected by abuse that begins in infancy (Bernard et al., 2014; Cicchetti, 2013a). Indeed, the entire immune system is affected as well (Hostinar et al., 2017).

Thus, all of the infant emotions begin in the brain and are affected by early experiences. Links between the amygdala—the center for fear and other emotions—and the prefrontal cortex are particularly plastic during infancy, which means that experience has a decided impact (Callaghan & Tottenham, 2016).

Although infant brains are particularly moldable, adult brains are also affected by experience. Consequently, caregiver–infant relationships occur in adults' brains, not just in their actions, and the brain activity of caregivers and of infants can be mutually reinforcing (Schore, 2015). Infant crying increases caregivers' cortisol: Some respond with rage, others with tenderness. That brain reaction in the adult affects the baby's brain. Both suffer, or thrive, from their early experiences.

Joseph Farris/CartoonStock

**Empathy Wins** Crying babies whose caregivers sympathize often become confident, accomplished, caring children. Sleep deprivation makes anyone unhappy, but this man's response is much better for both of them than anger or neglect.

 **LaunchPad**
macmillan learning

**Video: Temperament in Infancy and Adulthood** explores the unique ways infants respond to their environment.

⬤ **Especially for Nurses** Parents come to you with their fussy 3-month-old. They say they have read that temperament is "fixed" before birth, and they are worried that their child will always be difficult. What do you tell them? (see response, p. 196)

**Feliz Navidad** Not only is every language and culture distinct, but each individual also has a unique temperament. Here children watch the Cortylandia Christmas show in Madrid, Spain, where the Christmas holiday begins on December 24 and lasts through January 6 (Three Kings Day). As you see from the three fathers and children, each person has their own reaction to the same event.

⬤ **Observation Quiz** What indicates that each father has his own child on his shoulders? (see answer, p. 196) ⬆

Denis Doyle/Getty Images

## Temperament over the Years

In laboratory studies of temperament, infants are exposed to events that are frightening or attractive. Four-month-olds might see spinning mobiles or hear unusual sounds. Older babies might confront a noisy, moving robot or a clown who approaches quickly. During such experiences, some children laugh, some cry, others are quiet, and still others exhibit some combination of these reactions that might be signs of one of four types of babies: easy (40 percent), difficult (10 percent), slow-to-warm-up (15 percent), and hard-to-classify (35 percent).

These four categories originate from the *New York Longitudinal Study* (NYLS). Begun in the 1960s, the NYLS was the first large study to recognize that each newborn has distinct inborn traits (Thomas & Chess, 1977). According to the NYLS, by 3 months, infants manifest nine traits that cluster into the four categories just listed.

Although the NYLS began a rich research endeavor, its nine dimensions have not held up in later studies. Generally, only three (not nine) dimensions of temperament are found (Hirvonen et al., 2013; van den Akker et al., 2010; Degnan et al., 2011), each of which affects later personality and school performance. The following three dimensions of temperament are apparent:

> Effortful control (able to regulate attention and emotion, to self-soothe)
> Negative mood (fearful, angry, unhappy)
> Exuberant (active, social, not shy)

Each of these dimensions is associated with distinctive brain patterns as well as behavior. The last of these (exuberance versus shyness) is most strongly traced to genes (Wolfe et al., 2014).

One longitudinal study analyzed temperament in children as they grew, at 4, 9, 14, 24, and 48 months and in middle childhood, adolescence, and adulthood. The scientists designed laboratory experiments with specifics appropriate for the age of the children, collected detailed reports from the mothers and later from the participants themselves, and gathered observational data and physiological evidence, including brain scans.

Past data on each person were reevaluated each time, and cross-sectional and international studies were considered (Fox et al., 2001, 2005, 2013; Hane et al., 2008; Williams et al., 2010; Jarcho et al., 2013).

Half of the participants did not change much over time, reacting the same way and having similar brain-wave patterns when confronted with frightening experiences. Curiously, the participants most likely to change from infancy to age 4 were the inhibited, fearful ones. Least likely to change were the exuberant babies (see Figure 7.1). Apparently, adults coax frightened infants to be brave but let exuberant children stay happy.

The researchers found unexpected gender differences. As teenagers, the formerly inhibited boys were more likely than the average adolescent to use drugs, but the inhibited girls were less likely to do so (Williams et al., 2010). The most likely explanation is cultural: Shy boys seek to become less anxious by using drugs, but shy girls may be more accepted as they are, or more likely to obey their parents.

Examination of these children in adulthood found, again, intriguing differences between brain and behavior. Those who were inhibited in childhood still showed, in brain scans, evidence of their infant temperament. That confirms that genes affected their traits.

However, learning (specifically cognitive control) was evident: Their behavior was similar to those with a more outgoing temperament, unless other factors caused serious emotional problems. Apparently, most of them had learned to override their initial temperamental reactions—not to erase their innate impulses, but to keep them from impairing adult action (Jarcho et al., 2013).

Continuity and change were also seen in another study, which found that angry infants were likely to make their mothers hostile toward them, and, if that happened, such infants became antisocial children. However, if the mothers were loving and patient despite the difficult temperament of the children, hostile traits were not evident later on (Pickles et al., 2013).

Infants with difficult temperaments are at risk for later emotional problems, however, especially if their mothers had a difficult pregnancy and birth and became depressed or anxious (Garthus-Niegel et al., 2017). This is another example of the cascade of development—no single factor determines later outcomes, but several problems combine to increase risk.

Other studies confirm that difficult infants often become easier—*if* their parents provide excellent, patient care (Belsky & Pluess, 2009). How could this be? Some scientists suggest that because fussy and scared children often come to the parents for comfort or reassurance, they are particularly likely to flourish with responsive parenting, but they wither if their parents are rejecting (Stupica et al., 2011). This is differential susceptibility again. If the home is chaotic and the parenting erratic, inborn temperament traits are evident, but if the family is responsive, temperament seems less heritable (Saudino & Micalizzi, 2015).

All the research finds that traces of childhood temperament endure, blossoming into adult personality, but it also confirms that innate tendencies are only part of the story. Context always shapes behavior.

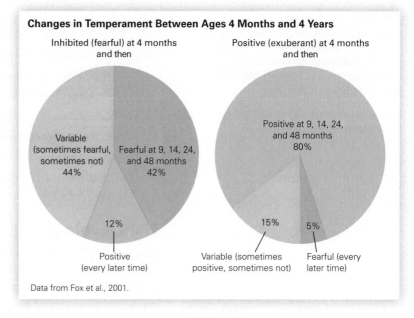

**Changes in Temperament Between Ages 4 Months and 4 Years**

Data from Fox et al., 2001.

**FIGURE 7.1**

**Do Babies' Temperaments Change?** Sometimes it is possible— especially if they were fearful babies. Adults who provide reassurance help children overcome fearfulness. If fearful children do not change, it is not known whether that's because their parents are not sufficiently reassuring (nurture) or because the babies themselves are temperamentally more fearful (nature).

**Faith, Not Fear** It is natural for infants to be frightened when swung upside down, but it is also common for fathers to teach their offspring the joy of safe adventures. This boy is unlikely to be a shy, timid toddler, thanks to his active, loving father.

● **Response for Nurses** (from p. 194): It's too soon to tell. Temperament is not truly "fixed" but variable, especially in the first few months. Many "difficult" infants become happy, successful adolescents and adults, if their parents are responsive.

● **Answer to Observation Quiz** (from p. 194): Watch the facial expressions.

> **WHAT HAVE YOU LEARNED?**
>
> **1.** What are the first emotions to appear in infants?
>
> **2.** What experiences trigger anger and sadness in infants?
>
> **3.** What do typical 1-year-olds fear?
>
> **4.** How do emotions differ between the first and second year of life?
>
> **5.** What is the significance of the toddler's reaction to seeing him- or herself in a mirror?
>
> **6.** Do traits of temperament endure or change as development continues?
>
> **7.** Give some examples of how context might affect temperament.

# The Development of Social Bonds

Humans are, by nature, social creatures, and thus nurture (other people) is crucial. The specifics during infancy depend on the age of the baby, with three kinds of social interactions—synchrony, attachment, and social referencing—each evident in the first two years of life (see Visualizing Development, p. 203).

## Synchrony

**synchrony** A coordinated, rapid, and smooth exchange of responses between a caregiver and an infant.

Early parent–child interactions are described as **synchrony,** a mutual exchange that requires split-second timing. Metaphors for synchrony are often musical—a waltz, a jazz duet—to emphasize that each partner must be attuned to the other, with moment-by-moment responses. Synchrony becomes more frequent and elaborate as the infant matures (Feldman, 2007).

To be specific, long before they can reach out and grab, infants respond excitedly to caregiver attention by waving their arms. Remember that focus is best on objects about 10 inches away, so adults need to move close so that the infant can make eye contact. Babies are delighted if a waving arm can touch a face or, even better, a hand can grab hair. This is the eagerness to "make interesting events last" that was described in Chapter 6.

**Open Wide** Synchrony is evident worldwide. Everywhere, babies watch their parents carefully, hoping for exactly what these two parents—each from quite different cultures—express, and responding with such delight that adults relish these moments.

Guylain Doyle/Getty Images

**Hold Me Tight** Synchrony is evident not only in facial expressions and noises but also in body positions. Note the mother's strong hands and extended arms, and her daughter's tucked in legs and arms. This is a caregiving dance that both have executed many times.

For their part, adults open their eyes wide, raise their eyebrows, smack their lips, and emit nonsense sounds. Hair-grabbing might make adults bob their head back and forth, in a playful attempt to shake off the grab, to the infants' joy, as Isaac did to Bethany in the chapter opening. That is synchrony.

## Both Partners Active

Detailed research reveals the symbiosis of adult–infant partnerships. Adults rarely smile at young infants until the infants smile at them, several weeks after birth. That tentative baby smile is like a switch that turns on the adult, who usually grins broadly and talks animatedly (Lavelli & Fogel, 2005).

Direct observation reveals synchrony; anyone can see it when watching a caregiver play with an infant who is far too young to talk. It is also evident in computer measurement of the millisecond timing of smiles, arched eyebrows, and so on (Messinger et al., 2010), as well as in measurements that are not visible, such as heart rate and brain waves.

Synchrony is a powerful learning experience for the new human. In every interaction, infants read others' emotions and develop social skills, such as taking turns and watching expressions.

Synchrony usually begins with adults imitating infants (not vice versa) in tone and rhythm. With young infants, adults should more often be responsive to their babies rather than vice versa (Beebe et al., 2016). Adults respond to barely perceptible infant facial expressions and body motions. This helps infants connect their internal state with behaviors that are understood within their family and culture.

This relationship is crucial when the infant is at medical risk. The necessity of time-consuming physical care might overwhelm concern about psychosocial needs, yet those needs are as important for long-term health as are the biological ones (Newnham et al., 2009). Responsiveness to the individual, not simply to the impaired human, leads to a strong, mutual love between parents and child (Solomon, 2012).

**still-face technique** An experimental practice in which an adult keeps his or her face unmoving and expressionless in face-to-face interaction with an infant.

> **THINK CRITICALLY:** What will happen if no one plays with an infant?

**attachment** According to Ainsworth, "an affectional tie" that an infant forms with a caregiver—a tie that binds them together in space and endures over time.

## Neglected Synchrony

Experiments involving the **still-face technique** suggest that synchrony is experience-expectant (needed for normal growth) (Tronick, 1989; Tronick & Weinberg, 1997). [**Developmental Link:** Experience-expectant and experience-dependent brain function are described in Chapter 5.]

In still-face studies, at first an infant faces an adult who responds while two video cameras simultaneously record their interpersonal reactions. Frame-by-frame analysis reveals that parents instinctively synchronize their responses to the infants' movements, with exaggerated tone and expression. Babies reciprocate with smiles and flailing limbs.

Then the adult stops all expression on cue, staring quietly with a "still face" for a minute or two. Sometimes by 2 months, and clearly by 6 months, infants are upset when their parents are unresponsive. Babies frown, fuss, drool, look away, kick, cry, or suck their fingers. By 5 months, they also vocalize, as if to say, "React to me" (Goldstein et al., 2009).

Many studies reach the same conclusion: Synchrony is experience-expectant, not simply experience-dependent. Responsiveness aids psychosocial and biological development, evident in heart rate, weight gain, and brain maturation. Particularly in the first year, mothers who are depressed and anxious are less likely to synchronize their responses, and then babies become less able to respond to social cues (Atzil et al., 2014).

For example, one study looked in detail at 4-month-old infants during and immediately after the still-face episode (Montirosso et al., 2015). The researchers found three clusters, which they called "socially engaged" (33 percent), "disengaged" (60 percent), and "negatively engaged" (7 percent).

When the mothers were still-faced, the socially engaged babies remained active, looking around at other things. When the still face was over, they quickly reengaged. The disengaged group became passive, taking longer to return to normal. The negatively engaged babies were angry, crying even after the still face ended.

The mothers of each type differed, with the engaged mothers matching the infants' actions (bobbing heads, opening mouth, and so on) and the negative mothers almost never matching and sometimes expressing anger that their baby cried (Montirosso et al., 2015). A lack of synchrony is a troubling sign.

## Attachment

Responsive and mutual relationships are important throughout childhood and beyond. However, once infants can walk, the moment-by-moment, face-to-face synchrony is less common. Instead, **attachment** becomes evident.

Attachment is the connection between one person and another, measured by how they respond to each other. Research on mother–infant attachment began with John Bowlby (1983) in England and Mary Ainsworth (1967) in Uganda. It has now been studied on every continent and in virtually every nation, in both atypical populations (e.g., infants with Down syndrome, autism spectrum disorder, and so on) and typical ones. Attachment is lifelong, beginning before birth and influencing relationships during early and late childhood, adolescence, and adulthood (e.g., Simpson & Rholes, 2015; Grossmann et al., 2014; Tan et al., 2016; Hunter & Maunder, 2016). (See At About This Time.)

Attachment is also universal, part of the inborn social nature of the human species, with specific manifestations dependent on the culture and age. For instance, Ugandan mothers never kiss their infants, but they often massage them, contrary to Westerners. Adults may phone their mothers every day—even when

## AT ABOUT THIS TIME

### Stages of Attachment

| | |
|---|---|
| Birth to 6 weeks | *Preattachment.* Newborns signal, via crying and body movements, that they need others. When people respond positively, the newborn is comforted and learns to seek more interaction. Newborns are also primed by brain patterns to recognize familiar voices and faces. |
| 6 weeks to 8 months | *Attachment in the making.* Infants respond preferentially to familiar people by smiling, laughing, babbling. Their caregivers' voices, touch, expressions, and gestures are comforting, often overriding the infant's impulse to cry. Trust (Erikson) develops. |
| 8 months to 2 years | *Classic secure attachment.* Infants greet the primary caregiver, play happily when he or she is present, show separation anxiety when the caregiver leaves. Both infant and caregiver seek to be close to each other (proximity) and frequently look at each other (contact). In many caregiver–infant pairs, physical touch (patting, holding, caressing) is frequent. |
| 2 to 6 years | *Attachment as launching pad.* Young children seek their caregiver's praise and reassurance as their social world expands. Interactive conversations and games (hide-and-seek, object play, reading, pretending) are common. Children expect caregivers to comfort and entertain. |
| 6 to 12 years | *Mutual attachment.* Children seek to make their caregivers proud by learning whatever adults want them to learn, and adults reciprocate. In concrete operational thought (Piaget), specific accomplishments are valued by adults and children. |
| 12 to 18 years | *New attachment figures.* Teenagers explore and make friendships independent from parents, using their working models of earlier attachments as a base. With formal operational thinking (Piaget), shared ideals and goals become influential. |
| 18 years on | *Attachment revisited.* Adults develop relationships with others, especially relationships with romantic partners and their own children, influenced by earlier attachment patterns. Past insecure attachments from childhood can be repaired rather than repeated, although this does not always happen. |

Information from Grobman, 2008.

the mothers are a thousand miles away. Or attached adults may sit in the same room of a large house, each reading quietly.

In recent decades, an application called *attachment parenting* has prioritized the mother–infant relationship during the first three years of life far more than Ainsworth or Bowlby did (Sears & Sears, 2001; Komisar, 2017). Some experts suggest that this approach has come too far from the original message of the research (Ennis, 2014). The basic criticism of attachment parenting is that it mandates that mothers are always nearby (co-sleeping, "wearing" the baby in a wrap or sling, breast-feeding on demand). That creates two problems: (1) Mothers feel guilty if they are not available 24/7, and (2) other caregivers (alloparents) are less appreciated.

## Signs of Attachment

Infants show their attachment through *proximity-seeking* (such as approaching and following their caregivers) and through *contact-maintaining* (such as touching,

**Stay in Touch** In early infancy, physical contact is often part of secure attachment. No wonder many happy babies travel next to their caregivers in slings, wraps, and snuggles. Note that attachment is mutual—she holds on to the thumb that her father provides.

**secure attachment** A relationship in which an infant obtains both comfort and confidence from the presence of his or her caregiver.

**insecure-avoidant attachment** A pattern of attachment in which an infant avoids connection with the caregiver, as when the infant seems not to care about the caregiver's presence, departure, or return.

**insecure-resistant/ambivalent attachment** A pattern of attachment in which an infant's anxiety and uncertainty are evident, as when the infant becomes very upset at separation from the caregiver and both resists and seeks contact on reunion.

**disorganized attachment** A type of attachment that is marked by an infant's inconsistent reactions to the caregiver's departure and return.

snuggling, and holding). Those attachment expressions are evident when a baby cries if the caregiver closes the door when going to the bathroom, or fusses if a back-facing car seat prevents the baby from seeing the parent.

To maintain contact when driving in a car, some caregivers in the front seat reach back to give a hand to reassure the baby, or they install a mirror angled so that driver and baby can see each other. Some caregivers take the baby into the bathroom: One mother complained that she hadn't been alone in the bathroom for two years (Senior, 2014). Contact need not be physical: Visual or verbal connections are often sufficient.

Attachment is mutual. Caregivers often keep a watchful eye on their baby, initiating contact with expressions, gestures, and sounds. Before going to sleep at midnight they might tiptoe to the crib to gaze at their sleeping infant, or, in daytime, absentmindedly smooth their toddler's hair.

## Secure and Insecure Attachment

Attachment is classified into four types: A, B, C, and D (see Table 7.1). Infants with **secure attachment** (type B) feel comfortable and confident. The caregiver is a *base for exploration*, providing assurance and enabling discovery. A toddler might, for example, scramble down from the caregiver's lap to play with an intriguing toy but periodically look back and vocalize (contact-maintaining) or bring the toy to the caregiver for inspection (proximity-seeking).

The caregiver's presence gives the child courage to explore; the caregiver's departure causes distress; the caregiver's return elicits positive social contact (such as smiling or hugging) and then more playing. This balanced reaction—being concerned but not overwhelmed by comings and goings—indicates security.

By contrast, insecure attachment (types A and C) is characterized by fear, anxiety, anger, or indifference. Some insecure children play independently without maintaining contact; this is **insecure-avoidant attachment** (type A). The opposite reaction is **insecure-resistant/ambivalent attachment** (type C). Children with this type of attachment cling to their caregivers and are angry at being left.

Early research was on mothers and infants. Later, fathers and other caregivers were included. They also may have secure or insecure attachments to an infant, and studies explored the role of infant temperament—which has some effect but does not determine attachment status (Groh et al., 2017).

Ainsworth's original schema differentiated only types A, B, and C. Later researchers discovered a fourth category (type D), **disorganized attachment.** Type D infants may shift suddenly from hitting to kissing their mothers, from staring blankly to crying hysterically, from pinching themselves to freezing in place.

Among the general population, almost two-thirds of infants are secure (type B). About one-third of infants are insecure, either indifferent (type A) or unduly anxious (type C). About 5 to 10 percent of infants fit into none of these categories; they are disorganized (type D), with no consistent strategy for social interaction, even avoidance or resistance. Sometimes they become hostile and aggressive, difficult for anyone to relate to (Lyons-Ruth et al., 1999).

Unlike the first three types, disorganized infants have elevated levels of cortisol in reaction to stress (Bernard & Dozier, 2010). A meta-analysis of 42 studies of more than 4,000 infants found that insecure attachment and especially disorganized attachment predict emotional problems, both externalizing (such as aggression) and internalizing (such as depression) (Groh et al., 2012).

## TABLE 7.1

### Patterns of Infant Attachment

| Type | Name of Pattern | In Playroom | Mother Leaves | Mother Returns | Toddlers* (%) |
|------|-----------------|-------------|---------------|----------------|---------------|
| A | Insecure-avoidant | Child plays happily. | Child continues playing. | Child ignores her. | 10–20 |
| B | Secure | Child plays happily. | Child pauses, is not as happy. | Child welcomes her, returns to play. | 50–70 |
| C | Insecure-resistant/ ambivalent | Child clings, is preoccupied with mother. | Child is unhappy, may stop playing. | Child is angry; may cry, hit mother, cling. | 10–20 |
| D | Disorganized | Child is cautious. | Child may stare or yell; looks scared, confused. | Child acts oddly; may scream, hit self, throw things. | 5–10 |

*Percents vary, depending on culture and personality. These are for typical children; some atypical groups have fewer secure infants.

## Measuring Attachment

Ainsworth (1973) developed a now-classic laboratory procedure called the **Strange Situation** to measure attachment. In a well-equipped playroom, an infant is observed for eight episodes, each lasting no more than three minutes. First, the child and mother are together. Next, according to a set sequence, the mother and then a stranger come and go. Infants' responses to their mother indicate which type of attachment they have formed.

Researchers are trained to distinguish types A, B, C, and D. They focus on the following:

> *Exploration of the toys.* A secure toddler plays happily.
> *Reaction to the caregiver's departure.* A secure toddler notices when the caregiver leaves and shows some sign of missing him or her.
> *Reaction to the caregiver's return.* A secure toddler welcomes the caregiver's reappearance, usually seeking contact, and then plays again.

Research measuring attachment has revealed that some behaviors that might seem normal are, in fact, a sign of insecurity. For instance, an infant who clings to the caregiver and refuses to explore the toys might be type C. Likewise, adults

**Strange Situation** A laboratory procedure for measuring attachment by evoking infants' reactions to the stress of various adults' comings and goings in an unfamiliar playroom.

**Excited, Troubled, Comforted** This sequence is repeated daily for 1-year-olds, which is why the same sequence is replicated to measure attachment. As you see, toys are no substitute for mother's comfort if the infant or toddler is secure, as this one seems to be. Some, however, cry inconsolably or throw toys angrily when left alone.

**THINK CRITICALLY:** Is the Strange Situation a valid way to measure attachment in every culture, or is it biased toward the Western idea of the ideal mother–child relationship?

who say their childhood was happy and their mother was a saint, especially if they provide few specific memories, might be insecure. And young children who are immediately friendly to strangers may never have formed a secure attachment (Tarullo et al., 2011).

## Insecure Attachment and the Social Setting

At first, developmentalists expected secure attachment to "predict all the outcomes reasonably expected from a well-functioning personality" (Thompson & Raikes, 2003, p. 708). But this expectation turned out to be naive.

Securely attached infants *are* more likely to become secure toddlers, socially competent preschoolers, high-achieving schoolchildren, and capable parents. Attachment affects early brain development, one reason these outcomes occur (Diamond & Fagundes, 2010). But insecure attachment does not always lead to later problems (Keller, 2014), and the links from one generation to another are weaker than originally thought (Fearon & Roisman, 2017).

Attachment forms in infancy (see Table 7.2), but it may change when the family context changes, such as a new caregiver who is unusually responsive or abusive. The underlying premise—that responsive early parenting buffers stress and encourages exploration—seems valid. However, attachment behaviors in the Strange Situation provide only one measurement of the quality of the parent–child relationship.

### Insights from Romania

No scholar doubts that close human relationships should develop in the first year of life and that the lack of such relationships risks dire consequences. Unfortunately, thousands of children born in Romania are proof.

When Romanian dictator Nicolae Ceausesçu forbade birth control and abortions in the 1980s, illegal abortions became the leading cause of death for Romanian women aged 15 to 45 (Verona, 2003), and 170,000 children were abandoned and sent to crowded, impersonal, state-run orphanages (Marshall, 2014). The children were severely deprived of social contact, experiencing virtually no synchrony, play, or conversation.

---

### TABLE 7.2

#### Predictors of Attachment Type

*Secure* **attachment (type B) is more likely if:**
- The parent is usually sensitive and responsive to the infant's needs.
- The infant–parent relationship is high in synchrony.
- The infant's temperament is "easy."
- The parents are not stressed about income, other children, or their marriage.
- The parents have a working model of secure attachment to their own parents.

*Insecure* **attachment is more likely if:**
- The parent mistreats the child. (Neglect increases type A; abuse increases types C and D.)
- The mother is mentally ill. (Paranoia increases type D; depression increases type C.)
- The parents are highly stressed about income, other children, or their marriage. (Parental stress increases types A and D.)
- The parents are intrusive and controlling. (Parental domination increases type A.)
- The parents have alcohol use disorder. (Father with alcoholism increases type A; mother with alcoholism increases type D.)
- The child's temperament is "difficult." (Difficult children tend to be type C.)
- The child's temperament is "slow-to-warm-up." (This correlates with type A.)

# Developing Attachment

Attachment begins at birth and continues lifelong. Much depends not only on the ways in which parents and babies bond, but also on the quality and consistency of caregiving, the safety and security of the home environment, and individual and family experience. While the patterns set in infancy may echo in later life, they are not determinative.

## HOW MANY CHILDREN ARE SECURELY ATTACHED?

The specific percentages of children who are secure and insecure vary by culture, parent responsiveness, context, and specific temperament and needs of both the child and the caregiver. Generally, about a third of all 1-year-olds seem insecure.

| 50–70% | 10–20% | 10–20% | 5–10% |
|---|---|---|---|
| Secure Attachment (Type B) | Avoidant Attachment (Type A) | Ambivalent Attachment (Type C) | Disorganized Attachment (Type D) |

## ATTACHMENT IN THE STRANGE SITUATION MAY INFLUENCE RELATIONSHIPS THROUGH THE LIFE SPAN

Attachment patterns formed in infancy affect adults lifelong, but later experiences of love and rejection may change early patterns. Researchers measure attachment by examining children's behaviors in the Strange Situation where they are separated from their parent and play in a room with an unfamiliar caregiver. These early patterns can influence later adult relationships. As life goes on, people become more or less secure, avoidant, or disorganized.

**Securely Attached [Type B]**
In the Strange Situation, children are able to separate from caregiver but prefer caregiver to strangers.

> Later in life, they tend to have supportive relationships and positive self-concept.

**Insecure-Avoidant [Type A]**
In the Strange Situation, children avoid caregiver.

> Later in life, they tend to be aloof in personal relationships, loners who are lonely.

**Insecure-Resistant/Ambivalent [Type C]**
In the Strange Situation, children appear upset and worried when separated from caregiver; they may hit or cling.

> Later in life, their relationships may be angry, stormy, unpredictable. They have few long-term friendships.

**Disorganized [Type D]**
In the Strange Situation, children appear angry, confused, erratic, or fearful.

> Later in life, they can demonstrate odd behavior—including sudden emotions. They are at risk for serious psychological disorders.

## THE CONTINUUM OF ATTACHMENT

Avoidance and anxiety occur along a continuum. Neither genes nor cultural variations were understood when the Strange Situation was first developed (in 1965). Some contemporary researchers believe the link between childhood attachment and adult personality is less straightforward than this table suggests.

Low Avoidance

Secure    Resistant

Low Anxiety    High Anxiety

Avoidant    Disorganized

High Avoidance

**Now Adults** These three infants were photographed in Romania in 1990. They were later adopted by Western families and now, as adults, may or may not carry emotional and cognitive scars.

● ● **Observation Quiz** What three possible dangers do you see? (see answer, p. 207) ➜

Josef Polleross/The Image Works

In the two years after Ceausescu was ousted and killed in 1989, thousands of those children were adopted by North American, western European, and Australian families. Those who were adopted before 6 months of age fared best; the adoptive parents established synchrony via play and caregiving. Most of these children developed well. Many of those adopted between 6 and 18 months also fared well.

For those adopted later, early signs were encouraging: Skinny infants gained weight and grew faster than other children, developing motor skills they had lacked (H. Park et al., 2011). However, if social deprivation had lasted a year or more, their emotions and intellect suffered.

Many were overly friendly to strangers, a sign of insecure attachment as previously mentioned. At age 11, their average IQ was only 85, which is 15 points lower than the statistical norm. The older they had been at adoption, the worse their cognition was (Rutter et al., 2010). Some became impulsive, angry teenagers. Apparently, the stresses of adolescence and emerging adulthood exacerbated the cognitive and social strains of growing up (Merz & McCall, 2011).

These children are now adults, many with serious emotional or conduct problems (Sonuga-Barke et al., 2017). Other research on children adopted nationally and internationally finds that many develop quite well, but every stress—from rejection in infancy to early institutionalization to the circumstances of the adoption process—makes it more difficult for the infant to become a happy, well-functioning adult (Grotevant & McDermott, 2014).

Romania no longer permits international adoption, even though some infants are still institutionalized. Research confirms that early emotional deprivation, not genes or nutrition, is their greatest problem. Romanian infants develop best in their own families, second best in foster families, and worst in institutions (Nelson et al., 2014). As best we know, this applies to infants everywhere: Families usually nurture their babies better than strangers who are not emotionally connected. The more years children spend in hospitals and orphanages, the more risk of becoming socially and intellectually impaired (Julian, 2013).

Fortunately, many institutions have improved or have been shuttered, although an estimated 8 million children are in orphanages worldwide (Marshal, 2014). More-recent adoptees are not as impaired as those Romanian orphans (Grotevant & McDermott, 2014). Many families with adopted children are as strongly attached as any biological family, as shown by the following.

## Can We Bear This Commitment?

Parents and children capture my attention, wherever they are. Today I saw one mother ignoring her stroller-bound toddler on a crowded subway (I wanted to tell her to talk to her child) and another mother breast-feed a happy 7-month-old in a public park (which was illegal three decades ago). I look for signs of secure or insecure attachment—the contact-maintaining and proximity-seeking moves that parents do, seemingly unaware that they are responding to primordial depths of human love.

I particularly observe families I know. I am struck by the powerful bond between parent and child, as strong (or stronger) in adoptive families as in genetic ones.

One adoptive couple is Macky and Nick. I see them echoing my own experiences with my biological daughters. Two examples: When Alice was a few days old, I overheard Nick phone another parent, asking which detergent is best for washing baby clothes. That reminded me that I also switched detergents for my newborn. When Macky was engrossed in conversation, Nick interrupted to insist that it was time to get the girls home for their nap. Parents everywhere do the same—with one parent telling the other parent it is time to get the children home.

My appreciation of their attachment was cemented by a third incident. In Macky's words:

I'll never forget the Fourth of July at the spacious home of my mother-in-law's best friend. It was a perfect celebration on a perfect day. Kids frolicked in the pool. Parents socialized nearby, on the sun-drenched lawn or inside the cool house. Many guests had published books on parenting; we imagined they admired our happy, thriving family.

My husband and I have two daughters, Alice who was then 7 and Penelope who was 4. They learned to swim early and are always the first to jump in the pool and the last to leave. Great children, and doesn't that mean great parents?

After hours of swimming, the four of us scrambled up to dry land. I went inside to the library to talk with my father, while most people enjoyed hot dogs, relish, mustard, and juicy watermelon.

Suddenly we heard a heart-chilling wail. Panicked, I raced to the pool's edge to see the motionless body of a small child who had gone unnoticed underwater for too long. His blue-face was still. Someone was giving CPR. His mother kept wailing, panicked, pleading, destroyed. I had a shameful thought—thank God that is not my child.

He lived. He regained his breath and was whisked away by ambulance. The party came to a quick close. We four, skin tingling from the summer sun, hearts beating from the near-death of a child who was my kids' playmate an hour before, drove away.

Turning to Nick, I asked, "Can we bear this commitment we have made? Can we raise our children in the face of all hazards—some we try to prevent, others beyond our control?"

That was five years ago. Our children are flourishing. Our confidence is strong and so are our emotions. But it takes only a moment to recognize just how entwined our well-being is with our children and how fragile life is. We are deeply grateful.

**A Grateful Family** This family photo shows (from *left* to *right*) Nick, Penelope, Macky, and Alice with their dog Cooper. When they adopted Alice as a newborn, the parents said, "This is a miracle we feared would never happen."

Many nations now restrict international adoptions, in part because some children were literally snatched from their biological parents to be sent abroad. According to government records, the number of international adoptees in the United States was 6,441 in 2014, down from 22,884 in 2004.

Those statistics are influenced more by international politics than by infant needs. Some infants in every nation are deprived of healthy interaction, sometimes within their own families. Ideally, no infant is institutionalized, but if that ideal is not reached, institutions need to change so that psychological health is as important as physical health (McCall, 2013).

## Social Referencing

**Social referencing** refers to seeking emotional responses or information from other people, much as a student might consult a dictionary or other reference work.

**social referencing** Seeking information about how to react to an unfamiliar or ambiguous object or event by observing someone else's expressions and reactions. That other person becomes a social reference.

**Rotini Pasta?** Look again. Every family teaches their children to relish delicacies that other people avoid. Examples are bacon (not in Arab nations), hamburgers (not in India), and, as shown here, a witchetty grub. This Australian aboriginal boy is about to swallow an insect larva.

Someone's reassuring glance, cautionary words, or a facial expression of alarm, pleasure, or dismay—those are social references.

Even at 8 months, infants notice where other people are looking and use that information to look in the same direction themselves (Tummeltshammer et al., 2014). After age 1, when infants can walk and are "little scientists," their need to consult others becomes urgent as well as more accurate.

Toddlers search for clues in gazes, faces, and body position, paying close attention to emotions and intentions. They focus on their familiar caregivers, but they also use relatives, other children, and even strangers to help them assess objects and events. They are remarkably selective, noticing that some strangers are reliable references and others are not (Fusaro & Harris, 2013).

Social referencing has many practical applications for the infant. Consider mealtime. Caregivers the world over smack their lips, pretend to taste, and say "yum-yum," encouraging toddlers to eat beets, liver, or spinach. Toddlers read expressions, insisting on the foods that the adults *really* like. If mother likes it, and presents it on the spoon, then they eat it—otherwise not (Shutts et al., 2013).

Through this process, some children develop a taste for raw fish or curried goat or smelly cheese—foods that children in other cultures refuse. Similarly, toddlers use social cues to understand the difference between real and pretend eating, as well as to learn which objects, emotions, and activities are forbidden.

## Fathers as Social Partners

Synchrony, attachment, and social referencing are sometimes more apparent with fathers than with mothers. Indeed, fathers often elicit more smiles and laughter from their infants than mothers do. They tend to play more exciting games, swinging and chasing, while mothers do more caregiving and comforting (Fletcher et al., 2013).

Although these generalities hold, and although women do more child care than men in every nation, both parents often work together to raise their children (Shwalb et al., 2013). One researcher who studied many families reports "fathers and mothers showed patterns of striking similarity: they touched, looked, vocalized, rocked, and kissed their newborns equally" (Parke, 2013, p. 121). Differences

**Not Manly?** Where did that idea come from? Fathers worldwide provide excellent care for their toddlers and enjoy it, evident in the United States *(left)* and India *(right)* and in every other nation.

were apparent from one couple to another, but not from one gender to another—except for smiling (women did it more).

Usually, mothers are caregivers and fathers are playmates, but not always. Each couple, given their circumstances (perhaps immigrant or same-sex), finds some way to help their infant thrive (Lamb, 2010). Traditional mother–father roles may be switched, with no harm to the baby (Parke, 2013).

Another study, this one of U.S. parents having a second child, found that mothers used slightly more techniques to soothe their crying infants than fathers did (7.7 versus 5.9), but the study also found that mothers were less distressed by infant crying if their partners were active soothers (Dayton et al., 2015). Women generally respond more intensely to infant cries than men do, but this varies by parental status (Parsons et al., 2017; Rigo et al., 2017).

As with humans of all ages, social contexts are influential: Fathers are influenced by other fathers (Roopnarine & Hossain, 2013; Qin & Chang, 2013). Thus, fathers of every ethnic group may be aware of what other men are doing, and that affects their own behavior. Stress decreases parent involvement for both sexes. Particularly if income is low, fathers sometimes choose to be uninvolved, a choice less open to mothers (Roopnarine & Hossain, 2013; Qin & Chang, 2013).

Close father–infant relationships teach infants (especially boys) appropriate expressions of emotion, particularly anger. The results may endure: Teenagers are less likely to lash out at friends and authorities if, as infants, they experienced a warm, responsive relationship with their father (Hoeve et al., 2011).

It is a stereotype that African American, Latin American, and Asian American fathers are less nurturing and stricter than other men (Parke, 2013). The opposite may be more accurate. Within the United States, contemporary fathers in all ethnic groups are, typically, more involved with their children than their own fathers were.

A constructive parental alliance can take many forms, but it cannot be taken for granted, no matter what the family configuration. Single-parent families, same-sex families, grandparent families, and nuclear families all function best when caregivers cooperate. No form is always constructive. [**Developmental Link:** Family forms are discussed in Chapter 13.]

Family members affect each other. Paternal depression correlates with maternal depression and with sad, angry, disobedient toddlers (see Figure 7.2). Cause and consequence are intertwined. When anyone is depressed or hostile, everyone (mother, father, baby, sibling) needs help.

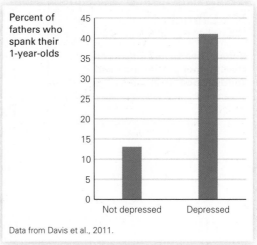

Data from Davis et al., 2011.

**FIGURE 7.2**

**Shame on Who?** Not on the toddlers, who are naturally curious and careless, but maybe not on the fathers either. Both depression and spanking are affected by financial stress, marital conflict, and cultural norms. Who is responsible for those?

**Answer to Observation Quiz** (from p. 204) Social isolation (the sheet around the crib), lead poisoning (note that two babies are biting the painted bars), and injured limbs and even strangulation (note the bent crib slats, farther apart than U.S. law allows).

## WHAT HAVE YOU LEARNED?

1. Why does synchrony affect early emotional development?

2. How is proximity-seeking and contact-maintaining attachment expressed by infants and caregivers?

3. What is the difference in behavior of infants in each of the four types of attachment?

4. How might each of the four types of attachment be expressed in adulthood?

5. What has been learned from the research on Romanian orphans?

6. How is social referencing important in toddlerhood?

7. What distinctive contributions do fathers make to infant development?

**Especially for Nursing Mothers** You have heard that if you wean your child too early he or she will overeat or develop alcohol use disorder. Is it true? (see response, p. 210)

**All Together Now** Toddlers in an employees' day-care program at a flower farm in Colombia learn to use the potty on a schedule. Will this experience lead to later personality problems? Probably not.

**trust versus mistrust** Erikson's first crisis of psychosocial development. Infants learn basic trust if the world is a secure place where their basic needs (for food, comfort, attention, and so on) are met.

**autonomy versus shame and doubt** Erikson's second crisis of psychosocial development. Toddlers either succeed or fail in gaining a sense of self-rule over their actions and their bodies.

# Theories of Infant Psychosocial Development

The fact that infants are emotional, social creatures is recognized by everyone who studies babies. However, each of the theories discussed in Chapter 2 has a distinct perspective on this universal reality, as you will now see.

## Psychoanalytic Theory

Psychoanalytic theory connects biosocial and psychosocial development. Sigmund Freud and Erik Erikson each described two distinct stages of early development, one in the first year and one beginning in the second year.

### Freud: Oral and Anal Stages

According to Freud (1935/1989, 2001), the first year of life is the *oral stage*, so named because the mouth is the young infant's primary source of gratification. In the second year, with the *anal stage*, pleasure comes from the anus—particularly from the sensual satisfaction of bowel movements and, eventually, the psychological pleasure of controlling them.

Freud believed that the oral and anal stages are fraught with potential conflicts. If a mother frustrates her infant's urge to suck—weaning too early or too late, for example, or preventing the baby from sucking a thumb or a pacifier—that may later lead to an *oral fixation*. A person with an oral fixation is stuck (fixated) at the oral stage, and therefore, as an adult, he or she eats, drinks, chews, bites, or talks excessively, still seeking the mouth-related pleasures of infancy.

Similarly, if toilet training is overly strict or if it begins before the infant is mature enough, then the toddler's refusal—or inability—to comply will clash with the wishes of the adult, who denies the infant normal anal pleasures. That may lead to an *anal personality*—an adult who seeks self-control, with an unusually strong need for regularity and cleanliness in all aspects of life. [**Developmental Link:** Theory of toilet training is discussed in Chapter 2.]

### Erikson: Trust and Autonomy

According to Erikson, the first crisis of life is **trust versus mistrust,** when infants learn whether or not the world can be trusted to satisfy basic needs. Babies feel secure when food and comfort are provided with "consistency, continuity, and sameness of experience" (Erikson, 1993a, p. 247). If social interaction inspires trust, the child (later the adult) confidently explores the social world.

The second crisis is **autonomy versus shame and doubt,** beginning at about 18 months, when self-awareness emerges. Toddlers want autonomy (self-rule) over their own actions and bodies. Without it, they feel ashamed and doubtful. Like Freud, Erikson believed that problems in early infancy could last a lifetime, creating adults who are suspicious and pessimistic (mistrusting) or easily shamed (lacking autonomy).

## Behaviorism

From the perspective of behaviorism, emotions and personality are molded as parents reinforce or punish a child. Behaviorists believe that parents who respond joyously to every glimmer of a grin will have children with a sunny disposition. The opposite is also true:

> Failure to bring up a happy child, a well-adjusted child—assuming bodily health—falls squarely upon the parents' shoulders. [By the time the child is 3] parents have already determined . . . [whether the child] is to grow into a happy

*JOSE MIGUEL GOMEZ/REUTERS/Newscom*

person, wholesome and good-natured, whether he is to be a whining, complaining neurotic, an anger-driven, vindictive, over-bearing slave driver, or one whose every move in life is definitely controlled by fear.

*[Watson, 1928/1972, pp. 7, 45]*

Later behaviorists recognized that infants' behavior also reflects social learning, as infants learn from other people. You already saw an example, social referencing. Social learning occurs throughout life, not necessary via direct teaching but often through observation (Shneidman & Woodward, 2016). Toddlers express emotions in various ways—from giggling to cursing—just as their parents or older siblings do.

For example, a boy might develop a hot temper if his father's outbursts seem to win his mother's respect; a girl might be coy, or passive-aggressive, if that is what she has seen at home. These examples are deliberately sexist: Gender roles, in particular, are learned, according to social learning. [**Developmental Link:** Social learning theory is discussed in Chapter 2.]

Parents often unwittingly encourage certain traits in their children. Should babies have many toys, or will that make them too greedy? Should you pick up your crying baby or give her a pacifier? Should you breast-feed until age 2 or longer or switch to bottle-feeding before 6 months?

These questions highlight the distinction between **proximal parenting** (being physically close to a baby, often holding and touching) and **distal parenting** (keeping some distance—providing toys, encouraging self-feeding, talking face-to-face instead of communicating by touch). Caregivers tend to behave in proximal or distal ways very early, when infants are only 2 months old (Kärtner et al., 2010).

Variations in proximal and distal parenting lead to variations in toddler behavior. For instance, toddlers who, as infants, were often held, patted, and hushed (proximal) became toddlers who are more obedient to their parents but less likely to recognize themselves in a mirror (Keller et al., 2010; Keller et al., 2004).

The long-term impact of responses to the behavior of infants is evident when researchers compare child-rearing practices of the Nso people of Cameroon (very proximal) with those of the Greeks in Athens (very distal). In Greece, Cameroon, Italy, Israel, and many other places, how much adults value individual rather than collective action is related to how much distal or proximal child care they experienced (Scharf, 2014; Carra et al., 2013; Borke et al., 2007; Kärtner et al., 2011).

**Only in America** Toddlers in every nation of the world sometimes cry when emotions overwhelm them, but in the United States young children are encouraged to express emotions—and Halloween is a national custom, unlike in other nations. Candy, dress-up, ghosts, witches, and ringing doorbells after sunset—no wonder many young children are overwhelmed.

**proximal parenting** Caregiving practices that involve being physically close to the baby, with frequent holding and touching.

**distal parenting** Caregiving practices that involve remaining distant from the baby, providing toys, food, and face-to-face communication with minimal holding and touching.

**Amusing or Neglectful?** Depends on the culture. In proximal cultures this father would be criticized for not interacting with his daughter, and the mother would be blamed for letting him do so. But in distal cultures, Dad might be admired for multitasking: simultaneously reading the paper, waiting for the bus, and taking the baby to day care.

## Cognitive Theory

Cognitive theory holds that thoughts determine a person's perspective. Early experiences are important because beliefs, perceptions, and memories make them so, not because they are buried in the unconscious (psychoanalytic theory) or burned into the brain's patterns (behaviorism).

According to many cognitive theorists, early experiences help infants develop a **working model,** which is a set of assumptions that becomes a frame of reference for later life (S. Johnson et al., 2010). It is a "model" because early relationships form a prototype, or blueprint; it is "working" because it is a work in progress, not fixed or final.

Ideally, infants develop "a working model of the self as lovable and competent" because the parents are "emotionally available, loving, and supportive of their mastery efforts" (Harter, 2012, p. 12). However, reality does not always conform to this ideal. A 1-year-old girl might develop a model, based on her parents' inconsistent responses to her, that people are unpredictable. She will continue to apply that model to everyone: Her childhood friendships will be insecure, and her adult relationships will be guarded.

The crucial idea, according to cognitive theory, is that an infant's early experiences themselves are not necessarily pivotal, but the interpretation of those experiences is (Olson & Dweck, 2009). Children may misinterpret their experiences, or parents may offer inaccurate explanations, and these form ideas that affect later thinking and behavior.

In this way, working models formed in childhood echo lifelong. A hopeful message from cognitive theory is that people can rethink and reorganize their thoughts, developing new models. Our mistrustful girl might marry someone who is faithful and loving, so she may gradually develop a new working model. The form of psychotherapy that seems most successful at the moment is called cognitive-behavioral, in which new thoughts about how to behave are developed. In other words, a new working model is developed.

## Evolutionary Theory

Remember that evolutionary theory stresses two needs: survival and reproduction. Human brains are extraordinarily adept at those tasks. However, not until after about two decades of maturation is the human brain fully functioning. A child must be nourished, protected, and taught much longer than offspring of any other species. Infant and parent emotions ensure this lengthy protection (Hrdy, 2009).

### Emotions for Survival

Infant emotions are part of this evolutionary mandate. All of the reactions described in the first part of this chapter—from the hunger cry to the temper tantrum—can be seen from this perspective (Konner, 2010).

For example, newborns are extraordinarily dependent, unable to walk or talk or even sit up and feed themselves for months after birth. They must attract adult devotion—and they do. That first smile, the sound of infant laughter, and their role in synchrony are all powerfully attractive to adults—especially to parents.

Adults call their hairless, chinless, round-faced, big-stomached, small-limbed offspring "cute," "handsome," "beautiful," "adorable," yet all these characteristics are often considered ugly in adults. Parents willingly devote hours to carrying, feeding, changing, and cleaning their infants, who never express their gratitude.

Adaptation is evident. Adults have the genetic potential to be caregivers, and grandparents have done it before, but, according to evolutionary psychology,

**working model** In cognitive theory, a set of assumptions that the individual uses to organize perceptions and experiences. For example, a person might assume that other people are trustworthy and be surprised by an incident in which this working model of human behavior is erroneous.

**Especially for Pediatricians** A mother complains that her toddler refuses to stay in the car seat, spits out disliked foods, and almost never does what she says. How should you respond? (see response, p. 212)

**Response for Nursing Mothers** (from p. 208): Freud thought so, but there is no experimental evidence that weaning, even when ill-timed, has such dire long-term effects.

whether or not that potential is expressed, turning busy adults into devoted care-givers and dependent infants into emotional magnets, is ruled by basic survival needs of the species. If humans were motivated solely by money or power, no one would have children. Yet evolution has created adults who find parenting worth every sacrifice.

### The Cost of Child Rearing

The financial costs of parenting are substantial: Food, diapers, clothes, furniture, medical bills, toys, and child care (whether paid or unpaid) are just a start. Before a child becomes independent, many parents buy a bigger residence and pay for edu-cation—including such luxuries as violin lessons or basketball camp. The emotional costs are greater—worry, self-doubt, fear. A book about parenting is titled *All Joy and No Fun*, highlighting the paradox: People choose to sacrifice time, money, and fun because they find parenting deeply satisfying (Senior, 2014).

Evolutionary theory holds that the emotions of attachment—love, jealousy, even clinginess and anger—keep toddlers near caregivers who remain vigilant. Infants fuss at still faces, fear separation, and laugh when adults play with them—all to sustain caregiving. Emotions are our genetic legacy; we would die without them.

Evolutionary social scientists note that if mothers were the exclusive caregivers of each child until children were adults, a given woman could rear only one or two offspring—not enough for the species to survive. Instead, before the introduction of reliable birth control, the average interval between births for humans was two to four years. Humans birth children at relatively short intervals because of **allocare**—the care of children by **alloparents,** caregivers who are not the biological parents (Hrdy, 2009).

Allocare is essential for *Homo sapiens'* survival. Compared with many other species (mother chimpanzees space births by four or five years and never let another chimp hold their babies), human mothers have evolved to let other people help with child care (Kachel et al., 2011). That may be universal for our species—but to understand the varieties of allocare, the next theory is needed.

### Sociocultural Theory

Cultural variations are vast in every aspect of infant care. You have read many examples: breast-feeding, co-sleeping, and language development among them.

Each theory just described can be used to justify or criticize certain varia-tions. For example, Westerners expect toddlers to go through the stubborn and

**allocare** Literally, "other-care"; the care of children by people other than the biological parents.

**alloparents** Literally, "other parents"; people who provide care for children but who are not the child's parents. In the twenty-first century, not only neighbors and relatives (grandparents, siblings, and so on) but also professionals (pediatricians, teachers, day-care aides, and nurses) can be alloparents.

**Same Situation, Far Apart: Safekeep-ing** Historically, grandmothers were some-times crucial for child survival. Now, even though medical care has reduced child mortality, grandmothers still do their part to keep children safe, as shown by these two—in the eastern United States *(left)* and Vietnam *(right)*.

Ted Richardson/Raleigh News & Observer/ MCT via Getty Images

**Contrast This with That** Three infants again, but this infant day-care center provides excellent care, as can be seen by comparing this scene with what is depicted in the photo on page 204.

**Observation Quiz** What three things do you see that suggest good care? (see answer, p. 214) ↑

**Response for Pediatricians** (from p. 210): Consider the origins of the misbehavior—probably a combination of the child's inborn temperament and the mother's distal parenting. Acceptance and consistent responses (e.g., avoiding disliked foods but always using the car seat) is more warranted than anger. Perhaps this mother is expressing hostility toward the child—a sign that intervention may be needed. Find out.

defiant "terrible twos"; that is a sign of autonomy, as Erikson described it and as distal parenting encourages. By contrast, parents in some other places expect toddlers to be obedient.

The result is that North American parents are urged to be patient, to lock up valuables, and to have the number for Poison Control ready. Other cultures use shame, guilt, or severe physical punishment (which U.S. authorities consider abuse) to enforce compliance. A study of children in three nations found that the Japanese were highest in shame, the Koreans highest in guilt, and the U.S. children highest in pride (Furukawa et al., 2012).

## Infant Day Care

The best way to illustrate the vast cultural differences in infant care is to look closely at one example, infant day care. People have opposite ideas about this topic, depending largely on their cultural background.

About 134 million babies will be born worldwide each year from 2010 to 2021 (United Nations, Department of Economic and Social Affairs, Population Division, 2015). Most newborns are cared for primarily by their mothers, but sociocultural differences in allocare soon are evident. Fathers and grandmothers typically provide care from the first days of life, although not in every culture.

In Western cultures, infant care provided by a nonrelative (usually in a day-care center) has increased since 1980. Since paid maternal leave is uncommon in the United States, 58 percent of the mothers of infants under 1 year of age were in the labor force in 2015 (U.S. Bureau of Labor Statistics, April 22, 2016).

Virtually no infant in the poorest nations receives regular nonmaternal care unless the mother is incapable, and then a close relative takes over. By contrast, by age 1, 90 percent of infants of the wealthiest families within developed nations are cared for regularly by a nanny or babysitter at home, or by a family day-care provider in her (almost never his) home, or by a trained professional in a day-care center. In France, the government subsidizes day care from 3 months on for every infant, rich or poor.

Almost every developmentalist agrees with three conclusions.

1. Attachment to someone is beneficial. That someone could be a mother and/or someone else, and the attachment can develop with a variety of care arrangements.
2. Frequent changes and instability are problematic. If an infant is cared for by a neighbor, a grandmother, a day-care center, and then another grandmother, each for only a month or two, or if an infant is with the biological mother, then a foster mother, then back with the biological mother, that is harmful. By age 3, children with unstable care histories are likely to be more aggressive than those with stable care, such as being at the same center with the same caregiver for years (Pilarz & Hill, 2014).
3. Babies benefit from a strong relationship with their parents. Accordingly, most nations provide some paid leave for mothers, lasting from a few days to 15 months (see Figure 7.3). Increasingly, paid leave is allowed for fathers, or family leave can be taken by either parent. In most nations, employed mothers must be allowed to return to the same job and salary when maternity leave ends.

Beyond the need for attachment and stability, experts are split on whether infant day care is beneficial or harmful or neutral. As one review explained: "This evidence now indicates that early nonparental care environments sometimes pose risks to

## FIGURE 7.3

**A Changing World**   No one was offered maternity leave a century ago because the only jobs that mothers had were unregulated ones. Now, virtually every nation except the United States has a maternity leave policy, revised every decade or so. (The data on this chart are from 2014—already outdated.) Since 2014, 65 nations have enacted 94 reforms increasing women's economic opportunities, and 18 nations have no legal differences between women and men. This may be the next innovation in many nations.

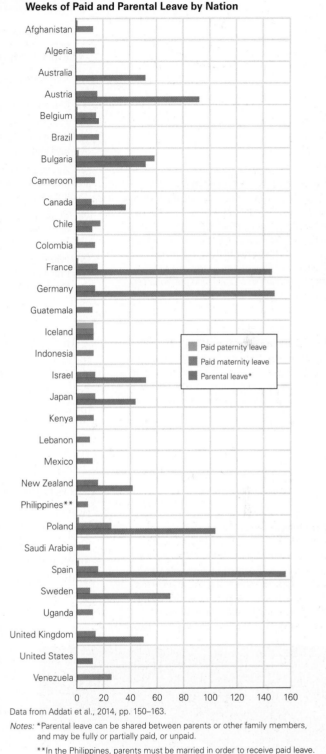

**Weeks of Paid and Parental Leave by Nation**

Data from Addati et al., 2014, pp. 150–163.

*Notes:* *Parental leave can be shared between parents or other family members, and may be fully or partially paid, or unpaid.

**In the Philippines, parents must be married in order to receive paid leave.

young children and sometimes confer benefits" (Phillips et al., 2011, p. 44). The same is true for parental care: Some mothers and fathers are wonderful, some not.

People tend to believe that the practices of their own family or culture are best and that other patterns harm the infant and the parent. Because of the difference-equals-deficit error, assumptions flourish, and adults disagree.

## International Variations

For ideological as well as economic reasons, center-based infant care is common in France, Israel, China, Chile, Norway, and Sweden, where it is heavily subsidized by the governments. Many families in those nations believe that subsidized infant care is a public right, in much the same way they assume that a public fire department is available if needed. By contrast, center care is scarce in South Asia, Africa, and Latin America, where many parents believe it is harmful. (Table 7.3 lists five essential characteristics of high-quality infant day care, wherever it is located.)

Most nations are between those two extremes. Germany recently began offering paid infant care as a successful strategy to increase the birth rate. In the United States, infant care is paid for almost exclusively by parents, which makes quality infant care from nonrelatives unaffordable for most families.

One detailed example comes from Australia, where the government attempted to increase the birth rate. Parents were given $5,000 for each newborn, parental leave was paid, and public subsidies provided child-care centers. Yet many Australians still believed that babies need exclusive maternal care (Harrison et al., 2014).

Parents are caught in the middle. For example, one Australian mother of a 12-month-old boy used center care, but said:

> I spend a lot of time talking with them about his day and what he's been doing and how he's feeling and they just seem to have time to do that, to make the effort to communicate. Yeah they've really bonded with him and he's got close to them. But I still don't like leaving him there.

*[quoted in Boyd et al., 2013, p. 172]*

Underlying every policy and practice are theories about what is best. In the United States, marked variations are apparent by state and by employer, with some employers being quite generous. Almost no U.S. company pays for paternal leave, with one exception: The U.S. military allows 10 days of paid leave for fathers.

## TABLE 7.3

### High-Quality Day Care

**High-quality day care during infancy has five essential characteristics:**

1. *Adequate attention to each infant*
   A small group of infants (no more than five) needs two reliable, familiar, loving caregivers. Continuity of care is crucial.

2. *Encouragement of language and sensorimotor development*
   Infants need language—songs, conversations, and positive talk—and easily manipulated toys with no small parts.

3. *Attention to health and safety*
   Cleanliness routines (e.g., handwashing), accident prevention, and safe areas to explore are essential.

4. *Professional caregivers*
   Caregivers should have experience and degrees/certificates in early-childhood education. Turnover should be low, morale high, and enthusiasm evident.

5. *Warm and responsive caregivers*
   Providers should engage the children in active play and guide them in problem solving. Quiet, obedient children may indicate unresponsive care.

**● Answer to Observation Quiz** (from p. 212) Remontia Green is holding the feeding baby in just the right position as she rocks back and forth—no propped-up bottle here. The two observing babies are at an angle and distance that makes them part of the social interaction, and they are strapped in. Finally, look at the cribs—no paint, close slats, and positioned so the babies can see each other.

**● Especially for Day-Care Providers** A mother who brings her child to you for day care says that she knows she is harming her baby, but economic necessity compels her to work. What do you say? (see response, p. 216)

**Double Winner** Baby and victory in the same month! These women are advocating for six weeks of paid maternity leave. The San Francisco Board of Supervisors voted yes, making this the first jurisdiction in the United States to mandate fully paid leave. The law went into effect in 2017—too late for this woman now. Perhaps her next baby?

In the United States, only 20 percent of infants are cared for *exclusively* by their mothers (i.e., no other relatives or babysitters) throughout their first year. This is in contrast to Canada, with far more generous maternal leave and lower rates of maternal employment. In the first year of life, most Canadians are cared for only by their mothers (Babchishin et al., 2013). Obviously, these differences are affected by culture, economics, and politics more than by any universal needs of babies.

## Recent Past and Present

Research two decades ago, led primarily by Jay Belsky, raised questions about the long-term consequences of infant day care (Belsky & Rovine, 1988; Belsky, 2001). Other studies were more positive. For instance, a large study in Canada found that infant girls seemed to develop equally well in various care arrangements. However, results for boys varied. Canadian boys from high-SES families, whose mothers were not exclusive caregivers, fared less well than high-SES boys whose mothers provided all of their care. By age 4, those who had been in day care were slightly more assertive or aggressive, with more emotional problems (e.g., a teacher might note that a kindergarten boy "seems unhappy").

The opposite was true for Canadian boys from low-SES families: On average, they benefited from nonmaternal care, again according to teacher reports. The researchers insist that no policy implications can be derived from this study, partly because care varied so much in quality, location, and provider (Côté et al., 2008).

Research in the United States has also found that center care benefits children of low-SES families (Peng & Robins, 2010). For wealthier children, questions arise. An ongoing longitudinal study by the Early Child Care Network of the National Institute of Child Health and Human Development (NICHD) has followed the development of more than 1,300 children born in 1991. Early day care correlated with many cognitive advances, especially in language.

Jeff Chiu/AP Images

The social consequences were less clear, however. Most analyses find that secure attachment to the mother was as common among infants in center care as among infants cared for at home. Like other, smaller studies, the NICHD research confirms that the mother–child relationship is pivotal.

However, infant day care seemed detrimental if the mother was insensitive *and* the infant spent more than 20 hours a week in a poor-quality program with too many children per group (McCartney et al., 2010). Again, boys in such circumstances had more conflicts with their teachers than did the girls or other boys with a different mix of maternal traits and day-care experiences.

Notice, however, that those children were born more than 25 years ago, when infant day-care centers were less common and often less able to meet the needs of small babies. More recent work finds that high-quality care in infancy benefits the cognitive skills of children of both sexes and all income groups, with no evidences of emotional harm, especially when it is followed by good preschool care (Li et al., 2013; Huston et al., 2015). Maybe earlier studies reflect cohort, not infant needs.

Nonetheless, the link between infant day care and later psychosocial problems, although not found in every study, raises concern. For that reason, the experience of Norway is particularly interesting.

## Norway

In Norway, new mothers are paid at full salary to stay home with their babies for 47 weeks, and high-quality, free center day care is available from age 1 on. Most (62 percent) Norwegian 1-year-olds are in center care, as are 84 percent of the 2-year-olds and 93 percent of the 3-year-olds.

In the United States, reliable statistics are not kept on center care for infants, but only 42 percent of all U.S. 3-year-olds were in educational programs in 2012, according to the National Center for Education Statistics (Kena et al., 2014). Rates increase slightly as maternal education rises, as mothers with more education are more likely to appreciate and afford early education.

Longitudinal results in Norway find no detrimental results of infant center care that begins at age 1. Too few children were in center care before their first birthday to find significant longitudinal results. By kindergarten, Norwegian day-care children had slightly more conflicts with caregivers, but the authors suggest that may be the result of shy children becoming bolder as a result of day care (Solheim et al., 2013). Some assertiveness may be an asset.

**Same Situation, Far Apart: Instead of Mothers** Casper, Wyoming *(left)*, is on the opposite side of Earth from Dhaka, Bangladesh *(right)*, but day care is needed in both places, as shown here.

**Observation Quiz** How do the two photographs reflect that the United States values individuality and Bangladesh values the group? (see answer, p. 217)

● **Response for Day-Care Providers** (from p. 214): Reassure the mother that you will keep her baby safe and will help to develop the baby's mind and social skills by fostering synchrony and attachment. Also tell her that the quality of mother–infant interaction at home is more important than anything else for psychosocial development; mothers who are employed full-time usually have wonderful, secure relationships with their infants. If the mother wishes, you can discuss ways to be a responsive mother.

## Quality Care

The issue of the quality of care has become crucial. A professional organization in the United States, the National Association for the Education of Young Children, updated its standards for care of babies from birth to 15 months, based on current research (NAEYC, 2014). Breast-feeding is encouraged (via bottles of breast milk that mothers have expressed earlier), babies are always put to sleep on their backs, group size is small (no more than eight infants), and the ratio of adults to babies is 1:4 or fewer.

Many specific practices are recommended to keep infant minds growing and bodies healthy. For instance, "before walking on surfaces that infants use specifically for play, adults and children remove, replace, or cover with clean foot coverings any shoes they have worn outside that play area. If children or staff are barefoot in such areas, their feet are visibly clean" (NAEYC, 2014, p. 59). Another recommendation is to "engage infants in frequent face-to-face social interactions"—including talking, singing, smiling, and touching (NAEYC, 2014, p. 4).

All of the research on infant day care confirms that sociocultural differences matter. What seems best for one infant, in one culture, may not be best for another infant elsewhere. Good infant care—whether by mother, father, grandmother, or day-care center—depends on specifics, not generalities.

## Conclusion

No matter what form of care is chosen or what theory is endorsed, individualized care with stable caregivers seems best (Morrissey, 2009). Caregiver change is especially problematic for infants because each simple gesture or sound that a baby makes not only merits an encouraging response but also requires interpretation by someone who knows that particular baby well.

For example, "baba" could mean bottle, baby, blanket, banana, or some other word that does not even begin with *b*. This example is an easy one, but similar communication efforts—requiring individualized emotional responses, preferably from a familiar caregiver—are evident even in the first smiles and cries.

A related issue is the growing diversity of baby care providers. Especially when the home language is not the majority language, parents hesitate to let people of another background care for their infants. That is one reason that immigrant parents in the United States often prefer care by relatives instead of by professionals (P. Miller et al., 2014). Relationships are crucial, not only between caregiver and infant but also between caregiver and parent (Elicker et al., 2014).

However, for immigrant families in particular, young children need to learn the language and customs of the new nation in order to thrive. Many immigrant families understand this, and they try to help the children adjust while maintaining cultural pride. A study of West African immigrants in Italy, for instance, found that the mothers were more verbal than they would have been in their native country, but they retained some of their home culture as well (Carra et al., 2013). Obviously, the success of parents in raising successful, bicultural children depends on the attitudes within the host nation as well as their own practices.

As is true of many topics in child development, questions remain. But one fact is without question: Each infant needs personal responsiveness. Someone should serve as a partner in the synchrony duet, a base for secure attachment, and a social reference who encourages exploration. Then, infant emotions and experiences—cries and laughter, fears and joys—will ensure that development goes well.

1. According to Freud, what might happen if a baby's oral needs are not met?

2. How might Erikson's crisis of "trust versus mistrust" affect later life?

3. How do behaviorists explain the development of emotions and personality?

4. What does a "working model" mean within cognitive theory?

5. What is the difference between proximal and distal parenting?

6. How does evolution explain the parent–child bond?

7. Why is allocare necessary for survival of the human species?

8. Why do cultures differ on the benefits of infant nonmaternal care?

9. What aspects of infant care are agreed on by everyone?

● **Answer to Observation Quiz** (from p. 215): The children in Bangladesh, unlike the U.S. children, are close in age, with close-cropped hair and standard, cotton uniforms. All focus on the same collection of balls, while the Wyoming teacher seems to appreciate the girl who does not want to look at the book.

# SUMMARY

## Emotional Development

**1.** Two emotions, contentment and distress, appear as soon as an infant is born. Smiles and laughter are evident in the early months. Between 4 and 8 months of age, anger emerges in reaction to restriction and frustration, and it becomes stronger by age 1.

**2.** Reflexive fear is apparent in very young infants. Fear of something specific, including fear of strangers and of separation, typically arise in the second half of the first year, and it is strong by age 1.

**3.** In the second year, social awareness produces more selective fear, anger, and joy. As infants become increasingly self-aware, emotions emerge that encourage an interface between the self and others—specifically, pride, shame, and affection. Self-recognition (measured by the mirror/rouge test) emerges at about 18 months.

**4.** Temperament is inborn, but the expression of temperament is influenced by the context, with evident plasticity. At least in the United States, parents tend to encourage exuberance and discourage fear.

## The Development of Social Bonds

**5.** Often by 2 months, and clearly by 6 months, infants become more responsive and social, and synchrony is evident. Caregivers and infants engage in reciprocal interactions, with split-second timing.

**6.** Infants are disturbed by a still face because they expect and need social interaction. Babies of depressed or rejecting parents become depressed or disturbed themselves.

**7.** Attachment is the relationship between two people who try to be close to each other (proximity-seeking and contact-maintaining). It is measured in infancy by a baby's reaction to the caregiver's presence, departure, and return in the Strange Situation.

**8.** Secure attachment provides encouragement for infant exploration, and it may influence the person lifelong. Some infants seem indifferent (type A—insecure-avoidant attachment) or overly dependent (type C—insecure-resistant/ambivalent attachment) instead of secure (type B). Disorganized attachment (type D) is the most worrisome.

**9.** As they become more mobile and engage with their environment, toddlers use social referencing (looking to other people's facial expressions and body language) to detect what is safe, frightening, or fun. Fathers help toddlers become more adventuresome.

**10.** Infants frequently use fathers as partners in synchrony, as attachment figures, and as social references, developing emotions and exploring their world. Contemporary fathers often play with their infants.

## Theories of Infant Psychosocial Development

**11.** According to all major theories, caregivers are especially influential in the first two years. Freud stressed the mother's impact on oral and anal pleasure; Erikson emphasized trust and autonomy. Both believed that the impact of these is lifelong.

**12.** Behaviorists focus on learning. They note that parents teach their babies many things, including when to be fearful or joyful, and how much physical and social distance (proximal or distal parenting) is best.

**13.** Cognitive theory holds that infants develop working models based on their experiences. Interpretation is crucial, and that can change with maturation.

**14.** Evolutionary theorists recognize that both infants and caregivers have impulses and emotions that have developed over millennia to foster the survival of each new member of the human species. Attachment is one example.

**15.** Sociocultural theory notes that infant care varies tremendously from one culture or era to another. The impact of nonmaternal care depends on many factors that change from one nation, one family, and even one child to another. For example, attitudes about infant day care vary a great deal, with the impact dependent on the quality of care (responsive, individualized, stable).

**16.** All theories agree with one conclusion from research in many nations: The relationship between the infant and caregiver is crucial. All aspects of early development are affected by policy and practice.

## KEY TERMS

social smile (p. 190)
separation anxiety (p. 190)
stranger wariness (p. 190)
self-awareness (p. 192)
temperament (p. 192)
synchrony (p. 196)
still-face technique (p. 198)

attachment (p. 198)
secure attachment (p. 200)
insecure-avoidant attachment
  (p. 200)
insecure-resistant/ambivalent
  attachment (p. 200)
disorganized attachment (p. 200)

Strange Situation (p. 201)
social referencing (p. 205)
trust versus mistrust (p. 208)
autonomy versus shame and
  doubt (p. 208)
proximal parenting (p. 209)
distal parenting (p. 209)

working model (p. 210)
allocare (p. 211)
alloparents (p. 211)

## APPLICATIONS

**1.** One cultural factor that influences infant development is how infants are carried from place to place. Ask four mothers whose infants were born in each of the past four decades how they transported them—front or back carriers, facing out or in, strollers or carriages, in car seats or on mother's laps, and so on. Why did they choose the mode(s) they chose? What are their opinions and yours on how such cultural practices might affect infants' development?

**2.** Record video of synchrony for three minutes. Ideally, ask the parent of an infant under 8 months of age to play with the infant.

If no infant is available, observe a pair of lovers as they converse. Note the sequence and timing of every facial expression, sound, and gesture of both partners.

**3.** Contact several day-care centers to try to assess the quality of care they provide. Ask about factors such as adult/child ratio, group size, and training for caregivers of children of various ages. Is there a minimum age? Why or why not? Analyze the answers, using Table 7.3 as a guide.

# The Developing Person So Far:
## The First Two Years

## BIOSOCIAL

twomeows/Moment/Getty Images

**Body Changes** Over the first two years, body weight quadruples and brain weight triples. Connections between brain cells grow dense, with complex networks of dendrites and axons. Experiences that are universal (experience-expectant) and culture-bound (experience-dependent) aid brain growth, partly by pruning unused connections between neurons.

**Perceiving and Moving** Brain maturation as well as culture underlies the development of all of the senses. Seeing, hearing, and mobility progress from reflexes to coordinated voluntary actions, including focusing, grasping, and walking.

**Surviving in Good Health** Infant health depends on immunization, parental practices (including "back to sleep"), and nutrition. Breast milk protects health. Survival rates are much higher today than even a few decades ago.

## COGNITIVE

hadynyah/E+/Getty Images

**Sensorimotor Intelligence** As Piaget describes it, in the first two years, infants progress from knowing their world through immediate sensory experiences to "experimenting" on that world through actions and mental images.

**Information Processing** Information-processing theory stresses the links between sensory experiences and perception. Infants develop their own ideas regarding the possibilities offered by the objects and events of the world.

**Language: What Develops in the First Two Years?** Interaction with responsive adults exposes infants to the structures of communication and language. By age 1, infants usually speak a word or two; by age 2, language has exploded—toddlers talk in short sentences and add vocabulary each day.

## PSYCHOSOCIAL

Westend61/Getty Images

**Emotional Development** Babies soon progress to smiling and laughing at pleasurable objects and events, and they also experience anger, sadness, and fear. Toddlers develop self-awareness and social awareness, and they experience new emotions: pride, shame, embarrassment, disgust, and guilt. Temperament varies, as do the links between emotions and the brain.

**The Development of Social Bonds** Parents and infants respond to each other by synchronizing their behavior. Toward the end of the first year, secure attachment to the parent sets the stage for the child's increasingly independent exploration of the world. Insecure attachment—avoidant, resistant, or disorganized—signifies a parent–child relationship that hinders learning. Infants' self-awareness and independence are shaped by parents.

**Theories of Infant Psychosocial Development** All of the theories of psychosocial development find that the infant–caregiver relationship is crucial. Infant day care is considered a fundamental right in some places, a luxury in others, and harmful in still others. All aspects of early development are affected by policy and practice.

Top: Jose Luis Pelaez Inc/Getty Images

## APPLICATION TO DEVELOPING LIVES PARENTING SIMULATION EARLY CHILDHOOD

As you progress through the Early Childhood simulation module, how you decide the following will impact the biosocial, cognitive, and psychosocial development of your child.

| | Biosocial | Cognitive | Psychosocial |
|---|---|---|---|
| | • How does your child's height and weight compare to national norms?<br>• What foods will your child eat at this stage of development?<br>• How much physical activity will you encourage? | • Which of Piaget's stages of cognitive development is your child in?<br>• In what kind of school will you enroll your child?<br>• Will your child be able to demonstrate impulse control?<br>• How will your child compare to national averages in reading, math, and language? | • In what kind of social environment will you place your child?<br>• How will your child react if you and your partner split up?<br>• How will you discipline your child at this age?<br>• How does your stress level impact your child's emotional health? |

# Early Childhood

**F**rom ages 2 to 6, children spend most of their waking hours discovering, creating, laughing, and imagining—all the while acquiring the skills they need. They chase each other and attempt new challenges (developing their bodies); they play with sounds, words, and ideas (developing their minds); they invent games and dramatize fantasies (learning social skills and morals).

These were once called the *preschool years* because school started in first grade. But first grade is no longer first; most children begin school long before age 6. Now these years are called *early childhood*. By whatever name, the years from ages 2 to 6 are a time for extraordinary growth, impressive learning, and spontaneous play, joyful not only for young children but also for anyone who knows them. ●●

# Early Childhood: Biosocial Development

## What Will You Know?

1. Do young children eat too much, too little, or the right amount?
2. If children never climb trees or splash in water, do they suffer?
3. Why is injury control more needed than accident prevention?
4. Which is worse, neglect or abuse?

+ **Body Changes**
  Growth Patterns
  Nutrition
  Brain Growth
  INSIDE THE BRAIN: Connected
    Hemispheres

+ **Advancing Motor Skills**
  Gross Motor Skills
  A VIEW FROM SCIENCE: Eliminating
    Lead
  Fine Motor Skills

+ **Injuries and Abuse**
  Avoidable Injury
  A CASE TO STUDY: "My Baby
    Swallowed Poison"
  Prevention

+ **Child Maltreatment**
  Definitions and Statistics
  Frequency of Maltreatment
  Consequences of Maltreatment
  Preventing Maltreatment

I often took 5-year-old Asa and his female friend, Ada, by subway from kindergarten in Manhattan to their homes in Brooklyn. Their bodies were quite similar (no visible sex differences yet), but they were a marked contrast to the hundreds of fellow subway riders. Of course they were shorter, thinner, with rounder heads and smaller hands, and their feet did not touch the floor when they sat, but that was not the most distinctive difference. Movement was.

I tried to keep their swinging feet from kicking other riders; I told them again and again to hold on to the pole; I asked them to sit beside me instead of careening up and down the subway car, looking out the window, oblivious to the strangers they bumped into or squeezed by. Enforcing proper subway behavior with 5-year-olds is difficult; I often failed.

That is how nature makes young children: full of energy and action. Adults must guide them and keep them safe while enjoying their exuberance. Most tired subway riders did just that; they smiled, admired, and seemed to sympathize with me. This chapter describes growth during early childhood—in body, brain, and motor skills—and what adults can do to protect it.

## Body Changes

In early childhood, as in infancy, the body and brain grow according to powerful epigenetic forces—biologically driven and socially guided, experience-expectant and experience-dependent. [**Developmental Link:** Experience-expectant and experience-dependent brain development are explained in Chapter 5.] Children's bodies and brains mature in size and function.

## Growth Patterns

Compare an unsteady 24-month-old with a cartwheeling 6-year-old. Physical differences are obvious. Height and weight increase in those four years (by about a foot and 16 pounds, or almost 30 centimeters and 8 kilograms), but that is not the most remarkable change. During early childhood, proportions shift radically: Children slim down as the lower body lengthens and fat gives way to muscle.

**Short and Chubby Limbs No Longer**
Siblings in New Mexico, ages 7 and almost 1, illustrate the transformation of body shape and skills during early childhood. Head size is almost the same, but arms are twice as long, evidence of proximo-distal growth.

In fact, the average body mass index (BMI, a ratio of weight to height) is lower at ages 5 and 6 than at any other time of life. [**Developmental Link:** Body mass index is defined in Chapter 11.] Gone are the infant's protruding belly, round face, short limbs, and large head. The center of gravity moves from the breast to the belly, enabling cartwheels, somersaults, and many other accomplishments. The joys of dancing, gymnastics, and pumping legs on a swing become possible; changing proportions enable new achievements.

During each year of early childhood, well-nourished children grow about 3 inches (about 7½ centimeters) and gain almost 4½ pounds (2 kilograms). By age 6, the average child in a developed nation:

- is at least 3½ feet tall (more than 110 centimeters).
- weighs between 40 and 50 pounds (between 18 and 23 kilograms).
- looks lean, not chubby.
- has adultlike body proportions (legs constitute about half the total height).

## Nutrition

Although they rarely starve, preschool children sometimes are malnourished, even in nations with abundant food. Small appetites are often satiated by unhealthy snacks, crowding out needed vitamins.

### Obesity Among Young Children

Older adults often encourage children to eat, instinctively protecting them against famine that was common a century ago. Unfortunately, that encouragement may be destructive.

As family income decreases, both malnutrition and obesity increase. Indeed, obesity is a sign of poor nutrition, likely to reduce immunity and later increase disease (Rook et al., 2014).

There are many explanations for the connection between obesity and low SES. Many family habits—less exercise, more television, fewer vegetables, more fast food—are more common in low-SES families than in those with wealthier, more educated parents (Cespedes et al., 2013). In addition, low-income children may live with grandmothers who know firsthand the dangers of inadequate body fat, so they promote eating patterns that, in other times and places, protected against starvation.

Immigrant elders do not realize that traditional diets in low-income nations are healthier than foods advertised in developed nations (de Hoog et al., 2014). Sadly, many of those regions are adopting Western diets and, as a result, "childhood obesity is one of the most serious public health challenges of the twenty-first century. The problem is global and is steadily affecting many low and middle income countries, particularly in urban settings" (Sahoo et al., 2015, pp. 187–88).

A life-span explanation links childhood stress to adult obesity. Children who lived in low-SES families became less attuned to hunger and satiety signals in their bodies, and, as adults, eat when they are not hungry (Hill et al., 2016).

For all children, appetite decreases between ages 2 and 6. Rates of obesity increase every year from birth through adolescence. To be specific, U.S. data finds 8 percent of 2- to 5-year-olds, 18 percent of 6- to 11-year-olds, and 21 percent of 12- to 19-year-olds were obese in 2012 (Ogden et al., 2014). There were interesting ethnic differences, with African American and Hispanic American children heavier than European American children—a difference often attributed to SES.

Rates for Asian American children show a distinct pattern: Infants and toddlers of Asian descent tend to be relatively heavy, but as older children they tend to have lower rates of obesity.

In former times, when most U.S. children lived in rural areas and played outside all day, the growth slowdown in early childhood was not noticed. Children did not come inside and had no snacks until their parents called them in for dinner, and then they ate whatever was put before them. Now, many adults fret, threaten, and cajole children to overeat ("Eat all your dinner and you can have ice cream").

One reason parents urge children to eat is that they underestimate their children's weight. A review of 69 studies found that half the parents of overweight children believe their children are thinner than they actually are. This problem was particularly likely for children ages 2 to 5 (Lundahl et al., 2014).

Surprisingly, parental recognition that their child is overweight may lead to an *increase* in that child's weight, according to research on 2,823 Australian 4- and 5-year-olds followed until mid-adolescence. Similar results were found in Ireland and the United States. The authors speculate that parents who recognize that their children are overweight may criticize the child rather than develop healthy eating and exercise habits for the family. Then their children may develop destructive eating habits—dieting and then bingeing, for instance—that result in more weight gain, not less (Robinson & Sutin, 2017).

There is some good news in the United States, however. Young children are eating more fruit and are obese less often, from 12.1 percent of 2- to 5-year-olds in 2010 to 8.4 percent in 2012 (Ogden et al., 2014). Both public education and parental action are credited with improvement. Many day-care centers have successfully prevented obesity increasing from ages 2 to 5 by increasing exercise and improving snacks (Sisson et al., 2016).

**Catching Up, Slimming Down** China has transformed its economy and family life since 1950, with far fewer poor families and malnourished children. Instead, problems and practices of the West are becoming evident, as in these two boys. They are attending a weight-loss camp in Zhengzhou, where the average 8- to 14-year-old child loses 14 pounds in one month.

## Nutritional Deficiencies

Although many young children consume more than enough calories, they do not always obtain adequate iron, zinc, and calcium. For example, North American children now drink less milk than formerly, which means they ingest less calcium and have weaker bones later on.

Eating a wide variety of fresh foods may be essential for optimal health. Compared with the average child, those preschoolers who eat more dark-green and orange vegetables and less fried food benefit in many ways. They gain bone mass but not fat, according to a study that controlled for other factors that might correlate with body fat, such as gender (girls have more), ethnicity (people of some ethnic groups are genetically thinner), and income (poor children have worse diets) (Wosje et al., 2010).

Sugar is a major problem. Many customs entice children to eat sweets—in birthday cake, holiday candy, desserts, sweetened juice, soda, and so on. Sweetened cereals and drinks (advertised as containing 100 percent of daily vitamins) are a poor substitute for a balanced, varied diet, partly because some nutrients have not yet been identified, much less listed on food labels.

The American Heart Association recommends no more than 6 teaspoons of natural and added sugars, such as high-fructose corn syrup, in early childhood. That recommendation is about one-third of what the average child consumes. Too much sugar causes poor circulation—with heart attacks likely 50 years later (M. Vos et al., 2016).

**Especially for Early-Childhood Teachers** You know that young children are upset if forced to eat a food they hate, but you have eight 3-year-olds with eight different preferences. What do you do? (see response, p. 226)

**Apples or Blueberries?** During early childhood, boys and girls love having a choice, so it is the adults' task to offer good options. Which book before bed? Which colored shirt before school? Which healthy snack before going out to play?

lostinbids/E+/Getty Images

The most immediate harm from sugar is cavities and decaying teeth before age 6. Thus, all children should see a dentist and brush their teeth regularly during early childhood—both practices that were unnecessary before widespread sugar consumption (Gibbons, 2012). Sweetened foods are a problem for families and culture, not just children.

## Allergies and Food

An estimated 3 to 8 percent of children are allergic to a specific food, almost always a common, healthy one: Cow's milk, eggs, peanuts, tree nuts (such as almonds and walnuts), soy, wheat, fish, and shellfish are the usual culprits. Diagnostic standards for allergies vary (which explains the range of estimates), and treatment varies even more (Chafen et al., 2010).

Some experts advocate total avoidance of the offending food—there are peanut-free schools, where no one is allowed to bring a peanut-butter sandwich for lunch. However, carefully giving children who are allergic to peanuts a tiny bit of peanut powder (under medical supervision) is usually a safe and effective way to decrease allergic reaction in preschool children (Vickery et al., 2017).

Indeed, exposure to peanuts can begin before birth: A study of pregnant women who ingested peanuts found that their children were less likely to be allergic (Frazier et al., 2014). Fortunately, many childhood food allergies are outgrown, but ongoing allergies make a balanced diet even harder.

Other allergies may increase as children grow older. This may also be related to diet: Children who eat more fruit and fewer fast foods (which have relatively high levels of saturated fatty acids, trans fatty acids, sodium, carbohydrates, and sugar) are less likely to have asthma, nasal congestion, watery eyes, and itchy skin allergies (Ellwood et al., 2013).

**Response for Early-Childhood Teachers** (from p. 225): Remember to keep food simple and familiar. Offer every child the same food, allowing refusal but no substitutes—unless for all eight. Children do not expect school and home routines to be identical; they eventually taste whatever other children enjoy.

## Brain Growth

By age 2, most neurons have connected to other neurons and substantial pruning has occurred. The 2-year-old's brain already weighs 75 percent of what it will weigh in adulthood; the 6-year-old's brain is 90 percent of adult weight.

Since most of the brain is already present and functioning by age 2, what remains to develop? The most important parts! Most important for people, that is.

Although the brains and bodies of other primates are better than those of humans in some ways (they climb trees earlier and faster, for instance), and although many animals have abilities that humans lack (smell in dogs, for instance), humans have intellectual capacities far beyond any other animal. Although evolution is sometimes thought to mean survival of the fittest, the human species developed "a mode of living built on social cohesion, cooperation and efficient planning. It was a question of survival of the smartest" (Corballis, 2011, p. 194).

As the prefrontal cortex matures, social understanding develops. For example, a careful series of tests, given to 106 chimpanzees, 32 orangutans, and 105 human 2½-year-olds, found that young children were "equivalent . . . to chimpanzees on tasks of physical cognition but far outstripped both chimpanzees and orang-utans on tasks of social cognition" such as pointing or following someone's gaze (Herrmann et al., 2007, p. 1365).

Children gradually become better at controlling their emotions when they are with other people. This is directly connected to brain development as time passes and family experiences continue, although how much of such control is due to brain maturation directly and how much is due to learning is disputed (DeLisi, 2014; Kochanska et al., 2009). Nonetheless, gradual self-control and development of the prefrontal cortex is apparent.

After infancy, most of the increase in brain weight occurs because of **myelination.** *Myelin* (sometimes called the *white matter* of the brain; the *gray matter* is the neurons themselves) is a fatty coating on the axons that protects and speeds signals between neurons (see Figure 8.1).

Myelin helps every part of the brain, especially the connections between neurons that are far from each other. It is far more than mere insulation around the axons: "Myelin organizes the very structure of network connectivity . . . and regulates the timing of information flow through individual circuits" (Fields, 2014, p. 266). This is evident in the major link between the left and the right halves of the brain, the corpus callosum, as Inside the Brain explains on the following page.

## Maturation of the Prefrontal Cortex

The entire frontal lobe continues to develop for many years after early childhood; dendrite density and myelination are still increasing in emerging adulthood. Nonetheless, neurological control advances significantly between ages 2 and 6, evident in several ways:

- Sleep becomes more regular.
- Emotions become more nuanced and responsive.
- Temper tantrums subside.
- Uncontrollable laughter and tears are less common.

One example of the maturing brain is evident in the game Simon Says. Players are supposed to follow the leader *only* when orders are preceded by the words "Simon says." Thus, if leaders touch their noses and say, "Simon says touch your nose," players are supposed to touch their noses; but when leaders touch their noses and say, "Touch your nose," no one is supposed to follow the example. Young children lose at this game because they impulsively do what they see and hear.

## Impulsiveness and Perseveration

Neurons have only two kinds of impulses: on–off or, in neuroscience terms, activate–inhibit. Each is signaled by biochemical messages from dendrites to

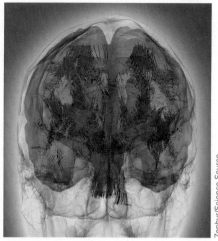

**FIGURE 8.1**

**Mental Coordination?** This brain scan of a 38-year-old depicts areas of myelination (the various colors) within the brain. As you see, the two hemispheres are quite similar, but not identical. For most important skills and concepts, both halves of the brain are activated.

**Especially for Early-Childhood Teachers** You know you should be patient, but frustration rises when your young charges dawdle on the walk to the playground a block away. What should you do? (see response, p. 230)

**myelination** The process by which axons become coated with myelin, a fatty substance that speeds the transmission of nerve impulses from neuron to neuron.

# Connected Hemispheres

The brain is divided into two halves, connected by the **corpus callosum,** a long, thick band of nerve fibers that grows particularly rapidly in early childhood (Ansado et al., 2015). For that reason, compared to toddlers, young children become much better at coordinating the two sides of their brains and, hence, both sides of their bodies. They can hop, skip, and gallop at age 5, unlike at age 2.

Serious disorders result when the corpus callosum fails to develop, which almost always results in intellectual disability (Cavalari & Donovick, 2014). Abnormal growth of the corpus callosum is one symptom of autism spectrum disorder, as well as dozens of other disorders (Al-Hashim et al., 2016; Travers et al., 2015; Wolff et al., 2015).

To appreciate the corpus callosum, note that each side of the body and brain specializes and is therefore dominant for certain functions. This is **lateralization,** literally, "sidedness."

The entire human body is lateralized, apparent not only in right- or left-handedness but also in the feet, the eyes, the ears, and the brain itself. People prefer to kick a ball, wink an eye, or listen on the phone with their preferred foot, eye, or ear, respectively. Genes, prenatal hormones, and early experiences all affect which side does what.

Astonishing studies of humans whose corpus callosa were severed to relieve severe epilepsy, as well as research on humans and other vertebrates with intact corpus callosa, reveal how the brain's hemispheres specialize. Typically, the left half controls the body's right side as well as areas dedicated to logical reasoning, detailed analysis, and the basics of language. The brain's right half controls the body's left side and areas dedicated to emotional and creative impulses, including appreciation of music, art, and poetry. Thus, the left side notices details and the right side grasps the big picture.

This left–right distinction has been exaggerated, especially when broadly applied to people (Hugdahl & Westerhausen, 2010). No one is exclusively left-brained or right-brained, except individuals with severe brain injury in childhood, who may use half of their brain to do all of the necessary thinking.

For everyone else, both sides of the brain are usually involved in every skill. That is why the corpus callosum is crucial. As myelination progresses, signals between the two hemispheres become quicker and clearer, enabling children to become better thinkers and to be less clumsy. For example, no 2-year-old can hop on one foot, but most 6-year-olds can—an example of brain balancing. Many songs, dances, and games that young children love involve moving their bodies in some coordinated way—challenging, but fun because of that. Logic (left brain) without emotion (right brain) is a severe impairment, as is the opposite (Damasio, 2012).

**corpus callosum**  A long, thick band of nerve fibers that connects the left and right hemispheres of the brain and allows communication between them.

**lateralization**  Literally, sidedness, referring to the specialization in certain functions by each side of the brain, with one side dominant for each activity. The left side of the brain controls the right side of the body, and vice versa.

Left-handed people tend to have thicker corpus callosa than right-handed people do, perhaps because they often need to readjust the interaction between the two sides of their bodies, depending on the task. For example, most left-handed people brush their teeth with their left hand because using their dominant hand is more natural, but they shake hands with their right hand because that is what social convention requires.

Acceptance of left-handedness is more widespread now than a century ago. More adults in Great Britain and the United States claim to be left-handed today (about 10 percent) than in 1900 (about 3 percent) (McManus et al., 2010). Developmentalists advise against trying to force a left-handed child to become right-handed, since the brain is the origin of handedness.

Left lateralization is an advantage in some professions, especially those involving creativity and split-second actions. A disproportionate number of artists, musicians, and sports stars were/are left-handed, including Pele, Babe Ruth, Monica Seles, Bill Gates, Oprah Winfrey, Jimi Hendrix, Lady Gaga, and Justin Bieber. Five of the past eight presidents of the United States were lefties: Gerald Ford, Ronald Reagan, George H.W. Bush, Bill Clinton, and Barack Obama.

powershot/iStock/Getty Images

**Dexterity in Evidence**  She already holds the pen at the proper angle with her thumb, index finger, and middle finger—an impressive example of dexterity for a 3-year-old. However, *dexter* is Latin for "right"—evidence of an old prejudice no longer apparent here.

axons to neurons. The consequences are evident in *executive function* and *emotional regulation*, both discussed in the next two chapters (Barrasso-Catanzaro & Eslinger, 2016; Holmes et al., 2016).

Activation and inhibition are necessary lifelong. Don't leap too quickly or hesitate too long. One sign of cognitive loss in late adulthood is when an elderly person becomes too cautious or too impulsive.

Many young children are notably unbalanced neurologically. They are impulsive, flitting from one activity to another. That explains why many 3-year-olds cannot stay quietly on one task, even in "circle time" in preschool, where each child is supposed to sit in place, not talking or touching anyone.

Poor **impulse control** signifies a personality disorder in adulthood but not in early childhood. Few 3-year-olds are capable of sustained attention to tasks that adults organize. However, some preschoolers pay too much attention to things that capture their interest. They might show **perseveration,** which is to stick to, or **persevere** in, one thought or action, such as playing with one toy or holding one fantasy for hours.

Young children may repeat one phrase or question again and again, or they do not stop giggling once they start. That is perseveration. Crying may become uncontrollable because the child is stuck in whatever triggered the tantrum.

No young child is perfect at regulating attention, because immaturity of the prefrontal cortex makes it impossible to moderate the limbic system. Impulsiveness and perseveration are evident. Because the amygdala is not well connected to more reflective parts of the brain, many children become suddenly terrified—even of something that exists only in imagination. Gradually preschoolers are less likely to perseverate, especially if they are taught to switch tasks (Zelazo, 2015).

A study of children from ages 3 to 6 found that the ability to attend to what adults requested gradually increased. That correlated with academic learning and behavioral control (fewer outbursts or tears) (Metcalfe et al., 2013). Development continues as brain maturation (innate) and emotional regulation (learned) allow most children to pay attention and switch activities as needed,

Stephanie Rausser/Getty Images

**Ready to Learn?** He is 5 years old, able to sit at a desk with impressive control of fine motor muscles in his upper lip, but probably not able to read the text on the board behind him. Should he be praised or punished? Perhaps neither; in another year or two, he will no longer be admired by his classmates for this trick.

**impulse control** The ability to postpone or deny the immediate response to an idea or behavior.

**perseveration** The tendency to persevere in, or stick to, one thought or action for a long time.

Barbara Smaller/The New Yorker Collection/Cartoonbank.com

*"I would share, but I'm not there developmentally."*

**Good Excuse** It is true that emotional control of selfish instincts is difficult for young children because the prefrontal cortex is not yet mature enough to regulate some emotions. However, family practices can advance social understanding.

● **Especially for Neurologists** Why do many experts think the limbic system is an oversimplified explanation of brain function? (see response, p. 233)

with neurological maturation related to cultural demands (Posner & Rothbart, 2017). By adolescence, most North American teenagers are able to change tasks at the sound of the school bell.

## Stress and the Brain

The relationship between stress and brain activity depends partly on the age of the person and partly on the degree of stress. Both too much and too little impair learning.

In an experiment, brain scans and hormone measurements were taken of 4- to 6-year-olds immediately after a fire alarm (Teoh & Lamb, 2013). As measured by their cortisol levels, some children were upset and some were not. Two weeks later, they were questioned about the event. Those with higher cortisol reactions to the alarm remembered more details than did those with less stress. That conclusion is found in other research as well—some stress, but not too much, aids cognition (Keller et al., 2012).

However, especially with children, when an adult demands answers in a stern, yes-or-no, stressful manner, memories are less accurate. There are good evolutionary reasons for that: People need to remember experiences that arouse their emotions so that they can avoid, or adjust to, similar experiences in the future. On the other hand, the brain protects itself from too much stress by shutting down.

**LaunchPad**
macmillan learning

**Video Activity: The Childhood Stress-Cortisol Connection** examines how high cortisol levels can negatively impact a child's overall health.

Generally, a balance between arousal and reassurance is needed, again requiring speedy coordination among many parts of the brain. For instance, if children are witnesses to a crime (a stressful experience) or experience abuse, memory is more accurate when an interviewer is warm and attentive, listening carefully but not suggesting answers (Johnson et al., 2016).

Studies of maltreated children suggest that excessive stress-hormone levels in early childhood permanently damage brain pathways, blunting or accelerating emotional responses lifelong (Evans & Kim, 2013; Wilson et al., 2011). Sadly, this topic leads again to the Romanian children mentioned in Chapter 7.

When some adopted Romanian children saw pictures of happy, sad, frightened, or angry faces, their limbic systems were less reactive than were those of Romanian children who were never institutionalized. Their brains were also less lateralized, suggesting less efficient thinking (C. Nelson et al., 2014). Thus, institutional life, without the stress reduction of loving caretakers, impaired their brains.

● **Response for Early-Childhood Teachers** (from p. 227): One solution is to remind yourself that the children's brains are not yet myelinated enough to enable them to quickly walk, talk, or even button their jackets. Maturation has a major effect, as you will observe if you can schedule excursions in September and again in November. Progress, while still slow, will be several seconds faster.

### WHAT HAVE YOU LEARNED?

1. About how much does a well-nourished child grow in height and weight from ages 2 to 6?

2. Why do many adults overfeed children?

3. How do childhood allergies affect nutrition?

4. Why are today's children more at risk of obesity than children 50 years ago?

5. How much does the brain grow from ages 2 to 6?

6. Why is myelination important for thinking and motor skills?

7. How does brain maturation affect impulsivity and perseveration?

# Advancing Motor Skills

Maturation and myelination allow children to move with greater speed, agility, and grace as they age (see Visualizing Development, p. 232). Brain growth, motivation, and guided practice undergird all motor skills.

## Gross Motor Skills

Gross motor skills improve dramatically during early childhood. When playing, many 2-year-olds fall down and bump clumsily into each other. By contrast, some 5-year-olds perform coordinated dance steps, tumbling tricks, or sports moves.

There remains much for them to learn, especially in the ability to adjust to other people and new circumstances. Thus, a 5-year-old can sometimes kick a ball with precision, but it is much harder for that child to be a good team player on a soccer team.

### Specific Skills

Many North American 5-year-olds can ride a tricycle, climb a ladder, and pump a swing, as well as throw, catch, and kick a ball. A few can do these things by age 3, and some 5-year-olds can already skate, ski, dive, and ride a bike—activities that demand balanced coordination and both brain hemispheres. Elsewhere, some 5-year-olds swim in oceans or climb cliffs.

Adults need to make sure children have a safe space to play, with time, appropriate equipment, and playmates. Children learn best from peers who demonstrate whatever the child is ready to try, from catching a ball to climbing a tree. Of course, culture and locale influence particulars: Some small children learn to skateboard, others to sail.

Recent urbanization concerns many scientists (Acuto & Parnell, 2016). A century ago, children with varied skill levels played together in empty lots or fields without adult supervision, but now most of the world's children live in cities and have few safe places for active play, such as ball games and tag.

Busy or violent streets not only impede development of gross motor skills but also add to the natural fears of the immature amygdala, compounded by the learned fears of adults. Gone are the days when parents told their children to go out and play, only to return when hunger, rain, or nightfall brought them home.

**Practice with the Big Kids** Ava is unable to stand as Carlyann can (*left*), but she is thrilled to be wearing her tutu in New York City's Central Park, with 230 other dancers in a highly organized attempt to break a record for the most ballerinas on pointe at the same moment. Motor skills are developing in exactly the same way on the other side of the world (*right*) as children in Beijing perform in ballet class.

# Developing Motor Skills

Every child can do more with each passing year. These examples detail what one child might be expected to accomplish from ages 2 to 6. But each child is unique, and much depends on culture, practice, and maturity.

**SKILLS**

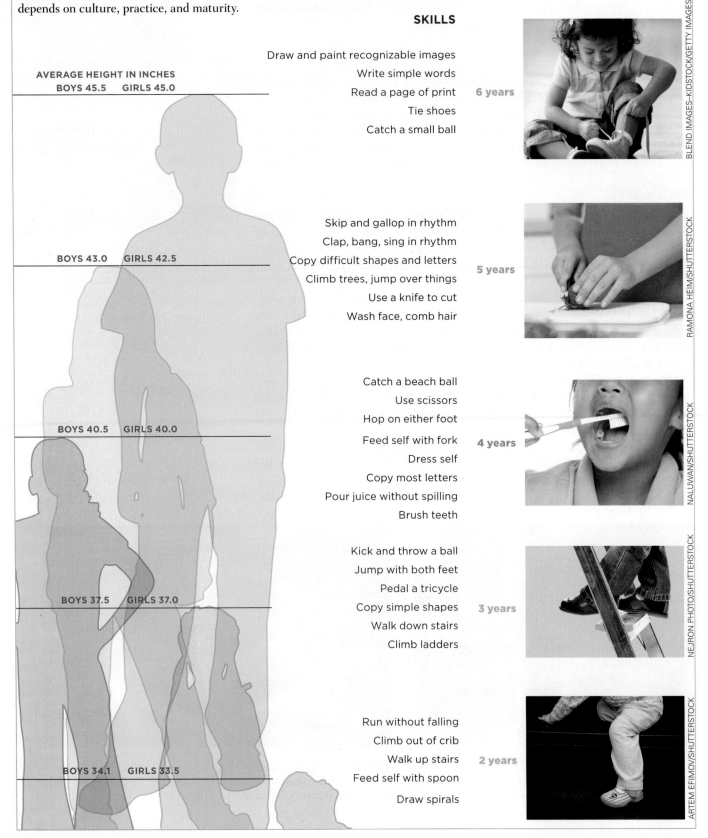

AVERAGE HEIGHT IN INCHES
BOYS 45.5    GIRLS 45.0

Draw and paint recognizable images
Write simple words
Read a page of print    **6 years**
Tie shoes
Catch a small ball

BOYS 43.0    GIRLS 42.5

Skip and gallop in rhythm
Clap, bang, sing in rhythm
Copy difficult shapes and letters    **5 years**
Climb trees, jump over things
Use a knife to cut
Wash face, comb hair

BOYS 40.5    GIRLS 40.0

Catch a beach ball
Use scissors
Hop on either foot
Feed self with fork    **4 years**
Dress self
Copy most letters
Pour juice without spilling
Brush teeth

BOYS 37.5    GIRLS 37.0

Kick and throw a ball
Jump with both feet
Pedal a tricycle
Copy simple shapes    **3 years**
Walk down stairs
Climb ladders

BOYS 34.1    GIRLS 33.5

Run without falling
Climb out of crib
Walk up stairs    **2 years**
Feed self with spoon
Draw spirals

BLEND IMAGES-KIDSTOCK/GETTY IMAGES

RAMONA HEIM/SHUTTERSTOCK

NALUWAN/SHUTTERSTOCK

NEJRON PHOTO/SHUTTERSTOCK

ARTEM EFIMOV/SHUTTERSTOCK

232

Now many parents fear strangers and traffic, keeping their 3- to 5-year-olds inside (R. Taylor et al., 2009).

That worries many childhood educators who believe that children need space and freedom to play in order to develop well (Moore & Sabo-Risley, 2017). Indeed, many agree that environment is the third teacher, "because the environment is viewed as another teacher having the power to enhance children's sense of wonder and capacity for learning" (Stremmel, 2012, p. 136). Balancing on branches and jumping over fences, squeezing mud and throwing pebbles, chasing birds and catching bugs—each forbidden now by some adults—educated millions of children in former cohorts.

## Environmental Hazards

Observable dangers and restricted exploration are not the only reasons some children are slow to develop motor skills. In addition, children who breathe heavily polluted air exercise less. Often they live in crowded neighborhoods and attend poor schools. Can we be certain that dirty air harms their learning?

Scientists have grappled with this question and answered yes: Environmental substances directly impair brain development in young children, especially those in low-SES families. Of course, many factors impact learning, but the conclusion that pollution harms the brain seems valid. Consider asthma, which keeps some children from playing and reduces oxygen to the brain.

In the United States, asthma is more prevalent among children who live in poverty than among those who do not. Worldwide, children who live in high-pollution cities have far higher rates of asthma than their peers elsewhere in their nation. Unfortunately, the World Health Organization reports that increasing numbers of children, often in megacities where air pollution is getting worse, suffer from asthma (World Health Organization, May 7, 2014). [**Developmental Link:** Asthma is defined and discussed in Chapter 11.]

A study in British Columbia, where universal public health care and detailed birth records allow solid longitudinal research, confirmed the connection. Pollution from traffic and industry during early childhood was a cause, not just a correlate, of asthma (N. Clark et al., 2010).

This study began with all 37,401 births in 1999 and 2000 in southwest British Columbia (which includes a major city, Vancouver). By age 3, almost 10 percent (3,482) of these children were asthmatic. Each of those 3,482 was matched on SES, gender, and so on with five other children from the same birth group. Exposure to air pollution (including carbon monoxide, nitric oxide, nitrogen dioxide, particulate matter, ozone, sulfur dioxide, black carbon, wood smoke, car exhausts, and smoke from parents' cigarettes) was measured.

Parents did not always protect their children, partly because they did not know which substances caused poor health. For example, because wood smoke is easy to see and smell, some parents tried to avoid it, but burning wood did not increase asthma.

However, although carbon monoxide emissions are not visible, when compared to their five matched peers, those children who were diagnosed with asthma were more likely to live near major highways, where carbon monoxide is prevalent. Other research finds that cigarette smoke affects a child's brain as well as their breath—a problem not recognized a decade ago (Swan & Lessov-Schlaggar, 2015).

From this and other research, we now know that hundreds of substances in air, food, and water affect the brain and thus impede balance, motor skills, and motivation. Many substances have not been tested, but some—including lead in the water and air, pesticides in the soil or on clothing, bisphenol A (BPA) in plastic, and secondhand cigarette smoke—are known to be harmful.

**Response for Neurologists** (from p. 230): The more we discover about the brain, the more complex we realize it is. Each part has specific functions and is connected to every other part.

One new concern is *e-waste*, which refers to discarded computers, cell phones, and other outmoded electronic devices. E-waste may spew pollutants that affect the brains of infants and children.

Many sources suggest that environmental pollutants of all kinds are especially harmful early in life. There are two main reasons: (1) Children take in more air, food, and water per pound of body weight; and (2) their organs are still developing. In addition, preschoolers are naturally active—taking apart old computers, tasting unknown substances, running during days of poor air quality and high heat.

Chronic disease and brain impairment are evident years after such kinds of childhood exposure to toxic chemicals (Suk et al., 2016). Further, children who are already at risk because of their tender age and their family structure (with single mothers, for instance) are most likely to live in polluted places (Downey et al., 2017).

Testing substances is complex, because literally thousands of chemical combinations have been developed in the past decades and virtually none of them has been studied scientifically with groups of humans or lower animals of any age. New methods of testing, at a molecular level, are now used, but again the problem of assuring safety in living creatures remains (Nel & Malloy, 2017).

Lead, however, has been thoroughly researched, and there is no doubt that it is severely toxic. The history of lead exposure in the following illustrates the tortuous path from science to practice.

---

**A VIEW FROM SCIENCE**

## Eliminating Lead

Lead was recognized as a poison a century ago (Hamilton, 1914). The symptoms of *plumbism*, as lead poisoning is called, were obvious—intellectual disability, hyperactivity, and even death if the level reached 70 micrograms per deciliter of blood.

The lead industry defended the heavy metal. Manufacturers argued that low levels were harmless, and they blamed parents for letting their children eat flaking chips of lead paint (which tastes sweet).

Further, since children with high levels of lead in their blood were often from low-SES families, some argued that malnutrition, inadequate schools, family conditions, or a host of other causes were the reasons for their reduced IQ (Scarr, 1985). I am chagrined to confess that this argument made sense to me when I wrote the first edition of this textbook (Berger, 1980).

Lead remained a major ingredient in paint (it speeds drying) and in gasoline (it raises octane) for most of the twentieth century. Finally, chemical analyses of blood and teeth, with careful longitudinal and replicated research, proved that lead was indeed a poison for all children (Needleman et al., 1990; Needleman & Gatsonis, 1990).

The United States banned lead in paint (in 1978) and automobile fuel (in 1996). The blood level that caused plumbism was set at 40 micrograms per deciliter, then 20, and then 10. Danger is now thought to begin at 5 micrograms, but no level has been proven to be risk-free (MMWR, April 5, 2013). Part of the problem is that the fetus and infant absorb lead at a much

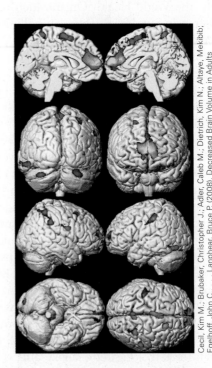

Cecil, Kim M.; Brubaker, Christopher J.; Adler, Caleb M.; Dietrich, Kim N.; Altaye, Mekibib; Egelhoff, John C.; . . . Lanphear, Bruce P. (2008). Decreased Brain Volume in Adults with Childhood Lead Exposure. Plos Medicine, 5(5), 741–750. doi: 10.1371/Journal. Pmed.0050112

**Toxic Shrinkage** A composite of 157 brains of adults—who, as children, had high lead levels in their blood—shows reduced volume. The red and yellow hot spots are all areas that are smaller than areas in a normal brain. No wonder lead-exposed children have multiple intellectual and behavioral problems.

higher rate than adults do, so lead's neurotoxicity is especially destructive of developing brains (Hanna-Attisha et al., 2016).

Regulation has made a difference: The percentage of U.S. 1- to 5-year-olds with more than 5 micrograms of lead per deciliter of blood was 8.6 percent in 1999–2001, 4.1 percent in 2003–2006, and 2.6 percent in 2007–2010 (see Figure 8.2). Children who are young, low-SES, and/or living in old housing tend to have higher levels (MMWR, April 5, 2013).

Many parents now know to increase their children's calcium intake, wipe window ledges clean, avoid child exposure to construction dust, test drinking water, discard lead-based medicines and crockery (available in some other nations), and make sure children never eat chips of lead-based paint. However, as evident many times in the study of development, private actions alone are not sufficient to protect health. Parents are blamed for obesity, injury, abuse, and neglect, but often the larger community is also to blame.

A stark recent example occurred in Flint, Michigan, where in April 2014 cost-saving officials (appointed by the state to take over the city when the tax base shrunk as the auto industry left) changed the municipal drinking water from Lake Huron to the Flint River. That river contained chemicals that increased lead leaching from old pipes, contaminating the water supply—often used for drinking and mixing infant formula.

The percent of young children in Flint with blood lead levels above 5 micrograms per deciliter doubled in two years, from 2.4 to 4.9 percent, and more than tripled in one neighborhood from 4.6 to 15.7 percent (Hanna-Attisha et al., 2016). Apparently, the state-appointed emergency manager focused on saving money, ignoring possible brain damage to children who, unlike him, are mostly low-income and African American. This oversight is considered an "abject failure to protect public health" (Bellinger, 2016, p. 1101).

The consequences may harm the community for decades. Remember from Chapter 1 that scientists sometimes use data collected for other reasons to draw new conclusions. This is the case with lead.

About 15 years after the sharp decline in blood lead levels in preschool children, the rate of violent crime committed by teenagers and young adults fell sharply. This seems more than coincidence, since some nations reduced lead before others, and those nations saw a reduction in teenage crime earlier than others.

A scientist comparing these trends concluded that some teenagers commit impulsive, violent crimes because their brains were poisoned by lead years earlier. The correlation is found in every nation that has reliable data on lead and crime—Canada, Germany, Italy, Australia, United States, New Zealand, France, and Finland (Nevin, 2007). Moreover, blood lead levels in early childhood predict later attention deficits and school suspensions (Amato et al., 2013; Goodlad et al., 2013).

There is no doubt that lead, even at low levels in the blood of a young child, harms the brain. That raises questions about the long-term effects of hundreds, perhaps thousands, of new chemicals in the air, water, or soil. It also makes the Flint tragedy more troubling. Developmentalists have known about the dangers of lead for decades. Why didn't the Michigan administrator know better?

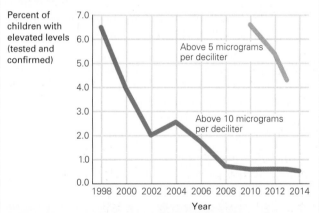

**Lead Concentration in Blood of Children Ages 6 and Under, United States**

Data from Child Trends Data Bank, 2015; Centers for Disease Control and Prevention, 2016.

### FIGURE 8.2

**Dramatic Improvement in a Decade** When legislators finally accepted the research establishing the damage from lead in paint, gasoline, and water, they passed laws making it exceedingly rare for any child to die or suffer intellectual disability because of plumbism. A decade ago, 10 micrograms in the blood was thought to be completely safe; now less than 1 child in 200 tests at that level, and even 5 micrograms alerts pediatricians and parents to find the source. These national data make the tragedy in Flint, Michigan, especially shocking.

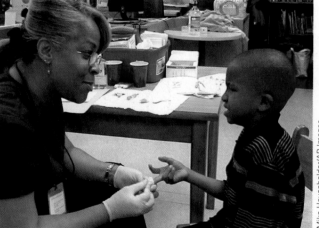

Mike Householder/AP Images

**Too Late?** Veronica Robinson is a University of Michigan nursing professor who volunteered to provide free lead testing for the children of Flint, Michigan. If 7-year-old Zyontae's level is high, brain damage in early life will trouble him lifelong.

## Fine Motor Skills

Fine motor skills are harder to master than gross motor skills. Whistling, winking, and especially writing are difficult in early childhood. Pouring juice into a glass, cutting food with a knife, and achieving anything more artful than a scribble all require a level of muscular control, patience, and judgment that is beyond most 2-year-olds. These skills still require concentration at age 6.

Many fine motor skills involve two hands and thus both sides of the brain: The fork stabs the meat while the knife cuts it; one hand steadies the paper while the other writes; tying shoes, buttoning shirts, cutting paper, and zipping zippers require both hands. Brain lateralization is needed. Short, stubby fingers add to the problem. As a result, shoelaces get knotted, paper gets ripped, and zippers get stuck. Parents and teachers need to provide good learning tools (large, wooden puzzles, art supplies, etc.) with much patience.

**Especially for Immigrant Parents** You and your family eat with chopsticks at home, but you want your children to feel comfortable in Western culture. Should you change your family's eating customs? (see response, p. 238)

### Academics Before Age 6

Traditional school necessitates fine motor skills and body control. Writing requires finger control, reading print requires eye control, classroom schedules require bladder control, and so on. Consequently, even the brightest 3-year-old is not ready for first grade.

Slow maturation is one reason many 6-year-olds are frustrated if their teachers demand that they write neatly and cut straight. Some educators suggest waiting until a child is "ready" for school; some suggest that preschools should focus on readiness; still others suggest that schools should adjust to children, not vice versa.

Fine motor skills—like many other biological characteristics, such as bones, brains, and teeth—mature about six months earlier in girls than in boys. By contrast, boys often are ahead of girls in gross motor skills. These gender differences may be biological, or they may result from practice: Young girls more often dress up and play with dolls (fine motor skills), while boys more often climb and kick (gross motor skills) (Saraiva et al., 2013).

In grade school, girls are, on average, ahead of boys in behavior and reading because of fine motor maturation. Boys, of course, catch up, and they should not be blamed if they are not as accomplished as their female classmates.

### Artistic Expression

Young children are imaginative, creative, and not yet self-critical. They love to express themselves, especially if their parents applaud their performances, display

**Same Situation, Far Apart: Finger Skills** Children learn whatever motor skills their culture teaches. Some master chopsticks, with fingers to spare; others cut sausage with a knife and fork. Unlike these children in Japan (*below left*) and Germany (*below right*), some never master either, because about one-third of adults worldwide eat directly with their hands.

their artwork, and otherwise communicate approval. The fact that their fine motor skills are immature, and thus their drawings lack precision, is irrelevant. Perhaps the immaturity of the prefrontal cortex is a blessing, allowing creativity without self-criticism.

All forms of artistic expression blossom during early childhood: 2- to 6-year-olds love to dance around the room, build an elaborate tower of blocks, make music by pounding in rhythm, and put bright marks on shiny paper. In every artistic domain, skill takes both practice and maturation.

For example, when drawing a person, 2- to 3-year-olds usually draw a "tadpole"—a circle head, dots for eyes, sometimes a smiling mouth, and then a line or two beneath to indicate the rest of the body. Gradually, tadpoles get bodies, limbs, hair, and so on. Children's artwork is not intended to be realistic: It communicates thoughts and self-expression (Papandreou, 2014). It is a mistake for adults to say "that looks like a . . ." or worse, "you forgot the feet."

Cultural and cohort differences are apparent in all artistic skills. Some parents enroll their preschool children in music lessons, hoping they will learn to play. As a result, those preschoolers become better at listening to sounds, evident in listening to speech as well as music. Neurological evidence finds that their brains reflect their new auditory abilities, a remarkable testimony to the role of family and culture (Strait et al., 2013).

Klaus Vedfelt/Getty Images

**What Is It?** Wrong question! Better to say "tell me about it" and then perhaps this 4-year-old will explain the fringe she carefully added to the . . .

---

### WHAT HAVE YOU LEARNED?

1. What three factors help children develop their motor skills?

2. How have cohort changes affected the development of gross motor skills?

3. What is known and unknown about the effects on young children of chemicals in food, air, and water?

4. What are conflicting interpretations of gender differences in motor skills?

5. How does brain maturation affect children's artistic expression?

---

## Injuries and Abuse

In almost all families of every income, ethnicity, and nation, parents want to protect their children while fostering their growth. Yet far more children die from violence—either accidental or deliberate—than from any specific disease.

The contrast between disease and violent (usually accidental) death is most obvious in developed nations, where medical prevention, diagnosis, and treatment make fatal illness rare until late adulthood. In the United States, four times as many 1- to 4-year-olds die of accidents than of cancer, which is the leading cause of disease death during these years (National Center for Health Statistics, 2015).

Indeed, in recent years, more 1- to 4-year-old U.S. children have been murdered than have died of cancer. (In 2013, for instance, there were 337 homicides and 328 cancer deaths.)

●● **Response for Immigrant Parents** (from p. 236): Children develop the motor skills that they see and practice. They will soon learn to use forks, spoons, and knives. Do not abandon chopsticks completely, because young children can learn several ways of doing things, and the ability to eat with chopsticks is a social asset.

## Avoidable Injury

Worldwide, injuries cause millions of premature deaths among adults as well as children: Not until age 40 does any specific disease overtake accidents as a cause of mortality.

In some nations, malnutrition, malaria, and other infectious diseases *combined* cause more infant and child deaths than injuries do, but those nations also have high rates of child injury. Southern Asia and sub-Saharan Africa have the highest rates of motor-vehicle deaths, even though the number of cars is relatively low (World Health Organization, 2015). Most children who die in such accidents are pedestrians, or are riding—without a helmet—on motorcycles.

### Age-Related Dangers

In accidents overall, 2- to 6-year-olds are more often seriously hurt than 6- to 10-year-olds. Why are young children so vulnerable? Many reasons.

Immaturity of the prefrontal cortex makes young children impulsive; they plunge into danger. Unlike infants, their motor skills allow them to run, leap, scramble, and grab in a flash, before a caregiver can stop them. Their curiosity is boundless; their impulses are uninhibited. Then, if they do something that becomes dangerous, such as lighting a fire while playing with matches, fear and stress might make them slow to get help.

Age-related trends are apparent in particulars. Falls are more often fatal for the youngest (under 24 months) and oldest people (over 80 years); preschoolers have high rates of poisoning and drowning; motor-vehicle deaths peak during ages 15 to 25.

Generally, as income falls, accident rates rise, but this is not always true. Not only are 1- to 4-year-olds more likely to die of drowning than any other age group, they drown in swimming pools six times more often than older children and adults (MMWR, May 16, 2014). Usually the deadly pool is in their own backyard, a luxury less likely for low-income families.

**Same Situation, Far Apart: Keeping Everyone Safe** Preventing child accidents requires action by both adults and children. In the United States (*above left*), adults passed laws and taught children to use seat belts—including this boy who buckles his stuffed companion. In France (*above right*), teachers stop cars while children hold hands to cross the street—each child keeping his or her partner moving ahead.

## Injury Control

Instead of using the term *accident prevention*, public health experts prefer **injury control (or harm reduction).** Consider the implications. *Accident* implies that an injury is random, unpredictable; if anyone is at fault, it's a careless parent or an accident-prone child. Instead, *injury control* suggests that the impact of an injury can be limited if appropriate controls are in place, and *harm reduction* implies that harm can be minimized.

If young children are allowed to play to develop their skills, minor mishaps (scratches and bruises) are bound to occur. Children need to play, yet communities need to protect them. A child with no scrapes may be overprotected, but serious injury is unlikely if a child falls on a safety surface instead of on concrete, if a car seat protects the body in a crash, if a bicycle helmet cracks instead of a skull, or if swallowed pills come from a tiny bottle. Reducing harm requires effort from professionals and parents, as I know too well from my own experience described in the following.

> **injury control/harm reduction** Practices that are aimed at anticipating, controlling, and preventing dangerous activities; these practices reflect the beliefs that accidents are not random and that injuries can be made less harmful if proper controls are in place.

---

**A CASE TO STUDY**

## "My Baby Swallowed Poison"

Many people think that the way to prevent injury to young children is to educate parents. However, public health research finds that laws that apply to everyone are more effective than education, especially if parents are overwhelmed by the daily demands of child care and money management. Injury rates rise when parents have more than one small child, and not enough money.

For example, thousands of lives have been saved by infant car seats. However, few parents voluntarily install car seats. Research has found that parents are more likely to use car seats if given them to take their newborn home from the hospital, and if an expert installs the seat and shows the parents how to use it—not simply tells them or makes them watch a video (Tessier, 2010).

New laws mandating car seats and new programs at hospitals have had an effect. In 2013, in the entire United States, only 60 infant passengers died in car accidents, about one-eighth the number in 2003.

The research concludes that motivation and education help, but laws mandating primary prevention are more effective. I know this firsthand. Our daughter Bethany, at age 2, climbed onto the kitchen counter to find, open, and swallow most of a bottle of baby aspirin. Where was I? In the next room, nursing our second child and watching television. I did not notice what Bethany was doing until I checked on her during a commercial.

Bethany is alive and well today, protected by all three levels of prevention (described on next page). *Primary prevention* included laws limiting the number of baby aspirin per container; *secondary prevention* included my pediatrician's written directions when Bethany was a week old to buy syrup of ipecac; *tertiary prevention* was my phone call to Poison Control.

I told the helpful stranger who answered the phone, "My baby swallowed poison." He calmly asked me a few questions and then advised me to give Bethany ipecac to make her throw up. I did, and she did.

I had bought that ipecac two years before, when I was a brand-new mother and ready to follow every bit of my pediatrician's advice. If the doctor had waited until Bethany was able to climb before he recommended it, I might not have followed his advice because by then I had more confidence in my ability to prevent harm.

I still blame myself, but I am grateful for all three levels of prevention that protected my child. In some ways, my own education helped avert a tragedy. I had chosen a wise pediatrician; I knew the number for Poison Control (FYI: 1-800-222-1222).

As I remember all the mistakes I made in parenting (only a few are mentioned in this book), I am grateful for every level of prevention. Without protective laws and a national network to help parents, the results might have been tragic.

---

Less than half as many 1- to 5-year-olds in the United States were fatally injured in 2014 as in 1984, thanks to laws that limit poisons, prevent fires, and regulate cars. Control has not yet caught up with newer hazards, however. For instance, many new homes in California, Florida, Texas, and Arizona have swimming pools: In those states drowning is a leading cause of child death. According

**Forget Baby Henry?** Infants left in parked cars on hot days can die from the heat. Henry's father invented a disc to be placed under the baby that buzzes his cell phone if he is more than 20 feet away from the disc. He hopes all absent-minded parents will buy one.

**primary prevention** Actions that change overall background conditions to prevent some unwanted event or circumstance, such as injury, disease, or abuse.

**secondary prevention** Actions that avert harm in a high-risk situation, such as stopping a car before it hits a pedestrian.

**tertiary prevention** Actions, such as immediate and effective medical treatment, that are taken after an illness or injury and that are aimed at reducing harm or preventing disability.

**Especially for Urban Planners** Describe a neighborhood park that would benefit 2- to 5-year-olds. (see response, p. 242)

to the American Association of Poison Control Centers' National Poison Data System, children under age 5 are now less often poisoned from pills and more often poisoned because of cosmetics or personal care products (deodorant, hair colorant, etc.) (Mowry et al., 2015, p. 968).

## Prevention

Prevention begins long before any particular child, parent, or legislator does something foolish. Unfortunately, no one notices injuries and deaths that did not happen.

### Finding the Cause

For developmentalists, two types of analysis are useful to predict and prevent danger. The first is to use a dynamic-systems or ecological approach. Every level must be considered: Causes can be found in the child, the microsystem, the exosystem, and the macrosystem.

For example, when a child is hit by a car, the child might have been impulsive, the parents neglectful (microsystem), the community without parks, traffic lights, sidewalks, or curbs (all exosystem), and/or the culture may have prioritized fast cars over slow pedestrians (macrosystem). Once all of those factors are recognized, preventive measures on every level become clear, from holding the hand of a young child when crossing the street up to enforcing national speed limits.

The second type of analysis involves understanding statistics. The data show that childhood poisoning decreased markedly when pill manufacturers adopted bottles with safety caps that are difficult for children to open. That statistic undercuts complaints about inconvenience.

New statistics show a rise in the number of children being poisoned by taking adult recreational drugs (such as cocaine, alcohol, or marijuana) or adult prescription drugs (such as opioids), or being shot by household guns not locked away. Those data can lead to new strategies for prevention (Fine et al., 2012). Pediatricians are now allowed to ask parents about home firearms (Rivera & Fan, 2017).

### Levels of Prevention

Three levels of prevention apply to every health and safety issue.

- In **primary prevention,** the overall conditions are structured to make harm less likely. Primary prevention reduces everyone's chance of injury.
- **Secondary prevention** is more targeted, averting harm in high-risk situations or for vulnerable individuals.
- **Tertiary prevention** begins after an injury has already occurred, limiting damage.

In general, tertiary prevention is the most visible of the three levels, but primary prevention is the most effective (L. Cohen et al., 2010). An example comes from data on pedestrian deaths. As compared with 20 years ago, fewer children in the United States today die after being hit by a motor vehicle (see Figure 8.3). How does each level of prevention contribute?

*Primary prevention* includes sidewalks, pedestrian overpasses, streetlights, and traffic circles. Cars have been redesigned (e.g., better headlights, windows, and brakes), and drivers' competence has improved (e.g., stronger penalties for drunk driving). Reduction of traffic via improved mass transit provides additional primary prevention.

*Secondary prevention* reduces danger in high-risk situations. School crossing guards and flashing lights on stopped schoolbuses are secondary prevention, as are

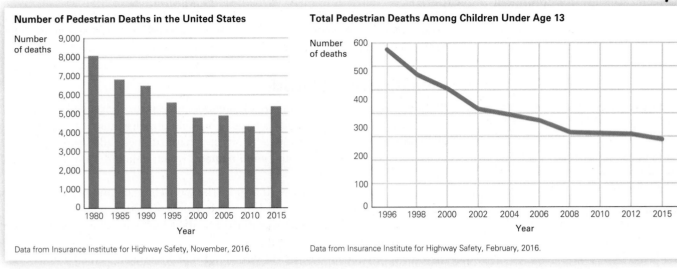

**Number of Pedestrian Deaths in the United States**

Data from Insurance Institute for Highway Safety, November, 2016.

**Total Pedestrian Deaths Among Children Under Age 13**

Data from Insurance Institute for Highway Safety, February, 2016.

**FIGURE 8.3**

**No Matter What Statistic**  Motor-vehicle fatalities of pedestrians, passengers, and drivers, from cars, trucks and motorcycles, for people of all ages, are all markedly lower in 2015 than in 1985, an especially dramatic difference since the population has increased by a third and the number of cars has doubled. The increase since 2010 is caused by better (not worse) prevention: Health-care improvements prevent many premature deaths, so more older people are crossing busy streets. Since the elderly are more likely to die if they are hit, overall *numbers* (not *rates*) of pedestrian deaths are rising.

salt on icy roads, warning signs before blind curves, speed bumps, and walk/don't walk signals at busy intersections.

Finally, *tertiary prevention* reduces damage after an accident. Examples include speedy ambulances, efficient emergency room procedures, effective follow-up care, and laws against hit-and-run drivers, all of which have been improved from decades ago. Medical personnel speak of the *golden hour*, the hour following an accident, when a victim should be treated. Of course, there is nothing magical about 60 minutes in contrast to 61 minutes, but the faster an injury victim reaches a trauma center, the better the chance of recovery (Dinh et al., 2013).

### WHAT HAVE YOU LEARNED?

1. What can be concluded from the data on rates of childhood injury?

2. How do injury deaths compare in developed and developing nations?

3. What are some examples of primary prevention?

4. What are some examples of secondary prevention?

## Child Maltreatment

Until about 1960, people thought child maltreatment was rare and consisted of a sudden attack by a disturbed stranger, usually a man. Today we know better, thanks to a pioneering study based on careful observation in one Boston hospital (Kempe & Kempe, 1978).

Maltreatment is neither rare nor sudden, and 92 percent of the time the perpetrators are one or both of the child's parents—more often the mother than the father (U.S. Department of Health and Human Services, January 25, 2016). That makes it much worse: Ongoing home abuse, with no protector, is much more damaging than a single outside incident, however injurious.

## Definitions and Statistics

**Child maltreatment** now refers to all intentional harm to, or avoidable endangerment of, anyone under 18 years of age. Thus, child maltreatment includes both **child abuse,** which is deliberate action that is harmful to a child's physical, emotional, or sexual well-being, and **child neglect,** which is failure to meet essential needs.

Neglect is worse than abuse. It also is "the most common and most frequently fatal form of child maltreatment" (Proctor & Dubowitz, 2014, p. 27). About three times as many neglect cases occur in the United States as abuse cases, a ratio probably found in many other nations.

To be specific, data on cases of *substantiated* maltreatment in the United States in 2014 indicate that 77 percent were neglect, 17 percent physical abuse, 6 percent emotional abuse, and 8 percent sexual abuse. (A few were tallied in two categories [U.S. Department of Health and Human Services, January 25, 2016].) Ironically, neglect is too often ignored by the public, who are "stuck in an overwhelming and debilitating" concept of maltreatment as something that causes immediate bodily harm (Kendall-Taylor et al., 2014, p. 810).

**Substantiated maltreatment** means that a case has been reported, investigated, and verified (see Figure 8.4). In 2014, about 800,000 children suffered substantiated abuse in the United States. Substantiated maltreatment harms about 1 in every 90 children aged 2 to 5 annually.

**Reported maltreatment** (technically a referral) means simply that the authorities have been informed. Since 1993, the number of children referred to authorities in the United States has ranged from about 2.7 million to 3.6 million per year, with 3.6 million in 2014 (U.S. Department of Health and Human Services, January 25, 2016).

**child maltreatment** Intentional harm to or avoidable endangerment of anyone under 18 years of age.

**child abuse** Deliberate action that is harmful to a child's physical, emotional, or sexual well-being.

**child neglect** Failure to meet a child's basic physical, educational, or emotional needs.

**substantiated maltreatment** Harm or endangerment that has been reported, investigated, and verified.

**reported maltreatment** Harm or endangerment about which someone has notified the authorities.

● **Response for Urban Planners** (from p. 240): The adult idea of a park—a large, grassy open place—is not best for young children. For them, you would design an enclosed area, small enough and with adequate seating to allow caregivers to socialize while watching their children. The playground surface would have to be protective (since young children are clumsy), with equipment that encourages motor skills. Teenagers and dogs should have their own designated areas, far from the youngest children.

**FIGURE 8.4**

**Getting Better?** As you can see, the number of victims of child maltreatment in the United States has declined in the past decades, an especially good result because the total number of children has increased. One possible explanation is that the legal, social work, and community responses have improved, so fewer children are mistreated. Other less sanguine explanations are possible, however.

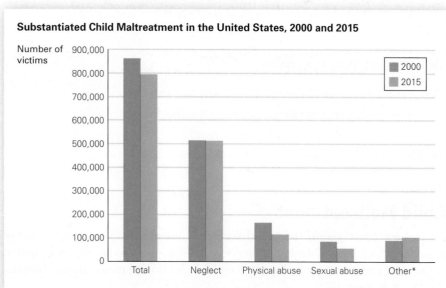

**Substantiated Child Maltreatment in the United States, 2000 and 2015**

Data from U.S. Department of Health and Human Services, December 31, 2000, p. 24, January 19, 2017, p. 45.
*Includes emotional and medical abuse, educational neglect, and maltreatment not specified by the state records.

The 4-to-1 ratio of reported versus substantiated cases occurs because:

1. Each child is counted only once, so four verified reports about a single child result in one substantiated case.
2. Substantiation requires proof. Most investigations do not find unmistakable harm or a witness.
3. Many professionals are *mandated reporters*, required to report any signs of *possible* maltreatment. In 2014, two-thirds of all reports came from professionals. Usually an investigation finds no harm (Pietrantonio et al., 2013).
4. Some reports are "screened out" as belonging to another jurisdiction, such as the military or a Native American tribe, who have their own systems. In 2014, many (about 39 percent) referrals were screened out.
5. A report may be false or deliberately misleading (though few are) (Sedlak & Ellis, 2014).

## Frequency of Maltreatment

How often does maltreatment actually occur? No one knows. Not all instances are noticed, not all that are noticed are reported, and not all reports are substantiated. Part of the problem is in drawing the line between harsh discipline and abuse, and between momentary and ongoing neglect. If the standard were perfect parenting all day and all night from birth to age 18, as judged by neighbors, professionals, as well as the parent, then every child has been mistreated. Only the most severe cases are tallied.

If we rely on official U.S. statistics, positive trends are apparent. Substantiated child maltreatment increased from about 1960 to 1990 but decreased thereafter (see Figure 8.5). Other sources also report declines, particularly in sexual abuse, over the past two decades (Finkelhor, 2008). Perhaps national awareness has led to better reporting and then more effective prevention.

Unfortunately, official reports raise doubt. For example, Pennsylvania reports fewer victims than Maine (3,262 compared to 3,823 in 2014), but the child population of Pennsylvania is more than 10 times that of Maine. Why the discrepancy? One hypothesis might be lack of sufficient personnel, but that hypothesis has been proven false: Pennsylvania has 20 times more employees screening

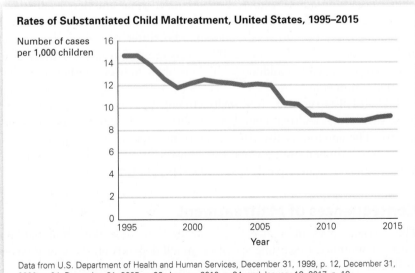

Rates of Substantiated Child Maltreatment, United States, 1995–2015

Number of cases per 1,000 children

Year

Data from U.S. Department of Health and Human Services, December 31, 1999, p. 12, December 31, 2000, p. 24, December 31, 2005, p. 26, January, 2010, p. 34, and January 19, 2017, p. 19.

**FIGURE 8.5**

**Still Far Too Many** The number of substantiated cases of maltreatment of children under age 18 in the United States is too high, but there is some good news: The rate has declined significantly from its peak (15.3) in 1993.

and investigating than Maine (2,803 to 145). There is another oddity in the data: Only 3 percent of the Pennsylvania victims are classified as neglected, but 62 percent suffered sexual abuse. (National rates are 75 percent neglect and 8 percent sexual abuse.)

Pennsylvania has the lowest child maltreatment rate of any of the 50 states, but Maine is not highest—Massachusetts is. Does Pennsylvania ignore thousands of maltreated children who would be substantiated victims if they lived in Massachusetts?

How maltreatment is defined is powerfully influenced by culture (one of my students asked, "When is a child too old to be beaten?"). Willingness to report also varies. The United States has become more culturally diverse, and people have become more suspicious of government. Does that reduce reporting but not abuse?

From a developmental perspective, beyond the difficulty in getting accurate data, another problem is that most maltreatment occurs early in life, before children are required to attend school, where a teacher would notice a problem. One infant in 45 is substantiated as maltreated, as is 1 preschooler in 90 (U.S. Department of Health and Human Services, January 25, 2016). Those are substantiated cases; some of the youngest victims never reach outsiders' attention.

An additional problem is that some children are abused in many ways by many people. Many studies have found that a single episode of child abuse followed by parental protection and love—never blaming the child—allows such children to recover. By contrast, repeated victimization causes lifelong harm, largely because such children are not protected by their parents. Indeed, often a family member is one of the abusers (Turner et al., 2016).

## Warning Signs

Instead of relying on official statistics and mandated reporters, every reader of this book can recognize developmental problems and prevent maltreatment. Often the first sign is delayed development, such as slow growth, immature communication, lack of curiosity, or unusual social interactions. These are all evident in infancy and early childhood, before a child comes to the notice of a professional.

Maltreated young children may seem fearful, easily startled by noise, defensive and quick to attack, and confused between fantasy and reality. These are symptoms of **post-traumatic stress disorder (PTSD),** first identified in combat veterans, then in adults who had experienced some emotional injury or shock (after a serious accident, natural disaster, or violent crime). More recently, PTSD is evident in some maltreated children, who suffer neurologically, emotionally, and behaviorally (Neigh et al., 2009; Weiss et al., 2013). Particularly if a child is abused during early childhood, PTSD is likely to occur, either immediately or later on (Dunn et al., 2017).

Table 8.1 lists signs of child maltreatment, both neglect and abuse. None of these signs *proves* maltreatment, but whenever any of them occurs, investigation is needed. The opposite is also true: Some things that many young children do (not eating much dinner, crying when they must stop playing, imagining things that are not true) are quite typical, not usually signs of abuse.

## Consequences of Maltreatment

The consequences of maltreatment involve not only the child but also the entire community. Regarding specifics, much depends on the culture as well as resilience—not only in the child but also in the social context.

---

**THINK CRITICALLY:** Why might Pennsylvania have so few cases of neglect?

---

🕐 **Especially for Nurses** While weighing a 4-year-old, you notice several bruises on the child's legs. When you ask about them, the child says nothing and the parent says that the child bumps into things. What should you do? (see response, p. 246)

---

**post-traumatic stress disorder (PTSD)** An anxiety disorder that develops as a delayed reaction to having experienced or witnessed a profoundly shocking or frightening event, such as rape, severe beating, war, or natural disaster. Its symptoms include flashbacks, hyperactivity, hypervigilance, displaced anger, sleeplessness, nightmares, sudden terror or anxiety, and confusion between fantasy and reality.

## TABLE 8.1

### Signs of Maltreatment in Children Aged 2 to 10

Injuries that are unlikely to be accidents, such as bruises on both sides of the face or body; burns with a clear line between burned and unburned skin

Repeated injuries, especially broken bones not properly tended (visible on X-ray)

Fantasy play with dominant themes of violence or sex

Slow physical growth

Unusual appetite or lack of appetite

Ongoing physical complaints, such as stomachaches, headaches, genital pain, sleepiness

Reluctance to talk, to play, or to move, especially if development is slow

No close friendships; hostility toward others; bullying of smaller children

Hypervigilance, with quick, impulsive reactions, such as cringing, startling, or hitting

Frequent absence from school

Frequent change of address

Frequent change in caregivers

Child seems fearful, not joyful, on seeing caregiver

Certain customs (such as circumcision, pierced ears, and spanking) are considered abusive among some groups but not in others; their effects vary accordingly. Children suffer if their parents seem to care less than most parents in their neighborhood, or if their parents are hostile to each other. If a parent forbids something other children have or punishes more severely or not at all, children might feel unloved.

The long-term effects of maltreatment depend partly on the child's interpretation at the time (punishment considered unfair is especially harmful) and, in adulthood, on the current relationship between the adult and the punishing parent. If the grown child has a good relationship with the formerly abusive parent (more common if abuse was not chronic), then the adult may recover from past maltreatment (Schafer et al., 2014). It has been said that abused children become abusive parents, but this is not necessarily true (Widom et al., 2015a). Many people avoid the mistakes of their parents, especially if their friends or partners show them a better way.

Nonetheless, the consequences of maltreatment may last for decades. The immediate impairment may be obvious, as when a child is bruised, broken, afraid to talk, or failing in school. However, when researchers follow maltreated children over the years, deficits in social skills and self-esteem seem more crippling than physical or intellectual damage.

Maltreated children tend to hate themselves and then hate everyone else. Even if the child was mistreated in the early years and then not after age 5, emotional problems (externalizing for the boys and internalizing for the girls) linger (Godinet et al., 2014). Adult drug abuse, social isolation, and poor health may result from maltreatment decades earlier (Mersky et al., 2013; Sperry & Widom, 2013).

Hate is corrosive. A warm and enduring friendship can repair some damage, but maltreatment makes such friendships less likely. Many studies find that mistreated children typically regard other people as hostile and exploitative; hence, they are less friendly, more aggressive, and more isolated than other children. They need friends but are unlikely to have them.

Photo Japan/Alamy

David Jakle/Getty Images

**Family Protection** Relatives are a safety net. Ideally, they feed and play with the young members of the family (as these grandfathers do). This is secondary prevention, allowing parents to provide good care. Rarely is tertiary prevention needed. About 1 percent of all U.S. grandparents are foster or adoptive parents of their grandchildren. This does not benefit the adults, but it may be the best solution for mistreated children.

⬤ **Response for Nurses** (from p. 244): Any suspicion of child maltreatment must be reported, and these bruises are suspicious. Someone in authority must find out what is happening so that the parent as well as the child can be helped.

The earlier that abuse starts and the longer it continues, the worse the children's relationships are. Physically and sexually abused children are likely to be irrationally angry and neglected children are often withdrawn (Petrenko et al., 2012). That makes healthy romances and friendships difficult.

Further, finding and keeping a job is a critical aspect of adult well-being, yet adults who were maltreated suffer in this way as well. One study carefully matched 807 children who had experienced substantiated abuse with other children who were of the same sex, ethnicity, and family SES. About 35 years later, long after maltreatment had stopped, those who had been mistreated were 14 percent less likely to be employed than those who had not been abused. The researchers concluded: "abused and neglected children experience large and enduring economic consequences" (Currie & Widom, 2010, p. 111).

In this study, women had more difficulty finding and keeping a job than men. It may be that self-esteem, emotional stability, and social skills are even more important for female employees than for male ones. This study is just one of hundreds of longitudinal studies, all of which find that maltreatment affects people decades after broken bones, or skinny bodies, or medical neglect.

## Preventing Maltreatment

Just as with injury control, the ultimate goal with regard to child maltreatment is *primary prevention*, a social network of customs and supports that help parents, neighbors, and professionals protect every child. Neighborhood stability, parental education, income support, and fewer unwanted children all reduce maltreatment.

All these are examples of primary prevention. Such measures are more effective in the long run, but governments and private foundations are more likely to fund projects that focus on high-risk families (Nelson & Caplan, 2014). The media's focus on shocking examples of parental abuse or social worker neglect ignores the many ways families, communities, and professionals stop maltreatment before it begins.

*Secondary prevention* involves spotting warning signs and intervening to keep a risky situation from getting worse. For example, insecure attachment, especially of the disorganized type, is a sign of a disrupted parent–child relationship. Thus, insecure attachment should be repaired before it becomes harmful. [**Developmental Link:** Attachment types are explained in detail in Chapter 7.]

An important aspect of secondary prevention is reporting the first signs of maltreatment. Unfortunately, relatively few reports come from neighbors (5 percent) or relatives (7 percent), who are usually the first to notice when a young child is mistreated.

One reason is that not everyone knows what is normal and what is not. Another reason is that many abusers hide from outsiders, deliberately changing residences and isolating themselves from relatives. Social isolation itself is a worrisome sign. Finally, many people are afraid that the abusers will turn on them if they report an abused child. They need to consider the consequences for the child, not only for themselves, and then either report or rescue.

*Tertiary prevention* limits harm after maltreatment has occurred. Reporting is the first step; investigating and substantiating is second. The final step, however, is helping the caregiver provide better care (specifics may include treating addiction, assigning a housekeeper, locating family helpers, securing better living quarters) and helping the child recover (with better home care, or with another family).

The priority must be child protection. In every case, **permanency planning** is needed: planning how to nurture the child until adulthood (Scott et al., 2013). Uncertainty, moving, a string of temporary placements, and frequent changes in schools are all destructive.

When children are taken from their parents and entrusted to another adult, that is **foster care.** The other adult might be a stranger or might be a relative, in which case it is called **kinship care.**

Foster parents are paid for the child's expenses and trained to provide good care, although specifics vary from state to state. Every year for the past decade in the United States, almost half a million children have been officially in foster care. At least another million are unofficially in kinship care, because relatives realize that the parents are unable or unwilling to provide good care.

In every nation, most foster children are from low-income, ethnic-minority families—a statistic that reveals problems in the macrosystem as well as the microsystem. In the United States, most foster children have physical, intellectual, and emotional problems that arose in their original families—evidence of their abuse and neglect (Jones & Morris, 2012). Obviously, foster parents need much more than financial subsidies to become good caregivers.

In many cases, the best permanency plan for children is to be adopted by another family, who will care for them lifelong. However, adoption is difficult, for many reasons:

- Judges and biological parents are reluctant to release children for adoption.
- Most adoptive parents prefer infants, but few maltreating adults recognize how hard child care can be until they have tried, and failed, to provide for their children.
- Some agencies screen out families not headed by heterosexual couples.
- Some professionals seek adoptive parents of the same ethnicity and/or religion as the child.

As detailed many times in this chapter, caring for young children is not easy. Parents shoulder most of the burden, and their love and protection usually result in strong and happy children. However, when parents are inadequate and the community is not supportive, complications abound. We all benefit from well-nurtured people; how to achieve that goal is a question we all must answer.

**permanency planning** An effort by child-welfare authorities to find a long-term living situation that will provide stability and support for a maltreated child. A goal is to avoid repeated changes of caregiver or school, which can be particularly harmful to the child.

**foster care** A legal, publicly supported system in which a maltreated child is removed from the parents' custody and entrusted to another adult or family, who is reimbursed for expenses incurred in meeting the child's needs.

**kinship care** A form of foster care in which a relative of a maltreated child, usually a grandparent, becomes the approved caregiver.

**Mother–Daughter Love, Finally** After a difficult childhood, 7-year-old Alexia is now safe and happy in her mother's arms. Maria Luz Martinez was her foster parent and has now become her adoptive mother.

# SUMMARY

## Body Changes

1. Well-nourished children gain weight and height during early childhood at a lower rate than infants do. Proportions change, allowing better body control.

2. Culture, income, and family customs all affect children's growth. Worldwide, an increasing number of children are eating too much unhealthy food, which puts them at risk for many health problems.

3. Although obesity has increased in every nation, in the United States, fewer young children are overweight than a decade ago. However, many young children consume too much sugar, which harms their teeth.

4. The brain continues to grow in early childhood, reaching about 75 percent of its adult weight at age 2 and 90 percent by age 6. Much of the increase is in myelination, which speeds transmission of messages from one part of the brain to another.

5. Maturation of the prefrontal cortex allows more reflective, coordinated thought and memory, better planning, and quicker responses. All of this is part of executive function. Many young children gradually become less impulsive and less likely to perseverate, although that process continues for many years.

6. The expression and regulation of emotions are fostered by better connections within the limbic system and between that system and other parts of the brain. Childhood trauma may create a flood of stress hormones (especially cortisol) that damage the brain and interfere with learning.

## Advancing Motor Skills

7. Gross motor skills continue to develop; clumsy 2-year-olds become 6-year-olds who move their bodies well, guided by their peers, practice, motivation, and opportunity—all varying by culture. Playing with other children helps develop skills that benefit children's physical, intellectual, and social development.

8. Urbanization and chemical pollutants are two factors that hamper development. More research is needed for many elements, but lead is now a proven neurotoxin, and many chemicals increase asthma, decrease oxygen, and impair the brain.

9. Fine motor skills are difficult to master during early childhood. Young children enjoy expressing themselves artistically, which helps them develop their body and finger control. Fortunately, self-criticism is not yet strong.

## Injuries and Abuse

10. Accidents cause more child deaths than diseases, with young children more likely to suffer a serious injury or premature death than older children. Close supervision and public safeguards can protect young children from their own eager, impulsive curiosity.

11. In the United States, various preventive measures have reduced the rate of serious injury, but medical measures have reduced disease deaths even faster. Four times as many young children die of injuries than of cancer, the leading cause of disease death in childhood.

12. Injury control occurs on many levels, including long before and immediately after each harmful incident. Primary prevention protects everyone, secondary prevention focuses on high-risk conditions and people, and tertiary prevention occurs after an injury. All three are needed.

## Child Maltreatment

13. Child maltreatment includes ongoing abuse and neglect, usually by a child's own parents. Each year, about 3 million cases of child maltreatment are reported in the United States; fewer than 1 million are substantiated, and rates of substantiated abuse have decreased in the past decade.

14. Physical abuse is the most obvious form of maltreatment, but neglect is more common and more harmful. Health, learning, and social skills are all impeded by abuse and neglect, not only during childhood but also decades later.

15. Primary prevention is needed to stop child maltreatment before it starts. Secondary prevention should begin when someone first notices a possible problem.

16. Tertiary prevention may include placement of a child in foster care, including kinship care. Permanency planning is required because frequent changes are harmful to children.

## KEY TERMS

myelination (p. 227)
corpus callosum (p. 228)
lateralization (p. 228)
impulse control (p. 229)
perseveration (p. 229)

injury control/harm reduction (p. 239)
primary prevention (p. 240)
secondary prevention (p. 240)
tertiary prevention (p. 240)
child maltreatment (p. 242)

child abuse (p. 242)
child neglect (p. 242)
substantiated maltreatment (p. 242)
reported maltreatment (p. 242)

post-traumatic stress disorder (PTSD) (p. 244)
permanency planning (p. 247)
foster care (p. 247)
kinship care (p. 247)

## APPLICATIONS

**1.** Keep a food diary for 24 hours, writing down what you eat, how much, when, how, and why. Did you eat at least five servings of fruits and vegetables, and very little sugar or fat? Did you get too hungry, or eat when you were not hungry? Then analyze when and why your food habits began.

**2.** Go to a playground or another place where young children play. Note the motor skills that the children demonstrate, including abilities and inabilities, and keep track of age and sex. What differences do you see among the children?

**3.** Ask several parents to describe each accidental injury of each of their children, particularly how it happened and what the consequences were. What primary, secondary, or tertiary prevention measures were in place, and what measures were missing?

**4.** Think back to your childhood and the friends you had at that time. Was there any maltreatment? Considering what you have learned in this chapter, why or why not?

# Early Childhood:
## Cognitive Development

## What Will You Know?

1. Are young children selfish or just self-centered?
2. Do children get confused if they hear two languages?
3. Is preschool for play or learning?

A sa, not yet 3 feet tall, held a large rubber ball. He wanted me to play basketball with him.

"We can't play basketball; we don't have a hoop," I told him.

"We can imagine a hoop," he answered, throwing up the ball.

"I got it in," he said happily. "You try."

I did.

"You got it in, too," he announced, and did a little dance.

Soon I was tired, and sat down.

"I want to sit and think my thoughts," I told him.

"Get up," he urged. *"You can play basketball and think your thoughts."*

Asa is typical. Imagination comes easily to him, and he aspires to the skills of older, taller people in his culture. He thinks by doing, and his vocabulary is impressive, but he does not yet understand that my feelings differ from his, that I would rather sit than throw a ball at an imaginary basket. He does know, however, that I usually respond to his requests.

This chapter describes these characteristics of the young child—imagination, active learning, vocabulary—but also their difficulty in understanding another person's perspective. I hope it also conveys the joy that adults gain when they understand how young children think. When that happens, you might do what I did—get up and play.

+ **Thinking During Early Childhood**
  Piaget: Preoperational Thought
  A CASE TO STUDY: Stones in the Belly
  Vygotsky: Social Learning
  Children's Theories
  Brain and Context

+ **Language Learning**
  A Sensitive Time
  The Vocabulary Explosion
  Acquiring Grammar
  Learning Two Languages

+ **Early-Childhood Schooling**
  Homes and Schools
  Child-Centered Programs
  Teacher-Directed Programs
  Intervention Programs
  Long-Term Gains from Intensive Programs

## Thinking During Early Childhood

You learned in Chapter 8 about the rapid advances in motor skills, brain development, and impulse control between ages 2 and 6, enabling the young child to do somersaults by kindergarten. Now you will see how each of these developmental advances affects cognition; young children are active learners, with new brain connections enabling new thoughts. The 6-year-old does the mental equivalent of somersaults.

## Piaget: Preoperational Thought

Early childhood is the time of **preoperational intelligence,** the second of Piaget's four periods of cognitive development (described in Table 2.3 on p. 46). Piaget called early-childhood thinking *pre*operational because children do not yet use logical operations (reasoning processes) (Inhelder & Piaget, 1964/2013a).

Left: Peathegee Inc/Blend Images/Getty Images
Top: Christopher Hope-Fitch/Getty Images

**Red Hot Anger** Emotions are difficult for young children to understand, since they are not visible. The Disney-Pixar movie *Inside Out* uses symbolic thought to remedy that—here with green Disgust, red Anger, and purple Fear. What colors are Joy and Sadness?

**preoperational intelligence**
Piaget's term for cognitive development between the ages of about 2 and 6; it includes language and imagination (which involve symbolic thought). Logical, operational thinking is not yet possible.

**symbolic thought** A major accomplishment of preoperational intelligence that allows a child to think symbolically, including understanding that words can refer to things not seen and that an item, such as a flag, can symbolize something else (in this case, a country).

**animism** The belief that natural objects and phenomena are alive, moving around, and having sensations and abilities that are human-like.

**centration** A characteristic of preoperational thought in which a young child focuses (centers) on one idea, excluding all others.

**egocentrism** Piaget's term for children's tendency to think about the world entirely from their own personal perspective.

**focus on appearance** A characteristic of preoperational thought in which a young child ignores all attributes that are not apparent.

Preoperational children are no longer limited to sensorimotor intelligence because they think in symbols, not just via senses and motor skills. In **symbolic thought,** an object or word can stand for something else, including something out of sight or imagined. Language is the most apparent example of symbolic thought. Words make it possible to think about many things at once.

However, although vocabulary and imagination soar in early childhood, logical connections between ideas are not yet *operational*, which means that Piaget found that young children cannot yet apply their impressive new linguistic ability to comprehend reality.

Consider how the word *dog*, for instance, changes in Piaget's description of cognition. During the sensorimotor level, *dog* means only the family dog sniffing at the child, not yet a symbol (Callaghan, 2013). By age 2, in preoperational thought, the word *dog* becomes a symbol: It can refer to a remembered dog, or a plastic dog, or an imagined dog. Symbolic thought allows for a language explosion (detailed later), which enables children to talk about thoughts and memories. Nonetheless, because they are not yet operational, if asked the differences between dogs and cats, preschoolers have difficulty contrasting the essential qualities of "dogness" from those of "catness."

Symbolic thought helps explain **animism,** the belief of many young children that natural objects (such as trees or clouds) are alive and that nonhuman animals have the same characteristics as human ones, especially the human each child knows best (him- or herself). Many children's stories include animals or objects that talk and listen (Aesop's fables, *Winnie-the-Pooh*, *Goodnight Gorilla*, *The Day the Crayons Quit*). Preoperational thought is symbolic and magical, not logical and realistic.

Among contemporary children, animism gradually disappears as the mind becomes more mature, by age 10 if not earlier (Kesselring & Müller, 2011). However, scholars contend that many preindustrial peoples believed in animism—praying to the sky and to trees, for instance—and that human history is best understood by considering Piaget's understanding of cognitive development (e.g., Oesterdiekhoff, 2014).

## Obstacles to Logic

Piaget described symbolic thought as characteristic of preoperational thought. He also noted four limitations that make logic difficult: centration, focus on appearance, static reasoning, and irreversibility.

**Centration** is the tendency to focus on one aspect of a situation to the exclusion of all others. Young children may, for example, insist that Daddy is a father, not a brother, because they center on the role that he fills for them. This illustrates a particular type of centration that Piaget called **egocentrism**—literally, "self-centeredness." Egocentric children contemplate the world exclusively from their personal perspective.

Egocentrism is *not* selfishness. One 3-year-old chose to buy a model car as a birthday present for his mother: His "behavior was not selfish or greedy; he carefully wrapped the present and gave it to his mother with an expression that clearly showed that he expected her to love it" (Crain, 2011, p. 133).

A second characteristic of preoperational thought is a **focus on appearance** to the exclusion of other attributes. For instance, a girl given a short haircut might worry that she has turned into a boy. In preoperational thought, a thing is whatever it appears to be—evident in the joy young children have in wearing the hats or shoes of a grown-up, clomping noisily and unsteadily around the house.

Third, preoperational children use **static reasoning.** They believe that the world is stable, unchanging, always in the state in which they currently encounter it.

Many children cannot imagine that their own parents were ever children. If they are told that Grandma is their mother's mother, they still do not understand how people change with maturation. One preschooler asked his grandmother to tell his mother not to spank him because "she has to do what her mother says."

The fourth characteristic of preoperational thought is **irreversibility.** Preoperational thinkers fail to recognize that reversing a process might restore whatever existed before. A young girl might cry because her mother put lettuce on her sandwich. She might reject the food even after the lettuce is removed because she believes that what is done cannot be undone.

## Conservation and Logic

Piaget described the ways in which preoperational intelligence disregards logic. A famous set of experiments involved **conservation,** the notion that the amount of something remains the same (is conserved) despite changes in its appearance.

Suppose two identical glasses contain the same amount of pink lemonade, and the liquid from one of these glasses is poured into a taller, narrower glass. When young children are asked whether one glass contains more or, alternatively, if both glasses contain the same amount, those younger than 6 answer that the narrower glass (with the higher level) has more. (See Figure 9.1 for other examples.)

**static reasoning** A characteristic of preoperational thought in which a young child thinks that nothing changes. Whatever is now has always been and always will be.

**irreversibility** A characteristic of preoperational thought in which a young child thinks that nothing can be undone. A thing cannot be restored to the way it was before a change occurred.

**conservation** The principle that the amount of a substance remains the same (i.e., is conserved) even when its appearance changes.

**Video Activity: Achieving Conservation** focuses on the cognitive changes that enable older children to pass Piaget's conservation-of-liquid task.

---

### Tests of Various Types of Conservation

| Type of Conservation | Initial Presentation | Transformation | Question | Preoperational Child's Answer |
|---|---|---|---|---|
| Volume | Two equal glasses of pink lemonade.  | Pour one into a taller, narrower glass.  | Which glass contains more? | The taller one.  |
| Number | Two equal lines of candy. 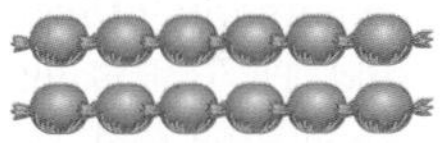 | Increase spacing of candy in one line.  | Which line has more candy? | The longer one.  |
| Matter | Two equal balls of cookie dough.  | Squeeze one ball into a long, thin shape.  | Which piece has more dough? | The long one.  |
| Length | Two pencils of equal length. 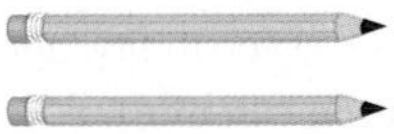 | Move one pencil. 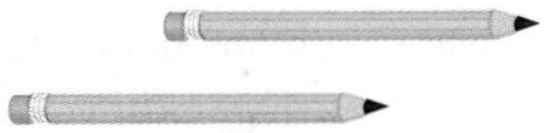 | Which pencil is longer? | The one that is farther to the right.  |

**FIGURE 9.1**

**Conservation, Please** According to Piaget, until children grasp the concept of conservation at (he believed) about age 6 or 7, they cannot understand that the transformations shown here do not change the total amount of liquid, candies, cookie dough, and pencils.

All four characteristics of preoperational thought are evident in this mistake. Young children fail to understand conservation because they focus (*center*) on what they see (*appearance*), noticing only the immediate (*static*) condition. It does not occur to them that they could pour the lemonade back into the wider glass and re-create the level of a moment earlier (*irreversibility*).

Piaget's original tests of conservation required children to respond verbally to an adult's questions. Contemporary researchers have made tests of logic simple and playful. In such tests young children sometimes succeed.

Moreover, before age 6, children indicate via eye movements or gestures that they are logical, even though they cannot yet put their understanding into words (Goldin-Meadow & Alibali, 2013). Further, conservation and many other logical ideas can be grasped bit by bit, with active, guided experience. Glimmers of understanding may be apparent as early as age 4 (Sophian, 2013).

As with an infant's sensorimotor intelligence, Piaget underestimated preoperational children. Piaget was right about his basic idea, however: Young children are not very logical (Lane & Harris, 2014). Their cognitive limits make smart 3-year-olds sometimes foolish, as Caleb is.

**⬤ Especially for Nutritionists**
How can Piaget's theory help you encourage children to eat healthy foods? (see response, p. 256)

---

**A CASE TO STUDY**

## Stones in the Belly

As we were reading a book about dinosaurs, my 3-year-old grandson, Caleb, told me that some dinosaurs (*sauropods*) have stones in their bellies. It helps them digest their food and then poop and pee.

"I didn't know that dinosaurs ate stones," I said.

"They don't eat them."

"Then how do they get the stones in their bellies? They must swallow them."

"They don't eat them."

"Then how do they get in their bellies?"

"They are just there."

"How did they get there?"

"They don't eat them," said Caleb. "Stones are dirty. We don't eat them."

I dropped it, as I knew that his mother had warned him not to eat pebbles, and I didn't want to confuse him. However, my question apparently puzzled him. Later he asked my daughter, "Do dinosaurs eat stones?"

"Yes, they eat stones so they can grind their food," she answered.

At that, Caleb was quiet.

In all of this, preoperational cognition is evident. Caleb is bright; he can name several kinds of dinosaurs, as can many young children.

But logic eluded Caleb. He was preoperational, not operational.

It seemed obvious to me that dinosaurs must have swallowed the stones. However, in his static thinking, Caleb said the stones "are just there." He rejected the thought that dinosaurs ate stones because he has been told that stones are too dirty to eat.

Caleb is egocentric, reasoning from his own experience, and animistic, in that he thinks other creatures think and act as he himself does. He trusts his mother, who told him never to eat stones, or, for that matter, sand from the sandbox, or food that fell on the floor. My authority as grandmother was clearly less than the authority of his mother, but at least he considered what I said. He was skeptical that a dinosaur would do something he had been told not to do, but the idea lingered rather than being completely rejected. Of course, the implications of my status as his mother's mother are beyond his static thinking.

Like many young children, Caleb is curious, and my question raised his curiosity.

Should I have expected him to tell me that I was right, when his mother agreed with me? No. That would have required far more understanding of reversibility and far less egocentrism than most young children can muster.

© 2016 Macmillan

## Vygotsky: Social Learning

For decades, the magical, illogical, and self-centered aspects of cognition dominated our conception of early-childhood thought. Scientists were understandably awed by Piaget, who demonstrated many aspects of egocentric thought in children.

Vygotsky emphasized another side of early cognition—that each person's thinking is shaped by other people. His focus on the sociocultural context contrasts with Piaget's emphasis on the individual.

### Mentors

Vygotsky believed that cognitive development is embedded in the social context at every age (Vygotsky, 1987). He stressed that children are curious and observant of everything in their world. They ask questions—about how machines work, why weather changes, where the sky ends—and seek answers from more knowledgeable mentors, who might be their parents, teachers, older siblings, or just a stranger. The answers they get are affected by the mentors' perceptions and assumptions—that is, their culture—which shapes their thought.

As you remember from Chapter 2, children learn through *guided participation*, because mentors teach them. Parents are their first guides, although children are guided by many others, especially in an interactive preschool (Broström, 2017).

According to Vygotsky, children learn because their mentors do the following:

- Present challenges.
- Offer assistance (without taking over).
- Add crucial information.
- Encourage motivation.

Learning from mentors indicates intelligence; according to Vygotsky, "What children can do with the assistance of others might be in some sense even more indicative of their mental development than what they can do alone" (Vygotsky, 1980, p. 85).

### Scaffolding

Vygotsky believed that all individuals learn within their **zone of proximal development (ZPD),** an intellectual arena in which new ideas and skills can be mastered. *Proximal* means "near," so the ZPD includes the ideas and skills children are close to mastering but cannot yet demonstrate independently. Learning depends, in part, on the wisdom and willingness of mentors to provide **scaffolding,** or temporary sensitive support, to help children within their developmental zone (Mermelshtine, 2017).

**Easy Question; Obvious Answer** *(above left)* Sadie, age 5, carefully makes sure both glasses contain the same amount. *(above right)* When one glass of pink lemonade is poured into a wide jar, she triumphantly points to the tall glass as having more. Sadie is like all 5-year-olds; only a developmental psychologist or a 7-year-old child knows better.

**zone of proximal development (ZPD)** Vygotsky's term for the skills—cognitive as well as physical—that a person can exercise only with assistance, not yet independently.

**scaffolding** Temporary support that is tailored to a learner's needs and abilities and aimed at helping the learner master the next task in a given learning process.

**Learning to Button** Most shirts for 4-year-olds are wide-necked without buttons, so preschoolers can put them on themselves. But the skill of buttoning is best learned from a mentor, who knows how to increase motivation.

Hero Images/DigitalVision/Getty Images

Good mentors provide plenty of scaffolding, encouraging children to look both ways before crossing the street (pointing out speeding trucks, cars, and buses while holding the child's hand) or letting them stir the cake batter (perhaps covering the child's hand on the spoon handle, in guided participation). Crucial in every activity is joint engagement, when both learner and mentor are actively involved together in the zone of proximal development (Adamson et al., 2014).

Culture matters. In some families and cultures, book-reading is a time for conversation and questions; in others, it is a time for telling the child to be quiet and listen. Parents scaffold whatever they deem important.

One study of U.S. parents found that many book-reading parents who were Chinese Americans pointed out how misbehavior caused problems for the book's characters, while many Mexican Americans highlighted the emotions of the characters (Luo et al., 2014). From this contrast, a possible conclusion is that Chinese Americans teach their children to become well-behaved adults, while Mexican Americans encourage their children to notice the emotions that accompany behavior.

## Overimitation

Sometimes scaffolding is inadvertent, as when children copy something that adults would rather the child not do. Young children curse, kick, and worse because someone else showed them how.

More benignly, children imitate meaningless habits and customs, a trait called **overimitation.** Children are eager to learn from mentors, allowing "rapid, high-fidelity intergenerational transmission of tool-use skills and for the perpetuation and generation of cultural forms" (Nielsen & Tomaselli, 2010, p. 735).

Overimitation was demonstrated in a series of experiments with 3- to 6-year-olds, 64 of them from San communities (pejoratively called Bushmen) in South Africa and Botswana, and, for comparison, 64 from cities in Australia and 19 from aboriginal communities within Australia. Australian middle-class adults often scaffold for children with words and actions, but San adults rarely do. The researchers expected the urban Australian children but not the San children to follow adult demonstrations (Nielsen et al., 2014). The researchers were wrong.

**overimitation** When a person imitates an action that is not a relevant part of the behavior to be learned. Overimitation is common among 2- to 6-year-olds when they imitate adult actions that are irrelevant and inefficient.

**Especially for Driving Instructors** Sometimes your students cry, curse, or quit. How would Vygotsky advise you to proceed? (see response, p. 258)

**Response for Nutritionists** (from p. 254): Take each of the four characteristics of preoperational thought into account. Because of egocentrism, having a special place and plate might assure the child that this food is exclusively his or hers. Since appearance is important, food should look tasty. Since static thinking dominates, if something healthy is added (e.g., grate carrots into the cake, add milk to the soup), do it before the food is given to the child. In the reversibility example in the text, the lettuce should be removed out of the child's sight and the "new" hamburger presented.

In part of the study, one by one, some children in each group watched an adult open a box, which could be opened easily and efficiently by pulling down a knob by hand. Instead, the adult waved a red stick above the box three times and used that stick to push down the knob to open the box.

Then children were given the stick and asked to open the box. No matter what their culture, they followed the adult example, waving the stick three times and not using their hands directly on the knob.

Other San and Australian children did not see the demonstration. When they were given the stick and asked to open the box, they simply pulled the knob. Then they observed an adult do the stick-waving opening—and they copied those inefficient actions, even though they already knew the easy way. Apparently, children everywhere learn from others, not only through explicit guidance but also through observation. Across cultures, overimitation is striking. It generalizes to other similar situations.

Overimitation is universal: Young children follow what adults do. They are naturally "socially motivated," which allows them to learn as long as the adults structure and guide that learning. Adults worldwide teach children in that way, using eye contact and facial expressions to facilitate learning (Heyes, 2016).

The process is exquisitely designed. Adults enjoy transmitting knowledge and, for their part, children are automatic imitators—especially when copying is not too difficult: They imitate adults who seem to know what they are doing, even if the adults are not deliberately teaching (Tomasello, 2016; Keupp et al., 2016).

That is exactly what Vygotsky expected and explained: Children are attuned to culture.

## Language as a Tool

Although all of the objects of a culture guide children, Vygotsky thought language is pivotal.

First, talking to oneself, called **private speech,** is evident when young children talk aloud to review, decide, and explain events to themselves (and, incidentally, to anyone else within earshot) (Al-Namlah et al., 2012). Older preschoolers are more circumspect, sometimes whispering. Audible or not, private speech aids cognition and self-reflection; adults should encourage it (Perels et al., 2009; Benigno et al., 2011). Many adults use private speech as they talk to themselves when alone; they write down ideas to help them think.

Tim Hall/Getty Images

**Count by Tens** A large, attractive abacus could be a scaffold. However, in this toy store the position of the balls suggests that no mentor is nearby. Children are unlikely to grasp the number system without a motivating guide.

**Observation Quiz** Is the girl above right-handed or left-handed? (see answer, p. 258) ↑

**private speech** The internal dialogue that occurs when people talk to themselves (either silently or out loud).

© Jose Luis Pelaez Inc/Corbis

© arabianEye/Corbis

**Same or Different?** Which do you see? Most people focus on differences, such as ethnicity or sex. But a developmental perspective appreciates similarities: book-reading to a preliterate child cradled on a parent's lap.

**social mediation** Human interaction that expands and advances understanding, often through words that one person uses to explain something to another.

Second, language advances thinking by facilitating social interaction, which is vital to learning (Vygotsky, 2012). This **social mediation** function of speech occurs as mentors guide mentees in their zone of proximal development, learning numbers, recalling memories, and following routines. Words are scaffolds.

### STEM Learning

**Answer to Observation Quiz** (from p. 257): Right-handed. Her dominant hand is engaged in something more comforting than exploring the abacus. Like all children, she uses both hands.

A practical use of Vygotsky's theory concerns STEM (science, technology, engineering, math) education. Many adults are concerned that too few college students choose a STEM career.

Developmentalists find that a person's interest in such vocations begins with learning about numbers and science (counting, shapes, fractions, molecular structure, the laws of motion) in early childhood. Spatial understanding—how one object fits with another—is an accomplishment of early childhood that enhances later math skills (Veridne et al., 2017). During the preschool years, an understanding of math and physics develops month by month. Before first grade, children learn to:

- Count objects, with one number per item (called *one-to-one correspondence*).
- Remember times and ages (bedtime at 8 P.M., a child is 4 years old, and so on).
- Understand sequence (first child wins, last child loses).
- Know which numbers are greater than others (e.g., that 7 is greater than 4).
- Understand how to make things move, from toy cars to soccer balls.
- Appreciate temperature effects, from ice to steam.

By age 3 or 4, children's brains are mature enough to comprehend numbers, store memories, and recognize routines. Whether or not children actually demonstrate such understanding depends on what they hear and how they participate in various activities within their families, schools, and cultures. "Scaffolding and elaboration from parents and teachers provides crucial input to spatial development," which itself leads to the math understanding that underpins STEM expertise (Verdine et al., 2017, p. 25).

**Response for Driving Instructors** (from p. 256): Use guided participation to scaffold the instruction so that your students are not overwhelmed. Be sure to provide lots of praise and days of practice. If emotion erupts, do not take it as an attack on you.

Some 2-year-olds hear sentences such as "One, two, three, takeoff," "Here are two cookies," or "Dinner in five minutes" several times a day. They are encouraged to touch an interesting bit of moss, or are alerted to the phases of the moon outside

**I Want a Pet** Young children are more fascinated than afraid of snakes, spiders, and—as shown here at the London Pet Show—scorpions. Although some children are temporarily cautious, phobias are more learned than innate. Many children want a pet; science education may begin here.

© Paul Brown/Corbis

their window, or play with toys that fit shapes, or learn about the relationship between pace and steepness of a hill they are climbing.

Other children never have such experiences—and they have a harder time with math in first grade, with science in third grade, and with physics in high school. If words mediate between brain potential and comprehension, STEM education begins long before formal education.

## Executive Function

One manifestation of children's impressive learning ability is in the development of **executive function,** the ability to use the mind to plan, remember, inhibit some impulses, and execute others. Executive function (also called *executive control* and closely related to *emotional regulation*, explained in Chapter 10) is an ability that develops throughout life, allowing students of all ages to learn from experience. It is first evident and measured during early childhood (Eisenberg & Zhou, 2016; Espy, 2016).

Usually, three components comprise executive function: (1) working memory, (2) cognitive flexibility, and (3) inhibitory control—which is the ability to focus on a task and ignore distractions. To combine memory, flexibility, and inhibition, researchers use scores on many tasks.

For instance, 3- to 5-year-olds are shown a series of barnyard animals and asked to remember them in order, to alternate stamping on a picture of a dog and one of a bone (both are presented repeatedly together), and to push a button when they see a fish but not a shark (Espy, 2016). Scores improve during early childhood.

Scientists have found that executive function benefits from practice as well as maturation. Consequently, targeted educational programs inspired by Vygotsky (e.g., Tools of the Mind) are used in preschools (Liew, 2012; Blair, 2016). Executive function is a better predictor of later learning in kindergarten than how old a child is and how advanced the child's language is (Pellicano et al., 2017).

Especially in math, computers can promote learning. Educational software becomes "a conduit for collaborative learning" (Cicconi, 2014, p. 58), as Web 2.0 (interactive) programs respond to the particular abilities and needs of each child. In preschool classrooms, several children can work together, each mentoring the others, talking aloud as the computer prompts them.

However, for executive function, interactive software must be chosen carefully. Video games, for instance, usually encourage rapid responses—the opposite of planning, inhibition, and memory that are the bedrock of executive function.

More broadly, educators disapprove if a screen replaces human interaction, but they also recognize that computers, carefully used (no more than an hour a day), might be learning tools, just as books might be (Alper, 2013; American Academy of Pediatrics, 2016). The crucial factor with educational technology and programming, as explained in Opposing Perspectives in Chapter 6, is evidence (not testimonials).

A study that compared 226 children who used the "Bedtime Math" app with 167 matched children who used "Bedtime Reading" found that the former had significantly higher math scores after a year (Berkowitz et al., 2015). The authors cite four reasons that this well-designed app is helpful:

1. The app required parents and children to discuss math together.
2. The app had stories but few distracting noises or animations.
3. The app gave math-phobic parents a way to talk about numbers and shapes with their children.
4. The app followed each story with questions that encouraged memory and reflection (both of which aid executive function).

**executive function** The cognitive ability to organize and prioritize the many thoughts that arise from the various parts of the brain, allowing the person to anticipate, strategize, and plan behavior.

# Children's Theories

Piaget and Vygotsky both recognized that children work to understand their world. No contemporary developmental scientist doubts that. They recognize that young children do more than gain words and concepts; they develop theories to help them understand and remember—theories that arise from both brain maturation and personal experience (Baron-Cohen et al., 2013).

## Theory-Theory

**theory-theory** The idea that children attempt to explain everything they see and hear by constructing theories.

Humans of all ages seek explanations, as Chapter 2 emphasizes. **Theory-theory** refers to the idea that children naturally construct theories to explain whatever they see and hear. In other words, the theory about how children think is that they construct a theory.

According to theory-theory, the best explanation for cognition is that humans seek reasons, causes, and underlying principles to make sense of their experience. That requires curiosity and thought, connecting bits of knowledge and observations, which is what young children do. Humans always want theories (even false ones sometimes suffice) to help them understand the world. Especially in childhood, theories are subject to change as new evidence accumulates (Meltzoff & Gopnik, 2013; Bridgers et al., 2016).

Exactly how do children seek explanations? They ask questions, and, if they are not satisfied with the answers, they develop their own theories. For example, one child thought his grandpa died because God was lonely; another thought thunder occurred because God was rearranging the furniture.

Children follow the same processes that scientists do: asking questions, developing hypotheses, gathering data, and drawing conclusions. As a result, "preschoolers have intuitive theories of the physical, biological, psychological, and social world" (Gopnik, 2012, p. 1623).

Of course, the cognitive methods of preschoolers lack the rigor of scientific experiments, but "infants and young children not only detect statistical patterns, they use those patterns to test hypotheses about people and things" (Gopnik, 2012, p. 1625). Their conclusions are not always correct: Like all good scientists, they allow new data to promote revision, although, like all humans, they sometimes stick to their old theories instead of newer versions.

One common theory-theory is that everyone intends to do things correctly. For that reason, when asked to repeat something ungrammatical that an adult says, children often correct the grammar. They theorize that the adult intended to speak grammatically but failed to do so (Over & Gattis, 2010).

This is an example of a general principle: Children theorize about intentions before they imitate what they see. As you have read, when children saw an adult wave a stick before opening a box, the children theorized that, since the adult did it deliberately, stick-waving must somehow be important.

## Theory of Mind

**theory of mind** A person's theory of what other people might be thinking. In order to have a theory of mind, children must realize that other people are not necessarily thinking the same thoughts that they themselves are. That realization seldom occurs before age 4.

Mental processes—thoughts, emotions, beliefs, motives, and intentions—are among the most complicated and puzzling phenomena that humans encounter every day. Adults wonder why people fall in love with the particular persons they do, why they vote for the candidates they do, or why they make foolish choices—from signing for a huge mortgage to buying an overripe cucumber. Children are likewise puzzled about a playmate's unexpected anger, a sibling's generosity, or an aunt's too-wet kiss.

To know what goes on in another person's mind, people develop a *folk psychology*, which includes ideas about other people's thinking, called **theory of mind.** Theory of mind is an emergent ability, slow to develop but typically evident in most children by about age 4 (Carlson et al., 2013).

Some aspects of theory of mind develop sooner, and some later. Longitudinal research finds that the preschool years typically begin with 2-year-olds not knowing that other people think differently than they do but end with 6-year-olds having a well-developed theory of mind (Wellman et al., 2011).

Part of theory of mind is an understanding that someone else might have a mistaken belief. For example, a child watches a puppet named Max put a toy dog into a red box. Then Max leaves and the child sees the dog taken out of the red box and put in a blue box.

When Max returns, the child is asked, "Where will Max look for the dog?" Without a theory of mind, most 3-year-olds confidently say, "In the blue box"; most 6-year-olds correctly say, "In the red box."

© Macmillan Archives/Jellybean Pictures

**Candies in the Crayon Box** Anyone would expect crayons in a crayon box, but once a child sees that candy is inside, he expects that everyone else will also know that candies are inside!

Theory of mind actually develops gradually, progressing from knowing that someone else might have different desires (at about age 3) to knowing that someone might hide their true feelings (about age 6). Culture matters. Even within one nation, regional differences appear, not in the universal progression but in specific examples (Duh et al., 2016). The most notable variations, however, are neurological, not cultural: Children who are deaf or have autism are remarkably slow to develop theory of mind (Carlson et al., 2013).

The development of theory of mind can be seen when young children try to escape punishment by lying. Their faces often betray them: worried or shifting eyes, pursed lips, and so on. Parents sometimes say, "I know when you are lying," and, to the consternation of most 3-year-olds, parents are usually right.

In one experiment, 247 children, aged 3 to 5, sat at a table that had an upside-down cup covering dozens of candies (Evans et al., 2011). The children were told *not* to look to see what was under the cup, and the experimenter left the room.

For 142 children (57 percent), curiosity overcame obedience. They peeked, spilling so many candies onto the table that they could not put them back under the cup. The examiner returned, asking how the candies got on the table. Only one-fourth of the participants (more often the younger ones) told the truth.

The rest lied, and their skill increased with their age. The 3-year-old liars typically told hopeless lies (e.g., "The candies got out by themselves"); the 4-year-olds told unlikely lies (e.g., "Other children came in and knocked over the cup"). Some of the 5-year-olds, however, told plausible lies (e.g., "My elbow knocked over the cup accidentally").

A study of prosocial lies (saying that a disappointing gift was appreciated) found that children who were advanced in theory of mind and in executive function were also better liars, able to stick to the lie that they liked the gift (S. Williams et al., 2016). This study was of 6- to 12-year-olds, not preschoolers, but the underlying abilities are first evident at about age 4.

**Especially for Social Scientists** Can you think of any connection between Piaget's theory of preoperational thought and 3-year-olds' errors in this theory-of-mind task? (see response, p. 262)

## Brain and Context

Generally, between ages 3 and 12, older children are better liars (see Figure 9.2) as they advance in theory of mind and executive control. A notable advance in

**LaunchPad**
macmillan learning

**Video: Theory of Mind: False-Belief Tasks** demonstrates how children's theory of mind develops with age.

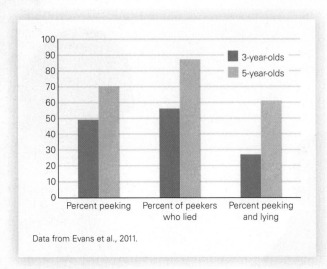

Data from Evans et al., 2011.

**FIGURE 9.2**

**Better with Age?** Could an obedient and honest 3-year-old become a disobedient and lying 5-year-old? Apparently yes, as the proportion of peekers and liars in this study more than doubled over those two years. Does maturation make children more able to think for themselves or less trustworthy?

**Response for Social Scientists**

(from p. 261): According to Piaget, preschool children focus on appearance and on static conditions (so they cannot mentally reverse a process). Furthermore, they are egocentric, believing that everyone shares their point of view. No wonder they believe that they had always known the dog was in the blue box and that Max would know that, too.

all of these abilities occurs between ages 4 and 5, probably because the prefrontal cortex matures markedly at this point (Devine & Hughes, 2014).

Children who are slow in language development are also slow in theory of mind, a finding that makes developmentalists suggest that underlying deficits—genetic or neurological—may be crucial for both. Developmentalists suggest that, in addition to specific efforts to improve language skills, therapists and teachers need to consider ways to advance executive function (Nilsson & de López, 2016). Remember the plasticity of the brain: The preschool years may be particularly important for neurological control.

Indeed, many studies have found that a child's ability to develop theories correlates with neurological maturation, which also correlates with advances in executive processing—the reflective, anticipatory capacity of the mind (Mar, 2011; Baron-Cohen et al., 2013). Detailed studies find that theory of mind activates several brain regions (Koster-Hale & Saxe, 2013). This makes sense, as theory of mind is a complex ability that humans develop in social contexts, so it is not likely to reside in just one neurological region.

Evidence for crucial brain maturation comes from the other research on the same 3- to 5-year-olds whose lying was studied. The children were asked to say "day" when they saw a picture of the moon and "night" when they saw a picture of the sun. They needed to inhibit their automatic reaction. Their success indicated advanced executive function, which correlated with maturation of the prefrontal cortex.

Even when compared to other children who were the same age, those who failed the day–night tests typically told impossible lies. Their age-mates who were higher in executive function told more plausible lies (Evans et al., 2011).

Does the crucial role of neurological maturation make culture and context irrelevant? Not at all: Nurture is always important. The reason that formal education traditionally began at about age 6 is that this is when maturation of the prefrontal cortex naturally allows sustained attention. However, experiences before age 6 advance brain development and thus prepare children for school (Blair & Raver, 2015).

Many educators and parents focus on young children's intelligence and vocabulary. That is not wrong: Children's minds need to be engaged, and their language development needs to be encouraged. However, for success in kindergarten and beyond, executive function seems especially crucial. It correlates more with brain development than do scores on intelligence tests (Friedman & Miyake, 2017).

Some helpful experiences before age 6 occur naturally: Children develop theory of mind in talking with adults and in playing with other children. Games that require turn-taking encourage memory and inhibitory control, two crucial components of executive control. In daily life, as brothers and sisters argue, agree, compete, and cooperate, and as older siblings fool younger ones, it dawns on 3-year-olds that not everyone thinks as they do, a thought that advances theory of mind.

By age 5, children have learned how to persuade their younger brothers and sisters to give them a toy. Meanwhile, younger siblings figure out how to gain sympathy by complaining that their older brothers and sisters have victimized them. Parents, beware: Asking, "Who started it?" may be irrelevant.

Social interactions with other children promote brain development, advancing theory of mind and executive function. This is especially evident when those other children are siblings of about the same age (McAlister & Peterson, 2013). As one expert in theory of mind quipped, "Two older siblings are worth about a year of chronological age" (Perner, 2000, p. 383).

# Language Learning

Learning language is often considered the premier cognitive accomplishment of early childhood. Two-year-olds use short, telegraphic sentences ("Want cookie," "Where Daddy go?"), omitting adjectives, adverbs, and articles. By contrast, 5-year-olds seem to be able to say almost anything (see At About This Time) using every part of speech. Some preschoolers understand and speak two or three languages, an accomplishment that many adults struggle for years to achieve.

## A Sensitive Time

Brain maturation, myelination, scaffolding, and social interaction make early childhood ideal for learning language. As you remember from Chapter 1, scientists once thought that early childhood was a *critical period* for language learning—the *only* time when a first language could be mastered and the best time to learn a second or third one.

It is easy to understand why they thought so. Young children have powerful motivation and ability to sort words and sounds into meaning (theory-theory). That makes them impressive language learners. However, the critical-period hypothesis is false: A new language can be learned after age 6.

Still, while new language learning in adulthood is possible, it is not easy. Early childhood is a *sensitive period* for language learning—for rapidly mastering vocabulary, grammar, and pronunciation. Young children are language sponges; they soak up every verbal drop they encounter.

One of the valuable (and sometimes frustrating) traits of young children is that they talk about many things to adults, to each other, to themselves, to their toys—unfazed by misuse, mispronunciation, ignorance, stuttering, and so on (Marazita & Merriman, 2010). Language comes easily partly because preoperational children are not self-critical about what they say. Egocentrism has advantages; this is one of them.

## The Vocabulary Explosion

The average child knows about 500 words at age 2 and more than 10,000 at age 6 (Herschensohn, 2007). That's more than six new words a day. As with many averages in development, the range is vast: The number of root words (e.g., *run* is a root word, not *running* or *runner*) that 5-year-olds know ranges from 2,000

### AT ABOUT THIS TIME

**Language in Early Childhood**

| Approximate Age | Characteristic or Achievement in First Language |
| --- | --- |
| 2 years | *Vocabulary:* 100–2,000 words <br> *Sentence length:* 2–6 words <br> *Grammar:* Plurals; pronouns; many nouns, verbs, adjectives <br> *Questions:* Many "What's that?" questions |
| 3 years | *Vocabulary:* 1,000–5,000 words <br> *Sentence length:* 3–8 words <br> *Grammar:* Conjunctions, adverbs, articles <br> *Questions:* Many "Why?" questions |
| 4 years | *Vocabulary:* 3,000–10,000 words <br> *Sentence length:* 5–20 words <br> *Grammar:* Dependent clauses, tags at sentence end ("... didn't I?" "... won't you?") <br> *Questions:* Peak of "Why?" questions; many "How?" and "When?" questions |
| 6 years and up | *Vocabulary:* 5,000–30,000 words <br> *Sentence length:* Some seem unending ("... and ... who ... and ... that ... and ...") <br> *Grammar:* Complex, depending on what the child has heard, with some children correctly using the passive voice ("Man bitten by dog") and subjunctive ("If I were ...") <br> *Questions:* Some about social differences (male–female, old–young, rich–poor) and many other issues |

to 6,000 (Biemiller, 2009). In fact, it is very difficult to determine vocabulary size, although almost everyone agrees that building vocabulary is crucial (Milton & Treffers-Daller, 2013).

To understand why vocabulary is difficult to measure, consider the following: Children listened to a story about a raccoon that saw its reflection in the water, and then they were asked what *reflection* means. Five answers:

1. "It means that your reflection is yourself. It means that there is another person that looks just like you."
2. "Means if you see yourself in stuff and you see your reflection."
3. "Is like when you look in something, like water, you can see yourself."
4. "It mean your face go in the water."
5. "That means if you the same skin as him, you blend in." (Hoffman et al., 2014, pp. 471–472)

In another example, a story included "a chill ran down his spine." Children were asked what *chill* meant. One answer: "When you want to lay down and watch TV—and eat nachos" (Hoffman et al., 2014, p. 473).

Which of the five listed responses indicated that the child knew what *reflection* means? None? All? Some number in between? The last child was given no credit for *chill*; is that fair?

lady so fat?" or "I don't want to kiss Grandpa because his breath smells."): The pragmatics of polite speech requires more social understanding than many young children possess.

## Learning Two Languages

Language-minority people (those who speak a language that is not their nation's dominant one) suffer if they do not also speak the majority language (Rosselli et al., 2016). In the United States, those who lack fluency in English often have lower school achievement, diminished self-esteem, and inadequate employment. Some of the problem is prejudice from those who speak English well, but some is directly connected to language. Fluency in English erases some liabilities; fluency in another language then becomes an asset.

Early childhood is the best time to learn languages; ideally every young child learns two languages. Neuroscience finds that if adults mastered two languages before age 6, both languages are located in the same areas of the brain with no detriment to the cortex structure (Klein et al., 2014). Being bilingual seems to benefit the brain lifelong, further evidence for plasticity (Bialystok, 2017). Indeed, the bilingual brain may provide some resistance to neurocognitive disorder due to Alzheimer's disease in old age (Costa & Sebastián-Gallés, 2014).

When adults learn a new language, their pronunciation, idioms, and exceptions to the rules usually lag behind their grammar and vocabulary. Thus, many immigrants speak the majority language with an accent but are proficient in comprehension and reading (difference is not deficit).

From infancy on, hearing is more acute than vocalization. Almost all young children mispronounce whatever language they speak, blithely unaware of their mistakes. They comprehend more than they say, they hear better than they speak, and they learn rapidly as long as people speak to them.

## Language Loss and Gains

Language-minority parents have a legitimate fear: Their children might make a *language shift*, becoming fluent in the school language and not in their home language. Language shift occurs whenever theory-theory leads children to conclude that their first language is inferior to another one (Bhatia & Ritchie, 2013).

Some language-minority children in Mexico shift to Spanish; some children of Canada's First Nations shift to French; some children in the United States shift to English. In China, all speak some form of Chinese, but some shift from Mandarin, Cantonese, and so on, troubling parents.

Remember that young children are preoperational: They center on the immediate status of their language (not on future usefulness or past glory), on appearance more than substance. No wonder many shift toward the language of the dominant culture. Since language is integral to culture, if a child is to become fluently bilingual, everyone who speaks with the child should respect both cultures, in song, books, and daily conversation. Children learn from

**Bilingual Learners** These are Chinese children learning a second language. Could this be in the United States? No, this is a class in the first Chinese-Hungarian school in Budapest. There are three clues: the spacious classroom, the letters on the book, and the trees outside.

ATTILA KISBENEDEK/Getty Images

**Especially for Immigrant Parents** You want your children to be fluent in the language of your family's new country, even though you do not speak that language well. Should you speak to your children in your native tongue or in the new language? (see response, p. 270)

listening and talking, so a child needs to hear twice as much talk to become fluent in two languages (Hoff et al., 2012). The extra effort on the part of the adults will benefit the child later on: Learning one language well makes it easier to learn another (Hoff et al., 2014).

The same practices make a child fluently trilingual, as some 5-year-olds are. Young children who are immersed in three languages may speak all three with no accent—except the accent of their mother, father, and friends. [**Developmental Link:** Bilingual education is also discussed in Chapter 12.]

## Listening, Talking, and Reading

Because understanding the printed word is crucial, a meta-analysis of about 300 studies analyzed which activities in early childhood aided reading later on. Both vocabulary and phonics (precise awareness of spoken sounds) predicted literacy (Shanahan & Lonigan, 2010). Five specific strategies and experiences were particularly effective for children of all income levels, languages, and ethnicities.

1. *Code-focused teaching*. In order for children to read, they must "break the code" from spoken to written words. One step is to connect letters and sounds (e.g., "A, alligators all around" or "B is for baby").
2. *Book-reading*. Vocabulary and print-awareness develop when adults read to children.
3. *Parent education*. When parents know how to encourage cognition (such as encouraging conversation in book-reading), children become better readers. Adult vocabulary expands children's vocabulary.
4. *Language enhancement*. Within each child's zone of proximal development, mentors help the child expand vocabulary. That requires teachers who know each child's zone.
5. *Preschool programs*. Children learn from teachers, songs, excursions, and other children. (We discuss variations of early education next, but every study finds that preschools advance language acquisition.)

---

### WHAT HAVE YOU LEARNED?

1. What is the evidence that early childhood is a sensitive time for learning language?
2. How does fast-mapping aid the language explosion?
3. How does overregularization signify a cognitive advance?
4. What in language learning shows the limitations of logic in early childhood?
5. What are the advantages of teaching a child two languages?
6. How can the language shift be avoided?

---

# Early-Childhood Schooling

Today, virtually every nation provides some early-childhood education, sometimes financed by the government, sometimes private, sometimes for a privileged few, and sometimes for every child (Georgeson & Payler, 2013).

In France, Denmark, Norway, and Sweden, more than 95 percent of all 3- to 5-year-olds are enrolled in government-sponsored schools. Norway also pays for education of 1- and 2-year-olds, and 80 percent of them attend (Ellingsaeter,

"We teach them that the world can be an unpredictable, dangerous, and sometimes frightening place, while being careful not to spoil their lovely innocence. It's tricky."

**Tricky Indeed** Young children are omnivorous learners, picking up habits, curses, and attitudes that adults would rather not transmit. Deciding what to teach—by actions more than words—is essential.

2014). The reasons for international variations are historical, economic, and political, but one message from research has reached almost every parent and politician worldwide—young children are amazingly capable and eager to learn.

## Homes and Schools

Developmental research does not translate directly into specific practices in early education, so no program can legitimately claim to follow Piaget or Vygotsky exactly (Hatch, 2012). This general finding should reassure parents: Young children learn in a variety of settings, and parents are influential even when a young child is in a day-care center from 8 A.M. to 6 P.M., five days a week. Nonetheless, developmental theories and scientific research inform educators, suggest hypotheses, and shape the curriculum of every program.

Beyond the amazing potential of young children to learn, another robust conclusion from research on children's learning seems not yet universally understood: Quality matters (Gambaro et al., 2014). If the home learning environment is poor, a good preschool program aids health, cognition, and social skills. If, instead, a family provides excellent learning, children still learn in a high-quality preschool, but their advances are not as dramatic as those of less fortunate children.

Indeed, it is better for children to be in excellent home care than in a low-quality, overcrowded day-care center. One expert criticizes inadequate government support that reduces quality: "Parents can find cheap babysitting that's bad for their kids on their own. They don't need government help with that" (Barnett, quoted in Samuels & Klein, 2013, p. 21).

Quality is notoriously difficult to judge (Votruba-Drzal & Dearing, 2017). "[B]ecause quality is hard for parents to observe, competition seems to be dominated by price" (Gambaro et al., 2014, p. 22). That is a problem, because to make a profit, programs hire fewer teachers—so low cost may indicate low quality.

● **Response for Immigrant Parents** (from p. 268): Children learn by listening, so it is important to speak with them often. Depending on how comfortable you are with the new language, you might prefer to read to your children, sing to them, and converse with them primarily in your native language and find a good preschool where they will learn the new language. The worst thing you could do is to restrict speech in either tongue.

● **Especially for Teachers** In trying to find a preschool program, what should parents look for? (see response, p. 272)

● **Especially for Unemployed Early-Childhood Teachers** You are offered a job in a program that has ten 3-year-olds for every adult. You know that is too many, but you want a job. What should you do? (see response, p. 272)

However, high cost does not necessarily mean high quality. As you have learned, children are active learners who benefit from social interaction with other children and with adults who guide them. A quiet preschool with adults who are not actively engaged with the children is low quality.

Quality cannot be judged by the name of a program or by its sponsorship. Educational institutions for 3- to 5-year-olds are called preschools, nursery schools, day-care centers, pre-primary programs, pre-K classes, and kindergartens. Sponsors can be public (federal, state, or city), private, religious, or corporate. Each child is an individual and cultures differ; an excellent program for one child might be less effective for another.

Professional assessment of quality also seems inadequate (Sabol et al., 2013). However, one aspect—child–teacher interaction—correlates with learning. A bad sign is a teacher who sits and watches; effective teachers talk, laugh, guide, and play with the children.

In order to sort through this variety, we review some distinctions among types of programs. One broad distinction concerns the program goals. Is the goal to encourage each child's creative individuality (*child-centered*) or to prepare the child for formal education (*teacher-directed*), or is it to prepare low-SES children for school (*intervention*, such as *Head Start*)?

## Child-Centered Programs

Many programs are called *child-centered*, or *developmental*, because they stress each child's development and growth. Teachers in such programs believe children need to follow their own interests rather than adult directions. For example, they agree that "children should be allowed to select many of their own activities from a variety of learning areas that the teacher has prepared" (Lara-Cinisomo et al., 2011). The physical space and the materials (such as dress-up clothes, art supplies, puzzles, blocks, and other toys) are arranged to allow exploration.

Most child-centered programs encourage artistic expression, including music and drama (Bassok et al., 2016). Some educators argue that young children are gifted in seeing the world more imaginatively than older people do. According to advocates of child-centered programs, this peak of creative vision should be

**Tibet, China, India, and . . . Italy?** Over the past half-century, as China increased its control of Tibet, thousands of refugees fled to northern India. Tibet traditionally had no preschools, but young children adapt quickly, as in this preschool program in Ladakh, India. This Tibetan boy is working a classic Montessori board.

Malie Rich-Griffith/Infocusphotos.com/Alamy

encouraged; children need many opportunities to tell stories, draw pictures, dance, and make music for their own delight.

That does not mean that academics are ignored. Advocates of math learning, for instance, believe that children have a natural interest in numbers and that child-centered schools can guide those interests as children grow (Stipek, 2013).

Child-centered programs are often influenced by Piaget, who emphasized that each child will discover new ideas if given a chance, or by Vygotsky, who thought that children learn from playing, especially with other children, with adult guidance.

## Montessori Schools

One type of child-centered school began in the slums of Rome in 1907, when Maria Montessori opened a nursery school (Standing, 1998). She believed that children needed structured, individualized projects to give them a sense of accomplishment. Her students completed puzzles, used sponges and water to clean tables, traced shapes, and so on.

Contemporary **Montessori schools** still emphasize individual pride and achievement, presenting many literacy-related tasks (e.g., outlining letters and looking at books) to young children. Specific materials differ from those that Montessori developed, but the underlying philosophy is the same. Children seek out learning tasks; they do not sit quietly in groups while a teacher instructs them. That makes Montessori programs child-centered (Lillard, 2013).

> **Montessori schools** Schools that offer early-childhood education based on the philosophy of Maria Montessori, which emphasizes careful work and tasks that each young child can do.

## Reggio Emilia

Another form of early-childhood education is **Reggio Emilia,** named after the town in Italy where it began. In Reggio Emilia, children are encouraged to master skills that are not usually taught in North American schools until age 7 or so, such as writing and using tools. Although many educators worldwide admire the Reggio philosophy and practice, it is expensive to duplicate in other nations—there are few dedicated Reggio Emilia schools in the United States.

Reggio schools do not provide large-group instruction, with lessons in, say, forming letters or cutting paper. Instead, hands-on activities chosen by individual children—such as drawing, cooking, and gardening—are stressed. Measurement of achievement, such as standardized testing to see whether children recognize the 26 letters of the alphabet, is antithetical to the conviction that each child should explore and learn in his or her own way. Each child's learning is documented via scrapbooks, photos, and daily notes—not to measure progress but to help the child and the parent take pride in accomplishments (Caruso, 2013).

Appreciation of the arts is evident. Every Reggio Emilia school originally had a studio, an artist, and space to encourage creativity (Forbes, 2012). Children's art is displayed on white walls and hung from high ceilings, and floor-to-ceiling windows open to a spacious, plant-filled playground. Big mirrors are part of the schools' décor—again, with the idea of fostering individuality and self-expression. However, individuality does not mean that children do not work together. On the contrary, group projects are encouraged.

> **Reggio Emilia** A program of early-childhood education that originated in the town of Reggio Emilia, Italy, and that encourages each child's creativity in a carefully designed setting.

> **Child-Centered Pride** How could Rachel Koepke, a 3-year-old from a Wisconsin town called Pleasant Prairie, seem so pleased that her hands (and cuffs) are blue? The answer arises from northern Italy—Rachel attends a Reggio Emilia preschool that encourages creative expression.

● **Response for Teachers** (from p. 270): Tell parents to look at the people more than the program. Parents should see the children in action and note whether the teachers show warmth and respect for each child.

● **Response for Unemployed Early-Childhood Teachers** (from p. 270): It would be best for you to wait for a job in a program in which children learn well, organized along the lines explained in this chapter. You would be happier, as well as learn more, in a workplace that is good for children. Realistically, though, you might feel compelled to take the job. If you do, change the child/adult ratio—find a helper, perhaps a college intern or a volunteer grandmother. But choose carefully—some adults are not helpful at all. Before you take the job, remember that children need continuity: You can't leave simply because you find something better.

**Learning from One Another** Every nation creates its own version of early education. In this scene in Kuala Lumpur, Malaysia, note the head coverings, uniforms, and distance between the sexes. None of these elements would be found in most early-childhood-education classrooms in North America or Europe, but none of them enhances or inhibits learning for these children.

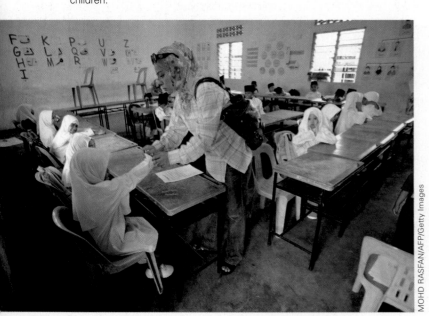

MOHD RASFAN/AFP/Getty Images

Often those group projects include exploring some aspect of the natural world. One analysis of Reggio Emilia in the United States found "a science-rich context that triggered and supported preschoolers' inquiries and effectively engaged preschoolers' hands, heads, and hearts with science" (Inan et al., 2010, p. 1186).

## Teacher-Directed Programs

Teacher-directed preschools stress academics, often taught by one adult to the entire group. The curriculum includes learning the names of letters, numbers, shapes, and colors according to a set timetable; every child naps, snacks, and goes to the bathroom on schedule as well. Children learn to sit quietly and listen to the teacher. Praise and other reinforcements are given for good behavior, and time-outs (brief separation from activities) are imposed to punish misbehavior.

The goal of teacher-directed programs is to make all children "ready to learn" when they enter elementary school. For that reason, basic skills are stressed, including precursors to reading, writing, and arithmetic, perhaps through teachers asking questions that children answer together in unison. Behavior is also taught, as children learn to respect adults, to follow schedules, to hold hands when they go on outings, and so on.

Children practice forming letters, sounding out words, counting objects, and writing their names. If a 4-year-old learns to read, that is success. (In a child-centered program, that might arouse suspicion that there was too little time to play or socialize.)

Many teacher-directed programs were inspired by behaviorism, which emphasizes step-by-step learning and repetition, with reinforcement (praise, gold stars, prizes) for accomplishment. Another inspiration for teacher-directed programs comes from information-processing research indicating that children who have not learned basic vocabulary and listening skills by kindergarten often fall behind in primary school. Many state legislatures mandate that preschoolers master specific concepts, an outcome best achieved by teacher-directed learning (Bracken & Crawford, 2010).

### Comparing Child-Centered and Teacher-Directed Learning

Most developmentalists advocate child-centered programs (Christakis, 2016; Golinkoff & Hirsh-Pasek, 2016). They believe that, from ages 2 to 6, young children learn best when they can interact in their own way with materials and ideas (Sim & Xu, 2017). They fear that the child's joy and creativity will be squashed if there are specific goals set for all children.

On the other hand, many parents and legislators want proof that children are learning things that will help them read, add, and so on. The developmental critics contend that this will "trade emotional grounding and strong language skills known to support learning for assembly-line schooling that teaches children isolated factoids" (Hirsh-Pasek & Golinkoff, 2016, p. 1158).

As Penelope Leach wrote, "Goals come from the outside. . . . It is important that people see early learning as coming from inside children because that's what makes clear its interconnectedness with play, and therefore the inappropriateness of many 'learning goals'" (Leach, 2011, p. 17). More specifically, one developmentalist writes, "why should we settle for unimaginative goals . . . like being able to identify triangles and squares, or recalling the names of colors and seasons" (Christakis, 2016).

Many developmentalists resist legislative standards and academic tests for young children, arguing that social skills and creative play are essential for healthy development but difficult to measure. A truly brilliant child is characterized by all the complex skills of executive function, not the easy-to-measure skills of letter recognition (Golinkoff & Hirsh-Pasek, 2016). [**Developmental Link:** Children's play is discussed in Chapter 10.]

Finding the right balance between formal and informal assessment, and between child-centered and teacher-directed learning, is a goal of many educators who hope each child has the education that works best for him or her (Fuligni et al., 2012). The current trend seems to be more toward teacher-directed than child-centered learning, according to a survey of kindergarten teachers (Bassok et al., 2016). (See Figure 9.3.)

## Intervention Programs

Several programs designed for children from low-SES families were established in the United States decades ago. Some solid research on the results of these programs is now available.

### Head Start

In the early 1960s, millions of young children in the United States were thought to need a "head start" on their formal education to foster better health and cognition before first grade. Consequently, since 1965, the federal government has funded a massive program for 4-year-olds called **Head Start.**

**Head Start** A federally funded early-childhood intervention program for low-income children of preschool age.

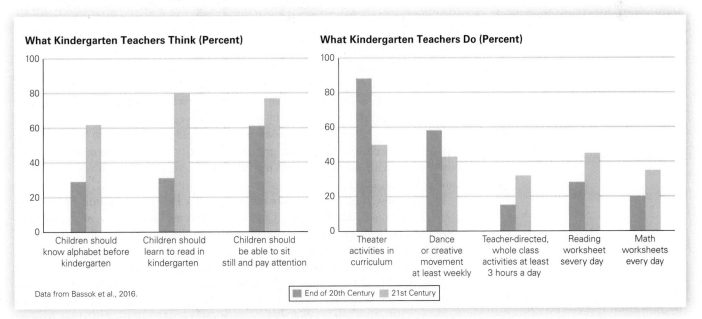

**FIGURE 9.3**

**Less Play, More Work** These data come from a large survey of more than 5,000 public school teachers throughout the United States. In 1998 and 2010, kindergarten teachers were asked identical questions but gave different answers. Smaller, more recent surveys suggest that these trends continue, and they now involve preschool teachers. Some use worksheets for 3-year-olds.

**If You're Happy and You Know It** Gabby Osborne (pink shirt) has her own way of showing happiness, not the hand-clapping that Lizalia Garcia tries to teach. The curriculum of this Head Start class in Florida includes learning about emotions, contrary to the wishes of some legislators, who want proof of academics.

© Octavio Jones/ZUMA Press/Corbis

The goals for Head Start have changed over the decades, from lifting families out of poverty to promoting literacy, from providing dental care and immunizations to teaching Standard English, from focusing on 4-year-olds to including 2- and 3-year-olds. In 2015, more than 8 billion dollars in federal funds were allocated to Head Start, which enrolled almost 1 million children.

Head Start is a massive program, but there are about 8 million 3- and 4-year-olds in the United States, which means that relatively few U.S. children of that age attend Head Start. Many other children are in private programs (about 83 percent of 4-year-olds from the wealthiest families are enrolled in private preschools). Many more are in state-sponsored programs, which range in quality from excellent to woefully inadequate (Barnett et al., 2016).

Although initially most Head Start programs were child-centered, they have become increasingly teacher-directed as waves of legislators have approved and shaped them. Children learn whatever their particular teachers emphasize. Not surprisingly, specific results vary by program and cohort.

For example, many low-income 3- and 4-year-olds in the United States are not typically exposed to math. After one Head Start program engaged children in a board game with numbers, their mathematical understanding advanced significantly (Siegler, 2009).

In 2016, new requirements were put in place for Head Start, requiring that programs be open at least 6 hours a day and 180 days a year (initially, most programs were half-day) and giving special supports to children who are homeless, or have special needs, or are learning English.

Such changes were made partly because federal research found that Head Start is most beneficial for children in poverty, or in rural areas, or with disabilities (U.S. Department of Health and Human Services, 2010). Those children are least likely to find other sources of early education, largely because of their parents' income, location, and stress (Crosnoe et al., 2016).

Historical data show that most Head Start children of every background advanced in language and social skills, but by elementary school non–Head Start children often caught up. However, there was one area in which the Head Start children maintained their superiority—vocabulary.

That finding also supports what you just learned about language development. Almost every preschool introduces children to words they would not learn at home. Children will fast-map those words, gaining a linguistic knowledge base that facilitates expanded vocabulary throughout life.

A longitudinal study of children born in 2001 found that those who went to Head Start were advanced in math and language, but, compared to similar children who had only their mother's care, they had more behavior problems, according to their teachers in kindergarten and first grade (R. Lee et al., 2014). One interpretation of that result is that the teachers did not know how to respond to the self-assertion of the Head Start children: They blamed the children instead of welcoming their independence.

## Long-Term Gains from Intensive Programs

This discussion of philosophies, practices, and programs may give the impression that the research on early-childhood cognition is contradictory. That is not true. Specifics are debatable, but empirical evidence and longitudinal evaluation find that preschool education advances learning and that learning concepts and executive control is more important than remembering facts. Ideally, each program has a curriculum that guides practice, all of the adults collaborate, and experienced teachers respond to each child.

The best longitudinal evidence comes from three intensive programs that enrolled children for years—sometimes beginning with home visits in infancy, sometimes continuing in after-school programs through first grade. One program, called *Perry* (or *High/Scope*), was spearheaded in Michigan (Schweinhart & Weikart, 1997); another, called *Abecedarian*, got its start in North Carolina (Campbell et al., 2001); a third, called *Child–Parent Centers*, began in Chicago (Reynolds, 2000). All focused on children from low-SES families.

All three programs compared experimental groups of children with matched control groups, and all reached the same conclusion: Early education has substantial long-term benefits that become most apparent when children are in third grade or later. By age 10, children who had been enrolled in any one of these three programs scored higher on math and reading achievement tests than did other children from the same backgrounds, schools, and neighborhoods. They were less likely to be placed in classes for children with special needs, or to repeat a year of school, or to drop out of high school before graduation.

An advantage of decades of longitudinal research is that teenagers and adults who received early education can be compared with those who did not. For all three programs, early investment paid off. In adolescence, the children who had undergone intensive preschool education had higher aspirations, possessed a greater sense of achievement, and were less likely to have been abused. As young adults, they were more likely to attend college and less likely to go to jail. As middle-aged adults, they were more often employed, paying taxes, healthy, and not needing government subsidies (Reynolds & Ou, 2011; Schweinhart et al., 2005; Campbell et al., 2014).

All three research projects found that providing direct cognitive training, with specific instruction in various school-readiness skills, was useful. Each child's needs and talents were considered—

**Lifetime Achievement** The baby in the framed photograph escaped the grip of poverty. The woman holding it proved that early education can transform children. She is Frances Campbell, who spearheaded the Abecedarian Project. The baby's accomplishments may be the more impressive of the two.

Frank Porter Graham Child Development Institute

a circumstance made possible because the child/adult ratio was low. This combination of child-centered and teacher-directed curricula, with all of the teachers working together on the same goals, benefited children. The parents reinforced what the children learned. In all three, teachers deliberately involved parents, and each program included strategies to enhance the home–school connection.

These programs were expensive (ranging from $6,500 to $20,000 annually per young child in 2016 dollars). From a developmental perspective, the decreased need for special education and other social services later on made early education a "wise investment" (Duncan & Magnuson, 2013, p. 128). Additional benefits to society over the child's lifetime, including increased employment and tax revenues, as well as reduced crime, are worth much more than the cost of the programs.

Among developed nations, the United States is an outlier, least likely to support new mothers or young children. However, since 2010, some states (e.g., Oklahoma, Georgia, Florida, New Jersey, and Illinois) and some cities (e.g., New York, Boston, Cleveland, San Antonio, and Los Angeles) have offered preschool to every 4-year-old. Although this investment generally results in fewer children needing special education later on, implementation and results are controversial—a topic for further research.

As of 2014, 40 states sponsored some public education for young children—usually only for 4-year-olds. More than a million children (1,347,072) attended state-sponsored preschools. Although these numbers include some 3-year-olds, it is estimated that 29 percent of all 4-year-olds were in state-sponsored preschool, twice as many as a decade earlier (Barnett et al., 2015). About another 10 percent attended the federal program, Head Start, and an estimated 3 percent were in special publicly funded programs for children with disabilities (U.S. Department of Education, 2015).

Most state programs pay only for children living in poverty, but many wealthy families pay tuition for preschool education. Private schools are expensive—as much as $30,000 a year. Not surprisingly, in the United States, families in the highest income quartile are more likely to have their 3- and 4-year-olds in an educational program than the national average (see Visualizing Development, p. 277).

The increases in government-sponsored preschool for 4-year-olds is good news, but developmentalists note that in the United States, unlike in Europe, almost half of all 4-year-olds and most 3-year-olds are not in any educational program. The children least likely to be in such programs are Spanish-speaking, or from families with income slightly above the poverty level, or have mothers who are not employed. In all three situations, a good early-education program would be especially helpful.

The other problem is that states save money in ways that do not promote learning. Spending per child has been decreasing. In inflation-adjusted dollars, per-pupil spending by states was $5,129 per child in 2002 and $4,121 in 2014 (Barnett et al., 2015). That means less child-centered learning (which is more expensive) and more teacher-directed education.

Compared to a decade ago, much more is known about early cognition: 2- to 4-year-olds are capable of learning languages, concepts, math, theory of mind, and much more. What a child learns before age 6 is pivotal for later schooling and adult life. The amazing potential of young children is also a theme of the next chapter, where we discuss other kinds of learning, such as in emotional regulation and social skills.

# Early-Childhood Schooling

Preschool can be an academic and social benefit to children. Around the world, increasing numbers of children are enrolled in early-childhood education.

Programs are described as "teacher-directed" or "child-centered," but in reality, most teachers' styles reflect a combination of both approaches. Some students benefit more from the order and structure of a teacher-directed classroom, while others work better in a more collaborative and creative environment.

### TEACHER-DIRECTED APPROACH
**Focused on Getting Preschoolers Ready to Learn**
Direct instruction
Teacher as formal authority
Students learn by listening
Classroom is orderly and quiet
Teacher fully manages lesssons
Rewards individual achievement
Encourages academics
Students learn from teacher

### CHILD-CENTERED APPROACH
**Focused on Individual Development and Growth**
Teacher as facilitator
Teacher as delegator
Students learn actively
Classroom is designed for collaborative work
Students influence content
Rewards collaboration among students
Encourages artistic expression
Students learn from each other

Worth Publishers

## DIFFERENT STUDENTS, DIFFERENT TEACHERS

There is clearly no "one right way" to teach children. Each approach has potential benefits and pitfalls. A classroom full of creative, self-motivated students can thrive when a gifted teacher acts as a competent facilitator. But students who are distracted or annoyed by noise, or who are shy or intimidated by other children, can blossom under an engaging and encouraging teacher in a more traditional environment.

**Done Well**

| Teacher-Directed (Done Well) | Child-Centered (Done Well) |
| --- | --- |
| • engaging teacher | • emphasizes social skills and emotion regulation |
| • clear, consistent assessment | • encourages critical thinking |
| • reading and math skills emphasized | • builds communication skills |
| • quiet, orderly classroom | • fosters individual achievement |
| • all students treated equally | • encourages creativity and curiosity |

**Teacher-Directed** ←→ **Child-Centered**

| Teacher-Directed (Done Poorly) | Child-Centered (Done Poorly) |
| --- | --- |
| • bored students | • chaotic/noisy classrooms |
| • passive learning | • students may miss important knowledge and skills |
| • less independent, critical thinking | • inconclusive assessment of student progress |
| • teacher may dominate | • some students may dominate others |

**Done Poorly**

**WHAT HAVE YOU LEARNED?**

1. What do most preschools provide that most homes do not?

2. In child-centered programs, what do the teachers do?

3. What makes the Reggio Emilia program different from most other preschool programs?

4. Why are Montessori schools still functioning 100 years after the first such schools opened?

5. What are the advantages and disadvantages of teacher-directed preschools?

6. What are the goals of Head Start?

7. What are the long-term results of intervention preschools?

## SUMMARY

### Thinking During Early Childhood

1. Piaget stressed the egocentric and illogical aspects of thought during early childhood. He called this stage of thinking preoperational intelligence because young children do not yet use logical operations to think about their observations and experiences.

2. Young children, according to Piaget, sometimes focus on only one thing (centration) and see things only from their own viewpoint (egocentrism), remaining stuck on appearances and current conditions. They may believe that living spirits reside in inanimate objects and that nonhuman animals have the same characteristics they themselves have, a belief called animism.

3. Vygotsky stressed the social aspects of childhood cognition, noting that children learn by participating in various experiences, guided by more knowledgeable adults or peers. Such guidance assists learning within the zone of proximal development, which encompasses the knowledge children are close to understanding and the skills they can almost master.

4. According to Vygotsky, the best teachers use various hints, guidelines, and other tools to provide a child with a scaffold for new learning. Language is a bridge that provides social mediation between the knowledge that the child already has and the learning that the society hopes to impart. For Vygotsky, words are tools for learning.

5. An important part of developing cognition during early childhood is the emergence of executive function, or cognitive control, as children learn to regulate and control their sensory impulses in order to use their minds more effectively.

6. Computers can aid cognitive advancement, but they also can impede it. Too much screen time and too little time for individualized human interaction slow down learning.

7. Children develop theories, especially to explain the purpose of life and their role in it. One theory about children's thinking is called "theory-theory"—the hypothesis that children develop theories because all humans innately seek explanations for everything they observe.

8. An example of the developing cognition of young children is theory of mind—an understanding of what others may be thinking. Theory of mind begins at around age 4, partly as a result of maturation of the brain. Culture and experiences also influence its development.

### Language Learning

9. Language develops rapidly during early childhood, a sensitive period but not a critical one for language learning. Vocabulary increases dramatically, with thousands of words added between ages 2 and 6. In addition, basic grammar is mastered.

10. The child's ability to learn language is evident in fast-mapping (the quick use of new vocabulary words) and in overregularization (applying the rules of grammar even when they are not valid).

11. Many children learn to speak more than one language, gaining cognitive as well as social advantages. Early childhood is the best time to learn two languages. The benefits of bilingualism are lifelong. Pronunciation lags behind production, which lags behind comprehension.

### Early-Childhood Schooling

12. Organized educational programs during early childhood advance cognitive and social skills, although specifics vary a great deal. The quality of a program cannot be judged by the name or by appearance.

13. Montessori and Reggio Emilia are two child-centered programs that began in Italy and are now offered in many nations. They stress individual interests of each child, including creative play, inspired by Piaget and Vygotsky.

14. Behaviorist principles led to many specific practices of teacher-directed programs. Children learn to listen to teachers and become ready for kindergarten. Teacher-directed programs are preferred by many parents and legislators, and they are increasingly popular—to the consternation of many child developmentalists.

**15.** Head Start is a U.S. federal government program primarily for low-income children. Longitudinal research finds that early-childhood education reduces the risk of later problems, such as needing special education. High-quality programs increase the likelihood that a child will become a law-abiding, gainfully employed adult.

**16.** Many types of preschool programs are successful. It is the quality of early education that matters. The training, warmth, and continuity of early-childhood teachers benefit children in many ways.

**17.** Some nations provide early education for all 3- and 4-year-olds. The United States is behind on this metric, with only about half of all 4-year-olds in preschool, and far fewer 3-year-olds.

## KEY TERMS

preoperational intelligence (p. 252)
symbolic thought (p. 252)
animism (p. 252)
centration (p. 252)
egocentrism (p. 252)
focus on appearance (p. 252)

static reasoning (p. 253)
irreversibility (p. 253)
conservation (p. 253)
zone of proximal development (ZPD) (p. 255)
scaffolding (p. 255)
overimitation (p. 256)

private speech (p. 257)
social mediation (p. 258)
executive function (p. 259)
theory-theory (p. 260)
theory of mind (p. 260)
fast-mapping (p. 265)
overregularization (p. 266)

pragmatics (p. 266)
Montessori schools (p. 271)
Reggio Emilia (p. 271)
Head Start (p. 273)

## APPLICATIONS

The best way to understand thinking in early childhood is to listen to a child, as Applications 1 and 2 require. If some students have no access to children, they should do Application 3 or 4.

**1.** Replicate one of Piaget's conservation experiments. The easiest one is conservation of liquids (Figure 9.1). Work with a child under age 5 who tells you that two identically shaped glasses contain the same amount of liquid. Then carefully pour one glass of liquid into a narrower, taller glass. Ask the child if one glass now contains more or if the glasses contain the same amount.

**2.** To demonstrate how rapidly language is learned, show a preschool child several objects and label one with a nonsense word that the child has never heard. (*Toma* is often used; so is *wug*.) Or choose a word the child does not know, such as *wrench*, *spatula*, or the name of a coin from another nation. Test the child's fast-mapping.

**3.** Theory of mind emerges at about age 4, but many adults still have trouble understanding other people's thoughts and motives. Ask several people why someone in the news did whatever he or she did (e.g., a scandal, a crime, a heroic act). Then ask your informants how sure they are of their explanation. Compare and analyze the reasons as well as the degrees of certainty. (One person may be sure of an explanation that someone else thinks is impossible.)

**4.** Think about an experience in which you learned something that was initially difficult. To what extent do Vygotsky's concepts (guided participation, zone of proximal development) explain the experience? Write a detailed, step-by-step account of your learning process as Vygotsky would have described it.

# Early Childhood:
## Psychosocial Development

## What Will You Know?

1. Why do 2-year-olds have more sudden tempers, tears, and terrors than 6-year-olds?
2. What do children learn from playing with each other?
3. What happens if parents let their children do whatever they want?

I was early to pick up my grandson, so I waited while the after-school teacher tried to encourage imagination in a circle of 4-year-olds.

"What would you like to be?" she asked, expecting them to say some sort of animal, perhaps a bear or a lion, or some sort of professional, perhaps a teacher or a police officer.

One girl said "princess"; another said "ballerina." All of the girls smiled approvingly. One boy said "Superman"; my grandson said "Spider-Man." Smiles from the boys. The teacher kept trying. She asked another boy.

"Spider-Man," he said.

"Think of something else," she said.

"I can't," he answered, and his best friend laughed.

That was not what the teacher expected. She switched activities; she had them all sing a song they knew.

I was surprised, too. This was 2014, in Brooklyn, New York. The parents of these children resist gender stereotypes. I once asked my son-in-law to use his "man hands" to open a stubborn jar of tomato sauce, and my daughter, scowling, said "that's sexist, Mom."

If I had remembered this chapter, I might not have been surprised. Preschoolers have definite ideas of male–female roles, often more rigid than their parents. They insist on their own opinions even when adults ask them to think of something else. Their self-confidence and the importance of peer approval are part of growing up, as is the fact that these children sat in a circle and listened to each other. The social world of the young child expands, sometimes in ways that adults do not expect.

✦ **Emotional Development**
Initiative Versus Guilt
Motivation

✦ **Play**
Playmates
Active Play
Learning Emotional Regulation

✦ **Challenges for Caregivers**
Styles of Caregiving
A VIEW FROM SCIENCE: Culture and Parenting Style
Discipline
OPPOSING PERSPECTIVES: Is Spanking OK?
Becoming Boys or Girls: Sex and Gender
A CASE TO STUDY: The Berger Daughters
What Is Best?

## Emotional Development

Controlling the expression of feelings, called **emotional regulation,** is the preeminent psychosocial task between ages 2 and 6. Emotional regulation is a lifelong endeavor, a crucial aspect of executive function, which develops most rapidly in early childhood (Gross, 2014; Lewis, 2013).

By age 6, most children can be angry, frightened, sad, anxious, or proud without the explosive outbursts of temper, terror, or tears of 2-year-olds. Depending on a child's training and temperament, some emotions are easier to control than others, but even temperamentally angry or fearful children learn to regulate their emotions (Moran et al., 2013; Tan et al., 2013; Suurland et al., 2016).

Left: Worth Archive/Ellie Miller
Top: Christopher Hope-Fitch/Getty Images

**emotional regulation** The ability to control when and how emotions are expressed.

**self-concept** A person's understanding of who he or she is, in relation to self-esteem, appearance, personality, and various traits.

**effortful control** The ability to regulate one's emotions and actions through effort, not simply through natural inclination.

**initiative versus guilt** Erikson's third psychosocial crisis, in which children undertake new skills and activities and feel guilty when they do not succeed at them.

In the process of emotional regulation, children develop their **self-concept,** which is their idea of who they are. Remember that 1-year-olds begin to recognize themselves in the mirror, the start of self-awareness. By age 6, children can describe some of their characteristics, including what emotions they feel and how they express them. That is probably true for all children everywhere, although parental guidance and encouragement aid in self-awareness (LeCuyer & Swanson, 2016).

Indeed, for all aspects of self-concept and emotional regulation, culture and family matter. Children may be encouraged to laugh/cry/yell, or the opposite, to hide their emotions. Some adults guffaw, slap their knees, and stomp their feet for joy; others cover their mouths if a smile spontaneously appears. Anger is regulated in almost every culture, but the expression of it—when, how, and to whom—varies a great deal. No matter what the specifics, parents teach emotional regulation (Kim & Sasaki, 2014).

Emotional regulation is also called **effortful control** (Eisenberg et al., 2014), a term that emphasizes that controlling outbursts is not easy. Effortful control is more difficult when people—of any age—are in pain, or tired, or hungry.

Effortful control, executive function, and emotional regulation are similar constructs, with much overlap. Executive function emphasizes cognition; effortful control emphasizes temperament; both undergird the ability to express emotions appropriately.

## Initiative Versus Guilt

Emotional regulation is part of Erikson's third developmental stage, **initiative versus guilt.** *Initiative* includes saying something new, expanding an ability, beginning a project, expressing an emotion. Depending on what happens when they try a new action, children feel proud or guilty.

Usually, North American adults encourage enthusiasm, effort, and pride in their 2- to 6-year-olds. If a project fails—the block tower falls down, the playmate turns away—adults usually suggest trying again and blame the block or the playmate, thus helping the child to avoid feeling guilty.

If parents ignore, rather than guide, joy and pride, or worse, if they blame the child for being ignorant, clumsy, or so on, the child may not learn emotional regulation. For both genetic and behavioral reasons, parents who blame their children and who have poor emotional regulation themselves are likely to have children who do not learn how to regulate their own emotions (Bridgett et al., 2015).

Guidance, yes; brutal honesty, no. Preschool children are usually proud of themselves, overestimating their skills. As one team expressed it:

> Compared to older children and adults, young children are the optimists of the world, believing they have greater physical abilities, better memories, are more skilled at imitating models, are smarter, know more about how things work, and rate themselves as stronger, tougher, and of higher social standing than is actually the case.

> [Bjorklund & Ellis, 2014, p. 244]

That *protective optimism* helps young children try new things, and thus, preschooler's initiative advances learning. As Erikson predicted, their optimistic self-concept protects them from guilt and shame.

If young children knew the true limits of their ability, they would not imagine becoming an NBA forward, a Grammy winner, a billionaire inventor. That might discourage them from trying to learn new things (Bjorklund & Ellis, 2014). Initiative is a driving force for young children, as it should be.

kirin_photo/Getty Images

**Genuinely Helpful** Children of all ages can be helpful to their families, but their actions depend on family and cohort. Thirty years ago, more children gathered freshly laid eggs than recycled plastic milk bottles. Indeed, no blue recycling bins existed until tens of thousands of environmentalists advocated reducing our carbon footprint.

● **Observation Quiz** Does this mother deserve praise? (see answer, p. 285) ↑

## Pride and Prejudice

In the United States, a young child's pride usually includes being proud of gender, size, and heritage. In most cases, girls are happy to be girls; boys to be boys—the nuances and complexities of gender are beyond them.

Similar reactions occur regarding how old they are. They are very glad that they aren't babies. "Crybaby" is an insult; praise for being "a big kid" is welcomed; pride in doing something better than a younger child is expressed. Bragging is common.

Indeed, many young children believe that whatever they are is good. They may feel superior to children of another nationality or religion. This arises because of maturation: Cognition enables them to understand group categories, not only of ethnicity, gender, and nationality but even categories that are irrelevant. They remember more about cartoon characters whose names begin with the same letter as theirs (Ross et al., 2011). If their parents or other adults express prejudice against people of another group, they may mirror those prejudices (Tagar et al., 2017).

One amusing example occurred when preschoolers were asked to explain why one person would steal from another, as occurred in a story about two fictional tribes, the Zaz and the Flurps. As you would expect from theory-theory, the preschoolers readily found reasons. Their first explanation illustrated their belief that group loyalty was more important than any personal characteristic.

> "Why did a Zaz steal a toy from a Flurp?"
> "Because he's a Zaz, but he's a Flurp . . . They're not the same kind . . ."

Only when asked to explain a more difficult case, when group loyalty was insufficient, did they consider character and fairness.

> "Why did a Zaz steal a toy from a Zaz?"
> "Because he's a very mean boy."

[Rhodes, 2013, p. 259]

**Proud Peruvian** In rural Peru, a program of early education (Pronoei) encourages community involvement and traditional culture. Preschoolers, like this girl in a holiday parade, are proud to be themselves, and that helps them become healthy and strong.

Mike Theiss/Corbis

**THINK CRITICALLY:** At what age, if ever, do people understand when pride becomes prejudice?

## Brain Maturation

The new initiative that Erikson described results from myelination of the limbic system, growth of the prefrontal cortex, and a longer attention span—all results of neurological maturation. Emotional regulation and cognitive maturation develop together, each enabling the other to advance (Bell & Calkins, 2011; Lewis, 2013; Bridgett et al., 2015). The entire brain works to regulate emotions: It is an error to think that emotions arise from only one part.

The prefrontal cortex coordinates and regulates all sensations. Normally, as the prefrontal cortex matures at about age 4 or 5, and as family and preschool experiences guide them, children less often throw tantrums, pick fights, or giggle during prayer. Throughout early childhood, violent outbursts, uncontrolled crying, and terrifying *phobias* (irrational, crippling fears) diminish.

The capacity for self-control, such as *not* opening a present immediately if asked to wait and *not* expressing disappointment at an undesirable gift, becomes more evident. Consider the most recent time you gave someone a gift. If the receiver was a young child, you probably could tell whether the child liked the present. If the receiver was an adult, you might not know: Adults blithely give unwanted gifts, not realizing the reaction (Galak et al., 2016). As you remember from Chapter 9, children are better at hiding disappointment as they become more socially aware.

In one study, researchers asked children to wait eight minutes before opening a wrapped present in front of them, while their mothers did some paperwork (Cole et al., 2010). The children used strategies to help them wait, including distractions and private speech.

**LaunchPad**
macmillan learning

**Video Activity: Can Young Children Delay Gratification?** illustrates how most young children are unable to overcome temptation even when promised an award.

Keisha was one of the study participants:

"Are you done, Mom?" . . . "I wonder what's in it" . . . "Can I open it now?"

Each time her mother reminds Keisha to wait, eventually adding, "If you keep interrupting me, I can't finish and if I don't finish . . ." Keisha plops in her chair, frustrated. "I really want it," she laments, aloud but to herself. "I want to talk to Mommy so I won't open it. If I talk, Mommy won't finish. If she doesn't finish, I can't have it." She sighs deeply, folds her arms, and scans the room. . . . The research assistant returns. Keisha looks at her mother with excited anticipation. Her mother says, "OK, now." Keisha tears open the gift.

[Cole et al., 2010, p. 59]

This is a more recent example of the famous marshmallow test, which now has longitudinal results (Mischel et al., 1972; Mischel, 2014). Children could eat one marshmallow immediately or get two marshmallows if they waited—sometimes as long as 15 minutes. Young children who delayed gobbling up a marshmallow became more successful as teenagers, young adults, and even middle-aged adults—doing well in college, for instance, and having happy marriages.

Of course, this is correlation, not causation: Some preschoolers who did not wait nonetheless became successful. However, emotional regulation in preschool predicts academic achievement and later success. Many factors are crucial.

- **Maturation matters.** Three-year-olds are poor at impulse control. They improve by age 6.
- **Learning matters.** In the zone of proximal development, children learn from mentors, who offer tactics for delaying gratification.
- **Culture matters.** Recent research finds that children in Cameroon are much better at waiting than Mischel's California children (Lamm et al., 2017).

In all aspects of emotional regulation, brain plasticity is evident. Children express and develop their emotions in response to the emotions of other people, and that molds their neuronal connections. The process is reciprocal and dynamic: Anger begets anger, which leads again to anger; joy begets joy, and so on.

The synergy of emotional regulation was found in brain scans when 3-year-olds did a puzzle with their mothers, some of whom became frustrated. As the scientists explain, "mothers and children regulate or deregulate each other" (Atzaba-Poria et al., 2017, p. 551).

Allen Brown/dbimages/Alamy

**Learning Emotional Regulation** Like this girl in Hong Kong, all 2-year-olds burst into tears when something upsets them—a toy breaks, a pet refuses to play, or it's time to go home. A mother who comforts them and helps them calm down is teaching them to regulate their emotions.

**intrinsic motivation** A drive, or reason to pursue a goal, that comes from inside a person, such as the desire to feel smart or competent.

**extrinsic motivation** A drive, or reason to pursue a goal, that arises from the need to have one's achievements rewarded from outside, perhaps by receiving material possessions or another person's esteem.

## Motivation

Motivation is the impulse that propels someone to act. It comes either from a person's own desires or from the social context.

**Intrinsic motivation** arises from within, when people do something for the joy of doing it: A musician might enjoy making music even if no one else hears it. Intrinsic motivation is thought to advance creativity, innovation, and emotional well-being (Weinstein & DeHaan, 2014). Erikson's psychosocial needs are intrinsic: The young child feels inwardly compelled to initiate things, such as walking along a ledge or exploring an anthill, when no one else suggested such activity.

**Extrinsic motivation** comes from outside the person, when people do something to gain praise or some other reinforcement. A musician might play for applause or money. Social rewards are powerful lifelong: Four-year-olds hold an adult's hand to cross the street because they are praised —and punished if they forget. If an extrinsic reward stops, the behavior may stop unless it has become a habit. Then it has become intrinsic: It feels good.

Intrinsic motivation is evident in every child. Young children play, question, exercise, create, destroy, and explore for the sheer joy of it. That serves them well. For example, a longitudinal study found that 3-year-olds who were strong in intrinsic motivation were, two years later, advanced in early math and literacy (Mokrova et al., 2013).

Children enjoy activity for its own pleasure. When playing a game, few young children keep score; intrinsic joy is the goal, more than winning. In fact, young children often claim to have won when objective scoring would say they lost; in this case, the children may really be winners.

Intrinsic motivation is apparent when children invent dialogues for their toys, concentrate on creating a work of art or architecture, or converse with **imaginary friends.** Such conversations with invisible companions are rarely encouraged by adults (thus no extrinsic motivation). Nevertheless, from about age 2 to 7, imaginary friends are increasingly common, although far from universal—most children do not have an imaginary friend.

An international study of 3- to 8-year-olds found that about 1 child in 5 said that they had one or more invisible companions, with notable variation by culture: 38 percent of children in the Dominican Republic, but only 5 percent in Nepal, had such a friend (Wigger, 2017). Is that because some families discourage imagination? American psychologists believe that children know that their imaginary friends are invisible and pretend, but conjuring them up meets various intrinsic psychosocial needs (M. Taylor et al., 2009).

The distinction between extrinsic and intrinsic motivation may be crucial in understanding how and when to praise something a child has done. Praise may be effective when it is connected to the particular production, not to a general trait. For example, an adult might say, "You worked hard and created a good drawing," not "You are a great artist." The goal is to help the child feel happy that effort paid off, which is what children are inclined to think. That motivates future action (Zentall & Morris, 2010).

In a set of experiments which suggest that specific praise for effort is better than generalized statements, some 4- to 7-year-old boys were told that boys are good at a particular game. Knowing this *decreased* their scores on the game. The same thing happened when girls were told that girls were good at the game. The children apparently feared that they would not be as good as most children of their sex. They "felt less happy and less competent, liked the game less, [and] were less persistent" (Cimpian, 2013, p. 272).

By contrast, other children were told that one particular child was good at the game. That led them to believe that personal effort mattered. That belief was motivating; their scores were higher than those who had been told that boys or girls in general were good.

**Especially for College Students** Is extrinsic or intrinsic motivation more influential in your study efforts? (see response, p. 286)

**imaginary friends** Make-believe friends who exist only in a child's imagination; increasingly common from ages 3 through 7. They combat loneliness and aid emotional regulation.

**Answer to Observation Quiz** (from p. 282): Yes—even if you don't consider recycling important. Notice her face and body: She is smiling and kneeling, and her hands are on her legs, all suggesting that she knows how to encourage without interfering. Even more commendable is her boys' behavior: Many brothers would be grabbing, shoving, and throwing, but, at least at this moment, shared cooperation is evident. Kudos to Mom.

**Especially for Professors** One of your students tells you about a child who plays, sleeps, and talks with an imaginary friend. Does this mean that child is emotionally disturbed? (see response, p. 286)

**Especially for Teachers of Young Children** Should you put gold stars on children's work? (see response, p. 286)

## WHAT HAVE YOU LEARNED?

1. How might protective optimism lead to a child's acquisition of new skills and competencies?
2. What did Erikson think was crucial for young children?
3. What is an example (not in the text) of intrinsic motivation?
4. What is an example (not in the text) of extrinsic motivation?
5. Why do child-centered preschools need children to be intrinsically motivated?

**Real or Fake?** This photo may be staged, but the children show the power of imagination—each responding to his or her cape in a unique way. Sociodramatic play is universal; children do it if given half a chance.

# Play

Play is timeless and universal—apparent in every part of the world over thousands of years. Many developmentalists believe that play is the most productive as well as the most enjoyable activity that children undertake (Elkind, 2007; Bateson & Martin, 2013; P. Smith, 2010). Others disagree. Whether play is essential for normal growth or is merely fun is "a controversial topic of study" (Pellegrini, 2011, p. 3).

This controversy underlies many of the disputes regarding preschool education, which increasingly stresses academic skills. One consequence is that "play in school has become an endangered species" (Trawick-Smith, 2012, p. 259). Among the leading theorists of human development, Vygotsky is well known for his respect for child's play, which makes a playing child "a head taller" than his or her actual height (Vygotsky, 1980).

Some educators want children to play less in order to focus on reading and math; others predict emotional and academic problems for children who rarely play (Golinkoff & Hirsh-Pasek, 2016). Children want to be active. If children are kept quiet for a long time, they tend to play more vigorously when they finally have the chance (Pellegrini, 2013).

## Playmates

Young children play best with *peers,* that is, people of about the same age and social status. Although infants are intrigued by other children, most infant play is either solitary or with a parent. Some maturation is required for play with peers (Bateson & Martin, 2013).

### The Historical Context

Children everywhere have always played, but specifics vary with culture and cohort (Roopnarine et al., 2015). Some developmentalists fear that play is subverted currently by three factors: (1) the current push toward early mastery of academic skills, (2) the "swift and pervasive rise of electronic media," and (3) adults who lean "more toward control than freedom" (Chudacoff, 2011, p. 108).

As you remember, one dispute in preschool education is the proper balance between unstructured, creative play and teacher-directed learning. Before the electronic age, most families had several children, and few mothers worked outside the home. The children played outside with all of their neighbors, boys and girls, of several ages. A century ago, American sociologist Mildred Parten described five stages of play, each more advanced than the previous one:

1. *Solitary:* A child plays alone, unaware of other children playing nearby.
2. *Onlooker:* A child watches other children play.
3. *Parallel:* Children play in similar ways but not together.
4. *Associative:* Children interact, sharing toys, but not taking turns.
5. *Cooperative:* Children play together, creating dramas or taking turns.

Parten (1932) described play as intrinsic, with children gradually advancing, from age 1 to 6, from solitary to cooperative play.

Research on contemporary children finds much more age variation than Parten did, perhaps because family size is smaller and parents invest heavily in each child. Many Asian parents successfully teach 3-year-olds to take turns, share, and otherwise

● **Response for College Students** (from p. 285): Both are important. Extrinsic motivation includes parental pressure and the need to get a good job after graduation. Intrinsic motivation includes the joy of learning, especially if you can express that learning in ways others recognize. Have you ever taken a course that was not required and was said to be difficult? That was intrinsic motivation.

● **Response for Professors** (from p. 285): No, unless the child is over age 10. In fact, imaginary friends are quite common, especially among creative children. The child may be somewhat lonely, though; you could suggest helping him or her find a friend.

● **Response for Teachers of Young Children** (from p. 285): Perhaps, but only after the work is completed and if the child has put genuine effort into it. You do not want to undercut intrinsic motivation, as happens with older students who know a particular course will be an "easy A."

# Less Play, Less Safe?

Play is universal—all young children do it when they are with each other, if they can. For children, play takes up more time than anything else, whether their family is rich or poor.

## WHAT 3-YEAR-OLDS DO WITH THEIR TIME

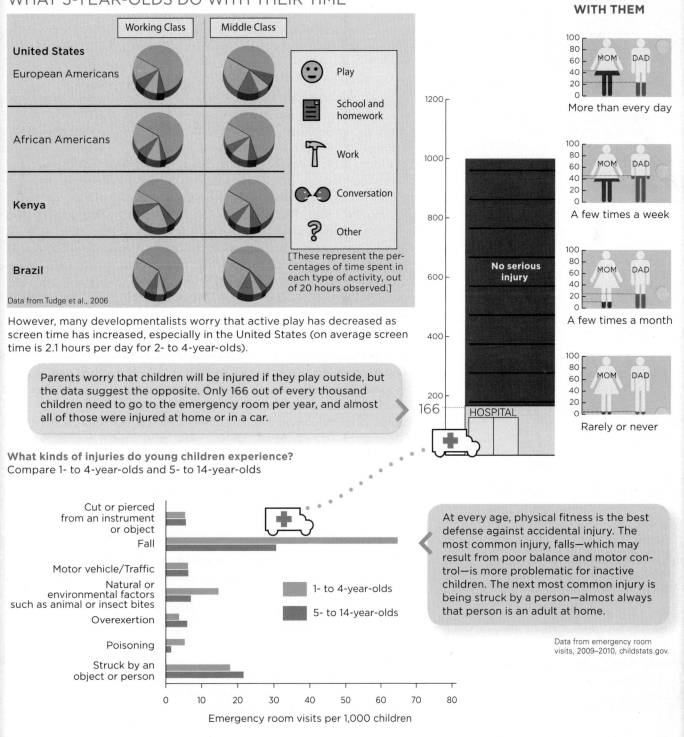

| | Working Class | Middle Class |
|---|---|---|
| **United States** European Americans | | |
| African Americans | | |
| Kenya | | |
| Brazil | | |

😊 Play

📄 School and homework

🔨 Work

Conversation

❓ Other

[These represent the percentages of time spent in each type of activity, out of 20 hours observed.]

Data from Tudge et al., 2006

However, many developmentalists worry that active play has decreased as screen time has increased, especially in the United States (on average screen time is 2.1 hours per day for 2- to 4-year-olds).

Parents worry that children will be injured if they play outside, but the data suggest the opposite. Only 166 out of every thousand children need to go to the emergency room per year, and almost all of those were injured at home or in a car.

No serious injury

166 ...... HOSPITAL

**PERCENT OF KIDS WHOSE PARENTS PLAY OUTDOORS WITH THEM**

MOM    DAD
More than every day

MOM    DAD
A few times a week

MOM    DAD
A few times a month

MOM    DAD
Rarely or never

**What kinds of injuries do young children experience?**
Compare 1- to 4-year-olds and 5- to 14-year-olds

- Cut or pierced from an instrument or object
- Fall
- Motor vehicle/Traffic
- Natural or environmental factors such as animal or insect bites
- Overexertion
- Poisoning
- Struck by an object or person

■ 1- to 4-year-olds
■ 5- to 14-year-olds

Emergency room visits per 1,000 children

At every age, physical fitness is the best defense against accidental injury. The most common injury, falls—which may result from poor balance and motor control—is more problematic for inactive children. The next most common injury is being struck by a person—almost always that person is an adult at home.

Data from emergency room visits, 2009–2010, childstats.gov.

Giulio_Fornasar/Getty Images

**Finally Cooperating** The goal of social play—cooperation—is shown by these two boys who, at ages 8 and 11, are long past the associative, self-absorbed play of younger children. Note the wide-open mouths of laughter over a shared video game—a major accomplishment.

cooperate (stage 5). Many North American children, encouraged to be individuals, still engage in parallel play at age 6 (stage 3).

## Social Play

Play can be divided into two kinds: *pretend play* when a child is alone and *social play* that occurs with playmates. One meta-analysis of the research on pretend play and social play (Lillard et al., 2013) reports that evidence is weak or mixed regarding pretend play but that social play has much to commend it. If social play is prevented, children are less happy and less able to learn, which suggests that social play is one way that children develop their minds and social skills.

Such an advance can be seen over the years of early childhood. Toddlers are too self-absorbed to be good playmates, but they learn quickly. By age 6, most children are quite skilled: Some know how to join a peer group, manage conflict, take turns, find friends, and keep the action going (Şendil & Erden, 2014; Göncü & Gaskins, 2011). Parents need to find playmates, because even the most playful parent is outmatched by another child at negotiating the rules of tag, at play-fighting, pretending to be sick, or killing dragons.

As they become better playmates, children learn emotional regulation, empathy, and cultural understanding. Specifics vary, but "play with peers is one of the most important areas in which children develop positive social skills" (Xu, 2010, p. 496). Look again at the introductory photo of this chapter on page 280. They all seek social play, and the front two found it.

## Active Play

Children need physical activity to develop muscle strength and control. Peers provide an audience, role models, and sometimes competition. For instance, running skills develop best when children chase or race each other, not when a child runs alone.

Active social play—not solitary play—correlates with peer acceptance and a healthy self-concept, and it may help regulate emotions (Becker et al., 2014; Sutton-Smith, 2011). Adults need to remember this when they want children to sit still and be quiet.

Among nonhuman primates, deprivation of social play warps later life, rendering some monkeys unable to mate, to make friends, or even to survive alongside other monkeys (Herman et al., 2011; Palagi, 2011). Might the same be true for human primates?

## Rough and Tumble

**rough-and-tumble play** Play that mimics aggression through wrestling, chasing, or hitting, but in which there is no intent to harm.

The most common form of active play is called **rough-and-tumble,** because it looks quite rough and because the children seem to tumble over one another. The term was coined by British scientists who studied animals in East Africa (Blurton-Jones, 1976). They noticed that young monkeys often chased, attacked, rolled over in the dirt, and wrestled quite roughly without injuring one another, all while seeming to smile (showing a *play face*).

When these scientists returned to London, they saw that puppies, kittens, and even their own children engaged in rough-and-tumble play, like baby monkeys. Children chase, wrestle, and grab each other, developing games like tag and cops-and-robbers, with various conventions, facial expressions, and gestures to signify "just pretend."

Rough-and-tumble play happens everywhere (although cops-and-robbers can be "robots-and-humans" or many other iterations) and has probably been common

**THINK CRITICALLY:** Is "play" an entirely different experience for adults than for children?

among children for thousands of years (Fry, 2014). It is much more common among boys than girls and flourishes best in ample space with minimal supervision (Pellegrini, 2013).

Many scientists think that rough-and-tumble play helps the prefrontal cortex develop, as children learn to regulate emotions, practice social skills, and strengthen their bodies (Pellis & Pellis, 2011). Indeed father–child play in childhood, especially rough-and-tumble between father and son, may prevent antisocial behavior and foster better parenting later on (Fry, 2014; Raeburn, 2014).

## Sociodramatic Play

Another major type of active play is **sociodramatic play,** in which children act out various roles and plots. Through such acting, children:

- explore and rehearse social roles.
- learn to explain their ideas and persuade playmates.
- practice emotional regulation by pretending to be afraid, angry, brave, and so on.
- develop self-concept in a nonthreatening context.

Sociodramatic play builds on pretending, which emerges in toddlerhood. But remember that solitary pretending may not advance various skills; dramatic pretending with peers does. As children combine their imagination with that of their friends, they advance in theory of mind (Kavanaugh, 2011).

Everywhere, as they age from 2 to 6, children increasingly prefer to play with children of their own gender. For example, a day-care center in Finland allowed extensive free play. The boys often enacted dramas of good guys versus bad guys. In this episode, four boys did so, with Joni as the bad guy. Tuomas directed the drama and acted in it.

> **Tuomas:** . . . and now he [Joni] would take me and would hang me. . . . this would be the end of all of me.
> **Joni:** Hands behind!
> **Tuomas:** I can't help it . . . I have to.
> *[The two other boys follow his example.]*
> **Joni:** I would put fire all around them.
> *[All three brave boys lie on the floor with hands tied behind their backs. Joni piles mattresses on them, and pretends to light a fire, which crackles closer and closer.]*
> **Tuomas:** Everything is lost!
> *[One boy starts to laugh.]*
> **Petterl:** Better not to laugh, soon we will all be dead. . . . I am saying my last words.
> **Tuomas:** Now you can say your last wish. . . . And now I say I wish we can be terribly strong.
> *[At that point, the three boys suddenly gain extraordinary strength, pushing off the mattresses and extinguishing the fire. Good triumphs over evil, but not until the last moment, because, as one boy explains, "Otherwise this playing is not exciting at all."]*
> *[adapted from Kalliala, 2006, p. 83]*

As with this example, boys' sociodramatic play often includes danger and then victory over evil. By contrast, girls typically act out domestic scenes, with themselves as the adults. In the same day-care center where Joni piled mattresses on his playmates, preparing to burn them, the girls say their play is "more beautiful and peaceful . . . [but] boys play all kinds of violent games" (Kalliala, 2006, p. 110).

**Joy Supreme** Pretend play in early childhood is thrilling and powerful. For this dancing 7-year-old from Park Slope, Brooklyn, pretend play overwhelms mundane realities, such as an odd scarf or awkward arm.

2016 Macmillan

**sociodramatic play** Pretend play in which children act out various roles and themes in stories that they create.

**Good Over Evil or Evil Over Good?** Boys everywhere enjoy "strong man" fantasy play, as the continued popularity of Spider-Man and Superman attests. These boys follow that script. Both are Afghan refugees now in Pakistan.

**Video: The Impact of Media on Early Childhood** explores how screen time can affect young children's cognition.

**empathy** The ability to understand the emotions and concerns of another person, especially when they differ from one's own.

**prosocial behavior** Actions that are helpful and kind but are of no obvious benefit to oneself.

The prevalence of sociodramatic play varies by culture, with parents often following cultural norms. Some cultures find make-believe frivolous and discourage it; in other cultures, parents teach toddlers to be lions, or robots, or ladies drinking tea. Then children elaborate on those themes (Kavanaugh, 2011). Many young children are avid television watchers, and they act out superhero themes.

In North America, most children have more than an hour of screen time every day (Carson et al., 2013; Fletcher et al., 2014). That troubles developmentalists for many reasons. One is simply time—the more children are glued to screens, especially when the screen is their own hand-held device, the less they spend in active, social play (see Figure 10.1).

Overall, the American Academy of Pediatrics (2016) recommends no more than an hour a day of any screen time for preschoolers. That time should be carefully monitored, to avoid violent or suggestive media, with racist and sexist stereotypes. However, many programs promote violence, and many young children watch more than recommended, unsupervised, not only in the United States but also in Canada, Great Britain, and Australia. Pediatricians, psychologists, and teachers all note that screen time reduces conversation, imagination, and outdoor play (Downing et al., 2017).

## Learning Emotional Regulation

Emotional regulation develops with social interaction. Young children enjoy playing together, and they gradually learn the actions and reactions that make them good playmates.

### Empathy and Antipathy

As theory of mind develops and children have experience with other children, they develop **empathy,** an understanding of other people's feelings and concerns. Empathy leads to compassion and **prosocial behavior**—helpfulness and kindness

**FIGURE 10.1**

**Learning by Playing** Fifty years ago, the average child spent three hours a day in outdoor play. Video games and television have largely replaced that playtime, especially in cities. Children seem safer if parents can keep an eye on them, but what are the long-term effects on brain and body?

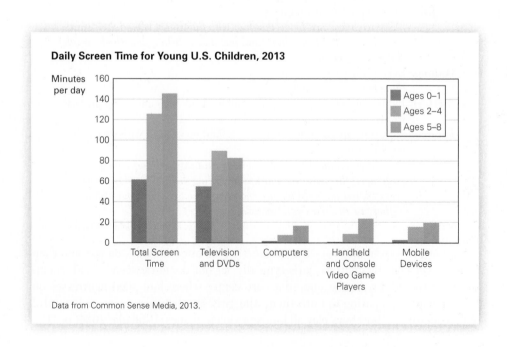

**Daily Screen Time for Young U.S. Children, 2013**

Data from Common Sense Media, 2013.

**Pinch, Poke, or Pat** Antisocial and prosocial responses are actually a sign of maturation: Babies do not recognize the impact of their actions. These children have much more to learn, but they already are quite social.

without any obvious personal benefit. Prosocial actions and preferences increase from ages 1 to 6. Empathetic preschoolers become first-graders who are likely to share, help, and play with other children (Z. Taylor et al., 2013).

The opposite can also happen. Children dislike other children, especially those who are mean in rough-and-tumble play, or who insist on their own way in sociodramatic play. Antipathy may lead to **antisocial behavior,** which includes verbal insults, social exclusion, and physical assault.

Both prosocial and antisocial behavior are innate and universal (Séguin & Tremblay, 2013). Two-year-olds find it hard to share, even to let another child use a crayon that they have already used. Preschool children have a sense of ownership: A teacher's crayon should be shared, but if a child owns it, the other children believe that he or she is allowed to be selfish (Neary & Friedman, 2014).

Generally, antisocial behavior diminishes over the preschool years, especially as social understanding increases. Parents and teachers help children learn how to take turns and share, increasing emotional maturity, or slowing it down if they neither discuss nor respond to emotions (Z. Taylor et al., 2013; Richards et al., 2014). Stress within the neighborhood and preschool can decrease empathy and increase antipathy, fueling emotional problems (Flouri & Sarmadi, 2016). In other words, context is crucial.

**antisocial behavior** Actions that are deliberately hurtful or destructive to another person.

**Video: Interview with Lawrence Walker** discusses what parents can do to encourage their children's moral development.

## Aggression

The most immediately troubling emotional problems are externalizing ones, when anger leads children to hit, kick, and hurt other people. Researchers recognize four general types of aggression, each evident in early childhood (see Table 10.1 on the following page). Two forms decrease over the years, one increases, and the fourth can become worse, harming both victim and perpetrator.

**Instrumental aggression** is common among 2-year-olds, who often want something and try to get it. This is called *instrumental* because the aggression is a tool, or instrument, to get something that is desired. The harm in grabbing a toy, and hitting, if someone resists, is not understood.

Because instrumental aggression naturally occurs, **reactive aggression** is also common among young children. Almost every child reacts when hurt, whether or not the hurt was deliberate. The reaction may not be controlled—a child might

**instrumental aggression** Behavior that hurts someone else because the aggressor wants to get or keep a possession or a privilege.

**reactive aggression** An impulsive retaliation for another person's intentional or accidental action, verbal or physical.

### TABLE 10.1

#### The Four Forms of Aggression

| Type of Aggression | Definition | Comments |
|---|---|---|
| Instrumental aggression | Hurtful behavior that is aimed at gaining something (such as a toy, a place in line, or a turn on the swing) that someone else has | Often increases from age 2 to 6; involves objects more than people; quite normal; more egocentric than antisocial. |
| Reactive aggression | An impulsive retaliation for a hurt (intentional or accidental) that can be verbal or physical | Indicates a lack of emotional regulation, characteristic of 2-year-olds. A 5-year-old can usually stop and think before reacting. |
| Relational aggression | Nonphysical acts, such as insults or social rejection, aimed at harming the social connections between the victim and others | Involves a personal attack and thus is directly antisocial; can be very hurtful; more common as children become socially aware. |
| Bullying aggression | Unprovoked, repeated physical or verbal attack, especially on victims who are unlikely to defend themselves | In both bullies and victims, a sign of poor emotional regulation; adults should intervene before the school years. (Bullying is discussed in Chapter 13.) |

**relational aggression** Nonphysical acts, such as insults or social rejection, aimed at harming the social connection between the victim and other people.

**bullying aggression** Unprovoked, repeated physical or verbal attacks, especially on victims who are unlikely to defend themselves.

punch in response to an unwelcome remark—but as the prefrontal cortex matures, the impulse to strike back becomes modified. Both instrumental aggression and reactive aggression are less often physical when children develop emotional regulation and theory of mind (Olson et al., 2011).

**Relational aggression** (usually verbal) destroys self-esteem and disrupts social networks, becoming more common as well as more hurtful as children mature. A child might spread rumors or tell others not to play with so-and-so.

In early childhood, relational aggression is usually quite direct: A young child might say "You can't be my friend" or comment about appearance, hurting another child's feelings. However, the sting of relational aggression is far less painful at age 3 than age 8. In adolescence, when it occurs via social media, it correlates with depression and even suicide (Underwood & Ehrenreich, 2017).

Relational as well as physical aggression may be part of the fourth and most ominous type, **bullying aggression,** which is intentionally done to dominate. Bullying aggression occurs among young children but should be stopped by kindergarten, before it becomes more harmful. Not only does it destroy self-esteem and thus learning, it eventually harms the bullies, who learn destructive habits. A 4-year-old bully may be friendless; a 10-year-old bully may be feared and admired; a 20-year-old bully may be hated and lonely. [**Developmental Link:** An in-depth discussion of bullying appears in Chapter 13.]

Between ages 2 and 6, as the brain matures and empathy increases, children learn to use aggression selectively, which decreases both internalizing and externalizing problems (Ostrov et al., 2014). Parents, peers, and preschool teachers are pivotal mentors in this learning process.

A longitudinal study found that close teacher–student relationships in preschool predicted less aggression and less victimization in elementary school. The probable reason—children wanted to please their teachers, who guide them toward prosocial, not antisocial, behavior (Runions & Shaw, 2013).

---

**WHAT HAVE YOU LEARNED?**

1. Why might playing with peers help children build muscles and develop self-control?

2. What do children learn from rough-and-tumble play?

3. What do children learn from sociodramatic play?

4. Why do experts want to limit children's screen time?

5. What is the connection between empathy and prosocial behavior?

6. What is the relationship between antipathy and aggression?

7. How do the four kinds of aggression differ?

8. What developmental changes occur in each form of aggression?

---

# Challenges for Caregivers

Every developmentalist realizes that caring for a young child is challenging. At this age, children are energetic and curious. That helps them learn but also tests the emotions and skills of caregivers.

## Styles of Caregiving

The more developmentalists study parents, the more styles of parenting they see. International variations are stark—from those who are so strict that they seem abusive to those who are so lenient that they seem neglectful. Variations are also apparent within each nation, within each ethnic group, and even within each neighborhood. Appreciation of culture makes developmentalists hesitate to say one style is best, but appreciation of children makes it hard not to judge.

### Baumrind's Categories

Although thousands of researchers have traced the effects of parenting on child development, the work of one person, 50 years ago, is especially influential. In her original research, Diana Baumrind (1967, 1971) studied 100 preschool children, all from California, almost all middle-class European Americans.

**Especially for Political Scientists** Many observers contend that children learn their political attitudes at home, from the way their parents teach them. Is this true? (see response, p. 295)

Erik de Castro/REUTERS/Corbis

**Protect Me from the Water Buffalo** These two are at the Carabao Kneeling Festival. In rural Philippines, hundreds of these large but docile animals kneel on the steps of the church, part of a day of gratitude for the harvest.

**Observation Quiz** Is the father to the left authoritarian, authoritative, or permissive? (see answer, p. 294) ←

● **Answer to Observation Quiz** (from p. 293): It is impossible to be certain based on one moment, but the best guess is authoritative. He seems patient and protective, providing comfort and guidance, neither forcing (authoritarian) nor letting the child do whatever he wants (permissive).

**authoritarian parenting** An approach to child rearing that is characterized by high behavioral standards, strict punishment for misconduct, and little communication from child to parent.

**permissive parenting** An approach to child rearing that is characterized by high nurturance and communication but little discipline, guidance, or control. (Also called *indulgent parenting*.)

**authoritative parenting** An approach to child rearing in which the parents set limits but listen to the child and are flexible.

**neglectful/uninvolved parenting** An approach to child rearing in which the parents are indifferent toward their children and unaware of what is going on in their children's lives.

She found that parents differed on four important dimensions:

1. *Expressions of warmth.* Some parents are warm and affectionate; others are cold and critical.
2. *Strategies for discipline.* Parents vary in how they explain, criticize, persuade, and punish.
3. *Expectations for maturity.* Parents vary in expectations for responsibility and self-control.
4. *Communication.* Some parents listen patiently; others demand silence.

On the basis of these dimensions, Baumrind identified three parenting styles (summarized in Table 10.2). A fourth style, not described by Baumrind, was suggested by other researchers.

**Authoritarian parenting.** The authoritarian parent's word is law, not to be questioned. Misconduct brings strict punishment, usually physical. Authoritarian parents set clear rules and hold high standards. They do not expect children to offer opinions; discussion about emotions and expressions of affection are rare. One adult raised by authoritarian parents said that "How do you feel?" had only two possible answers: "Fine" and "Tired."

**Permissive parenting.** Permissive parents (also called *indulgent*) make few demands, hiding any impatience they feel. Discipline is lax, partly because expectations for maturity are low. Permissive parents are nurturing and accepting, listening to whatever their offspring say, even allowing their children to curse at them.

**Authoritative parenting.** Authoritative parents set limits, but they are flexible. They encourage maturity, but they usually listen and forgive (not punish) if the child falls short. They consider themselves guides, not authorities (unlike authoritarian parents) and not friends (unlike permissive parents).

**Neglectful/uninvolved parenting** Neglectful parents are oblivious to their children's behavior; they seem not to care. Their children do whatever they want. This is quite different from permissive parents, who care very much.

The following long-term effects of parenting styles have been reported, not only in the United States but in many other nations as well (Fernandes, 2016; Baumrind et al., 2010; Chan & Koo, 2011; Huver et al., 2010; Deater-Deckard, 2013).

- *Authoritarian* parents raise children who become conscientious, obedient, and quiet but not especially happy. Such children may feel guilty or depressed, internalizing their frustrations and blaming themselves when things don't go well. As adolescents, they sometimes rebel, leaving home before age 20. As adults, they are quick to punish.

**TABLE 10.2**

### Characteristics of Parenting Styles Identified by Baumrind

| Style | Warmth | Discipline | Expectations of Maturity | Communication | |
|---|---|---|---|---|---|
| | | | | Parent to Child | Child to Parent |
| Authoritarian | Low | Strict, often physical | High | High | Low |
| Permissive | High | Rare | Low | Low | High |
| Authoritative | High | Moderate, with much discussion | Moderate | High | High |

- *Permissive* parents raise children who lack self-control, especially in the give-and-take of peer relationships. Inadequate emotional regulation makes these children immature and impedes friendships, so they are unhappy. They tend to continue to live at home, still dependent on their parents in adulthood.
- *Authoritative* parents raise children who are successful, articulate, happy with themselves, and generous with others. These children are usually liked by teachers and peers, especially in cultures that value individual initiative (e.g., the United States).
- *Neglectful/uninvolved* parents raise children who are immature, sad, lonely, and at risk of injury and abuse, not only in childhood but also lifelong.

## Problems with the Research

Baumrind's classification schema has been soundly criticized. You can probably already see some of the ways in which her research was flawed:

- She did not consider socioeconomic differences.
- She was unaware of cultural differences.
- She focused more on parent attitudes than on parent actions.
- She overlooked children's genetic differences.
- She did not recognize that some "authoritarian" parents are also affectionate.
- She did not realize that some "permissive" parents provide extensive verbal guidance.

More recent research finds that a child's temperament powerfully affects caregivers. Good caregivers treat each child as an individual who needs personalized care. For example, fearful children require reassurance, while impulsive ones need strong guidelines. Parents of fearful children may, to outsiders, seem permissive; parents of impulsive children may seem authoritarian.

Overprotection may be a consequence, not a cause, of childhood anxiety (McShane & Hastings, 2009; Deater-Deckard, 2013). Every child needs protection and guidance; some more than others. The right balance depends on the particular child, as differential susceptibility makes clear.

A study of parenting at age 2 and children's competence in kindergarten (including emotional regulation and friendships) found "multiple developmental pathways," with the best outcomes dependent on both the child and the adult (Blandon et al., 2010). Such studies suggest that simplistic advice—from a book, a professional, or a neighbor who does not know the child—may be misguided. Longitudinal, careful observation of parent–child interactions is needed before judging that a caregiver is too lax or too rigid.

As A View from Science on p. 296 suggests, given a multicultural and multicontextual perspective, developmentalists realize that many parenting practices are sometimes effective. But that does not mean that all families function equally well—far from it. Signs of emotional distress, including a child's anxiety, aggression, and inability to play with others, indicate that the family may not be the safe haven of support and guidance that it should be.

**Response for Political Scientists** (from p. 293): There are many parenting styles, and it is difficult to determine each one's impact on children's personalities. At this point, attempts to connect early child rearing with later political outlook are speculative.

**Pay Attention** Children develop best with lots of love and attention. They shouldn't have to ask for it!

"He's just doing that to get attention."

Harry Bliss/The New Yorker Collection/The Cartoon Bank

**A VIEW FROM SCIENCE**

## Culture and Parenting Style

Culture powerfully affects caregiving style. This is obvious internationally. In some nations, parents are expected to beat their children; in other nations, parents are arrested if they hit, slap, or spank. Some parents think they should never praise their children; elsewhere parents tell their children they are wonderful, even when they are not. Fifty nations have laws forbidding physical punishment of children; 145 (including the United States) do not.

A detailed study of Mexican American mothers of 4-year-olds noted 1,477 instances when the mothers tried to change their children's behavior. Most of the time the mothers simply uttered a command and the children complied (Livas-Dlott et al., 2010).

This simple strategy, with the mother asserting authority and the children obeying without question, might be considered authoritarian. Almost never, however, did the mothers use physical punishment or even harsh threats when the children did not immediately do as they were told—which happened 14 percent of the time. For example:

> Hailey [the 4-year-old] decided to look for another doll and started digging through her toys, throwing them behind her as she dug. Maricruz [the mother] told Hailey she should not throw her toys. Hailey continued to throw toys, and Maricruz said her name to remind her to stop. Hailey continued her misbehavior, and her mother repeated "Hailey" once more. When Hailey continued, Maricruz raised her voice but calmly directed, "Hailey, look at me." Hailey continued but then looked at Maricruz as she explained, "You don't throw toys; you could hurt someone." Finally, Hailey complied and stopped.

[Livas-Dlott et al., 2010, p. 572]

Note that the mother's first three efforts failed, and then a "look" accompanied by an explanation (albeit inaccurate in that setting, as no one could be hurt) succeeded. In this study, the Mexican American families did not fit any of Baumrind's categories; respect (*respeto*) for adult authority did not mean an authoritarian relationship. Instead, the relationship shows evident caring (*cariño*) (Livas-Dlott et al., 2010).

As with *respeto* and *cariño* (values evident in Latino parents), parenting in every culture includes strategies that need to be recognized and appreciated (Butler & Titus, 2015). However, the research finds that harsh or cold parenting is always harmful (Dyer et al., 2014). (The consequences of harsh punishment are discussed at the end of this chapter.) Parental affection allows children to develop self-respect and to become compassionate adults, no matter what the parenting styles or culture (Deater-Deckard, 2013; Eisenberg et al., 2013).

## Discipline

Children misbehave. They do not always do what adults think they should do. Sometimes they do not know better, but sometimes they deliberately ignore a request, perhaps doing exactly what they have been told not to do. Since misbehavior is part of growing up, and since children need guidance to keep them safe and strong, parents must respond. The research does not recommend doing nothing, but every form of discipline has critics as well as defenders (Larzelere et al., 2017).

### Physical Punishment

In the United States, young children are slapped, spanked, or beaten more often than are infants or older children, and more often than children in Canada or western Europe. Spanking is more frequent:

- in the southern United States than in New England.
- by mothers than by fathers.
- among conservative Christians than among nonreligious families.
- among African Americans than among European Americans.
- among European Americans than among Asian Americans.
- among U.S.-born Hispanics than among immigrant Hispanics.
- in low-SES families than in high-SES families.

[MacKenzie et al., 2011; S. Lee et al., 2015; Lee & Altschul, 2015]

These are generalities: Contrary to these generalizations, many African American mothers living in the South never spank, and many secular, European American, high-SES fathers in New England routinely do. In the generalities just listed, it is clear that local norms matter, but parents do not always follow them.

Most adults believe that their upbringing helped them become the person they are, and consequently they think that their own past was proper. Moreover, physical punishment (called **corporal punishment** because it hurts the body) usually succeeds momentarily because immediately afterward children are quiet.

However, longitudinal research finds that children who are physically punished are more likely to be disobedient and to become bullies, delinquents, and then abusive adults (Gershoff et al., 2012). They also learn less in school and quit before college (Straus & Paschall, 2009).

In fact, longitudinal research finds that children who are *not* spanked are *more* likely to develop self-control. As spanking increases, so does misbehavior (Gershoff, 2013). The correlation between spanking and later aggression holds for children of all ethnic groups, in many nations (Lansford et al., 2014).

In 43 nations (mostly in Europe), corporal punishment is illegal; in many nations on other continents, it is the norm. A massive international study of low- and moderate-income nations found that 63 percent of 2- to 5-year-olds had been physically punished (slapped, spanked, hit with an object) in the past month (Deater-Deckard & Lansford, 2016).

In more than 100 nations, physical punishment is illegal in schools, but each state of the United States sets laws, and teachers may legally paddle children in 19 of them. Overall, in the United States in one recent year, 218,466 children were corporally punished at school. Sixteen percent of those children had intellectual disabilities, and a disproportionate number were African American boys (Morones, 2013; Gershoff et al., 2015). Worldwide, boys are punished slightly more often than girls.

Although some adults believe that physical punishment will "teach a lesson" of doing the right thing, others argue that the lesson that children learn is that "might makes right." It is true that children who were physically disciplined tend to use corporal punishment on others—first on their classmates, later on their wives or husbands and children. However, many people believe that children sometimes need spanking.

Many studies of children from all family constellations and backgrounds find that physical punishment of young children correlates with delayed theory of mind and increased aggression (Olson et al., 2011). To prove cause without a doubt would require many parents of monozygotic twins to raise them identically, except that one twin would be spanked often and the other never. Of course, that is unethical as well as impossible.

Nonetheless, most developmentalists wonder why parents would take the chance. The best argument in favor of spanking is that alternative punishments may be worse (Larzelere et al., 2010; Larzelere & Cox, 2013). Let us consider alternatives.

## Alternatives to Spanking

Another common method of discipline is called **psychological control,** in which children's shame, guilt, and gratitude are used to control their behavior. Psychological control may reduce academic achievement and emotional understanding, just as spanking is thought to do.

Consider Finland, one of the nations where corporal punishment is now forbidden. Parents were asked about psychological control (Aunola et al., 2013).

**corporal punishment** Punishment that physically hurts the body, such as slapping, spanking, etc.

**THINK CRITICALLY:** The varying rates of physical punishment in schools could be the result of prejudice, or could be because some children misbehave more often. Which is it?

**Especially for Parents** Suppose you agree that spanking is destructive, but you sometimes get so angry at your child's behavior that you hit him or her. Is your reaction appropriate? (see response, p. 299)

**psychological control** A disciplinary technique that involves threatening to withdraw love and support and that relies on a child's feelings of guilt and gratitude to the parents.

# Is Spanking OK?

Opinions about spanking are influenced by past experience and cultural norms. That makes it hard for opposing perspectives to be understood by people on the other side (Ferguson, 2013). Try to suspend your own assumptions as you read this.

*What might be right with spanking?* Over the centuries, many parents have done it, so it has stood the test of time. Indeed, in the United States, parents who never spank are unusual. Spanking may seem less common now than in the twentieth century (Taillieu et al., 2014), but 85 percent of U.S. young adults who were children at the end of the twentieth century remember being slapped or spanked by their mothers (Bender et al., 2007). More than one-third of the mothers in low- and middle-income nations believe that to raise a child well, physical punishment is essential (Deater-Deckard & Lansford, 2016).

One pro-spanking argument is that the correlations reported by developmentalists (between spanking and later depression, low achievement, aggression, crime, and so on) may be caused by a third variable, not spanking itself. A suggested third variable is child misbehavior: Perhaps disobedient children cause spanking, not vice versa. Such children may become delinquent, depressed, and so on not because they were spanked but in spite of being spanked.

Noting problems with correlational research, one team explains, "Quite simply, parents do not need to use corrective actions when there are no problems to correct" (Larzelere & Cox, 2013, p. 284). These authors point out that every disciplinary technique, if used frequently, correlates with misbehavior, but the punishment may be the result, not the cause. Further, since parents who spank their children tend to have less education and less money than other parents, SES may be the underlying reason spanked children average lower academic achievement. Spanking may be a symptom of poor parenting, not the cause.

If that is true, the solution is to reduce poverty, not to forbid spanking. When researchers try to eliminate the effect of every third variable, especially SES, they find a smaller correlation between spanking and future problems than most other studies do (Ferguson, 2013).

*What might be wrong with spanking?* One problem is adults' emotions: Angry spankers may become abusive. Children are sometimes seriously injured and even killed by parents who use corporal punishment.

One pediatrician who hesitates to argue against all spanking, everywhere, nonetheless has observed that physical injury is common when parents discipline children. He says that parents should never spank in anger, cause bruises that last more than 24 hours, use an object, or spank a child under age 2 (Zolotor, 2014).

Another problem is the child's immature cognition. Many children do not understand why they are spanked. Parents assume that the transgression is obvious, but children may think that the parents' anger, not the child's actions, caused spanking (Harkness et al., 2011). Most parents tell their children why they are being spanked, but when they are hit, children are less likely to listen or understand.

Almost all of the research finds that children who are physically punished suffer in many ways (Grogan-Kaylo et al., 2018). They are more depressed, more antisocial, more likely to hate school, and less likely to have close friends. Many continue to suffer in adulthood.

As you might expect, many spanked children have parents who are relatively cold toward them. That certainly is one reason for this correlation. Surprisingly, however, if their parents are warm and loving, spanked children often are unusually anxious, worried that they did something wrong (Lansford et al., 2014).

Of course, there are exceptions. Some spanked children become happy and successful adults. For example, one U.S. study found that conservative Protestant parents spanked their children more often than other parents, but if that spanking occurred only in early (not middle) childhood, the children did not develop low self-esteem nor increased aggression (Ellison et al., 2011).

The authors of the study suggest that, since spanking was the norm in that group, the children did not think they were unloved. Moreover, religious leaders tell parents never to spank in anger. As a result, their children may "view mild-to-moderate corporal punishment as legitimate, appropriate, and even an indicator of parental involvement, commitment, and concern" (Ellison et al., 2011, p. 957).

As you remember, scientists respect evidence. Since empirical data, not cultural opinions, are crucial, some scientists criticize the methods of the anti-spanking research (e.g., Larzelere et al., 2017), and some criticize that criticism (Holden et al.,

**Smack** Will the doll learn never to disobey her mother again?

2017). Currently, the preponderance of evidence suggests that parents should avoid spanking their children.

As I write these words, I realize which perspective is mine. I am one of many developmentalists who believe that alternatives to spanking are better for the child and a safeguard against abuse. Indeed, the same study that found spanking common in developing nations also reported that 17 percent of the children experienced severe violence (Bornstein et al., 2016). That alone is reason to stop.

I am not persuaded by the research on conservative Protestant parents. The biblical advice against "sparing the rod" referred to the guiding rod that sheepherders use, not a punishing stick. I want parents to be good shepherds who guide children but do not hit them.

Nonetheless, a dynamic-systems, multicultural perspective reminds me that everyone is influenced by background and context. I know that I am; so is every scientist, and so are you.

If parents strongly agreed with the following statements, they were considered to use psychological control:

1. "My child should be aware of how much I have done for him/her."
2. "I let my child see how disappointed and shamed I am if he/she misbehaves."
3. "My child should be aware of how much I sacrifice for him/her."
4. "I expect my child to be grateful and appreciate all the advantages he/she has."

The higher the parents scored on these four measures of psychological control, the lower the children's math scores were—and this correlation grew stronger over time. Moreover, the children tended to have negative emotions (depression, anger, and so on). Thus, psychological control may have some of the same consequences as corporal punishment.

Another disciplinary technique often used with young children in North America is the **time-out,** in which a misbehaving child is required to sit quietly, without toys or playmates, for a short time. Time-out is not to be done in anger, or for too long; it is recommended that parents use a calm voice and that the time-out last only one to five minutes (Morawska & Sanders, 2011). Time-out is a punishment if the child really enjoys "time-in," when the child is happily engaged with the parents or with peers.

Time-out is favored by many experts. For example, in the large, longitudinal evaluation of the Head Start program highlighted in Chapter 9, an increase in time-outs and a decrease in spankings were considered signs of improved parental discipline (U.S. Department of Health and Human Services, January 2010).

However, the same team who criticized the correlation between spanking and misbehavior also criticized the research favoring time-out. They added, "misbehavior is motivated by wanting to escape from the situation . . . time-out reinforces the misbehavior" (Larzelere & Cox, 2013, p. 289).

Often combined with the time-out is another alternative to physical punishment and psychological control—**induction,** in which the parents talk extensively with the offender, helping the child understand why his or her behavior was wrong.

Ideally, time-out allows children to calm down. Then a strong and affectionate parent–child relationship means that children explain their emotions and parents listen carefully. Children can explain what they *might have* done instead of what *was* done, although such hypothetical reasoning is difficult—maybe impossible—for young children.

Induction takes time and patience. Since 3-year-olds confuse causes with consequences, they cannot answer "Why did you do that?" or appreciate a long explanation. Simple induction ("Why did he cry?") may be more appropriate, but even that is hard before a child develops theory of mind. Nonetheless, induction seems to pay off over time. Children whose parents used induction when they were 3-year-olds became children with fewer externalizing problems in elementary school (Choe et al., 2013b).

**Bad Boy or Bad Parent?** For some children in some cultures, standing in the corner may be an effective punishment. Much depends on whether this boy knows whether his parents' anger or his own behavior put him there.

**time-out** A disciplinary technique in which a child is separated from other people for a specified time.

**induction** A disciplinary technique in which the parent tries to get the child to understand why a certain behavior was wrong. Listening, not lecturing, is crucial.

**Response for Parents** (from p. 297): No. The worst time to spank a child is when you are angry. You might seriously hurt the child, and the child will associate anger with violence. You would do better to learn to control your anger and develop other strategies for discipline and for prevention of misbehavior.

## Becoming Boys or Girls: Sex and Gender

Another challenge for caregivers is to promote a healthy understanding of sex and gender (Wilcox & Kline, 2013). This is difficult for every parent, but it may be most difficult when children identify as transgender, experiencing a gender identity that is different than their biological sex. This presents their parents with a challenge that almost no parent anticipated a decade ago (Rahilly, 2015).

Biology determines whether an embryo is male or female (except in rare cases): Those XX or XY chromosomes normally shape organs and produce hormones. But genes create **sex differences**, which are biological, not **gender differences**, which are culturally prescribed. Theoretically, the distinction between sex and gender seems straightforward, but complexity is evident in practice. Scientists need to "treat culture and biology not as separate influences but as interacting components of nature and nurture" (Eagly & Wood, 2013, p. 349).

Although the 23rd pair of chromosomes are crucial, the entire culture creates gender differences, beginning with the blue or pink caps put on newborns' heads. Before age 2, children use gender labels (*Mrs., Mr., lady, man*) consistently. By age 4, children believe that certain toys (such as dolls or trucks) and roles (Daddy, Mommy, nurse, teacher, police officer, soldier) are reserved for one sex or the other.

There is much that young children do not yet understand. One little girl said that she would grow a penis when she got older, and one little boy felt sorry for his mother so he offered to buy a penis for her. A 3-year-old went with his father to see a neighbor's newborn kittens. Returning home, he told his mother that there were three girl kittens and two boy kittens. "How do you know?" she asked. "Daddy picked them up and read what was written on their tummies," he replied.

In one preschool, the children themselves decided that one wash-up basin was for boys and the other for girls. A girl started to use the boys' basin.

**sex differences** Biological differences between males and females, in organs, hormones, and body type.

**gender differences** Differences in the roles and behaviors of males and females that are prescribed by the culture.

**Same Situation, Far Apart: Culture Clash?** He wears the orange robes of a Buddhist monk, and she wears the hijab of a Muslim girl. Although he is at a week-long spiritual retreat led by the Dalai Lama and she is in an alley in Pakistan, both carry universal toys—a pop gun and a bride doll, identical to those found almost everywhere.

DIPTENDU DUTTA/Getty Images

Ilyas Dean/The Image Works

mandate by trying to look attractive to the other sex—walking, talking, and laughing in gendered ways. If girls see their mothers wearing makeup and high heels, they want to do likewise.

This evolutionary drive may explain why, already in early childhood, boys have a powerful urge to become like the men, and girls like the women. This will prepare them, later on, to mate and conceive a new generation.

Thus, according to this theory, over millennia of human history, genes, chromosomes, and hormones have evolved to allow survival of the species. Genes dictate that young boys are more active (rough-and-tumble play) and girls more domestic (playing house) because that prepares them for adulthood, when fathers defend against predators and mothers care for the home and children. To deny that is to deny nature. This means that transgender children have a difficult childhood. The entire culture pushes them to be whatever sex is on their birth certificate.

> **THINK CRITICALLY:** Should children be encouraged to combine both male and female characteristics (called *androgyny*), or is learning male and female roles crucial for becoming a happy man or woman?

## What Is Best?

Each major developmental theory strives to explain the ideas that young children express and the roles they follow. No consensus has been reached. That challenges caregivers because they know they should not blindly follow the norms of their culture, yet they also know that they need to provide guidance regarding male–female differences and everything else.

Regarding sex or gender, those who contend that nature (sex) is more important than nurture tend to design, cite, and believe studies that endorse their perspective. That has been equally true for those who believe that nurture (gender) is more important than nature. Only recently has a true interactionist perspective, emphasizing how nature affects nurture and vice versa, been endorsed (Eagly & Wood, 2013).

Some of the latest research suggests that our culture's emphasis on sex differences blinds us to the reality, a *gender similarities hypothesis,* that the two sexes have far more in common than traditional theories recognize. Perhaps instead of looking for sex differences, we should notice sex similarities, as they far outweigh differences in the brain, body, and behavior (Hyde, 2016).

Indeed, in early childhood, children are alike in many ways. No matter which sex or ethnic group or culture, these three chapters emphasize that all children need good nutrition, intellectual stimulation, and other children to play with, always protected and encouraged by adults. The results are evident: By age 6, children everywhere are eager to grow and learn beyond the familiar comfort of their homes, as the next three chapters explain.

---

### WHAT HAVE YOU LEARNED?

1. Describe the parenting that seems to promote the happiest, most successful children.

2. What are the limitations of Baumrind's description of parenting styles?

3. How does culture affect parenting style?

4. Why have many nations made corporal punishment illegal?

5. What are the arguments for and against psychological control?

6. When is time-out an effective punishment and when is it not?

7. What are the advantages and problems of induction?

8. What does psychoanalytic theory say about the origins of sex and gender differences?

9. What do behaviorists say about sex and gender roles?

10. What is the difference between the cognitive, sociocultural, and evolutionary perspectives on sex differences?

# SUMMARY

### Emotional Development

**1.** Emotional regulation is crucial during early childhood. It occurs in Erikson's third developmental stage, initiative versus guilt. Children normally feel pride when they demonstrate initiative but feel guilt or even shame at an unsatisfactory outcome.

**2.** Emotional regulation is made possible by maturation of the brain, particularly of the prefrontal cortex, as well as by experiences with parents and peers.

**3.** Intrinsic motivation is apparent in a preschooler's concentration on a drawing or a conversation with an imaginary friend. It may endure when extrinsic motivation stops.

### Play

**4.** All young children enjoy playing—preferably with other children of the same sex, who teach them lessons in social interaction that their parents do not.

**5.** Active play takes many forms, with rough-and-tumble play fostering social skills and sociodramatic play developing emotional regulation.

**6.** Prosocial emotions lead to caring for others; antisocial behavior includes instrumental, reactive, relational, and bullying aggression.

### Challenges for Caregivers

**7.** Three classic styles of parenting have been identified: authoritarian, permissive, and authoritative. Generally, children are more

successful and happy when their parents express warmth and set guidelines.

**8.** A fourth style of parenting, neglectful/uninvolved, is always harmful. The particulars of parenting reflect the culture as well as the temperament of the child.

**9.** Parental punishment can have long-term consequences, with both corporal punishment and psychological control teaching lessons that few parents want their children to learn.

**10.** Even 2-year-olds correctly use sex-specific labels. Young children become aware of gender differences in clothes, toys, playmates, and future careers.

**11.** Freud emphasized that children are attracted to the other-sex parent and eventually seek to identify, or align themselves, with the same-sex parent. Behaviorists hold that gender-related behaviors are learned through reinforcement and punishment (especially for males) and social modeling.

**12.** Cognitive theorists note that simplistic preoperational thinking leads to gender schemas and therefore stereotypes. Sociocultural theory explains that every society and culture organizes life in gendered ways. By belonging to that culture, children learn those social norms. Evolutionary theory contends that biological sex differences are crucial for the survival and reproduction of the species.

**13.** All five theories of gender-role development are plausible, which poses a challenge for caregivers who must determine which set of values they choose to teach.

# KEY TERMS

emotional regulation (p. 282)
self-concept (p. 282)
effortful control (p. 282)
initiative versus guilt (p. 282)
intrinsic motivation (p. 284)
extrinsic motivation (p. 284)
imaginary friends (p. 285)
rough-and-tumble play (p. 288)

sociodramatic play (p. 289)
empathy (p. 290)
prosocial behavior (p. 290)
antisocial behavior (p. 291)
instrumental aggression (p. 291)
reactive aggression (p. 291)
relational aggression (p. 292)
bullying aggression (p. 292)

authoritarian parenting (p. 294)
permissive parenting (p. 294)
authoritative parenting (p. 294)
neglectful/uninvolved parenting (p. 294)
corporal punishment (p. 297)
psychological control (p. 297)
time-out (p. 299)

induction (p. 299)
sex differences (p. 300)
gender differences (p. 300)
phallic stage (p. 301)
Oedipus complex (p. 301)
superego (p. 302)
identification (p. 302)
gender schema (p. 304)

# APPLICATIONS

**1.** Adults tend to believe that the way their parents raised them helped them become the people they are. Ask three people how their parents encouraged and disciplined them, and assess whether that indeed had an impact on adult personality.

**2.** Gender indicators often go unnoticed. Go to a public place (park, restaurant, busy street) and spend at least 10 minutes recording examples of gender differentiation, such as articles of clothing, mannerisms, interaction patterns, and activities. Quantify what you see, such as baseball hats on eight males and

two females. Or (better, but more difficult) describe four male–female conversations, indicating gender differences in length and frequency of talking, interruptions, vocabulary, and so on.

**3.** Analyze the intrinsic and extrinsic motivation for attending college. Do you think that one type or the other is more influential in your achievement? Explain.

# The Developing Person So Far:
## Early Childhood

## BIOSOCIAL

Worth Archive/Ellie Miller

**Body Changes** Children continue to grow from ages 2 to 6, but at a slower rate. Normally, the BMI (body mass index) is lower at about ages 5 and 6 than at any other time of life. Children often eat too much unhealthy food, putting themselves at risk for obesity and other problems. Myelination continues. Parts of the brain connect, allowing lateralization and coordination of the left and right sides of the brain and body. Impulsivity and perseveration gradually decline, allowing better emotional expression and regulation.

**Advancing Motor Skills** Play is important for development; increasingly children are getting too little. Urbanization and pollution are also problematic, causing asthma, lead poisoning, and other impairments.

**Injuries and Abuse** Far more children worldwide die of avoidable accidents than of diseases. To prevent harm, three kinds of prevention are needed: primary, secondary, and tertiary—with primary (before harm has occurred) the most crucial.

**Child Maltreatment** Maltreated children suffer ongoing abuse (most obvious) and neglect (most common), usually by their own parents. Both tertiary prevention and permanency planning are needed to mitigate the ill effects of maltreatment.

## COGNITIVE

Peathegee Inc/Blend Images/Getty Images

**Thinking During Early Childhood** Piaget described the young child's egocentric, illogical perspective, which prevents the child from grasping concepts such as conservation. Vygotsky stressed the cultural context, noting that children learn from mentors—which include parents, teachers, peers—and from the social context. Children develop their own theories, including a theory of mind, as they realize that not everyone thinks as they do.

**Language Learning** Language develops rapidly. By age 6, the average child knows 10,000 words and demonstrates extensive grammatical knowledge. Young children can become balanced bilinguals during these years if their social context is encouraging.

**Early-Childhood Education** Young children are avid learners. Child-centered, teacher-directed, and intervention programs, such as Head Start, can all nurture learning.

## PSYCHOSOCIAL

Worth Archive/Ellie Miller

Top: Christopher Hope-Fitch/Getty Images

**Emotional Development** Self-esteem is usually high during early childhood. Self-concept emerges in Erikson's stage of initiative versus guilt, as does the ability to regulate emotions. Externalizing problems may be the result of too little emotional regulation; internalizing problems may result from too much control.

**Play** All young children play, and they play best with peers. Play helps children develop physically and teaches emotional regulation, empathy, and cultural understanding. Instrumental and reactive aggression gradually decrease; relational aggression becomes more harmful; bullying aggression is most troubling.

**Challenges for Caregivers** A caregiving style that is warm and encouraging, with good communication as well as high expectations (called authoritative), is most effective in promoting the child's self-esteem, autonomy, and self-control. The authoritarian and permissive styles are less beneficial, although cultural variations are apparent. Young children become aware of sex and gender differences; many theories explain how this occurs.

## APPLICATION TO DEVELOPING LIVES PARENTING SIMULATION MIDDLE CHILDHOOD

As you progress through the Middle Childhood simulation module, how you answer the following questions will impact the biosocial, cognitive, and psychosocial development of your child.

| Biosocial | Cognitive | Psychosocial |
|---|---|---|
| • How will you adjust your child's diet and activity level in middle childhood?<br>• Will you follow the recommended immunization schedule?<br>• Will you regulate your child's screen time? | • Which of Piaget's stages of cognitive development is your child in?<br>• How will your child score on an intelligence test?<br>• Will you put your child in tutoring if needed?<br>• Will you help with your child's homework? | • Will you eat meals as a family around the table or have a different routine?<br>• What kind of elementary school will you choose for your child?<br>• What stage of moral development is your child in?<br>• Will your child be popular? |

# Middle Childhood

**E**very age has joys and sorrows, gains and losses. But if you were pushed to choose one best period, you might select middle childhood. From ages 6 to 11, children grow steadily as they master new athletic skills, learn thousands of words, and enter a wider social world. Life is simple, safe, and healthy; the dangers of adolescence (drugs, early sex, violence) are still distant.

But not always. For some children, these years are the worst, not the best. They hate school or fear home; they suffer with asthma or learning disorders; they are bullied or isolated; their parents fight or disappear. Nor do adults—caregivers, educators, politicians—always see these years as simple ones. Instead, some argue about food and school, about treatment for children with special needs, about the effects of single parenthood or divorce or poverty. The next three chapters describe both joys and complications. ●●

# Middle Childhood:
## Biosocial Development

## What Will You Know?

1. Does physical activity affect psychological health?
2. Why are IQ tests not used as often as they were a few decades ago?
3. Should children who are special—with unusual gifts or disabilities—be in special classes?

+ **A Healthy Time**
Slower Growth, Greater Strength
Physical Activity
Health Problems in Middle Childhood
A VIEW FROM SCIENCE: What Causes Childhood Obesity?

+ **Children with Special Brains and Bodies**
Measuring the Mind
Special Needs in Middle Childhood
Specific Learning Disorders
OPPOSING PERSPECTIVES: Drug Treatment for ADHD and Other Disorders

+ **Special Education**
A CASE TO STUDY: Unexpected and Odd
Labels, Laws, and Learning
Early Intervention
Gifted and Talented

**M**y daughter seemed lonely in the early weeks of first grade. Her teacher reassured me that she was admired, not rejected, and that she might become friends with Alison, who was also shy and bright. I spoke to Alison's mother, a friendly woman named Sharon, and we arranged a play date. Soon Bethany and Alison became best friends, as the teacher had predicted.

Unpredicted, however, is that Sharon became my friend. She and her husband, Rick (an editor of a fashion magazine), had one other child, a pudgy boy two years older than Alison. When my daughter and Alison were in fifth grade, I mentioned to Rick my interest in longitudinal research. He recalled a friend, a professional photographer, who took pictures of Alison and her brother every year. The friend wanted the pictures for his portfolio; Rick was happy to oblige. Rick then retrieved an old album with stunning portrayals of brother–sister relationships and personality development from infancy on. Alison was smiling and coy, even as an infant, and her brother was gaunt and serious until Alison was born, when he seemed to relax.

Rick welcomed my interest; Sharon did not.

"I hate that album," she said, slamming it shut. She explained that she told the pediatrician that she thought her baby boy was hungry, but the doctor insisted she stick to a four-hour breast-feeding schedule and told her to never give him formula. That's why she hated that album; it was evidence of an inexperienced mother heeding a doctor while starving her son.

Decades later, I am still friends with Sharon. Her genes and early life made her a large woman, but she carries her large frame well—she is neither too heavy nor too thin. Her adult son, however, is not only big—he is obese. His photo as a thin, serious infant haunts me now as well.

Did Sharon cause his obesity by underfeeding him when he was little, or by overfeeding him later on? Or did genes and culture interact in a destructive way? Or was he rebelling against his father, whose profession glorifies appearance?

Middle childhood is usually a happy time. But this chapter describes some biosocial problems, including obesity, asthma, and a host of intellectual disabilities, all caused by the complex interaction of genes and environment, nature and nurture. Consequences and solutions are also complex: Sharon and Rick are not the only parents who wonder what they could have done differently. I wonder, too.

# A Healthy Time

**middle childhood** The period between early childhood and early adolescence, approximately from ages 6 to 11.

Genes and environment safeguard **middle childhood,** as the years from about 6 to 11 are called (Konner, 2010). Fatal diseases and accidents are rare; both nature and nurture make these years the healthiest of the entire life span. In the United States, the death rate for 5- to 14-year-olds is one-half the rate for 1- to 4-year-olds and one-sixth the rate for 15- to 24-year-olds. From then on, disease fatalities increase steadily every year (National Center for Health Statistics, 2016).

Relatively good health has always been true everywhere in middle childhood, but this is even more apparent today. Worldwide, the current death rate in middle childhood is about one-fourth what it was in 1950 (United Nations, Department of Economic and Social Affairs, Population Division, 2015). In the United States in 1950, the death rate per 100,000 children aged 5 to 14 was 60; in 2014, it was 12. Likewise, minor illnesses, such as ear infections, infected tonsils, measles, and flu, are much less common than a few decades ago (National Center for Health Statistics, 2016).

REUTERS/Corbis

**Expert Eye-Hand Coordination** The specifics of motor-skill development in middle childhood depend on the culture. These flute players are carrying on the European Baroque musical tradition that thrives among the poor, remote Guarayo people of Bolivia.

## Slower Growth, Greater Strength

Unlike infants or adolescents, school-age children grow slowly and steadily, in body and brain. That makes self-care easy—from dressing to bathing, from making lunch to getting to school. Brain maturation allows children to sit in class without breaking pencils, tearing papers, or elbowing classmates. In these middle years, children are more self-sufficient than they were in early childhood, and, in most cases, they are not yet troubled by adolescent body changes.

### Teeth

Important to the individual child is the loss of baby teeth. Some children are eager for the Tooth Fairy to replace a lost tooth with money—and some are told to brush carefully because the Tooth Fairy likes clean teeth. Each permanent tooth arrives on schedule, from about ages 6 to 12, with girls a few months ahead of boys.

In earlier times, many children neither brushed their teeth nor saw a dentist, and fluoride was never added to water. That's why many of the oldest-old have missing teeth, replaced with implants or dentures—no longer common among younger cohorts.

Currently, most school-age children brush their teeth, and many communities—including all of the larger U.S. cities—add fluoride to drinking water. According to a national survey, about 75 percent of U.S. children saw a dentist for preventive care in the past year. For most (70 percent), their teeth were in good shape (Ida & Rozier, 2013). In 2011, one city in Canada (Calgary) stopped adding fluoride to the water. The teeth of second-grade children suffered compared to those of children in a similar city (Edmonton) (McLaren et al., 2016).

Aijaz Rahi/AP Images

**Global Decay** Thousands of children in Bangalore, India, gathered to brush their teeth together, part of an oral health campaign. Music, fast food, candy bars, and technology have been exported from the United States, and many developing nations have their own versions (Bollywood replaces Hollywood). Western diseases have also reached many nations; preventive health now follows.

● **Observation Quiz** Beyond toothbrushes, what other health tools do most children here have that their parents did not? (see answer, p. 314) ↑

### Children's Health Habits

The good health that most school-age children naturally enjoy depends on daily habits, including diet, exercise, and sleep. Unfortunately, children who have poor health for economic or social reasons (such as no regular medical care) are vulnerable lifelong, even if their socioeconomic status improves. Childhood experiences—especially prolonged stress and unhealthy food—affect physical and mental health in adulthood (McEwen & McEwen, 2017; Juster et al., 2016).

Peers and parents are crucial. If children see that others routinely care for their own health, social learning pushes them to do the same. Camps for children with asthma, cancer, diabetes, sickle-cell disease, and other chronic illnesses are beneficial because the example of other children, and the guidance of knowledgeable adults, help children learn self-care. Ideally, that becomes a habit in childhood—not a matter of parental insistence—lest teenage rebellion leads to ignoring special diets, pills, warning signs, and doctors (Dean et al., 2010; Naughton et al., 2014).

## Physical Activity

Beyond the sheer fun of playing, the benefits of physical activity—especially games with rules, which children are now able to follow—can last a lifetime. Exercise not only improves physical health and reduces depression but may also improve academic achievement (Ridgers et al., 2012).

### Brain Development

How could body movement improve intellectual functioning? A review of the research suggests several possible mechanisms, including direct benefits of better cerebral blood flow and increased neurotransmitters, as well as indirect results of better moods (Singh et al., 2012). Many studies have found that cognition and action are connected in children, an example of *embodied cognition,* the idea that thinking is closely allied with physical actions and health (Pexman, 2017).

Underlying body functioning is brain functioning. Remember *executive control,* the ability to inhibit some impulses to focus on others. Neurological advances allow children to pay special heed to the most important elements of their environment. **Selective attention,** the ability to concentrate on some stimuli while ignoring others, improves markedly at about age 7.

Selective attention is partly the result of maturation, but it is also greatly affected by experience, particularly the experience of playing with others. School-age children not only notice various stimuli (which is one form of attention) but also select appropriate responses when several possibilities conflict (Wendelken et al., 2011).

For example, in kickball, soccer, basketball, and baseball, it is crucial to attend to the ball, not to dozens of other stimuli. Thus, in baseball, young batters learn to ignore the other team's attempts to distract them, fielders start moving into position as soon as the bat connects, and pitchers adjust to the height, handedness, and past performance of the players. Another physical activity that seems to foster *executive function* is karate, which requires inhibition of some reactions in order to execute others (Alesi et al., 2014).

**LaunchPad**
macmillan learning

**Video Activity: Brain Development: Middle Childhood** depicts the changes that occur in a child's brain from age 6 to age 11.

Henning Dalhoff/Bonnier Publications/Science Source

**selective attention** The ability to concentrate on some stimuli while ignoring others.

Pressmaster/Shutterstock

**Pay Attention** Some adults think that computers make children lazy, because they can look up whatever they don't know. But imagine the facial expressions of these children if they were sitting at their desks with 30 classmates, listening to a lecture.

**reaction time** The time it takes to respond to a stimulus, either physically (with a reflexive movement such as an eyeblink) or cognitively (with a thought).

Similar advances occur in **reaction time,** which is how long it takes to respond to a stimulus. Preschoolers are sometimes frustratingly slow in putting on their pants, eating their cereal, throwing a ball. Reaction time is shorter every year of childhood, thanks to increasing myelination. Skill at games is an obvious example, from scoring on a video game, to swinging at a pitch, to kicking a soccer ball toward a teammate—all of which improve every year from 6 to 11, depending partly on practice.

## Neighborhood Play

In addition to brain development, playing games teaches cooperation, problem solving, and respect for teammates and opponents of many backgrounds. Where can children reap these benefits?

Neighborhood play is an ideal way to develop those skills. Rules and boundaries are adapted to the context (out of bounds is "past the tree" or "behind the truck"). Dozens of running and catching games go on forever—or at least until dark. Neighborhood play is active, interactive, and inclusive—any child can play. One scholar notes:

> Children play tag, hide and seek, or pickup basketball. They compete with one another but always according to rules, and rules that they enforce themselves without recourse to an impartial judge. The penalty for not playing by the rules is not playing, that is, social exclusion.

[Gillespie, 2010, p. 298]

For school-age children, "social exclusion" is a steep price. Most learn to cooperate, playing for hours every day.

Unfortunately, modern life has undercut informal neighborhood play. Vacant lots and empty fields have largely disappeared, and parents fear "stranger danger"—thinking that a stranger might hurt their child (which is exceedingly rare) and ignoring the many benefits of outside play, which are universal. Developmentalists seek to reduce parents' fears in order to increase children's active play (Carver, 2016; Depeau, 2016). As one advocate of more unsupervised, creative childhood play sadly notes:

> Actions that would have been considered paranoid in the '70s—walking third-graders to school, forbidding your kid to play ball in the street, going down the slide with your child in your lap—are now routine.

[Rosin, 2014]

Many parents enroll their children in organizations that offer—depending on the culture—tennis, karate, cricket, rugby, baseball, or soccer. Unfortunately, in every nation, childhood sports leagues are less likely to include children with special needs or low SES. Neighborhood leagues—Little League and so on—are scarce in inner-city neighborhoods. As a result, the children most likely to benefit are least likely to participate. The reasons are many, the consequences sad (Dearing et al., 2009). Another group with low participation is older girls, again a group particularly likely to benefit from athletic activity (Kremer et al., 2014).

**Answer to Observation Quiz** (from p. 312): Water bottles, sun visors, and I.D. badges—although the last item might not be considered a healthy innovation.

Henrik Weis/Corbis

**Idyllic** Two 8-year-olds, each with a 6-year-old sister, all four daydreaming or exploring in a very old tree beside a lake in Denmark—what could be better? Ideally, all of the world's children would be so fortunate, but most are not.

## Exercise in School

When opportunities for neighborhood play are scarce, physical education in school is a logical alternative. However, schools in the United States are pressured to focus on test scores, so time for physical education and recess has declined. According to a nationwide survey of 10,000 third-graders, about one-third of all U.S. schoolchildren have less than 15 minutes of recess each day. Some have no recess at all, a deprivation more likely in low-SES, urban, public schools.

**Are They Having Fun?** Helmets, uniforms, and competition—more appropriate for adults? Children everywhere want to do what the adults do, so probably these ones are proud of their ice hockey team.

The researchers write: "many children from disadvantaged backgrounds are not free to roam their neighborhoods or even their own yards unless they are accompanied by adults. . . . recess periods may be the only opportunity for them to practice their social skills with other children" (Barros et al., 2009, p. 434). In 2013, the American Academy of Pediatricians released a policy statement that "recess is a crucial and necessary component of a child's development," imploring educators never to punish children by reducing recess (Council on School Health, 2013).

The same schools that eliminate recess often cut physical education to allow more time for reading and math. Even when gym class is required, schools find reasons to cancel it. For instance, although Alabama law requires at least 30 minutes of physical education each day, a study of all primary schools in one low-income district found that cancellations resulted in an average of only 22 minutes of gym per day. No school in this district had after-school sports (Robinson et al., 2014).

Paradoxically, eliminating recess may reduce children's mastery of reading and math, contrary to what many in the United States believe. Other nations make different choices.

## Health Problems in Middle Childhood

Although health generally improves in middle childhood, some chronic conditions, including Tourette syndrome, stuttering, and allergies, often worsen. Even minor problems—glasses, coughing, nose blowing, a visible birthmark—can make children self-conscious, interfering with friendship formation.

Not always, of course. Researchers increasingly recognize "that the expression and outcome for any problem will depend on the configuration and timing of a host of surrounding circumstances" (Hayden & Mash, 2014, p. 49). Parents and children are not merely reactive: In a dynamic-systems manner, individuals and contexts influence each other. Consider two examples: obesity and asthma.

### Childhood Obesity

**Childhood overweight** is usually defined as a BMI above the 85th percentile, and **childhood obesity** is defined as a BMI above the 95th percentile for children of a particular age. In 2012, 18 percent of 6- to 11-year-olds in the United States were obese (Ogden et al., 2014). At the beginning of middle childhood, healthy children are active and relatively thin: The proportion of the body that is fat, not bone or muscle, is less than at any other stage.

Childhood obesity is increasing worldwide, having more than doubled since 1980 in all three nations of North America (Mexico, the United States, and Canada) (Ogden et al., 2011). Since 2000, rates have leveled off in the United States and have even been reduced in younger children. However, rates continue to increase in most other nations. In China, in only two de-

**Especially for Medical Professionals** You notice that a child is overweight, but you are hesitant to say anything to the parents, who are also overweight, because you do not want to offend them. What should you do? (see response, p. 319)

**childhood overweight** In a child, having a BMI above the 85th percentile, according to the U.S. Centers for Disease Control and Prevention's 1980 standards for children of a given age.

**childhood obesity** In a child, having a BMI above the 95th percentile, according to the U.S. Centers for Disease Control and Prevention's 1980 standards for children of a given age.

**Same Situation, Far Apart** Children have high energy but small stomachs, so they enjoy frequent snacks more than big meals. Yet snacks are typically poor sources of nutrition. Who is healthier: the American boy crunching buttered popcorn as he watches a 3-D movie, or the Japanese children eating *takoyaki* (an octopus dumpling) as part of a traditional celebration near Tokyo?

cades (from 1991 to 2011), overweight (which includes children who are obese and those who are heavy but not yet obese) among 6- to 12-year-olds more than doubled (from 11 percent to 26 percent) (Jia et al., 2017). (See Visualizing Development, p. 318.)

Childhood overweight correlates with asthma, high blood pressure, and elevated cholesterol (especially LDL, the "lousy" cholesterol). If a child is critically ill (rare in middle childhood), obesity adds to the risk, making death more likely (P. Ross et al., 2016). But for the vast majority of children, obesity is not a medical problem as much as a social one. As excessive weight builds, school achievement decreases, self-esteem falls, and loneliness rises (Harrist et al., 2012).

Loneliness may be the worst of these for school-age children, since during these years friends are particularly important. A reciprocal relationship is apparent: Children with poor social skills and few friends are more likely to become obese and vice versa (Jackson & Cunningham, 2015; Vandewater et al., 2015).

**asthma** A chronic disease of the respiratory system in which inflammation narrows the airways from the nose and mouth to the lungs, causing difficulty in breathing. Signs and symptoms include wheezing, shortness of breath, chest tightness, and coughing.

## Asthma

**Asthma** is a chronic inflammatory disorder of the airways that makes breathing difficult. Sufferers have periodic attacks, sometimes requiring a rush to the hospital emergency room, a frightening experience for children who know that asthma might kill them (although it almost never does in childhood).

Childhood asthma continues in adulthood about half the time, when it can be fatal (Banks & Andrews, 2015). But the most serious problem in middle childhood is social, not medical. Childhood friendships thrive between children who are almost never absent, yet asthma is the most common reason children miss school.

**Pride and Prejudice** In some city schools, asthma is so common that using an inhaler is a sign of pride, as suggested by the facial expressions of these two boys. The "prejudice" is beyond the walls of this school nurse's room, in a society that allows high rates of childhood asthma.

In the United States, childhood asthma rates have tripled since 1980, with 14 percent of U.S. 5- to 11-year-olds diagnosed with asthma at some time. Rates increase as income falls, and they reflect ethnic differences as well: Children whose parents were born in Puerto Rico have especially high rates (Loftus & Wise, 2016).

# What Causes Childhood Obesity?

The biological development of children is affected by many aspects of the microsystem, exosystem, and macrosystem. Here, we delve into the causes of childhood obesity to illustrate the larger issues surrounding the health of children.

There are "hundreds if not thousands of contributing factors" for childhood obesity, from the cells of the body to the norms of the society (Harrison et al., 2011, p. 51). Dozens of genes affect weight by influencing activity level, hunger, food preferences, body type, and metabolism. New genes and alleles that affect obesity—and that never act alone—are discovered virtually every month (Dunmore, 2013).

Knowing that genes are involved may slow down the impulse to blame people for being overweight. However, genes cannot explain why obesity rates have increased dramatically, since genes change little from one generation to the next. Instead, cultural and cohort changes must be responsible, evident not only in North America but worldwide. For example, a review in India acknowledges genes but focuses on sugary drinks, portion sizes, chips, baked goods, and candy (Sahoo et al., 2015).

Look at the figure on obesity among 6- to 11-year-olds in the United States (see Figure 11.1).

At first glance, one might think that the large ethnic gaps (such as only 9 percent of Asian Americans but 26 percent of Hispanic Americans) might be genetic. But look at gender: Non-Hispanic White *girls* are twice as likely to be obese as boys, but in the other groups *boys* are more often obese than girls. Something cultural, not biological, must be the reason.

Further evidence that social context affects obesity was found in a study that controlled for family income and early parenting: Ethnic differences in childhood obesity almost disappeared (Taveras et al., 2013).

What are those parenting practices that make children too heavy? Obesity rates rise if

- infants drink formula and eat solid foods before 4 months
- preschoolers have televisions in their bedrooms and drink large quantities of soda
- school-age children sleep too little but have several hours each day of screen time (TV, videos, games), rarely playing outside (Hart et al., 2011; Taveras et al., 2013).

### FIGURE 11.1

**Heavier and Heavier** The incidence of obesity (defined here as the 95th percentile or above, per the Centers for Disease Control and Prevention 2000 growth charts) is about 1 school child in 6. Rates are lower in younger children but higher in adolescents and adults, and differ by ethnicity which suggests that nurture is critical.

● **Observation Quiz** Are boys more likely to be overweight than girls? (see answer, p. 319) ➜

Although family habits in infancy and early childhood can set a child on the path to obesity, during middle childhood children themselves have *pester power*—the ability to get adults to do what they want (Powell et al., 2011). Often they pester their parents to buy calorie-dense foods that are advertised on television.

On average, all of these family practices changed for the worse toward the end of the twentieth century in North America and are spreading worldwide. For instance, family size has decreased, and, as a result, pester power has increased and more food is available for each child. That makes childhood obesity collateral damage of a reduction in birth rate—a worldwide trend in the early twenty-first century.

Attempts to limit sugar and fat clash with the goals of many corporations, since snacks and processed foods are very profitable. On the plus side, many schools now have policies that foster good nutrition. A national survey in the United States found that schools are reducing all types of commercial food advertising. However, vending machines are still prevalent in high schools, and free food coupons are often used as incentives in elementary schools (Terry-McElrath et al., 2014).

Overall, simply offering healthy food is not enough to convince children to change their diet; context and culture are crucial (Hanks et al., 2013). Communities can build parks, bike paths, and sidewalks, and nations can decrease subsidies for sugar and corn oil and syrup.

Rather than trying to zero in on any single factor, a dynamic-systems approach is needed: Many factors, over time, affect the health of every child. Changing just one factor is not enough.

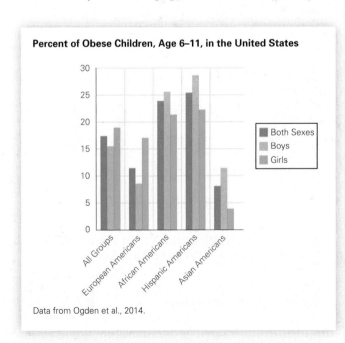

**Percent of Obese Children, Age 6–11, in the United States**

Data from Ogden et al., 2014.

# Childhood Obesity Around the Globe

Obesity now causes more deaths worldwide than malnutrition. Reductions are possible. A multi-faceted prevention effort—including mothers, preschools, pediatricians, grocery stores, and even the White House—has reduced obesity in the United States for 2- to 5-year-olds. It was 13.9 percent in 2002 and was 8.4 percent in 2012. However, obesity rates from age 6 to 60 remain high everywhere.

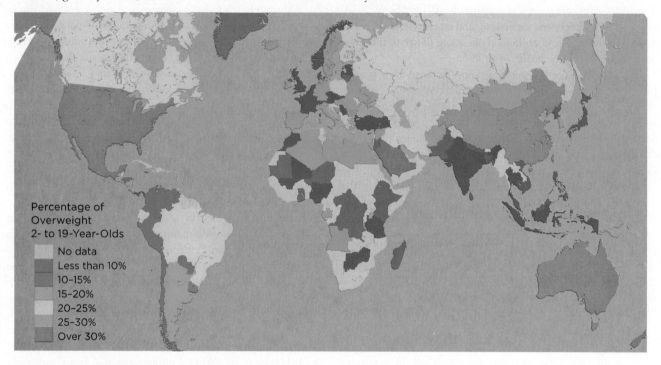

Percentage of
Overweight
2- to 19-Year-Olds

- No data
- Less than 10%
- 10–15%
- 15–20%
- 20–25%
- 25–30%
- Over 30%

DATA FROM M. NG ET AL., 2014.

## ADS AND OBESITY

Nations differ in children's exposure to televised ads for unhealthy food. The amount of this advertising continues to correlate with childhood obesity (e.g., Hewer, 2014). Parents can reduce overweight by limiting screen time and playing outside with their children. The community matters as well: When neighborhoods have no safe places to play, rates of obesity soar.

DATA FROM LOBSTEIN AND DIBB, 2005.

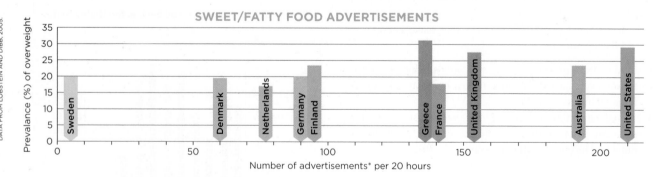

SWEET/FATTY FOOD ADVERTISEMENTS

Prevalance (%) of overweight — Number of advertisements* per 20 hours

Sweden, Denmark, Netherlands, Germany, Finland, Greece, France, United Kingdom, Australia, United States

## WORLD HEALTH ORGANIZATION (WHO) RECOMMENDATIONS FOR PHYSICAL ACTIVITY FOR CHILDREN

 **1** Children ages 5 to 17 should be active for at least an hour a day.

**2** More than an hour of exercise each day brings additional benefits.

 **3** Most physical activity should be aerobic. Vigorous activities should occur 3 times per week or more.

WHO also recommends daily exercise for adults of every age—including centenarians.

INFORMATION FROM WORLD HEALTH ORGANIZATION, 2011.

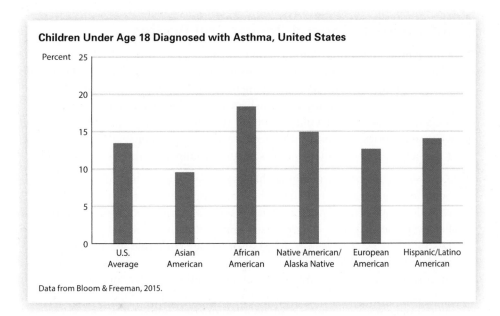

**Children Under Age 18 Diagnosed with Asthma, United States**

Data from Bloom & Freeman, 2015.

**FIGURE 11.2**

**Not Breathing Easy** Of all U.S. children younger than 18, almost 14 percent have been diagnosed at least once with asthma. Why do African American children have the highest rates? Puerto Rican children have even higher rates (not shown). Is that nature or nurture, genetics or pollution?

While some children outgrow asthma, about two-thirds do not (National Center for Health Statistics, 2014). (See Figure 11.2.)

Researchers have found many causes. Some alleles have been identified, as have many aspects of modern life—carpets, pollution, house pets, airtight windows, parental smoking, cockroaches, dust mites, less outdoor play. None acts in isolation. A combination of genetic sensitivity to allergies, early respiratory infections, and compromised lung functioning increases wheezing and shortness of breath (Mackenzie et al., 2014).

Some experts suggest a *hygiene hypothesis:* that "the immune system needs to tangle with microbes when we are young" (Leslie, 2012, p. 1428). Children may be overprotected from viruses and bacteria. In their concern about hygiene, parents prevent exposure to minor infections, diseases, and family pets that would strengthen their child's immunity.

This hypothesis is supported by data showing that (1) first-born children develop asthma more often than later-born ones; (2) asthma and allergies are less common among farm-dwelling children; and (3) children born by cesarean delivery (very sterile) have a greater incidence of asthma. Overall, it may be "that despite what our mothers told us, cleanliness sometimes leads to sickness" (Leslie, 2012, p. 1428).

Remember the microbiome—those bacteria that are within our bodies. Some are in the lungs and act to increase or decrease asthma (Singanayagam et al., 2017). Accordingly, changing the microbiome—via diet, drugs, or exposure to animals—may treat asthma. However, since asthma has multiple and varied causes and types, no single kind of treatment will help everyone.

**Response for Medical Professionals** (from p. 315): Speak to the parents, not accusingly but helpfully. Alert them to potential social and health problems that their child's weight poses. Most parents are concerned about their child's well-being and will work with you to improve the child's snacks and exercise levels.

**Answer to Observation Quiz** (from p. 317): Not always, but sometimes. Rates of obesity among Asian American boys are almost three times higher than among Asian American girls.

## WHAT HAVE YOU LEARNED?

1. How do childhood health habits affect adult health?

2. What are the advantages of physical play during middle childhood?

3. How could the brain be affected by playing with other children?

4. Why does a thin (but not too skinny) 6-year-old not need to eat more?

5. What roles do nature and nurture play in childhood asthma?

6. What are the hazards of asthma in childhood?

**developmental psychopathology** The field that uses insights into typical development to understand and remediate developmental disorders.

**comorbid** Refers to the presence of two or more disease conditions at the same time in the same person.

**aptitude** The potential to master a specific skill or to learn a certain body of knowledge.

**intelligence** The ability to learn and understand various aspects of life, traditionally focused on reading and math, and more recently on the arts, movement, and social interactions.

**Typical 7-Year-Old?** In many ways, this boy is typical. He likes video games and school, he usually appreciates his parents, and he gets himself dressed every morning. This photo shows him using blocks to construct a design to match a picture, one of the 10 kinds of challenges that comprise the WISC, a widely used IQ test. His attention to the task is not unusual for children his age, but his actual performance is more like that of an older child. That makes his IQ score significantly above 100.

# Children with Special Brains and Bodies

**Developmental psychopathology** links usual with unusual development, especially when the unusual results in special needs (Cicchetti, 2013b; Hayden & Mash, 2014). This topic is relevant lifelong because "[e]ach period of life, from the prenatal period through senescence, ushers in new biological and psychological challenges, strengths, and vulnerabilities" (Cicchetti, 2013b, p. 458). Turning points, opportunities, and past influences are always apparent.

At the outset, four general principles should be emphasized.

1. *Abnormality is normal,* meaning that everyone typically has some aspects of behavior that are quite unusual. Thus, most people sometimes act oddly. The opposite is also true: Everyone with a serious disorder is, in many respects, like everyone else. This is particularly apparent with children.
2. *Disability changes year by year.* Most disorders are **comorbid,** which means that more than one problem is evident in the same person. The disorder that seems most severe may become much milder, but another problem may appear.
3. *Life may get better or worse.* Prognosis is uncertain. Many children with severe disabilities (e.g., blindness) become productive adults. Conversely, some conditions (e.g., conduct disorder) become more disabling.
4. *Diagnosis and treatment reflect the social context.* Each individual interacts with the surrounding setting—including family, school, community, and culture—to modify, worsen, or even create psychopathology.

## Measuring the Mind

The importance of this last item is evident in a basic question—does a particular person have a disorder or not? In ancient times, if adults were strong and hardworking, that made them solid members of the community, not disordered. No one was singled out if they could not think quickly, read well, or sit still. If someone had an obvious disability, such as being blind or deaf, he or she received special care; no need for diagnosis.

Over the centuries, however, humans have placed more value on brain functioning. Books were printed so that everyone might read them; money was exchanged for daily food and housing; voters chose leaders instead of kings inheriting kingdoms. This all required learning, and some people were much better at reading, at math, at analysis. Schools were built for children, and it became apparent that some children learned more quickly than others. It became important to measure intelligence.

Currently, only about 1 percent of all children are diagnosed with obvious physical impairments. But in many nations, another 10 to 20 percent might need special education because of something amiss in their thinking. For that, the social context matters.

### Aptitude, Achievement, and IQ

The potential to master a specific skill or to learn a certain body of knowledge is called **aptitude.** A child's brain has the potential to read and write (true for most people), or an adult has the aptitude for becoming a talented soccer player, seamstress, chef, artist, or whatever (potentials that only some people have).

People assumed that, for **intelligence,** one general aptitude (often referred to as *g,* for general intelligence) could be assessed by answers to a series of questions testing vocabulary, memory, puzzle completion, and so on. The number of correct answers was compared to the average for children of a particular age, and an IQ score was found. The advantage of intelligence tests is that scores correlated with school achievement and often predicted which children would have difficulty mastering the regular curriculum.

Originally, IQ tests produced a score that was literally a quotient: Mental age (the average chronological age of children who answer a certain number of questions correctly) was divided by the chronological age of a child taking the test. The answer from that division (the quotient) was multiplied by 100.

Thus, if the average 9-year-old answered, say, exactly 60 questions correctly, then everyone who got 60 questions correct—no matter what their chronological age—would have a mental age of 9. Obviously, for children whose mental age was the same as their chronological age (such as a 9-year-old who got 60 questions right), the IQ would be 100 ($9 \div 9 = 1 \times 100 = 100$), exactly average.

If a 6-year-old answered the questions as well as a typical 9-year-old, the score would be $9 \div 6 \times 100$, or 150. If a 12-year-old answered only 60 questions correctly, the IQ would be 75 ($9 \div 12 \times 100$). The current method of calculating IQ is more complex, but the basic idea is the same: $g$ is calculated based on the average mental age of people of a particular chronological age. (See Figure 11.3.)

What is actually learned, not one's learning potential (aptitude), is called achievement. School **achievement tests** compare scores to norms established for each grade. For example, children of any age who read as well as the average third-grader would be at the third-grade level in reading achievement.

It was once assumed that aptitude was a fixed characteristic, present at birth. Longitudinal data show otherwise. Young children with a low IQ can become above average or even gifted adults, like my nephew David (discussed in Chapter 1).

## The Flynn Effect

Crucial for all IQ tests is vocabulary, which reflects the emphasis of family and culture as well as the brain of the child. Traditionally, IQ tests were validated by how well they predicted school achievement. We now know that school learning depends on family, school, and culture, as well as the mind of the child.

Indeed, the average IQ scores of entire nations have risen substantially every decade for the past century—a phenomenon called the **Flynn effect,** named after the researcher who described it (Flynn, 1999, 2012). The Flynn effect is more apparent for women than for men, and in southern Europe more than northern Europe, probably because educational opportunities for women and for southern Europeans improved markedly in the twentieth century (Weber et al., 2017).

Most psychologists now agree that the brain is like a muscle, affected by mental exercise—which often is encouraged or discouraged by the social setting. This is proven in language and music (brains literally grow with childhood music training) and is probably true in other domains (Moreno et al., 2015; Zatorre, 2013). Both speed and memory are crucial for $g$, and they are affected by experience, evident in the Flynn effect.

**achievement test** A measure of mastery or proficiency in reading, mathematics, writing, science, or some other subject.

**Flynn effect** The rise in average IQ scores that has occurred over the decades in many nations.

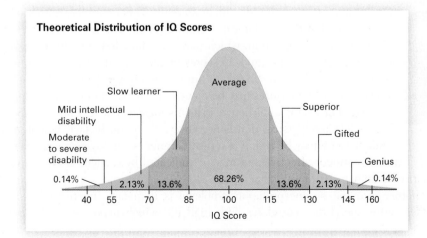

**Theoretical Distribution of IQ Scores**

Average

Slow learner

Mild intellectual disability

Moderate to severe disability

Superior

Gifted

Genius

0.14%        2.13%   13.6%      68.26%      13.6%   2.13%      0.14%

40   55      70        85      100      115     130      145   160

IQ Score

**FIGURE 11.3**

**In Theory, Most People Are Average**
Almost 70 percent of IQ scores fall within the "normal" range. Note, however, that this is a norm-referenced test. In fact, actual IQ scores have risen in many nations; 100 is no longer exactly the midpoint. Furthermore, in practice, scores below 50 are slightly more frequent than indicated by the normal curve (shown here) because severe disability is the result not of normal distribution but of genetic and prenatal factors.

**Observation Quiz** If a person's IQ is 110, what category is he or she in? (see answer, p. 322)

## Many Intelligences

Since scores change over time, IQ tests are much less definitive than they were once thought to be. Some scientists doubt whether any single test can measure the complexities of the human brain, especially if the test is designed to measure $g$, one general aptitude. According to some experts, children inherit and develop many abilities, some high and some low, rather than any $g$ (e.g., Q. Zhu et al., 2010).

Two leading developmentalists (Robert Sternberg and Howard Gardner) are among those who believe that humans have **multiple intelligences,** not just one. Sternberg originally described three kinds of intelligence: analytic, creative, and practical (2008; 2011). Children who are unusually creative, or very practical, may not be considered the best students in school; but they may flourish later on.

Gardner originally described seven intelligences: linguistic, logical-mathematical, musical, spatial, bodily-kinesthetic (movement), interpersonal (social understanding), and intrapersonal (self-understanding), each associated with a particular brain region (Gardner, 1983). He subsequently added an eighth (naturalistic: understanding nature, as in biology, zoology, or farming) and a ninth (spiritual/existential: thinking about life and death) (Gardner, 1999, 2006; Gardner & Moran, 2006).

Although everyone has some of all nine intelligences, Gardner believes each individual excels in particular ones. For example, someone might be gifted spatially but not linguistically (a visual artist who cannot describe her work) or might have interpersonal but not naturalistic intelligence (an astute clinical psychologist whose houseplants die). Gardner's concepts influence teachers in many primary schools, where children might demonstrate their understanding of a historical event via a poster with drawings instead of writing a paper with a bibliography.

Schools, cultures, and families dampen or expand particular intelligences. If two children are born with musical aptitude, the child whose parents are musicians is more likely to develop musical intelligence than the child whose parents are tone deaf. Gardner (2011) believes that schools often are too narrow, teaching only some aspects of intelligence and thus stunting children's learning.

Increasing awareness of the sociocultural perspective has made educators aware that every test reflects the culture of the people who create, administer, and take it. [**Developmental Link:** The sociocultural perspective is discussed in Chapter 2.] This is obvious for achievement tests: A child may score low because of home, school, or culture, not because of ability. Indeed, IQ tests are still used partly because achievement tests do not necessarily reflect aptitude.

## Brain Scans

Another way to indicate aptitude is to measure the brain directly, avoiding cultural biases. In childhood, brain scans do not correlate with scores on IQ tests, but they do later on (Brouwer et al., 2014). Brain scans can measure speed of reaction, which may underlie adult IQ. However, the variation in brain scans and IQ scores in children suggests flaws in one or the other (or both) of these measures (Goddings & Giedd, 2014).

Neurological measures may be no more accurate than paper-and-pencil tests. For example, although it seems logical that less brain activity means less intelligence, that is not always the case. In fact, heightened brain activity may be a sign of a disorder, not of intelligence (e.g., Xiang et al., 2016). Treatment effectiveness may be indicated by reduced brain activity (Thomas & Viljoen, 2016).

Another example of interpretation problems is in measuring the cortex. A thicker cortex sometimes correlates with high IQ, which makes sense because

**multiple intelligences** The idea that human intelligence is composed of a varied set of abilities rather than a single, all-encompassing one.

⬤ **Answer to Observation Quiz** (from p. 321): He or she is average. Anyone with a score between 85 and 115 has an average IQ.

⬤ **Especially for Teachers** What are the advantages and disadvantages of using Gardner's nine intelligences to guide your classroom curriculum? (see response, p. 323)

Brownie Harris/Corbis

**A Gifted Child** Georgie Pocheptsov is an artist, and his family and culture recognized his talent by buying art supplies, giving him time and a place to paint, and selling his creations. Did he lose anything because of his talent, as Picasso did?

that is where most thinking occurs. However, in 9- to 11-year-olds, a thinner cortex predicts greater vocabulary (Menary et al., 2013; Karama et al., 2009). (Extensive vocabulary is pivotal for many aspects of intelligence and school achievement.)

Brain patterns in creative children differ from those of children who score high on IQ tests, again a result that is difficult to interpret (Jung & Ryman, 2013). Thus, there are many reasons psychologists do not rely on children's brain scans to indicate intelligence or diagnose psychopathology.

## Consensus on the Brain

Neuroscientists and psychologists agree, however, on three generalities:

1. *Brain development depends on experiences.* Thus, a brain scan is accurate only at the moment, not in the future.
2. *Dendrites form and myelination changes throughout life.* Middle childhood is crucial, but developments before and after these years are also significant.
3. *Children with disorders often have unusual brain patterns, and training may change those patterns.* However, brain complexity and normal variation mean that diagnosis and remediation are far from perfect.

A new concept is **neurodiversity,** the idea that everyone's brain functions in a particular way. The implication is that diverse neurological patterns are not necessarily better or worse; they are simply different, an example of the *difference is not deficit* idea explained first in Chapter 1 (Kapp et al., 2013). The neurodiversity perspective arose from an effort to understand autism spectrum disorder, but it is now applied more broadly to appreciate every difference between one person and another. It cautions reliance on brain scans, paper-and-pencil tests, or even behavior to indicate intelligence, psychopathology, or future development.

**neurodiversity** The idea that each person has neurological strengths and weaknesses that should be appreciated, in much the same way diverse cultures and ethnicities are welcomed. Neurodiversity seems particularly relevant for children with disorders on the autism spectrum.

## Special Needs in Middle Childhood

Problems with testing are not the only reason diagnosis of psychopathology is complex (Hayden & Mash, 2014; Cicchetti, 2013b). One cause can have many (multiple) final manifestations, a phenomenon called **multifinality** (many final forms). The opposite is also apparent: Many causes can result in one symptom, a phenomenon called **equifinality** (equal in final form). Thus, a direct line from cause to consequence cannot be drawn with certainty.

For example, an infant who has been flooded with stress hormones may become hypervigilant or irrationally placid, may be easily angered or quick to cry, or may not be affected (multifinality). Or, a nonverbal child may have autism spectrum disorder or a hearing impairment; be electively mute or pathologically shy (equifinality).

The complexity of diagnosis is evident in the *Diagnostic and Statistical Manual of Mental Disorders*, 5th edition (American Psychiatric Association, 2013), referred to as DSM-5. A major problem is differentiating typical childish behavior and pathology. The latter may need targeted intervention, as early as possible.

Some suggest that childhood psychopathology was underdiagnosed in early editions of the DSM and now is overdiagnosed (Hayden & Mash, 2014). Some suggest that when neurodiversity includes everyone, children who have truly special needs may be shortchanged: They are not simply another manifestation of the vast variations of human life; they are children who need special attention (Kauffman et al., 2017).

To illustrate the many complexities, we discuss three particularly common and troubling disorders, attention-deficit/hyperactivity disorder (ADHD), specific learning disorder, and autism spectrum disorder (ASD). The online DSM-5

**multifinality** A basic principle of developmental psychopathology, which holds that one cause can have many (multiple) final manifestations.

**equifinality** A basic principle of developmental psychopathology, which holds that one symptom can have many causes.

**LaunchPad**
macmillan learning

Download the **DSM-5 Appendix** to learn more about the terminology and classification of childhood psychopathology.

Appendix lists the criteria for these three; professionals know much more about these and dozens of other disorders.

## Attention-Deficit/Hyperactivity Disorder

**attention-deficit/hyperactivity disorder (ADHD)** A condition characterized by a persistent pattern of inattention and/or by hyperactive or impulsive behaviors; ADHD interferes with a person's functioning or development.

Someone with **attention-deficit/hyperactivity disorder (ADHD)** is often inattentive and unusually active and impulsive. That interferes with the ability to learn. DSM-5 says that symptoms must start before age 12 (in DSM-IV it was age 7) and must impact daily life. (DSM-IV said *impaired,* not just *impacted.*) Partly because the definition now includes many more people, the rate of children diagnosed with ADHD has increased worldwide (Polanczyk et al., 2014).

Some impulsive, overactive, and unusual behaviors are expected for all children. However, those with ADHD "are so active and impulsive that they cannot sit still, are constantly fidgeting, talk when they should be listening, interrupt people all the time, can't stay on task, . . .accidentally injure themselves." All of this makes them "difficult to parent or teach" (Nigg & Barkley, 2014, p. 75).

There is no biological marker for ADHD. Although some brain patterns are distinct, they are not proof of the disorder. Nor is there any definitive written test. Instead, diagnosis depends on parent and teacher reporting actual behavior, confirmed by careful observation by a professional who has seen many children that age. The origin is thought to be neurological, with problems in brain regulation either because of genes, complications of pregnancy, or toxins (such as lead) (Nigg & Barkley, 2014).

ADHD is often comorbid with other intellectual disabilities and depression. This means that a child who has been diagnosed with ADHD has a higher risk of being depressed, but we do not know whether both comorbidities were caused by the same genes, or whether the context (such as a child being punished for not paying attention) caused the depression. Similar issues arise if a child with ADHD has a specific learning disorder.

**Almost Impossible** The concentration needed to do homework is almost beyond Clint, age 11, who takes medication for ADHD. Note his furrowed brow, resting head, and sad face.

One surprising comorbidity is deafness: Children with severe hearing loss are affected in balance and activity, and they are likely to develop ADHD (Antoine et al., 2013). The path may be direct or indirect: Whatever caused their hearing loss may also affect their activity level. When one brain insult causes many symptoms, that is multifinality; when many causes (deafness, toxins, illnesses) produce one disorder (ADHD), that is equifinality.

## Prevalence Statistics

For every type of psychopathology, it is difficult to know how prevalent it is. For example in 1980 about 5 percent of all U.S. 4- to 17-year-olds were diagnosed with ADHD. More recent rates are 7 percent of 4- to 9-year-olds, 13 percent of 10- to 13-year-olds, and 15 percent of 14- to 17-year-olds (Schwarz & Cohen, 2013). These numbers are called "astronomical" by one pediatric neurologist (Graf, quoted in Schwarz & Cohen, 2013) and "preposterous . . . a concoction to justify the giving out of medicine at unprecedented and unjustifiable levels" (Conners, quoted in Schwarz, 2013, p. A1).

Rates of ADHD in most other nations are lower than in the United States, but they are rising everywhere (Polanczy et al., 2014). Most research finds the highest rates in North America and the lowest rates in East Asia (Erskine et al., 2013), but since diagnosis depends on judgment, and since the gold standard of judgment (from parents *and* teachers *and* professional observation) is rare, international

**Response for Teachers** (from p. 322): The advantages are that all of the children learn more aspects of human knowledge and that many children can develop their talents. Art, music, and sports should be an integral part of education, not just a break from academics. The disadvantage is that they take time and attention away from reading and math, which might lead to less proficiency in those subjects on standard tests and thus to criticism from parents and supervisors.

Sacramento Bee/Lezlie Sterling/ZUMA Press

comparisons may be invalid. Increases anywhere raise three concerns:

- *Misdiagnosis.* If ADHD is diagnosed when another disorder is the problem, treatment might make the problem worse (Miklowitz & Cicchetti, 2010). Many psychoactive drugs alter moods, so a child with disruptive mood dysregulation (formerly called bipolar disorder) might be harmed by ADHD medication.
- *Drug abuse.* Although drugs sometimes are therapeutic for true ADHD cases, some adolescents seek a diagnosis of ADHD in order to obtain legal amphetamines (McCabe et al., 2014).
- *Typical behavior considered pathological.* In young children, activity, impulsiveness, and curiosity are typical. If that results in a diagnosis of ADHD, exuberance and self-confidence may suffer.

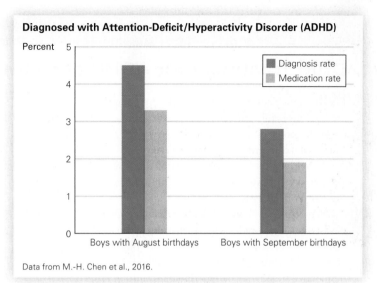

Data from M.-H. Chen et al., 2016.

**FIGURE 11.4**

**One Month Is One Year**  In the Taiwanese school system, the cutoff for kindergarten is September 1, so some boys enter school a year later because they were born a few days later. Those who are relatively young among their classmates are less able to sit still and listen. They are twice as likely to be given drugs to quiet them down.

"Typical considered pathological" is one interpretation of data on 378,000 children in Taiwan, a Chinese nation whose rates of ADHD are increasing (M.-H. Chen et al., 2016). Boys who were born in August, and hence entered kindergarten when they had just turned 5, were diagnosed with ADHD at the rate of 4.5 percent, whereas boys born in September, starting kindergarten when they were almost 6, were diagnosed at the rate of 2.8 percent. Diagnosis typically occurred years after kindergarten, but August birthday boys were at risk throughout their school years. (See Figure 11.4.)

This suggests that neurological immaturity, not neurological deficit, may be the problem. Changes in the school curriculum or adult expectations may be needed.

Regarding medication, one international difference is striking: In the United States, most children with ADHD are prescribed drugs; in most other developed nations, less than half of such children are medicated (Polanczyk et al., 2014).

Some interpret this as evidence that the United States treats problems with pills instead of helping children, parents, and teachers learn new behavior; others say that other nations need to catch up to the United States. The latter may be happening: Prescriptions are becoming more common for ADHD in England and elsewhere (Renoux et al., 2016; Bachmann et al., 2017).

A related issue regards the sex ratio: Boys are far more often diagnosed as having ADHD than girls, usually because their mothers and female teachers find them impossible to control. One review states "boys outnumber girls 3-to-1 in community samples and 9-to-1 in clinical samples" (Hasson & Fine, 2012, p. 190). Could typical male activity be one reason?

Treatment for ADHD involves (1) training for the family and the child, (2) special education for teachers, and (3) medication. But, as equifinality and multifinality stress, causes and symptoms vary, so treatment that helps one child may not work for another (Mulligan et al., 2013).

Drugs are one treatment method, but they are not always helpful. Adults sometimes disagree vehemently about whether a child should be medicated, as the following explains.

**Especially for Health Workers**  Parents ask that some medication be prescribed for their kindergarten child, who they say is much too active for them to handle. How do you respond? (see response, p. 328)

## Specific Learning Disorders

The DSM-5 diagnosis of **specific learning disorder** now includes problems in both perception and processing of information causing low achievement in reading, math, or writing (including spelling) (Lewandowski & Lovett, 2014). Disabilities in these areas undercut academic achievement, destroy self-esteem, and qualify a child for special education (according to U.S. law) or formal diagnosis (according to DSM-5). Hopefully, such children find (or are taught) ways to compensate, and other abilities shine.

**specific learning disorder**  A marked deficit in a particular area of learning that is not caused by an apparent physical disability, by an intellectual disability, or by an unusually stressful home environment.

# Drug Treatment for ADHD and Other Disorders

Because many adults are upset by children's moods and actions, and because any physician can write a prescription to quiet a child, thousands of U.S. children may be overmedicated. *But* because many parents do not recognize that their child needs help, or they are suspicious of drugs and psychologists (Moldavsky & Sayal, 2013; Rose, 2008), thousands of children may suffer needlessly.

Many child psychologists believe that the public discounts the devastation and lost learning that occur when a child's serious disorder is not recognized or treated. On the other hand, many parents are suspicious of drugs and psychotherapy and avoid recommended treatment (Gordon-Hollingsworth et al., 2015).

This controversy continues among experts. A leading book argues that ADHD is accurate for about one-third of the children diagnosed but that drug companies and doctors are far too quick to push pills, making ADHD "by far, the most misdiagnosed condition in American medicine" (Schwarz, 2016). A review of that book notes failure to mention the millions of people who have "experienced life-changing, positive results" from treatment—including medication (Zametkin & Solanto, 2017, p. 9).

In the United States, over 2 million people younger than 18 take prescription drugs to regulate emotions and behavior. The rates are about 14 percent for teenagers (Merikangas et al., 2013), about 10 percent for 6- to 11-year-olds, and less than 1 percent for 2- to 5-year-olds (Olfson et al., 2010).

In China, psychoactive medication is rarely prescribed for children: A Chinese child with ADHD symptoms is thought to need correction, not medication (Yang et al., 2013). An inattentive, overactive African child is more likely to be beaten than sent to the doctor. Wise or cruel?

The most common drug for ADHD is Ritalin (methylphenidate), but at least 20 other psychoactive drugs are prescribed for children to treat depression, anxiety, intellectual disability, autism spectrum disorder, disruptive mood dysregulation disorder, and many other conditions (see Figure 11.5). Some parents welcome the relief that drugs may provide; others refuse to medicate their children because they fear the consequences, among them later drug abuse or shorter height. Neither of those consequences has been proven. Indeed, long-term benefits including less drug abuse sometimes occur (Craig et al., 2015).

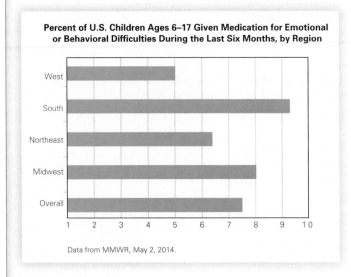

**Percent of U.S. Children Ages 6–17 Given Medication for Emotional or Behavioral Difficulties During the Last Six Months, by Region**

Data from MMWR, May 2, 2014.

**FIGURE 11.5**

**One Child in Every Classroom** Or maybe two, if the class has more than 20 students or is in Alabama. This figure shows the percent of 6- to 17-year-olds prescribed psychoactive drugs in the previous six months. About half of these children have been diagnosed with ADHD, and the rest have anxiety, mood, and other disorders. These data are averages, gathered from many communities. In fact, some schools, even in the South, have very few medicated children, and others, even in the West, have several in every class. The regional variations evident here are notable, but much more dramatic are rates by school, community, and doctor—some of whom are much quicker to medicate children than others.

Caitlin Teal Price/For The Washington Post via Getty Images

**A Family Learning** When Anthony Suppers was diagnosed with ADHD, his mother Michelle (shown here) realized she had it, too. That helps Anthony, because his mother knows how important it is to have him do his homework at his own desk as soon as he comes home from school.

Worrisome is that some research finds that medicating ADHD children increases the risk of severe mental illness in adulthood (Moran et al., 2015). On the other hand, one expert argues that teachers and doctors underdiagnose and undertreat African American children, and that increases another outcome—prison. If disruptive African American boys are punished, not treated, for ADHD symptoms, they may join the "school-to-prison pipeline" (Moody, 2016).

All professionals agree that finding the best drug at the right strength is difficult, in part because each child's genes and personality are unique, and in part because children's weight and metabolism change every year. Given all that, it is troubling that most children who are prescribed psychoactive drugs are seen only by a general practitioner, who does not follow up on dose and benefits (Patel et al., 2017).

Further, pharmaceutical companies may mislead parents about the benefits and liabilities of ADHD drugs. Most professionals believe that contextual interventions (instructing caregivers and schools on child management) should be tried before drugs (Daley et al., 2009; Leventhal, 2013). Many parents wonder whether professionals really understand.

Genes, culture, health care, education, religion, and stereotypes all affect ethnic and economic differences. As two experts explain, "disentangling these will be extremely valuable to improving culturally competent assessment in an increasingly diverse society" (Nigg & Barkley, 2014, p. 98). Given the emotional and practical implications of that tangle, opposing perspectives are not surprising.

---

The most commonly diagnosed learning disorder is **dyslexia**—unusual difficulty with reading. No single test accurately diagnoses dyslexia (or any learning disorder) because every academic achievement involves many distinct factors. One child with a reading disability might have trouble sounding out words but excel in comprehension; another child might have the opposite problem. Dozens of types and causes of dyslexia have been identified: No specific strategy helps every child (O'Brien et al., 2012). Historically, some children with dyslexia figured out themselves how to cope—as did Hans Christian Andersen and Winston Churchill.

Early theories hypothesized that visual difficulties—for example, letter reversals (reading *god* instead of *dog*) and mirror writing (*b* instead of *d*)—caused dyslexia. We now know that dyslexia more often originates with speech and hearing difficulties (Gabrieli, 2009; Swanson, 2013). An early warning occurs if a 3-year-old does not talk clearly or has not had a naming explosion. [**Developmental Link:** Language development in early childhood is explained in Chapter 6.]

Another common learning disorder is **dyscalculia,** unusual difficulty with math. For example, when asked to estimate the height of a normal room, second-graders with dyscalculia might answer "200 feet," or, when shown two cards, for example the 5 and 8 of hearts, and asked which is higher, children might correctly answer 8—but only after using their fingers to count the hearts on each card (Butterworth et al., 2011).

Some children have several learning disabilities; they may be diagnosed as having an intellectual disability (formerly called mental retardation). For them, as for children with only one learning disability, targeted help from teachers and guidance for parents makes life easier for the child and family and may remediate many learning problems (Crnic et al., 2017).

## Autism Spectrum Disorder

Of all the children with special needs, those with **autism spectrum disorder (ASD)** are especially puzzling. Causes and treatments are hotly disputed. Thomas Insel, director of the National Institute of Mental Health, describes the parents and other advocates of children with autism as "the most polarized, fragmented community I know" (quoted in Solomon, 2012, p. 280). Because of the controversies, variability, and uncertainty, many parents try several treatments, which may conflict with each other or may combine to be more helpful than any single treatment alone (Vivanti, 2017).

Learn more about how dyslexia affects children in **Video: Dyslexia: Expert and Children.**

**dyslexia** Unusual difficulty with reading; thought to be the result of some neurological underdevelopment.

**dyscalculia** Unusual difficulty with math, probably originating from a distinct part of the brain.

**Happy Reading** Those large prism glasses keep the letters from jumping around on the page, a boon for this 8-year-old French boy. Unfortunately, each child with dyslexia needs individualized treatment: These glasses help some, but not most, children who find reading difficult.

**autism spectrum disorder (ASD)** A developmental disorder marked by difficulty with social communication and interaction—including difficulty seeing things from another person's point of view—and restricted, repetitive patterns of behavior, interests, or activities.

**Video: Current Research into Autism Spectrum Disorder** explores why the causes of ASD are still largely unknown.

**Response for Health Workers** (from p. 325): Medication helps some hyperactive children but not all. It might be useful for this child, but other forms of intervention should be tried first. Compliment the parents on their concern about their child, but refer them to an expert in early childhood for an evaluation and recommendations. Behavior-management techniques geared to the particular situation, not medication, should be the first strategy.

Maarten de Boer/Getty Images

**Not a Cartoon** At age 3, Owen Suskind was diagnosed with autism. He stopped talking and spent hour after hour watching Disney movies. His father said his little boy "vanished," as chronicled in the Oscar-nominated documentary *Life Animated*. Now, at age 23 (shown here), Owen still loves cartoons, and he still has many symptoms of autism spectrum disorder. However, he also has learned to speak and has written a movie that reveals his understanding of himself, *The Land of the Lost Sidekicks*.

A century ago, autism was considered a rare disorder affecting fewer than 1 in 1,000 children with "an extreme aloneness that, whenever possible, disregards, ignores, shuts out anything . . . from the outside" (Kanner, 1943). Children with autism were usually nonverbal and severely impaired: They were considered profoundly *mentally retarded.* (The term "mental retardation," in DSM-IV, has been replaced with the term "intellectual disability" in DSM-5.) Treatment was thought to be hopeless: The child was fed and sheltered, sometimes at home or in an institution, and usually died young.

The DSM-5 expanded the term *autism* to *autism spectrum disorder,* which now includes mild, moderate, or severe categories. Children who were said to have Asperger syndrome now have "autism spectrum disorder without language or intellectual impairment" (American Psychiatric Association, 2013, p. 32).

No longer rare, many children are "on the spectrum." In the United States, among 8-year-olds, 1 child in every 68 (1 boy in 42; 1 girl in 189) is said to have ASD (MMWR, March 28, 2014). That's almost three times as many boys as girls. The other disparity is ethnic: The rates are higher among European American than Hispanic, Asian, or African American children.

Now, far more children are diagnosed with ASD, and far fewer with intellectual disability than twenty years ago. The reasons are disputed. The increase could be real: perhaps caused by the environment—chemicals in the food, pollution in the air and water. Or it could be that the rate of this disorder has not increased but that professionals are now aware of ASD and, in the United States, specialized education is now publicly funded (Klinger et al., 2014).

All children with ASD find it difficult to understand the emotions of others, which makes them feel alien, like "an anthropologist on Mars," as Temple Grandin, an educator and writer with ASD, expressed it (quoted in Sacks, 1995). Consequently, they are less likely to talk or play with other children, and they are delayed in developing theory of mind. However, they may have exceptional talents.

Some children with severe ASD never speak, rarely socialize, and play for hours with one object (such as a spinning top or a toy train). More often, however, children with ASD are less severely impaired. They have limited verbal and social skills but some strengths, such as drawing or geometry. Many (46 percent) score average or above on IQ tests (MMWR, March 28, 2014).

This wide range of abilities, with some children on the spectrum gifted as well as impaired, illustrates neurodiversity (Graf et al., 2017). Because of their diverse abilities, adults should neither be dazzled by their talents nor despairing at their deficiencies. Children with autism spectrum disorder are an extreme example of multiple intelligences: None of us excels at all nine.

Many scientists are searching for biological ways to detect ASD early in life, perhaps with blood tests or brain scans before age 1. At the moment, behavioral signs are the best we have. Most children with ASD show signs in early infancy (no social smile, for example, or less gazing at faces and eyes than most toddlers). Some improve by age 3; others deteriorate (Klinger et al., 2014).

Many children with ASD have an opposite problem—too much neurological activity, not too little. Their brains grow too fast, and by age 2 their heads are larger than average. Their sensory cortex is not only thicker than most but is hypersensitive, making them unusually upset by noise, light, and other sensations. Literally hundreds of genes and dozens of brain abnormalities are more common in people diagnosed with autism than in the general population.

As more children are diagnosed, some people wonder whether ASD is a disorder needing a cure or whether, instead, our culture needs to adjust to a society in which not everyone is outgoing, flexible, and a fluent talker—the opposite of people with autism. That question underlies the idea of neurodiversity. Instead of trying to make all children alike, we might welcome the neurological variation of human beings (Kapp et al., 2013; Silberman, 2015).

Neurodiversity is a logical extension of the criticism of IQ tests. If there are multiple intelligences, then it is restrictive and prejudicial to expect everyone to be the same. Some people are impaired in interpersonal intelligence (one of Gardner's nine), and they may suffer from ASD. But those same people might have other strengths to be appreciated, even celebrated.

The neurodiversity perspective leads to new criticisms of the many treatments for autism spectrum disorder. When a child is diagnosed with ASD, parental responses vary from irrational hope to deep despair, from blaming doctors and chemical additives to feeling guilty for their genes, for their behavior during pregnancy, or for the circumstances they allowed at their child's birth. Many parents sue schools, or doctors, or the government; many spend all of their money and change their lives; many subject their children to treatments that are, at best, harmless, and at worst, painful and even fatal.

A sympathetic observer describes one child who was medicated with

> Abilify, Topamax, Seroquel, Prozac, Ativan, Depakote, trazodone, Risperdal, Anafranil, Lamictal, Benadryl, melatonin, and the homeopathic remedy, Calms Forté. Every time I saw her, the meds were being adjusted again . . . [he also describes] physical interventions—putting children in hyperbaric oxygen chambers, putting them in tanks with dolphins, giving them blue-green algae, or megadosing them on vitamins . . . usually neither helpful nor harmful, though they can have dangers, are certainly disorienting, and cost a lot.

*[Solomon, 2012, pp. 229, 270]*

> **THINK CRITICALLY:** Many adults are socially inept, insensitive to other people's emotions, and poor at communication—might they have been diagnosed as on the spectrum if they had been born more recently?

Diagnosis and treatment are difficult; an intervention that seems to help one child proves worthless for another. It is known, however, that biology is crucial (genes, copy number abnormalities, birth complications, prenatal injury, perhaps chemicals during fetal or infant development). Family nurture is not the cause.

---

### WHAT HAVE YOU LEARNED?

**1.** When would an educator give an aptitude test instead of an achievement test?

**2.** Should traditional IQ tests be discarded? Why or why not?

**3.** What might be the explanation for the Flynn effect?

**4.** Should brain scans replace traditional intelligence tests? Why or why not?

**5.** What is the difference between multifinality and equifinality?

**6.** Why is medication used for some children with ADHD?

**7.** What is the difference between ADHD and normal child behavior?

**8.** What are dyslexia, dyscalculia, and dysgraphia?

**9.** How might an adult have a learning disorder that was never diagnosed?

**10.** What are the symptoms of autism spectrum disorder?

**11.** Who is likely to welcome the concept of neurodiversity?

---

## Special Education

The overlap of the biosocial, cognitive, and psychosocial domains is evident to developmentalists, as is the need for parents, teachers, therapists, and researchers to work together to help each child. However, deciding whether a child should be educated unlike the other children is not straightforward, nor is it closely related to individual needs. Parents, schools, and therapists often disagree about special education or even when and whether help is needed, as illustrated in A Case to Study on the following page.

## Unexpected and Odd

Scientists have traced the relationship between home, school, and academic achievement of more than 3,000 British children, beginning at age 3 and continuing until age 16. From what the scientists knew about gender, parents' education, and family income at age 3, they predicted test scores in adolescence. Because SES has such powerful effect on child achievement, most of their predictions were quite accurate.

However, a few children were markedly above or below expectations, such as low-SES boys who did well and high-SES girls who scored low. Researchers then delved into 50 cases, analyzing past data, visiting homes, and interviewing parents, teachers, and the adolescents themselves. Thus, they combined quantitative and qualitative methods (described in Chapter 1) to figure out why children achieved as they did (Siraj & Mayo, 2014).

Steven is a low-SES boy "succeeding against the odds." He is the second-born child of Carol, who cleaned houses for a living before becoming a mother, and John, whose salary as a postman was the sole income support for his wife and children. Both parents left school as soon as they could, at age 16. The interviewer reports that people find Steven a bit "odd," but that he is "bright, sweet-natured, and witty in a slightly awkward way" (p. 67).

As an infant, Steven

> never slept for more than twenty minutes at a time. If Carol was not holding him he would cry and scream. He never babbled or tried to talk, he would just grunt or scream. . . . He was always demanding her attention, clinging to her, wanting to be picked up and to be held. . . .
>
> Despite the screaming and clinging, Steven started playgroup when he turned two. . . . Typically when Steven saw another child, he would either slap or bite. At first, Carol would follow him around as he wandered through the room. She would try to stop him from hurting other children. . . . the other adults in the playgroup told her to just chill out and let the children work it out by themselves. So she did and he bit another child so badly that he drew blood. . . .
>
> The only child he did seem comfortable with was Oliver, a severely autistic boy. . . . Carol wondered if Steven's difficulties perhaps were similar to Oliver's autism. But she never dared voice her concern to anyone. She was afraid that once he had a disorder label attached to him his teachers would no longer feel they need to help him. . . .
>
> Finally, when Steven was two and a half, his hearing was tested. . . . Steven could barely hear. . . . An operation restoring his hearing followed just before his third birthday.
>
> [pp. 69–71]

At that point, the tantrums stopped, aggression receded, and speech began. Steven attended nursery school, five days a week.

(This was in England, where preschool is free for all 3- to 5-year-olds.) He received speech therapy, and Carol and Steven's older sister read to him for hours a day. His first two years as deaf, mute, and aggressive were not his only problems, however.

In elementary school, Steven fell behind, and his behavior "deteriorated." The teachers did not seem worried. But the test scores of several 7-year-old boys, including Steven, were very low.

> The headmistress swiftly set up a special education class. . . . Steven reports that she [his special needs teacher] was strict but fair. She took their questions seriously and taught them to patiently trace back their steps to determine what they found difficult or confusing. . . . When Steven returned to his regular class after nine weeks, his teachers and Carol were amazed at how much his performance and attitude had improved.
>
> [p. 71]

From then on, Steven became a good student. At age 12 he reacted to his parents' bitter divorce by deciding to separate school work from family life, telling his father not to put Mum down and to stop asking the children to take sides.

In adolescence, Steven tested within the top 20 percent in English and the top 5 percent in math. He relates well to both parents, particularly his mother, who always encouraged him to learn. He helps his older sister with her schoolwork, and he enjoys talking with Ethan, his best friend, for hours. That friend habitually carried a book with him. Following Ethan's example, Steven now carries something to read wherever he goes because he says that reading helps him with imagination, concentration, and relaxation.

Steven has his own computer, bought with his paper route earnings. Carol set it up on a desk near the kitchen, so Steven is not isolated from family interaction and so she can keep an eye on his work and his time.

His teachers say they welcome his inquisitive attention and questions—although the latter can be annoying. They say he "should have no trouble whatsoever getting into a good university and obtaining an advanced degree" (p. 69). Everyone seems to enjoy his company, especially Carol, who says "his poor attempts at telling a joke will often make you laugh until you have tears streaming down your face" (p. 67).

Steven credits Carol's dedication and that special education teacher with his success. His case is a wonderful example of the truism that children with special needs can get better with time and that social context is crucial. This case raises another question: How many other children like Steven had mothers who were less devoted, and teachers who were less skilled, and thus never exceeded expectations?

## Labels, Laws, and Learning

The distinction between typical and atypical is not clear-cut (the first principle of developmental psychopathology). That realization led to a series of reforms in the treatment and education of children with special needs in the United States. According to the 1975 Education of All Handicapped Children Act, all children can learn, and all must be educated in the **least restrictive environment (LRE).**

That law has been revised several times, but the goal remains the same. "No restrictions" means that children with special needs should not be educated apart from other children unless remediation within the regular classroom has been tried and failed. Further, every child merits schooling: None should be considered uneducable.

Consequently, LRE means keeping most children with special needs within a regular class (a practice once called *mainstreaming*) rather than in a special classroom or school. A child may be sent regularly to a *resource room,* with a teacher who provides targeted tutoring. A class may be an *inclusion class,* in which children with special needs are "included" in the general classroom, with "appropriate aids and services" (ideally from a trained teacher who works with the regular teacher).

A more recent educational strategy is called **response to intervention (RTI)** (Al Otaiba et al., 2015; Jimerson et al., 2016; Ikeda, 2012). First, all children are taught specific skills—for instance, learning the sounds that various letters make. Then the children are tested, and those who did not master the skill receive special "intervention"—practice and individualized teaching, within the regular class. Then they are tested again, and, if need be, intervention occurs again. Only when children do not respond adequately to repeated, focused intervention are they referred for special education.

If, after testing and consulting the family, a child is found to need special education, the school proposes an **individual education plan (IEP).** The idea is that schools need to "design learning pathways for each individual sufferer." The label, or specific diagnosis, is supposed to lead to effective remediation. Yet this may not actually occur: Educators do not always know the best way to remediate learning difficulties (Butterworth & Kovas, 2013).

Why don't educators know what to do? A major problem is that most research on remediation focuses on the less common problems. For example, in the United States, "research funding in 2008–2009 for autism spectrum disorder was 31 times greater than for dyslexia and 540 times greater than for dyscalculia" (Butterworth & Kovas, 2013, p. 304). Nor do educational categories necessarily reflect actual needs.

As Figure 11.6 shows, the proportion of children designated with special needs in the United States rose from 10 percent in 1980 to 13 percent in 2014, in part because more children are called "learning disabled" or "speech impaired" (Snyder & Dillow, 2015). It could be that there are more brain-damaging chemicals in the air, food, or water (as with lead in Flint, Michigan, examined in Chapter 8) or that families are less supportive.

However, many observers do not believe that the actual number of children with disorders has

**least restrictive environment (LRE)** A legal requirement that children with special needs be assigned to the most general educational context in which they can be expected to learn.

**response to intervention (RTI)** An educational strategy intended to help children who demonstrate below-average achievement in early grades, using special intervention.

**individual education plan (IEP)** A document that specifies educational goals and plans for a child with special needs.

**All Together Now** Kiemel Lamb *(top center)* leads children with ASD in song, a major accomplishment. For many of these children, music is soothing, words are difficult, and handholding in a group is almost impossible.

**Observation Quiz** What is the adult/child ratio here? (see answer, p. 333) ↓

The Tuscaloosa News, Dusty Compton/AP Images

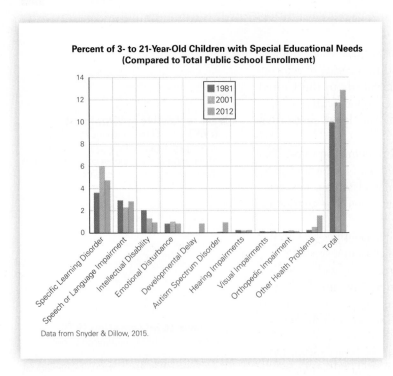

Percent of 3- to 21-Year-Old Children with Special Educational Needs
(Compared to Total Public School Enrollment)

Data from Snyder & Dillow, 2015.

**FIGURE 11.6**

**Nature or Nurture** Communities have always had some children with special needs, with physical, emotional, and neurological disorders of many kinds. In some eras, and even today in some nations, the education of such children was neglected. Indeed, many children were excluded from normal life. Now in the United States, every child is entitled to school. As you see, the specific label for such children has changed over the past decades, because of nurture, not nature. Thus, teratogens before and after birth, coupled with changing parental and community practice, probably caused the rise in autism spectrum disorder and developmental delay, the decrease in intellectual disability, and the fluctuation in learning disorders apparent here.

increased. Instead, teachers may be more likely to refer children who are hard to control, and parents may be more likely to want their children in smaller classes with less pressure to score high on tests. A more troubling explanation is implicit prejudice, since more schoolchildren are non-White or non-native speakers, and a disproportionate number of them are in special education (Harry & Klingner, 2014).

Internationally, the connection between special needs and education varies, again more for cultural and historical reasons than for child-related ones (Rotatori et al., 2014). In many African and Latin American nations, almost no child with special needs receives targeted public education; in many Asian nations, diagnosis depends primarily on physical disability.

The U.S. school system designates more children as having special needs than does any other nation: Whether this is a reason for national pride or shame depends on one's perspective. Some U.S. experts fear that the perspective of neurodiversity, RTI, and inclusion may actually reduce the help offered to children with special needs. If everyone is thought to be special in some way, will that neglect the very particular needs of some children (Kauffman et al., 2017)?

## Early Intervention

One conclusion from all of the research on special education is that diagnosis and intervention often occur too late, or not at all. The numbers of children in public schools who are designated as needing special education increase as children grow older, which is the opposite of what would occur if early intervention were successful. This is apparent in each of the disorders we have discussed.

To be specific, autism was not considered a reason for special education until passage of the Individuals with Disabilities Educational Act of 1997 (IDEA). There is still no separate education category for ADHD, though that disorder is most troubling to parents and teachers. To receive special services, teachers designate children with ADHD as having a specific learning disorder or as being emotionally disturbed. Since most disorders are comorbid, the particular special needs category chosen by a school psychologist may not be the diagnosis given by a private psychologist.

One result is that teachers, therapists, and parents may work at cross-purposes to educate a child. This problem may be greatest with autism spectrum disorder, since there are many types of ASD and many theories about what to do (Vivanti, 2017).

Those with ADHD have a similar problem. Even at age 4, children with ADHD symptoms tend to have difficulty making and keeping friends. Longitudinal research finds that poor early peer relationships worsen their ADHD more than ADHD characteristics worsen their peer relationships (Stenseng et al., 2016). A focus on helping them pay attention to schoolwork may be misplaced. A more important target for early schooling may be to help a young child learn how to be a good friend.

Traditionally, specific learning disorders were diagnosed *only* if a child had difficulty with a particular school subject that made his or her achievement scores at least two years below IQ (as a 9-year-old with an average IQ who read at the first-grade level). Also, for the diagnosis to be made, the child had to have adequate hearing and vision, with no other explanation for delayed reading, (such as that the family was abusive or the home language was not English).

All this meant a "wait to fail" approach, that learning disorders were not diagnosed until third grade or later, even though signs were apparent long before. It also provided no special help for children with dyslexia whose sensory, familial, or cultural problems affected their reading. This meant that poor learning strategies, low self-esteem, and hatred of school might already be established in first and second grade. As one expert says, "We need early identification, and . . . early intervention. If you wait until third grade, kids give up" (Shaywitz, cited in Stern, 2015, p. 1466).

A similar problem occurs with autism spectrum disorder. You read that signs of autism appear in infancy, but children are not usually diagnosed until age 4, on average (MMWR, March 28, 2014). This is long after many parents have noticed something amiss in their child, and years after the most effective intervention can begin.

In fact, some children diagnosed with autism spectrum disorder before age 4 no longer have it later on—an outcome that seems to be related to intense social intervention in the early years (Kroncke et al., 2016). Even with early intervention, most children with ASD have some deficits in adulthood, but the fact that some children overcome social and cognitive symptoms is another argument for early intervention. Plasticity of the brain and behavior is especially evident with special-needs children.

## Gifted and Talented

Children who are unusually gifted are often thought to have special educational needs, although federal laws in the United States do not include them as a special category. Instead, each U.S. state selects and educates gifted and talented children in a particular way.

Some children score very high on IQ tests, which qualifies them as gifted, and some are *divergent thinkers,* who find many solutions and even more questions for every problem. These two characteristics sometimes coincide in the same child, but not always. Instead, a high-IQ child might be a *convergent thinker,* quickly finding one, and only one, correct answer for every problem and being impatient, not only with children who think more slowly but also with children who are more creative.

This raises a question for educators: Should children who are unusually intelligent, talented, or imaginative be home-schooled, skipped, segregated, or enriched? Each of these solutions has been tried and found lacking.

Historically, most children did not attend school. If a family recognized their gifted or talented child, they taught the child themselves or hired a special coach or tutor. For example, Mozart composed music at age 3 and Picasso created works of art at age 4. Both boys had fathers who recognized their talent. Mozart's father transcribed his earliest pieces and toured Europe with his gifted son; Picasso's father removed him from school in second grade so that he could create all day.

Although intense early education nourished their talent, neither Mozart nor Picasso had a happy adult life. Mozart had a poor understanding of math and money. He had six children, only two of whom survived infancy, and he died in debt at age 35. Picasso regretted never learning to read or write. He married at age 17 and had a total of four children by three women.

**Answer to Observation Quiz** (from p. 331) About 1-to-1. The advantage of segregated classes for children with special needs is a low adult/child ratio.

Steve Granitz/Getty Images

**And Tomorrow?** The education of gifted children is controversial, as is the future of 8-year-old Sunny Pawar, "just a normal boy" from the slums of Mumbai and also a talented star in *Lion,* a 2016 Oscar-nominated film made in Australia. After a worldwide tour to promote the film, he returned to his one-room home and attends school, where he gets none of the perks of being a movie star. What next?

**acceleration** Educating gifted children alongside other children of the same mental, not chronological, age.

When school attendance became universal about a century ago, gifted children were allowed to skip early grades and join other children of the same mental age, not their chronological age. This practice was called **acceleration.** Today, it is rarely done because many accelerated children never learned how to get along with others. As one woman remembers:

> Nine-year-old little girls are so cruel to younger girls. I was much smaller than them, of course, and would have done anything to have a friend. Although I could cope with the academic work very easily, emotionally I wasn't up to it. Maybe it was my fault and I was asking to be picked on. I was a weed at the edge of the playground.

> *[Rachel, quoted in Freeman, 2010, p. 27]*

Calling herself a weed suggests that she never overcame her conviction that she was less cherished than the other children. Her intellectual needs may have been met by skipping two grades, but her emotional and social needs were severely neglected.

My own father skipped three grades, graduating from high school at age 14. Because he attended a one-room school, and because he was the middle child of five, his emotional and social needs were met until he began college—almost failing because of his immaturity. He recovered, but some other children do not. A chilling example comes from:

> Sufiah Yusof [who] started her maths degree at Oxford [the leading University in England] in 2000, at the age of 13. She too had been dominated and taught by her father. But she ran away the day after her final exam. She was found by police but refused to go home, demanding of her father in an email: "Has it ever crossed your mind that the reason I left home was because I've finally had enough of 15 years of physical and emotional abuse?" Her father claimed she'd been abducted and brainwashed. She refuses to communicate with him. She is now a very happy, high-class, high-earning prostitute.

> *[Freeman, 2010, p. 286]*

The fate of creative children may be worse than intellectually gifted ones. They joke in class, resist drudgery, ignore homework, and bedevil their teachers. They may become innovators, inventors, and creative forces in the future, but they also may become drug addicts or school dropouts. They may find it hard to earn a degree or get a steady job, because they are eager to try new things and feel stifled by normal life. Among the well-known creative geniuses who were poor students were Albert Einstein, Sigmund Freud, Isaac Newton, Oliver Sachs, Steve Jobs, and hundreds of thousands of others, probably some of whom you know personally.

One such person was Charles Darwin. His "school reports complained unendingly that he wasn't interested in studying, only shooting, riding, and beetle-collecting" (Freeman, 2010, p. 283). At the behest of his physician father, Darwin entered college to study medicine, but he found the instruction dull and dropped out. Without a degree, he began his famous five-year trip around South America at age 22, collecting specimens and developing the theory of evolution—which disputed conventional religious dogma as only a highly creative person could do.

Since both acceleration and intense home schooling have led to later social problems, a third education strategy has become popular, at least in the United States. Children who are bright, talented, and/or creative—all the same age but each with special abilities—are taught as a group in their own separate class. Ideally, such children are neither bored nor lonely; each is challenged and appreciated by classmates.

There is research that supports the idea that some children have talents and abilities that need to be nurtured during middle childhood. Children with exceptional musical, mathematical, or athletic gifts who are allowed to practice their talents with others who challenge them develop specialized brain structures (Moreno et al., 2015). Since plasticity means that children learn whatever their context teaches, perhaps some children need gifted-and-talented classes.

Such classes require unusual teachers, bright and creative, able to appreciate divergent thinking and to challenge the very intelligent. They must be flexible in individualizing instruction.

For example, a 7-year-old artist may need freedom, guidance, and inspiration for magnificent art but also patient, step-by-step instruction in sounding out simple words. Similarly, a 7-year-old classmate who already reads at the twelfth-grade level might have immature social skills, so the teacher must find another child to be a friend and then help both of them share, compromise, and take turns.

However, the argument against gifted-and-talented classes is that every child needs such teachers, no matter what the child's abilities or disabilities. If each school district, and sometimes each school, hires and assigns teachers, as occurs in the United States, then the best teachers may have the most able students. Should it be the opposite?

The trend for gifted students to have gifted teachers is furthered by *tracking*, putting children with special needs together, and allowing private or charter schools to select only certain students. The problem is worse if the gifted students are in a separate class within the same school as the other students. Then all of the students suffer: Some feel inferior and others superior—with neither group motivated to try new challenges and no one learning how to work together (Herrmann et al., 2016; Van Houtte, 2016).

Mainstreaming, IEPs, and so on were developed when parents and educators saw that segregation of children with special needs led to less learning and impaired adult lives. The same may happen if gifted and talented children are separated from the rest. Ideal school types are controversial and are discussed in the next chapter.

Some nations (China, Finland, Scotland, and many others) educate all children together, assuming that all children could become high achievers if they put in the effort and are guided by effective teachers. Every special and ordinary form of education can benefit by applying what we know about children's minds (De Corte, 2013). That is the topic of the next chapter.

**WHAT HAVE YOU LEARNED?**

**1.** What do mainstreaming and inclusion have in common?

**2.** Why is response to intervention considered an alternative to special education?

**3.** Why is it easier to help a child with special needs at age 6 than at age 10?

**4.** Why might children who have high IQs no longer skip grades?

**5.** What are the arguments for and against special classes for gifted children?

# SUMMARY

### A Healthy Time

1. Middle childhood is a time of steady growth and few serious illnesses. During these years, health habits, including daily oral care and good nutrition, protect children from later health problems.

2. Physical activity aids health and joy in many ways. However, current social and environmental conditions make informal neighborhood play uncommon and school exercise less prevalent than formerly. Children who most need physical activity may be least likely to have it.

3. Childhood obesity is a worldwide epidemic. Although the size and shape of a person's body is partly genetic, too little exercise and too much unhealthy food are the main reasons that today's youth are heavier than their counterparts of 50 years ago. Parents and policies share the blame.

4. The incidence of asthma is increasing overall. The causes include genes and the microbiome; the triggers include specific allergens such as pollution and house dust.

5. Brains continue to develop during middle childhood. Experience enhances coordination of brain impulses, and selective attention develops as children play.

### Children with Special Brains and Bodies

6. Developmental psychopathology uses an understanding of typical development to inform the study of unusual development. Four general lessons have emerged: Abnormality is normal; disability changes over time; a condition may get better or worse later on; diagnosis depends on context.

7. IQ tests quantify intellectual aptitude. Mental age rises as chronological age does, with children whose mental age is more than or less than their chronological age having high or low IQ scores. Most IQ tests emphasize language and logic, and they predict school achievement. Scores change over time, as culture and experience enhance particular abilities.

8. Achievement tests measure accomplishment, often in specific academic areas. Aptitude and achievement are correlated, both for individuals and for nations, and have risen in the past decades as Flynn documented.

9. Critics of IQ testing contend that intelligence is manifested in multiple ways, which makes g (general intelligence) too narrow and limited. Some psychologists stress that people have multiple intelligences, including creative and practical abilities. Gardner describes nine distinct intelligences.

10. Children with attention-deficit/hyperactivity disorder (ADHD) have potential problems in three areas: inattention, impulsiveness, and activity. Stimulant medication helps many children with ADHD to concentrate and learn, but any drug use by children is controversial.

11. DSM-5 recognizes learning disorders that impair learning in school, specifically dyslexia (unusual difficulty with reading), dyscalculia (unusual difficulty with math), and dysgraphia (unusual difficulty with writing).

12. Children on the autism spectrum typically have problems with social interaction and language. They often exhibit restricted, repetitive patterns of behavior, interests, and activities. Many causes are hypothesized. Autism spectrum disorder (ASD) originates in the brain, with genetic and prenatal influences.

### Special Education

13. About 13 percent of all school-age children in the United States receive special education services. These begin with an IEP (individual education plan) and assignment to the least restrictive environment (LRE), usually within the regular classroom.

14. Diagnosis and special education typically occur much later than seems best. Parents, teachers, and professionals need to come together to help children with special needs.

15. Some children are unusually intelligent, talented, or creative, and some states and nations provide special education for them. The traditional strategy—skipping a grade—no longer seems beneficial, but special classes for gifted and talented children are controversial.

# KEY TERMS

middle childhood (p. 312)
selective attention (p. 313)
reaction time (p. 314)
childhood overweight (p. 315)
childhood obesity (p. 315)
asthma (p. 316)
developmental psychopathology (p. 320)
comorbid (p. 320)

aptitude (p. 320)
intelligence (p. 320)
achievement test (p. 321)
Flynn effect (p. 321)
multiple intelligences (p. 322)
neurodiversity (p. 323)
multifinality (p. 323)
equifinality (p. 323)

attention-deficit/hyperactivity disorder (ADHD) (p. 324)
specific learning disorder (p. 325)
dyslexia (p. 327)
dyscalculia (p. 327)
autism spectrum disorder (ASD) (p. 327)

least restrictive environment (LRE) (p. 331)
response to intervention (RTI) (p. 331)
individual education plan (IEP) (p. 331)
acceleration (p. 334)

## APPLICATIONS

1. Compare play spaces for children in different neighborhoods—ideally, urban, suburban, and rural areas. Note size, safety, and use. How might children's weight and motor skills be affected by the differences you observe?

2. Should every teacher be skilled at teaching children with a wide variety of needs, or should some teachers specialize in particular kinds of learning difficulties? Ask professors in your education department. Then ask parents of children with special needs.

3. Parents of children with special needs often consult Internet sources. Pick one disorder and find 10 sites that describe causes and educational solutions. How valid, how accurate, and how objective is the information? What disagreements do you find? How might parents react to the information provided?

4. How inclusive are the elementary schools (public, charter, and private) in your community? Get data on ethnic, economic, and ability grouping. Then analyze whether this is best.

# Middle Childhood:
## Cognitive Development

## What Will You Know?

1. Does cognition improve naturally with age, or is teaching crucial to its development?
2. Why do children use slang, curse words, and bad grammar?
3. What type of school is best during middle childhood?

+ **Building on Theory**
Piaget and Concrete Thought
Vygotsky and Culture
A CASE TO STUDY: Is She Going to Die?
Information Processing
INSIDE THE BRAIN: Coordination and Capacity
Memory
Control Processes

+ **Language**
Vocabulary
Speaking Two Languages
Differences in Language Learning
OPPOSING PERSPECTIVES: Happiness or High Grades?

+ **Teaching and Learning**
International Schooling
Schooling in the United States
Choices and Complications

**A**t age 9, I wanted a puppy. My parents said no; we already had Dusty, a big family dog. I dashed off a poem, promising "to brush his hair as smooth as silk" and "to feed him milk." Twice wrong. Poor cadence, and cow's milk makes puppies sick. But my father praised my poem; I got Taffy, a blonde cocker spaniel.

At age 10, my daughter Sarah wanted her ears pierced. I said no, it would be unfair to her three older sisters, who had had to wait for ear-piercing until they were teenagers. Sarah wrote an affidavit and persuaded all three to sign "No objection." She got gold posts.

Children's wishes differ by cohort and their strategies by context. I knew that my father loved my childish poems, and Sarah knew that my husband and I wouldn't budge for doggerel but that signed documents might work. Sarah and I were both typical children, wanting something that we did not need and figuring out how to get it. Depending on their circumstances, children learn to divide fractions, text friends, memorize baseball stats, load rifles, and persuade parents.

This chapter describes the cognitive accomplishments that make all that possible. We begin with Piaget, Vygotsky, and information processing. Then we discuss applications of those theories to language and formal education, nationally and internationally. Everyone agrees that extensive learning occurs; adults disagree sharply about what and how to teach.

## Building on Theory

Learning is rapid. By age 11, some children beat their elders at chess, play music that adults pay to hear, publish poems, and win trophies for spelling or sports or some other learned skill. Others scavenge on the streets or kill in wars, mastering lessons that no child should know. How do they learn so quickly?

## Piaget and Concrete Thought

Piaget called middle childhood the time for **concrete operational thought,** characterized by new logical abilities. *Operational* comes from the Latin verb *operare,* meaning "to work; to produce." By calling this period operational, Piaget

Left: Marc Romanelli/Getty Images
Top: PhotoAlto/Jerome Gorin/Getty Images

**concrete operational thought** Piaget's term for the ability to reason logically about direct experiences and perceptions.

Sean De Burca/Getty Images

**How the Mind Works** The official dictionary used for the Scripps National Spelling Bee has 472,000 words, which makes rote memorization impossible. Instead, winners recognize patterns, roots, and exceptions—all possible in middle childhood.

**classification** The logical principle that things can be organized into groups (or categories or classes) according to some characteristic that they have in common.

emphasized productive thinking. Piaget's theory is a classic stage theory: Concrete operational thinking is the stage after preoperational thought and before formal operational cognition.

Piaget recognized that children do not leap wholesale to a new conceptual level but advance step by step within each stage. He called this *horizontal décalage*—the idea that at each level certain concepts appear in sequence over months or even years.

One example is with conservation (explained in Chapter 9). Preoperational children's focus on appearance prevents them from grasping conservation, but concrete operational children understand it. They apply it in sequence to liquids, length, and so on.

For instance, 7-year-olds typically know that two identical balls of clay contain the same amount when one is rolled into a long "snake." About two years later, children know that weight is conserved no matter what the shape. That is horizontal décalage.

In middle childhood, thinking is *concrete* operational, grounded in actual experience (like the solid concrete of a cement sidewalk). Concrete thinking arises from what is visible, tangible, and real, not abstract and theoretical (as at the next stage, formal operational thought). Children become more systematic, objective, scientific—and therefore educable.

## A Hierarchy of Categories

One logical operation is **classification,** the organization of things into groups (or *categories* or *classes*) according to some characteristic that they share. For example, *family* includes parents, siblings, and cousins. Other common classes are animals, toys, and food. Each class includes some elements and excludes others; each is part of a hierarchy.

Food, for instance, is an overarching category, with the next-lower level of the hierarchy being meat, grains, fruits, and so on. Most subclasses can be further divided: Meat includes poultry, beef, and pork, each of which can be divided again. Adults grasp that items at the bottom of a classification hierarchy belong to every higher level: Bacon is always pork, meat, and food. They also grasp that the higher categories include many items—that most food, meat, and pork are not bacon. This mental operation of moving up and down the hierarchy is beyond preoperational children but aids learning in school children.

Piaget devised many classification experiments. In one, he showed a child a bunch of nine flowers—seven yellow daisies and two white roses. Then the child is asked, "Are there more daisies or more flowers?" Until about age 7, most children answer, "More daisies." The youngest children offer no justification, but some 6-year-olds explain that "there are more yellow ones than white ones" or "because daisies are daisies, they aren't flowers" (Piaget et al., 2001). By age 8, most children can classify: "More flowers than daisies," they say.

## Application to Math

**seriation** The concept that things can be arranged in a logical series, such as the number sequence or the alphabet.

Another example of concrete logic is **seriation**, the knowledge that things can be arranged in a logical *series*. Seriation is crucial for using (not merely memorizing) the alphabet or the number sequence. By age 5, most children can count up to 100, but because they do not yet grasp seriation, they cannot correctly estimate where any particular two-digit number would be placed on a line that starts at 0 and ends at 100 (Meadows, 2006).

Logic allows children to understand math. A study of 6- and 7-year-olds testing their understanding of conservation of liquids found that those who understood it were much better at adding and subtracting than children of the same age who did not understand (Wubbena, 2013).

Indeed, every logical concept helps with math. Concrete operational thinkers begin to understand that 15 is always 15 (conservation), that numbers from 20 to 29 are all in the 20s (classification), that 134 is less than 143 (seriation), and that because $5 \times 3 = 15$, it follows that $15 \div 5$ must equal 3 (reversibility). By age 11, children use mental categories and subcategories flexibly, inductively, and simultaneously, unlike at age 7.

## Vygotsky and Culture

Like Piaget, Vygotsky felt that educators should consider children's thought processes, not just the products. He also believed that middle childhood was a time for much learning, with the specifics dependent on the family, school, and culture.

Vygotsky appreciated children's curiosity and creativity. For that reason, he believed that an educational system based on rote memorization rendered the child "helpless in the face of any sensible attempt to apply any of this acquired knowledge" (Vygotsky, 1994a, pp. 356–357).

### The Role of Instruction

Unlike Piaget, who thought children would discover most concepts themselves, Vygotsky stressed instruction from teachers and other mentors who provided the scaffold between potential and knowledge by engaging each child in his or her zone of proximal development. [**Developmental Link:** Vygotsky's theory is discussed in Chapters 2 and 9.]

Vygotsky would not be surprised at one finding of recent research: Internationally as well as nationally, children who begin school at age 4 or 5, not 6 or 7, tend to be ahead in academic achievement compared to those who enter later. This effect is still apparent at age 15, although not in every nation (Sprietsma, 2010). Vygotsky would explain the variation in impact by noting that in some nations early education is far more interactive, and hence better at guided participation, than in others.

Play with peers, screen time, dinner with families, neighborhood play—every experience, from birth on, teaches a child, according to Vygotsky. On their own, children gradually become more logical, but Vygotsky thought mentoring was helpful. Thus, when children are taught, they can master logical arguments (even counterfactual ones) by age 11. For example, they know that *if* birds can fly, and *if* elephants are birds, *then* elephants can fly (Christoforides et al., 2016). Vygotsky emphasized that the lessons a child learns vary by culture and school, not merely maturation.

### Cultural Variations

Culture and context affect more than academic learning. A stunning example comes from Varanasi, a city in northeast India. Many Varanasi children have an extraordinary sense of spatial orientation: They know whether they are facing north or south, even when they are inside a room with no windows. In one

**Math and Money** Third-grader Perry Akootchook understands basic math, so he might beat his mother at "spinning for money," shown here. Compare his concrete operational skills with those of a typical preoperational child, who would not be able to play this game and might give a dime for a nickel.

⬤ **Especially for Teachers** How might Piaget's and Vygotsky's ideas help in teaching geography to a class of third-graders? (see response, p. 345)

**Girls Can't Do It** As Vygotsky recognized, children learn whatever their culture teaches. Fifty years ago, girls were in cooking and sewing classes. No longer. This 2012 photo shows 10-year-olds Kamrin and Caitlin in a Kentucky school, preparing for a future quite different from that of their grandmothers.

# Is She Going to Die?

Philip is a delightful 7-year-old, with many intellectual skills. He speaks French to his mother and English to everyone else; he can already read fluently and calculate Pokemon trades. He is well liked, because he knows how to cooperate when he plays soccer, to use "bathroom words" to make his peers laugh, and to use polite phrases to make adults appreciate him. He switches easily from peer talk to teacher talk, and from French to English. All of this shows that his mind is developing just as it should in middle childhood.

Last year, his mother, Dora, needed open-heart surgery. She and her husband, Craig, told Philip who would take him to and from school and who would cook his dinner while she was recovering. Dora made Craig do the talking, because she was afraid she would cry when she spoke.

Philip was matter-of-fact, not emotional. He had few questions, mostly about exactly what the surgeon would cut. Later he told his parents that when he told his classmates that his mother was having an operation, one of them asked, "Is she going to die?" Philip reported this to illustrate his friend's foolishness.

His parents, wisely, exchanged wide-eyed glances but listened without comment. Privately, Craig asked Dora, "What is wrong with him? Does he have no heart?" She assured him that Philip was quite normal.

The fact that children are concrete operational thinkers (Piaget) and their perceptions arise from the immediate social context (Vygotsky) is illustrated not only by Philip but by every child in middle childhood. For instance, if they are told that their parents are divorcing, they might to ask "Is it my fault?" and "Where will I live?" instead of expressing sympathy, surprise, or anger. Aspects of cognition that adults take for granted—empathy, emotional sensitivity, hope and fears for the future—develop throughout these years.

I am glad to report that Dora's surgery went well. When he is 11, Philip might blame himself for not worrying; Craig and Dora will reassure him that he reacted appropriately. That happened to my daughter Sarah, who was upset in middle childhood that my husband and I ignored her when her older sister had cancer. A few years later, as a teenager, Sarah felt guilty that she had not been more sympathetic. Adolescents have more than enough "heart"; they get it during middle childhood.

REUTERS/Arko Datta/Corbis

**Never Lost** These children of Varanasi sleep beside the Ganges River in the daytime. At night, they use their excellent sense of direction to guide devotees from elsewhere.

experiment, children were blindfolded, spun around, and led to a second room, yet some still knew which way they were then facing (Mishra et al., 2009).

Further research in Varanasi found that some religious traditions emphasize north/south/east/west orientations instead of the Western left–right ones (Dasen & Mishra, 2013). For example, Christian children are taught that Jesus sits "at the right hand of God," but they do not know whether the Wicked Witch is from the north or some other direction (unless they read and reread *The Wizard of Oz*).

For children in Varanasi, compass directions are evident in language: Instead of "the dog is sleeping near the door," someone might say, "the dog is sleeping southeast." Learning north/south/east/west in order to communicate leads to an internal sense of direction by middle childhood.

Culture affects *how* children learn, not just what they learn. Many traditional Western schools expect children to learn directly, by listening to a teacher and demonstrating what they know on homework and tests: It is cheating to ask someone else for answers, and children are supposed to keep their eyes on their own papers. By contrast, in some other cultures learning occurs socially and indirectly, by observation and joint activity (Rogoff, 2016).

For example, one study tested children's ability to remember an overheard folktale. Children who grew up within Native American communities were accustomed to learning by observation, and thus they were better at remembering the folktale than other U.S. children (Tsethlikai & Rogoff, 2013).

## Information Processing

Contemporary educators and psychologists find both Piaget and Vygotsky insightful. International research confirms the merits of their theories (Griffin, 2011; Mercer & Howe, 2012). Piaget described universal changes; Vygotsky noted cultural impact. However, both grand theories of child cognition are limited, especially regarding

and directs business operations. For that reason, control processes are also called *executive processes*, and the ability to use them is called *executive function* (already mentioned in Chapter 9). Control processes allow a person to step back from the specifics to consider more general goals and cognitive strategies.

Executive function becomes more evident and significant among 10-year-olds than among 4- to 6-year-olds, although some older children still act impulsively (Masten, 2014; Bjorklund et al., 2009). Generally, however, students learn to listen to their teacher, ignoring classmates who are chewing gum or passing notes. That deliberate selectivity is a control process. Children can review their spelling words before bed and again at breakfast, creating mnemonics to remember the tricky ones. That signifies executive function.

Control processes improve with age and experience. For instance, in one study, children took a fill-in-the-blanks test and indicated how confident they were about each answer. Then they were allowed to delete some questions, with the remaining ones counting more. Already by age 9, they were able to estimate correctness; by age 11, they were skilled at knowing what to delete (Roebers et al., 2009).

Sometimes, experience that is not directly related has an impact. This seems to be true for fluently bilingual children, who must learn to inhibit one language while using another. They are advanced in control processes, obviously in language but also in more abstract measures of control (Bialystok, 2010). When bilingual individuals are asked to reason about something in their second language, they tend to be more rational and less emotional—which usually (but not always) leads to better thought (Costa et al., 2017).

Control processes develop spontaneously as the prefrontal cortex matures, but they can also be taught. Examples that may be familiar include spelling rules ("*i* before *e* except after *c*") and ways to remember how to turn a lightbulb ("lefty-loosey, righty-tighty").

Preschoolers ignore such rules; 7-year-olds begin to use them; 9-year-olds can create and master more complicated rules. Efforts to teach executive control succeed if the particular neurological maturation of the child is considered, as information processing would predict (Karbach & Unger, 2014).

**Fortunate Child or Too Fortunate?** Mothers everywhere help children with homework, as this mother does. Is it ever true that parents should let their children struggle, and fail?

## WHAT HAVE YOU LEARNED?

1. What did Piaget mean when he called cognition in middle childhood *concrete operational thought*?

2. What items would be in a class other than food or family, such as transportation or plants?

3. How do Vygotsky and Piaget differ in their explanation of cognitive advances in middle childhood?

4. How are the children of Varanasi an example of Vygotsky's theory?

5. How does information-processing theory differ from traditional theories of cognitive development?

6. According to Siegler, what is the pattern of learning math concepts?

7. What aspects of memory improve markedly during middle childhood?

8. How and why does the knowledge base increase in middle childhood?

9. How might control processes help a student learn?

# Language

As you remember, many aspects of language advance during early childhood. By age 6, children have mastered the basic vocabulary and grammar of their first language.

Many also speak a second language fluently. That increases their knowledge base, enabling more advanced learning and thinking in every subject and in every aspect of language—vocabulary, comprehension, speaking ability, and grammar (Language and Reading Research Consortium, 2015). Here are some specifics.

## Vocabulary

By age 6, children use every part of speech—adjectives, adverbs, interjections, and conjunctions, as well as thousands of nouns and verbs—to form sentences that may go on and on. Vocabulary builds during middle childhood because concrete operational children are logical; they can understand prefixes, suffixes, compound words, phrases, and metaphors, even if they have not heard them before. For example, 2-year-olds know *egg*, but 10-year-olds also know *egg salad, egg-drop soup, egghead, a good egg,* and *last one in is a rotten egg*—a phrase from my childhood that a 2017 Google search found still relevant today.

In middle childhood, some words become pivotal for understanding the curriculum, such as *negotiate, evolve, allegation, deficit, molecules*. Consequently, vocabulary is taught in every elementary school classroom.

### Understanding Metaphors

Metaphors, jokes, and puns are comprehended in middle childhood—and not earlier. Some jokes ("What is black and white and read all over?" and "Why did the chicken cross the road?") are funny only during middle childhood. Younger children don't get the jokes, and teenagers find them lame and stale.

But the new cognitive flexibility of 6- to 11-year-olds allows them to enjoy puns, unexpected answers to normal questions, as well as metaphors and similes. A lack of metaphorical understanding, or an inability to see the humor in a pun, indicates a cognitive problem (Thomas et al., 2010).

Metaphors are context specific, building on the knowledge base. An American who lives in China notes phrases that U.S. children understand but children in cultures without baseball do not, including "dropped the ball," "on the ball," "play ball," "throw a curve," "strike out" (Davis, 1999). If a teacher says "keep your eyes on the ball," some immigrant children might not pay attention because they are looking for that ball.

### Adjusting Language to the Context

Another aspect of language that advances markedly in middle childhood is pragmatics, defined in Chapter 9. Pragmatics is evident when a child knows which words to use with teachers (never calling them a *rotten egg*) and informally with friends (who can be called rotten eggs or worse). As children master pragmatics, they become more adept at making friends. Shy 6-year-olds cope far better with the social pressures of school if they use pragmatics well (Coplan & Weeks, 2009). By contrast, children with autism spectrum disorder are usually very poor at pragmatics (Klinger et al., 2014).

Mastery of pragmatics allows children to change styles of speech, or *linguistic codes*, depending on their audience. Each code includes many aspects of language—not just vocabulary but also tone, pronunciation, grammar, sentence

**Response for Teachers** (from p. 346):
Children this age can be taught strategies for remembering by forming links between working memory and long-term memory. You might break down the vocabulary list into word clusters, grouped according to root words, connections to the children's existing knowledge, applications, or (as a last resort) first letters or rhymes. Active, social learning is useful; perhaps in groups the students could write a story each day that incorporates 15 new words. Each group could read its story aloud to the class.

**Go with the Flow** This boat classroom in Bangladesh picks up students on shore and then uses solar energy to power computers linked to the Internet as part of instruction. The educational context will teach skills and metaphors that the students' peers will not understand.

length, idioms, and gestures. Sometimes the switch is between *formal code* (used in academic contexts) and *informal code* (used with friends); sometimes it is between standard (or proper) speech and dialect or vernacular (used on the street). Code is used in texting—numbers (411), abbreviations (LOL), emoticons (:-D), and spelling (r u ok?), which children do dozens of times a day.

Children may not realize that informal codes are wrong in formal language, nor what is gained by precise vocabulary. The peer group teaches the informal code, and each local community transmits dialect, metaphors, and pronunciation; schools must convey the formal code. All children need that instruction because the logic of grammar and spelling (whether *who* or *whom* is correct or how to spell *you*) is almost impossible to deduce, yet everyone is judged by their ability to speak and write the formal code.

## Speaking Two Languages

Code changes are obvious when children speak one language at home and another at school. Every nation includes many such children; most of the world's 6,000 languages are not school languages. In the United States, about one school-age child in four has a home language that is not English (see Figure 12.1); in other nations, almost every child has a home language and a school language.

In addition, many U.S. children speak 1 of the 20 or so English dialects with regional or ethnic word use, pronunciation, and grammar. Code-switching correlates with school achievement, so teachers need to respect the home language or dialect while teaching school speech (Terry et al., 2016). Children can learn several codes—it is easy before age 5, possible in middle childhood, and difficult after puberty.

If children learn two languages in the first three years of life, no brain differences are detectable between monolingual and bilingual children. However, from about age 4 through adolescence, the older children are when they learn a second language, the more likely their brains change to accommodate the second language, with greater cortical thickness on the left side (the language side) and thinness on the right (Klein et al., 2014). This reflects what we know about language learning: In infancy and early childhood, language is learned effortlessly; in middle childhood, some work (indicated by brain growth) is required.

Educators and political leaders in the United States argue about how to teach English to **English Language Learners (ELLs),** who are people whose first language is not standard English. One strategy is called **immersion,** in which instruction occurs entirely in the new language. The opposite strategy is to teach children in their first language initially and then to add instruction of the second language as a "foreign" tongue (a strategy rare in the United States but common elsewhere).

Between these extremes lies **bilingual education,** with instruction in two languages, and **ESL (English as a Second Language),** with all non-English speakers taught English in one multilingual group, preparing them to join English-only classes. Every method for teaching a second language sometimes succeeds and sometimes fails. A major problem is that language-learning abilities change with age: The youngest children learn a new language much more quickly than the older children (Stevens, 2015; Palacios & Kibler, 2016).

Language learning depends not only on the child but also on the literacy of the home environment (frequent reading, writing, and listening in any language helps); the warmth, training, and skill of the teacher; and the national context. If parents fear the possibility of deportation, that adds to stress and impairs learning, especially in middle childhood (Brabeck & Sibley, 2016; Dearing et al., 2016).

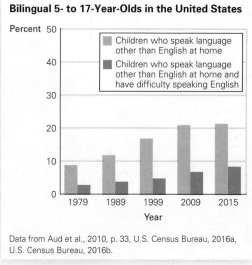

Data from Aud et al., 2010, p. 33, U.S. Census Bureau, 2016a, U.S. Census Bureau, 2016b.

**FIGURE 12.1**

**Increasing Treasure or Trouble?** This figure can be seen two ways. More U.S. children speak a language other than English at home, and most of them speak English well. Since bilingualism is increasingly needed for a global economy, that bodes well for the future. But more children do not speak English well. For their future and for the future of the nation, their education is crucial.

**English Language Learners (ELLs)** Children in the United States whose proficiency in English is low—usually below a cutoff score on an oral or written test. Many children who speak a non-English language at home are also capable in English; they are *not* ELLs.

**immersion** A strategy in which instruction in all school subjects occurs in the second (usually the majority) language that a child is learning.

**bilingual education** A strategy in which school subjects are taught in both the learner's original language and the second (majority) language.

**ESL (English as a Second Language)** A U.S. approach to teaching English that gathers all of the non-English speakers together and provides intense instruction in English. Students' first languages are never used; the goal is to prepare them for regular classes in English.

**Months or Years?** ESL classes, like this one in Canada, often use pictures and gestures to foster word learning. How soon will these children be ready for instruction?

Specifics differ for each state, grade, family, and child, but the general trends are discouraging. Unless a child is already bilingual at age 5, ELLs tend to fall further behind their peers with each passing year, leaving school at higher rates than other students their age. In the United States, children whose first language is Spanish are particularly stressed, with only 88 percent of 18- to 24-year-olds being high school graduates, compared to a national average of 95 percent (Krogstad, 2016).

Some of the problem for Hispanic American children arises from the exosystem, but even when the national context is benign, it takes time for kindergartners who speak a home language to catch up to their peers who already speak the school language. For example, in Edmonton, Canada, children who spoke Chinese as their first language needed four to six years to become as facile in academic English as their monolingual English peers (Paradis & Jia, 2017).

## Differences in Language Learning

Learning to speak, read, and write the school language is pivotal for primary school education. This is particularly difficult for children with an intellectual disability. Educators may make two opposite mistakes: Some assume that children who do not speak the school language are learning disabled, and others assume that every bilingual child who has a learning problem is held back solely by language. Difference is not necessarily deficit, but learning disabilities occur among children of every background.

To discover whether a child has difficulty learning language, that child should be tested in the home language—even when the child has been speaking the second language from kindergarten on (Erdos et al., 2014). If a language gap is found, two social factors must be considered: SES and expectations.

## Socioeconomic Status

Decades of research throughout the world have found a strong correlation between academic achievement and socioeconomic status. Language is a major reason. Not only do children from low-SES families usually have smaller vocabularies than those from higher-SES families, but their grammar is also simpler (fewer compound sentences, dependent clauses, and conditional verbs) and their sentences are shorter (Hart & Risley, 1995; Hoff, 2013). That slows down school learning.

Brain scans confirm that development of the hippocampus is particularly affected by SES, as is language learning (Jednoróg et al., 2012). That is correlation, not causation. Consequently, many researchers seek causes.

Possibilities include inadequate prenatal care, no breakfast, lead in the bloodstream, crowded households, few books at home, teenage parents, authoritarian child rearing, inexperienced teachers, air pollution, neighborhood violence, lack of role models . . . the list could go on and on (Van Agt et al., 2015; Kolb & Gibb, 2015; Rowe et al., 2016). All of these conditions correlate with low SES and less learning, but it is difficult to isolate the impact of any specific one.

However, one factor seems to be a cause, not just a correlate: language heard early on. Some parents use simpler vocabulary and talk much less to their infants and young children than other parents do. The mother's education is one crucial factor, especially if she continues her quest for learning by reading and asking questions. Children who grow up in homes with many books accumulate, on average, three more years of education than children who live in homes with no books (Evans et al., 2010).

Educated mothers and fathers are more likely to take their children to museums, zoos, and libraries, and to engage children in conversation about the interesting sights around them. Another way to surround children with language is to sing to a child, not just a few simple songs but dozens of songs with varied vocabulary in many stanzas. Then discussions about the meaning of words come naturally. Vocabulary is learned more quickly if the same words are heard from several people: Children benefit from conversations with relatives, teachers, and even strangers.

The second factor that seems to be crucial is expectations. Although substantial research has found that children are influenced by adults' positive expectations, the relationship between expectation and achievement becomes complicated as children grow older. One crucial factor seems to be whether parents and teachers share expectations, rather than working at cross-purposes.

It is also true that children may rebel against expectations if they feel that the expectations are unrealistic (Froiland & Davison, 2014). This is particularly likely with authoritarian parenting—high standards, without much warmth.

Teacher attitudes are significant in middle childhood. Fortunately, they are also malleable, and students respond to encouragement (Sparks, 2016). When teachers have high expectations while empathizing with students who must overcome problems, those students are less often absent or suspended. The same is true for parents, although opposing perspectives are evident regarding the tension between expectations and praise, apparent in Opposing Perspectives on the following page.

Expectations do not necessarily reflect SES, especially among immigrant families. Many first-generation children become excellent students: They try to validate their parents' decision to leave their native country (Ceballo et al., 2014; Fuller & García Coll, 2010). Their parents expect them to study hard, and they do.

**Especially for Parents** You've had an exhausting day but are setting out to buy groceries. Your 7-year-old son wants to go with you. Should you explain that you are so tired that you want to make a quick solo trip to the supermarket this time? (see response, p. 353)

JW LTD/Getty Images

**Priorities** This family in London has a low income, evident in the stained walls, peeling paint, and old toilet, but that does not necessarily limit the girl's future. More important is what she learns about values and behavior. If this scene is typical, this mother is teaching her daughter about appearance and obedience. What would happen if the child had to care for her own grooming? Tangles? Short hair? Independence? Linguistic advances?

**Observation Quiz** What in the daughter's behavior suggests that maternal grooming is a common event in her life? (see answer, p. 353)

# Happiness or High Grades?

Thousands of social scientists—psychologists, educators, sociologists, economists—have realized that, for cognitive development from middle childhood through late adulthood, characteristics beyond IQ scores, test grades, and family SES are sometimes pivotal.

One leading proponent of this idea is Paul Tough, who wrote: "We have been focusing on the wrong skills and abilities in our children, and we have been using the wrong strategies to help nurture and teach those skills" (Tough, 2012, p. xv). Instead of focusing on test scores, Tough believes we should focus on characteristics, particularly *grit* (persistence and effort).

Many scientists agree that executive control processes with many names (grit, emotional regulation, conscientiousness, resilience, executive function, effortful control) develop over the years of middle childhood. Over the long term, these aspects of character predict achievement.

Developmentalists disagree about exactly which qualities are crucial for achievement, with grit considered crucial by some and not others (Ivcevic & Brackett, 2014; Duckworth & Kern, 2011). However, no one denies that success depends on personal traits.

The opposing perspective is that parental encouragement is more important for academic achievement and that the focus on grit makes it seem as if the child is to be blamed for failure. Instead, parents, schools, and community may make learning very difficult for some children. Grit could make a child spend all the time studying and feeling inadequate, never enjoying life.

Remember that school-age children are ready for intellectual growth (Piaget) and are responsive to mentors (Vygotsky). These universals were evident in one study that occurred in two places, 12,000 miles apart: the northeastern United States and Taiwan.

More than 200 mothers were asked to recall and then discuss with their 6- to 10-year-olds two learning-related incidents that they knew their child had experienced. In one incident, the child had a "good attitude or behavior in learning"; in the other, "not perfect" (J. Li et al., 2014).

All of the mothers were married and middle-class, and all tried to encourage their children, stressing the value of education and the importance of doing well in school. The researchers noted that the mothers differed in the attitudes they were trying to encourage in their children. The Taiwanese mothers were far more likely to mention what the researchers called "learning virtues," such as practice, persistence, and concentration—all of which are part of grit. The American mothers were more likely to mention "positive affect," such as happiness and pride.

This distinction is evident in the following two excepts:

First, Tim and his American mother discussed a "not perfect" incident.

**MOTHER:** I wanted to talk to you about . . . that time when you had that one math paper that . . . mostly everything was wrong and you never bring home papers like that. . . .

**TIM:** I just had a clumsy day.

**MOTHER:** You had a clumsy day. You sure did, but there was, when we finally figured out what it was that you were doing wrong, you were pretty happy about it . . . and then you were happy to practice it, right? . . . Why do you think that was?

**TIM:** I don't know, because I was frustrated, and then you sat down and went over it with me, and I figured it out right with no distraction and then I got it right.

**MOTHER:** So it made you feel good to do well?

**TIM:** Uh-huh.

**MOTHER:** And it's okay to get some wrong sometimes.

**TIM:** And I, I never got that again, didn't I?

The next excerpt occurred when Ren and his Taiwanese mother discuss a "good attitude or behavior."

**MOTHER:** Oh, why does your teacher think that you behave well?

**REN:** It's that I concentrate well in class.

**MOTHER:** Is your good concentration the concentration to talk to your peer at the next desk?

**REN:** I listen to teachers.

**MOTHER:** Oh, is it so only for Mr. Chang's class or is it for all classes?

**REN:** Almost all classes like that. . . .

**MOTHER:** So you want to behave well because you want to get an . . . honor award. Is that so?

**REN:** Yes.

**MOTHER:** Or is it also that you yourself want to behave better?

**REN:** Yes. I also want to behave better myself.

*[J. Li et al., 2014, p. 1218]*

Both Tim and Ren are likely to be good students in their respective schools. When parents support and encourage their child's learning, almost always the child masters the basic skills required of elementary school students, and almost never does the child become crushed by life experiences. Instead, the child has sufficient strengths to overcome most challenges (Masten, 2014).

The specifics of parental encouragement affect the child's achievement. Some research has found that parents in Asia emphasize that education requires hard work, whereas parents in North America stress the joy of learning. Could it be, as one group of researchers contend, that U.S. children are happier but less accomplished than Asian ones (F. Ng et al., 2014)? If so, if a child cannot have both, which is more important: high self-esteem or high grades?

# Teaching and Learning

As we have just described, school-age children are great learners, using logic, developing strategies, accumulating knowledge, and expanding language. In every nation, new responsibilities and formal instruction begin at about age 6 because that is when the human body and brain are ready.

Traditionally, this learning occurred at home, as children learned to do the same work (herding goats, planting corn, tending children, cooking food) as their parents did. Currently, however, almost all (95 percent) of the world's 7-year-olds are in school. That is where their parents and political leaders want them to be. (See Visualizing Development on p. 363 for U.S. and international statistics on education in middle childhood.) Because the cost of school, and lost help to the parents, kept many children (especially girls) at home, almost every nation now makes education free, with 30 nations paying parents to send their children to school (Kremer et al., 2013).

Indeed, in many developing nations, the number of students in elementary school exceeds the number of school-age children, because many older children as well as adults now seek basic education. In 2014, Ghana, El Salvador, and China were among the nations with significantly more students in primary school than the total number of children in middle childhood (UNESCO, 2014).

## International Schooling

In every primary school, children are taught reading, writing, and arithmetic. Because of brain maturation, age 6 to age 11 is the best time for this. Some of the sequences recognized universally are listed in the accompanying At About This Time tables.

### Differences by Nation

Beyond literacy and math, nations vary in what they expect. For example, every nation wants children to become good citizens, but nations disagree about what good citizenship entails or how children can learn it (Cohen & Malin, 2010). Accordingly, many children simply follow their parents' example regarding everything from picking up trash to supporting a candidate for president.

Differences between one nation and another, and, in the United States, between one school and another, are stark in the **hidden curriculum**—all of the implicit values and assumptions that underlie the course offerings, schedules, tracking,

## AT ABOUT THIS TIME

### Math

| Age | Norms and Expectations |
| --- | --- |
| 4–5 years | ■ Count to 20.<br>■ Understand one-to-one correspondence of objects and numbers.<br>■ Understand *more* and *less*.<br>■ Recognize and name shapes. |
| 6 years | ■ Count to 100.<br>■ Understand *bigger* and *smaller*.<br>■ Add and subtract one-digit numbers. |
| 8 years | ■ Add and subtract two-digit numbers.<br>■ Understand simple multiplication and division.<br>■ Understand word problems with two variables. |
| 10 years | ■ Add, subtract, multiply, and divide multidigit numbers.<br>■ Understand simple fractions, percentages, area, and perimeter of shapes.<br>■ Understand word problems with three variables. |
| 12 years | ■ Begin to use abstract concepts, such as formulas and algebra. |

Math learning depends heavily on direct instruction and repeated practice, which means that some children advance more quickly than others. This list is only a rough guide, meant to illustrate the importance of sequence.

**hidden curriculum** The unofficial, unstated, or implicit patterns within a school that influence what children learn. For instance, teacher background, organization of the play space, and tracking are all part of the hidden curriculum—not formally prescribed, but instructive to the children.

## AT ABOUT THIS TIME

### Reading

| Age | Norms and Expectations |
|---|---|
| 4–5 years | ■ Understand basic book concepts. For instance, children learning English and many other languages understand that books are written from front to back, with print from left to right, and that letters make words that describe pictures.<br>■ Recognize letters—name the letters on sight.<br>■ Recognize and spell own name. |
| 6–7 years | ■ Know the sounds of the consonants and vowels, including those that have two sounds (e.g., *c, g, o*).<br>■ Use sounds to figure out words.<br>■ Read simple words, such as *cat, sit, ball, jump.* |
| 8 years | ■ Read simple sentences out loud, 50 words per minute, including words of two syllables.<br>■ Understand basic punctuation, consonant–vowel blends.<br>■ Comprehend what is read. |
| 9–10 years | ■ Read and understand paragraphs and chapters, including advanced punctuation (e.g., the colon).<br>■ Answer comprehension questions about concepts as well as facts.<br>■ Read polysyllabic words (e.g., *vegetarian, population, multiplication*). |
| 11–12 years | ■ Demonstrate rapid and fluent oral reading (more than 100 words per minute).<br>■ Vocabulary includes words that have specialized meaning in various fields.<br>■ For example, in civics, *liberties, federal, parliament*, and *environment* all have special meanings.<br>■ Comprehend paragraphs about unfamiliar topics.<br>■ Sound out new words, figuring out meaning using cognates and context.<br>■ Read for pleasure. |
| 13+ years | ■ Continue to build vocabulary, with greater emphasis on comprehension than on speech. Understand textbooks. |

Reading is a complex mix of skills, dependent on brain maturation, education, and culture. The sequence given here is approximate; it should not be taken as a standard to measure any particular child.

Aaron Bacall via Cartoonstock–www.cartoonstock.com

**Teacher Technique** Some children are riveted by TV but distracted at school. Has this teacher found a solution, or is she making the problem worse?

teacher characteristics, discipline, teaching methods, sports competitions, student government, extracurricular activities, and so on.

For example, whether and how students should talk in class is part of the hidden curriculum, taught from kindergarten on. In the United States, citizens are expected to voice and vote their opinions, so children are encouraged to say what they think—perhaps by raising their hands, but always by being active and talkative in class. Many teachers call on children and give points for participation. Children who sit quietly, never talking, are thought to be pathologically shy or even mute.

When I taught at United Nations International School, one student, newly arrived from India, was very quiet, so I called on him. He immediately stood up to answer—to the surprise of his classmates. Soon he learned to stay seated, but he never spoke in class unless required directly.

In general, North American students are expected to speak their minds, even when they are irrational. This correlates with later active citizenship (Lin, 2014). Some of my students at the United Nations school, encouraged to speak out, returned to their homelands to lead pro-democracy protests. I now wonder if

**Same Situation, Far Apart: Spot the Hidden Curriculum** Literacy is central to the curriculum for schoolchildren everywhere, no matter how far apart they live. However, in the U.S. classroom at the left, boys and girls learn together, clothes are casual, history books are paperback and illustrated, and children of every background read the same stories with the same patriotic—but not religious—themes. The hidden curriculum is quite different for the boy memorizing his holy book on the right.

their fellow countrymen thought them disrespectful, foolish, and ruined by their education abroad.

The hidden curriculum may also be the underlying reason for a disheartening difference in whether students ask their teachers for help. In one study, middle-class children requested special assistance more often than low-SES students did. The researchers found that the low-SES students sought to avoid special attention, fearing it would lead to criticism (Calarco, 2014). For that reason, the hidden curriculum meant that students who most needed help did not get it. Their middle-class teachers wanted to help these students, but they assumed that the students would request help.

Sadly, if teachers' gender, ethnicity, or economic background is unlike their students, children may conclude that education is irrelevant for them. If the school has gifted classes, the non-gifted may conclude that they are not capable of learning.

The physical environment also sends a hidden message. Some schools have spacious classrooms, wide hallways, and large, grassy playgrounds; others have cramped, poorly equipped classrooms and cement play yards. In some nations, school is held outdoors, with no chairs, desks, or books; classes are canceled when it rains. What does that tell the students?

**Room to Learn?** In the elementary school classroom in Florida *(left)*, the teacher is guiding two students who are working to discover concepts in physics—a stark contrast to the Filipino classroom *(right)* in a former storeroom. Sometimes the hidden curriculum determines the overt curriculum, as shown here.

## International Testing

Every nation now wants to improve education, because longitudinal data find that when achievement rises, the national economy advances (Hanushek & Woessmann, 2009). Apparently, better-educated adults are more productive workers. To evaluate the effectiveness of education, more than 50 nations have participated in at least one massive international test of children's learning.

Science and math achievement are tested in the **Trends in Math and Science Study (TIMSS)**. The main test of reading is the **Progress in International Reading Literacy Study (PIRLS)**. These tests are given every few years, with East Asian nations usually ranking at the top. The rank of the United States has risen over the past two decades, but in 2015 there were nine nations, in eastern and western Europe as well as in Asia, whose fourth-graders surpassed those in the United States (see Tables 12.2 and 12.3). Few developing nations give these tests, but when they do, their scores are low. Improvement is possible, however.

**Trends in Math and Science Study (TIMSS)** An international assessment of the math and science skills of fourth- and eighth-graders. Although the TIMSS is very useful, different countries' scores are not always comparable because sample selection, test administration, and content validity are hard to keep uniform.

**Progress in International Reading Literacy Study (PIRLS)** Inaugurated in 2001, a planned five-year cycle of international trend studies in the reading ability of fourth-graders.

### TABLE 12.2

**TIMSS Ranking and Average Scores of Math Achievement for Fourth-Graders, 2011 and 2015**

| Rank | Country | Score 2011 | Score 2015 |
|------|---------|------------|------------|
| 1. | Singapore | 606 | 618 |
| 2. | Hong Kong | 602 | 615 |
| 3. | Korea | 605 | 608 |
| 4. | Chinese Taipei | 591 | 597 |
| 5. | Japan | 585 | 593 |
| 6. | N. Ireland | 562 | 570 |
| 7. | Russian Federation | 542 | 564 |
| 8. | England | 542 | 546 |
| 9. | Belgium | 549 | 546 |
| 10. | United States | 541 | 539 |
| 11. | Canada (Quebec) | 533 | 533 |
| 12. | Finland | 545 | 532 |
| | Netherlands | 540 | 530 |
| | Germany | 528 | 522 |
| | Sweden | 504 | 519 |
| | Australia | 516 | 517 |
| | Canada (Ontario) | 518 | 512 |
| | Italy | 508 | 507 |
| | New Zealand | 486 | 491 |
| | Iran | 431 | 431 |
| | Kuwait | 342 | 353 |

Information from Mullis et al., 2016.

### TABLE 12.3

**PIRLS Distribution of Reading Achievement for Fourth-Graders, 2006 and 2011**

| Country | Score 2006 | Score 2011 |
|---------|------------|------------|
| Hong Kong | 564 | 571 |
| Russian Federation | 565 | 568 |
| Finland | ** | 568 |
| Singapore | 558 | 567 |
| N. Ireland | ** | 558 |
| United States | 540 | 556 |
| Denmark | 546 | 554 |
| Chinese Taipei | 535 | 553 |
| Ireland | ** | 552 |
| England | 539 | 552 |
| Canada | 549 | 548 |
| Italy | 551 | 541 |
| Germany | 548 | 541 |
| Israel | 512 | 541 |
| New Zealand | 532 | 531 |
| Australia | ** | 527 |
| Poland | 519 | 526 |
| France | 522 | 520 |
| Spain | 513 | 513 |
| Iran | 421 | 457 |
| Colombia | ** | 448 |
| Indonesia | 405 | 428 |
| Morocco | 323 | 310 |

Information from Mullis et al., 2007; Mullis et al., 2012b.

For example, Finland's scores on international tests increased dramatically after a wholesale reform of their public education system (see Figure 12.2). Reforms occurred in several waves (Sahlberg 2011, 2015). Finland abolished ability grouping in 1985; curriculum reform to encourage collaboration and active learning began in 1994. Now, during middle childhood, all children learn together—no tracking—and teachers are mandated to work with each child to make sure he or she masters the curriculum. Learning difficulties are remediated in the early grades, within the regular classroom.

Over the past two decades, strict requirements for becoming a teacher have been put in place. Only the top 3 percent of Finland's high school graduates are admitted to teachers' colleges. They study for five years at the university at no charge, earning a master's degree in the theory and practice of education.

Finnish teachers are granted more autonomy within their classrooms than is typical in other nations. Since the 1990s, they have had more time and encouragement to work with colleagues (Sahlberg, 2011, 2015). They are encouraged to respond to each child's temperament as well as skills. This strategy has led to achievement, particularly in math (Viljaranta et al., 2015).

## Problems with International Benchmarks

Elaborate and extensive measures are in place to make international tests valid. For instance, test items are designed to be fair and culture-free, and participating children represent the diversity (economic, ethnic, etc.) of each nation's child population. The design and implementation of the PIRLS and the TIMSS benefit from hundreds of researchers, who collaborate to ensure validity and reliability. Consequently, most social scientists respect the data gathered from these tests.

The tests are far from perfect, however. Designing test items that are equally challenging to every student in every nation is impossible. For example in math, should fourth-graders be expected to understand fractions, graphs, decimals, and simple geometry, or should the test examine only basic operations with whole numbers? Nations introduce these aspects of math at different ages: Is it fair to expect every fourth-grader to know them?

After such general issues are decided, items that are equally fair in every culture need to be written. That ideal is impossible, since culture affects us all. The following items were used to test fourth-grade math:

> Three thousand tickets for a basketball game are numbered 1 to 3,000. People with ticket numbers ending with 112 receive a prize. Write down all the prize-winning numbers.

Only 26 percent of fourth-graders worldwide got this one right (112, 1112, 2112—with no additional numbers). About half of the children in East Asian nations and 36 percent of the U.S. children were correct. Those national scores are not surprising; children in Singapore, Japan, and China have been close to the top on every international test for 20 years, and the United States has been above average but not by much.

On this test item, children from North Africa did especially poorly; only 2 percent of Moroccan fourth-graders were correct. Is basketball, or 3,000 tickets for one game, or giving random prizes as common in North Africa as in the United States and East Asia?

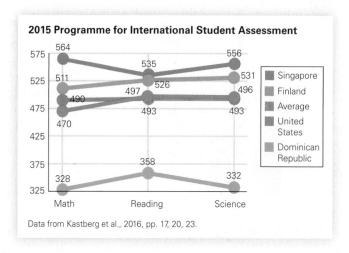

**2015 Programme for International Student Assessment**

Data from Kastberg et al., 2016, pp. 17, 20, 23.

**FIGURE 12.2**

**Lifelong Learning** Finnish and U.S. elementary school students score similarly on the TIMSS or PIRLS, but educators in Finland do not believe that these tests are the best measure of learning. Instead, they prefer to focus on using knowledge later on, measured by a test described in Chapter 15, the PISA. Shown here are PISA scores for 15-year-olds. Finland is among the highest scoring nations, and the United States is middling (just slightly below the overall average). For comparison, this graph also shows the highest (Singapore) and lowest (Dominican Republic) nations.

**Observation Quiz** In which of the three (math, reading, and science) is the United States lowest, and in which is Singapore lowest? (see answer, p. 358) ↑

**Sharing Answers** After individually subtracting 269 from 573, these two third-graders check their answers in two ways—first by adding and then by showing their work to each other. As you can see, he is not embarrassed at his mistake because students in this class enjoy learning from each other.

© Debbie Noda/Modesto Bee/ZUMAPRESS.com /Alamy

**"Big deal, an A in math. That would be a D in any other country."**

⬤ **Answer to Observation Quiz** (from p. 357): Math (United States) and reading (Singapore). Why do you think that is? (There is no right answer to this; experts debate it!)

Another item gives ingredients of a recipe—4 eggs, 8 cups of flour, ½ cup of milk—and then asks:

> The above ingredients are used to make a recipe for 6 people. Sam wants to make this recipe for only 3 people. Complete the table below to show what Sam needs to make the recipe for 3 people. The number of eggs he needs is shown.

The table lists 2 eggs, and the child needs to fill in measures for the flour and milk. Children in Ireland and England scored highest on this item (about half got it right), with Korea, China, and Japan lower than the United States (33 percent).

Many children everywhere have trouble with fractions, but almost always the East Asians do better than everyone else. Not with this item. Why not? Are English and Irish children experienced with recipes for baked goods that include eggs, flour, and milk, unlike Japanese children? Or were the Asian children distracted by the idea that a boy was using a recipe?

## Gender Differences in School Performance

In addition to marked national, ethnic, and economic differences, gender differences in achievement scores are reported. The PIRLS finds girls ahead of boys in verbal skills in every nation, by an average of 16 points. The female advantage is not that high in the United States, with the 2011 PIRLS finding girls 10 points ahead. Ten points is not much: Girls in the United States (and Canada, Germany, and the Netherlands) were ahead of boys, on average, by about 2 percent. Does that mean that those nations are more gender-equitable than those in Asia or most of Europe?

Historically, boys were ahead of girls in math and science. However, TIMSS reported that those gender differences among fourth-graders in math narrowed or disappeared in 2015. In most nations, boys are still slightly ahead, with the United States showing a significant male advantage (7 points—about 2 percent). However, in many nations, girls were ahead, sometimes by a great deal, such as 10 points in Indonesia and 20 points in Jordan. Such results support the *gender-similarities hypothesis* (see Chapter 10) that males and females are similar academically in middle childhood, with "trivial" exceptions later on (Hyde et al., 2008, p. 494).

**Future Engineers** After-school clubs now encourage boys to learn cooking and girls to play chess, and both sexes are active in every sport. The most recent push is for STEM (Science, Technology, Engineering, and Math) education—as in this after-school robotics club.

Unlike test results, classroom performance during elementary school finds that girls in every nation have higher report card grades, including in math and science. Is that biological (girls are better able to sit still, to manipulate a pencil)? Or within the culture (girls are more rewarded for "good" behavior, which includes quietly listening)? Or does the hidden curriculum within the school favor young girls (most elementary school teachers are women)?

The popularity of various explanations has shifted. Analysts once attributed girls' higher grades in school to their faster physical maturation. Now explanations are more often sociocultural. The same switch in explanations, from biology to culture, appears for male advantages. Is that change itself cultural?

## Schooling in the United States

Although most national tests indicate improvements in U.S. children's academic performance over the past decades, many other nations score higher on international tests. More troubling for the United States are large differences between income and ethnic groups (McNeil & Blad, 2014). Some high-scoring nations have more ethnic groups and immigrants, so diversity itself is not the reason.

Nonetheless, "federal civil rights data show persistent and widespread disparities among disadvantaged students from prekindergarten to high school" with low-SES children, English Language Learners, and minority ethnic groups all suffering (McNeil & Blad, 2014). For some statistics—high school graduation, for instance—Asian American children are an exception, but a closer look reveals that the "model minority" stereotype obscures some real disadvantages for many children of Asian heritage, and the stress of parental pressure and jealousy envy on the rest (Cherng & Liu, 2017).

Beginning in 2014, the United States' public schools have become "majority minority," which means that most students are from groups that once were called minorities—such as African American, Latino, or Asian American (Krogstad & Fry, 2014). (From a developmental perspective, the terms *majority* and *minority* are misleading, since the majority category includes many children whose ancestors came from distinct parts of Europe, and the minority category likewise includes many groups.)

Ethnic diversity could be beneficial. When ethnic minority children feel that their teachers and peers treat everyone equally, they are more engaged in learning—and that benefits everyone from every group (Baysu et al., 2016). Moreover, most parents want their children to learn about other backgrounds as well as to be proud of their own heritage. This is best done with personal contact between equals (e.g., students in the same classroom) and with teachers who guide students toward self-confidence and mutual respect. This ideal is difficult, however, partly because U.S. schools are more segregated than they were 40 years ago. Some classes are exclusively Latino, or African American, or European American (Rosiek & Kinslow, 2016).

Financial support for schools comes primarily from each local community in the United States, unlike in other nations. This may explain the large U.S. variations by race and income, since notable income disparities are apparent from one community to another, and those follow residential segregation. This is true from state to state as well: Massachusetts and Minnesota are consistently at the top of state achievement, and West Virginia, Mississippi, and New Mexico are at the bottom—in part because of the investment in education within those states and the proportion of students of high or low SES (which itself affects state spending) (Pryor, 2014).

**LaunchPad**
macmillan learning

**Video Activity: Educating the Girls of the World** examines the situation of girls' education around the world while stressing the importance of education for all children.

*Courtesy of Unicef*

## National Standards

For decades, the United States government has sponsored tests called the **National Assessment of Educational Progress (NAEP)** to measure achievement in reading, mathematics, and other subjects. The NAEP has high standards, rating fewer children proficient than do state tests. For example, New York's tests reported 62 percent proficient in math, but the NAEP found only 32 percent; 51 percent were proficient in reading on New York's state tests but only 35 percent according to NAEP (Martin, 2014).

Although many U.S. educators and political leaders try to eradicate performance disparities linked to a child's background, the NAEP finds that Latino and African American fourth-graders are about 12 percent lower than their European American peers in reading and 9 percent lower in math (Snyder et al., 2016).

**National Assessment of Educational Progress (NAEP)** An ongoing and nationally representative measure of U.S. children's achievement in reading, mathematics, and other subjects over time; nicknamed "the Nation's Report Card."

⬤⬤ **Especially for School Administrators** Children who wear uniforms in school tend to score higher on reading tests. Why? (see response, p. 362)

One explanation is that European Americans are, on average, higher in SES. However, the gap between low- and high-income U.S. students within ethnic groups is widening. A possibility is that the disparity in local funding for schools is at the root of the problem: High-SES children of all groups attend well-funded schools in the local school district.

It is difficult to compare results between states, because each state has particular standards and tests. For that reason, the governors of all 50 states designated a group of experts to develop high national standards, the *Common Core*, finalized in 2010. The standards are explicit, with half a dozen or more specific expectations for achievement in each subject for each grade. (Table 12.4 provides a sample of the specific standards.) Various testing companies have attempted to measure student accomplishments.

## Choices and Complications

Most states and teachers initially favored the Common Core, because high standards and accountability are goals shared by many. However, as testing increased, and implementation of the Common Core began in classrooms, many turned against it.

A poll by Education Next found only 12 percent of teachers were opposed to the Common Core in 2013; one year later, 40 percent were opposed (Gewertz, 2014). Likewise, many state legislators as well as members of the general public are critical of the Common Core. This illustrates a general finding: Issues regarding how best to teach children, and what they need to learn, are controversial among teachers, parents, and political leaders. Ten other controversial issues are listed on the next page.

| **TABLE 12.4** | | |
|---|---|---|
| **The Common Core: Sample Items for Each Grade** | | |
| **Grade** | **Reading and Writing** | **Math** |
| Kindergarten | Pronounce the primary sound for each consonant. | Know number names and the count sequence. |
| First | Decode regularly spelled one-syllable words. | Relate counting to addition and subtraction (e.g., by counting 2 more to add 2). |
| Second | Decode words with common prefixes and suffixes. | Measure the length of an object twice, using different units of length for the two measurements; describe how the two measurements relate to the size of the unit chosen. |
| Third | Decode multisyllabic words. | Understand division as an unknown-factor problem; for example, find 32 ÷ 8 by finding the number that makes 32 when multiplied by 8. |
| Fourth | Use combined knowledge of all letter–sound correspondences, syllable patterns, and morphology (e.g., roots and affixes) to read accurately unfamiliar multisyllabic words in context and out of context. | Apply and extend previous understandings of multiplication to multiply a fraction by a whole number. |
| Fifth | With guidance and support from peers and adults, develop and strengthen writing as needed by planning, revising, editing, and rewriting, or trying a new approach. | Graph points on the coordinate plane to solve real-world and mathematical problems. |

Information from National Governors Association, 2010.

## Ten Questions

1. Should public education be a priority for public funds, or should wealthy parents be able to pay for smaller class size, special curricula, and expensive facilities (e.g., a stage, a pool, a garden) in private education? All told, about 11 percent of students in the United States attend *private schools* (see Figure 12.3). Other nations have higher and lower rates. Economic factors are a major concern: Because they are funded primarily by tuition, private schools usually have few poor children.

2. Should parents be given **vouchers** to pay for some tuition at whatever private school they wish? That might make private school more affordable, but in Wisconsin only 20 percent of the parents who used vouchers for private schools had previously had their children in public schools. Most were already paying private school tuition, so the vouchers supplemented the tuition of children who were not in public school. If Wisconsin rates are true more generally, vouchers further increase inequality in schooling. In addition, vouchers in some states pay for religious schools, which some believe is contrary to the U.S. principle of separation of church and state.

3. Should more **charter schools** open or close? Charters are public schools funded and licensed by states or local districts, exempt from some regulations, especially those negotiated by teacher unions (hours, class size, etc.). Some admit students by lottery, but most have some control over admissions and expulsions, which makes them more ethnically segregated, enrolling fewer children with special needs (Stern et al., 2015). Some charter schools are remarkably successful; others are not (Peyser, 2011).

   Overall, more children (especially African American boys) and teachers leave or are expelled from charter schools than from other schools, a disturbing statistic. However, in some charters, children who stay learn more and are more likely to go to college than their peers in regular schools (Prothero, 2016).

4. **Home schooling** occurs when parents avoid both public and private schools by educating their children at home. In most states, authorities set standards for what a child must learn, but home-schooling families decide specifics of curriculum, schedules, and discipline. About 2 percent of all children were home-schooled in 2003, about 3 percent in 2007, and perhaps 4 percent in 2012 (Snyder & Dillow, 2013; Ray, 2013). Home schooling requires an adult at home, usually the mother in a two-parent family.

   The major criticism of home schooling is not academic (some mothers are conscientious teachers, especially in the early grades) but social: Children have no interaction with classmates. To compensate, many home-schooling parents plan activities with other home-schooling families, or they enroll their children in various classes (Sparks, 2012).

5. Should public education be free of *religion* to avoid bias toward one religion or another? In the United States, thousands of parochial schools were founded when Catholics perceived Protestant bias in public schools. In the past 20 years, many Catholic schools have closed, but schools teaching other religions—Judaism, Islam, conservative Christianity—have opened.

6. Should *the arts* be part of the curriculum? Music, drama, and the visual arts are essential in some places, not in others. Half of all U.S. 18- to 24-year-olds say that

**voucher** Public subsidy for tuition payment at a nonpublic school. Vouchers vary a great deal from place to place, not only in amount and availability but also in restrictions as to who gets them and what schools accept them.

**charter school** A public school with its own set of standards that is funded and licensed by the state or local district in which it is located.

**home schooling** Education in which children are taught at home, usually by their parents.

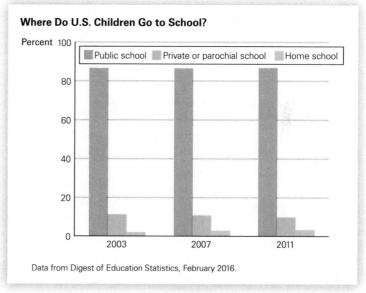

**Where Do U.S. Children Go to School?**

Percent

Data from Digest of Education Statistics, February 2016.

**FIGURE 12.3**

**Where'd You Go to School?** Home schooling remains the least chosen option, in part because it usually requires a stay-at-home parent who is able to teach the children. That also is the reason home schooling is far more common in the early grades than in high school. Recently, private and parochial schools are less favored, partly because more children are going to charter schools—a category within the public option. Whether this is an improvement or not is hotly contested.

**Plagiarism, Piracy, and Public School** Charter schools often have special support and unusual curricula, as shown here. These four children are learning about copyright law in a special summer school class at the ReNEW Cultural Arts Academy in New Orleans.

**Response for School Administrators** (from p. 360): The relationship reflects correlation, not causation. Wearing uniforms is more common when the culture of the school emphasizes achievement and study, with strict discipline in class and a policy of expelling disruptive students.

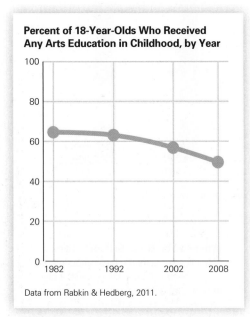

**Percent of 18-Year-Olds Who Received Any Arts Education in Childhood, by Year**

Data from Rabkin & Hedberg, 2011.

**FIGURE 12.4**

**Focus on Facts** As achievement test scores become the measure of learning, education in art, music, and movement has been squeezed out. Artists worry that creativity and imagination may be lost as well.

they had no arts education in childhood, either in school or anywhere else (Rabkin & Hedberg, 2011) (see Figure 12.4). By contrast, schools in Finland consider arts education essential, with a positive impact on learning (Nevanen et al., 2014).

7. Should children learn a *second language* in primary school? In Canada and in most European nations, almost every child studies two languages by age 10. Many African children know three languages before high school—their home language plus two other school languages. In the United States, less than 5 percent of children under age 11 study a language other than English in school (Robelen, 2011). Fears about immigration and globalization overtake the developmental benefits of learning new languages before puberty.

8. Can *computers* advance education? Some enthusiasts hope that connecting schools to the Internet or, even better, giving every child a laptop (as some schools do) will advance learning. The results are not dramatic, however. Sometimes computers improve achievement, but not always. Widespread, sustainable advances are elusive (Lim et al., 2013). Technology may be only a tool—a twenty-first-century equivalent of chalk—that depends on a creative, trained teacher to use well.

9. Are *class sizes* too big? Parents typically think that a smaller class size encourages more individualized education. That is a belief that motivates many parents to choose private schools or home schooling. However, mixed evidence comes from nations where children score high on international tests. Sometimes they have large student/teacher ratios (Korea's average is 28-to-1) and sometimes small (Finland's is 14-to-1).

10. Should teachers nurture *soft skills* such as empathy, cooperation, and integrity as part of the school curriculum, even though these skills cannot be tested by multiple-choice questions? Many scholars argue that soft skills are crucial not only for academic success but also for employment (Reardon, 2013). This idea is becoming increasingly popular, as was noted in Opposing Perspectives on page 352.

## Who Decides?

An underlying issue for almost any national or international school is the proper role of parents. In most nations, matters regarding public education—curriculum, funding, teacher training, and so on—are set by the central government. Almost

# Education in Middle Childhood Around the World

Only a decade ago, gender differences in education around the world were stark, with far fewer girls in school than boys. Now girls have almost caught up. However, many of today's children suffer from decades of past educational inequality: Recent data find that the best predictor of childhood health is an educated mother.

## WORLDWIDE PRIMARY SCHOOL ENROLLMENT, 2014

Enrollments in elementary school are increasing around the world, but poor countries still lag behind more wealthy ones, and in all countries, more boys attend school than girls.

Barbara Delgado/Shutterstock

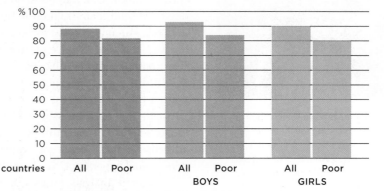

BOYS • GIRLS

Data from The World Bank, 2014.

## WORLDWIDE, BASIC ELEMENTARY EDUCATION LEADS TO:

**LESS –**
- Child and maternal mortality
- Transmission of HIV
- Early marriage and childbirth
- War

**MORE +**
- Better paying jobs
- Agricultural productivity
- Use of medical care
- Voting

Information from Hanushek & Woessmann, 2007.

## HOW ARE U.S. FOURTH-GRADERS DOING?

Primary school enrollment is high in the United States, but not every student is learning. While numbers are improving, less than half of fourth-graders are proficient in math and reading.

### PROFICIENCY LEVELS FOR U.S. FOURTH-GRADERS

**MATHEMATICS**

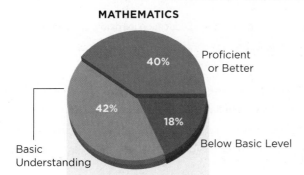

40% Proficient or Better
42%
18% Below Basic Level
Basic Understanding

**READING**

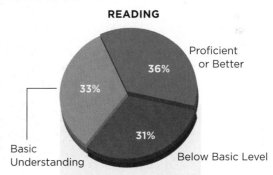

36% Proficient or Better
33%
31% Below Basic Level
Basic Understanding

NAEP (NATIONAL ASSESSMENT OF EDUCATIONAL PROGRESS)

Data from National Center for Education Statistics, 2015.

### CHANGE IN AVERAGE SCORES FOR FOURTH-GRADERS

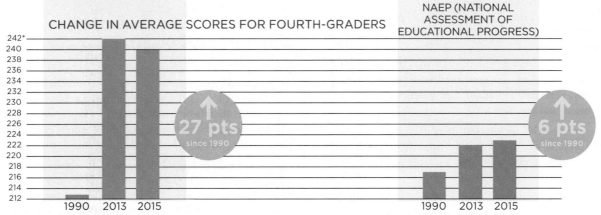

27 pts since 1990

6 pts since 1990

1990   2013   2015          1990   2013   2015

*The NAEP score ranges from 0–500.

Data from National Center for Education Statistics, 2015.

**Loved and Rewarded** Melissa Ochoa, a third-grade public school teacher near San Diego, California, is shown moments after she learned that she won $5,000 as a star educator. Which do you think is more rewarding to her, the money or the joy of her students?

all children attend the local school, whose resources and standards are similar to those of the other schools in that nation. The parents' job is to support the child's learning by checking homework and so on.

In the United States, however, local districts provide most of the funds and guidelines, and parents, as voters and volunteers, are often active in their child's school. Although most U.S. parents send their children to the nearest public school, almost one-third send their children to private schools or charter schools, or educate them at home. Parental choices may vary for each child, depending on the child's characteristics, the parents' current economic status, and the political rhetoric at the time. Every option has strengths and weaknesses, both for the child and for society.

It is difficult for parents to decide the best school for their child, partly because neither the test scores of students in any of these schools, nor the moral values a particular school espouses, correlate with the cognitive skills that developmentalists seek to foster (Finn et al., 2014). Thus, parents may choose a school that advertises what the parents value, but the school may not actually be the best educational experience for their child.

Statistical analysis raises questions about home schooling and about charter schools (Lubienski et al., 2013; Finn et al., 2014), but as our discussion of NAEP, Common Core, TIMSS, and so on makes clear, the evidence allows many interpretations. As one review notes, "the modern day, parent-led home-based education movement . . . stirs up many a curious query, negative critique, and firm praise" (Ray, 2013, p. 261).

Schoolchildren's ability to be logical and teachable, now that they are no longer preoperational and egocentric, makes this a good time to teach them—they will learn whatever adults deem important. Parents, politicians, and developmental experts all agree that school is vital for development, but disagreements about teachers and curriculum—hidden or overt—abound.

---

### WHAT HAVE YOU LEARNED?

1. What do all nations have in common regarding education in middle childhood?

2. How does the hidden curriculum differ from the stated school curriculum?

3. What are the TIMSS and the PIRLS?

4. What are the national and international differences in school achievement of girls and boys?

5. What are the strengths and liabilities of national and international tests?

6. What are the differences among charter schools, private schools, and home schools?

7. Which of the ten controversies are most contentious in your community, and why?

---

## SUMMARY

### Building on Theory

1. According to Piaget, middle childhood is the time of concrete operational thought, when egocentrism diminishes and logical thinking begins. School-age children can understand classification, conservation, and seriation.

2. Vygotsky stressed the social context of learning, including the specific lessons of school and learning from peers and adults. Culture affects not only what children learn but also how they learn.

3. An information-processing approach examines each step of the thinking process, from input to output, using the computer as a model. This approach is useful for understanding memory, perception, and expression.

4. Memory begins with information that reaches the brain from the sense organs. Then selection processes, benefiting from past experience, allow some information to reach working memory. Finally, long-term memory indefinitely stores images and ideas that can be retrieved when needed.

5. A broader knowledge base, logical strategies for retrieval, and faster processing advance every aspect of memory and cognition. Control processes are crucial. Children become better at controlling and directing their thinking as the prefrontal cortex matures.

## Language

**6.** Language learning advances in many practical ways, including expanded vocabulary, as words are logically linked together and as an understanding of metaphors begins.

**7.** Children excel at pragmatics during middle childhood, often using one code with their friends and another in school. Many children become fluent in the school language while speaking their first language at home.

**8.** Children of low SES are usually lower in linguistic skills, primarily because they hear less language at home and because adult expectations for their learning are low. This is not inevitable for low-SES families, however.

## Teaching and Learning

**9.** Nations and experts agree that education is critical during middle childhood. Almost all of the world's children now attend primary school and learn to read, write, and calculate. Many other aspects of curriculum vary from nation to nation and, within the United States, from school to school.

**10.** The hidden curriculum may be more influential on children's learning than the formal curriculum. Some believe elementary schools favor girls, although internationally, gender similarities seem to outweigh gender differences.

**11.** International assessments are useful as comparisons, partly because few objective measures of learning are available. Reading is assessed with the PIRLS, math and science with the TIMSS. On both measures, children in East Asia excel, and children in the United States are in the middle ranks.

**12.** In the United States, the National Assessment of Educational Progress (NAEP) is a test that may raise the standard of education. The Common Core, developed with the sponsorship of the governors of the 50 states, was an effort to raise national standards and improve accountability, but it is now controversial.

**13.** Nations differ in how much overall control the central government has on education and how much choice and influence parents have. Unlike almost all other countries, in the United States, each state, each district, and sometimes each school retains significant control. Education is a political issue more than a developmental one.

**14.** Disagreements about curriculum and sponsorship of school for young children are frequent. Some parents choose charter schools, others prefer private schools, and still others opt for home schooling. More research is needed to discover what is best.

## KEY TERMS

concrete operational thought (p. 340)
classification (p. 340)
seriation (p. 340)
automatization (p. 344)
sensory memory (p. 345)
working memory (p. 345)
long-term memory (p. 346)

knowledge base (p. 346)
control processes (p. 346)
English Language Learners (ELLs) (p. 349)
immersion (p. 349)
bilingual education (p. 349)
ESL (English as a Second Language) (p. 349)

hidden curriculum (p. 353)
Trends in Math and Science Study (TIMSS) (p. 356)
Progress in International Reading Literacy Study (PIRLS) (p. 356)

National Assessment of Educational Progress (NAEP) (p. 359)
voucher (p. 361)
charter school (p. 361)
home schooling (p. 361)

## APPLICATIONS

**1.** Visit a local elementary school and look for the hidden curriculum. For example, do the children line up? Why or why not, when, and how? Does gender, age, ability, or talent affect the grouping of children or the selection of staff? What is on the walls? Are parents involved? If so, how? For everything you observe, speculate about the underlying assumptions.

**2.** Interview a 6- to 11-year-old child to find out what he or she knows *and understands* about mathematics. Relate both correct and incorrect responses to the logic of concrete operational thought.

**3.** What do you remember about how you learned to read? Compare your memories with those of two other people, one at least 10 years older and the other at least 5 years younger than you are. Can you draw any conclusions about effective reading instruction? If so, what are they? If not, why not?

**4.** Talk to two parents of primary school children. What do they think are the best and worst parts of their children's education? Ask specific questions and analyze the results.

# Middle Childhood:
## Psychosocial Development

## What Will You Know?

1. What helps some children thrive in a difficult family, school, or neighborhood?
2. Should parents marry, risking divorce, or not marry, and thus avoid divorce?
3. What can be done to stop a bully?
4. Why would children lie to adults to protect a friend?

Neesha's fourth-grade teacher referred her to the school guidance team because Neesha often fell asleep in class, was late 51 days, and was absent 15 days. Yet she scored at the seventh-grade level in reading and writing, and at the fifth-grade level in math.

Something psychosocial was the problem. The school psychologist learned that Neesha's mother was a single parent, struggling to pay rent on the tiny apartment where she had moved when Neesha's father left three years earlier. Neesha's brother, also in middle childhood when their father left, was beaten up badly as part of his initiation into a gang, a group he considered "like a family."

> Neesha volunteered that she worried a lot about things and that sometimes when she worries she has a hard time falling asleep . . . it was hard to wake up. Her mom was sleeping late because she was working more nights cleaning offices. . . . Neesha said she got so far behind that she just gave up. She was also having problems with the other girls in the class, who were starting to tease her about sleeping in class and not doing her work. She said they called her names like "Sleepy" and "Dummy." . . . at first it made her very sad, and then it made her very mad. That's when she started to hit them to make them stop.
>
> [Wilmshurst, 2011, pp. 152–153]

Shortly after the counselor spoke with her,

> The school principal received a call from Neesha's mother, who asked that her daughter not be sent home from school because she was going to kill herself. . . . While the guidance counselor continued to keep the mother talking, the school contacted the police, who apprehended mom . . . The loaded gun was on her lap. . . . The mother was taken to the local psychiatric facility.
>
> [Wilmshurst, 2011, pp. 154–155]

This chapter describes the psychosocial development of children between ages 6 and 11. You will read about children who seem to cope with family and school problems—they are called resilient. But often they need help. Some find it, perhaps from a relative, a neighbor, a teacher.

Neesha thanked the school psychologist for working with her and added, "You know, sometimes it's hard being a kid."

+ **The Nature of the Child**
  Self-Concept
  OPPOSING PERSPECTIVES: Protect or Puncture Self-Esteem?
  Resilience and Stress

+ **Families and Children**
  Shared and Nonshared Environments
  Family Structure and Family Function
  A VIEW FROM SCIENCE: "I Always Dressed One in Blue Stuff . . ."
  Connecting Structure and Function
  Family Trouble

+ **The Peer Group**
  The Culture of Children
  A CASE TO STUDY: Ignorance All Around

+ **Children's Moral Values**
  Moral Reasoning
  What Children Value

# The Nature of the Child

As explained in the previous chapters, steady growth, brain maturation, and intellectual advances make middle childhood a time for more independence (see At About This Time). One practical result is that between ages 6 and 11, children learn to care for themselves. They not only hold their own spoon but also make their own lunch, not only zip their own pants but also pack their own suitcases, not only walk to school but also organize games with friends.

The tension between what has always been the nature of the child and what specific practices the cultural context encourages is evident in a 1979 list of signs of readiness for first grade (see Table 13.1).

Most parents today would not let a child walk several blocks without an adult. But the universals are still apparent: During these years, children become more capable and independent. Parent–child interactions shift from primarily physical care (bathing, dressing, and so on) to conversation about choices and values, a trend particularly apparent between boys and fathers, who now discuss many issues with their sons (Keown & Palmer, 2014). Girls as well as boys become conversation partners, not merely the recipient or instigator of demands.

The drive for independence expands the social world. School-age children venture outdoors alone to play with friends, if their parents let them. Some experts think that parents should do just that (Rosin, 2014). Schoolchildren have their own ideas and can argue with teachers, parents, friends, and others—no longer is their response either compliance or resistance. Instead negotiation and compromise are among their skills.

Images by Christina Kilgour/Getty Images

**Learning from Each Other**  Middle childhood is prime time for social comparison. Swinging is done standing, or on the belly, or twisted, or head down (as shown here) if someone else does it.

---

**TABLE 13.1**

**Signs of Readiness for First Grade, 1979**

Psychosocial development depends on what parents, schools, and communities expect. Unlike a few decades ago, today's children can do most of these by age 5, but their parents might be arrested if they sent their 6-year-old eight blocks to the store.

1. Will your child be 6 years, 6 months, or older when he begins first grade and starts receiving reading instruction?

2. Does your child have two to five permanent or second teeth?

3. Can your child tell, in such a way that his speech is understood by a school crossing guard or policeman, where he lives?

4. Can he draw and color and stay within the lines of the design being colored?

5. Can he stand on one foot with eyes closed for five to ten seconds?

6. Can he ride a small two-wheeled bicycle without helper wheels?

7. Can he tell left hand from right?

8. Can he travel alone in the neighborhood (four to eight blocks) to store, school, playground, or to a friend's home?

9. Can he be away from you all day without being upset?

10. Can he repeat an eight- to ten-word sentence, if you say it once, as "The boy ran all the way home from the store"?

11. Can he count eight to ten pennies correctly?

12. Does your child try to write or copy letters or numbers?

Information from Ames & Ilg, 1981, p. 76.

## Self-Concept

Throughout the centuries and in every culture, school-age children develop a much more realistic understanding of who they are and what they can do. They master whatever skills their community values.

### Social Comparison

The self-concept becomes more complex and logical when cognitive development and social awareness increase. Children realize they are not the fastest, smartest, prettiest, best. At some point between ages 6 and 11, when they win a race with their mother, it dawns on them that she could have run faster if she had tried.

Crucial during middle childhood is **social comparison**—comparing oneself to others (Davis-Kean et al., 2009; Dweck, 2013). Children's self-concept becomes influenced by the behavior and opinions of everyone else, even by other children whom they do not know (Thomaes et al., 2010).

Peers become crucial in many ways. A longitudinal study of almost 8,000 children, beginning when they were about 6 and ending when they were about 10, found that by age 10 self-concept correlated somewhat with emotional maturity in kindergarten but was affected much more strongly by a child's current relationship with other children (Guhn et al., 2016).

Over the years, children develop pride in their gender and background (Corenblum, 2014). Parents and teachers help by noting heroes who are female, African American, Latino, Muslim, Jewish, and so on. Of course, European American boys need heroes, too. According to a study of 9-year-olds, gender is particularly important as a source of identity, more so than race or family background (Rogers & Meltzoff, 2016).

Ideally, social comparison helps school-age children value themselves for who they are and abandon the imaginary, rosy self-evaluation of preschoolers. The self-concept becomes more realistic, attuned to other children and the culture. Often, self-esteem wanes.

Social comparison is not always benign: Children may focus on what they are rather than what they might become, on appearance rather than substance, on "performance rather than mastery," all of which undercuts motivation and aspiration (Wentzel & Muenks, 2016, p. 23). Affirming pride is an important counterbalance, because "by middle childhood . . . this [earlier] overestimate of their ability or judgments decreases" (Davis-Kean et al., 2009, p. 184).

> **social comparison** The tendency to assess one's abilities, achievements, social status, and other attributes by measuring them against those of other people, especially one's peers.

### Erikson's Insights

In the fourth psychosocial crisis, **industry versus inferiority,** Erikson noted that the child "must forget past hopes and wishes, while his exuberant imagination is tamed and harnessed to the laws of impersonal things," becoming "ready to apply himself to given skills and tasks" (Erikson, 1993a, pp. 258–259).

Think of learning to read and to add, both of which are painstaking and boring. Slowly sounding out "Jane has a dog" or writing "3 + 4 = 7" for the 100th time is not exciting. Yet school-age children busily practice reading and math: They are intrinsically motivated to read a page, finish a worksheet, memorize a spelling word, color a map, and so on. Adults can encourage this.

This was apparent in the mother–son dialogue in Chapter 12 on page 356. After Tim's mother wrote out many new math problems of the kind that had him "clumsy" in class, he did "the whole thing lickety split . . . [which made him] very happy" (J. Li et al., 2014, p. 1218). Similarly, children enjoy collecting, categorizing, and counting whatever they gather—perhaps stamps, stickers, stones, or seashells. That is industry.

> **industry versus inferiority** The fourth of Erikson's eight psychosocial crises, during which children attempt to master many skills, developing a sense of themselves as either industrious or inferior, competent or incompetent.

### Signs of Psychosocial Maturation over the Years of Middle Childhood*

These *develop* between ages 6 and 11, which means they might be present in older children but not yet in the youngest ones.

| |
|---|
| Children responsibly perform specific chores. |
| Children make decisions about a weekly allowance. |
| Children can tell time and have set times for various activities. |
| Children have homework, including some assignments over several days. |
| Children are punished less often than when they were younger. |
| Children try to conform to peers in clothes, language, and so on. |
| Children voice preferences about their after-school care, lessons, and activities. |
| Children are responsible for younger children, pets, and, in some places, work. |
| Children strive for independence from parents. |

*Of course, culture is crucial. For example, giving a child an allowance is typical for middle-class children in developed nations since about 1960. It was rare, or completely absent, in earlier times and other places.

Overall, children judge themselves as either *industrious* or *inferior*—deciding whether they are competent or incompetent, productive or useless, winners or losers. Honest affirmation from other people is crucial. As Erikson said:

> In this, children cannot be fooled by empty praise and condescending encouragement. They may have to accept artificial bolstering of their self-esteem in lieu of something better, but [they gain] . . . strength only from wholehearted and consistent recognition of real accomplishment, [that is] of achievement that has meaning in the culture.

[*Erikson, 1993a, pp. 235–236*]

Social rejection is both a cause and a consequence of feeling inferior (Rubin et al., 2013). The culture that is most salient in middle childhood is the culture of children, especially as developed by peers of the same sex. Indeed, boys who write "Girls stay out!" and girls who insist that "Boys stink!" are typical. From a developmental perspective, this temporary antipathy toward the other gender (which Freud called *latency*) is a dynamic and useful stage. Children strive to be

**Same Situation, Far Apart: Helping at Home** Sichuan, in China *(right)*, and Virginia, in the United States *(left)*, provide vastly different contexts for child development. Children everywhere help their families with household chores, as these two do, but expectations vary a great deal.

recognized for "real accomplishment" by their peers, shifting away from sexual interests until the hormones of puberty rise (Knight, 2014).

One component of self-concept has received considerable research attention (Dweck, 2013). As children become more self-aware, they benefit from praise for process not product, for *how* they learn and *how* they relate to others, not for static qualities such as intelligence and popularity. This encourages a **growth mindset.** Instead of being told that "failure is not an option," they are encouraged to "fail again, fail better" (Smith & Henriksen, 2016, p. 6).

The idea that change is possible is crucial. This concept (a growth mindset rather than a *fixed mindset*) does not come naturally to 6- to 11-year-olds, whose concrete operational thinking can lead to discouragement and quitting if they decide they are bad at sports, or math, or whatever.

For example, children who fail a test may be devastated *if* failure means they are not smart. However, children may consider failure a "learning opportunity," using metacognition to plan a better way to study, if they have a growth mindset. [**Developmental Link:** Dweck's research on whether intelligence is inborn or learned is further discussed in Chapter 15.]

Self-conscious emotions (pride, shame, guilt) develop during middle childhood, guiding social interaction. During these years, if those same emotions are uncontrolled, they can overwhelm a healthy self-concept, leading to psychopathology (Muris & Meesters, 2014).

**growth mindset** The idea that skills and abilities develop with practice and effort, instead of being fixed or inborn.

Watch **Video: Interview with Carol Dweck** to learn about how children's mindsets affect their intellectual development.

**THINK CRITICALLY:** When would a realistic, honest self-assessment be harmful?

---

## OPPOSING PERSPECTIVES

## Protect or Puncture Self-Esteem?

Unrealistically high self-esteem may reduce effortful control (described in Chapter 10), which leads to lower achievement and increased aggression. The same problems appear if self-esteem is unrealistically low. Children may be too self-critical or not self-critical enough (Baumeister, 2012; Robins et al., 2012).

Many cultures teach children to be modest, not prideful. For example, Australians say, "tall poppies are cut down"; the Chinese say, "the nail that sticks up is hammered"; and the Japanese discourage social comparison aimed at making oneself feel superior. That perspective is not held by everyone, even in those cultures.

But how much self-esteem is too high or too low, and what are the consequences? A trio of researchers, acknowledging that "whether high or low self-esteem is associated with increased aggression remains a topic of debate" (Teng et al., 2015, p. 45), surveyed 52 studies of self-esteem in Chinese children. They found that low self-esteem correlated with aggression, and thus they recommended that Chinese families and schools should not criticize children so much.

On the other hand, a study of fourth-grade students in the Netherlands found that "inflated self-esteem" (indicated by agreeing with items such as "I am a great example for other kids to follow") predicted bullying aggression among boys (not girls) (Reijntjes et al., 2015). These researchers were particularly concerned about child narcissism, an exaggerated pride that may be pathological.

Self-esteem is often encouraged in the United States. If 8-year-olds say that they want to be president when they grow up, adults usually smile and say, "That would be wonderful." Children's successes and ambitions are praised—even unlikely ones.

Teachers hesitate to criticize, especially in middle childhood. Some report card categories use phrases such as "on grade level" and "needs improvement" instead of letter grades. No child fails. This may lead to "social promotion," a much-criticized practice of passing children to the next grade whether or not they have mastered the work.

A backlash against age-based promotion is implicit when schools are closed because the children score low on achievement tests. A recent wave of educational reform in the United States tests children from the third grade on, promoting them only if they have achieved proficiency.

The wave has already produced an opposing counterwave, with parents opting out of testing and politicians criticizing Common Core standards. Obviously culture, cohort, and age all influence attitudes about achievement, standards, and self-esteem. Should children be praised less or criticized less?

This becomes especially crucial for children who have a disability or are of an ethnic minority in their schools. Experiencing prejudice from peers reduces self-esteem, but experiencing acceptance by peers and teachers protects self-esteem (Brown, 2017). In general, a realistic self-esteem is possible during middle childhood, with peers, teachers, and communities all influential.

**Same Situation, Far Apart: Play Ball** In the war in the Ukraine *(left),* volunteers guard the House of Parliament against a Russian takeover, and in Liberia *(right),* thousands have died from the Ebola epidemic. Nonetheless, one boy practices his soccer kick and four boys celebrate a soccer goal in 2015. Children can ignore national disasters as long as they have familiar caregivers nearby and a chance to play.

**Observation Quiz** How can you tell that the Liberian boys are celebrating a soccer victory instead of the end of an epidemic? (see answer, p. 374) ↑

**resilience** The capacity to adapt well to significant adversity and to overcome serious stress.

Thus, as with most developmental advances, the potential for psychological growth is evident. However, advance is not automatic—family and social context affect whether a more realistic, socially attuned self-concept will be a burden or a blessing, and cultures vary.

## Resilience and Stress

Although early experiences are powerful, some children seem unscathed by early stress. They have been called "resilient" or even "invincible." Current thinking about resilience, with insights from dynamic-systems theory, emphasizes that no one is impervious to past history or current context (see Table 13.2). Many suffer lifelong harm from maltreatment, some weather early storms, and a few become stronger (Masten, 2014).

One leading researcher defines **resilience** as "a dynamic process encompassing positive adaptation within the context of significant adversity" (Luthar et al., 2000, p. 543), and another writes that resilience is "the capacity of a dynamic system to adapt successfully to disturbances that threaten system function, viability, or development" (Masten, 2014, p. 10). Both definitions emphasize that:

- Resilience is *dynamic*, not a stable trait. A given person may be resilient at some periods but not at others. The effects from each earlier period reverberate as time goes on.
- Resilience is a *positive adaptation*. For example, if parental rejection leads a child to a closer relationship with another adult, that is positive adaptation.
- Adversity must be *significant*, a threat to the processes of development or even to life itself, not merely a minor stress.

### Cumulative Stress

One important discovery is that stress accumulates over time, with many minor disturbances (called "daily hassles") building to a major impact. That seems to have happened to Neesha, whose experience opened this chapter. She seemed to have coped well with the divorce, which is a major stress for some children. Her mother said that Neesha was "more like a little mother than a kid," and Neesha's academic accomplishments were stellar (Wilmshurst, 2011). Her fourth-grade schoolwork, however, suggested that the hassles of daily life were taking a toll.

## TABLE 13.2

### Dominant Ideas About Resilience, 1965 to Present

| Year | Idea |
|------|------|
| 1965 | All children have the same needs for healthy development. |
| 1970 | Some conditions or circumstances—such as "absent father," "teenage mother," "working mom," and "day care"—are harmful for every child. |
| 1975 | All children are *not* the same. Some children are resilient, coping easily with stressors that cause harm in other children. |
| 1980 | Nothing inevitably causes harm. Both maternal employment and preschool education, once thought to be risks, are often helpful. |
| 1985 | Factors beyond the family, both in the child (low birthweight, prenatal alcohol exposure, aggressive temperament) and in the community (poverty, violence), are very risky for children. |
| 1990 | Risk–benefit analysis finds that some children are "invulnerable" to, or even benefit from, circumstances that destroy others. |
| 1995 | No child is invincible. Risks are always harmful—if not in education, then in emotions; if not immediately, then long term. |
| 2000 | Risk–benefit analysis involves the interplay among many biological, cognitive, and social factors, some within the child (genes, disability, temperament), the family (function as well as structure), and the community (including neighborhood, school, church, and culture). |
| 2008 | Focus on strengths, not risks. Assets in child (intelligence, personality), family (secure attachment, warmth), community (schools, after-school programs), and nation (income support, health care) must be nurtured. |
| 2010 | Strengths vary by culture and national values. Both universal ideals and local variations must be recognized and respected. |
| 2012 | Genes as well as cultural practices can be either strengths or weaknesses; differential susceptibility means identical stressors can benefit one child and harm another. |
| 2015 | Communities are responsible for child resilience. Not every child needs help, but every community needs to encourage healthy child development. |
| 2017 | Resilience is seen not primarily as a trait in a child but as a characteristic of mothers and communities. Some are quite resilient, which fosters resilience in children. |

Almost every child can withstand one trauma. Repeated stresses, daily hassles, and multiple traumatic experiences make resilience difficult (Masten, 2014; Catani et al., 2010). The social context—especially supportive adults who do not blame the child—is crucial. If the school counselor and teachers are able to step in and find a good home for Neesha, she may become an accomplished, compassionate adult.

A chilling example comes from the "child soldiers" in the 1991–2002 civil war in Sierra Leone (Betancourt et al., 2013). Children witnessed and often participated in murder and rape. When the war was over, 529 war-affected youth, then aged 10 to 17, were interviewed. Many were pathologically depressed or anxious.

These war-damaged children were interviewed again two and six years later. Surprisingly, many had overcome their trauma and were functioning like typical children. Recovery was more likely if they were in middle childhood, not yet adolescence, when the war occurred. Furthermore, if at least one caregiver survived, if their communities did not reject them, and if their daily routines were restored, the children usually regained emotional normality.

**LaunchPad**
macmillan learning

**Video Activity: Child Soldiers and Child Peacemakers** examines the state of child soldiers in the world and then explores how adolescent cognition impacts the decisions of five teenage peace activists.

Courtesy of Unicef

**Same Situation, Far Apart: Praying Hands** Differences are obvious between the Northern Indian girls entering their Hindu school *(left)* and the West African boy in a Christian church *(right)*, even in their clothes and hand positions. But underlying similarities are more important. In every culture, many 8-year-olds are more devout than their elders. That is especially true if their community is under stress. Faith aids resilience.

**Answer to Observation Quiz** (from p. 372) They are hugging the ball.

An example from the United States comes from children living in a shelter for homeless families (Cutuli et al., 2013; Obradović, 2012). Compared with other children from the same kinds of families (typically high-poverty, single-parent), they were lower in academic achievement, self-concept, emotional stability, friendship networks, and worse on physiological measures such as cortisol levels, blood pressure, and weight.

The probable reason: Residential disruption, added to other stresses, was too much. Again, however, family protective factors buffered the impact: Having a parent with them who provided affection, hope, and stable routines enabled some homeless children to be resilient (Masten et al., 2014).

Similar results were found in a longitudinal study of children exposed to a sudden, wide-ranging, terrifying wildfire in Australia. Almost all of the children suffered stress reactions at the time, but 20 years later, the crucial factor for recovery was not their proximity to the blaze but whether they had been separated from their mothers (McFarlane & Van Hooff, 2009). Such research has caused the leading scientists studying resilience to advocate for more assistance to mothers, because that may advance child resilience more than programs aimed directly at children (Luthar & Eisenberg, 2017).

## Cognitive Coping

These examples are extreme, but the general finding appears in other research as well. Disasters take a toll, yet factors in the child (especially problem-solving ability), in the family (consistency and care), and in the community (good schools and welcoming religious institutions) all increase resilience (Masten, 2014). Even the impact of poverty on a child's brain can be markedly reduced. To think otherwise, as many Americans do, is "absurd" according to a neuroscientist in Spain and an ethicist in Sweden (Lipina & Evers, 2017).

A pivotal factor is the child's interpretation of events (Lagattuta, 2014). Cortisol increases in low-income children *if* they interpret circumstances connected to their family's poverty as a personal threat and *if* the family lacks order and routines (thus increasing daily hassles) (E. Chen et al., 2010). When low-SES children do not take things personally and their family is not chaotic, resilience is more likely.

Do you know adults who grew up in low-SES families but seem strengthened, not destroyed, by that experience? If so, they probably did not consider themselves poor, perhaps because their life was similar to that of every child they knew. They may have shared a bed with a sibling, eaten macaroni day after day, worn used clothes, and walked to school. However, if their family was loving and neither chaotic nor hostile, poverty did not harm them lifelong.

Overall, children's interpretation of circumstances (poverty, divorce, war, and so on) is crucial. Some consider their situation a temporary hardship; they look forward to leaving childhood behind. If they also can develop their strengths, such as creativity and intelligence, they may shine in adulthood—evident in thousands of success stories, from Abraham Lincoln to Oprah Winfrey. Lincoln studied by candlelight, Winfrey preached to the crows in her grandmother's backyard: Both of them eventually thrived.

The opposite reaction is **parentification,** when children feel responsible for the entire family. They become caretakers, including of their actual parents. Here again, interpretation is crucial. Children suffer if they feel burdened and unable to escape, but if they feel useful and respected, they may be resilient. The difference depends partly on community values: If everyone they know believes that children are supposed to help their families, then they may be proud of themselves (Khafi et al., 2014).

This conclusion comes from yet another group, Chinese American children who must interpret English for their parents. Some feel burdened; others are proud. The difference is more in their interpretation of what they do than in the actual work (Weisskirch, 2017).

> **THINK CRITICALLY:** Is there any harm in having the oldest child take care of the younger ones? Why or why not?

**parentification** When a child acts more like a parent than a child. Parentification may occur if the actual parents do not act as caregivers, making a child feel responsible for the family.

---

### WHAT HAVE YOU LEARNED?

1. How do Erikson's stages of cognition for preschool- and school-age children differ?
2. Why is social comparison particularly powerful during middle childhood?
3. Why do cultures differ in how they value pride or modesty?
4. What factors help a child become resilient?
5. Why and when might minor stresses be more harmful than major stresses?
6. How might a child's interpretation affect the ability to cope with repeated stress?

---

# Families and Children

No one doubts that genes affect personality as well as ability, that peers are vital, and that schools and cultures influence what, and how much, children learn. Some experts have gone further, suggesting that genes, peers, and communities are so influential that parents make no difference—unless they are grossly abusive (Harris, 1998, 2002; McLeod et al., 2007). This suggestion arose from studies about the impact of the nonshared environment on child development.

## Shared and Nonshared Environments

Many studies find that children are much less affected by *shared environment* (influences that arise from being in the same environment, such as two siblings living in one home, raised by their parents) than by *nonshared environment* (e.g., the experiences in the school or neighborhood that differ between one child and another).

Studies of siblings, especially of monozygotic and dizygotic twins, find that almost all personality traits and intellectual characteristics can be traced to the combination of genes and nonshared environments. Almost nothing is the result of shared influences. Even traits that are affected by upbringing, such

Masterfile/Masterfile

**Family Unity** Thinking about any family—even a happy, wealthy family like this one—makes it apparent that each child's family experiences differ. For instance, would you expect this 5-year-old boy to be treated the same way as his two older sisters? And how about each child's feelings toward the parents? Even though the 12-year-olds are twins, one may favor her mother while the other favors her father.

⬤ **Observation Quiz** The 12-year-olds are twins. Can you see any differences in their shared environment? (see answer, p. 378) ⬆

**family structure** The legal and genetic relationships among relatives living in the same home. Possible structures include nuclear family, extended family, stepfamily, single-parent family, and many others.

**family function** The way a family works to meet the needs of its members. Children need families to provide basic material necessities, to encourage learning, to help them develop self-respect, to nurture friendships, and to foster harmony and stability.

⬤ **Especially for Scientists** How would you determine whether or not parents treat all of their children the same? (see response, p. 378)

as psychopathology, happiness, sexual orientation, and romantic relationships (Bartels et al., 2013; Burt, 2009; Langstrom et al., 2010; Whisman & South, 2017) can be traced primarily to genes and nonshared environment.

Could it be that parents are merely caretakers, providing only the basics (food, shelter)? Might household restrictions, routines, values, and responses be irrelevant? If a child becomes a murderer or a hero, might that have been determined by genes and nonshared environment? If so, parents deserve neither blame nor credit!

Recent findings, however, reassert parent power. The analysis that nonshared influences are powerful was correct, but the assumption that siblings raised together share the same environment is false. This is apparent even for twins. If one twin abuses drugs or breaks the law, the other is more likely to do so (shared genes) but sometimes does neither (Laursen et al., 2017).

Many studies find that if a family experiences relocation, divorce, or unemployment, everyone is affected. However, the impact on each child depends on age, genes, and gender.

For example, moving to another town upsets school-age children more than infants; divorce harms boys more than girls; poverty hurts preschoolers the most. If siblings are raised in a dysfunctional family, one child may become antisocial, another pathologically anxious, and a third resilient (Beauchaine et al., 2009). Neesha and her brother shared their father's absence, stressful poverty, and their depressed mother. However, Neesha became a good student and her brother became a delinquent, already in juvenile detention at age 13.

Some of this may be gender and age. But in addition, even identical twins (same sex and age) might not share family experiences (see A View from Science on the next page).

## Family Structure and Family Function

**Family structure** refers to the legal and genetic connections among people who live together. Genetic connections (sometimes called "blood relations") are from parents to their biological children, or between siblings, cousins, grandparents and grandchildren, and so on. Legal connections may be via marriage, years of cohabitation ("common-law marriage"), or adoption.

**Family function** refers to how the people who live together as a family work together to care for each other. Some families function well; others are dysfunctional. Some family functions are needed by everyone at every age, such as love and encouragement. Other essential functions differ by age. A family functions well for infants who receive responsive caregiving, for teenagers who need encouragement and guidance, for young adults who are allowed independence, and for the aged if they are respected.

Family structures can vary dramatically without harming children, but always function is crucial.

### Family Function in Middle Childhood

What do school-age children need from their families? Ideally, five things:

1. *Physical necessities.* Although 6- to 11-year-olds eat, dress, and go to bed without help, families can provide basic needs, such as food, clothing, and shelter.
2. *Learning.* Middle childhood is prime learning time; families can encourage and guide education.
3. *Self-respect.* Because children from age 6 to 11 become self-critical and socially aware, families can foster success (in academics, sports, the arts, and so on) or shame (industry versus inferiority).

## A VIEW FROM SCIENCE

# "I Always Dressed One in Blue Stuff . . ."

To separate the effects of genes and environment, many researchers have studied twins. As you remember from Chapter 3, some twins are dizygotic (DZ), with only half of their genes in common, and some are monozygotic (MZ), genetically identical (some MZ twins differ because of epigenetic factors after conception, but genetically, MZ twins come from one ovum and one sperm producing one zygote). Typically MZ and DZ twins are raised together, so researchers assumed a shared environment.

In prior research, if MZ twins had the same trait but DZ twins did not, scientists assumed that the trait was genetic. However, if MZ and DZ twins were similar in any intellectual or personality characteristic, their shared environment was considered the reason. Studies of thousands of twins led to the conclusion that genes and nonshared environment were far more significant for intelligence and personality than shared environment—i.e., their parents' values and practices.

Comparing MZ and DZ twins is a useful research strategy. However, conclusions are now tempered by another finding: Siblings raised in the same households do not necessarily share the same home environment.

Researchers compared 1,000 sets of MZ twins reared by their biological parents. Their mothers' descriptions ranged from very positive ("my ray of sunshine") to very negative ("I wish I never had her. . . . She's a cow, I hate her.") (quoted in Caspi et al., 2004, p. 153). Many mothers saw personality differences between their twins. For example, one mother said:

> Susan can be very sweet. She loves babies . . . she can be insecure . . . she flutters and dances around. . . . There's not much between her

ears. . . . She's exceptionally vain, more so than Ann. Ann loves any game involving a ball, very sporty, climbs trees, very much a tomboy. One is a serious tomboy and one's a serious girlie girl. Even when they were babies I always dressed one in blue stuff and one in pink stuff.

> [quoted in Caspi et al., 2004, p. 156]

Some mothers rejected one twin and favored the other:

> He was in the hospital and everyone was all "poor Jeff, poor Jeff" and I started thinking, "Well, what about me? I'm the one's just had twins. I'm the one's going through this, he's a seven-week-old baby and doesn't know a thing about it . . ." I sort of detached and plowed my emotions into Mike. [Jeff's twin brother.]

> [quoted in Caspi et al., 2004, p. 156].

This same mother later blamed Jeff for favoring his father: "Jeff would do anything for Don but he wouldn't for me, and no matter what I did for either of them [Don or Jeff] it wouldn't be right" (p. 157). She said Mike was much more lovable.

The researchers measured each twin's personality at age 5 (assessing, among other things, antisocial behavior reported by teachers) and again two years later. They found that if a mother was more negative toward one of her twins, that twin *became* more antisocial, more likely to fight, steal, and hurt others at age 7 than at age 5, unlike the favored twin.

These researchers do not deny that many other nonshared factors—peers, teachers, and so on—have an impact. But parents matter. This will surprise no one who has a brother or a sister. Children from the same home do not always share the same experiences.

---

4. *Peer relationships*. Families can choose schools and neighborhoods with friendly children and arrange play dates, group activities, overnight trips, and so on.
5. *Harmony and stability*. Families can provide protective, predictable routines within a home that is a safe, peaceful haven.

The final item on the list above is especially desirable in middle childhood: Children cherish harmony and stability; they do not like conflict and change (Turner et al., 2012). Ironically, many parents move from one neighborhood or school to another during these years, not realizing that frequent moves may harm children academically and psychologically (Cutuli et al., 2013).

The need for continuity is evident for children in military families. Enlisted parents have higher incomes, better health care, and more education than do civilians from the same backgrounds. Children of career officers are more likely to

**Stay Home, Dad** The rate of battle deaths for U.S. soldiers is lower for those deployed in Iraq and Afghanistan than for any previous conflict, thanks to modern medicine and armor. However, psychological harm from repeated returns and absences is increasing, especially for children.

KidStock/Getty Images

● **Answer to Observation Quiz** (from p. 376) Their appearance and clothes are very similar. However, their relationship with their mother may differ.

● **Response for Scientists** (from p. 376): Proof is very difficult when human interaction is the subject of investigation, since random assignment is impossible. Ideally, researchers would find identical twins being raised together and would then observe the parents' behavior over the years.

**nuclear family** A family that consists of a father, a mother, and their biological children under age 18.

**single-parent family** A family that consists of only one parent and his or her children.

**extended family** A family of relatives in addition to the nuclear family, usually three or more generations living in one household.

**polygamous family** A family consisting of one man, several wives, and their children.

live in married families than other children are. But they move twice as often as other children if their military parent is a career officer, and more often than that if their parent is on active duty.

Analysis of all such research found that children of front-line soldiers have higher rates of depression, ADHD, and other behavioral disorders than their peers with more stable lives. Difficulties are worse in middle childhood (when harmony and stability are especially important) than earlier or later (Card et al., 2011). Compared to children of civilians, children of deployed parents are almost twice as likely to carry a knife or gun to school (Wadsworth et al., 2017).

To help these children, the U.S. military has instituted special programs, such as after-school sports that encourage positive friendships and abilities. Caregivers are advised to keep the child's life as stable as possible—no new homes, new rules, or new schools (Lester et al., 2011). Special attention is given to the caregivers, because they are likely to become anxious and depressed, which itself changes life for the child. As one report explains, deployment precipitates "unhealthy family functioning . . . marital instability . . . [and] a pattern of reverberating stress" (Lester et al., 2016, p. 947).

## Diverse Structures

Children flourish, or suffer, in many family structures. The most common structure during middle childhood is the **nuclear family,** which is made up of two parents and their biological children (see Table 13.3). Other two-parent structures include adoptive, foster, grandparent, stepparent, and same-sex couples. Probably the most complex two-parent structure is the *blended family,* with children from each of two remarried parents, who often then have a baby of their own. Blended families are idealized in the media, but relatively few children live within them.

One-third of U.S. children live in a **single-parent family.** Infants and adolescents are more often in single-parent households than are 6- to 11-year-olds.

**Extended families** consist of relatives residing with parents and children. Usually the additional persons are grandparents; sometimes they are uncles, aunts, or cousins. Shared households are common in some nations but less so in the United States. Rates vary depending on family culture: Extended families in the United States are more frequently low-SES, African American, and immigrant families. When they do not live in the same household, families in all of those groups tend to have more frequent interaction (R. Taylor et al., 2013).

In many nations, a **polygamous family** (one husband with two or more wives) is an acceptable family structure, although polygamous families are not common even in nations that condone them. In the United States, polygamy is illegal, and rare.

## Divorce

Scientists try to provide analysis and insight based on empirical data (of course), but the task goes far beyond reporting facts. Regarding divorce, thousands of studies and several opposing perspectives need to be considered, analyzed, and combined—no easy task. One scholar who has attempted to do so is Andrew Cherlin, who has written 13 books and more than 200 articles since 1988.

Among the facts that need interpretation are:

1. The United States leads the world in the rates of divorce, and remarriage, with almost one-half of all marriages ending in divorce.
2. Single parents, cohabiting parents, and stepparents sometimes provide good care for their estimated 40 million U.S. children, but children usually do best living with married parents who contributed genes and now provide intensive care and a shared home. Yet, this type is becoming less common.

3. Divorce is a process, not a decree: It affects children's academic achievement and psychosocial development for years, even decades, before and after the official end of marriage.
4. Custody disputes and outcomes frequently harm children. Noncustodial parents, especially fathers, often become less connected to their children.

## TABLE 13.3

### Family Structures (percent of U.S. 6- to 11-year-olds in each type)*

**Two-Parent Families (69%)**

1. **Nuclear family** (56%). Named after the nucleus (the tightly connected core particles of an atom), the nuclear family consists of a man and a woman and their biological offspring under 18 years of age. In middle childhood, about half of all children live in nuclear families. About 10 percent of such families also include a grandparent, and often an aunt or uncle, living under the same roof. Those are *extended* families.

2. **Stepparent family** (9%). Divorced fathers usually remarry; divorced mothers remarry about half the time. If the stepparent family includes children born to two or more couples (such as children from the spouses' previous marriages and/or children of the new couple), that is a *blended family*.

3. **Adoptive family** (2%). Although as many as one-third of infertile couples adopt children, they usually adopt only one or two. Thus, only 2 percent of children are adopted, although the overall percentage of adoptive families is higher than that.

4. **Grandparents alone** (1%). Grandparents take on parenting for some children when biological parents are absent (dead, imprisoned, sick, addicted, etc.). That is a *skipped-generation* family.

5. **Two same-sex parents** (1%). Some two-parent families are headed by a same-sex couple, whose legal status (married, step-, adoptive) varies.

**Single-Parent Families (31%)**

One-parent families are increasing, but they average fewer children than two-parent families. So in middle childhood, only 31 percent of children have a lone parent.

1. **Single mother—never married** (14%). In 2010, 41 percent of all U.S. births were to unmarried mothers; but when children are school age, many such mothers have married or have entrusted their children to their parents' care. Thus, only about 14 percent of 6- to 11-year-olds, at any given moment, are in single-mother, never-married homes.

2. **Single mother—divorced, separated, or widowed** (12%). Although many marriages end in divorce (almost half in the United States, fewer in other nations), many divorcing couples have no children. Others remarry. Thus, only 12 percent of school-age children currently live with single, formerly married mothers.

3. **Single father** (4%). About 1 father in 25 has physical custody of his children and raises them without their mother or a new wife. This category increased at the start of the twenty-first century but has decreased since 2005.

4. **Grandparent alone** (1%). Sometimes a single grandparent (usually the grandmother) becomes the sole caregiving adult for a child.

**More Than Two Adults (15%) [Also listed as two-parent or single-parent family]**

1. **Extended family** (15%). Some children live with a grandparent or other relatives, as well as with one (5 percent) or both (10 percent) of their parents. This pattern is most common with infants (20 percent) but occurs in middle childhood as well.

2. **Polygamous family** (0%). In some nations (not the United States), men can legally have several wives. This family structure is more favored by adults than children. Everywhere, polyandry (one woman, several husbands) is rare.

*Less than 1 percent of children under age 12 live without any caregiving adult; they are not included in this table.

The percentages in this table are estimates, based on data in U.S. Census Bureau (2011, 2015). The category "extended family" in this table is higher than most published statistics, since some families do not tell official authorities about relatives living with them.

Each of these is troubling. The underlying problem, Cherlin (2009) contends, is that the entire culture is conflicted: Marriage is idolized, but so is personal freedom. As a result, many North Americans assert their independence by marrying without consulting their parents or community. If they have a baby, child care becomes overwhelming and family support is lacking.

Added to that, the shrinking of the middle class means that many Americans cannot find jobs that adequately support their families. Often, both partners work to make ends meet, but even so, finding affordable housing and child care is difficult (Cherlin, 2014). That strains the marriage, precipitating conflict and sometimes divorce.

However, because marriage is the ideal, divorcing adults blame their former mate or their own poor choice, not the institution or the economy, according to Cherlin. Consequently, they seek another marriage, which may lead to another divorce. (Divorced adults marry more often than single adults their age, and the risk of divorce rises if a person has already been divorced.) Many young adults decide to avoid divorce by avoiding marriage and choosing cohabitation, a partnership that ends more often than marriage.

This leads to a related insight. Cherlin suggests that the main reason children are harmed by divorce, cohabitation, single parenthood, and stepparenthood is not the legal status of their parents but frequent changes in residence, school, and family members.

For instance, one common change in children's lives is that grandparents suddenly become more or less involved. Many newly divorced custodial parents live with their own parents temporarily; many noncustodial parents see their children infrequently, which may cut off the children from that set of grandparents.

The crucial factor for children is their relationship with both parents, and that often worsens when the parents separate. Recently divorced parents become stricter or more lenient, impose premature responsibility or allow too much freedom, keep family secrets or tell the child things that are confusing or troubling. Divorced parents may argue about child support, visitation, and child behavior—and each may tell the child that the other parent is wrong.

To make this more complex, sometimes divorce is better for children than an ongoing, destructive family, which makes it hard for a parent to know when to quit the marriage. As one scientist who has also studied divorced families for decades wrote:

> Although divorce leads to an increase in stressful life events, such as poverty, psychological and health problems in parents, and inept parenting, it also may be associated with escape from conflict, the building of new more harmonious fulfilling relationships, and the opportunity for personal growth and individuation.
>
> *[Hetherington, 2006, p. 204]*

Thus, some children fare better if their family structure is not a traditional nuclear family. But most do not.

## Connecting Structure and Function

The fact that family function is more influential than family structure does not make structure irrelevant. Structure powerfully affects function. Some structures make it easier for parents to provide the five family functions mentioned earlier (physical necessities, learning, self-respect, friendship, and harmony/stability).

### Two-Parent Families

On average, adults are better parents when they live with their own children, day after day, forming a strong and cooperative alliance. One scholar summarizes the conclusions of dozens of studies: "Children living with two biological married

**Didn't Want to Marry** This couple was happily cohabiting and strongly committed to each other but didn't wed until they learned that her health insurance would not cover him unless they were legally married. Twenty months after marriage, their son was born.

Macmillan Archive/Danny Goldfield

Charles Rex Arbogast/AP Images

Greg Elms/Getty Images

**Same Situation, Far Apart: Happy Families** The boys in both photos are about 4 years old. Roberto lives with his single mother in Chicago (*left*). She pays $360 a month for her two children to attend a day-care center. The youngest child in the Balmedina family (*right*) lives with his nuclear family—no day care needed—in the Philippines. Which boy has the better life? The answer is not known; family function is more crucial than family structure.

parents experience better educational, social, cognitive, and behavioral outcomes" (Brown, 2010, p. 1062).

Some of those benefits are correlates, not direct causes. For instance, education, earning potential, and emotional maturity all correlate with marriage, birth, and staying married. One data point is illustrative: Most highly educated women having their first baby are married (78 percent) at conception; most less educated women are not (only 11 percent) (Gibson-Davis & Rackin, 2014).

Thus, brides and grooms tend to have personal assets *before* marriage and parenthood, and they bring those assets to their new family. That means that the correlation between child success and married parents occurs partly because of *who* marries, not because of the wedding. Indeed, for some very low-SES women, marrying a man who is also a high-school dropout with no steady job would actually undercut their ability to give their baby attention. They may be better mothers not married!

Income also correlates with family structure. Usually, married couples live apart from their parents if everyone can afford it. This means that, at least in the United States, an extended family often occurs when someone is financially dependent, and that makes such families difficult for children.

These two factors—mate selection and income—explain some of the correlation between nuclear families and child well-being, but not all of it (Brown, 2010). The fact that the nuclear family is "not as strong as it appears" does not make marriage irrelevant. Ideally, marriage produces mutual affection and support, and then both partners become wealthier and healthier than either would alone. Further, when both parents live with their children day and night, a *parental alliance* may benefit the child.

Shared parenting decreases the risk of abuse and neglect. Having two parents in the house makes it more likely that someone will read to the children, check their homework, invite their friends over, buy them new clothes, and save for their college education. Of course, having two married parents does not guarantee an alliance. One of my students wrote:

> My mother externalized her feelings with outbursts of rage, lashing out and breaking things, while my father internalized his feelings by withdrawing, being silent and looking the other way. One could say I was being raised by bipolar parents. Growing up, I would describe my mom as the Tasmanian devil and my father as the ostrich, with his head in the sand. . . . My mother disciplined with corporal punishment as well as with psychological control, while my father was permissive. What a pair.
>
> [C, 2013]

DAVID MAXWELL/The New York Times/Redux

**Middle American Family** This photo seems to show a typical breakfast in Brunswick, Ohio—Cheerios for 1-year-old Carson, pancakes that 7-year-old Carter does not finish eating, and family photos crowded on the far table.

⬤ **Observation Quiz** What is unusual about this family? (see answer, p. 385) ↑

⬤ **Especially for Single Parents** You have heard that children raised in one-parent families will have difficulty in establishing intimate relationships as adolescents and adults. What can you do about this possibility? (see response, p. 385)

📖 **LaunchPad**
macmillan learning

Check out the Data Connections activity **Family Structure in the United States and Around the World.**

**Don't Judge** We know this is a mother and her child, but structure and function could be wonderful or terrible. These two could be half of a nuclear family, or a single mother with one adoptive child, or part of four other family structures. That does not matter as much as family function: If this scene is typical, with both enjoying physical closeness in the great outdoors, this family functions well.

This student never experienced a well-functioning parental alliance. That may help explain why she is now a single parent, having twice married, given birth, and divorced. For everyone, childhood family experiences echo in adulthood.

Adoptive and same-sex parents usually function well for children, not only in middle childhood but lifelong, again because a parental alliance is likely. Stepfamilies *can* also function well, if the biological parent chooses a partner who will be a good parent. Especially when children are under age 2 and the stepparent and biological parent form a healthy marriage, stepchildren may thrive (Ganong et al., 2011).

No structure is guaranteed to function well, but particular circumstances for all three family types—same-sex, adoptive, and step—nudge in one direction or the other. Unfortunately, a nudge toward instability occurs in these non-nuclear families. Compared to nuclear families, they are more likely to change neighborhoods and schools and to add or subtract family members. New babies arrive, older children come or go, and other relatives stay for a period and then move on. Stepchildren create "complex" structures, affecting every child (including the biological offspring of both parents) in school and in life (Brown et al., 2015).

Harmony is also more difficult in stepfamilies (Martin-Uzzi & Duval-Tsioles, 2013). Children may be expected to share a home and a bedroom with someone—introduced as the child's brother or sister—whose habits and values are alien from their own. Children are naturally loyal to both their original parents, yet those parents may have ongoing disputes. A solid parental alliance is difficult with three adults—two of whom had such profound disagreements that they divorced, and a third, a stranger who had no say in earlier discipline, education, or nurturance of a new stepchild.

Indeed, one observer suggests that, for children, polygamy is preferable to divorce, remarriage, and stepparenthood. The reason for this suggestion is that most remarried fathers are less involved with children from their first wife than they would be if they lived with both wives (Calder & Beaman, 2014).

Macmillan Archive/Danny Goldfield

Finally, the grandparent family is often idealized, but reality is much more complex. If a household has grandparents and parents, the grandparents may be care-receivers more than caregivers. The two adult generations often disagree about discipline, diet, and much else.

In about 2 percent of all U.S. families, grandparents provide full-time care with no parents present. The hope is that their experience and maturity will benefit the grandchildren. But that may not happen. Grandchildren whose parents have left them often have health or behavioral problems that are difficult for the grandparents to handle (Hayslip et al., 2014). Resentment, anger, and sadness may overwhelm the children. One grandmother said:

I had books thrown at me, chairs. I broke the blood vessels in my arms, but through it all, he always cried and said "Nana, I didn't mean to hurt you, I was so angry, I was so angry, I've been so hurt. I don't think I'll ever forgive mommy and daddy."

[quoted in Dunifon et al., 2016, p. 152]

## Single-Parent Families

On average, single parents have less income, time, and stability than do two adults together. Most single parents fill many roles—including wage earner, daughter, or son—making it hard to provide steady and extensive emotional and academic support for their children. About half have a live-in partner, who adds to the complexity of the parenting role.

Rates of single parenthood and single grandparenthood are far higher among African Americans than other ethnic groups (see Figure 13.1). This makes children from single-parent, African American families feel less stigmatized, but it does not lighten the burden. Many have crucial help from relatives (Parent et al., 2013). If a single parent is depressed (and many are), that compounds the problem.

Although family structure encourages or undercuts healthy function, every family structure is sometimes excellent and sometimes horrible. Contrary to the averages, thousands of stepparents provide excellent care, thousands of single-parent families are wonderful, and thousands of nuclear families are dysfunctional. Culture and national policy are always influential—providing support or shame (Abela & Walker, 2014).

For example, a study of children in the slums of Mumbai, India, found that children in nuclear families had *more* psychological disorders than children in extended families, presumably because grandparents, aunts, and uncles provided extra care and stability (Patil et al., 2013). However, another study in India found that college students who injured themselves (e.g., *cutting*) were more often from extended families than nuclear ones (Kharsati & Bhola, 2014). One explanation for these opposite results is that these two studies had different populations: College students were from wealthier families, unlike the children in Mumbai.

## Family Trouble

Two factors impair family function in every structure, ethnic group, and nation: low income and high conflict. Many families experience both: Financial stress increases conflict and vice versa.

> **THINK CRITICALLY:** Can you describe a situation in which having a single parent would be better for a child than having two parents?

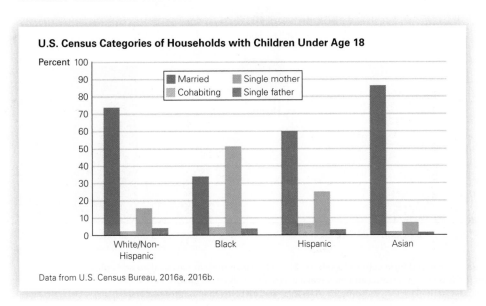

**U.S. Census Categories of Households with Children Under Age 18**

Data from U.S. Census Bureau, 2016a, 2016b.

**FIGURE 13.1**
**Possible Problems**  As the text makes clear, structure does not determine function, but raising children is more difficult as a single parent, in part because income is lower. African American families have at least one asset, however. They are more likely to have grandparents who are actively helping with child care.

# A Wedding, or Not? Family Structures Around the World

Children fare best when both parents actively care for them every day. This is most likely to occur if the parents are married, although there are many exceptions. Many developmentalists now focus on the rate of single parent-hood, shown on this map. Some single parents raise children well, but the risk of neglect, poverty, and instability in single-parent households increases the chances of child problems.

## RATES OF SINGLE PARENTHOOD

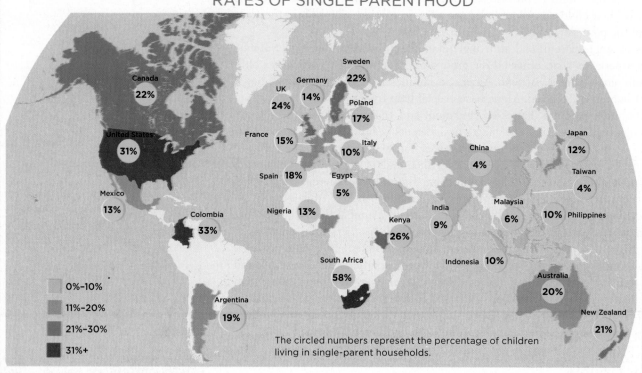

Canada 22%
United States 31%
Mexico 13%
Colombia 33%
Argentina 19%
UK 24%
Germany 14%
France 15%
Spain 18%
Italy 10%
Sweden 22%
Poland 17%
Egypt 5%
Nigeria 13%
South Africa 58%
Kenya 26%
India 9%
China 4%
Japan 12%
Taiwan 4%
Malaysia 6%
Philippines 10%
Indonesia 10%
Australia 20%
New Zealand 21%

0%–10%
11%–20%
21%–30%
31%+

The circled numbers represent the percentage of children living in single-parent households.

DATA FROM WILCOX, 2011; CHILD TRENDS, 2014.

A young couple in love and committed to each other—

## what next?

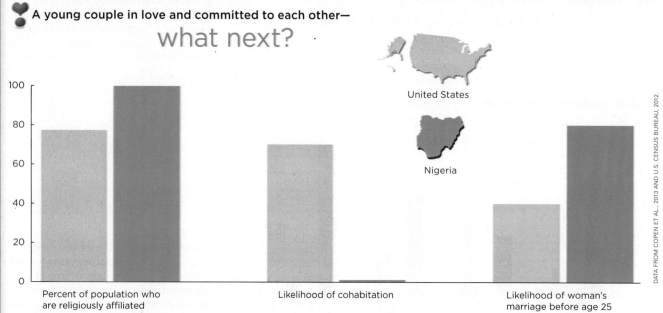

Percent of population who are religiously affiliated

Likelihood of cohabitation

Likelihood of woman's marriage before age 25

United States

Nigeria

DATA FROM COPEN ET AL., 2013 AND U.S. CENSUS BUREAU, 2012.

Cohabitation and marriage rates change from year to year and from culture to culture. These two examples are illustrative and approximate. Family-structure statistics like these often focus on marital status and may make it seem as if Nigerian children are more fortunate than American children. However, actual household functioning is more complex than that, and involves many other factors.

## Wealth and Poverty

Family income correlates with both function and structure. Marriage rates fall in times of recession. The current lower U.S. marriage rate is attributed to decreases in income over the past decades (Cherlin, 2014). Home foreclosure increases the rate of family dissolution (P. Cohen, 2014; Schaller, 2013).

Family function is also influenced by income. With low SES, "risk factors pile up in the lives of some children, particularly among the most disadvantaged" (Masten, 2014, p. 95). Several scholars have developed the *family-stress model*, which holds that any risk (such as low income, divorce, single parenthood, or unemployment) damages a family *only if* it increases stress on the parents, who then become less patient and responsive to their children.

If economic hardship is ongoing, if uncertainty about the future is high, if education is low—all of these may increase adult hostility and stress (D. Lee et al., 2013; Evans & Kim, 2013; Valdez et al., 2013). Reaction to wealth may also cause difficulty. If wealthy parents pressure their children to maintain high achievement, the stress can lead the children to use drugs, commit crimes, and fail in school—all of which are more common in children of very wealthy parents compared to parents with average income (Luthar & Barkin, 2012). Again, it is not the money itself; it is the money's effect on the parents.

## Conflict

Every researcher agrees that family conflict harms children, especially when adults fight about child rearing. Such fights are more common in stepfamilies, divorced families, and extended families, but nuclear families are not immune. Children suffer if they witness fights between the parents or among siblings (Cummings & Davies, 2010; Timmons & Margolin, 2015; Turner et al., 2012).

Some researchers wonder whether children are emotionally troubled in families with feuding parents because of their inherited genes, not because of what they see. Perhaps the parents' genes lead to marital problems and then their children have those same genes. If that is the case, then family conflict is not the source of the child's problems.

That hypothesis is plausible but was proven false. Researchers studied conflict in married adult twins (388 monozygotic pairs and 479 dizygotic pairs) who had an adolescent child. The researchers analyzed genes and family life for all of the pairs and all of the teenagers. Thus, they compared the problems of each child with those of his or her cousin, who had half (MZ parent) or a quarter (DZ parent) of the same genes (Schermerhorn et al., 2011).

Via complex statistical calculation, the researchers found that, although genes had some influence, witnessing family conflict and experiencing divorce had a more powerful effect. It correlated with externalizing problems in boys and internalizing problems in girls (Schermerhorn et al., 2011).

Other studies confirm this finding: Even if the parents never say a cross word directly to the child, witnessing conflict between the parents increases children externalizing and internalizing problems. The opposite is also true: When parents communicate well with each other, their children are less likely to have behavioral disorders (Knopp et al., 2017).

● **Answer to Observation Quiz** (from p. 382) Both parents are women. The evidence shows that families with same-sex parents are similar in many ways to families with opposite-sex parents, and children in such families develop well.

● **Response for Single Parents** (from p. 382): Do not get married mainly to provide a second parent for your child. If you were to do so, things would probably get worse rather than better. Do make an effort to have friends of both sexes with whom your child can interact.

Laurence Mouton/PhotoAlto/Alamy

**You Idiot!** Ideally, parents never argue in front of the children, as these two do here. However, *how* they argue is crucial. Every couple disagrees about specifics of family life; dysfunctional families call each other names. Hopefully, he said, "I know how to fit this bike into the car" and she answered, "I was just trying to help," rather than either one escalating the fight by saying, "It was your stupid idea to take this trip!"

E. Hanazaki Photography/Getty Images

**No Toys** Boys in middle childhood are happiest playing outside with equipment designed for work. This wheelbarrow is perfect, especially because at any moment the pusher might tip it.

**child culture** The idea that each group of children has games, sayings, clothing styles, and superstitions that are not common among adults, just as every culture has distinct values, behaviors, and beliefs.

# The Peer Group

Peers become increasingly important in middle childhood. With their new awareness of reality (concrete operations), children are painfully aware of their classmates' opinions, judgments, and accomplishments.

## The Culture of Children

**Child culture** includes customs, rules, and rituals that are passed down to younger children from slightly older ones. Jump-rope rhymes, insults, and superstitions are part of peer society. So are clothes: Many children reject clothes that parents buy as too loose, too tight, too long, too short, or wrong in color, style, brand, or decoration.

Language is another manifestation of child culture, because communication with peers is vital. Parents may proudly note how well their children speak a second language, but they may be distressed when their children spout their peers' curses, accents, and slang.

Independence from adults is acclaimed. Peers pity those (especially boys) whose parents kiss them ("mama's boy"), tease those who please the teachers ("teacher's pet," "suck-up"), and despise those who betray children to adults ("tattletale," "grasser," "snitch," "rat"). Keeping secrets from parents and teachers is a moral mandate.

Because they value independence, children find friends who defy authority, sometimes harmlessly (passing a note in class), sometimes not (shoplifting, smoking). If a bully teases or isolates a child, it is hard for the other children to defend the one who is shunned.

### Friendships

Teachers often try to separate friends, but developmentalists find that friends teach each other academic and social skills (Bagwell & Schmidt, 2011). Moreover, children learn faster and feel happier when they have friends. If they had to choose between being friendless but popular (looked up to by many peers) or having close friends but being unpopular (ignored by peers), most would choose to have friends (Bagwell & Schmidt, 2011). A wise choice.

Friendships become more intense and intimate over the years of middle childhood, as social cognition and effortful control advance. Six-year-olds may befriend anyone of the same sex and age who is willing to play with them. By age 10, children demand more of their friends. They share secrets and expect loyalty. Compared to younger children, older children change friends less often, become more upset when a friendship breaks up, and find it harder to make new friends.

Older children tend to choose friends whose interests, values, and backgrounds are similar to their own. By the end of middle childhood, close friendships are almost always between children of the same sex, age, ethnicity, and socioeconomic status (Rubin et al., 2013). This occurs not because children naturally become more prejudiced in middle childhood (they do not) but because they seek friends who understand and agree with them.

Gender differences persist in activities (girls converse more whereas boys play more active games), but children of all genders want best friends. During middle childhood, children develop skills that make them good friends, with boys more often laughing with their friends and girls more often expressing care and concern (Rose & Asher, 2017). Having no close friends at age 11 predicts depression at age 13 (Brendgen et al., 2010).

If adults focus only on academics, searching for the most demanding school and teacher, they may harm their children's friendship networks. For example, one mother worked as a school aide and saw that her daughter was not being academically challenged in a bilingual class. Accordingly, she got the child transferred to an English-only class, where she had no friends and the teacher resented having an additional student. This student became my student in college and remembers:

> When I was in elementary school from kindergarten to third grade I was in a bilingual class. However, my mother decided she wanted me in an English class, and I was immediately switched. When I was in the bilingual class I was never bullied but in my new class I was bullied every day. A lot of the kids would call me four eyes, ugly, a nerd, and a fly.
>
> I never really had any friends and the only time any of my peers would speak to me was if we had to do a group assignment. I was even bullied by the teacher because my mother worked in the school and she didn't really get along with my mother. One day she put me in the corner because I sneezed. She told me I was "disturbing the class". Another time I raised my hand to go to the bathroom and she told me I could not go. I was trying to obey her and hold it in until lunch time but I couldn't so I asked her again and she said no again. . . . I peed on myself. She then called the janitor to clean it up. I was so embarrassed I went into the closet and cried. The janitor called my mother and she came to the classroom with a change of clothes.
>
> Another day when going to lunch we were all lined up going down the stairs and I stood all the way in the back so I wouldn't get picked on. Huge mistake. Some of the boys pushed me down the stairs. I had a busted lip, broken glasses, a black eye, a huge knot on my forehead. . . . I hated to go to school, I wished to go back to the bilingual class where everyone treated me nice.
>
> *[Personal communication, 2016]*

**"Oh yeah? Well, my vocabulary is bigger than your vocabulary!"**

Johnny Hawkins/CartoonStock

**Better Than** Children of both sexes, all ethnic groups, and every religion, nation, and family think they are better than children of other groups. They can learn not to blurt out insults, but a deeper understanding of the diversity of human experience and abilities requires maturation.

**THINK CRITICALLY:** Do adults also choose friends who agree with them, or whose background is similar to their own?

## Popular and Unpopular Children

The particular qualities that make a child liked or disliked depend on culture, cohort, and sometimes the local region or school. For example, shyness is a detriment in North America, especially for boys in middle childhood, but this is not true everywhere.

Consider research in China. A 1990 survey in Shanghai found that shy children were liked and respected (X. Chen et al., 1992). Twelve years later, Chinese culture had shifted and a survey from the same schools found shy children less popular than their shy predecessors had been (X. Chen et al., 2005).

A few years later, a third study in rural China found that shyness was still valued; it predicted adult adjustment (X. Chen et al., 2009). By contrast, a fourth study from a Chinese city found that shyness in middle childhood predicted unhappiness later on—unless the shy child was also academically superior, in which case shyness was not a disability (X. Chen et al., 2013). Shyness is less of a problem if the child is not asocial, since cooperation with others is basic to Chinese culture (Sang et al., 2016).

Other traits also vary in how much they are admired. At every age, children who are outgoing, friendly, and cooperative are well liked. In the United States, by the end of middle childhood, a second set of traits also predicts popularity: being dominant and somewhat aggressive (Shi & Xie, 2012).

There are three types of unpopular children. Some are *neglected*, not rejected; they are ignored, but not shunned. The other two types are actively rejected: **aggressive-rejected,** disliked because they are antagonistic and confrontational, and **withdrawn-rejected,** disliked because they are timid and anxious.

Considerable change in social status occurs among children from year to year, as the class composition changes. Teachers can make a difference, if they are warm toward the disliked child (Hughes & Im, 2016). They also can make it worse, as occurred for my student.

Both aggressive-rejected and withdrawn-rejected children misinterpret social situations, lack emotional regulation, and may be mistreated at home, which increases the risk of rejection at school (Stenseng et al., 2015). Unless they are guided toward friendship with at least one other child, they may become bullies and/or victims.

## Bullies and Victims

**Bullying** is defined as repeated, systematic attacks intended to harm those who are unable or unlikely to defend themselves. It occurs in every nation, in every community, and in every kind of school (religious or secular, public or private, progressive or traditional, large or small). Victims are chosen because they are powerless, with many possible traits.

As one boy explained:

> You can get bullied because you are weak or annoying or because you are different. Kids with big ears get bullied. Dorks get bullied. You can also get bullied because you think too much of yourself and try to show off. Teacher's pet gets bullied. If you say the right answer too many times in class you can get bullied. There are lots of popular groups who bully each other and other groups, but you can get bullied within your group, too. If you do not want to get bullied, you have to stay under the radar, but then you might feel sad because no one pays attention to you.

*[quoted in Guerra et al., 2011, p. 306]*

Bullying may be any of four types:

- *Physical* (hitting, pinching, shoving, or kicking)
- *Verbal* (teasing, taunting, or name-calling)
- *Relational* (destroying peer acceptance)
- *Cyber* (bullying that uses cell phones, computers, and other electronic devices)

The first three types are common in primary school and begin even earlier, in preschool. (Cyberbullying is more common later on, and it is discussed in Chapter 15.)

A key word in the definition of bullying is *repeated*. Almost every child experiences an isolated attack or is called a derogatory name at some point. Victims of bullying, however, endure shameful experiences again and again—being forced to

**aggressive-rejected** A type of childhood rejection, when other children do not want to be friends with a child because of his or her antagonistic, confrontational behavior.

**withdrawn-rejected** A type of childhood rejection, when other children do not want to be friends with a child because of his or her timid, withdrawn, and anxious behavior.

**bullying** Repeated, systematic efforts to inflict harm through physical, verbal, or social attack on a weaker person.

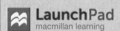
**LaunchPad**
macmillan learning

**Video: Bullying: Interview with Nikki Crick** explores the causes and repercussions of the different types of bullying.

hand over lunch money, to laugh at insults, to drink milk mixed with detergent, and so on—with no one defending them. Victims tend to be "cautious, sensitive, quiet . . . lonely and abandoned at school. As a rule, they do not have a single good friend in their class" (Olweus, 1999, p. 15).

Although it is often thought that victims are particularly unattractive or odd, this is not usually the case. Neesha was bullied because she fell asleep in class. The text does not say it, but probably Neesha's clothes were old and too small—a problem in middle childhood, when classmates tend to focus on external characteristics. Children who are new to a school or a class, or whose background and home culture are unlike that of their peers in some visible way, are especially vulnerable. So are children with special needs.

Remember the three types of unpopular children. Neglected children are not victimized; they are ignored, "under the radar." If their family relationships are good, they suffer less even if they are bullied (which they usually are not) (Bowes et al., 2010). Withdrawn-rejected children are often victims; they are isolated, feel depressed, and are friendless. Aggressive-rejected children are called **bully-victims** (or *provocative victims*), with neither friends nor sympathizers. They suffer the most because they strike back ineffectively, which increases the bullying (Dukes et al., 2009).

Unlike bully-victims, most bullies are *not* rejected. Although some have low self-esteem, others are proud; they are pleased with themselves and have friends who admire them and classmates who fear them (Guerra et al., 2011). As already mentioned, some are quite popular, with bullying seen as a form of social dominance and authority (Pellegrini et al., 2011).

Male bullies usually physically attack smaller, weaker boys. Female bullies usually use words to attack shyer, more soft-spoken girls. Young boys can sometimes bully girls, but by puberty (about age 11), boys who bully girls are not admired (Veenstra et al., 2010), although sexual teasing is. Especially in the final years of middle childhood, boys who are thought to be gay become targets, with suicide attempts being one consequence (Hong & Garbarino, 2012).

## Causes and Consequences of Bullying

Bullying may originate with a genetic predisposition or a brain abnormality, but when a toddler is aggressive, parents, teachers, and peers usually teach emotional regulation and effortful control. However, if home life is stressful, if discipline is ineffectual, if siblings are hostile, or if attachment is insecure, vulnerable young children develop externalizing and internalizing problems, becoming bullies or victims (Turner et al., 2012).

**Who Suffers More?** Physical bullying is typically the target of antibullying laws and policies, because it is easier to spot than relational bullying. But being rejected from the group, especially with gossip and lies, may be more devastating to the victim and harder to stop. It may be easier for the boy to overcome victimization than for the girl.

**bully-victim** Someone who attacks others and who is attacked as well. (Also called *provocative victims* because they do things that elicit bullying.)

Peers are crucial. Some peer groups approve of relational bullying, and then children entertain their classmates by mocking and insulting each other (Werner & Hill, 2010). On the other hand, when students themselves disapprove, the incidence of bullying plummets (Guerra & Williams, 2010). Television makes it worse. Programs designed for children often include admired characters with sharp tongues and high status—and the screen never shows the effect on the victims (Coyne, 2016).

Age matters. For most of childhood, bullies are disliked; but a switch occurs at about age 11, when bullying becomes a way to gain social status (Caravita & Cillessen, 2012). In addition, some behaviors that adults might consider bullying are accepted by children as part of social interaction, and some social dominance has been part of human development for centuries. It is crucial to understand when aggression is harmful (Bjorklund & Hawley, 2014). If children think teachers are clueless, punishing the wrong person for the wrong thing, that does not help the real victims.

The consequences of bullying can echo for years. Many victims become depressed; many bullies become increasingly cruel (Willoughby et al., 2014). Victims suffer for decades, especially if they blame themselves for their plight (Perren et al., 2013). Victims are chosen because of their emotional vulnerability and social isolation, not their appearance.

Unfortunately, if a young child is a victim, he or she is less likely to master the give-and-take of childhood interaction and has less practice coping with remarks, turning them into humor or stopping the repletion (Casper & Card, 2017). That impairs him or her lifelong. A longitudinal study found that children who were bullied in childhood are likely to become adults with emotional problems (Evans-Lacko et al., 2017).

Might those mental health problems predate bullying? If that were true, then childhood victimization does not cause later mental health issues in adults. This hypothesis was investigated in another study of monozygotic twins in which one was victimized and the twin—in another class or another school—was not. Longitudinal research found some genetic vulnerability to anxiety, depression, and so on, but it also found that the victimized child tends to suffer more than his or her twin—years later (Silberg et al., 2016). This proves that childhood victimization is a cause of later psychological difficulties.

It is obvious that victims need help, but bullies do, too. Unless they are stopped, bullies risk impaired social understanding, lower school achievement, and relationship difficulties. Decades later they have poor health habits and higher rates of psychological disorders (Copeland et al., 2013; Matthews et al., 2017; Ttofi et al., 2014). Compared to other adults the same age, former bullies are more likely to die young, be jailed, or have destructive marriages.

## Can Bullying Be Stopped?

Many victims find ways to halt ongoing bullying—by ignoring, retaliating, defusing, or avoiding. Friends defend each other and restore self-esteem (Bagwell & Schmidt, 2011). Thus, one way to protect victims is to encourage friendships. But what can change bullies?

We know what does not work: zero tolerance for fighting, passing state laws (especially when the emphasis is on punishment and reporting), and putting bullies together in a therapy group or a classroom (Hatzenbuehler et al., 2017; Smith, 2014). These may make daily life easier for some teachers, but they may also increase aggression. Without help, children themselves do not know why they are victims or bullies, or what they can do about it, as the following illustrates.

**THINK CRITICALLY:** The text says that both former bullies and former victims suffer in adulthood. Which would you rather be, and why?

**⬤ Especially for Parents of an Accused Bully** Another parent has told you that your child is a bully. Your child denies it and explains that the other child doesn't mind being teased. What should you do? (see response, p. 392)

Patrick Hardin/CartoonStock

"He followed me home — can I punch him?"

**Much to Learn** Children do not always know when something is hurtful, and adults do not always know when to intervene.

**A CASE TO STUDY**

## Ignorance All Around

Many adults tend to think of bullying as physical—a big boy beats up a smaller boy—and some think of the victims as suffering dramatically, perhaps driven to suicide. That actually is very rare. Much more common is social exclusion, and this is the bullying that may have consequences for later life.

Here is one example.

> One day I received a slip of paper from a group of girls (around seven of them) in which they wrote down several points about how I had to change. . . . (for example, they said I should change how I walked). I was very depressed . . . I recognised that one of the girls who sent the slip of paper was my friend who used to walk with me. . . . After I received the slip, she did not walk back with me, so I had to go back home alone, thinking "how can I change my walking?" . . .
>
> One week after I had received the slip, the girl (who had been my friend) began to keep company with me on the way home again. . . she said "because you changed yourself." . . . (What I can guess now is that I was a kind of a teacher's pet. . . . My depressed mood might have affected my behaviour toward the teacher, and the other girls may have considered it as a change.)

*[Smith, 2014, p. 3]*

Two years later, she saw another girl criticizing a third girl (P)—who was not very smart and who had dirty clothes. The former victim reacted by excluding P, refusing to interact with her, watching her get more and more depressed, for several months. She said, "I tried more and more ways to hurt her, and tried to justify everything about her as wrong."

As an adult she sought out the victim to apologize. She thought the other children probably could see that she was being cruel, but none of them said anything. She still wonders why she acted as she did. She also wonders why she told no one, even her mother, about her own experience as a victim. As a child, she was ashamed, she thought it was her fault that she was a victim, and she was bewildered by her friend's reactions.

Ignorance all around is the lesson from this case study: Children bully each other for reasons that they themselves do not understand; victims blame themselves; bystanders do not act; adults rarely are told. Both bullies and victims are caught in a vortex of irrational attack and self-blame; no one knows how to escape. That is why everyone in a school community needs to recognize the problem and know what to do. Punishment is not the solution: Friendship may be.

Some schools hire outsiders to talk to all of the teachers, or all of the children. That does not usually produce behavior change. Another strategy is to talk to the parents of the bully, but this may backfire. Since one cause of bullying is poor parent–child interaction, informing parents may "create even more problems for the child, for the parents, and for their relationship" (Rubin et al., 2013, p. 267).

The school community as a whole—teachers and bystanders, parents and aides, bullies and victims—needs to change. In fact, the entire school can either increase the rate of bullying or decrease it (Juvonen & Graham, 2014; Rosen et al., 2017).

Teachers especially need to be sensitive to the social dynamic of the class. For example, a Colorado study found that when the overall school climate encouraged learning and cooperation, children with high self-esteem were unlikely to be bullies; when the school climate was hostile, those with high self-esteem were often bullies (Gendron et al., 2011).

Again, peers are crucial: They must do more than simply notice bullying. It is worse to recognize bullying but not stop it. Some bystanders feel morally disengaged from the victims, which increases bullying. Others are sympathetic but feel powerless (Thornberg & Jungert, 2013).

Efforts to change the entire school are credited with successful efforts to decrease bullying in 29 schools in England (Cross et al., 2011). In the United States, teaching all of the children to intervene has led to reductions in bullying in a dozen schools in which careful before and after data were collected (Polanin et al., 2012). Another successful whole-school effort, called KiVa, has occurred in Finland and has spread to many other nations (Zych et al., 2017).

● **Response for Parents of an Accused Bully** (from p. 390) The future is ominous if the charges are true. Your child's denial is a sign that there is a problem. (An innocent child would be worried about the misperception instead of categorically denying that any problem exists.) You might ask the teacher what the school is doing about bullying. Family counseling might help. Because bullies often have friends who egg them on, you may need to monitor your child's friendships and perhaps befriend the victim. Talk about the situation with your child. Ignoring the situation might lead to heartache later on.

Further, the head of the school needs to encourage all of the teachers to focus on social interactions, not just on academics. Punishing the bullies might backfire, in that they may gain respect among their peers for defying adults. If adults target overt bullying, the result may be more bullying where adults might not see it, such as in bathrooms, at the edge of the playground, or on social media.

Evaluation is critical: Programs that seem good might be harmful. Longitudinal research on whole-school efforts finds that some programs make a difference and some do not, with variations depending on the age of the children and on the indicators (peer report of bullying or victimization, teacher report of incidents reported, and so on). Intervention is more effective in the earlier grades.

Objective follow-up efforts suggest that bullying can be reduced but not eliminated. It is foolhardy to blame only the bully and, of course, wrong to blame the victim: The entire school community—including the culture of the school—needs to change. That leads to the final topic of this chapter, the moral development of children.

---

### WHAT HAVE YOU LEARNED?

1. How does what children wear reflect the culture of children?

2. In what ways do friendships change from the beginning to the end of middle childhood?

3. How is a child's popularity affected by culture and cohort?

4. What are the similarities and differences between boy bullies and girl bullies?

5. How might bullying be reduced?

---

## Children's Moral Values

Middle childhood is prime time for moral development. Many forces drive children's growing interest in moral issues. Three of them are (1) child culture, (2) personal experience, and (3) empathy. The culture of children includes ethical mandates, such as loyalty to friends and keeping secrets. Fairness is seen as equality, not equity. Personal experiences also matter.

For all children, empathy increases in middle childhood as they become more socially perceptive. This increasing perception can backfire, however. One example was just described: Bullies become adept at picking victims. An increase in social understanding allows bystanders to notice and defend rejected children, but a deep understanding of social interaction is difficult for bullies, victims, and bystanders.

Without insight, children are self-protective. Bullies think they are doing no serious harm, victims think something is wrong with them, and bystanders ignore what they see, deciding to self-protect rather than to intervene (Pozzoli & Gini, 2013).

Children who are slow to develop theory of mind—which, as discussed in Chapter 9, is affected by family and culture—are also slow to develop empathy (Caravita et al., 2010). School-age children can think and act morally, but they do not always do so.

**Universal Morality** Remarkable? Not really. By the end of middle childhood, many children are eager to express their moral convictions, especially with a friend. Chaim Ifrah and Shai Reef believe that welcoming refugees is part of being a patriotic Canadian and a devout Jew, so they brought a welcoming sign to the Toronto airport where Syrian refugees (mostly Muslim) will soon deplane.

Steve Russell/Getty Images

The authors of a study of 7-year-olds "conclude that moral *competence* may be a universal human characteristic, but that it takes a situation with specific demand characteristics to translate this competence into actual prosocial performance" (van Ijzendoorn et al., 2010, p. 1).

## Moral Reasoning

Piaget wrote extensively about the moral development of children as they developed and enforced their own rules for playing games together (Piaget, 1932/2013b). His emphasis on how children think about moral issues led to a famous description of cognitive stages of morality (Kohlberg, 1963).

### Kohlberg's Levels of Moral Thought

Lawrence Kohlberg described three levels of moral reasoning and two stages at each level (see Table 13.4 on the following page), with parallels to Piaget's stages of cognition.

- **Preconventional moral reasoning** is similar to preoperational thought in that it is egocentric, with children most interested in their personal pleasure or avoiding punishment.
- **Conventional moral reasoning** parallels concrete operational thought in that it relates to current, observable practices: Children watch what their parents, teachers, and friends do, and they try to follow suit.
- **Postconventional moral reasoning** is similar to formal operational thought because it uses abstractions, going beyond what is concretely observed, willing to question "what is" in order to decide "what should be."

**preconventional moral reasoning** Kohlberg's first level of moral reasoning, emphasizing rewards and punishments.

**conventional moral reasoning** Kohlberg's second level of moral reasoning, emphasizing social rules.

**postconventional moral reasoning** Kohlberg's third level of moral reasoning, emphasizing moral principles.

According to Kohlberg, intellectual maturation advances moral thinking. During middle childhood, children's answers shift from being primarily preconventional to being more conventional: Concrete thought and peer experiences help children move past the first two stages (level I) to the next two (level II). Postconventional reasoning is not usually present until adolescence or adulthood, if then.

Kohlberg posed moral dilemmas to school-age boys (and eventually girls, teenagers, and adults). The most famous example of these dilemmas involves a poor man named Heinz, whose wife was dying. He could not pay for the only drug that could cure his wife, a drug that a local druggist sold for 10 times what it cost to make.

> Heinz went to everyone he knew to borrow the money, but he could only get together about half of what it cost. He told the druggist that his wife was dying and asked him to sell it cheaper or let him pay later. But the druggist said "no." The husband got desperate and broke into the man's store to steal the drug for his wife. Should the husband have done that? Why?
>
> *[Kohlberg, 1963, p. 19]*

The crucial element in Kohlberg's assessment of moral stages is not what a person answers but the reasons given. For instance, suppose a child says that Heinz should steal the drug. That itself does not indicate the child's level of moral reasoning. The reason could be that Heinz needs his wife to care for him (preconventional), or that people will blame him if he lets his wife die (conventional), or that a human life is more important than obeying a law (postconventional).

Or suppose another child says that Heinz should not steal. The reason could be that he will go to jail (preconventional), or that stealing is against the law (conventional), or that for a community to function, no one should take another person's livelihood (postconventional).

**TABLE 13.4**

**Kohlberg's Three Levels and Six Stages of Moral Reasoning**

**Level I: Preconventional Moral Reasoning**

The goal is to get rewards and avoid punishments; this is a self-centered level.

- *Stage one: Might makes right* (a punishment-and-obedience orientation). The most important value is to maintain the appearance of obedience to authority, avoiding punishment while still advancing self-interest. Don't get caught!
- *Stage two: Look out for number one* (an instrumental and relativist orientation). Everyone prioritizes his or her own needs. The reason to be nice to other people is so that they will be nice to you.

**Level II: Conventional Moral Reasoning**

Emphasis is placed on social rules; this is a parent- and community-centered level.

- *Stage three: Good girl and nice boy.* The goal is to please other people. Social approval is more important than any specific reward.
- *Stage four: Law and order.* Everyone must be a dutiful and law-abiding citizen, even when no police are nearby.

**Level III: Postconventional Moral Reasoning**

Emphasis is placed on moral principles; this level is centered on ideals.

- *Stage five: Social contract.* Obey social rules because they benefit everyone and are established by mutual agreement. If the rules become destructive or if one party doesn't live up to the agreement, the contract is no longer binding. Under some circumstances, disobeying the law is moral.
- *Stage six: Universal ethical principles.* Universal principles, not individual situations (level I) or community practices (level II), determine right and wrong. Ethical values (such as "life is sacred") are established by individual reflection and religious ideas, which may contradict egocentric (level I) or social and community (level II) values.

## Criticisms of Kohlberg

Kohlberg has been criticized for not appreciating cultural or gender differences. For example, in some cultures, loyalty to family overrides any other value, so moral people avoid postconventional actions that hurt their family. Also, Kohlberg's original participants were all boys. He may have discounted nurturance and relationships, thought to be more valued by females than males (Gilligan, 1982).

Overall, Kohlberg valued abstract principles and rational thinking more than individual needs and emotions. He did not recognize that emotions may be more influential than logic in moral development (Haidt, 2013). Thus, according to critics of Kohlberg, emotional regulation, empathy, and social understanding, all of which develop throughout childhood, may be more crucial for morality than intellectual development is. Smart people are not always moral people.

Later research finds that cultural contexts as well as maturation are important, with politics and religion having a major influence (Haidt, 2013). Considering both age and religion, one study compared mainline and evangelical Protestants, two groups thought to have different perspectives on ethics. Yet children of both groups were similar; fairness was important and individual rights and needs were considered. In other words, their conclusions about ethics were similar, even though the justification was not.

For example, when asked if money should be given to a panhandler, a child from an evangelical home said no "because they could go out to the store and buy like cigarettes or something that's not good for them" and one from a mainline background also said no because you should give them "food and water . . . they'll be able to live for a longer amount of time" (Jensen & McKenzie, 2016, p. 458).

Divergence on rationale was evident even for children, but it was more apparent with age, as evangelical adults were more likely to assert that God and religion were influential in their moral decisions. One conclusion is that middle childhood is the time for religious education of some sort—with the outcome evident later on, but basic human values are universal.

## What Children Value

Many lines of research have shown that children develop their own morality, guided by peers, parents, and culture (Killen & Smetana, 2014). Some prosocial values are evident in early childhood. Among these values are caring for close family members, cooperating with other children, and not hurting anyone intentionally. Even very young children think stealing is wrong, and even infants seem to appreciate social support and to punish mean behavior (Hamlin, 2014).

As children become more aware of themselves and others in middle childhood, they realize that one person's values may conflict with another's. Concrete operational cognition gives children the ability to understand and use logic, propelling them to think about moral rules and advance their theory of mind (Devine et al., 2016).

In some ways, as children become more aware of the social dynamic and of their own position in the social hierarchy, they are *less* likely to be prosocial, not more likely. To be specific, a study found that children were less likely to help other people (did they realize that helping is not always helpful?) but more likely to cooperate (Malti et al., 2016).

## Adults Versus Peers

When child culture conflicts with adult morality, children often align themselves with peers. A child might lie to protect a friend, for instance. Friendship itself has a hostile side: Many close friends reject other children who want to join their game or conversation (Rubin et al., 2013). They may protect a bully if he or she is a friend. Almost no child will answer a substitute teacher's angry "who threw that spitball?" because no child wants to be called a "tattletale," a term that signifies the value of loyalty to peers over responsiveness to adults.

The conflict between the morality of children and that of adults is evident in the value that children place on education. Adults usually prize school and respect teachers, but children may encourage one another to skip class, cheat on tests, harass a substitute teacher, and so on.

Three common imperatives among 6- to 11-year-olds are the following:

- Protect your friends.
- Don't tell adults what is happening.
- Conform to peer standards of dress, talk, behavior.

These principles can explain both apparent boredom and overt defiance, as well as standards of dress that mystify adults (such as jeans so loose that they fall off or so tight that they impede digestion—both styles worn by my children, who grew up in different cohorts). Clothing choices may seem like mere social conformity, but children may elevate it to a standard of right and wrong, not unlike adults who might consider it immoral if a woman does not wear a head covering or does wear a revealing dress. Children might call such criticism itself immoral: one daughter accused her mother of "slut-shaming" when the mother told the girl that her skirt was too short.

This conflict between adult values and peer friendship is evident in one boy. Paul said:

> I think right now about going Christian, right? Just going Christian, trying to do good, you know? Stay away from drugs, everything. And every time it seems like I think about that, I think about the homeboys. And it's a trip because a lot of the homeboys are my family, too, you know?

[quoted in Nieto, 2000, p. 249]

Kinzie Riehm/Getty Images

**Heavy Lift** Carrying your barefoot little sister across a muddy puddle is not easy, but this 7-year-old has internalized family values. Note her expression: She and many other children her age are proud to do what they consider the right thing.

**Observation Quiz** What indicates that this sister often carries her younger sibling? (see answer, p. 396) ↑

Paul chose friends, and he ended up in jail. Fortunately, peers sometimes may help one another act ethically, so if several children band together to stop a bully, they usually succeed, teaching bullies that their actions are not admired.

All of this does not mean that parents, teachers, and religious institutions are irrelevant. During middle childhood, morality can be scaffolded just as cognitive skills are, with mentors—peers or adults—using moral dilemmas to advance moral understanding while also advancing the underlying moral skills of empathy and emotional regulation (Hinnant et al., 2013).

## Developing Moral Values

Over the years of middle childhood, moral judgment becomes more comprehensive. Children gradually become better at taking psychological as well as physical harm into account, considering intentions as well as consequences.

For example, in one study 5- to 11-year-olds saw pictures depicting situations in which a child hurt another in order to prevent further harm (such as stopping a friend from climbing on a roof to retrieve a ball) or when one child was simply mean (such as pushing a friend off the swings so that the child could swing). The younger children were more likely to judge based on results—if anyone got hurt that was wrong—but the older children considered intention, so some hurt was acceptable.

When the harm was psychological, not physical (hurting the child's feelings, not hitting), more than half of the older children considered intentions, but only about 5 percent of the younger children did. Compared to the younger children, the older children were more likely to say justifiable harm was OK but unjustifiable harm should be punished (Jambon & Smetana, 2014).

Another detailed examination of morality began with an update of one of Piaget's moral issues: whether punishment should seek *retribution* (hurting the transgressor) or *restitution* (restoring what was lost). Piaget found that children advance from retribution to restitution between ages 8 and 10 (Piaget, 1932/2013b).

To learn how this occurs, researchers asked 133 children who were 9 years old to consider this scenario:

> Late one afternoon there was a boy who was playing with a ball on his own in the garden. His dad saw him playing with it and asked him not to play with it so near the house because it might break a window. The boy didn't really listen to his dad, and carried on playing near the house. Then suddenly, the ball bounced up high and broke the window in the boy's room. His dad heard the noise and came to see what had happened. The father wonders what would be the fairest way to punish the boy. He thinks of two punishments. The first is to say: "Now, you didn't do as I asked. You will have to pay for the window to be mended, and I am going to take the money from your pocket money." The second is to say: "Now, you didn't do as I asked. As a punishment you have to go to your room and stay there for the rest of the evening." Which of these punishments do you think is the fairest?
>
> *[Leman & Björnberg, 2010, p. 962]*

The children were split almost equally, half for paying for the window and half for being sent to the room, in their initial responses. Then, 24 pairs were formed of children who had opposite views. Each pair was asked to discuss the issue and try to reach an agreement. (The other 85 children did not discuss it.) Six pairs were boy–boy, six were boy–girl with the boy favoring restitution, six were boy–girl with the girl favoring restitution, and six were girl–girl.

The conversations typically took only five minutes, and the retribution side was more often chosen. Piaget would consider that a moral backslide, since more restitution advocates than retribution advocates switched sides. However, several weeks later, all of the children were queried again. At that point, many responses changed toward the more advanced restitution response (see Figure 13.2).

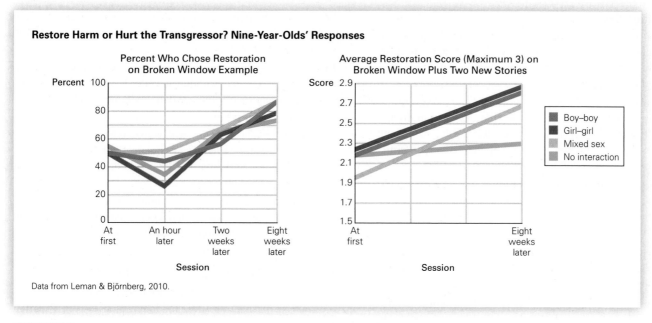

**FIGURE 13.2**

**Benefits of Time and Talking**   The graph on the left shows that most children, after their initial response, became even more likely to seek punishment rather than to repair damage. However, after some time and reflection, they affirmed the response that Piaget would consider more mature. The graph on the right indicates that children who had talked about the broken window example moved toward restorative justice even in examples that they had not heard before, which was not true for those who had not discussed the first story.

The researchers wrote, "conversation on a topic may stimulate a process of individual reflection that triggers developmental advances" (Leman & Björnberg, 2010, p. 969). Parents and teachers take note: Raising moral issues, and letting children discuss them, advances morality—not immediately, but soon, as described in the next three chapters.

## WHAT HAVE YOU LEARNED?

1. Using your own example, illustrate Kohlberg's three levels of moral reasoning.

2. What are the main criticisms of Kohlberg's theory?

3. What three values are common among school-age children?

4. What seems to advance moral thought from the beginning to the end of middle childhood?

# SUMMARY

## The Nature of the Child

**1.** Children develop their self-concept during middle childhood, basing it on a more realistic assessment of their competence than they had in earlier years. They strive for independence from parents and admiration from peers: Social comparison is evident.

**2.** Erikson emphasized industry, when children busily strive to master various tasks. If they are unable to do so, they feel inferior. Self-respect is always helpful, but high self-esteem may reduce

effortful control and is not valued in every culture. Low self-esteem is also harmful.

**3.** Both daily hassles and major stresses take a toll on children, with accumulated stresses more likely to impair development than any single event on its own. Resilience is aided by the child's interpretation of the situation and the availability of supportive adults, peers, and institutions.

## Families and Children

**4.** Families influence children in many ways, as do genes and peers. Although most siblings share a childhood home and parents, each sibling experiences different (nonshared) circumstances within the family.

**5.** The five functions of a supportive family are: (1) meet children's physical needs; (2) encourage learning; (3) nurture friendships; (4) foster self-respect; and (5) provide a safe, stable, and harmonious home. Function is more important than structure, but structure may make it easier to function well.

**6.** The most common family structure is the nuclear family. Other two-parent families include adoptive, same-sex, grandparent, and stepfamilies, each of which sometimes functions well for children. However, each also has vulnerabilities.

**7.** On average, children have fewer emotional problems and learn more in school if they live with two parents rather than one, especially if the parents cooperate, forming a strong parental alliance.

**8.** Single-parent families have higher rates of instability—for example, in where they live and in who is in the household. On average, such families have less income, which may cause stress. Nonetheless, some children fare better than they would if the child's other parent were present.

**9.** Income affects family function, for two-parent as well as single-parent households. Poor children are at greater risk for emotional and behavioral problems if the stresses that often accompany poverty hinder effective parenting.

**10.** No matter what the family SES, instability and conflict are harmful. Children suffer when their parents or siblings fight, even if the conflict does not involve them directly.

## The Peer Group

**11.** Peers teach crucial social skills during middle childhood. Each cohort of children has a culture, passed down from slightly older children. Close friends are wanted and needed.

**12.** Popular children may be cooperative and easy to get along with or may be competitive and aggressive. Much depends on the age and social context.

**13.** Rejected children may be neglected, aggressive, or withdrawn. Aggressive and withdrawn children have difficulty with social cognition; their interpretation of the normal give-and-take of childhood is impaired.

**14.** Bullying of all sorts—physical, verbal, relational, and cyber—is common, with long-term consequences for both bullies and victims. Bullies themselves may be admired, which makes their behavior more difficult to stop.

**15.** Overall, a multifaceted, long-term, whole-school approach, with parents, teachers, and bystanders working together, seems to be the best way to halt bullying. Careful evaluation is needed to discover whether a particular strategy changes the school culture.

## Children's Moral Values

**16.** School-age children seek to differentiate right from wrong. Peer values, cultural standards, and family practices are all part of their personal morality.

**17.** Children advance in moral thinking as they mature. Kohlberg described three levels of moral reasoning, each related to cognitive maturity. His description has been criticized for ignoring cultural and gender differences and for stressing rationality at the expense of emotions.

**18.** When values conflict, children often choose loyalty to peers over adult standards of behavior. As children grow older, especially when they discuss moral issues, they develop more thoughtful answers to moral questions, considering intentions as well as consequences.

# KEY TERMS

........................................

social comparison (p. 369)
industry versus inferiority (p. 369)
growth mindset (p. 371)
resilience (p. 372)
parentification (p. 375)

family structure (p. 376)
family function (p. 376)
nuclear family (p. 378)
single-parent family (p. 378)
extended family (p. 378)
polygamous family (p. 378)

child culture (p. 386)
aggressive-rejected (p. 388)
withdrawn-rejected (p. 388)
bullying (p. 388)
bully-victims (p. 389)

preconventional moral reasoning (p. 393)
conventional moral reasoning (p. 393)
postconventional moral reasoning (p. 393)

# APPLICATIONS

........................................

**1.** Go someplace where many school-age children congregate (such as a schoolyard, a park, or a community center) and use naturalistic observation for at least half an hour. Describe what popular, average, withdrawn, and rejected children do. Note at least one potential conflict. Describe the sequence and the outcome.

**2.** Focusing on verbal bullying, describe at least two times when someone said something hurtful to you and two times when you said something that might have been hurtful to someone else. What are the differences between the two types of situations?

**3.** How would your childhood have been different if your family structure had been different, such as if you had (or had not) lived with your grandparents, if your parents had (or had not) gotten divorced, if you had (or had not) been adopted, if you had lived with one parent (or two), if your parents were both the same sex (or not)? Avoid blanket statements: Appreciate that every structure has advantages and disadvantages.

# The Developing Person So Far:
## Middle Childhood

## BIOSOCIAL

**A Healthy Time** During middle childhood, children grow more slowly than they did earlier or will during adolescence. Physical play is crucial for development. Genes as well as immunization protect against contagious diseases, and medical awareness and care have improved over the past decades. Obesity and asthma have genetic roots and psychosocial consequences. Brain maturation continues, leading to faster reactions and better self-control.

**Children with Special Brains and Bodies** Children have multiple intellectual abilities, many that are not reflected in standard IQ tests. Some children have ADHD, a specific learning disorder, or autism spectrum disorder, but diagnosis, treatment, and outcome vary and depend on context. The same is true for gifted children.

Alberto Coto/Getty Images

## COGNITIVE

**Building on Theory** Beginning at about age 7, Piaget noted, children attain concrete operational thought, including the ability to understand the logical principles of classification. Vygotsky emphasized that children become more open to learning from mentors, both teachers and peers. Information-processing abilities increase, including greater memory, knowledge, control, and metacognition. Executive function improves.

**Language** Children's increasing ability to understand the structures and possibilities of language enables them to become more analytical and expressive in vocabulary, mastering the formal and informal codes. Children can become bilingual and bicultural, although much depends on the social context.

**Teaching and Learning** International comparisons reveal marked variations in the overt and hidden curricula, as well as in learning, between one nation and another. In recent years, the Common Core standards have been adapted *and* criticized. Many types of schools—public, charter, religious, private, home—are available, although SES determines options and hidden curriculum.

Marc Romanelli/Getty Images

## PSYCHOSOCIAL

**The Nature of the Child** Theorists agree that many school-age children develop competencies, emotional control, and attitudes to defend against stress. Some children are resilient, coping well with problems and finding support in friends, family, school, religion, and community, although no child is invincible.

**Families and Children** Parents continue to influence children, especially as they exacerbate or buffer problems in school and the community. During these years, families need to meet basic needs, encourage learning, foster self-respect, nurture friendship, and—most important—provide harmony and stability. Nuclear families often provide this, but one-parent, foster, same-sex, or grandparent families can also function well for children. Household income, low conflict, and family stability benefit children of all ages.

**The Peer Group** Children depend on friends for help, loyalty, and sharing of mutual interests. Rejection and bullying become serious problems.

**Children's Moral Values** Moral development, influenced by peers, advances during these years. Children develop moral standards that they try to follow, although these differ from the moral standards of adults.

Top: PhotoAlto/Jerome Gorin/Getty Images

knape Images/Getty Images

## APPLICATION TO DEVELOPING LIVES PARENTING SIMULATION ADOLESCENCE

As you progress through the Adolescence simulation module, how you answer the following questions will impact the biosocial, cognitive, and psychosocial development of your adolescent.

| Biosocial | Cognitive | Psychosocial |
|---|---|---|
| • Will your child experiment with smoking, drinking, or drugs during adolescence?<br>• How will you respond if you learn your child is experimenting with drugs?<br>• How will you encourage your child to spend his or her free time after school (sports, part-time job)? | • Which of Piaget's stages of cognitive development is your child in?<br>• What kind of path do you see your teenager pursuing after high school (college, military, work program)? | • How will you respond if your adolescent is struggling to fit in with peers?<br>• How often do you think you and your teenager will have conflicts?<br>• How social will your child be during his or her teen years?<br>• How much privacy will you grant your teenager?<br>• How will you respond when your teenager starts dating? |

# Adolescence

**A** century ago, puberty began at age 15 or so. Soon after that age, most girls married and most boys found work. It is said that *adolescence begins with biology and ends with culture.* If so, then a hundred years ago, adolescence lasted a few months.

Now adolescence lasts for years. Puberty starts at age 10 or so, and adult responsibilities are avoided for decades. Indeed, a few observers describe a *Peter Pan Syndrome*—men who "won't grow up," too self-absorbed to love and care for anyone else (Kiley, 1983; Snow, 2015). That is unfair to men and to teenagers, but even at age 18, almost no adolescent is ready for all of the responsibilities of adulthood. If high school seniors want marriage, parenthood, and a lifelong career, they should wait at least a few years.

In the next three chapters (covering ages 11 to 18), we begin with biology (Chapter 14), consider cognition (Chapter 15), and then discuss culture (Chapter 16). Adolescence attracts extremes, arousing the highest hopes and the worst fears of parents, teachers, police officers, social workers, and children themselves. Patterns and events can push a teenager toward early death or a happy life, or can simply move them along the path forged in childhood. Understanding the possibilities and pitfalls described in these chapters will help us all make this a fulfilling, not devastating, time of life.

# Adolescence:
## Biosocial Development

## What Will You Know?

1. How can you predict when puberty will begin for a particular child?
2. Why do many teenagers ignore their nutritional needs?
3. What makes teenage sex often a problem instead of a joy?

I overheard a conversation among three teenagers, including my daughter Rachel, all of them past their awkward years and now becoming beautiful. They were discussing the imperfections of their bodies. One spoke of her fat stomach (what stomach? I could not see it), another of her long neck (hidden by her silky, shoulder-length hair). Rachel complained about her fingers and her feet!

The reality that boys and girls become men and women is no shock to any adult. But for teenagers, heightened self-awareness often triggers surprise or even horror, joy, and despair at the details of their growth. Like these three, adolescents pay attention to each part of their bodies. Girls bond as they discuss their flaws; boys more often boast, yet almost all are both self-focused and social, needing each other.

This chapter describes the biosocial specifics of growing bodies and emerging sexuality. It all begins with hormones, but other invisible changes may be even more potent—such as the timing of neurological maturation that had not yet allowed these three to realize that minor imperfections are insignificant.

## Puberty Begins

**Puberty** refers to the years of rapid physical growth and sexual maturation that end childhood, producing a person of adult size, shape, and sexuality. Puberty begins with a cascade of hormones that produce external growth and internal changes, including heightened emotions and sexual desires.

The process normally starts sometime between ages 8 and 14. Most biological growth ends about four years after the first signs appear, although some individuals (especially boys) add height, weight, and muscle until age 20 or so. Over the past decades, the age of puberty has decreased, perhaps for both sexes, although the evidence is more solid for girls (Biro et al., 2013; Herman-Giddens, 2013).

For girls, the observable changes of puberty usually begin with nipple growth. Soon a few pubic hairs are visible, followed by a peak growth spurt, widening of the hips, the first menstrual period (**menarche**), a full pubic-hair pattern, and breast maturation (Susman et al., 2010). The average age of menarche is about 12 years, 4 months (Biro et al., 2013), with any age from 10 to 15 considered neither precocious nor delayed.

+ **Puberty Begins**
  Unseen Beginnings
  Brain Growth
  When Will Puberty Begin?
  INSIDE THE BRAIN: Lopsided Growth
  A VIEW FROM SCIENCE: Stress and Puberty
  Too Early, Too Late

+ **Growth and Nutrition**
  Growing Bigger and Stronger
  Diet Deficiencies
  Eating Disorders

+ **Sexual Maturation**
  Sexual Characteristics
  Sexual Activity
  Sexual Problems in Adolescence

**puberty** The time between the first onrush of hormones and full adult physical development. Puberty usually lasts three to five years. Many more years are required to achieve psychosocial maturity.

**menarche** A girl's first menstrual period, signaling that she has begun ovulation. Pregnancy is biologically possible, but ovulation and menstruation are often irregular for years after menarche.

**spermarche** A boy's first ejaculation of sperm. Erections can occur as early as infancy, but ejaculation signals sperm production. Spermarche may occur during sleep (in a "wet dream") or via direct stimulation.

**pituitary** A gland in the brain that responds to a signal from the hypothalamus by producing many hormones, including those that regulate growth and sexual maturation.

**adrenal glands** Two glands, located above the kidneys, that respond to the pituitary, producing hormones.

**HPA (hypothalamus–pituitary–adrenal) axis** A sequence of hormone production originating in the hypothalamus and moving to the pituitary and then to the adrenal glands.

**gonads** The paired sex glands (ovaries in females, testicles in males). The gonads produce hormones and mature gametes.

**HPG (hypothalamus–pituitary–gonad) axis** A sequence of hormone production originating in the hypothalamus and moving to the pituitary and then to the gonads.

**estradiol** A sex hormone, considered the chief estrogen. Females produce much more estradiol than males do.

**testosterone** A sex hormone, the best known of the androgens (male hormones); secreted in far greater amounts by males than by females.

For boys, the usual sequence is growth of the testes, initial pubic-hair growth, growth of the penis, first ejaculation of seminal fluid (**spermarche**), appearance of facial hair, a peak growth spurt, deepening of the voice, and final pubic-hair growth (Biro et al., 2001; Herman-Giddens et al., 2012; Susman et al., 2010). The typical age of spermarche is 13 years, almost a year later than menarche.

Age varies markedly. The averages here are for well-nourished adolescents in the United States. Malnutrition delays the start; stress advances it; genes always matter.

## Unseen Beginnings

The changes just listed are visible, but the entire process begins with an invisible event—a marked increase in hormones. *Hormones* are body chemicals that regulate hunger, sleep, moods, stress, sexual desire, immunity, reproduction, and many other bodily functions and processes, including puberty. Throughout adolescence, hormone levels correlate with physiological changes, brain restructuring, and self-reported developments (Goddings et al., 2012; Shirtcliff et al., 2009).

Hormone production is regulated deep within the brain, where biochemical signals from the hypothalamus signal another brain structure, the **pituitary.** The pituitary produces hormones that stimulate the **adrenal glands,** located above the kidneys at either side of the lower back. The adrenal glands produce more hormones. Many hormones that regulate puberty follow this route, known as the **HPA (hypothalamus–pituitary–adrenal) axis** (see Figure 14.1).

### Sex Hormones

Late in childhood, the pituitary activates not only the adrenal glands—the HPA axis—but also the **gonads,** or sex glands (ovaries in females; testes, or testicles, in males), following another sequence called the **HPG (hypothalamus–pituitary–gonad) axis.** One hormone in particular, GnRH (gonadotropin-releasing hormone), causes the gonads to enlarge and dramatically increase their production of sex hormones, chiefly **estradiol** in girls and **testosterone** in boys. These hormones affect the body's shape and function and produce additional hormones that regulate stress and immunity.

*Estrogens* (including estradiol) are female hormones and *androgens* (including testosterone) are male hormones, although both sexes have some of each. The ovaries produce high levels of estrogens, and the testes produce dramatic increases in androgens. This "surge of hormones" affects bodies, brains, and behavior before any visible signs of puberty appear, "well before the teens" (Peper & Dahl, 2013, p. 134).

The activated gonads soon produce mature ova or sperm, released in menarche or spermarche. Conception is possible, although peak fertility occurs four to six years later. This is crucial information for teenagers who are sexually active: Some mistakenly think they cannot become pregnant because they once had unprotected sex without conceiving. A few years later, that same one-time carelessness may lead to pregnancy.

Hormonal increases may also precipitate psychopathology. In both genders, adolescence is the peak time for the emergence of many disorders (Powers & Casey, 2015). The rush of hormones at puberty puts some vulnerable children over the edge, although hormones are never the sole cause (Remington & Seeman, 2015; Rudolph, 2014; Tackett et al., 2014).

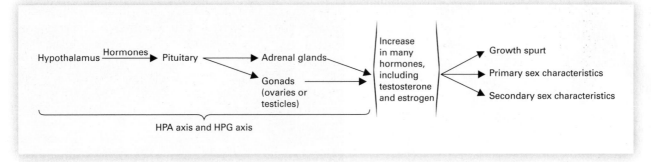

**FIGURE 14.1**

**Biological Sequence of Puberty** Puberty begins with a hormonal signal from the hypothalamus to the pituitary gland, both deep within the brain. The pituitary, in turn, sends a hormonal message through the bloodstream to the adrenal glands and the gonads to produce more hormones.

**LaunchPad**
macmillan learning

**Video: The Timing of Puberty** depicts the usual sequence of physical development for adolescents.

**THINK CRITICALLY:** If a child seems to be unusually short or unusually slow in reaching puberty, would you give the child hormones? Why or why not?

Probably because of sex differences in hormones, adolescent males are almost twice as likely as females to develop schizophrenia, and females are more than twice as likely to become severely depressed. The influence of hormones—a biological phenomenon—does not mean that the social context is irrelevant, however.

If a teenager has emotional problems, no matter what the origin, psychotherapy during adolescence has a good track record. About two-thirds of patients report becoming markedly better than those who sought therapy but were put on a waiting list. Success seems about equally likely for both sexes and for adolescents of all ethnic groups, although some conditions (anxiety) have a better improvement rate than others (depression) (Weisz et al., 2017).

For everyone, one psychological effect of estrogen and testosterone is new interest in sexuality. When puberty starts, most children become interested in the other gender (who used to be avoided or disparaged), and some find themselves attracted to same-sex partners.

Usually the object of a young adolescent's first attraction is safely unattainable—a film star, a popular singer, a teacher—but by mid-adolescence, fantasies may settle on another young person. Hormones also direct adolescents toward typical sexual roles, perhaps a product of selective fitness for the human species (Sisk, 2016). Of course, sexual identity and gender roles are increasingly complex because of the combination of puberty, norms, and variations—a topic discussed in Chapter 16.

Although emotional surges, nurturant impulses, and lustful urges arise with hormones, remember that body, brain, and behavior always interact. Sexual thoughts themselves can *cause* physiological and neurological processes, not just result from them. Cortisol levels rise at puberty, and that makes adolescents quick to react with passion, fury, or ecstasy (Goddings et al., 2012; Klein & Romeo, 2013). Then those emotions, in turn, increase levels of various hormones. Bodies, brains, and behavior all affect one another.

For example, when adults react to a young person's emerging breasts or beards, those reactions evoke adolescent thoughts and frustrations, which then raise hormone levels, propel physiological development, and trigger more emotions. Because of hormones, emotions are more likely to be expressed during adolescence (with shouts and tears), and that affects everyone's next reactions. Thus, the internal and external changes of puberty are cyclical and reciprocal, each affecting the other.

**Especially for Teenagers** Some 14-year-olds have unprotected sex and then are relieved to realize that conception did not occur. Does this mean they do not need to worry about contraception? (see response, p. 407)

**Do They See Beauty?** Both young women—the Mexican 15-year-old preparing for her Quinceañara and the Malaysian teen applying a rice facial mask—look wistful, even worried. They are typical of teenage girls everywhere, who do not realize how lovely they are.

## Body Rhythms

Because of hormones, the brain of every living creature responds to environmental changes over the hours, days, and seasons. For example, time of year affects body weight and height: Children gain weight more rapidly in winter and grow taller more quickly in summer. Another example is seasonal affective disorder (SAD), when people become depressed in winter. Those are seasonal changes, but many *biorhythms* are on a 24-hour cycle, called the **circadian rhythm.** (*Circadian* means "about a day.") Puberty interacts with biorhythms.

**circadian rhythm** A day–night cycle of biological activity that occurs approximately every 24 hours.

For most people, daylight awakens the brain. That's why people experiencing jet lag are urged to take an early-morning walk. But at puberty, night may be more energizing, making some teens wide awake and hungry at midnight but half asleep, with no appetite or energy, all morning.

In addition to circadian changes at puberty, some individuals (especially males) are naturally more alert in the evening than in the morning, a trait called *eveningness*. To some extent, this is genetic: Among people who are natural larks or night owls, 15 genes differ (Hu et al., 2016). Puberty plus eveningness increases risk (drugs, sex, delinquency), in part because teenagers are awake when adults are asleep. If they must wake up in the morning, many teenagers are sleep deprived (Roenneberg et al., 2012).

Added to the circadian sleep debt, "the blue spectrum light from TV, computer, and personal-device screens may have particularly strong effects on the human circadian system" (Peper & Dahl, 2013, p. 137). Watching late-night TV, working on a computer, or texting friends at 10 P.M. interferes with sleepiness. As a result, many adolescents find early bedtime and early rising almost impossible.

Schools that provide each student a tablet for homework warn against bedroom use. However, the powerful adolescent urge to stay in touch with friends results in sleeping next to electronic devices—and sleeping in class.

Sleep deprivation and irregular sleep schedules increase several proven dangers, including insomnia, nightmares, mood disorders (depression, conduct disorder, anxiety), and falling asleep while driving. Adolescents are particularly vulnerable to all of these, and sleepiness makes it worse (see Figure 14.2). In addition, sleepy students do not learn as well as well-rested ones.

earlier. For example, girls in northern Ghana reach menarche more than a year later (almost age 14) than African American girls in the United States (just past 12). Ghanaian girls in rural areas—where malnutrition is more common—are behind those in urban areas (Ameade & Garti, 2016). A more dramatic example arises from sixteenth-century Europe, where puberty is thought to have begun several years later than it does today.

All of the data suggest that in recent centuries puberty has begun at younger and younger ages. This is an example of what is called the **secular trend,** which is earlier or greater growth as nutrition and medicine improved. Increased food availability has led to more weight gain in childhood, promoting earlier puberty and taller average height. Over the nineteenth and twentieth centuries, because of the secular trend, every generation reached puberty before the previous one (Floud et al., 2011; Fogel & Grotte, 2011).

One curious bit of evidence of the secular trend is in the height of U.S. presidents. James Madison, the fourth president, was shortest at 5 feet, 4 inches; recent presidents have been much taller. The secular trend has stopped in most nations because childhood nutrition allows everyone to attain their genetic potential. Young men no longer look down at their short fathers, or girls at their short mothers, unless their parents were born in nations where hunger was common. Future presidents will most likely not be taller than those in the recent past.

Some scientists suspect that precocious (before age 8) or delayed (after age 14) puberty may be caused by hormones in the food supply. Cattle are fed steroids to increase bulk and milk production, and hundreds of chemicals and hormones are used to produce most of the food that children consume. All of these substances *might* affect appetite, body fat, and sex hormones, with effects at puberty (Clayton et al., 2014; Synovitz & Chopak-Foss, 2013; Wiley, 2011).

**Leptin,** a hormone that is naturally produced by the human body, definitely affects the onset of puberty. Leptin is essential for appetite, energy, and puberty. However, too much leptin correlates with obesity, early puberty, and then early termination of growth. Thus, the heaviest third-grade girl may become the tallest fifth-grader and then the shortest high school graduate.

Most research on leptin has been done with mice; the effects are more complicated for humans (Bohlen, 2016). In fact, the data on the effects on humans of hormones and other chemicals, whether natural or artificial, are not easy to interpret. It seems that the female body is especially sensitive not only to leptin but also to many other influences. Precise details are controversial, but it is known that many hormones and chemicals, both natural and artificial, affect puberty (M. Wolff et al., 2015).

## Stress

Stress hastens puberty, especially if a child's parents are sick, drug-addicted, or divorced, or if the neighborhood is violent and impoverished. One study of sexually abused girls found that they began puberty as much as a year earlier than they otherwise would have, a result attributed not only to stress but also to the hormones activated by sexual abuse (Noll et al., 2017). Particularly for girls who are genetically sensitive, puberty comes early if their family interaction is stressful but late if their family is supportive (Ellis et al., 2011; James et al., 2012).

This may explain the fact that many internationally adopted children experience early puberty, especially if their first few years of life were in an institution or an abusive home. An alternative explanation is that their age at adoption was underestimated: Puberty then seems early but actually is not (Hayes, 2013).

Developmentalists have known for decades that puberty is influenced by genes, hormones, and body fat. The effect of stress is a newer discovery, as the following explains.

**Response for Health Practitioners** (from p. 408): Many adolescents are intensely concerned about privacy and fearful of adult interference. This means that your first task is to convince the teenagers that you are nonjudgmental and that everything is confidential.

**secular trend** The long-term upward or downward direction of a certain set of statistical measurements, as opposed to a smaller, shorter cyclical variation. As an example, over the past two centuries, because of improved nutrition and medical care, children have tended to reach their adult height earlier and their adult height has increased.

**leptin** A hormone that affects appetite and is believed to affect the onset of puberty. Leptin levels increase during childhood and peak at around age 12.

# Stress and Puberty

Emotional stress, particularly when it has a sexual component, precipitates puberty. Girls growing up in dysfunctional families or chaotic neighborhoods reach menarche sooner than girls in more isolated, peaceful homes.

For example, a large longitudinal study in England found that when a girl's biological father was not in the home (which often meant a stressed mother and other men in the child's life), not only were daughters more often depressed but also menarche occurred earlier (Culpin et al., 2015).

This connection has been found in developing nations as well as developed ones. For example, in Peru, if a girl was physically and sexually abused, she was much more likely (odds ratio 1.56) to have her first period before age 11 than if she had not been abused (Barrios et al., 2015).

Hypothetically, the connection between stress and early puberty could be indirect. For example, perhaps children in dysfunctional families eat worse and watch TV more and that makes them overweight, which correlates with early menarche. Or, perhaps they inherit genes for early puberty from their distressed mothers, and those genes led the mothers to become pregnant too young, creating a stressful family environment. Either obesity or genes could cause early puberty, and then stress would be a by-product, not a cause. Plausible hypotheses—but not correct.

Several longitudinal studies show a direct link between stress and puberty. For example, one longitudinal study of 756 children found that parents who demanded respect, who often spanked, and who rarely hugged their babies were, a decade later, likely to have daughters who reached puberty earlier than other girls in the same study (Belsky et al., 2007). Perhaps harsh parenting increases cortisol, which precipitates puberty.

A follow-up of the same girls at age 15, controlling for genetic differences, found that harsh treatment in childhood increased sexual problems (more sex partners, pregnancies, sexually transmitted infections) but *not* other risks (drugs, crime) (Belsky et al., 2010). This suggests that stress triggers earlier increases of sex hormones but not generalized rebellion. The direct impact of stress on puberty seems proven.

Why would higher cortisol accelerate puberty? The opposite effect—delayed puberty—makes more sense. In such a scenario, stressed teens would still look and act childlike, which might evoke adult protection rather than lust or anger.

Protection is especially needed in conflict-ridden or stressed single-parent homes, yet such homes produce earlier puberty and less parental nurturance. Is this a biological mistake? Not according to evolutionary theory:

> Maturing quickly and breeding promiscuously would enhance reproductive fitness more than would delaying development, mating cautiously, and investing heavily in parenting. The latter strategy, in contrast, would make biological sense, for virtually the same reproductive-fitness-enhancing reasons, under conditions of contextual support and nurturance.
>
> [Belsky et al., 2010, p. 121]

In other words, thousands of years ago, when harsh conditions threatened survival of the species, adolescents needed to reproduce early and often, lest the entire community become extinct. By contrast, in peaceful times with plentiful food, puberty could occur later, allowing children to postpone maturity and instead enjoy extra years of nurturance from their parents and grandparents. Genes evolved to respond differently to war and peace.

Of course, this evolutionary benefit no longer applies. Today, early sexual activity and reproduction are more destructive than protective of communities. However, since the genome has been shaped over millennia, a puberty-starting allele that responds to social conditions responds in the twenty-first century as it did thousands of years ago. This idea complements current behavioral genetic understanding of differential susceptibility (Harkness, 2014). Because of genetic protections, not every distressed girl experiences early puberty, but also for genetic reasons, family stress may speed up age of menarche.

**Response for Parents Worried About Early Puberty** (from p. 410): Probably not. If she is overweight, her diet should change, but the hormone hypothesis is speculative. Genes are the main factor; she shares only one-eighth of her genes with her cousin.

## Too Early, Too Late

For a society's health, early puberty is problematic: It increases the rate of emotional and behavioral problems (Dimler & Natsuaki, 2015). For most adolescents, these links between puberty, stress, and hormones are irrelevant. Only one aspect of timing matters: their friends' schedules. No one wants to be too early or too late.

schools to encourage healthy eating, but effects are more apparent in elementary schools than in high schools (Mâsse et al., 2013; Terry-McElrath et al., 2014).

Rates of obesity are falling in childhood but not in adolescence. In 2003, only three U.S. states (Kentucky, Mississippi, Tennessee) had high school obesity rates at 15 percent or more; in 2015, 30 states did (MMWR, June 10, 2016). In Latin America, the nutritional focus is still on preventing underweight, not preventing overweight; yet overall, about one teenager in four is overweight or obese (Rivera et al., 2014).

## Body Image

One reason for poor nutrition among teenagers is anxiety about **body image**— that is, a person's idea of how his or her body looks. Few teenagers welcome every change in their bodies. Instead, they tend to focus on and exaggerate imperfections (as did the three girls in the anecdote that opens this chapter). Two-thirds of U.S. high school girls are trying to lose weight, one-third think they are overweight, and only one-sixth are actually overweight or obese (MMWR, June 10, 2016).

Few adolescents are happy with their bodies, partly because almost none of them have bodies like those portrayed online and in other media that are marketed to teenagers (Bell & Dittmar, 2011). Unhappiness with appearance— especially with weight for girls—is documented worldwide: in South Korea, China, and Greece (Argyrides & Kkeli, 2015; Chen & Jackson, 2009; Kim & Kim, 2009).

Dissatisfaction with body image is not only depressing but also can be dangerous. Many teenagers eat erratically and take drugs to change their bodies.

Teenagers try new diets, go without food for 24 hours (as did 19 percent of U.S. high school girls in one typical month), or take diet drugs (6.6 percent) (MMWR, June 13, 2014). Many eat oddly (e.g., only rice or only carrots), begin unusual diets, or exercise intensely.

**body image** A person's idea of how his or her body looks.

**Binging, Cutting, Starving Stardom** Both Demi Lovato (*left*) and Zayn Malik (*right*) are world-famous stars, with best-selling albums and world tours. Demi starred in *Camp Rock* (a Disney film) and Zayn was integral to One Direction (a leading "boy band" group from England). Yet, both suffered serious eating disorders while millions of fans adored them, a sobering lesson for us all.

## Eating Disorders

Dissatisfaction with body image can be dangerous, even deadly. Many teenagers, mostly girls, eat erratically or ingest drugs (especially diet pills) to lose weight; others, mostly boys, take steroids to increase muscle mass. [**Developmental Link:** Teenage drug abuse is discussed in Chapter 16.] Eating disorders are rare in childhood but increase dramatically at puberty, accompanied by distorted body image, food obsession, and depression (Le Grange & Lock, 2011). (See Visualizing Development, page 419.)

Adolescents sometimes switch from obsessive dieting to overeating to overexercising and back again. Although girls are most vulnerable, boys are too, especially those who aspire to be pop stars or who train to be wrestlers. Here, we describe two eating disorders that are particularly likely to begin in adolescence.

### Anorexia Nervosa

**anorexia nervosa** An eating disorder characterized by self-starvation. Affected individuals voluntarily undereat and often overexercise, depriving their vital organs of nutrition. Anorexia can be fatal.

A body mass index (BMI) of 18 or lower, or a loss of more than 10 percent of body weight within a month or two, indicates **anorexia nervosa,** a disorder characterized by voluntary starvation and a destructive, distorted attitude about one's own body fat. The affected person becomes very thin, risking death by organ failure. Staying too thin becomes an obsession.

Although anorexia existed earlier, it was not identified until about 1950, when some high-achieving, upper-class young women became so emaciated that they died. Soon anorexia was evident among teenagers and young adults of every income, nation, and ethnicity; the rate spikes at puberty and again in emerging adulthood. Certain alleles increase the risk of developing anorexia (Young, 2010), with higher risk among girls with close relatives who suffer from eating disorders or severe depression. Although far more common in girls, some boys are also at risk.

### Bulimia Nervosa and Binge Eating Disorder

**bulimia nervosa** An eating disorder characterized by binge eating and subsequent purging, usually by induced vomiting and/or use of laxatives.

About three times as common as anorexia is **bulimia nervosa.** This disorder is clinically present in 1 to 3 percent of female teenagers and young adults in the United States. They overeat compulsively, consuming thousands of calories within an hour or two, and then purge through vomiting or laxatives. Most are close to normal in weight and therefore unlikely to starve. However, they risk serious health problems, including damage to their gastrointestinal systems and cardiac arrest from electrolyte imbalance.

Bingeing and purging are common among adolescents. For instance, a 2013 survey found that *in the last 30 days,* 6.6 percent of U.S. high school girls and 2.2 percent of boys vomited or took laxatives to lose weight, with marked variation by state, from 3.6 percent in Nebraska to 9 percent in Arizona (MMWR, June 13, 2014).

A disorder that is newly recognized (DSM-5) is *binge eating disorder.* Some adolescents periodically and compulsively overeat, quickly consuming large amounts of ice cream, cake, or any snack food until their stomachs hurt. When bingeing becomes a disorder, overeating is typically done in private, at least weekly for several months. The sufferer does not purge (hence this is not bulimia) but feels out of control, distressed, and depressed.

### Life-Span Causes and Consequences

From a life-span perspective, teenage eating disorders are not limited to adolescence, even though this is when first signs typically appear. The origins begin much earlier, in family eating patterns if parents do not help their children eat

FRED DUFOUR/Getty Images

**Not Just Dieting** Elize, seen here sitting in a café in France, believes that she developed anorexia after she went on an extreme diet. Success with that diet led her to think that even less food would be better. She is recovering, but, as you can see, she is still too thin.

# Satisfied with Your Body?

Probably not, if you are a teenager. At every age, accepting who you are—not just ethnicity and gender, but also body shape, size, and strength—correlates with emotional health. During the adolescent years, when everyone's body changes dramatically, body dissatisfaction rises. As you see, this is particularly true for girls—but if the measure were satisfaction with muscles, more boys would be noted as unhappy.

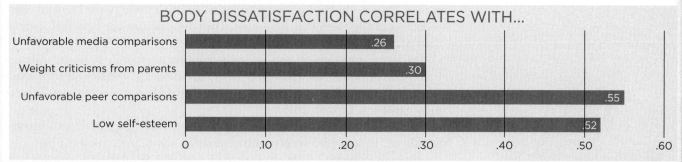

## BODY DISSATISFACTION CORRELATES WITH...

| | |
|---|---|
| Unfavorable media comparisons | .26 |
| Weight criticisms from parents | .30 |
| Unfavorable peer comparisons | .55 |
| Low self-esteem | .52 |

Scale: 0 .10 .20 .30 .40 .50 .60

Data from Van Vonderen & Kinnally, 2012.

## GENDER DIFFERENCES IN BODY DISSATISFACTION

Females of all ages tend to be dissatisfied with their bodies, but the biggest leap in dissatisfaction occurs when girls transition from early to mid-adolescence (Makinen et al., 2012).

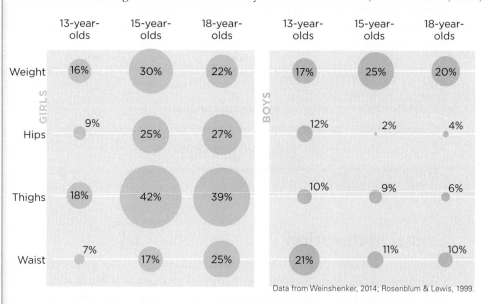

GIRLS

| | 13-year-olds | 15-year-olds | 18-year-olds |
|---|---|---|---|
| Weight | 16% | 30% | 22% |
| Hips | 9% | 25% | 27% |
| Thighs | 18% | 42% | 39% |
| Waist | 7% | 17% | 25% |

BOYS

| | 13-year-olds | 15-year-olds | 18-year-olds |
|---|---|---|---|
| Weight | 17% | 25% | 20% |
| Hips | 12% | 2% | 4% |
| Thighs | 10% | 9% | 6% |
| Waist | 21% | 11% | 10% |

Data from Weinshenker, 2014; Rosenblum & Lewis, 1999.

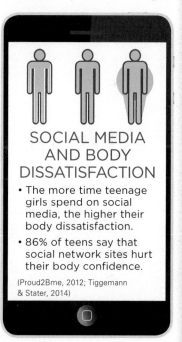

### SOCIAL MEDIA AND BODY DISSATISFACTION

• The more time teenage girls spend on social media, the higher their body dissatisfaction.

• 86% of teens say that social network sites hurt their body confidence.

(Proud2Bme, 2012; Tiggemann & Stater, 2014)

## NUTRITION AND EXERCISE

High school students are told, at home and at school, to eat their vegetables and not care about their looks. But they listen more to their peers and follow social norms. Fortunately, some eventually learn that, no matter what their body type, good nutrition and adequate exercise make a person feel more attractive, energetic, and happy.

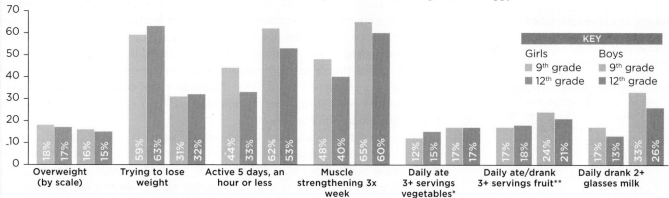

**KEY**

| | Girls | Boys |
|---|---|---|
| 9th grade | ■ | ■ |
| 12th grade | ■ | ■ |

| | Girls 9th | Girls 12th | Boys 9th | Boys 12th |
|---|---|---|---|---|
| Overweight (by scale) | 18% | 17% | 16% | 15% |
| Trying to lose weight | 59% | 63% | 31% | 32% |
| Active 5 days, an hour or less | 44% | 33% | 62% | 53% |
| Muscle strengthening 3x week | 48% | 40% | 65% | 60% |
| Daily ate 3+ servings vegetables* | 12% | 15% | 17% | 17% |
| Daily ate/drank 3+ servings fruit** | 17% | 18% | 24% | 21% |
| Daily drank 2+ glasses milk | 17% | 13% | 33% | 26% |

*Vegetables includes salad greens, and excludes French fries.
**Fruits include a glass of 100% fruit juice.

Data from MMWR, June 10, 2016.

sensibly—when they are hungry, without food being a punishment or a reward. Indeed, the origin could be at conception, since a genetic vulnerability is evident for anorexia.

For all eating disorders, family function (not structure) is crucial (Tetzlaff & Hilbert, 2014). During the teen years, many parents are oblivious to eating disorders. They might have given up trying to get their child to eat breakfast before school, or to join the family for dinner. They delay getting the help that their children need (Thomson et al., 2014).

The social emphasis on appearance is hard for any family to ignore. Since pubescent children add body fat before height and muscles, and since most teenagers develop a body type unlike the Hollywood cultural ideal, disordered eating is common (Smolak & Levine, 2015).

Problems continue. Many eating disorders are unrecognized until emerging adulthood. Unless adolescents with disordered eating patterns learn better habits, they are vulnerable later on. Perhaps 5 percent eventually die of organ failure related to anorexia. Death from eating disorders almost never occurs in adolescence: Instead, victims die 10 years or more after initial symptoms. Most survive but many experience depression, anxiety, and health complications such as heart disease, infertility, or osteoporosis. The chance of recovery is better if diagnosis and treatment occur during early adolescence (not adulthood), and hospitalization is brief (Errichiello et al., 2016; Meczekalski et al., 2013).

---

**WHAT HAVE YOU LEARNED?**

1. What is the pattern of growth in adolescent bodies?

2. What complications result from the sequence of growth (weight/height/muscles)?

3. Why are many teenagers deficient in iron and calcium?

4. Why are many adolescents unhappy with their appearance?

---

# Sexual Maturation

Sexuality is multidimensional, complicated, and variable—not unlike human development overall. Here, we consider biological changes at puberty and some cohort variations. Other aspects of sexuality are discussed in Chapter 16 and the Epilogue.

## Sexual Characteristics

**primary sex characteristics** The parts of the body that are directly involved in reproduction, including the vagina, uterus, ovaries, testicles, and penis.

**secondary sex characteristics** Physical traits that are not directly involved in reproduction but that indicate sexual maturity, such as a man's beard and a woman's breasts.

The body characteristics that are directly involved in conception and pregnancy are called **primary sex characteristics.** During puberty, every primary sex organ (the ovaries, the uterus, the penis, and the testes) increases dramatically in size and matures in function. Reproduction becomes possible.

At the same time that maturation of the primary sex characteristics occurs, secondary sex characteristics develop. **Secondary sex characteristics** are bodily features that do not directly affect reproduction (hence they are secondary) but that signify masculinity or femininity.

One secondary characteristic is body shape. Young boys and girls have similar shapes, but at puberty males widen at the shoulders and grow about 5 inches taller than females, while girls widen at the hips and develop breasts. Those female curves are often considered signs of womanhood, but neither breasts nor wide hips are required for reproduction; thus, they are secondary, not primary, sex characteristics.

The pattern of hair growth at the scalp line (widow's peak), the prominence of the larynx (Adam's apple), and several other anatomical features differ for men and women; all are secondary sex characteristics that few people notice. Facial and body hair increases in both sexes, affected by sex hormones as well as genes. Girls often shave their legs and pluck or wax any facial hair that they notice, while boys may proudly grow sideburns, soul patches, chinstraps, moustaches, and so on—with specifics dependent on culture and cohort. Hair on the head is cut and styled to be spikey, flat, curled, long, short, or shaved. Hair is far more than a growth characteristic; it is a display of sexuality, a mark of independence.

Secondary sex characteristics are important psychologically, if not biologically. Breasts are an obvious example. Many adolescent girls buy "minimizer," "maximizer," "training," or "shaping" bras in the hope that their breasts will conform to an idealized body image.

During the same years, many overweight boys are horrified to notice a swelling around their nipples—a temporary result of the erratic hormones of early puberty. If a boy's breast growth is very disturbing, tamoxifen or plastic surgery can reduce the swelling, although many doctors prefer to let time deal with the problem (Morcos & Kizy, 2012).

**LaunchPad**
macmillan learning

**Video: Romantic Relationships in Adolescence** explores teens' attitudes and assumptions about romance and sexuality.

## Sexual Activity

Primary and secondary sex characteristics such as menarche, spermarche, hair, and body shape are not the only evidence of sex hormones. Fantasizing, flirting, hand-holding, staring, standing, sitting, walking, displaying, and touching are all done in particular ways to reflect sexuality. As already explained, hormones trigger sexual thoughts, but the culture shapes thoughts into enjoyable fantasies, shameful obsessions, frightening impulses, or actual contact (see Figure 14.5).

Masturbation is common in both sexes, for instance, but culture determines attitudes, from private sin to mutual pleasure (Driemeyer et al., 2016). Caressing, oral sex, nipple stimulation, and kissing are all taboo in some cultures, expected in others.

The distinction between early and later sexual experience during adolescence may be significant. A detailed longitudinal study in Finland found that depressed and rebellious 13-year-olds were more likely to use drugs and have sex (Kaltiala-Heino et al., 2015). That had flipped by age 19, when those who had

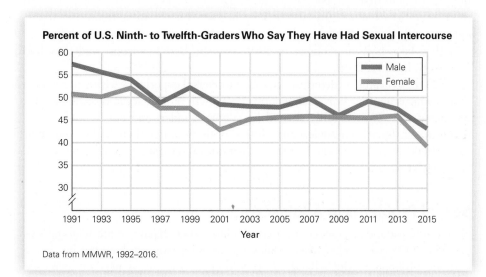

Percent of U.S. Ninth- to Twelfth-Graders Who Say They Have Had Sexual Intercourse

Data from MMWR, 1992–2016.

**FIGURE 14.5**

**Boys and Girls Together** Boys tend to be somewhat more sexually experienced than girls during the high school years, but since the Youth Risk Behavior Survey began in 1991, the overall trend has been toward equality in rates of sexual activity.

experienced intercourse were less likely to be depressed (Savioja et al., 2015). Emotions regarding sexual experience, like the rest of puberty, are strongly influenced by social norms regarding what is expected at what age.

Indeed, everyone is influenced by hormones and society, biology and culture. All adolescents have sexual interests that they did not previously have (biology), which propel teenagers in some nations to do things that teenagers of other nations would never do (culture).

Social norms regarding male–female differences are powerful. Traditionally, males were thought to have stronger sexual urges than females, which is why adolescent boys are supposed to "make the first move," from asking for a date to trying for a kiss. Then, girls were supposed to slow down the boys' advances. This was called the *double standard*, in that behaviors of boys and girls were held to different standards. Many adolescents still expect boys and girls to approach heterosexual interactions differently, with boys more insistent and girls more hesitant. As one teen explained, "that's just how it is" (Tolman et al., 2016).

The double standard is less powerful that it was. In many nations, including the United States, female rates of sexual activity are almost even with male rates. For example, among high school seniors, 57 percent of the girls and 59 percent of the boys have had sexual intercourse, with most of them sexually active in the past three months. The one notable difference among high school students is in the number of partners: 9 percent of the girls and 14 percent of the boys have had four or more (MMWR, June 10, 2016).

Over the past two decades in the United States, every gender, ethnic, and age group is *less* sexually active than the previous cohort. Between 1991 and 2015, intercourse experience among African American high school students decreased 40 percent (to 49 percent); among European Americans, down 20 percent (to 40 percent); and among Latinos, down 19 percent (to 43 percent) (MMWR, June 10, 2016).

These were responses to an anonymous questionnaire. As you know from Chapter 1, some inaccuracies may have occurred, but the trends are solid because the same questions were asked over the decades. Many reasons for the trends have been suggested: sex education, fear of HIV/AIDS, awareness of the hazards of pregnancy, more female education, less male–female intimacy. To explore these hypotheses, more research is needed.

The trend toward earlier puberty yet later sexual activity is international. More teenagers worldwide are virgins than was true a decade ago, a trend documented in China where first intercourse occurs at age 20, on average (Yu et al., 2013). In the United States, most 20-year-olds have had sex, but the same trends are apparent at younger ages. For example, in 2015, half (50 percent) of eleventh-graders said they have had intercourse; in 1991, two-thirds (62 percent) said they had (MMWR, June 10, 2016).

All of these examples demonstrate that a universal experience (rising hormones) that produces another universal experience (growth of primary and secondary sex characteristics) is powerfully shaped by cohort, gender, and culture. The most important influence on adolescents' sexual activity is not their bodies but their close friends, who have more influence than do sex or ethnic group norms (van de Bongardt et al., 2015).

## Sexual Problems in Adolescence

Sexual interest and interaction are part of adolescence; healthy adult relationships are more likely to develop when adolescent impulses are not haunted by shame and fear (Tolman & McClelland, 2011). Although guidance is needed, teenagers are neither depraved nor degenerate in experiencing sexual urges. Before focusing

Steve Coleman/Getty Images

**Everywhere** Glancing, staring, and—when emotions are overwhelming—averting one's eyes are part of the universal language of love. Although the rate of intercourse among teenagers is lower than it was, passion is expressed in simple words, touches, and, as shown here, the eyes on a cold day.

**LaunchPad**
macmillan learning

Check out the Data Connections activity **Sexual Behaviors of U.S. High School Students,** which examines how sexually active teens really are.

on the hazards of adolescent sex, we should note that several "problems" are less troubling now than in earlier decades. Here are three specifics:

- *Teen births have decreased.* In the United States, births to teenage mothers (aged 15 to 19) decreased 50 percent between 2007 and 2015 across race and ethnicity, with the biggest drop among Hispanic teens (J. Martin et al., 2017). [The 2015 rate was the lowest in 50 years.] Similar declines are evident in other nations. The most dramatic results are from China, where the 2015 teen pregnancy rate was about one-tenth of the rate 50 years ago (reducing the 2015 projection of the world's population by about 1 billion).
- *The use of "protection" has risen.* Contraception, particularly condom use among adolescent boys, has increased markedly in most nations since 1990. The U.S. Youth Risk Behavior Survey found that 63 percent of sexually active ninth-grade boys used a condom during their most recent intercourse (MMWR, June 10, 2016) (see Table 14.1).
- *The teen abortion rate is down.* In general, the teen abortion rate in the United States has declined every year since abortion became legal. The rate today is about half that of 20 years earlier (Kost & Henshaw, 2013), even as the rate among older women has increased. The reason is not only that intercourse is less frequent but also that contraception is more prevalent.

These are positive trends, but many aspects of adolescent sexual activity remain problematic.

## Sex Too Soon

Sex can, of course, be thrilling and affirming, providing a bonding experience. However, compared to a century ago, adolescent sexual activity—especially if it results in birth—is more hazardous because four circumstances have changed:

1. Earlier puberty and weaker social taboos result in some very young teens having sex. Early sex correlates with depression, drug abuse, and lifelong problems (Kastbom et al., 2015).
2. If early sex leads to pregnancy and birth, most teenage girls have no partners to help. A century ago, teenage mothers were often married; now, in the United States, 86 percent are unwed (Shattuck & Kreider, 2013).
3. Raising a child has become more complex and expensive, and family helpers are scarce. The strategy that most teenage mothers used in former times—having their mother raise the child—is less available, as most young grandmothers are employed (Meyer, 2014).

**Who Should Teens Talk to About Contraception?** This teenage girl is discussing contraception with her gynecologist.

**◖◗ Especially for Parents Worried About Their Teenager's Risk Taking** You remember the risky things you did at the same age, and you are alarmed by the possibility that your child will follow in your footsteps. What should you do? (see response, p. 426)

| TABLE 14.1 | | |
|---|---|---|
| **Condom Use Among 15-Year-Olds (Tenth Grade)** | | |
| National differences are apparent, even among nations that are similar in ethnicity and demographic values. Theories abound, and so does controversy. | | |
| **Country** | **Sexually Active (% of total)** | **Used Condom at Last Intercourse (% of those sexually active)** |
| France | 20 | 84 |
| England | 29 | 83 |
| Canada | 23 | 78 |
| Russia | 33 | 75 |
| Israel | 14 | 72 |
| United States | 41 | 60 |
| Data from MMWR, June 4, 2010, June 10, 2016; Nic Gabhainn et al., 2009. | | |

4. Sexually transmitted infections are more common and more dangerous (Satterwhite et al., 2013).

As you read, teen births are declining, as are teen abortions. However, the U.S. rate of adolescent pregnancy is the highest of any developed nation (true among every ethnic group). If a pregnant girl is under 16 (most are not), she is more likely than older pregnant teenagers to experience complications—including spontaneous or induced abortion, high blood pressure, stillbirth, preterm birth, and low birthweight. This is true worldwide, in wealthy as well as low-income nations (Ganchimeg et al., 2014).

There are many reasons for these hazards besides age. Poverty and lack of education correlate with teen pregnancy and with every problem just listed (Santelli & Melnikas, 2010). Beyond that, younger pregnant teenagers are often malnourished and postpone prenatal care. After birth, adolescents are less often the responsive mothers that newborns need, so insecure attachment is more common. [**Developmental Link:** Attachment types and the importance of early attachment were discussed in Chapter 7.]

Even if sexually active adolescents avoid pregnancy, early intercourse increases psychosocial problems. A study of 3,923 adult women in the United States found that those who *voluntarily* had sex before age 16 were more likely to divorce later on, whether or not they became pregnant or later married their first sexual partner. The same study found that adolescents of any age whose first sexual experience was unwanted (either "really didn't want it" or "had mixed feelings about it") were also more likely to later experience divorce (Paik, 2011).

Forced sex is much worse, of course, as now explained.

## Sexual Abuse

Teenage births are risky, but sometimes mother and baby develop well. Indeed, although most teenagers suffer in many ways if they have a baby, a minority of young mothers become more responsible, avoiding drugs and seeking more education (Gregson, 2010). Teenage pregnancy should be discouraged for many reasons, but we also should recognize many variations.

Abuse, however, is always devastating: It harms development lifelong. **Child sexual abuse** is defined as any sexual activity (including fondling and photographing) between a juvenile and an adult. Age 18 is the usual demarcation between adult and child, although legal age varies by state. Girls are particularly vulnerable, although boys are also at risk.

Although sexual abuse of younger children gathers most headlines, young adolescents are, by far, the most frequent victims. The rate of sexual abuse increases at puberty, a particularly sensitive time because many young adolescents are confused about their own sexual urges and identity (Graber et al., 2010). Virtually every adolescent problem, including pregnancy, drug abuse, eating disorders, and suicide, is more frequent in adolescents who are sexually abused.

This is true worldwide. Although solid numbers are unknown for obvious reasons, it is apparent that millions of girls in their early teens are forced into marriage or prostitution each year. Adolescent girls are common victims of sex trafficking, not only because their youth makes them more alluring but also because their immaturity makes them more vulnerable (McClain & Garrity, 2011). Some believe they are helping their families by earning money to support them; others are literally sold by their families (Montgomery, 2015).

It is virtually impossible to know how common child sexual abuse is. The problem begins with definition—would you consider it sexual abuse when a 14-year-old marries a man chosen by her parents? What about a 16-year-old who has sex with

*quavondo/Getty Images*

**See the Joy** Some young mothers are wonderful, as seems the case here. This mother–infant pair have many advantages, not only their mutual love but also a supportive community. (Note the floor of the playroom—colorful, nontoxic, and soft—perfect for toddlers.)

**child sexual abuse** Any erotic activity that arouses an adult and excites, shames, or confuses a child, whether or not the victim protests and whether or not genital contact is involved.

her 19-year-old boyfriend? Estimates of how many children are trafficked for sex in the United States range from 1,000 to 336,000 (Miller-Perrin & Wurtele, 2017).

When U.S.–born children suffer sexual abuse, they are usually not trafficked but instead are abused in their own homes. Typically, the victims are young adolescents who are not allowed friendships and romances that teach them how to develop a healthy and satisfying life. Sometimes the abuser is a biological parent, but more often it is a stepparent, older sibling, or uncle. Young people who are sexually exploited tend to fear sex and to devalue themselves lifelong, with higher rates of virtually every developmental problem (Pérez-Fuentes et al., 2013).

For example, in one longitudinal study in Washington, D.C., of 84 reported victims of child sexual abuse (all girls), each of them was interviewed six times over 23 years (Trickett et al., 2011). In order to isolate the effects of abuse, the researchers also followed the development of individuals from the same backgrounds (SES, ethnicity, and so on) who were not sexually abused.

Every problem examined was worse in the victims than in their peers who were not victimized. Among the examples: Sex was thought of as dirty, shameful, and dangerous; few were overweight as children, but 42 percent were obese in their 20s; school achievement was lower; rates of self-harm were higher; repeated victimization—both sexual and physical—was more common in adulthood (Trickett et al., 2011).

From a developmental perspective, their ability to care for their children is particularly important. Almost half of the girls who were abused became mothers, having a total of 78 children. Of those children, three died in infancy and nine were permanently removed from their mothers, who had severely maltreated them. These rates were much higher than rates among the mothers from the same income and ethnic groups who were not victimized.

Early in this chapter, we noted that the HPA axis regulates puberty and many other physiological responses. Many of the formerly abused women had abnormal HPA regulation, with alteration of their cortisol responses. That condition produced heightened stress reactions in early adolescence but then abnormally low stress responses in adulthood.

Fortunately, now that child sexual abuse is recognized and reported more often, it has become less common, with "large declines in sexual abuse from 1992 to 2010" in the United States (Finkelhor & Jones, 2012, p. 3). Worldwide, about 13 percent of women say they were sexually abused as children (Stoltenborgh et al., 2011). Of course, even one instance is too many.

Our discussion of sexual abuse focuses on girls because they are the most common victims. However, teenage boys may be sexually abused as well, a direct attack on their fledgling identity as men (Dorais, 2009). Disclosure of past abuse is particularly difficult for men, which makes reliable statistics difficult (Collin-Vézina et al., 2015).

Remember that perpetrators of all kinds of abuse are often people known to the child. After puberty, although sometimes abusers are parents, coaches, or other authorities, often they are other teenagers. In the most recent U.S. Youth Risk Behavior Survey of high school students, 15 percent of the girls and 5 percent of the boys said that they had been kissed, touched, or forced to have sex within a dating relationship when they did not want to (MMWR, June 10, 2016). Sex education is discussed in Chapter 16; obviously teenagers have much to learn.

## Sexually Transmitted Infections

Unlike teen pregnancy and sexual abuse, the other major problem of teenage sex shows no signs of abating. A **sexually transmitted infection (STI)** (sometimes called a sexually transmitted disease [STD]) is any infection transmitted through

**Could It Happen to You?** Lady Gaga sang "Til It Happens to You" at the 2016 Academy Awards, holding hands with fellow victims of sexual assault. As explained in the film *The Hunting Ground*, unwanted sexual comments and actions have been part of the college experience for decades, but now thousands of victims say, "No more."

**sexually transmitted infection (STI)** A disease spread by sexual contact, including syphilis, gonorrhea, genital herpes, chlamydia, and HIV.

**Response for Parents Worried About Their Teenager's Risk Taking** (from p. 423): You are right to be concerned, but you cannot keep your child locked up for the next decade or so. Since you know that some rebellion and irrationality are likely, try to minimize them by not boasting about your own youthful exploits, by reacting sternly to minor infractions to nip worse behavior in the bud, and by making allies of your child's teachers and the parents of your child's friends.

**LaunchPad**
macmillan learning

The Data Connections activity **Major Sexually Transmitted Infections: Some Basics** offers more information about the causes, symptoms, and rates of various STIs.

sexual contact. Worldwide, sexually active teenagers have higher rates of the most common STIs—gonorrhea, genital herpes, and chlamydia—than do sexually active people of any other age group.

In the United States, half of all new STIs occur in people ages 15 to 25, even though this age group has less than one-fourth of the sexually active people (Satterwhite et al., 2013). Rates are particularly high among sexually active adolescents, ages 15 to 19 (Gavin et al., 2009). Biology provides one reason: Pubescent girls are particularly likely to catch an STI compared to fully developed women, probably because adult women have more vaginal secretions that reduce infections. Further, if symptoms appear, teens are less likely to alert their partners or seek treatment unless pain requires it.

A survey of adolescents in a U.S. pediatric emergency department found that half of the teenagers (average age 15) were sexually active and 20 percent of those had an STI—although that was not usually the reason they came for medical help (M. Miller et al., 2015).

There are hundreds of STIs. *Chlamydia* is the most frequently reported one; it often begins without symptoms, yet it can cause permanent infertility.

Worse is *human papillomavirus (HPV)*, which has no immediate consequences but increases the risk of "serious, life-threatening cancer" in both sexes (MMWR, July 25, 2014, p. 622). Immunization before the first intercourse has reduced the rate of HPV, but in 2013, among 13- to 17-year-olds, only 38 percent of the girls and 14 percent of the boys had received all three recommended doses (MMWR, July 25, 2014).

National variations in laws and rates of STIs are large. Rates among U.S. teenagers are higher than those in any other medically advanced nation but lower than rates in some developing nations. HIV rates are not declining, despite increased awareness.

Once again, it is apparent that a universal experience (the biology of puberty) varies remarkably depending on national and family context. As we stated earlier, adolescence begins with biology and ends with culture. You will see more examples in the next chapter, as you learn that schools for adolescents vary a great deal in how and what they teach.

---

**WHAT HAVE YOU LEARNED?**

1. What are examples of the difference between primary and secondary sex characteristics?

2. Why are there fewer problems caused by adolescent sexuality now than a few decades ago?

3. What are the problems with adolescent pregnancy?

4. Among sexually active people, why do adolescents have more STIs than adults?

5. What are the effects of child sexual abuse?

---

# SUMMARY

## Puberty Begins

**1.** Puberty refers to the various changes that transform a child's body into an adult one. Even before the teenage years, biochemical signals from the hypothalamus to the pituitary gland to the adrenal glands (the HPA axis) increase production of testosterone, estrogen, and various other hormones, which cause the body to grow rapidly and become capable of reproduction.

**2.** Some emotional reactions, such as quick mood shifts, are directly caused by hormones, as are thoughts about sex.

The reactions of others to adolescents and the adolescents' own reactions to the physical changes they are undergoing also trigger emotional responses, which, in turn, affect hormones.

**3.** Hormones regulate all of the body rhythms of life, by day, by season, and by year. Changes in these rhythms in adolescence often result in sleep deprivation, partly because the natural circadian rhythm makes teenagers wide awake at night. Sleep deprivation causes numerous health and learning problems.

**4.** Various parts of the brain mature during puberty and in the following decade. The regions dedicated to emotional arousal (including the amygdala) mature before those that regulate and rationalize emotional expression (the prefrontal cortex).

**5.** Puberty normally begins anytime from about age 8 to about age 14. The young person's sex, genetic background, body fat, and level of stress all contribute to this variation in timing.

**6.** Girls generally begin and end puberty before boys do, although the time gap in sexual maturity is much shorter than the two-year gap in reaching peak height. Girls from divorced families or stressful neighborhoods are likely to reach puberty earlier.

### Growth and Nutrition

**7.** The growth spurt is an acceleration of growth in every part of the body. Peak weight usually precedes peak height, which is then followed by peak muscle growth. This sequence makes adolescents particularly vulnerable to sports injuries. The lungs and the heart also increase in size and capacity.

**8.** All of the changes of puberty depend on adequate nourishment, yet adolescents do not always make healthy food choices. One reason for poor nutrition is the desire to lose (or, less often, gain) weight because of anxiety about body image. This is a worldwide problem, involving cultural as well as biological factors.

**9.** The precursors of eating disorders are evident during puberty. Many adolescents eat too much of the wrong foods or too little food overall. Deficiencies of iron, vitamin D, and calcium are common, affecting bone growth and overall development.

**10.** Because of the sequence of brain development, many adolescents seek intense emotional experiences, unchecked by rational thought. For the same reason, adolescents are quick to react, explore, and learn. As a result, adolescents take risks, bravely or foolishly, with potential for harm as well as for good.

### Sexual Maturation

**11.** Male–female differences in bodies and behavior become apparent at puberty. The maturation of primary sex characteristics means that by age 13 or so, after experiencing menarche or spermarche, teenagers are capable of reproducing, although peak fertility is several years later.

**12.** Secondary sex characteristics are not directly involved in reproduction but signify that the child is becoming a man or a woman. Body shape, breasts, voice, body hair, and numerous other features differentiate males from females. Sexual activity is influenced more by culture than by physiology.

**13.** In the twenty-first century, teenage sexual behavior has changed for the better in several ways. Hormones and growth may cause sexual thoughts and behaviors at younger ages, but teen pregnancy is far less common, condom use has increased, and the average age of first intercourse has risen.

**14.** Among the problems that adolescents still face is the urge to become sexually active before their bodies and minds are ready. Giving birth before age 16 takes a physical toll on a growing girl; it also puts her baby at risk of physical and psychological problems.

**15.** Sexual abuse is more likely to occur in early adolescence than at other ages. Girls are more often the victims than boys are. The perpetrators are often family members or close friends of the family. Rates of child sexual abuse are declining in the United States, but globalization has probably increased international sex trafficking.

**16.** Untreated STIs at any age can lead to infertility and even death. Rates among sexually active teenagers are rising for many reasons, with HIV/AIDS not yet halted. Immunization to prevent HPV is decreasing rates of vaginal cancer in adulthood, but most teenagers are not immunized.

## KEY TERMS

puberty (p. 404)
menarche (p. 404)
spermarche (p. 404)
pituitary (p. 404)
adrenal glands (p. 404)
HPA (hypothalamus–pituitary–adrenal) axis (p. 404)

gonads (p.404)
HPG (hypothalamus–pituitary–gonad) axis (p. 404)
estradiol (p. 404)
testosterone (p. 404)
circadian rhythm (p. 406)
secular trend (p. 411)

leptin (p. 411)
growth spurt (p. 414)
body image (p. 417)
anorexia nervosa (p. 418)
bulimia nervosa (p. 418)
primary sex characteristics (p. 420)

secondary sex characteristics (p. 420)
child sexual abuse (p. 424)
sexually transmitted infection (STI) (p. 425)

## APPLICATIONS

**1.** Visit a fifth-, sixth-, or seventh-grade class. Note variations in the size and maturity of the students. Do you see any patterns related to gender, ethnicity, body fat, or self-confidence?

**2.** Interview two to four of your friends who are in their late teens or early 20s about their memories of menarche or spermarche, including their memories of others' reactions. Do their comments indicate that these events are or are not emotionally troubling for young people?

**3.** Talk with someone who became a teenage parent. Were there any problems with the pregnancy, the birth, or the first years of parenthood? Would the person recommend teen parenthood? What would have been different had the baby been born three years earlier or three years later?

**4.** Adult reactions to puberty can be reassuring or frightening. Interview two or three people about how adults prepared, encouraged, or troubled their development. Compare that with your own experience.

# Adolescence:
## Cognitive Development

## What Will You Know?

1. Why are young adolescents often egocentric?
2. Why does emotion sometimes overwhelm reason?
3. Is cyberbullying worse than direct bullying?
4. What kind of school is best for teenagers?

+ **Logic and Self**
Egocentrism
Formal Operational Thought
Two Modes of Thinking
A CASE TO STUDY: Biting the Policeman
INSIDE THE BRAIN: Impulses, Rewards, and Reflection

+ **Digital Natives**
Technology and Cognition
Sexual Abuse?
Addiction
Cyber Danger

+ **Secondary Education**
Definitions and Facts
Middle School
High School
OPPOSING PERSPECTIVES: Testing Variability

I have taught at four universities, educating thousands of college students. The basic curriculum is standard. That allows me to focus on updating, adding current examples, and adjusting to the particular class. Depending on the topic and the students, my methods change—lecture, discussion, polls, groups, video clips, pair/share, role-play, written responses, quizzes, and more.

No class is exactly like any other. Groups are dynamic: The particular students and their interactions affect the whole. Ideally, I recognize who needs encouragement ("Good question"), who needs prompts ("Do you agree with . . . ?"), who should think before they speak ("What is your evidence?"), whose background needs to be understood by others ("Is that what it was like when you were a child in . . . ?). Deciding who should learn what, when, and how is my challenge and my joy.

A few years ago, I taught an introductory course for college credit to advanced high school students. They grasped concepts quickly, they studied diligently, they completed papers on time—in all of those ways they were good students. But they presented unfamiliar challenges. One day I introduced psychoanalysis.

> **Student:** I don't agree with Freud.
> **Me:** You don't have to agree, just learn the terms and ideas.
> **Student:** Why should I do that?
> **Me:** You need to understand Freud, so you can then disagree.
> **Student:** But I have my own ideas, and I like them better than Freud's.

I was taken aback. None of my students had ever been so egocentric as to claim that their own ideas were so great that they didn't need to bother with Freud. Of course, many of my college students disagree with psychoanalytic theory. Some express insightful critiques. But none have resisted learning about Freud, deciding in advance that they liked their ideas so much that they did not need to learn other ideas.

Then I remembered: Bright as they were, these students were adolescents. I needed to adjust in order to reach them.

This chapter describes adolescent cognition, sometimes brilliant, sometimes theoretical, and sometimes egocentric. Teenagers can switch in a heartbeat from rapid, emotional thoughts to slower, logical ones: Those dual processes coexist but do not combine. Then this chapter explores how adolescents are taught—in middle school, in high school, and around the world—and how that may clash with adolescent cognition.

Image Source/Getty Images

**All Eyes on Me** Egocentrism and obsession with appearance are hallmarks of adolescence, as shown by these high school cheerleaders. Given teenage thinking, it is not surprising that many boys and girls seek stardom, sometimes making competition within teams and between schools fierce. Cooperation and moderation are more difficult.

**adolescent egocentrism** A characteristic of adolescent thinking that leads young people (ages 10 to 13) to focus on themselves to the exclusion of others.

# Logic and Self

Brain maturation, additional years of schooling, moral challenges, increased independence, and intense conversations all occur between the ages of 11 and 18. These aspects of adolescents' development propel cognitive growth, beginning with intense focus on oneself and moving toward impressive rational thought.

## Egocentrism

During puberty, young people center on themselves, in part because maturation of the brain and body heightens self-consciousness. Young adolescents grapple with conflicting feelings about their parents and friends, examine details of their physical changes, and think deeply (but not always realistically) about their future.

Some *ruminate*, going over problems via phone, text, conversation, social media, and private, quiet self-talk (as when they lie in bed, unable to sleep) about each nuance of everything they have done, are doing, might do, and should have done if only they had thought quickly enough. Others act impulsively without any rumination at all, blurting out words that they later regret. And most do both, zigzagging from thoughtfulness to thoughtlessness.

**Adolescent egocentrism**—that is, adolescents thinking intensely about themselves and about what others think of them—was first described by David Elkind (1967). He found that, egocentrically, adolescents regard themselves as much more unique, special, admired, or hated than anyone else considers them to be. Egocentric adolescents have trouble understanding other points of view.

For example, few girls are attracted to boys with pimples and braces, but one boy's eagerness to be seen as growing up kept him from realizing this, according to his older sister:

> Now in the 8th grade, my brother has this idea that all the girls are looking at him in school. He got his first pimple about three months ago. I told him to wash it with my face soap but he refused, saying, "Not until I go to school to show it off." He called the dentist, begging him to approve his braces now instead of waiting for a year. The perfect gifts for him have changed from action figures to a bottle of cologne, a chain, and a fitted baseball hat like the rappers wear.
>
> *[adapted from E., personal communication]*

Egocentrism leads adolescents to interpret everyone else's behavior as if it were a judgment on them. A stranger's frown or a teacher's critique can make a teenager conclude that "No one likes me" and then deduce that "I am unlovable" or even "I can't leave the house." More positive casual reactions—a smile from a sales clerk or an extra-big hug from a younger brother—could lead to "I am great" or "Everyone loves me."

Acute self-consciousness about physical appearance may be more prevalent between the ages of 10 and 14 than at any other time, in part because adolescents notice changes in their body that do not exactly conform to social norms and ideals (Guzman & Nishina, 2014). Adolescents also instigate changes that they think other teenagers will admire.

For example, piercings, shaved heads, torn jeans—all contrary to adult conventions—signify connection to youth culture, and wearing suits and ties, or dresses and pearls, would attract unwelcome attention from other youth. Notice groups of adolescents waiting in line for a midnight show, or clustering near their high school, and you will see appearance that may seem rebellious to adults but that conforms to teen culture.

**THINK CRITICALLY:** How should you judge the validity of the idea of adolescent egocentrism?

Because adolescents are focused on their own perspectives, their emotions may not be grounded in reality. A study of 1,310 Dutch and Belgian adolescents found that egocentrism was strong. For many of these teenagers, self-esteem and loneliness were closely tied to their *perception* of how others saw them, not to their actual popularity or acceptance among their peers. Gradually, after about age 15, some gained more perspective and became less depressed (Vanhalst et al., 2013).

## The Imaginary Audience

Egocentrism creates an **imaginary audience** in the minds of many adolescents. They believe they are at center stage, with all eyes on them, and they imagine how others might react to their appearance and behavior.

One woman remembers:

> When I was 14 and in the 8th grade, I received an award at the end-of-year school assembly. Walking across the stage, I lost my footing and stumbled in front of the entire student body. To be clear, this was not falling flat on one's face, spraining an ankle, or knocking over the school principal—it was a small misstep noticeable only to those in the audience who were paying close attention. As I rushed off the stage, my heart pounded with embarrassment and self-consciousness, and weeks of speculation about the consequence of this missed step were set into motion. There were tears and loss of sleep. Did my friends notice? Would they stop wanting to hang out with me? Would a reputation for clumsiness follow me to high school?

*[Somerville, 2013, p. 121]*

This woman became an expert on the adolescent brain. She remembered from personal experience that "adolescents are hyperaware of others' evaluations and feel they are under constant scrutiny by an imaginary audience" (Somerville, 2013, p. 124).

## Fables

Egocentrism leads naturally to a **personal fable,** the belief that one is unique, destined to have a heroic, fabled, even legendary life. Some 12-year-olds plan to star in the NBA, or to become billionaires, or to cure cancer. Some believe they are destined to die an early, tragic death. For that reason, statistics about smoking, junk food, vaping, or other destructive habits are of no import. One of my young students said "that's just a statistic," dismissing its relevance.

Adolescents markedly overestimate the chance that they will die soon. One study found that teens estimate 1 chance in 5 that they will die before age 20, when, in fact, the odds are less than 1 in 1,000. Even those most at risk of early death (urban African American males) survive at least to age 20 more than 99 times in 100. Sadly, if adolescents think that they will die young, they are likely to risk jail, HIV, drug addiction, and so on (Haynie et al., 2014). If someone dies, the response is fatalistic ("his number was up"), unaware that a self-fulfilling prophecy became a nail in the coffin.

The personal fable may coexist with the **invincibility fable,** the idea that death will not occur unless it is destined. This is another reason that some adolescents believe that fast driving, unprotected sex, or addictive drugs will spare them. Believing that one is invincible removes any impulse to control one's behavior, because personal control is impossible (Lin, 2016).

Similarly, teens post comments on Snapchat, Instagram, Facebook, and so on, and they expect others to understand, laugh, admire, or sympathize.

**imaginary audience** The other people who, in an adolescent's egocentric belief, are watching and taking note of his or her appearance, ideas, and behavior. This belief makes many teenagers very self-conscious.

**personal fable** An aspect of adolescent egocentrism characterized by an adolescent's belief that his or her thoughts, feelings, and experiences are unique, more wonderful, or more awful than anyone else's.

**invincibility fable** An adolescent's egocentric conviction that he or she cannot be overcome or even harmed by anything that might defeat a normal mortal, such as unprotected sex, drug abuse, or high-speed driving.

**Duck, Duck, Goose** Far more teens are injured in bicycle accidents than hunting ones, because almost all young people ride bicycles and relatively few are hunters. However, especially when no adult is present, young hunters are less likely to wear blaze orange, to attend safety classes, and to be licensed to hunt. Most likely these boys will return home safe, without the duck they seek. However, guns and off-road vehicles are leading causes of death for those under age 18, so this scene is not a comforting one.

**Typical or Extraordinary?** Francisca Vasconcelos, a San Diego high school senior, demonstrates formal operational thought. She used origami principles to create a 3D printed robot. She calls herself an "aspiring researcher," and her project won second place in the INTEL 2016 Science Fair. Is she typical of older adolescents, or extraordinarily advanced?

**formal operational thought** In Piaget's theory, the fourth and final stage of cognitive development, characterized by more systematic logical thinking and by the ability to understand and systematically manipulate abstract concepts.

 **LaunchPad**
macmillan learning

**Video Activity: The Balance Scale Task** shows children of various ages completing the task and gives you an opportunity to try it as well.

Their imaginary audience is other teenagers, not parents, teachers, college admission officers, or future employers who might have another interpretation (boyd, 2014).

Too much can be made of these fables and adolescent egocentrism overall. Indeed, one team of researchers considers adolescent egocentrism a "largely discredited notion" (Laursen & Hartl, 2013, p. 1266). Nonetheless, they and many others find some truth in it.

## Formal Operational Thought

Piaget described a shift in early adolescence to **formal operational thought** as adolescents move past concrete operational thinking and consider abstractions, including "assumptions that have no necessary relation to reality" (Piaget, 1950/2001, p. 163). Is Piaget correct? Many educators think so. They adjust the curriculum between primary and secondary school, reflecting a shift from concrete thought to formal, logical thought. Here are three examples:

- *Math.* Younger children multiply real numbers, such as $4 \times 3 \times 8$; adolescents multiply unreal numbers, such as $(2x)(3y)$ or even $(25xy^2)(-3zy^3)$.
- *Social studies.* Younger children study other cultures by considering daily life—drinking goat's milk or building an igloo, for instance. Adolescents consider the effects of GNP (gross national product) and TFR (total fertility rate) on global politics.
- *Science.* Younger students grow carrots and feed gerbils; adolescents study invisible particles and distant galaxies.

### Piaget's Experiments

Piaget and his colleagues devised a number of tasks to assess formal operational thought (Inhelder & Piaget, 1958/2013b). In these tasks, "in contrast to concrete operational children, formal operational adolescents imagine all possible determinants . . . [and] systematically vary the factors one by one, observe the results correctly, keep track of the results, and draw the appropriate conclusions" (P. Miller, 2011, p. 57).

One of their experiments (diagrammed in Figure 15.1) required balancing a scale by hooking weights onto the scale's arms. To master this task, a person must realize the reciprocal interaction between distance from the center and heaviness of the weight.

Balancing was not understood by the 3- to 5-year-olds. By age 7, children balanced the scale by putting the same amount of weight on each arm, but they didn't realize that the distance from the center mattered. By age 10, children experimented with the weights, using trial and error, not logic. Finally, by about age 13 or 14, some children hypothesized about reciprocity, realizing that a heavy weight close to the center can be counterbalanced with a light weight far from the center on the other side (Piaget & Inhelder, 1972).

### Hypothetical-Deductive Reasoning

One hallmark of formal operational thought is the capacity to think of possibility, not just reality. "Here and now" is only one of many possibilities, including "there and then," "long, long ago," "not yet," and "never." As Piaget said:

> The adolescent . . . thinks beyond the present and forms theories about everything, delighting especially in considerations of that which is not. . . .

*[Piaget, 1950/2001, p. 163]*

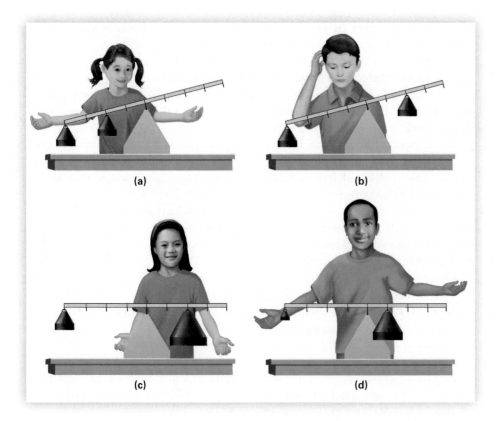

**FIGURE 15.1**

**How to Balance a Scale** Piaget's balance-scale test of formal reasoning, as it is attempted by (a) 4-year-old, (b) 7-year-old, (c) 10-year-old, and (d) 14-year-old. The key to balancing the scale is to make weight times distance from the center equal on both sides of the center; the realization of that principle requires formal operational thought.

**hypothetical thought** Reasoning that includes propositions and possibilities that may not reflect reality.

**deductive reasoning** Reasoning from a general statement, premise, or principle, through logical steps, to figure out (deduce) specifics. (Also called *top-down reasoning*.)

**inductive reasoning** Reasoning from one or more specific experiences or facts to reach (induce) a general conclusion. (Also called *bottom-up reasoning*.)

Adolescents are therefore primed to engage in **hypothetical thought,** reasoning about *if–then* propositions. Consider the following question, adapted from De Neys & Van Gelder (2009):

> If all mammals can walk,
> And whales are mammals,
> Can whales walk?

Children answer "No!" They know that whales swim, not walk; the logic escapes them. Some adolescents answer "Yes." They understand the conditional *if*, and therefore the counterfactual phrase "if all mammals."

> *Possibility* no longer appears merely as an extension of an empirical situation or of action actually performed. Instead, it is *reality* that is now secondary to *possibility*.
>
> *[Inhelder & Piaget, 1958/2013b, p. 251; emphasis in original]*

Hypothetical thought transforms perceptions, not necessarily for the better. Adolescents might criticize everything from their mother's spaghetti (it's not *al dente*) to the Gregorian calendar (it's not the Chinese or Jewish one). They criticize what *is* because of their hypothetical thinking about what might be and their growing awareness of other families and cultures (Moshman, 2011).

In developing the capacity to think hypothetically, by age 14 or so adolescents become more capable of **deductive reasoning,** or *top-down reasoning*, which begins with an abstract idea or premise and then uses logic to draw specific conclusions. In the example above, "if all mammals can walk" is a premise. By contrast, **inductive reasoning,** or *bottom-up reasoning*, predominates during the school years, as children accumulate facts and experiences

**Triple Winners** Sharing the scholarship check of $100,000, these high school students are not only high achievers but also have learned to collaborate within a comprehensive public school (Hewlett) in Long Island, New York. They were taught much more than formal operational logic.

(the knowledge base) to aid their thinking. Since they know whales cannot walk, that knowledge trumps the logic.

In essence, a child's reasoning goes like this: "This creature waddles and quacks. Ducks waddle and quack. Therefore, this must be a duck." This is inductive: It progresses from particulars ("waddles" and "quacks") to a general conclusion ("a duck"). By contrast, deduction progresses from the general to the specific: "If it's a duck, it will waddle and quack."

An example of the progress toward deductive reasoning comes from how children, adolescents, and adults change in their understanding of the causes of racism. Even before adolescence, almost every American is aware that racism exists—and almost everyone opposes it. However, children tend to think the core problem is that some people are prejudiced. Using inductive reasoning, they think that the remedy is to argue against racism when they hear other people express it. By contrast, older adolescents think, deductively, that racism is a society-wide problem that requires policy solutions.

This example arises from a study of adolescent opinions regarding policies to remedy racial discrimination (Hughes & Bigler, 2011). Not surprisingly, most students of all ages in an interracial U.S. high school recognized disparities between African and European Americans and believed that racism was a major cause.

**Especially for Natural Scientists** Some ideas that were once universally accepted, such as the belief that the sun moved around Earth, have been disproven. Is it a failure of inductive or deductive reasoning that leads to false conclusions? (see response, p. 437)

However, development of more advanced cognition made a difference. Among those who recognized marked inequalities, older adolescents (ages 16 to 17) more often supported systemic solutions (e.g., affirmative action and desegregation) than did younger adolescents (ages 14 to 15).

Similarly, in another study, when adolescents were asked how a person might overcome poverty, younger adolescents were more likely to emphasize personal hard work (an egocentric notion), while older adolescents used more complex analysis, noting systemic problems (formal operational thought), such as in national laws (Arsenio & Willems, 2017).

As you know, many researchers criticize Piaget's description of the stages of cognition. Nonetheless, something shifts in cognition after puberty. Piaget recognized that many older adolescents think more logically and hypothetically than most children do.

## Two Modes of Thinking

As you see, Piagetians emphasized the sequence of thought, not only from egocentric to formal but throughout all four stages. Another group of scholars disagrees. They suggest that thinking does not develop in sequence but in parallel, with two processes that are not tightly coordinated within the brain (Baker et al., 2015).

**dual processing** The notion that two networks exist within the human brain, one for emotional processing of stimuli and one for analytical reasoning.

To be specific, advanced logic in adolescence is counterbalanced by the increasing power of intuition. Thus, thinking occurs in two ways, called **dual processing.** The terms and descriptions of these two processes vary, including intuitive/analytic, implicit/explicit, creative/factual, contextualized/decontextualized, unconscious/conscious, gist/quantitative, emotional/intellectual, experiential/rational, hot/cold, systems 1 and 2. Although they interact and can overlap, each mode is independent (Kuhn, 2013) (see Visualizing Development, p. 436).

The thinking described by the first half of each pair is easier and quicker, preferred in everyday life. Sometimes, however, circumstances necessitate the second mode, when deeper thought is demanded. The discrepancy between the maturation of the limbic system and the prefrontal cortex reflects this duality. [**Developmental Link:** Timing differences in brain maturation are discussed in Chapter 14.]

To some extent, both modes of thinking reflect inborn temperament. Most children who are impulsive by nature learn to regulate their reactions in childhood, but a dual-processing perspective suggests that this regulation may break down during adolescence (Henderson et al., 2015).

## Intuitive and Analytic Processing

In describing adolescent cognition, we use the terms *intuitive* and *analytic*, defined as follows:

- **Intuitive thought** begins with a belief, assumption, or general rule (called a *heuristic*) rather than logic. Intuition is quick and powerful; it feels "right."
- **Analytic thought** is the formal, logical, hypothetical-deductive thinking described by Piaget. It involves rational analysis of many factors whose interactions must be calculated, as in the scale-balancing problem.

When the two modes of thinking conflict, people of all ages sometimes use one and sometimes the other: We are all "predictably irrational" at times (Ariely, 2010), but adolescent brains are increasingly myelinated, which makes thought occur with lightning speed. That may make them "fast and furious" intuitive thinkers, unlike their teachers and parents, who prefer slower, analytic thinking. The result: "people who interact with adolescents often are frustrated by the mercurial quality of their decisions" (Hartley & Somerville, 2015, p. 112).

To test yourself on intuitive and analytic thinking, answer the following:

1. A bat and a ball cost $1.10 in total. The bat costs $1 more than the ball. How much does the ball cost?
2. If it takes 5 minutes for 5 machines to make 5 widgets, how long would it take 100 machines to make 100 widgets?
3. In a lake, there is a patch of lily pads. Every day the patch doubles in size. If it takes 48 days for the patch to cover the entire lake, how long would it take for the patch to cover half the lake?

*[from Gervais & Norenzayan, 2012, p. 494]*

Answers are on page 438. As you see, the quick, intuitive responses may be wrong.

Paul Klaczynski conducted dozens of studies comparing the thinking of children, young adolescents, and older adolescents (usually 9-, 12-, and 15-year-olds) (Holland & Klaczynski, 2009; Klaczynski, 2001, 2011; Klaczynski et al., 2009). Variation in thinking was evident at every age.

Klaczynski reports that almost every adolescent is analytical and logical on some problems but not on others, with some passing the same questions that others fail. As they grow older, adolescents sometimes gain in logic and sometimes regress, with the social context and training in statistics becoming major influences on cognition (Klaczynski & Felmban, 2014).

That finding has been confirmed by dozens of other studies (Kail, 2013). Being smarter as measured by an intelligence test does not advance cognition as much as having more experience, in school and in life, and studying statistics and linguistics that emphasize logic. However, even though the adolescent mind is capable of logic, sometimes "social variables are better predictors . . . than cognitive abilities" (Klaczynski & Felmban, 2014, pp. 103–104).

**intuitive thought** Thought that arises from an emotion or a hunch, beyond rational explanation, and is influenced by past experiences and cultural assumptions.

**analytic thought** Thought that results from analysis, such as a systematic ranking of pros and cons, risks and consequences, possibilities and facts. Analytic thought depends on logic and rationality.

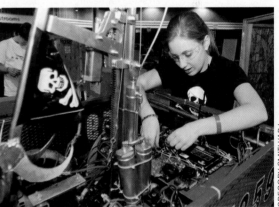

GREGORY SMITH/AP Images

**Impressive Connections** This robot is about to compete in the Robotics Competition in Atlanta, Georgia, but much more impressive are the brains of the Oregon high school team (including Melissa, shown here) who designed the robot.

**Observation Quiz** Melissa seems to be working by herself, but what sign do you see that suggests she is part of a team who built this robot? (see answer, p. 437) ↑

# Thinking in Adolescence

We are able to think both intuitively and analytically, but adolescents tend to rely more on intuitive thinking than do adults.

## INDUCTIVE vs. DEDUCTIVE REASONING

**INDUCTIVE:** Conclusion reached after many of the following. Note that the problem is that the adolescent's nimble mind can rationalize many specifics. Only when the evidence is overwhelming is the conclusion reached.

**DEDUCTIVE:** The principle is the starting point, not the end point.

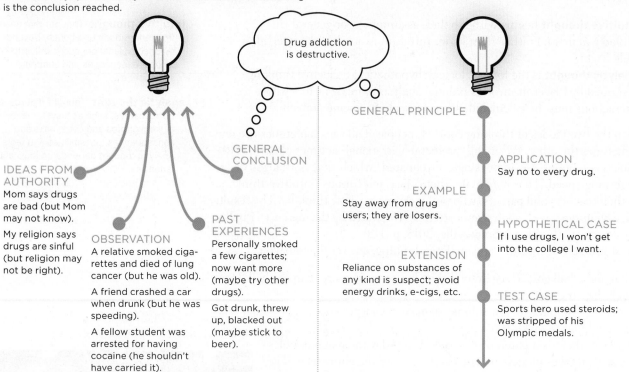

Drug addiction is destructive.

GENERAL CONCLUSION

GENERAL PRINCIPLE

**IDEAS FROM AUTHORITY**
Mom says drugs are bad (but Mom may not know).

My religion says drugs are sinful (but religion may not be right).

**OBSERVATION**
A relative smoked cigarettes and died of lung cancer (but he was old).

A friend crashed a car when drunk (but he was speeding).

A fellow student was arrested for having cocaine (he shouldn't have carried it).

**PAST EXPERIENCES**
Personally smoked a few cigarettes; now want more (maybe try other drugs).

Got drunk, threw up, blacked out (maybe stick to beer).

**APPLICATION**
Say no to every drug.

**HYPOTHETICAL CASE**
If I use drugs, I won't get into the college I want.

**EXAMPLE**
Stay away from drug users; they are losers.

**EXTENSION**
Reliance on substances of any kind is suspect; avoid energy drinks, e-cigs, etc.

**TEST CASE**
Sports hero used steroids; was stripped of his Olympic medals.

## CHANGES IN AGE

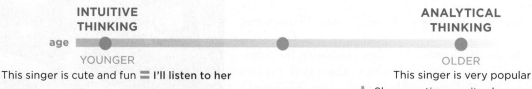

**INTUITIVE THINKING**

**ANALYTICAL THINKING**

age

YOUNGER

OLDER

This singer is cute and fun **= I'll listen to her**

This singer is very popular
**+** She sometimes writes her own songs
**+** She makes creative videos
**+** I agree with her morals **= I'll listen to her music**

JUPITERIMAGES/THINKSTOCK/GETTY IMAGES

As people age, their thinking tends to move from intuitive processing to more analytic processing. Virtually all cognitive psychologists note these two alternative processes and describe a developmental progression toward more dispassionate logic with maturity. However, the terms used and the boundaries between the two vary. They are roughly analogous to Kahneman's System 1 (which "operates automatically and quickly") and System 2 (which "are often associated with the subjective experience of agency, choice, and concentration") (Kahneman, 2011, pp. 20–21), as well as to the traditional distinction between inductive and deductive reasoning, and to Piaget's concrete operational versus formal operational thought. Although experts vary in their descriptions, and individuals vary in when and how they use these two processes, overall adolescents tend to favor intuitive rather than analytic thinking.

## Preferring Emotions

Why not use formal operational thinking? Klaczynski's young adolescents had all learned the scientific method in school, so they knew that scientists use empirical evidence and deductive reasoning. But they did not always think like scientists. Why not?

Dozens of experiments and extensive theorizing have found some answers (Albert & Steinberg, 2011). Essentially, logic is more difficult than intuition, and it requires questioning ideas that are comforting and familiar. Once people of any age reach an emotional conclusion (sometimes called a "gut feeling"), they resist changing their minds. Prejudice is not seen as prejudice; people develop reasons to support their feelings.

As people gain experience in making decisions and thinking things through, they may become better at knowing when analysis is needed (Milkman et al., 2009). For example, in contrast to younger students, when judging whether a rule is legitimate, older adolescents are more suspicious of authority and more likely to consider mitigating circumstances (Klaczynski, 2011). That may be wise—sometimes.

## Rewards and Reasons

More than 7,000 adolescents, beginning at age 12 and ending at age 24, were repeatedly queried about their ideas, activities, and plans. The results were "consistent with neurobiological research indicating that cortical regions involved in impulse control and planning continue to mature through early adulthood [and that] subcortical regions that respond to emotional novelty and reward are more responsive in middle adolescence than in either children or adults" (Harden & Tucker-Drob, 2011, p. 743).

**Response for Natural Scientists** (from p. 434): Probably both. Our false assumptions are not logically tested because we do not realize that they might need testing.

**Answer to Observation Quiz** (from p. 435): The flag on the robot matches her T-shirt. Often teenagers wear matching shirts to signify their joint identity.

**THINK CRITICALLY:** When might an emotional response to a problem be better than an analytic one?

**A CASE TO STUDY**

## Biting the Policeman

Both suspicion of authority and awareness of context advance reasoning, but both also complicate simple issues and lead to impulsive, destructive actions. Indeed, suspicion of authority may propel adolescents to respond illogically.

One day, a student of mine, herself only 18, was with her younger cousin. A police officer stopped them and asked why the cousin was not in school. He patted down the boy and asked for identification. That cousin was visiting from another state, and he did not have an ID.

My student cited a U.S. Supreme Court case that proved the officer did not have authority to "stop and frisk." When the officer grabbed her cousin, she bit his hand—and was arrested. After she spent weeks in jail, she finally was brought before the judge. Perhaps the time in jail caused her more analytic mind to activate. She had written an apology to the officer, which she read out loud. He did not press charges.

I appeared in court on her behalf; the judge released her to me. She was shivering; the first thing I did was put a warm coat on her. I found it ironic that the judge listened to me but that

the justice system did not understand the developmental cognition of my student.

This was dual-processing. In her education, my student had gained a formal understanding of the laws regarding police authority. However, there was a disconnect between her analysis and her emotions. She was still impulsive, intuitively defending her cousin in a way that an adult would not.

It is easy to conclude that more mature thought processes are wiser. The judge thought that I understood things that my student did not. Certainly she should not have bitten the officer. But also true is that the entire context shows that the authorities did not understand the adolescent mind. However unwise at the moment, my student's childhood experiences—learning that the authorities are suspect and family members must be protected—primed her to act as she did.

She is not alone in that. Most readers of the book can probably think of something they did in adolescence that arose from emotions and that, with the wisdom of time and maturity, they wish they had not done.

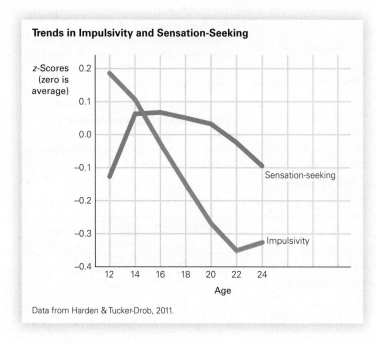

**Trends in Impulsivity and Sensation-Seeking**

Data from Harden & Tucker-Drob, 2011.

**FIGURE 15.2**

**Look Before You Leap** As you can see, adolescents become less impulsive as they mature, but they still enjoy the thrill of a new sensation.

| Answers (from p. 435) | Intuitive | Analytic |
|---|---|---|
| 1. | 10 cents | 5 cents |
| 2. | 100 minutes | 5 minutes |
| 3. | 24 days | 47 days |

Specifically, this longitudinal survey traced sensation-seeking (e.g., "I enjoy new and exciting experiences") from early adolescence to the mid-20s. Increases were notable from ages 12 to 14 (see Figure 15.2). Sensation-seeking leads to intuitive thinking, direct from the gut to the brain. The researchers also studied impulsivity, as indicated by agreement with statements such as "I often get in a jam because I do things without thinking." Impulsive action declined gradually as analytic thinking increased.

On average, sensation-seeking increased rapidly at puberty, and both sensation-seeking and impulsivity slowly declined with maturation. However, trajectories varied individually: Sensation-seeking did not necessarily correlate with impulsivity. Thus, biology (the HPA axis) is not necessarily linked to experience (the prefrontal cortex) (Harden & Tucker-Drob, 2011). Both affect behavior: Risky sex correlates with sensation-seeking and with impulsivity (Charnigo et al., 2013), but each has an independent impact.

This later finding is crucial as developmentalists try to understand adolescent cognition. It is true that brain regions associated with the joy of various sensations, specifically the *nucleus accumbens* (part of the *ventral striatum*), are more activated during adolescence than earlier or later (Braams et al., 2014). But, a strong response does not necessarily produce foolish risks (Chick, 2015). Adolescents think quickly and impulsively, but experience and education can elicit analytic thought.

Because of their thinking processes, adolescents are impulsive and do foolish things, but we need to avoid the stereotype. Logic, caution, and analytic thought are possible as well.

## Better Thinking

A developmental approach suggests that the adolescent way of thinking may have merit. For example, why do teenagers risk addiction by trying drugs, or risk HIV/AIDS by not using a condom? Of course, drug use is foolish and condom use is wise. But perhaps we should not blame teenage irrationality and impulsiveness for those actions.

Perhaps adolescents are rational, but their priorities are not the same as those of their parents. Parents want healthy, long-lived children, so they blame faulty reasoning when adolescents risk their lives. Judges want law-abiding citizens. Adolescents, however, value social warmth and friendship, and their hormones and brains are more attuned to those values than to long-term consequences (Crone & Dahl, 2012). It may not be that they do not know better; it may be that they evaluate differently (Hartley & Somerville, 2015).

A 15-year-old who is offered a cigarette, for example, might rationally choose peer acceptance and the possibility of romance over the distant risk of cancer. Think of a teenager who wants to be "cool" or "bad," and then decide whether he or she might say, "No, thank you, I promised my mother not to smoke."

Furthermore, weighing alternatives and thinking of future possibilities can be paralyzing. The systematic, analytic thought that Piaget described is slow and costly, not fast and frugal, wasting precious time when a young person wants to act. Some risks are taken impulsively, and that is not always bad.

Indeed, some experts suggest that the adolescent impulse to take risks, respond to peers, and explore new ideas is adaptive in some contexts (Ernst, 2016). It may

# Impulses, Rewards, and Reflection

The brain maturation process described in Chapter 14 is directly related to the dual processes just explained. Because the limbic system is activated by puberty while the prefrontal cortex is "developmentally constrained," maturing more gradually, adolescents are swayed by their intuition instead of by analysis (Hartley & Somerville, 2015, p. 109).

One specific is that the connection between the ventral striatum and the prefrontal cortex changes during puberty, and that increases risk-taking. Hormones, especially testosterone (rapidly increasing in boys but also increasing in girls), fuel new adolescent emotional impulses (Peper & Dahl, 2013). According to one review, many studies confirm that adolescents show "heightened activity in the striatum, both when anticipating rewards and when receiving rewards" (Crone et al., 2016, p. 360).

In choosing between a small but guaranteed reward and a large, possible reward, adolescent brains show more activity for the larger reward than the brains of children or adults. This means that when teenagers weigh the possible results of a particular risky action, their brains make them more inclined to imagine success than to fear failure. Whether this makes them brave and bold, or foolish and careless, is a matter of judgment, but the judge should know that neurological circuits tip the balance toward action.

Another crucial aspect of adolescent brains is that social rejection by peers is deeply felt, with activation throughout the limbic system as well as other subcortical areas. Social impulses are crucial for humans lifelong, but the brain is sensitive to particular kinds at particular ages (Nelson et al., 2016). For example, mother rejection is especially hurtful in infancy, as is a breakup with a romantic partner in adulthood. Adolescents are particularly sensitive to peer rejection.

Neurological sensitivity may further explain why teens readily follow impulses that promise social approval from friends. In experiments in which adults and adolescents, alone or with peers, play video games in which taking risks might lead to crashes or gaining points, adolescents are much more likely than adults are to risk crashing, especially when they are with peers.

There are notable differences in brain activity (specifically in the ventral striatum) between adolescents and adults. When they are with other adults, the adults' brains give more signals of caution (inhibition)—opposite to adolescents' brains when they are with peers (Albert et al., 2013) (see Figure 15.3).

This peer influence is apparent in both sexes but is stronger in boys—particularly when they are with other boys (de Boer et al., 2016). This explains why boys die accidental deaths during adolescence twice as often as girls. Teenage drivers like to fill (or overfill) their cars with teen passengers who will admire them for speeding, for passing trucks, for beating trains at railroad crossings, and so on. Of course, that is not true for every young driver, but passengers aged 15 to 17 are more likely to be injured

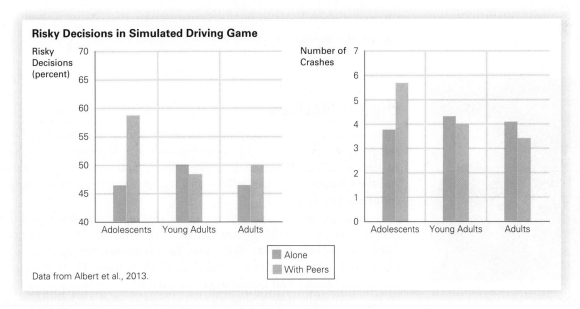

**FIGURE 15.3**

**Losing Is Winning** In this game, risk-taking led to more crashes and fewer points. As you see, adolescents were strongly influenced by the presence of peers, so much so that they lost points they would have kept if they had played alone. In fact, sometimes they laughed when they crashed instead of bemoaning their loss. Note the contrast with emerging adults, who were more likely to take risks when alone.

in a motor-vehicle crash than passengers of other ages (Bergen et al., 2014), and fatal accidents are more likely to occur if the driver is a teenager.

The accident rate in adolescence is aided by a third brain change in adolescence. Compared to children, there is a substantial increase in myelination between the emotional and action parts of the brain. This increase in white matter means rapid responses. As a result, adolescents act before slower-thinking adults can stop them (Hartley & Somerville, 2015).

Don't blame teen crashes on inexperience; blame it on the brain. Some states now prohibit teen drivers from transporting other teenagers, reducing deaths and banning one source of adolescent excitement. Teens advocate some laws, such as those that protect the environment; they do not advocate this one. Now that you understand the teen brain, perhaps you will.

be that "the fundamental task of adolescence—to achieve adult levels of social competence—requires a great deal of learning about the social complexities of human social interactions" (Peper & Dahl, 2013, p. 135).

Societies need some people who question assumptions, and adolescents impulsively question everything, sometimes raising important issues. As social and ecological circumstances change, traditions need reexamination, lest old customs ossify and societies die.

### WHAT HAVE YOU LEARNED?

1. How does adolescent egocentrism differ from early-childhood egocentrism?
2. What perceptions arise from belief in the imaginary audience?
3. Why are the personal fable and the invincibility fable called "fables"?
4. What are the advantages of using inductive rather than deductive reasoning?
5. When might intuition and analysis lead to contrasting conclusions?
6. How might intuitive thinking increase risk-taking?
7. When is intuitive thinking better than analytic thinking?

**Not All Thumbs** After two days of competition among 22 qualified contestants, with tests of texting speed, clarity, and knowledge, 15-year-old Kate Moore of Des Moines, Iowa, was declared champion. She won a trophy and $50,000. She has texted hundreds of friends for years.

ERIC THAYER/Reuters/Newscom

## Digital Natives

Adults over age 50 grew up without the Internet, instant messaging, Twitter, blogs, cell phones, smartphones, MP3 players, tablets, 3-D printers, or digital cameras. At first, the Internet was only for the military and then primarily for businesses and the educated elite. Until 2006, only students at a few highly selective colleges could join Facebook.

In contrast, today's teenagers are called *digital natives*, although if that implies that they know everything about digital communication, it is a misnomer (boyd, 2014). No doubt, however, adolescents have been networking, texting, and clicking for definitions, directions, and data all their lives. Their phones are always within reach; some text hundreds of times a day.

This isn't really new. Connection to peers has always been important to teenagers. In earlier generations, adults predicted that the automobile, or the shopping mall, or rock and roll would lead their children astray. Now Internet connection is omnipresent in developed nations, and it is widespread in developing nations as well. Teens who formerly felt isolated, such as those with Down syndrome, or who are LGBTQ, or deaf, or simply at odds with their neighbors, now can find peers.

As costs tumble, adolescents of every ethnic and economic group have smartphones, used primarily to connect with friends (Madden et al., 2013). African American and Latino American teenagers are more likely than European American teens to say they are online "almost constantly" (34 percent, 32 percent, 19 percent) (Lenhart, 2015, p. 2). Fewer low-SES families have desktops and high-speed connections at home, however, which limits the ability of some adolescents to access and analyze information.

## Technology and Cognition

In general, educators accept—even welcome—students' facility with technology. In most high schools, teachers use laptops, smartphones, digital projectors, Smart Boards, and so on as tools for learning. In some districts, students are required to take at least one class completely online. There are "virtual" schools in which students earn all of their credits via the Internet, never entering a school building, and school districts that give everyone a tablet instead of a textbook.

Some computer programs and games have been designed for high school classes. For example, 10 teachers were taught how to use a game (Mission Biotech) to teach genetics and molecular biology. Their students—even in advanced classes but especially in general education—scored higher on tests of the standard biology curriculum than students who did not use the game (Sadler et al., 2013). It seems that, when carefully used, computer games enhance learning.

Most secondary students check facts, read explanations, view videos, and thus grasp concepts that they would not have understood without technology. Almost every high school student in the United States uses the Internet for research, finding it quicker and more extensive than books on library shelves. And for some adolescents, the Internet is their only source of information about health and sex.

For decades, developmentalists have recognized that instruction, practice, discussion, and experience within the zone of proximal development advance adolescent thought. Technology may simply speed up the process. However, it may also subvert some kinds of learning. It encourages rapid shifts of attention, multitasking without reflection, and visual learning instead of invisible analysis (Greenfield, 2009).

A major concern is that adolescents need to activate their analytic minds to evaluate what they see on the screen. Adults make the same mistake, believing "fake news" because they saw it on the Internet (Mihailidis & Viotty, 2017). Not only do adolescents fail to evaluate what they read, they do not evaluate what they send. Messages impulsively sent to friends can endure for later viewing by thousands of unintended recipients, such as future employers and college admissions officers (boyd, 2014).

Watch **Video: The Impact of Media on Adolescent Development** to learn more about how technology affects cognition during adolescence.

## Sexual Abuse?

Parents worry about sexual abuse via the Internet. Research is reassuring: Although predators lurk online, most teens never encounter them. Sexual abuse is a serious problem, but if sexual abuse is defined as a perverted older stranger taking technological advantage of an innocent teen, it is "extremely rare" (Mitchell et al., 2013, p. 1226).

### Warnings

Contemporary teenagers have been warned by teachers and parents about the possibility of strangers trying to seduce them online, and forewarned seems forearmed: The percent of adolescents who have been asked online to talk about sex,

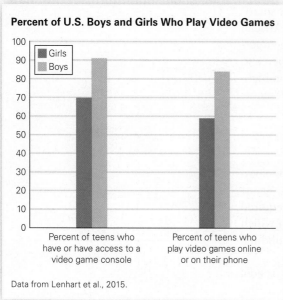

**Percent of U.S. Boys and Girls Who Play Video Games**

Legend: Girls, Boys

- Percent of teens who have or have access to a video game console
- Percent of teens who play video games online or on their phone

Data from Lenhart et al., 2015.

**FIGURE 15.4**

**Access or Addiction?** As we know from research on substance use disorder, use is not necessarily addiction. As you see, teenagers have no trouble accessing video games, and most decide to play. When does play become a compulsion, no longer a choice?

**Something Worth Sharing** But what is it? Is it the same as boys everywhere, or is it something specific to their culture? The four are in England: We do not know if they see a football (soccer) score, a prime minister's proclamation, or a sexy female.

or send a naked photo, is less than 1 percent. Those 1 percent were almost always solicited by another young person whom the teenager knew—a Facebook friend, for instance (Mitchell et al., 2013). Teenagers are actually more suspicious of strangers than they were before the Internet, and perhaps not suspicious enough of friends, coaches, clergy, and relatives.

The possibility of sexual predators is a major reason that more than half of all parents restrict their 13- to 17-year-olds' technology use (see Figure 15.4). More than 90 percent of parents discuss online behavior and appropriate Web sites with their teenagers, and "nearly half (48 percent) of parents know the password to their teen's email account, while 43 percent know the password to their teen's cell phone and 35 percent know the password to at least one of their teen's social media accounts" (Anderson, 2016, p. 3).

A study of media coverage of damaging sexual attacks on the Internet found that thoughtful discussion of sexism and homophobia, and of adolescent vulnerability to unwanted sexual comments, was missing. Instead, the focus too often was on "moral outrage" against an individual—as if the social context was free of blame (Milosevic, 2015).

## Harassment

While direct soliciting, either from a stranger or a friend, is rare, sexual harassment in social networking is not. Surveys in Belgium, Spain, and elsewhere find that between 4 and 84 percent of adolescents have experienced it in the past six months. The reasons for the wide range of estimates is that the definition is unclear: Some ask if the teenager has encountered any unwanted comments about appearance, body, or sexuality (Van Royen et al., 2016; Vega-Gea et al., 2016). Most have. Younger adolescents are bothered by comments that older teens brush off, LGBTQ teens are often targeted, and teens themselves do not know what might trouble someone else (Van Royen et al., 2015).

Texting—dozens of times a day—is common, and those in romantic relationships flirt online. Although teenagers enjoy staying in touch with their dating partners via the Internet—and most do it several times a day—when the relationship ends, it may turn ugly. After a breakup, 15 percent report being threatened online (Lenhart et al., 2015). (Sexual harassment may be part of a larger problem, cyberbullying, which is discussed soon.)

## Addiction

For some adolescents, online chats, message boards, gaming, and Internet gambling undercut active play, schoolwork, and friendship—a concern in every wired nation (Tang et al., 2014). Almost all (92 percent) 13- to 17-year-olds in the United States go online every day, and 24 percent say they are online "almost constantly" (Lenhart, 2015, p. 16).

When does this become addictive? Many adolescents report that playing video games takes time away from household chores and homework. Worse, one-fourth used video games as an escape, and one-fifth had "done poorly on a school assignment or test" because of time spent on video games. The heaviest users got lower school grades and had more physical fights than did the average users (Gentile, 2011).

Using criteria for addiction developed by psychiatrists for other addictions (gambling, drugs, and so on), an estimated 3 percent of U.S. adolescents suffer from Internet addiction, almost always with other disorders as well (Jorgenson et al., 2016)

| TABLE 15.1 | |
|---|---|
| **Signs of Substance Use Disorder** | |
| **In General** | **How It Might Apply to Internet Addiction*** |
| 1. Impairs desired activity and accomplishment, notable in failed personal goals and broken promises to oneself. | 1. Person denies, or lies about, how much time is spent online, which interferes with study, homework completion, household chores, or job-related concentration. |
| 2. Normal cognitive processes—memory, motivation, logic—are impaired. | 2. Person is less able to think deeply and analytically, or to remember things not online, such as personal phone numbers or appointment times. |
| 3. Social interactions disrupted, either disconnections when in a social group or isolation from other people. | 3. Person spends less time with family or in face-to-face communication with friends. Person ignores social interactions to check texts. |
| 4. Basic body maintenance and health disturbed, such as loss of sleep, changed appetite, hygiene. | 4. Person does not remember or care to do usual health maintaining activities. Internet interferes with sleep, healthy eating, and so on. |
| 5. Withdrawal symptoms: Person is agitated, physically or mentally, when unable to attain substance. | 5. Person is angry or depressed when Internet is not available, as when cell phones are banned from class, or parents restrict use, or connections are broken. |
| 6. Increasing dependence: Need for substance or activity increases over time, as brain patterns change. | 6. Person increases time spent; wants more devices (laptop, watch, tablet). |

*This list is speculative. DSM-5 finds insufficient evidence of Internet addiction, and does not use the word "addiction" because of "uncertain definition and its potentially negative connotation" (American Psychiatric Association, 2013, p. 485).

(see Table 15.1). Those rates are low according to research in other nations, with rates of 15 percent in Turkey, 12 percent in India, and 22 percent in Hong Kong (Şaşmaz et al., 2014; Yadav et al., 2013; Shek & Yu, 2016).

Reviewing research from many nations, one team of researchers reports addiction rates from 0 to 26 percent (Y.-H. Lee et al., 2015). The variation was caused more by differing definitions and methods of research than by differences among students in any particular place. But that is exactly the problem.

Remember that correlation is not causation. Might low school achievement, depression, aggression, and so on lead to video game playing and social media obsession rather than vice versa? Some scholars think that adults pathologize normal teen behavior, particularly in China, where rehabilitation centers are strict—some would say abusive—in keeping teenagers from Internet use (Bax, 2014).

In the United States, some parents may inadvertently increase problems. They are oblivious to actual use, because most adolescents have screens in their bedrooms, and their parents assume they are safe when at home. Other parents restrict contact with peers, online or in person, at home or in a public place. To socialize, their children may sneak out of the home at night, or log in privately and secretly (boyd, 2014).

Parents, educators, and developmentalists have not yet settled on guidelines about addiction. The psychiatrists who wrote the DSM-5, after careful consideration of the evidence, did not include Internet use as an addiction. Instead they wrote that further study is needed.

## Cyber Danger

Now we consider an Internet use that everyone agrees is harmful, although again the solution is not obvious. That is **cyberbullying,** when electronic devices are used to harass someone, with rumors, lies, embarrassing truths, or threats. Cyberbullies are usually already bullies, victims, or both: Bully-victims are especially

**cyberbullying** Bullying that occurs when one person spreads insults or rumors about another by means of social media posts, e-mails, text messages, or cell phone videos.

Spencer Grant/Alamy

**Consequences Unknown** Few adolescents think about the consequences of their impulsive rage, responses, or retorts on social media or smartphones. This educator at a community center tries to explain that victims can be devastated—rarely suicidal, but often depressed.

likely to engage in, and suffer from, cyberbullying. [**Developmental Link:** Bullying is discussed in Chapter 13.]

Abuse can be devastating. Ten years out of high school, adolescent bullies and victims—online or offline, sexual or otherwise—are less likely to have graduated from high school or college and less likely to have good jobs or any job at all (Sigurdson et al., 2014).

## Worst in Adolescence

Technology does not create bullies, but it allows another means to act and a larger audience, expanding the hurt (Giumetti & Kowalski, 2015). Moreover, although the standard definition of bullying is *repeated*, cyberbullying can be devastating with only one incident (Underwood & Ehrenreich, 2017).

Texted and posted rumors and insults can instantly reach thousands, day and night, with shame magnified by the imaginary audience. Photos and videos of someone drunk, naked, or crying are sometimes sent to dozens of others, who may send the material further or post it on public sites. Since younger adolescents act quickly without reflection, cyberbullying is particularly prevalent and thoughtlessly cruel between ages 11 and 14.

Cyberbullying is most damaging when the self-concept is fragile, when sexual impulses are new, and when impulsive thoughts precede analytic ones—all of which characterize many young adolescents. The most serious consequence is deep depression, added to the typical rise in depression at puberty. In extreme cases, cyberbullying may trigger suicide (Bonanno & Hymel, 2013; Geoffroy et al., 2016).

The school climate can be a powerful antidote for cyberbullying (Guo, 2016). When students consider school a good place to be—with supportive teachers, friendly students, opportunities for growth (clubs, sports, theater, music), and the like—those with high self-esteem are less likely to engage in cyberbullying. They not only disapprove of it, they stop it by blocking bullies and deleting messages. However, when the school climate is negative, those with high self-esteem may become bullies (Gendron et al., 2011).

Most adults are ignorant about cyberbullying—sometimes overreacting, sometimes oblivious, sometimes feeling powerless. However, adults can reduce cyberbullying, in part by helping adolescents see the harm. Adolescents themselves can protect each other and stop the bullies (Underwood & Ehrenreich, 2017).

## Sexting

The vulnerability of adolescence was tragically evident in the suicide of a California 15-year-old, Audrie Pott (Sulek, 2013). At a weekend sleepover, Audrie and her friends found alcohol. She got so drunk that she blacked out, or passed out. The next Monday, three boys in her school bragged that they had had sex with her, showing pictures on their cell phones to classmates. The next weekend, Audrie hanged herself. Only then did her parents and teachers learn what had happened.

**sexting** Sending sexual content, particularly photos or videos, via cell phones or social media.

One aspect of this tragedy will not surprise adolescents: **sexting,** as sending sexual photographs is called. As many as 30 percent of adolescents report having received sexting photos, with marked variation by school, gender, and ethnicity and often in attitude: Many teens send their own sexy "selfies" and are happy to receive them (Temple et al., 2014). Of those in romantic relationships, 63 percent have sent flirtatious messages online, and 23 percent have sent sexual pictures or videos (Lenhart et al., 2015). As with Internet addiction, researchers disagree regarding the best way to measure sexting and about who is harmed and by how much.

Two dangers are often not anticipated by teenagers who sext: (1) Pictures may be forwarded without the person's knowledge, and (2) senders of erotic self-images risk serious depression if the recipient's reaction is not what they wished (Temple et al., 2014). Remember body image (discussed in Chapter 14). Many teens have distorted self-concepts and unrealistic fantasies—no wonder sexting is fraught with trouble.

### Other Hazards

Internet connections allow troubled adolescents to connect with others who share their prejudices and self-destructive obsessions, such as anorexia, gun use, or cutting. The people they connect with are those who confirm and inform their twisted cognition. This is another reason that parents and teachers need to continue their close relationships with their adolescents. Note the absence of adults at Audrie's alcohol-fueled sleepover, rape, cyberbullying, and suicide.

One careful observer claims that, instead of being *native* users of technology, many teenagers are *naive* users—believing they have privacy settings that they do not have, trusting sites that are markedly biased, believing news that is fake, misunderstanding how to search for and verify information (boyd, 2014). Educators can help with all of this—but only if they themselves understand technology and teens.

Teens are intuitive, impulsive, and egocentric, often unaware of the impact of what they send, overestimating the validity of what they read, choosing immediate attraction over eventual gain. Adults should know better.

> **THINK CRITICALLY:** The older people are, the more likely they are to be critical of social media. Is that wisdom or ignorance? Why?

---

### WHAT HAVE YOU LEARNED?

1. What benefits come from adolescents' use of technology?
2. Why is adult fear of online adult predators exaggerated?
3. How do video games affect student learning?
4. Who is most apt and least apt to be involved in cyberbullying?
5. Why might sexting be a problem?
6. How might the term "digital native" be misleading?

---

## Secondary Education

What does our knowledge of adolescent thought imply about school? Educators, developmentalists, political leaders, and parents wonder exactly which curricula and school structures are best for 11- to 18-year-olds. There are dozens of options: academic or practical skills, single-sex or co-ed, competitive or cooperative, large or small, public or private, and more.

To complicate matters, adolescents are far from a homogeneous group. As a result,

> some youth thrive at school—enjoying and benefiting from most of their experiences there; others muddle along and cope as best they can with the stress and demands of the moment; and still others find school an alienating and unpleasant place to be.
>
> *[Eccles & Roeser, 2011, p. 225]*

Given all of these variations, no school structure or pedagogy is best for everyone. Various scientists, nations, schools, and teachers try many strategies, some based on opposite but logical hypotheses. To begin to analyze this complexity, we present definitions, facts, issues, and possibilities.

# Definitions and Facts

Each year of school advances human potential, a fact recognized by leaders and scholars in every nation and discipline. As you have read, adolescents are capable of deep and wide-ranging thought, no longer limited by concrete experience, yet they are often egocentric and impulsive. Quality matters: A year can propel thinking forward or can have little impact (Hanushek & Woessmann, 2010).

**Secondary education**—traditionally grades 7 through 12—denotes the school years after elementary or grade school (known as *primary education*) and before college or university (known as *tertiary education*). Adults are healthier and wealthier if they complete primary education, learning to read and write, and then continue on through secondary and tertiary education. This is true within nations and between them.

Even cigarette smoking by European American adults—seemingly unrelated to education—is almost three times as common among those with no high school diploma than it is among those with bachelor's degrees (40 percent versus 14 percent, respectively) (National Center for Health Statistics, 2016). This is typical: Data on almost every condition, from every nation and ethnic group, confirm that high school and college graduation correlates with better health, wealth, and family life. Some reasons are indirectly related to education (e.g., income and place of residence), but even when poverty and toxic neighborhoods are equalized, education confers benefits.

Partly because political leaders recognize that educated adults advance national wealth and health, every nation is increasing the number of students in secondary schools. Education is compulsory until at least age 12 almost everywhere, and new high schools and colleges open daily in developing nations. The two most populous countries, China and India, are characterized by massive growth in education.

In many nations, two levels of secondary education are provided. Traditionally, secondary education was divided into junior high (usually grades 7 and 8) and senior high (usually grades 9 through 12). As the average age of puberty declined, **middle schools** were created for grades 5 or 6 through 8. This makes sense, as you have learned: The pubescent 12-year-old is, cognitively as well as in many other ways, a quite different human being from the 17-year-old.

**secondary education** Literally, the period after primary education (elementary or grade school) and before tertiary education (college). It usually occurs from about ages 12 to 18, although there is some variation by school and by nation.

**middle school** A school for children in the grades between elementary school and high school. Middle school usually begins with grade 6 and ends with grade 8.

**Now Learn This** Educators and parents disagree among themselves about how and what middle school children need to learn. Accordingly, some parents send their children to a school where biology is taught via dissecting a squid (*left*), others where obedience is taught via white shirts and lining up (*right*).

**Observation Quiz** Although the philosophy and strategy of these two schools are quite different, both share one aspect of the hidden curriculum, what is it? (see answer, p. 448) ↑

## Middle School

Adjusting to middle school is bound to be stressful, as teachers, classmates, and expectations are quite different from primary school. Developmentalists agree that "teaching is likely to be particularly complex for middle school teachers because it happens amidst a critical period of cognitive, socioemotional, and biological development of students who confront heightened social pressures from peers and gradual decline of parental oversight" (Ladd & Sorensen, 2017).

Regarding learning, "researchers and theorists commonly view early adolescence as an especially sensitive developmental period" (McGill et al., 2012, p. 1003). Yet many developmentalists find middle schools to be "developmentally regressive" (Eccles & Roeser, 2010, p. 13), which means learning goes backward.

### Increasing Behavioral Problems

For many middle school students, academic achievement slows down and behavioral problems increase. Puberty itself is part of the problem. At least for other animals studied, especially when they are under stress, learning is reduced at puberty (McCormick et al., 2010).

For people, the biological and psychological stresses of puberty are not the only reason learning suffers in early adolescence. Cognition matters, too: How much new middle school students like their school affects how much they learn (Riglin et al., 2013). This applies to students of every ethnic group, with declines in academics particularly steep for young adolescents of ethnic minorities as they become more aware of low social expectations for them (Dotterer et al., 2009; McGill et al., 2012; Hayes et al., 2015).

Even if there were no discrimination in the larger society, students have reasons to dislike middle school. Bullying is common, particularly in the first year (Baly et al., 2014). Parents are less involved than in primary school, partly because students want more independence. Unlike primary school, when each classroom had one teacher, middle school teachers have hundreds of students. They become impersonal and distant, opposite to the direct, personal engagement that young adolescents need (Meece & Eccles, 2010).

The early signs of a future high school dropout are found in middle school. Student absenteeism is one sign, and experienced teachers are best at stopping this problem before it becomes chronic (Ladd & Sorensen, 2017). Those students most at risk are low-SES boys from minority ethnic groups, yet almost no middle school has male guidance counselors or teachers who are African American or Latino American men. Given the egocentric and intuitive thinking of many young adolescents, boys may stop trying to achieve if they do not see role models of successful, educated men (Morris & Morris, 2013).

### Finding Acclaim

To pinpoint the developmental mismatch between students' needs and the middle school context, note that just when egocentrism leads young people to feelings of shame or fantasies of stardom (the imaginary audience), schools typically require them to change rooms, teachers, and classmates every 40 minutes or so. That limits both public acclaim and new friendships.

Recognition for academic excellence is especially elusive because middle school teachers grade more harshly than their primary school counterparts. Effort without accomplishment is not recognized, and achievement that was earlier "outstanding" is now only average. Acclaim for after-school activities is also elusive,

**Especially for Teachers** You are stumped by a question your student asks. What do you do? (see response, p. 448)

**More Like Him Needed** In 2014 in the United States, half of the public school students were tallied as non-White and non-Hispanic, and half are male. Meanwhile, only 17 percent of teachers are non-White and non-Hispanic, and only 24 percent are male. This Gardena, California, high school teacher is a welcome exception in two other ways—he rarely sits behind his desk, and he uses gestures as well as his voice to explain.

Hill Street Studios/Blend Images/Newscom

● **Answer to Observation Quiz** (from p. 446): Both are single-sex. What does that teach these students?

● **Response for Teachers** (from p. 447): Praise a student by saying, "What a great question!" Egos are fragile, so it's best to always validate the question. Seek student engagement, perhaps asking whether any classmates know the answer or telling the student to discover the answer online or saying you will find out. Whatever you do, don't fake it; if students lose faith in your credibility, you may lose them completely.

**entity theory of intelligence** An approach to understanding intelligence that sees ability as innate, a fixed quantity present at birth; those who hold this view do not believe that effort enhances achievement. Also called a fixed mindset.

**incremental theory of intelligence** An approach to understanding intelligence which holds that intelligence can be directly increased by effort; those who subscribe to this view believe they can master whatever they seek to learn if they pay attention, participate in class, study, complete their homework, and so on. Also called a growth mindset.

**THINK CRITICALLY:** Would there be less bullying if more schools were multiethnic?

because many art, drama, dance, and other programs put adolescents of all ages together, and 11- to 13-year-olds are not as skilled as older adolescents.

Finally, when athletic teams become competitive, those with fragile egos protect themselves by not trying out. If sports require public showers, that is another reason for students in early puberty to avoid them: They do not feel at ease with their changing bodies and fear comments from their peers. Special camps for basketball, soccer, and so on are usually expensive—beyond the reach of low-SES families. Ironically, one factor that keeps students engaged in secondary school is participation on a sports team: Those who most need engagement may be least likely to get it.

As noted in the discussion of the brain, peer acceptance is more cherished at puberty than at any other time. Physical appearance—from eyebrows to foot size—suddenly becomes significant. Status symbols—from gang colors to trendy sunglasses—take on new meaning. Expensive clothes are coveted. Sexual conquests are flaunted, which may be thoughtlessly destructive to fragile egos. All of this adds stress to middle school students, who may have no psychic energy left for homework.

## Coping with Middle School

One way in which middle school students avoid feelings of failure in academics is to quit trying. Then they can blame a low grade on their choice ("I didn't study") rather than on their ability. Pivotal is how they think of their potential.

Educators write about a *fixed mindset* versus a *growth mindset*. The same idea is described by psychologists as the **entity theory of intelligence** (i.e., that ability is innate, a fixed quantity present at birth) versus an **incremental theory of intelligence** (i.e., that intelligence can increase if students work to master whatever they seek to understand) (Dweck, 1999).

If students hold the entity theory, they conclude that nothing they do can improve their academic skill. If they think they are "born stupid" at math, or language, or whatever, they mask their self-assessment by claiming not to study, try, or care. Thus, entity belief relieves stress, but it also reduces learning.

By contrast, if adolescents adopt the incremental theory, they will pay attention, participate in class, study, complete their homework, and learn. That is also called *mastery motivation*, an example of intrinsic motivation. [**Developmental Link:** Intrinsic and extrinsic motivation are discussed in Chapter 10.]

This is not hypothetical. In the first year of middle school, students with entity beliefs do not achieve much, whereas those with mastery motivation improve academically, true in many nations (e.g., Burnette et al, 2013; Diseth et al., 2014; Zhao & Wang, 2014). Middle school is a time when children can learn how to cope with challenges, both academic and social. Coping style—solving problems rather than blaming oneself—is crucial for middle school achievement (Monti et al., 2017).

This is found between ethnic groups within nations as well. For example, in Australia, indigenous (Maori) youth tend to have much lower achievement scores than Australian youth of British descent, but the difference is more attitudinal than ethnic. Most Maori youth, and most of their teachers, hold the entity theory, but Maori students who subscribe to the incremental theory achieve as much as their nonindigenous peers (Tarbetsky et al., 2016).

Believing that skills can be mastered and that effort pays off is also crucial for learning social skills (Dweck, 2013). Students want good peer relationships, but some are convinced that no one likes them. That self-perception may lead to social avoidance and a downward spiral of feelings of rejection (Zimmer-Gembeck, 2016). Adults must first change these students' attitudes and then help them change their behavior.

Teachers, parents, schools, and cultures allow the hidden curriculum to express the entity theory, encouraging children to compete, not to learn from each other (Eccles & Roeser, 2011). International comparisons reveal that educational systems that track students into higher or lower classes, that expel low-achieving students, and that allow competition between schools for the brightest students (all reflecting entity, not incremental, theory) also show lower average achievement and a larger gap between the scores of students at the highest and lowest score quartiles (OECD, 2011).

## High School

Many of the patterns and problems of middle school continue in high school, although once the sudden growth and unfamiliar sex impulses of puberty are less acute, and with maturation and experience, adolescents are better able to cope with school. They become increasingly able to think abstractly, analytically, hypothetically, and logically (all formal operational thought), as well as subjectively, emotionally, intuitively, and experientially. High school curricula and teaching methods often require the formal mode.

### The College-Bound

From a developmental perspective, the fact that high schools emphasize formal thinking makes sense, since many older adolescents are capable of abstract logic. In several nations, attempts are underway to raise standards so that all high school graduates will be ready for college, where analysis is required.

A mantra in the United States is "college for all," intended to encourage low achievers to aspire for tertiary education, although some authors believe the effect may be the opposite (Carlson, 2016). One result of the emphasis on college is that more students take classes that are assessed by externally scored exams, either the International Baccalaureate (IB) or the Advanced Placement (AP) tests. Such classes have high standards and satisfy some college requirements if the student scores well.

In 2016, AP classes were taken by about one-third of all high school graduates, compared to less than one-fifth (19 percent) in 2003. The increase was particularly notable among low-income students, because the cost of taking the exam ($53) was subsidized by the federal government (students still paid part of the fee).

**Especially for High School Teachers** You are much more interested in the nuances and controversies than in the basic facts of your subject, but you know that your students will take high-stakes tests on the basics and that their scores will have a major impact on their futures. What should you do? (see response, p. 451)

**Same Situation, Far Apart: How to Learn** Although developmental psychologists find that adolescents learn best when they are actively engaged with ideas, most teenagers are easier to control when they are taking tests (*left*, Winston-Salem, North Carolina, United States) or reciting scripture (*right*, Kabul, Afghanistan).

The College Board reports that, in recent years, even though more students are taking the exam (1.1 million in 2016), the proportion who pass remains about 65 percent (Zubrzycki, 2017).

Other indicators of increasing standards are requirements for an academic diploma and restrictions on vocational or general diplomas. Most U.S. schools require two years of math beyond algebra, two years of laboratory science, three years of history, four years of English, and two years of a language other than English.

In addition to mandated courses, 74 percent of U.S. public high school students are required to pass a **high-stakes test** in order to graduate. (Any exam for which the consequences of failing are severe is called "high-stakes.") A decade ago, no state required exit exams. Increased testing is evident in every state, but it is controversial, as the following explains.

**high-stakes test** An evaluation that is critical in determining success or failure. If a single test determines whether a student will graduate or be promoted, it is a high-stakes test.

---

**OPPOSING PERSPECTIVES**

## Testing

Secondary students in the United States take many more tests than they did even a decade ago. This includes many high-stakes tests—not only tests to earn a high school diploma but also tests to get into college (the SAT and ACT, achievement and aptitude) and tests to earn college credits (the AP and IB) while in high school.

High-stakes tests have become part of the culture, necessary to pass third, fifth, and eighth grades, and even to enter special kindergarten classes. Further, the Common Core, explained in Chapter 12, requires testing in reading and math, and the 2016 federal educational reform, the ESSA (Every Student Succeeds Act) requires standardized testing from the third grade on.

Tests also have high stakes for teachers, who may earn extra pay or lose their jobs based on how their students score, and for schools, which gain resources or are shuttered because of test scores. Entire school systems are rated on test scores. This is said to be one reason that widespread cheating on high-stakes tests occurred in Atlanta beginning in 2009 (Severson & Blinder, 2014).

Opposing perspectives on testing are voiced in many schools, parent groups, and state legislatures. In 2013, Alabama dropped its high-stakes test for graduation in the same year that Pennsylvania instituted such a test, but opposing voices have postponed implementation of that requirement. A 2007 law in Texas required 15 tests for graduation; in 2013, Texas law reduced that to 4 tests (Rich, 2013).

Overall, high school graduation rates in the United States have increased every year for the past decade, reaching 83.2 percent in 2016 after four years in high school. A careful analysis finds that those increases represent real improvement (Gewertz, 2017). It is possible that graduation has been made harder, and that the challenge results in better performance. Others contend that the high-stakes tests discourage some students while making graduation too easy for others who are adept at test-taking (Hyslop, 2014).

Students who fail high-stakes tests are often those with intellectual disabilities, one-third of whom do not graduate (Samuels, 2013), and those who attend schools in low-income neighborhoods. Some argue that the tests punish these students, when the real culprit is the school, the community, or the entire nation. Passing graduation exit exams does not correlate with excellence in college, but failing them increases the risk of harm—including prison later on (Baker & Lang, 2013).

Ironically, in the same decade during which U.S. schools are raising requirements, many East Asian nations, including China, Singapore, and Japan (all with high scores on international tests), have moved in the opposite direction. Particularly in Singapore, national high-stakes tests are being phased out, and local autonomy is increasing (Hargreaves, 2012).

International data support both sides of this controversy. One nation whose children generally score well is South Korea, where high-stakes tests have resulted in extensive studying. Many South Korean parents hire tutors to teach their children after school and on weekends to improve their test scores (Lee & Shouse, 2011). Almost all Korean students graduate from high school, and most attend college—but that accomplishment is not valued by many Korean educators, including Seongho Lee, a professor of education in Korea. He says that "oversupply in college education is a very serious social problem" creating an "army of the unemployed" (quoted in Fischer, 2016, p. A25).

On the opposite side of the globe, students in Finland also score well on international tests but have no national tests until the end of high school. Nor do they spend much time on homework or after-school education. A Finnish expert proudly states that "schoolteachers teach in order to help their students learn, not to pass tests" (Sahlberg, 2011, p. 26).

The most recent international data suggest that U.S. high school students are not doing well, despite more high-stakes tests. As reviewed in Chapter 12, two international tests, the Trends in International Mathematics and Science Study (TIMSS) and the Progress in International Reading Literacy Study (PIRLS ), find that the United States is far from the top on student learning. A third test, the PISA (described soon), also shows the United States lagging.

Graduation rates are increasing in the United States (see Figure 15.5). That is leading to a reexamination of U.S. education policies and practices, yet opposing perspectives are evident.

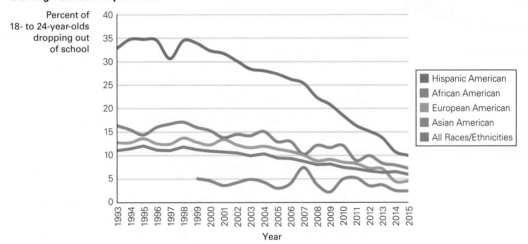

**U.S. High School Dropout Rate**

Data from Digest of Education Statistics, February 2017.

**FIGURE 15.5**

**Mostly Good News** This depicts wonderful improvements in high school graduation rates, especially among Hispanic youth, who drop out less than half as often as they did 20 years ago. However, since high school graduation is increasingly necessary for lifetime success, even the rates shown here may not have kept pace with the changing needs of the economy. Future health, income, and happiness may be in jeopardy for anyone who drops out.

## Alternatives to College

In the United States, a sizable minority (about 30 percent) of high school graduates do not enter college. Moreover, of those who enter public community colleges, most (about three-fourths) do not complete their associate's degree within three years, and almost half of those entering public or private four-year schools do not graduate. Some simply take longer or enter the job market first, but even 10 years after the usual age for high school graduation, only 37 percent of U.S. young adults have earned a bachelor's degree (Kena et al., 2016).

Rates are much lower in many of the largest cities. For example, only 18 percent of the approximately 60,000 ninth-grade students entering public schools in the district of Philadelphia managed to graduate on time from high school and then complete at least two years of college (Center for Education Policy, 2013).

The 82 percent who fell off track are often a disappointment to their parents: In Philadelphia and nationwide, almost all parents hope their children will graduate from college. The students may be a disappointment to themselves as well. Many quit high school before their senior year, but among the graduating Philadelphia seniors, 84 percent plan to go to college but only 47 percent enroll the following

**Response for High School Teachers** (from p. 449): It would be nice to follow your instincts, but the appropriate response depends partly on pressures within the school and partly on the expectations of the parents and administration. A comforting fact is that adolescents can think about and learn almost anything if they feel a personal connection to it. Look for ways to teach the facts your students need for the tests as the foundation for the exciting and innovative topics you want to teach. Everyone will learn more, and the tests will be less intimidating to your students.

San Diego Union-Tribune/ZUMAPress/Vista/ CA/USA/Newscom

**What Do They Need to Learn?** Jesse Olascoaga and José Perez here assemble a desk as part of a class in Trade Tech High School in Vista, California. Are they mastering skills that will lead to a good job? Much depends on what else they are learning. It may be collaboration and pride in work well done, in which case this is useful education.

**THINK CRITICALLY:** Is it more important to prepare high school students for jobs or for college?

**PISA (Programme for International Student Assessment)** An international test taken by 15-year-olds in 50 nations that is designed to measure problem solving and cognition in daily life.

September. Some will begin college later, but their chance of college completion is low.

These sobering statistics underlie another debate among educators. Should students be encouraged to "dream big" early in high school, aspiring for tertiary learning? This suggestion originates from studies that find a correlation between dreaming big in early adolescence and going to college years later (Domina et al., 2011a, 2011b). Others suggest that college is a "fairy tale dream" that may lead to low self-esteem (Rosenbaum, 2011). If adolescents fail academic classes, will they feel bored, stupid, and disengaged?

Business leaders have another concern—that high school graduates are not ready for the demands of work because their education has been too abstract, or the standards for writing and analyzing too low. They have not learned enough through discussion, emotional maturation, and real-world experience.

Internationally, vocational education that explicitly prepares students for jobs via a combination of academic classes and practical experience seems to succeed better than a general curriculum (Eichhorst et al., 2012). On the other hand, many students whose test scores suggest that they could succeed at a four-year college do not enroll. Some high schools are more encouraging than others. For example, students who entered high school with high achievement scores in two major cities in neighboring states (Albuquerque, New Mexico and Fort Worth, Texas) had markedly different college enrollment rates (about 83 percent compared to 58 percent) (Center for Education Policy, 2012).

Overall, the data present a dilemma for educators. Suggesting that a student should *not* go to college may be racist, classist, sexist, or worse. On the other hand, many students who begin college do not graduate, so they lose time and gain debt when they could have advanced in a vocation. Everyone agrees that adolescents need to be educated for life as well as for employment, but it is difficult to decide what that means.

## Measuring Practical Cognition

Employers usually provide on-the-job training, which is much more specific and current than what high schools can provide. They hope their future employees will have learned in secondary school how to think, explain, write, concentrate, and get along with other people.

As one executive of Boeing (which hired 33,000 new employees in two years) wrote:

> We believe that professional success today and in the future is more likely for those who have practical experience, work well with others, build strong relationships, and are able to think and do, not just look things up on the Internet.

*[Stephens & Richey, 2013, p. 314]*

Those skills are hard to measure, especially on national high-stakes tests or on the two international tests explained in Chapter 12, the PIRLS and the TIMSS.

The third in the set of international tests mentioned above, the **Programme for International Student Assessment (PISA)** was designed to measure students' ability to apply what they have learned. The PISA is taken by 15-year-olds, an age chosen because some 15-year-olds are close to the end of their formal school career. The questions are supposed to be practical, measuring knowledge that might apply at home or on the job. As a PISA report described it:

> The tests are designed to generate measures of the extent to which students can make effective use of what they have learned in school to deal with various problems and challenges they are likely to experience in everyday life.

*[PISA, 2009, p. 13]*

For example, among the 2012 math questions is this one:

Chris has just received her car driving license and wants to buy her first car. The table below shows the details of four cars she finds at a local car dealer. What car's engine capacity is the smallest?

A. Alpha     B. Bolte     C. Castel     D. Dezal

| Model | Alpha | Bolte | Castel | Dezal |
|---|---|---|---|---|
| Year | 2003 | 2000 | 2001 | 1999 |
| Advertised price (zeds) | 4800 | 4450 | 4250 | 3990 |
| Distance travelled (kilometers) | 105 000 | 115 000 | 128 000 | 109 000 |
| Engine capacity (liters) | 1.79 | 1.796 | 1.82 | 1.783 |

For that and the other questions on the PISA, the calculations are quite simple—most 10-year-olds can do them; no calculus, calculators, or complex formulas required. However, almost half of the 15-year-olds worldwide got that question wrong. (The answer is D.) One problem is decimals: Some students do not remember how to interpret them when a practical question, not an academic one, is asked. Even in Singapore and Hong Kong, one out of five 15-year-olds got this question wrong. Another problem is that distance traveled is irrelevant, yet many students are distracted by it.

Overall the U.S. students score lower on the PISA compared to many other nations, including Canada, the nation most similar to the United States in ethnicity and location. Compared to peers in other nations, the 2012 results rank the U.S. 15-year-olds 36th in math, 28th in science, and 24th in reading—all lower than in 2009, when the U.S. scores were 31st, 23rd, and 17th.

Some 2012 results were not surprising (China, Japan, Korea, and Singapore were all high), but some were unexpected (high scores for Finland, Poland, and Estonia). The lowest results were Peru, Indonesia, and Qatar. The results reflect the educational systems, not geography, since low-scoring Indonesia is close to Singapore.

International analysis finds that the following items correlate with high achievement of high school students on the PISA (OECD, 2010, p. 4):

- Leaders, parents, and citizens value education overall, with individualized approaches to learning so that all students learn what they need.
- Standards are high and clear, so every student knows what he or she must do, with a "focus on the acquisition of complex, higher-order thinking skills."
- Teachers and administrators are valued, and they are given "considerable discretion . . . in determining content" and sufficient salary as well as time for collaboration.
- Learning is prioritized "across the entire system," with high-quality teachers assigned to the most challenging schools.

The PISA and international comparisons of high school dropout rates suggest that U.S. secondary education can be improved, especially for those who do not go to college. Surprisingly, students who are capable of passing their classes, at least as measured on IQ tests, drop out almost as often as those who are less capable. Persistence, engagement, and motivation seem to be more crucial than intellectual ability alone (Archambault et al., 2009; Tough, 2012). Again, as in middle school, the incremental (growth mindset) theory of education may be crucial.

## Variability

An added complication is that adolescents themselves vary: Some are thoughtful, some are impulsive, some are ready for analytic challenges, some are egocentric. All of them, however, need personal encouragement.

A study of student emotional and academic engagement from fifth grade to eighth grade found that, as expected, the overall average was a slow and steady decline of engagement, but a distinctive group (about 18 percent) were highly engaged throughout while another distinctive group (about 5 percent) experienced precipitous disengagement year by year (Li & Lerner, 2011). The 18 percent are likely to do well in high school; the 5 percent are likely to drop out, but some of them are late bloomers who could succeed in college if given time and encouragement. Thus, schools and teachers need many strategies if they hope to reach every adolescent.

Similar complications are evident in one recent strategy for advancing academic achievement—separating the boys and the girls. Some studies find that teenagers benefit from being with others of their own sex, but other studies find the opposite. The data are complicated by selection effects: Single-sex schools are more often private, not public, and have smaller class size, wealthier families, and more selective admissions. All of those factors improve achievement—so the single-sex characteristic may be irrelevant.

Perhaps the age of the students is a crucial variable. A meta-analysis found some academic advantage to single-sex education in middle school but none in high school (Pahlke et al., 2014). As one review states, "both proponents and critics of single-sex schooling have studies that support their positions, stagnating the policy debate" (Pahlke & Hyde, 2016, p. 83). It also may be that the emphasis on academic achievement is too narrow: If the goal of secondary education is to prepare students for life, then coeducation may be better.

Now let us return to general conclusions for this chapter. The cognitive skills that boost national economic development and personal happiness are creativity, flexibility, relationship building, and analytic ability. Whether or not an adolescent is college-bound, those skills are exactly what the adolescent mind can develop—with proper education and guidance. Every cognitive theorist and researcher believes that adolescents' logical, social, and creative potential is not always realized, but that it can be. Does that belief end this chapter on a hopeful note?

---

### WHAT HAVE YOU LEARNED?

1. Why have most junior high schools disappeared?

2. What characteristics of middle schools make them more difficult for students than elementary schools?

3. Why does puberty affect a person's ability to learn?

4. How do beliefs about intelligence affect motivation and learning?

5. What are the advantages and disadvantages of high-stakes testing?

6. What are the problems with Advanced Placement classes and tests?

7. Should high schools prepare everyone for college? Why or why not?

8. How does the PISA differ from other international tests?

# SUMMARY

### Logic and Self

**1.** Cognition in early adolescence may be egocentric, a kind of self-centered thinking. Adolescent egocentrism gives rise to the personal fable, the invincibility fable, and the imaginary audience.

**2.** Formal operational thought is Piaget's term for the last of his four periods of cognitive development. He tested and demonstrated formal operational thought with various problems that students in a high school science or math class might encounter.

**3.** Piaget realized that adolescents are no longer earthbound and concrete in their thinking; they imagine the possible, the probable, and even the impossible, instead of focusing only on what is real. They develop hypotheses and explore, using deductive reasoning. However, few developmentalists find that adolescents move suddenly from concrete thinking to formal thinking.

**4.** Many cognitive theories describe two types of thinking during adolescence. One set of names for these two types is intuitive and analytic. Both become more forceful during adolescence, but brain development means that intuitive, emotional thinking matures before analytic, logical thought.

**5.** Few teenagers always use logic, although they are capable of doing so. Emotional, intuitive thinking is quicker and more satisfying, and sometimes better, than analytic thought.

**6.** Neurological as well as survey research finds that adolescent thinking is characterized by more rapid development of the limbic system and slower development of the prefrontal cortex. Peers further increase emotional impulses, so adolescents may make choices that their parents believe to be foolish.

### Digital Natives

**7.** Adolescents use technology, particularly the Internet, more than people of any other age. They reap many educational benefits.

Most teachers welcome the accessibility of information and the research advances made possible by the Internet. Social connections are encouraged as well.

**8.** However, technology can be destructive. Some adolescents may be addicted to video games, some use smartphones and instant messages for cyberbullying, some find like-minded peers to support eating disorders and other pathologies, some engage in sexting. Overall, adults may mistakenly attribute normal teen behavior to technology use.

### Secondary Education

**9.** Achievement in secondary education—after primary education (grade school) and before tertiary education (college)—correlates with the health and wealth of individuals and nations.

**10.** In middle school, many students struggle both socially and academically. One reason may be that middle schools are not structured to accommodate egocentrism or intuitive thinking. Students' beliefs about the nature of intelligence—entity or incremental—may also affect their learning.

**11.** Education in high school emphasizes formal operational thinking. In the United States, the demand for more accountability has led to an increase in the requirements for graduation and to more Advanced Placement (AP) classes and high-stakes testing.

**12.** A sizable number of high school students do not graduate or go on to college, and many more leave college without a degree. Current high school education does not seem to meet their needs.

**13.** The PISA test, taken by many 15-year-olds in 50 nations, measures how well students can apply the knowledge they have been taught. Students in the United States seem to have particular difficulty with such tests.

# KEY TERMS

adolescent egocentrism (p. 430)
imaginary audience (p. 431)
personal fable (p. 431)
invincibility fable (p. 431)
formal operational thought (p. 432)

hypothetical thought (p. 433)
deductive reasoning (p. 433)
inductive reasoning (p. 433)
dual processing (p. 434)
intuitive thought (p. 435)
analytic thought (p. 435)

cyberbullying (p. 443)
sexting (p. 444)
secondary education (p. 446)
middle school (p. 446)
entity theory of intelligence (p. 448)

incremental theory of intelligence (p. 448)
high-stakes test (p. 450)
PISA (Programme for International Student Assessment) (p. 452)

# APPLICATIONS

**1.** Describe a time when you overestimated how much other people were thinking about you. How was your mistake similar to and different from adolescent egocentrism?

**2.** Talk to a teenager about politics, families, school, religion, or any other topic that might reveal the way he or she thinks. Do you hear any adolescent egocentrism? Intuitive thinking? Systematic thought? Flexibility? Cite examples.

**3.** Think of a life-changing decision you have made. How did logic and emotion interact? What would have changed if you had given the matter more thought—or less?

**4.** Describe what happened and what you thought in the first year you attended a middle school or a high school. What made it better or worse than later years in that school?

# Adolescence:
## Psychosocial Development

## What Will You Know?

1. Why might a teenager be into sports one year and into books the next?
2. Should parents back off when their teenager disputes every rule, wish, or suggestion they make?
3. Who are the best, and worst, sources of information about sex?
4. Should we worry more about teen suicide or juvenile delinquency?
5. Why are adolescents forbidden to drink and smoke, but adults can do so?

+ **Identity**
Not Yet Achieved
Four Arenas of Identity
Formation

+ **Relationships with Adults**
A VIEW FROM SCIENCE: Teenagers,
Genes, and Drug Use
Parents

+ **Peer Power**
Peer Pressure
A CASE TO STUDY: The Naiveté of
Your Author
Romance
Sex Education

+ **Sadness and Anger**
Depression
Delinquency and Defiance

+ **Drug Use and Abuse**
Variations in Drug Use
OPPOSING PERSPECTIVES:
E-Cigarettes: Path to
Addiction or Healthy Choice?
Harm from Drugs
Preventing Drug Abuse: What
Works?

It's not easy being a teenager, as the previous chapters make clear, but neither is it easy being the parent of one. Sometimes I was too lenient. For example, once my daughter came home late. I was worried and angry but did not think about punishing her until she asked, "How long am I grounded?" And sometimes I was too strict. For years, I insisted that my children wash the dinner dishes—until they told me, again and again, that none of their friends had such mean mothers.

At times, my husband and I reacted emotionally, not rationally. When our children were infants, we decided how we would deal with adolescent problems. We were ready to be firm, united, and consistent regarding illicit drugs, unsafe sex, and serious lawbreaking. More than a decade later, when our children actually reached that stage, none of those issues appeared. Instead, questions of clothing, neatness, and homework took us by surprise. My husband said, "I knew they would become adolescents. I didn't expect us to become parents of adolescents."

This chapter is about adolescents' behavior and relationships with friends, parents, and the larger society. It begins with identity and ends with drugs, both of which seem to be the result of personal choice but actually are strongly affected by social norms. I know now that my children's actions and my reactions were influenced by personal history (I washed family dishes) and by current norms (their friends did not).

## Identity

Psychosocial development during adolescence is often understood as a search for a consistent understanding of oneself. Self-expression and self-concept become increasingly important at puberty. Each young person wants to know, "Who am I?"

According to Erik Erikson, life's fifth psychosocial crisis is **identity versus role confusion:** Working through the complexities of finding one's own identity is the primary task of adolescence (Erikson, 1968/1994). He said that this crisis is resolved with **identity achievement,** when adolescents have reconsidered the goals and values of their parents and culture, accepting some and discarding others, forging their own identity.

Sara Caldwell/Staff/The Augusta Chronicle/ZUMAPRESS.com/Alamy

**No Role Confusion** These are high school students in Junior ROTC training camp. For many youths who cannot afford college, the military offers a temporary identity, complete with haircut, uniform, and comrades.

**identity versus role confusion** Erikson's term for the fifth stage of development, in which the person tries to figure out "Who am I?" but is confused as to which of many possible roles to adopt.

**identity achievement** Erikson's term for the attainment of identity, or the point at which a person understands who he or she is as a unique individual, in accord with past experiences and future plans.

**role confusion** A situation in which an adolescent does not seem to know or care what his or her identity is. (Sometimes called *identity* or *role diffusion*.)

**foreclosure** Erikson's term for premature identity formation, which occurs when an adolescent adopts his or her parents' or society's roles and values wholesale, without questioning or analysis.

**moratorium** An adolescent's choice of a socially acceptable way to postpone making identity-achievement decisions. Going to college is a common example.

**THINK CRITICALLY:** Since identity is formed lifelong, is your identity now different from what it was five years ago?

Identity achievement is neither wholesale rejection nor unquestioning acceptance of social norms. Teenagers maintain continuity with the past so that they can move to the future, establishing their own identity. Simply following parental footsteps does not work, because the social context of each generation differs.

## Not Yet Achieved

Erikson's insights have inspired thousands of researchers. Notable among those was James Marcia, who described and measured four specific ways in which young people cope with the identity crisis: (1) role confusion, (2) foreclosure, (3) moratorium, and finally (4) identity achievement (Marcia, 1966).

Over the past half-century, major psychosocial shifts have lengthened the duration of adolescence and made identity achievement more complex (Côté & Levine, 2015). However, the above three way-stations on the road to identity achievement still seem evident (Kroger & Marcia, 2011).

**Role confusion** is the opposite of identity achievement. It is characterized by lack of commitment to any goals or values. Erikson originally called this *identity diffusion* to emphasize that some adolescents seem diffuse, unfocused, and unconcerned about their future. Perhaps worse, adolescents in role confusion see no goals or purpose in their life, and thus they flounder, unable to move forward (Hill et al., 2013).

Identity **foreclosure** occurs when, in order to avoid the confusion of not knowing who they are, young people lump traditional roles and values together, to be swallowed whole or rejected totally (Marcia, 1966; Marcia et al., 1993). They might follow customs transmitted from their parents or culture, never exploring alternatives. Or they might foreclose on an oppositional, *negative identity*—the direct opposite of whatever their parents want—again without thoughtful questioning. Foreclosure is comfortable, but it is limiting. That is why it is a temporary shelter for many young people, to be followed by more exploration (Meeus, 2011).

A more mature shelter is **moratorium,** a time-out that includes some exploration, either in breadth (trying many things) or in depth (following one path but with a tentative, temporary commitment). Moratoria are rare before age 18, and hence, they are discussed in the Epilogue, on emerging adulthood.

Erikson originally placed the identity crisis in adolescence; but we will establish identity is a lifelong process. Indeed, many scholars are now examining identity development in adulthood (Fadjukoff & Kroger, 2016).

Puberty and cognitive advances start the identity search in early adolescence. A study of almost 8,000 Belgian 14- to 30-year-olds confirms that young adolescents are often uncertain and confused about their identity. With maturation, people are more likely to reach identity achievement (Verschueren et al., 2017).

## Four Arenas of Identity Formation

Erikson (1968/1994) highlighted four aspects of identity: religious, political, vocational, and sexual. Terminology and timing have changed, yet the crucial question remains: Does the person ponder the possibilities and actively seek an identity (Lillevoll et al., 2013)?

### Religious Identity

Most adolescents begin to question some aspects of their faith, but their *religious identity* is similar to that of their parents. Few reject religion if they have grown up following a particular faith, especially if they have a good relationship with their parents (Kim-Spoon et al., 2012).

They may express their religious identity more devoutly. A Muslim girl might start to wear a headscarf, a Catholic boy might study for the priesthood, or a Baptist teenager might join a Pentecostal youth group, all surprising their parents.

The more common pattern is in the opposite direction: Although adolescents identify with the religion of their childhood, attendance at worship gradually decreases (Lopez et al., 2011). Major shifts are rare. Almost no young Muslims convert to Judaism, and almost no teenage Baptists become Hindu—although such conversions can occur in adulthood.

**Same Situation, Far Apart: Religious Identity** Awesome devotion is characteristic of adolescents, whether devotion is to a sport, a person, a music group, or—as shown here—a religion. This boy *(left)* praying on a Kosovo street is part of a dangerous protest against the town's refusal to allow building another mosque. This girl *(right)* is at a stadium rally for young Christians in Michigan, declaring her faith for all to see. While adults see differences between the two religions, both teens share not only piety but also twenty-first-century clothing. Her T-shirt is a recent innovation, and on his jersey is Messi 10, for a soccer star born in Argentina.

## Political Identity

Parents also influence their children's *political identity*. In the twenty-first century in the United States, more adults identify as independent than Republican, Democrat, or any other party. Their teenage children reflect their lack of party affiliation. Some adolescents boast that they do not care about politics, echoing the parents' generation without realizing it.

Others proudly vote for the first time at age 18—an event that is much more likely if they are living at home and their parents are voting than if they have already left home. Just like other aspects of political involvement, voting is a social activity, not an isolated, individual one (Hart & van Goethem, 2017).

In general, adolescents' interest in politics is predicted by their parents' involvement and current events, just as the identity search would predict (Stattin et al., 2017). Adolescents tend to be more liberal than their elders, especially on social issues (LGBTQ rights, reproduction, the environment), but major political shifts do not usually occur until later (P. Taylor, 2014). For example, Hillary Clinton's parents were Republican and she was a Young Republican at age 17, not becoming a Democrat until age 21. As a young adult, President Trump was a Democrat.

Related to political identity is *ethnic identity*, a topic not discussed by Erikson. In the United States and Canada, about half of all current adolescents are of African, Asian, Latino, or Native American (Aboriginal in Canada) heritage. Many of them also have ancestors of another ethnic group.

Official government categories are too broad; teenagers must forge a personal ethnic identity that is more specific. Hispanic youth, for instance, must figure out how having grandparents from Mexico, Peru, or Cuba, and/or California, Texas, or New York, affects them. Many Latinos (some identifying as *Chicano*) also have ancestors from Spain, Africa, Germany, and/or indigenous groups such as the Maya or Inca. Similarly, those who are European American must decide the significance of having grandparents from, say, Italy, Ireland, or Sweden. Youth with Asian or African ancestors also become much more specific in ethnic identity.

In general, pride in ethnic identity correlates with academic achievement, but the relationship is "complex and nuanced" (Miller-Cotto & Byrnes, 2016). Most studies find that ethnic identity correlates with well-being, although not every study comes to that conclusion (Smith & Silva, 2011).

## Vocational Identity

*Vocational identity* originally meant envisioning oneself as a worker in a particular occupation. Choosing a vocation made sense a century ago, when most girls

**Video Activity: Adolescence Around the World: Rites of Passage** presents a comparison of adolescent initiation customs in industrialized and developing societies.

**gender identity** A person's acceptance of the roles and behaviors that society associates with the biological categories of male and female.

became housewives and most boys became farmers, small businessmen, or factory workers. Those few in professions were mostly generalists (doctors did family medicine, lawyers handled all kinds of cases, teachers taught all subjects).

Early vocational identity is no longer appropriate. No teenager can realistically choose among the tens of thousands of careers. The typical young adult changes jobs every year, part of the search for meaningful and satisfying work (Gardner & Chao, 2017). The large Belgian study already referenced found that teenagers who choose employment, rather than higher education, are most likely in foreclosure. Currently, vocational identity is best seen as a dynamic, flexible exploration: Adults eventually find a career, or, even better, a calling, that can lead to a variety of specific jobs (Skorikov & Vondracek, 2011).

It is a myth that having a job will keep teenagers out of trouble and establish vocational identity (Staff & Schulenberg, 2010). Research that controlled for SES found that adolescents who are employed more than 20 hours a week during the school year tend to quit school, fight with parents, smoke cigarettes, and hate their jobs—not only when they are teenagers but also later on (although sometimes work that is steady and not too time-consuming may be beneficial) (Osilla et al., 2015; Mortimer, 2010).

Typically, employed teenagers spend their wages on clothes, cars, drugs, fast food, and music, not on supporting their families or saving for college (Mortimer, 2013). Grades fall: Employment interferes with schoolwork and attendance. This is true not only in the United States; similar results are found in South Korea (Lee et al., 2016).

## Gender Identity

The fourth type of identity described by Erikson is *sexual identity*. As you remember from Chapter 10, *sex* and *sexual* refer to biological characteristics, whereas *gender* refers to cultural and social attributes that differentiate males and females. A half-century ago, Erikson and other theorists thought of the two sexes as opposites (Miller & Simon, 1980). They assumed that adolescents who were confused about sexual identity would soon adopt "proper" male or female roles (Erikson, 1968/1994; A. Freud, 1958/2000).

Thus, adolescence was once a time for "gender intensification," when people increasingly identified as male or female. No longer (Priess et al., 2009). Erikson's term *sexual identity* has been replaced by **gender identity** (Denny & Pittman, 2007), which refers primarily to a person's self-definition as male, female, or transgender.

Gender identity often (but not always) begins with the person's biological sex and leads to a gender role, but many adolescents (who display the analytic, hypothetical thinking that Piaget described) question aspects of gender roles and expression. This may trouble their parents and grandparents, who grew up with more traditional expectations. I know a mother who thought she was being helpful when she suggested that her daughter's skirt was too short and too tight. Her daughter retorted, "Stop slut-shaming me."

Gender roles once meant that only men were employed; they were *breadwinners* (good providers) and women were *housewives* (married

**Sisters and Brothers** Gender equality has become important to both sexes, as evidenced by the thousands of men who joined the Women's March on January 21, 2017—the day after President Trump's inauguration. Many who attended took exception with his positions on sex and gender issues, and the result was one of the largest protest marches ever: an estimated 4 million people in more than one hundred towns and cities. This shows Washington, D.C., where more than half a million gathered.

to their houses). As women entered the labor market, gender roles expanded but were still strong (nurse/doctor, secretary/businessman, pink collar/blue collar). Even today, women in every nation do far more child care and elder care than men. There is a "slow but steady pace of change in gender divisions of domestic labor . . . combined with a persistence of gender differences and inequalities" (Doucet, 2015, p. 224).

Now, gender roles are changing everywhere. The speed and specifics of the change vary dramatically by culture and cohort. A new term, *cisgender*, refers to people whose gender identity is the same as their natal sex, but the fact that such a term exists is evidence of the complexity of gender identity.

All adolescents are vulnerable to feelings of depression and anxiety as they try to sort out how to express their sex and gender, but this is particularly true of those who are transgender or nonconforming in other ways (Reisner et al., 2016). Fluidity and uncertainty regarding sex and gender are especially common during early adolescence, when hormones increase and fluctuate. That adds to the difficulty of self-acceptance.

Among Western psychiatrists in former decades, people who had "a strong and persistent cross-gender identification" were said to have *gender identity disorder*, a serious diagnosis according to DSM-IV. However, the DSM-5 instead describes *gender dysphoria*, when people are distressed at their biological sex. This is not simply a change in words: A "disorder" means something is amiss with the individual, no matter how he or she feels about it, whereas "dysphoria" means the problem is in the distress, which can be mitigated by social conditions, by cognitive framing, or by transitioning to the other gender (Zucker et al., 2013).

What has not changed are sexual drives as hormone levels increase. As Erikson recognized, many adolescents are confused regarding when, how, and with whom to express those drives. Some foreclose by expressing male or female stereotypes; others seek a moratorium by avoiding all sexual contact, telling others via their clothes and mannerisms that they are not interested.

Some who feel uncertain about gender identity may aspire to a gender-stereotypic career (Sinclair & Carlsson, 2013). Choosing a career to establish gender identity, rather than to use skills, follow interests, and affirm values, is another reason why settling on a vocational identity during adolescence may be premature.

---

### WHAT HAVE YOU LEARNED?

1. What is Erikson's fifth psychosocial crisis, and how is it resolved?

2. How does identity foreclosure differ from identity moratorium?

3. What has changed over the past decades regarding political identity in the United States?

4. What role do parents play in the formation of an adolescent's religious and political identity?

5. Why is it premature for today's adolescents to achieve vocational identity?

6. What assumptions about gender identity did most adults hold 50 years ago?

7. What is the difference between gender identity disorder and gender dysphoria?

---

## Relationships with Adults

Adolescence is often depicted as a period of waning adult influence, when children distance themselves from their elders. This picture is only half true. Adult influence is less immediate but no less important.

# Teenagers, Genes, and Drug Use

A major challenge for developmentalists is to combine knowledge of effective prevention with laboratory analysis of molecular genetics. It is apparent, as explained in Chapter 3, that genes affect every behavior, including whether or not a person is likely to abuse drugs. It is also apparent, however, that parents and community contexts influence every teenage behavior, not only drug use but also sex, delinquency, and academic achievement.

The challenge is to understand the relationship between genes and environment, avoiding the danger of blaming all destructive behavior on genes, or on parents, or on the society. One of the leading researchers in this field is Gene Brody, who warns of overreliance on genetic analysis, even as he also lauds the use of genetic research (Brody, 2017).

Brody's work began with his lifelong interest in helping African American boys achieve their potential despite growing up in rural Georgia (Brody et al., 2009). Half of a group of 611 parents and their 11-year-old sons were assigned to a comparison group, with no special intervention, and the other half were the experimental group, invited to seven two-hour training sessions. Fewer than twenty boys were in each training group. Leaders were carefully chosen and educated to be were good role models, often because they had grown up in similar communities. Parents and sons were taught separately for an hour and then brought together. Teaching was active, with discussion and role-playing, because research has found that social interaction is crucial for effective education.

*The parents learned the following:*

- The importance of being nurturing and involved
- The importance of conveying pride in being African American (called *racial socialization*)
- How monitoring and control benefit adolescents
- Why clear norms and expectations reduce substance use
- Strategies for communication about sex

*The 11-year-olds learned the following:*

- The importance of having household rules
- Adaptive behaviors when encountering racism
- The need for making plans for the future
- The differences between them and peers who use alcohol

After that first hour, the parents and 11-year-olds were led in games, structured interactions, and modeling designed to improve family communication and cohesion. Three years after the intervention, both the experimental and comparison groups were reassessed regarding sex and alcohol/drug activity. The results were disappointing: The intervention helped, but not very much.

Then, four years after the study began, Brody read new research which found that people with the short allele of the 5-HTTLPR gene had heightened risks of depression, delinquency, and other problems. Might this apply to African American teenagers? Brody tracked down his original group, who were now 16-year-olds. He convinced them to donate saliva to be analyzed for the 5-HTTLPR allele. As Figure 16.1 shows, the training had almost no impact on those with the long allele, but it had a major impact on those with the short one.

That parent–son training lasting 14 or fewer hours (some families skipped sessions) had an impact is astonishing, given all of the other influences surrounding these boys. Apparently, since the parent–child relationship is crucial throughout adolescence, those seven sessions provided insights and connections that affected each vulnerable dyad from then on.

Differential susceptibility was apparent. In a follow-up study at age 19, the boys with the short 5-HTTLPR gene who did not experience the parent–son training had many indicators of poor health—physical and psychological (Brody et al., 2013). Further research with other teenagers and parents again found differential effects of inherited genes (Cho et al., 2016). Again, nature and nurture work together.

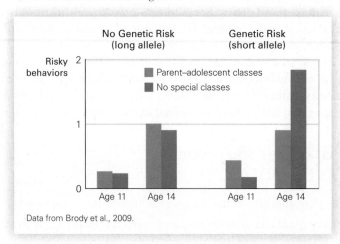

Data from Brody et al., 2009.

**FIGURE 16.1**

**Not Yet** The risk score was a simple one point for each of the following: had drunk alcohol, had smoked marijuana, had had sex. As shown, most of the 11-year-olds had done none of these. By age 14, most had done one (usually had drunk beer or wine)—except for those at genetic risk who did not have the seven-session training. Some of them had done all three, and many had done at least two. As you see, for those youths without genetic risk, the usual parenting was no better or worse than the parenting that benefited from the special classes: The average 14-year-old in either group had tried only one risky behavior. But for those at genetic risk, the special program made a decided difference.

**A Study in Contrasts?**  These two teenagers appear to be opposites: one yelling at his mother and the other conscientiously helping his father. However, adolescent moods can change in a flash, especially with parents. Later in the day, these two might switch.

## Parents

Caregiver–adolescent relationships are pivotal, affecting identity, expectations, and daily life. That does not mean that they are peaceful (Laursen & Collins, 2009). Disputes are common because the adolescent's drive for independence, arising from biological forces, psychological impulses, and social expectations, clashes with the adult's desire for control.

Normally, conflict peaks in early adolescence, especially between mothers and daughters. Usually this is not fighting but instead it is *bickering*—repeated, petty arguments (more nagging than fighting) about routine, day-to-day concerns such as cleanliness, clothes, chores, and schedules. Each generation tends to misjudge the other, and that increases conflict. Parents (usually biological parents, but this includes anyone in a parental role) think that their offspring resent them more than they actually do, and adolescents imagine that their parents want to dominate them more than they actually do (Sillars et al., 2010).

Unspoken concerns need to be aired so that both generations better understand each other. Bickering begins with squabbling and nagging, but ideally it leads to each person understanding what the adolescent needs. This is not simple, especially for parents who think they know their one, because puberty awakens new thoughts, worries, and concerns in almost every one (McLaren & Sillars, 2014).

Some bickering may indicate a healthy family, since close relationships almost always include conflict. A study of mothers and their adolescents suggested that "although too much anger may be harmful . . . some expression of anger may be adaptive" (Hofer et al., 2013, p. 276). In this study, as well as generally, the parent–child relationship usually improved with time (Tighe et al., 2016; Tsai et al., 2013).

Crucial is that caregivers avoid becoming much stricter or too lenient, and they instead maintain support while adapting to the adolescent's need for increased independence. One review of dozens of studies found that the effects of conflict varied a great deal but that "parent–adolescent conflict might signal the need for families to adapt and change . . . to accommodate adolescents' increasing needs for independence and egalitarianism" (Weymouth et al., 2016, p. 107).

**THINK CRITICALLY:** When do parents forbid an activity they should approve of, or ignore a behavior that should alarm them?

## Cultural Differences

Several researchers have compared parent–child relationships in various cultures: Everywhere, parent–child communication and encouragement reduce teenage depression, suicide, and low self-esteem, and increase aspirations and achievements. However, expectations, interactions, and behavior vary by culture (Brown & Bakken, 2011).

Parent–child conflict is less evident in cultures that stress **familism,** the belief that family members should sacrifice personal freedom and success to care for one another. Most refugee youth (Palestinian, Syrian, Iraqi) in Jordan agreed that parents had a right to decide their children's hairstyles, clothes, and music—contrary to what most U.S. teenagers believe (Smetana et al., 2016). In many traditional cultures, if adolescents do something that their parents would not approve, the teens keep it quiet.

By contrast, U.S. adolescents might deliberately provoke an argument by boldly advocating marijuana legalization, transgender rights, or abortion access, even if they themselves would not be affected (Cumsille et al., 2010). The parents' job is to listen, not overreact.

Cultural differences are evident not only between nations and among ethnic groups in the United States but also within nations and ethnic groups. This is illustrated by a longitudinal study of Mexican American adolescents (Wheeler et al., 2017). Those who strongly endorse familism were less likely than those who were more Americanized to defy their parents. Instead, they behaved as expected—attending school, avoiding gangs, not carrying a weapon.

Within each culture, as evident in the study of Hispanic youth, adolescent development is dynamic. Over the years, teenagers vary in how devoted they are to their parents: When familism becomes relatively low, risk-taking increases.

Overall, when impulsive, fearful, or adventurous children are raised in a supportive family, they are less likely to do drugs or otherwise break the law than the average adolescent. The opposite is true in a harsh family (Rioux et al., 2016). Thus, parents should engage, not explode.

**familism** The belief that family members should support one another, sacrificing individual freedom and success, if necessary, in order to preserve family unity and protect the family from outside forces.

Barbara Smaller/The New Yorker Collection/Cartoonbank.com

*"So I blame you for everything—whose fault is that?"*

## Closeness Within the Family

Parent–child relationships are crucial. Specifically:

1. Communication (Do family members talk openly and honestly?)
2. Support (Do they rely on each other?)
3. Connectedness (How emotionally close are family members?)
4. Control (Do parents restrict autonomy?)

No social scientist doubts that the first two, communication and support, are crucial for healthy development. Patterns set in place during childhood continue, ideally buffering some of the turbulence of adolescence. Regarding the next two, connectedness and control, consequences vary and observers differ in what they see. How do you react to this example, written by one of my students?

> I got pregnant when I was sixteen years old, and if it weren't for the support of my parents, I would probably not have my son. And if they hadn't taken care of him, I wouldn't have been able to finish high school or attend college. My parents also helped me overcome the shame that I felt when . . . my aunts, uncles, and especially my grandparents found out that I was pregnant.

> [I., personal communication]

**LaunchPad**
macmillan learning

**Video: Parenting in Adolescence** examines how family structure can help or hinder parent–teen relationships.

My student is grateful that she still lives with her parents, who provide most of the care for her son. However, did teenage motherhood give them too much control, preventing her from establishing her own identity? Indeed, had they unconsciously encouraged her dependence by neither chaperoning nor explaining contraception? I's parents were immigrants from South America, and culture may be a factor. Does her situation illustrate the best or the worst of familism?

A related issue is **parental monitoring**—that is, parental knowledge about each child's whereabouts, activities, and companions. Many studies have shown that when parental knowledge is the result of a warm, supportive relationship, adolescents usually become confident, well-educated adults, avoiding drugs and risky sex. However, if the parents are cold, strict, and punitive, monitoring may lead to rebellion.

Adolescents affect the accuracy and impact of monitoring. A "dynamic interplay between parent and child behaviors" is evident: Teenagers choose what to reveal (Abar et al., 2014, p. 2177). They are more likely to drink alcohol and lie about it if their parents are controlling and cold (Lushin et al., 2017).

Thus, monitoring may be part of a mutual, close interaction (Kerr et al., 2010). But if adolescents resist telling their parents anything, they may develop problems such as aggression against peers, lawbreaking, and drug abuse (Laird et al., 2013). Lack of communication is a symptom more than the cause.

> **parental monitoring** Parents' ongoing awareness of what their children are doing, where, and with whom.

---

### WHAT HAVE YOU LEARNED?

1. Why do parents and adolescents often bicker?

2. How do parent–adolescent relationships change over time?

3. When is parental monitoring a sign of a healthy parent–adolescent relationship?

4. How might a parent–child relationship be too close?

> **peer pressure** Encouragement to conform to one's friends or contemporaries in behavior, dress, and attitude; usually considered a negative force, as when adolescent peers encourage one another to defy adult authority.

## Peer Power

Adolescents rely on peers to help them navigate the physical changes of puberty, the intellectual challenges of high school, and the social changes of leaving childhood. Friendships are important at every stage, but during early adolescence popularity (not just friendship) is coveted. Especially when parents are harsh or neglectful, peer support can be crucial (Birkeland et al., 2014; LaFontana & Cillessen, 2010).

Peers do not negate the need for parental support: Healthy relationships with parents during childhood enhance later peer friendships. However, adolescents need more than parental support.

For example, in one experiment, children and adolescents had to give a speech, with or without their parents. For 9-year-olds, their parents' presence relieved stress, as indicated by cortisol reduction as well as visible signs. For 15-year-olds, however, the parents' presence was no help (Hostinar et al., 2015).

**More Familiar Than Foreign?** Even in cultures with strong and traditional family influence, teenagers choose to be with peers whenever they can. These boys play at Cherai Beach in India.

## Peer Pressure

**Peer pressure** is usually depicted as peers pushing a teenager to do something that adults disapprove, such as using drugs or breaking laws. Peer pressure is

> ● **Observation Quiz** What evidence do you see that traditional norms remain in this culture? (see answer, p. 466) ↑

especially strong in early adolescence, when adults seem clueless about biological and social stresses. However, peer pressure can be more helpful than harmful.

For example, many caregivers fear that social media corrupts innocent youth, but adolescents use social media to strengthen existing friendships (boyd, 2014). Of course, since most people post successes, not failures, some teens feel that they are less attractive, less social, or less competent than their peers, but that danger does not originate with the computer. Teens who have supportive friends offline are likely to benefit from online social interaction (Khan et al., 2016). Much depends on who the adolescent's social contacts are, a variable that is not determined by social media. Friends are chosen.

Peers may be particularly important for adolescents of minority and immigrant groups as they strive to achieve ethnic identity (not confused or foreclosed). The larger society provides stereotypes and prejudice, and parents may be stuck in past experiences, but peers bolster self-esteem as well as advise about romance, homework, and future education.

Given the myelination and maturation of parts of the brain, it is not surprising that the most influential peers are those nearby at the moment. This was found in a study in which all eleventh-graders in several public schools in Los Angeles were offered a free online SAT prep course (worth $200) that they could take if they signed up on a paper distributed by the organizers (Bursztyn & Jensen, 2015).

In this study, students were *not* allowed to talk before deciding whether or not to accept the offer. So they did not know that, although all of the papers had identical, detailed descriptions of the SAT program, one word differed in who would learn of their decision—either no other students or only the students in that particular class.

The two versions were:

*Your decision to sign up for the course will be kept completely private from everyone, <u>except</u> the other students in the room.*

*Your decision to sign up for the course will be kept completely private from everyone, <u>including</u> the other students in the room.*

A marked difference was found if students thought their classmates would learn of their decision: The honors students were *more* likely to sign up and the non-honors students *less* likely. To make sure this was a peer effect, not just divergent motivation and ability between honors and non-honors students, the researchers compared 107 students who took exactly two honors classes and several non-honors classes. Some happened to be sitting in an honors classroom when they signed up for SAT prep; others were not.

When the decisions of the 107 two-honors subgroup were kept totally private, acceptance rates were similar (72 and 79 percent) no matter which class students were in at the moment. But, if students thought their classmates might know their decision, imagined peer pressure affected them. When in an honors class, 97 percent signed up for the SAT program. Of those in a non-honors class, only 54 percent signed up, a 43-percent difference (Bursztyn & Jensen, 2015).

## Selecting Friends

Of course, peers *can* lead one another into trouble. A study of substance misuse and delinquency among twins found that—even controlling for genes and environment—when one twin became a delinquent, the other was more likely to do so (Laursen et al., 2017).

**Everyday Danger** After cousins Alex and Arthur, ages 16 and 20, followed family wishes to shovel snow around their Denver home, they followed their inner risk impulses and jumped from the roof. Not every young man can afford the expense of motocross or hang gliding, but almost every one of them leaps into risks that few 40-year-olds would dare.

**Answer to Observation Quiz** (from p. 465): The girls are only observers, keeping a respectful distance.

**Especially for Parents of a Teenager** Your 13-year-old comes home after a sleepover at a friend's house with a new, weird hairstyle—perhaps cut or colored in a bizarre manner. What do you say and do? (see response, p. 468)

## The Naiveté of Your Author

Adults are sometimes unaware of adolescents' desire for respect from their contemporaries. I did not recognize this at the time with my own children:

- Our oldest daughter wore the same pair of jeans in tenth grade, day after day. She washed them each night by hand, and I put them in the dryer early each morning. My husband was bewildered. "Is this some weird female ritual?" he asked. Years later, she explained that she was afraid that if she wore different pants each day, her classmates would think she cared about her clothes, which would prompt them to criticize her choices. To avoid imagined criticism, she wore only one pair of jeans.

- Our second daughter, at 16, pierced her ears for the third time. I asked if this meant she would do drugs; she laughed

at my foolishness. I later saw that many of her friends had multiple holes in their ear lobes.

- At age 15, our third daughter was diagnosed with cancer. My husband and I weighed opinions from four physicians, each explaining treatment that would minimize the risk of death. She had other priorities: "I don't care what you choose, as long as I keep my hair." (Now her health is good; her hair grew back.)

- Our youngest, in sixth grade, refused to wear her jacket (it was new; she had chosen it), even in midwinter. Years later she told me why—she wanted her classmates to think she was tough.

In retrospect, I am amazed that I was unaware of the power of peers.

---

Collectively, peers provide **deviancy training,** whereby one person shows another how to resist social norms (Dishion et al., 2001; Van Ryzin & Dishion, 2013). However, innocent teens are not corrupted by deviants. Adolescents choose their friends and models—not always wisely, but never randomly.

A developmental progression can be traced: The combination of "problem behavior, school marginalization, and low academic performance" at age 11 leads to gang involvement two years later, deviancy training two years after that, and violent behavior at age 18 or 19 (Dishion et al., 2010, p. 603).

This cascade is not inevitable; adults need to engage marginalized 11-year-olds instead of blaming their friends years later. Teachers are crucial: If young adolescents are mildly disruptive (e.g., they don't follow directions), they are more likely to align with other troublemakers and their behavior worsens if their teachers are not supportive (e.g., sarcastic, rigid, insensitive to student needs) (Shin & Ryan, 2017).

To further understand the impact of peers, examination of two concepts is helpful: *selection* and *facilitation*. Teenagers *select* friends whose values and interests they share, abandoning former friends who follow other paths. Then, friends *facilitate* destructive or constructive behaviors. It is easier to do wrong ("Let's all skip school on Friday") or right ("Let's study together for the chem exam") with friends. Peer facilitation helps adolescents do things they are unlikely to do alone.

Thus, adolescents select and facilitate, choose and are chosen. Happy, energetic, and successful teens have close friends who themselves are high achievers, with no major emotional problems. The opposite also holds: Those who are drug users, sexually active, and alienated from school choose compatible friends.

Research on teenage cigarette smoking finds that selection precedes peer pressure (Kiuru et al., 2010), and another study found that young adolescents tend to select peers who drink alcohol and then start drinking themselves (Osgood et al., 2013). Finally, a third study, of teenage sexual activity, again found that selection

**deviancy training** Destructive peer support in which one person shows another how to rebel against authority or social norms.

**THINK CRITICALLY:** Why is peer pressure thought to be much more sinister than it actually is?

Preappy/Moment/Getty Images

**Social or Solitary?** Adults have criticized the Internet for allowing teenagers to keep friends at a distance. By contrast, sitting around an outdoor fire is romanticized as a bonding experience. Which is more accurate here? Are these two girls about to talk about what they are reading?

⬤ **Response for Parents of a Teenager**
(from p. 466): Remember: Communicate, do not control. Let your child talk about the meaning of the hairstyle. Remind yourself that a hairstyle in itself is harmless. Don't say "What will people think?" or "Are you on drugs?" or anything that might give your child reason to stop communicating.

**LaunchPad**
macmillan learning

**Video: Romantic Relationships in Adolescence** explores teens' attitudes and assumptions about romance and sexuality.

**sexual orientation** A term that refers to whether a person is sexually and romantically attracted to others of the same sex, the opposite sex, or both sexes.

**FIGURE 16.2**

**Many Virgins** For 30 years, the Youth Risk Behavior Survey has asked high school students from all over the United States dozens of confidential questions about their behavior. As you can see, about one-fourth of all students have already had sex by the ninth grade, and more than one-third have not yet had sex by their senior year—a group whose ranks have been increasing in recent years. Other research finds that sexual behaviors are influenced by peers, with some groups all sexually experienced by age 14 and others not until age 18 or older.

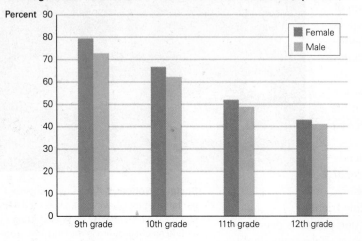

**U.S. High School Students Who Have Not Had Intercourse (by Grade)**

Data from MMWR, June 10, 2016.

was the crucial peer influence on behavior (van de Bongardt et al., 2015). In general, peers provide opportunity, companionship, and encouragement for what young adolescents already might do.

Selection and facilitation are evident lifelong, but the balance between the two shifts. Early adolescence is a time of selection; facilitation is more evident in later adolescence. From ages 20 to 29, selection processes are more influential again, as young adults abandon some high school friends and establish new ones (Samek et al., 2016).

## Romance

Selection is obvious in romance. Adolescents choose and are chosen by romantic partners, and then they influence each other on almost everything—sex, music, work, play, education, food, and so on. Even small things matter: If one gets a new jacket, or tattoo, or sunglasses, the other might too.

### First Love

Teens' first romances typically occur in high school, with girls having a steady partner more often than boys. Exclusive commitment is the ideal, but the fluidity and rapidity of the selection process mitigate against permanency. Cheating, flirting, switching, and disloyalty are rife. Breakups are common, as are unreciprocated crushes. Emotions range from exhilaration to despair, leading to impulsive sex, cruel revenge, and deep depression. Peer support can be vital: Friends help adolescents cope with romantic ups and downs (Mehta & Strough, 2009).

Contrary to adult fears, many teenagers have platonic friends of both sexes (Kreager et al., 2016). They also have romances that do not include intercourse. In the United States in 2015, more than 40 percent of all graduating seniors were virgins. Most of them had dated someone but not had sex with them (see Figure 16.2). Norms vary markedly from group to group, school to school, city to city, and nation to nation.

For instance, twice as many high school students in Philadelphia as in San Francisco say they have had intercourse (52 percent versus 26 percent) (MMWR, June 10, 2016). Obviously, within every city are many subgroups, each with specific norms. For example, girls from religious families who are closely connected to their parents tend to be romantically involved with boys from similar families, and their shared values slow down sexual activity (Kim-Spoon et al., 2012).

### Same-Sex Romances

Some adolescents are attracted to peers of the same sex. **Sexual orientation** refers to the direction of a person's erotic desires. One meaning of *orient* is "to turn toward"; thus, sexual orientation refers to whether a person is romantically attracted to (turned on by) people of the other sex, the same sex, or both sexes. Sexual orientation can be strong, weak, overt, secret, or unconscious.

Obviously, culture and cohort are powerful (Bailey et al., 2016). Some cultures accept youth who are gay, lesbian, bisexual, or transgender (the census in India gives people three choices: male, female, or Hijra [transgender]). Other cultures criminalize LGBTQ youth (38 of the 53 African nations), even killing them (Uganda).

Worldwide, many gay youths date the other sex to hide their orientation; deception puts them at risk for binge drinking, suicidal thoughts, and drug use. Those hazards are less common in cultures where same-sex partnerships are accepted, especially when parents affirm their offspring's sexuality (see Figure 16.3).

At least in the United States, adolescents have similar difficulties and strengths whether they are gay or straight (Saewyc, 2011). However, lesbian, gay, bisexual, and transgender youth have a higher risk of depression and anxiety, for reasons from every level of Bronfenbrenner's ecological-systems approach (Mustanski et al., 2014). [**Developmental Link:** Ecological systems are described in Chapter 1.]

As with gender identity, sexual orientation is surprisingly fluid during adolescence. In one study, 10 percent of sexually active teenagers had had same-sex partners, but many of those 10 percent nonetheless identified as heterosexual (Pathela & Schillinger, 2010). In that study, those most at risk of sexual violence and sexually transmitted infections had partners of both sexes, a correlation found in other studies (e.g., Russell et al., 2014).

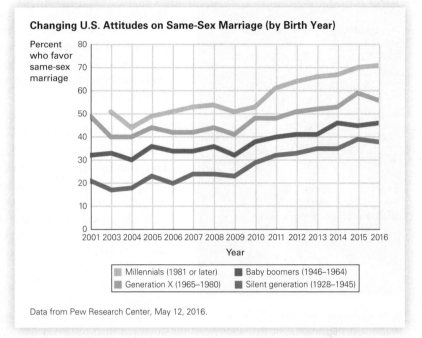

Data from Pew Research Center, May 12, 2016.

**FIGURE 16.3**

**Young and Old** Everyone knows that attitudes about same-sex relationships are changing. Less well known is that cohort differences are greater than the shift over the first decade of the twenty-first century.

## Sex Education

Many adolescents have strong sexual urges but minimal logic about pregnancy and disease, as might be expected from the 10-year interval between maturation of the body and of the brain. Millions of teenagers think they are oversexed, undersexed, or deviant, unaware that thousands, maybe millions, of people are just like them.

As a result, "students seem to waffle their way through sexually relevant encounters driven both by the allure of reward and the fear of negative consequences" (Wagner, 2011, p. 193). They have much to learn. Where do they learn it?

### From the Media

Many adolescents learn about sex from the media. The Internet is a common source, particularly regarding sexually transmitted infections (Simon & Daneback, 2013). Unfortunately, Web sites are often frightening (featuring pictures of diseased organs), mesmerizing (pornography), or misleading (offering false information about contraception). One team of medical professionals is particularly critical of information on pregnancy crisis sites (Bryant-Comstock et al., 2016). If that information is believed, unplanned pregnancies will increase—which may be the subtle goal of those sites.

Media consumption peaks at puberty. The television shows most watched by teenagers include sexual content almost seven times per hour (Steinberg & Monahan, 2011). That content is deceptive: Almost never does a character develop an STI, deal with an unwanted pregnancy, or mention (much less use) a condom.

Adolescents with intense exposure to sex in the media are more often sexually active, but the direction of this correlation is controversial (R. Collins et al., 2011;

**Girls Together** These two girls from Sweden are comfortable lying close to one another. Many boys of this age wouldn't want their photograph taken if they were this close to each other. Around the world, there are cultural and gender norms about what are acceptable expressions of physical affection among friends during adolescence.

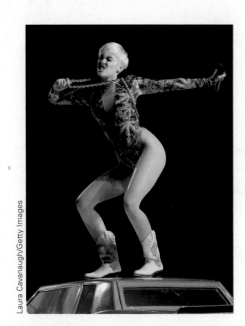

**To Be a Woman** Here, Miley Cyrus performs for thousands of fans in Brooklyn, New York. Does pop culture make it difficult for teenagers of both sexes to reconcile their own sexual impulses with the images of their culture?

**LaunchPad**
macmillan learning

The Data Connections activity **Sexual Behaviors of U.S. High School Students** examines how sexually active teens really are.

Steinberg & Monahan, 2011). The connection is not immediate and direct. Instead, the sexual media may increase an adolescent's focus on external appearance, objectifying the body, which may lead to greater sexual activity (Vandenbosch & Eggermont, 2015). One analysis concludes that "the most important influences on adolescents' sexual behavior may be closer to home than to Hollywood" (Steinberg & Monahan, 2011, p. 575).

## From Parents and Peers

As that quote implies, sex education begins at home. Every study finds that parental communication influences adolescents' behavior, and many programs of sex education explicitly require parental participation (Silk & Romero, 2014). However, embarrassment and ignorance are common on both sides.

Many parents underestimate their own child's sexual activity while fearing that the child's social connections are far too sexual (Elliott, 2012). According to young women aged 15 to 24 chosen to represent the U.S. population, only 25 percent of adolescents receive any sex education from either parent (Vanderberg et al., 2016).

More qualitative studies also report that communication about the sexual aspects of romance are rare between parents and children. Mothers and daughters are more likely than fathers or sons to have detailed conversations, but the emphasis is on pregnancy and diseases, not on pleasure and intimacy.

Ironically, although mothers are worried about their daughters' sexual experiences and knowledge, and although daughters want to learn more about sex from someone they trust, both mothers and daughters consider such information private—and almost never share personal details (Coffelt, 2017).

Especially when parents are silent, forbidding, or vague, adolescent sexual behavior is strongly influenced by peers. Boys learn about sex from other boys (Henry et al., 2012), girls from other girls, with the strongest influence being what peers say they have done, not something abstract (Choukas-Bradley et al., 2014).

Partners also teach each other. However, their lessons are more about pleasure than consequences: Few U.S. adolescent couples decide together *before* they have sex how they will prevent pregnancy and disease, and what they will do if their efforts fail. When adolescents were asked with whom they discussed sexual issues, friends were the most common confidants, then parents, and last of all dating partners. Indeed, only half of them had *ever* discussed anything about sex with their sexual partner (Widman et al., 2014).

## From Educators

Sex education from teachers varies dramatically by nation. The curriculum for middle schools in most European nations includes information about masturbation, same-sex romance, oral and anal sex, and specific uses and failures of various methods of contraception—subjects rarely covered in U.S. classes, even in high school. Rates of teenage pregnancy in most European nations are less than half of those in the United States. Obviously, curriculum is part of the larger culture, and cultural differences regarding sex are vast, but sex education in schools is part of the reason.

Within the United States, the timing and content of sex education vary by state and community. Some high schools provide comprehensive education, free condoms, and medical treatment; others provide nothing. Some schools begin sex education in primary school; others wait until senior year of high school. Because of the HIV/AIDS crisis, most adolescents (95 percent) receive sex education in school (Vanderberg et al., 2016), but content and timing limit effectiveness. Students listen to their peers who have already begun sexual activity, and they consult the Internet more than they listen to teachers of a school curriculum.

One controversy has been whether sexual abstinence should be taught as the only acceptable strategy. It is true, of course, that abstaining from sex (including oral and anal sex) prevents STIs, and that abstinence avoids pregnancy, but longitudinal data on abstinence-only education, four to six years after adolescents were taught, find that it does more harm than good. It does not postpone the age when students become sexually active, but, compared to more comprehensive education, students in abstinence-only classes are more likely to contract STIs (Trenholm et al., 2007).

Some social scientists contend that U.S. educators and parents present morals and facts to adolescents, yet teen behavior is driven by social norms and emotions. Sexual behavior does not spring from the prefrontal cortex: Knowing how and why to use a condom does not guarantee a careful, wise choice when passions run high. Consequently, effective sex education must engage emotions more than logic, and it should include role-playing with other teens, with required parental discussion (Suleiman & Brindis, 2014).

Most educators and developmentalists agree that sex education should begin earlier than it does and should convey more practical information (Hall et al., 2016; Lindberg et al., 2016). However, a vocal minority within state legislatures (almost never including parents of adolescents) blocks evidence-based sex education. One review reports that although sex education is part of the school curriculum in 49 of the 50 states, the emphasis is still on abstinence and male–female marriage (Hall et al., 2016). Only eight states mandate that sex education be medically accurate.

"Smirking or non-smirking?"

**Laugh and Learn** Emotions are as crucial as facts in sex education.

 **Especially for Sex Educators**
Suppose adults in your community never talk to their children about sex or puberty. Is that a mistake? (see response, p. 472)

### WHAT HAVE YOU LEARNED?

1. How does the influence of peers and parents differ for adolescents?
2. Why do many adults misunderstand the role of peer pressure?
3. What is the role of parents, peers, and society in helping an adolescent develop an ethnic identity?
4. How do adolescents choose romantic partners, and what do they do together?
5. How does culture affect sexual orientation?
6. From whom do adolescents usually learn about sex?
7. What does the research say about sex education in schools?

## Sadness and Anger

Adolescence can be a wonderful time. Nonetheless, troubles plague about 20 percent of youths. For instance, one specific survey of more than 10,000 13- to 17-year-olds in the United States found that 23 percent had a psychological disorder in the past month (Kessler et al., 2012). Most disorders are comorbid, with several problems occurring at once, and some are temporary—not too serious and soon outgrown.

We need to differentiate between pathology and normal moodiness, between behavior that is seriously troubled versus merely unsettling. Sometimes sadness and anger become intense, chronic, even deadly.

**LaunchPad** macmillan learning
Download the **DSM-5 Appendix** to learn more about the terminology and classification of various disorders.

**Blot Out the World** Teenagers sometimes despair at their future, as Anthony Ghost-Redfeather did in South Dakota. He tried to kill himself, and, like many boys involved in parasuicide, he is ashamed that he failed.

**Response for Sex Educators** (from p. 471): Yes, but forgive them. Ideally, parents should talk to their children about sex, presenting honest information and listening to the child's concerns. However, many parents find it very difficult to do so because they feel embarrassed and ignorant. You might schedule separate sessions for adults over 30, for emerging adults, and for adolescents.

**major depression** Feelings of hopelessness, lethargy, and worthlessness that last two weeks or more.

**rumination** Repeatedly thinking and talking about past experiences; can contribute to depression.

# Depression

The general emotional trend from early childhood to early adolescence is toward less confidence and higher rates of depression. Then, gradually, self-esteem increases. A dip in self-esteem at puberty is found for children of every ethnicity and gender (Fredricks & Eccles, 2002; Greene & Way, 2005; Kutob et al., 2010; Zeiders et al., 2013b), with notable individual differences.

Universal trends, as well as gender and family effects, are apparent. As in North America, a report from China also finds a dip in self-esteem at seventh grade (when many Chinese adolescents experience puberty) and then a gradual rise. Recent cohorts of Chinese teenagers have lower self-esteem than earlier cohorts. The authors ascribe this to reduced social connections: Many youth have no siblings or cousins, many parents are employed far from their children, and divorce has become more common (Liu & Xin, 2014).

Self-esteem tends to be higher in boys than in girls, in African Americans than in European Americans, who themselves have higher self-esteem than Latino and Asian Americans. All studies find notable variability among people of the same age and gender, and not every study finds the ethnic differences just delineated.

All observers find increasing depression in early adolescence compared to late childhood, and all find continuity within each person. Severe depression soon after puberty's onset may lift with maturation, but it rarely disappears (Huang, 2010).

The cultural norm of familism seems protective. For immigrant Latino youth with strong familism, self-esteem and ethnic pride are higher than for most other groups, and a rise over the years of adolescence is common. When compared to the high rates of depression among European American girls, the Latina rise in self-esteem from about age 16 is particularly notable (Zeiders et al., 2013b). Perhaps familism is the reason: Latinas with high familism become increasingly helpful at home, which makes their parents appreciative and them proud, unlike other U.S. teenage girls.

On the other hand, some families expect high achievement for every adolescent, and then teens are quick to criticize themselves and everyone else when any sign of failure appears (Bleys et al., 2016). The danger is perfectionism: When a teenager realizes that it is impossible to be perfect, depression may result (Damian et al., 2013). Perfectionism is considered one cause of teenage eating disorders (Wade et al., 2016).

## Major Depressive Disorder

Some adolescents sink into **major depression**, a deep sadness and hopelessness that disrupts all normal, regular activities. The causes, including genes and early care, predate adolescence. Then puberty—with its myriad physical and emotional ups and downs—pushes vulnerable children, especially girls, into despair.

The rate of serious depression more than doubles during this time, to an estimated 15 percent, affecting about one in five girls and one in ten boys, for many reasons, biological (hormonal) and cultural. One study found that the short allele of the serotonin transporter promoter gene (5-HTTLPR) increased the rate of depression among girls everywhere but increased depression among boys only if they lived in low-SES communities (Uddin et al., 2010).

It is not surprising that vulnerability to depression is partly genetic, but why does neighborhood affect boys more than girls? Perhaps hormones depress females everywhere, but cultures protect boys unless jobs, successful adult men, and encouragement within their community are scarce.

A cognitive explanation for gender differences in depression focuses on **rumination**—talking about, brooding, and mentally replaying past experiences. Girls ruminate much more than boys, and rumination often leads to depression (Michl et al., 2013). However, when rumination occurs with a close friend after

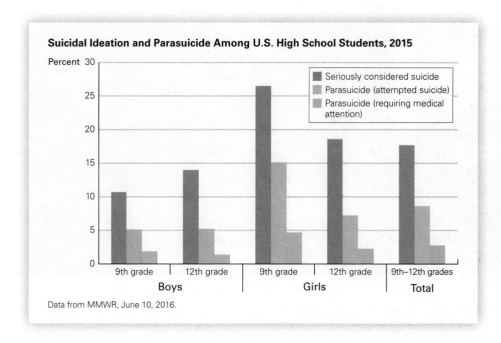

**FIGURE 16.4**

**Sad Thoughts** Completed suicide is rare in adolescence, but serious thoughts about killing oneself are frequent. Depression and parasuicide are more common in girls than in boys, but rates are high even in boys. There are three reasons to suspect that the rates for boys are underestimated: (1) Boys tend to be less aware of their emotions than girls are; (2) boys consider it unmanly to try to kill themselves and to fail; and (3) completed suicide is also higher in males than in females.

⬤⬤ **Observation Quiz** Does thinking seriously about suicide increase or decrease from the beginning to the end of high school? (see answer, p. 474) ⬅

a stressful event, the friend's support may be helpful (Rose et al., 2014). This is thought to be one reason girls are less likely to die by suicide. Differential susceptibility again.

## Suicide

Serious, distressing thoughts about killing oneself (called **suicidal ideation**) are most common at about age 15. More than one-third (40 percent) of U.S. high school girls felt so hopeless that they stopped doing some usual activities for two weeks or more in the previous year (an indication of depression), and nearly one-fourth (23 percent) seriously thought about suicide. The corresponding rates for boys were 20 percent and 12 percent (MMWR, June 10, 2016).

Suicidal ideation can lead to **parasuicide,** also called *attempted suicide* or *failed suicide.* Parasuicide includes any deliberate self-harm that could have been lethal. *Parasuicide* is the best word to use because "failed" suicide implies that to die is to succeed (!). "Attempt" is likewise misleading because, especially in adolescence, the difference between attempt and completion may be luck and treatment, not intent.

As you see in Figure 16.4, parasuicide can be divided according to instances that require medical attention (surgery, pumped stomach, etc.) and those that do not, but any parasuicide is a warning. Among U.S. high school students in 2015, 11.6 percent of the girls and 5.5 percent of the boys attempted suicide in the previous year (MMWR, June 10, 2016). If there is a next time, the person may die.

Thus, parasuicide—even if it seems half-hearted—must be taken seriously. Also serious are thoughts about suicide, even if not accompanied by any action. An ominous sign, particularly for adolescent boys from low-SES families, is a Google search for "how to kill yourself" (Ma-Kellams et al., 2016).

Although suicidal ideation during adolescence is common, completed suicides are not. The U.S. annual rate of completed suicide for people aged 15 to 19 (in school or not) is less than 8 per 100,000, or 0.008 percent, which is only half the rate for adults aged 20 and older (Parks et al., 2014). This is an important statistic to keep in mind whenever someone claims that adolescent suicide is "epidemic." It is not.

**suicidal ideation** Thinking about suicide, usually with some serious emotional and intellectual or cognitive overtones.

**parasuicide** Any potentially lethal action against the self that does not result in death. (Also called *attempted suicide* or *failed suicide.*)

⬤⬤ **Especially for Journalists** You just heard that a teenage cheerleader jumped off a tall building and died. How should you report the story? (see response, p. 474)

**THINK CRITICALLY:** Suicide rates increase with income. Why?

**In Every Nation** Everywhere, older adolescents are most likely to protest against government authority. *(left)* Younger adolescents in Alabama celebrate the 50-year anniversary of the historic Selma-to-Montgomery march across the Pettus Bridge. In that historic movement, most of those beaten and killed were under age 25. *(right)* In the fall of 2014, thousands of students in Hong Kong led pro-democracy protests, which began peacefully but led, days later, to violent confrontations, shown here as they began.

**cluster suicides** Several suicides committed by members of a group within a brief period.

🔵 **Answer to Observation Quiz** (from p. 473): Both. It increases for boys but decreases for girls.

🔵 **Response for Journalists** (from p. 473): Since teenagers seek admiration from their peers, be careful not to glorify the victim's life or death. Facts are needed, as is, perhaps, inclusion of warning signs that were missed or cautions about alcohol abuse. Avoid prominent headlines or anything that might encourage another teenager to do the same thing.

Because they are more emotional and egocentric than logical and analytical, adolescents are particularly affected when they hear about someone's suicide, either through the media or from peers (Niedzwiedz et al., 2014). They are susceptible to **cluster suicides,** which are several suicides within a group over a brief span of time. For that reason, media portrayals of a tragic suicide may inadvertently trigger more deaths.

## Delinquency and Defiance

Like low self-esteem and suicidal ideation, bouts of anger are common in adolescence. In fact, a moody adolescent could be both depressed and delinquent because externalizing and internalizing behavior are closely connected during these years (Loeber & Burke, 2011). This may explain suicide in jail: Teenagers jailed for assault (externalizing) are higher suicide risks (internalizing) than adult prisoners.

Externalizing actions are obvious. Many adolescents slam doors, curse parents, and tell friends exactly how badly other teenagers (or siblings or teachers) have behaved. Some teenagers—particularly boys—"act out" by breaking laws. They steal, damage property, or injure others.

One issue is whether teenage anger is not only common but also necessary for normal development. That is what Anna Freud (Sigmund's daughter, herself a prominent psychoanalyst) thought. She wrote that adolescent resistance to parental authority was "welcome . . . beneficial . . . inevitable." She explained:

> We all know individual children who, as late as the ages of fourteen, fifteen or sixteen, show no such outer evidence of inner unrest. They remain, as they have been during the latency period, "good" children, wrapped up in their family relationships, considerate sons of their mothers, submissive to their fathers, in accord with the atmosphere, idea and ideal of their childhood background. Convenient as this may be, it signifies a delay of their normal development and is, as such, a sign to be taken seriously.
>
> *[A. Freud, 1958/2000, p. 37]*

However, most contemporary psychologists, teachers, and parents are quite happy with well-behaved, considerate teenagers, who often become happy adults. A 30-year longitudinal study found that adults who had never been arrested usually earned degrees, "held high-status jobs, and expressed optimism about their own futures" (Moffitt, 2003, p. 61).

## Breaking the Law

Both the *prevalence* (how widespread) and the *incidence* (how frequent) of criminal actions are higher during adolescence than earlier or later. Arrest statistics in every nation reflect this fact. In the United States, 30 percent of African American males and 22 percent of European American males are arrested at least once before age 18 (Brame et al., 2014).

Many more adolescents have broken the law but have not been caught, or they have been caught but not arrested. Confidential self-reports suggest that most adolescents (male or female) break the law at least once before age 20. Boys are three times as likely as girls to be caught, arrested, and convicted. In general, youth of minority ethnic groups, and low-SES families, are more likely to be arrested.

Regarding gender, boys are more overtly aggressive and rebellious at every age, but this may be nurture, not nature (Loeber et al., 2013). Some studies find that female aggression is typically limited to family and friends, and thus, it is less likely to lead to an arrest. Parents hesitate to call the police to arrest their daughters.

Determining accurate gender, ethnic, and income differences in actual lawbreaking, not just in arrests, is complex. Both self-reports and police responses may be biased. For instance, research in the Netherlands found that one-third of those interrogated by the police later denied any police contact (van Batenburg-Eddes et al., 2012).

On the other hand, adolescents sometimes say that they committed a crime when they did not. Overall, in the United States, about 20 percent of confessions are false, and that is more likely before age 20. There are many reasons that a young person might confess falsely: Brain immaturity makes them less likely to consider long-term consequences, and they may prioritize protecting family members, defending friends, and pleasing adults—including the police (Feld, 2013; Steinberg, 2009).

One dramatic case involved 13-year-old Tyler Edmonds, who said he murdered his brother-in-law. He was convicted and sentenced to life in prison. He then said that he confessed falsely to protect his 26-year-old sister, whom he admired. His conviction was overturned—after he spent four years locked up.

The researchers who cited Tyler's case interviewed 194 boys, aged 14 to 17, all convicted of serious crimes. More than one-third (35 percent) said they had confessed falsely to a crime (not necessarily the one for which they were serving time). False confessions were more likely after two hours of intense interrogation—the adolescents wanted it to stop; acting on impulse, they said they were guilty (Malloy et al., 2014).

Many researchers distinguish between two kinds of teenage lawbreakers (Jolliffe et al., 2017; Monahan et al., 2013), as first proposed by Terri Moffitt (2001, 2003). Both types are usually arrested for the first time in adolescence, for similar crimes, but their future diverges.

1. Most juvenile delinquents are **adolescence-limited offenders,** whose criminal activity stops by age 21. They break the law with their friends, facilitated by their chosen antisocial peers.
2. Some delinquents are **life-course-persistent offenders,** who become career criminals. Their lawbreaking is more often done alone than as part of a gang, and the cause is neurological impairment (either inborn or caused by early experiences). Symptoms include not only childhood defiance but also early disabilities with language and learning.

**Change Their Uniforms** Juvenile offenders wear prison orange—easy to spot should they try to escape—as they listen to an ex-offender, Tony Allen, who grew up on the rough streets of Chicago. When this photo was taken, he earned 5 million dollars a years as star basketball player for the Memphis Grizzlies. If an adolescent-limited offender is imprisoned, talks like this have little effect unless at least two of these four are also present: a supportive family, a dedicated teacher, a strong religious community, and a circle of friends and neighbors who encourage another path.

> **THINK CRITICALLY:** If parents and society became more appreciative of this stage of life, rather than fearful of it, might that lead to healthier and more peaceful teenagers?

**adolescence-limited offender**
A person whose criminal activity stops by age 21.

**life-course-persistent offender**
A person whose criminal activity typically begins in early adolescence and continues throughout life; a career criminal.

During adolescence, the criminal records of both types may be similar. However, if adolescence-limited delinquents can be protected from various snares (such as quitting school, entering prison, drug addiction), they outgrow their criminal behavior. This is confirmed by other research: Few delinquent youths who are not imprisoned continue to be criminals in early adulthood (Monahan et al., 2009).

## Causes of Delinquency

The best way to reduce adolescent crime is to notice early behavior that predicts lawbreaking and to change patterns before puberty. Strong and protective social relationships, emotional regulation, and moral values from childhood keep many teenagers from jail. In early adolescence, three signs predict delinquency:

1. *Stubbornness* can lead to defiance, which can lead to running away. Runaways are often victims as well as criminals (e.g., falling in with human traffickers and petty thieves).
2. *Shoplifting* can lead to arson and burglary. Things become more important than people.
3. *Bullying* can lead to assault, rape, and murder.

Each of these pathways demands a different response. Stubbornness responds to social support—the rebel who feels understood, not punished, will gradually become less impulsive and irrational. The second pathway requires strengthening human relationships and moral education. Those who exhibit the third behavior present the most serious problem. Bullying should have been stopped in childhood, as Chapters 10 and 13 explained, and these adolescents need to develop other ways to connect with people.

In all cases, early warning signs are present, and intervention is more effective earlier than later (Loeber & Burke, 2011). Childhood family relationships are crucial, particularly for girls (Rhoades et al., 2016).

Adolescent crime in the United States and many other nations has decreased in the past 20 years. Only half as many juveniles under age 18 are currently arrested for murder as compared to 1990. No explanation for this decline is accepted by all scholars. Among the possibilities:

- fewer high school dropouts (more education means less crime);
- wiser judges (using more community service than prison);
- better policing (arrests for misdemeanors are up, which may warn parents);
- smaller families (parents are more attentive to each of 2 children than each of 12);
- better contraception and safer abortion (wanted children are less likely to become criminals);
- stricter drug laws (binge drinking and crack use increase crime);
- more immigrants (who are more law-abiding);
- less lead in the blood (early lead poisoning reduces brain functioning);
- and more.

Nonetheless, adolescents remain more likely to break the law than adults: The arrest rate for 15- to 17-year-olds is twice that for those over 18. The disproportion is true for almost every crime except fraud, forgery, and embezzlement, which fewer adolescents commit (FBI, 2015).

JASON LEE/Reuters

**A Man Now** This boy in Tibet is proud to be a smoker—in many Asian nations, smoking is considered manly.

# Drug Use and Abuse

Hormonal surges, the brain's reward centers, and cognitive immaturity combine to make adolescents particularly attracted to the sensations produced by psychoactive drugs. But their immature bodies and brains make drug use especially hazardous.

## Variations in Drug Use

Most teenagers try *psychoactive drugs*, that is, drugs that activate the brain. Cigarettes, alcohol, and many prescription medicines are as addictive and damaging as illegal drugs such as cocaine and heroin.

### Age Trends

For many developmental reasons, adolescence is a sensitive time for experimentation, daily use, and eventual addiction to psychoactive drugs (Schulenberg et al., 2014). Both prevalence and incidence increase from about ages 10 to 25 and then decrease when adult responsibilities and experiences make drugs less attractive. Most worrisome is drinking alcohol and smoking cigarettes before age 15, because early use escalates. That makes depression, sexual abuse, bullying, and later addiction more likely (Mennis & Mason, 2012; Merikangas & McClair, 2012).

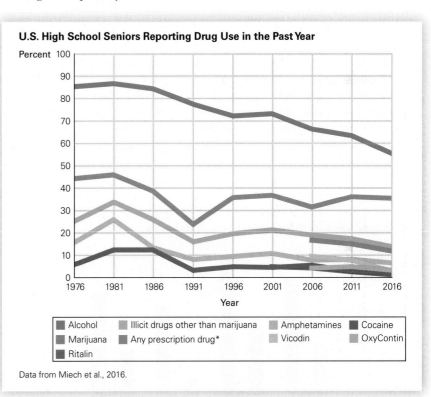

**U.S. High School Seniors Reporting Drug Use in the Past Year**

Data from Miech et al., 2016.

Although drug use increases every year from puberty until adulthood, one drug follows another pattern—*inhalants* (fumes from aerosol containers, glue, cleaning fluid, etc.). Sadly, the youngest adolescents are most likely to try inhalants, because inhalants are easy to get (hardware stores, drug stores, and supermarkets stock them) and cognitive immaturity means that few pubescent children have a realistic understanding of the risks—brain damage and even death (Nguyen et al., 2016).

Cohort differences are evident, even over a few years. Use of most drugs has decreased in the United States since 1976 (see Figure 16.5), with the most recent decreases in synthetic narcotics and prescription drugs (Miech et al., 2016). Data from the past few years show that cigarette smoking in down, but vaping is escalating. As described in Opposing Perspectives (p. 478), this bodes ill for later cigarette use (Park et al., 2016).

**FIGURE 16.5**

**Rise and Fall** By asking the same questions year after year, the Monitoring the Future study shows notable historical effects. It is encouraging that something in society, not in the adolescent, makes drug use increase and decrease and that the most recent data show a continued decline in the drug most commonly abused—alcohol.

*\*Includes use of amphetamines, sedatives (barbiturates), narcotics other than heroin, or tranquilizers—without a doctor's prescription.*

# E-Cigarettes: Path to Addiction or Healthy Choice?

Controversial is the use of *e-cigarettes*, which adolescents increasingly use. If e-cigs help adult smokers quit, then they save lives. Smokers with asthma, heart disease, or lung cancer who find it impossible to stop smoking cigarettes may switch to vaping with notable health benefits (Burstyn, 2014; Franck et al., 2014; Hajek et al., 2014).

However, will adolescents who try e-cigarettes become addicted to nicotine? Will vaping make them more likely to use other drugs later on? E-cigs themselves are not harmless. They deliver fewer harmful chemicals than combustible cigarettes (Goniewicz et al., 2017), but one by-product is benzene, a known carcinogen (Pankow et al., 2017). If the choice is between combustible cigarettes and e-cigarettes, then e-cigs are better; but if the choice is between no drugs and using e-cigarettes, e-cigs are far worse.

A victory of North American public health has been a marked reduction in smoking of regular cigarettes. Not only are there only half as many adult smokers as there were in 1950, there are numerous public places where smoking in forbidden, and many people now forbid anyone to smoke in their homes. In the United States, such homes are the majority (87 percent), an increase from almost zero in 1970 and 43 percent in 1992. Most

of those homes have no smoking residents, but cigarettes are banned in 46 percent of the homes where a smoker lives (Homa et al., 2015).

The best news of all is that far fewer teens begin smoking. Adolescents once thought smoking was cool; now they know it is harmful to their health, and ads remind them of immediate problems, such as bad breath (see Figure 16.6). Instead of being seen as cool, smokers may be seen as smelly.

That is a reason to celebrate. But will e-cigarettes make smoking more acceptable? Will adolescent smoking increase again? Nicotine is addictive, no matter how it is delivered.

E-cigs are illegal for people under age 18, but they are marketed in flavors like bubble gum, can be placed for a fee in Hollywood movies, and are permitted in many places where cigarettes are banned. If the image of smoking changes from a "cancer stick" to a "glamour accessory," will public health progress stop?

The evidence confirms that teenagers who try e-cigs are likely to smoke tobacco later (Miech et al., 2017b). Is that because e-cigs open a door or because those adolescents would be drug users no matter what, now starting with e-cigs but destined to do other drugs?

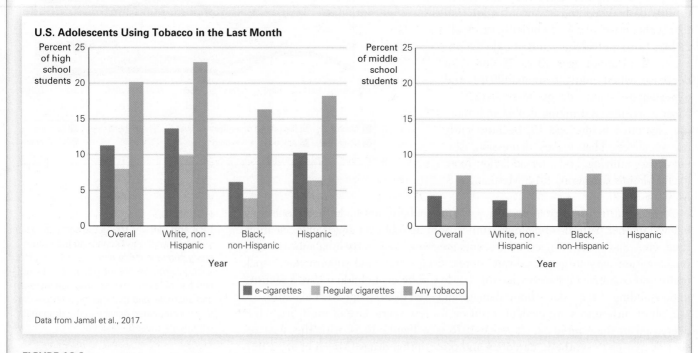

**U.S. Adolescents Using Tobacco in the Last Month**

Data from Jamal et al., 2017.

**FIGURE 16.6**

**Getting Better** The fact that more than one in five high school students (that's 3 million people) use tobacco—even though purchase of any kind is illegal—in the past month, is troubling. That means that more that 3 million students are at risk for addiction and poor health. The surprise (not shown) is that all these rates are lower than a year earlier. Is that because laws are stricter or teenagers are getting wiser?

The argument from distributors of e-cigarettes is that their products are healthier than cigarettes, that people should make their own choices, and that the fear of adolescent vaping is exaggerated—part of the irrational fear that everything teenagers do is trouble.

Teenagers themselves, by the millions, use e-cigarettes, with use skyrocketing in many nations and restricted in about half of them. Adults with chronic diseases, especially former smokers with chronic obstructive pulmonary disease, often use e-cigarettes (Kruse et al., 2017). Public health workers advise against them. As with all opposing perspectives, attitudes depend on who is judging.

**Choose Your Flavor** Mint- and chocolate-flavored e-cigarettes are particularly popular among adolescents.

Longitudinal data show that availability does not have much impact on use: Most high school students say that they could easily get alcohol, cigarettes, and marijuana. Most U.S. states prohibit purchase of e-cigarettes by those under age 18, but younger teens can buy them from 116 Internet vendors with no problem (Nikitin et al., 2016). Availability does not affect use, but perception of risks does, and that varies markedly from cohort to cohort (Miech et al., 2016).

## Harm from Drugs

Many researchers find that drug use before maturity is particularly likely to harm body and brain growth. However, adolescents typically deny that they ever could become addicted. Few adolescents notice when they or their friends move past *use* (experimenting) to *abuse* (experiencing harm) and then to *addiction* (needing the drug to avoid feeling nervous, anxious, sick, or in pain).

Each drug is harmful in a particular way. An obvious negative effect of *tobacco* is that it impairs digestion and nutrition, slowing down growth. This is true not only for cigarettes but also for bidis, cigars, pipes, chewing tobacco, and probably e-cigarettes. Since internal organs continue to mature after the height spurt, drug-using teenagers who appear to be fully grown may damage their developing hearts, lungs, brains, and reproductive systems.

*Alcohol* is the most frequently abused drug in North America. Heavy drinking impairs memory and self-control by damaging the hippocampus and the prefrontal cortex, perhaps distorting the reward circuits of the brain lifelong (Guerri & Pascual, 2010). Adolescence is a particularly sensitive period, because the regions of the brain that are connected to pleasure are more strongly affected by alcohol during adolescence than at later ages. That makes teenagers less conscious of the "intoxicating, aversive, and sedative effects" of alcohol (Spear, 2013, p. 155).

*Marijuana* seems harmless to many people (especially teenagers), partly because users seem more relaxed than inebriated. Yet adolescents who regularly smoke marijuana are more likely to drop out of school, become teenage parents, be depressed, and later be unemployed. As Chapter 1 explains, some of this may be correlation, not causation, but a longitudinal study that used neurological evidence showed decreasing brain connections as well as lower intelligence among adolescents who

**Especially for Police Officers** You see some 15-year-olds drinking beer in a local park when they belong in school. What do you do? (see response, p. 481)

**Especially for Parents Who Drink Socially** You have heard that parents should allow their children to drink at home, to teach them to drink responsibly and not get drunk elsewhere. Is that wise? (see response, p. 480)

**Relaxing on Marijuana?** Synthetic marijuana ("K-2," or "Spice") can be a deadly drug, evident in this unconscious young man on a Harlem sidewalk. Since secret chemicals are mixed and added in manufacturing, neither laws nor hospitals can keep up with new toxic substances.

**◐ Response for Parents Who Drink Socially** (from p. 479): No. Alcohol is particularly harmful for young brains. It is best to drink only when your children are not around. Children who are encouraged to drink with their parents are more likely to drink when no adults are present. It is true that adolescents are rebellious, and they may drink even if you forbid it. But if you allow alcohol, they might rebel with other drugs.

used marijuana habitually, compared to a control group who did not (Camchong et al., 2017).

Canada will legalize marijuana in 2018, with health researchers wishing there were more solid evidence but hoping that, once the brain is mature, benefits outweighed risks (Lake & Kerr, 2017). Marijuana will remain illegal in Canada for those under 18, although some doctors wish 21 were the cutoff (Rankin, 2017).

One problem with age restrictions is that most adolescents covet the drugs used by slightly older youth. Many young adults who can legally buy drugs do so for younger siblings and classmates, supposedly being kind. However, when New Zealand lowered the age for legal purchase of alcohol from 20 to 18, that nation experienced an uptick in hospital admissions for intoxication, car crashes, and injuries from assault, not only for 18- to 19-year-olds but also for 16- to 17-year-olds (Kypri et al., 2006, 2014).

As noted, some people suggest that the connection between drug use (including cigarettes, alcohol, marijuana, and illegal drugs) and later low achievement, depression, and poor health are correlations, not causes. Might stress lead to drug use, and then might intoxication reduce anxiety rather than make problems worse? Such self-medication is a plausible hypothesis, but it has been disproven.

Research suggests that drug use may make the user temporarily forget unpleasant emotions, but it *causes* more problems than it solves, often *preceding* anxiety disorders, depression, and rebellion (Maslowsky et al., 2014). Further, adolescents who use alcohol, cigarettes, and marijuana recreationally are likely to abuse these and other drugs after age 20 (Moss et al., 2014).

Longitudinal studies of twins (thus controlling for genes and early child care) confirm that many problems predate drug use: Genes and neighborhoods are, in part, the cause of addiction and rebellion. However, this research finds that although drugs do not cause all later problems, they do not help. Over the long term, the hypothesis that drugs relieve stress is false (Korhonen et al., 2012; Lynskey et al., 2012; Verweij et al., 2016).

## Preventing Drug Abuse: What Works?

Evidence in the United States finds that adolescent drug use, legal and illegal, bought on the street and prescribed by doctors, has decreased in recent years. (E-cigs are an exception.) The most valid reporting refers to alcohol, because it is a legal substance that adolescents readily admit to consuming. When asked if they drank alcohol in the past month, half said yes in 1991 but only one-third said yes in 2015 (Esser et al., 2017).

However, the same report found that binge drinking is still prevalent—and that binge drinkers usually found an older person to buy alcohol for them. That is dangerous. In the United States, an estimated 860 people under age 21 die every year by drinking too much (Esser et al., 2017). Peer pressure, and inexperience, probably leads them to keep drinking long after they should stop.

The Monitoring the Future study found that in 2016:

**Choose Your Weed** No latte or beer offered here, although this looks like the place where previous generations bought drinks. Instead, at A Greener Today in Seattle, Washington, customers ask for 1 of 20 possibilities—all marijuana.

- 16 percent of high school seniors report having had five drinks in a row in the past two weeks.
- 5 percent smoked cigarettes every day for the past month.
- 6 percent smoked marijuana every day.

[Miech et al., 2017b]

These figures suggest that addiction is the next step for these high school students. They are not the only ones in trouble. This survey did not include students who were absent or truant or had dropped out, yet they have higher rates of daily drug use and addiction. Compared to three decades ago, teenagers are wiser—or adults have made drug use more difficult—but the problem is still with us. Is further reduction possible?

Developmentalists are concerned not only about e-cigarettes but also about misuse of addictive prescription drugs—both stimulants (such as Ritalin and Adderall) and opioids (such as OxyContin) (Zosel et al., 2013). Should laws be more restrictive, or does that itself encourage drug use?

Remember that most adolescents think they are exceptions, sometimes feeling invincible, sometimes fearing social disapproval, but almost never realistic about their own potential addiction. Instead, some get a thrill from breaking the law, and some use stimulants to improve cognition or other drugs to relieve stress. They do not see that over time stress and depression increase, and achievement decreases (Bagot, 2017; McCabe et al., 2017).

Every psychoactive drug excites the limbic system and interferes with the prefrontal cortex. Because of these neurological reactions, drug users are more emotional (varying from euphoria to terror, from paranoia to rage) than they would otherwise be. They are also less reflective. Moodiness and impulsivity are characteristic of adolescents, and drugs make that worse. Every hazard—including car crashes, unsafe sex, and suicide—is more common among teens who have taken a psychoactive drug.

With harmful drugs, as with many other aspects of life, people of each generation prefer to learn things for themselves. A common phenomenon is **generational forgetting,** that each new cohort forgets what the previous cohort learned (Chassin et al., 2014; Johnston et al., 2012). Mistrust of the older generation, added to loyalty to one's peers, leads not only to generational forgetting but also to a backlash. When adults forbid something, that is a reason to try it, especially if adults exaggerate the dangers. If a friend passes out from drug use, adolescents may be slow to get medical help—a dangerous hesitancy.

Some antidrug curricula and advertisements make drugs seem exciting. Antismoking announcements produced by cigarette companies (such as a clean-cut young person advising viewers to think before they smoke) actually increase use (Strasburger et al., 2009).

This does not mean that trying to halt early drug use is hopeless. Massive ad campaigns by public health advocates in Florida and California cut adolescent smoking almost in half, in part because the publicity appealed to the young. Teenagers respond to graphic images. In one example:

> A young man walks up to a convenience store counter and asks for a pack of cigarettes. He throws some money on the counter, but the cashier says "that's not enough." So the young man pulls out a pair of pliers, wrenches out one of his teeth, and hands it over. . . . A voiceover asks: "What's a pack of smokes cost? Your teeth."
>
> [Krisberg, 2014]

Parental example and social changes also make a difference. Throughout the United States, higher prices, targeted warnings, and better law enforcement have led to a marked decline in smoking among younger adolescents. Looking internationally, laws have an effect. In Canada, cigarette advertising is outlawed, and cigarette packs have lurid pictures

**Response for Police Officers** (from p. 479): Avoid both extremes: Don't let them think this situation is either harmless or serious. You might take them to the police station and call their parents. These adolescents are probably not life-course-persistent offenders; jailing them or grouping them with other lawbreakers might encourage more crime.

**THINK CRITICALLY:** Might the fear of adolescent drug use be foolish, if most adolescents use drugs whether or not they are forbidden?

**generational forgetting** The idea that each new generation forgets what the previous generation learned. As used here, the term refers to knowledge about the harm drugs can do.

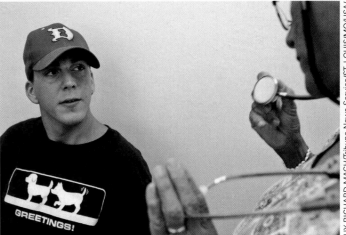

**Serious Treatment** A nurse checks Steve Duffer's blood pressure after a dose of Naltrexone, a drug with many side effects that combats severe addiction, in this case addiction to heroin. Steve is now 24.

HUY RICHARD MACH/Tribune News Service/ST. LOUIS/MO/USA/ Newscom

# Highlights in the Journey to Adulthood

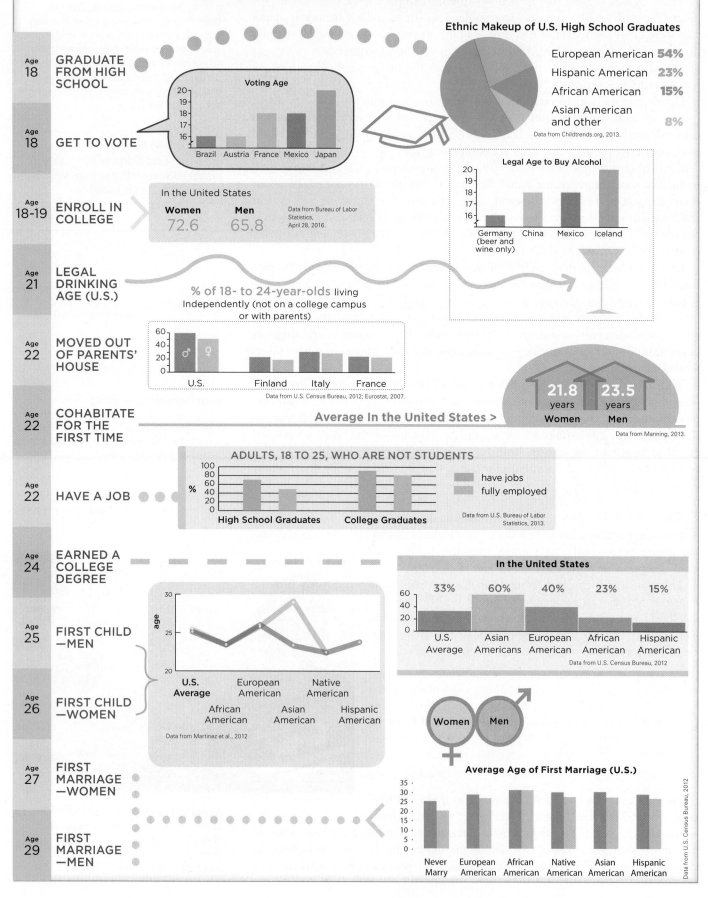

**Age 18** GRADUATE FROM HIGH SCHOOL

**Age 18** GET TO VOTE

**Voting Age**

| Brazil | Austria | France | Mexico | Japan |

**Ethnic Makeup of U.S. High School Graduates**

European American **54%**
Hispanic American **23%**
African American **15%**
Asian American and other **8%**

Data from Childtrends.org, 2013.

**Age 18-19** ENROLL IN COLLEGE

In the United States

**Women** 72.6   **Men** 65.8

Data from Bureau of Labor Statistics, April 28, 2016.

**Legal Age to Buy Alcohol**

Germany (beer and wine only)   China   Mexico   Iceland

**Age 21** LEGAL DRINKING AGE (U.S.)

% of 18- to 24-year-olds living Independently (not on a college campus or with parents)

**Age 22** MOVED OUT OF PARENTS' HOUSE

♂ ♀

U.S.   Finland   Italy   France

Data from U.S. Census Bureau, 2012; Eurostat, 2007.

**Age 22** COHABITATE FOR THE FIRST TIME

Average In the United States >

21.8 years **Women**   23.5 years **Men**

Data from Manning, 2013.

**ADULTS, 18 TO 25, WHO ARE NOT STUDENTS**

High School Graduates   College Graduates

have jobs
fully employed

Data from U.S. Bureau of Labor Statistics, 2013.

**Age 22** HAVE A JOB

**Age 24** EARNED A COLLEGE DEGREE

**In the United States**

| 33% | 60% | 40% | 23% | 15% |

U.S. Average   Asian Americans   European American   African American   Hispanic American

Data from U.S. Census Bureau, 2012

**Age 25** FIRST CHILD —MEN

age

U.S. Average   European American   Native American
African American   Asian American   Hispanic American

Data from Martinez et al., 2012

**Age 26** FIRST CHILD —WOMEN

Women   Men

**Age 27** FIRST MARRIAGE —WOMEN

**Average Age of First Marriage (U.S.)**

Never Marry   European American   African American   Native American   Asian American   Hispanic American

**Age 29** FIRST MARRIAGE —MEN

Data from U.S. Census Bureau, 2012

of diseased lungs, rotting teeth, and so on; fewer Canadian 15- to 19-year-olds smoke. The effect on teenagers when Canada legalizes marijuana for adults is not yet known.

In the past three chapters, we see that the universal biological processes do not lead to universal psychosocial problems. Biology does not change, but context matters. Rates of teenage births and abortions are declining sharply (Chapter 14), more students are graduating from high school (Chapter 15), and fewer teens drink or smoke (this chapter). Yet each of these chapters shows that much more needs to be done.

As explained at the beginning of these three chapters, adolescence starts with puberty; that much is universal. But what happens next depends on parents, peers, schools, communities, and cultures. In other words, the future of adolescents depends, in part, on you.

---

### WHAT HAVE YOU LEARNED?

**1.** Why are psychoactive drugs particularly attractive in adolescence?

**2.** Why are psychoactive drugs particularly destructive in adolescence?

**3.** What specific harm occurs with tobacco products?

**4.** How has adolescent drug use changed in the past decade?

**5.** What methods to reduce adolescent drug use are successful?

---

## SUMMARY

### Identity

**1.** Adolescence is a time for self-discovery. According to Erikson, adolescents seek their own identity, sorting through the traditions and values of their families and cultures.

**2.** Many young adolescents foreclose on their options without exploring possibilities, and many experience role confusion. Older adolescents might seek a moratorium. Identity achievement takes longer for contemporary adolescents than it did a half-century ago when Erikson first described it.

**3.** Identity achievement occurs in many domains, including religion, politics, vocation, and gender. Each of these remains important over the life span, but timing, contexts, and often terminology have changed since Erikson and Marcia first described them. Achieving vocational and gender identity is particularly difficult.

### Relationships with Adults

**4.** Parents continue to influence their growing children, despite bickering over minor issues. Ideally, communication and warmth remain high within the family, while parental control decreases and adolescents develop autonomy.

**5.** There are cultural differences in the timing of conflicts and in the particulars of parental monitoring. Too much parental control is harmful, as is neglect. Parents need to find a balance between granting freedom and providing guidance.

### Peer Power

**6.** Peers and peer pressure can be beneficial or harmful, depending on who the peers are. Adolescents select their friends, includ-

ing friends of the other sex, who then facilitate constructive and/or destructive behavior. Peer approval is particularly potent during adolescence.

**7.** Adolescents experience diverse sexual needs and may be involved in short-term or long-term romances, depending in part on their peer group. Contemporary teenagers are less likely to have intercourse than was true a decade ago.

**8.** Some youths are sexually attracted to people of the same sex. Social acceptance of same-sex relationships is increasing, but in some communities and nations, gay, lesbian, and transgender youth are bullied, rejected, or worse.

**9.** Many adolescents learn about sex from peers and the media—sources that do not provide a balanced picture. Ideally, parents are the best teachers about sex, but many are silent and naive.

**10.** Education about sex varies from nation to nation, with some nations providing comprehensive education beginning in the early grades. In the United States, most parents want schools to teach adolescents about sex, although accurate and effective sex education is prevented by many legislators. Abstinence-only education does not affect the age at which adolescents become sexually active, and it may increase teenage pregnancy and STIs.

### Sadness and Anger

**11.** Almost all adolescents become self-conscious and self-critical. A few become chronically sad and depressed. Many adolescents (especially girls) think about suicide, and some attempt it. Few adolescents actually kill themselves; most who do so are boys.

**12.** At least in Western societies, almost all adolescents become more independent and angry as part of growing up, although most still respect their parents. Breaking the law as well as bursts of anger are common; boys are more likely to be arrested for violent offenses than are girls.

**13.** Adolescence-limited delinquents should be prevented from hurting themselves or others; their criminal behavior disappears with maturation. Life-course-persistent offenders may continue to be so in adulthood. Early intervention—before the first arrest—is crucial.

### Drug Use and Abuse

**14.** Most adolescents experiment with drugs, especially alcohol and tobacco, although such substances impair growth of the body and the brain. Age, gender, community, and parental factors are influential.

**15.** Solid longitudinal data on use of e-cigarettes and marijuana during adolescence are not yet available, but many developmentalists are concerned that these substances may affect learning and habits.

**16.** All psychoactive drugs are particularly harmful in adolescence, as they affect the developing brain and threaten the already shaky impulse control. However, adults who exaggerate harm or who abuse drugs themselves are unlikely to prevent teen drug use.

**17.** Prevention and moderation of adolescent drug use and abuse are possible. Antidrug programs and messages need to be carefully designed to avoid a backlash or generational forgetting. Price, perception, and parents have an effect.

## KEY TERMS

identity versus role confusion (p. 458)
identity achievement (p. 458)
role confusion (p. 458)
foreclosure (p. 458)
moratorium (p. 458)

gender identity (p. 460)
familism (p. 464)
parental monitoring (p. 465)
peer pressure (p. 465)
deviancy training (p. 467)
sexual orientation (p. 468)

major depression (p. 472)
rumination (p. 472)
suicidal ideation (p. 473)
parasuicide (p. 473)
cluster suicides (p. 474)

adolescence-limited offender (p. 475)
life-course-persistent offender (p. 475)
generational forgetting (p. 481)

## APPLICATIONS

**1.** Interview people who spent their teenage years in U.S. schools of various sizes, or in another nation, about the peer relationships in their high schools. Describe and discuss any differences you find.

**2.** Locate a news article about a teenager who committed suicide. Were there warning signs that were ignored? Does the report inadvertently encourage cluster suicides?

**3.** Research suggests that most adolescents have broken the law but that few have been arrested or incarcerated. Ask 10 of your fellow students whether they broke the law when they were under 18

and, if so, how often, in what ways, and with what consequences. (Assure them of confidentiality; remind them that drug use, breaking curfew, and skipping school were illegal.) Do you see any evidence of gender or ethnic differences in lawbreaking or police responses? What additional research needs to be done?

**4.** Cultures vary in expectations for drug use. Interview three people from different backgrounds (not necessarily from different nations; each SES, generation, or religion has different standards) about their culture's drug use, including reasons for what is allowed and when. (Legal drugs should be included in your study.)

# The Developing Person So Far:
## Adolescence

## BIOSOCIAL

**Puberty Begins** Puberty begins adolescence, as the child's body becomes much bigger (the growth spurt) and male/female differentiation occurs, including menarche and spermarche. Hormones of the HPA and HPG axes influence growth and sexual maturation as well as body rhythms, which change so that adolescents are more wakeful at night. The normal range for the beginning of puberty is age 8 to age 14.

**Growth and Nutrition** The limbic system typically matures faster than the prefrontal cortex. As a result, adolescents are more likely to act impulsively. Many teens do not get enough iron or calcium because they often consume fast food and soda instead of family meals and milk. Some suffer from serious eating disorders such as anorexia, bulimia, and bingeing.

**Sexual Maturation** Both sexes experience increased hormones, new reproductive potential, and primary as well as secondary sexual characteristics. Every adolescent is more interested in sexual activities, with possible hazards of sexual infections and sexual abuse.

## COGNITIVE

**Logic and Self** Adolescents think differently than younger children do. Piaget stressed the adolescent's new analytical ability—using abstract logic (part of formal operational thought).

**Two Modes of Thinking** Adolescents use dual processing—both intuitive reasoning and analytic thought. Intuitive thinking is experiential, quick, and impulsive, unlike formal operational thought; intuitive processes sometimes crowd out analytical ones. Technology has both positive and negative aspects, including reduced isolation, access to information, but also cyberbullying and sexting.

**Secondary Education** Secondary education promotes individual and national success. International tests find marked differences in achievement. In the United States, high-stakes tests and more rigorous course requirements before high school graduation are intended to improve standards. Graduation rates are rising.

## PSYCHOSOCIAL

**Identity** Adolescent development includes a search for identity, as Erikson described. Adolescents combine childhood experiences, cultural values, and their unique aspirations in forming an identity. The contexts of identity are religion, politics/ethnicity, vocation, and gender.

**Adults and Peers** Families continue to be influential, despite rebellion and bickering. Adolescents seek autonomy but also rely on parental support. Parental guidance and ongoing communication promote adolescents' psychosocial health. The influence of friends and peers of both sexes is increasingly powerful. Parents are the best teachers when it comes to sex, but many adolescents get their information primarily from peers and the media.

**Sadness and Anger** Depression and rebellion may become serious problems. Thinking about suicide is common, but actual suicide is not. Many adolescents break the law, but delinquency may be limited to adolescent years. Some, however, are life-course-persistent offenders.

**Drug Use and Abuse** Adolescents are attracted to psychoactive drugs, yet such drugs are particularly harmful during the teen years. Rates of substance use are decreasing, except for a dramatic increase in e-cigarettes (vaping).

# Epilogue:
## Emerging Adulthood

## What Will You Know?

1. Is risk-taking an asset or a liability?
2. Does college make you think?
3. Is cohabiation a good alternative to marriage?

This epilogue is both a review and a preview. It follows the same sequence as earlier chapters at each stage—body, mind, and social world—always noting the impact of genetic, prenatal, and early experiences. You will see many familiar themes—family, friends, culture, context, and cohort. **Emerging adulthood** is the time after adolescence when people continue to learn and explore, postponing marriage, parenthood, and career. They are at the edge of the ocean, preparing to swim.

I followed this path myself. Between ages 18 and 25, I attended four colleges or universities, changed majors three times, rejected marriage offers from four young men, lived in ten different places (four states, two nations), and started several jobs—none lasting more than 18 months.

Following that period of rapid change, I stayed put. Now decades later, I have had just one husband, one neighborhood, one career, and since age 30, one main employer. The restlessness of my early 20s is now typical worldwide (Padilla-Walker & Nelson, 2017).

## Biosocial Development

Biologically, the years from ages 18 to 25 are prime time for hard physical work and safe reproduction. However, the ability of young adults to carry rocks, plow fields, or haul water is no longer admired, nor is their fertility. If a contemporary young couple had a baby every year, their neighbors would be appalled, not approving.

### Strong and Active Bodies

Maximum height is usually reached by age 16 for girls and age 18 for boys. Maximum strength soon follows. During emerging adulthood, muscles grow, bones strengthen, and shape changes, with males gaining more arm muscle and females more fat (Whitbourne & Whitbourne, 2014).

Every body system—including the digestive, respiratory, circulatory, muscular, and sexual-reproductive systems—functions optimally. Serious diseases are not yet apparent, and some childhood ailments are outgrown.

* **Biosocial Development**
  Strong and Active Bodies
  Taking Risks

* **Cognitive Development**
  Countering Stereotypes
  Cognitive Growth and Higher Education

* **Psychosocial Development**
  Identity Achievement
  Intimacy Needs
  Concluding Questions and Hopes

**emerging adulthood** The period of life between the ages of 18 and 25. Emerging adulthood is now widely thought of as a distinct developmental stage.

**What a Body Can Do** Here, at age 27, Tobin Heath leaps to celebrate her goal at the soccer World Cup final in Vancouver following seven years of star performances. All young adults can have moments when their bodies and minds crescendo to new heights.

FRANCK FIFE/AFP/Getty Images

## Keep Moving

Neighborhoods, genes, and health habits from childhood have an impact. Laboratory analysis of blood, urine, and body fat finds that some people experience aging three times faster than others, with about half of the difference between fast and slow aging already evident by age 26 (Belsky et al., 2015).

Many of the reasons for variation in health have already been explained. Low SES in childhood impacts health lifelong. Adequate sleep is needed, with effects apparent in midlife health (Carroll et al., 2014; McEwen & Karatsoreos, 2015).

Nutrition is always important. Most young people learn to eat well, but some do not, making "emerging adulthood . . . a critical risk period in the development and prevention of disordered eating" (Goldschmidt et al., 2016, p. 480). Exercise habits are crucial. If young adults stop exercising once high school is over, that is a serious mistake.

One study (CARDIA—Coronary Artery Risk Development in Adulthood) began with healthy 18- to 30-year-olds, most of them (3,154) reexamined 7 and 20 years later. Those who were the least fit at the first assessment (more than 400 of them) were four times more likely to have diabetes and high blood pressure in middle age. Problems began, unnoticed (except in blood work), when participants were in their 20s. However, unless their daily habits changed, death rates of those 400 began to climb later in life (Camhi et al., 2013).

## Taking Risks

Remember that each age group has its own gains and losses. This is apparent with risk-taking. Some emerging adults bravely, or foolishly, take risks—actions that are gender- and age-related, as well as genetic and hormonal. Those who are genetically impulsive *and* male *and* emerging adults are most likely to be brave and foolish.

Societies as well as individuals benefit because emerging adults take chances. Enrolling in college, moving to a new state or nation, getting married, having a

Kevin Foy/Alamy

**Fastest Increase** Obesity rates are rising faster in China than in any other nation as new American restaurants open every day. McDonald's and Starbucks each have about 5,000 outlets, catering especially to upwardly mobile young adults like these women in Beijing.

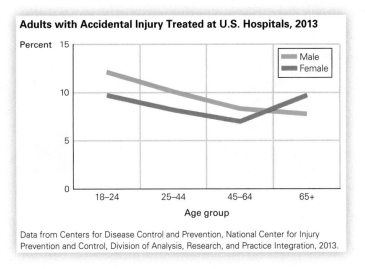

Data from Centers for Disease Control and Prevention, National Center for Injury Prevention and Control, Division of Analysis, Research, and Practice Integration, 2013.

**FIGURE EP.1**

**Send Them Home** Accidents, homicides, and suicides occur more frequently during emerging adulthood than later. Note that the age range of more patients falls within the six years of emerging adulthood than within the 20 years of adulthood. If all of the data were reported by six-year age groups, the chart would be much starker. Fewer young adults stay in the hospital, however. They are usually stitched, bandaged, injected, and sent home.

baby—all are risky. So is starting a business, filming a documentary, entering a sports competition, enlisting in the military, or traveling abroad.

Yet risk-taking may be destructive. Accidents, homicides, and suicides are the three leading causes of death among people aged 15 to 25—killing more of them than all diseases combined (see Figure EP.1). This is the case even in nations where infectious diseases and malnutrition are rampant. It was also true historically: Young males have always experienced what demographers call an *accident hump* at about age 20 (Goldstein, 2011).

Emerging-adult men are the most common killers and victims, murdered at three times the rate of men 20 years older (the U.S. annual rate per 100,000 is 20 compared to 7 for adults aged 45). As you can see, good health in emerging adulthood depends, not primarily on biology, but primarily on the mind, which makes the next topic particularly important.

## WHAT HAVE YOU LEARNED?

1. What are the biological strengths of emerging adulthood?
2. What affects the speed of the aging process?
3. How can risk-taking be beneficial?
4. How can risk-taking be harmful?

## Cognitive Development

Over the past century, Piaget changed our understanding of cognitive development by recognizing that maturation does not simply add knowledge. Cognition leaps forward at each stage, first from sensorimotor to preoperational (because of symbolic thought), and then from preoperational to concrete to formal (each with new logic).

Although formal operational thought is the final stage of Piaget's theory, some cognitive psychologists describe **postformal cognition,** which combines both

**postformal cognition** A proposed adult stage of cognitive development, following Piaget's four stages, that goes beyond adolescent thinking by being more practical, more flexible, and more dialectical (i.e., more capable of combining contradictory elements into a comprehensive whole).

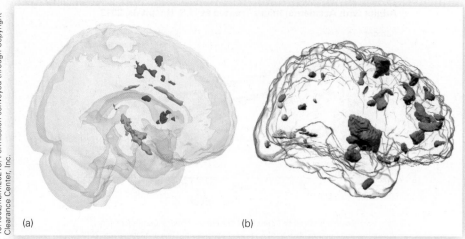

(a)                                                                    (b)

**Thinking Away from Home**  *(a)* Entering a residential college means experiencing new foods, new friends, and new neurons. A longitudinal study of 18-year-old students at the beginning and end of their first year in college (Dartmouth) found increases in the brain areas that integrate emotion and cognition—namely, the cingulate (blue and yellow), caudate (red), and insula (orange). Researchers also studied one-year changes in the brains of students over age 25 at the same college and found no dramatic growth. *(b)* Shown here are the areas of one person's brain changes from age 14 to 25. The frontal cortex (purple) demonstrated many changes in particular parts, as did the areas for processing speech (green and blue)—a crucial aspect of young-adult learning. Areas for visual processing (yellow) showed less change.

Researchers now know that brains mature in many ways between adolescence and adulthood; scientists are not yet sure of the cognitive implications.

---

**LaunchPad**
macmillan learning

Try **Video Activity: Brain Development: Emerging Adulthood** for a quick look at the changes that occur in a person's brain between ages 18 and 25.

aspects of dual-processing (intuition and analysis), when "thinking needs to be integrated with emotional and pragmatic aspects, rather than only dealing with the purely abstract" (Labouvie-Vief, 2015, p. 89). Postformal thought is a "type of logical, adaptive problem-solving that is a step more complex than scientific formal-level Piagetian tasks" (Sinnott, 2014, p. 3).

This idea is suggested by research on the brain. As described in Chapter 14, the prefrontal cortex is not fully mature until the early 20s, and new dendrites connect throughout life. Thinking changes as the brain matures (Lemieux, 2012). As is evident throughout childhood, adult brains benefit from better neurological connections and greater experience of the social world (Grayson & Fair, 2017).

## Countering Stereotypes

Cognitive flexibility, particularly the ability to change childhood assumptions, helps counter stereotypes. Young adults show many signs of such flexibility, evidence of their intellectual growth. The very fact that emerging adults marry later than did previous generations suggests that, couple by couple, thinking processes are not determined by childhood culture or by traditional norms. Postformal reasoning allows rational thinking to overcome emotional reactions, with responses dependent on reality, not stereotypes (Sinnott, 2014).

Unfortunately, many people do not recognize their stereotypes, even when false beliefs harm them. One of the most pernicious results is **stereotype threat,** arising in people who worry that other people might judge them as stupid, lazy, oversexed, or worse because of their ethnicity, sex, age, or appearance. Even the *possibility* of being stereotyped arouses emotions and hijacks memory, disrupting cognition (Schmader, 2010). That is stereotype threat.

Stereotype threat is more than a hypothesis. Hundreds of studies show that it harms almost all humans. African American men become poor students; women

**stereotype threat** The thought in a person's mind that one's appearance or behavior will be misread to confirm another person's oversimplified, prejudiced attitudes.

underperform in math; older people are more forgetful; bilingual students stumble with English, all because they worry about what other people are thinking about them.

Thus, members of stigmatized minorities in every nation might handicap themselves because of what they imagine others might think (Inzlicht & Schmader, 2012). The worst part is that stereotype threat is self-imposed. People who are alert to the *possibility* of prejudice are not only hypersensitive when it occurs but allow it to hijack their minds, undercutting ability. Fortunately, the creativity of adult cognition allows people to "challenge your stigma," reframing stereotypes to make them empowering, not debilitating (Wang et al., 2017).

**The Threat of Bias** If students fear that others expect them to do poorly because of their ethnicity or gender, they might not identify with academic achievement and therefore do worse on exams than they otherwise would have.

## Cognitive Growth and Higher Education

Education improves health and wealth. The data on virtually every physical condition, and every indicator of material success, show that college graduates are ahead of high school graduates, who themselves are ahead of those without a high school diploma.

### Selection and Facilitation

Remember that adolescents select their friends and then their friends encourage them to behave in certain ways. The same is true in emerging adulthood.

Selection effects *are* powerful in the connection between college and later life. A young person's family background influences the college experience. According to the U.S. Center for Education Statistics, parental SES is the strongest predictor of whether or not someone will earn a college degree, with 60 percent of those of high SES earning a bachelor's degree compared to 14 percent of those with low family SES (Kena et al., 2015).

Both money and role models make college seem essential for some young adults and irrelevant for others. One young man said:

> People always ask me, why don't you go to college. My dad, he never went. You work, you pay your bills, you help with the rent. My priority right now is to be responsible, to know how adult life works. It might go bad for me, or it might go good. It's going to be hard…. I'm scared one day we'll wake up some day and say "We don't got nothing to eat."

> [Maldonado, quoted in Healy, 2017]

However, selection effects are not the only reason college graduates have healthier and wealthier lives. When students of equal ability and family background are compared, education still makes a notable difference in later health and wealth. The average 25- to 34-year-old makes $20,000 a year more with a bachelor's degree compared to those with only a high school diploma (Kena et al., 2015) (see Visualizing Development, p. 492). The benefits are especially apparent when those from low-SES families are compared to each other.

However, there is a problem. Many students drop out of college. The financial benefits come primarily from graduation, yet the costs come from enrolling. Money is a major reason that many of those who choose to begin college do not earn a degree (McKinney & Burridge, 2015).

One effort to improve graduation rates has been to make college loans easier to obtain. In 2013, 59 percent of students borrowed money to pay for tuition (Chronicle of Higher Education, August 17, 2015). The interest on those loans is high, as is the default rate—about 25 percent.

**THINK CRITICALLY:** What imagined criticisms impair your own achievement, and how can you overcome them?

# Why Study?

From a life-span perspective, college graduation is a good investment, for individuals (they become healthier and wealthier) and for nations (national income rises). That long-term perspective is the main reason why nations that control enrollment, such as China, have opened dozens of new colleges in the past two decades. However, when the effort and cost of higher education depend on immediate choices made by students and families, as in the United States, many decide it is not worth it, as illustrated by the number of people who earn bachelor's degrees.

## EDUCATION IN THE UNITED STATES

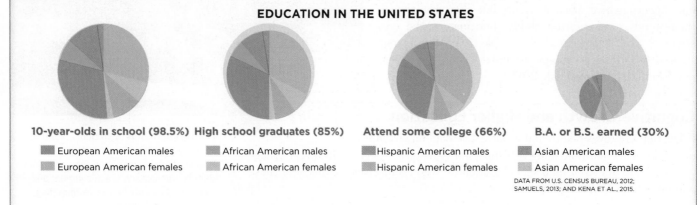

**10-year-olds in school (98.5%)** **High school graduates (85%)** **Attend some college (66%)** **B.A. or B.S. earned (30%)**

- ■ European American males
- ■ European American females
- ■ African American males
- ■ African American females
- ■ Hispanic American males
- ■ Hispanic American females
- ■ Asian American males
- ■ Asian American females

DATA FROM U.S. CENSUS BUREAU, 2012; SAMUELS, 2013; AND KENA ET AL., 2015.

## AMONG ALL ADULTS

The percentage of U.S. residents with high school and college diplomas is increasing as more of the oldest cohort (often without degrees) dies and the youngest cohorts aim for college. However, many people are insufficiently educated and less likely to find good jobs.

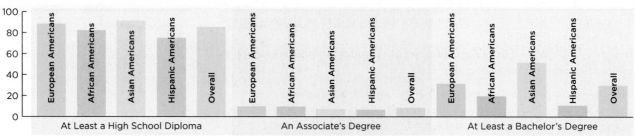

At Least a High School Diploma — An Associate's Degree — At Least a Bachelor's Degree

DATA FROM U.S. CENSUS BUREAU, 2013B.

## INCOME IMPACT

Over an average of 40 years of employment, someone who completes a master's degree earns $500,000 more than someone who leaves school in eleventh grade. That translates into about $90,000 for each year of education from twelfth grade to a master's. The earnings gap is even wider than those numbers indicate because this chart includes only adults who have jobs, yet finding work is more difficult for those with less education.

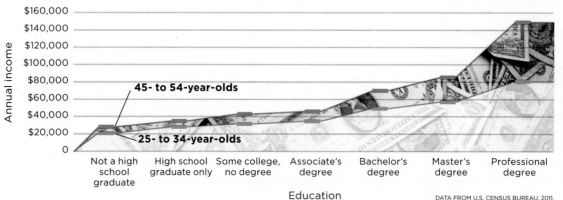

45- to 54-year-olds

25- to 34-year-olds

Annual income

Not a high school graduate | High school graduate only | Some college, no degree | Associate's degree | Bachelor's degree | Master's degree | Professional degree

Education

DATA FROM U.S. CENSUS BUREAU, 2011.

JUPITERIMAGES/THINKSTOCK/PHOTOS. COM/GETTY IMAGES PLUS

Students at for-profit colleges are more likely to obtain loans and more likely to default on them, perhaps because those colleges have the lowest graduation rates. That is one reason some analysts suggest that federal loans may burden students, taxpayers, and society without increasing learning, graduation, or later employment (Best & Best, 2014; Webber, 2015).

> **THINK CRITICALLY:** When is financial help a path toward accomplishment, and when is it destructive?

## College and Cognition

Developmentalists are more concerned about lifetime cognition than about lifetime income. Does college lead to better thinking? According to one comprehensive review:

> Compared to freshmen, seniors have better oral and written communication skills, are better abstract reasoners or critical thinkers, are more skilled at using reason and evidence to address ill-structured problems for which there are no verifiably correct answers, have greater intellectual flexibility in that they are better able to understand more than one side of a complex issue, and can develop more sophisticated abstract frameworks to deal with complexity.
>
> *[Pascarella & Terenzini, 1991, p. 155]*

Note that many of these abilities characterize postformal thinking.

But wait. Did you notice the date on that summary? Since you know that cohort and culture are influential, you might wonder whether those findings are still valid. Good question!

Many recent books suggest that the college experience has changed for the worse. Notably, a longitudinal study of U.S. college students found only half as much growth in critical thinking, analysis, and communication over the four years than had occurred two decades earlier. These scholars found that, over the first two years, almost half of the students made no cognitive advances at all (Arum & Roksa, 2011).

They offered many explanations, each confirmed by data. Compared to decades ago, students study less, professors expect less, and students avoid classes that require reading 40 pages a week or writing 20 pages a semester. Administrators and faculty still profess hope for intellectual growth, but they do not follow policies that would accomplish that. Instead, rigorous classes are optional, canceled, or chosen by few. Most students major in business, fewer in history or literature (which require more writing, reading, and analysis).

Some observers of the current college scene blame the exosystem for forcing colleges to follow a corporate model, considering students as customers to be satisfied rather than youth to be challenged (Deresiewicz, 2014). Customers, apparently, demand new dormitories and expensive sports facilities, and students borrow money to pay for them.

> **Especially for Those Considering Studying Abroad** Given the effects of college, would it be better for a student to study abroad in the first year or the last year of college education? (see response, p. 494)

**Culture and Cohort** Ideally, college brings together people of many backgrounds who learn from each other. This scene from a college library in the United Arab Emirates would not have happened a few decades ago. The dress of these three suggests that culture still matters, but education is recognized worldwide as benefiting every young person in every nation.

## Diversity

A century ago, virtually all college graduates, in the United States and elsewhere, were men of European American descent who attended institutions in their home country.

As Asian and African nations became independent of colonial rule, and as political leaders recognized the power of education, the number and diversity of college students increased dramatically. The result is **massification,** the idea

> **massification** The idea that establishing institutions of higher learning and encouraging college enrollment can benefit everyone (the masses).

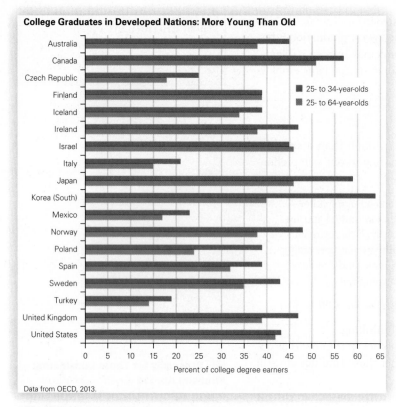

**College Graduates in Developed Nations: More Young Than Old**

Data from OECD, 2013.

**FIGURE EP.2**

**How Things Have Changed** This chart reveals two things. First, it shows whether young college graduates have grandparents and parents who did not attend college—dramatically true in Korea and Poland. Second, it reveals whether public support for college has increased in the past 20 years—not true in the United States, Israel, and Finland. In the United States, although more people begin college, fewer graduate, partly because the income gap is wider than it once was while public funding is reduced. Finding four years of tuition money is increasingly difficult for North Americans, and college loans are seen as a boon to banks but not individuals—making young adults wary of signing on the dotted line.

**Response for Those Considering Studying Abroad** (from p. 493): Since one result of college is that students become more open to other perspectives while developing their commitment to their own values, foreign study might be most beneficial after several years of college. If they study abroad too early, some students might be either too narrowly patriotic (they are not yet open) or too quick to reject everything about their national heritage (they have not yet developed their own commitments).

that college is not just for the elite but for almost everyone (the masses) (Altbach et al., 2010).

The United States was the first major nation to endorse massification, beginning with federal legislation to establish land-grant colleges in every state. (Iowa was the first, in 1864.) Now all 50 states have publicly-supported universities. One result: Throughout the twentieth century, the United States led the world in the percentage of college graduates (see Figure EP.2). This is no longer the case, however, because other nations have increased public funding for tertiary education while the United States has decreased it.

The result is greater economic disparity among those who attend college and those who do not. Other forms of diversity have increased. Women now attend college more than men, and African American, Latino, and immigrant college students in the United States are increasing. As laws and policies have made discrimination based on disabilities illegal, many students have classmates who are blind, are in wheelchairs, are intellectually disabled, and so on—again making it possible for the college experience to expand the mind.

In addition, thousands of LGBTQ college students have made their identities known. The latest diversity to be recognized is political: Both conservative and liberal students who are in the minority at their institutions are demanding recognition.

All diversity *can* advance cognition. Honest conversations among people of varied backgrounds and perspectives lead to intellectual challenge and deeper thought, with benefits lasting for years after graduation (Pascarella et al., 2014). Colleges that make use of their diversity—via curriculum, assignments, discussions, cooperative education, learning communities, residence halls, and so on—advance cognition of emerging adults (Harper & Yeung, 2013).

Of course, the presence of students of color, or with disabilities, or who are LGBTQ does not necessarily mean that other students learn from them. Moreover, the numbers overstate diversity: The fact that one-third of U.S. college *students* are non–European American does not mean that most *colleges* are one-third non–European American.

Instead, some colleges are almost exclusively African American or Latino American or Native American, and many others are 90 percent or more European American. Furthermore, few students study far from home: Not only do most community college students live with their parents, but most students at residential colleges live less than 100 miles away from their hometowns. They befriend students from their same region.

Students with distinct backgrounds—very rich or very poor, politically conservative or liberal, disabled or not, and so on—seek colleges with similar students. Then they befriend students who are most like themselves. People tend to be quiet about their atypical experiences—such as having fought in a war, or being transgender, or having a disability. Humans all seek comfort and social acceptance; they avoid the intellectual challenge of diversity.

Thus, they might miss an opportunity for intellectual growth. Remember postformal cognition. People need to engage others of many backgrounds: That is how humans learn. But the challenge of diversity needs to be sought.

---

**WHAT HAVE YOU LEARNED?**

**1.** What is the difference between formal and postformal thinking?

**2.** How does stereotype threat differ from stereotype?

**3.** How does earning a college degree affect later life?

**4.** What is the difference between college 50 years ago and college today?

**5.** What kinds of diversity are evident among college students?

**6.** Give an example of a time when you learned something new from a conversation with another student whose background was unlike yours.

---

> **LaunchPad**
> macmillan learning
>
> **Video: The Effects of Mentoring on Intellectual Development: The University-Community Links Project** shows how an after-school study enhancement program has proven beneficial for both its mentors and the at-risk students who attend it.

## Psychosocial Development

A theme of human development is that continuity and change are evident throughout life. Psychosocial continuity is apparent amidst new achievements, with emerging adulthood called the "crucible of personality development" (Roberts & Davis, 2016).

### Identity Achievement

As you remember, the identity crisis may begin in adolescence, but "identity development in the areas of love, work, and worldviews is a central task of the third decade of life" (Padilla-Walker & Nelson, 2017, p. 5). The identity crisis sometimes causes confusion or foreclosure (see Table EP.1). A more mature response is to seek a moratorium, postponing identity achievement, avoiding marriage and parenthood while exploring possibilities.

Moratoria include attending college; joining the military; taking on religious mission work; working as an intern in government, academia, or industry; and finding temporary work. All moratoria advance exploration and reduce the pressure to achieve identity.

---

**TABLE EP.1**

**Erikson's Eight Stages of Development**

| Stage | Virtue / Pathology | Possible in Emerging Adulthood If Not Successfully Resolved |
|---|---|---|
| Trust vs. mistrust | Hope / withdrawal | Suspicious of others, making close relationships difficult |
| Autonomy vs. shame and doubt | Will / compulsion | Obsessively driven, single-minded, not socially responsive |
| Initiative vs. guilt | Purpose / inhibition | Fearful, regretful (e.g., very homesick in college) |
| Industry vs. inferiority | Competence / inertia | Self-critical of any endeavor, procrastinating, perfectionistic |
| Identity vs. role diffusion | Fidelity / repudiation | Uncertain and negative about values, lifestyle, friendships |
| Intimacy vs. isolation | Love / exclusivity | Anxious about close relationships, jealous, lonely |
| Generativity vs. stagnation | Care / rejection | [In the future] Fear of failure |
| Integrity vs. despair | Wisdom / disdain | [In the future] No "mindfulness," no life plan |

Information from Erikson, 1982/1998.

**Grown Up Now?** In Korean tradition, age 19 signifies adulthood, when people can drink alcohol and, in modern times, vote. In 2011, administrators invited 100 19-year-olds to a public Coming of Age ceremony, shown here, that had begun centuries before. Emerging adults are torn between old and new. For example, in many nations, coming of age ceremonies are exclusive to one gender, but here young men and women participate.

**Ordinary Workers** Most children and adolescents want to be sports heroes, star entertainers, billionaires, or world leaders—yet fewer than one in 1 million succeed in doing so.

**intimacy versus isolation** The sixth of Erikson's eight stages of development. Adults seek someone with whom to share their lives in an enduring and self-sacrificing commitment. Without such commitment, they risk profound aloneness and isolation.

## Ethnic Identity

One crucial aspect of identity formation is ethnic identity, which is "not a matter of one's idiosyncratic self-perception but rather is profoundly shaped by one's social context, including one's social role and place in society" (Seaton et al., 2017, p. 683). In other words, how people see themselves is deeply affected by family, friends, and the wider culture—and that becomes increasingly important as each young person prepares to enter the adult world.

About half of all emerging adults in the United States have ancestors who were not European, but that simply describes who they are not—they need to figure out the specifics of having ancestors from China, or Colombia, or Cameroon, or wherever. Many young people have forebears from more than one heritage and group—again posing challenges in establishing their own unique identity.

At the same time, young adults of European backgrounds also seek to figure out their ethnic identity—as Irish or Italian or whatever—and what it means to be from a particular region (e.g., deep South, far West). As emerging adults enter colleges and workplaces in a global economy, interacting with people of many backgrounds, they need to know their own roots so that they can be proud of themselves and respect the roots of others (Rivas-Drake et al., 2014).

This is true internationally as well as nationally. In Chile, youth of both Mapuche (indigenous) and mainstream Chilean descent benefited when they respected themselves and each other (González et al., 2017). Similarly, in the United States, Hispanic college students who resisted both assimilation and alienation fared best: They were most likely to maintain their ethnic identity, deflect stereotype threat, and become good students (Rivas-Drake & Mooney, 2009).

## Vocational Identity

As explained in Chapter 16, vocational identity is so complex that adolescents are wise to postpone selecting a particular career. Today's job market has made development of vocational identity even harder.

Many young people take a series of temporary jobs. Between ages 18 and 25, the average U.S. worker has held seven jobs, with the college-educated changing jobs more than those with less education (U.S. Bureau of Labor Statistics, 2015). They want to try various kinds of work, and the recent economic recession led to a greater number of older adults keeping their jobs, making fewer openings for younger workers. Emerging adults may be "sagely avoiding foreclosure and premature commitment in a treacherous job market" (Konstam, 2015, p. 95).

## Intimacy Needs

In Erikson's theory, after achieving identity, people experience the crisis of **intimacy versus isolation.** Social isolation is harmful at every age and in every culture (Holt-Lunstad et al., 2015). Humans have a powerful inborn need to share their personal lives with someone else. Without intimacy, adults suffer from loneliness. Erikson explains:

> The young adult, emerging from the search for and the insistence on identity, is eager and willing to fuse his identity with others. He is ready for intimacy, that is, the capacity to commit himself to concrete affiliations and partnerships and to develop the ethical strength to abide by such commitments, even though they call for significant sacrifices and compromises.

*[Erikson, 1993a, p. 263]*

**New Jobs, New Workers** This barista in Germany *(left)* and these app developers in India *(right)* work at very different jobs. Yet they may have much in common: If they are like other emerging adults, their current employment is not what they imagined in high school, and not what they will be doing in 10 years.

Other theorists have different words for the same human need— *affiliation, affection, interdependence, communion, belonging, love*—but all developmentalists note the importance of social connections lifelong. Infant synchrony and attachment become precursors to adult intimacy, especially if the child develops a positive working model of social connections (Chow & Ruhl, 2014; Phillips et al., 2013).

## Emerging Adults and Their Parents

It is hard to overestimate the importance of family. Although composed of individuals, a family is much more than the people in it. In the dynamic synergy of a well-functioning family, children grow, adults find support, and everyone is part of a unit that gives meaning to, and provides models for, aspirations and decisions.

Parents may be more important to emerging adults than they were in former times. Two experts in human development write, "with delays in marriage, more Americans choosing to remain single, and high divorce rates, a tie to a parent may be the most important bond in a young adult's life" (Fingerman & Furstenberg, 2012).

Emerging adults hope to set out on their own, often leaving their childhood home and parents behind. They strive for independence. But all members of each family have **linked lives;** that is, the experiences and needs of family members at one stage of life are affected by those at other stages (Elder, 1998; Macmillan & Copher, 2005; Settersten, 2015). We have already described many examples. If parents fight, children suffer— even if no one lays a hand on them. Family financial stress and parental alliances shape children's lives.

Many emerging adults still live at home, though the percentage varies from nation to nation. Almost all unmarried young adults in Italy and Japan live with their parents. Fewer do so in the United States, but the rates are rising: In 2016, more emerging adults lived with their parents than in any other setting (e.g., with a spouse, with roommates, alone).

Those who are living with their parents are often depressed, especially if they are in the "boomerang" group who once were independent and who now need to save money because they are unemployed. However, if those living with their

"This property comes complete with grown-up children left behind by the vendors."

**No Thanks** Even living with one's own children is problematic.

**linked lives** Lives in which the success, health, and well-being of each family member are connected to those of other members, including those of another generation, as in the relationship between parents and children.

**Especially for Family Therapists** More emerging-adult children today live with their parents than ever before, yet you have learned that families often function better when young adults live on their own. What would you advise? (see response, p. 500)

parents have jobs and are saving money so that they can move out, they may be quite happy (Copp et al., 2015). The details of family interaction continue to be more important than who lives where.

## Friendship

Friendships may "reach their peak of functional significance during emerging adulthood" (Tanner & Arnett, 2011, p. 27). Unlike relatives, friends are chosen. They are selected because they are loyal, trustworthy, supportive, and enjoyable, and the choice is mutual, not obligatory.

Thus, friends understand and comfort each other when romance turns sour, and they share experiences and provide useful information about everything: how to study, where jobs might be, whether to go on a date with someone, what shoes to wear.

People tend to make more friends during emerging adulthood than at any later period, and they rely on these friends. Unlike in former cohorts, many have friends of both sexes. They often use social media to extend and deepen friendships that begin face-to-face, becoming more aware of the day-to-day tribulations and celebrations of their friends (Burstein, 2013).

## Romance

All close relationships have much in common—not only in the psychic needs they satisfy but also in the behaviors they require. Each ongoing relationship demands some personal sacrifice, including vulnerability that brings deeper self-understanding and shatters the isolation of too much self-protection. To establish intimacy, the young adult must

> face the fear of ego loss in situations which call for self-abandon: in the solidarity of close affiliations [and] sexual unions, in close friendship and in physical combat, in experiences of inspiration by teachers and of intuition from the recesses of the self. The avoidance of such experiences . . . may lead to a deep sense of isolation and consequent self-absorption.

[Erikson, 1993a, pp. 263–264]

We have already shown how family and friends can meet intimacy needs. Beyond that, many emerging adults seek, and find, a romantic partner—or several of them in sequence. Falling in love is a common experience, as is sexual attraction, but exactly what that means is affected by many particulars—personality, age, and gender among them (Sanz Cruces et al., 2015).

**Same Situation, Far Apart: Good Friends Together** These smiling emerging adults show that friendship matters everywhere. Culture matters, too. Would the eight Florida college students celebrating a 21st birthday at a Tex-Mex restaurant *(left)* be willing to switch places with the two Tibetan workers *(right)*?

It seems that love occurs everywhere, and passion, intimacy, and commitment have been built into every culture. However, cultural differences and cohort effects are apparent.

The impact of culture and cohort is apparent in the **hookup,** a sexual interaction between partners who know little about each other, perhaps having met a few hours before. If that happened a few decades ago, it was prostitution, a fling, or a dirty secret. No longer.

The desire for sex without emotional commitment is stronger in young men than in young women, for reasons that might be hormonal (testosterone) or cultural (women want committed fathers if children are born). In a U.S. survey of 18- to 24-year-olds who had completed at least one year of college, 56 percent of the men but only 31 percent of the women say they had had a hookup (Monto & Carey, 2014). Hookups are also more common at the beginning of emerging adulthood—for 19-year-olds new to college, not 25-year-olds in graduate school or at the workplace.

Some of the current awareness of campus sexual assault may be fueled by women's reluctance to be involved in casual sex and men's assumption that their dates share their sexual desires. While the complexities of sexual interaction during emerging adulthood cannot be described in a few paragraphs here, many old myths and falsehoods further complicate the issue (Deming et al., 2013). The following myths are still held by some older adults:

- Men can't control themselves.
- Women want sex even when they don't admit it.
- Rape is an attack by a stranger, or involving a woman who is drugged, not an aggressive act between acquaintances.

Most emerging adults know that these three are false.

Emerging adults differ from past generations in another way: They use the Internet to strengthen friendships and to seek romance, often requesting partners of particular ethnicity, political values, gender identity, sexual preferences, religious beliefs. When online connections lead to face-to-face interactions and then to marriage, happy marriages are as likely as when the first contact was made in person (Cacioppo et al., 2013).

Despite the media attention to "hookup culture," committed romantic relationships are still primary goals for most emerging adults. Marriage, however, may not be. Now sex almost always begins before marriage, and 40 percent of all babies are born to unmarried women (J. Martin et al., 2015).

One reason that marriage rates are down is that young adults expect more from marriage than previous cohorts did; they see marriage as a marker of maturity and success (Cherlin, 2009). The efforts that gay and lesbian couples made to achieve marriage equality, the backlash in "defense of marriage," and the 400,000 same-sex couples who wed suggest the power of the institution.

The fact that marriage is often postponed, and that sex often occurs without commitment, has led to the rise of another practice, **cohabitation,** as living with an unmarried partner is called (see Figure EP.3 on the following page). Almost everyone in some nations cohabits at some point—perhaps later marrying someone else.

Cohabitation is sometimes considered a way to avoid the pain of divorce, but cohabiting couples who marry are at least as likely to divorce as other married couples. Two-thirds of all newly married couples in the United States live with their partner before marriage (Manning et al., 2014), as do most couples in Canada (especially Quebec), northern Europe, England, and Australia. Many couples in Sweden, France, Jamaica, and Puerto Rico cohabit for decades, never marrying.

In the United States, the differences between couples who cohabit for years and those who cohabit for a shorter time and then either split up or marry is affected powerfully by education. Although marriage rates are down and cohabitation up in

**hookup** A sexual encounter between two people who are not in a romantic relationship. Neither intimacy nor commitment is expected.

---

**THINK CRITICALLY:** Does the success of marriages between people who met online indicate that something is amiss with more traditional marriages?

---

**LaunchPad**
macmillan learning

The Data Connections activity
**Technology and Romance: Trends for U.S. Adults** examines how emerging adults find romantic partners.

---

**cohabitation** An arrangement in which a couple lives together in a committed romantic relationship but are not formally married.

## FIGURE EP.3

**More Together, Fewer Married** As you see, the number of cohabiting male–female households in the United States has increased dramatically over the past decades. These numbers are an underestimate: Couples do not always tell the U.S. Census that they are living together, nor are cohabitants counted within their parents' households. Same-sex couples (not tallied until 2000) are also not included here.

⬤⬤ **Observation Quiz** Usually the rate of cohabitation increased at a steady rate, but there is one exception. When was that? (see answer, p. 502) ➜

⬤ **Response for Family Therapists** (from p. 498): Remember that family function is more important than family structure. Sharing a home can work out well if contentious issues—like privacy, money, and household chores—are clarified before resentments arise. You might offer a three-session preparation package to explore assumptions and guidelines.

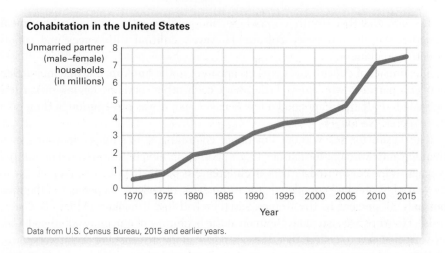

**Cohabitation in the United States**

Data from U.S. Census Bureau, 2015 and earlier years.

every demographic group, education increases the chance of marriage and marital childbearing.

Cohabiting couples without college degrees have children about five times as often as couples the same age who have graduated from college (Lundberg et al., 2016). The probable reason is not that college graduates know something that others do not; instead they are more likely to have a steady, well-paying job. Some young women decide that they would rather have a child with an unmarried partner than an unemployable husband.

In all patterns of sexual and romantic development, culture matters. Research in 30 nations finds that acceptance of cohabitation affects the happiness of those who cohabit and the success of their children. Within each of those 30 nations, demographic differences (such as education, income, age, and religion) matter (Soons & Kalmijn, 2009). Generally, those who are within a community where everyone cohabits are least likely to be harmed by it.

The importance of the social context during emerging adulthood was emphasized in the analysis of a survey of 2,195 18- to 25-year-olds in the United States. The researchers recommend that parents talk with their adult children about love and respect in sexual interactions rather than worrying about hookups and premarital sex (Weissbourd et al., 2017).

## Concluding Questions and Hopes

One question not yet addressed in this Epilogue is whether or not emerging adulthood is really a stage. Jeffrey Arnett was a college professor in Missouri who listened to his students and realized that they were neither adolescents nor adults. As a good researcher, he then queried young adults of many backgrounds elsewhere, read published research about "youth" or "late adolescence," and he thought about his own life. That led him to name a new stage, *emerging adulthood*.

**How to Find Your Soul Mate** Tiago and Mariela met on a dating site for people with tattoos, connected on Skype, moved in together, and soon were engaged to marry.

**WEIRD** An acronym for Western, Educated, Industrialized, Rich, Democracy referring to emerging adults. The criticism is that conclusions about human development based on people in such nations may not apply to most people in the world, who do not live in WEIRD nations.

Some other scientists disagree. Instead of a universal stage, might emerging adulthood be a cultural phenomenon for privileged youth who can afford to postpone work and family commitments? (Munson et al., 2013). Is it valid for professors at U.S. universities to study their own students and then draw conclusions about all humankind.

Instead, such conclusions may apply only to people who are **WEIRD**—from Western, Educated, Industrialized, Rich Democracies (Henrich et al., 2010). Most of the world's people are poor (even low-SES Americans are rich by global measures), never reach college, and live in nations without democratic elections. WEIRD people are unusual compared to most of the 7 billion people of the world.

If WEIRD people are unusual, perhaps emerging adulthood—when young adults become autonomous and independent, forging a future untethered by parents, postponing marriage, parenthood, and work commitments—is a WEIRD anomaly. Another set of experiences and expectations may be evident in cultures where social interdependence—not independence—is the ideal (Yeung & Alipio, 2013).

That is a topic now explored by many researchers. A study of personality development among youth in 62 nations found that an emerging-adult transition was evident everywhere, although how old youth were when emerging adulthood ended was affected by job responsibility. When work began at age 20 or earlier (as in Pakistan, Malaysia, and Zimbabwe), personality maturation was rapid. When work began late (as in the Netherlands, Canada, and the United States), emerging adulthood sometimes extended past age 25 (Bleidorn et al., 2013).

Data suggest that emerging adulthood is a trend in every nation, not just the WEIRD ones. Consider average marriage age. A century ago, most women everywhere married in their teens. Now, in sub-Saharan Africa the average marriage age is 21 for women and 25 for men; in East Asia, 26 and 28; in Western Europe, 31 and 33. North Americans have been marrying later in every recent decade: The current average is 27 for women and 29 for men (American Community Survey, 2014).

Data on childbearing, college attendance, and career commitment show similar worldwide trends. This leads most scholars to believe that although emerging adulthood was first recognized in Missouri, it is now evident worldwide.

Most emerging adults everywhere, like humans of all ages, have strengths as well as liabilities. Many survive risks, overcome substance abuse, think more deeply, combat loneliness, and deal with problems with the help of education, maturation, friends, and family. If they postpone marriage, prevent pregnancy, and avoid a set career until their identity is firmly established and their education is complete, they may be ready and eager to raise the next generation well, using all of the insights you have gained from Chapters 1 through 16.

**Same Situation, Far Apart: The Bride and Groom** Weddings everywhere involve special gowns and apparel—notice the gloves in Bali *(left)* and the headpiece in Malaysia *(right)*. They also involve families. In many places, the ceremony includes the new couple promising to care for their parents—a contrast to the U.S. custom of a father giving away his daughter to the groom.

⬤ **Answer to Observation Quiz** (from p. 500) Between 2005 and 2010. The probable reason: economic recession.

**WHAT HAVE YOU LEARNED?**

1. How might a moratorium help an emerging adult achieve identity?
2. How does ethnic identity affect achievement and self-esteem?
3. Do emerging adults still need their parents?
4. How does friendship in emerging adulthood differ from friendship at other times in life?
5. What is the relationship between intimacy needs and the Internet?
6. What are the advantages and disadvantages of cohabitation?
7. What is wrong with basing conclusions on WEIRD people?

# SUMMARY

## Biosocial Development

**1.** Emerging adulthood, from about age 18 to age 25, is a newly recognized period of development characterized by postponing parenthood, marriage, and career commitment, while attaining additional education.

**2.** Most emerging adults are strong and healthy. Good eating and exercise habits are crucial. Every body system functions optimally during these years; immunity is strong; death from disease is rare.

**3.** Risk-taking increases. Some risks are worthwhile, but many are dangerous. Young adults are far more likely to die of accidents, homicide, or suicide than from diseases.

## Cognitive Development

**4.** Many researchers believe that the complex and conflicting demands of adult life produce a new cognitive perspective. Postformal thinking is characterized by thinking that is flexible and practical, combining emotion and logic, intuition and analysis.

**5.** Stereotypes and stereotype threat interrupt thinking processes and thus can make people seem intellectually less capable. Ideally, adults find ways to overcome such liabilities.

**6.** How much college education advances cognition in current times is debatable. Research over the past several decades indicates not only that college increases wealth and health but also that college teaches adults to develop more critical thinking.

**7.** Students in college are far more diverse than college students were a few decades ago. Learning from people of different perspectives can advance cognition.

## Psychosocial Development

**8.** For today's youth, the identity crisis continues. In multiethnic nations, ethnic identity becomes important. Vocational identity is difficult to establish in the current economy.

**9.** Family support is needed lifelong. Family members have linked lives, always affected by one another and often helping one another at every age.

**10.** Friends are particularly crucial in emerging adulthood. Many emerging adults use social networking and matchmaking sites on the Internet to expand and deepen their friendship circles and mating options.

**11.** Hooking up and cohabitation are increasingly common. However, they do not usually improve long-term happiness or marital satisfaction.

**12.** Emerging adulthood, as a stage, does not seem confined to WEIRD people. Worldwide, marriage occurs later and education takes longer, which may prepare young adults to raise the next generation well.

# KEY TERMS

| | | | |
|---|---|---|---|
| emerging adulthood (p. 487) | massification (p. 493) | linked lives (p. 497) | WEIRD (p. 500) |
| postformal cognition (p. 489) | intimacy versus | hookup (p. 499) | |
| stereotype threat (p. 490) | isolation (p. 496) | cohabitation (p. 499) | |

# APPLICATIONS

**1.** Describe an incident during your emerging adulthood when taking a risk could have led to disaster. What were your feelings at the time? What would you do if you knew that a child of yours was about to do the same thing?

**2.** Read a biography or autobiography that includes information about the person's thinking from adolescence through adulthood. How did personal experiences, education, and maturation affect the person's thinking?

**3.** Statistics on cohort and culture in students and in colleges are fascinating, but only a few are reported here. Compare your nation, state, or province with another. Analyze the data and discuss causes and implications of differences.

**4.** Talk to three people you would expect to have contrasting views on love and marriage (differences in age, gender, upbringing, experience, and religion might affect attitudes). Ask each of them the same questions and then compare their answers.

# Appendix:
## More About Research Methods

This appendix explains how to learn about any topic. It is crucial that you distinguish valid conclusions from wishful thinking. Such learning begins with your personal experience.

## Make It Personal

Think about your life, observe your behavior, and watch the people around you. Pay careful attention to details of expression, emotion, and behavior. The more you see, the more fascinated, curious, and reflective you will become. Ask questions and listen carefully and respectfully to what other people say regarding development.

Whenever you ask specific questions as part of an assignment, **remember that observing ethical standards (see Chapter 1) comes first.** *Before* you interview anyone, inform the person of your purpose and assure him or her of confidentiality. Promise not to identify the person in your report (use a pseudonym) and do not repeat any personal details that emerge in the interview to anyone (friends or strangers). Your instructor will provide further ethical guidance. If you might publish what you've learned, get in touch with your college's Institutional Review Board (IRB).

## Read the Research

No matter how deeply you think about your own experiences, and no matter how intently you listen to others whose background is unlike yours, you also need to read scholarly published work in order to fully understand any topic that interests you. Be skeptical about magazine or newspaper reports; some are bound to be simplified, exaggerated, or biased.

### Professional Journals and Books

Part of the process of science is that conclusions are not considered solid until they are corroborated in many studies, which means that you should consult several sources on any topic. **Five journals in human development** are:

- *Developmental Psychology* (published by the American Psychological Association)
- *Child Development* (Society for Research in Child Development)
- *Developmental Review* (Elsevier)
- *Human Development* (Karger)
- *Developmental Science* (Wiley)

These journals differ in the types of articles and studies they publish, but all are well respected and peer-reviewed, which means that other scholars review each article submitted and recommend that it be accepted, rejected, or revised. Every article includes references to other recent work.

Also look at journals that specialize in longer reviews from the perspective of a researcher.

- *Child Development Perspectives* (from Society for Research in Child Development)
- *Perspectives on Psychological Science* (This is published by the Association for Psychological Science. APS publishes several excellent journals, none specifically on development but every issue has at least one article that is directly relevant.)

Beyond these seven are literally thousands of other professional journals, each with a particular perspective or topic, including many in sociology, family studies, economics, and so on. To judge them, look for journals that are peer-reviewed. Also consider the following details: the background of the author (research funded by corporations tends to favor their products); the nature of the publisher (professional organizations, as in the first two journals above, protect their reputations); how long the journal has been published (the volume number tells you that). Some interesting work does not meet these criteria, but these are guides to quality.

Many **books** cover some aspect of development. Single-author books are likely to present only one viewpoint. That view may be insightful, but it is limited. You might consult a *handbook,* which is a book that includes many authors and many topics. One good handbook in development, now in its seventh edition (a sign that past scholars have found it useful) is:

- *Handbook of Child Psychology and Developmental Science* (7th ed.), edited by Richard M. Lerner, 2015, Hoboken, NJ: Wiley.

Dozens of other good handbooks are available, many of which focus on a particular age, perspective, or topic.

## The Internet

The **Internet** is a mixed blessing, useful to every novice and experienced researcher but dangerous as well. Every library worldwide and most homes in North America, Western Europe, and East Asia have computers that provide access to journals and other information. If you're doing research in a library, ask for help from the librarians; many of them can guide you in the most effective ways to conduct online searches. In addition, other students, friends, and even strangers can be helpful.

Virtually everything is on the Internet, not only massive national and international statistics but also accounts of very personal experiences. Photos, charts, quizzes, ongoing experiments, newspapers from around the world, videos, and much more are available at a click. Every journal has a Web site, with tables of contents, abstracts, and sometimes full texts. (An abstract gives the key findings; for the full text, you may need to consult the library's copy of the print version.)

Unfortunately, you can spend many frustrating hours sifting through information that is useless, trash, or tangential. *Directories* (which list general topics or areas and then move you step by step in the direction you choose) and *search engines* (which give you all the sites that use a particular word or words) can help you select appropriate information. Each directory or search engine provides somewhat different lists; none provides only the most comprehensive and accurate sites. Sometimes organizations figure out ways to make their links appear first, even though they are biased. With experience and help, you will find the best sites for you, but you will also encounter some junk no matter how experienced you are.

Anybody can put anything online, regardless of its truth or fairness, so you need a very critical eye. Make sure you have several divergent sources for every "fact" you find; consider who provided the information and why. Every controversial issue has sites that forcefully advocate opposite viewpoints, sometimes with biased statistics and narrow perspectives.

Here are four Internet sites that are quite reliable:

- *embryo.soad.umich.edu* The Multidimensional Human Embryo. Presents MRI images of a human embryo at various stages of development, accompanied by brief explanations.
- *childdevelopmentinfo.com* Child Development Institute. A useful site, with links and articles on child development and information on common childhood psychological disorders.
- *eric.ed.gov* Education Resources Information Center (ERIC). Provides links to many education-related sites and includes brief descriptions of each.
- *www.cdc.gov/nchs/hus.htm* The National Center for Health Statistics issues an annual report on health trends, called *Health, United States.*

Every source—you, your interviewees, journals, books, and the Internet—is helpful. Do not depend on any particular one. Avoid plagiarism and prejudice by citing every source and noting objectivity, validity, and credibility. Your own analysis, opinions, words, and conclusions are crucial, backed up by science.

## Additional Terms and Concepts

As emphasized throughout the text, the study of development is a science. Social scientists spend years in graduate school, studying methods and statistics. Chapter 1 touches on some of these matters (observation and experiments; correlation and statistical significance; independent and dependent variables; experimental and control groups; cross-sectional, longitudinal, and cross-sequential research), but there is much more. A few additional aspects of research are presented here to help you evaluate research wherever you find it.

## Who Participates?

The entire group of people about whom a scientist wants to learn is called a **population.** Generally, a research population is quite large—not usually the world's entire population of more than 7 billion, but perhaps all the 4 million babies born in the United States last year, or all the 31 million Japanese currently over age 65.

The particular individuals who are studied in a specific research project are called the **participants.** They are used as a **sample** of the larger group. Ideally, the participants are a **representative sample,** that is, a sample that reflects the entire population. Every peer-reviewed, published study reports details on the sample.

Selection of the sample is crucial. People who volunteer, or people who have telephones, or people who have some particular condition are not a *random sample;*

**population** The entire group of individuals who are of particular concern in a scientific study, such as all the children of the world or all newborns who weigh less than 3 pounds.

**participants** The people who are studied in a research project. Participants is the term now used in psychology; other disciplines still call these people "subjects."

**sample** A group of individuals drawn from a specified population. A sample might be the low-birthweight babies born in four particular hospitals that are representative of all hospitals.

**representative sample** A group of research participants who reflect the relevant characteristics of the larger population whose attributes are under study.

in a random sample, everyone in a particular population is equally likely to be selected. To avoid *selection bias,* some studies are *prospective,* beginning with an entire cluster of people (for instance, every baby born on a particular day) and then tracing the development of some particular characteristic.

For example, prospective studies find the antecedents of heart disease, or child abuse, or high school dropout rates—all of which are much harder to find if the study is *retrospective,* beginning with those who had heart attacks, experienced abuse, or left school. Thus, although retrospective research finds that most high school dropouts say they disliked school, prospective research finds that some who like school still decide to drop out and then later say they hated school, while others dislike school but stay to graduate. Prospective research discovers how many students are in these last two categories; retrospective research on people who have already dropped out does not.

## Research Design

Every researcher begins not only by formulating a hypothesis but also by learning what other scientists have discovered about the topic in question and what methods might be useful and ethical in designing research. Often they include measures to guard against inadvertently finding only the results they expect. For example, the people who actually gather the data may not know the purpose of the research. Scientists say that these data gatherers are **blind** to the hypothesized outcome. Participants are sometimes "blind" as well, because otherwise they might, for instance, respond the way they think they should.

Another crucial aspect of research design is to define exactly what is to be studied. Researchers establish an **operational definition** of whatever phenomenon they will be examining, defining each variable by describing specific, observable behavior. This is essential in quantitative research, but it is also useful in qualitative research. For example, if a researcher wants to know when babies begin to walk, does walking include steps taken while holding on? Is one unsteady step enough? Some parents say yes, but the usual operational definition of *walking* is "takes at least three steps without holding on." This operational definition allows comparisons worldwide, making it possible to discover, for example, that well-fed African babies tend to walk earlier than well-fed European babies.

Operational definitions are difficult to formulate, but they are essential when personality traits are studied. How should *aggression* or *sharing* or *shyness* be defined? Lack of an operational definition leads to contradictory results. For instance, critics report that infant day care makes children more aggressive, but advocates report that it makes them less passive. In this case, both may be seeing the same behavior but defining it differently. For any scientist, operational definitions are crucial, and studies usually include descriptions of how they measured attitudes or behavior.

## Reporting Results

You already know that results should be reported in sufficient detail so that another scientist can analyze the conclusions and replicate the research. Various methods, populations, and research designs may produce divergent conclusions. For that reason, handbooks, some journals, and some articles are called *reviews:* They summarize past research. Often, when studies are similar in operational definitions and methods, the review is a **meta-analysis,** which combines the findings of many studies to present an overall conclusion.

Table 1.3 (p. 22) describes some statistical measures. One of them is *statistical significance,* which indicates whether or not a particular result could have occurred by chance.

**blind** The condition of data gatherers (and sometimes participants, as well) who are deliberately kept ignorant of the purpose of the research so that they cannot unintentionally bias the results.

**operational definition** A description of the specific, observable behavior that will constitute the variable that is to be studied, so that any reader will know whether that behavior occurred or not. Operational definitions may be arbitrary (e.g., an IQ score at or above 130 is operationally defined as "gifted"), but they must be precise.

**meta-analysis** A technique of combining results of many studies to come to an overall conclusion. Meta-analysis is powerful, in that small samples can be added together to lead to significant conclusions, although variations from study to study sometimes make combining them impossible.

A crucial statistic is **effect size,** a way of measuring how much impact one variable has on another. Effect size ranges from 0 (no effect) to 1 (total transformation, never found in actual studies). Effect size may be particularly important when the sample size is large, because a large sample often leads to highly "significant" results (results that are unlikely to have occurred by chance) that have only a tiny effect on the variable of interest.

Hundreds of statistical measures are used by developmentalists. Often the same data can be presented in many ways: Some scientists examine statistical analysis intently before they accept conclusions as valid. A specific example involved methods to improve students' writing ability between grades 4 and 12. A meta-analysis found that many methods of writing instruction have a significant impact, but effect size is much larger for some methods (teaching strategies and summarizing) than for others (prewriting exercises and studying models). For teachers, this statistic is crucial, for they want to know what has a big effect, not merely what is better than chance (significant).

Numerous articles published in the past decade are meta-analyses that combine similar studies to search for general trends. Often effect sizes are also reported, which is especially helpful for meta-analyses since standard calculations almost always find some significance if the number of participants is in the thousands.

An added problem is the "file drawer" problem—that studies without significant results tend to be filed away rather than published. Thus, an accurate effect size may be much smaller than the published meta-analysis finds, or may be nonexistent. For this reason, replication is an important step.

Overall, then, designing and conducting valid research is complex yet crucial. Remember that with your own opinions: As this appendix advises, it is good to "make it personal," but do not stop there.

**effect size** A way of indicating statistically how much of an impact the independent variable in an experiment had on the dependent variable.

# Glossary

**23rd pair** The chromosome pair that, in humans, determines sex. The other 22 pairs are autosomes, inherited equally by males and females.

## A

**acceleration** Educating gifted children alongside other children of the same mental, not chronological, age.

**accommodation** The restructuring of old ideas to include new experiences.

**achievement test** A measure of mastery or proficiency in reading, mathematics, writing, science, or some other subject.

**adolescence-limited offender** A person whose criminal activity stops by age 21.

**adolescent egocentrism** A characteristic of adolescent thinking that leads young people (ages 10 to 13) to focus on themselves to the exclusion of others.

**adrenal glands** Two glands, located above the kidneys, that respond to the pituitary, producing hormones.

**affordance** An opportunity for perception and interaction that is offered by a person, place, or object in the environment.

**age of viability** The age (about 22 weeks after conception) at which a fetus might survive outside the mother's uterus if specialized medical care is available.

**aggressive-rejected** A type of childhood rejection, when other children do not want to be friends with a child because of his or her antagonistic, confrontational behavior.

**allele** A variation that makes a gene different in some way from other genes for the same characteristics. Many genes never vary; others have several possible alleles.

**allocare** Literally, "other-care"; the care of children by people other than the biological parents.

**alloparents** Literally, "other parents"; people who provide care for children but who are not the child's parents. In the twenty-first century, not only neighbors and relatives (grandparents, siblings, and so on) but also professionals (pediatricians, teachers, day-care aides, and nurses) can be alloparents.

**amygdala** A tiny brain structure that registers emotions, particularly fear and anxiety.

**analytic thought** Thought that results from analysis, such as a systematic ranking of pros and cons, risks and consequences, possibilities and facts. Analytic thought depends on logic and rationality.

**animism** The belief that natural objects and phenomena are alive, moving around, and having sensations and abilities that are human-like.

**anorexia nervosa** An eating disorder characterized by self-starvation. Affected individuals voluntarily undereat and often overexercise, depriving their vital organs of nutrition. Anorexia can be fatal.

**anoxia** A lack of oxygen that, if prolonged, can cause brain damage or death.

**antisocial behavior** Actions that are deliberately hurtful or destructive to another person.

**Apgar scale** A quick assessment of a newborn's health, from 0 to 10. Below 5 is an emergency—a neonatal pediatrician is summoned immediately. Most babies are at 7, 8, or 9—almost never a perfect 10.

**apprenticeship in thinking** Vygotsky's term for how cognition is stimulated and developed in people by more skilled members of society.

**aptitude** The potential to master a specific skill or to learn a certain body of knowledge.

**assimilation** The reinterpretation of new experiences to fit into old ideas.

**asthma** A chronic disease of the respiratory system in which inflammation narrows the airways from the nose and mouth to the lungs, causing difficulty in breathing. Signs and symptoms include wheezing, shortness of breath, chest tightness, and coughing.

**attachment** According to Ainsworth, "an affectional tie" that an infant forms with a caregiver—a tie that binds them together in space and endures over time.

**attention-deficit/hyperactivity disorder (ADHD)** A condition characterized by a persistent pattern of inattention and/or by hyperactive or impulsive behaviors; ADHD interferes with a person's functioning or development.

**authoritarian parenting** An approach to child rearing that is characterized by high behavioral standards, strict punishment for misconduct, and little communication from child to parent.

**authoritative parenting** An approach to child rearing in which the parents set limits but listen to the child and are flexible.

**autism spectrum disorder (ASD)** A developmental disorder marked by difficulty with social communication and interaction—including difficulty seeing things from another person's point of view—and restricted, repetitive patterns of behavior, interests, or activities.

**automatization** A process in which repetition of a sequence of thoughts and actions makes the sequence routine so that it no longer requires conscious thought.

**autonomy versus shame and doubt** Erikson's second crisis of psychosocial development. Toddlers either succeed or fail in gaining a sense of self-rule over their actions and their bodies.

**axon** A fiber that extends from a neuron and transmits electrochemical impulses from that neuron to the dendrites of other neurons.

## B

**babbling** An infant's repetition of certain syllables, such as *ba-ba-ba*, that begins when babies are between 6 and 9 months old.

**bed-sharing** When two or more people sleep in the same bed.

**behavioral teratogens** Agents and conditions that can harm the prenatal brain, impairing the future child's intellectual and emotional functioning.

**behaviorism** A grand theory of human development that studies observable behavior. Behaviorism is also called *learning theory* because it describes the laws and processes by which behavior is learned.

**bilingual education** A strategy in which school subjects are taught in both the learner's original language and the second (majority) language.

**binocular vision** The ability to focus the two eyes in a coordinated manner in order to see one image.

**blind** The condition of data gatherers (and sometimes participants, as well) who are deliberately kept ignorant of the purpose of the research so that they cannot unintentionally bias the results.

**body image** A person's idea of how his or her body looks.

**Brazelton Neonatal Behavioral Assessment Scale (NBAS)** A test that is often administered to newborns which measures responsiveness and records 46 behaviors, including 20 reflexes.

**bulimia nervosa** An eating disorder characterized by binge eating and subsequent purging, usually by induced vomiting and/or use of laxatives.

**bully-victim** Someone who attacks others and who is attacked as well. (Also called *provocative victims* because they do things that elicit bullying.)

**bullying** Repeated, systematic efforts to inflict harm through physical, verbal, or social attack on a weaker person.

**bullying aggression** Unprovoked, repeated physical or verbal attacks, especially on victims who are unlikely to defend themselves.

# C

**carrier** A person whose genotype includes a gene that is not expressed in the phenotype. The carried gene occurs in half of the carrier's gametes and thus is passed on to half of the carrier's children. If such a gene is inherited from both parents, the characteristic appears in the phenotype.

**centration** A characteristic of preoperational thought in which a young child focuses (centers) on one idea, excluding all others.

**cephalocaudal development** Growth and development that occurs from the head down.

**cerebral palsy** A disorder that results from damage to the brain's motor centers. People with cerebral palsy have difficulty with muscle control, so their speech and/or body movements are impaired.

**cesarean section (c-section)** A surgical birth, in which incisions through the mother's abdomen and uterus allow the fetus to be removed quickly, instead of being delivered through the vagina. (Also called *section*.)

**charter school** A public school with its own set of standards that is funded and licensed by the state or local district in which it is located.

**child abuse** Deliberate action that is harmful to a child's physical, emotional, or sexual well-being.

**child culture** The idea that each group of children has games, sayings, clothing styles, and superstitions that are not common among adults, just as every culture has distinct values, behaviors, and beliefs.

**child maltreatment** Intentional harm to or avoidable endangerment of anyone under 18 years of age.

**child neglect** Failure to meet a child's basic physical, educational, or emotional needs.

**child sexual abuse** Any erotic activity that arouses an adult and excites, shames, or confuses a child, whether or not the victim protests and whether or not genital contact is involved.

**child-directed speech** The high-pitched, simplified, and repetitive way adults speak to infants and children. (Also called *baby talk* or *motherese*.)

**childhood obesity** In a child, having a BMI above the 95th percentile, according to the U.S. Centers for Disease Control and Prevention's 1980 standards for children of a given age.

**childhood overweight** In a child, having a BMI above the 85th percentile, according to the U.S. Centers for Disease Control and Prevention's 1980 standards for children of a given age.

**chromosome** One of the 46 molecules of DNA (in 23 pairs) that virtually every cell of the human body contains and that, together, contain all the genes. Other species have more or fewer chromosomes.

**circadian rhythm** A day–night cycle of biological activity that occurs approximately every 24 hours.

**classical conditioning** The learning process in which a meaningful stimulus (such as the smell of food to a hungry animal) is connected with a neutral stimulus (such as the sound of a tone) that had no special meaning before conditioning. (Also called *respondent conditioning*.)

**classification** The logical principle that things can be organized into groups (or categories or classes) according to some characteristic that they have in common.

**cluster suicides** Several suicides committed by members of a group within a brief period.

**co-sleeping** A custom in which parents and their children (usually infants) sleep together in the same room.

**cognitive equilibrium** In cognitive theory, a state of mental balance in which people are not confused because they can use their existing thought processes to understand current experiences and ideas.

**cognitive theory** A grand theory of human development that focuses on changes in how people think over time. According to this theory, our thoughts shape our attitudes, beliefs, and behaviors.

**cohabitation** An arrangement in which a couple lives together in a committed romantic relationship but are not formally married.

**cohort** People born within the same historical period who therefore move through life together, experiencing the same events, new technologies, and cultural shifts at the same ages. For example, the effect of the Internet varies depending on what cohort a person belongs to.

**comorbid** Refers to the presence of two or more disease conditions at the same time in the same person.

**concrete operational thought** Piaget's term for the ability to reason logically about direct experiences and perceptions.

**conservation** The principle that the amount of a substance remains the same (i.e., is conserved) even when its appearance changes.

**control processes** Mechanisms (including selective attention, metacognition, and emotional regulation) that combine memory, processing speed, and knowledge to regulate the analysis and flow of information within the information-processing system. (Also called *executive processes*.)

**conventional moral reasoning** Kohlberg's second level of moral reasoning, emphasizing social rules.

**copy number variations** Genes with various repeats or deletions of base pairs.

**corporal punishment** Punishment that physically hurts the body, such as slapping, spanking, etc.

**corpus callosum** A long, thick band of nerve fibers that connects the left and right hemispheres of the brain and allows communication between them.

**correlation** A number between +1.0 and −1.0 that indicates the degree of relationship between two variables, expressed in terms of the likelihood that one variable will (or will not) occur when the other variable does (or does not). A correlation indicates only that two variables are somehow related, not that one variable causes the other to occur.

**cortex** The outer layers of the brain in humans and other mammals. Most thinking, feeling, and sensing involves the cortex.

**cortisol** The primary stress hormone; fluctuations in the body's cortisol level affect human emotions.

**couvade** Symptoms of pregnancy and birth experienced by fathers.

**critical period** A crucial time when a particular type of developmental growth (in body or behavior) must happen for normal development to occur, or when harm (such as a toxic substance or destructive event) can occur.

**cross-sectional research** A research design that compares groups of people who differ in age but are similar in other important characteristics.

**cross-sequential research** A hybrid research design in which researchers first study several groups of people of different ages (a cross-sectional approach) and then follow those groups over the years (a longitudinal approach). (Also called *cohort-sequential research* or *time-sequential research*.)

**culture** A system of shared beliefs, norms, behaviors, and expectations that persist over time and prescribe social behavior and assumptions.

**cyberbullying** Bullying that occurs when one person spreads insults or rumors about another by means of social media posts, e-mails, text messages, or cell phone videos.

## D

**deductive reasoning** Reasoning from a general statement, premise, or principle, through logical steps, to figure out (deduce) specifics. (Also called *top-down reasoning*.)

**dendrite** A fiber that extends from a neuron and receives electrochemical impulses transmitted from other neurons via their axons.

**deoxyribonucleic acid (DNA)** The chemical composition of the molecules that contain the genes, which are the chemical instructions for cells to manufacture various proteins.

**dependent variable** In an experiment, the variable that may change as a result of whatever new condition or situation the experimenter adds. In other words, the dependent variable *depends* on the independent variable.

**developmental psychopathology** The field that uses insights into typical development to understand and remediate developmental disorders.

**developmental theory** A group of ideas, assumptions, and generalizations that interpret and illuminate the thousands of observations that have been made about human growth. A developmental theory provides a framework for explaining the patterns and problems of development.

**deviancy training** Destructive peer support in which one person shows another how to rebel against authority or social norms.

**differential susceptibility** The idea that people vary in how sensitive they are to particular experiences. Often such differences are genetic, which makes some people affected "for better or for worse" by life events. (Also called *differential sensitivity*.)

**difference-equals-deficit error** The mistaken belief that a deviation from some norm is necessarily inferior to behavior or characteristics that meet the standard.

**disorganized attachment** A type of attachment that is marked by an infant's inconsistent reactions to the caregiver's departure and return.

**distal parenting** Caregiving practices that involve remaining distant from the baby, providing toys, food, and face-to-face communication with minimal holding and touching.

**dizygotic (DZ) twins** Twins who are formed when two separate ova are fertilized by two separate sperm at roughly the same time. (Also called *fraternal twins*.)

**dominant–recessive pattern** The interaction of a heterozygous pair of alleles in such a way that the phenotype reflects one allele (the dominant gene) more than the other (the recessive gene).

**doula** A woman who helps with the birth process. Traditionally in Latin America, a doula was the only professional who attended childbirth. Now doulas are likely to arrive at the woman's home during early labor and later work alongside a hospital's staff.

**Down syndrome** A condition in which a person has 47 chromosomes instead of the usual 46, with 3 rather than 2 chromosomes at the 21st site. People with Down syndrome typically have distinctive characteristics, including unusual facial features, heart abnormalities, and language difficulties. (Also called *trisomy-21*.)

**dual processing** The notion that two networks exist within the human brain, one for emotional processing of stimuli and one for analytical reasoning.

**dynamic-systems approach** A view of human development as an ongoing, ever-changing interaction between the physical, cognitive, and psychosocial influences. The crucial understanding is that development is never static but is always affected by, and affects, many systems of development.

**dyscalculia** Unusual difficulty with math, probably originating from a distinct part of the brain.

**dyslexia** Unusual difficulty with reading; thought to be the result of some neurological underdevelopment.

## E

**eclectic perspective** The approach taken by most developmentalists, in which they apply aspects of each of the various theories of development rather than adhering exclusively to one theory.

**ecological-systems approach** A perspective on human development that considers all of the influences from the various contexts of development. (Later renamed *bioecological theory*.)

**effect size** A way of indicating statistically how much of an impact the independent variable in an experiment had on the dependent variable.

**effortful control** The ability to regulate one's emotions and actions through effort, not simply through natural inclination.

**egocentrism** Piaget's term for children's tendency to think about the world entirely from their own personal perspective.

**embryo** The name for a developing human organism from about the third week through the eighth week after conception.

**embryonic period** The stage of prenatal development from approximately the third week through the eighth week after conception. The basic forms of all body structures, including internal organs, develop.

**emerging adulthood** The period of life between the ages of 18 and 25. Emerging adulthood is now widely thought of as a distinct developmental stage.

**emotional regulation** The ability to control when and how emotions are expressed.

**empathy** The ability to understand the emotions and concerns of another person, especially when they differ from one's own.

**empirical evidence** Evidence that is based on observation, experience, or experiment; not theoretical.

**English Language Learners (ELLs)** Children in the United States whose proficiency in English is low—usually below a cutoff score on an oral or written test. Many children who speak a non-English language at home are also capable in English; they are *not* ELLs.

**entity theory of intelligence** An approach to understanding intelligence that sees ability as innate, a fixed quantity present at birth; those who hold this view do not believe that effort enhances achievement. Also called a fixed mindset.

**epigenetics** The study of how environmental factors affect genes and genetic expression—enhancing, halting, shaping, or altering the expression of genes.

**equifinality** A basic principle of developmental psychopathology, which holds that one symptom can have many causes.

**ESL (English as a Second Language)** A U.S. approach to teaching English that gathers all of the non-English speakers together and provides intense instruction in English. Students' first languages are never used; the goal is to prepare them for regular classes in English.

**estradiol** A sex hormone, considered the chief estrogen. Females produce much more estradiol than males do.

**ethnic group** People whose ancestors were born in the same region and who often share a language, culture, and religion.

**executive function** The cognitive ability to organize and prioritize the many thoughts that arise from the various parts of the brain, allowing the person to anticipate, strategize, and plan behavior.

**experience-dependent** Brain functions that depend on particular, variable experiences and therefore may or may not develop in a particular infant.

**experience-expectant** Brain functions that require certain basic common experiences (which an infant can be expected to have) in order to develop normally.

**experiment** A research method in which the researcher tries to determine the cause-and-effect relationship between two variables by manipulating one (called the *independent variable*) and then observing and recording the ensuing changes in the other (called the *dependent variable*).

**extended family** A family of relatives in addition to the nuclear family, usually three or more generations living in one household.

**extremely low birthweight (ELBW)** A body weight at birth of less than 1,000 grams (2 pounds, 3 ounces).

**extrinsic motivation** A drive, or reason to pursue a goal, that arises from the need to have one's achievements rewarded from outside, perhaps by receiving material possessions or another person's esteem.

## F

**false positive** The result of a laboratory test that reports something as true when in fact it is not true. This can occur for pregnancy tests, when a woman might not be pregnant even though the test says she is, or during pregnancy, when a problem is reported that actually does not exist.

**familism** The belief that family members should support one another, sacrificing individual freedom and success, if necessary, in order to preserve family unity and protect the family from outside forces.

**family function** The way a family works to meet the needs of its members. Children need families to provide basic material necessities, to encourage learning, to help them develop self-respect, to nurture friendships, and to foster harmony and stability.

**family structure** The legal and genetic relationships among relatives living in the same home. Possible structures include nuclear family, extended family, stepfamily, single-parent family, and many others.

**fast-mapping** The speedy and sometimes imprecise way in which children learn new words by tentatively placing them in mental categories according to their perceived meaning.

**fetal alcohol syndrome (FAS)** A cluster of birth defects, including abnormal facial characteristics, slow physical growth, and reduced intellectual ability, that may occur in the fetus of a woman who drinks alcohol while pregnant.

**fetal period** The stage of prenatal development from the ninth week after conception until birth. The fetus gains about 7 pounds (more than 3,000 grams) and organs become more mature, gradually able to function on their own.

**fetus** The name for a developing human organism from the start of the ninth week after conception until birth.

**fine motor skills** Physical abilities involving small body movements, especially of the hands and fingers, such as drawing and picking up a coin. (The word *fine* here means "small.")

**Flynn effect** The rise in average IQ scores that has occurred over the decades in many nations.

**focus on appearance** A characteristic of preoperational thought in which a young child ignores all attributes that are not apparent.

**foreclosure** Erikson's term for premature identity formation, which occurs when an adolescent adopts his or her parents' or society's roles and values wholesale, without questioning or analysis.

**formal operational thought** In Piaget's theory, the fourth and final stage of cognitive development, characterized by more systematic logical thinking and by the ability to understand and systematically manipulate abstract concepts.

**foster care** A legal, publicly supported system in which a maltreated child is removed from the parents' custody and entrusted to another adult or family, who is reimbursed for expenses incurred in meeting the child's needs.

**fragile X syndrome** A genetic disorder in which part of the X chromosome seems to be attached to the rest of it by a very thin string of molecules. The cause is a single gene that has more than 200 repetitions of one triplet.

## G

**gender differences** Differences in the roles and behaviors of males and females that are prescribed by the culture.

**gender identity** A person's acceptance of the roles and behaviors that society associates with the biological categories of male and female.

**gender schema** A cognitive concept or general belief based on one's experiences—in this case, a child's understanding of sex differences.

**gene** A small section of a chromosome; the basic unit for the transmission of heredity. A gene consists of a string of chemicals that provide instructions for the cell to manufacture certain proteins.

**generational forgetting** The idea that each new generation forgets what the previous generation learned. As used here, the term refers to knowledge about the harm drugs can do.

**genetic counseling** Consultation and testing by trained experts that enables individuals to learn about their genetic heritage, including harmful conditions that they might pass along to any children they may conceive.

**genome** The full set of genes that are the instructions to make an individual member of a certain species.

**genotype** An organism's entire genetic inheritance, or genetic potential.

**germinal period** The first two weeks of prenatal development after conception, characterized by rapid cell division and the beginning of cell differentiation.

**gonads** The paired sex glands (ovaries in females, testicles in males). The gonads produce hormones and mature gametes.

**grammar** All of the methods—word order, verb forms, and so on—that languages use to communicate meaning, apart from the words themselves.

**gross motor skills** Physical abilities involving large body movements, such as walking and jumping. (The word *gross* here means "big.")

**growth mindset** The idea that skills and abilities develop with practice and effort, instead of being fixed or inborn.

**growth spurt** The relatively sudden and rapid physical growth that occurs during puberty. Each body part increases in size on a schedule: Weight usually precedes height, and growth of the limbs precedes growth of the torso.

**guided participation** The process by which people learn from others who guide their experiences and explorations.

## H

**habituation** The process of becoming accustomed to an object or event through repeated exposure to it, and thus becoming less interested in it.

**Head Start** A federally funded early-childhood intervention program for low-income children of preschool age.

**head-sparing** A biological mechanism that protects the brain when malnutrition disrupts body growth. The brain is the last part of the body to be damaged by malnutrition.

**heritability** A statistic that indicates what percentage of the variation in a particular trait within a particular population, in a particular context and era, can be traced to genes.

**heterozygous** Referring to two genes of one pair that differ in some way. Typically one allele has only a few base pairs that differ from the other member of the pair.

**hidden curriculum** The unofficial, unstated, or implicit patterns within a school that influence what children learn. For instance, teacher background, organization of the play space, and tracking are all part of the hidden curriculum—not formally prescribed, but instructive to the children.

**high-stakes test** An evaluation that is critical in determining success or failure. If a single test determines whether a student will graduate or be promoted, it is a high-stakes test.

**hippocampus** A brain structure that is a central processor of memory, especially memory for locations.

**holophrase** A single word that is used to express a complete, meaningful thought.

**home schooling** Education in which children are taught at home, usually by their parents.

**homozygous** Referring to two genes of one pair that are exactly the same in every letter of their code. Most gene pairs are homozygous.

**hookup** A sexual encounter between two people who are not in a romantic relationship. Neither intimacy nor commitment is expected.

**HPA (hypothalamus–pituitary–adrenal) axis** A sequence of hormone production originating in the hypothalamus and moving to the pituitary and then to the adrenal glands.

**HPG (hypothalamus–pituitary–gonad) axis** A sequence of hormone production originating in the hypothalamus and moving to the pituitary and then to the gonads.

**Human Genome Project** An international effort to map the complete human genetic code. This effort was essentially completed in 2001, though analysis is ongoing.

**hypothalamus** A brain area that responds to the amygdala and the hippocampus to produce hormones that activate other parts of the brain and body.

**hypothesis** A specific prediction that can be tested.

**hypothetical thought** Reasoning that includes propositions and possibilities that may not reflect reality.

## I

**identification** An attempt to defend one's self-concept by taking on the behaviors and attitudes of someone else.

**identity achievement** Erikson's term for the attainment of identity, or the point at which a person understands who he or she is as a unique individual, in accord with past experiences and future plans.

**identity versus role confusion** Erikson's term for the fifth stage of development, in which the person tries to figure out "Who am I?" but is confused as to which of many possible roles to adopt.

**imaginary audience** The other people who, in an adolescent's egocentric belief, are watching and taking note of his or her appearance, ideas, and behavior. This belief makes many teenagers very self-conscious.

**imaginary friends** Make-believe friends who exist only in a child's imagination; increasingly common from ages 3 through 7. They combat loneliness and aid emotional regulation.

**immersion** A strategy in which instruction in all school subjects occurs in the second (usually the majority) language that a child is learning.

**immigrant paradox** The surprising, paradoxical fact that low-SES immigrant women tend to have fewer birth complications than native-born peers with higher incomes.

**immunization** A process that stimulates the body's immune system by causing production of antibodies to defend against attack by a particular contagious disease. Creation of antibodies may be accomplished either naturally (by having the disease), by injection, by drops that are swallowed, or by a nasal spray.

**implantation** The process, beginning about 10 days after conception, in which the developing organism burrows into the uterus, where it can be nourished and protected as it continues to develop.

**impulse control** The ability to postpone or deny the immediate response to an idea or behavior.

**in vitro fertilization (IVF)** Fertilization that takes place outside a woman's body (as in a glass laboratory dish). The procedure involves mixing sperm with ova that have been surgically removed from the woman's ovary. If a zygote is produced, it is inserted into a woman's uterus, where it may implant and develop into a baby.

**incremental theory of intelligence** An approach to understanding intelligence which holds that intelligence can be directly increased by effort; those who subscribe to this view believe they can master whatever they seek to learn if they pay attention, participate in class, study, complete their homework, and so on. Also called a growth mindset.

**independent variable** In an experiment, the variable that is introduced to see what effect it has on the dependent variable. (Also called *experimental variable*.)

**individual education plan (IEP)** A document that specifies educational goals and plans for a child with special needs.

**induction** A disciplinary technique in which the parent tries to get the child to understand why a certain behavior was wrong. Listening, not lecturing, is crucial.

**inductive reasoning** Reasoning from one or more specific experiences or facts to reach (induce) a general conclusion. (Also called *bottom-up reasoning*.)

**industry versus inferiority** The fourth of Erikson's eight psychosocial crises, during which children attempt to master many skills, developing a sense of themselves as either industrious or inferior, competent or incompetent.

**information-processing theory** A perspective that compares human thinking processes, by analogy, to computer analysis of data, including sensory input, connections, stored memories, and output.

**initiative versus guilt** Erikson's third psychosocial crisis, in which children undertake new skills and activities and feel guilty when they do not succeed at them.

**injury control/harm reduction** Practices that are aimed at anticipating, controlling, and preventing dangerous activities; these practices reflect the beliefs that accidents are not random and that injuries can be made less harmful if proper controls are in place.

**insecure-avoidant attachment** A pattern of attachment in which an infant avoids connection with the caregiver, as when the infant seems not to care about the caregiver's presence, departure, or return.

**insecure-resistant/ambivalent attachment** A pattern of attachment in which an infant's anxiety and uncertainty are evident, as when the infant becomes very upset at separation from the caregiver and both resists and seeks contact on reunion.

**instrumental aggression** Behavior that hurts someone else because the aggressor wants to get or keep a possession or a privilege.

**intelligence** The ability to learn and understand various aspects of life, traditionally focused on reading and math, and more recently on the arts, movement, and social interactions.

**intimacy versus isolation** The sixth of Erikson's eight stages of development. Adults seek someone with whom to share their lives in an enduring and self-sacrificing commitment. Without such commitment, they risk profound aloneness and isolation.

**intrinsic motivation** A drive, or reason to pursue a goal, that comes from inside a person, such as the desire to feel smart or competent.

**intuitive thought** Thought that arises from an emotion or a hunch, beyond rational explanation, and is influenced by past experiences and cultural assumptions.

**invincibility fable** An adolescent's egocentric conviction that he or she cannot be overcome or even harmed by anything that might defeat a normal mortal, such as unprotected sex, drug abuse, or high-speed driving.

**irreversibility** A characteristic of preoperational thought in which a young child thinks that nothing can be undone. A thing cannot be restored to the way it was before a change occurred.

## K

**kangaroo care** A form of newborn care in which mothers (and sometimes fathers) rest their babies on their naked chests, like kangaroo mothers that carry their immature newborns in a pouch on their abdomen.

**kinship care** A form of foster care in which a relative of a maltreated child, usually a grandparent, becomes the approved caregiver.

**knowledge base** A body of knowledge in a particular area that makes it easier to master new information in that area.

## L

**language acquisition device (LAD)** Chomsky's term for a hypothesized mental structure that enables humans to learn language, including the basic aspects of grammar, vocabulary, and intonation.

**lateralization** Literally, sidedness, referring to the specialization in certain functions by each side of the brain, with one side dominant for each activity. The left side of the brain controls the right side of the body, and vice versa.

**least restrictive environment (LRE)** A legal requirement that children with special needs be assigned to the most general educational context in which they can be expected to learn.

**leptin** A hormone that affects appetite and is believed to affect the onset of puberty. Leptin levels increase during childhood and peak at around age 12.

**life-course-persistent offender** A person whose criminal activity typically begins in early adolescence and continues throughout life; a career criminal.

**life-span perspective** An approach to the study of human development that takes into account all phases of life, not just childhood or adulthood.

**limbic system** The parts of the brain that interact to produce emotions, including the amygdala, the hypothalamus, and the hippocampus. Many other parts of the brain also are involved with emotions.

**linked lives** Lives in which the success, health, and well-being of each family member are connected to those of other members, including those of another generation, as in the relationship between parents and children.

**"little scientist"** The stage-five toddler (age 12 to 18 months) who experiments without anticipating the results, using trial and error in active and creative exploration.

**long-term memory** The component of the information-processing system in which virtually limitless amounts of information can be stored indefinitely.

**longitudinal research** A research design in which the same individuals are followed over time, as their development is repeatedly assessed.

**low birthweight (LBW)** A body weight at birth of less than 2,500 grams (5½ pounds).

## M

**major depression** Feelings of hopelessness, lethargy, and worthlessness that last two weeks or more.

**massification** The idea that establishing institutions of higher learning and encouraging college enrollment can benefit everyone (the masses).

**mean length of utterance (MLU)** The average number of words in a typical sentence (called utterance because children may not talk in complete sentences). MLU is often used to measure language development.

**menarche** A girl's first menstrual period, signaling that she has begun ovulation. Pregnancy is biologically possible, but ovulation and menstruation are often irregular for years after menarche.

**meta-analysis** A technique of combining results of many studies to come to an overall conclusion. Meta-analysis is powerful, in that small samples can be added together to lead to significant conclusions, although variations from study to study sometimes make combining them impossible.

**microbiome** All of the microbes (bacteria, viruses, and so on) with all of their genes in a community; here, the millions of microbes of the human body.

**middle childhood** The period between early childhood and early adolescence, approximately from ages 6 to 11.

**middle school** A school for children in the grades between elementary school and high school. Middle school usually begins with grade 6 and ends with grade 8.

**modeling** The central process of social learning, by which a person observes the actions of others and then copies them.

**monozygotic (MZ) twins** Twins who originate from one zygote that splits apart very early in development. (Also called *identical twins*.) Other monozygotic multiple births (such as triplets and quadruplets) can occur as well.

**Montessori schools** Schools that offer early-childhood education based on the philosophy of Maria Montessori, which emphasizes careful work and tasks that each young child can do.

**moratorium** An adolescent's choice of a socially acceptable way to postpone making identity-achievement decisions. Going to college is a common example.

**motor skill** The learned abilities to move some part of the body, in actions ranging from a large leap to a flicker of the eyelid. (The word *motor* here refers to movement of muscles.)

**multifactorial** Referring to a trait that is affected by many factors, both genetic and environmental, that enhance, halt, shape, or alter the expression of genes, resulting in a phenotype that may differ markedly from the genotype.

**multifinality** A basic principle of developmental psychopathology, which holds that one cause can have many (multiple) final manifestations.

**multiple intelligences** The idea that human intelligence is composed of a varied set of abilities rather than a single, all-encompassing one.

**myelin** The coating on axons that speeds transmission of signals from one neuron to another.

**myelination** The process by which axons become coated with myelin, a fatty substance that speeds the transmission of nerve impulses from neuron to neuron.

## N

**naming explosion** A sudden increase in an infant's vocabulary, especially in the number of nouns, that begins at about 18 months of age.

**National Assessment of Educational Progress (NAEP)** An ongoing and nationally representative measure of U.S. children's achievement in reading, mathematics, and other subjects over time; nicknamed "the Nation's Report Card."

**nature** In development, nature refers to the traits, capacities, and limitations that each individual inherits genetically from his or her parents at the moment of conception.

**neglectful/uninvolved parenting** An approach to child rearing in which the parents are indifferent toward their children and unaware of what is going on in their children's lives.

**neurodiversity** The idea that each person has neurological strengths and weaknesses that should be appreciated, in much the same way diverse cultures and ethnicities are welcomed. Neurodiversity seems particularly relevant for children with disorders on the autism spectrum.

**neuron** One of billions of nerve cells in the central nervous system, especially in the brain.

**neurotransmitter** A brain chemical that carries information from the axon of a sending neuron to the dendrites of a receiving neuron.

**nuclear family** A family that consists of a father, a mother, and their biological children under age 18.

**nurture** In development, nurture includes all of the environmental influences that affect the individual after conception. This includes everything from the mother's nutrition while pregnant to the cultural influences in the nation.

## O

**object permanence** The realization that objects (including people) still exist when they can no longer be seen, touched, or heard.

**Oedipus complex** The unconscious desire of young boys to replace their father and win their mother's romantic love.

**operant conditioning** The learning process by which a particular action is followed by something desired (which makes the person or animal more likely to repeat the action) or by something unwanted (which makes the action less likely to be repeated). (Also called *instrumental conditioning.*)

**operational definition** A description of the specific, observable behavior that will constitute the variable that is to be studied, so that any reader will know whether that behavior occurred or not. Operational definitions may be arbitrary (e.g., an IQ score at or above 130 is operationally defined as "gifted"), but they must be precise.

**overimitation** When a person imitates an action that is not a relevant part of the behavior to be learned. Overimitation is common among 2- to 6-year-olds when they imitate adult actions that are irrelevant and inefficient.

**overregularization** The application of rules of grammar even when exceptions occur, making the language seem more "regular" than it actually is.

## P

**parasuicide** Any potentially lethal action against the self that does not result in death. (Also called *attempted suicide* or *failed suicide.*)

**parent–infant bond** The strong, loving connection between parents and their baby.

**parental alliance** Cooperation between a mother and a father based on their mutual commitment to their children. In a parental alliance, the parents support each other in their shared parental roles.

**parental monitoring** Parents' ongoing awareness of what their children are doing, where, and with whom.

**parentification** When a child acts more like a parent than a child. Parentification may occur if the actual parents do not act as caregivers, making a child feel responsible for the family.

**participants** The people who are studied in a research project. Participants is the term now used in psychology; other disciplines still call these people "subjects."

**peer pressure** Encouragement to conform to one's friends or contemporaries in behavior, dress, and attitude; usually considered a negative force, as when adolescent peers encourage one another to defy adult authority.

**percentile** A point on a ranking scale of 0 to 100. The 50th percentile is the midpoint; half the people in the population being studied rank higher and half rank lower.

**permanency planning** An effort by child-welfare authorities to find a long-term living situation that will provide stability and support for a maltreated child. A goal is to avoid repeated changes of caregiver or school, which can be particularly harmful to the child.

**permissive parenting** An approach to child rearing that is characterized by high nurturance and communication but little discipline, guidance, or control. (Also called *indulgent parenting.*)

**perseveration** The tendency to persevere in, or stick to, one thought or action for a long time.

**personal fable** An aspect of adolescent egocentrism characterized by an adolescent's belief that his or her thoughts, feelings, and experiences are unique, more wonderful, or more awful than anyone else's.

**phallic stage** Freud's third stage of development, when the penis becomes the focus of concern and pleasure.

**phenotype** The observable characteristics of a person, including appearance, personality, intelligence, and all other traits.

**PISA (Programme for International Student Assessment)** An international test taken by 15-year-olds in 50 nations that is designed to measure problem solving and cognition in daily life.

**pituitary** A gland in the brain that responds to a signal from the hypothalamus by producing many hormones, including those that regulate growth and sexual maturation.

**pituitary** A gland in the brain that responds to a signal from the hypothalamus by producing many hormones, including those that regulate growth and that control other glands, among them the adrenal and sex glands.

**plasticity** The idea that abilities, personality, and other human characteristics can change over time. Plasticity is particularly evident during childhood, but even older adults are not always "set in their ways."

**polygamous family** A family consisting of one man, several wives, and their children.

**polygenic** Referring to a trait that is influenced by many genes.

**population** The entire group of individuals who are of particular concern in a scientific study, such as all the children of the world or all newborns who weigh less than 3 pounds.

**post-traumatic stress disorder (PTSD)** An anxiety disorder that develops as a delayed reaction to having experienced or witnessed a profoundly shocking or frightening event, such as rape, severe beating, war, or natural disaster. Its symptoms include flashbacks, hyperactivity, hypervigilance, displaced anger, sleeplessness, nightmares, sudden terror or anxiety, and confusion between fantasy and reality.

**postconventional moral reasoning** Kohlberg's third level of moral reasoning, emphasizing moral principles.

**postformal cognition** A proposed adult stage of cognitive development, following Piaget's four stages, that goes beyond adolescent thinking by being more practical, more flexible, and more dialectical (i.e., more capable of combining contradictory elements into a comprehensive whole).

**postpartum depression** A new mother's feelings of inadequacy and sadness in the days and weeks after giving birth.

**pragmatics** The practical use of language that includes the ability to adjust language communication according to audience and context.

**preconventional moral reasoning** Kohlberg's first level of moral reasoning, emphasizing rewards and punishments.

**prefrontal cortex** The area of the cortex at the very front of the brain that specializes in anticipation, planning, and impulse control.

**preoperational intelligence** Piaget's term for cognitive development between the ages of about 2 and 6; it includes language and imagination (which involve symbolic thought). Logical, operational thinking is not yet possible.

**preterm** A birth that occurs two or more weeks before the full 38 weeks of the typical pregnancy—that is, at 36 or fewer weeks after conception.

**primary circular reactions** The first of three types of feedback loops in sensorimotor intelligence, this one involving the infant's own body. The infant senses motion, sucking, noise, and other stimuli and tries to understand them.

**primary prevention** Actions that change overall background conditions to prevent some unwanted event or circumstance, such as injury, disease, or abuse.

**primary sex characteristics** The parts of the body that are directly involved in reproduction, including the vagina, uterus, ovaries, testicles, and penis.

**private speech** The internal dialogue that occurs when people talk to themselves (either silently or out loud).

**Progress in International Reading Literacy Study (PIRLS)** Inaugurated in 2001, a planned five-year cycle of international trend studies in the reading ability of fourth-graders.

**prosocial behavior** Actions that are helpful and kind but are of no obvious benefit to oneself.

**protein-calorie malnutrition** A condition in which a person does not consume sufficient food of any kind. This deprivation can result in several illnesses, severe weight loss, and even death.

**proximal parenting** Caregiving practices that involve being physically close to the baby, with frequent holding and touching.

**proximodistal development** Growth or development that occurs from the center or core in an outward direction.

**pruning** When applied to brain development, the process by which unused connections in the brain atrophy and die.

**psychoanalytic theory** A grand theory of human development that holds that irrational, unconscious drives and motives, often originating in childhood, underlie human behavior.

**psychological control** A disciplinary technique that involves threatening to withdraw love and support and that relies on a child's feelings of guilt and gratitude to the parents.

**puberty** The time between the first onrush of hormones and full adult physical development. Puberty usually lasts three to five years. Many more years are required to achieve psychosocial maturity.

## Q

**qualitative research** Research that considers qualities instead of quantities. Descriptions of particular conditions and participants' expressed ideas are often part of qualitative studies.

**quantitative research** Research that provides data that can be expressed with numbers, such as ranks or scales.

## R

**race** A group of people who are regarded by themselves or by others as distinct from other groups on the basis of physical appearance, typically skin color. Social scientists think race is a misleading concept, as biological differences are not signified by outward appearance.

**reaction time** The time it takes to respond to a stimulus, either physically (with a reflexive movement such as an eyeblink) or cognitively (with a thought).

**reactive aggression** An impulsive retaliation for another person's intentional or accidental action, verbal or physical.

**reflex** An unlearned, involuntary action or movement in response to a stimulus. A reflex occurs without conscious thought.

**Reggio Emilia** A program of early-childhood education that originated in the town of Reggio Emilia, Italy, and that encourages each child's creativity in a carefully designed setting.

**reinforcement** When a behavior is followed by something desired, such as food for a hungry animal or a welcoming smile for a lonely person.

**relational aggression** Nonphysical acts, such as insults or social rejection, aimed at harming the social connection between the victim and other people.

**REM (rapid eye movement) sleep** A stage of sleep characterized by flickering eyes behind closed lids, dreaming, and rapid brain waves.

**reminder session** A perceptual experience that helps a person recollect an idea, a thing, or an experience.

**replication** Repeating a study, usually using different participants, sometimes of another age, socioeconomic status (SES), or culture.

**reported maltreatment** Harm or endangerment about which someone has notified the authorities.

**representative sample** A group of research participants who reflect the relevant characteristics of the larger population whose attributes are under study.

**resilience** The capacity to adapt well to significant adversity and to overcome serious stress.

**response to intervention (RTI)** An educational strategy intended to help children who demonstrate below-average achievement in early grades, using special intervention.

**role confusion** A situation in which an adolescent does not seem to know or care what his or her identity is. (Sometimes called *identity* or *role diffusion*.)

**rough-and-tumble play** Play that mimics aggression through wrestling, chasing, or hitting, but in which there is no intent to harm.

**rumination** Repeatedly thinking and talking about past experiences; can contribute to depression.

# S

**sample** A group of individuals drawn from a specified population. A sample might be the low-birthweight babies born in four particular hospitals that are representative of all hospitals.

**scaffolding** Temporary support that is tailored to a learner's needs and abilities and aimed at helping the learner master the next task in a given learning process.

**science of human development** The science that seeks to understand how and why people of all ages change or remain the same over time.

**scientific method** A way to answer questions using empirical research and data-based conclusions.

**scientific observation** A method of testing a hypothesis by unobtrusively watching and recording participants' behavior in a systematic and objective manner—in a natural setting, in a laboratory, or in searches of archival data.

**secondary circular reactions** The second of three types of feedback loops in sensorimotor intelligence, this one involving people and objects. Infants respond to other people, to toys, and to any other object that they can touch or move.

**secondary education** Literally, the period after primary education (elementary or grade school) and before tertiary education (college). It usually occurs from about ages 12 to 18, although there is some variation by school and by nation.

**secondary prevention** Actions that avert harm in a high-risk situation, such as stopping a car before it hits a pedestrian.

**secondary sex characteristics** Physical traits that are not directly involved in reproduction but that indicate sexual maturity, such as a man's beard and a woman's breasts.

**secular trend** The long-term upward or downward direction of a certain set of statistical measurements, as opposed to a smaller, shorter cyclical variation. As an example, over the past two centuries, because of improved nutrition and medical care, children have tended to reach their adult height earlier and their adult height has increased.

**secure attachment** A relationship in which an infant obtains both comfort and confidence from the presence of his or her caregiver.

**selective adaptation** The process by which living creatures (including people) adjust to their environment. Genes that enhance survival and reproductive ability are selected, over the generations, to become more prevalent.

**selective attention** The ability to concentrate on some stimuli while ignoring others.

**self-awareness** A person's realization that he or she is a distinct individual whose body, mind, and actions are separate from those of other people.

**self-concept** A person's understanding of who he or she is, in relation to self-esteem, appearance, personality, and various traits.

**self-righting** The inborn drive to remedy a developmental deficit; literally, to return to sitting or standing upright after being tipped over. People of all ages have self-righting impulses, for emotional as well as physical imbalance.

**sensation** The response of a sensory organ (eyes, ears, skin, tongue, nose) when it detects a stimulus.

**sensitive period** A time when a certain type of development is most likely, although it may still happen later with more difficulty. For example, early childhood is considered a sensitive period for language learning.

**sensorimotor intelligence** Piaget's term for the way infants think—by using their senses and motor skills—during the first period of cognitive development.

**sensory memory** The component of the information-processing system in which incoming stimulus information is stored for a split second to allow it to be processed. (Also called the *sensory register*.)

**separation anxiety** An infant's distress when a familiar caregiver leaves; most obvious between 9 and 14 months.

**seriation** The concept that things can be arranged in a logical series, such as the number sequence or the alphabet.

**sex differences** Biological differences between males and females, in organs, hormones, and body type.

**sexting** Sending sexual content, particularly photos or videos, via cell phones or social media.

**sexual orientation** A term that refers to whether a person is sexually and romantically attracted to others of the same sex, the opposite sex, or both sexes.

**sexually transmitted infection (STI)** A disease spread by sexual contact, including syphilis, gonorrhea, genital herpes, chlamydia, and HIV.

**shaken baby syndrome** A life-threatening injury that occurs when an infant is forcefully shaken back and forth, a motion that ruptures blood vessels in the brain and breaks neural connections.

**single-parent family** A family that consists of only one parent and his or her children.

**small for gestational age (SGA)** A term for a baby whose birthweight is significantly lower than expected, given the time since conception. For example, a 5-pound (2,265-gram) newborn is considered SGA if born on time but not SGA if born two months early. (Also called *small-for-dates*.)

**social comparison** The tendency to assess one's abilities, achievements, social status, and other attributes by measuring them against those of other people, especially one's peers.

**social construction** An idea that arises from shared perceptions, not on objective reality. Many age-related terms (such as *childhood, adolescence, yuppie,* and *senior citizen*) are social constructions, strongly influenced by social assumptions.

**social learning theory** An extension of behaviorism that emphasizes the influence that other people have over a person's behavior. Even without specific reinforcement, every individual learns many things through observation and imitation of other people. (Also called *observational learning*.)

**social mediation** Human interaction that expands and advances understanding, often through words that one person uses to explain something to another.

**social referencing** Seeking information about how to react to an unfamiliar or ambiguous object or event by observing someone else's expressions and reactions. That other person becomes a social reference.

**social smile** A smile evoked by a human face, normally first evident in infants about 6 weeks after birth.

**sociocultural theory** A newer theory which holds that development results from the dynamic interaction of each person with the surrounding social and cultural forces.

**sociodramatic play** Pretend play in which children act out various roles and themes in stories that they create.

**socioeconomic status (SES)** A person's position in society as determined by income, occupation, education, and place of residence. (Sometimes called *social class*.)

**specific learning disorder** A marked deficit in a particular area of learning that is not caused by an apparent physical disability, by an intellectual disability, or by an unusually stressful home environment.

**spermarche** A boy's first ejaculation of sperm. Erections can occur as early as infancy, but ejaculation signals sperm production. Spermarche may occur during sleep (in a "wet dream") or via direct stimulation.

**static reasoning** A characteristic of preoperational thought in which a young child thinks that nothing changes. Whatever is now has always been and always will be.

**stem cells** Cells from which any other specialized type of cell can form.

**stereotype threat** The thought in a person's mind that one's appearance or behavior will be misread to confirm another person's oversimplified, prejudiced attitudes.

**still-face technique** An experimental practice in which an adult keeps his or her face unmoving and expressionless in face-to-face interaction with an infant.

**Strange Situation** A laboratory procedure for measuring attachment by evoking infants' reactions to the stress of various adults' comings and goings in an unfamiliar playroom.

**stranger wariness** An infant's expression of concern—a quiet stare while clinging to a familiar person, or a look of fear—when a stranger appears.

**stunting** The failure of children to grow to a normal height for their age due to severe and chronic malnutrition.

**substantiated maltreatment** Harm or endangerment that has been reported, investigated, and verified.

**sudden infant death syndrome (SIDS)** A situation in which a seemingly healthy infant, usually between 2 and 6 months old, suddenly stops breathing and dies unexpectedly while asleep.

**suicidal ideation** Thinking about suicide, usually with some serious emotional and intellectual or cognitive overtones.

**superego** In psychoanalytic theory, the judgmental part of the personality that internalizes the moral standards of the parents.

**survey** A research method in which information is collected from a large number of people by interviews, written questionnaires, or some other means.

**symbolic thought** A major accomplishment of preoperational intelligence that allows a child to think symbolically, including understanding that words can refer to things not seen and that an item, such as a flag, can symbolize something else (in this case, a country).

**synapse** The intersection between the axon of one neuron and the dendrites of other neurons.

**synchrony** A coordinated, rapid, and smooth exchange of responses between a caregiver and an infant.

## T

**temperament** Inborn differences between one person and another in emotions, activity, and self-regulation. It is measured by the person's typical responses to the environment.

**teratogen** An agent or condition, including viruses, drugs, and chemicals, that can impair prenatal development and result in birth defects or even death.

**teratology** The scientific study of birth abnormalities, especially on causes of biological disabilities and impairments.

**tertiary circular reactions** The third of three types of feedback loops in sensorimotor intelligence, this one involving active exploration and experimentation. Infants explore a range of new activities, varying their responses as a way of learning about the world.

**tertiary prevention** Actions, such as immediate and effective medical treatment, that are taken after an illness or injury and that are aimed at reducing harm or preventing disability.

**testosterone** A sex hormone, the best known of the androgens (male hormones); secreted in far greater amounts by males than by females.

**theory of mind** A person's theory of what other people might be thinking. In order to have a theory of mind, children must realize that other people are not necessarily thinking the same thoughts that they themselves are. That realization seldom occurs before age 4.

**theory-theory** The idea that children attempt to explain everything they see and hear by constructing theories.

**threshold effect** In prenatal development, when a teratogen is relatively harmless in small doses but becomes harmful once exposure reaches a certain level (the threshold).

**time-out** A disciplinary technique in which a child is separated from other people for a specified time.

**transient exuberance** The great but temporary increase in the number of dendrites that develop in an infant's brain during the first two years of life.

**Trends in Math and Science Study (TIMSS)** An international assessment of the math and science skills of fourth- and eighth-graders. Although the TIMSS is very useful, different countries' scores are not always comparable because sample selection, test administration, and content validity are hard to keep uniform.

**trust versus mistrust** Erikson's first crisis of psychosocial development. Infants learn basic trust if the world is a secure place where their basic needs (for food, comfort, attention, and so on) are met.

## U

**ultrasound** An image of a fetus (or an internal organ) produced by using high-frequency sound waves. (Also called *sonogram*.)

## V

**very low birthweight (VLBW)** A body weight at birth of less than 1,500 grams (3 pounds, 5 ounces).

**visual cliff** An experimental apparatus that gives the illusion of a sudden drop-off between one horizontal surface and another.

**voucher** Public subsidy for tuition payment at a nonpublic school. Vouchers vary a great deal from place to place, not only in amount and availability but also in restrictions as to who gets them and what schools accept them.

## W

**wasting** The tendency for children to be severely underweight for their age as a result of malnutrition.

**WEIRD** An acronym for Western, Educated, Industrialized, Rich, Democracy referring to emerging adults. The criticism is that conclusions about human development based on people in such nations may not apply to most people in the world, who do not live in WEIRD nations.

**withdrawn-rejected** A type of childhood rejection, when other children do not want to be friends with a child because of his or her timid, withdrawn, and anxious behavior.

**working memory** The component of the information-processing system in which current conscious mental activity occurs. (Formerly called *short-term memory*.)

**working model** In cognitive theory, a set of assumptions that the individual uses to organize perceptions and experiences. For example, a person might assume that other people are trustworthy and be surprised by an incident in which this working model of human behavior is erroneous.

# X

**X-linked** A gene carried on the X chromosome. If a male inherits an X-linked recessive trait from his mother, he expresses that trait because the Y from his father has no counteracting gene. Females are more likely to be carriers of X-linked traits but are less likely to express them.

**XX** A 23rd chromosome pair that consists of two X-shaped chromosomes, one each from the mother and the father. XX zygotes become females.

**XY** A 23rd chromosome pair that consists of an X-shaped chromosome from the mother and a Y-shaped chromosome from the father. XY zygotes become males.

# Z

**zone of proximal development** In sociocultural theory, Vygotsky's term for a metaphorical area, or "zone," surrounding a learner that includes all of the skills, knowledge, and concepts that the person is close ("proximal") to acquiring but cannot yet master without help.

**zygote** The single cell formed from the union of two gametes, a sperm and an ovum.

# References

**Aarnoudse-Moens, Cornelieke S. H.; Smidts, Diana P.; Oosterlaan, Jaap; Duivenvoorden, Hugo J. & Weisglas-Kuperus, Nynke.** (2009). Executive function in very preterm children at early school age. *Journal of Abnormal Child Psychology*, 37(7), 981–993. doi: 10.1007/s10802-009-9327-z

**Abar, Caitlin C.; Jackson, Kristina M. & Wood, Mark.** (2014). Reciprocal relations between perceived parental knowledge and adolescent substance use and delinquency: The moderating role of parent–teen relationship quality. *Developmental Psychology*, 50(9), 2176–2187. doi: 10.1037/a0037463

**Abela, Angela & Walker, Janet (Eds.).** (2014). *Contemporary issues in family studies: Global perspectives on partnerships, parenting and support in a changing world.* Malden, MA: Wiley.

**Accardo, Pasquale.** (2006). Who's training whom? *The Journal of Pediatrics*, 149(2), 151–152. doi: 10.1016/j.jpeds.2006.04.026

**Acharya, Kartikey; Leuthner, Stephen; Clark, Reese; Nghiem-Rao, Tuyet-Hang; Spitzer, Alan & Lagatta, Joanne.** (2017). Major anomalies and birth-weight influence NICU interventions and mortality in infants with trisomy 13 or 18. *Journal of Perinatology*, 37(4), 420–426. doi: 10.1038/jp.2016.245

**Acuto, Michele & Parnell, Susan.** (2016). Leave no city behind. *Science*, 352(6288), 873. doi: 10.1126/science.aag1385

**Adamson, Lauren B. & Bakeman, Roger.** (2006). Development of displaced speech in early mother-child conversations. *Child Development*, 77(1), 186–200. doi: 10.1111/j.1467-8624.2006.00864.x

**Adamson, Lauren B.; Bakeman, Roger; Deckner, Deborah F. & Nelson, P. Brooke.** (2014). From interactions to conversations: The development of joint engagement during early childhood. *Child Development*, 85(3), 941–955. doi: 10.1111/cdev.12189

**Addati, Laura; Cassirer, Naomi & Gilchrist, Katherine.** (2014). *Maternity and paternity at work: Law and practice across the world.* Geneva: International Labour Office.

**Adolph, Karen E.; Cole, Whitney G.; Komati, Meghana; Garciaguirre, Jessie S.; Badaly, Daryaneh; Lingeman, Jesse M., . . . Sotsky, Rachel B.** (2012). How do you learn to walk? Thousands of steps and dozens of falls per day. *Psychological Science*, 23(11), 1387–1394. doi: 10.1177/0956797612446346

**Adolph, Karen E. & Franchak, John M.** (2017). The development of motor behavior. *WIREs*, 8(1–2), e1430. doi: 10.1002/wcs.1430

**Adolph, Karen E. & Kretch, Kari S.** (2012). Infants on the edge: Beyond the visual cliff. In Alan M. Slater & Paul C. Quinn (Eds.), *Developmental psychology: Revisiting the classic studies.* Thousand Oaks, CA: Sage.

**Adolph, Karen E. & Robinson, Scott.** (2013). The road to walking: What learning to walk tells us about development. In Philip D. Zelazo (Ed.), *The Oxford handbook of developmental psychology* (Vol. 1, pp. 402–447). New York, NY: Oxford University Press. doi: 10.1093/oxfordhb/9780199958450.013.0015

**Ainsworth, Mary D. Salter.** (1967). *Infancy in Uganda: Infant care and the growth of love.* Baltimore, MD: Johns Hopkins Press.

**Ainsworth, Mary D. Salter.** (1973). The development of infant-mother attachment. In Bettye M. Caldwell & Henry N. Ricciuti (Eds.), *Child development and social policy* (pp. 1–94). Chicago, IL: University of Chicago Press.

**Aizer, Anna & Currie, Janet.** (2014). The intergenerational transmission of inequality: Maternal disadvantage and health at birth. *Science*, 344(6186), 856–861. doi: 10.1126/science.1251872

**Akhtar, Nameera & Jaswal, Vikram K.** (2013). Deficit or difference? Interpreting diverse developmental paths: An introduction to the special section. *Developmental Psychology*, 49(1), 1–3. doi: 10.1037/a0029851

**Aksglaede, Lise; Link, Katarina; Giwercman, Aleksander; Jørgensen, Niels; Skakkebæk, Niels E. & Juul, Anders.** (2013). 47,XXY Klinefelter syndrome: Clinical characteristics and age-specific recommendations for medical management. *American Journal of Medical Genetics Part C: Seminars in Medical Genetics*, 163(1), 55–63. doi: 10.1002/ajmg.c.31349

**Al Otaiba, Stephanie; Wanzek, Jeanne & Yovanoff, Paul.** (2015). Response to intervention. *European Scientific Journal*, 1, 260–264.

**Al-Hashim, Aqeela H.; Blaser, Susan; Raybaud, Charles & MacGregor, Daune.** (2016). Corpus callosum abnormalities: Neuroradiological and clinical correlations. *Developmental Medicine & Child Neurology*, 58(5), 475–484. doi: 10.1111/dmcn.12978

**Al-Namlah, Abdulrahman S.; Meins, Elizabeth & Fernyhough, Charles.** (2012). Self-regulatory private speech relates to children's recall and organization of autobiographical memories. *Early Childhood Research Quarterly*, 27(3), 441–446. doi: 10.1016/j.ecresq.2012.02.005

**Al-Sayes, Fatin; Gari, Mamdooh; Qusti, Safaa; Bagatian, Nadiah & Abuzenadah, Adel.** (2011). Prevalence of iron deficiency and iron deficiency anemia among females at university stage. *Journal of Medical Laboratory and Diagnosis*, 2(1), 5–11.

**Albert, Dustin; Chein, Jason & Steinberg, Laurence.** (2013). The teenage brain: Peer influences on adolescent decision making. *Current Directions in Psychological Science*, 22(2), 114–120. doi: 10.1177/0963721412471347

**Albert, Dustin & Steinberg, Laurence.** (2011). Judgment and decision making in adolescence. *Journal of Research on Adolescence*, 21(1), 211–224. doi: 10.1111/j.1532-7795.2010.00724.x

**Aleccia, JoNel.** (2014, February 5). Genetic tool delivers healthy babies to mom with fatal disease. *NBC News.*

**Alegre, Alberto.** (2011). Parenting styles and children's emotional intelligence: What do we know? *The Family Journal*, 19(1), 56–62. doi: 10.1177/1066480710387486

**Alesi, Marianha; Bianco, Antonino; Padulo, Johnny; Vella, Francesco Paolo; Petrucci, Marco; Paoli, Antonio, . . . Pepi, Annamaria.** (2014). Motor and cognitive development: the role of karate. *Muscle, Ligaments and Tendons Journal*, 4(2), 114–120. doi: 10.11138/mltj/2014.4.2.114

**Alexander, Karl L.; Entwisle, Doris R. & Olson, Linda Steffel.** (2014). *The long shadow: Family background, disadvantaged urban youth, and the transition to adulthood.* New York, NY: Russell Sage Foundation.

**Almond, Douglas.** (2006). Is the 1918 influenza pandemic over? Long-term effects of in utero influenza exposure in the post-1940 U.S. population. *Journal of Political Economy*, 114(4), 672–712. doi: 10.1086/507154

**Alpár, Alán; Di Marzo, Vincenzo & Harkany, Tibor.** (2016). At the tip of an iceberg: Prenatal marijuana and its possible relation to neuropsychiatric outcome in the offspring. *Biological Psychiatry*, 79(7), e33–e45. doi: 10.1016/j.biopsych.2015.09.009

**Alper, Meryl.** (2013). Developmentally appropriate New Media Literacies: Supporting cultural competencies and social skills in early childhood education. *Journal of Early Childhood Literacy*, 13(2), 175–196. doi: 10.1177/1468798411430101

**Altbach, Philip G.; Reisberg, Liz & Rumbley, Laura E.** (2010). Tracking a global academic revolution. *Change: The Magazine of Higher Learning*, 42(2), 30–39. doi: 10.1080/00091381003590845

**Amato, Michael S.; Magzamen, Sheryl; Imm, Pamela; Havlena, Jeffrey A.; Anderson, Henry A.; Kanarek, Marty S. & Moore, Colleen F.** (2013). Early lead exposure (<3 years old) prospectively predicts fourth grade school suspension in Milwaukee, Wisconsin (USA). *Environmental Research*, 126, 60–65. doi: 10.1016/j.envres.2013.07.008

**Ameade, Evans Paul Kwame & Garti, Helene Akpene.** (2016). Age at menarche and factors that influence it: A study among female university students in Tamale, northern Ghana. *PLoS ONE*, 11(5), e0155310. doi: 10.1371/journal.pone.0155310

**American Academy of Pediatrics.** (2016). Media and young minds. *Pediatrics*, 138(5). doi: 10.1542/peds.2016-2591

**American College of Obstetricians and Gynecologists Committee on Obstetric Practice.** (2011). Committee opinion no. 476: Planned home birth. *Obstetrics & Gynecology*, 117(2), 425–428. doi: 10.1097/AOG.0b013e31820eee20

**American Community Survey.** (2014). Washington, DC: U.S. Census Bureau.

**American Psychiatric Association.** (2013). *Diagnostic and statistical manual of mental disorders: DSM-5* (5th ed.). Washington, DC: American Psychiatric Association.

**Ames, Louise Bates & Ilg, Frances L.** (1981). *Your six-year-old: Loving and defiant.* New York, NY: Dell.

**Anderson, Daniel R. & Hanson, Katherine G.** (2016). Screen media and parent–child interactions. In Rachel Barr & Deborah Nichols Linebarger (Eds.), *Media exposure during infancy and early childhood: The effects of content and context on learning and development* (pp. 173–194). Switzerland: Springer. doi: 10.1007/978-3-319-45102-2_11

**Anderson, Monica.** (2016, January 7). *Parents, teens and digital monitoring. Numbers, Facts and Trends Shaping the World.* Washington, DC: Pew Research Center.

**Andreas, Nicholas J. ; Kampmann, Beate & Le-Doare, Kirsty Mehring.** (2015). Human breast milk: A review on its composition and bioactivity. *Early Human Development*, 91(11), 629–635. doi: 10.1016/j.earlhumdev.2015.08.013

**Ansado, Jennyfer; Collins, Louis; Fonov, Vladimir; Garon, Mathieu; Alexandrov, Lubomir; Karama, Sherif, . . . Beauchamp, Miriam H.** (2015). A new template to study callosal growth shows specific growth in anterior and posterior regions of the corpus callosum in early childhood. *European Journal of Neuroscience*, 42(1), 1675–1684. doi: 10.1111/ejn.12869

**Antenucci, Antonio.** (2013, November 26). Cop who bought homeless man boots promoted. *New York Post.*

**Antoine, Michelle W.; Hübner, Christian A; Arezzo, Joseph C. & Hébert, Jean M.** (2013). A causative link between inner ear defects and long-term striatal dysfunction. *Science*, 341(6150), 1120–1123. doi: 10.1126/science.1240405

**Apgar, Virginia.** (1953). A proposal for a new method of evaluation of the newborn infant. *Current Researches in Anesthesia and Analgesia*, 32, 260–267.

**Apgar, Virginia.** (2015). A proposal for a new method of evaluation of the newborn infant. *Anesthesia & Analgesia*, 120(5), 1056–1059. doi: 10.1213/ANE.0b013e31829bdc5c

**Archambault, Isabelle; Janosz, Michel; Fallu, Jean-Sébastien & Paganim, Linda S.** (2009). Student engagement and its relationship with early high school dropout. *Journal of Adolescence*, 32(3), 651–670. doi: 10.1016/j.adolescence.2008.06.007

**Argyrides, Marios & Kkeli, Natalie.** (2015). Predictive factors of disordered eating and body image satisfaction in Cyprus. *International Journal of Eating Disorders*, 48(4), 431–435. doi: 10.1002/eat.22310

**Ariely, Dan.** (2010). *Predictably Irrational: The hidden forces that shape our decisions* (Revised and Expanded ed.). New York, NY: Harper Perennial.

**Arigo, Danielle; Butryn, Meghan L.; Raggio, Greer A.; Stice, Eric & Lowe, Michael R.** (2016). Predicting change in physical activity: A longitudinal investigation among weight-concerned college women. *Annals of Behavioral Medicine*, 50(5), 629–641. doi: 10.1007/s12160-016-9788-6

**Arnheim, Norman & Calabrese, Peter.** (2016). Germline stem cell competition, mutation hot spots, genetic disorders, and older fathers. *Annual Review of Genomics and Human Genetics*, 17, 219–243. doi: 10.1146/annurev-genom-083115-022656

**Arsenio, William F. & Willems, Chris.** (2017). Adolescents' conceptions of national wealth distribution: Connections with perceived societal fairness and academic plans. *Developmental Psychology*, 53(3), 463–474. doi: 10.1037/dev0000263

**Arshad, S. Hasan; Karmaus, Wilfried; Zhang, Hongmei & Holloway, John W.** (2017). Multigenerational cohorts in patients with asthma and allergy. *Journal of Allergy and Clinical Immunology*, 139(2), 415–421. doi: 10.1016/j.jaci.2016.12.002

**Arum, Richard & Roksa, Josipa.** (2011). *Academically adrift: Limited learning on college campuses.* Chicago, IL: University of Chicago Press.

**Ashraf, Quamrul & Galor, Oded.** (2013). The 'Out of Africa' hypothesis, human genetic diversity, and comparative economic development. *American Economic Review*, 103(1), 1–46. doi: 10.1257/aer.103.1.1

**Aslin, Richard N.** (2012). Language development: Revisiting Eimas et al.'s /ba/ and /pa/ study. In Alan M. Slater & Paul C. Quinn (Eds.), *Developmental psychology: Revisiting the classic studies* (pp. 191–203). Thousand Oaks, CA: Sage.

**Asma, Stephen T.** (2013). *Against fairness.* Chicago, IL: University of Chicago Press.

**Associated Press.** (2004). David Reimer, 38, subject of the John/Joan case. *New York Times.* https://nyti.ms/2jXVgtI

**Atzaba-Poria, Naama; Deater-Deckard, Kirby & Bell, Martha Ann.** (2017). Mother-child interaction: Links between mother and child frontal electroencephalograph asymmetry and negative behavior. *Child Development*, 88(2), 544–554. doi: 10.1111/cdev.12583

**Atzil, Shir; Hendler, Talma & Feldman, Ruth.** (2014). The brain basis of social synchrony. *Social Cognitive and Affective Neuroscience*, 9(8), 1193–1202. doi: 10.1093/scan/nst105

**Aud, Susan; Hussar, William; Planty, Michael; Snyder, Thomas; Bianco, Kevin; Fox, Mary Ann, . . . Drake, Lauren.** (2010). *The condition of education 2010.* Washington, DC: National Center for Education Statistics, Institute of Education Sciences, U.S. Department of Education.

**Aunola, Kaisa; Tolvanen, Asko; Viljaranta, Jaana & Nurmi, Jari-Erik.** (2013). Psychological control in daily parent–child interactions increases children's negative emotions. *Journal of Family Psychology*, 27(3), 453–462. doi: 10.1037/a0032891

**Aven, Terje.** (2011). On some recent definitions and analysis frameworks for risk, vulnerability, and resilience. *Risk Analysis*, 31(4), 515–522. doi: 10.1111/j.1539-6924.2010.01528.x

**Ayyanathan, Kasirajan (Ed.).** (2014). *Specific gene expression and epigenetics: The interplay between the genome and its environment.* Oakville, Canada: Apple Academic Press.

**Azrin, Nathan H. & Foxx, Richard M.** (1974). *Toilet training in less than a day.* New York, NY: Simon & Schuster.

**Babchishin, Lyzon K.; Weegar, Kelly & Romano, Elisa.** (2013). Early child care effects on later behavioral outcomes using a Canadian nationwide sample. *Journal of Educational and Developmental Psychology*, 3(2), 15–29. doi: 10.5539/jedp.v3n2p15

**Babineau, Vanessa; Green, Cathryn Gordon; Jolicoeur-Martineau, Alexis; Minde, Klaus; Sassi, Roberto; St-André, Martin, . . . Wazana, Ashley.** (2015). Prenatal depression and 5-HTTLPR interact to predict dysregulation from 3 to 36 months – A differential susceptibility model. *Journal of Child Psychology and Psychiatry*, 56(1), 21–29. doi: 10.1111/jcpp.12246

**Bachmann, Christian J.; Wijlaars, Linda P.; Kalverdijk, Luuk J.; Burcu, Mehmet; Glaeske, Gerd; Schuiling-Veninga, Catharina C. M., . . . Zito, Julie M.** (2017). Trends in ADHD medication use in children and adolescents in five Western countries, 2005–2012. *European Neuropsychopharmacology*, 27(5), 484–493. doi: 10.1016/j.euroneuro.2017.03.002

**Bagot, Kara.** (2017). Making the grade: Adolescent prescription stimulant use. *Journal of the American Academy of Child & Adolescent Psychiatry*, 56(3), 189–190. doi: 10.1016/j.jaac.2016.12.011

**Bagwell, Catherine L. & Schmidt, Michelle E.** (2011). *Friendships in childhood & adolescence.* New York, NY: Guilford Press.

**Bailey, J. Michael; Vasey, Paul L.; Diamond, Lisa M.; Breedlove, S. Marc; Vilain, Eric & Epprecht, Marc.** (2016). Sexual orientation, controversy, and science. *Psychological Science in the Public Interest*, 17(2), 45–101. doi: 10.1177/1529100616637616

**Baillargeon, Renée & DeVos, Julie.** (1991). Object permanence in young infants: Further evidence. *Child Development*, 62(6), 1227–1246. doi: 10.1111/j.1467-8624.1991.tb01602.x

**Baker, Jeffrey P.** (2000). Immunization and the American way: 4 childhood vaccines. *American Journal of Public Health*, 90(2), 199–207. doi: 10.2105/AJPH.90.2.199

**Baker, Olesya & Lang, Kevin.** (2013). *The effect of high school exit exams on graduation, employment, wages and incarceration.* Cambridge, MA: National Bureau of Economic Research. doi: 10.3386/w19182

**Baker, Simon T. E.; Lubman, Dan I.; Yücel, Murat; Allen, Nicholas B.; Whittle, Sarah; Fulcher, Ben D., . . . Fornito, Alex.** (2015). Developmental changes in brain network hub connectivity in late adolescence. *Journal of Neuroscience*, 35(24), 9078–9087. doi: 10.1523/JNEUROSCI.5043-14.2015

**Balari, Sergio & Lorenzo, Guillermo.** (2015). Should it stay or should it go? A critical reflection on the critical period for language. *Biolinguistics*, 9, 8–42.

**Ball, Helen L. & Volpe, Lane E.** (2013). Sudden Infant Death Syndrome (SIDS) risk reduction and infant sleep location – Moving the discussion forward. *Social Science & Medicine*, 79(1), 84–91. doi: 10.1016/j.socscimed.2012.03.025

**Baltes, Paul B.** (1987). Theoretical propositions of life-span developmental psychology: On the dynamics between growth and decline. *Developmental Psychology, 23*(5), 611–626. doi: 10.1037/0012-1649.23.5.611

**Baltes, Paul B.; Lindenberger, Ulman & Staudinger, Ursula M.** (2006). Life span theory in developmental psychology. In William Damon & Richard M. Lerner (Eds.), *Handbook of child psychology* (6th ed., Vol. 1, pp. 569–664). Hoboken, NJ: Wiley.

**Baly, Michael W.; Cornell, Dewey G. & Lovegrove, Peter.** (2014). A longitudinal investigation of self- and peer reports of bullying victimization across middle school. *Psychology in the Schools, 51*(3), 217–240. doi: 10.1002/pits.21747

**Bandura, Albert.** (1986). *Social foundations of thought and action: A social cognitive theory.* Englewood Cliffs, NJ: Prentice-Hall.

**Bandura, Albert.** (1997). The anatomy of stages of change. *American Journal of Health Promotion, 12*(1), 8–10. doi: 10.4278/0890-1171-12.1.8

**Bandura, Albert.** (2006). Toward a psychology of human agency. *Perspectives on Psychological Science, 1*(2), 164–180. doi: 10.1111/j.1745-6916.2006.00011.x

**Bandura, Albert.** (2016). *Moral disengagement: How people do harm and live with themselves.* New York, NY: Worth.

**Banks, James R. & Andrews, Timothy.** (2015). Outcomes of childhood asthma to the age of 50 years. *Pediatrics, 136*(Suppl. 3). doi: 10.1542/peds.2015-2776JJJJ

**Bannon, Michael J.; Johnson, Magen M.; Michelhaugh, Sharon K.; Hartley, Zachary J.; Halter, Steven D.; David, James A., . . . Schmidt, Carl J.** (2014). A molecular profile of cocaine abuse includes the differential expression of genes that regulate transcription, chromatin, and dopamine cell phenotype. *Neuropsychopharmacology, 39*(9), 2191–2199. doi: 10.1038/npp.2014.70

**Baqui, Abdullah H.; Mitra, Dipak K.; Begum, Nazma; Hurt, Lisa; Soremekun, Seyi; Edmond, Karen, . . . Manu, Alexander.** (2016). Neonatal mortality within 24 hours of birth in six low- and lower-middle-income countries. *Bulletin of the World Health Organization, 94*, 752–758B. doi: 10.2471/BLT.15.160945

**Barber, Brian K. (Ed.).** (2002). *Intrusive parenting: How psychological control affects children and adolescents.* Washington, DC: American Psychological Association.

**Barnett, W. Steven; Carolan, Megan E.; Squires, James H.; Brown, Kirsty Clarke & Horowitz, Michelle.** (2015). *The state of preschool 2014: State preschool yearbook.* New Brunswick, NJ: National Institute for Early Education Research.

**Barnett, W. Steven; Weisenfeld, G. G.; Brown, Kirsty; Squires, Jim & Horowitz, Michelle.** (2016, July 29). *Implementing 15 essential elements for high quality: A state and local policy scan.* New Brunswick, NJ: National Institute for Early Education Research.

**Baron-Cohen, Simon; Tager-Flusberg, Helen & Lombardo, Michael (Eds.).** (2013). *Understanding other minds: Perspectives from developmental social neuroscience* (3rd ed.). New York, NY: Oxford University Press.

**Barone, Joseph.** (2015). *It's not your fault!: Strategies for solving toilet training and bedwetting problems.* New Brunswick, NJ: Rutgers University Press.

**Barr, Rachel.** (2013). Memory constraints on infant learning from picture books, television, and touchscreens. *Child Development Perspectives, 7*(4), 205–210. doi: 10.1111/cdep.12041

**Barrasso-Catanzaro, Christina & Eslinger, Paul J.** (2016). Neurobiological bases of executive function and social-emotional development: Typical and atypical brain changes. *Family Relations, 65*(1), 108–119. doi: 10.1111/fare.12175

**Barrett, Anne E. & Montepare, Joann M.** (2015). "It's about time": Applying life span and life course perspectives to the study of subjective age. *Annual Review of Gerontology and Geriatrics, 35*(1), 55–77. doi: 10.1891/0198-8794.35.55

**Barrett, Jon F. R.; Hannah, Mary E.; Hutton, Eileen K.; Willan, Andrew R.; Allen, Alexander C.; Armson, B. Anthony, . . . Asztalos, Elizabeth V.** (2013). A randomized trial of planned cesarean or vaginal delivery for twin pregnancy. *New England Journal of Medicine, 369,* 1295–1305. doi: 10.1056/NEJMoa1214939

**Barrios, Yasmin V.; Sanchez, Sixto E.; Nicolaidis, Christina; Garcia, Pedro J.; Gelaye, Bizu; Zhong, Qiuyue & Williams, Michelle A.** (2015). Childhood abuse and early menarche among Peruvian women. *Journal of Adolescent Health, 56*(2), 197–202. doi: 10.1016/j.jadohealth.2014.10.002

**Barros, Romina M.; Silver, Ellen J. & Stein, Ruth E. K.** (2009). School recess and group classroom behavior. *Pediatrics, 123*(2), 431–436. doi: 10.1542/peds.2007-2825

**Bartels, Meike; Cacioppo, John T.; van Beijsterveldt, Toos C. E. M. & Boomsma, Dorret I.** (2013). Exploring the association between well-being and psychopathology in adolescents. *Behavior Genetics, 43*(3), 177–190. doi: 10.1007/s10519-013-9589-7

**Bassok, Daphna; Latham, Scott & Rorem, Anna.** (2016). Is kindergarten the new first grade? *AERA Open, 2*(1). doi: 10.1177/2332858415616358

**Bateson, Patrick & Martin, Paul.** (2013). *Play, playfulness, creativity and innovation.* New York, NY: Cambridge University Press.

**Bauer, Patricia J.; San Souci, Priscilla & Pathman, Thanujeni.** (2010). Infant memory. *Wiley Interdisciplinary Reviews: Cognitive Science, 1*(2), 267–277. doi: 10.1002/wcs.38

**Baumeister, Roy F. (Ed.).** (2012). *Self-esteem: The puzzle of low self-regard.* New York, NY: Springer. doi: 10.1007/978-1-4684-8956-9

**Baumrind, Diana.** (1967). Child care practices anteceding three patterns of preschool behavior. *Genetic Psychology Monographs, 75*(1), 43–88.

**Baumrind, Diana.** (1971). Current patterns of parental authority. *Developmental Psychology, 4*(1, Pt. 2), 1–103. doi: 10.1037/h0030372

**Baumrind, Diana.** (2013). Authoritative parenting revisited: History and current status. In Robert E. Larzelere et al. (Eds.), *Authoritative parenting: Synthesizing nurturance and discipline for optimal child development* (pp. 11–34). Washington, D.C.: American Psychological Association.

**Baumrind, Diana; Larzelere, Robert E. & Owens, Elizabeth B.** (2010). Effects of preschool parents' power assertive patterns and practices on adolescent development. *Parenting, 10*(3), 157–201. doi: 10.1080/15295190903290790

**Bax, Trent.** (2014). *Youth and Internet addiction in China.* New York, NY: Routledge.

**Baysu, Gülseli; Celeste, Laura; Brown, Rupert; Verschueren, Karine & Phalet, Karen.** (2016). Minority adolescents in ethnically diverse schools: Perceptions of equal treatment buffer threat effects. *Child Development, 87*(5), 1352–1366. doi: 10.1111/cdev.12609

**Bazinger, Claudia & Kühberger, Anton.** (2012). Theory use in social predictions. *New Ideas in Psychology, 30*(3), 319–321. doi: 10.1016/j.newideapsych.2012.02.003

**Beal, Susan.** (1988). Sleeping position and sudden infant death syndrome. *The Medical Journal of Australia, 149*(10), 562.

**Beauchaine, Theodore P.; Klein, Daniel N.; Crowell, Sheila E.; Derbidge, Christina & Gatzke-Kopp. Lisa.** (2009). Multifinality in the development of personality disorders: A Biology × Sex × Environment interaction model of antisocial and borderline traits. *Development and Psychopathology, 21*(3), 735–770. doi: 10.1017/S0954579409000418

**Beck, Melinda.** (2009, May 26). How's your baby? Recalling the Apgar score's namesake. *Wall Street Journal,* p. D1.

**Beck, Martha N.** (1999). *Expecting Adam: A true story of birth, rebirth, and everyday magic.* New York, NY: Times Books.

**Becker, Derek R.; McClelland, Megan M.; Loprinzi, Paul & Trost, Stewart G.** (2014). Physical activity, self-regulation, and early academic achievement in preschool children. *Early Education and Development, 25*(1), 56–70. doi: 10.1080/10409289.2013.780505

**Beebe, Beatrice; Messinger, Daniel; Bahrick, Lorraine E.; Margolis, Amy; Buck, Karen A. & Chen, Henian.** (2016). A systems view of mother–infant face-to-face communication. *Developmental Psychology, 52*(4), 556–571. doi: 10.1037/a0040085

**Beilin, Lawrence & Huang, Rae-Chi.** (2008). Childhood obesity, hypertension, the metabolic syndrome and adult cardiovascular disease. *Clinical and Experimental Pharmacology and Physiology, 35*(4), 409–411. doi: 10.1111/j.1440-1681.2008.04887.x

**Bell, Beth T. & Dittmar, Helga.** (2011). Does media type matter? The role of identification in adolescent girls' media consumption and the impact of different thin-ideal media on body image. *Sex Roles, 65*(7/8), 478–490. doi: 10.1007/s11199-011-9964-x

**Bell, Martha Ann & Calkins, Susan D.** (2011). Attentional control and emotion regulation in early development. In Michael I. Posner (Ed.), *Cognitive neuroscience of attention* (2nd ed., pp. 322–330). New York, NY: Guilford Press.

**Bellinger, David C.** (2016). Lead contamination in Flint — An abject failure to protect public health. *New England Journal of Medicine*, 374(12), 1101–1103. doi: 10.1056/NEJMp1601013

**Belsky, Daniel W.; Caspi, Avshalom; Houts, Renate; Cohen, Harvey J.; Corcoran, David L.; Danese, Andrea, . . . Moffitt, Terrie E.** (2015). Quantification of biological aging in young adults. *Proceedings of the National Academy of Sciences of the United States of America*, 112(30), E4104–E4110. doi: 10.1073/pnas.1506264112

**Belsky, Jay.** (2001). Emanuel Miller lecture: Developmental risks (still) associated with early child care. *Journal of Child Psychology and Psychiatry*, 42(7), 845–859. doi: 10.1111/1469-7610.00782

**Belsky, Jay; Bakermans-Kranenburg, Marian J. & van IJzendoorn, Marinus H.** (2007). For better and for worse: Differential susceptibility to environmental influences. *Current Directions in Psychological Science*, 16(6), 300–304. doi: 10.1111/j.1467-8721.2007.00525.x

**Belsky, Jay & Pluess, Michael.** (2009). The nature (and nurture?) of plasticity in early human development. *Perspectives on Psychological Science*, 4(4), 345–351. doi: 10.1111/j.1745-6924.2009.01136.x

**Belsky, Jay & Rovine, Michael J.** (1988). Nonmaternal care in the first year of life and the security of infant-parent attachment. *Child Development*, 59(1), 157–167. doi: 10.2307/1130397

**Belsky, Jay; Steinberg, Laurence; Houts, Renate M. & Halpern-Felsher, Bonnie L.** (2010). The development of reproductive strategy in females: Early maternal harshness → earlier menarche → increased sexual risk taking. *Developmental Psychology*, 46(1), 120–128. doi: 10.1037/a0015549

**Bem, Sandra L.** (1981). Gender schema theory: A cognitive account of sex typing. *Psychological Review*, 88(4), 354–364. doi: 10.1037/0033-295X.88.4.354

**Bender, Heather L.; Allen, Joseph P.; Mcelhaney, Kathleen Boykin; Antonishak, Jill; Moore, Cynthia M.; Kelly, Heather O'beirne & Davis, Steven M.** (2007). Use of harsh physical discipline and developmental outcomes in adolescence. *Development and Psychopathology*, 19(1), 227–242. doi: 10.1017/S0954579407070125

**Benigno, Joann P.; Byrd, Dana L.; McNamara, Joseph P. H.; Berg, W. Keith & Farrar, M. Jeffrey.** (2011). Talking through transitions: Microgenetic changes in preschoolers' private speech and executive functioning. *Child Language Teaching and Therapy*, 27(3), 269–285. doi: 10.1177/0265659010394385

**Benn, Peter.** (2016). Prenatal diagnosis of chromosomal abnormalities through chorionic villus sampling and amniocentesis. In Aubrey Milunsky & Jeff M. Milunsky (Eds.), *Genetic disorders and the fetus: Diagnosis, prevention, and treatment* (7th ed., pp. 178–266). Hoboken, NJ: Wiley-Blackwell.

**Bennett, Craig M. & Baird, Abigail A.** (2006). Anatomical changes in the emerging adult brain: A voxel-based morphometry study. *Human Brain Mapping*, 27(9), 766–777. doi: 10.1002/hbm.20218

**Benoit, Amelie; Lacourse, Eric & Claes, Michel.** (2013). Pubertal timing and depressive symptoms in late adolescence: The moderating role of individual, peer, and parental factors. *Development and Psychopathology*, 25(2), 455–471. doi: 10.1017/S0954579412001174

**Bentley, Gillian R. & Mascie-Taylor, C. G. Nicholas.** (2000). Introduction. In Gillian R. Bentley & C. G. Nicholas Mascie-Taylor (Eds.), *Infertility in the modern world: Present and future prospects* (pp. 1–13). New York, NY: Cambridge University Press.

**Bergen, Gwen; Peterson, Cora; Ederer, David; Florence, Curtis; Haileyesus, Tadesse; Kresnow, Marcie-Jo & Xu, Likang.** (2014). *Vital signs: Health burden and medical costs of non-fatal injuries to motor vehicle occupants—United States, 2012. Morbidity and Mortality Weekly Report 63*(40), 894–900. Atlanta, GA: Centers for Disease Control and Prevention.

**Berger, Kathleen S.** (1980). *The developing person* (1st ed.). New York, NY: Worth.

**Berkowitz, Talia; Schaeffer, Marjorie W.; Maloney, Erin A.; Peterson, Lori; Gregor, Courtney; Levine, Susan C. & Beilock, Sian L.** (2015). Math at home adds up to achievement in school. *Science*, 350(6257), 196–198. doi: 10.1126/science.aac7427

**Bernard, Kristin & Dozier, Mary.** (2010). Examining infants' cortisol responses to laboratory tasks among children varying in attachment disorganization: Stress reactivity or return to baseline? *Developmental Psychology*, 46(6), 1771–1778. doi: 10.1037/a0020660

**Bernard, Kristin; Lind, Teresa & Dozier, Mary.** (2014). Neurobiological consequences of neglect and abuse. In Jill E. Korbin & Richard D. Krugman (Eds.), *Handbook of child maltreatment* (pp. 205–223). New York, NY: Springer. doi: 10.1007/978-94-007-7208-3_11

**Bernier, Annie; Calkins, Susan D. & Bell, Martha Ann.** (2016). Longitudinal associations between the quality of mother–infant interactions and brain development across infancy. *Child Development*, 87(4), 1159–1174. doi: 10.1111/cdev.12518

**Best, Joel & Best, Eric.** (2014). *The student loan mess: How good intentions created a trillion-dollar problem*. Berkeley, CA: University of California Press.

**Betancourt, Theresa S.; McBain, Ryan; Newnham, Elizabeth A. & Brennan, Robert T.** (2013). Trajectories of internalizing problems in war-affected Sierra Leonean youth: Examining conflict and postconflict factors. *Child Development*, 84(2), 455–470. doi: 10.1111/j.1467-8624.2012.01861.x

**Bhatia, Tej K. & Ritchie, William C. (Eds.).** (2013). *The handbook of bilingualism and multilingualism* (2nd ed.). Malden, MA: Wiley-Blackwell.

**Bhatnagar, Aruni; Whitsel, Laurie P.; Ribisl, Kurt M.; Bullen, Chris; Chaloupka, Frank; Piano, Mariann R., . . . Benowitz, Neal.** (2014). Electronic cigarettes: A policy statement from the American Heart Association. *Circulation*, 130(16), 1418–1436. doi: 10.1161/CIR.0000000000000107

**Bialystok, Ellen.** (2010). Global-local and trail-making tasks by monolingual and bilingual children: Beyond inhibition. *Developmental Psychology*, 46(1), 93–105. doi: 10.1037/a0015466

**Bialystok, Ellen.** (2017). The bilingual adaptation: How minds accommodate experience. *Psychological Bulletin*, 143(3), 233–262. doi: 10.1037/bul0000099

**Bianconi, Eva; Piovesan, Allison; Facchin, Federica; Beraudi, Alina; Casadei, Raffaella; Frabetti, Flavia, . . . Canaider, Silvia.** (2013). An estimation of the number of cells in the human body. *Annals of Human Biology*, 40(6), 463–471. doi: 10.3109/03014460.2013.807878

**Biemiller, Andrew.** (2009). Parent/caregiver narrative: Vocabulary development (0–60 Months). In Linda M. Phillips (Ed.), *Handbook of language and literacy development: A Roadmap from 0–60* (Online ed.). London, ON: Canadian Language and Literacy Research Network.

**Birkeland, Marianne S.; Breivik, Kyrre & Wold, Bente.** (2014). Peer acceptance protects global self-esteem from negative effects of low closeness to parents during adolescence and early adulthood. *Journal of Youth and Adolescence*, 43(1), 70–80. doi: 10.1007/s10964-013-9929-1

**Biro, Frank M.; Greenspan, Louise C.; Galvez, Maida P.; Pinney, Susan M.; Teitelbaum, Susan; Windham, Gayle C., . . . Wolff, Mary S.** (2013). Onset of breast development in a longitudinal cohort. *Pediatrics*, 132(6), 1019–1027. doi: 10.1542/peds.2012-3773

**Biro, Frank M.; McMahon, Robert P.; Striegel-Moore, Ruth; Crawford, Patricia B.; Obarzanek, Eva; Morrison, John A., . . . Falkner, Frank.** (2001). Impact of timing of pubertal maturation on growth in Black and White female adolescents: The National Heart, Lung, and Blood Institute Growth and Health Study. *Journal of Pediatrics*, 138(5), 636–643. doi: 10.1067/mpd.2001.114476

**Bjorklund, David F.; Dukes, Charles & Brown, Rhonda D.** (2009). The development of memory strategies. In Mary L. Courage & Nelson Cowan (Eds.), *The development of memory in infancy and childhood* (2nd ed., pp. 145–175). New York, NY: Psychology Press.

**Bjorklund, David F. & Ellis, Bruce J.** (2014). Children, childhood, and development in evolutionary perspective. *Developmental Review*, 34(3), 225–264. doi: 10.1016/j.dr.2014.05.005

**Bjorklund, David F. & Hawley, Patricia H.** (2014). Aggression grows up: Looking through an evolutionary developmental lens to understand the causes and consequences of human aggression. In Todd K. Shackelford & Ranald D. Hansen (Eds.), *The Evolution of Violence* (pp. 159–186). New York, NY: Springer. doi: 10.1007/978-1-4614-9314-3_9

**Bjorklund, David F. & Sellers, Patrick D.** (2014). Memory development in evolutionary perspective. In Patricia Bauer & Robyn Fivush (Eds.), *The Wiley handbook on the development of children's memory* (Vol. 1, pp. 126–150). Malden, MA: Wiley.

**Black, Robert E.; Victora, Cesar G.; Walker, Susan P.; Bhutta, Zulfiqar A.; Christian,**

**Parul; Onis, Mercedes de & Ezzati, Majid.** (2013). Maternal and child undernutrition and overweight in low-income and middle-income countries. *The Lancet, 382*(9809), 427–451. doi: 10.1016/S0140-6736(13)60937-X

**Blad, Evie.** (2014). Some states overhauling vaccine laws. *Education Week, 33*(31), 1, 23.

**Blair, Clancy.** (2016). Developmental science and executive function. *Current Directions in Psychological Science, 25*(1), 3–7. doi: 10.1177/0963721415622634

**Blair, Clancy & Raver, C. Cybele.** (2015). School readiness and self-regulation: A developmental psychobiological approach. *Annual Review of Psychology, 66,* 711–731. doi: 10.1146/annurev-psych-010814-015221

**Blandon, Alysia Y.; Calkins, Susan D. & Keane, Susan P.** (2010). Predicting emotional and social competence during early childhood from toddler risk and maternal behavior. *Development and Psychopathology, 22*(1), 119–132. doi: 10.1017/S0954579409990307

**Bleidorn, Wiebke; Klimstra, Theo A.; Denissen, Jaap J. A.; Rentfrow, Peter J.; Potter, Jeff & Gosling, Samuel D.** (2013). Personality maturation around the world: A cross-cultural examination of social-investment theory. *Psychological Science, 24*(12), 2530–2540. doi: 10.1177/0956797613498396

**Bleys, Dries; Soenens, Bart; Boone, Liesbet; Claes, Stephan; Vliegen, Nicole & Luyten, Patrick.** (2016). The role of intergenerational similarity and parenting in adolescent self-criticism: An actor–partner interdependence model. *Journal of Adolescence, 49,* 68–76. doi: 10.1016/j.adolescence.2016.03.003

**Blomqvist, Ylva Thernström; Nyqvist, Kerstin Hedberg; Rubertsson, Christine & Funkquist, Eva-Lotta.** (2017). Parents need support to find ways to optimise their own sleep without seeing their preterm infant's sleeping patterns as a problem. *Acta Paediatrica, 106*(2), 223–228. doi: 10.1111/apa.13660

**Bloom, Barbara & Freeman, Gulnur.** (2015). *Tables of summary health statistics for U.S. Children: 2014 national health interview survey.* Atlanta, GA: U.S. Department of Health & Human Services, Centers for Disease Control and Prevention, National Center for Health Statistics.

**Blurton-Jones, Nicholas G.** (1976). Rough-and-tumble play among nursery school children. In Jerome S. Bruner et al. (Eds.), *Play: Its role in development and evolution* (pp. 352–363). New York, NY: Basic Books.

**Bögels, Susan M.; Knappe, Susanne & Clark, Lee Anna.** (2013). Adult separation anxiety disorder in DSM-5. *Clinical Psychology Review, 33*(5), 663–674. doi: 10.1016/j.cpr.2013.03.006

**Bohlen, Tabata M.; Silveira, Marina A.; Zampieri, Thais T.; Frazão, Renata & Donato, Jose.** (2016). Fatness rather than leptin sensitivity determines the timing of puberty in female mice. *Molecular and Cellular Endocrinology, 423,* 11–21. doi: 10.1016/j.mce.2015.12.022

**Bombard, Jennifer M.; Robbins, Cheryl L.; Dietz, Patricia M. & Valderrama, Amy L.** (2013). Preconception care: The perfect opportunity for health care providers to advise lifestyle changes for hypertensive women. *American Journal of Health Promotion, 27*(3), S43–S49. doi: 10.4278/ajhp.120109-QUAN-6

**Bonanno, Rina A. & Hymel, Shelley.** (2013). Cyber bullying and internalizing difficulties: Above and beyond the impact of traditional forms of bullying. *Journal of Youth and Adolescence, 42*(5), 685–697. doi: 10.1007/s10964-013-9937-1

**Borke, Jörn; Lamm, Bettina; Eickhorst, Andreas & Keller, Heidi.** (2007). Father-infant interaction, paternal ideas about early child care, and their consequences for the development of children's self-recognition. *Journal of Genetic Psychology, 168*(4), 365–379. doi: 10.3200/GNTP.168.4.365-380

**Bornstein, Marc H.** (2017). The specificity principle in acculturation science. *Perspectives on Psychological Science, 12*(1), 3–45. doi: 10.1177/1745691616655997

**Bornstein, Marc H.; Arterberry, Martha E. & Mash, Clay.** (2005). Perceptual development. In Marc H. Bornstein & Michael E. Lamb (Eds.), *Developmental science: An advanced textbook* (5th ed., pp. 283–325). Mahwah, NJ: Lawrence Erlbaum Associates.

**Bornstein, Marc H. & Colombo, John.** (2012). Infant cognitive functioning and mental development. In Sabina Pauen (Ed.), *Early childhood development and later outcome.* New York, NY: Cambridge University Press.

**Bornstein, Marc H. & Putnick, Diane L.** (2016). Mothers' and fathers' parenting practices with their daughters and sons in low- and middle-income countries. *Monographs of the Society for Research in Child Development, 81*(1), 60–77. doi: 10.1111/mono.12226

**Bornstein, Marc H.; Putnick, Diane L.; Bradley, Robert H.; Deater-Deckard, Kirby & Lansford, Jennifer E.** (2016). Gender in low- and middle-income countries: Introduction. *Monographs of the Society for Research in Child Development, 81*(1), 7–23. doi: 10.1111/mono.12223

**Boundy, Ellen O.; Dastjerdi, Roya; Spiegelman, Donna; Fawzi, Wafaie W.; Missmer, Stacey A.; Lieberman, Ellice, . . . Chan, Grace J.** (2016). Kangaroo mother care and neonatal outcomes: A meta-analysis. *Pediatrics, 137*(1), e20152238. doi: 10.1542/peds.2015-2238

**Bouter, Lex M.** (2015). Commentary: Perverse incentives or rotten apples? *Accountability in Research, 22*(3), 148–161. doi: 10.1080/08989621.2014.950253

**Bowes, Lucy; Maughan, Barbara; Caspi, Avshalom; Moffitt, Terrie E. & Arseneault, Louise.** (2010). Families promote emotional and behavioural resilience to bullying: Evidence of an environmental effect. *Journal of Child Psychology and Psychiatry, 51*(7), 809–817. doi: 10.1111/j.1469-7610.2010.02216.x

**Bowlby, John.** (1983). *Attachment* (2nd ed.). New York, NY: Basic Books.

**boyd, danah.** (2014). *It's complicated: The social lives of networked teens.* New Haven, CT: Yale University Press.

**Boyd, Wendy; Walker, Susan & Thorpe, Karen.** (2013). Choosing work and care: Four Australian women negotiating return to paid work in the first year of motherhood. *Contemporary Issues in Early Childhood, 14*(2), 168–178. doi: 10.2304/ciec.2013.14.2.168

**Braams, Barbara R.; Güroğlu, Berna; de Water, Erik; Meuwese, Rosa; Koolschijn, P. Cédric; Peper, Jiska S. & Crone, Eveline A.** (2014). Reward-related neural responses are dependent on the beneficiary. *Social Cognitive and Affective Neuroscience, 9*(7), 1030–1037. doi: 10.1093/scan/nst077

**Braams, Barbara R.; van Duijvenvoorde, Anna C. K.; Peper, Jiska S. & Crone, Eveline A.** (2015). Longitudinal changes in adolescent risk-taking: A comprehensive study of neural responses to rewards, pubertal development, and risk-taking behavior. *The Journal of Neuroscience, 35*(18), 7226–7238. doi: 10.1523/JNEUROSCI.4764-14.2015

**Brabeck, Kalina M. & Sibley, Erin.** (2016). Immigrant parent legal status, parent–child relationships, and child social emotional wellbeing: A middle childhood perspective. *Journal of Child and Family Studies, 25*(4), 1155–1167. doi: 10.1007/s10826-015-0314-4

**Bracken, Bruce A. & Crawford, Elizabeth.** (2010). Basic concepts in early childhood educational standards: A 50-state review. *Early Childhood Education Journal, 37*(5), 421–430. doi: 10.1007/s10643-009-0363-7

**Bradley, Rachel & Slade, Pauline.** (2011). A review of mental health problems in fathers following the birth of a child. *Journal of Reproductive and Infant Psychology, 29*(1), 19–42. doi: 10.1080/02646838.2010.513047

**Brame, Robert; Bushway, Shawn D.; Paternoster, Ray & Turner, Michael G.** (2014). Demographic patterns of cumulative arrest prevalence by ages 18 and 23. *Crime & Delinquency, 60*(3), 471–486. doi: 10.1177/0011128713514801

**Brandone, Amanda C.; Horwitz, Suzanne R.; Aslin, Richard N. & Wellman, Henry M.** (2014). Infants' goal anticipation during failed and successful reaching actions. *Developmental Science, 17*(1), 23–34. doi: 10.1111/desc.12095

**Brazelton, T. Berry & Sparrow, Joshua D.** (2006). *Touchpoints, birth to 3: Your child's emotional and behavioral development* (2nd ed.). Cambridge, MA: Da Capo Press.

**Bremner, J. Gavin & Wachs, Theodore D. (Eds.).** (2010). *The Wiley-Blackwell handbook of infant development* (2nd ed.). Malden, MA: Wiley-Blackwell.

**Brémond-Gignac, Dominique; Copin, Henri; Lapillonne, Alexandre & Milazzo, Solange.** (2011). Visual development in infants: physiological and pathological mechanisms. *Current Opinion in Ophthalmology, 22*(Suppl), S1–S8. doi: 10.1097/01.icu.0000397180.37316.5d

**Brendgen, Mara; Lamarche, Véronique; Wanner, Brigitte & Vitaro, Frank.** (2010). Links between friendship relations and early adolescents' trajectories of depressed mood. *Developmental Psychology, 46*(2), 491–501. doi: 10.1037/a0017413

**Brennan, Arthur; Ayers, Susan; Ahmed, Hafez & Marshall-Lucette, Sylvie.** (2007).

A critical review of the Couvade syndrome: The pregnant male. *Journal of Reproductive and Infant Psychology*, 25(3), 173–189. doi: 10.1080/02646830701467207

**Bribiescas, Richard G. & Burke, Erin E.** (2017). Health, evolution, and reproductive strategies in men: New hypotheses and directions. In Grazyna Jasienska et al. (Eds.), *The arc of life: Evolution and health across the life course.* New York, NY: Springer. doi: 10.1007/978-1-4939-4038-7_6

**Bridgers, Sophie; Buchsbaum, Daphna; Seiver, Elizabeth; Griffiths, Thomas L. & Gopnik, Alison.** (2016). Children's causal inferences from conflicting testimony and observations. *Developmental Psychology*, 52(1), 9–18. doi: 10.1037/a0039830

**Bridgett, David J.; Burt, Nicole M.; Edwards, Erin S. & Deater-Deckard, Kirby.** (2015). Intergenerational transmission of self-regulation: A multidisciplinary review and integrative conceptual framework. *Psychological Bulletin*, 141(3), 602–654. doi: 10.1037/a0038662

**Brody, Gene H.** (2017). Using genetically informed prevention trials to test gene × environment hypotheses. In Patrick H. Tolan & Bennett L. Leventhal (Eds.), *Gene-environment transactions in developmental psychopathology: The role in intervention research* (pp. 211–233). Switzerland: Springer. doi: 10.1007/978-3-319-49227-8_11

**Brody, Gene H.; Beach, Steven R. H.; Philibert, Robert A.; Chen, Yi-fu & Murry, Velma McBride.** (2009). Prevention effects moderate the association of 5-HTTLPR and youth risk behavior initiation: Gene × environment hypotheses tested via a randomized prevention design. *Child Development*, 80(3), 645–661. doi: 10.1111/j.1467-8624.2009.01288.x

**Brody, Gene H.; Yu, Tianyi; Chen, Yi-fu; Kogan, Steven M.; Evans, Gary W.; Windle, Michael, . . . Philibert, Robert A.** (2013). Supportive family environments, genes that confer sensitivity, and allostatic load among rural African American emerging adults: A prospective analysis. *Journal of Family Psychology*, 27(1), 22–29. doi: 10.1037/a0027829

**Brody, Jane E.** (2012, July 24). The ideal and the real of breast-feeding. *New York Times*. http://nyti.ms/1damBS9

**Brody, Jane E.** (2013, February 26). Too many pills in pregnancy. *New York Times*, p. D5. http://nyti.ms/1eXwQtk

**Bronfenbrenner, Urie & Morris, Pamela A.** (2006). The bioecological model of human development. In William Damon & Richard M. Lerner (Eds.), *Handbook of child psychology* (6th ed., Vol. 1, pp. 793–828). Hoboken, NJ: Wiley.

**Broström, Stig.** (2017). A dynamic learning concept in early years' education: A possible way to prevent schoolification. *International Journal of Early Years Education*, 25(1), 3–15. doi: 10.1080/09669760.2016.1270196

**Brouwer, Rachel M.; van Soelen, Inge L. C.; Swagerman, Suzanne C.; Schnack, Hugo G.; Ehli, Erik A.; Kahn, René S., . . . Boomsma,**

**Dorret I.** (2014). Genetic associations between intelligence and cortical thickness emerge at the start of puberty. *Human Brain Mapping*, 35(8), 3760–3773. doi: 10.1002/hbm.22435

**Brown, B. Bradford & Bakken, Jeremy P.** (2011). Parenting and peer relationships: Reinvigorating research on family–peer linkages in adolescence. *Journal of Research on Adolescence*, 21(1), 153–165. doi: 10.1111/j.1532-7795.2010.00720.x

**Brown, Christia Spears.** (2017). Perceptions of intergroup discrimination. In Adam Rutland et al. (Eds.), *The Wiley handbook of group processes in children and adolescents* (pp. 269–291). Malden, MA: Wiley-Blackwell.

**Brown, Steven D. & Lent, Robert W.** (2016). Vocational psychology: Agency, equity, and well-being. *Annual Review of Psychology*, 67, 541–565. doi: 10.1146/annurev-psych-122414-033237

**Brown, Susan L.** (2010). Marriage and child well-being: Research and policy perspectives. *Journal of Marriage and Family*, 72(5), 1059–1077. doi: 10.1111/j.1741-3737.2010.00750.x

**Brown, Susan L.; Manning, Wendy D. & Stykes, J. Bart.** (2015). Family structure and child well-being: Integrating family complexity. *Journal of Marriage and Family*, 77(1), 177–190. doi: 10.1111/jomf.12145

**Bryant-Comstock, Katelyn; Bryant, Amy G.; Narasimhan, Subasri & Levi, Erika E.** (2016). Information about sexual health on crisis pregnancy center web sites: Accurate for adolescents? *Journal of Pediatric and Adolescent Gynecology*, 29(1), 22–25. doi: 10.1016/j.jpag.2015.05.008

**Bueno, Clarissa & Menna-Barreto, Luiz.** (2016). Environmental factors influencing biological rhythms in newborns: From neonatal intensive care units to home. *Sleep Science*, 9(4), 295–300. doi: 10.1016/j.slsci.2016.10.004

**Bureau of Labor Statistics.** (2016, April 28). College enrollment and work activity of 2015 high school graduates [Press release]. Washington, DC: United States Department of Labor. USDL–16–0822.

**Burnette, Jeni L.; O'Boyle, Ernest H.; VanEpps, Eric M.; Pollack, Jeffrey M. & Finkel, Eli J.** (2013). Mind-sets matter: A meta-analytic review of implicit theories and self-regulation. *Psychological Bulletin*, 139(3), 655–701. doi: 10.1037/a0029531

**Burstein, David D.** (2013). *Fast future: How the millennial generation is shaping our world.* Boston, MA: Beacon Press.

**Burstyn, Igor.** (2014). Peering through the mist: Systematic review of what the chemistry of contaminants in electronic cigarettes tells us about health risks. *BMC Public Health*, 14(1), 18. doi: 10.1186/1471-2458-14-18

**Bursztyn, Leonardo & Jensen, Robert.** (2015). How does peer pressure affect educational investments? *Quarterly Journal of Economics*, 130(3), 1329–1367. doi: 10.1093/Qje/Qjv021

**Burt, S. Alexandra.** (2009). Rethinking environmental contributions to child and adolescent psychopathology: A meta-analysis of shared environmental influences. *Psychological Bulletin*, 135(4), 608–637. doi: 10.1037/a0015702

**Buss, David M.** (2015). *Evolutionary psychology: The new science of the mind* (5th ed.). New York, NY: Routledge.

**Butler, Ashley M. & Titus, Courtney.** (2015). Systematic review of engagement in culturally adapted parent training for disruptive behavior. *Journal of Early Intervention*, 37(4), 300–318. doi: 10.1177/1053815115620210

**Buttelmann, David; Zmyj, Norbert; Daum, Moritz & Carpenter, Malinda.** (2013). Selective imitation of in-group over out-group members in 14-month-old infants. *Child Development*, 84(2), 422–428. doi: 10.1111/j.1467-8624.2012.01860.x

**Butterworth, Brian & Kovas, Yulia.** (2013). Understanding neurocognitive developmental disorders can improve education for all. *Science*, 340(6130), 300–305. doi: 10.1126/science.1231022

**Butterworth, Brian; Varma, Sashank & Laurillard, Diana.** (2011). Dyscalculia: From brain to education. *Science*, 332(6033), 1049–1053. doi: 10.1126/science.1201536

**Byard, Roger W.** (2014). "Shaken baby syndrome" and forensic pathology: An uneasy interface. *Forensic Science, Medicine, and Pathology*, 10(2), 239–241. doi: 10.1007/s12024-013-9514-7

**Byers-Heinlein, Krista; Burns, Tracey C. & Werker, Janet F.** (2010). The roots of bilingualism in newborns. *Psychological Science*, 21(3), 343–348. doi: 10.1177/0956797609360758

**Cabrera, Natasha.** (2015). Why do fathers matter for children's development? In Susan M. McHale et al. (Eds.), *Gender and Couple Relationships* (pp. 161–168). New York, NY: Springer. doi: 10.1007/978-3-319-21635-5_9

**Cacioppo, John T.; Cacioppo, Stephanie; Gonzaga, Gian C.; Ogburn, Elizabeth L. & VanderWeele, Tyler J.** (2013). Marital satisfaction and break-ups differ across on-line and off-line meeting venues. *PNAS*, 110(25), 10135–10140. doi: 10.1073/pnas.1222447110

**Cacioppo, Stephanie; Capitanio, John P. & Cacioppo, John T.** (2014). Toward a neurology of loneliness. *Psychological Bulletin*, 140(6), 1464–1504. doi: 10.1037/a0037618

**Calarco, Jessica McCrory.** (2014). The inconsistent curriculum: Cultural tool kits and student interpretations of ambiguous expectations. *Social Psychology Quarterly*, 77(2), 185–209. doi: 10.1177/0190272514521438

**Calder, Gillian & Beaman, Lori G. (Eds.).** (2014). *Polygamy's rights and wrongs: Perspectives on harm, family, and law.* Vancouver, BC: University of British Columbia Press.

**Callaghan, Bridget L. & Tottenham, Nim.** (2016). The neuro-environmental loop of plasticity: A cross-species analysis of parental effects on emotion circuitry development following typical and adverse caregiving. *Neuropsychopharmacology*, 41, 163–176. doi: 10.1038/npp.2015.204

**Callaghan, Tara.** (2013). Symbols and symbolic thought. In Philip D. Zelazo (Ed.), *The Oxford handbook of developmental psychology* (Vol. 1). New York, NY: Oxford University Press. doi: 10.1093/oxfordhb/9780199958450.013.0034

Camchong, Jazmin; Lim, Kelvin O. & Kumra, Sanjiv. (2017). Adverse effects of cannabis on adolescent brain development: A longitudinal study. *Cerebral Cortex*, 27(3), 1922–1930. doi: 10.1093/cercor/bhw015

Camhi, Sarah M.; Katzmarzyk, Peter T.; Broyles, Stephanie; Church, Timothy S.; Hankinson, Arlene L.; Carnethon, Mercedes R., . . . Lewis, Cora E. (2013). Association of metabolic risk with longitudinal physical activity and fitness: Coronary artery risk development in young adults (CARDIA). *Metabolic Syndrome and Related Disorders*, 11(3), 195–204. doi: 10.1089/met.2012.0120

Campbell, Frances; Conti, Gabriella; Heckman, James J.; Moon, Seong H.; Pinto, Rodrigo; Pungello, Elizabeth & Pan, Yi. (2014). Early childhood investments substantially boost adult health. *Science*, 343(6178), 1478–1485. doi: 10.1126/science.1248429

Campbell, Frances A.; Pungello, Elizabeth P.; Miller-Johnson, Shari; Burchinal, Margaret & Ramey, Craig T. (2001). The development of cognitive and academic abilities: Growth curves from an early childhood educational experiment. *Developmental Psychology*, 37(2), 231–242. doi: 10.1037/0012-1649.37.2.231

Cantor, Patricia & Cornish, Mary M. (2016). *Techwise infant and toddler teachers: Making sense of screen media for children under 3.* Charlotte, NC: Information Age Publishing.

Caravita, Simona C. S. & Cillessen, Antonius H. N. (2012). Agentic or communal? Associations between interpersonal goals, popularity, and bullying in middle childhood and early adolescence. *Social Development*, 21(2), 376–395. doi: 10.1111/j.1467-9507.2011.00632.x

Caravita, Simona C. S.; Di Blasio, Paola & Salmivalli, Christina. (2010). Early adolescents' participation in bullying: Is ToM involved? *The Journal of Early Adolescence*, 30(1), 138–170. doi: 10.1177/0272431609342983

Card, Noel A.; Bosch, Leslie; Casper, Deborah M.; Wiggs, Christine Bracamonte; Hawkins, Stacy Ann; Schlomer, Gabriel L. & Borden, Lynne M. (2011). A meta-analytic review of internalizing, externalizing, and academic adjustment among children of deployed military service members. *Journal of Family Psychology*, 25(4), 508–520. doi: 10.1037/a0024395

Carey, Nessa. (2012). *The epigenetics revolution: How modern biology is rewriting our understanding of genetics, disease, and inheritance.* New York, NY: Columbia University Press.

Carlson, Daniel L. & Lynch, Jamie L. (2017). Purchases, penalties, and power: The relationship between earnings and housework. *Journal of Marriage and Family*, 79(1), 199–224. doi: 10.1111/jomf.12337

Carlson, Scott. (2016, May 1). Should everyone go to college?: For poor kids, 'College for all' isn't the mantra it was meant to be. *The Chronicle of Higher Education.*

Carlson, Stephanie M.; Koenig, Melissa A. & Harms, Madeline B. (2013). Theory of mind. *Wiley Interdisciplinary Reviews: Cognitive Science*, 4(4), 391–402. doi: 10.1002/wcs.1232

Carra, Cecilia; Lavelli, Manuela; Keller, Heidi & Kärtner, Joscha. (2013). Parenting infants: Socialization goals and behaviors of Italian mothers and immigrant mothers from West Africa. *Journal of Cross-Cultural Psychology*, 44(8), 1304–1320. doi: 10.1177/0022022113486004

Carroll, Linda J.; Cassidy, David; Cancelliere, Carol; Côté, Pierre; Hincapié, Cesar A.; Kristman, Vicki L., . . . Hartvigsen, Jan. (2014). Systematic review of the prognosis after mild traumatic brain injury in adults: Cognitive, psychiatric, and mortality outcomes: Results of the international collaboration on mild traumatic brain injury prognosis. *Archives of Physical Medicine and Rehabilitation*, 95(3, Suppl.), S152–S173. doi: 10.1016/j.apmr.2013.08.300

Carson, Valerie & Kuzik, Nicholas. (2017). Demographic correlates of screen time and objectively measured sedentary time and physical activity among toddlers: A cross-sectional study. *BMC Public Health*, 17. doi: 10.1186/s12889-017-4125-y

Carson, Valerie; Tremblay, Mark S.; Spence, John C.; Timmons, Brian W. & Janssen, Ian. (2013). The Canadian Sedentary Behaviour Guidelines for the Early Years (zero to four years of age) and screen time among children from Kingston, Ontario. *Paediatrics & Child Health*, 18(1), 25–28.

Caruso, Federica. (2013). Embedding early childhood education and care in the socio-cultural context: The case of Italy. In Jan Georgeson & Jane Payler (Eds.), *International perspectives on early childhood education and care.* New York, NY: Open University Press.

Carver, Alison. (2016). Parental perceptions of risk and children's physical activity. In Claire Freeman et al. (Eds.), *Risk, protection, provision and policy* (pp. 241–259). Singapore: Springer Singapore. doi: 10.1007/978-981-287-035-3_8

Carwile, Jenny L.; Willett, Walter C.; Spiegelman, Donna; Hertzmark, Ellen; Rich-Edwards, Janet W.; Frazier, A. Lindsay & Michels, Karin B. (2015). Sugar-sweetened beverage consumption and age at menarche in a prospective study of US girls. *Human Reproduction*, 30(3), 675–683. doi: 10.1093/humrep/deu349

Casey, B. J. & Caudle, Kristina. (2013). The teenage brain: Self control. *Current Directions in Psychological Science*, 22(2), 82–87. doi: 10.1177/0963721413480170

Casper, Deborah M. & Card, Noel A. (2017). Overt and relational victimization: A meta-analytic review of their overlap and associations with social–psychological adjustment. *Child Development*, 88(2), 466–483. doi: 10.1111/cdev.12621

Caspi, Avshalom; Moffitt, Terrie E.; Morgan, Julia; Rutter, Michael; Taylor, Alan; Arseneault, Louise, . . . Polo-Tomas, Monica. (2004). Maternal expressed emotion predicts children's antisocial behavior problems: Using monozygotic-twin differences to identify environmental effects on behavioral development. *Developmental Psychology*, 40(2), 149–161. doi: 10.1037/0012-1649.40.2.149

Cassia, Viola Macchi; Kuefner, Dana; Picozzi, Marta & Vescovo, Elena. (2009). Early experience predicts later plasticity for face processing: Evidence for the reactivation of dormant effects. *Psychological Science*, 20(7), 853–859. doi: 10.1111/j.1467-9280.2009.02376.x

Cassina, Matteo; Cagnoli, Giulia A.; Zuccarello, Daniela; Gianantonio, Elena Di & Clementi, Maurizio. (2017). Human teratogens and genetic phenocopies. Understanding pathogenesis through human genes mutation. *European Journal of Medical Genetics*, 60(1), 22–31. doi: 10.1016/j.ejmg.2016.09.011

Catani, Claudia; Gewirtz, Abigail H.; Wieling, Elizabeth; Schauer, Elizabeth; Elbert, Thomas & Neuner, Frank. (2010). Tsunami, war, and cumulative risk in the lives of Sri Lankan schoolchildren. *Child Development*, 81(4), 1176–1191. doi: 10.1111/j.1467-8624.2010.01461.x

Cavalari, Rachel N. S. & Donovick, Peter J. (2014). Agenesis of the corpus callosum: Symptoms consistent with developmental disability in two siblings. *Neurocase: The Neural Basis of Cognition*, 21(1), 95–102. doi: 10.1080/13554794.2013.873059

Ceballo, Rosario; Maurizi, Laura K.; Suarez, Gloria A. & Aretakis, Maria T. (2014). Gift and sacrifice: Parental involvement in Latino adolescents' education. *Cultural Diversity and Ethnic Minority Psychology*, 20(1), 116–127. doi: 10.1037/a0033472

Cecil, Kim M.; Brubaker, Christopher J.; Adler, Caleb M.; Dietrich, Kim N.; Altaye, Mekibib; Egelhoff, John C., . . . Lanphear, Bruce P. (2008). Decreased brain volume in adults with childhood lead exposure. *PloS Medicine*, 5(5), 741–750. doi: 10.1371/journal.pmed.0050112

Center for Education Policy. (2012). *SDP strategic performance indicator: The high school effect on college-going. The SDP College-Going Diagnostic Strategic Performance Indicators.* Cambridge, MA: Harvard University, Center for Education Policy Research.

Center for Education Policy. (2013). *SDP college-going diagnostic: The school district of Philadelphia.* Cambridge, MA: Harvard University, Center for Education Policy Research.

Centers for Disease Control and Prevention. (2014). Underlying cause of death 1999–2012. Retrieved January 21, 2015, from CDC WONDER Online Database http://wonder.cdc.gov/ucd-icd10.html

Centers for Disease Control and Prevention. (2014, October 10). *Updates on CDC's polio eradication efforts. Global Health — Polio.* Atlanta, GA: Centers for Disease Control and Prevention.

Centers for Disease Control and Prevention. (2015). Atlanta, GA: Division for Heart Disease and Stroke Prevention.

Centers for Disease Control and Prevention. (2015, January 9). *Updates on CDC's polio eradication efforts. Global Health – Polio.* Atlanta, GA: Centers for Disease Control and Prevention.

Centers for Disease Control and Prevention. (2015, May 15). *Epidemiology and prevention of vaccine-preventable diseases* (Jennifer Hamborsky et al. Eds. 13th ed.). Washington DC: Public Health Foundation.

**Centers for Disease Control and Prevention.** (2016). *Number of children tested and confirmed bll's ≥10 μg/dl by state, year, and bll group, children < 72 months old. CDC's National Surveillance Data (1997–2014)*: U.S. Department of Health & Human Services.

**Centers for Disease Control and Prevention.** (2016, August). *Breastfeeding report card — United States, 2016.* Atlanta, GA: Centers for Disease Control and Prevention.

**Centers for Disease Control and Prevention, National Center for Injury Prevention and Control, Division of Analysis, Research, and Practice Integration.** (2013). *Fatal Injury Reports, 1999–2013, for National, Regional, and States.* Atlanta, GA: Centers for Disease Control and Prevention.

**Cerdá, Magdalena; Moffitt, Terrie E.; Meier, Madeline H.; Harrington, Hona Lee; Houts, Renate; Ramrakha, Sandhya, . . . Caspi, Avshalom.** (2016). Persistent cannabis dependence and alcohol dependence represent risks for midlife economic and social problems: A longitudinal cohort study. *Clinical Psychological Science, 4*(6), 1028–1046. doi: 10.1177/2167702616630958

**Cespedes, Elizabeth M.; McDonald, Julia; Haines, Jess; Bottino, Clement J.; Schmidt, Marie Evans & Taveras, Elsie M.** (2013). Obesity-related behaviors of US- and non-US-born parents and children in low-income households. *Journal of Developmental & Behavioral Pediatrics, 34*(8), 541–548. doi: 10.1097/DBP.0b013e3182a509fb

**Chafen, Jennifer J. S.; Newberry, Sydne J.; Riedl, Marc A.; Bravata, Dena M.; Maglione, Margaret; Suttorp, Marika J., . . . Shekelle, Paul S.** (2010). Diagnosing and managing common food allergies. *JAMA, 303*(18), 1848–1856. doi: 10.1001/jama.2010.582

**Champagne, Frances A. & Curley, James P.** (2010). Maternal care as a modulating influence on infant development. In Mark S. Blumberg et al. (Eds.), *Oxford handbook of developmental behavioral neuroscience* (pp. 323–341). New York, NY: Oxford University Press. doi: 10.1093/oxfordhb/9780195314731.013.0017

**Chan, Tak Wing & Koo, Anita.** (2011). Parenting style and youth outcomes in the UK. *European Sociological Review, 27*(3), 385–399. doi: 10.1093/esr/jcq013

**Chang, Alicia; Sandhofer, Catherine M. & Brown, Christia S.** (2011). Gender biases in early number exposure to preschool-aged children. *Journal of Language and Social Psychology, 30*(4), 440–450. doi: 10.1177/0261927X11416207

**Charnigo, Richard; Noar, Seth M.; Garnett, Christopher; Crosby, Richard; Palmgreen, Philip & Zimmerman, Rick S.** (2013). Sensation seeking and impulsivity: Combined associations with risky sexual behavior in a large sample of young adults. *The Journal of Sex Research, 50*(5), 480–488. doi: 10.1080/00224499.2011.652264

**Chartier, Karen G.; Scott, Denise M.; Wall, Tamara L.; Covault, Jonathan; Karriker-Jaffe, Katherine J.; Mills, Britain A., . . . Arroyo, Judith A.** (2014). Framing ethnic variations in alcohol outcomes from biological pathways to neighborhood context. *Alcoholism: Clinical and Experimental Research, 38*(3), 611–618. doi: 10.1111/acer.12304

**Chassin, Laurie; Bountress, Kaitlin; Haller, Moira & Wang, Frances.** (2014). Adolescent substance use disorders. In Eric J. Mash & Russell A. Barkley (Eds.), *Child psychopathology* (3rd ed., pp. 180–124). New York, NY: Guilford Press.

**Chen, Edith; Cohen, Sheldon & Miller, Gregory E.** (2010). How low socioeconomic status affects 2-year hormonal trajectories in children. *Psychological Science, 21*(1), 31–37. doi: 10.1177/0956797609355566

**Chen, Hong & Jackson, Todd.** (2009). Predictors of changes in weight esteem among mainland Chinese adolescents: A longitudinal analysis. *Developmental Psychology, 45*(6), 1618–1629. doi: 10.1037/a0016820

**Chen, Mu-Hong; Lan, Wen-Hsuan; Bai, Ya-Mei; Huang, Kai-Lin; Su, Tung-Ping; Tsai, Shih-Jen, . . . Hsu, Ju-Wei.** (2016). Influence of relative age on diagnosis and treatment of Attention-deficit hyperactivity disorder in Taiwanese children. *The Journal of Pediatrics, 172*, 162–167. e161. doi: 10.1016/j.jpeds.2016.02.012

**Chen, Xinyin; Cen, Guozhen; Li, Dan & He, Yunfeng.** (2005). Social functioning and adjustment in Chinese children: The imprint of historical time. *Child Development, 76*(1), 182–195. doi: 10.1111/j.1467-8624.2005.00838.x

**Chen, Xinyin; Rubin, Kenneth H. & Sun, Yuerong.** (1992). Social reputation and peer relationships in Chinese and Canadian children: A cross-cultural study. *Child Development, 63*(6), 1336–1343. doi: 10.1111/j.1467-8624.1992.tb01698.x

**Chen, Xinyin; Wang, Li & Wang, Zhengyan.** (2009). Shyness-sensitivity and social, school, and psychological adjustment in rural migrant and urban children in China. *Child Development, 80*(5), 1499–1513. doi: 10.1111/j.1467-8624.2009.01347.x

**Chen, Xinyin; Yang, Fan & Wang, Li.** (2013). Relations between shyness-sensitivity and internalizing problems in Chinese children: Moderating effects of academic achievement. *Journal of Abnormal Child Psychology, 41*(5), 825–836. doi: 10.1007/s10802-012-9708-6

**Cheng, Diana; Kettinger, Laurie; Uduhiri, Kelechi & Hurt, Lee.** (2011). Alcohol consumption during pregnancy: Prevalence and provider assessment. *Obstetrics & Gynecology, 117*(2), 212–217. doi: 10.1097/AOG.0b013e3182078569

**Cheng, Yvonne W.; Shaffer, Brian; Nicholson, James & Caughey, Aaron B.** (2014). Second stage of labor and epidural use: A larger effect than previously suggested. *Obstetrics & Gynecology, 123*(3), 527–535. doi: 10.1097/AOG.0000000000000134

**Cherlin, Andrew J.** (2009). *The marriage-go-round: The state of marriage and the family in America today.* New York, NY: Knopf.

**Cherlin, Andrew J.** (2014). *Labor's love lost: The rise and fall of the working-class family in America.* New York, NY: Russell Sage.

**Cherng, Hua-Yu Sebastian & Liu, Jia-Lin.** (2017). Academic social support and student expectations: The case of second-generation Asian Americans. *Asian American Journal of Psychology, 8*(1), 16–30. doi: 10.1037/aap0000072

**Cheslack-Postava, Keely; Liu, Kayuet & Bearman, Peter S.** (2011). Closely spaced pregnancies are associated with increased odds of autism in California sibling births. *Pediatrics, 127*(2), 246–253. doi: 10.1542/peds.2010-2371

**Chick, Christina F.** (2015). Reward processing in the adolescent brain: Individual differences and relation to risk taking. *Journal of Neuroscience, 35*(40), 13539–13541. doi: 10.1523/JNEUROSCI.2571-15.2015

**Child Trends.** (2014). *World family map 2014: Mapping family change and child well-being outcome.* Bethesda, MD: Child Trends.

**Child Trends Data Bank.** (2015, March). *Lead poisoning: Indicators on children and youth.* Bethesda, MD: Child Trends.

**Cho, Junhan; Kogan, Steven M. & Brody, Gene H.** (2016). Genetic moderation of transactional relations between parenting practices and child self-regulation. *Journal of Family Psychology, 30*(7), 780–790. doi: 10.1037/fam0000228

**Choe, Daniel E.; Lane, Jonathan D.; Grabell, Adam S. & Olson, Sheryl L.** (2013a). Developmental precursors of young school-age children's hostile attribution bias. *Developmental Psychology, 49*(12), 2245–2256. doi: 10.1037/a0032293

**Choe, Daniel E.; Olson, Sheryl L. & Sameroff, Arnold J.** (2013b). The interplay of externalizing problems and physical and inductive discipline during childhood. *Developmental Psychology, 49*(11), 2029–2039. doi: 10.1037/a0032054

**Chomsky, Noam.** (1968). *Language and mind.* New York, NY: Harcourt Brace & World.

**Chomsky, Noam.** (1980). *Rules and representations.* New York, NY: Columbia University Press.

**Chong, Jessica X.; Buckingham, Kati J.; Jhangiani, Shalini N.; Boehm, Corinne; Sobreira, Nara; Smith, Joshua D., . . . Bamshad, Michael J.** (2015). The genetic basis of mendelian phenotypes: Discoveries, challenges, and opportunities. *American Journal of Human Genetics, 97*(2), 199–215. doi: 10.1016/j.ajhg.2015.06.009

**Choukas-Bradley, Sophia; Giletta, Matteo; Widman, Laura; Cohen, Geoffrey L. & Prinstein, Mitchell J.** (2014). Experimentally measured susceptibility to peer influence and adolescent sexual behavior trajectories: A preliminary study. *Developmental Psychology, 50*(9), 2221–2227. doi: 10.1037/a0037300

**Chow, Chong Man & Ruhl, Holly.** (2014). Friendship and romantic stressors and depression in emerging adulthood: Mediating and moderating roles of attachment representations. *Journal of Adult Development, 21*(2), 106–115. doi: 10.1007/s10804-014-9184-z

**Christakis, Erika.** (2016). *The importance of being little: What preschoolers really need from grownups.* New York, NY: Viking.

**Christian, Cindy W. & Block, Robert.** (2009). Abusive head trauma in infants and children. *Pediatrics, 123*(5), 1409–1411. doi: 10.1542/peds.2009-0408

**Christoforides, Michael; Spanoudis, George & Demetriou, Andreas.** (2016). Coping with logical fallacies: A developmental training program for learning to reason. *Child Development*, 87(6), 1856–1876. doi: 10.1111/cdev.12557

**Chronicle of Higher Education.** (2015, August 17). *The almanac of higher education 2015–16*. Washington, DC.

**Chudacoff, Howard P.** (2011). The history of children's play in the United States. In Anthony D. Pellegrini (Ed.), *The Oxford handbook of the development of play* (pp. 101–109). New York, NY: Oxford University Press. doi: 10.1093/oxfordhb/9780195393002.013.0009

**Cicchetti, Dante.** (2013a). Annual Research Review: Resilient functioning in maltreated children – past, present, and future perspectives. *Journal of Child Psychology and Psychiatry*, 54(4), 402–422. doi: 10.1111/j.1469-7610.2012.02608.x

**Cicchetti, Dante.** (2013b). An overview of developmental psychopathology. In Philip D. Zelazo (Ed.), *The Oxford handbook of developmental psychology* (Vol. 2, pp. 455–480). New York, NY: Oxford University Press. doi: 10.1093/oxfordhb/9780199958474.013.0018

**Cicconi, Megan.** (2014). Vygotsky meets technology: A reinvention of collaboration in the early childhood mathematics classroom. *Early Childhood Education Journal*, 42(1), 57–65. doi: 10.1007/s10643-013-0582-9

**Cimpian, Andrei.** (2013). Generic statements, causal attributions, and children's naive theories. In Mahzarin R. Banaji & Susan A. Gelman (Eds.), *Navigating the social world: What infants, children, and other species can teach us* (pp. 269–274). New York, NY: Oxford University Press.

**Clark, Caron A. C.; Fang, Hua; Espy, Kimberly A.; Filipek, Pauline A.; Juranek, Jenifer; Bangert, Barbara, . . . Taylor, H. Gerry.** (2013). Relation of neural structure to persistently low academic achievement: A longitudinal study of children with differing birth weights. *Neuropsychology*, 27(3), 364–377. doi: 10.1037/a0032273

**Clark, Nina A.; Demers, Paul A.; Karr, Catherine J.; Koehoorn, Mieke; Lencar, Cornel; Tamburic, Lillian & Brauer, Michael.** (2010). Effect of early life exposure to air pollution on development of childhood asthma. *Environmental Health Perspectives*, 118(2), 284–290. doi: 10.1289/ehp.0900916

**Clayton, P. E.; Gill, M. S.; Tillmann, V. & Westwood, M.** (2014). Translational neuroendocrinology: Control of human growth. *Journal of Neuroendocrinology*, 26(6), 349–355. doi: 10.1111/jne.12156

**Coffelt, Tina A.** (2017). Deciding to reveal sexual information and sexuality education in mother-daughter relationships. *Sex Education*, 17(5), 571–587. doi: 10.1080/14681811.2017.1326377

**Cohen, Joel E. & Malin, Martin B. (Eds.).** (2010). *International perspectives on the goals of universal basic and secondary education*. New York, NY: Routledge.

**Cohen, Jon.** (2014). Saving lives without new drugs. *Science*, 346(6212), 911. doi: 10.1126/science.346.6212.911

**Cohen, Larry; Chávez, Vivian & Chehimi, Sana (Eds.).** (2010). *Prevention is primary: Strategies for community well-being* (2nd ed.). San Francisco, CA: Jossey-Bass.

**Cohen, Philip N.** (2014). Recession and divorce in the United States, 2008–2011. *Population Research and Policy Review*, 33(5), 615–628. doi: 10.1007/s11113-014-9323-z

**Colaco, Marc; Johnson, Kelly; Schneider, Dona & Barone, Joseph.** (2013). Toilet training method is not related to dysfunctional voiding. *Clinical Pediatrics*, 52(1), 49–53. doi: 10.1177/0009922812464042

**Cole, Pamela M.; Armstrong, Laura Marie & Pemberton, Caroline K.** (2010). The role of language in the development of emotion regulation. In Susan D. Calkins & Martha Ann Bell (Eds.), *Child development at the intersection of emotion and cognition* (pp. 59–78). Washington, DC: American Psychological Association.

**Coleman-Jensen, Alisha; Rabbitt, Matthew P.; Gregory, Christian & Singh, Anita.** (2015). *Household food security in the United States in 2014*. Washington, DC: U.S. Department of Agriculture, Economic Research Service.

**Collin-Vézina, Delphine; De La Sablonnière-Griffin, Mireille; Palmer, Andrea M. & Milne, Lise.** (2015). A preliminary mapping of individual, relational, and social factors that impede disclosure of childhood sexual abuse. *Child Abuse & Neglect*, 43, 123–134. doi: 10.1016/j.chiabu.2015.03.010

**Collins, Christine E.; Turner, Emily C.; Sawyer, Eva Kille; Reed, Jamie L.; Young, Nicole A.; Flaherty, David K. & Kaas, Jon H.** (2016). Cortical cell and neuron density estimates in one chimpanzee hemisphere. *Proceedings of the National Academy of Sciences*, 113(3), 740–745. doi: 10.1073/pnas.1524208113

**Collins, Rebecca L.; Martino, Steven C.; Elliott, Marc N. & Miu, Angela.** (2011). Relationships between adolescent sexual outcomes and exposure to sex in media: Robustness to propensity-based analysis. *Developmental Psychology*, 47(2), 585–591. doi: 10.1037/a0022563

**Colson, Eve R.; Willinger, Marian; Rybin, Denis; Heeren, Timothy; Smith, Lauren A.; Lister, George & Corwin, Michael J.** (2013). Trends and factors associated with infant bed sharing, 1993–2010: The National Infant Sleep Position study. *JAMA Pediatrics*, 167(11), 1032–1037. doi: 10.1001/jamapediatrics.2013.2560

**Common Sense Media.** (2013). *Zero to eight: Children's media use in America 2013*. San Francisco, CA: Common Sense Media.

**Compian, Laura J.; Gowen, L. Kris & Hayward, Chris.** (2009). The interactive effects of puberty and peer victimization on weight concerns and depression symptoms among early adolescent girls. *The Journal of Early Adolescence*, 29(3), 357–375. doi: 10.1177/0272431608323656

**Confer, Jaime C.; Easton, Judith A.; Fleischman, Diana S.; Goetz, Cari D.; Lewis, David M. G.; Perilloux, Carin & Buss, David M.** (2010). Evolutionary psychology: Controversies, questions, prospects, and limitations. *American Psychologist*, 65(2), 110–126. doi: 10.1037/a0018413

**Coovadia, Hoosen M. & Wittenberg, Dankwart F. (Eds.).** (2004). *Paediatrics and child health: A manual for health professionals in developing countries* (5th ed.). New York, NY: Oxford University Press.

**Copeland, William E.; Wolke, Dieter; Angold, Adrian & Costell, E. Jane.** (2013). Adult psychiatric outcomes of bullying and being bullied by peers in childhood and adolescence. *JAMA Psychiatry*, 70(4), 419–426. doi: 10.1001/jamapsychiatry.2013.504

**Copen, Casey E.; Daniels, Kimberly & Mosher, William D.** (2013). *First premarital cohabitation in the United States: 2006–2010 national survey of family growth*. National Health Statistics Report. Hyattsville, MD: U.S. Department of Health and Human Services, Centers for Disease Control and Prevention, National Center for Health Statistics.

**Coplan, Robert J. & Weeks, Murray.** (2009). Shy and soft-spoken: Shyness, pragmatic language, and socio-emotional adjustment in early childhood. *Infant and Child Development*, 18(3), 238–254. doi: 10.1002/icd.622

**Copp. Jennifer E.; Giordano, Peggy C.; Longmore, Monica A. & Manning, Wendy D.** (2015). Living with parents and emerging adults' depressive symptoms. *Journal of Family Issues*, (In Press). doi: 10.1177/0192513X15617797

**Corballis, Michael C.** (2011). *The recursive mind: The origins of human language, thought, and civilization*. Princeton, NJ: Princeton University Press.

**Corenblum, Barry.** (2014). Relationships between racial–ethnic identity, self-esteem and in-group attitudes among first nation children. *Journal of Youth and Adolescence*, 43(3), 387–404. doi: 10.1007/s10964-013-0081-8

**Costa, Albert & Sebastián-Gallés, Núria.** (2014). How does the bilingual experience sculpt the brain? *Nature Reviews Neuroscience*, 15(5), 336–345. doi: 10.1038/nrn3709

**Costa, Albert; Vives, Marc–Lluís & Corey, Joanna D.** (2017). On language processing shaping decision making. *Current Directions in Psychological Science*, 26(2), 146–151. doi: 10.1177/0963721416680263

**Côté, James E. & Levine, Charles.** (2015). *Identity formation, youth, and development: A simplified approach*. New York, NY: Psychology Press.

**Côté, Sylvana M.; Borge, Anne I.; Geoffroy, Marie-Claude; Rutter, Michael & Tremblay, Richard E.** (2008). Nonmaternal care in infancy and emotional/behavioral difficulties at 4 years old: Moderation by family risk characteristics. *Developmental Psychology*, 44(1), 155–168. doi: 10.1037/0012-1649.44.1.155

**Council on School Health.** (2013). The crucial role of recess in school: From the American Academy of Pediatrics policy statement. *Pediatrics*, 131(1), 183–188. doi: 10.1542/peds.2012-2993

**Couzin-Frankel, Jennifer.** (2013a). Return of unexpected DNA results urged. *Science*, 339(6127), 1507–1508. doi: 10.1126/science.339.6127.1507

**Couzin-Frankel, Jennifer.** (2013b). How does fetal environment influence later health? *Science*, 340(6137), 1160–1161. doi: 10.1126/science.340.6137.1160

**Couzin-Frankel, Jennifer.** (2016). A cancer legacy. *Science, 351*(6272), 440–443. doi: 10.1126/science.351.6272.440

**Couzin-Frankel, Jennifer.** (2017). Fateful imprints. *Science, 355*(6321), 122–125. doi: 10.1126/science.355.6321.122

**Cowan, Nelson.** (2014). Working memory underpins cognitive development, learning, and education. *Educational Psychology Review, 26*(2), 197–223. doi: 10.1007/s10648-013-9246-y

**Cowan, Nelson & Alloway, Tracy.** (2009). Development of working memory in childhood. In Mary L. Courage & Nelson Cowan (Eds.), *The development of memory in infancy and childhood* (2nd ed., pp. 303–342). New York, NY: Psychology Press.

**Coyne, Sarah M.** (2016). Effects of viewing relational aggression on television on aggressive behavior in adolescents: A three-year longitudinal study. *Developmental Psychology, 52*(2), 284–295. doi: 10.1037/dev0000068

**Craig, Stephanie G.; Davies, Gregory; Schibuk, Larry; Weiss, Margaret D. & Hechtman, Lily.** (2015). Long-term effects of stimulant treatment for ADHD: What can we tell our patients? *Current Developmental Disorders Reports, 2*(1), 1–9. doi: 10.1007/s40474-015-0039-5

**Crain, William C.** (2011). *Theories of development: Concepts and applications* (6th ed.). Boston, MA: Prentice–Hall.

**Creswell, John W.** (2009). *Research design: Qualitative, quantitative, and mixed methods approaches* (3rd ed.). Thousand Oaks, CA: Sage.

**Cristia, Alejandrina; Seidl, Amanda; Junge, Caroline; Soderstrom, Melanie & Hagoort, Peter.** (2014). Predicting individual variation in language from infant speech perception measures. *Child Development, 85*(4), 1330–1345. doi: 10.1111/cdev.12193

**Crnic, Keith A.; Neece, Cameron L.; McIntyre, Laura Lee; Blacher, Jan & Baker, Bruce L.** (2017). Intellectual disability and developmental risk: Promoting intervention to improve child and family well-being. *Child Development, 88*(2), 436–445. doi: 10.1111/cdev.12740

**Crone, Eveline A. & Dahl, Ronald E.** (2012). Understanding adolescence as a period of social–affective engagement and goal flexibility. *Nature Reviews Neuroscience, 13*(9), 636–650. doi: 10.1038/nrn3313

**Crone, Eveline A.; van Duijvenvoorde, Anna C. K. & Peper, Jiska S.** (2016). Annual research review: Neural contributions to risk-taking in adolescence–developmental changes and individual differences. *Journal of Child Psychology and Psychiatry, 57*(3), 353–368. doi: 10.1111/jcpp.12502

**Crosnoe, Robert; Purtell, Kelly M.; Davis-Kean, Pamela; Ansari, Arya & Benner, Aprile D.** (2016). The selection of children from low-income families into preschool. *Developmental Psychology, 52*(4), 599–612. doi: 10.1037/dev0000101

**Cross, Donna; Monks, Helen; Hall, Marg; Shaw, Thérèse; Pintabona, Yolanda; Erceg, Erin, . . . Lester, Leanne.** (2011). Three-year results of the Friendly Schools whole-of-school intervention on children's bullying behaviour. *British Educational Research Journal, 37*(1), 105–129. doi: 10.1080/01411920903420024

**Crossley, Nicolas A.; Mechelli, Andrea; Scott, Jessica; Carletti, Francesco; Fox, Peter T.; McGuire, Philip & Bullmore, Edward T.** (2014). The hubs of the human connectome are generally implicated in the anatomy of brain disorders. *Brain, 137*(8), 2382–2395. doi: 10.1093/brain/awu132

**Cubillo, Ana; Halari, Rozmin; Smith, Anna; Taylor, Eric & Rubia, Katya.** (2012). A review of fronto-striatal and fronto-cortical brain abnormalities in children and adults with Attention deficit hyperactivity disorder (ADHD) and new evidence for dysfunction in adults with ADHD during motivation and attention. *Cortex, 48*(2), 194–215. doi: 10.1016/j.cortex.2011.04.007

**Culotta, Elizabeth.** (2009). On the origin of religion. *Science, 326*(5954), 784–787. doi: 10.1126/science.326_784

**Culpin, Iryna; Heron, Jon; Araya, Ricardo & Joinson, Carol.** (2015). Early childhood father absence and depressive symptoms in adolescent girls from a UK cohort: The mediating role of early menarche. *Journal of Abnormal Child Psychology, 43*(5), 921–931. doi: 10.1007/s10802-014-9960-z

**Cummings, E. Mark & Davies, Patrick T.** (2010). *Marital conflict and children: An emotional security perspective.* New York, NY: Guilford Press.

**Cumsille, Patricio; Darling, Nancy & Martínez, M. Loreto.** (2010). Shading the truth: The patterning of adolescents' decisions to avoid issues, disclose, or lie to parents. *Journal of Adolescence, 33*(2), 285–296. doi: 10.1016/j.adolescence.2009.10.008

**Cunningham, F. Gary; Leveno, Kenneth; Bloom, Steven; Spong, Catherine Y.; Dashe, Jodi; Hoffman, Barbara, . . . Sheffield, Jeanne S.** (2014). *Williams obstetrics* (24th ed.). New York, NY: McGraw-Hill Education.

**Currie, Janet & Widom, Cathy S.** (2010). Long-term consequences of child abuse and neglect on adult economic well-being. *Child Maltreatment, 15*(2), 111–120. doi: 10.1177/1077559509355316

**Cutuli, J. J.; Desjardins, Christopher David; Herbers, Janette E.; Long, Jeffrey D.; Heistad, David; Chan, Chi-Keung, . . . Masten, Ann S.** (2013). Academic achievement trajectories of homeless and highly mobile students: Resilience in the context of chronic and acute risk. *Child Development, 84*(3), 841–857. doi: 10.1111/cdev.12013

**Daley, Dave; Jones, Karen; Hutchings, Judy & Thompson, Margaret.** (2009). Attention deficit hyperactivity disorder in pre-school children: Current findings, recommended interventions and future directions. *Child: Care, Health and Development, 35*(6), 754–766. doi: 10.1111/j.1365-2214.2009.00938.x

**Dalman, Christina; Allebeck, Peter; Gunnell, David; Harrison, Glyn; Kristensson, Krister; Lewis, Glyn, . . . Karlsson, Håkan.** (2008). Infections in the CNS during childhood and the risk of subsequent psychotic illness: A cohort study of more than one million Swedish subjects. *American Journal of Psychiatry, 165*(1), 59–65. doi: 10.1176/appi.ajp.2007.07050740

**Damasio, Antonio R.** (2012). *Self comes to mind: Constructing the conscious brain.* New York, NY: Vintage.

**Damian, Lavinia E.; Stoeber, Joachim; Negru, Oana & Băban, Adriana.** (2013). On the development of perfectionism in adolescence: Perceived parental expectations predict longitudinal increases in socially prescribed perfectionism. *Personality and Individual Differences, 55*(6), 688–693. doi: 10.1016/j.paid.2013.05.021

**Darwin, Charles.** (1859). *On the origin of species by means of natural selection.* London, UK: J. Murray.

**Darwin, Zoe; Galdas, Paul; Hinchliff, Sharron; Littlewood, Elizabeth; McMillan, Dean; McGowan, Linda & Gilbody, Simon.** (2017). Fathers' views and experiences of their own mental health during pregnancy and the first postnatal year: A qualitative interview study of men participating in the UK Born and Bred in Yorkshire (BaBY) cohort. *BMC Pregnancy and Childbirth, 17*(45). doi: 10.1186/s12884-017-1229-4

**Dasen, Pierre R. & Mishra, Ramesh C.** (2013). Cultural differences in cognitive styles. In Bhoomika Rastogi Kar (Ed.), *Cognition and brain development: Converging evidence from various methodologies* (pp. 231–249). Washington, DC: American Psychological Association. doi: 10.1037/14043-012

**Daum, Moritz M.; Ulber, Julia & Gredebäck, Gustaf.** (2013). The development of pointing perception in infancy: Effects of communicative signals on covert shifts of attention. *Developmental Psychology, 49*(10), 1898–1908. doi: 10.1037/a0031111

**Davis, Linell.** (1999). *Doing culture: Cross-cultural communication in action.* Beijing, China: Foreign Language Teaching & Research Press.

**Davis, R. Neal; Davis, Matthew M.; Freed, Gary L. & Clark, Sarah J.** (2011). Fathers' depression related to positive and negative parenting behaviors with 1-year-old children. *Pediatrics, 127*(4), 612–618. doi: 10.1542/peds.2010-1779

**Davis-Kean, Pamela E.; Jager, Justin & Collins, W. Andrew.** (2009). The self in action: An emerging link between self-beliefs and behaviors in middle childhood. *Child Development Perspectives, 3*(3), 184–188. doi: 10.1111/j.1750-8606.2009.00104.x

**Dayalu, Praveen & Albin, Roger L.** (2015). Huntington disease: Pathogenesis and treatment. *Neurologic Clinics, 33*(1), 101–114. doi: 10.1016/j.ncl.2014.09.003

**Dayanim, Shoshana & Namy, Laura L.** (2015). Infants learn baby signs from video. *Child Development, 86*(3), 800–811. doi: 10.1111/cdev.12340

**Dayton, Carolyn Joy; Walsh, Tova B.; Oh, Wonjung & Volling, Brenda.** (2015). Hush now baby: Mothers' and fathers' strategies for soothing their infants and associated parenting outcomes. *Journal of Pediatric Health Care, 29*(2), 145–155. doi: 10.1016/j.pedhc.2014.09.001

**de Boer, Anouk; Peeters, Margot & Koning, Ina.** (2016). An experimental study of risk taking behavior among adolescents: A closer look at peer and sex influences. *The Journal of Early Adolescence*, (In Press). doi: 10.1177/0272431616648453

De Corte, Erik. (2013). Giftedness considered from the perspective of research on learning and instruction. *High Ability Studies*, 24(1), 3–19. doi: 10.1080/13598139.2013.780967

de Heering, Adelaide; de Liedekerke, Claire; Deboni, Malorie & Rossion, Bruno. (2010). The role of experience during childhood in shaping the other-race effect. *Developmental Science*, 13(1), 181–187. doi: 10.1111/j.1467-7687.2009.00876.x

de Hoog, Marieke L. A.; Kleinman, Ken P.; Gillman, Matthew W.; Vrijkotte, Tanja G. M.; van Eijsden, Manon & Taveras, Elsie M. (2014). Racial/ethnic and immigrant differences in early childhood diet quality. *Public Health Nutrition*, 17(6), 1308–1317. doi: 10.1017/S1368980013001183

de Jonge, Ank; Mesman, Jeanette A. J. M.; Manniën, Judith; Zwart, Joost J.; van Dillen, Jeroen & van Roosmalen, Jos. (2013). Severe adverse maternal outcomes among low risk women with planned home versus hospital births in the Netherlands: Nationwide cohort study. *BMJ*, 346, f3263. doi: 10.1136/bmj.f3263

de la Croix, David. (2013). *Fertility, education, growth, and sustainability*. New York, NY: Cambridge University Press.

De Lee, Joseph Bolivar. (1938). *The principles and practice of obstetrics* (7th ed.). Philadelphia, PA: W. B. Saunders Co.

De Neys, Wim & Van Gelder, Elke. (2009). Logic and belief across the lifespan: The rise and fall of belief inhibition during syllogistic reasoning. *Developmental Science*, 12(1), 123–130. doi: 10.1111/j.1467-7687.2008.00746.x

de Vrieze, Jop. (2017). Big studies clash over fetal growth rates. *Science*, 355(6323), 336. doi: 10.1126/science.355.6323.336

Dean, Angela J.; Walters, Julie & Hall, Anthony. (2010). A systematic review of interventions to enhance medication adherence in children and adolescents with chronic illness. *Archives of Disease in Childhood*, 95(9), 717–723. doi: 10.1136/adc.2009.175125

Dearing, Eric; Walsh, Mary E.; Sibley, Erin; Lee St. John, Terry; Foley, Claire & Raczek, Anastacia E. (2016). Can community and school-based supports improve the achievement of first-generation immigrant children attending high-poverty schools? *Child Development*, 87(3), 883–897. doi: 10.1111/cdev.12507

Dearing, Eric; Wimer, Christopher; Simpkins, Sandra D.; Lund, Terese; Bouffard, Suzanne M.; Caronongan, Pia, . . . Weiss, Heather. (2009). Do neighborhood and home contexts help explain why low-income children miss opportunities to participate in activities outside of school? *Developmental Psychology*, 45(6), 1545–1562. doi: 10.1037/a0017359

Deater-Deckard, Kirby. (2013). The social environment and the development of psychopathology. In Philip D. Zelazo (Ed.), *The Oxford handbook of developmental psychology* (Vol. 2, pp. 527–548).

New York, NY: Oxford University Press. doi: 10.1093/oxfordhb/9780199958474.013.0021

Deater-Deckard, Kirby & Lansford, Jennifer E. (2016). Daughters' and sons' exposure to childrearing discipline and violence in low- and middle-income countries. *Monographs of the Society for Research in Child Development*, 81(1), 78–103. doi: 10.1111/mono.12227

Degnan, Kathryn A.; Hane, Amie Ashley; Henderson, Heather A.; Moas, Olga Lydia; Reeb-Sutherland, Bethany C. & Fox, Nathan A. (2011). Longitudinal stability of temperamental exuberance and social–emotional outcomes in early childhood. *Developmental Psychology*, 47(3), 765–780. doi: 10.1037/a0021316

Dehaene-Lambertz, Ghislaine. (2017). The human infant brain: A neural architecture able to learn language. *Psychonomic Bulletin & Review*, 24(1), 48–55. doi: 10.3758/s13423-016-1156-9

Delaunay-El Allam, Maryse; Soussignan, Robert; Patris, Bruno; Marlier, Luc & Schaal, Benoist. (2010). Long-lasting memory for an odor acquired at the mother's breast. *Developmental Science*, 13(6), 849–863. doi: 10.1111/j.1467-7687.2009.00941.x

DeLisi, Matt. (2014). Low self-control is a brain-based disorder. In Kevin M. Beaver et al. (Eds.), *The nurture versus biosocial debate in criminology: On the origins of criminal behavior and criminality* (pp. 172–183). Thousand Oaks, CA: Sage.

DeLoache, Judy S.; Chiong, Cynthia; Sherman, Kathleen; Islam, Nadia; Vanderborght, Mieke; Troseth, Georgene L., . . . O'Doherty, Katherine. (2010). Do babies learn from baby media? *Psychological Science*, 21(11), 1570–1574. doi: 10.1177/0956797610384145

Deming, Michelle E.; Covan, Eleanor Krassen; Swan, Suzanne C. & Billings, Deborah L. (2013). Exploring rape myths, gendered norms, group processing, and the social context of rape among college women a qualitative analysis. *Violence Against Women*, 19(4), 465–485. doi: 10.1177/1077801213487044

Denny, Dallas & Pittman, Cathy. (2007). Gender identity: From dualism to diversity. In Mitchell Tepper & Annette Fuglsang Owens (Eds.), *Sexual Health* (Vol. 1, pp. 205–229). Westport, CT: Praeger.

Depeau, Sandrine. (2016). Children in cities: The delicate issue of well-being and quality of urban life. In Ghozlane Fleury-Bahi et al. (Eds.), *Handbook of environmental psychology and quality of life research* (pp. 345–368). Switzerland: Springer International Publishing. doi: 10.1007/978-3-319-31416-7_19

Deresiewicz, William. (2014). *Excellent sheep: The miseducation of the American elite and the way to a meaningful life*. New York, NY: Free Press.

Desai, Rishi J.; Hernandez-Diaz, Sonia; Bateman, Brian T. & Huybrechts, Krista F. (2014). Increase in prescription opioid use during pregnancy among Medicaid-enrolled women. *Obstetrics & Gynecology*, 123(5), 997–1002. doi: 10.1097/AOG.0000000000000208

Devaraj, Sridevi; Hemarajata, Peera & Versalovic, James. (2013). The human gut microbiome and body metabolism: Implications for

obesity and diabetes. *Clinical Chemistry*, 59(4), 617–628. doi: 10.1373/clinchem.2012.187617

Devine, Rory T. & Hughes, Claire. (2014). Relations between false belief understanding and executive function in early childhood: A meta-analysis. *Child Development*, 85(5), 1777–1794. doi: 10.1111/cdev.12237

Devine, Rory T.; White, Naomi; Ensor, Rosie & Hughes, Claire. (2016). Theory of mind in middle childhood: Longitudinal associations with executive function and social competence. *Developmental Psychology*, 52(5), 758–771. doi: 10.1037/dev0000105

Diamond, Lisa M. & Fagundes, Christopher P. (2010). Psychobiological research on attachment. *Journal of Social and Personal Relationships*, 27(2), 218–225. doi: 10.1177/0265407509360906

Diamond, Milton & Sigmundson, H. Keith. (1997). Sex reassignment at birth: Long-term review and clinical implications. *Archives of Pediatric Adolescent Medicine*, 151(3), 298–304. doi: 10.1001/archpedi.1997.02170400084015

Diamond, Marian C. (1988). *Enriching heredity: The impact of the environment on the anatomy of the brain*. New York, NY: Free Press.

Digest of Education Statistics. (2014, November). *Table 206.10. Number and percentage of homeschooled students ages 5 through 17 with a grade equivalent of kindergarten through 12th grade, by selected child, parent, and household characteristics: 2003, 2007, and 2012*. Washington, DC: National Center for Education Statistics.

Digest of Education Statistics. (2016, February). *Table 205.10. Private elementary and secondary school enrollment and private enrollment as a percentage of total enrollment in public and private schools, by region and grade level: Selected years, fall 1995 through fall 2013*. Washington, DC: National Center for Education Statistics.

Digest of Education Statistics. (2017, February). *Table 219.80: Percentage of high school dropouts among persons 16 to 24 years old (status dropout rate) and number of status dropouts, by noninstitutionalized or institutionalized status, birth in or outside of the United States, and selected characteristics: Selected years, 2006 through 2015*. Washington, DC: National Center for Education Statistics.

Dimler, Laura M. & Natsuaki, Misaki N. (2015). The effects of pubertal timing on externalizing behaviors in adolescence and early adulthood: A meta-analytic review. *Journal of Adolescence*, 45, 160–170. doi: 10.1016/j.adolescence.2015.07.021

Dinh, Michael M.; Bein, Kendall; Roncal, Susan; Byrne, Christopher M.; Petchell, Jeffrey & Brennan, Jeffrey. (2013). Redefining the golden hour for severe head injury in an urban setting: The effect of prehospital arrival times on patient outcomes. *Injury*, 44(5), 606–610. doi: 10.1016/j.injury.2012.01.011

DiPietro, Janet A.; Costigan, Kathleen A. & Voegtline, Kristin M. (2015). Fetal motor activity. *Monographs of the Society for Research in Child Development*, 80(3), 33–42. doi: 10.1111/mono.12176

Diseth, Åge; Meland, Eivind & Breidablik, Hans J. (2014). Self-beliefs among students:

Grade level and gender differences in self-esteem, self-efficacy and implicit theories of intelligence. *Learning and Individual Differences*, 35, 1–8. doi: 10.1016/j.lindif.2014.06.003

**Dishion, Thomas J.; Poulin, François & Burraston, Bert.** (2001). Peer group dynamics associated with iatrogenic effects in group interventions with high-risk young adolescents. In Douglas W. Nangle & Cynthia A. Erdley (Eds.), *The role of friendship in psychological adjustment* (pp. 79–92). San Francisco, CA: Jossey-Bass.

**Dishion, Thomas J.; Véronneau, Marie-Hélène & Myers, Michael W.** (2010). Cascading peer dynamics underlying the progression from problem behavior to violence in early to late adolescence. *Development and Psychopathology*, 22(3), 603–619. doi: 10.1017/S0954579410000313

**Dix, Theodore & Yan, Ni.** (2014). Mothers' depressive symptoms and infant negative emotionality in the prediction of child adjustment at age 3: Testing the maternal reactivity and child vulnerability hypotheses. *Development and Psychopathology*, 26(1), 111–124. doi: 10.1017/S0954579413000898

**Dobson, Velma; Candy, T. Rowan; Hartmann, E. Eugenie; Mayer, D. Luisa; Miller, Joseph M. & Quinn, Graham E.** (2009). Infant and child vision research: Present status and future directions. *Optometry & Vision Science*, 86(6), 559–560. doi: 10.1097/OPX.0b013e3181aa06d5

**Domina, Thurston; Conley, AnneMarie & Farkas, George.** (2011a). The case for dreaming big. *Sociology of Education*, 84(2), 118–121. doi: 10.1177/0038040711401810

**Domina, Thurston; Conley, AnneMarie & Farkas, George.** (2011b). The link between educational expectations and effort in the college-for-all era. *Sociology of Education*, 84(2), 93–112. doi: 10.1177/1941406411401808

**Dominguez-Bello, Maria G.; De Jesus-Laboy, Kassandra M.; Shen, Nan; Cox, Laura M.; Amir, Amnon; Gonzalez, Antonio, . . . Clemente, Jose C.** (2016). Partial restoration of the microbiota of cesarean-born infants via vaginal microbial transfer. *Nature Medicine*, 22, 250–253. doi: 10.1038/nm.4039

**Dorais, Michel.** (2009). *Don't tell: The sexual abuse of boys* (2nd ed.). Montreal, Canada: McGill-Queen's University Press.

**Dotterer, Aryn M.; McHale, Susan M. & Crouter, Ann C.** (2009). The development and correlates of academic interests from childhood through adolescence. *Journal of Educational Psychology*, 101(2), 509–519. doi: 10.1037/a0013987

**Doucet, Andrea.** (2015). Parental responsibilities: Dilemmas of measurement and gender equality. *Journal of Marriage and Family*, 77(1), 224–242. doi: 10.1111/jomf.12148

**Downey, Liam; Crowder, Kyle & Kemp, Robert J.** (2017). Family structure, residential mobility, and environmental inequality. *Journal of Marriage and Family*, 79(2), 535–555. doi: 10.1111/jomf.12355

**Downing, Katherine L.; Hinkley, Trina; Salmon, Jo; Hnatiuk, Jill A. & Hesketh, Kylie D.** (2017). Do the correlates of screen time and sedentary time differ in preschool children? *BMC Public Health*, 17(285). doi: 10.1186/s12889-017-4195-x

**Driemeyer, Wiebke; Janssen, Erick; Wiltfang, Jens & Elmerstig, Eva.** (2016). Masturbation experiences of Swedish senior high school students: Gender differences and similarities. *The Journal of Sex Research*, (In Press). doi: 10.1080/00224499.2016.1167814

**Dubicka, Bernadka; Carlson, Gabrielle A.; Vail, Andy & Harrington, Richard.** (2008). Prepubertal mania: Diagnostic differences between US and UK clinicians. *European Child & Adolescent Psychiatry*, 17(3), 153–161. doi: 10.1007/s00787-007-0649-5

**Dubois, Jessica; Poupon, Cyril; Thirion, Bertrand; Simonnet, Hina; Kulikova, Sofya; Leroy, François, . . . Dehaene-Lambertz, Ghislaine.** (2016). Exploring the early organization and maturation of linguistic pathways in the human infant brain. *Cerebral Cortex*, 26(5), 2283–2298. doi: 10.1093/cercor/bhv082

**Duch, Helena; Fisher, Elisa M.; Ensari, Ipek; Font, Marta; Harrington, Alison; Taromino, Caroline, . . . Rodriguez, Carmen.** (2013). Association of screen time use and language development in Hispanic toddlers: A cross-sectional and longitudinal study. *Clinical Pediatrics*, 52(9), 857–865. doi: 10.1177/0009922813492881

**Duckworth, Angela L. & Kern, Margaret L.** (2011). A meta-analysis of the convergent validity of self-control measures. *Journal of Research in Personality*, 45(3), 259–268. doi: 10.1016/j.jrp.2011.02.004

**Dugas, Lara R.; Fuller, Miles; Gilbert, Jack & Layden, Brian T.** (2016). The obese gut microbiome across the epidemiologic transition. *Emerging Themes in Epidemiology*, 13(1). doi: 10.1186/s12982-015-0044-5

**Duggan, Maeve & Brenner, Joanna.** (2013). *The demographics of social media users — 2011*. Washington, DC: Pew Research Center Internet & American Life Project, Pew Research Center.

**Duh, Shinchieh; Paik, Jae H.; Miller, Patricia H.; Gluck, Stephanie C.; Li, Hui & Himelfarb, Igor.** (2016). Theory of mind and executive function in Chinese preschool children. *Developmental Psychology*, 52(4), 582–591. doi: 10.1037/a0040068

**Dukes, Richard L.; Stein, Judith A. & Zane, Jazmin I.** (2009). Effect of relational bullying on attitudes, behavior and injury among adolescent bullies, victims and bully-victims. *The Social Science Journal*, 46(4), 671–688. doi: 10.1016/j.soscij.2009.05.006

**Dumas, A.; Simmat-Durand, L. & Lejeune, C.** (2014). Pregnancy and substance use in France: A literature review. *Journal de Gynécologie Obstétrique et Biologie de la Reproduction*, 43(9), 649–656. doi: 10.1016/j.jgyn.2014.05.008

**Duncan, Greg J. & Magnuson, Katherine.** (2013). Investing in preschool programs. *Journal of Economic Perspectives*, 27(2), 109–132. doi: 10.1257/jep.27.2.109

**Dunifon, Rachel; Kopko, Kimberly; Chase-Lansdale, P. Lindsay & Wakschlag, Lauren.** (2016). Multigenerational relationships in families with custodial grandparents. In Madonna Harrington Meyer & Ynesse Abdul-Malak (Eds.), *Grandparenting in the United States* (pp. 133–160). Amityville, NY: Baywood.

**Dunmore, Simon J.** (2013). Of fat mice and men: The rise of the adipokines. *Journal of Endocrinology*, 216(1), E1–E2. doi: 10.1530/JOE-12-0513

**Dunn, Erin C.; Nishimi, Kristen; Powers, Abigail & Bradley, Bekh.** (2017). Is developmental timing of trauma exposure associated with depressive and post-traumatic stress disorder symptoms in adulthood? *Journal of Psychiatric Research*, 84, 119–127. doi: 10.1016/j.jpsychires.2016.09.004

**DuPont, Robert L. & Lieberman, Jeffrey A.** (2014). Young brains on drugs. *Science*, 344(6184), 557. doi: 10.1126/science.1254989

**Dutra, Lauren M. & Glantz, Stanton A.** (2014). Electronic cigarettes and conventional cigarette use among US adolescents: A cross-sectional study. *JAMA Pediatrics*, 168(7), 610–617. doi: 10.1001/jamapediatrics.2013.5488

**Dvornyk, Volodymyr & Waqar-ul-Haq.** (2012). Genetics of age at menarche: A systematic review. *Human Reproduction Update*, 18(2), 198–210. doi: 10.1093/humupd/dmr050

**Dweck, Carol S.** (1999). *Self-theories: Their role in motivation, personality, and development*. Philadelphia, PA: Psychology Press.

**Dweck, Carol S.** (2013). Social Development. In Philip D. Zelazo (Ed.), *The Oxford handbook of developmental psychology* (Vol. 2, pp. 167–190). New York, NY: Oxford University Press. doi: 10.1093/oxfordhb/9780199958474.013.0008

**Dyer, Nazly; Owen, Margaret T. & Caughy, Margaret O'Brien.** (2014). Ethnic differences in profiles of mother–child interactions and relations to emerging school readiness in African American and Latin American children. *Parenting*, 14(3/4), 175–194. doi: 10.1080/15295192.2014.972756

**Eagly, Alice H. & Wood, Wendy.** (2013). The nature–nurture debates: 25 years of challenges in understanding the psychology of gender. *Perspectives on Psychological Science*, 8(3), 340–357. doi: 10.1177/1745691613484767

**Earth Policy Institute.** (2011). *Two stories of disease: Smallpox and polio*. Washington, DC: Earth Policy Institute.

**Eccles, Jacquelynne S. & Roeser, Robert W.** (2010). An ecological view of schools and development. In Judith L. Meece & Jacquelynne S. Eccles (Eds.), *Handbook of research on schools, schooling, and human development* (pp. 6–22). New York, NY: Routledge.

**Eccles, Jacquelynne S. & Roeser, Robert W.** (2011). Schools as developmental contexts during adolescence. *Journal of Research on Adolescence*, 21(1), 225–241. doi: 10.1111/j.1532-7795.2010.00725.x

**Eckholm, Erik.** (2013, October 24). Case explores rights of fetus versus mother. *New York Times*, pp. A1, A16. https://nyti.ms/2jS0Nld

**Ehrenberg, Rachel.** (2016). GMOs under scrutiny. *Science News*, 189(3), 22–27.

**Ehrlich, Sara Z. & Blum-Kulka, Shoshana.** (2014). 'Now I said that Danny becomes Danny again': A multifaceted view of kindergarten children's peer argumentative discourse. In Asta Cekaite et al. (Eds.), *Children's peer talk: Learning from each other* (pp. 23–41). New York, NY: Cambridge University Press.

**Eichhorst, Werner; Rodríguez-Planas, Núria; Schmidl, Ricarda & Zimmermann, Klaus F.** (2012). *A roadmap to vocational education and training systems around the world.* Bonn, Germany: Institute for the Study of Labor.

**Eimas, Peter D.; Siqueland, Einar R.; Jusczyk, Peter & Vigorito, James.** (1971). Speech perception in infants. *Science, 171*(3968), 303–306. doi: 10.1126/science.171.3968.303

**Eisenberg, Nancy; Hofer, Claire; Sulik, Michael J. & Liew, Jeffrey.** (2013). The development of prosocial moral reasoning and a prosocial orientation in young adulthood: Concurrent and longitudinal correlates. *Developmental Psychology, 50*(1), 58–70. doi: 10.1037/a0032990

**Eisenberg, Nancy; Hofer, Claire; Sulik, Michael J. & Spinrad, Tracy L.** (2014). Self-regulation, effortful control, and their socioemotional correlates. In James J. Gross (Ed.), *Handbook of emotion regulation* (2nd ed., pp. 157–172). New York, NY: Guilford Press.

**Eisenberg, Nancy & Zhou, Qing.** (2016). Conceptions of executive function and regulation: When and to what degree do they overlap? In James A. Griffin et al. (Eds.), *Executive function in preschool-age children: Integrating measurement, neurodevelopment, and translational research* (pp. 115–136). Washington, DC: American Psychological Association. doi: 10.1037/14797-006

**Elder, Glen H.** (1998). The life course as developmental theory. *Child Development, 69*(1), 1–12. doi: 10.1111/j.1467-8624.1998.tb06128.x

**Elicker, James; Ruprecht, Karen M. & Anderson, Treshawn.** (2014). Observing infants' and toddlers' relationships and interactions in group care. In Linda J. Harrison & Jennifer Sumsion (Eds.), *Lived spaces of infant-toddler education and care: Exploring diverse perspectives on theory, research and practice* (pp. 131–145). Dordrecht, Netherlands: Springer. doi: 10.1007/978-94-017-8838-0_10

**Elkind, David.** (1967). Egocentrism in adolescence. *Child Development, 38*(4), 1025–1034.

**Elkind, David.** (2007). *The power of play: How spontaneous, imaginative activities lead to happier, healthier children.* Cambridge, MA: Da Capo Press.

**Ellefson, Michelle R.; Ng, Florrie Fei-Yin; Wang, Qian & Hughes, Claire.** (2017). Efficiency of executive function: A two-generation cross-cultural comparison of samples from Hong Kong and the United Kingdom. *Psychological Science, 28*(5), 555–566. doi: 10.1177/0956797616687812

**Ellingsaeter, Anne L.** (2014). Towards universal quality early childhood education and care: The Norwegian model. In Ludovica Gambaro et al. (Eds.), *An equal start?: Providing quality early education and care for disadvantaged children* (pp. 53–76). Chicago, IL: Policy Press.

**Elliott, Sinikka.** (2012). *Not my kid: What parents believe about the sex lives of their teenagers.* New York, NY: New York University Press.

**Ellis, Bruce J. & Boyce, W. Thomas.** (2008). Biological sensitivity to context. *Current Directions in Psychological Science, 17*(3), 183–187. doi: 10.1111/j.1467-8721.2008.00571.x

**Ellis, Bruce J.; Shirtcliff, Elizabeth A.; Boyce, W. Thomas; Deardorff, Julianna & Essex, Marilyn J.** (2011). Quality of early family relationships and the timing and tempo of puberty: Effects depend on biological sensitivity to context. *Development and Psychopathology, 23*(1), 85–99. doi: 10.1017/S0954579410000660

**Ellison, Christopher G.; Musick, Marc A. & Holden, George W.** (2011). Does conservative Protestantism moderate the association between corporal punishment and child outcomes? *Journal of Marriage and Family, 73*(5), 946–961. doi: 10.1111/j.1741-3737.2011.00854.x

**Ellwood, Philippa; Asher, M. Innes; García-Marcos, Luis; Williams, Hywel; Keil, Ulrich; Robertson, Colin & Nagel, Gabriele.** (2013). Do fast foods cause asthma, rhinoconjunctivitis and eczema? Global findings from the International Study of Asthma and Allergies in Childhood (ISAAC) Phase Three. *Thorax, 68*(4), 351–360. doi: 10.1136/thoraxjnl-2012-202285

**Engelberts, Adèle C. & de Jonge, Guustaaf Adolf.** (1990). Choice of sleeping position for infants: Possible association with cot death. *Archives of Disease in Childhood, 65*(4), 462–467. doi: 10.1136/adc.65.4.462

**Ennis, Linda Rose (Ed.).** (2014). *Intensive mothering: The cultural contradictions of modern motherhood.* Toronto: Demeter Press.

**Enserink, Martin.** (2011). Can this DNA sleuth help catch criminals? *Science, 331*(6019), 838–840. doi: 10.1126/science.331.6019.838

**Epps, Chad & Holt, Lynn.** (2011). The genetic basis of addiction and relevant cellular mechanisms. *International Anesthesiology Clinics, 49*(1), 3–14. doi: 10.1097/AIA.0b013e3181f2bb66

**Erdos, Caroline; Genesee, Fred; Savage, Robert & Haigh, Corinne.** (2014). Predicting risk for oral and written language learning difficulties in students educated in a second language. *Applied Psycholinguistics, 35*(2), 371–398. doi: 10.1017/S0142716412000422

**Erickson, Anders C.; Ostry, Aleck; Chan, Hing Man & Arbour, Laura.** (2016). Air pollution, neighbourhood and maternal-level factors modify the effect of smoking on birth weight: A multilevel analysis in British Columbia, Canada. *BMC Public Health, 16*(1). doi: 10.1186/s12889-016-3273-9

**Erikson, Erik H.** (1968). *Identity: Youth and crisis.* New York, NY: Norton.

**Erikson, Erik H.** (1982). *The life cycle completed: A review.* New York, NY: Norton.

**Erikson, Erik H.** (1993a). *Childhood and society* (2nd ed.). New York, NY: Norton.

**Erikson, Erik H.** (1993b). *Gandhi's truth: On the origins of militant nonviolence.* New York, NY: Norton.

**Erikson, Erik H.** (1994). *Identity: Youth and crisis.* New York, NY: Norton.

**Erikson, Erik H.** (1998). *The life cycle completed.* New York, NY: Norton.

**Ernst, Monique.** (2016). A tribute to the adolescent brain. *Neuroscience & Biobehavioral Reviews, 70*, 334–338. doi: 10.1016/j.neubiorev.2016.06.017

**Errichiello, Luca; Iodice, Davide; Bruzzese, Dario; Gherghi, Marco & Senatore, Ignazio.** (2016). Prognostic factors and outcome in anorexia nervosa: A follow-up study. *Eating and Weight Disorders, 21*(1), 73–82. doi: 10.1007/s40519-015-0211-2

**Erskine, Holly E.; Ferrari, Alize J.; Nelson, Paul; Polanczyk, Guilherme V.; Flaxman, Abraham D.; Vos, Theo, . . . Scott, James G.** (2013). Research Review: Epidemiological modelling of Attention-deficit/hyperactivity disorder and conduct disorder for the Global Burden of Disease Study 2010. *Journal of Child Psychology and Psychiatry, 54*(12), 1263–1274. doi: 10.1111/jcpp.12144

**Espy, Kimberly Andrews.** (2016). *Monographs of the society for research in child development: The changing nature of executive control in preschool, 81*(4), 1–179. doi: 10.1111/mono.12267

**Esser, Marissa B.; Clayton, Heather; Demissie, Zewditu; Kanny, Dafna & Brewer, Robert D.** (2017, May 12). *Current and binge drinking among high school students — United States, 1991–2015. Morbidity and Mortality Weekly Report 66*(18), 474–478. Atlanta, GA: Centers for Disease Control and Prevention.

**Estroff, Todd Wilk & Gold, Mark S.** (1986). Psychiatric presentations of marijuana abuse. *Psychiatric Annals, 16*(4), 221–224. doi: 10.3928/0048-5713-19860401-08

**Evans, Angela D.; Xu, Fen & Lee, Kang.** (2011). When all signs point to you: Lies told in the face of evidence. *Developmental Psychology, 47*(1), 39–49. doi: 10.1037/a0020787

**Evans, Gary W. & Kim, Pilyoung.** (2013). Childhood poverty, chronic stress, self-regulation, and coping. *Child Development Perspectives, 7*(1), 43–48. doi: 10.1111/cdep.12013

**Evans, M. D. R.; Kelley, Jonathan; Sikora, Joanna & Treiman, Donald J.** (2010). Family scholarly culture and educational success: Books and schooling in 27 nations. *Research in Social Stratification and Mobility, 28*(2), 171–197. doi: 10.1016/j.rssm.2010.01.002

**Evans-Lacko, Sara; Takizawa, Ryu; Brimblecombe, Nicola; King, Derek; Knapp, Martin; Maughan, Barbara & Arseneault, Louise.** (2017). Childhood bullying victimization is associated with use of mental health services over five decades: A longitudinal nationally representative cohort study. *Psychological Medicine, 47*(1), 127–135. doi: 10.1017/S0033291716001719

**Everett, Caleb.** (2017). *Numbers and the making of us: Counting and the course of human cultures.* Cambridge, MA: Harvard University Press.

**Eyer, Diane E.** (1992). *Mother-infant bonding: A scientific fiction.* New Haven, CT: Yale University Press.

**Fadjukoff, Päivi & Kroger, Jane.** (2016). Identity development in adulthood: Introduction. *Identity, 16*(1), 1–7. doi: 10.1080/15283488.2015.1121821

**Fairhurst, Merle T.; Löken, Line & Grossmann, Tobias.** (2014). Physiological and behavioral responses reveal 9-month-old infants' sensitivity to pleasant touch. *Psychological Science, 25*(5), 1124–1131. doi: 10.1177/0956797614527114

**Fareed, Mohd; Anwar, Malik Azeem & Afzal, Mohammad.** (2015). Prevalence and gene frequency of color vision impairments among children of six populations from North Indian region. *Genes & Diseases, 2*(2), 211–218. doi: 10.1016/j.gendis.2015.02.006

**Fazzi, Elisa; Signorini, Sabrina G.; Bomba, Monica; Luparia, Antonella; Lanners, Josée & Balottin, Umberto.** (2011). Reach on sound: A key to object permanence in visually impaired children. *Early Human Development, 87*(4), 289–296. doi: 10.1016/j.earlhumdev.2011.01.032

**FBI.** (2015). *Crime in the United States, 2014.* Clarksburg, WV: U.S. Department of Justice, Federal Bureau of Investigation, Criminal Justice Information Services Division.

**Feeley, Nancy; Sherrard, Kathyrn; Waitzer, Elana & Boisvert, Linda.** (2013). The father at the bedside: Patterns of involvement in the NICU. *Journal of Perinatal & Neonatal Nursing, 27*(1), 72–80. doi: 10.1097/JPN.0b013e31827fb415

**Feld, Barry C.** (2013). *Kids, cops, and confessions: Inside the interrogation room.* New York, NY: New York University Press.

**Feldman, Ruth.** (2007). Parent-infant synchrony and the construction of shared timing; physiological precursors, developmental outcomes, and risk conditions. *Journal of Child Psychology and Psychiatry, 48*(3/4), 329–354. doi: 10.1111/j.1469-7610.2006.01701.x

**Ferguson, Christopher J.** (2013). Spanking, corporal punishment and negative long-term outcomes: A meta-analytic review of longitudinal studies. *Clinical Psychology Review, 33*(1), 196–208. doi: 10.1016/j.cpr.2012.11.002

**Fernandes, Eulalia.** (2016). Resilience and emotional intelligence among adolescents as a function of perceived parenting style. *International Educational Scientific Research Journal, 2*(7), 29–31.

**Ferrari, Marco & Quaresima, Valentina.** (2012). A brief review on the history of human functional near-infrared spectroscopy (fNIRS) development and fields of application. *NeuroImage, 63*(2), 921–935. doi: 10.1016/j.neuroimage.2012.03.049

**Fewtrell, Mary; Wilson, David C.; Booth, Ian & Lucas, Alan.** (2011). Six months of exclusive breast feeding: How good is the evidence? *BMJ, 342,* c5955. doi: 10.1136/bmj.c5955

**Fields, R. Douglas.** (2014). Myelin—More than insulation. *Science, 344*(6181), 264–266. doi: 10.1126/science.1253851

**Filová, Barbora; Ostatníková, Daniela; Celec, Peter & Hodosy, Július.** (2013). The effect of testosterone on the formation of brain structures. *Cells Tissues Organs, 197*(3), 169–177. doi: 10.1159/000345567

**Fine, J. S.; Calello, D. P.; Marcus, S. M. & Lowry, J. A.** (2012). 2011 Pediatric fatality review of the National Poison Center Database. *Clinical Toxicology, 50*(10), 872–874. doi: 10.3109/15563650.2012.752494

**Finer, Lawrence B. & Zolna, Mia R.** (2016). Declines in unintended pregnancy in the United States, 2008–2011. *New England Journal of Medicine, 374,* 843–852. doi: 10.1056/NEJMsa1506575

**Fingerman, Karen L.; Berg, Cynthia; Smith, Jacqui & Antonucci, Toni C.** (2011). *Handbook of lifespan development.* New York, NY: Springer.

**Fingerman, Karen L. & Furstenberg, Frank F.** (2012, May 30). You can go home again. *New York Times,* p. A29. https://nyti.ms/2vDsBih

**Finkelhor, David.** (2008). *Childhood victimization: Violence, crime, and abuse in the lives of young people.* New York, NY: Oxford University Press.

**Finkelhor, David & Jones, Lisa.** (2012). *Have sexual abuse and physical abuse declined since the 1990s?* Durham, NH: Crimes Against Children Research Center, University of New Hampshire.

**Finn, Amy S.; Kraft, Matthew A.; West, Martin R.; Leonard, Julia A.; Bish, Crystal E.; Martin, Rebecca E., . . . Gabrieli, John D. E.** (2014). Cognitive skills, student achievement tests, and schools. *Psychological Science, 25*(3), 736–744. doi: 10.1177/0956797613516008

**Fischer, Karin.** (2016, May 1). When everyone goes to college: A lesson from South Korea. *The Chronicle of Higher Education.*

**Fiset, Sylvain & Plourde, Vickie.** (2013). Object permanence in domestic dogs (Canis lupus familiaris) and gray wolves (Canis lupus). *Journal of Comparative Psychology, 127*(2), 115–127. doi: 10.1037/a0030595

**Fitzgerald, Maria.** (2015). What do we really know about newborn infant pain? *Experimental Physiology, 100*(12), 1451–1457. doi: 10.1113/EP085134

**Fletcher, Erica N.; Whitaker, Robert C.; Marino, Alexis J. & Anderson, Sarah E.** (2014). Screen time at home and school among low-income children attending Head Start. *Child Indicators Research, 7*(2), 421–436. doi: 10.1007/s12187-013-9212-8

**Fletcher, Richard; St. George, Jennifer & Freeman, Emily.** (2013). Rough and tumble play quality: Theoretical foundations for a new measure of father–child interaction. *Early Child Development and Care, 183*(6), 746–759. doi: 10.1080/03004430.2012.723439

**Floud, Roderick; Fogel, Robert W.; Harris, Bernard & Hong, Sok Chul.** (2011). *The changing body: Health, nutrition, and human development in the Western world since 1700.* New York, NY: Cambridge University Press.

**Flouri, Eirini & Sarmadi, Zahra.** (2016). Prosocial behavior and childhood trajectories of internalizing and externalizing problems: The role of neighborhood and school contexts. *Developmental Psychology, 52*(2), 253–258. doi: 10.1037/dev0000076

**Flynn, James R.** (1999). Searching for justice: The discovery of IQ gains over time. *American Psychologist, 54*(1), 5–20. doi: 10.1037/0003-066X.54.1.5

**Flynn, James R.** (2012). *Are we getting smarter?: Rising IQ in the twenty-first century.* New York, NY: Cambridge University Press.

**Fogel, Robert W. & Grotte, Nathaniel.** (2011). *An overview of the changing body: Health, nutrition, and human development in the Western world since 1700. NBER working paper series.* Cambridge, MA: National Bureau of Economic Research.

**Forbes, Deborah.** (2012). The global influence of the Reggio Emilia Inspiration. In Robert Kelly (Ed.), *Educating for creativity: A global conversation* (pp. 161–172). Calgary, Canada: Brush Education.

**Forget-Dubois, Nadine; Dionne, Ginette; Lemelin, Jean-Pascal; Pérusse, Daniel; Tremblay, Richard E. & Boivin, Michel.** (2009). Early child language mediates the relation between home environment and school readiness. *Child Development, 80*(3), 736–749. doi: 10.1111/j.1467-8624.2009.01294.x

**Foster, Eugene A.; Jobling, Mark A.; Taylor, P. G.; Donnelly, Peter; de Knijff, Peter; Mieremet, Rene, . . . Tyler-Smith, C.** (1998). Jefferson fathered slave's last child. *Nature, 396*(6706), 27–28. doi: 10.1038/23835

**Fox, Nathan A.; Henderson, Heather A.; Marshall, Peter J.; Nichols, Kate E. & Ghera, Melissa M.** (2005). Behavioral inhibition: Linking biology and behavior within a developmental framework. *Annual Review of Psychology, 56,* 235–262. doi: 10.1146/annurev.psych.55.090902.141532

**Fox, Nathan A.; Henderson, Heather A.; Rubin, Kenneth H.; Calkins, Susan D. & Schmidt, Louis A.** (2001). Continuity and discontinuity of behavioral inhibition and exuberance: Psychophysiological and behavioral influences across the first four years of life. *Child Development, 72*(1), 1–21. doi: 10.1111/1467-8624.00262

**Fox, Nathan A.; Reeb-Sutherland, Bethany C. & Degnan, Kathryn A.** (2013). Personality and emotional development. In Philip D. Zelazo (Ed.), *The Oxford handbook of developmental psychology* (Vol. 2, pp. 15–44). New York, NY: Oxford University Press. doi: 10.1093/oxfordhb/9780199958474.013.0002

**Franck, Caroline; Budlovsky, Talia; Windle, Sarah B.; Filion, Kristian B. & Eisenberg, Mark J.** (2014). Electronic cigarettes in North America: History, use, and implications for smoking cessation. *Circulation, 129*(19), 1945–1952. doi: 10.1161/CIRCULATIONAHA.113.006416

**Frankenburg, William K.; Dodds, Josiah; Archer, Philip; Shapiro, Howard & Bresnick, Beverly.** (1992). The Denver II: A major revision and restandardization of the Denver Developmental Screening Test. *Pediatrics, 89*(1), 91–97.

**Franklin, Sarah.** (2013). *Biological relatives: IVF, stem cells, and the future of kinship.* Durham, NC: Duke University Press.

**Frayer, David W.** (2017). Talking hyoids and talking Neanderthals. In Assaf Marom & Erella Hovers (Eds.), *Human Paleontology and Prehistory: Contributions in Honor of Yoel Rak* (pp. 233–237). Switzerland: Springer. doi: 10.1007/978-3-319-46646-0_17

**Frazier, A. Lindsay; Camargo, Carlos A.; Malspeis, Susan; Willett, Walter C. & Young, Michael C.** (2014). Prospective study of peripregnancy consumption of peanuts or tree nuts by mothers and the risk of peanut or tree nut allergy in their offspring. *JAMA Pediatrics, 168*(2), 156–162. doi: 10.1001/jamapediatrics.2013.4139

**Fredricks, Jennifer A. & Eccles, Jacquelynne S.** (2002). Children's competence and value beliefs from childhood through adolescence: Growth trajectories in two male-sex-typed domains. *Developmental Psychology, 38*(4), 519–533. doi: 10.1037/0012-1649.38.4.519

**Freeman, Joan.** (2010). *Gifted lives: What happens when gifted children grow up?* New York, NY: Routledge.

**Freud, Anna.** (1958). Adolescence. *Psychoanalytic Study of the Child, 13,* 255–278.

**Freud, Anna.** (2000). Adolescence. In James B. McCarthy (Ed.), *Adolescent development and psychopathology* (pp. 29–52). Lanham, MD: University Press of America.

**Freud, Sigmund.** (1935). *A general introduction to psychoanalysis.* New York, NY: Liveright.

**Freud, Sigmund.** (1938). *The basic writings of Sigmund Freud.* New York, NY: Modern Library.

**Freud, Sigmund.** (1989). *Introductory lectures on psycho-analysis.* New York, NY: Liveright.

**Freud, Sigmund.** (1995). *The basic writings of Sigmund Freud.* New York, NY: Modern Library.

**Freud, Sigmund.** (2001). An outline of psychoanalysis. *The standard edition of the complete psychological works of Sigmund Freud* (Vol. 23). London, UK: Vintage.

**Friedman, Naomi P. & Miyake, Akira.** (2017). Unity and diversity of executive functions: Individual differences as a window on cognitive structure. *Cortex, 86,* 186–204. doi: 10.1016/j.cortex.2016.04.023

**Friend, Stephen H. & Schadt, Eric E.** (2014). Clues from the resilient. *Science, 344*(6187), 970–972. doi: 10.1126/science.1255648

**Froiland, John M. & Davison, Mark L.** (2014). Parental expectations and school relationships as contributors to adolescents' positive outcomes. *Social Psychology of Education, 17*(1), 1–17. doi: 10.1007/s11218-013-9237-3

**Fry, Douglas P.** (2014). Environment of evolutionary adaptedness, rough-and-tumble play, and the selection of restraint in human aggression. In Darcia Narvaez et al. (Eds.), *Ancestral landscapes in human evolution: Culture, childrearing and social wellbeing* (pp. 169–188). New York, NY: Oxford University Press.

**Fuligni, Allison Sidle; Howes, Carollee; Huang, Yiching; Hong, Sandra Soliday & Lara-Cinisomo, Sandraluz.** (2012). Activity settings and daily routines in preschool classrooms: Diverse experiences in early learning settings for low-income children. *Early Childhood Research Quarterly, 27*(2), 198–209. doi: 10.1016/j.ecresq.2011.10.001

**Fuller, Bruce & García Coll, Cynthia.** (2010). Learning from Latinos: Contexts, families, and child development in motion. *Developmental Psychology, 46*(3), 559–565. doi: 10.1037/a0019412

**Furey, Terrence S. & Sethupathy, Praveen.** (2013). Genetics driving epigenetics. *Science, 342*(6159), 705–706. doi: 10.1126/science.1246755

**Furukawa, Emi; Tangney, June & Higashibara, Fumiko.** (2012). Cross-cultural continuities and discontinuities in shame, guilt, and pride: A study of children residing in Japan, Korea and the USA. *Self and Identity, 11*(1), 90–113. doi: 10.1080/15298868.2010.512748

**Fury, Gail; Carlson, Elizabeth A. & Sroufe, Alan.** (1997). Children's representations of attachment relationships in family drawings. *Child Development, 68*(6), 1154–1164. doi: 10.1111/j.1467-8624.1997.tb01991.x

**Fusaro, Maria & Harris, Paul L.** (2013). Dax gets the nod: Toddlers detect and use social cues to evaluate testimony. *Developmental Psychology, 49*(3), 514–522. doi: 10.1037/a0030580

**Gabrieli, John D. E.** (2009). Dyslexia: A new synergy between education and cognitive neuroscience. *Science, 325*(5938), 280–283. doi: 10.1126/science.1171999

**Galak, Jeff; Givi, Julian & Williams, Elanor F.** (2016). Why certain gifts are great to give but not to get: A framework for understanding errors in gift giving. *Current Directions in Psychological Science, 25*(6), 380–385. doi: 10.1177/0963721416656937

**Galván, Adriana.** (2013). The teenage brain: Sensitivity to rewards. *Current Directions in Psychological Science, 22*(2), 88–93. doi: 10.1177/0963721413480859

**Galvao, Tais F.; Silva, Marcus T.; Zimmermann, Ivan R.; Souza, Kathiaja M.; Martins, Silvia S. & Pereira, Mauricio G.** (2014). Pubertal timing in girls and depression: A systematic review. *Journal of Affective Disorders, 155,* 13–19. doi: 10.1016/j.jad.2013.10.034

**Gambaro, Ludovica; Stewart, Kitty & Waldfogel, Jane (Eds.).** (2014). *An equal start?: Providing quality early education and care for disadvantaged children.* Chicago, IL: Policy Press.

**Ganapathy, Thilagavathy.** (2014). Couvade syndrome among 1st time expectant fathers. *Muller Journal of Medical Science Research, 5*(1), 43–47. doi: 10.4103/0975-9727.128944

**Ganchimeg, Togoobaatar; Ota, Erika; Morisaki, Naho; Laopaiboon, Malinee; Lumbiganon, P.; Zhang, Jun, . . . Mori, Rintaro.** (2014). Pregnancy and childbirth outcomes among adolescent mothers: A World Health Organization multicountry study. *BJOG, 121*(Suppl. 1), 40–48. doi: 10.1111/1471-0528.12630

**Ganong, Lawrence H.; Coleman, Marilyn & Jamison, Tyler.** (2011). Patterns of stepchild–stepparent relationship development. *Journal of Marriage and Family, 73*(2), 396–413. doi: 10.1111/j.1741-3737.2010.00814.x

**Gao, Wei; Lin, Weili; Grewen, Karen & Gilmore, John H.** (2016). Functional connectivity of the infant human brain: Plastic and modifiable. *The Neuroscientist,* (In Press). doi: 10.1177/1073858416635986

**García Coll, Cynthia T. & Marks, Amy K.** (2012). *The immigrant paradox in children and adolescents: Is becoming American a developmental risk?* Washington, DC: American Psychological Association.

**Gardner, Howard.** (1983). *Frames of mind: The theory of multiple intelligences.* New York, NY: Basic Books.

**Gardner, Howard.** (1999). Are there additional intelligences? The case for naturalist, spiritual, and existential intelligences. In Jeffrey Kane (Ed.), *Education, information, and transformation: Essays on learning and thinking* (pp. 111–131). Upper Saddle River, NJ: Merrill.

**Gardner, Howard.** (2004). *The unschooled mind: How children think and how schools should teach.* New York, NY: Basic Books.

**Gardner, Howard.** (2006). *Multiple intelligences: New horizons in theory and practice.* New York, NY: Basic Books.

**Gardner, Howard & Moran, Seana.** (2006). The science of multiple intelligences theory: A response to Lynn Waterhouse. *Educational Psychologist, 41*(4), 227–232. doi: 10.1207/s15326985ep4104_2

**Gardner, Phil & Chao, Georgia.** (2017). Healthy transitions to work. In Laura M. Padilla-Walker & Larry J. Nelson (Eds.), *Flourishing in emerging adulthood: Positive development during the third decade of life* (pp. 104–128). New York, NY: Oxford University Press.

**Gardner, Paula & Hudson, Bettie L.** (1996). *Advance report of final mortality statistics, 1993. Monthly Vital Statistics Report, 44*(7, Suppl.). Hyattsville, MD: National Center for Health Statistics.

**Garthus-Niegel, Susan; Ayers, Susan; Martini, Julia; von Soest, Tilmann & Eberhard-Gran, Malin.** (2017). The impact of postpartum post-traumatic stress disorder symptoms on child development: A population-based, 2-year follow-up study. *Psychological Medicine, 47*(1), 161–170. doi: 10.1017/S003329171600235X

**Gash, Don M. & Deane, Andrew S.** (2015). Neuron-based heredity and human evolution. *Frontiers in Neuroscience, 9,* 209. doi: 10.3389/fnins.2015.00209

**Gavin, Lorrie; MacKay, Andrea P.; Brown, Kathryn; Harrier, Sara; Ventura, Stephanie J.; Kann, Laura, . . . Ryan, George.** (2009, July 17). *Sexual and reproductive health of persons aged 10–24 Years — United States, 2002–2007. Morbidity and Mortality Weekly Report 58*(SS06). Atlanta, GA: Centers for Disease Control and Prevention.

**Ge, Xinting; Shi, Yonggang; Li, Junning; Zhang, Zhonghe; Lin, Xiangtao; Zhan, Jinfeng, . . . Liu, Shuwei.** (2015). Development of the human fetal hippocampal formation during early second trimester. *NeuroImage, 119,* 33–43. doi: 10.1016/j.neuroimage.2015.06.055

**Geiger, Abigail.** (2016, October 12). *Support for marijuana legalization continues to rise. Fact Tank.* Washington, DC: Pew Research Center.

**Gendron, Brian P.; Williams, Kirk R. & Guerra, Nancy G.** (2011). An analysis of bullying among students within schools: Estimating the effects of individual normative beliefs, self-esteem, and school climate. *Journal of School Violence, 10*(2), 150–164. doi: 10.1080/15388220.2010.539166

**Gentile, Douglas A.** (2011). The multiple dimensions of video game effects. *Child Development Perspectives, 5*(2), 75–81. doi: 10.1111/j.1750-8606.2011.00159.x

**Geoffroy, Marie-Claude; Boivin, Michel; Arseneault, Louise; Turecki, Gustavo; Vitaro, Frank; Brendgen, Mara, . . . Côté, Sylvana M.** (2016). Associations between peer victimization and suicidal ideation and suicide attempt during adolescence: Results from a prospective population-based birth cohort. *Journal of the American Academy of Child and Adolescent Psychiatry*, 55(2), 99–105. doi: 10.1016/j.jaac.2015.11.010

**Georgeson, Jan & Payler, Jane (Eds.).** (2013). *International perspectives on early childhood education and care*. New York, NY: Open University Press.

**Gernhardt, Ariane; Keller, Heidi & Rübeling, Hartmut.** (2016). Children's family drawings as expressions of attachment representations across cultures: Possibilities and limitations. *Child Development*, 87(4), 1069–1078. doi: 10.1111/cdev.12516

**Gershoff, Elizabeth T.** (2013). Spanking and child development: We know enough now to stop hitting our children. *Child Development Perspectives*, 7(3), 133–137. doi: 10.1111/cdep.12038

**Gershoff, Elizabeth T.; Lansford, Jennifer E.; Sexton, Holly R.; Davis-Kean, Pamela & Sameroff, Arnold J.** (2012). Longitudinal links between spanking and children's externalizing behaviors in a national sample of White, Black, Hispanic, and Asian American families. *Child Development*, 83(3), 838–843. doi: 10.1111/j.1467-8624.2011.01732.x

**Gershoff, Elizabeth T.; Purtell, Kelly M. & Holas, Igor.** (2015). *Corporal punishment in U.S. public schools: Legal precedents, current practices, and future policy*. New York, NY: Springer. doi: 10.1007/978-3-319-14818-2

**Gerstenberg, Tobias & Tenenbaum, Joshua B.** (2017). Intuitive theories. In Michael R. Waldmann (Ed.), *The Oxford handbook of causal reasoning* (pp. 515–548). New York, NY: Oxford University Press. doi: 10.1093/oxfordhb/9780199399550.013.28

**Gervais, Will M. & Norenzayan, Ara.** (2012). Analytic thinking promotes religious disbelief. *Science*, 336(6080), 493–496. doi: 10.1126/science.1215647

**Gewertz, Catherine.** (2014, August 19). Support slipping for Common Core, especially among teachers, poll finds [Web log post]. *Education week: Curriculum matters*. Retrieved from http://blogs.edweek.org/edweek/curriculum/2014/08/education_next_poll_shows_comm.html

**Gewertz, Catherine.** (2017, May 3). Is the high school graduation rate inflated? No, study says [Web log post]. *Education Week*. Retrieved from http://blogs.edweek.org/edweek/high_school_and_beyond/2017/05/is_the_high_school_graduation_rate_inflated.html

**Gibbons, Ann.** (2012). An evolutionary theory of dentistry. *Science*, 336(6084), 973–975. doi: 10.1126/science.336.6084.973

**Gibson, Eleanor J.** (1969). *Principles of perceptual learning and development*. New York, NY: Appleton-Century-Crofts.

**Gibson, Eleanor J.** (1988). Exploratory behavior in the development of perceiving, acting, and the acquiring of knowledge. *Annual Review of Psychology*, 39, 1–42. doi: 10.1146/annurev.ps.39.020188.000245

**Gibson, Eleanor J.** (1997). An ecological psychologist's prolegomena for perceptual development: A functional approach. In Cathy Dent-Read & Patricia Zukow-Goldring (Eds.), *Evolving explanations of development: Ecological approaches to organism-environment systems* (1st ed., pp. 23–54). Washington, DC: American Psychological Association.

**Gibson, Eleanor J. & Walk, Richard D.** (1960). The "visual cliff". *Scientific American*, 202(4), 64–71. doi: 10.1038/scientificamerican0460-64

**Gibson, James J.** (1979). *The ecological approach to visual perception*. Boston, MA: Houghton Mifflin.

**Gibson-Davis, Christina & Rackin, Heather.** (2014). Marriage or carriage? Trends in union context and birth type by education. *Journal of Marriage and Family*, 76(3), 506–519. doi: 10.1111/jomf.12109

**Giles, Amy & Rovee-Collier, Carolyn.** (2011). Infant long-term memory for associations formed during mere exposure. *Infant Behavior and Development*, 34(2), 327–338. doi: 10.1016/j.infbeh.2011.02.004

**Gilles, Floyd H. & Nelson, Marvin D.** (2012). *The developing human brain: Growth and adversities*. London, UK: Mac Keith Press.

**Gillespie, Michael A.** (2010). Players and spectators: Sports and ethical training in the American university. In Elizabeth Kiss & J. Peter Euben (Eds.), *Debating moral education: Rethinking the role of the modern university* (pp. 293–316). Durham, NC: Duke University Press.

**Gilligan, Carol.** (1982). *In a different voice: Psychological theory and women's development*. Cambridge, MA: Harvard University Press.

**Gillon, Raanan.** (2015). Defending the four principles approach as a good basis for good medical practice and therefore for good medical ethics. *Journal of Medical Ethics*, 41(1), 111–116. doi: 10.1136/medethics-2014-102282

**Giuffrè, Mario; Piro, Ettore & Corsello, Giovanni.** (2012). Prematurity and twinning. *Journal of Maternal-Fetal and Neonatal Medicine*, 25(3), 6–10. doi: 10.3109/14767058.2012.712350

**Giumetti, Gary W. & Kowalski, Robin M.** (2015). Cyberbullying matters: Examining the incremental impact of cyberbullying on outcomes over and above traditional bullying in North America. In Raúl Navarro et al. (Eds.), *Cyberbullying across the globe: Gender, family, and mental health* (pp. 117–130). New York, NY: Springer. doi: 10.1007/978-3-319-25552-1_6

**Glenberg, Arthur M.; Witt, Jessica K. & Metcalfe, Janet.** (2013). From the revolution to embodiment: 25 years of cognitive psychology. *Perspectives on Psychological Science*, 8(5), 573–585. doi: 10.1177/1745691613498098

**Goddings, Anne-Lise & Giedd, Jay N.** (2014). Structural brain development during childhood and adolescence. In Michael S. Gazzaniga & George R. Mangun (Eds.), *The cognitive neurosciences* (5th ed., pp. 15–22). Cambridge, MA: MIT Press.

**Goddings, Anne-Lise; Heyes, Stephanie Burnett; Bird, Geoffrey; Viner, Russell M. & Blakemore, Sarah-Jayne.** (2012). The relationship between puberty and social emotion processing. *Developmental Science*, 15(6), 801–811. doi: 10.1111/j.1467-7687.2012.01174.x

**Godinet, Meripa T.; Li, Fenfang & Berg, Teresa.** (2014). Early childhood maltreatment and trajectories of behavioral problems: Exploring gender and racial differences. *Child Abuse & Neglect*, 38(3), 544–556. doi: 10.1016/j.chiabu.2013.07.018

**Golden, Neville H.; Yang, Wei; Jacobson, Marc S.; Robinson, Thomas N. & Shaw, Gary M.** (2012). Expected body weight in adolescents: Comparison between weight-for-stature and BMI methods. *Pediatrics*, 130(6), e1607–e1613. doi: 10.1542/peds.2012-0897

**Goldin-Meadow, Susan.** (2015). From action to abstraction: Gesture as a mechanism of change. *Developmental Review*, 38, 167–184. doi: 10.1016/j.dr.2015.07.007

**Goldin-Meadow, Susan & Alibali, Martha W.** (2013). Gesture's role in speaking, learning, and creating language. *Annual Review of Psychology*, 64, 257–283. doi: 10.1146/annurev-psych-113011-143802

**Goldschmidt, Andrea B.; Wall, Melanie M.; Zhang, Jun; Loth, Katie A. & Neumark-Sztainer, Dianne.** (2016). Overeating and binge eating in emerging adulthood: 10-year stability and risk factors. *Developmental Psychology*, 52(3), 475–483. doi: 10.1037/dev0000086

**Goldstein, Joshua R.** (2011). A secular trend toward earlier male sexual maturity: Evidence from shifting ages of male young adult mortality. *PLoS ONE*, 6(8), e14826. doi: 10.1371/journal.pone.0014826

**Goldstein, Michael H.; Schwade, Jennifer A. & Bornstein, Marc H.** (2009). The value of vocalizing: Five-month-old infants associate their own noncry vocalizations with responses from caregivers. *Child Development*, 80(3), 636–644. doi: 10.1111/j.1467-8624.2009.01287.x

**Golinkoff, Roberta M. & Hirsh-Pasek, Kathy.** (2016). *Becoming brilliant: What science tells us about raising successful children*. Washington, DC: American Psychological Association.

**Golombok, Susan.** (2015). *Modern families: Parents and children in new family forms*. New York, NY: Cambridge University Press. doi: 10.1017/CBO9781107295377

**Göncü, Artin & Gaskins, Suzanne.** (2011). Comparing and extending Piaget's and Vygotsky's understandings of play: Symbolic play as individual, sociocultural, and educational interpretation. In Anthony D. Pellegrini (Ed.), *The Oxford handbook of the development of play* (pp. 48–57). New York, NY: Oxford University Press. doi: 10.1093/oxfordhb/9780195393002.013.0005

**Goniewicz, Maciej L.; Gawron, Michal; Smith, Danielle M.; Peng, Margaret; Jacob, Peyton & Benowitz, Neal L.** (2017). Exposure to nicotine and selected toxicants in cigarette smokers who switched to electronic cigarettes: A longitudinal within-subjects observational study. *Nicotine & Tobacco Research*, 19(2), 160–167. doi: 10.1093/ntr/ntw160

**González, Roberto; Lickel, Brian; Gupta, Manisha; Tropp. Linda R.; Luengo Kanacri, Bernadette P.; Mora, Eduardo, . . . Bernardino, Michelle.** (2017). Ethnic identity development and acculturation preferences among minority and majority youth: Norms and contact. *Child Development*, 88(3), 743–760. doi: 10.1111/cdev.12788

**Gonzalez-Gomez, Nayeli; Hayashi, Akiko; Tsuji, Sho; Mazuka, Reiko & Nazzi, Thierry.** (2014). The role of the input on the development of the LC bias: A crosslinguistic comparison. *Cognition*, 132(3), 301–311. doi: 10.1016/j.cognition.2014.04.004

**Goodlad, James K.; Marcus, David K. & Fulton, Jessica J.** (2013). Lead and Attention-deficit/hyperactivity disorder (ADHD) symptoms: A meta-analysis. *Clinical Psychology Review*, 33(3), 417–425. doi: 10.1016/j.cpr.2013.01.009

**Gopnik, Alison.** (2012). Scientific thinking in young children: Theoretical advances, empirical research, and policy implications. *Science*, 337(6102), 1623–1627. doi: 10.1126/science.1223416

**Gordon-Hollingsworth, Arlene T.; Becker, Emily M.; Ginsburg, Golda S.; Keeton, Courtney; Compton, Scott N.; Birmaher, Boris B., . . . March, John S.** (2015). Anxiety disorders in Caucasian and African American children: A comparison of clinical characteristics, treatment process variables, and treatment outcomes. *Child Psychiatry & Human Development*, 46(5), 643–655. doi: 10.1007/s10578-014-0507-x

**Gostin, Lawrence O.** (2016). 4 Simple reforms to address mass shootings and other firearm violence. *JAMA*, 315(5), 453–454. doi: 10.1001/jama.2015.19497

**Gottesman, Irving I.; Laursen, Thomas Munk; Bertelsen, Aksel & Mortensen, Preben Bo.** (2010). Severe mental disorders in offspring with 2 psychiatrically ill parents. *Archives of General Psychiatry*, 67(3), 252–257. doi: 10.1001/archgenpsychiatry.2010.1

**Gough, Ethan K.; Moodie, Erica E. M.; Prendergast, Andrew J.; Johnson, Sarasa M. A.; Humphrey, Jean H.; Stoltzfus, Rebecca J., . . . Manges, Amee R.** (2014). The impact of antibiotics on growth in children in low and middle income countries: Systematic review and meta-analysis of randomised controlled trials. *BMJ*, 348, g2267. doi: 10.1136/bmj.g2267

**Graber, Julia A.; Nichols, Tracy R. & Brooks-Gunn, Jeanne.** (2010). Putting pubertal timing in developmental context: Implications for prevention. *Developmental Psychobiology*, 52(3), 254–262. doi: 10.1002/dev.20438

**Grady, Jessica S.; Ale, Chelsea M. & Morris, Tracy L.** (2012). A naturalistic observation of social behaviours during preschool drop-off. *Early Child Development and Care*, 182(12), 1683–1694. doi: 10.1080/03004430.2011.649266

**Graf, William D.; Miller, Geoffrey; Epstein, Leon G. & Rapin, Isabelle.** (2017). The autism "epidemic": Ethical, legal, and social issues in a developmental spectrum disorder. *Neurology*, 88(14), 1371–1380. doi: 10.1212/WNL.0000000000003791

**Grayson, David S. & Fair, Damien A.** (2017). Development of large-scale functional networks from birth to adulthood: A guide to the neuroimaging literature. *NeuroImage*, (In Press). doi: 10.1016/j.neuroimage.2017.01.079

**Green, James A.; Whitney, Pamela G. & Potegal, Michael.** (2011). Screaming, yelling, whining, and crying: Categorical and intensity differences in vocal expressions of anger and sadness in children's tantrums. *Emotion*, 11(5), 1124–1133. doi: 10.1037/a0024173

**Green, Ronald.** (2015). Designer babies. In Henk ten Have (Ed.), *Encyclopedia of global bioethics*. Living Reference Work: Springer International Publishing. doi: 10.1007/978-3-319-05544-2_138-1

**Greene, Melissa L. & Way, Niobe.** (2005). Self-esteem trajectories among ethnic minority adolescents: A growth curve analysis of the patterns and predictors of change. *Journal of Research on Adolescence*, 15(2), 151–178. doi: 10.1111/j.1532-7795.2005.00090.x

**Greenfield, Patricia M.** (2009). Technology and informal education: What is taught, what is learned. *Science*, 323(5910), 69–71. doi: 10.1126/science.1167190

**Greenough, William T.; Black, James E. & Wallace, Christopher S.** (1987). Experience and brain development. *Child Development*, 58(3), 539–559. doi: 10.1111/j.1467-8624.1987.tb01400.x

**Greenough, William T. & Volkmar, Fred R.** (1973). Pattern of dendritic branching in occipital cortex of rats reared in complex environments. *Experimental Neurology*, 40(2), 491–504. doi: 10.1016/0014-4886(73)90090-3

**Gregg, Norman McAlister.** (1941). Congenital cataract following German measles in the mother. *Transactions of the Ophthalmological Society of Australia*, 3, 35–46.

**Gregg, Norman McAlister.** (1991). Congenital cataract following German measles in the mother. *Epidemiology and Infection*, 107(1), iii–xiv. doi: 10.1017/S0950268800048627

**Gregson, Joanna.** (2010). *The culture of teenage mothers*. Albany, NY: SUNY.

**Griffin, Martyn.** (2011). Developing deliberative minds: Piaget, Vygotsky and the deliberative democratic citizen. *Journal of Public Deliberation*, 7(1).

**Griffiths, Thomas L.** (2015). Manifesto for a new (computational) cognitive revolution. *Cognition*, 135, 21–23. doi: 10.1016/j.cognition.2014.11.026

**Grobman, Kevin H.** (2008). Learning & teaching developmental psychology: Attachment theory, infancy, & infant memory development. http://www.devpsy.org/questions/attachment_theory_memory.html

**Grogan-Kaylor, Andrew; Ma, Julie & Graham-Bermann, Sandra A.** (2018). The case against physical punishment. *Current Opinion in Psychology*, 19, 22–27. doi: 10.1016/j.copsyc.2017.03.022

**Groh, Ashley M.; Narayan, Angela J.; Bakermans-Kranenburg, Marian J.; Roisman, Glenn I.; Vaughn, Brian E.; Fearon, R. M. Pasco & van IJzendoorn, Marinus H.** (2017). Attachment and temperament in the early life course: A meta-analytic review. *Child Development*, 88(3), 770–795. doi: 10.1111/cdev.12677

**Groh, Ashley M.; Roisman, Glenn I.; van IJzendoorn, Marinus H.; Bakermans-Kranenburg, Marian J. & Fearon, R. Pasco.** (2012).

The significance of insecure and disorganized attachment for children's internalizing symptoms: A meta-analytic study. *Child Development*, 83(2), 591–610. doi: 10.1111/j.1467-8624.2011.01711.x

**Gross, James J. (Ed.).** (2014). *Handbook of emotion regulation* (2nd ed.). New York, NY: Guilford Press.

**Grossmann, Klaus E.; Bretherton, Inge; Waters, Everett & Grossmann, Karin (Eds.).** (2014). *Mary Ainsworth's enduring influence on attachment theory, research, and clinical applications*. New York, NY: Routledge.

**Grossmann, Tobias.** (2013). Mapping prefrontal cortex functions in human infancy. *Infancy*, 18(3), 303–324. doi: 10.1111/infa.12016

**Grossmann, Tobias.** (2017). The eyes as windows into other minds: An integrative perspective. *Perspectives on Psychological Science*, 12(1), 107–121. doi: 10.1177/1745691616654457

**Grotevant, Harold D. & McDermott, Jennifer M.** (2014). Adoption: Biological and social processes linked to adaptation. *Annual Review of Psychology*, 65, 235–265. doi: 10.1146/annurev-psych-010213-115020

**Grünebaum, Amos; McCullough, Laurence B.; Sapra, Katherine J.; Brent, Robert L.; Levene, Malcolm I.; Arabin, Birgit & Chervenak, Frank A.** (2014). Early and total neonatal mortality in relation to birth setting in the United States, 2006–2009. *American Journal of Obstetrics and Gynecology*, 211(4), 390.e391–390.e397. doi: 10.1016/j.ajog.2014.03.047

**Guerra, Nancy G. & Williams, Kirk R.** (2010). Implementing bullying prevention in diverse settings: Geographic, economic, and cultural influences. In Eric M. Vernberg & Bridget K. Biggs (Eds.), *Preventing and treating bullying and victimization* (pp. 319–336). New York, NY: Oxford University Press.

**Guerra, Nancy G.; Williams, Kirk R. & Sadek, Shelly.** (2011). Understanding bullying and victimization during childhood and adolescence: A mixed methods study. *Child Development*, 82(1), 295–310. doi: 10.1111/j.1467-8624.2010.01556.x

**Guerri, Consuelo & Pascual, María.** (2010). Mechanisms involved in the neurotoxic, cognitive, and neurobehavioral effects of alcohol consumption during adolescence. *Alcohol*, 44(1), 15–26. doi: 10.1016/j.alcohol.2009.10.003

**Guhn, Martin; Gadermann, Anne M.; Almas, Alisa; Schonert-Reichl, Kimberly A. & Hertzman, Clyde.** (2016). Associations of teacher-rated social, emotional, and cognitive development in kindergarten to self-reported wellbeing, peer relations, and academic test scores in middle childhood. *Early Childhood Research Quarterly*, 35, 76–84. doi: 10.1016/j.ecresq.2015.12.027

**Guo, Siying.** (2016). A meta-analysis of the predictors of cyberbullying perpetration and victimization. *Psychology in the Schools*, 53(4), 432–453. doi: 10.1002/pits.21914

**Gutierrez-Galve, Leticia; Stein, Alan; Hanington, Lucy; Heron, Jon & Ramchandani, Paul.** (2015). Paternal depression in the postnatal period and child development: Mediators and moderators. *Pediatrics, 135*(2), e339–e347. doi: 10.1542/peds.2014-2411

**Guzman, Natalie S. de & Nishina, Adrienne.** (2014). A longitudinal study of body dissatisfaction and pubertal timing in an ethnically diverse adolescent sample. *Body Image, 11*(1), 68–71. doi: 10.1016/j.bodyim.2013.11.001

**Haden, Catherine A.** (2010). Talking about science in museums. *Child Development Perspectives, 4*(1), 62–67. doi: 10.1111/j.1750-8606.2009.00119.x

**Hagan, José E.; Wassilak, Steven G. F.; Craig, Allen S.; Tangermann, Rudolf H.; Diop, Ousmane M.; Burns, Cara C. & Quddus, Arshad.** (2015, May 22). *Progress toward polio eradication — Worldwide, 2014–2015. Morbidity and Mortality Weekly Report 64*(19), 527–531. Atlanta, GA: Centers for Disease Control and Prevention.

**Haidt, Jonathan.** (2013). *The righteous mind: Why good people are divided by politics and religion.* New York, NY: Vintage Books.

**Hajek, Peter; Etter, Jean-François; Benowitz, Neal; Eissenberg, Thomas & McRobbie, Hayden.** (2014). Electronic cigarettes: Review of use, content, safety, effects on smokers and potential for harm and benefit. *Addiction, 109*(11), 1801–1810. doi: 10.1111/add.12659

**Halim, May Ling; Ruble, Diane N.; Tamis-LeMonda, Catherine S.; Zosuls, Kristina M.; Lurye, Leah E. & Greulich, Faith K.** (2014). Pink frilly dresses and the avoidance of all things "girly": Children's appearance rigidity and cognitive theories of gender development. *Developmental Psychology, 50*(4), 1091–1101. doi: 10.1037/a0034906

**Hall, Kelli Stidham; Sales, Jessica McDermott; Komro, Kelli A. & Santelli, John.** (2016). The state of sex education in the United States. *Journal of Adolescent Health, 58*(6), 595–597. doi: 10.1016/j.jadohealth.2016.03.032

**Hall, Matthew L.; Eigsti, Inge-Marie; Bortfeld, Heather & Lillo-Martin, Diane.** (2017). Auditory deprivation does not impair executive function, but language deprivation might: Evidence from a parent-report measure in deaf native signing children. *Journal of Deaf Studies and Deaf Education, 22*(1), 9–21. doi: 10.1093/deafed/enw054

**Hallers-Haalboom, Elizabeth T.; Mesman, Judi; Groeneveld, Marleen G.; Endendijk, Joyce J.; van Berkel, Sheila R.; van der Pol, Lotte D. & Bakermans-Kranenburg, Marian J.** (2014). Mothers, fathers, sons and daughters: Parental sensitivity in families with two children. *Journal of Family Psychology, 28*(2), 138–147. doi: 10.1037/a0036004

**Hamdan, Noora & Gunderson, Elizabeth A.** (2017). The number line is a critical spatial-numerical representation: Evidence from a fraction intervention. *Developmental Psychology, 53*(3), 587–596. doi: 10.1037/dev0000252

**Hamerton, John L. & Evans, Jane A.** (2005). Sex chromosome anomalies. In Merlin G. Butler & F. John Meaney (Eds.), *Genetics of developmental disabilities* (pp. 585–650). Boca Raton, FL: Taylor & Francis.

**Hamilton, Alice.** (1914). Lead poisoning in the United States. *American Journal of Public Health, 4*(6), 477–480. doi: 10.2105/AJPH.4.6.477-a

**Hamlat, Elissa J.; Shapero, Benjamin G.; Hamilton, Jessica L.; Stange, Jonathan P.; Abramson, Lyn Y. & Alloy, Lauren B.** (2014a). Pubertal timing, peer victimization, and body esteem differentially predict depressive symptoms in African American and Caucasian girls. *The Journal of Early Adolescence, 35*(2), 378–402. doi: 10.1177/0272431614534071

**Hamlat, Elissa J.; Stange, Jonathan P.; Abramson, Lyn Y. & Alloy, Lauren B.** (2014b). Early pubertal timing as a vulnerability to depression symptoms: Differential effects of race and sex. *Journal of Abnormal Child Psychology, 42*(4), 527–538. doi: 10.1007/s10802-013-9798-9

**Hamlin, J. Kiley.** (2014). The origins of human morality: Complex socio-moral evaluations by preverbal infants. In Jean Decety & Yves Christen (Eds.), *New frontiers in social neuroscience* (pp. 165–188). New York, NY: Springer. doi: 10.1007/978-3-319-02904-7_10

**Hane, Amie Ashley; Cheah, Charissa; Rubin, Kenneth H. & Fox, Nathan A.** (2008). The role of maternal behavior in the relation between shyness and social reticence in early childhood and social withdrawal in middle childhood. *Social Development, 17*(4), 795–811. doi: 10.1111/j.1467-9507.2008.00481.x

**Hanks, Andrew S.; Just, David R. & Wansink, Brian.** (2013). Smarter lunchrooms can address new school lunchroom guidelines and childhood obesity. *The Journal of Pediatrics, 162*(4), 867–869. doi: 10.1016/j.jpeds.2012.12.031

**Hanna-Attisha, Mona; LaChance, Jenny; Sadler, Richard Casey & Schnepp, Allison Champney.** (2016). Elevated blood lead levels in children associated with the Flint drinking water crisis: A spatial analysis of risk and public health response. *American Journal of Public Health, 106*(2), 283–290. doi: 10.2105/AJPH.2015.303003

**Hannon, Erin E.; Schachner, Adena & Nave-Blodgett, Jessica E.** (2017). Babies know bad dancing when they see it: Older but not younger infants discriminate between synchronous and asynchronous audiovisual musical displays. *Journal of Experimental Child Psychology, 159*, 159–174. doi: 10.1016/j.jecp.2017.01.006

**Hanushek, Eric A. & Woessmann, Ludger.** (2007). *The role of education quality in economic growth. World Bank Policy Research Working Paper No. 4122.* Washington, DC: World Bank.

**Hanushek, Eric A. & Woessmann, Ludger.** (2009). Do better schools lead to more growth? Cognitive skills, economic outcomes, and causation. *Journal of Economic Growth, 17*(4), 267–321. doi: 10.1007/s10887-012-9081-x

**Hanushek, Eric A. & Woessmann, Ludger.** (2010). *The high cost of low educational performance: The long-run economic impact of improving PISA outcomes.* Paris: OECD Publishing. doi: 10.1787/9789264077485-en

**Harden, K. Paige & Tucker-Drob, Elliot M.** (2011). Individual differences in the development of sensation seeking and impulsivity during adolescence: Further evidence for a dual systems model. *Developmental Psychology, 47*(3), 739–746. doi: 10.1037/a0023279

**Hargreaves, Andy.** (2012). Singapore: The Fourth Way in action? *Educational Research for Policy and Practice, 11*(1), 7–17. doi: 10.1007/s10671-011-9125-6

**Harkness, Sara.** (2014). Is biology destiny for the whole family? Contributions of evolutionary life history and behavior genetics to family theories. *Journal of Family Theory & Review, 6*(1), 31–34. doi: 10.1111/jftr.12032

**Harkness, Sara; Super, Charles M. & Mavridis, Caroline J.** (2011). Parental ethnotheories about children's socioemotional development. In Xinyin Chen & Kenneth H. Rubin (Eds.), *Socioemotional development in cultural context* (pp. 73–98). New York, NY: Guilford Press.

**Harper, Casandra E. & Yeung, Fanny.** (2013). Perceptions of institutional commitment to diversity as a predictor of college students' openness to diverse perspectives. *The Review of Higher Education, 37*(1), 25–44. doi: 10.1353/rhe.2013.0065

**Harris, Judith R.** (1998). *The nurture assumption: Why children turn out the way they do.* New York, NY: Free Press.

**Harris, Judith R.** (2002). Beyond the nurture assumption: Testing hypotheses about the child's environment. In John G. Borkowski et al. (Eds.), *Parenting and the child's world: Influences on academic, intellectual, and social-emotional development* (pp. 3–20). Mahwah, NJ: Erlbaum.

**Harris, Michelle A.; Wetzel, Eunike; Robins, Richard W.; Donnellan, M. Brent & Trzesniewski, Kali H.** (2017). The development of global and domain self-esteem from ages 10 to 16 for Mexican-origin youth. *International Journal of Behavioral Development,* (In Press). doi: 10.1177/0165025416679744

**Harrison, Kristen; Bost, Kelly K.; McBride, Brent A.; Donovan, Sharon M.; Grigsby-Toussaint, Diana S.; Kim, Juhee, . . . Jacobsohn, Gwen Costa.** (2011). Toward a developmental conceptualization of contributors to overweight and obesity in childhood: The Six-Cs model. *Child Development Perspectives, 5*(1), 50–58. doi: 10.1111/j.1750-8606.2010.00150.x

**Harrison, Linda J.; Elwick, Sheena; Vallotton, Claire D. & Kappler, Gregor.** (2014). Spending time with others: A time-use diary for infant-toddler child care. In Linda J. Harrison & Jennifer Sumsion (Eds.), *Lived spaces of infant-toddler education and care: Exploring diverse perspectives on theory, research and practice* (pp. 59–74). Dordrecht, Netherlands: Springer. doi: 10.1007/978-94-017-8838-0_5

**Harrist, Amanda W.; Topham, Glade L.; Hubbs-Tait, Laura; Page, Melanie C.; Kennedy, Tay S. & Shriver, Lenka H.** (2012). What developmental science can contribute to a transdisciplinary understanding of childhood obesity: An interpersonal and intrapersonal risk model. *Child Development Perspectives, 6*(4), 445–455. doi: 10.1111/cdep.12004

**Harry, Beth & Klingner, Janette.** (2014). *Why are so many minority students in special education?:*

*Understanding race and disability in schools* (2nd ed.). New York, NY: Teachers College Press.

**Hart, Betty & Risley, Todd R.** (1995). *Meaningful differences in the everyday experience of young American children*. Baltimore, MD: P. H. Brookes.

**Hart, Chantelle N.; Cairns, Alyssa & Jelalian, Elissa.** (2011). Sleep and obesity in children and adolescents. *Pediatric Clinics of North America*, 58(3), 715–733. doi: 10.1016/j.pcl.2011.03.007

**Hart, Daniel & Van Goethem, Anne.** (2017). The role of civic and political participation in successful early adulthood. In Laura M. Padilla-Walker & Larry J. Nelson (Eds.), *Flourishing in emerging adulthood: Positive development during the third decade of life* (pp. 139–166). New York, NY: Oxford University Press.

**Harter, Susan.** (2012). *The construction of the self: Developmental and sociocultural foundations* (2nd ed.). New York, NY: Guilford Press.

**Hartley, Catherine A. & Somerville, Leah H.** (2015). The neuroscience of adolescent decision-making. *Current Opinion in Behavioral Sciences*, 5, 108–115. doi: 10.1016/j.cobeha.2015.09.004

**Hartman, Sarah & Belsky, Jay.** (2015). An evolutionary perspective on family studies: Differential susceptibility to environmental influences. *Family Process*, 55(4), 700–712. doi: 10.1111/famp.12161

**Hasson, Ramzi & Fine, Jodene Goldenring.** (2012). Gender differences among children with ADHD on continuous performance tests: A meta-analytic review. *Journal of Attention Disorders*, 16(3), 190–198. doi: 10.1177/1087054711427398

**Hatch, J. Amos.** (2012). From theory to curriculum: Developmental theory and its relationship to curriculum and instruction in early childhood education. In Nancy File et al. (Eds.), *Curriculum in early childhood education: Re-examined, rediscovered, renewed*. New York, NY: Routledge.

**Hatzenbuehler, Mark L.; Flores, Javier E.; Cavanaugh, Joseph E.; Onwuachi-Willig, Angela & Ramirez, Marizen R.** (2017). Anti-bullying policies and disparities in bullying: A state-level analysis. *American Journal of Preventive Medicine*, 53(2), 184–191. doi: 10.1016/j.amepre.2017.02.004

**Hawkes, Kristen & Coxworth, James E.** (2013). Grandmothers and the evolution of human longevity: A review of findings and future directions. *Evolutionary Anthropology*, 22(6), 294–302. doi: 10.1002/evan.21382

**Hawthorne, Joanna.** (2009). Promoting development of the early parent-infant relationship using the Neonatal Behavioural Assessment Scale. In Jane Barlow & P. O. Svanberg (Eds.), *Keeping the baby in mind: Infant mental health in practice* (pp. 39–51). New York, NY: Routledge.

**Hayden, Erika Check.** (2016, October 12). A radical revision of human genetics. *Nature*, 538(7624), 154–157. doi: 10.1038/538154a

**Hayden, Elizabeth P. & Mash, Eric J.** (2014). Child psychopathology: A developmental-systems perspective. In Eric J. Mash & Russell A. Barkley (Eds.), *Child psychopathology* (3rd ed., pp. 3–72). New York, NY: Guilford Press.

**Hayes, DeMarquis; Blake, Jamilia J.; Darensbourg, Alicia & Castillo, Linda G.** (2015). Examining the academic achievement of Latino adolescents: The role of parent and peer beliefs and behaviors. *The Journal of Early Adolescence*, 35(2), 141–161. doi: 10.1177/0272431614530806

**Hayes, Peter.** (2013). International adoption, "early" puberty, and underrecorded age. *Pediatrics*, 131(6), 1029–1031. doi: 10.1542/peds.2013-0232

**Haynie, Dana L.; Soller, Brian & Williams, Kristi.** (2014). Anticipating early fatality: Friends', schoolmates' and individual perceptions of fatality on adolescent risk behaviors. *Journal of Youth and Adolescence*, 43(2), 175–192. doi: 10.1007/s10964-013-9968-7

**Hayslip, Bert; Blumenthal, Heidemarie & Garner, Ashley.** (2014). Health and grandparent–grandchild well-being: One-year longitudinal findings for custodial grandfamilies. *Journal of Aging and Health*, 26(4), 559–582. doi: 10.1177/0898264314525664

**Healy, Jack.** (2017, June 23). Out of high school, into real life. *New York Times*. https://nyti.ms/2tVHdth

**Hein, Sascha; Tan, Mei; Aljughaiman, Abdullah & Grigorenko, Elena L.** (2014). Characteristics of the home context for the nurturing of gifted children in Saudi Arabia. *High Ability Studies*, 25(1), 23–33. doi: 10.1080/13598139.2014.906970

**Helle, Nadine; Barkmann, Claus; Bartz-Seel, Jutta; Diehl, Thilo; Ehrhardt, Stephan; Hendel, Astrid, . . . Bindt, Carola.** (2016). Very low birth-weight as a risk factor for postpartum depression four to six weeks postbirth in mothers and fathers: Cross-sectional results from a controlled multicentre cohort study. *Journal of Affective Disorders*, 180, 154–161. doi: 10.1016/j.jad.2015.04.001

**Hellerstein, Susan C.; Feldman, Sarah & Duan, Tao.** (2015). China's 50% caesarean delivery rate: Is it too high? *BJOG: An International Journal of Obstetrics & Gynaecology*, 122(2), 160–164. doi: 10.1111/1471-0528.12971

**Henderson, Heather A.; Pine, Daniel S. & Fox, Nathan A.** (2015). Behavioral inhibition and developmental risk: A dual-processing perspective. *Neuropsychopharmacology Reviews*, 40(1), 207–224. doi: 10.1038/npp.2014.189

**Hennessy-Fiske, Molly.** (2011, February 8). California; Concern about child obesity grows, poll finds; Many Californians support restricting unhealthful food and drink in schools. *Los Angeles Times*, p. AA3.

**Henrich, Joseph; Heine, Steven J. & Norenzayan, Ara.** (2010). The weirdest people in the world? *Behavioral and Brain Sciences*, 33(2/3), 61–83. doi: 10.1017/S0140525X0999152X

**Henry, David B.; Deptula, Daneen P. & Schoeny, Michael E.** (2012). Sexually transmitted infections and unintended pregnancy: A longitudinal analysis of risk transmission through friends and attitudes. *Social Development*, 21(1), 195–214. doi: 10.1111/j.1467-9507.2011.00626.x

**Herd, Pamela; Higgins, Jenny; Sicinski, Kamil & Merkurieva, Irina.** (2016). The implications of unintended pregnancies for mental health in later life. *American Journal of Public Health*, 106(3), 421–429. doi: 10.2105/AJPH.2015.302973

**Herman, Khalisa N.; Paukner, Annika & Suomi, Stephen J.** (2011). Gene × environment interactions and social play: Contributions from rhesus macaques. In Anthony D. Pellegrini (Ed.), *The Oxford handbook of the development of play* (pp. 58–69). New York, NY: Oxford University Press. doi: 10.1093/oxfordhb/9780195393002.013.0006

**Herman-Giddens, Marcia E.** (2013). The enigmatic pursuit of puberty in girls. *Pediatrics*, 132(6), 1125–1126. doi: 10.1542/peds.2013-3058

**Herman-Giddens, Marcia E.; Steffes, Jennifer; Harris, Donna; Slora, Eric; Hussey, Michael; Dowshen, Steven A., . . . Reiter, Edward O.** (2012). Secondary sexual characteristics in boys: Data from the pediatric research in office settings network. *Pediatrics*, 130(5), e1058–e1068. doi: 10.1542/peds.2011-3291

**Herrmann, Esther; Call, Josep; Hernàndez-Lloreda, María Victoria; Hare, Brian & Tomasello, Michael.** (2007). Humans have evolved specialized skills of social cognition: The cultural intelligence hypothesis. *Science*, 317(5843), 1360–1366. doi: 10.1126/science.1146282

**Herrmann, Julia; Schmidt, Isabelle; Kessels, Ursula & Preckel, Franzis.** (2016). Big fish in big ponds: Contrast and assimilation effects on math and verbal self-concepts of students in within-school gifted tracks. *British Journal of Educational Psychology*, 86(2), 222–240. doi: 10.1111/bjep.12100

**Herschensohn, Julia R.** (2007). *Language development and age*. New York, NY: Cambridge University Press.

**Hetherington, E. Mavis.** (2006). The influence of conflict, marital problem solving and parenting on children's adjustment in nondivorced, divorced and remarried families. In Alison Clarke-Stewart & Judy Dunn (Eds.), *Families count: Effects on child and adolescent development* (pp. 203–237). New York, NY: Cambridge University Press.

**Heyer, Djai B. & Meredith, Rhiannon M.** (2017). Environmental toxicology: Sensitive periods of development and neurodevelopmental disorders. *NeuroToxicology*, 58, 23–41. doi: 10.1016/j.neuro.2016.10.017

**Heyes, Cecilia.** (2016). Who knows? Metacognitive social learning strategies. *Trends in Cognitive Sciences*, 20(3), 204–213. doi: 10.1016/j.tics.2015.12.007

**Hill, Patrick L.; Burrow, Anthony L. & Sumner, Rachel.** (2013). Addressing important questions in the field of adolescent purpose. *Child Development Perspectives*, 7(4), 232–236. doi: 10.1111/cdep.12048

**Hill, Sarah E.; Prokosch, Marjorie L.; DelPriore, Danielle J.; Griskevicius, Vladas & Kramer, Andrew.** (2016). Low childhood socioeconomic status promotes eating in the absence of energy need. *Psychological Science*, 27(3), 354–364. doi: 10.1177/0956797615621901

**Hinnant, J. Benjamin; Nelson, Jackie A.; O'Brien, Marion; Keane, Susan P. & Calkins, Susan D.** (2013). The interactive roles of parenting, emotion regulation and executive functioning in moral reasoning during middle childhood. *Cognition and Emotion*, 27(8), 1460–1468. doi: 10.1080/02699931.2013.789792

**Hirsh-Pasek, Kathy & Golinkoff, Roberta M.** (2016, March 11). The preschool paradox: It's time to rethink our approach to early education [Review of the book *The importance of being little: What preschoolers really need from grownups*, by Erika Christakis]. *Science*, 351(6278), 1158. doi: 10.1126/science.aaf1173

**Hirvonen, Riikka; Aunola, Kaisa; Alatupa, Saija; Viljaranta, Jaana & Nurmi, Jari-Erik.** (2013). The role of temperament in children's affective and behavioral responses in achievement situations. *Learning and Instruction*, 27, 21–30. doi: 10.1016/j.learninstruc.2013.02.005

**Ho, Emily S.** (2010). Measuring hand function in the young child. *Journal of Hand Therapy*, 23(3), 323–328. doi: 10.1016/j.jht.2009.11.002

**Hoeve, Machteld; Dubas, Judith S.; Gerris, Jan R. M.; van der Laan, Peter H. & Smeenk, Wilma.** (2011). Maternal and paternal parenting styles: Unique and combined links to adolescent and early adult delinquency. *Journal of Adolescence*, 34(5), 813–827. doi: 10.1016/j.adolescence.2011.02.004

**Hofer, Claire; Eisenberg, Nancy; Spinrad, Tracy L.; Morris, Amanda S.; Gershoff, Elizabeth; Valiente, Carlos, . . . Eggum, Natalie D.** (2013). Mother-adolescent conflict: Stability, change, and relations with externalizing and internalizing behavior problems. *Social Development*, 22(2), 259–279. doi: 10.1111/sode.12012

**Hoff, Erika.** (2013). Interpreting the early language trajectories of children from low-SES and language minority homes: Implications for closing achievement gaps. *Developmental Psychology*, 49(1), 4–14. doi: 10.1037/a0027238

**Hoff, Erika; Core, Cynthia; Place, Silvia; Rumiche, Rosario; Señor, Melissa & Parra, Marisol.** (2012). Dual language exposure and early bilingual development. *Journal of Child Language*, 39(1), 1–27. doi: 10.1017/S0305000910000759

**Hoff, Erika; Rumiche, Rosario; Burridge, Andrea; Ribota, Krystal M. & Welsh, Stephanie N.** (2014). Expressive vocabulary development in children from bilingual and monolingual homes: A longitudinal study from two to four years. *Early Childhood Research Quarterly*, 29(4), 433–444. doi: 10.1016/j.ecresq.2014.04.012

**Hoffman, Jessica L.; Teale, William H. & Paciga, Kathleen A.** (2014). Assessing vocabulary learning in early childhood. *Journal of Early Childhood Literacy*, 14(4), 459–481. doi: 10.1177/1468798413501184

**Holden, Constance.** (2010). Myopia out of control. *Science*, 327(5961), 17. doi: 10.1126/science.327.5961.17-c

**Holden, George W.; Grogan-Kaylor, Andrew; Durrant, Joan E. & Gershoff, Elizabeth T.** (2017). Researchers deserve a better critique: Response to Larzelere, Gunnoe, Roberts, and Ferguson (2017). *Marriage & Family Review*, 53(5), 465–490. doi: 10.1080/01494929.2017.1308899

**Holland, James D. & Klaczynski, Paul A.** (2009). Intuitive risk taking during adolescence. *Prevention Researcher*, 16(2), 8–11.

**Hollich, George J.; Hirsh-Pasek, Kathy; Golinkoff, Roberta M.; Brand, Rebecca J.; Brown, Ellie; Chung, He Len, . . . Rocroi, Camille.** (2000). *Breaking the language barrier: An emergentist coalition model for the origins of word learning.* Malden, MA: Blackwell. doi: 10.1111/1540-5834.00090

**Holmes, Christopher J.; Kim-Spoon, Jungmeen & Deater-Deckard, Kirby.** (2016). Linking executive function and peer problems from early childhood through middle adolescence. *Journal of Abnormal Child Psychology*, 44(1), 31–42. doi: 10.1007/s10802-015-0044-5

**Holt-Lunstad, Julianne; Smith, Timothy B.; Baker, Mark; Harris, Tyler & Stephenson, David.** (2015). Loneliness and social isolation as risk factors for mortality: A meta-analytic review. *Perspectives on Psychological Science*, 10(2), 227–237. doi: 10.1177/1745691614568352

**Holzer, Jessica; Canavan, Maureen & Bradley, Elizabeth.** (2014). County-level correlation between adult obesity rates and prevalence of dentists. *JADA*, 145(9), 932–939. doi: 10.14219/jada.2014.48

**Homa, David M.; Neff, Linda J.; King, Brian A.; Caraballo, Ralph S.; Bunnell, Rebecca E.; Babb, Stephen D., . . . Wang, Lanqing.** (2015, February 6). Vital signs: Disparities in nonsmokers' exposure to secondhand smoke — United States, 1999–2012. *Morbidity and Mortality Weekly Report* 64(4), 103–108. Atlanta, GA: Centers for Disease Control and Prevention.

**Hong, David S. & Reiss, Allan L.** (2014). Cognitive and neurological aspects of sex chromosome aneuploidies. *The Lancet Neurology*, 13(3), 306–318. doi: 10.1016/S1474-4422(13)70302-8

**Hong, Jun Sung & Garbarino, James.** (2012). Risk and protective factors for homophobic bullying in schools: An application of the social–ecological framework. *Educational Psychology Review*, 24(2), 271–285. doi: 10.1007/s10648-012-9194-y

**Hook, Jennifer L.** (2017). Women's housework: New tests of time and money. *Journal of Marriage and Family*, 79(1), 179–198. doi: 10.1111/jomf.12351

**Horton, Megan K.; Kahn, Linda G.; Perera, Frederica; Barr, Dana B. & Rauh, Virginia.** (2012). Does the home environment and the sex of the child modify the adverse effects of prenatal exposure to chlorpyrifos on child working memory? *Neurotoxicology and Teratology*, 34(5), 534–541. doi: 10.1016/j.ntt.2012.07.004

**Hostinar, Camelia E.; Johnson, Anna E. & Gunnar, Megan R.** (2015). Parent support is less effective in buffering cortisol stress reactivity for adolescents compared to children. *Developmental Science*, 18(2), 281–297. doi: 10.1111/desc.12195

**Hostinar, Camelia E.; Nusslock, Robin & Miller, Gregory E.** (2017). Future directions in the study of early-life stress and physical and emotional health: Implications of the neuroimmune network hypothesis. *Journal of Clinical Child & Adolescent Psychology*, (In Press). doi: 10.1080/15374416.2016.1266647

**Howe, Tsu-Hsin; Sheu, Ching-Fan; Hsu, Yung-Wen; Wang, Tien-Ni & Wang, Lan-Wan.** (2016). Predicting neurodevelopmental outcomes at preschool age for children with very low birth weight. *Research in Developmental Disabilities*, 48, 231–241. doi: 10.1016/j.ridd.2015.11.003

**Howell, Diane M.; Wysocki, Karen & Steiner, Michael J.** (2010). Toilet training. *Pediatrics in Review*, 31(6), 262–263. doi: 10.1542/pir.31-6-262

**Hoyert, Donna L.; Kung, Hsiang-Ching & Smith, Betty L.** (2005). *Deaths: Preliminary data for 2003. National Vital Statistics Reports* 53(15). Hyattsville, MD: National Center for Health Statistics.

**Hoyert, Donna L. & Xu, Jiaquan.** (2012). *Deaths: Preliminary data for 2011. National Vital Statistics Reports* 61(6). Hyattsville, MD: National Center for Health Statistics.

**Hoyme, H. Eugene; Kalberg, Wendy O.; Elliott, Amy J.; Blankenship, Jason; Buckley, David; Marais, Anna-Susan, . . . May, Philip A.** (2016). Updated clinical guidelines for diagnosing fetal alcohol spectrum disorders. *Pediatrics*, 138(2), e20154256. doi: 10.1542/peds.2015-4256

**Hrdy, Sarah B.** (2009). *Mothers and others: The evolutionary origins of mutual understanding.* Cambridge, MA: Harvard University Press.

**Hu, Youna; Shmygelska, Alena; Tran, David; Eriksson, Nicholas; Tung, Joyce Y. & Hinds, David A.** (2016). GWAS of 89,283 individuals identifies genetic variants associated with self-reporting of being a morning person. *Nature Communications*, 7(10448). doi: 10.1038/ncomms10448

**Huang, Chiungjung.** (2010). Mean-level change in self-esteem from childhood through adulthood: Meta-analysis of longitudinal studies. *Review of General Psychology*, 14(3), 251–260. doi: 10.1037/a0020543

**Huang, Francis L.** (2017). Does attending a state-funded preschool program improve letter name knowledge? *Early Childhood Research Quarterly*, 38, 116–126. doi: 10.1016/j.ecresq.2016.08.002

**Huang, Z. Josh & Luo, Liqun.** (2015). It takes the world to understand the brain. *Science*, 350(6256), 42–44. doi: 10.1126/science.aad4120

**Hugdahl, Kenneth & Westerhausen, René (Eds.).** (2010). *The two halves of the brain: Information processing in the cerebral hemispheres.* Cambridge, MA: MIT Press.

**Hughes, Julie M. & Bigler, Rebecca S.** (2011). Predictors of African American and European American adolescents' endorsement of race-conscious social policies. *Developmental Psychology*, 47(2), 479–492. doi: 10.1037/a0021309

**Hughes, Jan N. & Im, Myung H.** (2016). Teacher–student relationship and peer disliking and liking across grades 1–4. *Child Development*, 87(2), 593–611. doi: 10.1111/cdev.12477

**Huh, Susanna Y.; Rifas-Shiman, Sheryl L.; Zera, Chloe A.; Edwards, Janet W. Rich; Oken, Emily; Weiss, Scott T. & Gillman, Matthew W.** (2012). Delivery by caesarean section and risk of obesity in preschool age children: A prospective cohort study. *Archives of the Diseases of Childhood, 97*(7), 610–616. doi: 10.1136/archdischild-2011-301141

**Hunter, Jonathan & Maunder, Robert (Eds.).** (2016). *Improving patient treatment with attachment theory: A guide for primary care practitioners and specialists.* New York, NY: Springer. doi: 10.1007/978-3-319-23300-0

**Huston, Aletha C.; Bobbitt, Kaeley C. & Bentley, Alison.** (2015). Time spent in child care: How and why does it affect social development? *Developmental Psychology, 51*(5), 621–634. doi: 10.1037/a0038951

**Hutchinson, Esther A.; De Luca, Cinzia R.; Doyle, Lex W.; Roberts, Gehan & Anderson, Peter J.** (2013). School-age outcomes of extremely preterm or extremely low birth weight children. *Pediatrics, 131*(4), e1053–e1061. doi: 10.1542/peds.2012-2311

**Huver, Rose M. E.; Otten, Roy; de Vries, Hein & Engels, Rutger C. M. E.** (2010). Personality and parenting style in parents of adolescents. *Journal of Adolescence, 33*(3), 395–402. doi: 10.1016/j.adolescence.2009.07.012

**Huynh, Jimmy L. & Casaccia, Patrizia.** (2013). Epigenetic mechanisms in multiple sclerosis: Implications for pathogenesis and treatment. *The Lancet Neurology, 12*(2), 195–206. doi: 10.1016/S1474-4422(12)70309-5

**Hvistendahl, Mara.** (2013). China heads off deadly blood disorder. *Science, 340*(6133), 677–678. doi: 10.1126/science.340.6133.677

**Hyde, Janet S.** (2016). Sex and cognition: Gender and cognitive functions. *Current Opinion in Neurobiology, 38*, 53–56. doi: 10.1016/j.conb.2016.02.007

**Hyde, Janet S.; Lindberg, Sara M.; Linn, Marcia C.; Ellis, Amy B. & Williams, Caroline C.** (2008). Gender similarities characterize math performance. *Science, 321*(5888), 494–495. doi: 10.1126/science.1160364

**Hyslop, Anne.** (2014). *The case against exit exams.* New American Education Policy Brief. Washington DC: New America Education Policy Program.

**Iida, Hiroko & Rozier, R. Gary.** (2013). Mother-perceived social capital and children's oral health and use of dental care in the United States. *American Journal of Public Health, 103*(3), 480–487. doi: 10.2105/AJPH.2012.300845

**Ikeda, Martin J.** (2012). Policy and practice considerations for response to intervention: Reflections and commentary. *Journal of Learning Disabilities, 45*(3), 274–277. doi: 10.1177/0022219412442170

**Imdad, Aamer; Sadiq, Kamran & Bhutta, Zulfiqar A.** (2011). Evidence-based prevention of childhood malnutrition. *Current Opinion in Clinical Nutrition & Metabolic Care, 14*(3), 276–285. doi: 10.1097/MCO.0b013e328345364a

**Inan, Hatice Z.; Trundle, Kathy C. & Kantor, Rebecca.** (2010). Understanding natural sciences education in a Reggio Emilia-inspired preschool. *Journal of Research in Science Teaching, 47*(10), 1186–1208. doi: 10.1002/tea.20375

**Inhelder, Bärbel & Piaget, Jean.** (1958). *The growth of logical thinking from childhood to adolescence: An essay on the construction of formal operational structures.* New York, NY: Basic Books.

**Inhelder, Bärbel & Piaget, Jean.** (1964). *The early growth of logic in the child: Classification and seriation.* New York, NY: Harper & Row.

**Inhelder, Bärbel & Piaget, Jean.** (2013a). *The early growth of logic in the child: Classification and seriation.* New York, NY: Routledge.

**Inhelder, Bärbel & Piaget, Jean.** (2013b). *The growth of logical thinking from childhood to adolescence: An essay on the construction of formal operational structures.* New York, NY: Routledge.

**Insel, Thomas R.** (2014). Mental disorders in childhood: Shifting the focus from behavioral symptoms to neurodevelopmental trajectories. *JAMA, 311*(17), 1727–1728. doi: 10.1001/jama.2014.1193

**Insurance Institute for Highway Safety.** (2013a). Older drivers. http://www.iihs.org/iihs/topics/t/older-drivers/fatalityfacts/older-people

**Insurance Institute for Highway Safety.** (2013b). Teenagers: Driving carries extra risks for them. http://www.iihs.org/iihs/topics/t/teenagers/fatalityfacts/teenagers/2013

**Insurance Institute for Highway Safety.** (2016, February). Fatality facts: Pedestrians 2014. http://www.iihs.org/iihs/topics/t/pedestrians-and-bicyclists/fatalityfacts/pedestrians

**Insurance Institute for Highway Safety.** (2016, November). Fatality facts: Pedestrians and bicyclists 2015. http://www.iihs.org/iihs/topics/t/pedestrians-and-bicyclists/fatalityfacts/pedestrians

**Inzlicht, Michael & Schmader, Toni.** (2012). *Stereotype threat: Theory, process, and application.* New York, NY: Oxford University Press.

**Irwin, Scott; Galvez, Roberto; Weiler, Ivan Jeanne; Beckel-Mitchener, Andrea & Greenough, William.** (2002). Brain structure and the functions of FMR1 protein. In Randi Jenssen Hagerman & Paul J. Hagerman (Eds.), *Fragile X syndrome: Diagnosis, treatment, and research* (3rd ed., pp. 191–205). Baltimore, MD: Johns Hopkins University Press.

**Ishii, Nozomi; Kono, Yumi; Yonemoto, Naohiro; Kusuda, Satoshi & Fujimura, Masanori.** (2013). Outcomes of infants born at 22 and 23 weeks' gestation. *Pediatrics, 132*(1), 62–71. doi: 10.1542/peds.2012-2857

**Ivcevic, Zorana & Brackett, Marc.** (2014). Predicting school success: Comparing conscientiousness, grit, and emotion regulation ability. *Journal of Research in Personality, 52*, 29–36. doi: 10.1016/j.jrp.2014.06.005

**Jackson, Sandra L. & Cunningham, Solveig A.** (2015). Social competence and obesity in elementary school. *American Journal of Public Health, 105*(1), 153–158. doi: 10.2105/AJPH.2014.302208

**Jaffe, Arthur C.** (2011). Failure to thrive: Current clinical concepts. *Pediatrics in Review, 32*(3), 100–108. doi: 10.1542/pir.32-3-100

**Jamal, Ahmed; Gentzke, Andrea; Hu, S. Sean; Cullen, Karen A.; Apelberg, Benjamin J.; Homa, David M. & King, Brian A.** (2017, June 16). Tobacco use among middle and high school students — United States, 2011–2016. *Morbidity and Mortality Weekly Report 66*(23), 597–603. Atlanta, GA: Centers for Disease Control and Prevention.

**Jambon, Marc & Smetana, Judith G.** (2014). Moral complexity in middle childhood: Children's evaluations of necessary harm. *Developmental Psychology, 50*(1), 22–33. doi: 10.1037/a0032992

**James, Jenée; Ellis, Bruce J.; Schlomer, Gabriel L. & Garber, Judy.** (2012). Sex-specific pathways to early puberty, sexual debut, and sexual risk taking: Tests of an integrated evolutionary–developmental model. *Developmental Psychology, 48*(3), 687–702. doi: 10.1037/a0026427

**Jarcho, Johanna M.; Fox, Nathan A.; Pine, Daniel S.; Etkin, Amit; Leibenluft, Ellen; Shechner, Tomer & Ernst, Monique.** (2013). The neural correlates of emotion-based cognitive control in adults with early childhood behavioral inhibition. *Biological Psychology, 92*(2), 306–314. doi: 10.1016/j.biopsycho.2012.09.008

**Jednoróg, Katarzyna; Altarelli, Irene; Monzalvo, Karla; Fluss, Joel; Dubois, Jessica; Billard, Catherine, . . . Ramus, Franck.** (2012). The influence of socioeconomic status on children's brain structure. *PLoS ONE, 7*(8), e42486. doi: 10.1371/journal.pone.0042486

**Jensen, Lene Arnett & McKenzie, Jessica.** (2016). The moral reasoning of U.S. Evangelical and mainline protestant children, adolescents, and adults: A cultural–developmental study. *Child Development, 87*(2), 446–464. doi: 10.1111/cdev.12465

**Jia, Peng; Xue, Hong; Zhang, Ji & Wang, Youfa.** (2017). Time trend and demographic and geographic disparities in childhood obesity prevalence in China—Evidence from twenty years of longitudinal data. *International Journal of Environmental Research and Public Health, 14*(4). doi: 10.3390/ijerph14040369

**Jimerson, Shane R.; Burns, Matthew K. & VanDerHeyden, Amanda M. (Eds.).** (2016). *Handbook of response to intervention: The science and practice of multi-tiered systems of support.* New York, NY: Springer. doi: 10.1007/978-1-4899-7568-3

**Johnson, Jonni L.; McWilliams, Kelly; Goodman, Gail S.; Shelley, Alexandra E. & Piper, Brianna.** (2016). Basic principles of interviewing the child eyewitness. In William T. O'Donohue & Matthew Fanetti (Eds.), *Forensic interviews regarding child sexual abuse* (pp. 179–195). New York, NY: Springer. doi: 10.1007/978-3-319-21097-1_10

**Johnson, Mark H. & de Haan, Michelle.** (2015). *Developmental cognitive neuroscience: An introduction* (4th ed.). Hoboken, NJ: Wiley.

**Johnson, Susan C.; Dweck, Carol S.; Chen, Frances S.; Stern, Hilarie L.; Ok, Su-Jeong & Barth, Maria.** (2010). At the intersection of social and cognitive development: Internal working models of attachment in infancy. *Cognitive Science, 34*(5), 807–825. doi: 10.1111/j.1551-6709.2010.01112.x

**Johnston, Lloyd D.; O'Malley, Patrick M.; Bachman, Jerald G. & Schulenberg, John E.** (2012). *Monitoring the future, national survey results on drug use, 1975–2011, Volume I: Secondary school students.* Ann Arbor, MI: Institute for Social Research, The University of Michigan.

**Jolles, Diana R.** (2017). Unwarranted variation in utilization of cesarean birth among low-risk childbearing women. *Journal of Midwifery & Women's Health, 62*(1), 49–57. doi: 10.1111/jmwh.12565

**Jolliffe, Darrick; Farrington, David P.; Piquero, Alex R.; MacLeod, John F. & van de Weijer, Steve.** (2017). Prevalence of life-course-persistent, adolescence-limited, and late-onset offenders: A systematic review of prospective longitudinal studies. *Aggression and Violent Behavior, 33,* 4–14. doi: 10.1016/j.avb.2017.01.002

**Jonas, Eric & Kording, Konrad Paul.** (2017). Could a neuroscientist understand a microprocessor? *PLoS Computational Biology, 13*(1), e1005268. doi: 10.1371/journal.pcbi.1005268

**Jones, Andrea M. & Morris, Tracy L.** (2012). Psychological adjustment of children in foster care: Review and implications for best practice. *Journal of Public Child Welfare, 6*(2), 129–148. doi: 10.1080/15548732.2011.617272

**Jones, Jeffrey M.** (2015, October 21). *In U.S., 58% back legal marijuana use.* Washington, DC: Gallup.

**Jones, Mary C.** (1965). Psychological correlates of somatic development. *Child Development, 36*(4), 899–911. doi: 10.2307/1126932

**Jong, Jyh-Tsorng; Kao, Tsair; Lee, Liang-Yi; Huang, Hung-Hsuan; Lo, Po-Tsung & Wang, Hui-Chung.** (2010). Can temperament be understood at birth? The relationship between neonatal pain cry and their temperament: A preliminary study. *Infant Behavior and Development, 33*(3), 266–272. doi: 10.1016/j.infbeh.2010.02.001

**Jonsson, Maria; Cnattingius, Sven & Wikström, Anna-Karin.** (2013). Elective induction of labor and the risk of cesarean section in low-risk parous women: A cohort study. *Acta Obstetricia et Gynecologica Scandinavica, 92*(2), 198–203. doi: 10.1111/aogs.12043

**Jorgenson, Alicia Grattan; Hsiao, Ray Chih-Jui & Yen, Cheng-Fang.** (2016). Internet addiction and other behavioral addictions. *Child & Adolescent Psychiatric Clinics, 25*(3), 509–520. doi: 10.1016/j.chc.2016.03.004

**Julian, Megan M.** (2013). Age at adoption from institutional care as a window into the lasting effects of early experiences. *Clinical Child and Family Psychology Review, 16*(2), 101–145. doi: 10.1007/s10567-013-0130-6

**Jung, Courtney.** (2015). *Lactivism: How feminists and fundamentalists, hippies and yuppies, and physicians and politicians made breastfeeding big business and bad policy.* New York, NY: Basic Books.

**Jung, Rex E. & Ryman, Sephira G.** (2013). Imaging creativity. In Kyung Hee Kim et al. (Eds.), *Creatively gifted students are not like other gifted students: Research, theory, and practice* (pp. 69–87). Rotterdam, The Netherlands: SensePublishers. doi: 10.1007/978-94-6209-149-8_6

**Juonala, Markus; Magnussen, Costan G.; Berenson, Gerald S.; Venn, Alison; Burns, Trudy L.; Sabin, Matthew A., . . . Raitakari, Olli T.** (2011). Childhood adiposity, adult adiposity, and cardiovascular risk factors. *New England Journal of Medicine, 365*(20), 1876–1885. doi: 10.1056/NEJMoa1010112

**Juster, Robert-Paul; Russell, Jennifer J.; Almeida, Daniel & Picard, Martin.** (2016). Allostatic load and comorbidities: A mitochondrial, epigenetic, and evolutionary perspective. *Development and Psychopathology, 28*(4), 1117–1146. doi: 10.1017/S0954579416000730

**Juvonen, Jaana & Graham, Sandra.** (2014). Bullying in schools: The power of bullies and the plight of victims. *Annual Review of Psychology, 65,* 159–185. doi: 10.1146/annurev-psych-010213-115030

**Kachel, A. Friederike; Premo, Luke S. & Hublin, Jean-Jacques.** (2011). Modeling the effects of weaning age on length of female reproductive period: Implications for the evolution of human life history. *American Journal of Human Biology, 23*(4), 479–487. doi: 10.1002/ajhb.21157

**Kahneman, Daniel.** (2011). *Thinking, fast and slow.* New York, NY: Farrar, Straus and Giroux.

**Kail, Robert V.** (2013). Influences of credibility of testimony and strength of statistical evidence on children's and adolescents' reasoning. *Journal of Experimental Child Psychology, 116*(3), 747–754. doi: 10.1016/j.jecp.2013.04.004

**Kaiser, Jocelyn.** (2014a). Gearing up for a closer look at the human placenta. *Science, 344*(6188), 1073. doi: 10.1126/science.344.6188.1073

**Kaiser, Jocelyn.** (2014b). Ambitious children's study meets disappointing end. *Science, 346* (6216), 1441. doi: 10.1126/science.346.6216.1441

**Kaiser, Jocelyn.** (2017). A yellow light for human embryo editing. *Science, 355*(6326), 675. doi: 10.1126/science.355.6326.675-b

**Kalliala, Marjatta.** (2006). *Play culture in a changing world.* Maidenhead, UK: Open University Press.

**Kaltiala-Heino, Riittakerttu; Fröjd, Sari & Marttunen, Mauri.** (2015). Depression, conduct disorder, smoking and alcohol use as predictors of sexual activity in middle adolescence: a longitudinal study. *Health Psychology and Behavioral Medicine, 3*(1), 25–39. doi: 10.1080/21642850.2014.996887

**Kang, Hye-Kyung.** (2014). Influence of culture and community perceptions on birth and perinatal care of immigrant women: Doulas' perspective. *The Journal of Perinatal Education, 23*(1), 25–32. doi: 10.1891/1058-1243.23.1.25

**Kanner, Leo.** (1943). Autistic disturbances of affective contact. *Nervous Child, 2,* 217–250.

**Kapp. Steven K.; Gillespie-Lynch, Kristen; Sherman, Lauren E. & Hutman, Ted.** (2013). Deficit, difference, or both? Autism and neurodiversity. *Developmental Psychology, 49*(1), 59–71. doi: 10.1037/a0028353

**Karama, Sherif; Ad-Dab'bagh, Yasser; Haier, Richard J.; Deary, Ian J.; Lyttelton, Oliver C.; Lepage, Claude & Evans, Alan C.** (2009). Positive association between cognitive ability and cortical thickness in a representative US sample of healthy 6 to 18-year-olds. *Intelligence, 37*(2), 145–155. doi: 10.1016/j.intell.2008.09.006

**Karbach, Julia & Unger, Kerstin.** (2014). Executive control training from middle childhood to adolescence. *Frontiers in Psychology, 5*(390). doi: 10.3389/fpsyg.2014.00390

**Karmiloff-Smith, Annette; Al-Janabi, Tamara; D'Souza, Hana; Groet, Jurgen; Massand, Esha; Mok, Kin, . . . Strydom, Andre.** (2016). The importance of understanding individual differences in Down syndrome. *F1000Research, 5*(389). doi: 10.12688/f1000research.7506.1

**Kärtner, Joscha; Borke, Jörn; Maasmeier, Kathrin; Keller, Heidi & Kleis, Astrid.** (2011). Sociocultural influences on the development of self-recognition and self-regulation in Costa Rican and Mexican toddlers. *Journal of Cognitive Education and Psychology, 10*(1), 96–112. doi: 10.1891/1945-8959.10.1.96

**Kärtner, Joscha; Keller, Heidi & Yovsi, Relindis D.** (2010). Mother–infant interaction during the first 3 months: The emergence of culture-specific contingency patterns. *Child Development, 81*(2), 540–554. doi: 10.1111/j.1467-8624.2009.01414.x

**Kastberg, David; Chan, Jessica Ying & Murray, Gordon.** (2016). *Performance of U.S. 15-year-old students in science, reading, and mathematics literacy in an international context: First look at PISA 2015.* Washington, DC: National Center for Education Statistics. NCES 2017-048.

**Kastbom, Åsa A.; Sydsjö, Gunilla; Bladh, Marie; Priebe, Gisela & Svedin, Carl-Göran.** (2015). Sexual debut before the age of 14 leads to poorer psychosocial health and risky behaviour in later life. *Acta Paediatrica, 104*(1), 91–100. doi: 10.1111/apa.12803

**Kauffman, James M.; Anastasiou, Dimitris & Maag, John W.** (2017). Special education at the crossroad: An identity crisis and the need for a scientific reconstruction. *Exceptionality, 25*(2), 139–155. doi: 10.1080/09362835.2016.1238380

**Kavanaugh, Robert D.** (2011). Origins and consequences of social pretend play. In Anthony D. Pellegrini (Ed.), *The Oxford handbook of the development of play* (pp. 296–307). New York, NY: Oxford University Press. doi: 10.1093/oxfordhb/9780195393002.013.0022

**Keil, Frank C.** (2011). Science starts early. *Science, 331*(6020), 1022–1023. doi: 10.1126/science.1195221

**Keller, Heidi.** (2014). Introduction: Understanding relationships. In Hiltrud Otto & Heidi Keller (Eds.), *Different faces of attachment: Cultural variations on a universal human need* (pp. 3–25). New York, NY: Cambridge University Press.

**Keller, Heidi; Borke, Jörn; Chaudhary, Nandita; Lamm, Bettina & Kleis, Astrid.** (2010). Continuity in parenting strategies: A cross-cultural comparison. *Journal of Cross-Cultural Psychology, 41*(3), 391–409. doi: 10.1177/0022022109359690

**Keller, Heidi; Yovsi, Relindis; Borke, Joern; Kärtner, Joscha; Jensen, Henning & Papaligoura, Zaira.** (2004). Developmental consequences of early parenting experiences: Self-recognition and self-regulation in three cultural communities. *Child Development, 75*(6), 1745–1760. doi: 10.1111/j.1467-8624.2004.00814.x

**Keller, Peggy S.; El-Sheikh, Mona; Granger, Douglas A. & Buckhalt, Joseph A.** (2012).

Interactions between salivary cortisol and alpha-amylase as predictors of children's cognitive functioning and academic performance. *Physiology & Behavior, 105*(4), 987–995. doi: 10.1016/j.physbeh.2011.11.005

**Kempe, Ruth S. & Kempe, C. Henry.** (1978). *Child abuse.* Cambridge, MA: Harvard University Press.

**Kena, Grace; Aud, Susan; Johnson, Frank; Wang, Xiaolei; Zhang, Jijun; Rathbun, Amy, . . . Kristapovich, Paul.** (2014, May). *The condition of education 2014.* Washington, DC: U.S. Department of Education, National Center for Education Statistics.

**Kena, Grace; Hussar, William; McFarland, Joel; de Brey, Cristobal; Musu-Gillette, Lauren; Wang, Xiaolei, . . . Dunlop Velez, Erin.** (2016). *The condition of education 2016.* Washington, DC: U.S. Department of Education, National Center for Education Statistics.

**Kena, Grace; Musu-Gillette, Lauren; Robinson, Jennifer; Wang, Xiaolei; Rathbun, Amy; Zhang, Jijun, . . . Dunlop Velez, Erin.** (2015). *The condition of education 2015.* Washington, DC: Department of Education, National Center for Education Statistics.

**Kendall-Taylor, Nathaniel; Lindland, Eric; O'Neil, Moira & Stanley, Kate.** (2014). Beyond prevalence: An explanatory approach to reframing child maltreatment in the United Kingdom. *Child Abuse & Neglect, 38*(5), 810–821. doi: 10.1016/j.chiabu.2014.04.019

**Keown, Louise J. & Palmer, Melanie.** (2014). Comparisons between paternal and maternal involvement with sons: Early to middle childhood. *Early Child Development and Care, 184*(1), 99–117. doi: 10.1080/03004430.2013.773510

**Kern, Margaret L.; Benson, Lizbeth; Larson, Emily; Forrest, Christopher B.; Bevans, Katherine B. & Steinberg, Laurence.** (2016). The anatomy of developmental predictors of healthy lives study (TADPOHLS). *Applied Developmental Science, 20*(2), 135–145. doi: 10.1080/10888691.2015.1095642

**Kerr, Margaret; Stattin, Håkan & Burk, William J.** (2010). A reinterpretation of parental monitoring in longitudinal perspective. *Journal of Research on Adolescence, 20*(1), 39–64. doi: 10.1111/j.1532-7795.2009.00623.x

**Kersken, Verena; Zuberbühler, Klaus & Gomez, Juan-Carlos.** (2017). Listeners can extract meaning from non-linguistic infant vocalisations cross-culturally. *Scientific Reports, 7.* doi: 10.1038/srep41016

**Kesselring, Thomas & Müller, Ulrich.** (2011). The concept of egocentrism in the context of Piaget's theory. *New Ideas in Psychology, 29*(3), 327–345. doi: 10.1016/j.newideapsych.2010.03.008

**Kessler, Ronald C.; Avenevoli, Shelli; Costello, E. Jane; Georgiades, Katholiki; Green, Jennifer G.; Gruber, Michael J., . . . Merikangas, Kathleen R.** (2012). Prevalence, persistence, and sociodemographic correlates of DSM-IV disorders in the National Comorbidity Survey Replication Adolescent Supplement. *Archives of General Psychiatry, 69*(4), 372–380. doi: 10.1001/archgenpsychiatry.2011.160

**Keupp. Stefanie; Bancken, Christin; Schillmöller, Jelka; Rakoczy, Hannes & Behne, Tanya.** (2016). Rational over-imitation: Preschoolers consider material costs and copy causally irrelevant actions selectively. *Cognition, 147*(3), 85–92. doi: 10.1016/j.cognition.2015.11.007

**Khafi, Tamar Y.; Yates, Tuppett M. & Luthar, Suniya S.** (2014). Ethnic differences in the developmental significance of parentification. *Family Process, 53*(2), 267–287. doi: 10.1111/famp.12072

**Khan, Shereen; Gagné, Monique; Yang, Leigh & Shapk, Jennifer.** (2016). Exploring the relationship between adolescents' self-concept and their offline and online social worlds. *Computers in Human Behavior, 55*(Part B), 940–945. doi: 10.1016/j.chb.2015.09.046

**Kharsati, Naphisabet & Bhola, Poornima.** (2014). Patterns of non-suicidal self-injurious behaviours among college students in India. *International Journal of Social Psychiatry, 61*(1), 39–49. doi: 10.1177/0020764014535755

**Kiley, Dan.** (1983). *The Peter Pan syndrome: Men who have never grown up.* New York, NY: Dodd Mead.

**Kilgore, Paul E.; Grabenstein, John D.; Salim, Abdulbaset M. & Rybak, Michael.** (2015). Treatment of Ebola virus disease. *Pharmacotherapy, 35*(1), 43–53. doi: 10.1002/phar.1545

**Killen, Melanie & Smetana, Judith G. (Eds.).** (2014). *Handbook of moral development* (2nd ed.). New York, NY: Psychology Press.

**Kim, Bo-Ram; Chow, Sy-Miin; Bray, Bethany & Teti, Douglas M.** (2017). Trajectories of mothers' emotional availability: relations with infant temperament in predicting attachment security. *Attachment & Human Development, 19*(1), 38–57. doi: 10.1080/14616734.2016.1252780

**Kim, Dong-Sik & Kim, Hyun-Sun.** (2009). Body-image dissatisfaction as a predictor of suicidal ideation among Korean boys and girls in different stages of adolescence: A two-year longitudinal study. *The Journal of Adolescent Health, 45*(1), 47–54. doi: 10.1016/j.jadohealth.2008.11.017

**Kim, Hojin I. & Johnson, Scott P.** (2013). Do young infants prefer an infant-directed face or a happ. face? *International Journal of Behavioral Development, 37*(2), 125–130. doi: 10.1177/0165025413475972

**Kim, Heejung S. & Sasaki, Joni Y.** (2014). Cultural neuroscience: Biology of the mind in cultural contexts. *Annual Review of Psychology, 65,* 487–514. doi: 10.1146/annurev-psych-010213-115040

**Kim, Joon Sik.** (2011). Excessive crying: Behavioral and emotional regulation disorder in infancy. *Korean Journal of Pediatrics, 54*(6), 229–233. doi: 10.3345/kjp.2011.54.6.229

**Kim, Pilyoung; Strathearn, Lane & Swain, James E.** (2016). The maternal brain and its plasticity in humans. *Hormones and Behavior, 77,* 113–123. doi: 10.1016/j.yhbeh.2015.08.001

**Kim-Spoon, Jungmeen; Longo, Gregory S. & McCullough, Michael E.** (2012). Parent-adolescent relationship quality as a moderator for the influences of parents' religiousness on adolescents' religiousness and adjustment. *Journal of Youth and Adolescence, 41*(12), 1576–1587. doi: 10.1007/s10964-012-9796-1

**King, Bruce M.** (2013). The modern obesity epidemic, ancestral hunter-gatherers, and the sensory/reward control of food intake. *American Psychologist, 68*(2), 88–96. doi: 10.1037/a0030684

**King, Martin Luther.** (1977). *Strength to love.* Cleveland, OH: Collins.

**Kinney, Hannah C. & Thach, Bradley T.** (2009). The sudden infant death syndrome. *New England Journal of Medicine, 361,* 795–805. doi: 10.1056/NEJMra0803836

**Kirk, Elizabeth; Howlett, Neil; Pine, Karen J. & Fletcher, Ben.** (2013). To sign or not to sign? The impact of encouraging infants to gesture on infant language and maternal mind-mindedness. *Child Development, 84*(2), 574–590. doi: 10.1111/j.1467-8624.2012.01874.x

**Kirschner, Paul A.** (2017). Stop propagating the learning styles myth. *Computers & Education, 106,* 166–171. doi: 10.1016/j.compedu.2016.12.006

**Kiuru, Noona; Burk, William J.; Laursen, Brett; Salmela-Aro, Katariina & Nurmi, Jari-Erik.** (2010). Pressure to drink but not to smoke: Disentangling selection and socialization in adolescent peer networks and peer groups. *Journal of Adolescence, 33*(6), 801–812. doi: 10.1016/j.adolescence.2010.07.006

**Klaczynski, Paul A.** (2001). Analytic and heuristic processing influences on adolescent reasoning and decision-making. *Child Development, 72*(3), 844–861. doi: 10.1111/1467-8624.00319

**Klaczynski, Paul A.** (2011). Age differences in understanding precedent-setting decisions and authorities' responses to violations of deontic rules. *Journal of Experimental Child Psychology, 109*(1), 1–24. doi: 10.1016/j.jecp.2010.10.010

**Klaczynski, Paul A.; Daniel, David B. & Keller, Peggy S.** (2009). Appearance idealization, body esteem, causal attributions, and ethnic variations in the development of obesity stereotypes. *Journal of Applied Developmental Psychology, 30*(4), 537–551. doi: 10.1016/j.appdev.2008.12.031

**Klaczynski, Paul A. & Felmban, Wejdan S.** (2014). Heuristics and biases during adolescence: Developmental reversals and individual differences. In Henry Markovits (Ed.), *The developmental psychology of reasoning and decision-making* (pp. 84–111). New York, NY: Psychology Press.

**Klaus, Marshall H. & Kennell, John H.** (1976). *Maternal-infant bonding: The impact of early separation or loss on family development.* St. Louis, MO: Mosby.

**Klein, Denise; Mok, Kelvin; Chen, Jen-Kai & Watkins, Kate E.** (2014). Age of language learning shapes brain structure: A cortical thickness study of bilingual and monolingual individuals. *Brain and Language, 131,* 20–24. doi: 10.1016/j.bandl.2013.05.014

**Klein, Hilary.** (1991). Couvade syndrome: Male counterpart to pregnancy. *International Journal of Psychiatry in Medicine, 21*(1), 57–69. doi: 10.2190/FLE0-92JM-C4CN-J83T

**Klein, Zoe A. & Romeo, Russell D.** (2013). Changes in hypothalamic–pituitary–adrenal stress responsiveness before and after puberty in rats. *Hormones and Behavior, 64*(2), 357–363. doi: 10.1016/j.yhbeh.2013.01.012

**Klinger, Laura G.; Dawson, Geraldine; Burner, Karen & Crisler, Megan.** (2014). Autism spectrum disorder. In Eric J. Mash & Russell A. Barkley (Eds.), *Child psychopathology* (3rd ed., pp. 531–572). New York, NY: Guilford Press.

**Knight, Rona.** (2014). A hundred years of latency: From Freudian psychosexual theory to dynamic systems nonlinear development in middle childhood. *Journal of the American Psychoanalytic Association, 62*(2), 203–235. doi: 10.1177/0003065114531044

**Knopik, Valerie S.; Neiderhiser, Jenae M.; DeFries, John C. & Plomin, Robert.** (2017). *Behavioral genetics* (7th ed.). New York, NY: Worth.

**Knopp. Kayla; Rhoades, Galena K.; Allen, Elizabeth S.; Parsons, Aleja; Ritchie, Lane L.; Markman, Howard J. & Stanley, Scott M.** (2017). Within- and between-family associations of marital functioning and child well-being. *Journal of Marriage and Family, 79*(2), 451–461. doi: 10.1111/jomf.12373

**Koch, Linda.** (2015). Shaping the gut microbiome. *Nature Reviews Genetics, 16*, 2–3. doi: 10.1038/nrg3869

**Kochanek, Kenneth D.; Xu, Jiaquan; Murphy, Sherry L.; Miniño, Arialdi M. & Kung, Hsiang-Ching.** (2011). *Deaths: Preliminary data for 2009. National Vital Statistics Reports 59*(4). Hyattsville, MD: National Center for Health Statistics.

**Kochanska, Grazyna; Barry, Robin A.; Jimenez, Natasha B.; Hollatz, Amanda L. & Woodard, Jarilyn.** (2009). Guilt and effortful control: Two mechanisms that prevent disruptive developmental trajectories. *Journal of Personality and Social Psychology, 97*(2), 322–333. doi: 10.1037/a0015471

**Kohlberg, Lawrence.** (1963). The development of children's orientations toward a moral order: I. Sequence in the development of moral thought. *Vita Humana, 6*(1/2), 11–33. doi: 10.1159/000269667

**Kohlberg, Lawrence; Levine, Charles & Hewer, Alexandra.** (1983). *Moral stages: A current formulation and a response to critics.* New York, NY: Karger.

**Kolb, Bryan & Gibb, Robbin.** (2015). Childhood poverty and brain development. *Human Development, 58*(4/5), 215–217. doi: 10.1159/000438766

**Kolb, Bryan & Whishaw, Ian Q.** (2015). *Fundamentals of human neuropsychology* (7th ed.). New York, NY: Worth Publishers.

**Komisar, Erica.** (2017). *Being there: Why prioritizing motherhood in the first three years matters.* New York, NY: TarcherPerigee.

**Konner, Melvin.** (2010). *The evolution of childhood: Relationships, emotion, mind.* Cambridge, MA: Harvard University Press.

**Konstam, Varda.** (2015). *Emerging and young adulthood: Multiple perspectives, diverse narratives.* New York, NY: Springer. doi: 10.1007/978-3-319-11301-2

**Kopp. Claire B.** (2011). Development in the early years: Socialization, motor development, and consciousness. *Annual Review of Psychology, 62*, 165–187. doi: 10.1146/annurev.psych.121208.131625

**Korhonen, Tellervo; Latvala, Antti; Dick, Danielle M.; Pulkkinen, Lea; Rose, Richard J.; Kaprio, Jaakko & Huizink, Anja C.** (2012). Genetic and environmental influences underlying externalizing behaviors, cigarette smoking and illicit drug use across adolescence. *Behavior Genetics, 42*(4), 614–625. doi: 10.1007/s10519-012-9528-z

**Kost, Kathryn & Henshaw, Stanley.** (2013). *U.S. teenage pregnancies, births and abortions, 2008: State trends by age, race and ethnicity.* New York, NY: Guttmacher Institute.

**Koster-Hale, Jorie & Saxe, Rebecca.** (2013). Functional neuroimaging of theory of mind. In Simon Baron-Cohen et al. (Eds.), *Understanding other minds: Perspectives from developmental social neuroscience* (3rd ed., pp. 132–163). New York, NY: Oxford University Press.

**Kouider, Sid; Stahlhut, Carsten; Gelskov, Sofie V.; Barbosa, Leonardo S.; Dutat, Michel; de Gardelle, Vincent, . . . Dehaene-Lambertz, Ghislaine.** (2013). A neural marker of perceptual consciousness in infants. *Science, 340*(6130), 376–380. doi: 10.1126/science.1232509

**Kozhimannil, Katy B. & Kim, Helen.** (2014). Maternal mental illness. *Science, 345*(6198), 755. doi: 10.1126/science.1259614

**Kozhimannil, Katy B.; Law, Michael R. & Virnig, Beth A.** (2013). Cesarean delivery rates vary tenfold among US hospitals; Reducing variation may address quality and cost issues. *Health Affairs, 32*(3), 527–535. doi: 10.1377/hlthaff.2012.1030

**Kreager, Derek A.; Molloy, Lauren E.; Moody, James & Feinberg, Mark E.** (2016). Friends first? The peer network origins of adolescent dating. *Journal of Research on Adolescence, 26*(2), 257–269. doi: 10.1111/jora.12189

**Krebs, John R.** (2009). The gourmet ape: Evolution and human food preferences. *American Journal of Clinical Nutrition, 90*(3), 707S–711S. doi: 10.3945/ajcn.2009.27462B

**Kremer, Michael; Brannen, Conner & Glennerster, Rachel.** (2013, April 19). The challenge of education and learning in the developing world. *Science, 340*(6130), 297–300. doi: 10.1126/science.1235350

**Kremer, Peter; Elshaug, Christine; Leslie, Eva; Toumbourou, John W.; Patton, George C. & Williams, Joanne.** (2014). Physical activity, leisure-time screen use and depression among children and young adolescents. *Journal of Science and Medicine in Sport, 17*(2), 183–187. doi: 10.1016/j.jsams.2013.03.012

**Kretch, Kari S. & Adolph, Karen E.** (2013). No bridge too high: Infants decide whether to cross based on the probability of falling not the severity of the potential fall. *Developmental Science, 16*(3), 336–351. doi: 10.1111/desc.12045

**Krisberg, Kim.** (2014). Public health messaging: How it is said can influence behaviors: Beyond the facts. *The Nation's Health, 44*(6), 1, 20.

**Kroger, Jane & Marcia, James E.** (2011). The identity statuses: Origins, meanings, and interpretations. In Seth J. Schwartz et al. (Eds.), *Handbook of identity theory and research* (pp. 31–53). New York, NY: Springer. doi: 10.1007/978-1-4419-7988-9_2

**Krogstad, Jens M.** (2017, July 28). *5 facts about Latinos and education. Fact Tank.* Washington, DC: Pew Research Center.

**Krogstad, Jens M. & Fry, Richard.** (2014, August 18). *Dept. of Ed. projects public schools will be 'majority-minority' this fall. Fact Tank.* Washington, DC: Pew Research Center.

**Kroncke, Anna P.; Willard, Marcy & Huckabee, Helena.** (2016). Optimal outcomes and recovery. In *Assessment of autism spectrum disorder: Critical issues in clinical, forensic and school settings* (pp. 23–33). New York, NY: Springer. doi: 10.1007/978-3-319-25504-0_3

**Kruse, Gina R.; Kalkhoran, Sara & Rigotti, Nancy A.** (2017). Use of electronic cigarettes among U.S. adults with medical comorbidities. *AJPM, 52*(6), 798–804. doi: 10.1016/j.amepre.2016.12.004

**Kuehn, Bridget M.** (2011). Scientists find promising therapies for fragile X and Down syndromes. *JAMA, 305*(4), 344–346. doi: 10.1001/jama.2010.1960

**Kuhn, Deanna.** (2013). Reasoning. In Philip D. Zelazo (Ed.), *The Oxford handbook of developmental psychology* (Vol. 1, pp. 744–764). New York, NY: Oxford University Press. doi: 10.1093/oxfordhb/9780199958450.013.0026

**Kundu, Tapas K. (Ed.).** (2013). *Epigenetics: Development and disease.* New York, NY: Springer. doi: 10.1007/978-94-007-4525-4

**Kushnerenko, Elena; Tomalski, Przemyslaw; Ballieux, Haiko; Ribeiro, Helena; Potton, Anita; Axelsson, Emma L., . . . Moore, Derek G.** (2013). Brain responses to audiovisual speech mismatch in infants are associated with individual differences in looking behaviour. *European Journal of Neuroscience, 38*(9), 3363–3369. doi: 10.1111/ejn.12317

**Kutob, Randa M.; Senf, Janet H.; Crago, Marjorie & Shisslak, Catherine M.** (2010). Concurrent and longitudinal predictors of self-esteem in elementary and middle school girls. *Journal of School Health, 80*(5), 240–248. doi: 10.1111/j.1746-1561.2010.00496.x

**Kuwahara, Keisuke; Kochi, Takeshi; Nanri, Akiko; Tsuruoka, Hiroko; Kurotani, Kayo; Pham, Ngoc Minh, . . . Mizoue, Tetsuya.** (2014). Flushing response modifies the association of alcohol consumption with markers of glucose metabolism in Japanese men and women. *Alcoholism: Clinical and Experimental Research, 38*(4), 1042–1048. doi: 10.1111/acer.12323

**Kvalvik, Liv G.; Haug, Kjell; Klungsøyr, Kari; Morken, Nils-Halvdan; Deroo, Lisa A. & Skjærven, Rolv.** (2017). Maternal smoking status in successive pregnancies and risk of having a small for gestational age infant. *Paediatric and Perinatal Epidemiology, 31*(1), 21–28. doi: 10.1111/ppe.12333

**Kypri, Kypros; Davie, Gabrielle; McElduff, Patrick; Connor, Jennie & Langley, John.**

(2014). Effects of lowering the minimum alcohol purchasing age on weekend assaults resulting in hospitalization in New Zealand. *American Journal of Public Health, 104*(8), 1396–1401. doi: 10.2105/AJPH.2014.301889

**Kypri, Kypros; Voas, Robert B.; Langley, John D.; Stephenson, Shaun C. R.; Begg, Dorothy J.; Tippetts, A. Scott & Davie, Gabrielle S.** (2006). Minimum purchasing age for alcohol and traffic crash injuries among 15- to 19-year-olds in New Zealand. *American Journal of Public Health, 96*(1), 126–131. doi: 10.2105/AJPH.2005.073122

**Labouvie-Vief, Gisela.** (2015). *Integrating emotions and cognition throughout the lifespan.* New York, NY: Springer. doi: 10.1007/978-3-319-09822-7

**Ladd, Helen F. & Sorensen, Lucy C.** (2017). Returns to teacher experience: Student achievement and motivation in middle school. *Education Finance and Policy, 12*(2), 241–279. doi: 10.1162/EDFP_a_00194

**LaFontana, Kathryn M. & Cillessen, Antonius H. N.** (2010). Developmental changes in the priority of perceived status in childhood and adolescence. *Social Development, 19*(1), 130–147. doi: 10.1111/j.1467-9507.2008.00522.x

**Lagattuta, Kristin H.** (2014). Linking past, present, and future: Children's ability to connect mental states and emotions across time. *Child Development Perspectives, 8*(2), 90–95. doi: 10.1111/cdep.12065

**Lai, Stephanie A.; Benjamin, Rebekah G.; Schwanenflugel, Paula J. & Kuhn, Melanie R.** (2014). The longitudinal relationship between reading fluency and reading comprehension skills in second-grade children. *Reading & Writing Quarterly: Overcoming Learning Difficulties, 30*(2), 116–138. doi: 10.1080/10573569.2013.789785

**Laird, Robert D.; Marrero, Matthew D.; Melching, Jessica A. & Kuhn, Emily S.** (2013). Information management strategies in early adolescence: Developmental change in use and transactional associations with psychological adjustment. *Developmental Psychology, 49*(5), 928–937. doi: 10.1037/a0028845

**Lake, Neil.** (2012). Labor, interrupted: Cesareans, "cascading interventions," and finding a sense of balance. *Harvard Magazine, 115*(2), 21–26.

**Lake, Stephanie & Kerr, Thomas.** (2017). The challenges of projecting the public health impacts of marijuana legalization in Canada. *International Journal of Health Policy Management, 6*(5), 285–287. doi: 10.15171/ijhpm.2016.124

**Lamb, Michael E.** (1982). Maternal employment and child development: A review. In Michael E. Lamb (Ed.), *Nontraditional families: Parenting and child development* (pp. 45–69). Hillsdale, NJ: Erlbaum.

**Lamb, Michael E. (Ed.).** (2010). *The role of the father in child development* (5th ed.). Hoboken, NJ: Wiley.

**Lamm, Bettina; Keller, Heidi; Teiser, Johanna; Gudi, Helene; Yovsi, Relindis D.; Freitag, Claudia, . . . Lohaus, Arnold.** (2017). Waiting for the second treat: Developing culture-specific modes of self-regulation. *Child Development,* (In Press). doi: 10.1111/cdev.12847

**Lander, Eric S.** (2016). The heroes of CRISPR. *Cell, 164*(1/2), 18–28. doi: 10.1016/j.cell.2015.12.041

**Landgren, Kajsa; Lundqvist, Anita & Hallström, Inger.** (2012). Remembering the chaos – But life went on and the wound healed: A four year follow up with parents having had a baby with infantile colic. *The Open Nursing Journal, 6,* 53–61. doi: 10.2174/1874434601206010053

**Lando, Amy M. & Lo, Serena C.** (2014). Consumer understanding of the benefits and risks of fish consumption during pregnancy. *American Journal of Lifestyle Medicine, 8*(2), 88–92. doi: 10.1177/1559827613514704

**Lane, Jonathan D. & Harris, Paul L.** (2014). Confronting, representing, and believing counterintuitive concepts: Navigating the natural and the supernatural. *Perspectives on Psychological Science, 9*(2), 144–160. doi: 10.1177/1745691613518078

**Långström, Niklas; Rahman, Qazi; Carlström, Eva & Lichtenstein, Paul.** (2010). Genetic and environmental effects on same-sex sexual behavior: A population study of twins in Sweden. *Archives of Sexual Behavior, 39*(1), 75–80. doi: 10.1007/s10508-008-9386-1

**Language and Reading Research Consortium.** (2015). The dimensionality of language ability in young children. *Child Development, 86*(6), 1948–1965. doi: 10.1111/cdev.12450

**Lansford, Jennifer E.; Sharma, Chinmayi; Malone, Patrick S.; Woodlief, Darren; Dodge, Kenneth A.; Oburu, Paul, . . . Di Giunta, Laura.** (2014). Corporal punishment, maternal warmth, and child adjustment: A longitudinal study in eight countries. *Journal of Clinical Child & Adolescent Psychology, 43*(4), 670–685. doi: 10.1080/15374416.2014.893518

**Lara-Cinisomo, Sandraluz; Fuligni, Allison Sidle & Karoly, Lynn A.** (2011). Preparing preschoolers for kindergarten. In DeAnna M. Laverick & Mary Renck Jalongo (Eds.), *Transitions to early care and education* (Vol. 4, pp. 93–105). New York, NY: Springer. doi: 10.1007/978-94-007-0573-9_9

**Laraway, Kelly A.; Birch, Leann L.; Shaffer, Michele L. & Paul, Ian M.** (2010). Parent perception of healthy infant and toddler growth. *Clinical Pediatrics, 49*(4), 343–349. doi: 10.1177/0009922809343717

**Larzelere, Robert E. & Cox, Ronald B.** (2013). Making valid causal inferences about corrective actions by parents from longitudinal data. *Journal of Family Theory & Review, 5*(4), 282–299. doi: 10.1111/jftr.12020

**Larzelere, Robert E.; Cox, Ronald B. & Smith, Gail.** (2010). Do nonphysical punishments reduce antisocial behavior more than spanking? A comparison using the strongest previous causal evidence against spanking. *BMC Pediatrics, 10*(10). doi: 10.1186/1471-2431-10-10

**Larzelere, Robert E.; Cox, Ronald B. & Swindle, Taren M.** (2015). Many replications do not causal inferences make: The need for critical replications to test competing explanations of nonrandomized studies. *Perspectives on Psychological Science, 10*(3), 380–389. doi: 10.1177/1745691614567904

**Larzelere, Robert E.; Gunnoe, Marjorie Lindner; Roberts, Mark W. & Ferguson, Christopher J.** (2017). Children and parents deserve better parental discipline research: Critiquing the evidence for exclusively "positive" parenting. *Marriage & Family Review, 53*(1), 24–35. doi: 10.1080/01494929.2016.1145613

**Lau, Carissa; Ambalavanan, Namasivayam; Chakraborty, Hrishikesh; Wingate, Martha S. & Carlo, Waldemar A.** (2013). Extremely low birth weight and infant mortality rates in the United States. *Pediatrics, 131*(5), 855–860. doi: 10.1542/peds.2012-2471

**Laurent, Heidemarie K.** (2014). Clarifying the contours of emotion regulation: Insights from parent–child stress research. *Child Development Perspectives, 8*(1), 30–35. doi: 10.1111/cdep.12058

**Laurino, Mercy Y.; Bennett, Robin L.; Saraiya, Devki S.; Baumeister, Lisa; Doyle, Debra L.; Leppig, Kathleen, . . . Raskind, Wendy H.** (2005). Genetic evaluation and counseling of couples with recurrent miscarriage: Recommendations of the National Society of Genetic Counselors. *Journal of Genetic Counseling, 14*(3), 165–181. doi: 10.1007/s10897-005-3241-5

**Laursen, Brett & Collins, W. Andrew.** (2009). Parent-child relationships during adolescence. In Richard M. Lerner & Laurence Steinberg (Eds.), *Handbook of adolescent psychology* (3rd ed., Vol. 2, pp. 3–42). Hoboken, NJ: Wiley.

**Laursen, Brett & Hartl, Amy C.** (2013). Understanding loneliness during adolescence: Developmental changes that increase the risk of perceived social isolation. *Journal of Adolescence, 36*(6), 1261–1268. doi: 10.1016/j.adolescence.2013.06.003

**Laursen, Brett; Hartl, Amy C.; Vitaro, Frank; Brendgen, Mara; Dionne, Ginette & Boivin, Michel.** (2017). The spread of substance use and delinquency between adolescent twins. *Developmental Psychology, 53*(2), 329–339. doi: 10.1037/dev0000217

**Lavelli, Manuela & Fogel, Alan.** (2005). Developmental changes in the relationship between the infant's attention and emotion during early face-to-face communication: The 2-month transition. *Developmental Psychology, 41*(1), 265–280. doi: 10.1037/0012-1649.41.1.265

**Le Grange, Daniel & Lock, James (Eds.).** (2011). *Eating disorders in children and adolescents: A clinical handbook.* New York, NY: Guilford Press.

**Leach, Penelope.** (2011). The EYFS and the real foundations of children's early years. In Richard House (Ed.), *Too much, too soon?: Early learning and the erosion of childhood.* Stroud, UK: Hawthorn.

**Leavitt, Judith W.** (2009). *Make room for daddy: The journey from waiting room to birthing room.* Chapel Hill, NC: University of North Carolina Press.

**LeCuyer, Elizabeth A. & Swanson, Dena Phillips.** (2016). African American and European American mothers' limit setting and their 36-month-old children's responses to limits, self-concept, and social competence. *Journal of Family Issues, 37*(2), 270–296. doi: 10.1177/0192513X13515883

Lee, Dohoon; Brooks-Gunn, Jeanne; McLanahan, Sara S.; Notterman, Daniel & Garfinkel, Irwin. (2013). The Great Recession, genetic sensitivity, and maternal harsh parenting. *Proceedings of the National Academy of Sciences*, *110*(34), 13780–13784. doi: 10.1073/pnas.1312398110

Lee, Jihyun & Porretta, David L. (2013). Enhancing the motor skills of children with autism spectrum disorders: A pool-based approach. *JOPERD: The Journal of Physical Education, Recreation & Dance*, *84*(1), 41–45. doi: 10.1080/07303084.2013.746154

Lee, Moosung; Oi-yeung Lam, Beatrice; Ju, Eunsu & Dean, Jenny. (2016). Part-time employment and problem behaviors: Evidence from adolescents in South Korea. *Journal of Research on Adolescence*, (In Press). doi: 10.1111/jora.12258

Lee, RaeHyuck; Zhai, Fuhua; Brooks-Gunn, Jeanne; Han, Wen-Jui & Waldfogel, Jane. (2014). Head Start participation and school readiness: Evidence from the early childhood longitudinal study–birth cohort. *Developmental Psychology*, *50*(1), 202–215. doi: 10.1037/a0032280

Lee, Soojeong & Shouse, Roger C. (2011). The impact of prestige orientation on shadow education in South Korea. *Sociology of Education*, *84*(3), 212–224. doi: 10.1177/0038040711411278

Lee, Shawna J. & Altschul, Inna. (2015). Spanking of young children: Do immigrant and U.S.-born Hispanic parents differ? *Journal of Interpersonal Violence*, *30*(3), 475–498. doi: 10.1177/0886260514535098

Lee, Shawna J.; Altschul, Inna & Gershoff, Elizabeth T. (2015). Wait until your father gets home? Mother's and fathers' spanking and development of child aggression. *Children and Youth Services Review*, *52*, 158–166. doi: 10.1016/j.childyouth.2014.11.006

Lee, Yuan-Hsuan; Ko, Chih-Hung & Chou, Chien. (2015). Re-visiting Internet addiction among Taiwanese students: A cross-sectional comparison of students' expectations, online gaming, and online social interaction. *Journal of Abnormal Child Psychology*, *43*(3), 589–599. doi: 10.1007/s10802-014-9915-4

Legerstee, Maria. (2013). The developing social brain: Social connections and social bonds, social loss, and jealousy in infancy. In Maria Legerstee et al. (Eds.), *The infant mind: Origins of the social brain* (pp. 223–247). New York, NY: Guilford Press.

Lehner, Ben. (2013). Genotype to phenotype: Lessons from model organisms for human genetics. *Nature Reviews Genetics*, *14*(3), 168–178. doi: 10.1038/nrg3404

Leiter, Valerie & Herman, Sarah. (2015). Guinea pig kids: Myths or modern Tuskegees? *Sociological Spectrum*, *35*(1), 26–45. doi: 10.1080/02732173.2014.978429

Leman, Patrick J. & Björnberg, Marina. (2010). Conversation, development, and gender: A study of changes in children's concepts of punishment. *Child Development*, *81*(3), 958–971. doi: 10.1111/j.1467-8624.2010.01445.x

Lemieux, André. (2012). Post-formal thought in gerontagogy or beyond Piage. *Journal of Behavioral and Brain Science*, *2*(3), 399–406. doi: 10.4236/jbbs.2012.23046

Lemish, Daphna & Kolucki, Barbara. (2013). Media and early childhood development. In Pia Rebello Britto et al. (Eds.), *Handbook of early childhood development research and its impact on global policy*. New York, NY: Oxford University Press.

Lenhart, Amanda. (2015, April 9). *Teen, social media and technology overview 2015: Smartphone facilitate shifts in communication landscape for teens*. Pew Research Center: Internet, Science & Tech. Washington, DC: Pew Research Center.

Leonard, Hayley C. & Hill, Elisabeth L. (2014). Review: The impact of motor development on typical and atypical social cognition and language: A systematic review. *Child and Adolescent Mental Health*, *19*(3), 163–170. doi: 10.1111/camh.12055

Lerner, Richard M. (2009). *On the nature of human plasticity*. New York, NY: Cambridge University Press.

Lerner, Richard M.; Agans, Jennifer P.; DeSouza, Lisette M. & Hershberg, Rachel M. (2014). Developmental science in 2025: A predictive review. *Research in Human Development*, *11*(4), 255–272. doi: 10.1080/15427609.2014.967046

Leslie, Mitch. (2012). Gut microbes keep rare immune cells in line. *Science*, *335*(6075), 1428. doi: 10.1126/science.335.6075.1428

Lester, Patricia; Aralis, Hilary; Sinclair, Maegan; Kiff, Cara; Lee, Kyung-Hee; Mustillo, Sarah & Wadsworth, Shelley MacDermid. (2016). The impact of deployment on parental, family and child adjustment in military families. *Child Psychiatry & Human Development*, *47*(6), 938–949. doi: 10.1007/s10578-016-0624-9

Lester, Patricia; Leskin, Gregory; Woodward, Kirsten; Saltzman, William; Nash, William; Mogil, Catherine, . . . Beardslee, William. (2011). Wartime deployment and military children: Applying prevention science to enhance family resilience. In Shelley MacDermid Wadsworth & David Riggs (Eds.), *Risk and resilience in U.S. military families* (pp. 149–173). New York, NY: Springer. doi: 10.1007/978-1-4419-7064-0_8

Leung, Sumie; Mareschal, Denis; Rowsell, Renee; Simpson, David; Laria, Leon; Grbic, Amanda & Kaufman, Jordy. (2016). Oscillatory activity in the infant brain and the representation of small numbers. *Frontiers in Systems Neuroscience*, *10*(4). doi: 10.3389/fnsys.2016.00004

Leventhal, Bennett L. (2013). Complementary and alternative medicine: Not many compliments but lots of alternatives. *Journal of Child and Adolescent Psychopharmacology*, *23*(1), 54–56. doi: 10.1089/cap.2013.2312

Lewallen, Lynne P. (2011). The importance of culture in childbearing. *Journal of Obstetric, Gynecologic, & Neonatal Nursing*, *40*(1), 4–8. doi: 10.1111/j.1552-6909.2010.01209.x

Lewandowski, Lawrence J. & Lovett, Benjamin J. (2014). Learning disabilities. In Eric J. Mash & Russell A. Barkley (Eds.), *Child psychopathology* (3rd ed., pp. 625–669). New York, NY: Guilford Press.

Lewin, Kurt. (1945). The Research Center for Group Dynamics at Massachusetts Institute of Technology. *Sociometry*, *8*(2), 126–136. doi: 10.2307/2785233

Lewin, Tamar. (2009, October 24). No Einstein in your crib? Get a refund. *New York Times*, p. A1. https://nyti.ms/2k8BI5m

Lewis, John D.; Theilmann, Rebecca J.; Townsend, Jeanne & Evans, Alan C. (2013). Network efficiency in autism spectrum disorder and its relation to brain overgrowth. *Frontiers in Human Neuroscience*, *7*, 845. doi: 10.3389/fnhum.2013.00845

Lewis, Michael. (2010). The emergence of human emotions. In Michael Lewis et al. (Eds.), *Handbook of emotions* (3rd ed.). New York, NY: Guilford Press.

Lewis, Michael & Brooks, Jeanne. (1978). Self-knowledge and emotional development. In Michael Lewis & L. A. Rosenblum (Eds.), *Genesis of behavior* (Vol. 1, pp. 205–226). New York, NY: Plenum Press.

Lewis, Michael & Kestler, Lisa (Eds.). (2012). *Gender differences in prenatal substance exposure*. Washington, DC: American Psychological Association.

Lewis, Marc D. (2013). The development of emotional regulation: Integrating normative and individual differences through developmental neuroscience. In Philip D. Zelazo (Ed.), *The Oxford handbook of developmental psychology* (Vol. 2, pp. 81–97). New York, NY: Oxford University Press. doi: 10.1093/oxfordhb/9780199958474.013.0004

Li, Jin; Fung, Heidi; Bakeman, Roger; Rae, Katharine & Wei, Wanchun. (2014). How European American and Taiwanese mothers talk to their children about learning. *Child Development*, *85*(3), 1206–1221. doi: 10.1111/cdev.12172

Li, Weilin; Farkas, George; Duncan, Greg J.; Burchinal, Margaret R. & Vandell, Deborah Lowe. (2013). Timing of high-quality child care and cognitive, language, and preacademic development. *Developmental Psychology*, *49*(8), 1440–1451. doi: 10.1037/a0030613

Li, Yibing & Lerner, Richard M. (2011). Trajectories of school engagement during adolescence: Implications for grades, depression, delinquency, and substance use. *Developmental Psychology*, *47*(1), 233–247. doi: 10.1037/a0021307

Liben, Lynn S. (2016). We've come a long way, baby (but we're not there yet): Gender past, present, and future. *Child Development*, *87*(1), 5–28. doi: 10.1111/cdev.12490

Libertus, Klaus & Needham, Amy. (2010). Teach to reach: The effects of active vs. passive reaching experiences on action and perception. *Vision Research*, *50*(24), 2750–2757. doi: 10.1016/j.visres.2010.09.001

Libertus, Melissa E.; Feigenson, Lisa & Halberda, Justin. (2013). Is approximate number precision a stable predictor of math ability? *Learning and Individual Differences*, *25*, 126–133. doi: 10.1016/j.lindif.2013.02.001

Liew, Jeffrey. (2012). Effortful control, executive functions, and education: Bringing self-regulatory and social-emotional competencies to the table. *Child Development Perspectives, 6*(2), 105–111. doi: 10.1111/j.1750-8606.2011.00196.x

Lillard, Angeline S. (2013). Playful learning and Montessori education. *American Journal of Play, 5*(2), 157–186.

Lillard, Angeline S.; Lerner, Matthew D.; Hopkins, Emily J.; Dore, Rebecca A.; Smith, Eric D. & Palmquist, Carolyn M. (2013). The impact of pretend play on children's development: A review of the evidence. *Psychological Bulletin, 139*(1), 1–34. doi: 10.1037/a0029321

Lillevoll, Kjersti R.; Kroger, Jane & Martinussen, Monica. (2013). Identity status and locus of control: A meta-analysis. *Identity, 13*(3), 253–265. doi: 10.1080/15283488.2013.799471

Lim, Cher Ping; Zhao, Yong; Tondeur, Jo; Chai, Ching Sing & Tsai, Chin-Chung. (2013). Bridging the gap: Technology trends and use of technology in schools. *Educational Technology & Society, 16*(2), 59–68.

Lin, Alex R. (2014). Examining students' perception of classroom openness as a predictor of civic knowledge: A cross-national analysis of 38 countries. *Applied Developmental Science, 18*(1), 17–30. doi: 10.1080/10888691.2014.864204

Lin, Phoebe. (2016). Risky behaviors: Integrating adolescent egocentrism with the theory of planned behavior. *Review of General Psychology, 20*(4), 392–398. doi: 10.1037/gpr0000086

Lindberg, Laura Duberstein; Maddow-Zimet, Isaac & Boonstra, Heather. (2016). Changes in adolescents' receipt of sex education, 2006–2013. *Journal of Adolescent Health, 58*(6), 621–627. doi: 10.1016/j.jadohealth.2016.02.004

Lipina, Sebastián J. & Evers, Kathinka. (2017). Neuroscience of childhood poverty: Evidence of impacts and mechanisms as vehicles of dialog with ethics. *Frontiers in Psychology, 8*(61). doi: 10.3389/fpsyg.2017.00061

Liu, Dong & Xin, Ziqiang. (2014). Birth cohort and age changes in the self-esteem of Chinese adolescents: A cross-temporal meta-analysis, 1996–2009. *Journal of Research on Adolescence.* doi: 10.1111/jora.12134

Livas-Dlott, Alejandra; Fuller, Bruce; Stein, Gabriela L.; Bridges, Margaret; Mangual Figueroa, Ariana & Mireles, Laurie. (2010). Commands, competence, and *cariño*: Maternal socialization practices in Mexican American families. *Developmental Psychology, 46*(3), 566–578. doi: 10.1037/a0018016

Lobstein, Tim & Dibb, Sue. (2005). Evidence of a possible link between obesogenic food advertising and child overweight. *Obesity Reviews, 6*(3), 203–208. doi: 10.1111/j.1467-789X.2005.00191.x

LoBue, Vanessa. (2013). What are we so afraid of? How early attention shapes our most common fears. *Child Development Perspectives, 7*(1), 38–42. doi: 10.1111/cdep.12012

Lock, Margaret. (2013). The lure of the epigenome. *The Lancet, 381*(9881), 1896–1897. doi: 10.1016/S0140-6736(13)61149-6

Loeber, Rolf & Burke, Jeffrey D. (2011). Developmental pathways in juvenile externalizing and internalizing problems. *Journal of Research on Adolescence, 21*(1), 34–46. doi: 10.1111/j.1532-7795.2010.00713.x

Loeber, Rolf; Capaldi, Deborah M. & Costello, Elizabeth. (2013). Gender and the development of aggression, disruptive behavior, and delinquency from childhood to early adulthood. In Patrick H. Tolan & Bennett L. Leventh (Eds.), *Disruptive behavior disorders* (pp. 137–160). New York, NY: Springer. doi: 10.1007/978-1-4614-7557-6_6

Loftus, Patricia A. & Wise, Sarah K. (2016). Epidemiology of asthma. *Current Opinion in Otolaryngology & Head & Neck Surgery, 24*(3), 245–249. doi: 10.1097/MOO.0000000000000262

Longo, Lawrence D. (2013). *The rise of fetal and neonatal physiology: Basic science to clinical care.* New York, NY: Springer.

Lopez, Anna B.; Huynh, Virginia W. & Fuligni, Andrew J. (2011). A longitudinal study of religious identity and participation during adolescence. *Child Development, 82*(4), 1297–1309. doi: 10.1111/j.1467-8624.2011.01609.x

Lubienski, Christopher; Puckett, Tiffany & Brewer, T. Jameson. (2013). Does homeschooling "work"? A critique of the empirical claims and agenda of advocacy organizations. *Peabody Journal of Education, 88*(3), 378–392. doi: 10.1080/0161956X.2013.798516

Luecken, Linda J.; Lin, Betty; Coburn, Shayna S.; MacKinnon, David P.; Gonzales, Nancy A. & Crnic, Keith A. (2013). Prenatal stress, partner support, and infant cortisol reactivity in low-income Mexican American families. *Psychoneuroendocrinology, 38*(12), 3092–3101. doi: 10.1016/j.psyneuen.2013.09.006

Luna, Beatriz; Paulsen, David J.; Padmanabhan, Aarthi & Geier, Charles. (2013). The teenage brain: Cognitive control and motivation. *Current Directions in Psychological Science, 22*(2), 94–100. doi: 10.1177/0963721413478416

Lundahl, Alyssa; Kidwell, Katherine M. & Nelson, Timothy D. (2014). Parental underestimates of child weight: A meta-analysis. *Pediatrics, 133*(3), e689–e703. doi: 10.1542/peds.2013-2690

Lundberg, Shelly; Pollak, Robert A. & Stearns, Jenna. (2016). Family inequality: Diverging patterns in marriage, cohabitation, and childbearing. *Journal of Economic Perspectives, 30*(2), 79–102. doi: 10.1257/jep.30.2.79

Luo, Rufan; Tamis-LeMonda, Catherine S.; Kuchirko, Yana; Ng, Florrie F. & Liang, Eva. (2014). Mother–child book-sharing and children's storytelling skills in ethnically diverse, low-income families. *Infant and Child Development, 23*(4), 402–425. doi: 10.1002/icd.1841

Lupski, James R. (2013). Genome mosaicism: One human, multiple genomes. *Science, 341*(6144), 358–359. doi: 10.1126/science.1239503

Lushin, Viktor; Jaccard, James & Kaploun, Victor. (2017). Parental monitoring, adolescent dishonesty and underage drinking: A nationally representative study. *Journal of Adolescence, 57*, 99–107. doi: 10.1016/j.adolescence.2017.04.003

Luthar, Suniya S. & Barkin, Samuel H. (2012). Are affluent youth truly "at risk"? Vulnerability and resilience across three diverse samples. *Development and Psychopathology, 24*(2), 429–449. doi: 10.1017/S0954579412000089

Luthar, Suniya S.; Cicchetti, Dante & Becker, Bronwyn. (2000). The construct of resilience: A critical evaluation and guidelines for future work. *Child Development, 71*(3), 543–562. doi: 10.1111/1467-8624.00164

Luthar, Suniya S. & Eisenberg, Nancy. (2017). Resilient adaptation among at-risk children: Harnessing science toward maximizing salutary environments. *Child Development, 88*(2), 337–349. doi: 10.1111/cdev.12737

Lyall, Donald M.; Inskip, Hazel M.; Mackay, Daniel; Deary, Ian J.; McIntosh, Andrew M.; Hotopf, Matthew, . . . Smith, Daniel J. (2016). Low birth weight and features of neuroticism and mood disorder in 83,545 participants of the UK Biobank cohort. *British Journal of Psychiatry Open, 2*(1), 38–44. doi: 10.1192/bjpo.bp.115.002154

Lynskey, Michael T.; Agrawal, Arpana; Henders, Anjali; Nelson, Elliot C.; Madden, Pamela A. F. & Martin, Nicholas G. (2012). An Australian twin study of cannabis and other illicit drug use and misuse, and other psychopathology. *Twin Research and Human Genetics, 15*(5), 631–641. doi: 10.1017/thg.2012.41

Lyons-Ruth, Karlen; Bronfman, Elisa & Parsons, Elizabeth. (1999). Maternal frightened, frightening, or atypical behavior and disorganized infant attachment patterns. *Monographs of the Society for Research in Child Development, 64*(3), 67–96. doi: 10.1111/1540-5834.00034

Ma-Kellams, Christine; Or, Flora; Baek, Ji Hyun & Kawachi, Ichiro. (2016). Rethinking suicide surveillance: Google search data and self-reported suicidality differentially estimate completed suicide risk. *Clinical Psychological Science, 4*(3), 480–484. doi: 10.1177/2167702615593475

Mac Dougall, Kristin; Beyene, Yewoubdar & Nachtigall, Robert D. (2013). Age shock: Misperceptions of the impact of age on fertility before and after IVF in women who conceived after age 40. *Human Reproduction, 28*(2), 350–356. doi: 10.1093/humrep/des409

MacDorman, Marian F.; Mathews, T. J.; Mohangoo, Ashna D. & Zeitlin, Jennifer. (2014). *International comparisons of infant mortality and related factors: United States and Europe, 2010. National Vital Statistics Reports 63*(5). Hyattsville, MD: National Center for Health Statistics.

MacDorman, Marian F. & Rosenberg, Harry M. (1993). *Trends in infant mortality by cause of death and other characteristics, 1960–88. Vital and Health Statistic 20*(20). Hyattsville, MD: National Center for Health Statistics.

Macgregor, Stuart; Lind, Penelope A.; Bucholz, Kathleen K.; Hansell, Narelle K.; Madden, Pamela A. F.; Richter, Melinda M., . . . Whitfield, John B. (2009). Associations of ADH and ALDH2 gene variation with self report alcohol reactions, consumption and dependence: An integrated analysis. *Human Molecular Genetics, 18*(3), 580–593. doi: 10.1093/hmg/ddn372

Mackenzie, Karen J.; Anderton, Stephen M. & Schwarze, Jürgen. (2014). Viral respiratory tract infections and asthma in early life: Cause and effect? *Clinical & Experimental Allergy*, 44(1), 9–19. doi: 10.1111/cea.12139

MacKenzie, Michael J.; Nicklas, Eric; Brooks-Gunn, Jeanne & Waldfogel, Jane. (2011). Who spanks infants and toddlers? Evidence from the fragile families and child well-being study. *Children and Youth Services Review*, 33(8), 1364–1373. doi: 10.1016/j.childyouth.2011.04.007

Macmillan, Ross & Copher, Ronda. (2005). Families in the life course: Interdependency of roles, role configurations, and pathways. *Journal of Marriage and Family*, 67(4), 858–879. doi: 10.1111/j.1741-3737.2005.00180.x

Macosko, Evan Z. & McCarroll, Steven A. (2013). Our fallen genomes. *Science*, 342(6158), 564–565. doi: 10.1126/science.1246942

MacWhinney, Brian. (2015). Language Development. In Richard M. Lerner (Ed.), *Handbook of child psychology and developmental science* (7th ed., Vol. 2, pp. 296–338). New York, NY: Wiley.

Madden, Mary; Lenhart, Amanda; Duggan, Maeve; Cortesi, Sandra & Gasser, Urs. (2013). *Teens and technology 2013*. Washington, DC: Pew Research Center, Pew Internet & American Life Project.

Mahmoudzadeh, Mahdi; Dehaene-Lambertz, Ghislaine; Fournier, Marc; Kongolo, Guy; Goudjil, Sabrina; Dubois, Jessica, . . . Wallois, Fabrice. (2013). Syllabic discrimination in premature human infants prior to complete formation of cortical layers. *Proceedings of the National Academy of Sciences*, 110(12), 4846–4851. doi: 10.1073/pnas.1212220110

Majdandžić, Mirjana; Möller, Eline L.; de Vente, Wieke; Bögels, Susan M. & van den Boom, Dymphna C. (2013). Fathers' challenging parenting behavior prevents social anxiety development in their 4-year-old children: A longitudinal observational study. *Journal of Abnormal Child Psychology*, 42(2), 301–310. doi: 10.1007/s10802-013-9774-4

Malina, Robert M.; Bouchard, Claude & Bar-Or, Oded. (2004). *Growth, maturation, and physical activity* (2nd ed.). Champaign, IL: Human Kinetics.

Mallett, Christopher A. (2016). The school-to-prison pipeline: A critical review of the punitive paradigm shift. *Child and Adolescent Social Work Journal*, 33(1), 15–24. doi: 10.1007/s10560-015-0397-1

Malloy, Lindsay C.; Shulman, Elizabeth P. & Cauffman, Elizabeth. (2014). Interrogations, confessions, and guilty pleas among serious adolescent offenders. *Law and Human Behavior*, 38(2), 181–193. doi: 10.1037/lhb0000065

Malloy, Michael H. (2009). Impact of cesarean section on intermediate and late preterm births: United States, 2000–2003. *Birth*, 36(1), 26–33. doi: 10.1111/j.1523-536X.2008.00292.x

Malti, Tina; Ongley, Sophia F.; Peplak, Joanna; Chaparro, Maria P.; Buchmann, Marlis; Zuffianò, Antonio & Cui, Lixian. (2016). Children's sympathy, guilt, and moral reasoning in helping, cooperation, and sharing:

A 6-year longitudinal study. *Child Development*, 87(6), 1783–1795. doi: 10.1111/cdev.12632

Mandelbaum, David E. & de la Monte, Suzanne M. (2017). Adverse structural and functional effects of marijuana on the brain: Evidence reviewed. *Pediatric Neurology*, 66, 12–20. doi: 10.1016/j.pediatrneurol.2016.09.004

Mandler, Jean M. & DeLoache, Judy. (2012). The beginnings of conceptual development. In Sabina M. Pauen (Ed.), *Early childhood development and later outcome*. New York, NY: Cambridge University Press.

Mann, Joshua R.; McDermott, Suzanne; Bao, Haikun & Bersabe, Adrian. (2009). Maternal genitourinary infection and risk of cerebral palsy. *Developmental Medicine & Child Neurology*, 51(4), 282–288. doi: 10.1111/j.1469-8749.2008.03226.x

Manning, Wendy D. (2013). Trends in cohabitation: Over twenty years of change, 1987–2010. *Family Profiles*, 13(12). Bowling Green, OH: National Center for Family & Marriage Research.

Manning, Wendy D.; Brown, Susan L. & Payne, Krista K. (2014). Two decades of stability and change in age at first union formation. *Journal of Marriage and Family*, 76(2), 247–260. doi: 10.1111/jomf.12090

Månsson, Johanna & Stjernqvist, Karin. (2014). Children born extremely preterm show significant lower cognitive, language and motor function levels compared with children born at term, as measured by the Bayley-III at 2.5 years. *Acta Paediatrica*, 103(5), 504–511. doi: 10.1111/apa.12585

Mar, Raymond A. (2011). The neural bases of social cognition and story comprehension. *Annual Review of Psychology*, 62, 103–134. doi: 10.1146/annurev-psych-120709-145406

Marazita, John M. & Merriman, William E. (2010). Verifying one's knowledge of a name without retrieving it: A U-shaped relation to vocabulary size in early childhood. *Language Learning and Development*, 7(1), 40–54. doi: 10.1080/15475441.2010.496099

Marcia, James E. (1966). Development and validation of ego-identity status. *Journal of Personality and Social Psychology*, 3(5), 551–558. doi: 10.1037/h0023281

Marcia, James E.; Waterman, Alan S.; Matteson, David R.; Archer, Sally L. & Orlofsky, Jacob L. (1993). *Ego identity: A handbook for psychosocial research*. New York, NY: Springer-Verlag.

Marcus, Gary F. & Rabagliati, Hugh. (2009). Language acquisition, domain specificity, and descent with modification. In John Colombo et al. (Eds.), *Infant pathways to language: Methods, models, and research disorders* (pp. 267–285). New York, NY: Psychology Press.

Maron, Dina Fine. (2015, June 8). Has maternal mortality really doubled in the U.S.? *Scientific American*.

Marschik, Peter B.; Kaufmann, Walter E.; Sigafoos, Jeff; Wolin, Thomas; Zhang, Dajie; Bartl-Pokorny, Katrin D., . . . Johnston, Michael V. (2013). Changing the perspective on early development of Rett syndrome. *Research in Developmental Disabilities*, 34(4), 1236–1239. doi: 10.1016/j.ridd.2013.01.014

Marshall, Eliot. (2014). An experiment in zero parenting. *Science*, 345(6198), 752–754. doi: 10.1126/science.345.6198.752

Martin, Carmel. (2014). *Common Core implementation best practices. New York State Office of the Governor Common Core Implementation Panel*. Washington, DC: Center for American Progress.

Martin, Carol L.; Fabes, Richard; Hanish, Laura; Leonard, Stacie & Dinella, Lisa. (2011). Experienced and expected similarity to same-gender peers: Moving toward a comprehensive model of gender segregation. *Sex Roles*, 65(5/6), 421–434. doi: 10.1007/s11199-011-0029-y

Martin, Joyce A.; Hamilton, Brady E. & Osterman, Michelle J. K. (2016, September). *Births in the United States, 2015. NCHS Data Brief 258*. Hyattsville, MD: National Center for Health Statistics.

Martin, Joyce A.; Hamilton, Brady E.; Osterman, Michelle J. K.; Curtin, Sally C. & Mathews, T. J. (2015). *Births: Final data for 2013. National Vital Statistics Reports* 64(1). Hyattsville, MD: National Center for Health Statistics.

Martin, Joyce A.; Hamilton, Brady E.; Osterman, Michelle J. K.; Driscoll, Anne K. & Mathews, T. J. (2017). *Births: Final data from 2015. National Vital Statistics Reports* 66(1). Hyattsville, MD: National Center for Health Statistics.

Martin-Uzzi, Michele & Duval-Tsioles, Denise. (2013). The experience of remarried couples in blended families. *Journal of Divorce & Remarriage*, 54(1), 43–57. doi: 10.1080/10502556.2012.743828

Martinez, Gladys; Daniels, Kimberly & Chandra, Anjani. (2012, April 12). *Fertility of men and women aged 15–44 years in the United States: National Survey of Family Growth, 2006–2010. National Health Statistics Reports 51*. Washington, DC: U.S. Department of Health And Human Services, Centers for Disease Control and Prevention National Center for Health Statistics.

Martinson, Melissa L. & Reichman, Nancy E. (2016). Socioeconomic inequalities in low birth weight in the United States, the United Kingdom, Canada, and Australia. *American Journal of Public Health*, 106(4), 748–754. doi: 10.2105/AJPH.2015.303007

Mascarelli, Amanda. (2013). Growing up with pesticides. *Science*, 341(6147), 740–741. doi: 10.1126/science.341.6147.740

Mascaro, Jennifer S.; Rentscher, Kelly E.; Hackett, Patrick D.; Mehl, Matthias R. & Rilling, James K. (2017). Child gender influences paternal behavior, language, and brain function. *Behavioral Neuroscience*, 131(3), 262–273. doi: 10.1037/bne0000199

Maski, Kiran P. & Kothare, Sanjeev V. (2013). Sleep deprivation and neurobehavioral functioning in children. *International Journal of Psychophysiology*, 89(2), 259–264. doi: 10.1016/j.ijpsycho.2013.06.019

Maslowsky, Julie; Schulenberg, John E. & Zucker, Robert A. (2014). Influence of conduct problems and depressive symptomatology on adolescent substance use: Developmentally proximal versus distal effects. *Developmental Psychology*, 50(4), 1179–1189. doi: 10.1037/a0035085

Mâsse, Louise C.; Perna, Frank; Agurs-Collins, Tanya & Chriqui, Jamie F. (2013).

Change in school nutrition-related laws from 2003 to 2008: Evidence from the School Nutrition-Environment State Policy Classification System. *American Journal of Public Health, 103*(9), 1597–1603. doi: 10.2105/AJPH.2012.300896

**Masten, Ann S.** (2014). *Ordinary magic: Resilience in development*. New York, NY: Guilford Press.

**Masten, Ann S.; Cutuli, J. J.; Herbers, Janette E.; Hinz, Elizabeth; Obradović, Jelena & Wenzel, Amanda J.** (2014). Academic risk and resilience in the context of homelessness. *Child Development Perspectives, 8*(4), 201–206. doi: 10.1111/cdep.12088

**Mathews, T. J.; Menacker, Fay & MacDorman, Marian F.** (2003). *Infant mortality statistics from the 2001 period linked birth/infant death data set. National Vital Statistics Reports 52*(2). Hyattsville, MD: National Center for Health Statistics.

**Mathison, David J. & Agrawal, Dewesh.** (2010). An update on the epidemiology of pediatric fractures. *Pediatric Emergency Care, 26*(8), 594–603. doi: 10.1097/PEC.0b013e3181eb838d

**Matthews, Karen A.; Jennings, J. Richard; Lee, Laisze & Pardini, Dustin A.** (2017). Bullying and being bullied in childhood are associated with different psychosocial risk factors for poor physical health in men. *Psychological Science, 28*(6), 808–821. doi: 10.1177/0956797617697700

**May, Lillian; Byers-Heinlein, Krista; Gervain, Judit & Werker, Janet F.** (2011). Language and the newborn brain: Does prenatal language experience shape the neonate neural response to speech? *Frontiers in Psychology, 2*, 222. doi: 10.3389/fpsyg.2011.00222

**McAlister, Anna R. & Peterson, Candida C.** (2013). Siblings, theory of mind, and executive functioning in children aged 3–6 years: New longitudinal evidence. *Child Development, 84*(4), 1442–1458. doi: 10.1111/cdev.12043

**McCabe, Sean Esteban; Veliz, Philip; Wilens, Timothy E. & Schulenberg, John E.** (2017). Adolescents' prescription stimulant use and adult functional outcomes: A national prospective study. *Journal of the American Academy of Child and Adolescent Psychiatry, 56*(3), 226–233. e224. doi: 10.1016/j.jaac.2016.12.008

**McCabe, Sean Esteban; West, Brady T.; Teter, Christian J. & Boyd, Carol J.** (2014). Trends in medical use, diversion, and nonmedical use of prescription medications among college students from 2003 to 2013: Connecting the dots. *Addictive Behaviors, 39*(7), 1176–1182. doi: 10.1016/j.addbeh.2014.03.008

**McCabe, Viki.** (2014). *Coming to our senses: Perceiving complexity to avoid catastrophes*. New York, NY: Oxford University Press.

**McCall, Robert B.** (2013). The consequences of early institutionalization: Can institutions be improved? – Should they? *Child and Adolescent Mental Health, 18*(4), 193–201. doi: 10.1111/camh.12025

**McCarthy, Neil & Eberhart, Johann K.** (2014). Gene–ethanol interactions underlying fetal alcohol spectrum disorders. *Cellular and Molecular Life Sciences, 71*(14), 2699–2706. doi: 10.1007/s00018-014-1578-3

**McCartney, Kathleen; Burchinal, Margaret; Clarke-Stewart, Alison; Bub, Kristen L.; Owen, Margaret T. & Belsky, Jay.** (2010). Testing a series of causal propositions relating time in child care to children's externalizing behavior. *Developmental Psychology, 46*(1), 1–17. doi: 10.1037/a0017886

**McClain, Natalie M. & Garrity, Stacy E.** (2011). Sex trafficking and the exploitation of adolescents. *Journal of Obstetric, Gynecologic, & Neonatal Nursing, 40*(2), 243–252. doi: 10.1111/j.1552-6909.2011.01221.x

**McCormick, Cheryl M.; Mathews, Iva Z.; Thomas, Catherine & Waters, Patti.** (2010). Investigations of HPA function and the enduring consequences of stressors in adolescence in animal models. *Brain and Cognition, 72*(1), 73–85. doi: 10.1016/j.bandc.2009.06.003

**McEwen, Bruce S. & Karatsoreos, Ilia N.** (2015). Sleep deprivation and circadian disruption: Stress, allostasis, and allostatic load. *Sleep Medicine Clinics, 10*(1), 1–10. doi: 10.1016/j.jsmc.2014.11.007

**McEwen, Craig A. & McEwen, Bruce S.** (2017). Social structure, adversity, toxic stress, and intergenerational poverty: An early childhood model. *Annual Review of Sociology, 43*, 445–472. doi: 10.1146/annurev-soc-060116-053252

**McFarland, Joel; Hussar, Bill; de Brey, Cristobal; Snyder, Tom; Wang, Xiaolei; Wilkinson-Flicker, Sidney, . . . Hinz, Serena.** (2017, May). *The condition of education 2017*. Washington, DC: National Center for Education Statistics. NCES 2017–144.

**McFarlane, Alexander C. & Van Hooff, Miranda.** (2009). Impact of childhood exposure to a natural disaster on adult mental health: 20-year longitudinal follow-up study. *The British Journal of Psychiatry, 195*(2), 142–148. doi: 10.1192/bjp.bp.108.054270

**McGill, Rebecca K.; Hughes, Diane; Alicea, Stacey & Way, Niobe.** (2012). Academic adjustment across middle school: The role of public regard and parenting. *Developmental Psychology, 48*(4), 1003–1018. doi: 10.1037/a0026006

**McGillion, Michelle; Herbert, Jane S.; Pine, Julian; Vihman, Marilyn; dePaolis, Rory; Keren-Portnoy, Tamar & Matthews, Danielle.** (2017). What paves the way to conventional language? The predictive value of babble, pointing, and socioeconomic status. *Child Development, 88*(1), 156–166. doi: 10.1111/cdev.12671

**McKeever, Pamela M. & Clark, Linda.** (2017). Delayed high school start times later than 8:30 am and impact on graduation rates and attendance rates. *Sleep Health, 3*(2), 119–125. doi: 10.1016/j.sleh.2017.01.002

**McKinney, Lyle & Burridge, Andrea Backscheider.** (2015). Helping or hindering? The effects of loans on community college student persistence. *Research in Higher Education, 56*(4), 299–324. doi: 10.1007/s11162-014-9349-4

**McLaren, Lindsay; Patterson, Steven; Thawer, Salima; Faris, Peter; McNeil, Deborah; Potestio, Melissa & Shwart, Luke.** (2016). Measuring the short-term impact of fluoridation cessation on dental caries in grade 2

children using tooth surface indices. *Community Dentistry and Oral Epidemiology, 44*(3), 274–282. doi: 10.1111/cdoe.12215

**McLaren, Rachel M. & Sillars, Alan.** (2014). Hurtful episodes in parent–adolescent relationships: How accounts and attributions contribute to the difficulty of talking about hurt. *Communication Monographs, 81*(3), 359–385. doi: 10.1080/03637751.2014.933244

**McLeod, Bryce D.; Wood, Jeffrey J. & Weisz, John R.** (2007). Examining the association between parenting and childhood anxiety: A meta-analysis. *Clinical Psychology Review, 27*(2), 155–172. doi: 10.1016/j.cpr.2006.09.002

**McManus, I. Chris; Moore, James; Freegard, Matthew & Rawles, Richard.** (2010). Science in the making: Right hand, left hand. III: Estimating historical rates of left-handedness. *Laterality: Asymmetries of Body, Brain and Cognition, 15*(1/2), 186–208. doi: 10.1080/13576500802565313

**McNeil, Michele & Blad, Evie.** (2014). U.S. comes up short on education equity, federal data indicate. *Education Week, 33*(26), 8.

**McRae, Daphne N.; Muhajarine, Nazeem; Stoll, Kathrin; Mayhew, Maureen; Vedam, Saraswathi; Mpofu, Deborah & Janssen, Patricia A.** (2016). Is model of care associated with infant birth outcomes among vulnerable women? A scoping review of midwifery-led versus physician-led care. *SSM – Population Health, 2*, 182–193. doi: 10.1016/j.ssmph.2016.01.007

**McShane, Kelly E. & Hastings, Paul D.** (2009). The New Friends Vignettes: Measuring parental psychological control that confers risk for anxious adjustment in preschoolers. *International Journal of Behavioral Development, 33*(6), 481–495. doi: 10.1177/0165025409103874

**Meadows, Sara.** (2006). *The child as thinker: The development and acquisition of cognition in childhood* (2nd ed.). New York, NY: Routledge.

**Meczekalski, Blazej; Podfigurna-Stopa, Agnieszka & Katulski, Krzysztof.** (2013). Long-term consequences of anorexia nervosa. *Maturitas, 75*(3), 215–220. doi: 10.1016/j.maturitas.2013.04.014

**Meece, Judith L. & Eccles, Jacquelynne S.** (Eds.). (2010). *Handbook of research on schools, schooling, and human development*. New York, NY: Routledge.

**Meeus, Wim.** (2011). The study of adolescent identity formation 2000–2010: A review of longitudinal research. *Journal of Research on Adolescence, 21*(1), 75–94. doi: 10.1111/j.1532-7795.2010.00716.x

**Mehta, Clare M. & Strough, JoNell.** (2009). Sex segregation in friendships and normative contexts across the life span. *Developmental Review, 29*(3), 201–220. doi: 10.1016/j.dr.2009.06.001

**Meltzoff, Andrew N. & Gopnik, Alison.** (2013). Learning about the mind from evidence: Children's development of intuitive theories of perception and personality. In Simon Baron-Cohen et al. (Eds.), *Understanding other minds: Perspectives from developmental social neuroscience* (3rd ed., pp. 19–34). New York, NY: Oxford University Press. doi: 10.1093/acprof:oso/9780199692972.001.0001

**Menary, Kyle; Collins, Paul F.; Porter, James N.; Muetzel, Ryan; Olson, Elizabeth A.; Kumar, Vipin, . . . Luciana, Monica.** (2013). Associations between cortical thickness and general intelligence in children, adolescents and young adults. *Intelligence, 41*(5), 597–606. doi: 10.1016/j.intell.2013.07.010

**Mendle, Jane; Harden, K. Paige; Brooks-Gunn, Jeanne & Graber, Julia A.** (2010). Development's tortoise and hare: Pubertal timing, pubertal tempo, and depressive symptoms in boys and girls. *Developmental Psychology, 46*(5), 1341–1353. doi: 10.1037/a0020205

**Mendle, Jane; Harden, K. Paige; Brooks-Gunn, Jeanne & Graber, Julia A.** (2012). Peer relationships and depressive symptomatology in boys at puberty. *Developmental Psychology, 48*(2), 429–435. doi: 10.1037/a0026425

**Mennis, Jeremy & Mason, Michael J.** (2012). Social and geographic contexts of adolescent substance use: The moderating effects of age and gender. *Social Networks, 34*(1), 150–157. doi: 10.1016/j.socnet.2010.10.003

**Mercer, Neil & Howe, Christine.** (2012). Explaining the dialogic processes of teaching and learning: The value and potential of sociocultural theory. *Learning, Culture and Social Interaction, 1*(1), 12–21. doi: 10.1016/j.lcsi.2012.03.001

**Merikangas, Kathleen R.; He, Jian-ping; Rapoport, Judith; Vitiello, Benedetto & Olfson, Mark.** (2013). Medication use in US youth with mental disorders. *JAMA Pediatrics, 167*(2), 141–148. doi: 10.1001/jamapediatrics.2013.431

**Merikangas, Kathleen R. & McClair, Vetisha L.** (2012). Epidemiology of substance use disorders. *Human Genetics, 131*(6), 779–789. doi: 10.1007/s00439-012-1168-0

**Mermelshtine, Roni.** (2017). Parent–child learning interactions: A review of the literature on scaffolding. *British Journal of Educational Psychology, 87*(2), 241–254. doi: 10.1111/bjep.12147

**Merriam, Sharan B.** (2009). *Qualitative research: A guide to design and implementation.* San Francisco, CA: Jossey-Bass.

**Mersky, Joshua P.; Topitzes, James & Reynolds, Arthur J.** (2013). Impacts of adverse childhood experiences on health, mental health, and substance use in early adulthood: A cohort study of an urban, minority sample in the U.S. *Child Abuse & Neglect, 37*(11), 917–925. doi: 10.1016/j.chiabu.2013.07.011

**Mertens, Donna M.** (2014). *Research and evaluation in education and psychology* (4th ed.). Thousand Oaks, CA: SAGE.

**Merz, Emily C. & McCall, Robert B.** (2011). Parent ratings of executive functioning in children adopted from psychosocially depriving institutions. *Journal of Child Psychology and Psychiatry, 52*(5), 537–546. doi: 10.1111/j.1469-7610.2010.02335.x

**Messinger, Daniel M.; Ruvolo, Paul; Ekas, Naomi V. & Fogel, Alan.** (2010). Applying machine learning to infant interaction: The development is in the details. *Neural Networks, 23*(8/9), 1004–1016. doi: 10.1016/j.neunet.2010.08.008

**Metcalfe, Lindsay A.; Harvey, Elizabeth A. & Laws, Holly B.** (2013). The longitudinal relation between academic/cognitive skills and externalizing behavior problems in preschool children. *Journal of Educational Psychology, 105*(3), 881–894. doi: 10.1037/a0032624

**Meyer, Madonna Harrington.** (2014). *Grandmothers at work: Juggling families and jobs.* New York, NY: New York University Press.

**Michl, Louisa C.; McLaughlin, Katie A.; Shepherd, Kathrine & Nolen-Hoeksema, Susan.** (2013). Rumination as a mechanism linking stressful life events to symptoms of depression and anxiety: Longitudinal evidence in early adolescents and adults. *Journal of Abnormal Psychology, 122*(2), 339–352. doi: 10.1037/a0031994

**Miech, Richard A.; Johnston, Lloyd D.; O'Malley, Patrick M.; Bachman, Jerald G. & Schulenberg, John E.** (2016). *Monitoring the future, national survey results on drug use, 1975–2015: Volume I, secondary school students.* Ann Arbor, Michigan: Institute for Social Research, The University of Michigan.

**Miech, Richard A.; Johnston, Lloyd D.; O'Malley, Patrick M.; Bachman, Jerald G.; Schulenberg, John E. & Patrick, Megan E.** (2017a). *Monitoring the future, national survey results on drug use, 1975–2016: Volume I, secondary school students.* Ann Arbor, Michigan: Institute for Social Research, The University of Michigan.

**Miech, Richard A.; Patrick, Megan E.; O'Malley, Patrick M. & Johnston, Lloyd D.** (2017b). E-cigarette use as a predictor of cigarette smoking: Results from a 1-year follow-up of a national sample of 12th grade students. *Tobacco Control,* (In Press). doi: 10.1136/tobaccocontrol-2016-053291

**Migliano, Andrea Bamberg & Guillon, Myrtille.** (2012). The effects of mortality, subsistence, and ecology on human adult height and implications for *Homo* evolution. *Current Anthropology, 53*(S6). doi: 10.1086/667694

**Mihailidis, Paul & Viotty, Samantha.** (2017). Spreadable spectacle in digital culture: Civic expression, fake news, and the role of media literacies in "post-fact" society. *American Behavioral Scientist, 61*(4), 441–454. doi: 10.1177/0002764217701217

**Miklowitz, David J. & Cicchetti, Dante (Eds.).** (2010). *Understanding bipolar disorder: A developmental psychopathology perspective.* New York, NY: Guilford Press.

**Miles, Lynden K.** (2009). Who is approachable? *Journal of Experimental Social Psychology, 45*(1), 262–266. doi: 10.1016/j.jesp.2008.08.010

**Milkman, Katherine L.; Chugh, Dolly & Bazerman, Max H.** (2009). How can decision making be improved? *Perspectives on Psychological Science, 4*(4), 379–383. doi: 10.1111/j.1745-6924.2009.01142.x

**Miller, Cindy F.; Martin, Carol Lynn; Fabes, Richard A. & Hanish, Laura D.** (2013). Bringing the cognitive and the social together: How gender detectives and gender enforcers shape children's gender development. In Mahzarin R. Banaji & Susan A. Gelman (Eds.), *Navigating the social world: What infants, children, and other species can teach us* (pp. 306–313). New York, NY: Oxford University Press.

**Miller, Greg.** (2016). Pot and pain. *Science, 354*(6312), 566–568. doi: 10.1126/science.354.6312.566

**Miller, Greg.** (2017). Pioneering study images activity in fetal brains. *Science, 355*(6321), 117–118. doi: 10.1126/science.355.6321.117-b

**Miller, Melissa K.; Dowd, M. Denise; Harrison, Christopher J.; Mollen, Cynthia J.; Selvarangan, Rangaraj & Humiston, Sharon.** (2015). Prevalence of 3 sexually transmitted infections in a pediatric emergency department. *Pediatric Emergency Care, 31*(2), 107–112. doi: 10.1097/PEC.0000000000000284

**Miller, Portia; Votruba-Drzal, Elizabeth; Coley, Rebekah Levine & Koury, Amanda S.** (2014). Immigrant families' use of early childcare: Predictors of care type. *Early Childhood Research Quarterly, 29*(4), 484–498. doi: 10.1016/j.ecresq.2014.05.011

**Miller, Patricia H.** (2011). *Theories of developmental psychology* (5th ed.). New York, NY: Worth Publishers.

**Miller, Patricia Y. & Simon, William.** (1980). The development of sexuality in adolescence. In Joseph Adelson (Ed.), *Handbook of adolescent psychology* (pp. 383–407). New York, NY: Wiley.

**Miller-Cotto, Dana & Byrnes, James P.** (2016). Ethnic/racial identity and academic achievement: A meta-analytic review. *Developmental Review, 41*, 51–70. doi: 10.1016/j.dr.2016.06.003

**Miller-Perrin, Cindy & Wurtele, Sandy K.** (2017). Sex trafficking and the commercial sexual exploitation of children. *Women & Therapy, 40*(1/2), 123–151. doi: 10.1080/02703149.2016.1210963

**Mills-Koonce, W. Roger; Garrett-Peters, Patricia; Barnett, Melissa; Granger, Douglas A.; Blair, Clancy & Cox, Martha J.** (2011). Father contributions to cortisol responses in infancy and toddlerhood. *Developmental Psychology, 47*(2), 388–395. doi: 10.1037/a0021066

**Milosevic, Tijana.** (2015). Cyberbullying in US mainstream media. *Journal of Children and Media, 9*(4), 492–509. doi: 10.1080/17482798.2015.1089300

**Milton, James & Treffers-Daller, Jeanine.** (2013). Vocabulary size revisited: The link between vocabulary size and academic achievement. *Applied Linguistics Review, 4*(1), 151–172. doi: 10.1515/applirev-2013-0007

**Milunsky, Aubrey & Milunsky, Jeff M.** (2016). *Genetic disorders and the fetus: Diagnosis, prevention, and treatment* (7th ed.). Hoboken, NJ: Wiley-Blackwell.

**Minagawa-Kawai, Yasuyo; van der Lely, Heather; Ramus, Franck; Sato, Yutaka; Mazuka, Reiko & Dupoux, Emmanuel.** (2011). Optical brain imaging reveals general auditory and language-specific processing in early infant development. *Cerebral Cortex, 21*(2), 254–261. doi: 10.1093/cercor/bhq082

**Mindell, Jodi A.; Sadeh, Avi; Wiegand, Benjamin; How, Ti Hwei & Goh, Daniel Y. T.** (2010). Cross-cultural differences in infant and toddler sleep. *Sleep Medicine, 11*(3), 274–280. doi: 10.1016/j.sleep.2009.04.012

**Miniño, Arialdi M.; Heron, Melonie P.; Murphy, Sherry L. & Kochanek, Kenneth D.** (2007). *Deaths: Final data for 2004. National Vital Statistics Reports* 55(19). Hyattsville, MD: National Center for Health Statistics.

Mischel, Walter. (2014). *The marshmallow test: Mastering self-control*. New York, NY: Little, Brown and Company.

Mischel, Walter; Ebbesen, Ebbe B. & Raskoff Zeiss, Antonette. (1972). Cognitive and attentional mechanisms in delay of gratification. *Journal of Personality and Social Psychology, 21*(2), 204–218. doi: 10.1037/h0032198

Mishra, Ramesh C.; Singh, Sunita & Dasen, Pierre R. (2009). Geocentric dead reckoning in Sanskrit- and Hindi-medium school children. *Culture & Psychology, 15*(3), 386–408. doi: 10.1177/1354067x09343330

Misra, Dawn P.; Caldwell, Cleopatra; Young, Alford A. & Abelson, Sara. (2010). Do fathers matter? Paternal contributions to birth outcomes and racial disparities. *American Journal of Obstetrics and Gynecology, 202*(2), 99–100. doi: 10.1016/j.ajog.2009.11.031

Missana, Manuela; Rajhans, Purva; Atkinson, Anthony P. & Grossmann, Tobias. (2014). Discrimination of fearful and happy body postures in 8-month-old infants: An event-related potential study. *Frontiers in Human Neuroscience, 8*, 531. doi: 10.3389/fnhum.2014.00531

Mitchell, Edwin A. (2009). SIDS: Past, present and future. *Acta Paediatrica, 98*(11), 1712–1719. doi: 10.1111/j.1651-2227.2009.01503.x

Mitchell, Kimberly J.; Jones, Lisa M.; Finkelhor, David & Wolak, Janis. (2013). Understanding the decline in unwanted online sexual solicitations for U.S. youth 2000–2010: Findings from three Youth Internet Safety Surveys. *Child Abuse & Neglect, 37*(12), 1225–1236. doi: 10.1016/j.chiabu.2013.07.002

Mitchell, Philip B.; Meiser, Bettina; Wilde, Alex; Fullerton, Janice; Donald, Jennifer; Wilhelm, Kay & Schofield, Peter R. (2010). Predictive and diagnostic genetic testing in psychiatry. *Psychiatric Clinics of North America, 33*(1), 225–243. doi: 10.1016/j.psc.2009.10.001

Miyata, Susanne; MacWhinney, Brian; Otomo, Kiyoshi; Sirai, Hidetosi; Oshima-Takane, Yuriko; Hirakawa, Makiko, . . . Itoh, Keiko. (2013). Developmental sentence scoring for Japanese. *First Language, 33*(2), 200–216. doi: 10.1177/0142723713479436

Mize, Krystal D.; Pineda, Melannie; Blau, Alexis K.; Marsh, Kathryn & Jones, Nancy A. (2014). Infant physiological and behavioral responses to a jealousy provoking condition. *Infancy, 19*(3), 338–348. doi: 10.1111/infa.12046

MMWR. (1992). *Youth risk behavior surveillance — United States, 1991. Morbidity and Mortality Weekly Report Surveillance Summaries*. Atlanta, GA: U.S. Department of Health and Human Services, Centers for Disease Control and Prevention.

MMWR. (1995, March 24). *Youth risk behavior surveillance — United States, 1993. Morbidity and Mortality Weekly Report Surveillance Summaries 44*(SS-1). Atlanta, GA: U.S. Department of Health and Human Services, Centers for Disease Control and Prevention.

MMWR. (1996, September 27). *Youth risk behavior surveillance — United States, 1995. Morbidity and Mortality Weekly Report Surveillance Summaries 45*(SS-4). Atlanta, GA: U.S. Department of Health and Human Services, Centers for Disease Control and Prevention.

MMWR. (1998, August 14). *Youth risk behavior surveillance — United States, 1997. Morbidity and Mortality Weekly Report Surveillance Summaries 47*(SS-3). Atlanta, GA: U.S. Department of Health and Human Services, Centers for Disease Control and Prevention.

MMWR. (2000, June 9). *Youth risk behavior surveillance — United States, 1999. Morbidity and Mortality Weekly Report Surveillance Summaries 49*(SS05). Atlanta, GA: U.S. Department of Health and Human Services, Centers for Disease Control and Prevention.

MMWR. (2002, June 28). *Youth risk behavior surveillance — United States, 2001. Morbidity and Mortality Weekly Report Surveillance Summaries 51*(SS04). Atlanta, GA: U.S. Department of Health and Human Services, Centers for Disease Control and Prevention.

MMWR. (2004, May 21). *Youth risk behavior surveillance — United States, 2003. Morbidity and Mortality Weekly Report Surveillance Summaries 53*(SS-2). Atlanta, GA: U.S. Department of Health and Human Services, Centers for Disease Control and Prevention.

MMWR. (2006, June 9). *Youth risk behavior surveillance — United States, 2005. Morbidity and Mortality Weekly Report Surveillance Summaries 55*(SS-5). Atlanta, GA: U.S. Department of Health and Human Services, Centers for Disease Control and Prevention.

MMWR. (2008, January 18). *School-associated student homicides — United States, 1992–2006. Morbidity and Mortality Weekly Report 57*(2), 33–36. Atlanta, GA: U.S. Department of Health and Human Services, Centers for Disease Control and Prevention.

MMWR. (2008, June 6). *Youth risk behavior surveillance — United States, 2007. Morbidity and Mortality Weekly Report Surveillance Summaries 57*(SS04). Atlanta, GA: U.S. Department of Health and Human Services, Centers for Disease Control and Prevention.

MMWR. (2010, June 4). *Youth risk behavior surveillance — United States, 2009. Morbidity and Mortality Weekly Report Surveillance Summaries 59*(SS05). Atlanta, GA: U.S. Department of Health and Human Services, Centers for Disease Control and Prevention.

MMWR. (2012, July 20). *Alcohol Use and Binge Drinking Among Women of Childbearing Age — United States, 2006–2010. Morbidity and Mortality Weekly Report 61*(28), 534–538. Atlanta, GA: U.S. Department of Health and Human Services, Centers for Disease Control and Prevention.

MMWR. (2012, June 8). *Youth risk behavior surveillance — United States, 2011. Morbidity and Mortality Weekly Report 61*(4). Atlanta, GA: U.S. Department of Health and Human Services, Centers for Disease Control and Prevention.

MMWR. (2013, April 5). *Blood lead levels in children aged 1–5 Years — United States, 1999–2010. Morbidity and Mortality Weekly Report 62*(13), 245–248. Atlanta, GA: U.S. Department of Health and Human Services, Centers for Disease Control and Prevention.

MMWR. (2013, May 3). *Progress toward eradication of polio — Worldwide, January 2011–March 2013. Morbidity and Mortality Weekly Report 62*(17), 335–338. Atlanta, GA: Centers for Disease Control and Prevention.

MMWR. (2014, July 25). *Human papillomavirus vaccination coverage among adolescents, 2007–2013, and postlicensure vaccine safety monitoring, 2006–2014 — United States. Morbidity and Mortality Weekly Report 63*(29). Atlanta, GA: U.S. Department of Health and Human Services, Centers for Disease Control and Prevention.

MMWR. (2014, June 13). *Youth risk behavior surveillance — United States, 2013. Morbidity and Mortality Weekly Report 63*(4). Atlanta, GA: U.S. Department of Health and Human Services, Centers for Disease Control and Prevention.

MMWR. (2014, March 7). *Impact of requiring influenza vaccination for children in licensed child care or preschool programs — Connecticut, 2012–13 influenza season. Morbidity and Mortality Weekly Report 63*(9), 181–185. Atlanta, GA: U.S. Department of Health and Human Services, Centers for Disease Control and Prevention.

MMWR. (2014, March 28). *Prevalence of autism spectrum disorder among children aged 8 years — Autism and Developmental Disabilities Monitoring Network, 11 sites, United States, 2010. Morbidity and Mortality Weekly Report 63*(2). Atlanta, GA: U.S. Department of Health and Human Services, Centers for Disease Control and Prevention.

MMWR. (2014, May 2). *QuickStats: Percentage of children aged 6–17 years prescribed medication during the preceding 6 months for emotional or behavioral difficulties, by census region — National Health Interview Survey, United States, 2011–2012. Morbidity and Mortality Weekly Report 63*(17), 389–389. Atlanta, GA: Centers for Disease Control and Prevention.

MMWR. (2014, May 16). *Racial/ethnic disparities in fatal unintentional drowning among persons aged ≤29 years — United States, 1999–2010. Morbidity and Mortality Weekly Report 63*(19), 421–426. Atlanta, GA: U.S. Department of Health and Human Services, Centers for Disease Control and Prevention.

MMWR. (2014, September 5). *Prevalence of smokefree home rules — United States, 1992–1993 and 2010–2011. Morbidity and Mortality Weekly Report 63*(35), 765–769. Atlanta, GA: Department of Health and Human Services, Centers for Disease Control and Prevention.

MMWR. (2016, January 8). *Notifiable diseases and mortality tables. Morbidity and Mortality Weekly Report 64*(52). Atlanta, GA: Centers for Disease Control and Prevention.

MMWR. (2016, June 10). *Youth risk behavior surveillance — United States, 2015. Morbidity and Mortality Weekly Report 65*(6). Atlanta, GA: U.S. Department of Health and Human Services, Centers for Disease Control and Prevention.

MMWR. (2016, October 14). *QuickStats: Gestational weight gain among women with full-term, singleton births, compared with recommendations — 48 states and the District of Columbia, 2015. Morbidity and Mortality Weekly Report 65*(40), 1121. Atlanta, GA: Centers for Disease Control and Prevention. doi: 10.15585/mmwr.mm6540a10

**Moffitt, Terrie E.** (2003). Life-course-persistent and adolescence-limited antisocial behavior: A 10-year research review and a research agenda. In Benjamin B. Lahey et al. (Eds.), *Causes of conduct disorder and juvenile delinquency* (pp. 49–75). New York, NY: Guilford Press.

**Moffitt, Terrie E.; Caspi, Avshalom; Rutter, Michael & Silva, Phil A.** (2001). *Sex differences in antisocial behaviour: Conduct disorder, delinquency, and violence in the Dunedin Longitudinal Study.* New York, NY: Cambridge University Press.

**Mokrova, Irina L.; O'Brien, Marion; Calkins, Susan D.; Leerkes, Esther M. & Marcovitch, Stuart.** (2013). The role of persistence at preschool age in academic skills at kindergarten. *European Journal of Psychology of Education, 28*(4), 1495–1503. doi: 10.1007/s10212-013-0177-2

**Moldavsky, Maria & Sayal, Kapil.** (2013). Knowledge and attitudes about Attention-deficit/hyperactivity disorder (ADHD) and its treatment: The views of children, adolescents, parents, teachers and healthcare professionals. *Current Psychiatry Reports, 15,* 377. doi: 10.1007/s11920-013-0377-0

**Moles, Laura; Manzano, Susana; Fernández, Leonides; Montilla, Antonia; Corzo, Nieves; Ares, Susana, . . . Espinosa-Martos, Irene.** (2015). Bacteriological, biochemical, and immunological properties of colostrum and mature milk from mothers of extremely preterm infants. *Journal of Pediatric Gastroenterology & Nutrition, 60*(1), 120–126. doi: 10.1097/MPG.0000000000000560

**Møller, Signe J. & Tenenbaum, Harriet R.** (2011). Danish majority children's reasoning about exclusion based on gender and ethnicity. *Child Development, 82*(2), 520–532. doi: 10.1111/j.1467-8624.2010.01568.x

**Monahan, Kathryn C.; Steinberg, Laurence & Cauffman, Elizabeth.** (2009). Affiliation with antisocial peers, susceptibility to peer influence, and antisocial behavior during the transition to adulthood. *Developmental Psychology, 45*(6), 1520–1530. doi: 10.1037/a0017417

**Monahan, Kathryn C.; Steinberg, Laurence; Cauffman, Elizabeth & Mulvey, Edward P.** (2013). Psychosocial (im)maturity from adolescence to early adulthood: Distinguishing between adolescence-limited and persisting antisocial behavior. *Development and Psychopathology, 25*(4), 1093–1105. doi: 10.1017/S0954579413000394

**Money, John & Ehrhardt, Anke A.** (1972). *Man & woman, boy & girl: The differentiation and dimorphism of gender identity from conception to maturity.* Baltimore, MD: Johns Hopkins University Press.

**Montgomery, Heather.** (2015). Understanding child prostitution in Thailand in the 1990s. *Child Development Perspectives, 9*(3), 154–157. doi: 10.1111/cdep.12122

**Monthly Vital Statistics Report.** (1980). *Final mortality statistics, 1978: Advance report. Monthly Vital Statistics Report, 29*(6, Suppl. 2). Hyattsville, MD: National Center for Health Statistics.

**Monti, Jennifer D.; Rudolph, Karen D. & Miernicki, Michelle E.** (2017). Rumination about social stress mediates the association between peer victimization and depressive symptoms during middle childhood. *Journal of Applied Developmental Psychology, 48,* 25–32. doi: 10.1016/j.appdev.2016.11.003

**Montirosso, Rosario; Casini, Erica; Provenzi, Livio; Putnam, Samuel P.; Morandi, Francesco; Fedeli, Claudia & Borgatti, Renato.** (2015). A categorical approach to infants' individual differences during the Still-Face paradigm. *Infant Behavior and Development, 38,* 67–76. doi: 10.1016/j.infbeh.2014.12.015

**Montirosso, Rosario; Tronick, Ed & Borgatti, Renato.** (2017). Promoting neuroprotective care in neonatal intensive care units and preterm infant development: Insights from the neonatal adequate care for quality of life study. *Child Development Perspectives, 11*(1), 9–15. doi: 10.1111/cdep.12208

**Monto, Martin A. & Carey, Anna G.** (2014). A new standard of sexual behavior? Are claims associated with the "hookup culture" supported by general social survey data? *The Journal of Sex Research, 51*(6), 605–615. doi: 10.1080/00224499.2014.906031

**Moody, Myles.** (2016). From under-diagnoses to over-representation: Black children, ADHD, and the school-to-prison pipeline. *Journal of African American Studies, 20*(2), 152–163. doi: 10.1007/s12111-016-9325-5

**Moore, Keith L.; Persaud, T. V. N. & Torchia, Mark G.** (2015). *The developing human: Clinically oriented embryology* (10th ed.). Philadelphia, PA: Saunders.

**Moore, Mary Ruth & Sabo-Risley, Constance (Eds.).** (2017). *Play in America: Essays in honor of Joe L. Frost.* Bloomington, IL: Archway Publishing.

**Morales, Michelle; Tangermann, Rudolf H. & Wassilak, Steven G. F.** (2016). *Progress toward polio eradication — Worldwide, 2015–2016. Morbidity and Mortality Weekly Report 65*(18), 470–473. Atlanta, GA: Centers for Disease Control and Prevention.

**Moran, Lyndsey R.; Lengua, Liliana J. & Zalewski, Maureen.** (2013). The interaction between negative emotionality and effortful control in early social-emotional development. *Social Development, 22*(2), 340–362. doi: 10.1111/sode.12025

**Moran, Lauren V.; Masters, Grace A.; Pingali, Samira; Cohen, Bruce M.; Liebson, Elizabeth; Rajarethinam, R. P. & Ongur, Dost.** (2015). Prescription stimulant use is associated with earlier onset of psychosis. *Journal of Psychiatric Research, 71,* 41–47. doi: 10.1016/j.jpsychires.2015.09.012

**Morawska, Alina & Sanders, Matthew.** (2011). Parental use of time out revisited: A useful or harmful parenting strategy? *Journal of Child and Family Studies, 20*(1), 1–8. doi: 10.1007/s10826-010-9371-x

**Morcos, Roy N. & Kizy, Thomas.** (2012). Gynecomastia: When is treatment indicated? *Journal of Family Practice, 61*(12), 719–725.

**Moreno, Sylvain; Lee, Yunjo; Janus, Monika & Bialystok, Ellen.** (2015). Short-term second language and music training induces lasting functional brain changes in early childhood. *Child Development, 86*(2), 394–406. doi: 10.1111/cdev.12297

**Morgan, Ian G.; Ohno-Matsui, Kyoko & Saw, Seang-Mei.** (2012). Myopia. *The Lancet, 379*(9827), 1739–1748. doi: 10.1016/S0140-6736(12)60272-4

**Morón, Cecilio & Viteri, Fernando E.** (2009). Update on common indicators of nutritional status: Food access, food consumption, and biochemical measures of iron and anemia. *Nutrition Reviews, 67*(Suppl. 1), S31–S35. doi: 10.1111/j.1753-4887.2009.00156.x

**Morones, Alyssa.** (2013). Paddling persists in U.S. schools. *Education Week, 33*(9), 1, 10–11.

**Morris, Vivian G. & Morris, Curtis L.** (2013). A call for African American male teachers: The supermen expected to solve the problems of low-performing schools. In Chance W. Lewis & Ivory A. Toldson (Eds.), *Black male teachers: Diversifying the United States' teacher workforce* (pp. 151–165). Bingley, UK: Emerald Group.

**Morrissey, Taryn.** (2009). Multiple child-care arrangements and young children's behavioral outcomes. *Child Development, 80*(1), 59–76. doi: 10.1111/j.1467-8624.2008.01246.x

**Mortimer, Jeylan T.** (2010). The benefits and risks of adolescent employment. *Prevention Researcher, 17*(2), 8–11.

**Mortimer, Jeylan T.** (2013). Work and its positive and negative effects on youth's psychosocial development. In Carol W. Runyan et al. (Eds.), *Health and safety of young workers: Proceedings of a U.S. and Canadian series of symposia* (pp. 66–79). Washington, DC: U.S. Department of Health and Human Services, Centers for Disease Control and Prevention, National Institute for Occupational Safety and Health.

**Mosher, William D.; Jones, Jo & Abma, Joyce C.** (2012). *Intended and unintended births in the United States: 1982–2010. National Health Statistics Reports 55,* 1–27. Hyattsville, MD: U.S. Department of Health and Human Services, Centers for Disease Control and Prevention, National Center for Health Statistics.

**Moshman, David.** (2011). *Adolescent rationality and development: Cognition, morality, and identity* (3rd ed.). New York, NY: Psychology Press.

**Moss, Howard B.; Chen, Chiung M. & Yi, Hsiao-ye.** (2014). Early adolescent patterns of alcohol, cigarettes, and marijuana polysubstance use and young adult substance use outcomes in a nationally representative sample. *Drug & Alcohol Dependence, 136*(Suppl. 1), 51–62. doi: 10.1016/j.drugalcdep.2013.12.011

**Moultrie, Fiona; Goksan, Sezgi; Poorun, Ravi & Slater, Rebeccah.** (2016). Pain in neonates and infants. In Anna A. Battaglia (Ed.), *An introduction to pain and its relation to nervous system disorders* (pp. 283–293). New York, NY: Wiley.

**Mowry, James B.; Spyker, Daniel A.; Brooks, Daniel E.; Mcmillan, Naya & Schauben, Jay L.** (2015). 2014 Annual report of the American Association of Poison Control Centers' National

Poison Data System (NPDS): 32nd Annual report. *Clinical Toxicology*, 53(10), 962–1146. doi: 10.3109/15563650.2015.1102927

**Mozaffarian, Dariush; Benjamin, Emelia J.; Go, Alan S.; Arnett, Donna K.; Blaha, Michael J.; Cushman, Mary, . . . Turner, Melanie B.** (2016). Heart disease and stroke statistics—2016 Update: A report from the American Heart Association. *Circulation*, 133(4), e38–e360. doi: 10.1161/CIR.0000000000000350

**Mrug, Sylvie; Elliott, Marc N.; Davies, Susan; Tortolero, Susan R.; Cuccaro, Paula & Schuster, Mark A.** (2014). Early puberty, negative peer influence, and problem behaviors in adolescent girls. *Pediatrics*, 133(1), 7–14. doi: 10.1542/peds.2013-0628

**Mullally, Sinéad L. & Maguire, Eleanor A.** (2014). Learning to remember: The early ontogeny of episodic memory. *Developmental Cognitive Neuroscience*, 9(13), 12–29. doi: 10.1016/j.dcn.2013.12.006

**Mulligan, Aisling; Anney, Richard; Butler, L.; O'Regan, M.; Richardson, T.; Tulewicz, E. M., . . . Gill, Michael.** (2013). Home environment: Association with hyperactivity/impulsivity in children with ADHD and their non-ADHD siblings. *Child: Care, Health & Development*, 39(2), 202–212. doi: 10.1111/j.1365-2214.2011.01345.x

**Mullis, Ina V. S.; Martin, Michael O.; Foy, Pierre & Arora, A.** (2012a). *TIMSS 2011 International results in mathematics*. Chestnut Hill, MA: TIMSS & PIRLS International Study Center, Boston College.

**Mullis, Ina V. S.; Martin, Michael O.; Foy, Pierre & Drucker, Kathleen T.** (2012b). *PIRLS 2011 international results in reading*. Chestnut Hill, MA: TIMSS & PIRLS International Study Center, Boston College.

**Mullis, Ina V. S.; Martin, Michael O.; Foy, Pierre & Hooper, Martin.** (2016). *TIMSS 2015 International results in mathematics*. Chestnut Hill, MA: TIMSS & PIRLS International Study Center, Boston College.

**Mullis, Ina V. S.; Martin, Michael O.; Kennedy, Ann M. & Foy, Pierre.** (2007). International student achievement in reading. In, *IEA's progress in international reading literacy study in primary school in 40 countries* (pp. 35–64). Chestnut Hill, MA: TIMSS & PIRLS International Study Center, Boston College.

**Munson, Michelle R.; Lee, Bethany R.; Miller, David; Cole, Andrea & Nedelcu, Cristina.** (2013). Emerging adulthood among former system youth: The ideal versus the real. *Children and Youth Services Review*, 35(6), 923–929. doi: 10.1016/j.childyouth.2013.03.003

**Muris, Peter & Meesters, Cor.** (2014). Small or big in the eyes of the other: On the developmental psychopathology of self-conscious emotions as shame, guilt, and pride. *Clinical Child and Family Psychology Review*, 17(1), 19–40. doi: 10.1007/s10567-013-0137-z

**Murphy, Sherry L.; Kochanek, Kenneth D.; Xu, Jiaquan & Arias, Elizabeth.** (2015, December). *Mortality in the United States, 2014. NCHS Data Brief* (229). Hyattsville, MD: National Center for Health Statistics.

**Murphy, Sherry L.; Xu, Jiaquan & Kochanek, Kenneth D.** (2012). *Deaths: Preliminary data for 2010. National Vital Statistics Reports* 60(4). Hyattsville, MD: National Center for Health Statistics.

**Murray, Thomas H.** (2014). Stirring the simmering "designer baby" pot. *Science*, 343(6176), 1208–1210. doi: 10.1126/science.1248080

**Mustanski, Brian; Birkett, Michelle; Greene, George J.; Hatzenbuehler, Mark L. & Newcomb, Michael E.** (2014). Envisioning an America without sexual orientation inequities in adolescent health. *American Journal of Public Health*, 104(2), 218–225. doi: 10.2105/AJPH.2013.301625

**Næss, Kari-Anne B.** (2016). Development of phonological awareness in Down syndrome: A meta-analysis and empirical study. *Developmental Psychology*, 52(2), 177–190. doi: 10.1037/a0039840

**NAEYC.** (2014). *NAEYC Early Childhood Program Standards and Accreditation Criteria & Guidance for Assessment*. Washington, DC: National Association for the Education of Young Children.

**Nanji, Ayaz.** (2005, February 8). World's smallest baby goes home. *CBS News*. http://www.cbsnews.com/stories/2005/02/08/health/main672488.shtml

**Narayan, Chandan R.; Werker, Janet F. & Beddor, Patrice Speeter.** (2010). The interaction between acoustic salience and language experience in developmental speech perception: Evidence from nasal place discrimination. *Developmental Science*, 13(3), 407–420. doi: 10.1111/j.1467-7687.2009.00898.x

**National Center for Education Statistics.** (2013a). *The Nation's report card: A first look: 2013 mathematics and reading*. Washington, DC: Institute of Education Sciences, U.S. Department of Education.

**National Center for Education Statistics.** (2013b). *Table 204.30: Children 3 to 21 years old served under Individuals with Disabilities Education Act (IDEA), Part B, by type of disability: Selected years, 1976–77 through 2011–12. Digest of Education Statistics*. Washington, DC: Institute of Education Sciences, U.S. Department of Education.

**National Center for Education Statistics.** (2013c). *Annual diploma counts and the Averaged Freshmen Graduation Rate (AFGR) in the United States by race/ethnicity: School years 2007–08 through 2011–12. Common Core Data*. Washington, DC: U.S. Department of Education, Institute of Education Sciences, National Center for Education Statistics.

**National Center for Education Statistics.** (2015). The nation's report card 2015: Mathematics and reading. https://www.nationsreportcard.gov/reading_math_2015

**National Center for Health Statistics.** (2014). *Health, United States, 2013: With special feature on prescription drugs*. Hyattsville, MD: U.S. Department of Health and Human Services, Centers for Disease Control and Prevention.

**National Center for Health Statistics.** (2015). *Health, United States, 2014: With a special feature on adults aged 55–64*. Hyattsville, MD: U.S. Department of Health and Human Services, Centers for Disease Control and Prevention.

**National Center for Health Statistics.** (2016). *Health, United States, 2015: With a special feature on racial and ethnic health disparities*. Hyattsville, MD: U.S. Department of Health and Human Services, Centers for Disease Control and Prevention.

**National Governors Association Center for Best Practices (NGA Center) and the Council of Chief State School Officers (CCSSO).** (2010, October 25). *Common Core state standards initiative*. Washington, DC: National Governors Association.

**Naughton, Michelle J.; Yi-Frazier, Joyce P.; Morgan, Timothy M.; Seid, Michael; Lawrence, Jean M.; Klingensmith, Georgeanna J., . . . Loots, Beth.** (2014). Longitudinal associations between sex, diabetes self-care, and health-related quality of life among youth with type 1 or type 2 diabetes mellitus. *The Journal of Pediatrics*, 164(6), 1376–1383.e1371. doi: 10.1016/j.jpeds.2014.01.027

**Neale, Joanne; Bradford, Julia & Strang, John.** (2017). Development of a proto-typology of opiate overdose onset. *Addiction*, 112(1), 168–175. doi: 10.1111/add.13589

**Neary, Karen R. & Friedman, Ori.** (2014). Young children give priority to ownership when judging who should use an object. *Child Development*, 85(1), 326–337. doi: 10.1111/cdev.12120

**Neary, Marianne T. & Breckenridge, Ross A.** (2013). Hypoxia at the heart of sudden infant death syndrome? *Pediatric Research*, 74(4), 375–379. doi: 10.1038/pr.2013.122

**Needleman, Herbert L. & Gatsonis, Constantine A.** (1990). Low-level lead exposure and the IQ of children: A meta-analysis of modern studies. *JAMA*, 263(5), 673–678. doi: 10.1001/jama.1990.03440050067035

**Needleman, Herbert L.; Schell, Alan; Bellinger, David; Leviton, Alan & Allred, Elizabeth N.** (1990). The long-term effects of exposure to low doses of lead in childhood. *New England Journal of Medicine*, 322(2), 83–88. doi: 10.1056/NEJM199001113220203

**Neggers, Yasmin & Crowe, Kristi.** (2013). Low birth weight outcomes: Why better in Cuba than Alabama? *Journal of the American Board of Family Medicine*, 26(2), 187–195. doi: 10.3122/jabfm.2013.02.120227

**Nel, Andre E. & Malloy, Timothy F.** (2017). Policy reforms to update chemical safety testing. *Science*, 355(6329), 1016–1018. doi: 10.1126/science.aak9919

**Nelson, Charles A.; Fox, Nathan A. & Zeanah, Charles H.** (2014). *Romania's abandoned children: Deprivation, brain development, and the struggle for recovery*. Cambridge, MA: Harvard University Press.

**Nelson, Eric E.; Jarcho, Johanna M. & Guyer, Amanda E.** (2016). Social re-orientation and brain development: An expanded and updated view. *Developmental Cognitive Neuroscience*, 17, 118–127. doi: 10.1016/j.dcn.2015.12.008

**Nelson, Geoffrey & Caplan, Rachel.** (2014). The prevention of child physical abuse and neglect: An update. *Journal of Applied Research on Children: Informing Policy for Children at Risk*, 5(1).

**Nevanen, Saila; Juvonen, Antti & Ruismäki, Heikki.** (2014). Does arts education develop school readiness? Teachers' and artists' points of view on an art education project. *Arts Education Policy Review, 115*(3), 72–81. doi: 10.1080/10632913.2014.913970

**Neville, Helen A.; Gallardo, Miguel E. & Sue, Derald Wing (Eds.).** (2016). *The myth of racial color blindness: Manifestations, dynamics, and impact.* Washington, DC: American Psychological Association.

**Nevin, Rick.** (2007). Understanding international crime trends: The legacy of preschool lead exposure. *Environmental Research, 104*(3), 315–336. doi: 10.1016/j.envres.2007.02.008

**Newnham, Carol A.; Milgrom, Jeannette & Skouteris, Helen.** (2009). Effectiveness of a modified mother-infant transaction program on outcomes for preterm infants from 3 to 24 months of age. *Infant Behavior and Development, 32*(1), 17–26. doi: 10.1016/j.infbeh.2008.09.004

**Ng, Florrie Fei-Yin; Pomerantz, Eva M. & Deng, Ciping.** (2014). Why are Chinese mothers more controlling than American mothers? "My child is my report card". *Child Development, 85*(1), 355–369. doi: 10.1111/cdev.12102

**Ng, Marie; Fleming, Tom; Robinson, Margaret; Thomson, Blake; Graetz, Nicholas; Margono, Christopher, . . . Gakidou, Emmanuela.** (2014). Global, regional, and national prevalence of overweight and obesity in children and adults during 1980—2013: A systematic analysis for the Global Burden of Disease Study 2013. *The Lancet, 384*(9945), 766–781. doi: 10.1016/S0140-6736(14)60460-8

**Ngui, Emmanuel; Cortright, Alicia & Blair, Kathleen.** (2009). An investigation of paternity status and other factors associated with racial and ethnic disparities in birth outcomes in Milwaukee, Wisconsin. *Maternal and Child Health Journal, 13*(4), 467–478. doi: 10.1007/s10995-008-0383-8

**Nguyen, Jacqueline; O'Brien, Casey & Schapp. Salena.** (2016). Adolescent inhalant use prevention, assessment, and treatment: A literature synthesis. *Drug Policy, 31*, 15–24. doi: 10.1016/j.drugpo.2016.02.001

**Niakan, Kathy K.; Han, Jinnuo; Pedersen, Roger A.; Simon, Carlos & Reijo Pera, Renee A.** (2012). Human pre-implantation embryo development. *Development, 139*, 829–841. doi: 10.1242/dev.060426

**Nic Gabhainn, Saoirse; Baban, Adriana; Boyce, William & Godeau, Emmanuelle.** (2009). How well protected are sexually active 15-year olds? Cross-national patterns in condom and contraceptive pill use 2002–2006. *International Journal of Public Health, 54*(Suppl. 2), 209–215. doi: 10.1007/s00038-009-5412-x

**Niclasen, Janni; Andersen, Anne-Marie N.; Strandberg-Larsen, Katrine & Teasdale, Thomas W.** (2014). Is alcohol binge drinking in early and late pregnancy associated with behavioural and emotional development at age 7 years? *European Child & Adolescent Psychiatry, 23*(12), 1175–1180. doi: 10.1007/s00787-013-0511-x

**Niedzwiedz, Claire; Haw, Camilla; Hawton, Keith & Platt, Stephen.** (2014). The definition and epidemiology of clusters of suicidal behavior: A systematic review. *Suicide and Life-Threatening Behavior, 44*(5), 569–581. doi: 10.1111/sltb.12091

**Nielsen, Mark & Tomaselli, Keyan.** (2010). Overimitation in Kalahari Bushman children and the origins of human cultural cognition. *Psychological Science, 21*(5), 729–736. doi: 10.1177/0956797610368808

**Nielsen, Mark; Tomaselli, Keyan; Mushin, Ilana & Whiten, Andrew.** (2014). Exploring tool innovation: A comparison of Western and Bushman children. *Journal of Experimental Child Psychology, 126*, 384–394. doi: 10.1016/j.jecp.2014.05.008

**Nieto, Sonia.** (2000). *Affirming diversity: The sociopolitical context of multicultural education* (3rd ed.). New York, NY: Longman.

**Nigg, Joel T. & Barkley, Russell A.** (2014). Attention-deficit/hyperactivity disorder. In Eric J. Mash & Russell A. Barkley (Eds.), *Child psychopathology* (3rd ed., pp. 75–144). New York, NY: Guilford Press.

**Nikitin, Dmitriy; Timberlake, David S. & Williams, Rebecca S.** (2016). Is the e-liquid industry regulating itself? A look at e-liquid Internet vendors in the United States. *Nicotine & Tobacco Research, 18*(10), 1967–1972. doi: 10.1093/ntr/ntw091

**Nilsson, Kristine Kahr & de López, Kristine Jensen.** (2016). Theory of mind in children with specific language impairment: A systematic review and meta-analysis. *Child Development, 87*(1), 143–153. doi: 10.1111/cdev.12462

**Noll, Jennie G.; Trickett, Penelope K.; Long, Jeffrey D.; Negriff, Sonya; Susman, Elizabeth J.; Shalev, Idan, . . . Putnam, Frank W.** (2017). Childhood sexual abuse and early timing of puberty. *Journal of Adolescent Health, 60*(1), 65–71. doi: 10.1016/j.jadohealth.2016.09.008

**O'Brien, Beth A.; Wolf, Maryanne & Lovett, Maureen W.** (2012). A taxometric investigation of developmental dyslexia subtypes. *Dyslexia, 18*(1), 16–39. doi: 10.1002/dys.1431

**O'Leary, Colleen M.; Nassar, Natasha; Zubrick, Stephen R.; Kurinczuk, Jennifer J.; Stanley, Fiona & Bower, Carol.** (2010). Evidence of a complex association between dose, pattern and timing of prenatal alcohol exposure and child behaviour problems. *Addiction, 105*(1), 74–86. doi: 10.1111/j.1360-0443.2009.02756.x

**O'Dougherty, Maureen.** (2013). Becoming a mother through postpartum depression: Narratives from Brazil. In Charlotte Faircloth et al. (Eds.), *Parenting in global perspective: Negotiating ideologies of kinship, self and politics* (pp. 184–199). New York, NY: Routledge.

**Oakes, J. Michael.** (2009). The effect of media on children: A methodological assessment from a social epidemiologist. *American Behavioral Scientist, 52*(8), 1136–1151. doi: 10.1177/0002764209331538

**Obradović, Jelena.** (2012). How can the study of physiological reactivity contribute to our understanding of adversity and resilience processes in development? *Development and Psychopathology, 24*(2), 371–387. doi: 10.1017/S0954579412000053

**OECD.** (2010). *PISA 2009 results: Learning to learn: Student engagement, strategies and practices* (Vol. 3): PISA, OECD Publishing. doi: 10.1787/9789264083943-en

**OECD.** (2011). *Education at a glance 2011: OECD indicators.* Paris, France: Organisation for Economic Cooperation and Development. doi: 10.1787/eag-2011-en

**OECD.** (2013). *Education at a glance 2013: OECD indicators.* Paris, France: Organisation for Economic Cooperation and Development. doi: 10.1787/19991487

**OECD.** (2014). *Education at a glance 2014: OECD Indicators.* Paris, France: Organisation for Economic Cooperation and Development. doi: 10.1787/eag-2014-en

**OECD.** (2017). *Obesity update.* Paris, France: Organisation for Economic Cooperation and Development.

**OECD.Stat.** (2017). *Income distribution and poverty.* OECD Income Distribution Database. Retrieved from: http://stats.oecd.org/index.aspx?queryid=66670

**Oesterdiekhoff, Georg W.** (2014). The role of developmental psychology to understanding history, culture and social change. *Journal of Social Sciences, 10*(4), 185–195. doi: 10.3844/jssp.2014.185.195

**Ogden, Cynthia L.; Carroll, Margaret D.; Kit, Brian K. & Flegal, Katherine M.** (2014). Prevalence of childhood and adult obesity in the United States, 2011–2012. *JAMA, 311*(8), 806–814. doi: 10.1001/jama.2014.732

**Ogden, Cynthia L.; Gorber, Sarah C.; Dommarco, Juan A. Rivera; Carroll, Margaret; Shields, Margot & Flegal, Katherine.** (2011). The epidemiology of childhood obesity in Canada, Mexico and the United States. In Luis A. Moreno et al. (Eds.), *Epidemiology of obesity in children and adolescents* (Vol. 2, pp. 69–93). New York, NY: Springer. doi: 10.1007/978-1-4419-6039-9_5

**Olfson, Mark; Crystal, Stephen; Huang, Cecilia & Gerhard, Tobias.** (2010). Trends in antipsychotic drug use by very young, privately insured children. *Journal of the American Academy of Child and Adolescent Psychiatry, 49*(1), 13–23. doi: 10.1016/j.jaac.2009.09.003

**Olson, Kristina R. & Dweck, Carol S.** (2009). Social cognitive development: A new look. *Child Development Perspectives, 3*(1), 60–65. doi: 10.1111/j.1750-8606.2008.00078.x

**Olson, Sheryl L.; Lopez-Duran, Nestor; Lunkenheimer, Erika S.; Chang, Hyein & Sameroff, Arnold J.** (2011). Individual differences in the development of early peer aggression: Integrating contributions of self-regulation, theory of mind, and parenting. *Development and Psychopathology, 23*(1), 253–266. doi: 10.1017/S0954579410000775

**Olweus, Dan.** (1999). Sweden. In Peter K. Smith et al. (Eds.), *The nature of school bullying: A cross-national perspective* (pp. 7–27). New York, NY: Routledge.

**Open Science Collaboration.** (2015). Estimating the reproducibility of psychological science. *Science, 349*(6251), 943. doi: 10.1126/science.aac4716

**Osgood, D. Wayne; Ragan, Daniel T.; Wallace, Lacey; Gest, Scott D.; Feinberg,**

Mark E. & Moody, James. (2013). Peers and the emergence of alcohol use: Influence and selection processes in adolescent friendship networks. *Journal of Research on Adolescence*, 23(3), 500–512. doi: 10.1111/jora.12059

Osher, David; Bear, George G.; Sprague, Jeffrey R. & Doyle, Walter. (2010). How can we improve school discipline? *Educational Researcher*, 39(1), 48–58. doi: 10.3102/0013189X09357618

Osilla, Karen Chan; Miles, Jeremy N. V.; Hunter, Sarah B. & Amico, Elizabeth J. D. (2015). The longitudinal relationship between employment and substance use among at-risk adolescents. *Journal of Child & Adolescent Behavior Genetics*, 3(3). doi: 10.4172/2375-4494.1000202

Ostfeld, Barbara M.; Esposito, Linda; Perl, Harold & Hegyi, Thomas. (2010). Concurrent risks in sudden infant death syndrome. *Pediatrics*, 125(3), 447–453. doi: 10.1542/peds.2009-0038

Ostrov, Jamie M.; Kamper, Kimberly E.; Hart, Emily J.; Godleski, Stephanie A. & Blakely-McClure, Sarah J. (2014). A gender-balanced approach to the study of peer victimization and aggression subtypes in early childhood. *Development and Psychopathology*, 26(3), 575–587. doi: 10.1017/S0954579414000248

Over, Harriet & Gattis, Merideth. (2010). Verbal imitation is based on intention understanding. *Cognitive Development*, 25(1), 46–55. doi: 10.1016/j.cogdev.2009.06.004

Padilla-Walker, Laura M. & Nelson, Larry J. (Eds.). (2017). *Flourishing in emerging adulthood: Positive development during the third decade of life.* New York, NY: Oxford University Press.

Pahlke, Erin & Hyde, Janet Shibley. (2016). The debate over single-sex schooling. *Child Development Perspectives*, 10(2), 81–86. doi: 10.1111/cdep.12167

Pahlke, Erin; Hyde, Janet Shibley & Allison, Carlie M. (2014). The effects of single-sex compared with coeducational schooling on students' performance and attitudes: A meta-analysis. *Psychological Bulletin*, 140(4), 1042–1072. doi: 10.1037/a0035740

Paik, Anthony. (2011). Adolescent sexuality and the risk of marital dissolution. *Journal of Marriage and Family*, 73(2), 472–485. doi: 10.1111/j.1741-3737.2010.00819.x

Palacios, Natalia & Kibler, Amanda. (2016). Oral English language proficiency and reading mastery: The role of home language and school supports. *The Journal of Educational Research*, 109(2), 122–136. doi: 10.1080/00220671.2014.927341

Palagi, Elisabetta. (2011). Playing at every age: Modalities and potential functions in non-human primates. In Anthony D. Pellegrini (Ed.), *The Oxford handbook of the development of play* (pp. 70–82). New York, NY: Oxford University Press. doi: 10.1093/oxfordhb/9780195393002.013.0007

Pankow, James F.; Kim, Kilsun; McWhirter, Kevin J.; Luo, Wentai; Escobedo, Jorge O.; Strongin, Robert M., . . . Peyton, David H. (2017). Benzene formation in electronic cigarettes. *PLoS ONE*, 12(3), e0173055. doi: 10.1371/journal.pone.0173055

Panksepp. Jaak & Watt, Douglas. (2011). What is basic about basic emotions? Lasting lessons from affective neuroscience. *Emotion Review*, 3(4), 387–396. doi: 10.1177/1754073911410741

Papandreou, Maria. (2014). Communicating and thinking through drawing activity in early childhood. *Journal of Research in Childhood Education*, 28(1), 85–100. doi: 10.1080/02568543.2013.851131

Papapetrou, Eirini P. (2016). Induced pluripotent stem cells, past and future. *Science*, 353(6303), 991–992. doi: 10.1126/science.aai7626

Paradis, Johanne & Jia, Ruiting. (2017). Bilingual children's long-term outcomes in English as a second language: Language environment factors shape individual differences in catching up with monolinguals. *Developmental Science*, 20(1), e12433. doi: 10.1111/desc.12433

Parent, Justin; Jones, Deborah J.; Forehand, Rex; Cuellar, Jessica & Shoulberg, Erin K. (2013). The role of coparents in african american single-mother families: The indirect effect of coparent identity on youth psychosocial adjustment. *Journal of Family Psychology*, 27(2), 252–262. doi: 10.1037/a0031477

Park, Hyun; Bothe, Denise; Holsinger, Eva; Kirchner, H. Lester; Olness, Karen & Mandalakas, Anna. (2011). The impact of nutritional status and longitudinal recovery of motor and cognitive milestones in internationally adopted children. *International Journal of Environmental Research and Public Health*, 8(1), 105–116. doi: 10.3390/ijerph8010105

Park, Ji-Yeun; Seo, Dong-Chul & Lin, Hsien-Chang. (2016). E-cigarette use and intention to initiate or quit smoking among US youths. *American Journal of Public Health*, 106(4), 672–678. doi: 10.2105/AJPH.2015.302994

Parke, Ross D. (2013). Gender differences and similarities in parental behavior. In Bradford Wilcox & Kathleen K. Kline (Eds.), *Gender and parenthood: Biological and social scientific perspectives* (pp. 120–163). New York, NY: Columbia University Press.

Parker, Andrew. (2012). *Ethical problems and genetics practice.* New York, NY: Cambridge University Press.

Parks, Sharyn E.; Johnson, Linda L.; McDaniel, Dawn D. & Gladden, Matthew. (2014, January 17). *Surveillance for violent deaths — National Violent Death Reporting System, 16 states, 2010. Morbidity and Mortality Weekly Report* 63(SS01), 1–33. Atlanta, GA: U.S. Department of Health and Human Services, Centers for Disease Control and Prevention, Morbidity and Mortality Weekly Report.

Parsons, Christine E.; Young, Katherine S.; Elmholdt, Else-Marie Jegindoe; Stein, Alan & Kringelbach, Morten L. (2017). Interpreting infant emotional expressions: Parenthood has differential effects on men and women. *The Quarterly Journal of Experimental Psychology*, 70(3), 554–564. doi: 10.1080/17470218.2016.1141967

Parten, Mildred B. (1932). Social participation among pre-school children. *The Journal of Abnormal and Social Psychology*, 27(3), 243–269. doi: 10.1037/h0074524

Pascarella, Ernest T.; Martin, Georgianna L.; Hanson, Jana M.; Trolian, Teniell L.; Gillig, Benjamin & Blaich, Charles. (2014). Effects of diversity experiences on critical thinking skills over 4 years of college. *Journal of College Student Development*, 55(1), 86–92. doi: 10.1353/csd.2014.0009

Pascarella, Ernest T. & Terenzini, Patrick T. (1991). *How college affects students: Findings and insights from twenty years of research.* San Francisco, CA: Jossey-Bass.

Pasco Fearon, R. M. & Roisman, Glenn I. (2017). Attachment theory: progress and future directions. *Current Opinion in Psychology*, 15, 131–136. doi: 10.1016/j.copsyc.2017.03.002

Patel, Ayush; Medhekar, Rohan; Ochoa-Perez, Melissa; Aparasu, Rajender R.; Chan, Wenyaw; Sherer, Jeffrey T., . . . Chen, Hua. (2017). Care provision and prescribing practices of physicians treating children and adolescents with ADHD. *Psychiatric Services*, 68(7), 681–688. doi: 10.1176/appi.ps.201600130

Pathela, Preeti & Schillinger, Julia A. (2010). Sexual behaviors and sexual violence: Adolescents with opposite-, same-, or both-sex partners. *Pediatrics*, 126(5), 879–886. doi: 10.1542/peds.2010-0396

Patil, Rakesh N.; Nagaonkar, Shashikant N.; Shah, Nilesh B. & Bhat, Tushar S. (2013). A cross-sectional study of common psychiatric morbidity in children aged 5 to 14 years in an urban slum. *Journal of Family Medicine and Primary Care*, 2(2), 164–168. doi: 10.4103/2249-4863.117413

Pellegrini, Anthony D. (2011). Introduction. In Anthony D. Pellegrini (Ed.), *The Oxford handbook of the development of play* (pp. 3–6). New York, NY: Oxford University Press. doi: 10.1093/oxfordhb/9780195393002.013.0001

Pellegrini, Anthony D. (2013). Play. In Philip D. Zelazo (Ed.), *The Oxford handbook of developmental psychology* (Vol. 2, pp. 276–299). New York, NY: Oxford University Press. doi: 10.1093/oxfordhb/9780199958474.013.0012

Pellegrini, Anthony D.; Roseth, Cary J.; Van Ryzin, Mark J. & Solberg, David W. (2011). Popularity as a form of social dominance: An evolutionary perspective. In Antonius H. N. Cillessen et al. (Eds.), *Popularity in the peer system* (pp. 123–139). New York, NY: Guilford Press.

Pellicano, Elizabeth; Kenny, Lorcan; Brede, Janina; Klaric, Elena; Lichwa, Hannah & McMillin, Rebecca. (2017). Executive function predicts school readiness in autistic and typical preschool children. *Cognitive Development*, 43, 1–13. doi: 10.1016/j.cogdev.2017.02.003

Pellis, Sergio M. & Pellis, Vivien C. (2011). Rough-and-tumble play: Training and using the social brain. In Anthony D. Pellegrini (Ed.), *The Oxford handbook of the development of play* (pp. 245–259). New York, NY: Oxford University Press. doi: 10.1093/oxfordhb/9780195393002.013.0019

Peng, Duan & Robins, Philip K. (2010). Who should care for our kids? The effects of infant child care on early child development. *Journal of Children and Poverty*, 16(1), 1–45. doi: 10.1080/10796120903575085

Peng, Peng; Yang, Xiujie & Meng, Xiangzhi. (2017). The relation between approximate number system and early arithmetic: The mediation role of numerical knowledge. *Journal of Experimental Child Psychology, 157*, 111–124. doi: 10.1016/j.jecp.2016.12.011

Pennisi, Elizabeth. (2016). The right gut microbes help infants grow. *Science, 351*(6275), 802. doi: 10.1126/science.351.6275.802

Peper, Jiska S. & Dahl, Ronald E. (2013). The teenage brain: Surging hormones — brain-behavior interactions during puberty. *Current Directions in Psychological Science, 22*(2), 134–139. doi: 10.1177/0963721412473755

Perels, Franziska; Merget-Kullmann, Miriam; Wende, Milena; Schmitz, Bernhard & Buchbinder, Carla. (2009). Improving self-regulated learning of preschool children: Evaluation of training for kindergarten teachers. *British Journal of Educational Psychology, 79*(2), 311–327. doi: 10.1348/000709908X322875

Pérez-Fuentes, Gabriela; Olfson, Mark; Villegas, Laura; Morcillo, Carmen; Wang, Shuai & Blanco, Carlos. (2013). Prevalence and correlates of child sexual abuse: A national study. *Comprehensive Psychiatry, 54*(1), 16–27. doi: 10.1016/j.comppsych.2012.05.010

Perner, Josef. (2000). Communication and representation: Why mentalistic reasoning is a life-long endeavour. In Peter Mitchell & Kevin John Riggs (Eds.), *Children's reasoning and the mind* (pp. 367–401). Hove, UK: Psychology Press.

Perren, Sonja; Ettekal, Idean & Ladd, Gary. (2013). The impact of peer victimization on later maladjustment: Mediating and moderating effects of hostile and self-blaming attributions. *Journal of Child Psychology and Psychiatry, 54*(1), 46–55. doi: 10.1111/j.1469-7610.2012.02618.x

Peters, Stacey L.; Lind, Jennifer N.; Humphrey, Jasmine R.; Friedman, Jan M.; Honein, Margaret A.; Tassinari, Melissa S., . . . Broussard, Cheryl S. (2013). Safe lists for medications in pregnancy: Inadequate evidence base and inconsistent guidance from Web-based information, 2011. *Pharmacoepidemiology and Drug Safety, 22*(3), 324–328. doi: 10.1002/pds.3410

Petrenko, Christie L. M.; Friend, Angela; Garrido, Edward F.; Taussig, Heather N. & Culhane, Sara E. (2012). Does subtype matter? Assessing the effects of maltreatment on functioning in preadolescent youth in out-of-home care. *Child Abuse & Neglect, 36*(9), 633–644. doi: 10.1016/j.chiabu.2012.07.001

Pew Research Center. (2016, May 12). *Changing attitudes on gay marriage. Religion & Public Life*. Washington, DC: Pew Research Center.

Pexman, Penny M. (2017). The role of embodiment in conceptual development. *Language, Cognition and Neuroscience*, (In Press). doi: 10.1080/23273798.2017.1303522

Peyser, James A. (2011). Unlocking the secrets of high-performing charters. *Education Next, 11*(4), 36–43.

Phillips, Deborah A.; Fox, Nathan A. & Gunnar, Megan R. (2011). Same place, different experiences: Bringing individual differences to research in child care. *Child Development Perspectives, 5*(1), 44–49. doi: 10.1111/j.1750-8606.2010.00155.x

Phillips, Tommy M.; Wilmoth, Joe D.; Wall, Sterling K.; Peterson, Donna J.; Buckley, Rhonda & Phillips, Laura E. (2013). Recollected parental care and fear of intimacy in emerging adults. *The Family Journal, 21*(3), 335–341. doi: 10.1177/1066480713476848

Piaget, Jean. (1932). *The moral judgment of the child*. London, UK: K. Paul, Trench, Trubner & Co.

Piaget, Jean. (1950). *The psychology of intelligence*. London, UK: Routledge & Paul.

Piaget, Jean. (1952). *The origins of intelligence in children*. Oxford, UK: International Universities Press.

Piaget, Jean. (1954). *The construction of reality in the child*. New York, NY: Basic Books.

Piaget, Jean. (2001). *The psychology of intelligence*. New York, NY: Routledge.

Piaget, Jean. (2011). *The origins of intelligence in children*. New York, NY: Routledge.

Piaget, Jean. (2013a). *The construction of reality in the child*. New York, NY: Routledge.

Piaget, Jean. (2013b). *The moral judgment of the child*. New York, NY: Routledge.

Piaget, Jean & Inhelder, Bärbel. (1972). *The psychology of the child*. New York, NY: Basic Books.

Piaget, Jean; Voelin-Liambey, Daphne & Berthoud-Papandropoulou, Ioanna. (2001). Problems of class inclusion and logical implication. In Robert L. Campell (Ed.), *Studies in reflecting abstraction* (pp. 105–137). Hove, UK: Psychology Press.

Pickles, Andrew; Hill, Jonathan; Breen, Gerome; Quinn, John; Abbott, Kate; Jones, Helen & Sharp, Helen. (2013). Evidence for interplay between genes and parenting on infant temperament in the first year of life: Monoamine oxidase A polymorphism moderates effects of maternal sensitivity on infant anger proneness. *Journal of Child Psychology and Psychiatry, 54*(12), 1308–1317. doi: 10.1111/jcpp.12081

Piekny, Jeanette & Maehler, Claudia. (2013). Scientific reasoning in early and middle childhood: The development of domain-general evidence evaluation, experimentation, and hypothesis generation skills. *British Journal of Developmental Psychology, 31*(2), 153–179. doi: 10.1111/j.2044-835X.2012.02082.x

Pietrantonio, Anna Marie; Wright, Elise; Gibson, Kathleen N.; Alldred, Tracy; Jacobson, Dustin & Niec, Anne. (2013). Mandatory reporting of child abuse and neglect: Crafting a positive process for health professionals and caregivers. *Child Abuse & Neglect, 37*(2/3), 102–109. doi: 10.1016/j.chiabu.2012.12.007

Pilarz, Alejandra Ros & Hill, Heather D. (2014). Unstable and multiple child care arrangements and young children's behavior. *Early Childhood Research Quarterly, 29*(4), 471–483. doi: 10.1016/j.ecresq.2014.05.007

Pinker, Steven. (1999). *Words and rules: The ingredients of language*. New York, NY: Basic Books.

Pinker, Steven. (2003). *The blank slate: The modern denial of human nature*. New York, NY: Penguin.

Pinker, Steven. (2011). *The better angels of our nature: Why violence has declined*. New York, NY: Viking.

PISA. (2009). *Learning mathematics for life: A perspective from PISA*. Paris, France: OECD. doi: 10.1787/9789264075009-en

Pittenger, Samantha L.; Huit, Terrence Z. & Hansen, David J. (2016). Applying ecological systems theory to sexual revictimization of youth: A review with implications for research and practice. *Aggression and Violent Behavior, 26*, 35–45. doi: 10.1016/j.avb.2015.11.005

Plomin, Robert; DeFries, John C.; Knopik, Valerie S. & Neiderhiser, Jenae M. (2013). *Behavioral genetics*. New York, NY: Worth Publishers.

Plows, Alexandra. (2011). *Debating human genetics: Contemporary issues in public policy and ethics*. New York, NY: Routledge.

Pluess, Michael. (2015). Individual differences in environmental sensitivity. *Child Development Perspectives, 9*(3), 138–143. doi: 10.1111/cdep.12120

Pogrebin, Abigail. (2010). *One and the same: My life as an identical twin and what I've learned about everyone's struggle to be singular*. New York, NY: Anchor.

Polanczyk, Guilherme V.; Willcutt, Erik G.; Salum, Giovanni A.; Kieling, Christian & Rohde, Luis A. (2014). ADHD prevalence estimates across three decades: An updated systematic review and meta-regression analysis. *International Journal of Epidemiology, 43*(2), 434–442. doi: 10.1093/ije/dyt261

Polanin, Joshua R.; Espelage, Dorothy & Pigott, Therese. (2012). A meta-analysis of school-based bullying prevention programs' effects on bystander intervention behavior. *School Psychology Review, 41*(1), 47–65.

Polirstok, Susan. (2015). Classroom management strategies for inclusive classrooms. *Creative Education, 6*, 927–933. doi: 10.4236/ce.2015.610094

Pons, Ferran & Lewkowicz, David J. (2014). Infant perception of audio-visual speech synchrony in familiar and unfamiliar fluent speech. *Acta Psychologica, 149*, 142–147. doi: 10.1016/j.actpsy.2013.12.013

Posner, Michael I. & Rothbart, Mary K. (2017). Integrating brain, cognition and culture. *Journal of Cultural Cognitive Science, 1*(1), 3–15. doi: 10.1007/s41809-017-0001-7

Powell, Cynthia M. (2013). Sex chromosomes, sex chromosome disorders, and disorders of sex development. In Steven L. Gersen & Martha B. Keagle (Eds.), *The principles of clinical cytogenetics* (pp. 175–211). New York, NY: Springer. doi: 10.1007/978-1-4419-1688-4_10

Powell, Kendall. (2006). Neurodevelopment: How does the teenage brain work? *Nature, 442*(7105), 865–867. doi: 10.1038/442865a

Powell, Shaun; Langlands, Stephanie & Dodd, Chris. (2011). Feeding children's desires? Child and parental perceptions of food promotion to the "under 8s". *Young Consumers: Insight and Ideas for Responsible Marketers, 12*(2), 96–109. doi: 10.1108/17473611111141560

Powers, Alisa & Casey, B. J. (2015). The adolescent brain and the emergence and peak of psychopathology. *Journal of Infant, Child, and Adolescent Psychotherapy*, *14*(1), 3–15. doi: 10.1080/15289168.2015.1004889

**Pozzoli, Tiziana & Gini, Gianluca.** (2013). Why do bystanders of bullying help or not? A multi-dimensional model. *The Journal of Early Adolescence*, *33*(3), 315–340. doi: 10.1177/0272431612440172

**Prather, Jonathan; Okanoya, Kazuo & Bolhuis, Johan J.** (2017). Brains for birds and babies: Neural parallels between birdsong and speech acquisition. *Neuroscience & Biobehavioral Reviews*, (In Press). doi: 10.1016/j.neubiorev.2016.12.035

**Priess, Heather A.; Lindberg, Sara M. & Hyde, Janet Shibley.** (2009). Adolescent gender-role identity and mental health: Gender intensification revisited. *Child Development*, *80*(5), 1531–1544. doi: 10.1111/j.1467-8624.2009.01349.x

**Proctor, Laura J. & Dubowitz, Howard.** (2014). Child neglect: Challenges and controversies. In Jill E. Korbin & Richard D. Krugman (Eds.), *Handbook of child maltreatment* (pp. 27–61). New York, NY: Springer. doi: 10.1007/978-94-007-7208-3_2

**Propper, Cathi B. & Holochwost, Steven J.** (2013). The influence of proximal risk on the early development of the autonomic nervous system. *Developmental Review*, *33*(3), 151–167. doi: 10.1016/j.dr.2013.05.001

**Prothero, Arianna.** (2016, April 20). Charters help alums stick with college. *Education Week*, *35*(28), 1, 13.

**Proud2Bme.** (2012, March 26). Overall, do social networking sites like Facebook and Twitter help or hurt your body confidence? Retrieved from PROUD2BME website: http://proud2bme.org.

**Pryor, Frederic L.** (2014). A note on the determinants of recent pupil achievement. *Scientific Research*, *5*, 1265–1268. doi: 10.4236/ce.2014.514143

**Pucher, Philip H.; Macdonnell, Michael & Arulkumaran, Sabaratnam.** (2013). Global lessons on transforming strategy into action to save mothers' lives. *International Journal of Gynecology & Obstetrics*, *123*(2), 167–172. doi: 10.1016/j.ijgo.2013.05.009

**Qin, Desiree B. & Chang, Tzu-Fen.** (2013). Asian fathers. In Natasha J. Cabrera & Catherine S. Tamis-LeMonda (Eds.), *Handbook of father involvement: Multidisciplinary perspectives* (2nd ed., pp. 261–281). New York, NY: Routledge.

**Qin, Jiabi; Sheng, Xiaoqi; Wang, Hua; Liang, Desheng; Tan, Hongzhuan & Xia, Jiahui.** (2015). Assisted reproductive technology and risk of congenital malformations: A meta-analysis based on cohort studies. *Archives of Gynecology and Obstetrics*, *292*(4), 777–798. doi: 10.1007/s00404-015-3707-0

**Qin, Jia-Bi; Sheng, Xiao-Qi; Wang, Hua; Chen, Guo-Chong; Yang, Jing; Yu, Hong & Yang, Tu-Bao.** (2017). Worldwide prevalence of adverse pregnancy outcomes associated with in vitro fertilization/intracytoplasmic sperm injection among multiple births: A systematic review and meta-analysis based on cohort studies. *Archives of Gynecology and Obstetrics*, *295*(3), 577–597. doi: 10.1007/s00404-017-4291-2

**Rabkin, Nick & Hedberg, Eric C.** (2011). *Arts education in America: What the declines mean for arts participation*. Washington, DC: National Endowment for the Arts.

**Raeburn, Paul.** (2014). *Do fathers matter?: What science is telling us about the parent we've overlooked*. New York, NY: Farrar, Straus and Giroux.

**Rahilly, Elizabeth P.** (2015). The gender binary meets the gender-variant child: Parents' negotiations with childhood gender variance. *Gender & Society*, *29*(3), 338–361. doi: 10.1177/0891243214563069

**Ramírez, Naja Ferjan; Ramírez, Rey R.; Clarke, Maggie; Taulu, Samu & Kuhl, Patricia K.** (2017). Speech discrimination in 11-month-old bilingual and monolingual infants: A magnetoencephalography study. *Developmental Science*, *20*(1), e12427. doi: 10.1111/desc.12427

**Ramo, Danielle E.; Young-Wolff, Kelly C. & Prochaska, Judith J.** (2015). Prevalence and correlates of electronic-cigarette use in young adults: Findings from three studies over five years. *Addictive Behaviors*, *41*, 142–147. doi: 10.1016/j.addbeh.2014.10.019

**Ramscar, Michael & Dye, Melody.** (2011). Learning language from the input: Why innate constraints can't explain noun compounding. *Cognitive Psychology*, *62*(1), 1–40. doi: 10.1016/j.cogpsych.2010.10.001

**Ranciaro, Alessia; Campbell, Michael C.; Hirbo, Jibril B.; Ko, Wen-Ya; Froment, Alain; Anagnostou, Paolo, . . . Tishkoff, Sarah A.** (2014). Genetic origins of lactase persistence and the spread of pastoralism in Africa. *The American Journal of Human Genetics*, *94*(4), 496–510. doi: 10.1016/j.ajhg.2014.02.009

**Rand, David G. & Nowak, Martin A.** (2016). Cooperation among humans. In Dirk Messner & Silke Weinlich (Eds.), *Global cooperation and the human factor in international relations* (pp. 113–138). New York, NY: Routledge.

**Rankin, Jay.** (2017). Physicians disagree on legal age for cannabis. *CMAJ*, *189*(4), E174–E175. doi: 10.1503/cmaj.1095378

**Raspberry, Kelly A. & Skinner, Debra.** (2011). Negotiating desires and options: How mothers who carry the fragile X gene experience reproductive decisions. *Social Science & Medicine*, *72*(6), 992–998. doi: 10.1016/j.socscimed.2011.01.010

**Ravallion, Martin.** (2014). Income inequality in the developing world. *Science*, *344*(6186), 851–855. doi: 10.1126/science.1251875

**Ray, Brian D.** (2013). Homeschooling rising into the twenty-first century: Editor's introduction. *Peabody Journal of Education*, *88*(3), 261–264. doi: 10.1080/0161956X.2013.796822

**Raz, Naftali & Lindenberger, Ulman.** (2013). Life-span plasticity of the brain and cognition: From questions to evidence and back. *Neuroscience & Biobehavioral Reviews*, *37*(9), 2195–2200. doi: 10.1016/j.neubiorev.2013.10.003

**Reardon, Sean F.** (2013). The widening income achievement gap. *Educational Leadership*, *70*(8), 10–16.

**Reavey, Daphne; Haney, Barbara M.; Atchison, Linda; Anderson, Betsi; Sandritter, Tracy & Pallotto, Eugenia K.** (2014). Improving pain assessment in the NICU: A quality improvement project. *Advances in Neonatal Care*, *14*(3), 144–153. doi: 10.1097/ANC.0000000000000034

**Reijntjes, Albert; Vermande, Marjolijn; Thomaes, Sander; Goossens, Frits; Olthof, Tjeert; Aleva, Liesbeth & Van der Meulen, Matty.** (2015). Narcissism, bullying, and social dominance in youth: A longitudinal analysis. *Journal of Abnormal Child Psychology*, *44*(1), 63–74. doi: 10.1007/s10802-015-9974-1

**Reilly, Steven K. & Noonan, James P.** (2016). Evolution of gene regulation in humans. *Annual Review of Genomics and Human Genetics*, *17*, 45–67. doi: 10.1146/annurev-genom-090314-045935

**Reisner, Sari L.; Katz-Wise, Sabra L.; Gordon, Allegra R.; Corliss, Heather L. & Austin, S. Bryn.** (2016). Social epidemiology of depression and anxiety by gender identity. *Journal of Adolescent Health*, *59*(2), 203–208. doi: 10.1016/j.jadohealth.2016.04.006

**Remington, Gary & Seeman, Mary V.** (2015). Schizophrenia and the influence of male gender. *Clinical Pharmacology & Therapeutics*, *98*(6), 578–581. doi: 10.1002/cpt.201

**Renoux, Christel; Shin, Ju-Young; Dell'Aniello, Sophie; Fergusson, Emma & Suissa, Samy.** (2016). Prescribing trends of Attention-deficit hyperactivity disorder (ADHD) medications in UK primary care, 1995–2015. *British Journal of Clinical Pharmacology*, *82*(3), 858–868. doi: 10.1111/bcp.13000

**Restrepo-Mesa, Sandra L.; Estrada-Restrepo, Alejandro; González-Zapata, Laura I. & Agudelo-Suárez, Andrés A.** (2015). Newborn birth weights and related factors of native and immigrant residents of Spain. *Journal of Immigrant and Minority Health*, *17*(2), 339–348. doi: 10.1007/s10903-014-0089-5

**Reynolds, Arthur J.** (2000). *Success in early intervention: The Chicago Child-Parent Centers*. Lincoln, NE: University of Nebraska Press.

**Reynolds, Arthur J. & Ou, Suh-Ruu.** (2011). Paths of effects from preschool to adult well-being: A confirmatory analysis of the Child-Parent Center Program. *Child Development*, *82*(2), 555–582. doi: 10.1111/j.1467-8624.2010.01562.x

**Rhoades, Kimberly A.; Leve, Leslie D.; Eddy, J. Mark & Chamberlain, Patricia.** (2016). Predicting the transition from juvenile delinquency to adult criminality: Gender-specific influences in two high-risk samples. *Criminal Behaviour and Mental Health*, *26*(5), 336–351. doi: 10.1002/cbm.1957

**Rhodes, Marjorie.** (2013). The conceptual structure of social categories: The social allegiance hypothesis. In Mahzarin R. Banaji & Susan A. Gelman (Eds.), *Navigating the social world: What infants, children, and other species can teach us* (pp. 258–262). New York, NY: Oxford University Press.

**Rich, Motoko.** (2013, April 11). Texas considers backtracking on testing. *New York Times*, p. 12. https://nyti.ms/2kOs1Nm

**Richards, Jennifer S.; Hartman, Catharina A.; Franke, Barbara; Hoekstra, Pieter J.; Heslenfeld, Dirk J.; Oosterlaan, Jaap, . . . Buitelaar, Jan K.** (2014). Differential susceptibility to maternal expressed emotion in children with ADHD and their siblings? Investigating plasticity genes, prosocial and antisocial behaviour. *European Child & Adolescent Psychiatry*, *24*(2), 209–217. doi: 10.1007/s00787-014-0567-2

Ridgers, Nicola D.; Salmon, Jo; Parrish, Anne-Maree; Stanley, Rebecca M. & Okely, Anthony D. (2012). Physical activity during school recess: A systematic review. *American Journal of Preventive Medicine*, 43(3), 320–328. doi: 10.1016/j.amepre.2012.05.019

Riglin, Lucy; Frederickson, Norah; Shelton, Katherine H. & Rice, Frances. (2013). A longitudinal study of psychological functioning and academic attainment at the transition to secondary school. *Journal of Adolescence*, 36(3), 507–517. doi: 10.1016/j.adolescence.2013.03.002

Rigo, Paola; De Pisapia, Nicola; Bornstein, Marc H.; Putnick, Diane L.; Serra, Mauro; Esposito, Gianluca & Venuti, Paola. (2017). Brain processes in women and men in response to emotive sounds. *Social Neuroscience*, 12(2), 150–162. doi: 10.1080/17470919.2016.1150341

Riordan, Jan & Wambach, Karen (Eds.). (2009). *Breastfeeding and human lactation* (4th ed.). Sudbury, MA: Jones and Bartlett Publishers.

Rioux, Charlie; Castellanos-Ryan, Natalie; Parent, Sophie & Séguin, Jean R. (2016). The interaction between temperament and the family environment in adolescent substance use and externalizing behaviors: Support for diathesis–stress or differential susceptibility? *Developmental Review*, 40(10), 117–150. doi: 10.1016/j.dr.2016.03.003

Rivas-Drake, Deborah & Mooney, Margarita. (2009). Neither colorblind nor oppositional: Perceived minority status and trajectories of academic adjustment among Latinos in elite higher education. *Developmental Psychology*, 45(3), 642–651. doi: 10.1037/a0014135

Rivas-Drake, Deborah; Seaton, Eleanor K.; Markstrom, Carol; Quintana, Stephen; Syed, Moin; Lee, Richard M., . . . Yip, Tiffany. (2014). Ethnic and racial identity in adolescence: Implications for psychosocial, academic, and health outcomes. *Child Development*, 85(1), 40–57. doi: 10.1111/cdev.12200

Rivera, Juan Ángel; de Cossío, Teresita González; Pedraza, Lilia S.; Aburto, Tania C.; Sánchez, Tania G. & Martorell, Reynaldo. (2014). Childhood and adolescent overweight and obesity in Latin America: A systematic review. *The Lancet Diabetes & Endocrinology*, 2(4), 321–332. doi: 10.1016/S2213-8587(13)70173-6

Robelen, Erik W. (2011). More students enrolling in Mandarin Chinese. *Education Week*, 30(27), 5.

Roberts, Brent W. & Davis, Jordan P. (2016). Young adulthood is the crucible of personality development. *Emerging Adulthood*, 4(5), 318–326. doi: 10.1177/2167696816653052

Roberts, Leslie. (2017, April 7). Nigeria's invisible crisis. *Science*, 356(6333), 18–23. doi: 10.1126/science.356.6333.18

Robins, Richard W.; Trzesniewski, Kali H. & Donnellan, M. Brent. (2012). A brief primer on self-esteem. *Prevention Researcher*, 19(2), 3–7.

Robinson, Eric & Sutin, Angelina R. (2017). Parents' perceptions of their children as overweight and children's weight concerns and weight gain. *Psychological Science*, 28(3), 320–329. doi: 10.1177/0956797616682027

Robinson, Leah E.; Wadsworth, Danielle D.; Webster, E. Kipling & Bassett, David R. (2014). School reform: The role of physical education policy in physical activity of elementary school children in Alabama's Black Belt region. *American Journal of Health Promotion*, 38(Suppl. 3), S72–S76. doi: 10.4278/ajhp.130430-ARB-207

Rochat, Philippe. (2013). Self-conceptualizing in development. In Philip D. Zelazo (Ed.), *The Oxford handbook of developmental psychology* (Vol. 2, pp. 378–397). New York, NY: Oxford University Press. doi: 10.1093/oxfordhb/9780199958474.013.0015

Roebers, Claudia M.; Schmid, Corinne & Roderer, Thomas. (2009). Metacognitive monitoring and control processes involved in primary school children's test performance. *British Journal of Educational Psychology*, 79(4), 749–767. doi: 10.1348/978185409X429842

Roenneberg, Till; Allebrandt, Karla; Merrow, Martha & Vetter, Céline. (2012). Social jetlag and obesity. *Current Biology*, 22(10), 939–943. doi: 10.1016/j.cub.2012.03.038

Rogers, Leoandra O. & Meltzoff, Andrew N. (2016). Is gender more important and meaningful than race? An analysis of racial and gender identity among Black, White, and mixed-race children. *Cultural Diversity and Ethnic Minority Psychology*. doi: 10.1037/cdp0000125

Rogoff, Barbara. (2003). *The cultural nature of human development*. New York, NY: Oxford University Press.

Rogoff, Barbara. (2016). Culture and participation: A paradigm shift. *Current Opinion in Psychology*, 8, 182–189. doi: 10.1016/j.copsyc.2015.12.002

Romeo, Russell D. (2013). The teenage brain: The stress response and the adolescent brain. *Current Directions in Psychological Science*, 22(2), 140–145. doi: 10.1177/0963721413475445

Rook, Graham A. W.; Lowry, Christopher A. & Raison, Charles L. (2014). Hygiene and other early childhood influences on the subsequent function of the immune system. *Brain Research*, (Corrected Proof). doi: 10.1016/j.brainres.2014.04.004

Roopnarine, Jaipaul; Patte, Michael; Johnson, James & Kuschner, David (Eds.). (2015). *International perspectives on children's play*. New York, NY: McGraw Hill.

Roopnarine, Jaipaul L. & Hossain, Ziarat. (2013). African American and African Caribbean fathers. In Natasha J. Cabrera & Catherine S. Tamis-LeMonda (Eds.), *Handbook of father involvement: Multidisciplinary perspectives* (2nd ed., pp. 223–243). New York, NY: Routledge.

Rose, Amanda J. & Asher, Steven R. (2017). The social tasks of friendship: Do boys and girls excel in different tasks? *Child Development Perspectives*, 11(1), 3–8. doi: 10.1111/cdep.12214

Rose, Amanda J.; Schwartz-Mette, Rebecca A.; Glick, Gary C.; Smith, Rhiannon L. & Luebbe, Aaron M. (2014). An observational study of co-rumination in adolescent friendships. *Developmental Psychology*, 50(9), 2199–2209. doi: 10.1037/a0037465

Rose, Nikolas. (2016). Reading the human brain: How the mind became legible. *Body & Society*, 22(2), 140–177. doi: 10.1177/1357034X15623363

Rose, Steven. (2008). Drugging unruly children is a method of social control. *Nature*, 451(7178), 521. doi: 10.1038/451521a

Roseberry, Sarah; Hirsh-Pasek, Kathy; Parish-Morris, Julia & Golinkoff, Roberta M. (2009). Live action: Can young children learn verbs from video? *Child Development*, 80(5), 1360–1375. doi: 10.1111/j.1467-8624.2009.01338.x

Rosen, Lisa H.; DeOrnellas, Kathy & Scott, Shannon R. (Eds.). (2017). *Bullying in school: Perspectives from school staff, students, and parents*. New York, NY: Palgrave Macmillan. doi: 10.1057/978-1-137-59298-9

Rosen, Meghan. (2016). Concern grows over Zika birth defects. *Science News*, 190(9), 14–15.

Rosenbaum, James E. (2011). The complexities of college for all. *Sociology of Education*, 84(2), 113–117. doi: 10.1177/0038040711401809

Rosenblum, Gianine D. & Lewis, Michael. (1999). The relations among body image, physical attractiveness, and body mass in adolescence. *Child Development*, 70(1), 50–64. doi: 10.1111/1467-8624.00005

Rosiek, Jerry & Kinslow, Kathy. (2016). *Resegregation as curriculum: The meaning of the new racial segregation in U.S. public schools*. New York, NY: Routledge.

Rosin, Hanna. (2014, March 19). The overprotected kid. *The Atlantic*.

Ross, Josephine; Anderson, James R. & Campbell, Robin N. (2011). *I remember me: Mnemonic self-reference effects in preschool children*. Boston, MA: Wiley-Blackwell.

Ross, Patrick A.; Newth, Christopher J. L.; Leung, Dennis; Wetzel, Randall C. & Khemani, Robinder G. (2016). Obesity and mortality risk in critically ill children. *Pediatrics*, 137(3), e20152035. doi: 10.1542/peds.2015-2035

Rosselli, Mónica; Ardila, Alfredo; Lalwani, Laxmi N. & Vélez-Uribe, Idaly. (2016). The effect of language proficiency on executive functions in balanced and unbalanced Spanish–English bilinguals. *Bilingualism: Language and Cognition*, 19(3), 489–503. doi: 10.1017/S1366728915000309

Rossignol, Michel; Chaillet, Nils; Boughrassa, Faiza & Moutquin, Jean-Marie. (2014). Interrelations between four antepartum obstetric interventions and cesarean delivery in women at low risk: A systematic review and modeling of the cascade of interventions. *Birth*, 41(1), 70–78. doi: 10.1111/birt.12088

Rotatori, Anthony; Bakken, Jeffrey P.; Burkhardt, Sandra A.; Obiakor, Festus E. & Sharma, Umesh. (2014). *Special education international perspectives: Practices across the globe*. Bingley, UK: Emerald.

Rothstein, Mark A. (2015). The moral challenge of Ebola. *American Journal of Public Health*, 105(1), 6–8. doi: 10.2105/AJPH.2014.302413

Rovee-Collier, Carolyn. (1987). Learning and memory in infancy. In Joy Doniger Osofsky (Ed.), *Handbook of infant development* (2nd ed., pp. 98–148). New York, NY: Wiley.

**Rovee-Collier, Carolyn.** (1990). The "memory system" of prelinguistic infants. *Annals of the New York Academy of Sciences, 608,* 517–542. doi: 10.1111/j.1749-6632.1990.tb48908.x

**Rovee-Collier, Carolyn & Cuevas, Kimberly.** (2009). The development of infant memory. In Mary L. Courage & Nelson Cowan (Eds.), *The development of memory in infancy and childhood* (2nd ed., pp. 11–41). New York, NY: Psychology Press.

**Rovee-Collier, Carolyn & Hayne, Harlene.** (1987). Reactivation of infant memory: Implications for cognitive development. In Hayne W. Reese (Ed.), *Advances in child development and behavior* (Vol. 20, pp. 185–238). London, UK: Academic Press.

**Rovner, Alisha J.; Nansel, Tonja R.; Wang, Jing & Iannotti, Ronald J.** (2011). Food sold in school vending machines is associated with overall student dietary intake. *Journal of Adolescent Health, 48*(1), 13–19. doi: 10.1016/j.jadohealth.2010.08.021

**Rowe, Meredith L.; Denmark, Nicole; Harden, Brenda Jones & Stapleton, Laura M.** (2016). The role of parent education and parenting knowledge in children's language and literacy skills among White, Black, and Latino families. *Infant and Child Development, 25*(2), 198–220. doi: 10.1002/icd.1924

**Rübeling, Hartmut; Keller, Heidi; Yovsi, Relindis D.; Lenk, Melanie & Schwarzer, Sina.** (2011). Children's drawings of the self as an expression of cultural conceptions of the self. *Journal of Cross-Cultural Psychology, 42*(3), 406–424. doi: 10.1177/0022022110363475

**Rubertsson, C.; Hellström, J.; Cross, M. & Sydsjö, G.** (2014). Anxiety in early pregnancy: Prevalence and contributing factors. *Archives of Women's Mental Health, 17*(3), 221–228. doi: 10.1007/s00737-013-0409-0

**Rubin, Kenneth H.; Bowker, Julie C.; McDonald, Kristina L. & Menzer, Melissa.** (2013). Peer relationships in childhood. In Philip D. Zelazo (Ed.), *The Oxford handbook of developmental psychology* (Vol. 2, pp. 242–275). New York, NY: Oxford University Press. doi: 10.1093/oxfordhb/9780199958474.013.0011

**Rudolph, Karen D.** (2014). Puberty as a developmental context of risk for psychopathology. In Michael Lewis & Karen D. Rudolph (Eds.), *Handbook of developmental psychopathology* (pp. 331–354). New York, NY: Springer. doi: 10.1007/978-1-4614-9608-3_17

**Runions, Kevin C. & Shaw, Thérèse.** (2013). Teacher–child relationship, child withdrawal and aggression in the development of peer victimization. *Journal of Applied Developmental Psychology, 34*(6), 319–327. doi: 10.1016/j.appdev.2013.09.002

**Russell, Charlotte K.; Robinson, Lyn & Ball, Helen L.** (2013). Infant sleep development: Location, feeding and expectations in the postnatal period. *The Open Sleep Journal, 6*(Suppl. 1: M9), 68–76. doi: 10.2174/1874620901306010068

**Russell, Stephen T.; Everett, Bethany G.; Rosario, Margaret & Birkett, Michelle.** (2014). Indicators of victimization and sexual orientation among adolescents: Analyses from youth risk behavior surveys. *American Journal of Public Health, 104*(2), 255–261. doi: 10.2105/AJPH.2013.301493

**Rutter, Michael; Sonuga-Barke, Edmund J.; Beckett, Celia; Castle, Jennifer; Kreppner, Jana; Kumsta, Robert, . . . Gunnar, Megan R.** (2010). Deprivation-specific psychological patterns: Effects of institutional deprivation. *Monographs of the Society for Research in Child Development, 75*(1). doi: 10.1111/j.1540-5834.2010.00547.x

**Ryan, Erin L.** (2012). "They are kind of like magic": Why U.S. mothers use baby videos with 12- to 24-month-olds. *Journalism and Mass Communication, 2*(7), 771–785.

**Sabol, T. J.; Soliday Hong, S. L.; Pianta, R. C. & Burchinal, M. R.** (2013). Can rating pre-K programs predict children's learning? *Science, 341*(6148), 845–846. doi: 10.1126/science.1233517

**Sacks, Oliver.** (1995). *An anthropologist on Mars: Seven paradoxical tales.* New York, NY: Knopf.

**Sadeh, Avi; Mindell, Jodi A.; Luedtke, Kathryn & Wiegand, Benjamin.** (2009). Sleep and sleep ecology in the first 3 years: A web-based study. *Journal of Sleep Research, 18*(1), 60–73. doi: 10.1111/j.1365-2869.2008.00699.x

**Sadler, Troy D.; Romine, William L.; Stuart, Parker E. & Merle-Johnson, Dominike.** (2013). Game-based curricula in biology classes: Differential effects among varying academic levels. *Journal of Research in Science Teaching, 50*(4), 479–499. doi: 10.1002/tea.21085

**Saewyc, Elizabeth M.** (2011). Research on adolescent sexual orientation: Development, health disparities, stigma, and resilience. *Journal of Research on Adolescence, 21*(1), 256–272. doi: 10.1111/j.1532-7795.2010.00727.x

**Saey, Tina Hesman.** (2016). Neandertal DNA poses health risks. *Science News, 189*(5), 18–19.

**Sahlberg, Pasi.** (2011). *Finnish lessons: What can the world learn from educational change in Finland?* New York, NY: Teachers College Press.

**Sahlberg, Pasi.** (2015). *Finnish lessons 2.0: What can the world learn from educational change in Finland?* (2nd. ed.). New York, NY: Teachers College.

**Sahoo, Krushnapriya; Sahoo, Bishnupriya; Choudhury, Ashok Kumar; Sofi, Nighat Yasin; Kumar, Raman & Bhadoria, Ajeet Singh.** (2015). Childhood obesity: Causes and consequences. *Journal of Family Medicine and Primary Care, 4*(2), 187–192. doi: 10.4103/2249-4863.154628

**Samek, Diana R.; Goodman, Rebecca J.; Erath, Stephen A.; McGue, Matt & Iacono, William G.** (2016). Antisocial peer affiliation and externalizing disorders in the transition from adolescence to young adulthood: Selection versus socialization effects. *Developmental Psychology, 52*(5), 813–823. doi: 10.1037/dev0000109

**Samuels, Christina A.** (2013). Study reveals gaps in graduation rates: Diplomas at risk. *Education Week, 32*(32), 5.

**Samuels, Christina A. & Klein, Alyson.** (2013). States faulted on preschool spending levels. *Education Week, 32*(30), 21, 24.

**Sanchez, Gabriel R. & Vargas, Edward D.** (2016). Taking a closer look at group identity: The link between theory and measurement of group consciousness and linked fate. *Political Research Quarterly, 69*(1), 160–174. doi: 10.1177/1065912915624571

**Sánchez, Virginia; Muñoz-Fernández, Noelia & Vega-Gea, Esther.** (2017). Peer sexual cybervictimization in adolescents: Development and validation of a scale. *International Journal of Clinical and Health Psychology, 17*(2), 171–179. doi: 10.1016/j.ijchp.2017.04.001

**Sang, Biao; Ding, Xuechen; Coplan, Robert J.; Liu, Junsheng; Pan, Tingting & Feng, Xingyi.** (2016). Assessment and implications of social avoidance in Chinese early adolescents. *The Journal of Early Adolescence,* (In Press). doi: 10.1177/0272431616678988

**Santelli, John S. & Melnikas, Andrea J.** (2010). Teen fertility in transition: Recent and historic trends in the United States. *Annual Review of Public Health, 31,* 371–383. doi: 10.1146/annurev.publhealth.29.020907.090830

**Sanz Cruces, José Manuel; Hawrylak, María Fernández & Delegido, Ana Benito.** (2015). Interpersonal variability of the experience of falling in love. *International Journal of Psychology and Psychological Therapy, 15*(1), 87–100.

**Saraiva, Linda; Rodrigues, Luís P.; Cordovil, Rita & Barreiros, João.** (2013). Influence of age, sex and somatic variables on the motor performance of pre-school children. *Annals of Human Biology, 40*(5), 444–450. doi: 10.3109/03014460.2013.802012

**Şaşmaz, Tayyar; Öner, Seva; Kurt, A. Öner; Yapıcı, Gülçin; Yazıcı, Aylin Ertekin; Buğdaycı, Resul & Şiş, Mustafa.** (2014). Prevalence and risk factors of Internet addiction in high school students. *European Journal of Public Health, 24*(1), 15–20. doi: 10.1093/eurpub/ckt051

**Satterwhite, Catherine Lindsey; Torrone, Elizabeth; Meites, Elissa; Dunne, Eileen F.; Mahajan, Reena; Ocfemia, M. Cheryl Bañez, . . . Weinstock, Hillard.** (2013). Sexually transmitted infections among US women and men: Prevalence and incidence estimates, 2008. *Sexually Transmitted Diseases, 40*(3), 187–193. doi: 10.1097/OLQ.0b013e318286bb53

**Saudino, Kimberly J. & Micalizzi, Lauren.** (2015). Emerging trends in behavioral genetic studies of child temperament. *Child Development Perspectives, 9*(3), 144–148. doi: 10.1111/cdep.12123

**Savioja, Hanna; Helminen, Mika; Fröjd, Sari; Marttunen, Mauri & Kaltiala-Heino, Riittakerttu.** (2015). Sexual experience and self-reported depression across the adolescent years. *Health Psychology and Behavioral Medicine, 3*(1), 337–347. doi: 10.1080/21642850.2015.1101696

**Saw, Seang-Mei; Cheng, Angela; Fong, Allan; Gazzard, Gus; Tan, Donald T. H. & Morgan, Ian.** (2007). School grades and myopia. *Ophthalmic and Physiological Optics, 27*(2), 126–129. doi: 10.1111/j.1475-1313.2006.00455.x

**Saxton, Matthew.** (2010). *Child language: Acquisition and development.* Thousand Oaks, CA: Sage.

**Scarr, Sandra.** (1985). Constructing psychology: Making facts and fables for our times. *American Psychologist, 40*(5), 499–512. doi: 10.1037/0003-066x.40.5.499

**Schafer, Markus H.; Morton, Patricia M. & Ferraro, Kenneth F.** (2014). Child maltreatment and adult health in a national sample: Heterogeneous relational contexts, divergent effects? *Child Abuse & Neglect, 38*(3), 395–406. doi: 10.1016/j.chiabu.2013.08.003

**Schaie, K. Warner.** (2005). *Developmental influences on adult intelligence: The Seattle Longitudinal Study.* New York, NY: Oxford University Press.

**Schaie, K. Warner.** (2013). *Developmental influences on adult intelligence: The Seattle Longitudinal Study* (2nd ed.). New York, NY: Oxford University Press.

**Schaller, Jessamyn.** (2013). For richer, if not for poorer? Marriage and divorce over the business cycle. *Journal of Population Economics, 26*(3), 1007–1033. doi: 10.1007/s00148-012-0413-0

**Schanler, Richard. J.** (2011). Outcomes of human milk-fed premature infants. *Seminars in Perinatology, 35*(1), 29–33. doi: 10.1053/j.semperi.2010.10.005

**Schardein, James L.** (1976). *Drugs as teratogens.* Cleveland, OH: CRC Press.

**Scharf, Miri.** (2014). Parenting in Israel: Together hand in hand, you are mine and I am yours. In Helaine Selin (Ed.), *Parenting across cultures: Childrearing, motherhood and fatherhood in non-Western cultures* (pp. 193–206). Dordrecht: Springer. doi: 10.1007/978-94-007-7503-9_14

**Schifrin, Barry S. & Cohen, Wayne R.** (2013). The effect of malpractice claims on the use of caesarean section. *Best Practice & Research Clinical Obstetrics & Gynaecology, 27*(2), 269–283. doi: 10.1016/j.bpobgyn.2012.10.004

**Schermerhorn, Alice C.; D'Onofrio, Brian M.; Turkheimer, Eric; Ganiban, Jody M.; Spotts, Erica L.; Lichtenstein, Paul, . . . Neiderhiser, Jenae M.** (2011). A genetically informed study of associations between family functioning and child psychosocial adjustment. *Developmental Psychology, 47*(3), 707–725. doi: 10.1037/a0021362

**Schmader, Toni.** (2010). Stereotype threat deconstructed. *Current Directions in Psychological Science, 19*(1), 14–18. doi: 10.1177/0963721409359292

**Schmidt, Marco F. H.; Butler, Lucas P.; Heinz, Julia & Tomasello, Michael.** (2016). Young children see a single action and infer a social norm promiscuous normativity in 3-year-olds. *Psychological Science, 27*(10), 1360–1370. doi: 10.1177/0956797616661182

**Schore, Allan & McIntosh, Jennifer.** (2011). Family law and the neuroscience of attachment, Part I. *Family Court Review, 49*(3), 501–512. doi: 10.1111/j.1744-1617.2011.01387.x

**Schore, Allan N.** (2015). *Affect regulation and the origin of the self: The neurobiology of emotional development.* New York, NY: Routledge.

**Schulenberg, John; Patrick, Megan E.; Maslowsky, Julie & Maggs, Jennifer L.** (2014). The epidemiology and etiology of adolescent substance use in developmental perspective.

In Michael Lewis & Karen D. Rudolph (Eds.), *Handbook of Developmental Psychopathology* (pp. 601–620). New York, NY: Springer. doi: 10.1007/978-1-4614-9608-3_30

**Schulz, Laura.** (2015). Infants explore the unexpected. *Science, 348*(6230), 42–43. doi: 10.1126/science.aab0582

**Schwarz, Alan.** (2013, December 15). The selling of Attention deficit disorder. *New York Times,* p. A1. https://goo.gl/amrRdX

**Schwarz, Alan.** (2016). *ADHD Nation: Children, doctors, big pharma, and the making of an American epidemic.* New York, NY: Scribner.

**Schwarz, Alan & Cohen, Sarah.** (2013, March 31). A.D.H.D. seen in 11% of U.S. children as diagnoses rise. *New York Times.* https://nyti.ms/2ktsPDB

**Schweinhart, Lawrence J.; Montie, Jeanne; Xiang, Zongping; Barnett, W. Steven; Belfield, Clive R. & Nores, Milagros.** (2005). *Lifetime effects: The High/Scope Perry Preschool Study through age 40.* Ypsilanti, MI: High/Scope Press.

**Schweinhart, Lawrence J. & Weikart, David P.** (1997). *Lasting differences: The High/Scope Preschool curriculum comparison study through age 23.* Ypsilanti, MI: High/Scope Educational Research Foundation.

**Schytt, Erica & Waldenström, Ulla.** (2010). Epidural analgesia for labor pain: Whose choice? *Acta Obstetricia et Gynecologica Scandinavica, 89*(2), 238–242. doi: 10.3109/00016340903280974

**Scott, Diane L.; Lee, Chang-Bae; Harrell, Susan W. & Smith-West, Mary B.** (2013). Permanency for children in foster care: Issues and barriers for adoption. *Child & Youth Services, 34*(3), 290–307. doi: 10.1080/0145935X.2013.826045

**Scott, Lisa S. & Monesson, Alexandra.** (2010). Experience-dependent neural specialization during infancy. *Neuropsychologia, 48*(6), 1857–1861. doi: 10.1016/j.neuropsychologia.2010.02.008

**Sears, William & Sears, Martha.** (2001). *The attachment parenting book: A commonsense guide to understanding and nurturing your baby.* Boston, MA: Little Brown.

**Seaton, Eleanor K.; Quintana, Stephen; Verkuyten, Maykel & Gee, Gilbert C.** (2017). Peers, policies, and place: The relation between context and ethnic/racial identity. *Child Development, 88*(3), 683–692. doi: 10.1111/cdev.12787

**Sedlak, Andrea J. & Ellis, Raquel T.** (2014). Trends in child abuse reporting. In Jill E. Korbin & Richard D. Krugman (Eds.), *Handbook of child maltreatment* (pp. 3–26). New York, NY: Springer. doi: 10.1007/978-94-007-7208-3_1

**Séguin, Jean R. & Tremblay, Richard E.** (2013). Aggression and antisocial behavior: A developmental perspective. In Philip D. Zelazo (Ed.), *The Oxford handbook of developmental psychology* (Vol. 2, pp. 507–526). New York, NY: Oxford University Press. doi: 10.1093/oxfordhb/9780199958474.013.0020

**Şendil, Çağla Öneren & Erden, Feyza Tantekin.** (2014). Peer preference: A way of evaluating social competence and behavioural well-being in early childhood. *Early Child Development and Care, 184*(2), 230–246. doi: 10.1080/03004430.2013.778254

**Senior, Jennifer.** (2014). *All joy and no fun: The paradox of modern parenthood.* New York, NY: Ecco.

**Seppa, Nathan.** (2013a). Urban eyes: Too much time spent indoors may be behind a surge in nearsightedness. *Science News, 183*(3), 22–25. doi: 10.1002/scin.5591830323

**Seppa, Nathan.** (2013b). Home births more risky than hospital deliveries: Records suggest babies born at home are more prone to unresponsiveness after five minutes. *Science News, 184*(8), 14. doi: 10.1002/scin.5591840813

**Settersten, Richard A.** (2015). Relationships in time and the life course: The significance of linked lives. *Research in Human Development, 12*(3/4), 217–223. doi: 10.1080/15427609.2015.1071944

**Severson, Kim & Blinder, Alan.** (2014, January 7). Test scandal in Atlanta brings more guilty pleas. *New York Times,* p. A9. https://nyti.ms/2wbJl3Z

**Shah, Nirvi.** (2011). Policy fight brews over discipline. *Education Week, 31*(7), 1, 12.

**Shanahan, Timothy & Lonigan, Christopher J.** (2010). The National Early Literacy Panel: A summary of the process and the report. *Educational Researcher, 39*(4), 279–285. doi: 10.3102/0013189x10369172

**Shattuck, Rachel M. & Kreider, Rose M.** (2013). *Social and economic characteristics of currently unmarried women with a recent birth: 2011. American Community Survey Reports.* Washington, DC: U.S. Department of Commerce.

**Sheeran, Paschal; Harris, Peter R. & Epton, Tracy.** (2014). Does heightening risk appraisals change people's intentions and behavior? A meta-analysis of experimental studies. *Psychological Bulletin, 140*(2), 511–543. doi: 10.1037/a0033065

**Shek, Daniel T. L. & Yu, Lu.** (2016). Adolescent internet addiction in Hong Kong: Prevalence, change, and correlates. *Journal of Pediatric & Adolescent Gynecology, 29*(1 Suppl.), S22–S30. doi: 10.1016/j.jpag.2015.10.005

**Shi, Bing & Xie, Hongling.** (2012). Popular and nonpopular subtypes of physically aggressive preadolescents: Continuity of aggression and peer mechanisms during the transition to middle school. *Merrill-Palmer Quarterly, 58*(4), 530–553. doi: 10.1353/mpq.2012.0025

**Shi, Rushen.** (2014). Functional morphemes and early language acquisition. *Child Development Perspectives, 8*(1), 6–11. doi: 10.1111/cdep.12052

**Shin, Huiyoung & Ryan, Allison M.** (2017). Friend influence on early adolescent disruptive behavior in the classroom: Teacher emotional support matters. *Developmental Psychology, 53*(1), 114–125. doi: 10.1037/dev0000250

**Shirtcliff, Elizabeth A.; Dahl, Ronald E. & Pollak, Seth D.** (2009). Pubertal development: Correspondence between hormonal and physical development. *Child Development, 80*(2), 327–337. doi: 10.1111/j.1467-8624.2009.01263.x

**Shneidman, Laura & Woodward, Amanda L.** (2016). Are child-directed interactions the cradle of social learning? *Psychological Bulletin, 142*(1), 1–17. doi: 10.1037/bul0000023

**Shulman, Cory.** (2016). *Research and practice in infant and early childhood mental health.* Switzerland: Springer. doi: 10.1007/978-3-319-31181-4

Shulman, Elizabeth P.; Monahan, Kathryn C. & Steinberg, Laurence. (2017). Severe violence during adolescence and early adulthood and its relation to anticipated rewards and costs. *Child Development*, 88(1), 16–26. doi: 10.1111/cdev.12684

Shutts, Kristin; Kinzler, Katherine D. & DeJesus, Jasmine M. (2013). Understanding infants' and children's social learning about foods: Previous research and new prospects. *Developmental Psychology*, 49(3), 419–425. doi: 10.1037/a0027551

Shwalb, David W.; Shwalb, Barbara J. & Lamb, Michael E. (Eds.). (2013). *Fathers in cultural context*. New York, NY: Psychology Press.

Siegal, Michael & Surian, Luca (Eds.). (2012). *Access to language and cognitive development*. New York, NY: Oxford University Press.

Siegel, Shepard. (2016). The heroin overdose mystery. *Current Directions in Psychological Science*, 25(6), 375–379. doi: 10.1177/0963721416664404

Siegler, Robert S. (2009). Improving the numerical understanding of children from low-income families. *Child Development Perspectives*, 3(2), 118–124. doi: 10.1111/j.1750-8606.2009.00090.x

Siegler, Robert S. (2016). Continuity and change in the field of cognitive development and in the perspectives of one cognitive developmentalist. *Child Development Perspectives*, 10(2), 128–133. doi: 10.1111/cdep.12173

Siegler, Robert S. & Braithwaite, David W. (2017). Numerical development. *Annual Review of Psychology*, 68, 187–213. doi: 10.1146/annurev-psych-010416-044101

Sigurdson, J. F.; Wallander, J. & Sund, A. M. (2014). Is involvement in school bullying associated with general health and psychosocial adjustment outcomes in adulthood? *Child Abuse & Neglect*, 38(10), 1607–1617. doi: 10.1016/j.chiabu.2014.06.001

Silberg, Judy L.; Copeland, William E.; Linker, Julie; Moore, Ashlee A.; Roberson-Nay, Roxann & York, Timothy P. (2016). Psychiatric outcomes of bullying victimization: A study of discordant monozygotic twins. *Psychological Medicine*, 46(9), 1875–1883. doi: 10.1017/S0033291716000362

Silberman, Steve. (2015). *Neurotribes: The legacy of autism and the future of neurodiversity*. New York, NY: Avery.

Silk, Jessica & Romero, Diana. (2014). The role of parents and families in teen pregnancy prevention: An analysis of programs and policies. *Journal of Family Issues*, 35(10), 1339–1362. doi: 10.1177/0192513X13481330

Sillars, Alan; Smith, Traci & Koerner, Ascan. (2010). Misattributions contributing to empathic (in)accuracy during parent-adolescent conflict discussions. *Journal of Social and Personal Relationships*, 27(6), 727–747. doi: 10.1177/0265407510373261

Sim, Zi L. & Xu, Fei. (2017). Learning higher-order generalizations through free play: Evidence from 2- and 3-year-old children. *Developmental Psychology*, 53(4), 642–651. doi: 10.1037/dev0000278

Simmons, Joseph P.; Nelson, Leif D. & Simonsohn, Uri. (2011). False-positive psychology: Undisclosed flexibility in data collection and analysis allows presenting anything as significant. *Psychological Science*, 22(11), 1359–1366. doi: 10.1177/0956797611417632

Simon, Laura & Daneback, Kristian. (2013). Adolescents' use of the internet for sex education: A thematic and critical review of the literature. *International Journal of Sexual Health*, 25(4), 305–319. doi: 10.1080/19317611.2013.823899

Simpson, Elizabeth A.; Jakobsen, Krisztina V.; Damon, Fabrice; Suomi, Stephen J.; Ferrari, Pier F. & Paukner, Annika. (2017). Face detection and the development of own-species bias in infant macaques. *Child Development*, 88(1), 103–113. doi: 10.1111/cdev.12565

Simpson, Jeffry A. & Kenrick, Douglas. (2013). *Evolutionary social psychology*. Hoboken, NJ: Taylor & Francis.

Simpson, Jeffry A. & Rholes, W. Steven (Eds.). (2015). *Attachment theory and research: New directions and emerging themes*. New York, NY: Guilford.

Sinclair, Samantha & Carlsson, Rickard. (2013). What will I be when I grow up? The impact of gender identity threat on adolescents' occupational preferences. *Journal of Adolescence*, 36(3), 465–474. doi: 10.1016/j.adolescence.2013.02.001

Singanayagam, Aran; Ritchie, Andrew I. & Johnston, Sebastian L. (2017). Role of microbiome in the pathophysiology and disease course of asthma. *Current Opinion in Pulmonary Medicine*, 23(1), 41–47. doi: 10.1097/MCP.0000000000000333

Singh, Amika; Uijtdewilligen, Léonie; Twisk, Jos W. R.; van Mechelen, Willem & Chinapaw, Mai J. M. (2012). Physical activity and performance at school: A systematic review of the literature including a methodological quality assessment. *Archives of Pediatrics & Adolescent Medicine*, 166(1), 49–55. doi: 10.1001/archpediatrics.2011.716

Singh, Leher. (2008). Influences of high and low variability on infant word recognition. *Cognition*, 106(2), 833–870. doi: 10.1016/j.cognition.2007.05.002

Sinnott, Jan D. (2014). *Adult development: Cognitive aspects of thriving close relationships*. New York, NY: Oxford University Press.

Siraj, Iram & Mayo, Aziza. (2014). *Social class and educational inequality: The impact of parents on schools*. New York, NY: Cambridge University Press. doi: 10.1017/CBO9781139086387

Sisk, Cheryl L. (2016). Hormone-dependent adolescent organization of socio-sexual behaviors in mammals. *Current Opinion in Neurobiology*, 38, 63–68. doi: 10.1016/j.conb.2016.02.004

Sisson, Susan B.; Krampe, Megan; Anundson, Katherine & Castle, Sherri. (2016). Obesity prevention and obesogenic behavior interventions in child care: A systematic review. *Preventive Medicine*, 87, 57–69. doi: 10.1016/j.ypmed.2016.02.016

Skinner, B. F. (1953). *Science and human behavior*. New York, NY: Macmillan.

Skinner, B. F. (1957). *Verbal behavior*. New York, NY: Appleton-Century-Crofts.

Skoog, Thérése & Stattin, Håkan. (2014). Why and under what contextual conditions do early-maturing girls develop problem behaviors? *Child Development Perspectives*, 8(3), 158–162. doi: 10.1111/cdep.12076

Skorikov, Vladimir B. & Vondracek, Fred W. (2011). Occupational identity. In Seth J. Schwartz et al. (Eds.), *Handbook of identity theory and research* (pp. 693–714). New York, NY: Springer. doi: 10.1007/978-1-4419-7988-9_29

Slavich, George M. & Cole, Steven W. (2013). The emerging field of human social genomics. *Clinical Psychological Science*, 1(3), 331–348. doi: 10.1177/2167702613478594

Slining, Meghan; Adair, Linda S.; Goldman, Barbara D.; Borja, Judith B. & Bentley, Margaret. (2010). Infant overweight is associated with delayed motor development. *The Journal of Pediatrics*, 157(1), 20–25.e21. doi: 10.1016/j.jpeds.2009.12.054

Sloan, Mark. (2009). *Birth day: A pediatrician explores the science, the history, and the wonder of childbirth*. New York, NY: Ballantine Books.

Smetana, Judith G.; Ahmad, Ikhlas & Wray-Lake, Laura. (2016). Beliefs about parental authority legitimacy among refugee youth in Jordan: Between- and within-person variations. *Developmental Psychology*, 52(3), 484–495. doi: 10.1037/dev0000084

Smith, Ashley R.; Chein, Jason & Steinberg, Laurence. (2014). Peers increase adolescent risk taking even when the probabilities of negative outcomes are known. *Developmental Psychology*, 50(5), 1564–1568. doi: 10.1037/a0035696

Smith, Michelle I.; Yatsunenko, Tanya; Manary, Mark J.; Trehan, Indi; Mkakosya, Rajhab; Cheng, Jiye, . . . Gordon, Jeffrey I. (2013). Gut microbiomes of Malawian twin pairs discordant for kwashiorkor. *Science*, 339(6119), 548–554. doi: 10.1126/science.1229000

Smith, Peter K. (2010). *Children and play: Understanding children's worlds*. Malden, MA: Wiley-Blackwell.

Smith, Peter K. (2014). *Understanding school bullying: Its nature and prevention strategies*. Thousand Oaks, CA: SAGE.

Smith, Shaunna & Henriksen, Danah. (2016). Fail again, fail better: Embracing failure as a paradigm for creative learning in the arts. *Art Education*, 69(2), 6–11.

Smith, Timothy B. & Silva, Lynda. (2011). Ethnic identity and personal well-being of people of color: A meta-analysis. *Journal of Counseling Psychology*, 58(1), 42–60. doi: 10.1037/a0021528

Smithells, R. W.; Sheppard, S.; Schorah, C. J.; Seller, M. J.; Nevin, N. C.; Harris, R., . . . Fielding, D. W. (2011). Apparent prevention of neural tube defects by periconceptional vitamin supplementation. *International Journal of Epidemiology*, 40(5), 1146–1154. doi: 10.1093/ije/dyr143

Smolak, Linda & Levine, Michael P. (Eds.). (2015). *The Wiley handbook of eating disorders*. Malden, MA: John Wiley & Sons.

Snider, Terra Ziporyn. (2012). Later school start times are a public-health issue. *Education Week*, 31(31), 25, 27.

Snow, J. B. (2015). *Narcissist and the Peter Pan syndrome: Emotionally unavailable and emotionally immature men.* Amazon Digital Services LLC: J. B. Snow Publishing.

**Snyder, Thomas D.; Brey, Cristobal de & Dillow, Sally A.** (2016). *Digest of education statistics, 2015.* Washington, DC: National Center for Education Statistics, Institute of Education Sciences, U.S. Department of Education.

**Snyder, Thomas D. & Dillow, Sally A.** (2013). *Digest of education statistics, 2012.* Washington, DC: National Center for Education Statistics, Institute of Education Sciences, U.S. Department of Education.

**Snyder, Thomas D. & Dillow, Sally A.** (2015, May). *Digest of education statistics, 2013.* Washington, DC: National Center for Education Statistics, Institute of Education Sciences, U.S. Department of Education.

**Soderstrom, Melanie; Ko, Eon-Suk & Nevzorova, Uliana.** (2011). It's a question? Infants attend differently to yes/no questions and declaratives. *Infant Behavior and Development, 34*(1), 107–110. doi: 10.1016/j.infbeh.2010.10.003

**Soley, Gaye & Hannon, Erin E.** (2010). Infants prefer the musical meter of their own culture: A cross-cultural comparison. *Developmental Psychology, 46*(1), 286–292. doi: 10.1037/a0017555

**Solheim, Elisabet; Wichstrøm, Lars; Belsky, Jay & Berg-Nielsen, Turid Suzanne.** (2013). Do time in child care and peer group exposure predict poor socioemotional adjustment in Norway? *Child Development, 84*(5), 1701–1715. doi: 10.1111/cdev.12071

**Solomon, Andrew.** (2012). *Far from the tree: Parents, children and the search for identity.* New York, NY: Scribner.

**Somerville, Leah H.** (2013). The teenage brain: Sensitivity to social evaluation. *Current Directions in Psychological Science, 22*(2), 121–127. doi: 10.1177/0963721413476512

**Sonuga-Barke, Edmund J. S.; Kennedy, Mark; Kumsta, Robert; Knights, Nicky; Golm, Dennis; Rutter, Michael, . . . Kreppner, Jana.** (2017). Child-to-adult neurodevelopmental and mental health trajectories after early life deprivation: the young adult follow-up of the longitudinal English and Romanian Adoptees study. *The Lancet, 389*(10078), 1539–1548. doi: 10.1016/S0140-6736(17)30045-4

**Soons, Judith P. M. & Kalmijn, Matthijs.** (2009). Is marriage more than cohabitation? Well-being differences in 30 European countries. *Journal of Marriage and Family, 71*(5), 1141–1157. doi: 10.1111/j.1741-3737.2009.00660.x

**Sophian, Catherine.** (2013). Vicissitudes of children's mathematical knowledge: Implications of developmental research for early childhood mathematics education. *Early Education and Development, 24*(4), 436–442. doi: 10.1080/10409289.2013.773255

**Soska, Kasey C.; Adolph, Karen E. & Johnson, Scott P.** (2010). Systems in development: Motor skill acquisition facilitates three-dimensional object completion. *Developmental Psychology, 46*(1), 129–138. doi: 10.1037/a0014618

**Sousa, David A.** (2014). *How the brain learns to read* (2nd ed.). Thousand Oaks, CA: SAGE.

**Sowell, Elizabeth R.; Thompson, Paul M.; Holmes, Colin J.; Jernigan, Terry L. & Toga, Arthur W.** (1999). In vivo evidence for post-adolescent brain maturation in frontal and striatal regions. *Nature Neuroscience, 2*(10), 859–862. doi: 10.1038/13154

**Sowell, Elizabeth R.; Thompson, Paul M. & Toga, Arthur W.** (2007). Mapping adolescent brain maturation using structural magnetic resonance imaging. In Daniel Romer & Elaine F. Walker (Eds.), *Adolescent psychopathology and the developing brain: Integrating brain and prevention science* (pp. 55–84). New York, NY: Oxford University Press.

**Sparks, Sarah D.** (2012). Form + function = Finnish schools. *Education Week, 31*(36), 9.

**Sparks, Sarah D.** (2016, July 20). Dose of empathy found to cut suspension rates. *Education Week, 35*(36), 1, 20.

**Spear, Linda.** (2013). The teenage brain: Adolescents and alcohol. *Current Directions in Psychological Science, 22*(2), 152–157. doi: 10.1177/0963721412472192

**Spelke, Elizabeth S.** (1993). Object perception. In Alvin I. Goldman (Ed.), *Readings in philosophy and cognitive science* (pp. 447–460). Cambridge, MA: MIT Press.

**Sperry, Debbie M. & Widom, Cathy S.** (2013). Child abuse and neglect, social support, and psychopathology in adulthood: A prospective investigation. *Child Abuse & Neglect, 37*(6), 415–425. doi: 10.1016/j.chiabu.2013.02.006

**Sprietsma, Maresa.** (2010). Effect of relative age in the first grade of primary school on long-term scholastic results: International comparative evidence using PISA 2003. *Education Economics, 18*(1), 1–32. doi: 10.1080/09645290802201961

**Staff, Jeremy & Schulenberg, John.** (2010). Millennials and the world of work: Experiences in paid work during adolescence. *Journal of Business and Psychology, 25*(2), 247–255. doi: 10.1007/s10869-010-9167-4

**Standing, E. M.** (1998). *Maria Montessori: Her life and work.* New York, NY: Plume.

**Starr, Christine R. & Zurbriggen, Eileen L.** (2016). Sandra Bem's gender schema theory after 34 years: A review of its reach and impact. *Sex Roles,* (In Press). doi: 10.1007/s11199-016-0591-4

**Stattin, Håkan; Hussein, Oula; Özdemir, Metin & Russo, Silvia.** (2017). Why do some adolescents encounter everyday events that increase their civic interest whereas others do not? *Developmental Psychology, 53*(2), 306–318. doi: 10.1037/dev0000192

**Steinberg, Laurence.** (2004). Risk taking in adolescence: What changes, and why? *Annals of the New York Academy of Sciences, 1021,* 51–58. doi: 10.1196/annals.1308.005

**Steinberg, Laurence.** (2009). Should the science of adolescent brain development inform public policy? *American Psychologist, 64*(8), 739–750. doi: 10.1037/0003-066x.64.8.739

**Steinberg, Laurence.** (2014). *Age of opportunity: Lessons from the new science of adolescence.* Boston, MA: Houghton Mifflin Harcourt.

**Steinberg, Laurence.** (2015). The neural underpinnings of adolescent risk-taking: The roles of reward-seeking, impulse control, and peers. In Gabriele Oettingen & Peter M. Gollwitzer (Eds.), *Self-regulation in adolescence* (pp. 173–192). New York, NY: Cambridge University Press.

**Steinberg, Laurence & Monahan, Kathryn C.** (2011). Adolescents' exposure to sexy media does not hasten the initiation of sexual intercourse. *Developmental Psychology, 47*(2), 562–576. doi: 10.1037/a0020613

**Stenseng, Frode; Belsky, Jay; Skalicka, Vera & Wichstrøm, Lars.** (2015). Social exclusion predicts impaired self-regulation: A 2-year longitudinal panel study including the transition from preschool to school. *Journal of Personality, 83*(2), 212–220. doi: 10.1111/jopy.12096

**Stenseng, Frode; Belsky, Jay; Skalicka, Vera & Wichstrøm, Lars.** (2016). Peer rejection and Attention deficit hyperactivity disorder symptoms: Reciprocal relations through ages 4, 6, and 8. *Child Development, 87*(2), 365–373. doi: 10.1111/cdev.12471

**Stephens, Rick & Richey, Mike.** (2013). A business view on U.S. education. *Science, 340*(6130), 313–314. doi: 10.1126/science.1230728

**Stern, Gavin.** (2015). For kids with special learning needs, roadblocks remain. *Science, 349*(6255), 1465–1466. doi: 10.1126/science.349.6255.1465

**Stern, Mark; Clonan, Sheila; Jaffee, Laura & Lee, Anna.** (2015). The normative limits of choice: Charter schools, disability studies, and questions of inclusion. *Educational Policy, 29*(3), 448–477. doi: 10.1177/0895904813510779

**Stern, Peter.** (2013). Connection, connection, connection... *Science, 342*(6158), 577. doi: 10.1126/science.342.6158.577

**Sternberg, Robert J.** (2008). Schools should nurture wisdom. In Barbara Z. Presseisen (Ed.), *Teaching for intelligence* (2nd ed., pp. 61–88). Thousand Oaks, CA: Corwin Press.

**Sternberg, Robert J.** (2011). The theory of successful intelligence. In Robert J. Sternberg & Scott Barry Kaufman (Eds.), *The Cambridge handbook of intelligence* (pp. 504–526). New York, NY: Cambridge University Press.

**Stevens, Gillian.** (2015). Trajectories of English acquisition among foreign-born Spanish-language children in the United States. *International Migration Review, 49*(4), 981–1000. doi: 10.1111/imre.12119

**Stevenson, Richard J.; Oaten, Megan J.; Case, Trevor I.; Repacholi, Betty M. & Wagland, Paul.** (2010). Children's response to adult disgust elicitors: Development and acquisition. *Developmental Psychology, 46*(1), 165–177. doi: 10.1037/a0016692

**Stiles, Joan & Jernigan, Terry.** (2010). The basics of brain development. *Neuropsychology Review, 20*(4), 327–348. doi: 10.1007/s11065-010-9148-4

**Stipek, Deborah.** (2013). Mathematics in early childhood education: Revolution or evolution? *Early Education & Development, 24*(4), 431–435. doi: 10.1080/10409289.2013.777285

Stolt, Suvi; Matomäki, Jaakko; Lind, Annika; Lapinleimu, Helena; Haataja, Leena & Lehtonen, Liisa. (2014). The prevalence and predictive value of weak language skills in children with very low birth weight – A longitudinal study. *Acta Paediatrica, 103*(6), 651–658. doi: 10.1111/apa.12607

Stoltenborgh, Marije; van IJzendoorn, Marinus H.; Euser, Eveline M. & Bakermans-Kranenburg, Marian J. (2011). A global perspective on child sexual abuse: Meta-analysis of prevalence around the world. *Child Maltreatment, 16*(2), 79–101. doi: 10.1177/1077559511403920

Strait, Dana L.; Parbery-Clark, Alexandra; O'Connell, Samantha & Kraus, Nina. (2013). Biological impact of preschool music classes on processing speech in noise. *Developmental Cognitive Neuroscience, 6*, 51–60. doi: 10.1016/j.dcn.2013.06.003

Strasburger, Victor C.; Wilson, Barbara J. & Jordan, Amy B. (2009). *Children, adolescents, and the media* (2nd ed.). Los Angeles, CA: Sage.

Straus, Murray A. & Paschall, Mallie J. (2009). Corporal punishment by mothers and development of children's cognitive ability: A longitudinal study of two nationally representative age cohorts. *Journal of Aggression, Maltreatment & Trauma, 18*(5), 459–483. doi: 10.1080/10926770903035168

Stremmel, Andrew J. (2012). A situated framework: The Reggio experience. In Nancy File et al. (Eds.), *Curriculum in early childhood education: Re-examined, rediscovered, renewed* (pp. 133–145). New York, NY: Routledge.

Striley, Katie & Field-Springer, Kimberly. (2016). When it's good to be a bad nurse: expanding risk orders theory to explore nurses' experiences of moral, social and identity risks in obstetrics units. *Health, Risk & Society, 18*(1–2), 77–96. doi: 10.1080/13698575.2016.1169254

Stroebe, Wolfgang & Strack, Fritz. (2014). The alleged crisis and the illusion of exact replication. *Perspectives on Psychological Science, 9*(1), 59–71. doi: 10.1177/1745691613514450

Strouse, Gabrielle A. & Ganea, Patricia A. (2017). Toddlers' word learning and transfer from electronic and print books. *Journal of Experimental Child Psychology, 156*, 129–142. doi: 10.1016/j.jecp.2016.12.001

Stupica, Brandi; Sherman, Laura J. & Cassidy, Jude. (2011). Newborn irritability moderates the association between infant attachment security and toddler exploration and sociability. *Child Development, 82*(5), 1381–1389. doi: 10.1111/j.1467-8624.2011.01638.x

Suchy, Frederick J.; Brannon, Patsy M.; Carpenter, Thomas O.; Fernandez, Jose R.; Gilsanz, Vicente; Gould, Jeffrey B., . . . Wolf, Marshall A. (2010). National Institutes of Health Consensus Development Conference: Lactose intolerance and health. *Annals of Internal Medicine, 152*(12), 792–796. doi: 10.7326/0003-4819-152-12-201006150-00248

Suk, William A.; Ahanchian, Hamid; Asante, Kwadwo Ansong; Carpenter, David O.; Diaz-Barriga, Fernando; Ha, Eun-Hee, . . . Landrigan, Philip J. (2016). Environmental pollution: An under-recognized threat to children's health, especially in low- and middle-income countries. *Environmental Health Perspectives, 124*(3), A41–A45. doi: 10.1289/ehp.1510517

Suleiman, Ahna B. & Brindis, Claire D. (2014). Adolescent school-based sex education: Using developmental neuroscience to guide new directions for policy and practice. *Sexuality Research and Social Policy, 11*(2), 137–152. doi: 10.1007/s13178-014-0147-8

Sulek, Julia P. (2013, April 30). Audrie Pott suicide: Parents share grief, quest for justice in exclusive interview. *San Jose Mercury News*.

Sun, Li; Guo, Xin; Zhang, Jing; Liu, Henghui; Xu, Shaojun; Xu, Yuanyuan & Tao, Fangbiao. (2016). Gender specific associations between early puberty and behavioral and emotional characteristics in children. *Zhonghua Liu Xing Bing Xue Za Zhi, 37*(1), 35–39. doi: 10.3760/cma.j.issn.0254-6450.2016.01.007

Sun, Min & Rugolotto, Simone. (2004). Assisted infant toilet training in a Western family setting. *Journal of Developmental & Behavioral Pediatrics, 25*(2), 99–101. doi: 10.1097/00004703-200404000-00004

Suomi, Steven J. (2002). Parents, peers, and the process of socialization in primates. In John G. Borkowski et al. (Eds.), *Parenting and the child's world: Influences on academic, intellectual, and social-emotional development* (pp. 265–279). Mahwah, NJ: Erlbaum.

Super, Charles M.; Harkness, Sara; Barry, Oumar & Zeitlin, Marian. (2011). Think locally, act globally: Contributions of African research to child development. *Child Development Perspectives, 5*(2), 119–125. doi: 10.1111/j.1750-8606.2011.00166.x

Susic, Dinko & Varagic, Jasmina. (2017). Obesity: A perspective from hypertension. *Medical Clinics of North America, 101*(1), 139–157. doi: 10.1016/j.mcna.2016.08.008

Susman, Elizabeth J.; Houts, Renate M.; Steinberg, Laurence; Belsky, Jay; Cauffman, Elizabeth; DeHart, Ganie, . . . Halpern-Felsher, Bonnie L. (2010). Longitudinal development of secondary sexual characteristics in girls and boys between ages 9-1/2 and 15-1/2 years. *Archives of Pediatrics & Adolescent Medicine, 164*(2), 166–173. doi: 10.1001/archpediatrics.2009.261

Sutton-Smith, Brian. (2011). The antipathies of play. In Anthony D. Pellegrini (Ed.), *The Oxford handbook of the development of play* (pp. 110–115). New York, NY: Oxford University Press. doi: 10.1093/oxfordhb/9780195393002.013.0010

Suurland, Jill; van der Heijden, Kristiaan B.; Huijbregts, Stephan C. J.; Smaling, Hanneke J. A.; de Sonneville, Leo M. J.; Van Goozen, Stephanie H. M. & Swaab, Hanna. (2016). Parental perceptions of aggressive behavior in preschoolers: Inhibitory control moderates the association with negative emotionality. *Child Development, 87*(1), 256–269. doi: 10.1111/cdev.12455

Swaab, D. F. & Hofman, M. A. (1984). Sexual differentiation of the human brain: A historical perspective. *Progress in Brain Research, 61*, 361–374. doi: 10.1016/S0079-6123(08)64447-7

Swain, James E.; Kim, Pilyoung; Spicer, Julie; Ho, Shao-Hsuan; Dayton, Carolyn J.; Elmadih, Alya & Abel, Kathryn M. (2014). Approaching the biology of human parental attachment: Brain imaging, oxytocin and coordinated assessments of mothers and fathers. *Brain Research, 1580*, 78–101. doi: 10.1016/j.brainres.2014.03.007

Swan, Gary E. & Lessov-Schlaggar, Christina N. (2015). The effects of tobacco smoke on cognition and the brain. In Shari R. Waldstein & Merrill F. Elias (Eds.), *Neuropsychology of cardiovascular disease* (2nd ed.). New York, NY: Psychology Press.

Swanson, H. Lee. (2013). Meta-analysis of research on children with learning disabilities. In H. Lee Swanson et al. (Eds.), *Handbook of learning disabilities* (2nd ed., pp. 627–642). New York, NY: Guilford Press.

Synovitz, Linda & Chopak-Foss, Joanne. (2013). Precocious puberty: Pathology, related risks, and support strategies. *Open Journal of Preventive Medicine, 3*(9), 504–509. doi: 10.4236/ojpm.2013.39068

Taber, Daniel R.; Stevens, June; Evenson, Kelly R.; Ward, Dianne S.; Poole, Charles; Maciejewski, Matthew L., . . . Brownson, Ross C. (2011). State policies targeting junk food in schools: Racial/ethnic differences in the effect of policy change on soda consumption. *American Journal of Public Health, 101*(9), 1769–1775. doi: 10.2105/ajph.2011.300221

Tackett, Jennifer L.; Herzhoff, Kathrin; Harden, K. Paige; Page-Gould, Elizabeth & Josephs, Robert A. (2014). Personality × hormone interactions in adolescent externalizing psychopathology. *Personality Disorders: Theory, Research, and Treatment, 5*(3), 235–246. doi: 10.1037/per0000075

Taga, Keiko A.; Markey, Charlotte N. & Friedman, Howard S. (2006). A longitudinal investigation of associations between boys' pubertal timing and adult behavioral health and well-being. *Journal of Youth and Adolescence, 35*(3), 380–390. doi: 10.1007/s10964-006-9039-4

Tagar, Michal Reifen; Hetherington, Chelsea; Shulman, Deborah & Koenig, Melissa. (2017). On the path to social dominance? Individual differences in sensitivity to intergroup fairness violations in early childhood. *Personality and Individual Differences, 113*, 246–250. doi: 10.1016/j.paid.2017.03.020

Taillieu, Tamara L.; Afifi, Tracie O.; Mota, Natalie; Keyes, Katherine M. & Sareen, Jitender. (2014). Age, sex, and racial differences in harsh physical punishment: Results from a nationally representative United States sample. *Child Abuse & Neglect, 38*(12), 1885–1894. doi: 10.1016/j.chiabu.2014.10.020

Tajalli, Hassan & Garba, Houmma A. (2014). Discipline or prejudice? Overrepresentation of minority students in disciplinary alternative education programs. *Urban Review, 46*(4), 620–631. doi: 10.1007/s11256-014-0274-9

Tamis-LeMonda, Catherine S.; Bornstein, Marc H. & Baumwell, Lisa. (2001). Maternal responsiveness and children's achievement of language milestones. *Child Development, 72*(3), 748–767. doi: 10.1111/1467-8624.00313

Tamis-LeMonda, Catherine S.; Kuchirko, Yana & Song, Lulu. (2014). Why is infant language learning facilitated by parental responsiveness? *Current Directions in Psychological Science*, 23(2), 121–126. doi: 10.1177/0963721414522813

Tamm, Leanne; Epstein, Jeffery N.; Denton, Carolyn A.; Vaughn, Aaron J.; Peugh, James & Willcutt, Erik G. (2014). Reaction time variability associated with reading skills in poor readers with ADHD. *Journal of the International Neuropsychological Society*, 20(3), 292–301. doi: 10.1017/S1355617713001495

Tan, Cheryl H.; Denny, Clark H.; Cheal, Nancy E.; Sniezek, Joseph E. & Kanny, Dafna. (2015, September 25). *Alcohol use and binge drinking among women of childbearing age — United States, 2011–2013. Morbidity and Mortality Weekly Report 64*(37), 1042–1046. Atlanta, GA: Centers for Disease Control and Prevention.

Tan, Joseph S.; Hessel, Elenda T.; Loeb, Emily L.; Schad, Megan M.; Allen, Joseph P. & Chango, Joanna M. (2016). Long-term predictions from early adolescent attachment state of mind to romantic relationship behaviors. *Journal of Research on Adolescence*, 26(4), 1022–1035. doi: 10.1111/jora.12256

Tan, Patricia Z.; Armstrong, Laura M. & Cole, Pamela M. (2013). Relations between temperament and anger regulation over early childhood. *Social Development*, 22(4), 755–772. doi: 10.1111/j.1467-9507.2012.00674.x

Tang, Jie; Yu, Yizhen; Du, Yukai; Ma, Ying; Zhang, Dongying & Wang, Jiaji. (2014). Prevalence of Internet addiction and its association with stressful life events and psychological symptoms among adolescent Internet users. *Addictive Behaviors*, 39(3), 744–747. doi: 10.1016/j.addbeh.2013.12.010

Tanner, Jennifer L. & Arnett, Jeffrey Jensen. (2011). Presenting emerging adulthood: What makes emerging adulthood developmentally distinctive. In Jeffrey Jensen Arnett et al. (Eds.), *Debating emerging adulthood: Stage or process?* (pp. 13–30). New York, NY: Oxford University Press. doi: 10.1093/acprof:oso/9780199757176.003.0002

Tanumihardjo, Sherry A.; Gannon, Bryan & Kaliwile, Chisela. (2016). Controversy regarding widespread vitamin A fortification in Africa and Asia. *Advances in Nutrition*, 7, 5A.

Tarbetsky, Ana L.; Collie, Rebecca J. & Martin, Andrew J. (2016). The role of implicit theories of intelligence and ability in predicting achievement for Indigenous (Aboriginal) Australian students. *Contemporary Educational Psychology*, 47, 61–71. doi: 10.1016/j.cedpsych.2016.01.002

Tarullo, Amanda R.; Garvin, Melissa C. & Gunnar, Megan R. (2011). Atypical EEG power correlates with indiscriminately friendly behavior in internationally adopted children. *Developmental Psychology*, 47(2), 417–431. doi: 10.1037/a0021363

Tarun, Kumar; Kumar, Singh Sanjeet; Manish, Kumar; Sunita & Ashok, Sharan. (2016). Study on relationship between Anemia and academic performance of adolescent girls. *International Journal of Physiology*, 4(1), 81–86. doi: 10.5958/2320-608X.2016.00017.2

Tattersall, Ian. (2017). Why was human evolution so rapid? In Assaf Marom & Erella Hovers (Eds.), *Human paleontology and prehistory: Contributions in Honor of Yoel Rak* (pp. 1–9). Switzerland: Springer. doi: 10.1007/978-3-319-46646-0_1

Taveras, Elsie M.; Gillman, Matthew W.; Kleinman, Ken P.; Rich-Edwards, Janet W. & Rifas-Shiman, Sheryl L. (2013). Reducing racial/ethnic disparities in childhood obesity: The role of early life risk factors. *JAMA Pediatrics*, 167(8), 731–738. doi: 10.1001/jamapediatrics.2013.85

Tay, Marc Tze-Hsin; Au Eong, Kah Guan; Ng, C. Y. & Lim, M. K. (1992). Myopia and educational attainment in 421,116 young Singaporean males. *Annals Academy of Medicine Singapore*, 21(6), 785–791.

Taylor, Marjorie; Shawber, Alison B. & Mannering, Anne M. (2009). Children's imaginary companions: What is it like to have an invisible friend? In Keith D. Markman et al. (Eds.), *Handbook of imagination and mental simulation* (pp. 211–224). New York, NY: Psychology Press.

Taylor, Paul. (2014). *The next America: Boomers, millennials, and the looming generational showdown*. New York, NY: PublicAffairs.

Taylor, Robert Joseph; Chatters, Linda M.; Woodward, Amanda Toler & Brown, Edna. (2013). Racial and ethnic differences in extended family, friendship, fictive kin, and congregational informal support networks. *Family Relations*, 62(4), 609–624. doi: 10.1111/fare.12030

Taylor, Rachael W.; Murdoch, Linda; Carter, Philippa; Gerrard, David F.; Williams, Sheila M. & Taylor, Barry J. (2009). Longitudinal study of physical activity and inactivity in preschoolers: The FLAME study. *Medicine & Science in Sports & Exercise*, 41(1), 96–102. doi: 10.1249/MSS.0b013e3181849d81

Taylor, Zoe E.; Eisenberg, Nancy; Spinrad, Tracy L.; Eggum, Natalie D. & Sulik, Michael J. (2013). The relations of ego-resiliency and emotion socialization to the development of empathy and prosocial behavior across early childhood. *Emotion*, 13(5), 822–831. doi: 10.1037/a0032894

Telzer, Eva H.; Ichien, Nicholas T. & Qu, Yang. (2015). Mothers know best: Redirecting adolescent reward sensitivity toward safe behavior during risk taking. *Social Cognitive and Affective Neuroscience*, 10(10), 1383–1391. doi: 10.1093/scan/nsv026

Temple, Jeff R.; Le, Vi Donna; van den Berg, Patricia; Ling, Yan; Paul, Jonathan A. & Temple, Brian W. (2014). Brief report: Teen sexting and psychosocial health. *Journal of Adolescence*, 37(1), 33–36. doi: 10.1016/j.adolescence.2013.10.008

Teng, Zhaojun; Liu, Yanling & Guo, Cheng. (2015). A meta-analysis of the relationship between self-esteem and aggression among Chinese students. *Aggression and Violent Behavior*, 21(6), 45–54. doi: 10.1016/j.avb.2015.01.005

Teoh, Yee San & Lamb, Michael E. (2013). Interviewer demeanor in forensic interviews of children. *Psychology, Crime & Law*, 19(2), 145–159. doi: 10.1080/1068316X.2011.614610

Terry, Nicole Patton; Connor, Carol McDonald; Johnson, Lakeisha; Stuckey,

Adrienne & Tani, Novell. (2016). Dialect variation, dialect-shifting, and reading comprehension in second grade. *Reading and Writing*, 29(2), 267–295. doi: 10.1007/s11145-015-9593-9

Terry-McElrath, Yvonne M.; Turner, Lindsey; Sandoval, Anna; Johnston, Lloyd D. & Chaloupka, Frank J. (2014). Commercialism in US elementary and secondary school nutrition environments: Trends from 2007 to 2012. *JAMA Pediatrics*, 168(3), 234–242. doi: 10.1001/jamapediatrics.2013.4521

Tessier, Karen. (2010). Effectiveness of hands-on education for correct child restraint use by parents. *Accident Analysis & Prevention*, 42(4), 1041–1047. doi: 10.1016/j.aap.2009.12.011

Tetzlaff, Anne & Hilbert, Anja. (2014). The role of the family in childhood and adolescent binge eating. A systematic review. *Appetite*, 76(1), 208. doi: 10.1016/j.appet.2014.01.050

Thaler, Richard H. & Sunstein, Cass R. (2008). *Nudge: Improving decisions about health, wealth, and happiness*. New Haven, CT: Yale University Press.

Thomaes, Sander; Reijntjes, Albert; Orobio de Castro, Bram; Bushman, Brad J.; Poorthuis, Astrid & Telch, Michael J. (2010). I like me if you like me: On the interpersonal modulation and regulation of preadolescents' state self-esteem. *Child Development*, 81(3), 811–825. doi: 10.1111/j.1467-8624.2010.01435.x

Thomas, Alexander & Chess, Stella. (1977). *Temperament and development*. New York, NY: Brunner/Mazel.

Thomas, Bianca Lee & Viljoen, Margaretha. (2016). EEG brain wave activity at rest and during evoked attention in children with Attention-deficit/hyperactivity disorder and effects of methylphenidate. *Neuropsychobiology*, 73(1), 16–22. doi: 10.1159/000441523

Thomas, Michael S. C.; Van Duuren, Mike; Purser, Harry R. M.; Mareschal, Denis; Ansari, Daniel & Karmiloff-Smith, Annette. (2010). The development of metaphorical language comprehension in typical development and in Williams syndrome. *Journal of Experimental Child Psychology*, 106(2/3), 99–114. doi: 10.1016/j.jecp.2009.12.007

Thomason, Moriah E.; Scheinost, Dustin; Manning, Janessa H.; Grove, Lauren E.; Hect, Jasmine; Marshall, Narcis; . . . Romero, Roberto. (2017). Weak functional connectivity in the human fetal brain prior to preterm birth. *Scientific Reports*, 7(39286). doi: 10.1038/srep39286

Thompson, Charis. (2014). Reproductions through technology. *Science*, 344(6182), 361–362. doi: 10.1126/science.1252641

Thompson, Leonard & Berat, Lynn. (2014). *A History of South Africa* (4th ed.). New Haven, CT: Yale University Press.

Thompson, Ross A. & Raikes, H. Abigail. (2003). Toward the next quarter-century: Conceptual and methodological challenges for attachment theory. *Development and Psychopathology*, 15(3), 691–718. doi: 10.1017/S0954579403000348

Thomson, Keith Stewart. (2015). *Private doubt, public dilemma: Religion and science since Jefferson and Darwin*. New Haven, CT: Yale University Press.

Thomson, Samuel; Marriott, Michael; Telford, Katherine; Law, Hou; McLaughlin, Jo & Sayal, Kapil. (2014). Adolescents with a diagnosis of anorexia nervosa: Parents' experience of recognition and deciding to seek help. *Clinical Child Psychology Psychiatry*, 19(1), 43–57. doi: 10.1177/1359104512465741

Thornberg, Robert & Jungert, Tomas. (2013). Bystander behavior in bullying situations: Basic moral sensitivity, moral disengagement and defender self-efficacy. *Journal of Adolescence*, 36(3), 475–483. doi: 10.1016/j.adolescence.2013.02.003

Tiggemann, Marika & Slater, Amy. (2014). NetTweens: The Internet and body image concerns in preteenage girls. *The Journal of Early Adolescence*, 34(5), 606–620. doi: 10.1177/0272431613501083

Tighe, Lauren A.; Birditt, Kira S. & Antonucci, Toni C. (2016). Intergenerational ambivalence in adolescence and early adulthood: Implications for depressive symptoms over time. *Developmental Psychology*, 52(5), 824–834. doi: 10.1037/a0040146

Timmons, Adela C. & Margolin, Gayla. (2015). Family conflict, mood, and adolescents' daily school problems: Moderating roles of internalizing and externalizing symptoms. *Child Development*, 86(1), 241–258. doi: 10.1111/cdev.12300

Tishkoff, Sarah A.; Reed, Floyd A.; Friedlaender, Françoise R.; Ehret, Christopher; Ranciaro, Alessia; Froment, Alain, . . . Williams, Scott M. (2009). The genetic structure and history of Africans and African Americans. *Science*, 324(5930), 1035–1044. doi: 10.1126/science.1172257

Tobey, Emily A.; Thal, Donna; Niparko, John K.; Eisenberg, Laurie S.; Quittner, Alexandra L. & Wang, Nae-Yuh. (2013). Influence of implantation age on school-age language performance in pediatric cochlear implant users. *International Journal of Audiology*, 52(4), 219–229. doi: 10.3109/14992027.2012.759666

Tolman, Deborah L.; Davis, Brian R. & Bowman, Christin P. (2016). "That's just how it is": A gendered analysis of masculinity and femininity ideologies in adolescent girls' and boys' heterosexual relationships. *Journal of Adolescent Research*, 31(1), 3–31. doi: 10.1177/0743558415587325

Tolman, Deborah L. & McClelland, Sara I. (2011). Normative sexuality development in adolescence: A decade in review, 2000–2009. *Journal of Research on Adolescence*, 21(1), 242–255. doi: 10.1111/j.1532-7795.2010.00726.x

Tomalski, Przemyslaw & Johnson, Mark H. (2010). The effects of early adversity on the adult and developing brain. *Current Opinion in Psychiatry*, 23(3), 233–238. doi: 10.1097/YCO.0b013e3283387a8c

Tomasello, Michael. (2006). Acquiring linguistic constructions. In William Damon & Richard M. Lerner (Eds.), *Handbook of child psychology* (6th ed., Vol. 2, pp. 255–298). Hoboken, NJ: Wiley.

Tomasello, Michael. (2016). The ontogeny of cultural learning. *Current Opinion in Psychology*, 8, 1–4. doi: 10.1016/j.copsyc.2015.09.008

Tomasello, Michael & Herrmann, Esther. (2010). Ape and human cognition. *Current Directions in Psychological Science*, 19(1), 3–8. doi: 10.1177/0963721409359300

Tonn, Jessica L. (2006). Later high school start times a reaction to research. *Education Week*, 25(28), 5, 17.

Torre, Lindsey A.; Bray, Freddie; Siegel, Rebecca L.; Ferlay, Jacques; Lortet-Tieulent, Joannie & Jemal, Ahmedin. (2015). Global cancer statistics. *CA: A Cancer Journal for Clinicians*, 65(2), 87–108. doi: 10.3322/caac.21262

Tough, Paul. (2012). *How children succeed: Grit, curiosity, and the hidden power of character.* Boston, MA: Houghton Mifflin Harcourt.

Travers, Brittany G.; Tromp, Do P. M.; Adluru, Nagesh; Lange, Nicholas; Destiche, Dan; Ennis, Chad, . . . Alexander, Andrew L. (2015). Atypical development of white matter microstructure of the corpus callosum in males with autism: A longitudinal investigation. *Molecular Autism*, 6. doi: 10.1186/s13229-015-0001-8

Trawick-Smith, Jeffrey. (2012). Teacher–child play interactions to achieve learning outcomes: Risks and opportunities. In Robert C. Pianta (Ed.), *Handbook of early childhood education* (pp. 259–277). New York, NY: Guilford Press.

Trenholm, Christopher; Devaney, Barbara; Fortson, Ken; Quay, Lisa; Wheeler, Justin & Clark, Melissa. (2007). *Impacts of four Title V, Section 510 abstinence education programs final report.* Washington, DC: U.S. Department of Health and Human Services, Mathematica Policy Research, Inc.

Trickett, Penelope K.; Noll, Jennie G. & Putnam, Frank W. (2011). The impact of sexual abuse on female development: Lessons from a multigenerational, longitudinal research study. *Development and Psychopathology*, 23(2), 453–476. doi: 10.1017/S0954579411000174

Tronick, Edward. (1989). Emotions and emotional communication in infants. *American Psychologist*, 44(2), 112–119. doi: 10.1037//0003-066X.44.2.112

Tronick, Edward & Weinberg, M. Katherine. (1997). Depressed mothers and infants: Failure to form dyadic states of consciousness. In Lynne Murray & Peter J. Cooper (Eds.), *Postpartum depression and child development* (pp. 54–81). New York, NY: Guilford Press.

Tsai, Kim M.; Telzer, Eva H. & Fuligni, Andrew J. (2013). Continuity and discontinuity in perceptions of family relationships from adolescence to young adulthood. *Child Development*, 84(2), 471–484. doi: 10.1111/j.1467-8624.2012.01858.x

Tsethlikai, Monica & Rogoff, Barbara. (2013). Involvement in traditional cultural practices and American Indian children's incidental recall of a folktale. *Developmental Psychology*, 49(3), 568–578. doi: 10.1037/a0031308

Ttofi, Maria M.; Bowes, Lucy; Farrington, David P. & Lösel, Friedrich. (2014). Protective factors interrupting the continuity from school bullying to later internalizing and externalizing problems: A systematic review of prospective longitudinal studies. *Journal of School Violence*, 13(1), 5–38. doi: 10.1080/15388220.2013.857345

Tummeltshammer, Kristen S.; Wu, Rachel; Sobel, David M. & Kirkham, Natasha Z. (2014). Infants track the reliability of potential informants. *Psychological Science*, 25(9), 1730–1738. doi: 10.1177/0956797614540178

Turner, Heather A.; Finkelhor, David; Ormrod, Richard; Hamby, Sherry; Leeb, Rebecca T.; Mercy, James A. & Holt, Melissa. (2012). Family context, victimization, and child trauma symptoms: Variations in safe, stable, and nurturing relationships during early and middle childhood. *American Journal of Orthopsychiatry*, 82(2), 209–219. doi: 10.1111/j.1939-0025.2012.01147.x

Turner, Heather A.; Shattuck, Anne; Finkelhor, David & Hamby, Sherry. (2016). Polyvictimization and youth violence exposure across contexts. *Journal of Adolescent Health*, 58(2), 208–214. doi: 10.1016/j.jadohealth.2015.09.021

U.S. Bureau of Labor Statistics. (2015). *The employment situation – July 2015.* Washington, DC: U.S. Department of Labor.

U.S. Bureau of Labor Statistics. (2016, April 22). *Employment characteristics of families – 2015.* Washington, DC: U.S. Department of Labor.

U.S. Census Bureau. (2000, January 13). *(NP-D1-A) Annual projections of the resident population by age, sex, race, and Hispanic origin: Lowest, middle, highest series and zero international migration series, 1999 to 2100: Middle series data (2011–2020).* Retrieved from: https://www.census.gov/population/projections/data/national/np-d1.html

U.S. Census Bureau. (2010a). *America's families and living arrangements: 2009.* U.S. Department of Commerce, Economics and Statistics Administration, U.S. Census Bureau.

U.S. Census Bureau. (2010b). *Age by language spoken at home by ability to speak English for the population 5 years and over: Population 5 years and over. 2010 American Community Survey 1-Year Estimates. American FactFinder.* Washington, DC: U.S. Department of Commerce.

U.S. Census Bureau. (2010c). *Annual estimates of the resident population by sex, race, and Hispanic origin for the United States: April 1, 2000 to July 1, 2009.* Washington, DC: U.S. Census Bureau.

U.S. Census Bureau. (2011). *America's families and living arrangements: 2011.* U.S. Department of Commerce, Economics and Statistics Administration, U.S. Census Bureau.

U.S. Census Bureau. (2012). *Statistical abstract of the United States: 2012.* Washington, DC: U.S. Department of Commerce.

U.S. Census Bureau. (2013a). *America's families and living arrangements: 2012.* Washington, DC: U.S. Department of Commerce, Economics and Statistics Administration, U.S. Census Bureau.

U.S. Census Bureau. (2013b). *2009–2013 American Community Survey 5-year estimates: Poverty. American FactFinder.* Washington, DC: U.S. Department of Commerce, United States Census Bureau.

U.S. Census Bureau. (2014). *America's families and living arrangements: 2014.* Washington, DC: U.S. Department of Commerce, Economics and Statistics Administration, U.S. Census Bureau.

U.S. Census Bureau. (2015). *America's families and living arrangements: 2015: Households (H table series). Table H3: Households by Race and Hispanic Origin of Household Reference Person and Detailed Type.* Washington, DC: U.S. Department of Commerce, Economics and Statistics Administration, U.S. Census Bureau.

U.S. Census Bureau. (2016a). *Selected population profile in the United States: 2014 American* community survey 1-year estimates. *American Fact-Finder*. Washington, DC: U.S. Department of Commerce.

**U.S. Census Bureau.** (2016b). *Selected population profile in the United States: 2009 American community survey 1-year estimates. American Fact-Finder*. Washington, DC: U.S. Department of Commerce.

**U.S. Department of Agriculture.** (2016, October 11). *Key statistics & graphics: Food insecurity by household characteristics*. Washington, DC: U.S. Department of Agriculture.

**U.S. Department of Education.** (2015, April). *A matter of equity: Preschool in America*. Washington, DC: U.S. Department of Education.

**U.S. Department of Health and Human Services.** (1999, December 31). *Child maltreatment 1999*. Washington, DC: Administration on Children, Youth and Families, Children's Bureau.

**U.S. Department of Health and Human Services.** (2000, December 31). *Child maltreatment 2000*. Washington, DC: Administration on Children, Youth and Families, Children's Bureau.

**U.S. Department of Health and Human Services.** (2005, December 31). *Child maltreatment 2005*. Washington, DC: Administration on Children, Youth and Families, Children's Bureau.

**U.S. Department of Health and Human Services.** (2010). *Head Start impact study: Final report*. Washington, DC: Administration for Children and Families.

**U.S. Department of Health and Human Services.** (2010, January). *Child maltreatment 2009*. Washington, DC: Administration for Children and Families, Administration on Children, Youth and Families, Children's Bureau.

**U.S. Department of Health and Human Services.** (2011). *The Surgeon General's call to action to support breastfeeding*. Washington, DC: U.S. Department of Health and Human Services, Office of the Surgeon General.

**U.S. Department of Health and Human Services.** (2016, January 25). *Child maltreatment 2014*. Washington, DC: Administration for Children and Families, Administration on Children, Youth and Families, Children's Bureau.

**U.S. Department of Health and Human Services.** (2017, January 19). *Child maltreatment 2015*. Washington, DC: Administration for Children and Families, Administration on Children, Youth and Families, Children's Bureau.

**Uddin, Monica; Koenen, Karestan C.; de los Santos, Regina; Bakshis, Erin; Aiello, Allison E. & Galea, Sandro.** (2010). Gender differences in the genetic and environmental determinants of adolescent depression. *Depression and Anxiety, 27*(7), 658–666. doi: 10.1002/da.20692

**Uflacker, Alice; Doraiswamy, Murali; Rechitsky, Svetlana; See, Tricia; Geschwind, Michael & Tur-Kaspa, Ilan.** (2014). Preimplantation genetic diagnosis (PGD) for genetic prion disorder due to F198S mutation in the PRNP gene. *JAMA Neurology, 71*(4), 484–486. doi: 10.1001/jamaneurol.2013.5884

**Underwood, Emily.** (2013). Why do so many neurons commit suicide during brain development? *Science, 340*(6137), 1157–1158. doi: 10.1126/science.340.6137.1157

**Underwood, Emily.** (2014, February 28). Can Down syndrome be treated? *Science, 343*(6174), 964–967. doi: 10.1126/science.343.6174.964

**Underwood, Marion K. & Ehrenreich, Samuel E.** (2017). The power and the pain of adolescents' digital communication: Cyber victimization and the perils of lurking. *American Psychologist, 72*(2), 144–158. doi: 10.1037/a0040429

**UNESCO.** (2014). *Country profiles. UNESCO Institute for Statistics Data Centre*. Montreal, Canada: UNESCO, Université de Montréal at the Montreal's École des hautes études.

**UNICEF.** (2014a, October). *Low birthweight: Percentage of infants weighing less than 2,500 grams at birth*. UNICEF global databases, based on DHS, MICS, other national household surveys, data from routine reporting systems, UNICEF and WHO. Retrieved from: http://data.unicef.org/nutrition/low-birthweight.html

**UNICEF.** (2017, February). *Maternal mortality fell by almost half between 1990 and 2015*. New York: NY: United Nations.

**UNICEF.** (2017, January 13). *Global overview child malnutrition 1990–2015. UNICEF Data and Analytics: Joint Malnutrition Estimates 2016 Edition*. New York: NY: United Nations.

**UNICEF; World Health Organization & World Bank.** (2017, May). *Child malnutrition estimates*. Retrieved from: https://data.unicef.org/wp-content/uploads/2017/05/JME-May-2017.xlsx

**United Nations.** (2015, July). *Probabilistic population projections based on the World Population Prospects: The 2015 Revision*. New York: Population Division, DESA.

**United Nations, Department of Economic and Social Affairs, Population Division.** (2015). *World population prospects: The 2015 revision*. New York, NY.

**Uppal, Preena; Holland, Andrew J. A.; Bajuk, Barbara; Abdel-Latif, Mohamed; Jaffe, Adam; Hilder, Lisa, . . . Oei, Ju Lee.** (2013). The association between maternal country of birth and neonatal intensive care unit outcomes. *Early Human Development, 89*(8), 607–614. doi: 10.1016/j.earlhumdev.2013.03.003

**Ursache, Alexandra; Blair, Clancy; Stifter, Cynthia & Voegtline, Kristin.** (2013). Emotional reactivity and regulation in infancy interact to predict executive functioning in early childhood. *Developmental Psychology, 49*(1), 127–137. doi: 10.1037/a0027728

**Vaala, Sarah E.; Linebarger, Deborah L.; Fenstermacher, Susan K.; Tedone, Ashley; Brey, Elizabeth; Barr, Rachel, . . . Calvert, Sandra L.** (2010). Content analysis of language-promoting teaching strategies used in infant-directed media. *Infant and Child Development, 19*(6), 628–648. doi: 10.1002/icd.715

**Valdez, Carmen R.; Chavez, Tom & Woulfe, Julie.** (2013). Emerging adults' lived experience of formative family stress: The family's lasting influence. *Qualitative Health Research, 23*(8), 1089–1102. doi: 10.1177/1049732313494271

**Valeri, Beatriz O.; Holsti, Liisa & Linhares, Maria B. M.** (2015). Neonatal pain and developmental outcomes in children born preterm: A systematic review. *Clinical Journal of Pain, 31*(4), 355–362. doi: 10.1097/AJP.0000000000000114

**Valsiner, Jaan.** (2006). Developmental epistemology and implications for methodology. In Richard M. Lerner & William Damon (Eds.), *Handbook of child psychology* (6th ed., Vol. 1, pp. 166–209). Hoboken, NJ: Wiley.

**Van Agt, H. M. E.; de Ridder-Sluiter, J. G.; Van den Brink, G. A.; de Koning, H. J. & Reep van den Bergh, C.** (2015). The predictive value of early childhood factors for language outcome in pre-school children. *Journal of Child and Adolescent Behaviour, 3*(6). doi: 10.4172/2375-4494.1000266

**van Batenburg-Eddes, Tamara; Butte, Dick & van de Looij-Jansen, Petra.** (2012). Measuring juvenile delinquency: How do self-reports compare with official police statistics? *European Journal of Criminology, 9*(1), 23–37. doi: 10.1177/1477370811421644

**van de Bongardt, Daphne; Reitz, Ellen; Sandfort, Theo & Deković, Maja.** (2015). A meta-analysis of the relations between three types of peer norms and adolescent sexual behavior. *Personality and Social Psychology Review, 19*(3), 203–234. doi: 10.1177/1088868314544223

**van den Akker, Alithe; Deković, Maja; Prinzie, Peter & Asscher, Jessica.** (2010). Toddlers' temperament profiles: Stability and relations to negative and positive parenting. *Journal of Abnormal Child Psychology, 38*(4), 485–495. doi: 10.1007/s10802-009-9379-0

**van den Pol, Anthony N.; Mao, Guochao; Yang, Yang; Ornaghi, Sara & Davis, John N.** (2017). Zika virus targeting in the developing brain. *Journal of Neuroscience, 37*(8), 2161–2175. doi: 10.1523/JNEUROSCI.3124-16.2017

**van Goozen, Stephanie H. M.** (2015). The role of early emotion impairments in the development of persistent antisocial behavior. *Child Development Perspectives, 9*(4), 206–210. doi: 10.1111/cdep.12134

**Van Hecke, Wim; Emsell, Louise & Sunaert, Stefan (Eds.).** (2016). *Diffusion tensor imaging: A practical handbook*. New York, NY: Springer. doi: 10.1007/978-1-4939-3118-7

**Van Horn, Linda V.; Bausermann, Robert; Affenito, Sandra; Thompson, Douglas; Striegel-Moore, Ruth; Franko, Debra & Albertson, Ann.** (2011). Ethnic differences in food sources of vitamin D in adolescent American girls: The National Heart, Lung, and Blood Institute Growth and Health Study. *Nutrition Research, 31*(8), 579–585. doi: 10.1016/j.nutres.2011.07.003

**Van Houtte, Mieke.** (2016). Lower-track students' sense of academic futility: Selection or effect? *Journal of Sociology, 52*(4), 874–889. doi: 10.1177/1440783315600802

**van IJzendoorn, Marinus H.; Bakermans-Kranenburg, Marian J.; Pannebakker, Fieke & Out, Dorothée.** (2010). In defence of situational morality: Genetic, dispositional and situational determinants of children's donating to charity. *Journal of Moral Education, 39*(1), 1–20. doi: 10.1080/03057240903528535

van Nunen, Karolien; Kaerts, Nore; Wyndaele, Jean-Jacques; Vermandel, Alexandra & Van Hal, Guido. (2015). Parents' views on toilet training (TT): A quantitative study to identify the beliefs and attitudes of parents concerning TT. *Journal of Child Health Care*, 19(2), 265–274. doi: 10.1177/1367493513508232

Van Royen, Kathleen; Poels, Karolien & Vandebosch, Heidi. (2016). Help, I am losing control! Examining the reporting of sexual harassment by adolescents to social networking sites. *Cyberpsychology, Behavior, and Social Networking*, 19(1), 16–22. doi: 10.1089/cyber.2015.0168

Van Royen, Kathleen; Vandebosch, Heidi & Poels, Karolien. (2015). Severe sexual harassment on social networking sites: Belgian adolescents' views. *Journal of Children and Media*, 9(4), 472–491. doi: 10.1080/17482798.2015.1089301

Van Ryzin, Mark J. & Dishion, Thomas J. (2013). From antisocial behavior to violence: A model for the amplifying role of coercive joining in adolescent friendships. *Journal of Child Psychology and Psychiatry*, 54(6), 661–669. doi: 10.1111/jcpp.12017

Van Vonderen, Kristen E. & Kinnally, William. (2012). Media effects on body image: Examining media exposure in the broader context of internal and other social factors. *American Communication Journal*, 14(2), 41–57.

Vandenbosch, Laura & Eggermont, Steven. (2015). The role of mass media in adolescents' sexual behaviors: Exploring the explanatory value of the three-step self-objectification process. *Archives of Sexual Behavior*, 44(3), 729–742. doi: 10.1007/s10508-014-0292-4

Vanderberg, Rachel H.; Farkas, Amy H.; Miller, Elizabeth; Sucato, Gina S.; Akers, Aletha Y. & Borrero, Sonya B. (2016). Racial and/or ethnic differences in formal sex education and sex education by parents among young women in the United States. *Journal of Pediatric and Adolescent Gynecology*, 29(1), 69–73. doi: 10.1016/j.jpag.2015.06.011

Vandewater, Elizabeth A.; Park, Seoung Eun; Hébert, Emily T. & Cummings, Hope M. (2015). Time with friends and physical activity as mechanisms linking obesity and television viewing among youth. *International Journal of Behavioral Nutrition and Physical Activity*, 12(Suppl. 1), S6. doi: 10.1186/1479-5868-12-S1-S6

Vanhalst, Janne; Luyckx, Koen; Scholte, Ron H. J.; Engels, Rutger C. M. E. & Goossens, Luc. (2013). Low self-esteem as a risk factor for loneliness in adolescence: Perceived – but not actual – social acceptance as an underlying mechanism. *Journal of Abnormal Child Psychology*, 41(7), 1067–1081. doi: 10.1007/s10802-013-9751-y

Vedantam, Shankar. (2011, December 5). *What's behind a temper tantrum? Scientists deconstruct the screams*. Hidden Brain. Washington DC: NPR.

Veenstra, René; Lindenberg, Siegwart; Munniksma, Anke & Dijkstra, Jan Kornelis. (2010). The complex relation between bullying, victimization, acceptance, and rejection: Giving special attention to status, affection, and sex differences. *Child Development*, 81(2), 480–486. doi: 10.1111/j.1467-8624.2009.01411.x

Vega-Gea, Esther; Ortega-Ruiz, Rosario & Sánchez, Virginia. (2016). Peer sexual harassment in adolescence: Dimensions of the sexual harassment survey in boys and girls. *International Journal of Clinical and Health Psychology*, 16(1), 47–57. doi: 10.1016/j.ijchp.2015.08.002

Vennemann, Mechtild M.; Hense, Hans-Werner; Bajanowski, Thomas; Blair, Peter S.; Complojer, Christina; Moon, Rachel Y. & Kiechl-Kohlendorfer, Ursula. (2012). Bed sharing and the risk of sudden infant death syndrome: Can we resolve the debate? *The Journal of Pediatrics*, 160(1), 44–48. doi: 10.1016/j.jpeds.2011.06.052

Verdine, Brian N.; Golinkoff, Roberta Michnick; Hirsh-Pasek, Kathy & Newcombe, Nora S. (2017). Spatial skills, their development, and their links to mathematics. *Monographs of the Society for Research in Child Development: Links between spatial and mathematical skills across the preschool*, 82(1), 7–30. doi: 10.1111/mono.12280

Verkuyten, Maykel. (2016). Further conceptualizing ethnic and racial identity research: The social identity approach and its dynamic model. *Child Development*, 87(6), 1796–1812. doi: 10.1111/cdev.12555

Verona, Sergiu. (2003). Romanian policy regarding adoptions. In Victor Littel (Ed.), *Adoption update* (pp. 5–10). New York, NY: Nova Science.

Verschueren, Margaux; Rassart, Jessica; Claes, Laurence; Moons, Philip & Luyckx, Koen. (2017). Identity statuses throughout adolescence and emerging adulthood: A large-scale study into gender, age, and contextual differences. *Psychologica Belgica*, 57(1), 32–42. doi: 10.5334/pb.348

Verweij, Karin J. H.; Creemers, Hanneke E.; Korhonen, Tellervo; Latvala, Antti; Dick, Danielle M.; Rose, Richard J., . . . Kaprio, Jaakko. (2016). Role of overlapping genetic and environmental factors in the relationship between early adolescent conduct problems and substance use in young adulthood. *Addiction*, 111(6), 1036–1045. doi: 10.1111/add.13303

Viadero, Debra. (2017, March 24). Assessment: A snapshot of a field in motion. *Education Week*, 36(32), 5.

Vickery, Brian P.; Berglund, Jelena P.; Burk, Caitlin M.; Fine, Jason P.; Kim, Edwin H.; Kim, Jung In, . . . Burks, A. Wesley. (2017). Early oral immunotherapy in peanut-allergic preschool children is safe and highly effective. *Journal of Allergy and Clinical Immunology*, 139(1), 173–181.e178. doi: 10.1016/j.jaci.2016.05.027

Viljaranta, Jaana; Aunola, Kaisa; Mullola, Sari; Virkkala, Johanna; Hirvonen, Riikka; Pakarinen, Eija & Nurmi, Jari-Erik. (2015). Children's temperament and academic skill development during first grade: Teachers' interaction styles as mediators. *Child Development*, 86(4), 1191–1209. doi: 10.1111/cdev.12379

Vitale, Susan; Sperduto, Robert D. & Ferris, Frederick L. (2009). Increased prevalence of myopia in the United States between 1971–1972 and 1999–2004. *Archives of Ophthalmology*, 127(12), 1632–1639. doi: 10.1001/archophthalmol.2009.303

Vivanti, Giacomo. (2017). Individualizing and combining treatments in autism spectrum disorder:

Four elements for a theory-driven research agenda. *Current Directions in Psychological Science*, 26(2), 114–119. doi: 10.1177/0963721416680262

Vöhringer, Isabel A.; Kolling, Thorsten; Graf, Frauke; Poloczek, Sonja; Fassbender, Ilna; Freitag, Claudia, . . . Knopf, Monika. (2017). The development of implicit memory from infancy to childhood: On average performance levels and interindividual differences. *Child Development*, (In Press). doi: 10.1111/cdev.12749

Volkow, Nora D.; Compton, Wilson M. & Wargo, Eric M. (2017). The risks of marijuana use during pregnancy. *JAMA*, 317(2), 129–130. doi: 10.1001/jama.2016.18612

Vos, Amber A.; van Voorst, Sabine F.; Steegers, Eric A. P. & Denktaş, Semiha. (2016). Analysis of policy towards improvement of perinatal mortality in the Netherlands (2004–2011). *Social Science & Medicine*, 157, 156–164. doi: 10.1016/j.socscimed.2016.01.032

Vos, Miriam B.; Kaar, Jill L.; Welsh, Jean A.; Van Horn, Linda V.; Feig, Daniel I.; Anderson, Cheryl A. M., . . . Johnson, Rachel K. (2016). Added sugars and cardiovascular disease risk in children: A scientific statement from the American Heart Association. *Circulation*, (In Press). doi: 10.1161/CIR.0000000000000439

Votruba-Drzal, Elizabeth & Dearing, Eric (Eds.). (2017). *Handbook of early childhood development programs, practices, and policies*. New York, NY: Wiley.

Vygotsky, Lev S. (1980). *Mind in society: The development of higher psychological processes*. Cambridge, MA: Harvard University Press.

Vygotsky, Lev S. (1987). Thinking and speech. In Robert W. Rieber & Aaron S. Carton (Eds.), *The collected works of L. S. Vygotsky* (Vol. 1, pp. 39–285). New York, NY: Springer.

Vygotsky, Lev S. (1994a). The development of academic concepts in school aged children. In René van der Veer & Jaan Valsiner (Eds.), *The Vygotsky reader* (pp. 355–370). Cambridge, MA: Blackwell.

Vygotsky, Lev S. (1994b). Principles of social education for deaf and dumb children in Russia. In Rene van der Veer & Jaan Valsiner (Eds.), *The Vygotsky reader* (pp. 19–26). Cambridge, MA: Blackwell.

Vygotsky, Lev S. (2012). *Thought and language*. Cambridge, MA: MIT Press.

Wade, Tracey D.; O'Shea, Anne & Shafran, Roz. (2016). Perfectionism and eating disorders. In Fuschia M. Sirois & Danielle S. Molnar (Eds.), *Perfectionism, health, and well-being* (pp. 205–222). New York, NY: Springer. doi: 10.1007/978-3-319-18582-8_9

Wadsworth, Shelley MacDermid; Bailey, Keisha M. & Coppola, Elizabeth C. (2017). U.S. military children and the wartime deployments of family members. *Child Development Perspectives*, 11(1), 23–28. doi: 10.1111/cdep.12210

Wagenaar, Karin; van Weissenbruch, Mirjam M.; van Leeuwen, Flora E.; Cohen-Kettenis, Peggy T.; Delemarre-van de Waal, Henriette A.; Schats, Roel & Huisman, Jaap. (2011). Self-reported behavioral and socioemotional functioning of 11- to 18-year-old adolescents conceived by in vitro fertilization. *Fertility and Sterility, 95*(2), 611–616. doi: 10.1016/j.fertnstert.2010.04.076

**Wagmiller, Robert L.** (2015). The temporal dynamics of childhood economic deprivation and children's achievement. *Child Development Perspectives, 9*(3), 158–163. doi: 10.1111/cdep.12125

**Wagner, Katie; Dobkins, Karen & Barner, David.** (2013). Slow mapping: Color word learning as a gradual inductive process. *Cognition, 127*(3), 307–317. doi: 10.1016/j.cognition.2013.01.010

**Wagner, Paul A.** (2011). Socio-sexual education: A practical study in formal thinking and teachable moments. *Sex Education: Sexuality, Society and Learning, 11*(2), 193–211. doi: 10.1080/14681811.2011.558427

**Wainer, Allison L.; Hepburn, Susan & Griffith, Elizabeth McMahon.** (2016). Remembering parents in parent-mediated early intervention: An approach to examining impact on parents and families. *Autism,* (In Press). doi: 10.1177/1362361315622411

**Walker, Christa L. Fischer; Rudan, Igor; Liu, Li; Nair, Harish; Theodoratou, Evropi; Bhutta, Zulfiqar A., . . . Black, Robert E.** (2013). Global burden of childhood pneumonia and diarrhoea. *The Lancet, 381*(9875), 1405–1416. doi: 10.1016/S0140-6736(13)60222-6

**Wallis, Claudia.** (2014). Gut reactions: Intestinal bacteria may help determine whether we are lean or obese. *Scientific American, 310*(6), 30–33. doi: 10.1038/scientificamerican0614-30

**Wambach, Karen & Riordan, Jan.** (2014). *Breastfeeding and human lactation* (5th ed.). Burlington, MA: Jones & Bartlett Publishers.

**Wang, Chao; Xue, Haifeng; Wang, Qianqian; Hao, Yongchen; Li, Dianjiang; Gu, Dongfeng & Huang, Jianfeng.** (2014). Effect of drinking on all-cause mortality in women compared with men: A meta-analysis. *Journal of Women's Health, 23*(5), 373–381. doi: 10.1089/jwh.2013.4414

**Wang, Cynthia S.; Whitson, Jennifer A.; Anicich, Eric M.; Kray, Laura J. & Galinsky, Adam D.** (2017). Challenge your stigma: How to reframe and revalue negative stereotypes and slurs. *Current Directions in Psychological Science, 26*(1), 75–80. doi: 10.1177/0963721416676578

**Wang, Jingyun & Candy, T. Rowan.** (2010). The sensitivity of the 2- to 4-month-old human infant accommodation system. *Investigative Ophthalmology and Visual Science, 51*(6), 3309–3317. doi: 10.1167/iovs.09-4667

**Warneken, Felix.** (2015). Precocious prosociality: Why do young children help? *Child Development Perspectives, 9*(1), 1–6. doi: 10.1111/cdep.12101

**Watson, John B.** (1924). *Behaviorism.* New York, NY: The People's Institute Pub. Co.

**Watson, John B.** (1928). *Psychological care of infant and child.* New York, NY: Norton.

**Watson, John B.** (1972). *Psychological care of infant and child.* New York, NY: Arno Press.

**Watson, John B.** (1998). *Behaviorism.* New Brunswick, NJ: Transaction.

**Webber, Douglas A.** (2015). *Are college costs worth it?: How individual ability, major choice, and debt affect optimal schooling decisions.* Bonn, Germany: Institute for the Study of Labor.

**Weber, Daniela; Dekhtyar, Serhiy & Herlitz, Agneta.** (2017). The Flynn effect in Europe—Effects of sex and region. *Intelligence, 60,* 39–45. doi: 10.1016/j.intell.2016.11.003

**Weinshenker, Naomi J.** (2010). Teenagers and body image: What's typical and what's not? www.education.com

**Weinstein, Netta & DeHaan, Cody.** (2014). On the mutuality of human motivation and relationships. In Netta Weinstein (Ed.), *Human motivation and interpersonal relationships: Theory, research, and applications* (pp. 3–25). New York, NY: Springer. doi: 10.1007/978-94-017-8542-6_1

**Weiss, Nicole H.; Tull, Matthew T.; Lavender, Jason & Gratz, Kim L.** (2013). Role of emotion dysregulation in the relationship between childhood abuse and probable PTSD in a sample of substance abusers. *Child Abuse & Neglect, 37*(11), 944–954. doi: 10.1016/j.chiabu.2013.03.014

**Weiss, Noel S. & Koepsell, Thomas D.** (2014). *Epidemiologic methods: Studying the occurrence of illness* (2nd ed.). New York, NY: Oxford University Press.

**Weissbourd, Richard; Ross Anderson, Trisha; Cashin, Alison & McIntyre, Joe.** (2017). *The talk: How adults can promote young people's healthy relationships and prevent misogyny and sexual harassment. Making Caring Common Project.* Cambridge, MA: Harvard Graduate School of Education.

**Weisskirch, Robert S.** (2017). A developmental perspective on language brokering. In Robert S. Weisskirch (Ed.), *Language brokering in immigrant families: Theories and contexts.* New York, NY: Routledge.

**Weisz, John R.; Kuppens, Sofie; Ng, Mei Yi; Eckshtain, Dikla; Ugueto, Ana M.; Vaughn-Coaxum, Rachel, . . . Fordwood, Samantha R.** (2017). What five decades of research tells us about the effects of youth psychological therapy: A multilevel meta-analysis and implications for science and practice. *American Psychologist, 72*(2), 79–117. doi: 10.1037/a0040360

**Wellman, Henry M.; Fang, Fuxi & Peterson, Candida C.** (2011). Sequential progressions in a theory-of-mind scale: Longitudinal perspectives. *Child Development, 82*(3), 780–792. doi: 10.1111/j.1467-8624.2011.01583.x

**Wendelken, Carter; Baym, Carol L.; Gazzaley, Adam & Bunge, Silvia A.** (2011). Neural indices of improved attentional modulation over middle childhood. *Developmental Cognitive Neuroscience, 1*(2), 175–186. doi: 10.1016/j.dcn.2010.11.001

**Wentzel, Kathryn R. & Muenks, Katherine.** (2016). Peer influence on students' motivation, academic achievement and social behavior. In Kathryn R. Wentzel & Geetha B. Ramani (Eds.), *Handbook of social influences in school contexts: Social-emotional, motivation, and cognitive outcomes.* New York, NY: Routledge.

**Werner, Nicole E. & Hill, Laura G.** (2010). Individual and peer group normative beliefs about relational aggression. *Child Development, 81*(3), 826–836. doi: 10.1111/j.1467-8624.2010.01436.x

**Weymouth, Bridget B.; Buehler, Cheryl; Zhou, Nan & Henson, Robert A.** (2016). A meta-analysis of parent–adolescent conflict: Disagreement, hostility, and youth maladjustment. *Journal of Family Theory & Review, 8*(1), 95–112. doi: 10.1111/jftr.12126

**Wheeler, Lorey A.; Zeiders, Katharine H.; Updegraff, Kimberly A.; Umaña-Taylor, Adriana J.; Rodríguez de Jesús, Sue A. & Perez-Brena, Norma J.** (2017). Mexican-origin youth's risk behavior from adolescence to young adulthood: The role of familism values. *Developmental Psychology, 53*(1), 126–137. doi: 10.1037/dev0000251

**Whisman, Mark A. & South, Susan C.** (2017). Gene–environment interplay in the context of romantic relationships. *Current Opinion in Psychology, 13,* 136–141. doi: 10.1016/j.copsyc.2016.08.002

**Whitbourne, Susan K. & Whitbourne, Stacey B.** (2014). *Adult development and aging: Biopsychosocial perspectives* (5th ed.). Hoboken, NJ: Wiley.

**White, Rebecca M. B.; Deardorff, Julianna; Liu, Yu & Gonzales, Nancy A.** (2013). Contextual amplification or attenuation of the impact of pubertal timing on Mexican-origin boys' mental health symptoms. *Journal of Adolescent Health, 53*(6), 692–698. doi: 10.1016/j.jadohealth.2013.07.007

**Whiteside-Mansell, Leanne; Bradley, Robert H.; Casey, Patrick H.; Fussell, Jill J. & Conners-Burrow, Nicola A.** (2009). Triple risk: Do difficult temperament and family conflict increase the likelihood of behavioral maladjustment in children born low birth weight and preterm? *Journal of Pediatric Psychology, 34*(4), 396–405. doi: 10.1093/jpepsy/jsn089

**Widman, Laura; Choukas-Bradley, Sophia; Helms, Sarah W.; Golin, Carol E. & Prinstein, Mitchell J.** (2014). Sexual communication between early adolescents and their dating partners, parents, and best friends. *The Journal of Sex Research, 51*(7), 731–741. doi: 10.1080/00224499.2013.843148

**Widom, Cathy Spatz; Czaja, Sally J. & DuMont, Kimberly A.** (2015a). Intergenerational transmission of child abuse and neglect: Real or detection bias? *Science, 347*(6229), 1480–1485. doi: 10.1126/science.1259917

**Widom, Cathy Spatz; Horan, Jacqueline & Brzustowicz, Linda.** (2015b). Childhood maltreatment predicts allostatic load in adulthood. *Child Abuse & Neglect, 47,* 59–69. doi: 10.1016/j.chiabu.2015.01.016

**Wigger, J. Bradley.** (2017). Invisible friends across four countries: Kenya, Malawi, Nepal and the Dominican Republic. *International Journal of Psychology,* (In Press). doi: 10.1002/ijop.12423

**Wilcox, W. Bradford (Ed.).** (2011). *The sustainable demographic dividend: What do marriage and fertility have to do with the economy?* New York, NY: Social Trends Institute.

**Wilcox, William B. & Kline, Kathleen K.** (2013). *Gender and parenthood: Biological and social scientific perspectives.* New York: NY: Columbia University Press.

**Wiley, Andrea S.** (2011). Milk intake and total dairy consumption: Associations with early menarche in NHANES 1999-2004. *PLoS ONE*, 6(2), e14685. doi: 10.1371/journal.pone.0014685

**Wilkinson, Stephen.** (2015). Prenatal screening, reproductive choice, and public health. *Bioethics*, 29(1), 26–35. doi: 10.1111/bioe.12121

**Williams, Anne M.; Chantry, Caroline; Geubbels, Eveline L.; Ramaiya, Astha K.; Shemdoe, Aloisia I.; Tancredi, Daniel J. & Young, Sera L.** (2016). Breastfeeding and complementary feeding practices among HIV-exposed infants in coastal Tanzania. *Journal of Human Lactation*, 32(1), 112–122. doi: 10.1177/0890334415618412

**Williams, Joshua L.; Corbetta, Daniela & Guan, Yu.** (2015). Learning to reach with "sticky" or "non-sticky" mittens: A tale of developmental trajectories. *Infant Behavior and Development*, 38, 82–96. doi: 10.1016/j.infbeh.2015.01.001

**Williams, Katie M. & Hammond, Christopher J.** (2016). GWAS in myopia: Insights into disease and implications for the clinic. *Expert Review of Ophthalmology*, 11(2), 101–110. doi: 10.1586/17469899.2016.1164597

**Williams, Lela Rankin; Fox, Nathan A.; Lejuez, C. W.; Reynolds, Elizabeth K.; Henderson, Heather A.; Perez-Edgar, Koraly E., . . . Pine, Daniel S.** (2010). Early temperament, propensity for risk-taking and adolescent substance-related problems: A prospective multi-method investigation. *Addictive Behaviors*, 35(2), 1148–1151. doi: 10.1016/j.addbeh.2010.07.005

**Williams, Shanna; Moore, Kelsey; Crossman, Angela M. & Talwar, Victoria.** (2016). The role of executive functions and theory of mind in children's prosocial lie-telling. *Journal of Experimental Child Psychology*, 141, 256–266. doi: 10.1016/j.jecp.2015.08.001

**Willoughby, Michael T.; Mills-Koonce, W. Roger; Gottfredson, Nisha C. & Wagner, Nicholas J.** (2014). Measuring callous unemotional behaviors in early childhood: Factor structure and the prediction of stable aggression in middle childhood. *Journal of Psychopathology and Behavioral Assessment*, 36(1), 30–42. doi: 10.1007/s10862-013-9379-9

**Wilmshurst, Linda.** (2011). *Child and adolescent psychopathology: A casebook* (2nd ed.). Thousand Oaks, CA: Sage.

**Wilson, Kathryn R.; Hansen, David J. & Li, Ming.** (2011). The traumatic stress response in child maltreatment and resultant neuropsychological effects. *Aggression and Violent Behavior*, 16(2), 87–97. doi: 10.1016/j.avb.2010.12.007

**Wolfe, Christy D.; Zhang, Jing; Kim-Spoon, Jungmeen & Bell, Martha Ann.** (2014). A longitudinal perspective on the association between cognition and temperamental shyness. *International Journal of Behavioral Development*, 38(3), 266–276. doi: 10.1177/0165025413516257

**Wolff, Mary S.; Teitelbaum, Susan L.; McGovern, Kathleen; Pinney, Susan M.; Windham, Gayle C.; Galvez, Maida, . . . Biro, Frank M.** (2015). Environmental phenols and pubertal development in girls. *Environment International*, 84, 174–180. doi: 10.1016/j.envint.2015.08.008

**Woodward, Amanda L. & Markman, Ellen M.** (1998). Early word learning. In Deanna Kuhn & Robert S. Siegler (Eds.), *Handbook of child psychology* (5th ed., Vol. 2, pp. 371–420). Hoboken, NJ: Wiley.

**Woolley, Jacqueline D. & Ghossainy, Maliki E.** (2013). Revisiting the fantasy–reality distinction: Children as naïve skeptics. *Child Development*, 84(5), 1496–1510. doi: 10.1111/cdev.12081

**World Bank.** (2014). *Table 2.11: World Development indicators, participation in education.* Washington, DC: World Bank.

**World Bank.** (2016). *World development indicators: Mortality rate, infant (per 1,000 live births).* Retrieved from: http://data.worldbank.org/indicator/SP.DYN.IMRT.IN

**World Bank.** (2017). *Net enrolment rate, primary, both sexes (%).* Retrieved from: http://data.worldbank.org/indicator/SE.PRM.NENR

**World Bank Group.** (2015). *Women, business and the law 2016: Getting to equal.* (License: Creative Commons Attribution CC BY 3.0 IGO). Washington, DC: World Bank. doi: 10.1596/978-1-4648-0677-3

**World Health Organization.** (2006). WHO Motor Development Study: Windows of achievement for six gross motor development milestones. *Acta Paediatrica*, 95(Suppl. 450), 86–95. doi: 10.1111/j.1651-2227.2006.tb02379.x

**World Health Organization.** (2011). *Global recommendations on physical activity for health: Information sheet: global recommendations on physical activity for health 5–17 years old.* Geneva, Switzerland: World Health Organization.

**World Health Organization.** (2014, May 7). *Air quality deteriorating in many of the world's cities. Media centre, News releases.* Geneva, Switzerland: World Health Organization.

**World Health Organization.** (2015). *Global status report on road safety 2015.* Geneva, Switzerland: World Health Organization.

**Wosje, Karen S.; Khoury, Philip R.; Claytor, Randal P.; Copeland, Kristen A.; Hornung, Richard W.; Daniels, Stephen R. & Kalkwarf, Heidi J.** (2010). Dietary patterns associated with fat and bone mass in young children. *American Journal of Clinical Nutrition*, 92(2), 294–303. doi: 10.3945/ajcn.2009.28925

**Wubbena, Zane C.** (2013). Mathematical fluency as a function of conservation ability in young children. *Learning and Individual Differences*, 26, 153–155. doi: 10.1016/j.lindif.2013.01.013

**Xiang, Jing; Korostenskaja, Milena; Molloy, Cynthia; deGrauw, Xinyao; Leiken, Kimberly; Gilman, Carley, . . . Murray, Donna S.** (2016). Multi-frequency localization of aberrant brain activity in autism spectrum disorder. *Brain and Development*, 38(1), 82–90. doi: 10.1016/j.braindev.2015.04.007

**Xu, Fei.** (2013). The object concept in human infants: Commentary on Fields. *Human Development*, 56(3), 167–170. doi: 10.1159/000351279

**Xu, Fei & Kushnir, Tamar.** (2013). Infants are rational constructivist learners. *Current Directions in Psychological Science*, 22(1), 28–32. doi: 10.1177/0963721412469396

**Xu, Jiaquan; Murphy, Sherry L.; Kochanek, Kenneth D. & Arias, Elizabeth.** (2016, December). *Mortality in the United States, 2015. NCHS Data Brief* (267). Hyattsville, MD: National Center for Health Statistics.

**Xu, Yaoying.** (2010). Children's social play sequence: Parten's classic theory revisited. *Early Child Development and Care*, 180(4), 489–498. doi: 10.1080/03004430802090430

**Yadav, Priyanka; Banwari, Girish; Parmar, Chirag & Maniar, Rajesh.** (2013). Internet addiction and its correlates among high school students: A preliminary study from Ahmedabad, India. *Asian Journal of Psychiatry*, 6(6), 500–505. doi: 10.1016/j.ajp.2013.06.004

**Yang, Rongwang; Zhang, Suhan; Li, Rong & Zhao, Zhengyan.** (2013). Parents' attitudes toward stimulants use in China. *Journal of Developmental & Behavioral Pediatrics*, 34(3), 225. doi: 10.1097/DBP.0b013e318287cc27

**Yeung, Wei-Jun Jean & Alipio, Cheryll.** (2013). Transitioning to adulthood in Asia: School, work, and family life. *The ANNALS of the American Academy of Political and Social Science*, 646(1), 6–27. doi: 10.1177/0002716212470794

**Young, Gerald.** (2016). Nature and nurture: Evolution and complexities. In, *Unifying causality and psychology* (pp. 275–302). Switzerland: Springer. doi: 10.1007/978-3-319-24094-7_12

**Young, John K.** (2010). Anorexia nervosa and estrogen: Current status of the hypothesis. *Neuroscience & Biobehavioral Reviews*, 34(8), 1195–1200. doi: 10.1016/j.neubiorev.2010.01.015

**Yu, Xiao-ming; Guo, Shuai-jun & Sun, Yuying.** (2013). Sexual behaviours and associated risks in Chinese young people: A meta-analysis. *Sexual Health*, 10(5), 424–433. doi: 10.1071/SH12140

**Yudell, Michael; Roberts, Dorothy; DeSalle, Rob & Tishkoff, Sarah.** (2016). Taking race out of human genetics. *Science*, 351(6273), 564–565. doi: 10.1126/science.aac4951

**Zachry, Anne H. & Kitzmann, Katherine M.** (2011). Caregiver awareness of prone play recommendations. *American Journal of Occupational Therapy*, 65(1), 101–105. doi: 10.5014/ajot.2011.09100

**Zametkin, Alan J. & Solanto, Mary V.** (2017). A Review of ADHD Nation. *The ADHD Report*, 25(2), 6–10. doi: 10.1521/adhd.2017.25.2.6

**Zapf, Jennifer A. & Smith, Linda B.** (2007). When do children generalize the plural to novel nouns? *First Language*, 27(1), 53–73. doi: 10.1177/0142723707070286

**Zatorre, Robert J.** (2013). Predispositions and plasticity in music and speech learning: Neural correlates and implications. *Science*, 342(6158), 585–589. doi: 10.1126/science.1238414

**Zeiders, Katharine H.; Umaña-Taylor, Adriana J. & Derlan, Chelsea L.** (2013a). Trajectories of depressive symptoms and self-esteem in Latino youths: Examining the role of gender and perceived discrimination. *Developmental Psychology*, 49(5), 951–963. doi: 10.1037/a0028866

**Zeiders, Katharine H.; Updegraff, Kimberly A.; Umaña-Taylor, Adriana J.; Wheeler, Lorey A.; Perez-Brena, Norma J. & Rodríguez, Sue A.** (2013b). Mexican-origin youths trajectories of depressive symptoms: The role of familism values. *Journal of Adolescent Health*, 53(5), 648–654. doi: 10.1016/j.jadohealth.2013.06.008

**Zeifman, Debra M.** (2013). Built to bond: Coevolution, coregulation, and plasticity in parent-infant bonds. In Cindy Hazan & Mary I. Campa (Eds.), *Human bonding: The science of affectional ties* (pp. 41–73). New York, NY: Guilford Press.

**Zelazo, Philip David.** (2015). Executive function: Reflection, iterative reprocessing, complexity, and the developing brain. *Developmental Review*, 38, 55–68. doi: 10.1016/j.dr.2015.07.001

**Zentall, Shannon R. & Morris, Bradley J.** (2010). "Good job, you're so smart": The effects of inconsistency of praise type on young children's motivation. *Journal of Experimental Child Psychology*, 107(2), 155–163. doi: 10.1016/j.jecp.2010.04.015

**Zhao, Jinxia & Wang, Meifang.** (2014). Mothers' academic involvement and children's achievement: Children's theory of intelligence as a mediator. *Learning and Individual Differences*, 35, 130–136. doi: 10.1016/j.lindif.2014.06.006

**Zhu, Qi; Song, Yiying; Hu, Siyuan; Li, Xiaobai; Tian, Moqian; Zhen, Zonglei, . . . Liu, Jia.** (2010). Heritability of the specific cognitive ability of face perception. *Current Biology*, 20(2), 137–142. doi: 10.1016/j.cub.2009.11.067

**Zieber, Nicole; Kangas, Ashley; Hock, Alyson & Bhatt, Ramesh S.** (2014). Infants' perception of emotion from body movements. *Child Development*, 85(2), 675–684. doi: 10.1111/cdev.12134

**Zimmer-Gembeck, Melanie J.** (2016). Peer rejection, victimization, and relational self-system processes in adolescence: Toward a transactional model of stress, coping, and developing sensitivities. *Child Development Perspectives*, 10(2), 122–127. doi: 10.1111/cdep.12174

**Zimmerman, Frederick J.; Christakis, Dimitri A. & Meltzoff, Andrew N.** (2007). Associations between media viewing and language development in children under age 2 years. *The Journal of Pediatrics*, 151(4), 364–368. doi: 10.1016/j.jpeds.2007.04.071

**Zimmerman, Julie B. & Anastas, Paul T.** (2015). Toward substitution with no regrets. *Science*, 347(6227). doi: 10.1126/science.aaa0812

**Zimmerman, Marc A.; Stoddard, Sarah A.; Eisman, Andria B.; Caldwell, Cleopatra H.; Aiyer, Sophie M. & Miller, Alison.** (2013). Adolescent resilience: Promotive factors that inform prevention. *Child Development Perspectives*, 7(4), 215–220. doi: 10.1111/cdep.12042

**Zolotor, Adam J.** (2014). Corporal punishment. *Pediatric Clinics of North America*, 61(5), 971–978. doi: 10.1016/j.pcl.2014.06.003

**Zosel, Amy; Bartelson, Becki Bucher; Bailey, Elise; Lowenstein, Steven & Dart, Rick.** (2013). Characterization of adolescent prescription drug abuse and misuse using the Researched Abuse Diversion and Addiction-Related Surveillance (RADARS[R]) System. *Journal of the American Academy of Child & Adolescent Psychiatry*, 52(2), 196-204.e192. doi: 10.1016/j.jaac.2012.11.014

**Zubrzycki, Jaclyn.** (2012). Experts fear handwriting will become a lost art. *Education Week*, 31(18), 1, 13.

**Zubrzycki, Jackie.** (2017). 1 in 5 public school students in the class of 2016 passed an AP exam [Web log post]. *Education Week: Curriculum Matters*. Retrieved from http://blogs.edweek.org/edweek/curriculum/2017/02/ap_results_release_2017.html

**Zucker, Kenneth J.; Cohen-Kettenis, Peggy T.; Drescher, Jack; Meyer-Bahlburg, Heino F. L.; Pfäfflin, Friedemann & Womack, William M.** (2013). Memo outlining evidence for change for Gender Identity Disorder in the DSM-5. *Archives of Sexual Behavior*, 42(5), 901–914. doi: 10.1007/s10508-013-0139-4

**Zych, Izabela; Farrington, David P.; Llorent, Vicente J. & Ttofi, Maria M. (Eds.).** (2017). *Protecting children against bullying and its consequences.* Switzerland: Springer. doi: 10.1007/978-3-319-53028-4

# Name Index

Aarnoudse-Moens, Cornelieke S. H., 122
Abar, Caitlin C., 465
Abbott, Kate, 195
Abdel-Latif, Mohamed, 122
Abel, Kathryn M., 105
Abela, Angela, 383
Abelson, Sara, 121
Abramson, Lyn Y., 413
Aburto, Tania C., 240, 417
Abuzenadah, Adel, 416
Acuto, Michele, 231
Adair, Linda S., 151
Adamson, Lauren B., 178, 256
Ad-Dab'bagh, Yasser, 323
Adluru, Nagesh, 228
Adolph, Karen E., 103, 148, 151, 152, 153, 171
Afifi, Tracie O., 298
Afzal, Mohammad, 83
Agans, Jennifer P., 8, 17
Agrawal, Arpana, 480
Agrawal, Dewesh, 415
Agudelo-Suárez, Andrés A., 122
Agurs-Collins, Tanya, 417
Ahanchian, Hamid, 234
Ahmad, Ikhlas, 464
Ahmed, Hafez, 127
Aiello, Allison E., 472
Ainsworth, Mary, 61, 198
Ainsworth, Mary D. Salter, 201
Aiyer, Sophie M., 17
Aizer, Anna, 14
Akers, Aletha Y., 470, 471
Akhtar, Nameera, 15
Aksglaede, Lise, 88
Alatupa, Saija, 194
Albert, Dustin, 410, 437, 439
Albin, Roger L., 90
Ale, Chelsea M., 23
Aleccia, JoNel, 90
Alesi, Marianha, 313
Aleva, Liesbeth, 371
Alexander, Andrew L, 228
Alexander, Karl L., 26
Alexandrov, Lubomir, 228
Al-Hashim, Aqeela H., 228
Alibali, Martha W., 254
Alicea, Stacey, 447
Alipio, Cheryll, 501
Aljughaiman, Abdullah, 346
Allebeck, Peter, 156
Allebrandt, Karla, 406
Allen, Alexander C., 111
Allen, Elizabeth S., 385
Allen, Joseph P., 198, 298
Allen, Nicholas B., 434
Allison, Carlie M., 454
Alloway, Tracy, 345
Alloy, Lauren B., 413
Almas, Alisa, 369
Almeida, Daniel, 313
Almond, Douglas, 112
Al-Namlah, Abdulrahman S., 257
Al Otaiba, Stephanie, 331
Alpár, Alán, 11
Alper, Meryl, 259
Al-Sayes, Fatin, 416
Altarelli, Irene, 350
Altschul, Inna, 297

Amato, Michael S., 235
Ambalavanan, Namasivayam, 119, 122
Ameade, Evans Paul Kwame, 411
American Academy of Pediatrics, 259, 290
American College of Obstetricians and Gynecologists, 121
American College of Obstetricians and Gynecologists Committee on Obstetric Practice, 111
American Community Survey, 501
American Psychiatric Association, 191, 323, 328
Amico, Elizabeth J. D., 460
Amir, Amnon, 109
Anagnostou, Paolo, 59
Anastas, Paul T., 27
Anastasiou, Dimitris, 332
Andersen, Anne-Marie N., 114
Anderson, Betsi, 149
Anderson, Cheryl A. M., 225
Anderson, Daniel R., 183, 442
Anderson, Henry A., 235
Anderson, James R., 283
Anderson, Peter J., 122
Anderson, Sarah E., 290
Anderton, Stephen M., 319
Andreas, Nicholas J., 158
Andrews, Timothy, 316
Angold, Adrian, 390
Anicich, Eric M., 491
Anney, Richard, 325
Ansado, Jennyfer, 228
Ansari, Arya, 274
Ansari, Daniel, 348
Antenucci, Antonio, 35, 36
Antoine, Michelle W., 324
Antonishak, Jill, 298
Antonucci, Toni C., 8, 463
Anundson, Katherine, 225
Anwar, Malik Azeem, 83
Aparasu, Rajender R., 327
Apgar, Virginia, 106
Arabin, Birgit, 111
Aralis, Hilary, 378
Araya, Ricardo, 412
Arbour, Laura, 121
Archambault, Isabelle, 453
Archer, Philip, 150
Archer, Sally L., 458
Ardila, Alfredo, 267, 316
Ares, Susana, 158
Aretakis, Maria T., 351
Arezzo, Joseph C., 324
Argyrides, Marios, 417
Arias, Elizabeth, 155
Ariely, Dan, 157, 435
Arigo, Danielle, 26
Aristotle, 60
Armson, B. Anthony, 111
Armstrong, Laura M., 281, 283, 284
Arnett, Donna K., 6
Arnett, Jeffrey, 61
Arnett, Jeffrey Jensen, 498
Arroyo, Judith A., 84
Arseneault, Louise, 377, 390, 444
Arsenio, William F., 434
Arshad, S. Hasan, 112
Arulkumaran, Sabaratnam, 107
Arum, Richard, 493

Asante, Kwadwo Ansong, 234
Asher, M. Innes, 226
Asher, Steven R, 387
Ashraf, Quamrul, 71
Aslin, Richard N., 166, 174
Asscher, Jessica, 192, 194
Associated Press, 8
Asztalos, Elizabeth V., 111
Atchison, Linda, 149
Atkinson, Anthony P., 193
Atzaba-Poria, Naama, 284
Atzil, Shir, 198
Aud, Susan, 215
Au Eong, Kah Guan, 85
Aunola, Kaisa, 194, 297, 357
Austin, S. Bryn, 461
Aven, Terje, 114
Avenevoli, Shelli, 471
Axelsson, Emma L., 176
Ayers, Susan, 127, 195
Ayyanathan, Kasirajan, 69
Azrin, Nathan H., 56
Băban, Adriana, 423, 472
Babchishin, Lyzon K., 214
Babineau, Vanessa, 8
Bachman, Jerald G., 10, 477, 481
Bachmann, Christian J., 325
Badaly, Daryaneh, 151
Baek, Ji Hyun, 473
Bagatian, Nadiah, 416
Bagot, Kara, 481
Bagwell, Catherine L., 386, 390
Bahrick, Lorraine E., 197
Bai, Ya-Mei, 325
Bailey, Elise, 481
Bailey, J. Michael, 468
Bailey, Keisha M., 378
Baillargeon, Renée, 167
Bajanowski, Thomas, 138
Bajuk, Barbara, 122
Bakeman, Roger, 178, 256, 352, 369
Baker, Bruce L., 327
Baker, Jeffrey P., 156
Baker, Mark, 496
Baker, Olesya, 450
Baker, Simon T. E., 434
Bakermans-Kranenburg, Marian J., 200, 303, 393, 412, 425
Bakken, Jeffrey P., 332
Bakken, Jeremy P., 464
Bakshis, Erin, 472
Balari, Sergio, 185
Ball, Helen L., 137, 138
Ballieux, Haiko., 176
Ballottin, Umberto, 174
Baltes, Paul B., 8, 9
Baly, Michael W., 447
Bamshad, Michael J., 86
Bancken, Christin, 257
Bandura, Albert, 45, 61
Bangert, Barbara, 122
Banks, James R., 316
Bannon, Michael J., 80
Banwari, Girish, 443
Bao, Haikun, 124
Baqui, Abdullah H., 110
Barbosa, Leonardo S., 169
Barkin, Samuel H., 385
Barkley, Russell A., 324, 327
Barkmann, Claus, 128

Asante, Kwadwo Ansong, 234
Barner, David, 265
Barnett, Melissa, 190
Barnett, W. Steven, 274, 275, 276
Baron-Cohen, Simon, 260, 262
Barone, Joseph, 57
Barr, Dana B., 117
Barr, Rachel, 181, 183
Barrasso-Catanzaro, Christina, 229
Barreiros, João, 236
Barrett, Anne E., 9
Barrett, Jon F. R., 111
Barrios, Yasmin V., 412
Barros, Romina M., 315
Barry, Oumar, 152
Barry, Robin A., 227
Bartels, Meike, 376
Bartelson, Becki Bucher, 481
Barth, Maria, 210
Bartz-Seel, Jutta, 128
Bassett, David R., 315
Bassok, Daphna, 270, 273
Bateman, Brian T., 118
Bateson, Patrick, 286
Bauer, Patricia J., 172
Baumeister, Roy F., 371
Baumrind, Diana, 61, 293
Bax, Trent, 443
Baym, Carol L., 313, 346
Baysu, Gülseli, 359
Bazerman, Max H., 437
Bazinger, Claudia, 35
Beach, Steven R. H., 462
Beaman, Lori G., 382
Beardslee, William, 378
Bearman, Peter S., 114
Beauchaine, Theodore P., 376
Beauchamp, Miriam H., 228
Beck, Martha N., 120, 128
Beck, Melinda, 106
Beckel-Mitchener, Andrea, 142
Becker, Bronwyn, 372
Becker, Derek R., 288
Becker, Emily M., 326
Beckett, Celia, 204
Beddor, Patrice Speeter, 175
Beebe, Beatrice, 197
Begum, Nazma, 110
Behne, Tanya, 257
Beilin, Lawrence, 158
Beilock, Sian L., 259
Bein, Kendall, 241
Belfield, Clive R., 275
Bell, Beth T., 417
Bell, Martha Ann, 140, 194, 283, 284
Bellinger, David C., 235
Belsky, Daniel W., 488
Belsky, Jay, 20, 195, 214, 215, 215, 332, 388, 403, 404, 412
Bem, Sandra L., 304
Bender, Heather L., 298
Benigno, Joann P., 257
Benjamin, Emelia J, 6
Benjamin, Rebekah G., 344
Benn, Peter, 87, 88
Benner, Aprile D, 274
Benoit, Amelie, 413
Benowitz, Neal L., 27, 478
Benson, Lizbeth, 27
Bentley, Alison, 215

Bentley, Margaret, 151
Berat, Lynn, 16
Beraudi, Alina, 75
Berenson, Gerald S., 5, 6
Berg, Cynthia, 8
Berg, Teresa, 245
Berg, W. Keith, 257
Bergen, Gwen, 440
Berger, Kathleen S., 234
Berglund, Jelena P., 226
Berg-Nielsen, Turid Suzanne, 215
Berkowitz, Talia, 259
Bernard, Kristin, 200
Bernier, Annie, 140
Bersabe, Adrian, 124
Bertelsen, Aksel, 91
Berthoud-Papandropoulou, Ioanna, 340
Best, Eric, 493
Best, Joel, 493
Betancourt, Theresa S., 373
Bevans, Katherine B., 27
Bhadoria, Ajeet Singh, 224, 317
Bhat, Tushar S., 383
Bhatia, Tej K., 267
Bhatnagar, Aruni, 27
Bhatt, Ramesh S., 171
Bhola, Poornima, 383
Bhutta, Zulfiqar A., 159
Bialystok, Ellen, 267, 321, 335, 347
Bianco, Antonino, 314
Bianconi, Eva, 75
Biemiller, Andrew, 264
Bigler, Rebecca S., 434
Billard, Catherine, 350
Billings, Deborah L., 499
Bindt, Carola, 128
Binet, Alfred, 60
Birch, Leann L., 5
Bird, Geoffrey, 404, 405
Birditt, Kira S., 463
Birkeland, Marianne S., 465
Birkett, Michelle, 469
Birmaher, Boris B., 326
Biro, Frank M., 228, 410, 411
Bish, Crystal E., 364
Bjorklund, David F., 171, 282, 390
Björnberg, Marina, 396
Blacher, Jan, 327
Black, James E., 142
Black, Robert E., 159
Blad, Evie, 156, 359
Bladh, Marie, 423
Blaha, Michael J., 6
Blaich, Charles, 494
Blair, Clancy, 190, 193, 259, 262, 344
Blair, Kathleen, 127
Blair, Peter S., 138
Blake, Jamilia J., 447
Blakely-McClure, Sarah J., 292
Blakemore, Sarah-Jayne, 404, 405
Blanco, Carlos, 425
Blandon, Alysia Y., 295
Blankenship, Jason, 113, 115
Blaser, Susan, 228
Blau, Alexis K., 191
Bleidorn, Wiebke, 501
Bleys, Dries, 472
Blinder, Alan, 450
Block, Robert, 146
Blomqvist, Ylva Thernström, 138
Bloom, Steven, 105
Blumenthal, Heidemarie, 382
Blum-Kulka, Shoshana, 301
Blurton-Jones, Nicholas G., 288
Bobbitt, Kaeley C., 215
Boehm, Corinne, 86
Bögels, Susan M., 101, 193

Bohlen, Tabata M., 411
Boisvert, Linda, 129
Boivin, Miche, 181
Boivin, Michel, 376, 444, 466
Bolhuis, Johan J., 144
Bolwby, John, 61, 198
Bomba, Monica, 174
Bonanno, Rina A., 444
Boomsma, Dorret I., 376
Boone, Liesbet, 472
Boonstra, Heather, 471
Borden, Lynne M., 378
Borgatti, Renato, 150, 198
Borge, Anne I., 214
Borja, Judith B., 151
Borke, Joern, 209
Borke, Jörn, 209
Bornstein, Marc H., 44, 169, 198, 207, 299, 301, 304
Borrero, Sonya B., 470, 471
Bortfeld, Heather, 177
Bosch, Leslie, 378
Bost, Kelly K., 317
Bothe, Denise, 204
Bottino, Clement J., 224
Bouffard, Suzanne M., 314
Boughrassa, Faiza, 112
Boundy, Ellen O., 129
Bountress, Kaitlin, 481
Bouter, Lex M., 5
Bower, Carol, 115
Bowes, Lucy, 390
Bowker, Julie C., 370, 387, 391, 395
Bowlby, John, 61, 198
Bowman, Christin P., 422
Boyce, William, 423
Boyd, Carol J., 325
boyd, danah, 432, 440, 441, 443, 445, 466
Boyd, Wendy, 213
Braams, Barbara R., 410, 438
Brabeck, Kalina M., 349
Bracken, Bruce A., 272
Brackett, Marc, 352
Bradford, Julia, 42
Bradley, Bekh, 244
Bradley, Elizabeth, 29
Bradley, Rachel, 127
Bradley, Robert H., 128, 299, 301, 304
Braithwaite, David W., 343
Brame, Robert, 475
Brand, Rebecca J., 185
Brandone, Amanda C., 166
Brannen, Conner, 353
Brannon, Patsy M., 59
Brauer, Michael, 233
Bravata, Dena M., 226
Bray, Bethany, 138
Bray, Freddie, 83
Brazelton, T. Berry, 56
Breckenridge, Ross A., 155
Brede, Janina, 259
Breedlove, S. Marc, 468
Breen, Gerome, 195
Breidablik, Hans J., 448
Breivik, Kyrre, 465
Bremner, J. Gavin, 179
Brémond-Gignac, Dominique, 148
Brendgen, Mara, 376, 387, 444, 466
Brennan, Arthur, 127
Brennan, Jeffrey, 241
Brennan, Robert T., 373
Brent, Robert L., 111
Bresnick, Beverly, 150
Bretherton, Inge, 198
Brewer, Robert, 480
Brey, Cristobal de, 359
Brey, Elizabeth, 181
Bribiescas, Richard G., 127

Bridgers, Sophie, 260
Bridges, Margaret, 296
Bridget, David J., 282, 283
Brimblecombe, Nicola, 390
Brindis, Claire D., 471
Brody, Gene H., 462, 463
Brody, Jane E., 118
Bronfenbrenner, Urie, 11, 12, 61
Bronfman, Elisa, 200
Brooks, Daniel E., 240
Brooks, Jeanne, 192
Brooks-Gunn, Jeanne, 275, 296, 385, 413, 424
Broström, Stig, 255
Broussard, Cheryl S., 119
Brown, B. Bradford, 464
Brown, Christia S., 302, 371
Brown, Edna, 378
Brown, Ellie, 185
Brown, Kathryn, 426
Brown, Kirsty Clarke, 274, 276
Brown, Louise, 76
Brown, Rupert, 359
Brown, Susan L., 381, 382, 499
Brownson, Ross C., 416
Broyles, Stephanie, 488
Bruzzese, Dario, 420
Bryant, Amy G., 469
Bryant-Comstock, Katelyn, 469
Bub, Kristen L., 215
Buchbinder, Carla, 257
Buchmann, Marlis, 395
Bucholz, Kathleen K., 84
Buchsbaum, Daphna, 260
Buck, Karen A., 197
Buckhalt, Joseph A., 230
Buckingham, Kati J., 86
Buckley, David, 113, 115
Buckley, Rhonda, 497
Budlovsky, Talia., 478
Buehler, Cheryl, 463
Bueno, Clarissa, 137
Buğdaycı, Resul, 443
Buitelaar, Jan K., 291
Bullen, Chris, 27
Bunge, Silvia A., 313, 346
Burchinal, Margaret R., 215, 270, 275
Burcu, Mehmet, 325
Burk, Caitlin M., 226
Burk, William J., 465, 467
Burke, Erin E., 127
Burke, Jeffrey D., 474, 476
Burkhardt, Sandra A., 332
Burks, A. Wesley, 226
Burner, Karen, 328, 348
Burner, Karen & Crisler, Megan, 328
Burnette, Jeni L., 448
Burns, Cara C., 156
Burns, Matthew K., 331
Burns, Tracey C., 174
Burns, Trudy L, 5, 6
Burraston, Bert, 467
Burridge, Andrea, 268
Burridge, Andrea Backscheider, 491
Burrow, Anthony L., 458
Burstein, David D., 478, 498
Bursztyn, Leonardo, 466
Burt, Nicole M., 282, 283
Burt, S. Alexandra, 376
Bushman, Brad J., 369
Bushway, Shawn D., 475
Buss, David M., 55, 57
Butler, Ashley M., 296
Butler, L., 325
Butler, Lucas P., 15
Butryn, Meghan L., 26
Butte, Dick, 475
Buttelmann, David, 174, 176

Butterworth, Brian, 327, 331
Byard, Roger W., 146
Byers-Heinlein, Krista, 50, 174
Byrd, Dana L., 257
Byrne, Christopher M., 241
Byrnes, James P., 459
Cabrera, Natasha, 19
Cacioppo, John T., 7, 376, 499
Cacioppo, Stephanie, 7, 499
Cagnoli, Giulia A., 86
Cairns, Alyssa, 317
Calarco, Jessica McCrory, 355
Calder, Gillian, 382
Caldwell, Cleopatra H., 17, 121
Calello, D. P., 240
Calkins, Susan D., 140, 194, 283, 285, 295, 396
Call, Josep, 227
Callaghan, Bridget L., 193
Callaghan, Tara, 252
Calvert, Sandra L., 181
Camargo, Carlos A., 226
Camchong, Jazmin, 480
Camhi, Sarah M., 488
Campbell, Frances A., 275
Campbell, Michael C., 59
Campbell, Robin N., 283
Canaider, Silvia, 75
Canavan, Maureen, 29
Cancelliere, Carol, 488
Candy, T. Rowan, 148
Cantor, Patricia, 183
Capaldi, Deborah M., 475
Caplan, Rachel, 246
Caravita, Simona C. S., 390, 392
Card, Noel A., 378, 390
Carey, Anna G., 499
Carey, Nessa, 19
Carlo, Waldemar A., 119, 122
Carlson, Daniel L., 36
Carlson, Elizabeth A., 54
Carlson, Scott, 449
Carlson, Stephanie M., 261
Carlsson, Rickard, 461
Carlström, Eva, 376
Carnethon, Mercedes R., 488
Carolan, Megan E., 276
Caronongan, Pia, 314
Carpenter, David O., 234
Carpenter, Malinda, 174, 176
Carpenter, Thomas O., 59
Carra, Cecilia, 209, 216
Carroll, Linda J., 488
Carroll, Margaret D., 224, 225, 315
Carson, Valerie, 183, 290
Carter, Philippa, 233, 285
Caruso, Federica, 271
Carver, Alison, 314
Carwile, Jenny L., 410
Casaccia, Patrizia, 72
Casadei, Raffaella, 75
Case, Trevor I., 192
Casey, B. J., 404, 409
Casey, Patrick H., 128
Cashin, Alison, 500
Casini, Erica, 198
Casper, Deborah M., 378, 390
Caspi, Avshalom, 11, 377, 475, 488
Cassia, Viola Macchi, 145
Cassidy, David, 488
Cassidy, Jude, 195
Cassina, Matteo, 86
Castellanos-Ryan, Natalie, 464
Castillo, Linda G., 447
Castle, Jennifer, 204
Castle, Sherri, 225
Catani, Claudia, 373
Caudle, Kristina, 409

Cauffman, Elizabeth, 475, 476
Caughey, Aaron B., 109
Caughy, Margaret O'Brien, 296
Cavalari, Rachel N. S., 228
Cavanaugh, Joseph E., 390
Ceausescu, Nicolae, 202
Ceballo, Rosario, 351
Celec, Peter, 100
Celeste, Laura, 359
Cen, Guozhen, 387
Center for Education Policy, 451, 452
Centers for Disease Control and
     Prevention, 74, 156, 157, 158
Cerdá, Magdalena, 11
Cespedes, Elizabeth M., 224
Chafen, Jennifer J. S., 226
Chai, Ching Sing, 362
Chaillet, Nils, 112
Chakraborty, Hrishikesh, 119, 122
Chaloupka, Frank J., 27, 317
Chamberlain, Patricia, 476
Champagne, Frances A., 129
Chan, Chi-Keung, 374, 377
Chan, Grace J., 129
Chan, Hing Man, 121
Chan, Tak Wing, 294
Chan, Wenyaw, 327
Chang, Alicia, 302
Chang, Hyein, 292, 297
Chang, Tzu-Fen, 207
Chango, Joanna M., 198
Chantry, Caroline, 158, 261
Chao, Georgia, 460
Chaparro, Maria P., 395
Charnigo, Richard, 438
Chartier, Karen G., 84
Chase-Lansdale, P. Lindsay, 383
Chassin, Laurie, 481
Chatters, Linda M., 378
Chaudhary, Nandita, 209
Chavez, Tom, 385
Cheah, Charissa, 194
Cheal, Nancy E., 118
Chein, Jason, 410, 439
Chen, Chiung M., 480
Chen, Edith, 374
Chen, Frances S., 210
Chen, Guo-Chong, 114
Chen, Henian, 197
Chen, Hong, 417
Chen, Hua, 327
Chen, Jen-Kai, 267, 349
Chen, Mu-Hong, 325
Chen, Xinyin, 387, 388
Chen, Yi-fu, 462
Cheng, Angela, 85
Cheng, Diana, 118
Cheng, Jiye, 70, 159, 160
Cheng, Yvonne W., 109
Cherlin, Andrew J., 380, 385, 499
Cherng, Hua-Yu Sebastian, 358
Chervenak, Frank A., 111
Cheslack-Postava, Keely, 114
Chess, Stella, 194
Chick, Christina F., 438
Chinapaw, Mai J. M., 313
Chiong, Cynthia, 182
Cho, Junhan, 463
Choe, Daniel E., 299
Chomsky, Noam, 184
Chong, Jessica X., 86
Chopak-Foss, Joanne, 411
Chou, Chien, 443
Choudhury, Ashok Kumar, 224, 317
Choukas-Bradley, Sophia, 470
Chow, Chong Man, 497
Chow, Sy-Miin, 138
Chriqui, Jamie F., 417
Christakis, Dimitri A., 182

Christakis, Erika, 272, 273
Christian, Cindy W., 146
Christian, Parul, 159
Christoforides, Michael, 341
Chronicle of Higher Education, 491
Chudacoff, Howard P., 286
Chugh, Dolly, 437
Chung, He Len, 185
Church, Timothy S., 488
Cicchetti, Dante, 320, 323, 325, 372
Cicconi, Megan, 259
Cillessen, Antonius H. N., 390, 392,
     465
Cimpian, Andrei, 285
Claes, Laurence, 458
Claes, Michel, 413
Claes, Stephan, 4472
Clark, Caron A. C., 122
Clark, Lee Anna, 191
Clark, Linda, 407
Clark, Nina A., 233
Clarke, Maggie, 177
Clarke-Stewart, Alison, 215
Clayton, Heather D., 480
Clayton, P. E., 411
Claytor, Randal P., 225
Clemente, Jose C., 109
Clementi, Maurizio, 86
Clonan, Sheila, 361
Cnattingius, Sven, 109
Coburn, Shayna S., 122
Coffelt, Tina A., 470
Cohen, Bruce M., 327
Cohen, Geoffrey L., 470
Cohen, Harvey J., 488
Cohen, Joel E., 240, 353
Cohen, Jon, 30
Cohen, P., 385
Cohen, Sarah, 324
Cohen, Sheldon, 374
Cohen, Wayne R., 111
Cohen-Kettenis, Peggy T., 76, 461
Colaco, Marc, 57
Cole, Andrea, 500
Cole, Pamela M., 281, 283, 284
Cole, Steven W., 80
Cole, Whitney G., 151
Coleman, Marilyn, 382
Coleman-Jensen, Alisha, 123
Coley, Rebekah Levine, 216
Collie, Rebecca J., 448
Collins, Christine E., 102
Collins, Louis, 228
Collins, Paul F., 323
Collins, Rebecca L., 469
Collins, W. Andrew, 369, 462
Collin-Vézina, Delphine, 425
Colombo, John, 169
Colson, Eve R., 138
Compian, Laura J., 413
Complojer, Christina, 138
Compton, Scott N., 326
Compton, Wilson M., 11
Confer, Jaime C., 57
Conley, AnneMarie, 452
Conners-Burrow, Nicola A., 128
Connor, Carol McDonald, 349
Connor, Jennie, 480
Conti, Gabriella, 275
Coovadia, Hoosen M., 150
Copeland, Kristen A., 225
Copeland, William E., 390
Copher, Ronda, 497
Copin, Henri, 148
Coplan, Robert J., 348, 388
Copp, Jennifer E., 498
Coppola, Elizabeth C., 378
Corballis, Michael C., 227
Corbetta, Daniela, 152

Corcoran, David L., 488
Cordovil, Rita, 236
Core, Cynthia, 268
Corenblum, Barry, 369
Corey, Joanna D., 347
Corliss, Heather L., 461
Cornell, Dewey G., 447
Cornish, Mary M., 183
Corsello, Giovanni, 79
Cortesi, Sandra, 441
Cortright, Alicia, 127
Corwin, Michael J., 138
Corzo, Nieves, 158
Costa, Albert, 267, 347
Costello, E. Jane, 390, 471
Costello, Elizabeth, 475
Costigan, Kathleen A., 103
Côté, James, E., 458
Côté, Pierre, 488
Côté, Sylvana M., 214, 444
Council on School Health, 315
Couzin-Frankel, Jennifer, 72, 90,
     93, 112
Covan, Eleanor Krassen, 499
Covault, Jonathan, 84
Cowan, Nelson, 345
Cox, Laura M., 109
Cox, Martha, 190
Cox, Ronald B., 297, 298, 299
Coxworth, James E., 58
Coyne, Sarah M., 390
Crago, Marjorie, 472
Craig, Allen S., 156
Craig, Stephanie G., 326
Crain, William C., 252
Crawford, Elizabeth, 272
Creemers, Hanneke E., 480
Creswell, John W., 30
Crisler, Megan, 328, 348
Cristia, Alejandrina, 184
Crnic, Keith A., 122, 327
Crone, Eveline A., 410, 438, 439
Crosby, Richard, 438
Crosnoe, Robert, 274
Cross, Donna, 391
Cross, M., 117
Crouter, Ann C., 447
Crowder, Kyle, 234
Crowe, Kristi, 123
Crowell, Sheila E., 376
Crystal, Stephen, 326
Cubillo, Ana, 48
Cuevas, Kimberly, 173
Cui, Lixian, 395
Culpin, Iryna, 412
Cummings, Hope M., 316
Cumsille, Patricio, 464
Cunningham, F. Gary, 105
Cunningham, Solveig A., 316
Curley, James P., 129
Currie, Janet, 14, 246
Curtin, Sally C., 499
Cushman, Mary, 6
Cutuli, J. J., 374, 377
Czaja, Sally J., 245
Dahl, Ronald E., 404, 406, 438, 439,
     440
Daley, Dave, 327
Dalman, Christina, 156
Damasio, Antonio R., 228
Damian, Lavinia E., 472
Damon, Fabrice, 145
Daneback, Kristian, 55, 469
Danese, Andrea, 488
Daniel, David B., 435
Daniels, Stephen R., 225
Darensbourg, Alicia, 447
Darling, Nancy, 464
Dart, Rick, 481

Darwin, Charles, 36, 54, 60
Darwin, Zoe, 127, 128
Dasen, Pierre R., 342
Dashe, Jodi, 105
Dastjerdi, Roya, 129
Daum, Moritz, 174, 176, 177
David, James A., 80
Davie, Gabrielle, 480
Davies, Gregory, 326
Davis, Brian R., 422
Davis, John N., 113
Davis, Linell, 348
Davis, Steven M., 298
Davis-Kean, Pamela E., 274, 369
Davison, Mark L., 351
Dawson, Geraldine, 328, 348
Dayalu, Praveen, 90
Dayanim, Shoshana, 182
Dayton, Carolyn J., 105, 207
Dean, Angela J., 313
Dean, Jenny, 460
Deane, Andrew S., 102
Deardorff, Julianna, 414
Dearing, Eric, 269, 314, 349
Deary, Ian J., 122, 323
Deater-Deckard, Kirby, 229, 282, 283,
     284, 294, 296, 298, 299, 301, 304
de Boer, Anouk, 439
Deboni, Malorie, 145
de Brey, Cristobal, 451
Deckner, Deborah F., 256
De Corte, Erik, 335
de Cossío, Teresita González,
     240, 417
DeFries, John C., 80, 89, 91
de Gardelle, Vincent, 169
Degnan, Kathryn A., 194
deGrauw, Xinyao, 322
DeHaan, Cody, 284
de Haan, Michelle, 140, 176
Dehaene-Lambertz, Ghislaine, 169,
     176, 185
de Heering, Adelaide, 145
de Hoog, Marieke L. A., 224
DeJesus, Jasmine M., 206
De Jesus-Laboy, Kassandra M., 109
de Jonge, Ank, 111
de Jonge, Guustaaf Adolf, 155
Dekhtyar, Serhiy, 321
de Knijff, Peter, 75
de Koning, H. J., 350
Deković, Maja, 192, 194, 422, 468
de la Croix, David, 153
de la Monte, Suzanne M., 11
De La Sablonnière-Griffin, Mireille,
     425
Delaunay-El Allam, 149
De Lee, Joseph Bolivar, 110
Delegido, Ana Benito, 499
Delemarre-van de Waal, Henriette
     A., 76
de Liedekerke, Claire, 145
DeLisi, Matt, 227
Dell'Aniello, Sophie, 325
DeLoache, Judy S., 169, 182
de López, Kristine Jensen, 262
de los Santos, Regina, 472
DelPriore, Danielle J., 224
De Luca, Cinzia R., 122
Demers, Paul A., 233
Deming, Michelle E., 499
Demetriou, Andreas, 341
Deming, Michelle E., 499
Demissie, Zewditu, 480
De Neys, Wim, 433
Deng, Ciping, 352
Denissen, Jaap J. A., 501
Denktaş, Semiha, 111
Denmark, Nicole, 350
Denny, Clark H., 118

Denny, Dallas, 460
DeOrnellas, Kathy, 391
Depeau, Sandrine, 314
De Pisapia, Nicola, 207
DePrimo, Larry, 36
Deptula, Daneen P., 470
Derbidge, Christina, 376
Deresiewicz, William, 493
de Ridder-Sluiter, J. G., 350
Deroo, Lisa A., 114
Desai, Rishi J., 118
DeSalle, Rob, 16
Desjardins, Christopher David, 374, 377
de Sonneville, Leo M. J., 281
DeSouza, Lisette M., 8, 17
Destiche, Dan, 228
Devaraj, Sridevi, 70
de Vente, Wieke, 193
Devine, Rory T., 262, 395
DeVos, Julie, 167
de Vries, Hein, 294
de Water, Erik, 438
Diamond, Lisa M., 202, 468
Diamond, Marian C., 145
Diamond, Milton, 8
Diaz-Barriga, Fernando, 234
Dick, Danielle M., 480
Diehl, Thilo, 128
Dijkstra, Jan Kornelis, 389
Dillow, Sally A., 359, 361
Di Marzo, Vincenzo, 11
Dimler, Laura M., 412
Dinella, Lisa, 304
Ding, Xuechen, 388
Dinh, Michael M., 241
Dionne, Ginette, 181, 376, 466
Diop, Ousmane M., 156
DiPietro, Janet A., 103
Diseth, Åge, 448
Dishion, Thomas J., 467
Dittmar, Helga, 417
Dix, Theodore, 190
Dobkins, Karen, 265
Dobson, Velma, 148
Dodd, Chris, 317
Dodds, Josiah, 150
Domina, Thurston, 452
Dominguez-Bello, Maria G., 109
Dommarco, Juan A. Rivera, 315
Donald, Jennifer, 91
Donato, Jose, 411
Donnellan, M. Brent, 371, 413
Donnelly, Peter, 75
Donovan, Sharon M., 317
Donovick, Peter J., 228
Dorais, Michel, 425
Doraiswamy, Murali, 90
Dotterer, Aryn M., 447
Doucet, Andrea, 461
Dowd, M. Denise, 426
Down, Langdon, 87
Downey, Liam, 234
Downing, Katherine L., 290
Doyle, Lex W., 122
Dozier, Mary, 200
Drescher, Jack, 461
Driemeyer, Wiebke, 421
Driscoll, Anne K., 43
Drucker, Kathleen T., 356
Du, Yukai, 442
Duan, Tao, 107
Dubas, Judith S., 207
Dubois, Jessica, 176, 350
Dubowitz, Howard, 242
Duch, Helena, 183
Duckworth, Angela L., 352
Dugas, Lara R., 70
Duggan, Maeve, 441

Duh, Shinchieh, 261
Duivenvoorden, Hugo J., 122
Dukes, Richard L., 389
Dumas, A., 115
DuMont, Kimberly A., 245
Duncan, Greg J., 215, 276
Dunifon, Rachel, 383
Dunlop Velez, Erin, 451, 491
Dunmore, Simon J., 317
Dunn, Erin C., 244
Dunne, Eileen F., 424
DuPont, Robert L., 11
Dupoux, Emmanuel, 174, 176
Durrant, Joan E., 298
Dutat, Michel, 169
Dutra, Lauren M., 27
Duval-Tsioles, Denise, 382
Dvornyk, Volodymyr, 410
Dweck, Carol S., 210, 369, 448
Dye, Melody, 266
Dyer, Nazly, 296
Eagly, Alice H., 7, 300, 302, 305
Earth Policy Institute, 157
Easton, Judith A., 57
Ebbesen, Ebbe B., 284
Eberhard-Gran, Malin, 195
Eberhart, Johann K., 116
Eccles, Jacquelynne S., 445, 447, 449, 472
Eckholm, Erik, 119
Eckshtain, Dikla, 405
Eddy, J. Mark, 476
Ederer, David, 440
Edmond, Karen, 110
Edwards, Erin S., 282, 283
Edwards, Janet W. Rich, 109
Eggermont, Steven, 470
Eggum, Natalie D., 291, 463
Ehrenberg, Rachel, 84
Ehrenreich, Samuel E., 292, 444
Ehret, Christopher, 16
Ehrhardt, Anke A., 8
Ehrhardt, Stephan, 128
Eichhorst, Werner, 452
Eigsti, Inge-Marie, 177
Eimas, Peter D., 176
Eisenberg, Laurie S., 148
Eisenberg, Mark J, 478
Eisenberg, Nancy, 259, 282, 291, 296, 374, 463
Eisman, Andria B., 17
Eissenberg, Thomas, 27, 478
Ekas, Naomi V., 196
Elbert, Thomas, 373
Elder, Glen H., 497
Elicker, James, 216
Elkind, David, 286, 430
Elliott, Amy J., 113, 115
Elliott, Marc N., 469
Elliott, Sinikka, 470
Ellis, Amy B., 358
Ellis, Bruce J., 7, 282, 411
Ellis, Raquel T., 243
Ellison, Christopher G., 298, 411
Ellwood, Philippa, 226
Elmadih, Alya, 105
Elmerstig, Eva, 421
Elmholdt, Else-Marie Jegindoe, 207
Elshaug, Christine, 314
El-Sheikh, Mona, 230
Elwick, Sheena, 213
Emsell, Louise, 50
Endendijk, Joyce J., 303
Engelberts, Adèle C., 155
Engels, Rutger C. M. E., 294, 431
Ennis, Chad, 228
Ennis, Linda Rose, 199
Ensari, Ipek, 183
Enserink, Martin, 81

Ensor, Rosie, 395
Entwisle, Doris R., 26
Epprecht, Marc, 468
Epps, Chad, 84
Epstein, Leon G., 328
Epton, Tracy, 114
Erath, Stephen A., 468
Erceg, Erin, 391
Erden, Feyza Tantekin, 288
Erdos, Caroline, 350
Erickson, Anders C., 121
Erikson, Erik, 39–41, 61, 199, 208, 212, 282–284, 300–303, 339–341, 369, 370, 457–458, 460–461, 496, 498
Ernst, Monique, 194, 195, 438
Errichiello, Luca, 420
Erskine, Holly E., 324
Escobedo, Jorge O., 478
Eslinger, Paul J., 229
Espelage, Dorothy, 391
Espinosa-Martos, Irene, 158
Esposito, Gianluca, 207
Esposito, Linda, 155
Espy, Kimberly A., 122, 259
Esser, Marissa B., 480
Estrada-Restrepo, Alejandro, 122
Estroff, Todd Wilk, 10
Etkin, Amit, 194, 195
Ettekal, Idean, 390
Etter, Jean-François, 27, 478
Euser, Eveline M., 425
Evans, Alan C., 142, 323
Evans, Angela D., 261, 262
Evans, Gary W., 230, 385
Evans, Jane A., 88
Evans, M. D. R., 351
Evans-Lacko, Sara, 390
Evenson, Kelly R., 416
Everett, Bethany G., 469
Everett, Caleb, 343
Evers, Kathinka, 374
Eyer, Diane E., 128
Ezzati, Majid, 159
Fabes, Richard A., 304
Facchin, Federica, 75
Fadjukoff, Päivi, 458
Fagundes, Christopher P., 202
Fair, Damien A., 490
Fallu, Jean-Sébastien, 453
Fang, Fuxi, 261
Fang, Hua, 122
Fareed, Mohd, 83
Faris, Peter, 312
Farkas, Amy H., 470, 471
Farkas, George, 215, 452
Farrar, M. Jeffrey, 257
Farrington, David P., 390, 391, 475
Fassbender, Iina, 172
Fawzi, Wafaie W., 129
Fazzi, Elisa, 174
FBI, 476
Fearon, R. M. Pasco, 200
Fedeli, Claudia, 198
Feeley, Nancy, 129
Feig, Daniel I., 225
Feigenson, Lisa, 343
Feinberg, Mark E., 467, 468
Feld, Barry C., 475
Feldman, Ruth, 196, 198
Feldman, Sarah, 107
Felmban, Wejdan S., 435
Feng, Xingyi, 388
Fenstermacher, Susan K., 181
Ferguson, Christopher J., 296, 298
Fergusson, Emma, 325
Ferlay, Jacques, 83
Fernandes, Eulalia, 294
Fernandez, Jose R., 59

Fernández, Leonides, 158
Fernyhough, Charles, 257
Ferrari, Alize J., 324
Ferrari, Marco, 50, 158
Ferrari, Pier F., 145
Ferraro, Kenneth F., 245
Ferris, Frederick L., 85
Fielding, D. W., 116
Fields, R. Douglas, 227
Field-Springer, Kimberly, 109
Filion, Kristian B., 478
Filipek, Pauline A., 122
Filová, Barbora, 100
Fine, J. S., 240
Fine, Jason P., 226
Fine, Jodene Goldenring, 325
Finer, Lawrence B., 76, 121, 123
Fingerman, Karen L., 8, 497
Finkel, Eli J., 448
Finkelhor, David, 243, 244, 385, 389, 425, 441, 442
Finn, Amy S., 364
Fischer, Karin, 450
Fiset, Sylvain, 167
Fisher, Elisa M., 183
Fitzgerald, Maria, 149
Flaherty, David K., 102
Flaxman, Abraham D., 324
Flegal, Katherine M., 224, 225, 315
Fleischman, Diana S, 57
Fletcher, Ben, 177
Fletcher, Erica N., 290
Fletcher, Richard, 206
Florence, Curtis, 440
Flores, Javier E., 390
Floud, Roderick, 411
Fluss, Joel, 350
Flynn, James R., 321
Fogel, Alan, 197
Fogel, Robert W., 411
Foley, Claire, 349
Fong, Allan, 85
Fonov, Vladimir, 228
Font, Marta, 183
Forbes, Deborah, 271
Fordwood, Samantha R., 405
Forget-Dubois, Nadine, 181
Fornito, Alex, 434
Forrest, Christopher B., 27
Foster, Eugene A., 75
Fournier, Marc, 176
Fox, Nathan A., 194, 195, 204, 213, 230, 435
Foxx, Richard M., 56
Foy, Pierre, 356
Frabetti, Flavia, 75
Franchak, John M., 103, 151, 152, 153
Franck, Caroline, 478
Franke, Barbara, 291
Frankenburg, William K., 150
Franklin, Sarah, 76
Frayer, David W., 68
Frazão, Renata, 411
Frazier, A. Lindsay, 226, 410
Frederickson, Norah, 447
Fredricks, Jennifer A., 472
Freegard, Matthew, 228
Freeman, Emily, 206
Freeman, Joan, 333
Freitag, Claudia, 172
Freud, Anna, 474
Freud, Sigmund, 39–41, 60, 208, 301–302, 370, 460
Friedlaender, Françoise R., 16
Friedman, Howard S., 413
Friedman, Jan M., 119
Friedman, Naomi P., 262
Friedman, Ori, 291

Froiland, John M., 351
Fröjd, Sari, 421, 422
Froment, Alain, 16, 59
Fry, Douglas P., 289
Fry, Richard, 359
Fujimura, Masanori, 103
Fulcher, Ben D., 434
Fuligni, Allison Sidle, 270, 273
Fuligni, Andrew J., 459, 463
Fuller, Bruce, 296, 351
Fuller, Miles, 70
Fullerton, Janice, 91
Fulton, Jessica J., 235
Fung, Heidi, 352, 369
Funkquist, Eva-Lotta, 138
Furey, Terrence S., 69
Furstenberg, Frank F., 497
Furukawa, Emi, 212
Fury, Gail, 54
Fusaro, Maria, 206
Fussell, Jill J., 128
Gabrieli, John D. E., 327, 364
Gadermann, Anne M., 369
Gagné, Monique, 466
Galak, Jeff, 283
Galdas, Paul, 127, 128
Galea, Sandro, 472
Galinsky, Adam D., 491
Gallardo, Miguel E., 17
Galor, Oded, 71
Galván, Adriana, 410
Galvao, Tais F., 413
Galvez, Maida, 228, 411
Galvez, Roberto, 142
Gambaro, Ludovica, 269
Ganapathy, Thilagavathy, 127
Ganchimeg, Togoobaatar, 424
Ganea, Patricia A., 182
Gannon, Bryan, 85
Ganong, Lawrence H., 382
Gao, Wei, 139, 140, 141, 142, 171
Garba, Houmma A., 44
Garbarino, James, 389
Garber, Judy, 411
Garcia, Pedro J., 412
García Coll, Cynthia, 122, 351
Garciaguirre, Jessie S., 151
García-Marcos, Luis, 226
Gardner, Howard, 61, 322
Gardner, Paula, 155
Gardner, Phil, 460
Garfinkel, Irwin, 385
Gari, Mamdooh, 416
Garner, Ashley, 382
Garnett, Christopher, 438
Garon, Mathieu, 228
Garrett-Peters, Patricia, 190
Garrity, Stacy E., 424
Garthus-Niegel, Susan, 195
Garti, Helene Akpene, 411
Garvin, Melissa C., 202
Gash, Don M., 102
Gaskins, Suzanne, 288
Gasser, Urs., 441
Gatsonis, Constantine A., 234
Gattis, Merideth, 260
Gatzke-Kopp, Lisa, 376
Gavin, Lorrie, 426
Gawron, Michal, 478
Gazzaley, Adam, 313, 346
Gazzard, Gus, 85
Ge, Xinting, 101
Gee, Gilbert C., 495
Geier, Charles, 409
Gelaye, Bizu, 412
Gelskov, Sofie V., 169
Gendron, Brian P., 391, 444
Genesee, Fred, 350
Gentile, Douglas A., 442

Geoffroy, Marie-Claude, 214, 444
Georgeson, Jan, 268
Georgiades, Katholiki, 471
Gerhard, Tobias, 326
Gernhardt, Ariane, 54
Gerrard, David F., 233, 285
Gerris, Jan R. M., 207
Gershoff, Elizabeth T., 297, 298, 463
Gerstenberg, Tobias, 35
Gervain, Judit, 50
Gervais, Will M., 435
Geschwind, Michael, 90
Gest, Scott D., 467
Geubbels, Eveline L., 158, 261
Gewertz, Catherine, 360, 450
Gewirtz, Abigail H., 373
Ghera, Melissa M., 194
Gherghi, Marco, 420
Ghossainy, Maliki E., 346
Gianantonio, Elena Di, 86
Gibb, Robbin, 350
Gibbons, Ann, 226
Gibson, Eleanor J., 170, 171
Gibson, J., 170
Gibson-Davis, Christina, 381
Giedd, Jay N., 322
Gilbert, Jack, 70
Gilbody, Simon, 127, 128
Giles, Amy, 171
Giletta, Matteo, 470
Gill, M. S., 411
Gill, Michael, 325
Gilles, Floyd H., 139
Gillespie, Charles F., 244
Gillespie, Michael A., 314
Gillespie-Lynch, Kristen, 323, 328
Gillig, Benjamin, 494
Gilligan, Carol, 394
Gillman, Matthew W., 109, 224, 317
Gillon, Raanan, 30
Gilman, Carley, 322
Gilmore, John H., 139, 140, 141, 142, 171
Gilsanz, Vicente, 59
Gini, Gianluca, 392
Ginsburg, Golda S., 326
Giordano, Peggy C., 498
Giuffrè, Mario, 79
Giumetti, Gary W., 444
Givi, Julian, 283
Giwercman, Aleksander, 88
Gladden, Matthew, 473
Glaeske, Gerd, 325
Glantz, Stanton A., 27
Glenberg, Arthur M., 45
Glennerster, Rachel, 353
Glick, Gary C., 473
Gluck, Stephanie C., 261
Go, Alan S., 6
Goddings, Anne-Lise, 322, 404, 405
Godeau, Emmanuelle., 423
Godinet, Meripa T., 245
Godleski, Stephanie A., 292
Goetz, Cari D., 57
Goh, Daniel Y. T., 138
Goksan, Sezgi, 150
Gold, Mark S., 10
Golden, Neville H., 415
Goldin-Meadow, Susan, 177, 254
Goldman, Barbara D., 151
Goldstein, Joshua R., 489
Goldstein, Michael H., 198
Golin, Carol E., 470
Golinkoff, Roberta M., 183, 185, 258, 272, 273, 286
Golm, Dennis, 204
Golombok, Susan, 76
Gomez, Juan-Carlos, 179
Göncü, Artin, 288

Goniewicz, Maciej L., 478
Gonzaga, Gian C., 7, 499
Gonzales, Nancy A., 122, 414
Gonzalez, Antonio, 109
Gonzalez-Gomez, Nayeli, 179
González-Zapata, Laura I., 122
Goodlad, James K., 235
Goodman, Gail S., 230
Goodman, Rebecca J., 468
Goossens, Frits, 371
Goossens, Luc, 431
Gopnik, Alison, 260, 266
Gorber, Sarah C., 315
Gordon, Allegra R., 461
Gordon, Jeffrey I., 70, 159, 160
Gordon-Hollingsworth, Arlene T., 326
Gosling, Samuel D., 501
Gostin, Lawrence O., 31
Gottesman, Irving I., 91
Gottfredson, Nisha C., 390
Gottman, John, 61
Goudjil, Sabrina, 176
Gough, Ethan K., 160
Gould, Jeffrey B., 59
Gowen, L. Kris, 413
Grabenstein, John D., 59
Graber, Julia A., 413, 424
Grady, Jessica S., 23
Graf, Frauke, 172
Graf, William D., 328
Graham, Sandra, 391
Graham-Bermann, Sandra A., 298
Granger, Douglas A., 190, 230
Gratz, Kim L., 244
Grayson, David S., 490
Grbic, Amanda, 171
Gredebäck, Gustaf, 177
Green, Cathryn Gordon, 8
Green, James A., 191
Green, Jennifer G., 471
Green, Ronald, 76
Greene, George J., 469
Greene, Melissa L., 472
Greenfield, Patricia M., 441
Greenough, William T., 142, 145
Gregg, Norman McAlister, 114
Gregor, Courtney, 259
Gregory, Christian, 123
Gregson, Joanna, 424
Greulich, Faith K., 304
Grewen, Karen, 139, 140, 141, 142, 171
Griffin, Martyn, 342
Griffiths, Thomas L., 45, 260
Grigorenko, Elena L., 346
Grigsby-Toussaint, Diana S., 317
Griskevicius, Vladas, 224
Groeneveld, Marleen G., 303
Grogan-Kaylor, Andrew, 298
Groh, Ashley M., 200
Gross, James J., 281
Grossmann, Karin, 198
Grossmann, Klaus E., 198
Grossmann, Tobias, 140, 148, 193
Grotevant, Harold D., 204
Grotte, Nathaniel, 411
Grove, Lauren E., 101
Gruber, Michael J., 471
Grünebaum, Amos, 111
Gu, Dongfeng, 84
Guan, Yu, 152
Guerra, Nancy G., 388, 389, 390, 391, 444
Guerri, Consuelo, 479
Guhn, Martin, 369
Gunderson, Elizabeth A., 343
Gunnar, Megan R., 202, 204, 213, 465
Gunnell, David, 156

Gunnoe, Marjorie Lindner, 296, 298
Guo, Cheng, 371
Guo, Siying., 444
Guo, Xin, 413
Güroğlu, Berna, 438
Gutierrez-Galve, Leticia, 127
Guyer, Amanda E., 439
Guzman, Natalie S. de, 430
Ha, Eun-Hee, 234
Haataja, Leena, 122
Hackett, Patrick D., 302
Haden, Catherine A., 53
Hagan, José E., 156
Hagoort, Peter, 184
Haidt, Jonathan, 45, 394
Haier, Richard J., 323
Haigh, Corinne, 350
Haileyesus, Tadesse, 440
Haines, Jess, 224
Hajek, Peter, 27, 478
Halari, Rozmin, 48
Halberda, Justin, 343
Halim, May Ling, 304
Hall, Anthony, 313
Hall, Kelli Stidham, 471
Hall, Marg, 391
Hall, Matthew L., 177
Haller, Moira, 481
Hallers-Haalboom, Elizabeth T.J., 303
Hallström, Inger, 146
Halpern-Felsher, Bonnie L., 412
Halter, Steven D., 80
Hamby, Sherry, 244, 385, 389
Hamdan, Noora, 343
Hamerton, John L., 88
Hamilton, Brady E., 25, 423, 499
Hamilton, Jessica L., 413
Hamlat, Elissa J., 413
Hamlin, J. Kiley, 395
Hammond, Christopher J., 84
Han, Jinnuo, 98
Han, Wen-Jui, 275
Hane, Amie Ashley, 194
Haney, Barbara M., 149
Hanington, Lucy, 127
Hanish, Laura D., 304
Hankinson, Arlene L., 488
Hanks, Andrew S., 317
Hanna-Attisha, Mona, 235
Hannah, Mary E., 111
Hannon, Erin E., 179, 191
Hansell, Narelle K., 84
Hansen, David J., 12, 230
Hanson, Jana M., 494
Hanson, Katherine G., 183, 442
Hanushek, Eric A., 356, 446
Hao, Yongchen, 84
Harden, Brenda Jones, 350
Harden, K. Paige, 404, 410, 413, 438
Hare, Brian, 227
Hargreaves, Andy, 450
Harkany, Tibor, 11
Harkness, Sara, 152, 298, 412
Harlwo, Harry, 61
Harms, Madeline B., 261
Harper, Casandra E., 494
Harrell, Susan W., 247
Harrier, Sara, 426
Harrington, Alison, 183
Harrington, Hona Lee, 11
Harris, Bernard, 411
Harris, Michelle A., 413
Harris, Paul L., 206, 254
Harris, Peter R., 114
Harris, R., 116
Harris, Tyler, 496
Harrison, Christopher J., 426
Harrison, Glyn, 156

Harrison, Kristen, 317
Harrison, Linda J., 213
Harry, Beth, 332
Hart, Betty, 350
Hart, Chantelle N., 317
Hart, Daniel, 459
Hart, Emily J., 292
Harter, Susan, 210
Hartl, Amy C., 376, 432, 466
Hartley, Catherine A., 409, 435, 438, 439, 440
Hartley, Zachary J., 80
Hartman, Catharina A., 291
Hartman, Sarah, 20
Hartmann, E. Eugenie, 148
Hartvigsen, Jan, 488
Harvey, Elizabeth A., 229
Hasson, Ramzi, 325
Hastings, Paul D., 295
Hatch, J. Amos, 269
Hatzenbuehler, Mark L., 390, 469
Haug, Kjell, 114
Havlena, Jeffrey A., 235
Haw, Camilla, 474
Hawkes, Kristen, 58
Hawkins, Stacy Ann, 378
Hawley, Patricia H., 390
Hawrylak, María Fernández, 499
Hawthorne, Joanna, 125
Hawton, Keith, 474
Hayashi, Akiko, 179
Hayden, Elizabeth P., 315, 320, 323
Hayden, Erika Check, 91
Hayes, DeMarquis, 447
Hayes, Peter, 411
Hayne, Harlene, 173
Haynie, Dana L., 431
Hayslip, Bert, 382
Hayward, Chris, 413
He, Jian-ping, 326
He, Yunfeng, 387
Hébert, Emily T., 316
Hébert, Jean M., 324
Hechtman, Lily, 326
Heckman, James J., 275
Hect, Jasmine, 101
Hedberg, Eric C., 362
Heeren, Timothy, 138
Hegyi, Thomas, 155
Hein, Sascha, 346
Heine, Steven J., 500
Heinz, Julia, 15
Heistad, David, 374, 377
Helle, Nadine, 128
Hellerstein, Susan C., 107
Hellström, J., 117
Helminen, Mika, 422
Helms, Sarah W., 470
Hemarajata, Peera, 70
Hendel, Astrid, 128
Henders, Anjali, 480
Henderson, Heather A., 194, 435
Hendler, Talma, 198
Hennessy-Fiske, Molly, 5
Henrich, Joseph, 500
Henriksen, Danah, 371
Henry, David B., 470
Hense, Hans-Werner, 138
Henshaw, Stanley, 423
Henson, Robert A., 463
Herbers, Janette E., 374, 377
Herlitz, Agneta, 321
Herman, Khalisa N., 288
Herman, Sarah, 30
Hernandez-Diaz, Sonia, 118
Hernández-Lloreda, María Victoria, 227
Heron, Jon, 127, 412
Herrmann, Esther, 183, 227

Herrmann, Julia, 335
Herschensohn, Julia R., 263
Hershberg, Rachel M., 8, 17
Hertzman, Clyde, 369
Hertzmark, Ellen, 410
Herzhoff, Kathrin, 404, 410
Hesketh, Kylie D., 290
Heslenfeld, Dirk J., 291
Hessel, Elenda T., 198
Hetherington, Chelsea, 283
Hetherington, E. Mavis, 380
Hewer, Alexandra, 303
Heyer, Djai B., 117
Heyes, Cecilia, 257
Heyes, Stephanie Burnett, 404, 405
Higashibara, Fumiko, 212
Hilbert, Anja, 420
Hilder, Lisa, 122
Hill, Elisabeth L., 152
Hill, Heather D., 212
Hill, Jonathan, 195
Hill, Laura G., 390
Hill, Patrick L., 458
Hill, Sarah E., 224
Himelfarb, Igor, 261
Hincapié, Cesar A., 488
Hinchliff, Sharron, 127, 128
Hinkley, Trina, 290
Hinnant, J. Benjamin, 396
Hinz, Elizabeth, 374
Hirakawa, Makiko, 179
Hirbo, Jibril B., 59
Hirsh-Pasek, Kathy, 183, 185, 258, 272, 273, 286
Hirvonen, Riikka, 194, 357
Hnatiuk, Jill A., 290
Ho, Emily S., 152
Ho, Shao-Hsuan, 105
Hock, Alyson, 171
Hodosy, Július, 100
Hoekstra, Pieter J., 291
Hoeve, Machteld, 207
Hofer, Claire, 282, 296, 463
Hoff, Erika, 268
Hoffman, Barbara, 105
Hoffman, Jessica L., 264
Hofman, M. A., 49
Holden, George W., 298, 411
Holland, Andrew J. A., 122
Holland, James D., 435
Hollatz, Amanda L., 227
Hollich, George J., 185
Holloway, John W., 112
Holmes, Christopher J., 229
Holochwost, Steven J., 146
Holsinger, Eva, 204
Holsti, Liisa, 149
Holt, Lynn, 84
Holt, Melissa, 385, 389
Holt-Lunstad, Julianne, 496
Holzer, Jessica, 29
Honein, Margaret A., 119
Hong, David S., 88
Hong, Jun Sung, 389
Hong, Sandra Soliday, 273
Hong, Sok Chul, 411
Hook, Jennifer L., 36
Hornung, Richard W., 225
Horowitz, Michelle, 274, 276
Horton, Megan K., 117
Horwitz, Suzanne R., 166
Hossain, Ziarat, 207
Hostinar, Camelia E., 193, 465
Hotopf, Matthew, 122
Houts, Renate, 11, 488
How, Ti Hwei, 138
Howe, Christine, 342
Howe, Tsu-Hsin, 122
Howell, Diane M., 57

Howes, Carollee, 273
Howlett, Neil, 177
Hoyert, Donna L., 155
Hoyme, H. Eugene, 113, 115
Hrdy, Sarah B., 58, 210, 211
Hsiao, Ray Chih-Jui, 442
Hsu, Ju-Wei, 325
Hsu, Yung-Wen, 122
Hu, Siyuan, 322
Huang, Cecilia, 326
Huang, Chiungjung, 472
Huang, Francis L., 5
Huang, Hung-Hsuan, 192
Huang, Jianfeng, 84
Huang, Kai-Lin, 325
Huang, Rae-Chi, 158
Huang, Yiching, 273
Huang, Z. Josh, 141
Hublin, Jean-Jacques, 211
Hübner, Christian A., 324
Huckabee, Helena, 333
Hudson, Bettie L., 155
Hugdahl, Kenneth, 228
Hughes, Claire, 262, 395
Hughes, Diane, 447
Hughes, Jan N., 388
Hughes, Julie M., 434
Huh, Susanna Y., 109
Huijbregts, Stephan C. J., 281
Huisman, Jaap, 76
Huit, Terrence Z., 12
Huizink, Anja C., 480
Humiston, Sharon, 426
Humphrey, Jasmine R., 119
Humphrey, Jean H., 160
Hunter, Jonathan, 198
Hunter, Sarah B., 460
Hurt, Lee, 118
Hurt, Lisa, 110
Hussar, William, 451
Hussein, Oula, 459
Huston, Aletha C., 215
Hutchings, Judy, 327
Hutchinson, Esther A., 122
Hutman, Ted, 323, 328
Hutton, Eileen K., 111
Huver, Rose M. E., 294
Huybrechts, Krista F., 118
Huynh, Jimmy L., 72
Huynh, Virginia W., 459
Hvistendahl, Mara, 92
Hyde, Janet S., 305, 358
Hyde, Janet Shibley, 454, 460
Hymel, Shelley, 444
Hyslop, Anne, 450
Iacono, William G., 468
Iannotti, Ronald J., 416
Ichien, Nicholas T., 410
Iida, Hiroko, 312
Ikeda, Martin J., 331
Im, Myung H., 388
Imm, Pamela, 235
Inan, Hatice Z., 272
Inhelder, Bärbel, 46, 251, 432, 433
Insel, Thomas R., 142
Inskip, Hazel M., 122
Insurance Institute for Highway Safety, 408
Inzlicht, Michael, 491
Iodice, Davide, 420
Irwin, Scott, 142
Ishii, Nozomi, 103
Islam, Nadia, 182
Itoh, Keiko, 179
Ivcevic, Zorana, 352
Jaccard, James, 465
Jackson, Kristina M., 465
Jackson, Sandra L., 316
Jackson, Todd, 417

Jacob, Peyton, 478
Jacobsohn, Gwen Costa, 317
Jacobson, Marc S., 415
Jaffe, Adam, 122
Jaffe, Arthur C., 136
Jaffee, Laura, 361
Jager, Justin, 369
Jakobsen, Krisztina V., 145
Jambon, Marc, 396
James, Jenée, 411
Jamison, Tyler, 382
Janosz, Michel, 453
Janssen, Erick, 421
Janssen, Ian, 290
Janssen, Patricia A., 107
Janus, Monika, 321, 335
Jarcho, Johanna M., 194, 195, 439
Jaswal, Vikram K., 15
Jednoróg, Katarzyna, 350
Jelalian, Elissa, 317
Jemal, Ahmedin, 83
Jenner, Edward, 60
Jennings, J. Richard, 390
Jensen, Henning, 209
Jensen, Lene Arnett, 394
Jensen, Robert, 466
Jernigan, Terry, 101, 144
Jhangiani, Shalini N., 86
Jia, Peng, 316
Jia, Ruiting, 350
Jimenez, Natasha B., 227
Jimerson, Shane R., 331
Jingzhou, Wu, 76, 77
Jobling, Mark A., 75
Johnson, Anna E., 465
Johnson, Frank, 215
Johnson, James, 286
Johnson, Jonni L., 230
Johnson, Kelly, 57
Johnson, Lakeisha, 349
Johnson, Linda L., 473
Johnson, Magen M., 80
Johnson, Mark H., 140, 146, 176
Johnson, Rachel K., 225
Johnson, Sarasa M. A., 160
Johnson, Scott P., 152, 190
Johnson, Susan C., 210
Johnston, Lloyd D., 10, 317, 477, 478, 481
Johnston, Sebastian L., 319
Joinson, Carol, 412
Jolicoeur-Martineau, Alexis, 8
Jolles, Diana R., 109
Jolliffe, Darrick, 475
Jonas, Eric, 48
Jones, Andrea M., 247
Jones, Helen, 195
Jones, Karen, 327
Jones, Lisa, 425
Jones, Lisa M., 441, 442
Jones, Mary C., 413
Jones, Nancy A., 191
Jong, Jyh-Tsorng, 192
Jonsson, Maria, 109
Joost J., 111
Jordan, Amy B., 481
Jørgensen, Niels, 88
Jorgenson, Alicia Grattan, 442
Josephs, Robert A., 404, 410
Ju, Eunsu, 460
Julian, Megan M., 204
Jung, Rex E., 323
Junge, Caroline, 184
Jungert, Tomas, 391
Juonala, Markus, 5, 6
Juranek, Jenifer, 122
Jusczyk, Peter, 176
Just, David R., 317
Juster, Robert-Paul, 312

Juul, Anders, 88
Juvonen, Antti, 362
Juvonen, Jaana, 391
Kaar, Jill L., 225
Kaas, Jon H., 102
Kachel, A. Friederike, 211
Kaerts, Nore, 57
Kahn, Linda G., 117
Kaiser, Jocelyn, 91, 98
Kalberg, Wendy O., 113, 115
Kaliwile, Chisela, 85
Kalkhoran, Sara, 479
Kalkwarf, Heidi J., 225
Kalliala, Marjatta, 289
Kalmijn, Matthijs, 500
Kaltiala-Heino, Riittakerttu, 421, 422
Kalverdijk, Luuk J., 325
Kamper, Kimberly E., 292
Kampmann, Beate, 158
Kanarek, Marty S., 235
Kang, Hye-Kyung, 107
Kangas, Ashley, 171
Kann, Laura, 426
Kanner, Leo, 328
Kanny, Dafna, 118, 480
Kantor, Rebecca, 272
Kao, Tsair, 192
Kaploun, Victor, 465
Kapp, Steven K., 323, 328
Kappler, Gregor, 213
Kaprio, Jaakko, 480
Karama, Sherif, 228, 323
Karatsoreos, Ilia N., 488
Karbach, Julia, 347
Karlsson, Håkan, 156
Karmaus, Wilfried, 112
Karmiloff-Smith, Annette, 348
Karoly, Lynn A., 270
Karr, Catherine J., 233
Karriker-Jaffe, Katherine J., 84
Kärtner, Joscha, 209, 216
Kastbom, Åsa A., 423
Katherine M., 298
Katulski, Krzysztof., 420
Katzmarzyk, Peter T., 488
Katz-Wise, Sabra L., 461
Kauffman, James M., 332
Kaufman, Jordy, 171
Kavanaugh, Robert D., 289, 290
Kawachi, Ichiro, 473
Keane, Susan P., 295, 396
Keeton, Courtney, 326
Keil, Frank C., 169, 173
Keil, Ulrich, 226
Keller, Heidi, 54, 202, 209, 216
Keller, Peggy S., 230, 435
Kelley, Jonathan, 351
Kelly, Heather O'Beirne, 298
Kemp, Robert J., 234
Kempe, C. Henry, 241
Kempe, Ruth S., 241
Kena, Grace, 215, 451, 491
Kendall-Taylor, Nathaniel, 242
Kennedy, Ann M., 356
Kennedy, Mark, 204
Kennell, John H., 128
Kenny, Lorcan, 259
Keown, Louise J., 368
Kern, Margaret L., 27, 352
Kerr, Margaret, 465
Kerr, Thomas, 480
Kersken, Verena, 179
Kesselring, Thomas, 252
Kessels, Ursula, 335
Kessler, Ronald C., 471
Kestler, Lisa, 116
Kettinger, Laurie, 118

Keupp, Stefanie, 257
Khafi, Tamar Y., 375
Khan, Shereen, 466
Kharsati, Naphisabet, 383
Khoury, Philip R., 225
Kibler, Amanda, 349
Kidwell, Katherine M., 225
Kiechl-Kohlendorfer, Ursula, 138
Kieling, Christian, 324, 325
Kiff, Cara, 378
Kiley, Dan, 401
Kilgore, Paul E., 59
Killen, Melanie, 395
Kim, Bo-Ram, 138
Kim, Dong-Sik, 417
Kim, Edwin H., 226
Kim, Heejung S., 282
Kim, Helen, 126
Kim, Hojin, 190
Kim, Hyun-Sun, 417
Kim, J., 190
Kim, Juhee, 317
Kim, Jung In, 226
Kim, Kilsun, 478
Kim, Pilyoung, 50, 105, 230, 385
Kim-Spoon, Jungmeen, 194, 229, 459, 468
King, Bruce M., 57
King, Derek, 390
King, Martin Luther, Jr., 36
Kinney, Hannah C., 155
Kinslow, Kathy, 359
Kinzler, Katherine D., 206
Kirchner, H. Lester, 204
Kirk, Elizabeth, 177
Kirkham, Natasha Z., 206
Kirschner, Paul A., 54
Kit, Brian K., 224, 225, 315
Kitzmann, Katherine M., 151
Kiuru, Noona, 467
Kizy, Thomas, 421
Kkeli, Natalie, 417
Klaczynsk, Paul A., 435, 437
Klaric, Elena, 259
Klaus, Marshall H., 128
Klein, Alyson, 269
Klein, Daniel N., 376
Klein, Denise, 267, 349
Klein, Zoe A., 405
Kleinman, Ken P., 224, 317
Kleis, Astrid, 209
Klimstra, Theo A., 501
Kline, Kathleen K., 300
Klingensmith, Georgeanna J., 313
Klinger, Laura G., 328, 348
Klingner, Janette, 332
Klungsøyr, Kari, 114
Knapp, Martin, 390
Knappe, Susanne, 191
Knight, Rona, 371
Knights, Nicky, 204
Knopf, Monika, 172
Knopik, Valerie S., 80, 89, 91
Knopp, Kayla, 385
Ko, Chih-Hung, 443
Ko, Eon-Suk, 184
Ko, Wen-Ya, 59
Koch, Linda, 70
Kochanek, Kenneth D., 155
Kochanska, Grazyna, 227
Kochi, Takeshi, 84
Koehoorn, Mieke, 233
Koenen, Karestan C., 472
Koenig, Melissa A., 261, 283
Koepsell, Thomas D., 89
Koerner, Ascan, 463
Kogan, Steven M., 463
Kohlberg, Lawrence, 303, 393
Kolb, Bryan, 140, 350

Kolling, Thorsten, 172
Kolucki, Barbara, 183
Komati, Meghana, 151
Komisar, Erica, 199
Komro, Kelli A., 471
Kongolo, Guy, 176
Koning, Ina, 439
Konner, Melvin, 57, 139, 144, 147, 193, 210, 312
Kono, Yumi, 103
Konstam, Varda, 496
Koo, Anita, 294
Koolschijn, P. Cédric, 438
Kopko, Kimberly, 383
Kopp, Claire B., 192
Kording, Konrad Paul, 48
Korhonen, Tellervo, 480
Korostenskaja, Milena, 322
Kost, Kathryn, 423
Koster-Hale, Jorie, 262
Kothare, Sanjeev V., 136
Kouider, Sid, 169
Koury, Amanda S., 216
Kowalski, Robin M., 444
Kozhimannil, Katy B., 109, 126
Kraft, Matthew A., 364
Kramer, Andrew, 224
Krampe, Megan, 225
Kraus, Nina, 237
Kray, Laura J., 491
Kreager, Derek A., 468
Krebs, John R., 148
Kreider, Rose M., 423
Kremer, Michael, 353
Kremer, Peter, 314
Kreppner, Jana, 204
Kresnow, Marcie-jo, 440
Kretch, Kari S., 148, 171
Kringelbach, Morten L., 207
Krisberg, Kim, 481
Kristapovich, Paul, 215
Kristensson, Krister, 156
Kristman, Vicki L., 488
Kroger, Jane, 458
Krogstad, Jens M., 350, 359
Kroncke, Anna P., 333
Kruse, Gina R., 479
Kuchirko, Yana, 181, 256
Kuefner, Dana, 145
Kühberger, Anton, 35
Kuhl, Patricia K., 177
Kuhn, Deanna, 87, 434
Kuhn, Emily S., 465
Kuhn, Melanie R., 344
Kulikova, Sofya, 176
Kumar, Raman, 224, 317
Kumar, Singh Sanjeet, 416
Kumar, Vipin, 323
Kumra, Sanjiv, 480
Kumsta, Robert, 204
Kundu, Tapas K., 80
Kung, Hsiang-Ching, 155
Kuppens, Sofie, 405
Kurinczuk, Jennifer J., 115
Kurotani, Kayo, 84
Kurt, A. Öner, 443
Kuschner, David, 286
Kushnerenko, Elena, 176
Kushnir, Tamar, 168
Kusuda, Satoshi, 103
Kutob, Randa M., 472
Kuwahara, Keisuke, 84
Kuzik, Nicholas, 183
Kvalvik, Liv G., 114
Kypri, Kypros, 480
Labouvie-Vief, Gisela, 489
LaChance, Jenny, 235
Lacourse, Eric, 413

Ladd, Gary, 390
Ladd, Helen F., 446, 447
LaFontana, Kathryn M., 465
Lagattuta, Kristin H., 374
Lai, Stephanie A., 344
Laird, Robert D., 465
Lake, Neil, 109
Lake, Stephanie, 480
Lalwani, Laxmi N., 267, 316
Lamarche, Véronique, 387
Lamb, Michael E., 128, 206, 207, 230
Lamm, Bettina, 209, 284
Lan, Wen-Hsuan, 325
Lander, Eric S., 75, 76
Landgren, Kajsa, 146
Lando, Amy M., 117
Landrigan, Philip J., 234
Lane, Jonathan D., 254
Lang, Kevin, 450
Lange, Nicholas, 228
Langlands, Stephanie, 317
Langley, John, 480
Långström, Niklas, 376
Language and Reading Research Consortium, 348
Lanners, Josée, 174
Lansford, Jennifer E., 298, 299, 301, 304
Laopaiboon, Malinee, 424
Lapillonne, Alexandre, 148
Lapinleimu, Helena, 122
Lara-Cinisomo, Sandraluz, 270, 273
Laraway, Kelly A., 5
Laria, Leon, 171
Larson, Emily, 27
Larzelere, Robert E., 294, 296, 297, 298, 299
Latham, Scott, 270, 273
Latvala, Antti, 480
Lau, Carissa, 119, 122
Laurillard, Diana, 327
Laursen, Brett, 376, 432, 462, 466, 467
Laursen, Thomas Munk, 91
Lavelli, Manuela, 197, 209, 216
Lavender, Jason, 244
Law, Hou, 420
Law, Michael R., 109
Lawrence, Jean M., 313
Laws, Holly B., 229
Layden, Brian T., 70
Le, Vi Donna, 444, 445
Leach, Penelope, 273
Leavitt, Judith W., 127
LeCuyer, Elizabeth A., 282
Le-Doare, Kirsty Mehring, 158
Lee, Anna, 361
Lee, Bethany R., 500
Lee, Chang-Bae, 247
Lee, Dohoon, 385
Lee, Jihyun, 19
Lee, Kang, 261, 262
Lee, Kyung-Hee, 378
Lee, Laisze, 390
Lee, Liang-Yi, 192
Lee, Moosung, 460
Lee, RaeHyuck, 275
Lee, Richard M., 496
Lee, Shawna J., 297
Lee, Soojeong, 450
Lee, Yuan-Hsuan, 443
Lee, Yunjo, 321, 335
Leeb, Rebecca T., 385, 389
Leerkes, Esther M., 285
Lee-St.John, Terry, 349
Legerstee, Maria, 193
Le Grange, Daniel, 418
Lehner, Ben, 80
Lehtonen, Lisa, 122

Leibenluft, Ellen, 194, 195
Leiken, Kimberly, 322
Leiter, Valerie, 30
Lejeune, C., 115
Lejuez, C. W., 194
Leman, Patrick J., 396
Lemelin, Jean-Pascal, 181
Lemieux, André, 490
Lemish, Daphna, 183
Lenberg, Arthur M., 48
Lencar, Cornel, 233
Lengua, Liliana J., 281
Lenhart, Amanda, 441, 442, 444
Lent, Robert W., 8
Leonard, Hayley C., 152
Leonard, Julia A., 364
Leonard, Stacie, 304
Lepage, Claude, 323
Lerner, Richard M., 8, 17, 19, 454
Leroy, François, 176
Leskin, Gregory, 378
Leslie, Eva, 314
Leslie, Mitch, 319
Lessov-Schlaggar, Christina N., 233
Lester, Leann, 391
Lester, Patricia, 378
Leung, Sumie, 171
Leve, Leslie D., 476
Levene, Malcolm I., 111
Leveno, Kenneth, 105
Leventhal, Bennett L., 327
Levi, Erika E., 469
Levine, Charles, 303, 458
Levine, Michael P., 420
Levine, Susan C., 259
Lewallen, Lynne P., 121
Lewandowski, Lawrence J., 325, 344
Lewin, Tamar, 182
Lewis, Cora E., 488
Lewis, David M. G., 57
Lewis, Glyn, 156
Lewis, John D., 142
Lewis, Marc D., 281, 283
Lewis, Michael, 116, 192
Lewkowicz, David J., 177
Li, Dan, 387
Li, Dianjiang, 84
Li, Fenfang, 245
Li, Hui, 261
Li, Jin, 352, 369
Li, Junning, 101
Li, Ming, 230
Li, Rong, 326
Li, Weilin, 215
Li, Xiaobai, 322
Li, Yibing, 454
Liang, Desheng, 76
Liang, Eva, 256
Liben, Lynn S., 303, 304
Libertus, Klaus, 152
Libertus, Melissa E., 343
Lichtenstein, Paul, 376
Lichwa, Hannah, 259
Lieberman, Ellice, 129
Lieberman, Jeffrey A., 11
Liebson, Elizabeth, 327
Liew, Jeffrey, 259, 296
Lillard, Angeline S., 271, 288
Lillevoll, Kjersti R., 458
Lillo-Martin, Diane, 177
Lim, Cher Ping, 362
Lim, Kelvin O., 480
Lim, M. K., 85
Lin, Alex R., 354
Lin, Betty, 122
Lin, Hsien-Chang, 27, 477
Lin, Phoebe, 431
Lin, Weili, 139, 140, 141, 142, 171
Lin, Xiangtao, 101

Lind, Annika, 122
Lind, Jennifer N., 119
Lind, Penelope A., 84
Lindberg, Laura Duberstein, 471
Lindberg, Sara M., 358, 460
Lindenberg, Siegwart, 389
Lindenberger, Ulman, 9
Lindland, Eric, 242
Linebarger, Deborah L., 181
Ling, Yan, 444, 445
Lingeman, Jesse M., 151
Linhares, Maria B. M., 149
Link, Katarina, 88
Linker, Julie, 390
Linn, Marcia C., 358
Lipina, Sebastián J., 374
Lister, George, 138
Littlewood, Elizabeth, 127, 128
Liu, Dong, 472
Liu, Henghui, 413
Liu, Jia, 322
Liu, Jia-Lin, 359
Liu, Junsheng, 388
Liu, Kayuet, 114
Liu, Li, 159
Liu, Shuwei, 101
Liu, Yanling, 371
Liu, Yu, 414
Livas-Dlott, Alejandra, 296
Llorent, Vicente J., 391
Lo, Po-Tsung, 192
Lo, Serena C., 117
LoBue, Vanessa, 171
Lock, James, 418
Locke, John, 60
Loeb, Emily L., 198
Loeber, Rolf, 474, 475, 476
Loftus, Patricia A., 316
Lombardo, Michael, 260, 262
Long, Jeffrey D., 374, 377, 411
Longmore, Monica A., 498
Longo, Gregory S., 459, 468
Longo, Lawrence D., 110
Lonigan, Christopher J., 268
Lopez, Anna B., 459
Lopez-Duran, Nestor, 292, 297
Loprinzi, Paul, 288
Lorenzo, Guillermo, 185
Lortet-Tieulent, Joannie, 83
Lösel, Friedrich, 390
Lovegrove, Peter, 447
Lovett, Benjamin J., 235, 344
Lovett, Maureen W., 327
Lowe, Michael R., 26
Lowenstein, Steven, 481
Lowry, Christopher A., 224
Lowry, J. A., 240
Lubman, Dan I., 434
Luciana, Monica, 323
Luebbe, Aaron M., 473
Luecken, Linda J., 122
Luedtke, Kathryn, 137
Lumbiganon, P., 424
Luna, Beatriz, 409
Lund, Terese, 314
Lundahl, Alyssa, 225
Lundberg, Shelly, 500
Lundqvist, Anita, 146
Lunkenheimer, Erika S., 292, 297
Luo, Liqun, 141
Luo, Rufan, 256
Luo, Wentai, 478
Luparia, Antonella, 174
Lupski, James R., 87
Lurye, Leah E., 304
Lushin, Viktor, 465
Luthar, Suniya S., 372, 374, 375, 385
Luyckx, Koen, 431, 458
Luyten, Patrick, 472

Lyall, Donald M., 122
Lynch, Jamie L., 36
Lynskey, Michael T., 480
Lyons-Ruth, Karlen, 200
Lyttelton, Oliver C., 323
Ma, Julie, 298
Ma, Ying, 442
Maag, John W., 332
Maasmeier, Kathrin, 209
Macdonnell, Michael, 107
MacDorman, Marian F., 105, 155
MacGregor, Daune, 228
Macgregor, Stuart, 84
Maciejewski, Matthew L., 416
MacKay, Andrea P., 426
Mackay, Daniel, 122
Mackenzie, Karen J., 319
MacKenzie, Michael J., 296
MacKinnon, David P., 122
MacLeod, John F., 475
Macmillan, Ross, 497
Macosko, Evan Z., 69, 70
MacWhinney, Brian, 177, 179
Madden, Mary, 441
Madden, Pamela A. F., 84, 480
Maddow-Zimet, Isaac, 471
Maehler, Claudia, 344
Maggs, Jennifer L, 477
Maglione, Margaret, 226
Magnuson, Katherine, 276
Magnussen, Costan G., 5, 6
Maguire, Eleanor A., 171
Magzamen, Sheryl, 235
Mahajan, Reena, 424
Mahmoudzadeh, Mahdi, 176
Majdandžić, Mirjana, 193
Ma-Kellams, Christine, 473
Malin, Martin B., 240, 353
Mallett, Christopher A., 44
Malloy, Lindsay C., 475
Malloy, Michael H., 109
Malloy, Timothy F., 234
Maloney, Erin A., 259
Malspeis, Susan, 226
Malti, Tina, 395
Manary, Mark J., 70, 159, 160
Mandalakas, Anna, 204
Mandelbaum, David E., 11
Mandler, Jean M., 169
Mangual Figueroa, Ariana, 296
Maniar, Rajesh, 443
Manish, Kumar, 416
Mann, Joshua R., 124
Manniën, Judith; Zwart, 111
Manning, Janessa H., 101
Manning, Wendy D., 382, 498, 499
Månsson, Johanna, 104
Manu, Alexander, 110
Manzano, Susana, 158
Mao, Guochao, 113
Mar, Raymond A., 262
Marais, Anna-Susan, 113, 115
Marazita, John M., 263
March, John S., 326
Marcia, James, E., 458
Marcovitch, Stuart, 285
Marcus, David K., 235
Marcus, Gary F., 185
Marcus, S. M., 240
Mareschal, Denis, 171, 348
Margolin, Gayla, 385
Margolis, Amy, 197
Marino, Alexis J., 290
Markey, Charlotte N., 413
Markman, Ellen M., 265
Markman, Howard J., 385
Marks, Amy K., 122
Markstrom, Carol, 496
Marlier, Luc, 149

Maron, Dina Fine, 110
Marrero, Matthew D., 465
Marriott, Michael, 420
Marsh, Kathryn, 191
Marshall, Eliot, 202, 204
Marshall, Narcis, 101
Marshall, Peter J., 194
Marshall-Lucette, Sylvie, 127
Martin, Andrew J., 448
Martin, Carmel, 359
Martin, Carol L., 304
Martin, Georgianna L., 494
Martin, Joyce A., 25, 423, 499
Martin, Michael O., 356
Martin, Nicholas G., 480
Martin, Paul, 286
Martin, Rebecca E., 364
Martínez, M. Loreto, 464
Martini, Julia, 195
Martino, Steven C., 469
Martins, Silvia S., 413
Martinson, Melissa L., 121
Martinussen, Monica, 458
Martin-Uzzi, Michele, 382
Martorell, Reynaldo, 240, 417
Marttunen, Mauri, 421, 422
Maryse; Soussignan, Robert, 149
Mascarelli, Amanda, 117
Mascaro, Jennifer S., 302
Mash, Eric J., 315, 320, 323
Maski, Kiran P., 136
Maslow, Abraham, 61
Maslowsky, Julie, 477, 480
Mason, Michael J., 477
Mâsse, Louise C., 417
Masten, Ann S., 347, 352, 372, 373, 374, 377, 385
Masters, Grace A., 327
Mathews, Iva Z., 447
Mathews, T. J., 105, 155, 423, 499
Mathison, David J., 415
Matomäki, Jaakko, 122
Matteson, David R., 458
Matthews, Karen A., 390
Maughan, Barbara, 390
Maunder, Robert, 198
Maurizi, Laura K., 351
Mavridis, Caroline J., 298
May, Lillian, 50
May, Philip A., 113, 115
Mayer, D. Luisa, 148
Mayhew, Maureen, 107
Mazuka, Reiko, 174, 176, 179
McAlister, Anna R., 262
McBain, Ryan, 373
McBride, Brent A., 317
McCabe, Sean Esteban, 325, 481
McCabe, Viki, 170
McCall, Robert B., 204, 205
McCarroll, Steven A., 69, 70
McCarthy, Neil, 116
McCartney, Kathleen, 215
McClain, Natalie M., 424
McClair, Vetisha L., 477
McClelland, Megan M., 288
McClelland, Sara I., 422
McCormick, Cheryl M., 447
McCullough, Laurence B., 111
McCullough, Michael E., 459, 468
McDaniel, Dawn D., 473
McDermott, Jennifer M., 204
McDermott, Suzanne, 124
McDonald, Julia, 224
McDonald, Kristina L., 370, 387, 391, 395
McElduff, Patrick, 480
Mcelhaney, Kathleen Boykin, 298
McEwen, Bruce S., 312, 488
McEwen, Craig A., 312

McFarland, Joel, 451
McFarlane, Alexander C., 374
McGill, Rebecca K., 447
McGovern, Kathleen, 228, 411
McGowan, Linda, 127, 128
McGue, Matt, 468
McHale, Susan M., 447
McIntosh, Andrew M., 122
McIntosh, Jennifer, 139
McIntyre, Joe, 500
McIntyre, Laura Lee, 327
McKeever, Pamela M., 407
McKenzie, Jessica, 394
McKinney, Lyle, 491
McLanahan, Sara S., 385
McLaren, Lindsay, 312
McLaren, Rachel M., 463
McLaughlin, Jo, 420
McLaughlin, Katie A., 472
McLeod, Bryce D., 375
McManus, I. Chris, 228
McMillan, Dean, 127, 128
Mcmillan, Naya, 240
McMillin, Rebecca, 259
McNamara, Joseph P. H., 257
McNeil, Deborah, 312
McNeil, Michele, 359
McRae, Daphne N., 107
McRobbie, Hayden, 27, 478
McShane, Kelly E., 295
McWhirter, Kevin J., 478
McWilliams, Kelly, 230
Meadows, Sara, 340
Meczekalski, Blazej, 420
Medhekar, Rohan, 327
Meece, Judith L., 447
Meesters, Cor., 371
Meeus, Wim, 458
Mehl, Matthias R., 302
Mehta, Clare M., 468
Meier, Madeline H., 11
Meins, Elizabeth, 257
Meiser, Bettina, 91
Meites, Elissa, 424
Meland, Eivind, 448
Melching, Jessica A., 465
Melnikas, Andrea J., 424
Meltzoff, Andrew N., 182, 260, 266, 369
Menacker, Fay, 155
Menary, Kyle, 323
Mendle, Jane, 413
Meng, Xiangzhi, 343
Menna-Barreto, Luiz, 137
Mennis, Jeremy, 477
Menzer, Melissa, 370, 387, 391, 395
Mercer, Neil, 342
Mercy, James A., 385, 389
Meredith, Rhiannon M., 117
Merget-Kullmann, Miriam, 257
Merikangas, Kathleen R., 326, 471, 477
Merle-Johnson, Dominike, 441
Mermelshtine, Roni, 255
Merriam, Sharan B., 30
Merriman, William E., 263
Merrow, Martha, 406
Mersky, Joshua P., 245
Mertens, Donna M., 30
Merz, Emily C., 204
Mesman, Jeanette A. J. M., 111
Mesman, Judi, 303
Messinger, Daniel M., 197
Metcalfe, Janet, 45, 48
Metcalfe, Lindsay A., 229
Meuwese, Rosa, 438
Meyer, Madonna Harrington, 423
Meyer-Bahlburg, Heino F. L., 461
Micalizzi, Lauren, 195

Michelhaugh, Sharon K., 80
Michels, Karin B., 410
Michl, Louisa C., 472
Miech, Richard A., 10, 477, 478
Mieremet, Rene, 75
Miernicki, Michelle E., 448
Mihailidis, Paul, 441
Miklowitz, David J., 325
Milazzo, Solange, 148
Miles, Jeremy N. V., 460
Miles, Lynden K., 170
Milgrom, Jeannette, 197
Milkman, Katherine L., 437
Miller, Alison, 17
Miller, Cindy F., 304
Miller, David, 500
Miller, Elizabeth, 470, 471
Miller, Geoffrey, 328
Miller, Greg, 11, 63, 101
Miller, Gregory E., 193, 374
Miller, Joseph M., 148
Miller, Melissa K., 426
Miller, P, 432
Miller, Patricia H., 47, 261
Miller, Patricia Y., 460
Miller, Portia, 216
Miller-Cotto, Dana, 459
Miller-Johnson, Shari, 275
Miller-Perrin, Cindy, 425
Mills, Britain A., 84
Mills-Koonce, W. Roger, 190, 390
Milne, Lise, 425
Milosevic, Tijana, 442
Milton, James, 264
Milunsky, Aubrey, 87, 88, 89
Milunsky, Jeff M., 87, 88, 89
Minagawa-Kawai, Yasuyo, 174, 176
Minde, Klaus, 8
Mindell, Jodi A., 137, 138
Miniño, Arialdi M., 155
Mireles, Laurie, 296
Mischel, Walter, 284
Mishra, Ramesh C., 342
Misra, Dawn P., 121
Missana, Manuela, 193
Missmer, Stacey A., 129
Mitchell, Edwin A., 155
Mitchell, Kimberly J., 441, 442
Mitchell, Philip B., 91
Mitra, Dipak K., 110
Miu, Angela, 469
Miyake, Akira, 262
Miyata, Susanne, 179
Mize, Krystal D., 191
Mizoue, Tetsuya, 84
Mkakosya, Rajhab, 70, 159, 160
MMWR, 25, 156, 157, 234, 235, 238, 328, 333, 415, 416, 417, 418, 422, 423, 425, 426, 468, 473
Moas, Olga Lydia, 194
Moffitt, Terrie E., 11, 377, 474, 475, 488
Mogil, Catherine, 378
Mohangoo, Ashna D., 105
Mok, Kelvin, 267, 349
Mokrova, Irina L., 285
Moldavsky, Maria, 326
Moles, Laura, 158
Mollen, Cynthia J., 426
Möller, Eline L., 193
Møller, Signe J., 301
Molloy, Cynthia, 322
Molloy, Lauren E., 468
Monahan, Kathryn C., 44, 469, 470, 475, 476
Monesson, Alexandra, 145
Money, John, 8
Monks, Helene, 391
Montepare, Joann M., 9

Montessori, Maria, 60
Montgomery, Heather, 424
Monthly Vital Statistics Report, 1980., 155
Monti, Jennifer D., 448
Montie, Jeanne, 275
Montilla, Antonia, 158
Montirosso, Rosario, 150, 198
Monto, Martin A., 499
Monzalvo, Karla, 350
Moodie, Erica E. M., 160
Moody, James, 467, 468
Moody, Myles, 327
Moon, Rachel Y., 138
Moon, Seong H., 275
Mooney, Margarita, 496
Moons, Philip, 458
Moore, Ashlee A., 390
Moore, Colleen F., 235
Moore, Cynthia M., 298
Moore, Derek G., 176
Moore, James, 228
Moore, Keith L., 9
Moore, Mary Ruth, 233
Moran, Lauren V., 327
Moran, Lyndsey R., 281
Moran, Seana, 322
Morandi, Francesco, 198
Morawska, Alina, 299
Morcillo, Carmen, 425
Morcos, Roy N., 421
Moreno, Sylvain, 321, 335
Morgan, Ian G., 85
Morgan, Julia, 377
Morgan, Timothy M., 313
Mori, Rintaro, 424
Morisaki, Naho, 424
Morken, Nils-Halvdan, 114
Morón, Cecilio, 416
Morris, Amanda S., 463
Morris, Bradley J., 285
Morris, Curtis L., 447
Morris, Pamela A., 12
Morris, Tracy L., 23
Morris, Vivian L., 447
Morrissey, Taryn, 216
Mortensen, Preben Bo, 91
Mortimer, Jeylan T., 460
Morton, Patricia M., 245
Moshman, David, 433
Moss, Howard B., 480
Mota, Natalie, 298
Moultrie, Fiona, 150
Moutquin, Jean-Marie, 112
Mowry, James B., 240
Mozaffarian, Dariush, 6
Mpofu, Deborah, 107
Muenks, Katherine, 369
Muetzel, Ryan, 323
Muhajarine, Nazeem, 107
Mullally, Sinéad L., 171
Müller, Ulrich, 252
Mulligan, Aisling, 325
Mullis, Ina V. S., 356
Mullola, Sari, 357
Mulvey, Edward P., 475
Munniksma, Anke, 389
Munson, Michelle R., 500
Murdoch, Linda, 233, 285
Muris, Peter, 371
Murphy, Sherry L., 155
Murray, Donna S., 322
Murray, Thomas H., 73, 74, 91
Murry, Velma McBride, 462
Mushin, Ilana, 256
Musick, Marc A., 298, 411
Mustanski, Brian, 469
Mustillo, Sarah, 378
Musu-Gillette, Lauren, 451, 491

Myers, Michael W., 467
Næss, Kari-Anne B., 87
NAEYC, 216
Nagaonkar, Shashikant N., 383
Nagel, Gabriele, 226
Nair, Harish, 159
Namy, Laura L., 182
Nanji, Ayaz, 103
Nanri, Akiko, 84
Nansel, Tonja R., 416
Narasimhan, Subasri, 469
Narayan, Chandan R., 175
Nash, William, 378
Nassar, Natasha, 115
National Center for Health Statistics, 237, 312, 319, 331, 446
Natsuaki, Misaki N., 412
Naughton, Michelle J., 313
Nave-Blodgett, Jessica E., 191
Nazzi, Thierry, 179
Neale, Joanne, 42
Neary, Karen R., 291
Neary, Marianne T., 155
Nedelcu, Cristina, 500
Neece, Cameron L., 327
Needham, Amy, 152
Needleman, Herbert L., 234
Neggers, Yasmin, 123
Negriff, Sonya, 411
Negru, Oana, 472
Neiderhiser, Jenae M., 80, 89, 91
Neigh, Gretchen N., 244
Nel, Andre E., 234
Nelson, Charles A., 204, 230
Nelson, Elliot C., 480
Nelson, Eric E., 439
Nelson, Geoffrey, 246
Nelson, Jackie A., 396
Nelson, Larry J., 495
Nelson, Leif D., 31
Nelson, Marvin D., 139
Nelson, P. Brooke, 256
Nelson, Paul, 324
Nelson, Timothy D., 225
Nemeroff, Charles B., 244
Neuner, Frank, 373
Nevanen, Saila, 362
Neville, Helen A., 17
Nevin, N. C., 116
Nevin, Rick, 235
Nevzorova, Uliana, 184
Newberry, Sydne J., 226
Newcomb, Michael E., 469
Newcombe, Nora S., 258
Newnham, Carol A., 197
Newnham, Elizabeth A., 373
Ng, C. Y., 85
Ng, Florrie Fei-Yin, 256, 352
Ng, Mei Yi, 405
Ngui, Emmanuel, 127
Nguyen, Jacqueline, 477
Niakan, Kathy K., 98
Nic Gabhainn, Saoirse, 423
Nichols, Kate E., 194
Nichols, Tracy R., 424
Nicholson, James, 109
Nicklas, Eric, 296
Niclasen, Janni, 114
Nicolaidis, Christina, 412
Niedzwiedz, Claire, 474
Nielsen, Mark, 256
Nieto, Sonia, 395
Nigg, Joel T., 324, 327
Nikitin, Dmitriy, 479
Nilsson, Kristine Kahr, 262
Niparko, John K., 148
Nishimi, Kristen, 244
Nishina, Adrienne, 430

Noar, Seth M., 438
Nolen-Hoeksema, Susan, 472
Noll, Jennie G., 411, 425
Norenzayan, Ara, 435, 500
Nores, Milagros, 275
Notterman, Daniel, 385
Nowak, Martin A., 58
Nurmi, Jari-Erik, 194, 297, 357, 467
Nusslock, Robin, 193
Nyqvist, Kerstin Hedberg, 138
Oaten, Megan J., 192
Obiakor, Festus E., 332
O'Boyle, Ernest H., 448
Obradović, Jelena, 374
O'Brien, Beth A., 327
O'Brien, Marion, 396
O'Brien, Casey, 477
O'Brien, Marion, 285
Ocfemia, M. Cheryl Bañez, 424
Ochoa-Perez, Melissa, 327
O'Connell, Samantha, 237
O'Doherty, Katherine, 182
O'Dougherty, Maureen, 125
OECD, 57, 449, 453
Oei, Ju Lee, 122
Oesterdiekhoff, Georg W., 252
Ogburn, Elizabeth L., 7, 499
Ogden, Cynthia L., 224, 225, 315
Oh, Wonjung, 207
Ohno-Matsui, Kyoko, 85
Oi-yeung Lam, Beatrice, 460
Ok, Su-Jeong, 210
Okanoya, Kazuo, 144
Okely, Anthony D., 313
Oken, Emily, 109
O'Leary, Colleen M., 115
Olfson, Mark, 326, 425
Olness, Karen, 204
Olson, Elizabeth A., 323
Olson, Kristina R., 210
Olson, Linda Steffel, 26
Olson, Sheryl L., 292, 297, 299
Olthof, Tjeert, 371
Olweus, Dan, 389
O'Malley, Patrick M., 10, 477, 478, 481
O'Neil, Moira, 242
Öner, Seva, 443
Ongley, Sophia F., 395
Ongur, Dost, 327
Onis, Mercedes de, 159
Onwuachi-Willig, Angela, 390
Oosterlaan, Jaap, 122, 291
Open Science Collaboration (2015), 5
Or, Flora, 473
O'Regan, M., 325
Orlofsky, Jacob L., 458
Ormrod, Richard, 385, 389
Ornaghi, Sara, 113
Orobio de Castro, Bram, 369
Ortega-Ruiz, Rosario, 442
Osgood, D. Wayne, 467
O'Shea, Anne, 472
Oshima-Takane, Yuriko, 179
Osilla, Karen Chan, 460
Ostatníková, Daniela, 100
Osterman, Michelle J. K., 25, 423, 499
Ostfeld, Barbara M., 155
Ostrov, Jamie M., 292
Ostry, Aleck, 121
Ota, Erika, 424
Otomo, Kiyoshi, 179
Otten, Roy, 294
Ou, Suh-Ruu, 275
Out, Dorothée, 393
Over, Harriet, 260
Owen, Margaret T., 215, 296
Owens, Elizabeth B., 294
Özdemir, Metin, 459

Paciga, Kathleen A., 264
Padilla-Walker, Laura M., 495
Padmanabhan, Aarthi, 409
Padulo, Johnny, 314
Paganim, Linda S., 453
Page-Gould, Elizabeth, 404, 410
Pahlke, Erin, 454
Paik, Anthony, 424
Paik, Jae H., 261
Pakarinen, Eija, 357
Palacios, Natalia, 349
Palagi, Elisabetta, 288
Pallotto, Eugenia K., 149
Palmer, Andrea M., 425
Palmer, Melanie, 368
Palmgreen, Philip, 438
Pan, Tingting, 388
Pan, Yi, 275
Pankow, James F., 478
Panksepp, Jaak, 189, 191
Pannebakker, Fieke, 393
Paoli, Antonio, 314
Papaligoura, Zaira, 209
Papandreou, Maria, 237
Paradis, Johanne, 350
Parbery-Clark, Alexandra, 237
Pardini, Dustin A., 390
Parent, Sophie, 464
Parish-Morris, Julia, 183
Park, Hyun, 204
Park, Ji-Yeun, 27, 477
Park, Seoung Eun, 316
Parke, Ross D., 206, 207
Parker, A., 92, 93
Parks, Sharyn E., 473
Parmar, Chirag, 443
Parnell, Susan, 231
Parra, Marisol, 268
Parrish, Anne-Maree, 313
Parsons, Aleja, 385
Parsons, Christine E., 207
Parsons, Elizabeth, 200
Parten, Mildred, 286
Pascarella, Ernest T., 493, 494
Pasco Fearon, R. M., 202
Pascual, María, 479
Patel, Ayush, 327
Paternoster, Ray, 475
Pathak, Preeti, 469
Pathman, Thanujeni, 172
Patil, Rakesh N., 383
Patrick, Megan E., 477, 478
Patris, Bruno, 149
Patte, Michael, 286
Patterson, Steven, 312
Patton, George C., 314
Paukner, Annika, 145, 288
Paul, Ian M., 5
Paul, Jonathan A., 444, 445
Paulsen, David J., 409
Pavlov, Ivan, 41, 42, 60
Payler, Jane, 268
Payne, Krista K., 499
Pedersen, Roger A., 98
Pedraza, Lilia S., 240, 417
Peeters, Margot, 439
Pellegrini, Anthony D., 286, 289, 389
Pellicano, Elizabeth, 259
Pellis, Sergio M., 289
Pellis, Vivien C., 289
Pemberton, Caroline K., 283, 284
Peng, Duan, 214
Peng, Margaret, 478
Peng, Peng, 343
Pennisi, Elizabeth, 70
Peper, Jiska S., 404, 406, 410, 438, 439, 440
Pepi, Annamaria, 314

Peplak, Joanna, 395
Pereira, Mauricio G., 413
Perels, Franziska, 257
Perera, Frederica, 117
Perez-Brena, Norma J., 464, 472
Perez-Edgar, Koraly E., 194
Pérez-Fuentes, Gabriela, 425
Perilloux, Carin, 57
Perl, Harold, 155
Perna, Frank, 417
Perren, Sonja, 390
Persaud, T. V. N., 9
Pérusse, Daniel, 181
Petchell, Jeffrey, 241
Peters, Stacey L., 119
Peterson, Candida C., 261, 262
Peterson, Cora, 440
Peterson, Donna J., 497
Peterson, Lori, 259
Petrucci, Marco, 314
Pexman, Penny M., 313
Peyser, James A., 361
Peyton, David H., 478
Pfäfflin, Friedemann, 461
Phalet, Karen, 359
Pham, Ngoc Minh, 84
Philibert, Robert A., 462
Phillips, Deborah A., 213
Phillips, Laura E., 497
Phillips, Tommy M., 493
Piaget, Jean, 45–48, 60, 164–168, 199, 251–254, 260, 339–341, 393, 396, 432–436
Piano, Mariann R., 27
Pianta, R. C., 270
Picard, Martin, 313
Pickles, Andrew, 195
Picozzi, Marta, 145
Piekny, Jeanette, 344
Pigott, Therese, 391
Pilarz, Alejandra Ros, 212
Pine, Daniel S., 194, 195, 434
Pine, Karen J., 177
Pineda, Melannie, 191
Pingali, Samira, 327
Pinker, Steven, 29, 56, 61, 185
Pinney, Susan M., 228, 403, 404, 411
Pintabona, Yolanda, 391
Pinto, Rodrigo, 275
Piovesan, Allison, 75
Piper, Brianna, 230
Piquero, Alex R., 475
Piro, Ettore, 79
PISA, 452
Pittenger, Samantha L., 12
Pittman, Cathy, 460
Place, Silvia, 268
Plato, 60
Platt, Stephen, 474
Plomin, Robert, 80, 89, 91
Plourde, Vickie, 167
Plows, Alexandra, 92
Pluess, Michael, 10, 195
Podfigurna-Stopa, Agnieszka, 420
Poels, Karolien, 442
Pogrebin, Abigail, 77
Polanczyk, Guilherme V., 324, 325
Polanin, Joshua R., 391
Polirstok, Susan, 44
Pollack, Jeffrey M., 448
Pollak, Robert A., 500
Pollak, Seth D., 404
Poloczek, Sonja, 172
Polo-Tomas, Monica, 377
Pomerantz, Eva M., 352
Pons, Ferran, 177
Poole, Charles, 416
Poorthuis, Astrid, 369
Poorun, Ravi, 150

Porretta, David L., 19
Porter, James N., 323
Posner, Michael I., 230
Potegal, Michael, 191
Potestio, Melissa, 312
Potter, Jeff, 501
Potton, Anita, 176
Poulin, François, 467
Poupon, Cyril, 176
Powell, Kendall, 409
Powell, Shaun, 317
Powers, Abigail, 244
Powers, Alisa, 404
Pozzoli, Tiziana, 392
Prather, Jonathan, 144
Preckel, Franzis, 335
Premo, Luke S., 211
Prendergast, Andrew J., 160
Priebe, Gisela, 423
Priess, Heather A., 460
Prinstein, Mitchell J., 470
Prinzie, Peter, 192, 194
Prochaska, Judith J., 27
Proctor, Laura J., 242
Prokosch, Marjorie L., 224
Propper, Cathi B., 146
Prothero, Arianna, 361
Provenzi, Livio, 198
Pryor, Frederic L., 359
Pucher, Philip H., 107
Pulkkinen, Lea, 480
Pungello, Elizabeth P., 275
Purser, Harry R. M., 348
Purtell, Kelly M., 274
Putnam, Frank W., 411, 425
Putnam, Samuel P., 198
Putnick, Diane L., 207, 299, 301, 304
Qin, Desiree B., 207
Qin, Jia-Bi, 76, 114
Qu, Yang, 410
Quaresima, Valentina, 50, 158
Quddus, Arshad, 156
Quinn, Graham E., 148
Quinn, John, 195
Quintana, Stephen, 495, 496
Quittner, Alexandra L., 148
Qusti, Safaa, 416
Rabagliati, Hugh, 185
Rabbitt, Matthew P., 123
Rabkin, Nick, 362
Rackin, Heather, 381
Raczek, Anastacia E., 349
Rae, Katharine, 352, 369
Raeburn, Paul, 127, 289
Ragan, Daniel T., 467
Raggio, Greer A., 26
Rahilly, Elizabeth P., 300, 301
Rahman, Qazi, 376
Raikes, H. Abigail, 202
Raison, Charles L., 224
Raitakari, Olli T., 5, 6
Rajarethinam, R. P., 327
Rajhans, Purva, 193
Rakoczy, Hannes, 257
Ramaiya, Astha K., 158, 261
Ramchandani, Paul, 127
Ramey, Craig T., 275
Ramirez, Marizen R., 390
Ramírez, Naja Ferjan, 177
Ramírez, Rey R., 177
Ramo, Danielle E., 27
Ramrakha, Sandhya, 11
Ramscar, Michael, 266
Ramus, Franck, 174, 176, 350
Ranciaro, Alessia, 16, 59
Rand, David G., 58
Rankin, Jay, 480
Rapin, Isabelle, 328

Rapoport, Judith, 326
Raskoff Zeiss, Antonette, 284
Raspberry, Kelly A., 93
Rassart, Jessica, 458
Rathbun, Amy, 215, 491
Rauh, Virginia, 117
Ravallion, Martin, 14
Raver, C. Cybele, 262
Rawles, Richard, 228
Ray, Brian D., 361, 364
Raybaud, Charles, 228
Raz, Naftali, 9
Reavey, Daphne, 149
Rechitsky, Svetlana, 90
Reeb-Sutherland, Bethany C., 194
Reed, Floyd A., 16
Reed, Jamie L., 102
Reep van den Bergh, C., 350
Reichman, Nancy E., 121
Reijntjes, Albert, 369, 371
Reijo Pera, Renee A., 98
Reisner, Sari L., 461
Reiss, Allan L., 88
Reitz, Ellen, 422, 468
Remington, Gary, 404
Renoux, Christel, 325
Rentfrow, Peter J., 501
Rentscher, Kelly E., 302
Repacholi, Betty M., 192
Restrepo-Mesa, Sandra L., 122
Reynolds, Arthur J., 245, 275
Reynolds, Elizabeth K., 194
Rhoades, Galena K., 385
Rhoades, Kimberly A., 476
Rhodes, Marjorie, 283
Rholes, W. Steven, 198
Ribeiro, Helena, 176
Ribisl, Kurt M., 27
Ribota, Krystal M., 268
Rice, Frances, 447
Rich, Motoko, 450
Richards, Jennifer S., 291
Richardson, T., 325
Rich-Edwards, Janet W., 317, 410
Richey, Mike, 452
Richter, Melinda M., 84
Ridgers, Nicola D., 313
Riedl, Marc A., 226
Rifas-Shiman, Sheryl L., 109, 317
Riglin, Lucy, 447
Rigo, Paola, 207
Rigotti, Nancy A., 479
Rilling, James K., 302
Riordan, Jan, 158
Rioux, Charlie, 464
Risley, Todd R., 350
Ritchie, Andrew I., 319
Ritchie, Lane L., 385
Ritchie, William C., 267
Rivas-Drake, Deborah, 496
Rivera, Juan Ángel, 240, 417
Rizzolatti, Giacomo, 61
Robelen, Erik W., 362
Roberson-Nay, Roxann, 390
Roberts, Dorothy, 16
Roberts, Gehan, 122
Roberts, Leslie, 159
Roberts, Mark W., 296, 298
Robertson, Colin, 226
Robins, Philip K., 214
Robins, Richard W., 371, 413
Robinson, Eric, 225
Robinson, Jennifer, 491
Robinson, Leah E., 315
Robinson, Lyn, 137
Robinson, Scott, 152
Robinson, Thomas N., 415
Rochat, Philippe, 192
Rocroi, Camille, 185

Roderer, Thomas, 347
Rodrigues, Luís P., 236
Rodriguez, Carmen, 183
Rodríguez, Sue A., 472
Rodríguez de Jesús, Sue A., 464
Rodríguez-Planas, Núria, 452
Roebers, Claudia M., 347
Roenneberg, Till, 406
Roeser, Robert W., 445, 447, 449
Rogers, Leoandra O., 369
Rogoff, Barbara, 52, 61, 342
Rohde, Luis A., 324, 325
Roisman, Glenn I., 200, 202
Roksa, Josipa, 493
Romano, Elisa, 214
Romeo, Russell D., 405, 408
Romero, Diana, 470
Romero, Roberto, 101
Romine, William L., 441
Roncal, Susan, 241
Rook, Graham A. W., 224
Roopnarine, Jaipaul L., 207, 286
Rorem, Anna, 270, 273
Rosario, Margaret, 469
Rose, Amanda J., 387, 473
Rose, Nikolas, 50
Rose, Richard J., 480
Rose, Steven, 326
Roseberry, Sarah, 183
Rosen, Lisa H., 391
Rosen, Meghan, 113
Rosenbaum, James E., 452
Rosenberg, Harry M., 155
Roseth, Cary J., 389
Rosiek, Jerry, 359
Rosin, Hanna, 314, 368
Ross, Josephine, 283
Ross Anderson, Trisha, 500
Rosselli, Mónica, 267, 316
Rossignol, Michel, 112
Rossion, Bruno, 145
Rotatori, Anthony, 332
Rothbart, Mary K., 230
Rothstein, Mark A., 30
Rousseau, Jean Jacques, 60
Rovee-Collier, Carolyn, 61, 171, 172, 173
Rovine, Michael J., 214
Rovner, Alisha J., 416
Rowe, Meredith L., 350
Rowsell, Renee, 171
Rozier, R. Gary, 312
Rübeling, Hartmut, 54
Rubertsson, C., 117
Rubertsson, Christine, 138
Rubia, Katya, 48
Rubin, Kenneth H., 194, 370, 387, 391, 395
Ruble, Diane N., 304
Rudan, Igor, 159
Rudolph, Karen D., 404, 448
Rugolotto, Simone, 56
Ruhl, Holly, 497
Ruismäki, Heikki, 362
Rumiche, Rosario, 268
Runions, Kevin C., 292
Ruprecht, Karen M., 216
Russell, Charlotte K., 137
Russell, Jennifer J., 313
Russell, Stephen T., 469
Russo, Silvia, 459
Rutter, Michael, 204, 214, 377, 475
Ruvolo, Paul, 196
Ryan, Allison M., 467
Ryan, Erin L., 182
Ryan, George, 426
Rybak, Michael, 59
Rybin, Denis, 138

Ryman, Sephira G., 323
Sabin, Matthew A., 5, 6
Sabol, T. J., 270
Sabo-Risley, Constance, 233
Sacks, Oliver, 328
Sadeh, Avi, 137, 138
Sadek, Shelly, 388, 389
Sadler, Richard Casey, 235
Sadler, Troy D., 441
Saewyc, Elizabeth M., 469
Saey, Tina Hesman, 89
Sahlberg, Pasi, 357, 450
Sahoo, Bishnupriya, 224, 317
Sahoo, Krushnapriya, 224, 317
Sales, Jessica McDermott, 471
Salim, Abdulbaset M., 59
Salmela-Aro, Katariina, 467
Salmon, Jo, 290, 313
Saltzman, William, 378
Salum, Giovanni A., 324, 325
Samek, Diana R., 468
Sameroff, Arnold J., 292, 297, 299
Samuels, Christina A., 269, 450
Sanchez, Gabriel R., 16
Sanchez, Sixto E., 412
Sánchez, Tania G., 240, 417
Sánchez, Virginia, 442
Sanders, Matthew, 299
Sandfort, Theo, 422, 468
Sandhofer, Catherine M., 302
Sandoval, Anna, 317
Sandritter, Tracy, 149
Sang, Biao, 388
San Souci, Priscilla, 172
Santelli, John S., 424, 471
Sanz Cruces, José Manuel, 498
Sapra, Katherine J., 111
Saraiva, Linda, 236
Sareen, Jitender, 298
Sasaki, Joni Y., 282
Sassi, Roberto, 8
Şaşmaz, Tayyar, 443
Sato, Yutaka, 174, 176
Satterwhite, Catherine Lindsey, 424
Saudino, Kimberly J., 195
Savage, Robert, 350
Savioja, Hanna, 422
Saw, Seang-Mei, 85
Sawyer, Eva Kille, 102
Saxe, Rebecca, 262
Saxton, Matthew, 183
Sayal, Kapil, 326, 420
Scarr, Sandra, 234
Schaal, Benoist, 149
Schachner, Adena, 191
Schad, Megan M., 198
Schadt, Eric E., 7
Schaeffer, Marjorie W., 259
Schafer, Markus H., 245
Schaie, K. Warner, 27, 61
Schaller, Jessamyn, 385
Schanler, Richard. J., 158
Schapp, Salena, 477
Schardein, James L., 114
Scharf, Miri, 209
Schats, Roel, 76
Schauben, Jay L., 240
Schauer, Elizabeth, 373
Scheinost, Dustin, 101
Schibuk, Larry, 326
Schifrin, Barry S., 111
Schillinger, Julia A., 469
Schillmöller, Jelka, 257
Schlomer, Gabriel L., 378, 411
Schmader, Toni, 490, 491
Schmid, Corinne, 347
Schmidl, Ricarda, 452
Schmidt, Carl J., 80
Schmidt, Isabelle, 335

Schmidt, Louis A., 194
Schmidt, Marco F. H., 15
Schmidt, Marie Evans, 224
Schmidt, Michelle E., 386, 390
Schmitz, Bernhard, 257
Schneider, Dona, 57
Schnepp, Allison Champney, 235
Schoeny, Michael E., 470
Schofield, Peter R., 91
Scholte, Ron H. J., 431
Schonert-Reichl, Kimberly A., 369
Schorah, C. J., 116
Schore, Allan N., 139, 193
Schuiling-Veninga, Catharina C. M., 325
Schulenberg, John E., 10, 460, 477, 480, 481
Schwade, Jennifer A., 198
Schwanenflugel, Paula J., 344
Schwartz-Mette, Rebecca A., 473
Schwarz, Alan, 324, 326
Schwarze, Jürgen, 319
Schweinhart, Lawrence J., 275
Schytt, Erica, 111
Scott, Denise M., 84
Scott, Diane L., 247
Scott, James G., 324
Scott, Lisa S., 145
Scott, Shannon R., 391
Sears, Martha, 138, 199
Sears, William, 138, 199
Seaton, Eleanor K., 496
Sebastián-Gallés, Núria, 267
Sedlak, Andrea J., 243
See, Tricia, 90
Seeman, Mary V., 404
Séguin, Jean R., 291, 464
Seid, Michael, 313
Seidl, Amanda, 184
Seiver, Elizabeth, 260
Seller, M. J., 116
Sellers, Patrick D., 171
Selvarangan, Rangaraj, 426
Senatore, Ignazio, 420
Şendil, Çağla Öneren, 288
Senf, Janet H., 472
Senior, Jennifer, 200, 211
Señor, Melissa, 268
Seo, Dong-Chul, 27, 477
Seppa, Nathan, 85
Serra, Mauro, 207
Sethupathy, Praveen, 69
Settersten, Richard A., 497
Severson, Kim, 450
Shaffer, Brian, 109
Shafran, Roz, 472
Shah, Nilesh B., 383
Shah, Nirvi, 44
Shalev, Idan, 411
Shanahan, Timothy, 268
Shapero, Benjamin G., 413
Shapiro, Howard, 150
Shapk, Jennifer, 466
Sharan, Ashok, 416
Sharan, Sunita, 416
Sharma, Umesh, 332
Sharp, Helen, 195
Shattuck, Anne, 244
Shattuck, Rachel M., 423
Shaw, Gary M., 415
Shaw, Thérèse, 292, 391
Shechner, Tomer, 194, 195
Sheeran, Paschal, 114
Sheffield, Jeanne S., 105
Shek, Daniel T. L., 443
Shekelle, Paul G., 226
Shelley, Alexandra E., 230
Shelton, Katherine H., 447
Shemdoe, Aloisia I., 158, 261

Shen, Nan, 109
Sheng, Xiao-Qi, 76, 114
Shepherd, Kathrine, 472
Sheppard, S., 116
Sherer, Jeffrey T., 327
Sherman, Kathleen, 182
Sherman, Laura J., 195
Sherman, Lauren E., 323, 328
Sherrard, Kathyrn, 129
Sheu, Ching-Fan, 122
Shi, Bing, 388
Shi, Rushen, 183
Shi, Yonggang, 101
Shields, Margot, 315
Shin, Huiyoung, 467
Shin, Ju-Young, 325
Shirtcliff, Elizabeth A., 404
Shisslak, Catherine M., 472
Shneidman, Laura, 209
Shouse, Roger C., 450
Shulman, Deborah, 283
Shulman, Elizabeth P., 44, 475
Shutts, Kristin, 206
Shwalb, Barbara J., 206
Shwalb, David W., 206
Shwart, Luke, 312
Sibley, Erin, 349
Siegal, Michael, 266
Siegel, Rebecca L., 83
Siegel, Shepard, 41
Siegler, Robert S., 274, 343
Sigmundson, H. Keith, 8
Signorini, Sabrina G., 174
Sigurdson, J. F., 444
Sikora, Joanna, 351
Silberg, Judy L., 390
Silberman, Steve, 328
Silk, Jessica, 470
Sillars, Alan, 463
Silva, Lynda, 459
Silva, Marcus T., 413
Silva, Phil A., 475
Silveira, Marina A., 411
Silver, Ellen J., 315
Sim, Zi L., 272
Simmat-Durand, L., 115
Simmons, Joseph P., 31
Simon, Carlos, 98
Simon, Laura, 55, 469
Simon, William, 460
Simonnet, Hina, 176
Simonsohn, Uri, 31
Simpkins, Sandra D., 314
Simpson, David, 171
Simpson, Elizabeth A., 145
Simpson, Jeffry A., 198
Sinclair, Maegan, 378
Sinclair, Samantha, 461
Singanayagam, Aran, 319
Singh, Amika, 313
Singh, Anita, 123
Singh, Leher, 175
Singh, Sunita, 342
Sinnott, Jan D., 490
Siqueland, Einar R., 176
Sirai, Hidetosi, 179
Şiş, Mustafa, 443
Sisk, Cheryl L., 405
Sisson, Susan B., 225
Skakkebæk, Niels E., 88
Skalicka, Vera, 332, 388
Skinner, B. F., 43, 61, 181
Skinner, Debra, 93
Skjærven, Rolv, 114
Skoog, Thérèse, 413
Skorikov, Vladimir B., 460
Skouteris, Helen, 197

Slade, Pauline, 127
Slater, Rebeccah, 150
Slavich, George M., 80
Slining, Meghan, 151
Sloan, M., 127
Smaling, Hanneke J. A., 281
Smeenk, Wilma, 207
Smetana, Judith G., 395, 396, 464
Smidts, Diana P., 122
Smith, Anna, 48
Smith, Betty L., 155
Smith, Daniel J., 122
Smith, Danielle M., 478
Smith, Gail, 297
Smith, Jacqui, 8
Smith, Joshua D., 86
Smith, Lauren A., 138
Smith, Michelle I., 70, 159, 160
Smith, P., 286
Smith, Peter K., 390, 391
Smith, Rhiannon L., 473
Smith, Shaunna, 371
Smith, Timothy B., 459, 496
Smith, Traci, 463
Smithells, R. W., 116
Smith-West, Mary B, 247
Smolak, Linda, 420
Snider, Terra Ziporyn, 407
Sniezek, Joseph E., 118
Snow, J. B., 401
Snyder, Thomas D., 359, 361
Sobel, David M., 206
Sobreira, Nara, 86
Soderstrom, Melanie, 184
Soenens, Bart, 472
Sofi, Nighat Yasin, 224, 317
Solanto, Mary V., 326
Solberg, David W., 389
Soley, Gaye, 179
Solheim, Elisabet, 215
Soliday Hong, S. L., 270
Soller, Brian, 431
Solomon, Andrew, 197, 327, 328
Somerville, Leah H., 409, 431, 435, 438, 439, 440
Song, Lulu, 181
Song, Yiying, 322
Sonuga-Barke, Edmund J. S., 204
Soons, Judith P. M., 500
Sophian, Catherine, 254
Soremekun, Seyi, 110
Sorensen, Lucy C., 446, 447
Soska, Kasey C., 152
Sotsky, Rachel B., 151
Sousa, David A., 344
South, Susan C., 376
Souza, Kathiaja M., 413
Spanoudis, George, 341
Sparks, Sarah D., 351, 361
Sparrow, Joshua D., 56
Spear, Linda, 479
Spelke, Elizabeth S., 167
Spence, John C., 290
Sperduto, Robert D., 85
Sperry, Debbie M., 245
Spicer, Julie, 105
Spiegelman, Donna, 129, 410
Spinrad, Tracy L., 282, 291, 463
Spong, Catherine Y., 105
Sprietsma, Maresa, 341
Spyker, Daniel A., 240
Squires, James H., 276
Squires, Jim, 274
Sroufe, Alan, 54
St. George, Jennifer, 206
Staff, Jeremy, 460
Stahlhut, Carsten, 169

Standing, E. M., 271
Stange, Jonathan P., 413
Stanley, Fiona, 115
Stanley, Kate, 242
Stanley, Rebecca M., 313
Stanley, Scott M., 385
Stapleton, Laura M., 350
Starr, Christine R., 304
Stattin, Håkan, 413, 459, 465
Staudinger, Ursula M., 9
Stearns, Jenna, 500
Steegers, Eric A. P., 111
Stein, Alan, 127, 207
Stein, Gabriela L., 296
Stein, Judith A., 389
Stein, Ruth E. K., 315
Steinberg, Laurence, 27, 44, 403, 404, 409, 410, 412, 437, 439, 469, 470, 475, 476
Steiner, Michael J., 57
Stenseng, Frode, 332, 388
Stephens, Rick, 452
Stephenson, David, 496
Stern, Gavin, 333
Stern, Hilarie L., 210
Stern, Mark, 361
Stern, P., 344
Sternberg, Robert, 322
Stevens, Gillian, 349
Stevens, June, 416
Stevenson, Richard J., 192
Stewart, Kitty, 269
Stice, Eric, 26
Stifter, Cynthia, 193
Stiles, Joan, 101, 144
Stipek, Deborah, 271
Stjernqvist, Karin, 104
Stoddard, Sarah A., 17
Stoeber, Joachim, 472
Stoll, Kathrin, 107
Stolt, Suvi, 122
Stoltenborgh, Marije, 425
Stoltzfus, Rebecca J., 160
Strack, Fritz, 5
Strandberg-Larsen, Katrine, 114
Strang, John, 42
Strasburger, Victor C., 481
Strathearn, Lane, 50
Stremmel, Andrew J., 233
Striley, Katie, 109
Stroebe, Wolfgang, 5
Strongin, Robert M., 478
Strough, JoNell, 468
Strouse, Gabrielle A., 182
Stuart, Parker E., 441
Stuckey, Adrienne, 349
Stupica, Brandi, 195
Stykes, J. Bart, 382
Su, Tung-Ping, 325
Suarez, Gloria A., 351
Sucato, Gina S., 470, 471
Suchy, Frederick J., 59
Sue, Derald Wing, 17
Suissa, Samy, 325
Suk, William A., 234
Suleiman, Ahna B., 471
Sulek, Julia P., 444
Suleman, Nadya, 76
Sulik, Michael J., 282, 291, 296
Sumner, Racgek, 458
Sun, Li, 413
Sun, Min, 56
Sun, Yuerong, 387
Sunaert, Stefan, 50
Sund, A. M., 444
Suomi, Stephen J., 129, 145, 288

Super, Charles M., 152, 298
Surian, Luca, 266
Susic, Dinko, 6
Susman, Elizabeth J., 403, 404, 411
Sutin, Angelina R., 225
Sutton-Smith, Brian, 288
Suttorp, Marika J., 226
Suurland, Jill, 281
Svedin, Carl-Göran, 423
Swaab, D. F., 49
Swaab, Hanna, 281
Swain, James E., 50, 105
Swan, Gary E., 233
Swan, Suzanne C., 499
Swanson, Dena Phillips, 282
Swanson, H. Lee, 327
Sydsjö, Gunilla, 117, 423
Syed, Moin, 496
Synovitz, Linda, 411
Taber, Daniel R., 416
Tackett, Jennifer L., 404, 410
Taga, Keiko A., 413
Tagar, Michal Reifen, 283
Tager-Flusberg, Helen, 260, 262
Taillieu, Tamara S., 298
Tajalli, Hassan, 44
Takizawa, Ryu, 390
Tamburic, Lillian, 233
Tamis-LeMonda, Catherine S., 181, 256, 304
Tan, Cheryl H., 118
Tan, Donald T. H., 85
Tan, Hongzhuan, 76
Tan, Joseph S., 198
Tan, Mei, 346
Tan, Patricia Z., 281
Tancredi, Daniel J., 158, 261
Tang, Jie, 442
Tangermann, Rudolf H., 156
Tangney, June, 212
Tani, Novell, 349
Tanner, Jennifer L., 498
Tanumihardjo, Sherry A., 85
Tao, Fangbiao, 413
Tarbetsky, Ana L., 448
Taromino, Caroline, 183
Tarullo, Amanda R., 202
Tarun, Kumar, 416
Tassinari, Melissa S., 119
Tattersall, Ian, 59
Taulu, Samu, 177
Taveras, Elsie M., 224, 317
Tay, Marc Tze-Hsin, 85
Taylor, Alan, 377
Taylor, Barry J., 233, 285
Taylor, Eric, 48
Taylor, H. Gerry, 122
Taylor, Paul, 75, 459
Taylor, Rachael W., 233, 285
Taylor, Robert Joseph, 378
Taylor, Zoe E., 291
Teale, William H., 264
Teasdale, Thomas W., 114
Tedone, Ashley, 181
Teitelbaum, Susan L., 228, 403, 404, 411
Telch, Michael J., 369
Telford, Katherine, 420
Telzer, Eva H., 410, 463
Temple, Brian W., 444, 445
Temple, Jeff R., 444, 445
Tenenbaum, Harriet R., 301
Tenenbaum, Joshua B., 35
Teng, Zhaojun, 371
Teoh, Yee San, 230
Terenzini, Patrick T., 493
Terry, Nicole Patton, 349

Terry-McElrath, Yvonne M., 317
Tessier, Karen, 239
Teter, Christian J., 325
Teti, Douglas M., 138
Tetzlaff, Anne, 420
Thach, Bradley T., 155
Thal, Donna, 148
Thawer, Salima, 312
Theilmann, Rebecca J., 142
Theodoratou, Evropi, 159
Thirion, Bertrand, 176
Thomaes, Sander, 369, 371
Thomas, Alexander, 194
Thomas, Bianca Lee, 322
Thomas, Catherine, 447
Thomas, Michael S. C., 348
Thomason, Moriah E., 101
Thompson, Charis, 76
Thompson, Leonard, 16
Thompson, Margaret, 327
Thompson, Ross A., 202
Thomson, Samuel, 420
Thornberg, Robert, 391
Thorpe, Karen, 213
Tian, Moqian, 322
Tighe, Lauren A., 463
Tillmann, V., 411
Timberlake, David S., 479
Timmons, Adela C., 385
Timmons, Brian W., 290
Tishkoff, Sarah A., 59
Titus, Courtney, 296
Tobey, Emily A., 148
Tolman, Deborah L., 422
Tolvanen, Asko, 297
Tomalski, Przemyslaw, 146, 176
Tomaselli, Keyan, 256
Tomasello, Michael, 15, 183, 185, 227, 257
Tondeur, Jo, 362
Tonn, Jessica L., 407
Topitzes, James, 245
Torchia, Mark G., 9
Torre, Lindsey A., 83
Torrone, Elizabeth, 424
Tottenham, Nim, 193
Tough, Paul, 352, 453
Toumbourou, John W., 314
Townsend, Jeanne, 142
Travers, Brittany G., 228
Trawick-Smith, Jeffrey, 286
Treffers-Daller, Jeanine, 264
Trehan, Indi, 70, 159, 160
Treiman, Donald J., 351
Tremblay, Mark S., 290
Tremblay, Richard E., 181, 214, 291
Trickett, Penelope K., 411, 425
Trolian, Teniell L., 494
Tromp, Do P. M., 228
Tronick, Edward, 150, 198
Troseth, Georgene L., 182
Trost, Stewart G., 288
Trundle, Kathy C., 272
Trzesniewski, Kali H., 371, 413
Tsai, Chin-Chung, 362
Tsai, Kim M., 463
Tsai, Shih-Jen, 325
Tsethlikai, Monica, 342
Tsuji, Sho, 179
Tsuruoka, Hiroko, 84
Ttofi, Maria M., 390, 391
Tucker-Drob, Elliot M., 438
Tulewicz, E. M., 325
Tull, Matthew T., 244
Tummeltshammer, Kristen S., 206
Turecki, Gustavo, 444

Tur-Kaspa, Ilan, 90
Turner, Emily C., 102
Turner, Heather A., 244, 385, 389
Turner, Lindsey, 317
Turner, Melanie B., 6
Turner, Michael G., 475
Twisk, Jos W. R., 313
Tyler-Smith, C., 75
Uddin, Monica, 472
Uduhiri, Kelechi, 118
Uflacker, Alice, 90
Ugueto, Ana M., 405
Uijtdewilligen, Léonie, 313
Ulber, Julia, 177
Umaña-Taylor, Adriana J., 464, 472
Underwood, Emily, 87, 101
Underwood, Marion K., 292, 444
UNESCO, 353
Unger, Kerstin, 347
UNICEF, 110, 123, 124, 159
United Nations, 2015, 153
United Nations, Department of Economic and Social Affairs, Population Division, 212, 312
Updegraff, Kimberly A., 464, 472
Uppal, Preena, 122
Ursache, Alexandra, 193
U.S. Bureau of Labor Statistics, 212, 496
U.S. Census Bureau, 127, 383, 500
U.S. Department of Education, 276
U.S. Department of Health and Human Services, 158, 242, 244, 274, 299
Vaala, Sarah E., 181
Valdez, Carmen R., 385
Valeri, Beatriz O., 149
Valiente, Carlos, 463
Vallotton, Claire D., 213
Valsiner, Jaan, 52
Van Agt, H. M. E., 350
van Batenburg-Eddes, Tamara, 475
van Beijsterveldt, Toos C. E. M., 376
van Berkel, Sheila R., 303
van de Bongardt, Daphne, 422, 468
Vandebosch, Heidi, 442
Vandell, Deborah Lowe, 215
van de Looij-Jansen, Petra, 475
van den Akker, Alithe, 192, 194
van den Berg, Patricia, 444, 445
van den Boom, Dymphna C., 193
Vandenbosch, Laura, 470
Van den Brink, G. A., 350
van den Pol, Anthony N., 113
Vanderberg, Rachel H., 470, 471
Vanderborght, Mieke, 182
van der Heijden, Kristiaan B., 281
VanDerHeyden, Amanda M., 331
van der Laan, Peter H., 207
van der Lely, Heather, 174, 176
Van der Meulen, Matty, 371
van der Pol, Lotte D., 303
VanderWeele, Tyler J., 7, 499
Vandewater, Elizabeth A., 316
van de Weijer, Steve, 475
van Dillen, Jeroen, 111
van Duijvenvoorde, Anna C. K., 410, 439
Van Duuren, Mike, 348
van Eijsden, Manon, 224
VanEpps, Eric M., 448
Van Gelder, Elke, 433
Van Goethem, Anne, 459
van Goozen, Stephanie H. M., 190, 281
Van Hal, Guido, 57

Vanhalst, Janne, 431
Van Hecke, Wim, 50
Van Hooff, Miranda, 374
Van Horn, Linda V., 225
Van Houtte, Mieke, 335
van IJzendoorn, Marinus H., 200, 393, 412, 425
van Leeuwen, Flora E., 76
van Mechelen, Willem, 313
van Nunen, Karolien, 57
van Roosmalen, Jos, 111
Van Royen, Kathleen, 442
Van Ryzin, Mark J., 389, 467
van Voorst, Sabine F., 111
van Weissenbruch, Mirjam M., 76
Vargas, Edward D., 16
Varma, Sashank, 327
Vasey, Paul L., 468
Vaughn, Brian E., 200
Vaughn-Coaxum, Rachel, 405
Vedam, Saraswathi, 107
Vedantam, Shankar, 191
Veenstra, René, 389
Vega-Gea, Esther, 442
Vélez-Uribe, Idaly, 267, 316
Veliz, Philip, 481
Vella, Francesco Paolo, 314
Venn, Alison, 5, 6
Vennemann, Mechtild M., 138
Ventura, Stephanie J., 426
Venuti, Paola, 207
Verdine, Brian N., 258
Verkuyten, Maykel, 16, 495
Vermande, Marjolijn, 371
Vermanel, Alexandra, 57
Verona, Sergiu, 202
Véronneau, Marie-Hélène, 467
Versalovic, James, 70
Verschueren, Karine, 359
Verschueren, Margaux, 458
Verweij, Karin J. H., 480
Vescovo, Elena, 145
Vetter, Céline, 406
Vickery, Brian P., 226
Victora, Cesar G., 159
Vigorito, James, 176
Vilain, Eric, 468
Viljaranta, Jaana, 194, 297, 357
Viljoen, Margaretha, 322
Villegas, Laura, 425
Viner, Russell M., 404, 405
Viotty, Samantha, 441
Virkkala, Johanna, 357
Virnig, Beth A., 109
Vitale, Susan, 85
Vitaro, Frank, 376, 387, 444, 466
Viteri, Fernando E., 416
Vitiello, Benedetto, 326
Vivanti, Giacomo, 332
Vives, Marc-Lluís, 347
Vliegen, Nicole, 472
Voegtlin, Kristin M., 103, 193
Voelin-Liambey, Daphne, 340
Vöhringer, Isabel A., 172
Volkmar, Fred R., 145
Volkow, Nora D., 11
Volling, Brenda, 207
Volpe, Lane E., 138
Vondracek, Fred W., 460
von Soest, Tilmann, 195
Vos, Amber A., 111
Vos, Miriam B., 225
Vos, Theo, 324
Votruba-Drzal, Elizabeth, 216, 269
Vrijkotte, Tanja G. M., 224
Vygotsky, Lev S., 51–54, 60, 255–260, 286, 341–343

Wachs, Theodore D., 179
Wade, Tracey D., 472
Wadsworth, Danielle D., 315
Wadsworth, Shelley MacDermid, 378
Wagenaar, Karin, 76
Wagland, Paul, 192
Wagner, Katie, 265
Wagner, Nicholas J., 390
Wagner, Paul A., 469
Waitzer, Elana, 129
Wakschlag, Lauren, 383
Waldenström, Ulla, 111
Waldfogel, Jane, 269, 275, 296
Walk, Richard D., 170
Walker, Christa L. Fischer, 159
Walker, Janet, 383
Walker, Susan P., 159, 213
Wall, Sterling K., 497
Wall, Tamara L., 84
Wallace, Christopher S., 142
Wallace, Lacey, 467
Wallander, J., 444
Wallis, Claudia, 109
Wallois, Fabrice, 176
Walsh, Mary E., 349
Walsh, Tova B., 207
Walters, Julie, 313
Wambach, Karen, 158
Wang, Chao, 84
Wang, Cynthia S., 491
Wang, Frances, 481
Wang, Hua, 76, 114
Wang, Hui-Chung, 192
Wang, Jiaji, 442
Wang, Jing, 416
Wang, Jingyun, 148
Wang, Lan-Wan, 122
Wang, Li, 388
Wang, Meifang, 448
Wang, Nae-Yuh, 148
Wang, Qianqian, 84
Wang, Shuai, 425
Wang, Tien-Ni, 122
Wang, Xiaolei, 215, 451, 491
Wang, Youfa, 316
Wang, Zhengyan, 388
Wanner, Brigitte, 387
Wansink, Brian, 317
Wanzek, Jeanne, 331
Waqar-ul-Haq, 410
Ward, Dianne S., 416
Wargo, Eric M., 11
Warneken, Felix, 192
Wassilak, Steven G. F., 156
Waterman, Alan S., 458
Waters, Everett, 198
Waters, Patti, 447
Watkins, Kate E., 267, 349
Watson, John B., 43, 60, 209
Watt, Douglas, 189, 191
Way, Niobe, 447, 472
Wazana, Ashley B., 8
Webber, Douglas A., 493
Weber, Daniela, 321
Weber, Max, 60
Webster, E. Kipling, 315
Weegar, Kelly, 214
Weeks, Murray, 348
Wei, Wanchun, 352, 369
Weikart, David P., 275
Weiler, Ivan Jeanne, 142
Weinberg, M. Katherine, 198
Weinstein, Netta, 284
Weinstock, Hillard, 424
Weisenfeld, G. G., 274
Weisglas-Kuperus, Nynke, 122
Weiss, Margaret D., 326

Weiss, Nicole H., 244
Weiss, Noel S., 89
Weiss, Scott T., 109
Weissbourd, Richard, 500
Weisskirch, Robert S., 375
Weisz, John R., 375, 405
Wellman, Henry M., 166, 261
Welsh, Jean A., 225
Welsh, Stephanie N., 268
Wende, Milena, 257
Wendelken, Carter, 313, 346
Wentzel, Kathryn R., 369
Wenzel, Amanda J., 374
Werker, Janet F., 50, 174, 175
Werner, Emmy, 61
Werner, Nicole E., 390
West, Brady T., 325
West, Martin R., 364
Westerhausen, René, 228
Westwood, M., 411
Wetzel, Eunike, 413
Weymouth, Bridget B., 463
Wheeler, Lorey A., 464, 472
Whishaw, Ian Q., 140
Whisman, Mark A., 376
Whitaker, Robert C., 290
White, Naomi, 395
White, Rebecca M. B., 414
Whiten, Andrew, 256
Whiteside-Mansell, Leanne, 128
Whitfield, John B., 84
Whitney, Pamela G., 191
Whitsel, Laurie P., 27
Whitson, Jennifer A., 491
Whittle, Sarah, 434
Wichstrøm, Lars, 215, 332, 388
Widman, Laura, 470
Widom, Cathy Spatz, 245, 246
Wiegand, Benjamin, 137, 138
Wieling, Elizabeth, 373
Wigger, J. Bradley, 285
Wiggs, Christine Bracamonte, 378
Wijlaars, Linda P., 325
Wikström, Anna-Karin, 109
Wilcox, William B., 300
Wilde, Alex, 91
Wilens, Timothy E., 481
Wiley, Andrea S., 411
Wilhelm, Kay, 91
Wilkinson, Stephen, 73
Willan, Andrew R., 111
Willard, Marcy, 333
Willcutt, Erik G., 324, 325
Willems, Chris, 434

Willett, Walter C., 226, 410
Williams, Anne M., 158, 261
Williams, Caroline C., 358
Williams, Elanor F., 283
Williams, Hywel, 226
Williams, Joshua L., 152
Williams, Katie M., 84
Williams, Kirk R., 388, 389, 390,
    391, 444
Williams, Kristi, 431
Williams, Lela Rankin, 194
Williams, Michelle A., 412
Williams, Rebecca S., 479
Williams, Scott M., 16
Williams, Sheila M., 233, 285
Willinger, Marian, 138
Willoughby, Michael T., 390
Wilmoth, Joe D., 497
Wilmshurst, Linda, 367, 372
Wilson, Barbara J., 481
Wilson, Kathryn R., 230
Wiltfang, Jens, 421
Wimer, Christopher, 314
Windham, Gayle C., 228, 403,
    404, 411
Windle, Sarah B., 478
Wingate, Martha S., 119, 122
Wise, Sarah K., 316
Witt, Jessica K., 45, 48
Wittenberg, Dankwart F., 150
Woessmann, Ludger, 356, 446
Wolak, Janis, 441, 442
Wold, Bente, 465
Wolf, Marshall A., 59
Wolf, Maryanne, 327
Wolfe, Christy D., 194
Wolff, Mary S., 228, 403, 404, 411
Wolke, Dieter, 390
Womack, William M., 461
Wood, Jeffrey J., 375
Wood, Mark, 465
Wood, Wendy, 7, 300, 302, 305
Woodard, Jarilyn, 227
Woodcock, Jennie, 108
Woodward, Amanda L., 209, 265, 378
Woodward, Kirsten, 378
Woolley, Jacqueline D., 346
World Bank, 121, 123
World Health Organization, 150,
    233, 238
Wosje, Karen S., 225
Woulfe, Julie, 385
Wray-Lake, Laura, 464
Wu, Rachel, 206

Wubbena, Zane C., 341
Wurtele, Sandy K., 425
Wyndaele, Jean-Jacques, 57
Wysocki, Karen, 57
Xia, Jiahui, 76
Xiang, Jing, 322
Xiang, Zongping, 275
Xie, Hongling, 388
Xin, Ziqiang, 472
Xu, Fei, 167, 168, 272
Xu, Fen, 261, 262
Xu, Jiaquan, 155
Xu, Likang, 440
Xu, Shaojun, 413
Xu, Yuanyuan, 413
Xue, Haifeng, 84
Xue, Hong, 316
Yadav, Priyanka, 443
Yan, Ni, 190
Yang, Jing, 114
Yang, Leigh, 466
Yang, Rongwang, 326
Yang, Tu-Bao, 114
Yang, Wei, 415
Yang, Xiujie, 343
Yang, Yang, 113
Yapıcı, Gülçin, 443
Yates, Tuppett M., 375
Yatsunenko, Tanya, 70, 159, 160
Yazıcı, Aylin Ertekin, 443
Yen, Cheng-Fang, 442
Yeung, Fanny, 494
Yeung, Wei-Jun Jean, 501
Yi, Hsiao-ye, 480
Yi-Frazier, Joyce P., 313
Yip, Tiffany, 496
Yonemoto, Naohiro, 103
York, Timothy P., 390
Young, Alford A., 121
Young, Gerald, 7
Young, Katherine S., 207
Young, Michael C., 226
Young, Nicole A., 102
Young, Sera L., 158, 261
Young-Wolff, Kelly C., 27
Yovanoff, Paul, 331
Yovsi, Relindisra, 209
Yu, Hong, 114
Yu, Lu, 443
Yu, Yizhen, 442
Yücel, Murat, 434
Yudell, Michael, 16
Zachry, Anne H., 151
Zalewski, Maureen, 281

Zametkin, Alan J., 326
Zampieri, Thais T., 411
Zane, Jazmin I., 389
Zatorre, Robert J., 20, 321
Zeanah, Charles H., 204, 230
Zeiders, Katharine H., 464, 472
Zeifman, Debra M., 125, 126, 145, 147
Zeitlin, Jennifer, 105
Zeitlin, Marian, 152
Zelazo, Philip David, 229
Zentall, Shannon R., 285
Zera, Chloe A., 109
Zhai, Fuhua, 275
Zhan, Jinfeng, 101
Zhang, Dongying, 442
Zhang, Hongmei, 112
Zhang, Ji, 316
Zhang, Jijun, 215, 491
Zhang, Jing, 194, 413
Zhang, Jun, 424
Zhang, Suhan, 326
Zhang, Zhonghe, 101
Zhao, Jinxia, 448
Zhao, Yong, 362
Zhao, Zhengyan, 326
Zhen, Zonglei, 322
Zhong, Qiuyue, 412
Zhou, Nan, 463
Zhou, Qing, 259
Zhu, Qi, 322
Zieber, Nicole, 171
Zimmer-Gembeck,
    Melanie J., 448
Zimmerman, Frederick J., 182
Zimmerman, Julie B., 27
Zimmerman, Marc A., 17
Zimmerman, Rick S., 438
Zimmermann, Ivan R., 413
Zimmermann, Klaus F., 452
Zito, Julie M., 325
Zmyj, Norbert, 174, 176
Zolna, Mia R., 76, 121, 123
Zolotor, Adam J., 298
Zosel, Amy, 481
Zosuls, Kristina M., 304
Zuberbühler, Klaus, 179
Zubrick, Stephen R., 115
Zubrzycki, Jackie, 450
Zuccarello, Daniela, 86
Zucker, Kenneth J., 461
Zucker, Robert A., 480
Zuffianò, Antonio, 395
Zurbriggen, Eileen L., 304
Zych, Izabela, 391

# Subject Index

Note: Page numbers followed by f, p, or t indicate figures, photographs, or tables respectively

Abecedarian Project, 275, 275p
Abnormality, 320, 328, 329, 336. *See also* Birth defects
Abortion
    in cases of birth defects, 86, 99t, 120
    rate for teens, 423
    reduction in adolescent crime due to, 476
    in Romania, 202
    sex selection by, 73–74
    spontaneous abortion, 87, 98, 424
Abstract thinking, 46t
Abuse. *See also* Bullying; Child maltreatment; Cyberbullying; Sexual abuse
    child, 242
    impact on adulthood, 37
    injuries and, 237–241
Abusive head trauma, 146
Academic achievement. *See also* Achievement tests; International tests
    before age 6, 236
    divorce and, 379
    employment affecting, 460
    family function related to, 379
    foundation in repetition, 343
    in high school, 453
    marijuana use affecting, 479–480
    in middle school, 447–449
    physical activity affecting, 313
    in secondary education, 455
    sleep deprivation inhibiting, 406, 407f
    stereotype threat affecting, 490–491
    of video game players, 442–443
Acceleration, 334
Accidents, 237, 238
Accommodation, 47, 47f, 165–166
Achievement tests, 320–321. *See also* International tests
    Advanced Placement, 449
    efficacy of, 320–321, 336
    high-stakes tests, 449, 451f, 455
    SAT and ACT, 450
Active apprenticeship, 52
Active labor, 105
Active learning, 251
Active play, 288–290, 306
Adaptation, 47, 47f, 165, 178p, 210–211
Adaptation, positive, 372
Adaptive cognition, 165–166
Addiction. *See also* Alcohol; Drug use and abuse; Smoking; Tobacco
    adolescents and, 442–443, 443t
    to drugs, 478, 479
    genetic/environmental contribution to, 83–84
    to video games, chat rooms, Internet gambling, 442–443, 442f, 443t
Additive heredity, 81
ADHD. *See* Attention-deficit/hyperactivity disorder (ADHD)

Adolescence. *See also* Puberty
    attachment, 199t
    attraction of extremes, 401
    body image, 417
    brain development, 407–408, 409f, 427, 430, 435, 438, 484
    cognitive learning stages, 46, 46t
    decision making, 435
    diet deficiencies, 415–416, 416p, 419
    digital natives, 440–445, 440p, 442f, 444p, 455, 485
    drug use and abuse, 406, 411–413, 416–417, 423, 464, 465, 476p, 477–483, 477f, 480p, 481p, 482f, 485
    education during, 445–454, 447p, 449p, 485
    egocentrism of, 430–432, 431p
    Erikson's stages of development, 40t
    Freud's stages of development, 40t
    growth and nutrition, 414–420, 415f, 415p, 427, 485
    identity formation, 457–461, 458p, 459p, 460p, 483, 485
    logic and self in, 430–440, 431p, 432p, 433f, 435p, 485
    motor vehicle crashes, 238, 408, 439–440, 439f, 480
    need for guidance, 376
    nutrition, 427
    peer relationships, 390p, 412–413, 439f, 465–471, 465p, 468p, 469f, 469p, 483, 485
    pregnancy during, 158t, 423–424, 424p, 427, 461, 470
    puberty, 401–414, 406p, 407f, 413p, 485
    relationships with adults, 461–465, 462p, 463f, 465p, 472–473, 483, 485
    sadness and anger in, 471–477, 472p, 473f, 474p
    same-sex romance, 468–469, 469f
    sexual activity, 25, 25f, 468f
    sexual maturation, 420–426, 421f, 422p, 424p, 485
    smoking behaviors, 478–479, 478f
    social learning during, 45
    as stage of life, 25p
    two modes of thinking, 434–440, 436f, 439f, 449, 484
Adolescence-limited offenders, 475, 483–484
Adolescent-adult relationships, 461–465, 462p, 463f, 465p, 483
Adolescent egocentrism, 430–432, 431p
Adoption
    of institutionalized children, 204, 230
    international adoption, 205
    of maltreated children, 247, 247p, 248
    of Romanian orphans, 204
Adoptive family, 379t, 382

Adrenal glands, 404, 405f, 427
Adulthood. *See also* Death and dying; Emerging adulthood; Fathers; Late adulthood; Mothers; Parents
    ADHD in, 48p
    attachment, 199t
    changes in eyes, 84
    formal operational stage, 47p
    Freud's stages of development, 40t
    language learning in, 267
    motor vehicle crashes, 439–440, 439f
    parents and, 497–498
    peer influence in, 439f
    percentage highlighting journey to, 482f
    relationships with adolescents, 461–465, 461p, 463f, 465p, 484
Advanced Placement, 449, 455
Advertising, 318f
Affordances, 170–171, 170p, 186
Africa
    ADHD treatment, 326
    age of walking in, 152
    bilingual education in, 362
    college graduates in, 494
    co-sleeping in, 138
    education for special needs children in, 332
    incidence of anemia, 415
    infant day care in, 213
    infant mortality in, 154f
    low birthweight in, 122
    onset of puberty, 410
    stunting of children in, 159f
    toilet training in, 56
    view of non-heterosexual behavior, 468
    vision heritability in, 84
    wasting and stunting in, 159, 159f
African Americans
    ADHD treatment for, 326
    caregiving style of, 296
    college students and, 494
    discipline styles associated with, 296
    education of, 359
    family structure, 383f
    high school graduation rate, 451f
    incidence of autism, 328
    low birthweight of, 16
    onset of puberty, 410, 413
    parent response to ADHD medications, 326
    self-esteem in adolescence, 471–473
    sexual activity of adolescents, 422
    sickle-cell anemia incidence, 89
    single-parent families, 383
    stereotype threat, 491
    suspension from school, 44
    3-year-old play, 287f

Age. *See also* Adolescence; Adulthood; Children; Early childhood (ages 2 to 6); Emerging adulthood; Infancy (first two years); Late adulthood; Middle childhood
    attachment related to, 198
    attitude toward bullying related to, 390
    birthweight related to, 123, 131
    bullying associated with, 390
    cultural differences in, 51
    dangers related to, 238
    eating habits associated with, 415–416
    gamete production affected by, 87–88
    incidence of multiple births related to, 79
    income differences, 14
    of language learning, 180f
    memory retention and, 173
    nearsightedness affected by, 84
    of new mothers, 99t
    prenatal development affected by, 99t
    of puberty, 408–412
    ranges for different stage of development, 8t
    self-esteem in adolescence related to, 471–473
    trends in drug use, 477–479
    vision affected by, 84
Age of viability, 103, 103p
Age periods, 9f
Aggression. *See also* Abuse; Bullying; Child maltreatment; Corporal punishment; Cyberbullying
    of adolescents, 465
    in early childhood, 291–292
    of early-maturing boys, 413
    effect of high/low self-esteem, 371
    effects of sexual abuse, 425
    of preschoolers, 306
    as result of disorganized attachment, 200
    as result of physical punishment, 297, 306
    types of, 291–292, 292t
    video games promoting, 443
Aggressive-rejected children, 388
Alcohol
    adolescent use of, 409, 484
    birthweight affected by, 124
    early-maturing children's risk of using, 413
    effect on fetus, 114–115
    epigenetic changes due to, 80
    harm to adolescent users, 479
    non-heterosexual teens' use of, 474
    prenatal development affected by, 112–119, 112p, 115f
    use in United States, 477f

Alcohol use disorder
  genetic/environmental contribution
      to, 82–83, 91
  preventative measures, 86
Alleles
  additive heredity, 81
  for alcohol use disorder, 83–84
  as carriers of disease, 88–89
  defined, 69
  for eye formation, 81–82
  genetic diversity associated with, 71
  for neural-tube defects, 116
  single-nucleotide polymorphisms, 69
Allergies, 158, 226, 315, 319
Allocare, 211, 211p, 212p, 218
Alpha-fetoprotein (AFP), 119
Alzheimer's disease (AD)
  bilingual brain's resistance to, 267
  dominant genetic disorder, 88
Amphetamines, 477f
Amygdala
  connection to prefrontal cortex, 193
  development of, 427
  functions of, 141, 229
  location of, 141f
  maturation in adolescence, 408
Anal stage, 39, 40t, 208
Analytical thought, 435–436, 436f,
      455
Androgens, 404
Anemia, 415
Anencephaly, 116
Angelman syndrome, 72, 72p
Anger
  in adolescence, 471–477, 474p,
      483–484
  brain growth enabling, 193
  of early-maturing boys, 413
  in infants, 190, 190t
  as learned response, 217
  in toddlers, 191
Animals
  abilities of, 227
  artificial production of twins, 77
  care of offspring, 210–211
  effect of deprivation of social play,
      288
  object permanence in, 167
  rough-and-tumble play of, 288
Animism, 252
Anorexia nervosa, 418, 418p, 427, 455
Anoxia, 124, 131
Antibodies, 156, 158t
Antipathy, 290–291, 306
Antisocial behavior
  in adolescence, 406
  defined, 291, 291p
Anxiety
  attachment related to, 203f
  sleep deprivation causing, 406
Anxiety disorders, post-traumatic
      stress disorder, 244
Apgar scale, 106, 106t
Apoptosis, 101
Appearance. See Physical appearance
Appetite, 245t
Apprenticeship in thinking, 52
Aptitude, 320, 336
Aptitude tests, 320–321, 336
Artistic expression, 236–237, 270
Arts, 361–362, 362f
Asia. See also specific Asian country
  child nutrition in, 159, 159t
  college graduates in, 494
  co-sleeping in, 138
  education in, 356
  incidence of anemia, 415
  low birthweight in, 122, 122f

motor-vehicle deaths in, 238
obesity in, 573
play in early childhood, 286, 288
preferred sex of children, 73–74
scores on international tests, 356t
smoking and alcohol use, 124
vision heritability in, 84
wasting and stunting in, 159f
Asian Americans
  childhood obesity among, 317
  discipline styles associated with, 296
  education of, 451f
  family structure, 383f
  incidence of autism, 328
  onset of puberty, 410
  self-esteem in adolescence,
      472–473
Asperger syndrome, 328
Assimilation, 47, 47f, 165–166
Associative play, 288p
Asthma
  in adolescence, 415
  effect of breast-feeding, 158, 158t
  effect on gross motor development,
      233–234
  in first-born children, 29
  in middle childhood, 316, 316p, 319,
      319f, 336
  socioeconomic effect on incidence
      of, 233
  in United States, 319f
Attachment
  allocare and, 212
  continuum of, 203f
  defined, 198
  disorganized attachment, 200, 201t,
      203f, 217
  with fathers, 206–207
  impact on adulthood, 37
  of infants in day care, 214
  insecure attachment and social
      setting, 202, 204
  insecure-avoidant attachment, 200,
      201t, 203f, 217
  insecure-resistant/ambivalent
      attachment, 200, 201t, 203f,
      217
  measurement of, 201–202, 201p
  patterns of, 200, 201t
  predictors of type, 202t
  secure attachment, 200, 201t, 203f,
      205, 217
  signs of, 199–200
  social setting and, 202t, 203–204
  stages of, 199t
  in Strange Situation, 203f
Attachment parenting, 199
Attempted suicide. See Parasuicide
Attention-deficit/hyperactivity
      disorder (ADHD)
  brain patterns associated with, 48p
  comorbid disorders, 324
  diagnosis of, 324–325, 332
  education and, 325f, 332
  effect of low birthweight, 122
  incidence in United States, 324,
      325f
  misdiagnosis of, 325
  possible causes of, 235
  problems associated with, 336
  treatment for, 324p, 325, 325f,
      326–327, 326f, 336
Auditory cortex, 141f
Australia
  ads for sweets in, 318f
  birth of blind babies, 114
  cohabitation in, 499
  co-sleeping in, 138f

effects of wildfire on children, 374
infant day care in, 213
international test scores, 356t
low birthweight in, 122f
maternal mortality in, 110f
paternity leave in, 213
scaffolding in, 256
view of pride in, 371
Authoritarian parenting, 294, 294t,
      306, 412, 465
Authoritative parenting, 294, 294t,
      306, 465
Autism spectrum disorder (ASD)
  abnormal growth of corpus callosum,
      227
  diagnosis and treatment of, 328–329,
      331p, 332, 333
  DSM-5 criteria, 328
  dynamic-systems approach to
      developing motor skills,
      19–20
  education for children with, 328,
      328p
  epigenetic influence on, 80
  increase in diagnoses of, 328–329
  lack of pruning, 142
  misinformation concerning, 91
  possible causes of, 336
  pragmatics and, 348–349
  research funding for, 332
  timing of birth and, 114
  treatment of, 19, 336
Automatization, 344
Autonomy, 208
Autonomy vs. shame and doubt, 40t,
      208
Autosomes, 71
Axons
  defined, 140
  function of, 140, 143f
  growth and refinement in first two
      years, 139
  photograph of, 140p


Babbling, 174p, 175t, 176–177, 181
Babies. See Infancy (first two years);
      Newborns
Babinski reflex, 126
Baby blues, 126
Baby talk, 175
Back-sleeping, 154, 154p, 155
Bandura, Albert, 45, 61
Base pairs, 68, 69, 70
Baumrind's styles of caregiving,
      293–294, 294t
Bed-sharing, 138, 139, 160
Beginning of pregnancy, 98t
Behavior. See also Antisocial behavior;
      Delinquency; Prosocial
      behavior; Risky behavior;
      Self-destructive behavior
  cultural influence on, 36
  friends' facilitation of, 466–468
  increasing problems in middle school
      years, 447
  in puberty, 404–405, 430
  self-concept's influence on,
      47, 430
Behavioral teratogens, 112–116
Behaviorism
  application to early childhood,
      302–303
  application to infant social
      development, 208–209,
      209p, 218
  area of focus and emphasis, 63t
  classical conditioning, 41–42, 44t

concepts of, 64
contribution of, 62
criticism of, 62
defined, 41
emergence of, 35–36
focus of, 39
influence on teacher-directed
      programs, 272
operant conditioning, 43–44, 44p,
      44t
social learning, 44t, 45
on toilet training, 56
in the United States, 42–43
view of gender development,
      302–303, 306
view of language development, 179,
      181, 185
Behavior modification, 163
Belgium, 213, 356t
Benchmarks, 357–358
Bickering, 463, 483
Bilingual children
  cognitive and social benefits, 348
  control processes of, 347
  reasons and process for learning two
      languages, 267
  in United States, 349, 349f
Bilingual learning, 267–268
Bilingual schooling, 349–350, 362
Binet, Alfred, 60
Binge drinking
  by adolescents, 469
  in childbearing years, 114, 116t
Binge eating disorder, 418
Binocular vision, 148
Bioecological theory. See Ecological
      systems
Biological development, 16–18, 18f
Biorhythms
  circadian rhythm, 406, 407f
  disruption of, 406–407, 407f
  seasonal, 406–407
Biosocial development, 32
  body changes in early childhood,
      223–230, 224p
  body size in first two years,
      136, 136f
  body strength and activity, 487–488
  brain development in adolescence,
      407–408, 409f
  brain development in early
      childhood, 226–230, 229p
  brain development in middle
      childhood, 313–314, 316p
  brain growth in first two years, 139,
      142–144
  child mistreatment in early
      childhood, 241–248, 242f,
      243f, 245t, 247p
  in early childhood, 306
  growth and nutrition in adolescence,
      414–420, 415f, 415p
  health in middle childhood, 312–
      319, 312p, 316p, 318f, 319f
  injury in early childhood, 237–241,
      238p, 241f
  motor skills in early childhood,
      231–237, 231p, 232f, 236p
  motor skills in first two years,
      150–153, 150p, 150t
  puberty, 403–414, 406p, 407f,
      413p, 485
  risk-taking in emerging adulthood,
      488–489, 489f
  senses in first two years, 147–150,
      149p
  sexual maturation in adolescence,
      420–426, 421f, 422p, 424p

survival in first two years, 153–160, 154f, 157f, 158t, 159f
Bipolar disorder, 122, 325
Birth
Apgar scale, 106, 106t
case study, 99t
changes in, 97
complications during, 124
by C-section, 109, 109p
development at, 104
doula's support, 107, 107p
epidural anesthesia, 109
full-term weight at, 104, 121
induced labor, 109
location of, 97, 110p, 111
low birthweight, 119, 121– 124, 122f, 124f, 131
newborn survival, 110
positions for, 105
preterm delivery, 103, 110, 119
uterine rupture, 111
vaginal, 105–107, 105f, 106p, 110p
vulnerability during, 99t
Birth control. See Contraception
Birth defects, 20–21, 88, 113, 115f, 120
Birthing centers, 105, 111
Birthweight, 104, 119, 121–123, 124. See also Low birthweight (LBW)
Bisphenol A (BPA), 27, 233
Blastocyst, 75, 98
Blind data gatherers, 506
Blind participants, 506
Block stacking, 152t
Bodily-kinesthetic intelligence, 322
Body fat
of adolescent girls, 414
effect on puberty, 410–411, 414–415, 427
role of leptin, 411
Body image
of adolescents, 415p, 417, 419, 421, 427, 444–445
of early-maturing girls, 413
eating disorders associated with, 418–420, 418p, 427
Body mass index (BMI)
in early childhood, 224
indications of anorexia nervosa, 418
in middle childhood, 315
Body shape, changes in puberty, 420, 427
Body size
growth during middle childhood, 312
growth in adolescence, 403–404, 410–411, 414–415, 415f, 427, 485
growth in early childhood, 223–230, 224p, 248
growth in first two years, 136, 136f, 137p, 139f, 219
malnutrition's effect on, 159–160, 159f
nutrition in early childhood, 224–226
Body temperature, 125
Bonding, 128–129, 129p
Book-reading, 268
Books for research, 503–504
Botswana, 256
Bottom-up reasoning, 433
Bowlby, John, 61
Boys. See also Males
addiction to video games, 442–443, 442f, 443t

with autism, 328
as bullies, 389, 389p
change in body shape at puberty, 403–404, 420–421
delinquency of, 474
depression in adolescence, 472–473
eating disorders among adolescents, 418, 419
externalization of problems, 385
gender development, 300–305, 300p
growth of, 403–404, 410, 415
incidence of anemia, 415
maturation of, 236
Oedipus complex, 301
puberty, 403, 404, 405f , 413, 427
school drop-out rates, 447
self-esteem in adolescence, 472–473
sex-related impulses of, 422
sexual abuse of, 424–425
social effect of early and late maturation of, 413
sociodramatic play, 289, 289p
suicide/parasuicide of, 472–473, 473f, 483–484
superego, 302
Brain. See also Cognition; Intelligence testing; specific brain structure
connected hemispheres, 228
consensus on, 323
context and, 261–262
control processes, 346–347
coordination and capacity, 344
dual processing, 434–436, 439–440, 439f
function, 467
fusiform face area, 145
lateralization, 228, 235
music's effect on, 321
myelination of, 227
neurons connecting, 227
scans, 322–323
special, children's with, 320
stress hormones effect on, 193, 230
structures of, 141f
Brain development/maturation. See also Limbic system; Prefrontal cortex
in adolescence, 407–408, 409f, 427, 430, 435, 485
at birth, 101–102
completion, 210
in early childhood, 221, 226–230, 227f, 228p, 229p, 247, 283–284
effect of stress on, 193
during emerging adulthood, 490, 490p
for emotional regulation, 227, 229–230
emotions and in first two years, 193, 194p, 195f, 217
environmental hazards, 233–234, 234f, 235p
epigenetics and, 7
experience-dependent development, 142
experience-expectant development, 142
experience promoting, 322–323
exuberance and pruning, 139, 142
in fetus, 101, 102f
in first two years, 151

growth in first two years, 133, 139, 139f, 142–144, 159, 219, 226–227
impulse control and perseveration, 227, 229–230
language acquisition and, 265
malnutrition's effect on, 159–160
maturation of, 50t
in middle childhood, 312, 313–314, 316p, 336, 343
needed for gross motor skills, 150–151
of prefrontal cortex (See Prefrontal cortex)
prenatal development, 99, 101–102
pruning, 226
sequence of, 408, 409f
use of drugs affecting, 479
Brain Research Through Advancing Innovative Neurotechnologies (BRAIN), 141
Brain scans, 322–323
Brain stem, 101
Brazelton Neonatal Behavioral Assessment Scale (NBAS), 125, 131, 149
Brazil
low birthweights in, 122f
paternity leave in, 213
three-year-old play, 287f
Breast-feeding
benefits of, 127, 157–159, 158p, 158t
at birth, 106
effect of C-sections on, 109, 109p
impact on adulthood, 37
in U.S., 158
Breathing reflex, 125, 158t
Broca's area, 147p
Bronfenbrenner, Urie, 11–12, 32, 61, 97
Bulimia nervosa, 418, 427
Bullying
causes and consequences, 297, 388–389, 398, 476
cyberbullying, 442, 443–444, 444p, 447, 455
in middle childhood, 386, 388–389, 389p, 398, 448
in middle school, 447
physical, 388, 388p, 398
reduction of, 390–392, 398
types of, 388
victims of, 388–389, 389p
Bullying aggression, 292, 292t, 306, 388–389, 389p
Bully-victims, 389

Cameroon, 209, 213
Camps for children with special needs, 313
Canada
childhood obesity in, 315
cohabitation in, 499
college graduates in, 494f
co-sleeping in, 138f
discipline styles in, 296
disparities between rich and poor, 13f
infant day care in, 214
infant mortality in, 154f
international test scores, 356t, 358, 453
language shifts in, 267
low birthweight in, 122f

maternal mortality in, 110f
paternity leave in, 213
Cancer
causes of, 70, 80
in early childhood, 237
CARDIA (Coronary Artery Risk Development in Adulthood), 488
Cardiovascular accident (CVA). See Stroke
Cardiovascular system. See also Heart; Heart disease; Stroke
aging of, 659
development of, 104
Career academies, 452
Caregivers. See also Family; Fathers; Grandparents; Mothers; Parents
challenges for with children 2-6, 293–305, 293p, 306
effect on infant sleep patterns, 137
foster care, 204, 247, 247p
frequent changes as indicator of maltreatment, 245t
kinship care, 247
Caregiving. See also Family; Fathers; Mothers; Parenting; Parents
allocare, 211–214, 212p, 218
attachment, 198–205, 199t, 201t, 202t, 217
Baumrind's styles of, 293–295
brain development affected by, 193, 193p
challenges with children 2-6, 306
culture effect on style, 296
discipline, 296–299
emotional development affected by, 190, 193
by fathers, 209p
foster care, 247p
infant day care, 211–214, 212p
infant growth and development affected by, 135
infant strategies for maintenance of, 210
proximal and distal parenting, 209, 209p
styles of, 293–295, 294t, 295p, 306
synchrony with infants, 196p, 196–197, 197p, 200p, 204
temperament affected by, 193, 196p, 197p
Carrier, 82, 82f, 89
Car seats, 239
Case to Study
Berger Daughters, 303, 303p
Biting the Policeman, 437
Can We Bear This Commitment?, 205
David, 20–21, 20p
Is She Going to Die?, 342
"My Baby Swallowed Poison," 239
Naiveté of Your Author, 467
Raising Healthy Children, 90–91
Scientist at Work (SIDS), 155
Stones in the Belly (early childhood cognition), 254
Unexpected and Odd, 330
What Were You Thinking?, 409–410
Cataracts, 115f
Catch-up growth, 146
Categorization, 340
Causation, 29, 32
Cell death, 101
Center-based infant care, 213
Central nervous system (CNS), 101, 140
Centration, 252

Cephalocaudal pattern of
    development, 100, 150
Cerebellum, 141f
Cerebral cortex, 141f, 322–323
Cerebral palsy, 124
Cesarean section (C-section), 107,
    109, 131
Charter schools, 361, 362, 362p, 365
Chemicals, 410–411. See also Toxins
Chickenpox, 156
Child-centered preschool programs
    assumptions of, 270–272, 270p, 284
    methodology of, 271p
    Montessori schools, 271, 278
    Reggio Emilia, 271–272, 271p, 278
    teacher-directed programs vs.,
        272–273, 277f
Child culture
    bullies and victims, 386, 388–389,
        389p
    conflict with adult morality,
        395–396
    development of moral values,
        392–397
    friendships, 386–387, 386p, 387p
    in middle childhood, 398
    popular and unpopular children,
        387–388
Child-directed speech, 175, 178–179,
    181
Child-directed videos, 182–183
Childhood. See also Early childhood
    (ages 2 to 6); Infancy
    (first two years); Middle
    childhood; Newborns
    attachment, 199t
    concrete operational stage, 47p
    effect of low birthweight, 122
    Erikson's stages of development, 40t
    evolutionary theory concerning, 58
    Freud's stages of development, 40t
    immunization, 156–157, 156p
    obesity in, 109
    social learning during, 45
Childhood obesity
    in adolescence, 416, 416p, 419
    breast-feeding reducing risk of, 158,
        158t, 336
    contributing factors, 109, 317, 318f
    in early childhood, 5–6, 6f, 224–226,
        225p, 248
    effect on onset of puberty,
        410–411
    in middle childhood, 315–316, 316p,
        318f
    role of leptin, 411
    in United States, 315, 317, 317f
Childhood overweight, 5, 315–316
Child maltreatment. See also Neglect
    attachment affected by, 202t
    brain development affected by, 193,
        217, 230
    consequences of, 244–247
    definitions and statistics, 242–243,
        242f
    in early childhood, 241–248, 242f,
        243f, 245t, 247p, 307
    effect on emotional development,
        230
    effect on neurobiological
        development, 193
    frequency of, 243–244, 243f
    impact on adulthood, 12–13
    levels of prevention, 247p, 248
    prevention of, 246–247, 246p, 247p,
        248
    by sexually abused mothers, 425
    warning signs, 244, 245t

Child neglect, 242, 248. See also
    Child maltreatment; Neglect
Child–Parent Centers, 275
Child pornography, 444–445
Childrearing costs, 211
Children. See also Bilingual children;
    Childhood; Childhood
    obesity; Child maltreatment;
    Children with special needs;
    Early childhood (ages 2 to
    6); Infancy (first two years);
    Middle childhood
    cognitive learning stages, 46, 46t
    overweight, 5
    overweight people in, 315–316
    theories, 260–261
Children with special needs
    education for, 331–332, 332f
    in middle childhood, 323–325
Child soldiers, 373
Chile
    infant mortality in, 153, 154f
    low birthweight in, 122f, 123
    paternity leave in, 213
China
    ADHD in, 326
    age of walking in, 152
    body image of adolescents in, 417
    book-reading parents in, 256
    childhood obesity in, 225p, 315–316
    co-sleeping in, 138f
    C-sections in, 109, 109p
    education in, 85p, 335, 353, 446
    high school graduation rate, 446
    high-stakes tests, 450
    infant day care in, 213
    infant mortality in, 153
    international test scores, 357f
    language shifts in, 267
    legality of sex determination, 73–74
    low birthweight in, 122f, 123
    obesity in, 488p
    one-child policy, 73–74
    PISA scores, 453
    popularity of shy children, 387
    regulation of pride, 371
    school's effect on vision in, 85
    sexual activity of adolescents in, 422
    teen pregnancy in, 423
Chlamydia, 425
Chlorpyrifos, 117
Cholera, 89
Chromosomes. See also Alleles;
    Genes; Heredity
    combinations of, 88
    at conception, 68p, 71, 72–73, 94
    copy number variations, 86–93, 87p,
        88t, 94
    defined, 68, 94
    effect of excess chromosomes,
        86–87, 87p, 88t, 94
    of normal human, 73p
    role in protein synthesis, 68, 68f
    23rd pair (sex chromosomes), 71,
        72f, 86–88, 88t, 94
Chronosystem, 12, 12f, 97. See also
    Cohort; Historical context
Cigarettes. See Smoking; Tobacco
Circadian rhythm
    disruption in adolescence, 406–407,
        407f, 427
    effect of electronic blue-spectrum
        light, 406
Citing sources, 505
Citizenship, 353
Class. See Social class
Classical conditioning, 41–42, 44t
Classification, 340

Cleft palate, 115f
Climbing, 150
Clothes, 386
Cluster suicides, 474
Cocaine, 477f
Cochlear implant, 148
Code-focused teaching, 268
Code of ethics, 30
Cognition
    adolescence in digital age, 455
    college and, 493
    dendrite pruning associated with,
        161
    effects of pesticides, 117
    low birthweight's effect on, 122
    measurement of, 452–453
    measurement of practical cognition,
        452–453
    perception leading to, 165
    postformal, 489–490, 502
    prenatal/postnatal brain growth
        affecting, 139
    technology and, 441
    teratogens' effect on, 112
Cognitive-behavioral therapy, 210
Cognitive coping, 374–375
Cognitive development
    of adolescence in digital age, 440–
        445, 440p, 442f, 444p, 485
    defined, 17, 17f, 19
    early-childhood education, 268–278,
        271p
    education in middle childhood,
        353–364, 353t, 354t, 355p,
        356f, 360t, 361f, 362f, 363f
    emotional regulation enabling and
        enabled by, 284
    information processing in first two
        years, 169–173, 170p, 171p,
        172f, 173p, 186, 219, 306
    information processing in middle
        childhood, 342–344, 345t,
        346p
    language development in first two
        years, 174–186, 174p, 175t,
        177p, 184p, 219
    language in middle childhood,
        348–349, 348p
    language learning in early childhood,
        263–268, 264t
    logic and self in adolescence,
        430–440, 431p, 432p,
        433f, 435p
    postformal thought of emerging
        adulthood, 489–490
    sensorimotor intelligence in first two
        years, 164–168, 164t, 168p,
        186, 219
    teaching and learning in adolescence,
        445–454, 447p, 449p
    theories applied to middle childhood,
        339–347, 340p, 345t
    thinking during early childhood,
        251–263, 253f, 256p, 261p
    on toilet training, 56
    two modes of thinking in
        adolescence, 434–435, 436f,
        439f
Cognitive disequilibrium, 46, 47f
Cognitive equilibrium, 46, 47f
Cognitive flexibility, 490
Cognitive theory
    application of, 45–49
    application to adolescence, 432–434,
        433f, 433p, 485
    application to early childhood,
        168p, 251–254, 253f, 276,
        303–304, 306

application to infant social
    development, 164–168, 164t
application to middle childhood,
    339–341, 340p
areas of focus and emphasis, 63t
concrete operational stage, 339–341,
    340p, 341p
contribution/criticism of, 62
emergence of, 35–36
information processing, 47–48,
    342–344
logic and self in adolescence, 485
Piaget's stages of development,
    45–48, 46t, 47f, 47p, 64
preoperational thought, 251–254,
    253f, 276
sensorimotor intelligence, 164–168,
    164t, 168p, 186
working model, 210
Cohabitation, 499–500, 502
    effect on children, 380
    in Nigeria, 384f
    in United States, 383f, 384f, 499
Cohort. See also Historical context
    artistic expression associated with,
        237
    co-sleeping and, 138
    culture and, 493p
    defined, 13
    early maturation of boys associated
        with, 413
    eating habits associated with,
        415–416
    effect on attitudes toward marijuana,
        10–11, 11f
    identity related to, 461
    play influenced by, 282, 286
    popularity of children related to, 387
    sexual activity in adolescence
        changing with, 422
    variation in drug use, 477–479, 484
    view of non-heterosexual behavior by,
        468–469
    weight affected by, 317
Cohort-sequential research, 27.
    See also Cross-sequential
        research
Colic, 190
College
    alternatives to, 451–452
    cognition and, 493
    cognitive growth associated with,
        491
    graduates in developed nations,
        494
    graduation rates, 450–451, 455
College-bound students, 449–450,
    451f
Colombia, 213, 356t
Colorblindness, 17, 82–83, 83t
Colostrum, 106, 157
Common Core standards, 360–362,
    360t, 365, 371
Communication
    in caregiving, 294
    within CNS, 140
    within families, 464–465
    between hemispheres of
        brain, 228
    personality affected by, 375–376
    role in childbearing/rearing, 128
    technology enabling, 440
Community
    contribution to clinical
        depression in adolescent
        boys, 472–473
    effect on self-esteem in adolescence,
        472

elements of developmental context, 11–12
resilience of child associated with, 372–374
teaching of language, 349
Comorbid disorders
in adolescence, 471
in middle childhood, 320
psychopathological disorders as, 320, 477
Comparison group, 23, 24, 24f
Competition, 449
Computers
for math learning, 259
use in middle childhood, 313p
use in schools, 362
Conception
determining date of, 98t
division creating multiple fetus, 77–79, 78f
genetic combination, 68p, 69–71, 88
in vitro fertilization, 76, 76p, 98
Concrete operational thought
of adolescents, 436f
characteristics of, 46t, 47p, 339–341, 340p, 341p, 365
classification, conservation, reversibility, and seriation, 339–340
moral development enabled by, 393, 395
Conflict
within families, 385, 385p, 398, 412
between parents and teens, 462–463
Connectedness, 464–465
Conservation
lacking in early childhood, 253–254, 253f, 255p
in middle childhood, 340
types of, 253f
Contact-maintaining, 199, 205
Contentment, 190, 190t, 217
Continuity and change, in development, 9–10
Contraception
adolescents' use of, 423, 423f
education concerning, 470–471
reduction in adolescent crime due to, 476
Control, 464–465
Control group, 24, 24f
Control processes, 346–347, 365
Conventional moral reasoning, 393, 394t
Convergent thinkers, 333
Conversation, 253, 430
Cooperative play, 286
Coordination, 140, 344
Coping, cognitive, 374–375
Copy number variations, 70, 86–89, 94
Corporal punishment, 297, 306
Corpus callosum, 141f, 227, 228, 344
Correlation, 29, 29t
Cortex
defined, 140
emotional development related to maturity of, 193
folding of, 101–102
language acquisition and, 176
prenatal development, 101, 102f
Cortisol
brain development affected by, 146, 193, 230
in disorganized attached infants, 200
effects of sexual abuse, 425
in infants, 190, 193

in low-income children, 374
onset of puberty affected by, 412
production in hypothalamus, 141
Co-sleeping, 138, 139f, 139p, 159
Cost-benefit analysis, 22t
Cot death. See Sudden infant death syndrome (SIDS)
Couvade, 127
Crawling, 150p, 150t, 151
Creative geniuses, 334
Creative intelligence
areas of brain controlling, 140
in early childhood, 235–237
Sternberg's theory, 322, 322p
Creativity. See also Artistic expression
in early childhood, 270–271
prefrontal cortex and, 236–237, 236p
Creeping, 150p, 150t, 151
Crime, 235, 475–476, 483–484. See also Delinquency; Homicide
CRISPR, 75, 94
Critical period, 9, 114, 115f, 263
Croatia, 122, 213
Cross-fostering, 129
Cross-sectional research
defined, 25–26
participants, 25p
process of, 25–27, 28f
Cross-sequential research
defined, 27
longitudinal vs., 25–27, 26f
process of, 28f
Crying
caregiver's response to, 193, 194p
in early childhood, 229, 283
in early infancy, 146, 190, 192, 192p, 193
as infant reflex, 125
as survival technique, 210
triggers for, 209p
C-section, 107, 109, 109p, 131
Cuba, 122, 122f
Cultural patterns, 52
Culture
artistic expression associated with, 237
attachment affected by, 198–199
behavior influenced by, 36
birth and, 105, 106p, 107p
birthweight affected by, 121
child-rearing practices affected by, 193, 209
of children in middle childhood, 386–392, 386p, 389p
cohort and, 493p
contribution to adolescent depression, 472–473
contribution to alcohol use disorder, 83–84
co-sleeping and, 138–139
defined, 14
definition of child maltreatment determined by, 244
as determinant of infant care, 209, 211–212
development affected by, 14–17
drug use associated with, 484
effect on genetic expression, 80
effect on international test scores, 357
effect on play, 289–290
emotional development affected by, 191, 282, 284
ethnicity/race related to, 16f
fine motor skills permitted by, 236, 236p

gender roles affected by, 303–304
impact on family function, 378, 380, 383
infant day care determined by, 212–213
influence on gross and fine motor skills, 152
influence on sex differences, 73, 74
language development differences, 178–179, 185p
learning affected by, 341–342
male-female relationships affected by, 466–468
math learning and, 258–259
memory influenced by, 345
metaphors related to, 348
moral development and empathy associated with, 394
moral values determined by, 394
parent–adolescent relationships related to, 464
parenting styles related to, 296
perception of affordances and, 170
personality influenced by, 375–376
play influenced by, 286
reduction of SIDS, 154
role in learning process, 51
schooling determined by, 365
sexual activity in adolescence affected by, 422
as social construct, 14–15, 32
strategies for working memory development influenced by, 345–346
temperament differences related to, 194–195
thought processes affected by, 255–257
view of non-heterosexual behavior associated with, 468
views of pride and, 371
vision affected by, 84–85
weight affected by, 317
Cumulative stress, 372–374
Curiosity, 4, 190, 190t, 254
Curriculum. See Education
Custody disputes, 379
Cutting, 445
Cyberbullying, 388, 398, 443–444, 444p, 455
Cyber danger, 443–444
Cystic fibrosis, 89, 93p

Daily hassles, 372–374
Darwin, Charles, 37, 54, 60, 334
Daycare, 269
Deafness, 115f, 324. See also Hearing
Death and dying
of children, 237
due to opioid, overdose, 41–42, 42f
infanticide, 58, 74, 74p
of males, 73–74
in middle childhood, 312
pedestrian deaths, 238, 240, 241f
sudden infant death syndrome, 154, 155f
in United States, 241f, 312
Decision making, 435, 437
Deductive reasoning, 433, 436f, 455
Deferred imitation, 168, 168p
Defiance, 474–476, 474p
Delinquency
of adolescents, 474–476, 474p, 483–484

causes of, 462, 466–468, 476
types of, 475–476
Delivery. See Labor and delivery
Dendrites
changes throughout life, 323
defined, 140
density in early childhood, 227
emotional development related to growth of, 193
experience altering, 173
function of, 140, 143f
growth and refinement in first two years, 141, 161
increased density, 227
photograph of, 139f
Denmark
ads for sweets in, 318f
early childhood education in, 268–269
international test scores, 356t
low birthweights in, 122f
maternal mortality in, 110f
schizophrenia study, 91
Dentists, 29
Deoxyribonucleic acid (DNA). See DNA
Dependent experiences, 142
Dependent variable, 23, 24, 24f
Depression. See also Postpartum depression
in adolescence, 413, 417, 472–473, 472p, 473f, 483, 484
bullying resulting in, 390, 444
causes of, 122
effect of mothers on infants, 7–8, 190, 198, 200, 202t, 207, 217
of fathers, 207, 207f, 217
of friendless teens, 387
from marijuana use, 479
misinformation concerning, 91
mother's effect on infants, 195
in people with short 5-HTTLPR gene, 463
postpartum depression, 126
as result of disorganized attachment, 200
sleep deprivation causing, 406
Depth perception, 148, 170, 170p
Development. See also Biosocial development; Cognitive development; Developmental theories; Psychosocial development; specific life stage
characteristics of, 20t–21t
critical period, 9
differential sensitivity, 21t
differential susceptibility, 7–8, 13
domains of, 17f
dynamic systems approach, 19–20
multicontexual nature of, 10–14, 21t
multicultural nature of, 14–17, 21t
multidirectional nature of, 9–10, 21t
multidisciplinary nature of, 17–19, 21t, 51
patterns of growth, 9f
plasticity of, 19–20, 20p, 21t, 32
sensitive period, 9–10
study of, 25–28, 28f, 503–507
Developmental crisis, 39. See also Psychosocial development
Developmental growth patterns, 9f
Developmental programs, 270–272, 270p
Developmental psychopathology, 320, 323, 336

Developmental theories
　application to middle childhood,
　　339–347, 345t, 365
　behaviorism (See Behaviorism)
　classical conditioning, 41–42
　cognitive theory (See Cognitive
　　theory; Piaget, Jean)
　defined, 37
　domains of, 32
　eclectic perspective, 62–63
　Erikson's psychosocial theory (See
　　Erikson, Erik; Psychosocial
　　theory)
　evolutionary theory (See Evolutionary
　　theory)
　Freud's psychosexual theory
　　(See Freud, Sigmund;
　　Psychosexual theory)
　grand theories, 38–51
　information processing theory
　　(See Information-processing
　　theory)
　newer theories, 51–62
　operant conditioning, 43–44,
　　44p, 44t
　psychoanalytic theory (See
　　Psychosexual theory;
　　Psychosocial development)
　questions and answers of, 37
　theory of the mind (See Theory of
　　mind)
　theory-theory, 260, 267
　universal perspective (See
　　Evolutionary theory;
　　Humanism)
Deviancy training, 467
Diabetes
　effect of breast-feeding, 158, 158t
　epigenetic influence on, 80
　low birthweight associated with, 122
　obesity associated with, 5–6
　in pregnant women, 123
Diagnostic and Statistical Manual of
　　Mental Disorders (American
　　Psychiatric Association)
　ADHD criteria, 325, 327
　complexity of diagnosis, 323–325
　gender dysphoria criteria, 461
Difference-equals-deficit error
　concerning infant care, 213
　defined, 15
　ethnicity and race, 16
　in language abilities, 350
Differential susceptibility
　age and, 13
　defined, 7–8
　in emotional development, 193
　individualized child-rearing and, 295
　onset of puberty, 412
　personality development and, 373t
　phenotype and, 80
　plasticity and, 19–20, 21t
　in responses to stress, 373
　role of Y chromosome, 116
　vulnerability to depression, 473
Differentiation of cells, 75, 98
Diffusion tensor imaging (DTI), 50t
Digital divide, 440–441
Digital natives, 440–445, 440p, 442f,
　　444p, 455
Disability, changing nature of, 320, 336
Discipline
　consequences of, 36
　induction, 299
　physical punishment, 296–297, 298p
　psychological control, 297, 299, 306
　strategies for, 294, 296–299
　time-out, 299
Discontinuity, 9

Discoveries, 37
Disease. See also Illness; Mental
　　illness; Psychopathology;
　　Sexually transmitted
　　infections (STIs); specific
　　disease
　genetic causes of, 70
　immunization against, 156–157,
　　336, 426
Disengaged infants, 198
Disequilibrium, 47f
Disgust, 191–192
Disorganized attachment, 200, 201t,
　　203f, 217, 246
Disruptive mood dysregulation, 325
Distal parenting, 209, 209p
Distress, 190, 190t, 217
Divergent thinkers, 335
Diversity. See also African Americans;
　　Age; Asian Americans;
　　Boys; Culture; Ethnic
　　identity; Ethnicity; European
　　Americans; Fathers;
　　Females; Gender; Gender
　　differences; Gender identity;
　　Girls; Hispanic Americans;
　　Immigrants; Latino
　　Americans; Men; Mexican
　　Americans; Mothers; Native
　　Americans; Prejudice; Race;
　　Racism; Religion; Religious
　　identity; Same-sex romance;
　　Socioeconomic status (SES);
　　specific continent; specific
　　nation
　biological advantage of, 81
　in college, 493–495
Divorce
　contributing factors, 380, 424
　effect on children, 378–380, 382,
　　385
　onset of puberty affected by,
　　411–412
　rates during recessions, 385
　in United States, 378
Dizygotic (DZ) twins, 78f, 79, 81p, 92,
　　116, 375–376
DNA. See also Chromosomes;
　　Epigenetics; Genes; Heredity
　defined, 68
　of microbiome, 70
　from mother and father, 75–76
　nature-nurture controversy, 6–8
　role in protein synthesis, 68, 68f
　testing, 75
Domains of human development, 17,
　　17f, 19
Dominant disorders, 88
Dominant genes, 81, 82f, 88, 94
Dominant-recessive heredity
　expression of, 94
　gene disorders with dominant genes,
　　88, 94
　gene disorders with recessive genes,
　　88–89, 94
　genotype/phenotype, 81–82, 82f, 94
　X-linked characteristics, 82
Doula, 107, 107p
Down syndrome, 87, 87p, 88, 120
Dress standards, 395
Drowning, 238, 239
Drug use and abuse
　ADHD treatment, 325, 326
　in adolescence, 406, 411–412, 417,
　　423, 465, 477–483, 477f,
　　480p, 481p, 482f, 484
　birthweight affected by, 121, 124,
　　125, 131
　breast-feeding and, 158

contribution to abusive relationships,
　　424
　early-maturing girls' risk of, 413
　eating disorders associated with, 418
　epigenetic changes due to, 80
　harm from, 479–480
　by non-heterosexual teens, 468
　prenatal development affected by,
　　112–113, 115f
　of prescription drugs, 477f
　prevention of, 480–483, 481p, 482f,
　　484
　as risk factor for schizophrenia, 481
　sleep deprivation causing, 406
　in United States, 477f
　variations in, 477, 477f, 479, 480p
DSM-5. See Diagnostic and Statistical
　　Manual of Mental Disorders
　　(American Psychiatric
　　Association)
DTI (diffusion tensor imaging), 50t
Dual-process model of cognition,
　　434–436, 436f
Duchenne muscular dystrophy, 89
Dynamic-systems perspective
　approach to autism, 19, 19p
　approach to childhood obesity, 317
　on impact of teratogens, 114
　on learning to walk, 151
　view of resilience and stress, 372
Dyscalculia, 327, 331, 336
Dysgraphia, 336
Dyslexia, 327, 327p, 331, 333, 336

Early adulthood. See Emerging
　　adulthood
Early childhood (ages 2 to 6)
　artistic expressions, 236–237, 236p
　body changes, 223–230, 224p
　brain development, 226–230, 229p,
　　283–284
　challenges for caregivers, 293–305,
　　293p
　development of impulse control, 227,
　　229–230
　effect of stress, 230
　emotional development, 263p,
　　281–285, 284p, 290–292
　emotions and brain development in,
　　230, 283–284, 283p
　environmental hazards, 233–234,
　　234f, 235p
　Erikson's stages of development, 40t
　Freud's stages of development, 40t
　impulsiveness and perseveration,
　　227, 229–230, 229p
　injury in, 237–241, 238p, 241f, 287f
　language learning, 263–268, 264t,
　　276
　maltreatment, 241–248, 242f, 243f,
　　245t, 247p
　moral development, 395
　motor skills development,
　　231–237, 231p, 232f, 234f,
　　235p, 236p
　nutrition during, 224–226, 224p
　oral health, 226
　play, 286–292, 286p, 287p, 288p,
　　290f, 290p, 291p
　psychosocial development,
　　281–305
　as stage of life, 26p
　STEM education and, 258–259
　thought processes during, 251–263,
　　253f, 255p, 256p, 257p,
　　258p, 261p
　as time of play and learning, 221
Early-childhood schooling, 277f

child-centered programs, 269p,
　　270–273, 271p, 276, 277f
　homes and schools, 269–270
　intensive preschool programs,
　　275–278
　teacher-directed programs, 272–273,
　　272p, 276, 277f
Eating disorders. See also Obesity
　in adolescence, 418–420, 418p, 427
　anorexia nervosa, 418, 418p, 420,
　　427, 445, 455
　associated with sexual abuse, 424
　binge eating disorder, 418
　bulimia nervosa, 418, 420, 427
　encouragement through social
　　networking, 445, 455
Ebola, 30, 31p, 59
E-cigarettes, 27, 478–479. See also
　　Smoking
Eclectic perspective, 62–63
Ecological systems, 11–14, 12f, 32
Education. See also Bilingual
　　schooling; College; Early-
　　childhood schooling; High
　　school; Learning; Middle
　　school; Teaching
　of adolescents, 445–456, 447p,
　　449p, 451f
　around the world, 363
　children vs. adult's view of, 395–396
　college-bound students, 449–450,
　　451f
　controversy over starting age, 236
　drop-out rates, 350
　effects of school climate on
　　cyberbullying, 443–444
　encouragement of healthy eating,
　　416
　exercise in schools, 314–315
　for gifted and talented children, 336
　high school graduation rate, 446
　homes and schools, 269–270
　influence on development, 14
　international schooling, 353–355,
　　354p
　international testing, 356–358, 356t,
　　357f, 365
　in middle childhood, 353–364, 353t,
　　354t, 356t, 357f, 357p, 363f,
　　365
　in middle school, 447–449, 447p
　national standards, 359–360
　norms for math and reading, 353t,
　　354t
　nutrition in schools, 317
　physical setting for, 355–356, 355p
　questions concerning, 361–364
　relationship to culture, 52
　religion and, 361
　role of encouragement, 362
　sex education, 469–471, 483, 484
　special education, 329–335
　teen pregnancy associated with, 424
　types of schools, 441
　in United States, 359–360, 360t,
　　361f, 362p, 363, 363f, 371,
　　491f
　use of technology, 441, 455
　vision affected by, 85, 85p
　vocational, 452
Education of All Handicapped
　　Children Act (1975), 331
Effect size, 22t, 507
Effortful control
　development in early childhood,
　　282, 389
　effect of high self-esteem, 371
　as inborn trait, 194
　in middle childhood, 389

Egocentrism
  of adolescents, 429, 430–432, 437,
    447, 453, 474
  aid to language learning, 263
  creation of fables, 431–432
  creation of imaginary audiences, 431
  of early childhood, 46t, 252, 254,
    256, 262
Egypt, 116, 122
Electra complex, 302
Electroencephalogram (EEG), 49t,
    144p
Electronic devices, 406
El Salvador, 353
Embarrassment, development in
    infancy, 190t
Embodied cognition, 313
Embryo, 75, 99, 100p
Embryonic growth, 1
Embryonic period
  defined, 98
  development, 9, 98–100, 99t, 100p,
    131
  effect of teratogens during, 114, 115f
  vulnerability during, 99t
Emerging adulthood
  defined, 487, 502
  friendship and, 498, 498p
  moratoria in, 458, 458p
  motor vehicle crashes, 439–440,
    439f
  parents and, 497–498
  peer influence in, 439f
  postformal thought, 489–490
  as stage of life, 25p
  substance abuse in, 27
Emotional development
  anger and sadness, 190, 190t
  brain development in first two years
    and, 193, 194p, 195f
  brain maturation in early childhood,
    227, 283–284
  in early childhood, 281–285, 283p,
    284p, 306
  fear, 190–191, 191p
  in first two years, 189–196, 190t,
    191p, 192p, 217, 219
  imaginary friends, 284–285
  initiative versus guilt, 282–284
  motivation for preschoolers,
    284–285
  protective optimism, 282
  in puberty, 404–405
  self-awareness, 192, 192p
  smiling and laughing, 190, 190p
  social awareness, 191–192
  temperament, 192, 194–196, 194p,
    195f
Emotional regulation
  in adolescence, 408, 409, 427
  brain maturation required for,
    409–410
  as control process in information
    processing, 346
  development in early childhood,
    227, 229–230, 229p, 248,
    281–285, 283p, 284p,
    290–292, 306, 389
  effects of drugs on, 481
  role of play, 288, 306
  use of imaginary friends, 284–285
Emotions
  adolescents' reliance on, 437
  areas of brain controlling, 140
  brain development in early childhood
    and, 227, 229–230, 252,
    252p
  development of normal responses,
    144, 229

stress hormones and, 230
  for survival, 210–211
Empathy
  development of, 192, 290–291, 306
  development of moral values, 392
Empirical evidence, 4
Employment
  consequences of maltreatment in
    childhood, 246
  in teen years, 460
Encouragement, 37
England. See United Kingdom
English as a second language (ESL),
    349–350
English language learners (ELLs),
    349–350
Entity theory of intelligence,
    448–449
Environment
  adaptations to changes in, 58–59
  alcohol use disorder contributed to,
    83–84
  gene expression affected by, 69, 80
  hazards for children, 233–234
  incidence of twins affected by, 80
  infant sleep patterns affected by, 137
  phenotype influenced by, 81p,
    83–85, 94
  schizophrenia influenced by, 91
Environmental hazards. See also Toxins
  gross motor development and,
    233–234
  lead, 233–234, 234f, 235p
Epidural, 109
Epigenetics
  defined, 7, 69, 94
  effect on genes, 80
  influence on development, 77
  role in brain development, 143
  role in psychological disorders, 91
Equifinality, 323, 325
Erikson, Erik, 61p
  arenas of identity, 458–461
  autonomy vs. shame and doubt, 40t,
    208, 218, 495t
  generativity vs. stagnation, 40t, 495t
  identity vs. role confusion, 40p, 40t,
    457, 495t
  industry vs. inferiority, 40t, 369–371,
    398, 495t
  initiative vs. guilt, 40t, 282–284,
    306, 495t
  integrity vs. despair, 40t, 495t
  intimacy vs. isolation, 40t, 495t
  photograph of, 40p
  stages of psychosocial development,
    39–40, 40t, 64, 208
  toilet training advice, 56–57
  trust vs. mistrust, 40–41, 40t, 495t
  view of sexes, 461
Estonia, 453
Estradiol, 404
Estrogen, 404, 405f, 427
Ethics
  of genetic counselors, 91–93
  genetic testing and, 89–90
  implications of research results,
    30–31
  of medical intervention for preterm
    infants, 110
  in research, 30–31, 503
Ethiopia, 122f, 153p
Ethnic group, 16
Ethnic identity
  in adolescence, 459
  formation in emerging adulthood,
    496, 496p
  peer pressure enabling formation of,
    465–466

Ethnicity. See also specific ethnic
    group
  age of puberty related to, 413–414
  childhood obesity and, 317
  early-/late-maturing children affected
    by, 413–414
  education affected by, 359
  ethnic make-up of the United States,
    18f
  high school graduation rate by, 451f
  incidence of autism related to, 328
  income differences, 14
  influence on development, 16, 193
  nutrition and, 225
  onset of puberty affected by, 410
  relationship to race/culture, 16f
  school drop-out rates related to, 447
  self-esteem related to, 472–473
  sexual activity in adolescence related
    to, 422
  as social construct, 32
  support and defense of members of
    group, 447
  in the United States, make-up of, 15
  United States regional differences
    in, 15
Europe. See also specific nation
  birth of thalidomide affected babies,
    114
  child nutrition in, 159–160
  cohabitation in, 499
  co-sleeping in, 138f
  low birthweight in, 122, 122f
  onset of puberty, 410
  punishment of poor behavior
    in, 296
  sex education in, 470
  wasting and stunting in,
    158t, 159f
European Americans
  age of walking, 152
  college students and, 494
  cystic fibrosis incidence, 89
  discipline styles associated with, 296
  family structure, 369
  incidence of autism, 328
  onset of puberty, 410
  self-esteem in adolescence,
    472–473
  sexual activity in adolescence, 422
  suspension from school, 44
  3-year-old play, 287f
Eveningness, 406
Event-related potential (ERP), 49t
Every Student Succeeds Act (ESSA),
    450
Evolutionary psychology, 54–56
Evolutionary theory
  on allocare, 210–211, 212p
  application to early childhood,
    304–305
  application to infant social
    development, 210–211, 218
  application to language acquisition,
    183–185
  area of focus and emphasis, 63t
  concepts of, 54–56, 57–58, 59, 62
  contribution of, 62
  criticism of, 62
  development of, 334
  on early onset of puberty, 412
  emergence of, 36
  on language development, 179
E-waste, 27, 234
Excitement, 409, 438, 438f
Executive control, 313, 352
Executive function, 229, 259, 261,
    273, 282, 346–347
Executive processes, 346–347

Exercise. See also Physical activity;
    Play
  benefits of, 312–315
  neighborhood games, 315, 336
  in schools, 314–315
  WHO recommendations for
    children, 318f
Exosystem, 12, 12f, 240. See also
    Community; Employment;
    Religion; Videos and young
    children
Expectant experiences, 142
Expectations. See also Norms
  for math and reading goals,
    353t, 354t
  of maturity in caregiving, 294
Experience
  brain growth and development
    associated with, 142, 161,
    173, 193, 323
  control processes affected
    by, 347
  decision making influenced by,
    434–435, 437
  development of moral values, 392
  fine motor skills associated
    with, 161
  increase in knowledge base,
    346–347
  misinterpretation of, 210
  moral development through, 392
  perception of affordances and,
    170, 171
  professional success associated with,
    452
  pruning of brain connections, 139,
    142
  selective attention developed by, 313
Experience-dependent brain
    development
  body growth in early childhood, 223
  brain development and, 142, 219
  language development, 184
  synchrony, 198
Experience-expectant brain
    development
  body growth in early childhood, 223
  brain development and, 142, 219
  language development, 176–177,
    184
  synchrony, 198
Experiment, 23–24, 23f, 24p
Experimental group, 23f, 23p, 24
Experimental laboratory, first, 60
Experimental variable. See
    Independent variable
Extended family, 378, 379t,
    381, 383
Externalization of problems, 385,
    389, 474
Extremely low birthweight (ELBW),
    119, 122
Extrinsic motivation, 284
Exuberance, 139, 194
Eye color, 81–82, 82f
Eye-hand coordination, 151
Eyes, 148. See also Vision


Fables of adolescence, 431–432
Face recognition, 144, 148
Facilitation of behavior, 467–468
Factor analysis, 22t
Failure to thrive, 136
Fairness, 392
Faith, 374, 374p
False negative, 120
False positive, 120
Familism, 464, 472

Family. *See also* Cohabitation;
        Divorce; Fathers; Marriage;
        Mothers; Parents; Same-sex
        parents
    adoption, 204–205, 248, 382
    benefits of breast-feeding, 158t
    birthweight affected by, 131
    bonding, 128–129, 129p
    conflict within, 385, 411–412
    elements of developmental context, 10
    father's role in pregnancy and birth, 127
    foster families, 204, 247, 248
    functions of, 376–378, 398
    kangaroo care, 129, 129p, 130
    middle childhood and, 375–386,
        376p, 384f, 385p, 398
    mothers following birth, 127
    newborns, 125–126
    parent–adolescent relationships,
        464, 464p, 483
    parental alliance, 128, 131, 207,
        381, 382, 398
    sexual abuse within, 425
    shared and unshared environments,
        375–376, 376p
    socioeconomic context, 385
    stepfamilies, 381–382, 385
    structure and function of, 376–380
    structure and low birthweight, 124f
    trouble within, 383, 385
    two-parent families, 379t, 380–383,
        380p
Family leave, 213
Family-stress model, 385
Fast-mapping, 265, 275
Fathers. *See also* Parents
    biological response to birth, 127, 131
    couvade, 127
    depression following birth, 127
    effect on birthweight, 121
    expectations, 126p
    kangaroo care, 129
    new, 127
    percentage who spank one-year-olds,
        207f
    response to infants, 126
    role in birth, 97
    role in child development, 19
    as social partners, 206–207, 206p,
        207f, 209p, 218
    support of mothers during/after
        birth, 127
Fear. *See also* Anxiety; Anxiety
        disorders
    brain growth enabling, 193
    development of hypothalamus
        effected by, 193
    effect of caregiver's response, 195,
        195p
    as indicator of maltreatment, 245t
    in infants, 190–191, 190t, 191p
    as learned response, 190t, 217
    regulation of, 229
    separation anxiety, 190–191
    stranger wariness, 190, 191p, 233
    in toddlers, 191
Females. *See also* Girls; Mothers
    chromosomes of, 71–73, 73p
    effect of child maltreatment, 246
    innate vulnerability of, 116
Fetal alcohol effects (FAE), 115
Fetal alcohol syndrome (FAS),
        112–113, 112p
Fetal monitoring, 125
Fetal period
    defined, 98
    development, 99t, 100–104, 100p,
        102f, 104p, 131

development of hearing, 147–148
effect of teratogens during, 112–113,
        115f
middle three months, 103
photographs of, 100p
third month, 100
vulnerability during, 99t
Fetus
    defined, 100
    development of, 75, 100–104
    photograph of, 100p, 104p
    preterm delivery, 103
    teratogen damage to, 112–116, 115f
File drawer problems, 507
Fine motor skills
    in early childhood, 232f, 236–237,
        236p, 248
    in first two years, 151–152
    norms for development, 152t
Finger movement skills, 151
Finland
    ads for sweets in, 318f
    college graduates in, 494f
    education in, 335, 362
    high-stakes tests in, 450
    infant mortality in, 153, 154f
    international test scores, 356t, 357,
        357f, 453
    low birthweight in, 122f
    sexual activity of adolescents
        in, 421
    style of discipline used in, 297
    view of teaching in, 357
First acquired adaptations, 164t,
        165–166
First-born children, 29
First words, 175t, 180p, 180t
5-HTTLPR genotype, 7–8, 463, 463f,
        472
Fixed mindset, 448
Fluoride, 312
Flying storks, 111
Flynn effect, 321
fMRI, 49t, 50t
fNIRS, 50, 50t
Focus on appearance, 252–253
Folic acid, 116–117
Folk psychology, 260
Folk theories, 35, 37
Fontanels, 102
Food, 148–149, 226
Food insecurity, 123
Forebrain, 101, 102f, 140
Foreclosure, 458, 460, 461
Formal code (language), 349
Formal operational thought
    in adolescence, 432–434, 433f,
        433p, 436f, 449, 455
    characteristics of, 45–46, 46p, 46t
    hypothetical-deductive reasoning,
        432–434
    moral development related to, 393
    Piaget's experiment, 432, 433f
Formula-feeding, 158, 159
Foster care
    advantages over institutions, 204
    kinship care, 248
    for maltreated children, 247, 247p,
        248
Fragile X syndrome, 89, 142
Framingham Heart Study, 5
France
    ads for sweets in, 318f
    cohabitation in, 499
    disparities between rich and poor,
        13f
    early-childhood education in,
        268–269

infant day care in, 213
international test scores, 356t
language preferences of infants, 179
paternity leave in, 213
Fraternal twins, 77p, 79
Freud, Sigmund, 60p
    background of, 51
    latency of middle childhood, 370
    oral and anal stages in infant social
        development, 208, 218
    phallic stage, 301, 306
    photograph of, 39p
    psychoanalytic theory, 35–36, 64
    psychosexual theory, 39, 40t
    toilet training advice, 39, 40t, 56–57
Friendship
    aid for bullied children, 390
    in emerging adulthood, 498, 502
    facilitation of bad/good behavior,
        467–468, 483
    hostile side of, 395
    importance of in adolescence,
        439–440, 465
    lack of as indicator of maltreatment,
        245t
    in middle childhood, 386–387, 386p
    in middle school setting, 447
    selection of friends, 466–468
Frontal lobe, 140, 227
Functional magnetic resonance
    imaging (fMRI), 49t
Functional near infrared spectroscopy
    (fNIRS), 50t
Fusiform face area of brain, 145

Gamete, 70
Gang involvement, 467, 475
Gardner, Howard, 61
Gender. *See also* Boys; Girls; Men; Sex
    ADHD diagnosis and, 325
    alcohol use related to, 83p, 84
    body fat associated with, 224
    childhood obesity and, 317
    cultural differences, 73–74
    differences in international test
        scores, 358, 365
    friendships related to, 387
    incidence of autism related to, 328
    onset of puberty affected by,
        410–411
    sexual activity in adolescence
        affected by, 421–422
    temperament differences related to,
        194–195
Gender development
    in early childhood, 300–305, 306
    genetic determination of age of
        onset, 410
    in puberty, 410
Gender differences, 300–305, 300p
Gender discrimination, 370
Gender dysphoria, 461
Gender identity
    behaviorist perspective, 303–304
    cognitive theory's perspective,
        303–304
    development in adolescence, 460–
        461, 483
    psychoanalytic perspective, 301–302
    sociocultural theory's perspective,
        303–304
Gender intensification, 460
Gender roles
    development in early childhood,
        300–305, 300p, 301p, 302p
    as social learning, 209
Gender schema, 304

Gender similarities hypothesis, 305, 358
Gene-gene interactions, 80
General intelligence (*g*), 320
Generational forgetting, 481
Generativity *vs.* stagnation, 40t
Generosity, 192
Genes. *See also* Alleles;
        Chromosomes; DNA;
        Epigenetics; Genotype
    additive heredity, 81, 94
    for alcohol use disorder, 83–84, 94
    for Alzheimer's disease, 686
    beneficial mutations of, 58–59, 58f
    for bullying, 389
    computer illustration of segment
        of, 68p
    at conception, 70, 72
    copy number variations, 87p, 88, 88t
    defined, 68, 94
    depression caused by, 472–473
    differential susceptibility of, 116–117,
        194–195, 412, 472–473
    dominant-recessive heredity, 81–82,
        82f, 83t, 89, 94
    editing of, 75
    effect of, 83–85
    epigenetic effect on, 69
    for experience-expectant growth, 142
    expression of, 69
    for gender development, 410, 427
    genetic counseling and testing,
        89–93, 90p
    heterozygous genes, 71
    homozygous genes, 71
    incidence of twins controlled by, 79
    influence on development, 19
    interaction of, 80–81
    for nearsightedness, 84–85
    number in humans, 80, 94
    parent–adolescent relationships
        affected by, 462–463, 463f
    personality affected by, 375–376
    problems caused by, 86–93, 87p,
        88t, 336
    protein synthesis, 68, 68f
    race and, 16
    role in brain development, 143
    role in family conflict, 385
    for senses, 147
    teratogens effects influenced by, 115
    uniformity in cells of individuals, 75
    weight affected by, 317
Genetic code, 68–74, 94
Genetic counseling and testing,
        89–93, 90p, 94, 120
Genetic diseases, 313
Genetic diversity, 59, 71
Genetics, 17, 19, 58–59
Genetic testing, 94
Genetic vulnerability, 116, 124
Genital herpes, 425
Genital stage, 39, 40t
Genome, 68
Genotype
    additive heredity, 81
    carrier of, 82, 82f
    defined, 71
    functions of, 79
    parental imprinting, 88t
    X-linked characteristics, 82, 83t
Germany
    ads for sweets in, 318f
    allocare in, 213
    education in, 358
    international test scores, 356t, 358
    low birthweight in, 122f
    maternal mortality in, 110f
    paternity leave in, 213

Germinal period
  defined, 98
  development, 75p, 98, 98t, 99p, 99t, 131
  effect of teratogens during, 114, 115f
  fertilization and implantation, 99f
  vulnerability during, 99t
Gerontology, 60
Gestational age, 98t
Gestures, 176–177, 177p
Ghana, 353
Gifted and talented children, 333–335, 333p
Girls. See also Females
  addiction to video games, 442–443, 442f, 443t
  anorexia nervosa, 418, 418p
  with autism, 328
  body image in adolescence, 413, 416p, 417
  as bullies, 389, 389p
  change in body shape at puberty, 403, 420–421
  delinquency of, 475–476
  depression in adolescence, 472–473
  determining sexual orientation, 469, 469p
  eating disorders among adolescents, 418–420
  Electra complex, 302
  gender development, 300–305, 300p
  growth of, 404, 410–411, 415
  incidence of anemia, 415
  internalization of problems, 385
  moral development of, 504
  puberty, 389, 404, 405f, 427
  self-esteem in adolescence, 472
  sex-related impulses of, 420–421
  sexual abuse of, 411, 424–425
  social effect of early or late maturation, 413, 413p
  sociodramatic play, 289, 289p
  suicide/parasuicide of, 473–474, 473f, 483
Glaucoma, 115f
Goals, infants' pursuit of, 166
Golden hour, 241
Gonadotropin-releasing hormones, 404
Gonads, 404
Gonorrhea, 425, 426
Grabbing, 152p
Grammar
  acquisition in early childhood, 256–266
  advancement in middle childhood, 348
  defined, 179
  overregularization, 266
Grandmother hypothesis, 58
Grandmothers, 211p, 212
Grandparents, 379t
  as foster parents, 246p
  raising grandchildren, 382
Grand theories, 35–36, 64. See also Behaviorism; Psychoanalytic theory
Grasping reflex, 108f, 151, 152t
Gray matter, 227
Great Britain. See United Kingdom
Greece, 209, 318f
Grimace response, 108f
Gross motor skills
  crawling, 150p
  defined, 150
  development in early childhood, 231–237, 231p, 232f, 236p, 248

development in first two years, 150–151, 161
effect of lead, 233–234, 234f
environmental hazards delaying, 233–234
Growth. See also Body size; Brain development/maturation
  in adolescence, 414–420, 415f, 415p, 427, 485
Growth mindset, 371, 448
Guatemala, 213
Guided participation, 52, 255–257, 256p
Guilt, 282, 297, 302, 306, 371
Gun regulation, 31
Gyri, 101

Habituation, 176
Hair, changes in puberty, 403–404, 415, 421
Haiti, 122f
Hand gestures, 177, 177p, 182
Hand skills, 151, 152t
Happiness
  arising from genes and nonshared environment, 376
  or high grades, 352
Harlow, Harry, 61
Harmony, 377, 382
Harm reduction, 239, 240p
Hate, 245
Head-sparing, 139
Head Start, 270, 273–274, 274p, 299, 307
Health
  benefits of exercise, 313
  level of education related to, 446
  during middle childhood, 312–319, 312p, 313p, 314p, 316p
Health habits
  in middle childhood, 312–313
  nutrition (See Nutrition)
  obesity (See Obesity)
Health problems. See also Diabetes; Heart disease; Illness; Mental illness; Psychopathology
  asthma, 316, 316p, 319, 319f
  childhood obesity, 315–316, 317, 317f
  in middle childhood, 315–319, 316p, 318f, 319f
Hearing
  area of brain controlling, 140
  deafness, 115f
  effect of low birthweight, 122
  fetal development of, 104, 104p, 147–148, 147p, 161
  as necessary for brain development, 146
Heart, prenatal development, 99
Heart disease
  effect of breast-feeding, 158, 158t
  effect of low birthweight, 122
  genetic causes of, 70
  obesity associated with, 5–6
Height
  functions of, 136
  growth in early childhood, 223–224, 232f
  growth in first two years, 139f
Hemophilia, 89
Herbal medication safety, 118
Herd immunity, 156
Heredity. See also Chromosomes; DNA; Genes; Genetic code
  of addiction, 83–84

additive heredity, 81
copy number variations, 86–93, 87p, 88t
dominant-recessive heredity, 81–82
effect on vision, 84–85
excess chromosomes, 86–93, 87p, 88t
genetic counseling and testing, 90p, 91–92
genetic disorders, 87p, 88–89, 88t
Heredity–environment debate. See Nature–nurture controversy
Heritability, 84–85
Heroin, 41
Heterozygous genes, 71
Heuristic, 435
Hiccups, 125
Hidden curriculum, 353–354, 355, 355p, 358, 365, 449
High blood pressure. See Hypertension
Higher education, cognitive growth and, 491–495
High school, 449–453, 449p, 451f, 455
High school graduation rate, 446, 450–451, 451f, 455
High-stakes tests, 450, 451f, 455
Hindbrain, 140
Hippocampus
  damage from alcohol, 479
  functions of, 140
  location of, 141f
  prenatal development, 101
  SES affecting development of, 350
Hispanic Americans. See also Latino Americans
  age of walking in, 152
  childhood obesity, 317, 394
  education of, 350, 451f
  family structure, 383f
  high school graduation rate, 451f
  incidence of autism, 328
  onset of puberty, 410
  race of, 14–15
  self-esteem in adolescence, 472–473
  sexual activity of adolescents, 422
Historical context. See also Chronosystem; Cohort
  attitudes toward marijuana, 10–11, 13f
  defined, 12–14
  identity related to, 457
  of onset of puberty, 411
HIV/AIDS
  breast-feeding and, 158
  genetic protection from, 59
  immunization and, 157, 158
  prenatal detection of, 119
Holophrase, 177, 179
Home birth, 105, 107, 111
Home foreclosure, 385
Home learning environment, 269
Homelessness, 14p, 374
Home schooling, 361, 364, 365
Homicide
  of children, 237
  infanticide, 58, 74, 74p
Homosexual people. See Same-sex marriage; Same-sex parents
Homozygous genes, 71
Hong Kong, 138f, 356t
Hookups, 499, 502
Horizontal décalage, 340
Hormones. See also Estrogen; Oxytocin; Testosterone
  defined, 404
  effect on mood, 427

regulation of body rhythms, 406–407, 407f, 427
released at birth, 105
role in sex development, 405–406, 405f, 411, 421, 427
stimulation of sexual activity, 421–422
HPA axis. See Hypothalamus-pituitary-adrenal cortex axis (HPA axis)
HPG axis. See Hypothalamus-pituitary-gonad axis (HPG axis)
Hubs, 344
Human development
  aspects of, 4
  in early childhood, 223–230
  in first two years, 219
  nutrition in early childhood, 224–226
  patterns of, 9f, 223–224, 224p
  perspectives of, 63t
  in puberty, 415, 485
  science of, highlights of, 60–61
Human genome, 94
Human Genome Project, 80
Human papillomavirus (HPV), 426
Human sexuality, 62
Huntington's disease, 88, 90
Hybrid theory of language development, 185
Hydrofracking, 27
Hygiene hypothesis, 319
Hyperactivity, 234, 244. See also Attention deficit hyperactivity disorder (ADHD)
Hypertension. See also Blood pressure
  breast-feeding and, 158t
  obesity associated with, 6
Hypervigilance, 245t
Hypothalamus
  effect of fear on development of, 193
  functions of, 140
  location of, 141f
  stimulation of puberty, 404, 405f, 427
Hypothalamus-pituitary-adrenal cortex axis (HPA axis)
  abnormalities causing psychopathology in adolescence, 404
  disruptions due to sexual abuse, 425
  link to experience, 438
  stimulation of puberty, 404, 408, 427
Hypothalamus-pituitary-gonad axis (HPG axis), 404
Hypothesis, 4, 6, 22, 23, 37, 506
Hypothetical-deductive reasoning, 432–434, 435
Hypothetical thought, 433

Iceland, 213, 494f
Identical twins. See Monozygotic (MZ) twins
Identification, 302
Identity. See also Ethnic identity; Political identity; Religious identity; Vocational identity
  formation in adolescence, 457–461, 458p, 459p, 460p, 475, 483, 485
  four arenas of, 458–461, 458p, 459p, 483, 484
Identity achievement, 457, 496
Identity crisis, 41p, 457, 458, 458p
Identity diffusion, 458

Identity *vs.* role confusion, 40t, 41p, 457, 483
Illness. *See also* Asthma; Diabetes; Heart disease; Psychopathology
  effect on birthweight, 123
  effect on prenatal development, 112–113, 115f, 116–117, 118
  malnutrition's effect on, 160
  in middle childhood, 312
  resistance in adolescence, 415–416
Imaginary audience, 431, 444, 447, 455
Imaginary friends, 284–285
Imagination, 140, 251, 286p
Immersion teaching, 349
Immigrant paradox, 121
Immigrants
  adult-adolescent relationships among, 465
  lawfulness of, 476
  peer pressure's effect on ethnic identity, 465–466
Immunization
  functions of, 156
  for HPV, 426
  problems caused by, 158–159
  success of, 156–157, 161
Implantation, 98, 99f
Impulse control
  of adolescents, 437
  brain maturation required for, 408, 409
  development in early childhood, 227, 229–230, 229p, 238, 248
Impulsivity, 437–438, 485
Inclusion classes, 331
Income. *See also* Socioeconomic status (SES)
  accident rates and, 238
  education affected by, 359
  family structure and function correlated with, 381, 385, 398
  influence on development, 14
  nutrition and, 225
Incremental theory of intelligence, 448
Independence
  in adolescence, 415, 421, 430
  in middle childhood, 386
Independent variable, 23, 23f, 24
India
  abortion of female fetuses, 74p
  childhood obesity in, 317
  colorblindness in, 82
  couvade in, 127
  education in, 354, 446
  infanticide, 74p
  infant mortality in, 154f
  low birthweights in, 122f, 123
Individual education plan (IEP), 331, 335
Indonesia, 138f, 213, 356t
Induced labor, 109
Induction, 299p, 306
Inductive reasoning, 433–434, 436f, 455
Industry *vs.* inferiority, 40t, 369–372, 376, 398
Infancy (first two years). *See also* Infant mortality; Newborns
  affordances, 170–171, 170p

attachment, 198–205, 199t, 201t, 202t, 217
biosocial development, 133
body growth, 136, 137p
bonding, 128–129
brain and emotions, 193, 194p, 195f, 217
brain growth, 160
Brazelton Neonatal Behavioral Assessment Scale, 125, 131, 149
breast-feeding, 157–159, 158p
cognitive development, 163, 219
cognitive learning stages, 46, 46t
co-sleeping, 138f
development of social bonds, 202t, 204p, 206p, 207f, 217, 219
emotional development, 189–196, 190p, 190t, 191p, 192p, 217, 219
Erikson's stages of development, 40t
face recognition, 145
failure to thrive, 136
father as social partner, 206–207, 206p, 207f, 218
Freud's stages of development, 39p, 40t
immunization, 156–157, 161
information processing theory, 169–173, 169p, 170f, 170p, 173p
kangaroo care, 129, 129p, 147–148
language development, 174–185, 174p, 175t, 177p, 184p, 219
low birthweight, 119, 121–123
malnutrition during, 159–160, 159f, 160p, 161
memory of, 171–173, 172f
motor skill development, 150–152, 150p, 150t
need for caregiving, 376
need for stimulation, 144–146
physical growth, 135–147, 136f
senses of, 147–150, 149p
sensorimotor intelligence, 47p, 164–168, 164t, 168p, 186
shaken baby syndrome, 146
sleep patterns, 137, 160
social referencing, 205–206, 206p
sudden infant death syndrome, 160
survival of, 153–160
synchrony with caregivers, 196–201, 196p, 197p, 217
temperament, 192, 192p, 194–195
theories of psychosocial development, 208–217, 219
vision during, 84
Infant amnesia, 171–172, 172f
Infant day care, 212–213, 212p, 214t, 215p, 218
Infanticide, 58, 74, 74p
Infant mortality
  from 1950-2010, 153, 154f
  by country, 154f
  due to SIDS, 160
  malnutrition associated with, 159–160
  reduction of, 129
  in United States, 110
Infection, 124. *See also* Sexually transmitted infections (STIs)
Inferiority, 369–371
Infertility
  causes of, 426
  chromosomal abnormalities associated with, 87–88
Informal code (language), 349
Information processing, 272

Information-processing theory
  affordances, 170–171
  concepts of, 47–48, 64, 342–344
  control processes during middle childhood, 346–347
  defined, 47
  in first two years, 169–173, 169p, 170p, 172f, 173p, 186, 219
  knowledge in middle childhood, 346
  memory advances from infancy to age 11, 345t
  memory in first two years, 171–173, 172f, 186
  memory in middle childhood, 345–346
  metacognition and metamemory, 346
  in middle childhood, 342–347, 342p, 345t, 346p, 347p, 365
Inhalant, 477
Inherited intellectual disability, 89
Initiative *vs.* guilt, 40, 40t, 282–284
Injury
  age-related dangers, 238
  avoidable injury, 238, 238p
  control of, 239, 248
  in early childhood, 237–241, 238p, 241f, 248, 287f, 307
  as indicator of maltreatment, 245t
  prevention of, 238p, 240–241, 240p, 241f, 248
  sports injuries, 415
Innate vulnerability, 116
Insecure attachment
  as indicator of maltreatment, 202t, 246
  of Romanian adoptees, 204p
  social setting and, 201t, 202, 202t, 203f, 204–205, 204p
  teen mothers associated with, 424
  types of, 217
Insecure-avoidant attachment, 202, 202t, 203f, 217
Insecure-resistant/ambivalent attachment, 201t, 202, 203f, 217
Inside the Brain
  Connected Hemispheres, 228
  Coordination and Capacity, 344
  Expressing Emotions, 193
  Impulses, Rewards, and Reflection, 439–440
  Lopsided Growth, 409–410
  Measuring Mental Activity, 49t–50t
  Neuronal Birth and Death, 101–102
  Neuroscience Vocabulary, 140–141
  Understanding Speech, 176
Instincts, 57, 58
Institutional Review Board (IRB), 30
Instrumental aggression, 291–292, 292t, 306
Instrumental conditioning, 43–44, 44p
Integrity *vs.* despair, 40t
Intellectual disabilities
  ADHD, 325–327
  behavioral teratogens causing, 112–114
  Down syndrome, 87
  high-stakes tests and, 450
  plumbism causing, 234–235
  recessive genetic disorders associated with, 89
Intelligence
  defined, 320
  multiple, 322, 328
  types of, 322

Intelligence testing. *See also* Achievement tests; International tests; IQ tests
  improvement over time, 320
  theoretical distribution of scores, 321f
Intensive preschool programs, 275–278
Internalization of problems, 385, 389, 474
International schooling, 353–355, 355p, 450–451
International tests. *See also* Programme for International Student Assessment (PISA); Progress in International Reading Literacy Study (PIRLS); Trends in Math and Science Study (TIMMS)
  gender differences, 358
  International Baccalaureate test, 449
  problems with benchmarks, 357–358
  scores, 356, 356t, 357f
Internet. *See also* Social networking
  availability of, 440, 455
  drug safety information, 119
  sexual abuse via, 441–442
  as source for research, 504–505
  as a source of sex education, 469–470
Interpersonal intelligence, 322, 329
Intervention programs, 273–275
Intimacy *vs.* isolation, 496t, 502
  characteristics of, 40t
  of emerging adulthood, 496–497, 497t
Intrapersonal intelligence, 322
Intrinsic motivation, 284–285, 448
Intuitive thinking, 436f
Intuitive thought, of adolescents, 435, 436f, 438, 455
Invincibility fable, 431, 455
In vitro fertilization (IVF), 76, 77, 94, 98
IQ. *See also* General intelligence (g); Intelligence
  benefits of breast-feeding, 158t
  drop-out rates related to, 453
  effect of ingested lead, 234–235
  effect of preterm birth, 122
  effect on thought processes, 437
  improvement over time, 320–321
  link to openness, 617
  testing for, 320–321, 321p
  theoretical distribution of scores, 321f
IQ tests
  criticism of, 329
  types of, 336
Iran, 356t
Iraq, 464
Ireland, 116, 494f
Irreversibility, 252, 253, 254
Islam, 346
Isolation. *See* Intimacy *vs.* isolation
Isolation, victimization of socially isolated children, 390
Israel
  college graduates in, 494f
  infant care in, 213
  infant day care in, 213
  international test scores, 356t
Italy
  college graduates in, 494f
  international test scores, 356t
  low birthweights in, 122f

Jacob's syndrome, 88t
Jamaica, 122f, 499
Japan
  childhood obesity in, 316, 316p
  college graduates in, 494f
  co-sleeping in, 138, 138f
  education in, 357
  high-stakes tests in, 450
  infant mortality in, 153, 154f
  language preferences of infants, 179
  low birthweights in, 122f, 124
  neonatal care in, 103
  paternity leave in, 213
  regulation of pride in, 371
  scores on international tests, 356t,
    357
Jealousy, 191, 193

Kahneman's Systems 1 and 2, 436f
Kangaroo care, 129, 129p, 130,
    147–148
Kenya, 122f, 213, 287f
Kicking, 151
Kindergarten, in Germany, 60
King, Martin Luther, Jr., 37
Kinship care, 247, 249
KiVa, 391
Klinefelter syndrome, 88t
Knowledge base, 346, 365
Kohlberg, Lawrence
  criticism of, 394–395
  levels and stages of moral thought,
    393–394, 394t, 398
Korea
  body image of adolescents in, 417
  college graduates in, 494f
  education in, 362
  incidence of twins, 79
  low birthweights in, 124
  scores on international tests, 356t
Kuwait, 356t
Kwashiorkor, 159, 161

Labor and delivery
  in birthing centers, 105, 111
  complications during, 124
  C-sections, 107, 109, 109p
  doula's support, 107, 107p
  epidural anesthesia, 109
  at home, 107p, 111
  induced labor, 109, 112
  low birthweight, 121–123, 122f,
    124f, 131
  preterm delivery, 103, 105–107,
    119, 131
  vaginal, 105–111, 105f,
    106p, 110p
Lactose intolerance, 59, 59p
Language. See also Bilingual children;
    Bilingual learning; Bilingual
    schooling
  loss and gain, 267–268
  math learning and, 258–259
  in middle childhood, 348–352, 348p,
    349f, 386
  as symbolic thought, 252
  as a tool in early childhood,
    263–268
  vocabulary, 348–349, 348p
Language acquisition device (LAD),
    184–185
Language development
  age of infants knowing 50 words,
    180f
  babbling, 176–177, 186

bilingual learning, 347, 349f (See also
    Bilingual children; Bilingual
    learning; Bilingual schooling)
child-directed speech, 178
communication milestones, 180t
cultural differences, 178–179, 185p
differences in middle childhood,
    350–351
in early childhood, 263–268, 264t,
    307
in first two years, 174–186, 174p,
    175t, 177p, 184p, 219
first words, 177–178, 180t, 186
grammar, 179
low birthweight affecting, 122
mean length of utterance (MLU),
    179
in middle childhood, 348–352, 348p,
    365
naming explosion, 178, 186
percent of infants knowing 50 words,
    184p
sensitive period for learning, 9–10,
    263, 264t
social-pragmatic theory, 183
socioeconomic context and, 350–
    351, 365
theories of, 179, 181, 183–185, 186
understanding speech, 176
universal sequence, 174–178, 175t
use of first-person pronouns, 192
videos and, 182–183
vocabulary explosion, 263–264
Language enhancement, 268
Language explosion, 252
Language shift, 267
Late adulthood
  driving ability, 439f
  need for respect, 376
Latency, 39, 40t, 302, 370
Lateralization, 228, 230, 236
Latin America
  child nutrition in, 158–159
  co-sleeping in, 138
  disparities between rich and poor, 13
  education for special needs children
    in, 332
  infant day care in, 213
  wasting and stunting in, 158t, 159f
Latino Americans, 494. See also
    Hispanic Americans;
    Mexican Americans
Laughter
  development in infancy, 190, 190t,
    193, 217
  in early childhood, 227
  as survival technique, 210
Law breaking, in adolescence, 475–
    476, 483–484
Laws
  Education of All Handicapped
    Children Act (1975), 331
  preventing injury, 240–241
  against teratogen use during
    pregnancy, 119
Learning. See also College; Early-
    childhood schooling;
    Education; High school;
    Middle school; Preschool
    programs; Teaching
  in adolescence, 445–456, 447p,
    449p
  apprenticeship in thinking, 52
  automatization in, 344
  behaviorist view of, 42–43

dependence on fine motor skills, 236
international schooling, 353–355
international tests, 356–358, 356t
in middle childhood, 339–347, 345p,
    347p, 353–364, 353t, 354t,
    356t, 365
national variations in curriculum,
    353–355
as need in middle childhood, 376
pruning in brain enabling, 139, 142
required factors, 37
types of, 44t
use of technology, 441
in zone of proximal development,
    52–53, 53f
Learning theory. See Behaviorism
Least restrictive environment (LRE),
    331, 336
Lebanon, 213
Left-handedness, 228
Leg tucking reflex, 125
Leptin, 411
Lewin, Kurt, 36
LGBTQ, college students, 494
Life-course-persistent offenders, 475,
    484
Life-span perspective, 8–21
Limbic system
  effects of drugs on, 481
  emotional regulation, 283–284
  functions of, 140, 141f
  maturation in adolescence, 408,
    409–410, 434, 439, 455, 484
  myelination of, 283–284
  in Romanian adoptees, 239
Linguistic codes, 348–349
Linguistic intelligence, 322
Linked lives, 497, 502
Listening, 174–176, 268
Little scientists, 168, 168p, 182, 186,
    206
Logic
  of adolescents, 430–440, 431p,
    432p, 433f, 435p, 454
  conservation in early childhood and,
    253f
  development of in middle childhood,
    339–341
  obstacles to in early childhood,
    252–253
  words and limits of, 264
Logical extension, 265
Logical-mathematical intelligence,
    322
Loneliness, 316
Longitudinal research
  cross-sectional research vs, 25–27
  defined, 26
  process of, 26, 28f
Long-term memory, 346, 348, 365
Low birthweight (LBW)
  causes, 114, 121–123, 424
  consequences, 122–124
  defined, 119
  family structure compared, 124f
  national statistics compared, 122f,
    123–124
  in United States, 122–124
Lungs, prenatal development, 104
Luxembourg, 739
Lying, 261, 262f
Lymphoid system, 415

Macrosystems, 12, 12f, 14, 240. See
    also Culture; Social bonds
Madagascar, 213

Magic Middle, 53f
Magnetic resonance imaging (MRI),
    49t
Mainstreaming, 331, 335
Malaria, 89
Malaysia, 138f, 272p
Male–female differences, 8
Males. See also Boys; Fathers
  chromosomes of, 71–72, 73p
  effect of child maltreatment, 246
  innate vulnerability of, 116
Malnutrition
  catch-up growth overcoming, 146
  delay of puberty, 410
  effect on birthweight, 121
  effect on brain growth, 139
  effect on infant survival, 159–160,
    160p, 161
  teen pregnancy associated with, 424
Mandated reporters, 243, 244
Marasmus, 159, 161
Marijuana
  attitude toward, 10–11, 11f, 480p
  harm to adolescent users, 479–480
  use in United States, 477f, 479–480
Marriage, 499. See also Divorce;
    Family; Family structure
Maslow, Abraham, 61
Massification, 493, 502
Mastering language utterances
    (MLU), 180f
Mastery motivation, 448
Masturbation, 421–422
Maternal education, 153, 381
Maternal mortality, 110, 110f
Maternity leave, 212, 213
Math
  acquisition of concepts, 343
  concrete operational thought
    necessary for, 341
  dyscalculia, 336
  international test scores, 356t, 357f
  norms for learning, 353t
  understanding in early childhood,
    258–259
  in United States, 356t, 357f
Maturation, 170, 171
Maturation, of prefrontal cortex, 227
Mean length of utterance (MLU), 179
Means to an end stage, 164t, 166
Measles, 156, 157
Media, 469–470
Medical checkups, 135
Medical practices, for newborns/
    mothers, 107, 107p, 109–111
Memory
  advances from infancy to age 11,
    345t
  areas of brain controlling, 140
  conditions of, 172
  cultural differences, 345–346
  in first two years, 171–173, 172f,
    173p, 186
  infant amnesia, 172f
  long-term memory, 346 348, 365
  in middle childhood, 345–346, 365
  motivation and, 172
  reminders and repetition affecting,
    172–173
  sensory memory, 345, 365
  working memory, 345–346, 365
Men. See Fathers; Males
Menarche, 403, 404, 405f, 410–411,
    412, 427
Menstruation, 415. See also Menarche
Mental activity measurement, 48p,
    49, 50t

Mental combination stage, 164t, 168
Mental illness, 70, 91. *See also* Psychopathology
Mentors
  facilitation of reading, 268
  role in learning process, 52–53, 255, 256p, 341
  scaffolding of learning, 255–256, 257p
  scaffolding of morality, 396
Mercury, 117
Mesosystem, 12, 12f
Meta-analysis, 21t, 506
Metacognition, 346
Metamemory, 346
Metaphors, 348
Methylation, 69
Mexican Americans, 256, 296, 472
Mexico
  childhood obesity in, 315
  disparities between rich and poor, 13f
  infant mortality in, 154f
  language shifts in, 267
  paternity leave in, 213
Microbiome, 70, 319
Microcephaly, 49
Microsystems, 12, 12f, 240. *See also* Education; Family; Peer relationships; Religion
Midbrain, 101, 102f, 140
Middle childhood
  bilinguals in the United States, 348–352, 348p, 349f
  brain development, 313–314, 316p, 343, 344
  challenges of, 309, 311, 320
  child culture, 386–392
  concrete operational stage, 339–341, 340p, 341p
  coordination and capacity, 344
  developmental theories applied to, 341p, 345t, 365, 398
  education during, 353–364, 353t, 354t, 355p, 356t, 357f, 363f
  family life, 375–386, 376p, 382p, 384f, 385p, 398
  friendships, 386–387
  growth during, 309
  health during, 312–319, 312p, 313p, 314p, 316p, 318f, 319f, 336
  health habits, 312–313
  inductive reasoning in, 433–434
  information processing in, 342–346, 345t, 346p, 347p
  moral development, 392–397, 392p, 394t, 395p, 397f, 398
  nature of the child, 368–375, 368t, 370p, 397
  needs of, 376–377, 398
  peer group, 386–392, 386p, 389p, 398
  special needs children, 323–325
Middle East, 158t, 159f
Middle school, 447–449, 447p, 455
Midwives, 107, 111
Military families, 377–378, 377p
Military service
  as form of moratorium, 458
  identity provided by, 458p
Mind, measuring, 320–323
Mirror/rouge test, 192, 192p, 217
Miscarriage, 86, 99t, 424
Misdiagnosis of ADHD, 325
Mitochondrial DNA, 75
Modeling, 45, 45p
Modesty, 191
Monozygotic (MZ) twins
  family experiences and, 376

process producing, 77, 78f, 79, 94
  psychological disorders in, 91
Montessori, Maria, 60
Montessori schools, 271, 278
Mood disorders, 406
Moral competence, 393
Moral development
  in early childhood, 302
  Kohlberg's levels of moral thought, 393–394, 394t
  in middle childhood, 392–397, 394t, 395p, 397f, 398
Moral reasoning, 393–395, 394t
Moral values
  conflict between children and adults over, 395–396
  development of, 37, 392–397, 397f
  in middle childhood, 391–397, 391p, 394t, 397f, 398
Moratorium, 458, 461, 483, 495
Moro reflex, 126
Morphine, 41
Morula, 75
Mosaicism, 87
Motherese, 175
Mother–infant interaction, 125
Mothers
  behavior causing low birthweight in infants, 119, 121
  breast-feeding, 157–159, 158p, 158t
  chromosomal abnormalities associated with age, 86
  difficulties following birth, 126
  effect of depression on infants, 7–8, 190, 198, 200, 202t, 207, 217
  expectations, 126p
  interaction with infants, 125
  new, 126–127
  postpartum depression, 127
  response to infants, 125–126
  responsiveness and infant language learning, 181, 181f
Motivation
  areas of brain controlling, 140
  extrinsic motivation, 284–285
  increase in knowledge base, 346
  intrinsic motivation, 284–285
  perception of affordances and, 170–171
  of preschoolers, 284–285
Motor skills
  artistic expressions, 236–237, 236p
  defined, 150
  development in early childhood, 231–237, 231p, 232f, 236p, 248, 307
  development in first two years, 150–152, 161, 219
  fine motor skills, 152t, 161, 219, 235–236, 236p
  gross motor skills, 150–151, 150p, 160–161, 219, 231–237, 231p, 232f, 236p
Motor-vehicle crashes
  of adolescents, 238, 408, 439–440, 439f, 481
  causing death of young children, 238
Movement, 147, 150–152
MRI (magnetic resonance imaging), 49t
Multicontexual nature of development, 9–12, 21t
Multicultural nature of development, 14–17, 21t
Multidirectional nature of development, 8–10, 201t

Multidisciplinary nature of development, 17, 19, 21t
Multifactorial traits, 80, 94
Multifinality, 323, 324
Multiple births. *See also* Twins
  causes of, 77, 78f, 79, 94
  low birthweights, 121
Multiple intelligences, 322, 328, 329
Multiple sclerosis, 72
Mumps, 156
Muscle strength, 151
Musical intelligence, 322
Muslims, 346
Mutations, 70
Myelin, 139, 140, 143f, 227
Myelination, 102
  changes throughout life, 323
  in early childhood, 227, 227f, 228, 283
  of limbic system, 283–284
  motor skills permitted by, 227
  in newborns, 102
  reaction time related to, 314
  speed of thought associated with, 344
Myopia, 84

Naming explosion, 175t, 178, 186
Narcissism, 371
National Assessment of Educational Progress (NAEP), 359, 363f, 365
National policies
  development affected by, 14
  paternity leave affected by, 213
  sex selection in pregnancy influenced by, 76
Native Americans, 342, 451f
Naturalistic intelligence, 322
Nature, 6. *See also* Nature–nurture interaction
Nature–nurture controversy, 6–8
Nature–nurture interaction
  in alcohol use disorder, 83–84
  in brain development, 143f
  in development, 6–8, 95
  in education, 67
  in gender identity, 300
  in health during middle childhood, 311, 312
  in middle childhood, 311, 312
  in moral development, 306
  in nearsightedness, 84–85
  predictions based on, 20–21
  in psychological disorders, 91
  relationship between genotype and phenotype, 83–85
  in temperament, 194–195
Nature of the child
  cognitive coping, 374–376
  Erikson's industry and inferiority stage, 369–372, 397
  Freud's latency stage, 370–372
  in middle childhood, 368–375, 368t, 370p, 397
  resilience and stress, 372–375, 372p, 373t
  response to cumulative stress, 372–374, 372p
  self-concept, 369–372
Nearsightedness, 84–85, 94
Negative correlation, 29
Negative identity, 458
Negatively engaged infants, 198
Negative mood, 194
Neglect. *See also* Child maltreatment
  of children, 243–244, 248
  effect on attachment, 202t, 204p
  effect on brain growth, 144–146

Neglected victims, 389, 398
Neglectful/uninvolved parenting, 294, 294t, 306, 465
Neighborhood games, 314, 314p, 336
Neocortex, 140
Netherlands
  ads for sweets in, 318f
  home births in, 111
  international test scores, 356t, 358
  maternal mortality in, 110f
Neural progenitor cells, 101
Neural tube, 99, 101, 102f
Neural-tube defects, 115f, 116
Neurodiversity, 323, 328, 329
Neurogenesis, 19p, 101
Neurological problems, 122
Neurons
  change with experience, 173
  communication, 143
  defined, 140
  developing connections, 227
  emotional development related to growth of, 193
  firing of, 140
  function of, 143
  kinds of impulses, 227, 229
  photograph of, 139f
  prenatal development, 101–102
  pruning of, 139, 142
Neurotransmitters, 140, 143
New adaptation and anticipation stage, 164t, 166
Newborns. *See also* Infancy (first two years)
  Apgar score, 106–107, 106t
  attachment, 199t
  attraction of adult devotion, 210
  birth of, 105–111, 105f, 106p
  birthweight, 104, 119, 121–123, 122f, 124f
  bonding, 128–129
  brain growth, 160–161
  Brazelton Neonatal Behavioral Assessment Scale, 125, 149
  breast-feeding, 157–159, 158p
  co-sleeping, 138f, 139p
  effect of C-section, 109
  effect of epidural anesthesia, 109
  effect of induced labor, 109
  effect on family, 125–126
  emotional development, 189–196
  face recognition, 145
  failure to thrive, 136
  first minutes after birth, 106–107
  growth, 135–147
  immunization and, 156
  infant mortality, 111, 122
  interaction with mother, 125
  kangaroo care, 129, 129p, 130, 147–148
  mortality rate, 122
  motor skill development, 150–152, 150p, 150t
  preterm delivery, 103, 119
  reflexes of, 108f, 125–126
  senses of, 84, 126, 147–150
  shaken baby syndrome, 146
  sleep patterns, 160
  sudden infant death syndrome, 160
  survival of, 110–111, 153–160, 154f, 156p
Newer theories, 36, 51–62, 64. *See also* Evolutionary theory; Sociocultural theory
New Guinea, 127
New means through active experimentation stage, 164t, 168

*New York Longitudinal Study* (NYLS), 194
New Zealand, 110f, 138, 138f, 213, 356t
Niger, 160p
Nigeria, 79, 122f, 154f, 156, 384f
Nightmares, 141
Nonshared environment, 375–376
Norms
  of attachment, 199t
  for body size, 136, 136f
  for development of fine motor skills, 152t
  for emotional development, 190t
  for fine motor skills, 152t
  for language learning, 180t, 264t
  for learning reading, 354t
  for math learning, 353t
  of psychosocial maturation in middle childhood, 370t
  theories and facts *vs.*, 64
North America. *See also* Canada; Mexico; United States
  childhood obesity in, 315
  play in early childhood, 288
  screen time of children in, 290
  self-concept of children in, 282
  wasting and stunting in, 158f, 159f
Norway
  early-childhood education in, 268–269
  infant day care in, 215
  low birthweight in, 122f
  maternal mortality in, 110f
Nr3c1 gene, 143
Nuclear family, 378, 379t, 380–383, 380p, 381p, 383f, 385, 398
Nurture, 6. *See also* Nature–nurture interaction
Nutrition
  of adults, 488
  birthweight affected by, 112
  breast-feeding, 37, 109, 157–159, 158p, 158t
  deficiencies in early childhood, 225–226
  diet deficiencies in adolescents, 415–416, 415p, 419, 427, 485
  in early childhood, 224–226, 224p, 248
  effect of chemicals in food, 410–411
  effect on infant sleep patterns, 137
  food insecurity, 123
  genetic expression affected by, 83
  height affected by, 84
  infant mortality associated with, 158–159
  oral health related to, 226
  prenatal development affected by, 125
  in United States, 123
  vision impacted by, 84

Obesity
  in adolescence, 416, 416p, 419, 427
  in adulthood, 311
  breast-feeding and, 158, 158t
  causes of weight gain, 136
  in childhood, 5–6, 6f, 224–226, 248, 315–316, 317, 318, 318f, 336
  of children born by C-section, 109
  as eating disorder, 418
  onset of puberty affected by, 410, 411
  in pregnant women, 123

role of leptin, 411
  of sexually abused girls, 425
Object permanence, 46t, 167, 167p, 186
Observation, 22
Observational learning, 45
Occipital lobe, 140, 141f
Oedipus complex, 301
Onlooker play, 286
On-the-job training, 452
Operant conditioning, 43–44, 44p, 44t, 181
Operational definition, 506
Opioid overdose death, 41–42, 42f
Opioids, 118
Opposing Perspectives
  E-Cigarettes: Past Addiction or Healthy Choice?, 479–480
  Is Spanking OK?, 298–299
  Protect or Puncture Self-Esteem?, 371
  Testing, 450–451
  Toilet Training-How and When?, 56–57
  Too Many Boys?, 73–74
  Using the Word *Race*, 16–17
  "What Do People Live to Do?," 120
Oral fixation, 208
Oral health, 226
Oral stage, 39, 39p, 40t, 56, 208
Organ growth, 415, 479
Orphanages, 202, 204, 204p
Osteoporosis, in adolescents, 416
Ovaries, 404, 420
Overimitation, 256–257
Overregularization, 266
Ovum
  abnormal genetic formation, 86–87, 87p, 88t
  effect of age, 86
  fertilization, 70, 70p
  sex chromosomes of, 72
Own-race effect, 145
Oxytocin, 104

Pain, 140, 149–150, 149p, 190
Pakistan, 123
Palestine, 464
Palmar grasping reflex, 126
Parallel play, 286
Parasuicide, 472, 473, 473f
Parent–adolescent relationships, 470, 472
Parental alliance, 128, 207, 381–382, 398
Parental imprinting, 72
Parental leave, 212, 213
Parental monitoring, 465, 483
Parent–child relationships, 299
Parent education, 268
Parentification, 375
Parent–infant bond, 128–129
Parenting, styles of, 294–295, 294t
Parents. *See also* Caregiving; Fathers; Mothers
  adolescents' peer relationships and, 465
  attachment, 198–205, 199t, 201t, 202t
  effect on child's personality, 375–376
  emerging adults and, 497–498
  facilitation of reading, 268
  influence on child's personality, 375–376
  influence on identity formation, 303–304, 458–459
  instinct to protect young, 57–58

maltreatment of children, 242–248, 242f, 245t
  as mentors, 255, 256p
  moral development and empathy associated with, 395
  proximal and distal parenting, 209, 209p
  reinforcement of gender roles, 302–303
  relationship with adolescent children, 461–465, 462p, 463f, 465p, 483, 484
  resilience of child associated with, 372–374
  role in learning process, 352
  as role models, 208–209
  sex education from, 470
  synchrony with infants, 196p, 196–198, 197p, 200p, 204
  as teachers of emotional regulation, 282, 284p
  view of newborns, 210
Parietal lobe, 140
Participants in studies, 505, 506
Paternal leave, 213
Patterns of growth, 9f
Pavlov, Ivan, 35–36, 41, 42p, 51, 60
Pedestrian deaths, 238, 240–241, 241f
Peer relationships
  in adolescence, 409–410, 439–440, 439f, 465–471, 465p, 467p, 468f, 469f, 469p, 483, 484
  bullies and victims, 388–389, 389p, 398
  child culture, 386–392, 386p
  effect on morality, 395
  effect on self-esteem in adolescence, 472
  facilitation of bad/good behavior, 466–468, 483
  friendships, 386–387, 386p, 483
  influence on sexual behavior, 470
  in middle childhood, 377, 386–392, 386p, 389p, 398
  moral development and empathy associated with, 394–395, 398
  onset of puberty and, 413, 413p
  parents and, 465
  peer pressure, 465–466, 467p
  personality affected by, 375
  popular and unpopular children, 387–388, 398
  romance, 468–469, 468f, 469f
  selection of friends, 466–468
  sex education from, 470
  social networking, 467p
  social skills necessary for, 448
Peers, 286
Penis, 420
Percentile, 136
Perception
  defined, 170
  development of, 161
  in first two years, 147–153, 219
  leading to cognition, 165
  sensations leading to, 148, 345
Permanency planning, 247, 247p, 259
Permissive parenting, 294, 294t, 306
Perseveration, 227, 229–230
Personal fable, 431, 455
Pester power, 317
Pesticides, 117, 233
PET (positron emission tomography), 50t
Phallic stage, 39, 40t, 301–302, 306
Phase delay, 407f
Phenotype
  additive heredity, 80p, 81, 94

copy number variations, 86–93, 87p, 88t
dominant-recessive heredity, 81–82, 82f, 89, 94
environmental influence on, 81p, 94
functions of, 80
parental imprinting, 88t
X-linked characteristics, 82, 83t
Philippines, 122f, 129p, 138f, 213
Phobias, 57, 283
Phrenology, 49
Phthalates, 27
Physical activity. *See also* Exercise; Play; Sports
  in adolescence, 414
  in middle childhood, 316p, 336
  running speed during adolescence, 415f
  WHO recommendations for children, 318f
Physical appearance
  adolescents' concern about, 417, 419, 430–432, 448
  focus on, 252–253
  genetic determination of, 77p, 79
  of newborns, 128
  race based on, 16
Physical bullying, 388, 388p, 398
Physical context of development, 11–12
Physical education, 314–315, 336
Physical necessities, 376
Physical punishment, 296–299, 298p, 306
Piaget, Jean, 60p
  application to middle childhood, 364
  background of, 45–46, 51
  on children's moral thinking, 393
  cognitive development theory, 35–36, 176, 343
  concrete operational thought, 339–341, 340p, 341p, 436f
  formal operational thought, 432–434, 433f, 433p, 435p, 438, 455, 485
  influence on child-centered programs, 271
  on moral issue of retribution or restitution, 396–397, 397f
  new research and, 47, 167, 168
  photograph of, 46p
  preoperational thought, 251–254, 255, 260, 269, 278
  sensorimotor intelligence, 164–168, 164t, 186
  stages of development, 45–47, 46t
  stages of sensorimotor intelligence, 164–168, 164t, 165p, 166p, 167p, 168p
Pincer movement, 152
PISA. *See* Programme for International Student Assessment (PISA)
Pituitary gland, 141, 141f, 404, 405f
Placenta, 98, 105f, 114
Plagiarism, avoiding, 505
Planning
  of adolescents, 437
  brain maturation required for, 409–410
Plasticity
  case study of David, 20–21, 20p
  defined, 19, 143
  of developmental process, 19–21, 21t, 217
  of fetal brain, 101
  of human brain, 146
  of infant brain, 141

Play
    aggression, 291–292, 292t
    in early childhood, 286–293, 306
    effect on vision, 85
    emotional regulation through, 290–
        292, 291p, 292t
    as indicator of maltreatment, 245t
    in middle childhood, 313–315, 314p,
        315p
    neighborhood, 314
    playmates, 286, 287, 289
    rough-and-tumble play, 288
    safety during, 287f
    social and pretend, 286, 288p, 289p
    sociodramatic, 289–290, 289p
    stages of, 286
Play face, 288
Playmates, 286, 288
Plumbism, 234–235, 234f, 235p
Pneumonia, 159
Pointing, 177, 177p
Poisoning, 239, 240
Poland
    college graduates in, 494f
    infant mortality in, 153, 154f
    international test scores, 356t, 453
Polio, 156, 157, 157f
Political identity, 459, 460p, 483, 484
Pollution
    asthma associated with, 233
    birthweight affected by, 121
    brain development affected by, 233
    gross motor development affected by,
        233–234
Polygamous family, 378, 379t, 382
Polygenic traits, 80, 81, 83–84, 94
Polymorphic genes, 69
Popularity, 387–388, 398, 465
Population, 505
Positive adaptation, 372
Positive correlation, 29
Positron emission tomography (PET),
    50t
Postconventional moral reasoning,
    393–394, 394t
Postformal cognition, 489, 502
Postformal reasoning, 489–490
Postformal thought, of emerging
    adulthood, 489–490
Postpartum depression, 126–127, 198
Postpartum psychosis, 126
Post-traumatic stress disorder (PTSD),
    244
Poverty. See also Socioeconomic status
    (SES)
    asthma rates associated with, 233
    defined, 14
    effect on academic achievement, 14
Practical guidance, 37
Practical intelligence, 322
Practice, 152
Prader-Willi syndrome, 72
Pragmatics, 266–267, 348–349, 365
Precocious puberty, 410
Preconventional moral reasoning,
    393–394, 394t
Prefrontal cortex
    ability to develop theories, 262
    connection to amygdala, 193
    damage from alcohol, 479
    defined, 140
    development of control processes,
        347
    development of in first two years,
        146
    effects of drugs on, 481
    emotional regulation, 283–284, 292,
        306
    executive function and, 262

functions of, 140
    growth in early childhood, 227
    injuries caused by immaturity of, 229
    location of, 141f
    maturation in adolescence, 408,
        409–410, 434, 438, 439, 484
    maturation in early childhood, 227,
        229, 285
    maturation of, 50
    play's role in development, 289
    role in development of theory of the
        mind, 262
Pregnancy. See also Abortion; Prenatal
        development
    advice from experts, 118–119
    associated with sexual abuse, 424
    beginning of, 98t
    choosing sex of zygote, 73–74
    due date, 98t
    effect of stress on incidence of in
        young girls, 412
    effect of teratogens, 112–113, 115f
    embryonic period, 98–100, 98t,
        100p, 115f
    father's role in, 127–128
    fetal period, 100–104, 100p, 102f,
        104p, 115f
    first trimester (See Embryonic
        period; Germinal period)
    germinal period, 98, 98t, 99, 99f, 99t
    health during, 118
    labor and delivery, 97p, 105–111,
        105f, 107p, 109p, 112
    last trimester, 104, 147
    length of, 98t
    miscarriage, 86, 87, 424
    prenatal diagnosis of problems, 119
    preparation for, 116t
    preterm delivery, 103
    problems and solutions, 112–125,
        115f
    second trimester, 103, 104p
    stillbirth, 92, 99t
    in teen years, 158t, 423–424, 424p,
        427, 465, 470
    third month, 100, 100p
    timing between, 114, 115
    trimesters of, 98t
    in vitro fertilization, 76, 94, 98
    vulnerability during prenatal
        development, 99t
    weight gain during, 118, 118f
Prejudice, racial, 437
Prenatal care, 118
Prenatal development
    effect of teratogens, 112–116,
        115f, 124
    embryonic period, 98, 98t, 99,
        99t, 115f
    of eyes, 148
    fetal period, 98, 98t, 100–104, 100p,
        102f, 104p, 115f, 131
    germinal period, 98, 98t, 99f, 131
    of hearing, 147–148
    low birthweight, 119, 121–123, 122f,
        123f
    risk analysis, 113–114
    in second trimester, 101–102, 104p
    stages of, 115f
    vulnerability during, 99t
Prenatal diagnosis of problems, 119
Preoperational thought
    aid to language learning, 263
    characteristics of, 44t, 46–47, 47p
    conservation and logic, 253–254,
        253f
    defined, 251–254, 256, 267, 278
    obstacles to logic, 252–253
    view of gender roles, 304

Preoperative intelligence, 251–252
Preschool programs. See Early-
        childhood schooling
Prescription drugs, 477f
Pretending, 192, 288, 289p
Pretend play, 288
Preterm delivery
    age of viability, 103
    birthweight, 122
    complications, 104
    defined, 121
    effect on emotional development,
        190
    of infant conceived by IVF, 79
    survival of infant, 110–111
    teen pregnancy associated
        with, 424
Prevention, 240–241
Pride
    of bullies, 389
    cultural norms for development of,
        191, 283
    development in early childhood, 306
    development in middle childhood,
        371–372
    development of in first two years,
        190
Primary circular reactions, 164t,
    165–166, 165f
Primary education, 446, 455
Primary prevention
    of injury, 240, 249
    of maltreatment of children, 246, 249
Primary school, 363, 363f
Primary sex characteristics, 420, 427
Primitive streak, 99
Private schools, 365
Private speech, 257
Problems
    externalization of, 385, 389, 474
    in families, 385, 385p
    internalization of, 385, 389, 474
Professional journals, 503–504
Progeria, 664
Programme for International
        Student Assessment (PISA),
        357f, 451, 452–453, 455
Progress in International Reading
        Literacy Study (PIRLS),
        356, 356t, 357, 365, 451
Prosocial behavior
    in adolescence, 476
    development in early childhood,
        290–291, 291p
    development in middle childhood, 395
    development of in early childhood,
        286, 306, 395
Prosopagnosia, 145
Prospective studies, 506
Protective optimism, 282
Protein-calorie malnutrition, 159, 161
Protein synthesis, 68, 68f
Provocative victims, 389
Proximal parenting, 209, 209p
Proximity-seeking, 199, 205
Proximodistal pattern, 100, 150
Pruning, 139, 161, 193, 226
Psychoactive drugs
    for ADHD, 325
    effect on birthweight, 121
    safety during pregnancy, 115
    use for psychopathologies, 325
Psychoanalytic theory. See also
        Psychosexual theory;
        Psychosocial theory
    application to early childhood,
        282–284, 301–302
    application to infant social
        development, 208

application to middle childhood,
        369–372
    concepts of, 39–41, 40t
    defined, 39
    emergence of, 35–36, 39–41
    Erikson's stages of development,
        39–41, 40t, 208, 282–284
    focus and emphasis of, 63t
    Freud's stages of development, 40t
    on toilet training, 56–57
Psychological control, 299, 306
Psychological disorders, 91
Psychopathology. See also Depression;
        Mental illness
    of bullies and victims, 390
    causes and consequences, 376,
        404–405
    comorbidity of, 320
    diagnosis and treatment of, 320,
        323–325
    increase in puberty, 455
Psychosexual theory
    Freud's stages of development, 39,
        40t
    latency in middle childhood,
        370–371
    oral and anal stages in infant social
        development, 208
    phallic stage and preschoolers'
        sexism, 306
    stages of development, 40t
Psychosocial development
    adolescent-adult relationships,
        461–465, 462p, 463f,
        465p, 485
    area of focus, 63t
    brain and emotions in first two years,
        193, 195f, 219, 1894p
    challenges for caregivers of 2- to
        6-year-olds, 293–305, 293p
    contribution of, 62
    criticism of, 62
    defined, 17f, 32
    development of social bonds in first
        two years, 187p, 196–207,
        199t, 200p, 201p, 201t,
        204p, 206p, 207f, 219
    drug use and abuse in adolescence,
        477–483, 477f, 480p, 481p,
        482f, 485
    in early childhood, 281–305
    emotional development in early
        childhood, 281–285, 283p,
        284p, 306
    emotional development in first two
        years, 189–196, 190p, 190t,
        191p, 192p, 219
    families and children, 375–386,
        376p, 384f, 385p
    identity achievement, 496
    identity formation in adolescence,
        458–461, 458p, 459p, 460p,
        484
    intimacy during emerging adulthood,
        496–497
    intimacy needs, 496–500
    moral values of middle childhood,
        307, 391–397, 394t, 395p,
        397f
    nature of the child in middle
        childhood, 368–375, 368t,
        370p
    peer group in middle childhood,
        386–392, 389p
    peer relationships in adolescence,
        465–471, 465p, 467p, 468f,
        469f, 469p, 485
    play in early childhood, 286–293,
        287f

sadness and anger in adolescence, 471–476, 472p, 473f, 474p
temperament, 192, 192p, 194–195
theories of infant psychosocial development, 208–217, 218
vocational identity, 496
Psychosocial problems, 424
Psychosocial theory
application to early childhood, 282–284, 306
application to infant social development, 208
application to middle childhood, 369–372
arenas of identity, 458–461
autonomy *vs.* shame and doubt, 208, 218
identity *vs.* role confusion, 457, 485
industry *vs.* inferiority, 369–372, 397
initiative *vs.* guilt, 282–284, 306
stages of psychosocial development, 40t
trust *vs.* mistrust, 208
view of sexes, 461
Puberty. *See also* Adolescence
age of onset, 403, 408–412, 427, 485
body fat, 410–411, 414, 427
body rhythms, 406–407, 407f
changes in eyes, 84
defined, 403–404
duration of, 403
effect of stress, 406–407, 412, 427
Freud's stages of development, 39
genes controlling age of onset, 410
hormones stimulating, 404–405, 405f, 406p
menarche and spermarche, 403–404, 427
peer relationships, 413, 413p, 427, 465–471, 465p, 467p, 468f, 469p
precocious puberty, 410
rise in depression, 472
sequence of, 403–404
sexual maturation, 420–421, 421f, 422p, 424p
stress of middle school, 447–449, 447p
Puerto Rico, 499
Punishment. *See* Discipline

Qualitative research, 29–30
Quantitative research, 30
Quickening, 103

Race, 16–17, 16f. *See also* Ethnicity; *specific ethnic group*
Racial socialization, 462
Racism, 16–17, 434
Random sample, 505, 506
Rational judgment, 437
Reaction time, 314
Reactive aggression, 291–292, 292t, 306
Reading
connections in the brain required for, 344
dyslexia, 327p, 336
international test scores, 356t, 357f
language acquisition through, 268
norms for learning, 354t
Programme for International Student Assessment, 452–453, 455
Progress in International Reading Literacy Study, 356t, 365

strategies facilitating, 268
in United States, 356t, 363f
working memory supporting, 345
Recess, 314–315
Recessive disorders, 89
Recessive genes
disorders associated with, 88, 89, 92, 93p, 94
X-linked characteristics, 81–82, 82f
Reflexes
of infants, 108f, 125–126, 140, 164t, 165
skills developed from, 150
Reflexive fear, 217
Reflux, 190
Refugees, 14p
Reggio Emilia, 271–272, 271p, 278
Reinforcement, 44
Rejected children, 398
Relational aggression, 292, 292t, 306
Relational bullying, 388, 389, 398
Religion
as aid to overcoming stress, 374–375, 374p
education and, 361
effect on marital status, 384f
moral development and, 394
Religious identity, 458–459, 458p, 483, 484
Reminder session, 173
REM (rapid eye movement) sleep, 137
Repetition, 172–173, 344
Replication, 4–5, 6
Reported maltreatment, 242, 244
Reporting results, 4, 5, 506–507
Representative sample, 505
Reproduction. *See also* Birth; Labor and delivery; Pregnancy; Sexual activity
as biological-based drive, 57–58
evolutionary theory applied to, 59
maturity of system in adolescence, 106–107, 427
in vitro fertilization, 76, 94, 98
Reproductive nurturance, 210
Reprogrammed cells, 75–76
Research
analysis of, 4
blind gatherers, 506
code of ethics, 30
correlation and causation, 29
cross-sectional, 25–27, 28f
cross-sequential, 28f
design of, 506
effect size, 507
experiment, 23–24, 24f, 32
file drawer problems, 507
Internet sources, 504–505
journals and books, 503–504
longitudinal, 26, 28f
meta-analysis, 506
observation, 22–23, 32
operational definition, 506
participants, 506, 507
personalization of, 503
population, 506
reporting results, 506–507
representative sample, 505
sample, 505
scientific method, 4–5, 32
statistical measures, 22t
study issues, 32
survey, 24–25, 32
on teratogen damage, 116–117, 118
Resilience, in middle childhood, 372–375, 372p, 372t, 398
Resource room, 331

Respiration of newborns, 108f
Respiratory development, 104
Respondent conditioning, 41
Response to intervention (RTI), 331
Restitution, 396, 397f
Retribution, 396, 397f
Retrieval of memories, 345
Retrospective studies, 506
Reversibility, 341
Reviews, 506
Rewards, 44, 437
Ribonucleic acid (RNA), 69
Risk analysis for teratogen exposure, 113–115, 124
Risky behavior. *See also* Drug use and abuse; Excitement; Parasuicide; Self-destructive behavior; Sexual activity; Suicidal ideation; Suicide
of adolescents, 430–431, 438
during emerging adulthood, 488–489, 489p
in people with short 5-HTTLPR gene, 463, 463f
Ritalin, 326, 477f
Role confusion, 458, 483
Role models
effect on learning, 37
effect on social learning, 209
influence on adolescents' decisions, 436, 438, 483
Romance
in adolescence, 468–469, 468f, 469f, 483
emerging adults and, 498–500
Romanian orphans, 146p, 202, 204, 204p, 230
Romantic partners. *See* Cohabitation; Marriage
Rooting reflex, 125
Rotavirus, 156
Rough-and-tumble play, 288–289, 304, 306
Rubella, 20–21, 113, 114, 156
Rubeola, 156
Rumination, 472–473
Running, 150t
Russia, 356t

Sadness
in adolescence, 471–476, 472p, 473f, 483–484
development in infancy, 190, 190t, 192, 192p
Safety, 287f
Same-sex parents, 382, 382p
Same-sex romance, 468–469, 468f, 469f, 483
Sample, 505
Saudi Arabia, 213, 416
Scaffolding
of language learning, 263, 265
mentor-assisted learning, 255–256, 257p, 278
in middle childhood, 341
of morality, 396
Schizophrenia
caused by mumps, 156
epigenetic influence on, 80
misinformation concerning, 91
Schools. *See* Education
Science, 4, 28–31, 258–259, 258p, 357f
Science of human development, 4
Scientific method/designing science
application of, 22–28
cautions and challenges, 28–31
defined, 4
process of, 4–6, 32, 117

Scientific observation, 22–23, 32
Scientific questions, 37
Scotland, 335
Screen time
in early childhood, 290, 290f, 290p
for infants, 182, 183
Seasonal rhythms, 406, 427
Seattle Longitudinal Study, 27
Secondary circular reactions, 164t, 165f, 166, 186
Secondary education, 446, 455. *See also* High school; Middle school
Secondary prevention
of injury, 240–241, 249
of maltreatment of children, 246, 249
Secondary sex characteristics, 420–421, 427
Secular trend, 411
Secure attachment, 200, 201, 202, 202t, 203f, 205, 217
Selection bias, avoiding, 506
Selection process, 364
Selective adaptation, 58, 58f, 59p
Selective attention, 313, 344
Self-awareness, 190t, 192, 192p, 193, 217
Self-care, 312, 336
Self-concept
of adolescents, 430–440, 431p, 432p, 433f, 435p, 444–445, 457
effect on behavior, 47
development in early childhood, 282, 288
in middle childhood, 369–372, 397
Self-conscious emotions, 371
Self-consciousness, 430–432
Self-control, 283–284
Self-criticism, 371
Self-definition, 77
Self-destructive behavior, 445, 455. *See also* Parasuicide; Risky behavior; Suicidal ideation; Suicide
Self-esteem
of bullies and victims, 389, 390
childhood overweight related to, 316
cultural influences on, 371
cyberbullying and, 443–444
depression associated with low self-esteem, 472–473
of early-maturing girls, 413
ethnic differences, 472–473
of maltreated children, 245
in middle childhood, 371
relationships affecting, 472–473
Self-expression, 457
Self-harm, 425
Self-recognition, 192p, 217
Self-respect, 376, 398
Self-righting, 146
Senior citizens. *See* Late adulthood
Sensations, 147, 165, 345
Sensation-seeking, 408, 438, 438f
Senses
areas of brain controlling, 140
hearing, 115f, 122, 147–148, 161
interaction with movement in infancy, 147
as necessary for brain development, 146
of newborns, 125, 147–150
perception of affordances and, 170
smell, 148–149
taste, 148–149
touch, 140
vision, 83t, 84–85, 148, 161

Sensitive guidance, 52
Sensitive period
    defined, 9–10, 32
    for language learning, 9–10, 263,
        264t
    predictions based on, 20–21
Sensorimotor intelligence
    characteristics of, 44–46, 46t, 47p
    defined, 164
    primary circular reactions, 165–166,
        165p
    secondary circular reactions, 165p,
        166
    stages of, 47p, 164t, 186, 219
    tertiary circular reactions, 165–166,
        165p, 168p
Sensory deprivation, 145, 146p
Sensory memory, 345, 346
Sensory register, 345, 346, 365
Sensory stimulation, 144–146
Separation anxiety, 190
Seriation, 340–341
Serotonin, 143, 193
Serotonin transporter promoter gene,
    463, 463f, 472
Sex. See also Boys; Gender; Girls
    chromosomes determining, 71–72,
        73p, 94
    commitment and, 499
    effect on onset of puberty, 427
    fetal development of, 100
    gender development, 300–305, 306
    parental choosing, 73–74
Sex characteristics, 422p
Sex chromosomes
    problems of, 87–88, 88t
    recessive genetic disorders associated
        with, 89
    role in puberty, 410
    sex determination, 8, 71–73, 72f,
        73p, 300
Sex differences, 73–74, 300–305,
    301p, 427
Sex education, 468–471, 483, 484
Sex hormones. See also Cortisol
    involvement in clinical depression,
        472
    role in puberty, 404–405, 405f
    stimulation of sexual activity,
        421–422
Sexism, 62
Sexting, 444–445
Sexual abuse
    of adolescents, 424–425
    of children, 242, 242f, 243, 424–425
    consequences of, 412
    via Internet, 441–442
Sexual activity
    in adolescence, 421–422, 421f, 427,
        468f, 483
    before age 13, 25, 25f
    contraception use, 423f, 424
    of early-maturing girls and boys, 413
    effect of sex education, 469–470
    effect of stress on age of initial
        encounters, 412
    effects of drug abuse, 481
    flaunting of in middle school years,
        448
    influence on, 469–471
    problem for adolescents, 421–424
Sexual identity, 460–461,
    483, 484
Sexual intercourse, 25, 25f. See also
    Sex
Sexual interests, 404–405
Sexuality, 468–469, 469p
Sexually transmitted infections (STIs).
    See also HIV/AIDS

    in adolescence, 424, 425–426, 469
    among bisexuals, 469
    effect of stress on incidence of in
        young girls, 412
Sexual maturation in adolescence,
    420–426, 421f, 422p, 424p,
    485
Sexual orientation, 376, 468–469,
    469p, 483
Sexual-reproductive system. See also
        Birth; Labor and delivery;
        Pregnancy; Reproduction;
        Sexual activity; Sexually
        transmitted infections (STIs)
    contraception, 423f, 424, 469–471,
        476
Sexual teasing, 389, 413
Shaken baby syndrome, 146
Shame
    adolescent's feelings of, 447
    cultural norms for development of,
        191
    development in early childhood,
        217, 306
    development in infancy, 190t
    development in middle childhood,
        371
Shared environment, 375–376, 376p
Shift work, 29
Shivering, 125
Shoplifting, 476
Short-term memory. See Working
        memory
Shyness, 387
Siblings, 375
Sickle-cell anemia, 89
SIDS. See Sudden infant death
        syndrome (SIDS)
Sierra Leone, 122f, 373
Significance, 22t
Sign language, 174, 177, 177p, 183,
        184p, 185
Singapore, 85, 110f, 356t, 450, 453
Single father, 379t
Single mother, 379t
Single-nucleotide polymorphisms
        (SNPs), 69
Single-parent families, 379, 379t,
        380, 381p, 383, 383f, 384f,
        385, 398
Sitting, 150t, 151
Skinner, B. F., 43, 44p, 61, 181, 184
Skin-to-skin contact, 128–129,
        129p, 149
Skipped-generation family, 379t
Sleep
    of newborns, 137–139, 160
    patterns in adolescents, 406–407,
        407f
    patterns in early childhood, 227
    patterns in infancy, 137
Sleep deprivation, 406
Slow wave sleep, 137
Small-for-dates, 121
Small for gestational age
        (SGA), 121
Smallpox, 156
Smell, 140, 148–149
Smile
    development of, 147, 148, 190,
        190p, 190t, 193, 217
    as survival technique, 210
Smoking
    birth complications due to, 114,
        114p
    birthweight affected by, 121, 124
    breast-feeding and, 158
    consequences of, 477, 478
    effect of second-hand smoke, 233

    effect on children, 233
    effect on prenatal development,
        112–113, 115f
    friends' facilitation of, 467–468
    national variation in use,
        479, 480p
    in United States, 477f
    as vestige of oral stage, 39
Social anxiety, 80, 193
Social awareness, 191–192, 217
Social bonds. See also Family;
        Friendships; Parents; Peer
        relationships
    attachment, 198–205, 199t, 200p,
        201p, 201t, 202t, 217
    of bullies and victims, 391
    development in first two years,
        192–200, 195p, 199t, 200p,
        201p, 201t, 202t, 204p,
        206p, 207f, 217, 219
    fathers as social partners, 206–207,
        206p, 207f, 218
    social referencing, 205–206, 206p,
        218
    synchrony, 196–198,196p, 197p,
        200p, 217
    theories of psychosocial
        development, 219
Social class, 12–14. See also
        Socioeconomic context
        (SES)
Social cognition, 387
Social comparison, 368p, 369
Social constructs, 14–15, 16
Social context. See also Culture;
        Exosystem; Historical
        context; Macrosystems;
        Microsystems
    adjusting language for, 348–349,
        348p
    childhood obesity and, 317
    as crucial element in overcoming
        stress, 373
    development of theory of mind
        associated with, 261–262
    diagnosis and treatment of special
        brain disorders dependent
        in, 320
    during emerging adulthood, 500
    fathers' caregiving of infants and, 207
    interplay of physical and
        psychological problems, 316
    language adjusted to, 348–349
    learning in early childhood affected
        by, 255–257, 256p, 258p
    learning in middle childhood related
        to, 364
    metaphors related to, 348
    peer pressure in ethnic groups,
        465–466
    popularity of children related to, 388
    social learning embedded in,
        255–257
    stimulation of sexual activity, 422
Social decisions, 37
Social deficit, 245
Social exclusion, 314
Social interaction. See also Social
        bonds
    advancement of executive function
        and theory of mind,
        261–262
    fostering of theory of mind, 262
    language development and, 263
    role of play, 306
    social learning theory, 45, 208–209,
        255–257, 256p, 257p
Social isolation, 245
Social learning, 208–209, 255–259

    Social learning theory, 45, 45p
        application to early childhood,
            208–209, 255–257, 256p,
            257p, 302–303
        concepts of, 44t, 45, 64
        mentors, 255–257, 256p
        scaffolding, 255–257, 257p
    Socially engaged infants, 198
    Social mediation, 258
    Social networking, of adolescents,
        440–441, 467p
    Social play, 288, 288p
    Social-pragmatic theory, 183
    Social promotion, 371
    Social referencing, 205–206, 206p,
        218
    Social rejection, 370
    Social setting, 202, 202t, 204–205,
        204p
    Social skills, 386, 448
    Social smile, 190, 190t, 193
    Social support. See also Family;
            Friendships
        at birth of child, 125
        within families, 464, 476
    Social understanding, 227, 392
    Social variables, 435
    Sociocultural theory
        application to achievement tests, 322
        application to early childhood, 304
        application to middle childhood,
            358, 364
        area of focus and emphasis, 63t
        concepts of, 36, 51–54, 64
        contribution of, 62
        criticism of, 62
        defined, 51
        social learning in infancy and,
            211–216
        STEM education and, 258–259
        on toilet training, 56
        view of language development, 179
        zone of proximal development,
            52–53, 255, 256, 258,
            265, 268
    Sociodramatic play, 286p, 289–290
    Socioeconomic status (SES). See also
            Income
        academic achievement correlated
            with, 350–351
        accident rates and, 237
        asthma rates associated with, 233
        availability of technology, 441
        childhood obesity and, 224
        contribution to clinical depression in
            adolescent boys, 472
        crime rate in adolescence effected
            by, 475
        defined, 13
        development affected by, 13–14, 32
        differences in thinking and, 51
        discipline styles associated with,
            297, 298
        early childhood schooling for low
            income families, 273–278
        education in United States
            determined by, 359, 360, 446
        environmental hazards related to, 233
        family structure and function
            correlated with, 385
        food choices base on, 416–417
        gap between rich and poor, 13f
        health and, 488
        language learning associated with,
            350–351, 365
        lead poisoning related to, 234–235
        low birthweight associated with, 121
        marriages affected by, 381
        neighborhood games and, 314

resilience affected by, 375
teen pregnancy associated with, 425
Soft skills, 362
Solitary play, 288
Sonogram, 100, 100p
South Africa, 256
South Asia, 159f, 213
South Korea, 122f, 450, 453
Spain
    birth rituals in, 127
    college graduates in, 494f
    international test scores, 356t
    paternity leave in, 213
Spanking, 207f, 297–298, 298p
Spatial intelligence, 322, 341–342
Spatial orientation, 140
Special education, 329–335
    early intervention, 332–333
    for gifted and talented children,
        333–335
    labels, laws, and learning, 331–332,
        331p, 332f
Specific learning disorder, 325–329
Speech, 147p
Sperm
    abnormal genetic formation, 86–87,
        87p, 88t
    effect of age, 86
    fertilization, 70, 70p
    inactivation of, 73
    sex chromosomes of, 72–73
Spermarche, 404, 410, 427
Spice (synthetic marijuana), 480p
Spina bifida, 116
Spinal cord, 141f
Spiritual/existential intelligence,
    322
Spitting up, 125
Sports
    injuries during puberty, 415
    in middle school, 448
SRY gene, 72–73, 100
Stability
    as need of middle childhood, 377,
        380, 398
    in permanent placement homes,
        237p, 246–247
    in step families, 382
Stage of first habits, 164t, 165–166
Stage of reflexes, 164t, 165
Stages of life, 26p
Standing, 150t
Static reasoning, 253, 254, 256
Statistical measures, 22t
Statistical significance, 506
Status symbols, 448
Stem cells, 75–76, 94
STEM (science, technology,
    engineering, math),
    258–259, 359p
Stepfamily, 379t, 380, 382, 385, 398
Stepparent family, 379t
Stepparents, 378, 383
Stepping reflex, 108f, 126
Stereotypes, 490, 502
    postformal thinking countering,
        489–490
    of race or ethnicity, 14–15
Stereotype threat, 490–491, 502
    deflection of, 490
Sterilization, 93
Stillbirth, 92, 99t
Still-face technique, 198, 217
Stimulation, lack of in infancy,
    144–146
Storage of memories, 345
Stranger wariness, 190, 191p,
    233, 314
Strange Situation, 201–202, 203f

Stress
    aggressive children affected by, 389
    attachment affected by, 200, 202t
    brain development affected by, 146,
        193, 217, 230, 248
    cumulative stress, 372–374
    of disorganized attached infants, 200
    effect during puberty, 405, 411–412
    effect in middle childhood, 372–375,
        372p, 398
    effect on parent involvement with
        infants, 207
    within families, 385
    in infants, 190
    maternal nurturing affected by, 7
    of middle school, 447
Stroke, 5–6
Stubborness, 476
Study of development
    correlation and causation, 29
    cross-sectional research, 25–27, 28f
    cross-sequential research, 25f, 28
    ethical issues, 30–31
    longitudinal research, 26, 28f
    scientific method, 4–6, 32
Stunting, 159, 159f, 160p
Stuttering, 315
Sub-Saharan Africa, 123, 159f, 238
Substance use disorder (SUD), 27,
    41, 443t
Substantiated maltreatment, 242, 243,
    243f, 244, 249
Sucking reflex, 108f, 125, 165f, 165p,
    166
Sudden infant death syndrome
    (SIDS), 138, 154, 155f, 160
Sugar, 225, 248
Suicidal ideation, 472p, 473–474, 473f
Suicide
    of adolescents and young adults,
        483, 484
    by bullied children, 389, 444
    cluster suicides, 474
    of cyberbullied adolescents, 444
    drug abuse related to, 481
    incidence of in U.S., 473
    internalization of problems
        associated with, 474
    of Native Americans, 472p
    of non-heterosexual teens, 469
    parent–adolescent relationships
        affecting, 473–474
    sexual abuse related to, 424, 444
Sulci, 101
Superego, 302
Survey, 24–25, 32
Survival
    allocare, 211
    combination of genes insuring, 94
    developmental theories concerning,
        37
    emotions for, 210–211
    evolutionary theory concerning,
        57–59, 62
    of newborns, 103, 110–111,
        153–154
    of the smartest, 227
Swallowing reflexes, 125
Sweden
    ads for sweets in, 318f
    cohabitation in, 499
    early childhood education in,
        268–269
    infant day care in, 213
    international test scores, 356t
    low birthweights in, 122f
    medical care in, 111
    paternity leave in, 213
Swimming reflex, 126, 150

Switzerland, 110f
Symbolic thought, 252
Synapses
    defined, 140
    function of, 140, 143
    growth and refinement in first two
        years, 140, 161
    increase in infancy, 140
    photograph of, 139f
Synaptic gap, 143f
Synchrony
    between adoptees and parents, 204
    defined, 196
    between infant and caregiver,
        196–198, 196p, 197p,
        206, 217
    as survival technique, 210–211
Synthetic marijuana, 480p
Syphilis, 119
Syria, 464

Tablet apps, 182
Taiwan, 352
Talking, 268. See also Language
    development
Taste, 148–149, 149p
Teacher-directed preschool programs,
    272–273, 277f
Teachers, 388
Teacher–student relationships, 292
Teaching. See also College; Early-
    childhood schooling;
    Education; High school;
    Learning; Middle school;
    Preschool programs
    adolescents, 429, 445–456, 447p,
        449p, 484
    children in middle childhood,
        352–364, 356t, 365
    international schooling, 353–358,
        353t, 354t, 355p
    international tests, 353–358, 356t
    in middle childhood, 353–364
    sex education, 470–471
    in the United States, 349–350,
        360–364
    use of technology, 441
Technology
    addiction to video games, 442–443,
        442f, 443t, 455
    adolescents' familiarity with,
        440–441, 455, 485
    cyberbullying, 443–444, 444p, 455
    educational applications, 441
    sexting, 444–445
    social networking, 440–441, 467p
Teenagers, 235. See also Adolescence
Teeth, 115f, 312, 312p
Temperament
    changes between ages 4 months and
        4 years, 195f
    defined, 192, 217
    effect on attachment, 202t
    effect on child-rearing practices, 295
    in first two years, 192, 194–195, 194p
Temperature, infants' sensitivity to,
    149
Temper tantrums, 191, 227, 283
Temporal lobe, 140
Teratogens
    advice from experts, 118–119
    applying research, 118
    complications during birth associated
        with, 124
    critical time, 114–115
    effect on prenatal development,
        112, 113
    prenatal diagnosis, 119

    preterm delivery, 121
    risk analysis, 113–114
    threshold effect, 114, 115f
Teratology, 114–115
Tertiary circular reactions, 164t,
    165–166, 165f, 168p, 186
Tertiary education, 446, 455. See also
    College; Higher education
Tertiary prevention
    of injury, 240, 241, 249
    of maltreatment of children, 246, 248
Testes, 404, 420
Testosterone
    increase in puberty, 404, 405f, 427
Texting, 408, 440, 440p
Thailand, 138f
Thalamus, 141f
Thalassemia, 89
Thalidomide, 9, 114
Theoretical reasoning, 46t
Theories, 35–38, 62–63, 64. See
    also Folk theories; Grand
    theories; Newer theories;
    specific theory
Theories of infant psychosocial
    development, 208–217
Theory of mind
    as cognitive development, 260–261,
        261p, 262, 262f, 278, 289
    development of empathy associated
        with, 392
    development of expertise associated
        with, 395
    development of in children with
        ASD, 328
    effect on corporal punishment on
        development of, 299
Theory-theory, 260, 263, 267, 304
Thinking. See also Cognition;
    Cognitive development
    area of brain controlling, 140
    during early childhood, 251–254,
        253f, 255p, 256p, 257p,
        258p, 261p
    during emerging adulthood, 490
    formal and postformal, 490, 490p
    during middle childhood, 342–344,
        345t
    pruning in brain enabling, 139
    two modes of in adolescence, 434–
        436, 436f, 438f, 449, 455
Third variable, 29t, 30
Thrashing reflex, 125
Threshold effect, 114–115
Time-out, 299, 306
Time-sequential research. See
    Cross-sequential research
TIMSS. See Trends in Math and
    Science Study (TIMMS)
Tobacco
    adolescent use of, 484
    effect on birthweight, 121
    harm from, 479
    national variation in use, 479
Toilet training, 39, 56–57, 208, 208p
Top-down reasoning, 433
Touch, 140, 148–149
Tourette syndrome, 315
Toxins
    effect on brain development,
        234–235, 234f, 235p, 476
    effect on fetus, 112–116
Tracking, 335
Traits
    genetic/environmental effect on, 83–85
    multifactorial, 80, 94
    polygenic, 80, 81–82, 83–84, 94
    temperament, 192, 192p, 194–
        195, 195f

Transgender children, 300, 301, 305
Transient exuberance, 142
Transitional sleep, 137
Trends in Math and Science Study
        (TIMMS), 356, 356t, 358,
        365, 451
Trimesters, 98t
Triple X syndrome, 88t
Trisomy-21, 87, 87p, 89
Trust vs. mistrust, 40, 40t, 208
Tummy time, 151
Turner syndrome, 88t
23rd pair of chromosomes
    defined, 71
    problems of, 87–88, 88t
    recessive genetic disorders associated
            with, 81–82, 83t, 89
    sex determination, 71–73, 73p, 94
Twins
    breast-feeding and, 158
    dizygotic, 72p, 77, 94, 116
    low birthweight, 122, 123
    monozygotic, 77, 78f, 79, 94,
            375–376
    schizophrenia and, 91
    shared and nonshared environments,
            375–376
Two-parent families, 379t, 380–383,
        380p, 398


Uganda, 213
Ultrasound image, 100, 100p
Umbilical cord, 106
United Kingdom
    ads for sweets in, 318f
    college graduates in, 494f
    co-sleeping in, 138f
    home births in, 111
    incidence of neural-tube defects,
            116
    low birthweights in, 122f
    paternity leave in, 213
    scores on international tests, 356t
    thalidomide babies, 114
    vision heritability in, 85
United States
    ADHD in, 324, 326–327, 326f
    adolescent crime in, 475
    ads for sweets in, 318f
    advice to pregnant women in,
            118–119
    asthma rates, 233, 319, 319f
    behaviorism in, 42–43
    bilingual school children in,
            349–350, 349f
    body image of adolescents in, 417
    book-reading parents in, 256
    brain research in, 141
    breast-feeding in, 158, 158t
    cardiovascular death rate, 74
    caregiving styles in, 296
    childhood obesity in, 316, 317, 317f
    child maltreatment in, 242, 242f, 243f
    cohabitation in, 383f, 499–500, 500f
    college graduates in, 494f
    co-sleeping in, 138, 138f
    couvade in, 127
    C-sections in, 107, 109
    cultural differences in, 51
    death in, 312
    discipline styles, 296, 297
    disparities between rich and poor,
            13, 13f

divorce rates in, 378
early childhood education in,
        273–276
eating disorders in, 418
eating habits in, 416
education in, 331, 332f, 353–354,
        357, 359–364, 360t, 361f,
        363f, 364p, 365, 371,
        450–451, 491f
education of children with
        disabilities, 52
epidural anesthesia use, 109
ethnic make-up, 18f
family structures in, 379t, 383f
father involvement with infants in,
        207
foster care in, 248
groups of popular and unpopular
        children in, 388
high school graduation rate, 450,
        451f
home births in, 111
incidence of autism in, 328
incidence of measles in, 156
induced labor, 109
infant care in, 213, 214, 215
infant deaths in car accidents, 240
infant mortality in, 110, 122, 154f
influence of family in, 384f
international adoption, 205
international test scores, 356t, 357,
        357f, 453, 455
language shifts in, 267
laws preventing injury, 239, 241
leave for infant care in, 212
legality of sex determination, 73–74
low birthweight in, 122–123, 122f
massification, 494
maternal leave in, 212, 215
maternal mortality in, 110f
parent–adolescent relationships, 464
paternity leave in, 213
pedestrian deaths, 241f
pride instilled in children, 282, 283
punishment of poor behavior
        in, 297
rate of STIs in, 426
regulation of lead, 234
restrictions on tobacco use, 479
school discipline in, 44
screen time of children in, 290f
secular trend in, 411
sex education in, 470–471
sexual activity of adolescents,
        422, 426
SIDS deaths, 155
stay-at-home mother in, 212
teen abortion rate, 423
teen pregnancy, 423
three-year-old play, 287f
toilet training in, 56–57
view of self-esteem, 371
vision heritability in, 85
Universal grammar, 184
Universal perspective. See
        Evolutionary theory
Universal sequence of language
        development, 174–178,
        174p, 175t
Urbanization, 231
U.S. Youth Risk Behavior Survey,
        423, 425
Uterine rupture, 111
Uterus, 420

Vaccination, 156
Vanishing twin, 79
Vaping, 27, 479
Varanasi children, 341–342, 342p
Variability, 454
Variables, 23, 24f
Varicella, 157
Ventral striatum, 439
Verbal bullying, 388, 398
Very low birthweight (VLBW), 119
Viability, 103, 103p
Victims. See also Abuse; Child
        maltreatment; Domestic
        abuse; Sexual abuse
    of bullying, 389, 389p, 391
Video games
    addiction to, 442f , 443t, 455
    dangers of, 29
Videos and young children, 182–183,
        290
Vietnam, 138, 138f
View from Science
    Culture and Parenting Style, 296
    Eliminating Lead, 234–235, 234f
    Face Recognition, 145
    Happiness or High Grades, 352
    "I Always Dressed One in
            Blue Stuff . . .," 377
    Object Permanence, 167
    Parents, Genes, and Risks, 462–463
    What Causes Childhood Obesity?,
            317
    What Is Safe? (during pregnancy), 117
Vision
    area of brain controlling, 140
    binocular vision, 148
    development in first two years, 148
    development of, 85, 148, 148p, 161
    effect of low birthweight, 122–123
    factors affecting, 86–89
    maturity at birth, 148
    nearsightedness, 84–85
    as necessary for brain development,
            146
Visual cliff, 170p, 171
Visual cortex, 141f, 148
Visualizing Development
    Childhood Obesity Around the
            Globe, 318, 318f
    Developing Attachment, 203f
    Developing Motor Skills, 232f
    Diverse Complexities, 18f
    Early Communication and Language
            Development, 180f
    Education in Middle Childhood
            Around the World, 363f
    Healthy Newborn, 108f
    Highlights in the Journey to
            Adulthood, 482f
    Nature, Nurture, and the Brain, 143
    A Wedding, or Not? Family
            Structures Around the
            World, 384f
    Why Study?, 492f
Vitamin A, 84
Vocabulary. See also Language
        development
    adjusting to context, 348–349, 348p
    in early childhood, 251
    pragmatics, 348–349
    understanding metaphors, 348
Vocabulary explosion, 263–264
Vocation. See Employment
Vocational education, 452

Vocational identity, 459–460, 483,
        484, 496
Vouchers (for schooling), 361
Vygotsky, Lev, 60
    influence on child-centered
            programs, 271
    photograph of, 52p
    on role of instruction, 341, 341p
    social learning in early childhood,
            255–257, 255p, 258p, 278
    social learning in middle childhood,
            341–342, 364
    sociocultural theory, 51–54
    STEM education and, 258–259


Walking
    development of motor skills for, 150,
            150t, 151p
    learning process, 135, 150, 151
Walking reflex, 150
Warmth, expression of
    in caregiving, 294, 306
    toward adolescents, 465, 470, 483
Wasting, 159–160, 160p
Watson, John B., 43, 60
Weight
    growth in early childhood,
            223–224
    growth in first two years,
            136, 139f
WEIRD, 500–501, 501p, 502
Well-baby checkups, 146
White matter, 227
Whooping cough, 156
Withdrawn-rejected children, 388,
        389
Word combination, 179
Working memory, development of,
        345–346, 365
Working model, 210


X chromosome, 71–72, 87
X-linked characteristics, 82, 83t
X-linked disorders, 89
XX chromosomes, 71, 72f, 94, 300
XY chromosomes, 71, 72f, 94, 300


Y chromosome, 82, 116


Zero correlation, 29
Zone of excitement, 54p
Zone of proximal development (ZPD)
    defined, 52, 255
    emotional regulation taught, 284
    as site of learning, 54p, 255, 256,
            258
    sociocultural theory, 52–53, 53f
    teaching of language, 265
Zygotes
    assisted reproductive technology, 94
    defined, 70
    differentiation, 98
    division creating twins, 77, 78f, 79
    duplication and division of, 75, 75p,
            77, 94
    fertilization, 70, 70p, 88, 94
    genes determining sex, 71–73, 73p
    genetic code in, 70, 75, 88
    implantation, 98, 99f, 99t
    in vitro fertilization, 73–74, 94, 98